S0-EKM-040
National
Security
Agency

UNITED STATES COAST GUARD
1790
COAST GUARD

DEPARTMENT OF DEFENSE
UNITED STATES OF AMERICA

DEPARTMENT OF JUSTICE
FEDERAL BUREAU OF PRISONS

ARMY
NATIONAL
GUARD

NSWC
NAVAL SURFACE WARFARE CENTER
A TRADITION OF EXCELLENCE
NAVAL
SURFACE
WARFARE
CENTER

DEPARTMENT OF THE NAVY
OFFICE OF THE COMPTROLLER

NAVY OFFICER

Franklin Mass Media Law 3rd Ed. UCB—1

University Casebook Series

October, 1986

ACCOUNTING AND THE LAW, Fourth Edition (1978), with Problems Pamphlet (Successor to Dohr, Phillips, Thompson & Warren)

George C. Thompson, Professor, Columbia University Graduate School of Business.
Robert Whitman, Professor of Law, University of Connecticut.
Ellis L. Phillips, Jr., Member of the New York Bar.
William C. Warren, Professor of Law Emeritus, Columbia University.

ACCOUNTING FOR LAWYERS, MATERIALS ON (1980)

David R. Herwitz, Professor of Law, Harvard University.

ADMINISTRATIVE LAW, Eighth Edition (1987), with 1983 Problems Supplement (Supplement edited in association with Paul R. Verkuil, Dean and Professor of Law, Tulane University)

Walter Gellhorn, University Professor Emeritus, Columbia University.
Clark Byse, Professor of Law, Harvard University.
Peter L. Strauss, Professor of Law, Columbia University.
Todd D. Rakoff, Professor of Law, Harvard University.

ADMIRALTY, Third Edition (1987), with Statute and Rule Supplement

Jo Desha Lucas, Professor of Law, University of Chicago.

ADVOCACY, see also Lawyering Process

AGENCY, see also Enterprise Organization

AGENCY—PARTNERSHIPS, Third Edition (1982)

Abridgement from Conard, Knauss & Siegel's Enterprise Organization, Third Edition.

ANTITRUST: FREE ENTERPRISE AND ECONOMIC ORGANIZATION, Sixth Edition (1983), with 1983 Problems in Antitrust Supplement and 1986 Case Supplement

Louis B. Schwartz, Professor of Law, University of Pennsylvania.
John J. Flynn, Professor of Law, University of Utah.
Harry First, Professor of Law, New York University.

BANKRUPTCY (1985)

Robert L. Jordan, Professor of Law, University of California, Los Angeles.
William D. Warren, Professor of Law, University of California, Los Angeles.

BUSINESS ORGANIZATION, see also Enterprise Organization

BUSINESS PLANNING, Temporary Second Edition (1984)

David R. Herwitz, Professor of Law, Harvard University.

BUSINESS TORTS (1972)

Milton Handler, Professor of Law Emeritus, Columbia University.

UNIVERSITY CASEBOOK SERIES—Continued

CHILDREN IN THE LEGAL SYSTEM (1983)

Walter Wadlington, Professor of Law, University of Virginia.
Charles H. Whitebread, Professor of Law, University of Southern California.
Samuel Davis, Professor of Law, University of Georgia.

CIVIL PROCEDURE, see Procedure

CLINIC, see also Lawyering Process

COMMERCIAL LAW (1983) with 1986 Bankruptcy Supplement

Robert L. Jordan, Professor of Law, University of California, Los Angeles.
William D. Warren, Professor of Law, University of California, Los Angeles.

COMMERCIAL LAW, CASES & MATERIALS ON, Fourth Edition (1985)

E. Allan Farnsworth, Professor of Law, Columbia University.
John Honnold, Professor of Law, University of Pennsylvania.

COMMERCIAL PAPER, Third Edition (1984)

E. Allan Farnsworth, Professor of Law, Columbia University.

COMMERCIAL PAPER (1983) (Reprinted from COMMERCIAL LAW)

Robert L. Jordan, Professor of Law, University of California, Los Angeles.
William D. Warren, Professor of Law, University of California, Los Angeles.

COMMERCIAL PAPER AND BANK DEPOSITS AND COLLECTIONS (1967), with Statutory Supplement

William D. Hawkland, Professor of Law, University of Illinois.

COMMERCIAL TRANSACTIONS—Principles and Policies (1982)

Alan Schwartz, Professor of Law, University of Southern California.
Robert E. Scott, Professor of Law, University of Virginia.

COMPARATIVE LAW, Fourth Edition (1980)

Rudolf B. Schlesinger, Professor of Law, Hastings College of the Law.

COMPETITIVE PROCESS, LEGAL REGULATION OF THE, Third Edition (1986), with 1986 Selected Statutes Supplement

Edmund W. Kitch, Professor of Law, University of Virginia.
Harvey S. Perlman, Dean of the Law School, University of Nebraska.

CONFLICT OF LAWS, Eighth Edition (1984), with 1986 Case Supplement

Willis L. M. Reese, Professor of Law, Columbia University.
Maurice Rosenberg, Professor of Law, Columbia University.

CONSTITUTIONAL LAW, Seventh Edition (1985), with 1986 Supplement

Edward L. Barrett, Jr., Professor of Law, University of California, Davis.
William Cohen, Professor of Law, Stanford University.

CONSTITUTIONAL LAW, CIVIL LIBERTY AND INDIVIDUAL RIGHTS, Second Edition (1982), with 1985 Supplement

William Cohen, Professor of Law, Stanford University.
John Kaplan, Professor of Law, Stanford University.

CONSTITUTIONAL LAW, Eleventh Edition (1985), with 1986 Supplement (Supplement edited in association with Frederick F. Schauer, Professor of Law, University of Michigan)

Gerald Gunther, Professor of Law, Stanford University.

CONSTITUTIONAL LAW, INDIVIDUAL RIGHTS IN, Fourth Edition (1986), (Reprinted from CONSTITUTIONAL LAW, Eleventh Edition), with 1986 Supplement (Supplement edited in association with Frederick F. Schauer, Professor of Law, University of Michigan)

Gerald Gunther, Professor of Law, Stanford University.

CONSUMER TRANSACTIONS (1983), with Selected Statutes and Regulations Supplement and 1987 Case Supplement

Michael M. Greenfield, Professor of Law, Washington University.

CONTRACT LAW AND ITS APPLICATION, Third Edition (1983)

The late Addison Mueller, Professor of Law, University of California, Los Angeles.
Arthur I. Rosett, Professor of Law, University of California, Los Angeles.
Gerald P. Lopez, Professor of Law, University of California, Los Angeles.

CONTRACT LAW, STUDIES IN, Third Edition (1984)

Edward J. Murphy, Professor of Law, University of Notre Dame.
Richard E. Speidel, Professor of Law, Northwestern University.

CONTRACTS, Fourth Edition (1982)

John P. Dawson, Professor of Law Emeritus, Harvard University.
William Burnett Harvey, Professor of Law and Political Science, Boston University.
Stanley D. Henderson, Professor of Law, University of Virginia.

CONTRACTS, Third Edition (1980), with Statutory Supplement

E. Allan Farnsworth, Professor of Law, Columbia University.
William F. Young, Professor of Law, Columbia University.

CONTRACTS, Second Edition (1978), with Statutory and Administrative Law Supplement (1978)

Ian R. Macneil, Professor of Law, Cornell University.

COPYRIGHT, PATENTS AND TRADEMARKS, see also Competitive Process; see also Selected Statutes and International Agreements

COPYRIGHT, PATENT, TRADEMARK AND RELATED STATE DOCTRINES, Second Edition (1981), with 1985 Case Supplement, 1986 Selected Statutes Supplement and 1981 Problem Supplement

Paul Goldstein, Professor of Law, Stanford University.

COPYRIGHT, Unfair Competition, and Other Topics Bearing on the Protection of Literary, Musical, and Artistic Works, Fourth Edition (1985), with 1985 Statutory Supplement

Ralph S. Brown, Jr., Professor of Law, Yale University.
Robert C. Denicola, Professor of Law, University of Nebraska.

CORPORATE ACQUISITIONS, The Law and Finance of (1986)

Ronald J. Gilson, Professor of Law, Stanford University.

CORPORATE FINANCE, Second Edition (1979), with 1984 Supplement

Victor Brudney, Professor of Law, Harvard University.
Marvin A. Chirelstein, Professor of Law, Columbia University.

CORPORATE READJUSTMENTS AND REORGANIZATIONS (1976)

Walter J. Blum, Professor of Law, University of Chicago.
Stanley A. Kaplan, Professor of Law, University of Chicago.

UNIVERSITY CASEBOOK SERIES—Continued

CORPORATION LAW, BASIC, Second Edition (1979), with 1983 Case and Documentary Supplement

Detlev F. Vagts, Professor of Law, Harvard University.

CORPORATIONS, see also Enterprise Organization

CORPORATIONS, Fifth Edition—Unabridged (1980), with 1986 Supplement

The late William L. Cary, Professor of Law, Columbia University.
Melvin Aron Eisenberg, Professor of Law, University of California, Berkeley.

CORPORATIONS, Fifth Edition—Abridged (1980), with 1986 Supplement

The late William L. Cary, Professor of Law, Columbia University.
Melvin Aron Eisenberg, Professor of Law, University of California, Berkeley.

CORPORATIONS, Second Edition (1982), with 1982 Corporation and Partnership Statutes, Rules and Forms

Alfred F. Conard, Professor of Law, University of Michigan.
Robert N. Knauss, Dean of the Law School, University of Houston.
Stanley Siegel, Professor of Law, University of California, Los Angeles.

CORPORATIONS COURSE GAME PLAN (1975)

David R. Herwitz, Professor of Law, Harvard University.

CORRECTIONS, SEE SENTENCING

CREDITORS' RIGHTS, see also Debtor-Creditor Law

CRIMINAL JUSTICE ADMINISTRATION, Third Edition (1986), with 1986 Case Supplement

Frank W. Miller, Professor of Law, Washington University.
Robert O. Dawson, Professor of Law, University of Texas.
George E. Dix, Professor of Law, University of Texas.
Raymond I. Parnas, Professor of Law, University of California, Davis.

CRIMINAL LAW, Third Edition (1983)

Fred E. Inbau, Professor of Law Emeritus, Northwestern University.
James R. Thompson, Professor of Law Emeritus, Northwestern University.
Andre A. Moenssens, Professor of Law, University of Richmond.

CRIMINAL LAW AND APPROACHES TO THE STUDY OF LAW (1986)

John M. Brumbaugh, Professor of Law, University of Maryland.

CRIMINAL LAW, Second Edition (1986)

Peter W. Low, Professor of Law, University of Virginia.
John C. Jeffries, Jr., Professor of Law, University of Virginia.
Richard C. Bonnie, Professor of Law, University of Virginia.

CRIMINAL LAW, Fourth Edition (1986)

Lloyd L. Weinreb, Professor of Law, Harvard University.

CRIMINAL LAW AND PROCEDURE, Sixth Edition (1984)

Rollin M. Perkins, Professor of Law Emeritus, University of California, Hastings College of the Law.
Ronald N. Boyce, Professor of Law, University of Utah.

CRIMINAL PROCEDURE, Second Edition (1980), with 1986 Supplement

Fred E. Inbau, Professor of Law Emeritus, Northwestern University.
James R. Thompson, Professor of Law Emeritus, Northwestern University.
James B. Haddad, Professor of Law, Northwestern University.
James B. Zagel, Chief, Criminal Justice Division, Office of Attorney General of Illinois.
Gary L. Starkman, Assistant U. S. Attorney, Northern District of Illinois.

CRIMINAL PROCESS, Third Edition (1978), with 1986 Supplement

Lloyd L. Weinreb, Professor of Law, Harvard University.

DAMAGES, Second Edition (1952)

Charles T. McCormick, late Professor of Law, University of Texas.
William F. Fritz, late Professor of Law, University of Texas.

DEBTOR–CREDITOR LAW (1984) with 1986 Supplement

Theodore Eisenberg, Professor of Law, Cornell University.

DEBTOR–CREDITOR LAW, Second Edition (1981), with Statutory Supplement

William D. Warren, Dean of the School of Law, University of California, Los Angeles.
William E. Hogan, Professor of Law, New York University.

DECEDENTS' ESTATES (1971)

Max Rheinstein, late Professor of Law Emeritus, University of Chicago.
Mary Ann Glendon, Professor of Law, Boston College.

DECEDENTS' ESTATES AND TRUSTS, Sixth Edition (1982)

John Ritchie, Emeritus Dean and Wigmore Professor of Law, Northwestern University.
Neill H. Alford, Jr., Professor of Law, University of Virginia.
Richard W. Effland, Professor of Law, Arizona State University.

DOMESTIC RELATIONS, see also Family Law

DOMESTIC RELATIONS, Successor Edition (1984) with 1987 Supplement

Walter Wadlington, Professor of Law, University of Virginia.

ELECTRONIC MASS MEDIA, Second Edition (1979)

William K. Jones, Professor of Law, Columbia University.

EMPLOYMENT DISCRIMINATION, Second Edition (1987)

Joel W. Friedman, Professor of Law, Tulane University.
George M. Strickler, Professor of Law, Tulane University.

ENERGY LAW (1983) with 1986 Case Supplement

Donald N. Zillman, Professor of Law, University of Utah.
Laurence Lattman, Dean of Mines and Engineering, University of Utah.

ENTERPRISE ORGANIZATION, Third Edition (1982), with 1982 Corporation and Partnership Statutes, Rules and Forms Supplement

Alfred F. Conard, Professor of Law, University of Michigan.
Robert L. Knauss, Dean of the Law School, University of Houston.
Stanley Siegel, Professor of Law, University of California, Los Angeles.

ENVIRONMENTAL POLICY LAW 1985 Edition, with 1985 Problems Supplement (Supplement in association with Ronald H. Rosenberg, Professor of Law, College of William and Mary)

Thomas J. Schoenbaum, Professor of Law, University of Georgia.

EQUITY, see also Remedies

EQUITY, RESTITUTION AND DAMAGES, Second Edition (1974)

Robert Childres, late Professor of Law, Northwestern University.
William F. Johnson, Jr., Professor of Law, New York University.

ESTATE PLANNING, Second Edition (1982), with 1985 Case, Text and Documentary Supplement

David Westfall, Professor of Law, Harvard University.

ETHICS, see Legal Profession, and Professional Responsibility

ETHICS AND PROFESSIONAL RESPONSIBILITY (1981) (Reprinted from THE LAWYERING PROCESS)

Gary Bellow, Professor of Law, Harvard University.
Bea Moulton, Legal Services Corporation.

EVIDENCE, Fifth Edition (1984)

John Kaplan, Professor of Law, Stanford University.
Jon R. Waltz, Professor of Law, Northwestern University.

EVIDENCE, Seventh Edition (1983) with Rules and Statute Supplement (1984)

Jack B. Weinstein, Chief Judge, United States District Court.
John H. Mansfield, Professor of Law, Harvard University.
Norman Abrams, Professor of Law, University of California, Los Angeles.
Margaret Berger, Professor of Law, Brooklyn Law School.

FAMILY LAW, see also Domestic Relations

FAMILY LAW Second Edition (1985)

Judith C. Areen, Professor of Law, Georgetown University.

FAMILY LAW AND CHILDREN IN THE LEGAL SYSTEM, STATUTORY MATERIALS (1981)

Walter Wadlington, Professor of Law, University of Virginia.

FEDERAL COURTS, Seventh Edition (1982), with 1986 Supplement

Charles T. McCormick, late Professor of Law, University of Texas.
James H. Chadbourn, late Professor of Law, Harvard University.
Charles Alan Wright, Professor of Law, University of Texas.

FEDERAL COURTS AND THE FEDERAL SYSTEM, Hart and Wechsler's Second Edition (1973), with 1981 Supplement

Paul M. Bator, Professor of Law, Harvard University.
Paul J. Mishkin, Professor of Law, University of California, Berkeley.
David L. Shapiro, Professor of Law, Harvard University.
Herbert Wechsler, Professor of Law, Columbia University.

FEDERAL PUBLIC LAND AND RESOURCES LAW, Second Edition (1987), with 1984 Statutory Supplement

George C. Coggins, Professor of Law, University of Kansas.
Charles F. Wilkinson, Professor of Law, University of Oregon.

FEDERAL RULES OF CIVIL PROCEDURE, 1986 Edition

FEDERAL TAXATION, see Taxation

FOOD AND DRUG LAW (1980), with Statutory Supplement

Richard A. Merrill, Dean of the School of Law, University of Virginia.
Peter Barton Hutt, Esq.

FUTURE INTERESTS (1958)

Philip Mechem, late Professor of Law Emeritus, University of Pennsylvania.

FUTURE INTERESTS (1970)

Howard R. Williams, Professor of Law, Stanford University.

FUTURE INTERESTS AND ESTATE PLANNING (1961), with 1962 Supplement

W. Barton Leach, late Professor of Law, Harvard University.
James K. Logan, formerly Dean of the Law School, University of Kansas.

GOVERNMENT CONTRACTS, FEDERAL, Successor Edition (1985)

John W. Whelan, Professor of Law, Hastings College of the Law.

GOVERNMENT REGULATION: FREE ENTERPRISE AND ECONOMIC ORGANIZATION, Sixth Edition (1985)

Louis B. Schwartz, Professor of Law, University of Pennsylvania.
John J. Flynn, Professor of Law, University of Utah.
Harry First, Professor of Law, New York University.

HINCKLEY JOHN W., TRIAL OF: A Case Study of the Insanity Defense

Peter W. Low, Professor of Law, University of Virginia.
John C. Jeffries, Jr., Professor of Law, University of Virginia.
Richard C. Bonnie, Professor of Law, University of Virginia.

INJUNCTIONS, Second Edition (1984)

Owen M. Fiss, Professor of Law, Yale University.
Doug Rendleman, Professor of Law, College of William and Mary.

INSTITUTIONAL INVESTORS, 1978

David L. Ratner, Professor of Law, Cornell University.

INSURANCE, Second Edition (1985)

William F. Young, Professor of Law, Columbia University.
Eric M. Holmes, Professor of Law, University of Georgia.

INTERNATIONAL LAW, see also Transnational Legal Problems, Transnational Business Problems, and United Nations Law

INTERNATIONAL LAW IN CONTEMPORARY PERSPECTIVE (1981), with Essay Supplement

Myres S. McDougal, Professor of Law, Yale University.
W. Michael Reisman, Professor of Law, Yale University.

INTERNATIONAL LEGAL SYSTEM, Second Edition (1981), with Documentary Supplement

Joseph Modeste Sweeney, Professor of Law, Tulane University.
Covey T. Oliver, Professor of Law, University of Pennsylvania.
Noyes E. Leech, Professor of Law, University of Pennsylvania.

INTRODUCTION TO LAW, see also Legal Method, On Law in Courts, and Dynamics of American Law

INTRODUCTION TO THE STUDY OF LAW (1970)

E. Wayne Thode, late Professor of Law, University of Utah.
Leon Lebowitz, Professor of Law, University of Texas.
Lester J. Mazor, Professor of Law, University of Utah.

JUDICIAL CODE and Rules of Procedure in the Federal Courts with Excerpts from the Criminal Code, 1984 Edition

Henry M. Hart, Jr., late Professor of Law, Harvard University.
Herbert Wechsler, Professor of Law, Columbia University.

JURISPRUDENCE (Temporary Edition Hardbound) (1949)

Lon L. Fuller, Professor of Law Emeritus, Harvard University.

JUVENILE, see also Children

JUVENILE JUSTICE PROCESS, Third Edition (1985)

Frank W. Miller, Professor of Law, Washington University.
Robert O. Dawson, Professor of Law, University of Texas.
George E. Dix, Professor of Law, University of Texas.
Raymond I. Parnas, Professor of Law, University of California, Davis.

LABOR LAW, Tenth Edition (1986), with 1986 Statutory Supplement

Archibald Cox, Professor of Law, Harvard University.
Derek C. Bok, President, Harvard University.
Robert A. Gorman, Professor of Law, University of Pennsylvania.

LABOR LAW, Second Edition (1982), with Statutory Supplement

Clyde W. Summers, Professor of Law, University of Pennsylvania.
Harry H. Wellington, Dean of the Law School, Yale University.
Alan Hyde, Professor of Law, Rutgers University.

LAND FINANCING, Third Edition (1985)

The late Norman Penney, Professor of Law, Cornell University.
Richard F. Broude, Member of the California Bar.
Roger Cunningham, Professor of Law, University of Michigan.

LAW AND MEDICINE (1980)

Walter Wadlington, Professor of Law and Professor of Legal Medicine, University of Virginia.
Jon R. Waltz, Professor of Law, Northwestern University.
Roger B. Dworkin, Professor of Law, Indiana University, and Professor of Biomedical History, University of Washington.

LAW, LANGUAGE AND ETHICS (1972)

William R. Bishin, Professor of Law, University of Southern California.
Christopher D. Stone, Professor of Law, University of Southern California.

LAW, SCIENCE AND MEDICINE (1984), with 1987 Supplement

Judith C. Areen, Professor of Law, Georgetown University.
Patricia A. King, Professor of Law, Georgetown University.
Steven P. Goldberg, Professor of Law, Georgetown University.
Alexander M. Capron, Professor of Law, Georgetown University.

LAWYERING PROCESS (1978), with Civil Problem Supplement and Criminal Problem Supplement

Gary Bellow, Professor of Law, Harvard University.
Bea Moulton, Professor of Law, Arizona State University.

LEGAL METHOD (1980)

Harry W. Jones, Professor of Law Emeritus, Columbia University.
John M. Kernochan, Professor of Law, Columbia University.
Arthur W. Murphy, Professor of Law, Columbia University.

LEGAL METHODS (1969)

Robert N. Covington, Professor of Law, Vanderbilt University.
E. Blythe Stason, late Professor of Law, Vanderbilt University.
John W. Wade, Professor of Law, Vanderbilt University.
Elliott E. Cheatham, late Professor of Law, Vanderbilt University.
Theodore A. Smedley, Professor of Law, Vanderbilt University.

LEGAL PROFESSION, THE, Responsibility and Regulation (1985)

Geoffrey C. Hazard, Jr., Professor of Law, Yale University.
Deborah L. Rhode, Professor of Law, Stanford University.

LEGISLATION, Fourth Edition (1982) (by Fordham)

Horace E. Read, late Vice President, Dalhousie University.
John W. MacDonald, Professor of Law Emeritus, Cornell Law School.
Jefferson B. Fordham, Professor of Law, University of Utah.
William J. Pierce, Professor of Law, University of Michigan.

LEGISLATIVE AND ADMINISTRATIVE PROCESSES, Second Edition (1981)

Hans A. Linde, Judge, Supreme Court of Oregon.
George Bunn, Professor of Law, University of Wisconsin.
Fredericka Paff, Professor of Law, University of Wisconsin.
W. Lawrence Church, Professor of Law, University of Wisconsin.

LOCAL GOVERNMENT LAW, Second Revised Edition (1986)

Jefferson B. Fordham, Professor of Law, University of Utah.

MASS MEDIA LAW, Third Edition (1987)

Marc A. Franklin, Professor of Law, Stanford University.

MENTAL HEALTH PROCESS, Second Edition (1976), with 1981 Supplement

Frank W. Miller, Professor of Law, Washington University.
Robert O. Dawson, Professor of Law, University of Texas.
George E. Dix, Professor of Law, University of Texas.
Raymond I. Parnas, Professor of Law, University of California, Davis.

MUNICIPAL CORPORATIONS, see Local Government Law

NEGOTIABLE INSTRUMENTS, see Commercial Paper

NEGOTIATION (1981) (Reprinted from THE LAWYERING PROCESS)

Gary Bellow, Professor of Law, Harvard Law School.
Bea Moulton, Legal Services Corporation.

NEW YORK PRACTICE, Fourth Edition (1978)

Herbert Peterfreund, Professor of Law, New York University.
Joseph M. McLaughlin, Dean of the Law School, Fordham University.

OIL AND GAS, Fifth Edition (1987)

Howard R. Williams, Professor of Law, Stanford University.
Richard C. Maxwell, Professor of Law, University of California, Los Angeles.
Charles J. Meyers, Dean of the Law School, Stanford University.
Stephen F. Williams, Professor of Law, University of Colorado.

ON LAW IN COURTS (1965)

Paul J. Mishkin, Professor of Law, University of California, Berkeley.
Clarence Morris, Professor of Law Emeritus, University of Pennsylvania.

UNIVERSITY CASEBOOK SERIES—Continued

PATENTS AND ANTITRUST (Pamphlet) (1983)

Milton Handler, Professor of Law Emeritus, Columbia University.
Harlan M. Blake, Professor of Law, Columbia University.
Robert Pitofsky, Professor of Law, Georgetown University.
Harvey J. Goldschmid, Professor of Law, Columbia University.

PERSPECTIVES ON THE LAWYER AS PLANNER (Reprint of Chapters One through Five of Planning by Lawyers) (1978)

Louis M. Brown, Professor of Law, University of Southern California.
Edward A. Dauer, Professor of Law, Yale University.

PLANNING BY LAWYERS, MATERIALS ON A NONADVERSARIAL LEGAL PROCESS (1978)

Louis M. Brown, Professor of Law, University of Southern California.
Edward A. Dauer, Professor of Law, Yale University.

PLEADING AND PROCEDURE, see Procedure, Civil

POLICE FUNCTION, Fourth Edition (1986), with 1986 Case Supplement

Reprint of Chapters 1–10 of Miller, Dawson, Dix and Parnas's CRIMINAL JUSTICE ADMINISTRATION, Third Edition.

PREPARING AND PRESENTING THE CASE (1981) (Reprinted from THE LAWYERING PROCESS)

Gary Bellow, Professor of Law, Harvard Law School.
Bea Moulton, Legal Services Corporation.

PREVENTIVE LAW, see also Planning by Lawyers

PROCEDURE—CIVIL PROCEDURE, Second Edition (1974), with 1979 Supplement

The late James H. Chadbourn, Professor of Law, Harvard University.
A. Leo Levin, Professor of Law, University of Pennsylvania.
Philip Shuchman, Professor of Law, Cornell University.

PROCEDURE—CIVIL PROCEDURE, Fifth Edition (1984), with 1986 Supplement

Richard H. Field, late Professor of Law, Harvard University.
Benjamin Kaplan, Professor of Law Emeritus, Harvard University.
Kevin M. Clermont, Professor of Law, Cornell University.

PROCEDURE—CIVIL PROCEDURE, Fourth Edition (1985)

Maurice Rosenberg, Professor of Law, Columbia University.
Hans Smit, Professor of Law, Columbia University.
Harold L. Korn, Professor of Law, Columbia University.

PROCEDURE—PLEADING AND PROCEDURE: State and Federal, Fifth Edition (1983), with 1986 Supplement

David W. Louisell, late Professor of Law, University of California, Berkeley.
Geoffrey C. Hazard, Jr., Professor of Law, Yale University.
Colin C. Tait, Professor of Law, University of Connecticut.

PROCEDURE—FEDERAL RULES OF CIVIL PROCEDURE, 1986 Edition

PRODUCTS LIABILITY (1980)

Marshall S. Shapo, Professor of Law, Northwestern University.

PRODUCTS LIABILITY AND SAFETY (1980), with 1985 Case and Documentary Supplement

W. Page Keeton, Professor of Law, University of Texas.
David G. Owen, Professor of Law, University of South Carolina.
John E. Montgomery, Professor of Law, University of South Carolina.

PROFESSIONAL RESPONSIBILITY, Third Edition (1984), with 1986 Selected National Standards Supplement

Thomas D. Morgan, Dean of the Law School, Emory University.
Ronald D. Rotunda, Professor of Law, University of Illinois.

PROPERTY, Fifth Edition (1984)

John E. Cribbet, Dean of the Law School, University of Illinois.
Corwin W. Johnson, Professor of Law, University of Texas.

PROPERTY—PERSONAL (1953)

S. Kenneth Skolfield, late Professor of Law Emeritus, Boston University.

PROPERTY—PERSONAL, Third Edition (1954)

Everett Fraser, late Dean of the Law School Emeritus, University of Minnesota.
Third Edition by Charles W. Taintor, late Professor of Law, University of Pittsburgh.

PROPERTY—INTRODUCTION, TO REAL PROPERTY, Third Edition (1954)

Everett Fraser, late Dean of the Law School Emeritus, University of Minnesota.

PROPERTY—REAL AND PERSONAL, Combined Edition (1954)

Everett Fraser, late Dean of the Law School Emeritus, University of Minnesota.
Third Edition of Personal Property by Charles W. Taintor, late Professor of Law, University of Pittsburgh.

PROPERTY—FUNDAMENTALS OF MODERN REAL PROPERTY, Second Edition (1982), with 1985 Supplement

Edward H. Rabin, Professor of Law, University of California, Davis.

PROPERTY—PROBLEMS IN REAL PROPERTY (Pamphlet) (1969)

Edward H. Rabin, Professor of Law, University of California, Davis.

PROPERTY, REAL (1984)

Paul Goldstein, Professor of Law, Stanford University.

PROSECUTION AND ADJUDICATION, Third Edition (1986), with 1986 Case Supplement

Reprint of Chapters 11–26 of Miller, Dawson, Dix and Parnas's CRIMINAL JUSTICE ADMINISTRATION, Third Edition.

PSYCHIATRY AND LAW, see Mental Health, see also Hinckley, Trial of

PUBLIC REGULATION OF DANGEROUS PRODUCTS (paperback) (1980)

Marshall S. Shapo, Professor of Law, Northwestern University.

PUBLIC UTILITY LAW, see Free Enterprise, also Regulated Industries

REAL ESTATE PLANNING (1980), with 1980 Problems, Statutes and New Materials Supplement

Norton L. Steuben, Professor of Law, University of Colorado.

UNIVERSITY CASEBOOK SERIES—Continued

REAL ESTATE TRANSACTIONS, Second Edition (1985), with 1985 Statute, Form and Problem Supplement

Paul Goldstein, Professor of Law, Stanford University.

RECEIVERSHIP AND CORPORATE REORGANIZATION, see Creditors' Rights

REGULATED INDUSTRIES, Second Edition, 1976

William K. Jones, Professor of Law, Columbia University.

REMEDIES (1982), with 1984 Case Supplement

Edward D. Re, Chief Judge, U. S. Court of International Trade.

RESTITUTION, Second Edition (1966)

John W. Wade, Professor of Law, Vanderbilt University.

SALES, Second Edition (1986)

Marion W. Benfield, Jr., Professor of Law, University of Illinois.
William D. Hawkland, Chancellor, Louisiana State Law Center.

SALES AND SALES FINANCING, Fifth Edition (1984)

John Honnold, Professor of Law, University of Pennsylvania.

SALES LAW AND THE CONTRACTING PROCESS (1982)

Reprint of Chapters 1–10 of Schwartz and Scott's Commercial Transactions.

SECURED TRANSACTIONS IN PERSONAL PROPERTY (1983) (Reprinted from COMMERCIAL LAW)

Robert L. Jordan, Professor of Law, University of California, Los Angeles.
William D. Warren, Professor of Law, University of California, Los Angeles.

SECURITIES REGULATION, Fifth Edition (1982), with 1986 Cases and Releases Supplement and 1986 Selected Statutes, Rules and Forms Supplement

Richard W. Jennings, Professor of Law, University of California, Berkeley.
Harold Marsh, Jr., Member of California Bar.

SECURITIES REGULATION (1982), with 1985 Supplement

Larry D. Soderquist, Professor of Law, Vanderbilt University.

SECURITY INTERESTS IN PERSONAL PROPERTY (1984)

Douglas G. Baird, Professor of Law, University of Chicago.
Thomas H. Jackson, Professor of Law, Stanford University.

SECURITY INTERESTS IN PERSONAL PROPERTY (1985) (Reprinted from Sales and Sales Financing, Fifth Edition)

John Honnold, Professor of Law, University of Pennsylvania.

SENTENCING AND THE CORRECTIONAL PROCESS, Second Edition (1976)

Frank W. Miller, Professor of Law, Washington University.
Robert O. Dawson, Professor of Law, University of Texas.
George E. Dix, Professor of Law, University of Texas.
Raymond I. Parnas, Professor of Law, University of California, Davis.

SOCIAL SCIENCE IN LAW, Cases and Materials (1985)

John Monahan, Professor of Law, University of Virginia.
Laurens Walker, Professor of Law, University of Virginia.

SOCIAL WELFARE AND THE INDIVIDUAL (1971)

Robert J. Levy, Professor of Law, University of Minnesota.
Thomas P. Lewis, Dean of the College of Law, University of Kentucky.
Peter W. Martin, Professor of Law, Cornell University.

TAX, POLICY ANALYSIS OF THE FEDERAL INCOME (1976)

William A. Klein, Professor of Law, University of California, Los Angeles.

TAXATION, FEDERAL INCOME, Successor Edition (1985)

Michael J. Graetz, Professor of Law, Yale University.

TAXATION, FEDERAL INCOME, Fifth Edition (1985)

James J. Freeland, Professor of Law, University of Florida.
Stephen A. Lind, Professor of Law, University of Florida.
Richard B. Stephens, Professor of Law Emeritus, University of Florida.

TAXATION, FEDERAL INCOME, Volume I, Personal Income Taxation, Successor Edition (1986), Volume II, Taxation of Partnerships and Corporations, Second Edition (1980), with 1985 Legislative Supplement

Stanley S. Surrey, late Professor of Law, Harvard University.
Paul R. McDaniel, Professor of Law, Boston College Law School.
Hugh J. Ault, Professor of Law, Boston College Law School.
Stanley A. Koppelman, Boston University

TAXATION, FEDERAL WEALTH TRANSFER, Second Edition (1982) with 1985 Legislative Supplement

Stanley S. Surrey, late Professor of Law, Harvard University.
William C. Warren, Professor of Law Emeritus, Columbia University.
Paul R. McDaniel, Professor of Law, Boston College Law School.
Harry L. Gutman, Instructor, Harvard Law School and Boston College Law School.

TAXATION, FUNDAMENTALS OF CORPORATE, Cases and Materials (1985)

Stephen A. Lind, Professor of Law, University of Florida.
Stephen Schwarz, Professor of Law, University of California, Hastings.
Daniel J. Lathrope, Professor of Law, University of California, Hastings.
Joshua Rosenberg, Professor of Law, University of San Francisco.

TAXATION, FUNDAMENTALS OF PARTNERSHIP, Cases and Materials (1985)

Stephen A. Lind, Professor of Law, University of California, Hastings.
Stephen Schwarz, Professor of Law, University of California, Hastings.
Daniel J. Lathrope, Professor of Law, University of California, Hastings.
Joshua Rosenberg, Professor of Law, University of San Francisco.

TAXATION, PROBLEMS IN THE FEDERAL INCOME TAXATION OF PARTNERSHIPS AND CORPORATIONS, Second Edition (1986)

Norton L. Steuben, Professor of Law, University of Colorado.
William J. Turnier, Professor of Law, University of North Carolina.

TAXATION, PROBLEMS IN THE FUNDAMENTALS OF FEDERAL INCOME, Second Edition (1985)

Norton L. Steuben, Professor of Law, University of Colorado.
William J. Turnier, Professor of Law, University of North Carolina.

TAXES AND FINANCE—STATE AND LOCAL (1974)

Oliver Oldman, Professor of Law, Harvard University.
Ferdinand P. Schoettle, Professor of Law, University of Minnesota.

UNIVERSITY CASEBOOK SERIES—Continued

TORT LAW AND ALTERNATIVES, Third Edition (1983)

Marc A. Franklin, Professor of Law, Stanford University.
Robert L. Rabin, Professor of Law, Stanford University.

TORTS, Seventh Edition (1982)

William L. Prosser, late Professor of Law, University of California, Hastings College.
John W. Wade, Professor of Law, Vanderbilt University.
Victor E. Schwartz, Professor of Law, American University.

TORTS, Third Edition (1976)

Harry Shulman, late Dean of the Law School, Yale University.
Fleming James, Jr., Professor of Law Emeritus, Yale University.
Oscar S. Gray, Professor of Law, University of Maryland.

TRADE REGULATION, Second Edition (1983), with 1985 Supplement

Milton Handler, Professor of Law Emeritus, Columbia University.
Harlan M. Blake, Professor of Law, Columbia University.
Robert Pitofsky, Professor of Law, Georgetown University.
Harvey J. Goldschmid, Professor of Law, Columbia University.

TRADE REGULATION, see Antitrust

TRANSNATIONAL BUSINESS PROBLEMS (1986)

Detlev F. Vagts, Professor of Law, Harvard University.

TRANSNATIONAL LEGAL PROBLEMS, Third Edition (1986) with Documentary Supplement

Henry J. Steiner, Professor of Law, Harvard University.
Detlev F. Vagts, Professor of Law, Harvard University.

TRIAL, see also Evidence, Making the Record, Lawyering Process and Preparing and Presenting the Case

TRIAL ADVOCACY (1968)

A. Leo Levin, Professor of Law, University of Pennsylvania.
Harold Cramer, of the Pennsylvania Bar.
Maurice Rosenberg, Professor of Law, Columbia University, Consultant.

TRUSTS, Fifth Edition (1978)

George G. Bogert, late Professor of Law Emeritus, University of Chicago.
Dallin H. Oaks, President, Brigham Young University.

TRUSTS AND SUCCESSION (Palmer's), Fourth Edition (1983)

Richard V. Wellman, Professor of Law, University of Georgia.
Lawrence W. Waggoner, Professor of Law, University of Michigan.
Olin L. Browder, Jr., Professor of Law, University of Michigan.

UNFAIR COMPETITION, see Competitive Process and Business Torts

UNITED NATIONS LAW, Second Edition (1967), with Documentary Supplement (1968)

Louis B. Sohn, Professor of Law, Harvard University.

WATER RESOURCE MANAGEMENT, Second Edition (1980), with 1983 Supplement

Charles J. Meyers, Dean of the Law School, Stanford University.
A. Dan Tarlock, Professor of Law, Indiana University.

WILLS AND ADMINISTRATION, Fifth Edition (1961)

Philip Mechem, late Professor of Law, University of Pennsylvania.
Thomas E. Atkinson, late Professor of Law, New York University.

WORLD LAW, see United Nations Law

University Casebook Series

CASES AND MATERIALS

ON

MASS MEDIA LAW

By

MARC A. FRANKLIN
Frederick I. Richman Professor of Law
Stanford University

THIRD EDITION

Mineola, New York
THE FOUNDATION PRESS, INC.
1987

Library of Congress Cataloging in Publication Data

Franklin, Marc A.
Cases and materials on mass media law.

(University casebook series)
Includes index.
1. Mass media—Law and legislation—United States—Cases. I. Title. II. Series.
KF2750.A7F7 1986 343.73'099 86–19440
ISBN 0–88277–350–X 347.30399

Franklin Mass Media Law 3rd Ed. UCB

For Ruth

PREFACE TO THIRD EDITION

In the five years since the second edition of this book, much has happened in media law, ranging from developments in libel law at the outset of the book to important new developments in broadcasting and cable television at the back of the book. Much attention has been devoted to bringing the materials up to date in all sections. As an example, the chapter on defamation has been much expanded to take account of recent developments. Overall, of the fifty principal cases in the book, twenty are making their first appearances. In addition, many of the notes discuss cases that have been decided since the last edition. The book refers to developments occurring as recently as September, 1986.

But this edition is not simply an updating of the second edition. Much has been reorganized. The material on the administration of justice has been allocated in terms of whether the issue relates to publication or to access. The material on national security has been moved to Chapter I in order to give more focus to a discussion of the role of prior restraint in the regulation of speech and press.

The material on access to government information and proceedings has undergone extensive change. First, the sequence has been reordered so that it now begins with the less important issues and progresses to the major constitutional questions about minimum access. Second, though, this is one of the few areas of the book in which simplification has occurred, largely as a result of the recent decision in *Press-Enterprise II.*

The material on broadcasting has been reorganized and shortened in order to sharpen the focus on constitutional matters and on relationships to print media. This has led to a reduction in the amount of attention given to issues more closely identified with administrative law. This shift occurs at the same time that the Federal Communications Commission is attempting to relieve licensees of many of their prior obligations. Although the coverage of broadcasting is now shorter, it contains new materials addressing the impact on broadcasting of the economic and technical development of other technologies, such as cable television.

Overall, the past few years have given no indication that the importance of media law is likely to wane. If anything, the increase in litigation, both public and private, suggests that courts will be spending larger percentages of their time on these matters in the next few years.

MARC A. FRANKLIN

San Francisco, California
October, 1986

*

ACKNOWLEDGMENTS

Several students have helped produce this third edition. Karen Klein, J.D. '87, worked extensively on revising the material on broadcasting. Fred Cate, J.D. '87 and Stephanie Turpin, J.D. '88, provided general assistance. Debra Somberg, A.B. '87, played the major part in the production process, supported by Scott Martin, A.B. '87. Among teachers of media law, David A. Anderson, Peter Linzer, and Ellen Solender all used the second edition and provided candid and useful suggestions for revision. For the second time in as many editions, David Sobelsohn has proposed several extensive changes, some of which are reflected in this edition. Carroll Rudy, with support from Zelda McDonald, provided able secretarial assistance during this revision.

Most of the student assistance was supported by the Stanford Legal Research Fund, made possible by a bequest from the Estate of Ira S. Lillick and by gifts from Roderick E. and Carla A. Hills and other friends of the Stanford Law School.

Thanks are also due the authors and copyright holders who permitted excerpts from the following works to be included in this book:

Abrams, Floyd, "In Defense of Tornillo." Reprinted by permission of The Yale Law Journal Company and Fred B. Rothman & Company from *The Yale Law Journal*, Vol. 86, p. 361.

Abrams, Floyd, "The Press *Is* Different: Reflections On Justice Stewart and the Autonomous Press," Hofstra Law Review, Vol. 7, (1979).

Anderson, David A., "The Origins of the Press Clause," originally published in 30 UCLA L.Rev. 455, Copyright © 1983, The Regents of the University of California. All Rights Reserved.

Cendali, Dale, "Of Things to Come," Harvard Journal of Legislation, Vol. 22 (1985).

Chafee, Zechariah, Free Speech in the United States, Cambridge, Mass.: Harvard University Press, Copyright © 1941 by the President and Fellows of Harvard College, renewed 1969 by Zechariah Chafee III; reprinted by permission of the publishers.

Emerson, Thomas I., "The System of Freedom of Expression." Copyright © 1970 by Thomas I. Emerson. Reprinted by permission of Random House, Inc. and Thomas I. Emerson.

Ingber, Stanley, "Defamation: A Conflict Between Reason and Decency," Virginia Law Review, Vol. 65 (1979).

Jeffries, John, Jr., "Rethinking Prior Restraint." Reprinted by permission of The Yale Law Journal and Fred B. Rothman & Company from *The Yale Law Journal*, Vol. 92, pp. 422–33.

Lange, David, "The Speech and Press Clauses," originally published in 23 UCLA L.Rev. 77, Copyright © 1975, The Regents of the University of California. All Rights Reserved.

Levy, Leonard W., "Emergence of a Free Press." Copyright © 1985 by Leonard W. Levy. Reprinted by permission of Oxford University Press, Inc.

Nimmer, Melville B., "Introduction—Is Freedom of the Press a Redundancy: What Does It Add to Freedom of Speech?" Copyright © 1975 Hastings College of the Law, The Hastings Law Journal.

Paul, Dan, "Why a Shield Law?" University of Miami Law Review, Vol. 29 (1975).

Sowle, Kathryn D., "Defamation and the First Amendment: The Case for a Constitutional Privilege of Fair Report," New York University Law Review, Vol. 54 (1979).

Wellington, Harry, "Freedom of Expression." Reprinted by permission of The Yale Law Journal and Fred B. Rothman & Company from *The Yale Law Journal*, Vol. 88, pp. 1105–16.

SUMMARY OF CONTENTS

CHAPTER VII. PROTECTING COMMUNITY MORALS—OBSCENITY

CHAPTER VIII. PROTECTING THE MARKETPLACE

CHAPTER IX. PROTECTING THE RIGHT TO AN IMPARTIAL JURY

PART THREE. LIMITS ON GATHERING

CHAPTER X. WILLING PRIVATE SOURCES

CHAPTER XI. UNWILLING PRIVATE SOURCES

CHAPTER XII. ACCESS TO GOVERNMENT SOURCES

PART FOUR. BROADCASTING

CHAPTER XIII. INTRODUCTION TO BROADCASTING

CHAPTER XIV. JUSTIFICATIONS FOR GOVERNMENT REGULATION

CHAPTER XV. LEGAL CONTROL OF BROADCAST PROGRAMMING

CHAPTER XVI. BROADCAST LICENSING

CHAPTER XVII. CABLE TELEVISION AND NEW TECHNOLOGIES

*

TABLE OF CONTENTS

PART ONE. INTRODUCTION

CHAPTER I. THE DEVELOPMENT OF THE CONCEPT OF FREEDOM OF EXPRESSION

PART TWO. LIMITS ON PUBLISHING

CHAPTER II. PROTECTING REPUTATION—DEFAMATION

CHAPTER III. PROTECTING PRIVACY

CHAPTER IV. PROTECTING PHYSICAL AND EMOTIONAL SECURITY

CHAPTER V. PROTECTING CREATIVE ACTIVITY

CHAPTER VI. THE PRESS AND THE POLITICAL PROCESS

CHAPTER VII. PROTECTING COMMUNITY MORALS—OBSCENITY

CHAPTER VIII. PROTECTING THE MARKETPLACE

CHAPTER IX. PROTECTING THE RIGHT TO AN IMPARTIAL JURY

PART THREE. LIMITS ON GATHERING

CHAPTER X. WILLING PRIVATE SOURCES

CHAPTER XI. UNWILLING PRIVATE SOURCES

CHAPTER XII. ACCESS TO GOVERNMENT SOURCES

PART FOUR. BROADCASTING

CHAPTER XIII. INTRODUCTION TO BROADCASTING

CHAPTER XIV. JUSTIFICATIONS FOR GOVERNMENT REGULATION

CHAPTER XV. LEGAL CONTROL OF BROADCAST PROGRAMMING

CHAPTER XVI. BROADCAST LICENSING

CHAPTER XVII. CABLE TELEVISION AND NEW TECHNOLOGIES

*

TABLE OF CASES

The principal cases are in italic type. Cases cited or discussed are in roman type. References are to Pages.

*

CASES AND MATERIALS

ON

MASS MEDIA LAW

*

Part One

INTRODUCTION

Chapter I

THE DEVELOPMENT OF THE CONCEPT OF FREEDOM OF EXPRESSION

A. THE CONFLICT BETWEEN MEDIA AND GOVERNMENT

Until only a few decades ago, most litigants in First Amendment free expression cases were dissidents—anarchists or members of splinter political or small religious groups, or others not in the mainstream of American thinking. They were contending, in part, that the First Amendment must protect everyone, including the most divergent speakers, if it was to protect anyone. Although such persons still sue if they are prevented from expressing their views or are punished for doing so despite the First or Fourteenth Amendment, a new class of litigants has appeared—the journalists and their employers, the print and broadcast media.

Few would deny that the mass media are part of the fabric of the country; some might suggest they are part of the "establishment." That status has not kept the press from frequent confrontations with government officials whose actions affect the gathering, publishing, or disseminating of information, or with courts that hold the press liable for harm inflicted on private citizens.

Most of what we learn about government and public officials comes via the mass media. Each of us has limited time and mobility for gathering such information for ourselves. To a large extent, the media determine what issues the public focuses upon. The extent of the impact of the media on public opinion is not clear; it has been the subject of much research, yielding often inconclusive or contradictory results. Sometimes, however, the impact is obvious, as when President Richard Nixon resigned in the face of allegations of wrongdoing first brought to public attention by the press.

Significantly, public officials believe the mass media have great power and influence. They accuse the press of using that power to inhibit efforts by elected and appointed officials to carry out their duties. The press, on the other hand, complains that officials interfere with efforts to gather and publish news about government. Since, as we shall see, some persons believe that the First Amendment authorizes the press to be a watchdog over government, it is not surprising that much First Amendment litigation involves press attempts to play that role.

Not many years ago, tension did not exist. Reporters considered government officials their natural allies in helping to provide stories and leads—and vice-versa. Reporters did little investigating into government, or into much else, and they accepted press releases at face value. Beginning in the 1960s, several developments changed the relationship to one that most observers would now see as adversary. Among these were the realization of government dishonesty or deviousness in informing the public about the Vietnam war; practices of state and local public officials responding to civil rights activities in the South; the revelations about practices of J. Edgar Hoover and the FBI generally in dealing with a variety of political movements; events surrounding the 1968 Democratic convention in Chicago; the "dirty tricks" occurring during presidential campaigns; and, of course, Watergate itself.

At the same time, styles of reporting were changing. The reporter who regularly accepted government handouts was being replaced by a reporter interested in what has come to be called "investigative" reporting. This challenging, aggressive approach was bound to lead to conflict with government in ways that will be explored in the course of this book. The growing power of television during this period brought into the field new types of news gatherers who emphasized the more explicit and intrusive visual dimension.

Each of these influences fed on the others. As each government misdeed (or corporation misdeed, for that matter) was revealed, more and more reporters saw the value of investigative reporting. Even those who did not become true investigators refused to take government's word at face value any more. The end result is that the press and the government have been involved in an unprecedented series of legal confrontations since the early 1970s that are of great moment for the future of the country. To better understand how courts resolve these questions, we begin by considering the nature of freedom of expression.

B. INTRODUCTION TO FREE EXPRESSION VALUES

1. INTRODUCTION

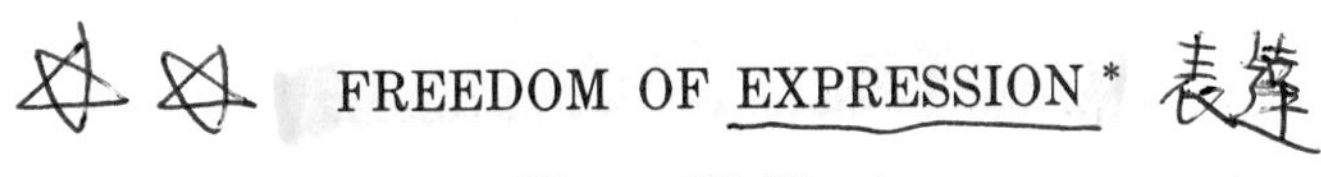

FREEDOM OF EXPRESSION *

Harry Wellington

88 Yale L.J. 1105, 1106–1110 (1979).

Intuition at first may suggest that an individual ought to have more freedom to speak than he has liberty in other areas. There would seem to be some truth in the adage, "sticks and stones can break my bones, but words will never hurt me." Yet speech often hurts. It can offend, injure reputation, fan prejudice or passion, and ignite the world. Moreover, a great deal of other conduct that the state regulates has less harmful potential. Victimless crimes and sexual relations between consenting adults have no direct effect on the public; much speech does. Indeed, some constitutionally valid regulation of innocent conduct may itself directly harm the public. Restrictions placed on the sale of eyeglasses, for example, can decrease the freedom of a class of vendors and increase the price of spectacles, while failing to afford protection to any group of purchasers. Moreover, the vendor forced out of business, the drug user, and the homosexual might happily exchange some free expression for other freedoms lost.

There are several well-known ways of separating expression from other freedoms—some more successful than others in establishing expression's relative immunity from regulation. Some appeal to the Constitution and particularly to the First Amendment; others do not.[7]

Consider the following from an interview between Edmond Cahn and Hugo L. Black. The speaker is the Justice:

> The beginning of the First Amendment is that "Congress shall make no law." I understand that it is rather old-fashioned and shows a slight naivete to say that "no law" means no law. It is one of the most amazing things about the ingeniousness of the times that strong arguments are made, which *almost* convince me, that it

* Text omissions are indicated by three dots. Omitted citations are indicated by [ ]. There is no indication when footnotes are omitted. When they do appear, footnotes are numbered as in the material quoted.—ed.

7. Compare C. Black, Structure and Relationship in Constitutional Law 39–45 (1969) (structure of Constitution requires uninhibited political expression) *and* A. Meiklejohn, Free Speech and Its Relation to Self-Government 27 (1948) (First Amendment "a deduction from the basic American agreement that public issues shall be decided by universal suffrage") *with* J.S. Mill, [On Liberty (R. McCallum, ed. 1946)] at 46 ("necessity to the mental well-being of mankind . . . of freedom of opinion, and freedom of the expression of opinion") *and* R. Wolff, The Poverty of Liberalism 3 (1968) (attempt at "analysis and clarification" of Mill's philosophy of free expression).

> is very foolish of me to think "no law" means no law. But what it *says* is "Congress shall make no law . . . ."[8]

And the Justice went on to say, "I believe [the Amendment] means what it says."[9]

In an earlier lecture, Black had maintained: "It is my belief that there *are* 'absolutes' in our Bill of Rights, and that they were put there on purpose by men who knew what words meant, and meant their prohibitions to be 'absolutes.' "[10] Yet historical research rejects absolutely the Justice's view of the founders' purpose. Nor can an appeal to the Amendment's language—"Congress shall make no law . . . abridging the freedom of speech"[12]—sustain the absolutist's position. Robert Bork is clearly correct when he insists that "[a]ny such reading is, of course, impossible. . . . Is Congress forbidden," he asks,

> to prohibit incitement to mutiny aboard a naval vessel engaged in action against an enemy, to prohibit shouted harangues from the visitors' gallery during its own deliberations or to provide any rules for decorum in federal courtrooms? Are the states forbidden, by the incorporation of the first amendment in the fourteenth, to punish the shouting of obscenities in the streets?[13]

One can back away from the extreme version of the absolutist's position without abandoning the claim that the language of the First Amendment elevates expression to a preferred freedom. Thus, for example, some of Bork's concerns were anticipated by Alexander Meiklejohn who insisted that the Amendment "does not forbid the abridging of *speech.* But . . . it does forbid the abridging of *the freedom of speech.*"[14] Meiklejohn argued that the phrase, "the freedom of speech" implies the existence of rules regarding procedure, order, forum, etc. He used the New England town meeting as his model: there could be no freedom of speech if everyone spoke at once. But any view relevant to the question before the meeting, no matter how unpopular, was protected by the strong language of the Amendment.

8. Justice Black and First Amendment "Absolutes": A Public Interview, 37 N.Y. U.L.Rev. 549, 553 (1962) (footnote omitted) [hereinafter cited as Public Interview].

9. Id. at 563. It should be noted that the Amendment refers only to Congress. If it means what it says (whatever that may mean) are we to assume that the Amendment does not bind the other branches of government? May the President abridge the freedom of speech by executive order? Justice Black would have been the first to say no.

10. Black, The Bill of Rights, 35 N.Y. U.L.Rev. 865, 867 (1960).

12. U.S. Const. Amend. I ("Congress shall make no law respecting an establishment of religion, or prohibiting the free exercise thereof; or abridging the freedom of speech, or of the press; or the right of the people peaceably to assemble, and to petition the Government for a redress of grievances.")

13. Bork, Neutral Principles and Some First Amendment Problems, 47 Ind.L.J. 1, 21 (1971).

14. *A. Meiklejohn,* supra note 7, at 19 (emphasis altered).

"The freedom of speech," of course, is not a self-defining phrase: what cannot be abridged is what is protected. Nor is the word "abridging" unambiguous. What is protected and how extensively it is protected must be determined through interpretive tools extrinsic to the language of the Amendment. As we shall see, Meiklejohn himself had a full kit of interpretive tools.

This much does seem clear. On the one hand, the language of the Amendment points to a special status for expression. It creates a stronger presumption against state regulation than weaker language would. To say "Congress shall make no *unreasonable* law . . . abridging the freedom of speech" adds an adjective that weakens a liberty.[17] On the other hand, the language does not tell a legislature or a court much. They must look elsewhere to determine the strength of the presumption.[18] And Justice Black knew this. Perhaps it explains his position:

> I have to be honest about it. I confess not only that I think the Amendment means what it says but also that I may be slightly influenced by the fact that I do not think Congress *should* make any law with respect to these subjects. That has become a rather bad confession to make in these days, the confession that one is actually for something because he believes in it.[19]

Moreover, it should be observed that total reliance on the language of the First Amendment in separating freedom of expression from less-protected freedoms not only fails in fact; it is inadequate in conception. For even if the language supported the conception, many would be left unsatisfied. The contemporary American lawyer has trouble resting his case exclusively on what was written almost two hundred years ago. Yet he knows that he has no case at all without legitimate authority. This is symptomatic of our constitutional law: the appeal to text is seen as important but generally in need of support; and satisfactory support is hard to find because it so frequently leads to indeterminate results. This is as true in the area of the freedom of speech as it is elsewhere.

We begin our search for support with English history. We then turn to philosophy and to American history and law.

17. See C. Black, The People and the Court 217–18 (1960) (absolute character of First Amendment's language creates presumption that any government regulation of expression is unconstitutional).

18. After looking, it may be that some will find justification for speaking in absolutes. Charles Black, for one, endorsed a variant of the absolutist position. See Black, *Mr. Justice Black, the Supreme Court, and the Bill of Rights,* Harper's, Feb. 1961, at 68 ("The 'absolutist' view, taken sensibly, would tend to carve out large areas of personal freedom to be enjoyed without regard to transient legislative views on the pressing necessity of shutting people up . . . .")

19. *Public Interview,* supra note 8, at 553.

2. THE ENGLISH BACKGROUND

EMERGENCE OF A FREE PRESS

Leonard W. Levy

5–13 (1985).

Just as many torts or private wrongs became crimes, or offenses against the king's peace, so too certain libels became the objects of criminal retribution. As early as 1275 Parliament outlawed "any slanderous News . . . or *false* News or Tales where by discord or occasion of discord or slander may grow between the King and his people or the great men of the Realm . . . " Parliament re-enacted the statute in 1379 for the prevention of the "subversion and destruction of the said realm" by means of false speech. The king's council, which later became the Court of Star Chamber, meted out punishment. These were the earliest statutes making dangerous utterances a crime, and together with the ecclesiastical laws against heresy, blasphemy, and other religious crimes intensified the long history of suppression of opinions deemed pernicious.

The invention of printing, of course, magnified the danger of such opinions. The Crown claimed an authority to control printing presses as a right of prerogative. Henry VIII took over a system for the censorship of heretical manuscripts, long established by the English church and approved by Parliament, and soon applied it to writings on any subject. The manuscript of any work intended for publication had to be submitted to royal officials empowered to censor objectionable passages and to approve or deny a license for the printing of the work. Anything published without an *imprimatur* was criminal. Under Elizabeth the government elaborated the system of prior restraints upon the press, dividing the administration of the complex licensing system among three Crown agencies: the Stationers' Company, a guild of master publishers chartered to monopolize the presses and vested with extraordinary powers of search and seizure; the Court of High Commission, the highest ecclesiastical tribunal, which controlled the Stationers' Company and did the actual licensing; and the Court of Star Chamber which issued decrees defining criminal matter and shared with the Court of High Commission jurisdiction over the trial of offenders. The agencies for enforcement changed during the Puritan Revolution, but the licensing system continued. Under the Restoration, the system was based principally on an act of Parliament, rather than royal prerogative; it continued until 1694.[7] But the expiration of the system at that time did not remotely mean that the press had become free. It remained subject to the restraints of the common law, so-called because

7. For an excellent discussion of the licensing system from its origins in England to its demise in 1694, see Frederick S. Siebert, *Freedom of the Press in England, 1476–1776* (Urbana, 1952), chaps. 2–3, 6–12.

it was the law shared in common throughout the realm to distinguish it from local law. The common law was a national or centralized body of non-statutory ("unwritten") and uncodified law devised mainly by the king's royal courts of record in London, especially the Court of Common Pleas (civil jurisdiction) and the Court of King's Bench (criminal jurisdiction), and applied in a supposedly uniform manner by royal judges who served everywhere in the realm.

One might publish without a license, but he did so at the peril of being punished for libel. The point of departure for the modern law of criminal libels was Sir Edward Coke's report of *De Libellis Famosis,* a Star Chamber case of 1606, in which the following propositions were stated. A libel against a private person might be punished criminally on the theory that it provokes revenge and therefore tends, however remotely, to a breach of the peace. But a libel against a government official comprises an even greater offense "for it concerns not only the breach of the peace, but also the scandal of government. . . . "[9] The medieval statutes fixed the falsity of the libel as the essence of the crime, but the Star Chamber ruled in 1606 that truth or falsity was not material, because a true statement that damages the reputation of the government or an official is the more dangerous to the public peace. The Star Chamber also ruled that the common law courts possessed concurrent jurisdiction over criminal libels. After Parliament abolished the Star Chamber in 1642, the common-law courts had exclusive jurisdiction and applied Star Chamber doctrines in libel prosecutions.

Four major classes of criminal libel emerged from subsequent decisions in the common-law courts. Blasphemous libel or defamation of religion, together with laws against heresy and the establishment of a state church, made freedom of religious expression a risk. The law of obscene libel protected public morality but crimped literary, artistic, and other forms of personal expression. The law of private libel protected individual reputations by making possible civil suits for damages; but the state could prosecute a gross private libel to prevent supposed bad tendencies toward breach of the peace. The use of the criminal law to avenge the defamation of a person made the libel, in such a case, to be known as a "criminal libel," although the same term referred collectively to four classes of libel. Thus criminal libel was a redundant subcategory of the broad offense of criminal libel.

By far the most repressive class of libel was seditious libel. It can be defined in a quite elaborate and technical manner in order to take into account the malicious or criminal intent of the accused, the bad tendency of his remarks, and their truth or falsity. But the crime has never been satisfactorily or consistently defined, the necessary result of its inherent vagueness. Seditious libel has always been an accordion-like concept, expandable or contractible at the whim of judges. Judged by actual prosecutions, the crime consisted of defaming or condemning or ridiculing the government: its form, constitution, officers, laws,

9. *De Libellis Famosis,* 3 Coke's *Reports* 254 (1606). . . .

conduct, or policies, to the jeopardy of the public peace. In effect, any malicious criticism about the government that could be construed to have the bad tendency of lowering it in the public's esteem, holding it up to contempt or hatred, or of disturbing the peace was seditious libel, exposing the speaker or writer to criminal prosecution. Words damaging to the government that tended, however remotely, to cause a breach of the peace, constituted seditious libel according to the courts, but such reasoning explained nothing because *every* crime theoretically breached the king's peace. Criticism of the government that went too far, not the tendency of the words to breach the peace, distinguished the crime of seditious libel, although loose judicial language sometimes suggested otherwise. Loose language invariably characterized the crime, because the government always alleged that the defendant spoke or wrote maliciously, falsely, scandalously, scurrilously, and seditiously, or some combination thereof.

. . .

The fact that seditious libel was a crime did not make criticism of the government illegal or even risky. By the early eighteenth century, partisanship and polemics characterized the English press. The press teemed with seditious libels, according to judicial standards, but suffered little from prosecutions. As a matter of practice it was remarkably free and unrestrained; prosecutions tended to be selective and exemplary. Judicial standards probably did not coincide with popular ones; juries sometimes rebelled against judicial instructions, refusing to return verdicts of guilty. Moreover, libelous writers frequently had the protection of powerful factional leaders.

Chief Justice John Holt in Tuchin's case (1704) explained the rationale underlying the concept of seditious libel: "a reflection on the government" must be punished because, "If people should not be called to account for possessing the people with an ill opinion of the government, no government can subsist. For it is very necessary for all governments that the people should have a good opinion of it. And nothing can be worse to any government than to endeavour to procure animosities as to the management of it; this has always been looked upon as a crime, and no government can be safe without it." [13]

. . . Treason as a purely verbal crime, unconnected with some overt act beyond the words themselves, died out after the execution of John Matthews in 1720, convicted under a special statute rather than at common law. Utterances once held to be treasonable became wholly assimilated within the concept of seditious libel. As a lesser crime or misdemeanor, seditious libel merited less severe punishment: imprisonment, fines, the pillory, and whipping.

13. *Rex v. Tuchin,* in Thomas Bayly Howell, comp., *A Complete Collection of State Trials to 1783,* continued by T. J. Howell to 1820 (London, 1816–28, 34 vols.), 14:1095, 1128 (1704), quoted in Stephen, *History of the Criminal Law in England,* 2:318.

But prosecution for seditious libel became the government's principal instrument for controlling the press. According to Frederick S. Siebert's excellent study of freedom of the press in England, "convictions for seditious libel ran into the hundreds" in both the seventeenth and eighteenth centuries. That probably exaggerated the number of eighteenth-century convictions for seditious libel. Of the period 1700–1730, Siebert said, "Only occasionally was it necessary for the government to crack the whip of seditious libel to remind printers and publishers of their proper function." Of the period 1730–60, he said, it "witnessed the beginning of the revolt of juries and the failure of prosecutions. . . . " A conviction in 1754 he described as "the first to be obtained from a London jury in twenty-seven years." A wide disparity existed between the number of informations filed for seditious libel and the actual number of prosecutions; there was also a disparity between the number of prosecutions and the actual number of convictions. The number of informations undoubtedly "ran into the hundreds." Being arrested, called into court, and forced to pay costs on the dismissal of the information could have an intimidating effect even if the prosecution proceeded no further. In other words, trials, let alone convictions, were not necessary for the law of seditious libel to operate oppressively. One prosecutorial trick was to charge a person with seditious libel, persuade him to leave the country in order to avoid trial, and then outlaw him if he left, thereby preventing his return.

The procedure in prosecuting a seditious libel was extremely objectionable to libertarian theorists, more so than the fact that the accused could be punished for words alone. From 1662 until a century later the secretary of state possessed the power of ferreting out seditious libels by issuing warrants that authorized a search of the homes and offices of all suspects and the arrest of anyone on the mere suspicion of being implicated in the writing, publishing, or circulation of such libels. General warrants, the use of which was severely restricted in felony cases, were employed promiscuously in cases of seditious libel, a misdemeanor. Search, seizure, and arrest were used to harass anti-administration writers and editors against whom the evidence might not warrant a trial. But the government did not remain restricted to trying only those indicted or presented by a grand jury. Alternatively, the attorney-general might proceed against all misdemeanors by an information, that is, by determining the libelous character of a publication, bringing it to the attention of the Court of the King's Bench, and securing a warrant for the arrest and trial of the offender. Prosecuting by information rather than by indictment bypassed the Englishman's beloved institution, the grand jury, which in felony cases stood between him and the government.

At the trial of a seditious libel, the defendant was not even judged by his peers in any meaningful way. Despite the ambiguity of earlier practice, judges in the eighteenth century permitted juries to decide only the fact of the publication. That is, the only question that the jury passed upon was whether the defendant did or did not publish the

remarks charged against him and whether they carried the innuendo as alleged. The judges reserved exclusively for themselves as a matter of law the decision on the crucial question whether the defendant's remarks were seditious because maliciously intended and of a bad tendency. . . .

The judges also refused to permit the defendant to plead the truth as a defense. Indeed, they proceeded on the theory that the truth of a libel made it even worse because it was more provocative, thereby increasing the tendency to breach of the peace or exacerbating the scandal against the government. As a result of these rules applicable to criminal or crown libels, a man might be arrested on a general warrant, prosecuted on an information without the consent of a grand jury, and convicted for his political opinions by judges appointed by the government he had aspersed.

Thus the disappearance of the prior restraints that had been imposed by the licensing system until 1694 did not meaningfully free the press. Theoretically one might say or print what he pleased, but he was responsible to the common law for allegedly malicious, scurrilous, scandalous, or derogatory utterances which supposedly tended towards the contempt, ridicule, hatred, scorn, or disrepute of other persons, religion, government, or morality. Blackstone, the oracle of the common law in the minds of the American Framers, summarized the law of Crown libels as follows:

> Where blasphemous, immoral, treasonable, schismatical, seditious, or scandalous libels are punished by the English law . . . the liberty of the press, properly understood, is by no means infringed or violated. The *liberty of the press* is indeed essential to the nature of a free state; but this consists in laying no *previous* restraints upon publications, and not in freedom from censure for criminal matter when published. Every freeman has an undoubted right to lay what sentiments he pleases before the public: to forbid this is to destroy the freedom of the press: but if he publishes what is improper, mischievous, or illegal, he must take the consequences of his own temerity. . . . But to punish (as the law does at present) any dangerous or offensive writings, which, when published, shall on a fair and impartial trial[23] be adjudged of a pernicious tendency, is necessary for the preservation of peace and good order, a government and religion, the only solid foundations of civil liberty. Thus the will of individuals is still left free; the abuse only of that free-will is the object of legal punishment. Neither is any restraint hereby laid upon freedom of thought or enquiry: liberty of private sentiment is still left; the disseminat-

23. Blackstone's endorsement of a "fair and impartial" trial was meaningless to the libertarians of the time, since he explicitly repudiated one of their two major gauges of fairness, the right of the defendant to prove the truth of his alleged libel; moreover, Blackstone ignored the other libertarian gauge of fairness at a time when it was the principal issue of contention: the right of the jury rather than of the judge to decide the criminality of the alleged libel.

> ing, or making public, of bad sentiments, destructive of the ends of society, is the crime which society corrects.[24]

Samuel Johnson believed the law too liberal. "It seems not more reasonable," he complained, "to leave the right of printing unrestrained, because writers may be afterwards restrained, than it would be to sleep with doors unbolted, because by our laws, we can hang a thief."

The common law's definition of freedom of the press meant merely the absence of censorship in advance of publication. But the presence of punishment afterwards, for "bad sentiments," oral or published, had an effect similar to a law authorizing previous restraints. A man who may be whipped and jailed for what he says or prints is not likely to feel free to express his opinions even if he does not need a government license to do so. The common-law definition of freedom of the press left the press at the mercy of the Crown's prosecutors and judges. Freedom of discussion and the law of libel simply conflicted; the first could not conceptually coexist with the second.

---

3. Bases for Freedom of Expression

---

a. *Individual Fulfillment*

In The System of Freedom of Expression (1970), Professor Thomas Emerson advanced a cluster of four basic premises upon which freedom of expression rests in a democratic society. The first is framed in terms of the individual:

> First, freedom of expression is essential as a means of assuring individual self-fulfillment. The proper end of man is the realization of his character and potentialities as a human being. For the achievement of this self-realization the mind must be free. Hence suppression of belief, opinion, or other expression is an affront to the dignity of man, a negation of man's essential nature. Moreover, man in his capacity as a member of society has a right to share in the common decisions that affect him. To cut off his search for truth, or his expression of it, is to elevate society and the state to a despotic command over him and to place him under the arbitrary control of others.

We return to Emerson's three other premises shortly. Emerson also observed that his premises yielded two "basic implications," the first of which is relevant here:

24. Sir William Blackstone, *Commentaries on the Laws of England* (London, 1765–69), book 4, chap. II, 151–152. . . .

> [I]t is not a general measure of the individual's right to freedom of expression that any particular exercise of that right may be thought to promote or retard other goals of the society. The theory asserts that freedom of expression, while not the sole or sufficient end of society, is a good in itself, or at least an essential element in a good society. The society may seek to achieve other or more inclusive ends—such as virtue, justice, equality, or the maximum realization of the potentialities of its members. These are not necessarily gained by accepting the rules for freedom of expression. But, as a general proposition, the society may not seek them by suppressing the beliefs or opinions of individual members. To achieve these other goals it must rely upon other methods: the use of counter-expression and the regulation or control of conduct which is not expression. Hence the right to control individual expression, on the ground that it is judged to promote good or evil, justice or injustice, equality or inequality, is not, speaking generally, within the competence of the good society.

Professor C. Edwin Baker believes individual self-fulfillment, which he calls a "liberty model," is "the most coherent theory of the first amendment":

> The liberty model holds that the free speech clause protects not a marketplace but rather an arena of individual liberty from certain types of governmental restrictions. Speech is protected not as a means to a collective good but because of the value of speech conduct to the individual. The liberty theory justifies protection because of the way the protected conduct fosters individual self-realization and self-determination without improperly interfering with the legitimate claims of others.

Baker, Scope of the First Amendment Freedom of Speech, 25 UCLA L.Rev. 964, 966 (1978).

In Baker's view, speech may aid in self-fulfillment in ways that are often not recognized:

> To engage voluntarily in a speech act is to engage in self-definition or expression. A Vietnam war protestor may explain that when she chants "Stop This War Now" at a demonstration, she does so without any expectation that her speech will affect the continuance of war or even that it will communicate anything to people in power; rather, she participates and chants in order to *define* herself publicly in opposition to the war. This war protestor provides a dramatic illustration of the importance of this self-expressive use of speech, independent of any effective communication to others, for self-fulfillment or self-realization. (p. 994).

Elsewhere, Baker observes that "Speech is not merely communicative but also creative." Here he discusses uses of speech for such things as coining new words, writing a poem, writing rules for a game, and teaching or developing new capabilities in another. "The creative aspect, the new aspect of the world which results, varies in these examples. But in each case either the speaker or the listener or both possess something new—new images, new capacities, new opportunities, new amusements—which did not exist before and which were created by people's speech activity." (pp. 994–95).

See also L. Tribe, American Constitutional Law 576 (1978) (freedom of speech is "in part . . . an end in itself, an expression of the sort of society we wish to become and the sort of persons we wish to be").

Some have been skeptical of self-fulfillment arguments, in part because they are potentially applicable, as Baker and others recognize, to "actions" as well as "words." These problems are discussed in Schauer, Must Speech Be Special? 78 Nw.U.L.Rev. 1284 (1983).

Most of the justifications for freedom of expression have emphasized the social aspects of expression and the importance to society of maintaining a structure of free expression. Professor Emerson's last three premises share this focus.

THE SYSTEM OF FREEDOM OF EXPRESSION

Thomas I. Emerson

6–8 (1970).

Second, freedom of expression is an essential process for advancing knowledge and discovering truth. An individual who seeks knowledge and truth must hear all sides of the question, consider all alternatives, test his judgment by exposing it to opposition, and make full use of different minds. Discussion must be kept open no matter how certainly true an accepted opinion may seem to be; many of the most widely acknowledged truths have turned out to be erroneous. Conversely, the same principle applies no matter how false or pernicious the new opinion appears to be; for the unaccepted opinion may be true or partially true and, even if wholly false, its presentation and open discussion compel a rethinking and retesting of the accepted opinion. The reasons which make open discussion essential for an intelligent individual judgment likewise make it imperative for rational social judgment.

Third, freedom of expression is essential to provide for participation in decision making by all members of society. This is particularly significant for political decisions. Once one accepts the premise of the Declaration of Independence—that governments "derive their just powers from the consent of the governed"—it follows that the governed must, in order to exercise their right of consent, have full freedom of expression both in forming individual judgments and in forming the common judgment. The principle also carries beyond the political realm. It embraces the right to participate in the building of the whole culture, and includes freedom of expression in religion, literature, art, science, and all areas of human learning and knowledge.

Finally, freedom of expression is a method of achieving a more adaptable and hence a more stable community, of maintaining the precarious balance between healthy cleavage and necessary consensus. This follows because suppression of discussion makes a rational judgment impossible, substituting force for reason; because suppression promotes inflexibility and stultification, preventing society from adjusting to changing circumstances or developing new ideas; and because suppression conceals the real problems confronting a society, diverting public attention from the critical issues. At the same time the process of open discussion promotes greater cohesion in a society because people are more ready to accept decisions that go against them if they have a part in the decision-making process. Moreover, the state at all times retains adequate powers to promote unity and to suppress resort to force. Freedom of expression thus provides a framework in which the conflict necessary to the progress of a society can take place without destroying the society. It is an essential mechanism for maintaining the balance between stability and change.

The validity of the foregoing premises has never been proved or disproved, and probably could not be. Nevertheless our society is based upon the faith that they hold true and, in maintaining a system of freedom of expression, we act upon that faith. . . .

. . .

The second implication, in a sense a corollary of the first, is that the theory rests upon a fundamental distinction between belief, opinion, and communication of ideas on the one hand, and different forms of conduct on the other. For shorthand purposes we refer to this distinction hereafter as one between "expression" and "action." As just observed, in order to achieve its desired goals, a society or the state is entitled to exercise control over action—whether by prohibiting or compelling it—on an entirely different and vastly more extensive basis. But expression occupies an especially protected position. In this sector of human conduct, the social right of suppression or compulsion is at its lowest point, in most respects nonexistent. A majority of one has the right to control action, but a minority of one has the right to talk.

This marking off of the special status of expression is a crucial ingredient of the basic theory for several reasons. In the first place, thought and communication are the fountainhead of all expression of the individual personality. To cut off the flow at the source is to dry up the whole stream. Freedom at this point is essential to all other freedoms. Hence society must withhold its right of suppression until the stage of action is reached. Secondly, expression is normally conceived as doing less injury to other social goals than action. It generally has less immediate consequences, is less irremediable in its impact. Thirdly, the power of society and the state over the individual is so pervasive, and construction of doctrines, institutions, and administrative practices to limit this power so difficult, that only by drawing such a protective line between expression and action is it possible to strike a safe balance between authority and freedom.

---

b. Marketplace of Ideas

The first glimmers of the view that freedom of expression enhances the social good came in John Milton's Areopagitica in 1644. Milton, the English poet and essayist, wanted a divorce and wrote an essay he hoped would lower the strict legal obstacles in his path. He was chastised for publishing without a license, and wrote Areopagitica to induce Parliament to allow unlicensed printing. Milton argued that licensing was unworkable and an affront to those who had views to express. Moreover, he said, it was harmful to society, since people are better able to function as citizens if they are knowledgeable and exposed to different points of view. Attempting to assuage official fears that the Crown's views would be overwhelmed if unlicensed printing were allowed, Milton wrote: "And though all the winds of doctrine were let loose to play upon the earth, so Truth be in the field, we do injuriously by licensing and prohibiting to misdoubt her strength. Let her and Falsehood grapple; who ever knew Truth put to the worse, in a free and open encounter?"

Milton, however, was not ready to give freedom of expression to everyone on every subject. As a Puritan, he would not allow free discussion of Catholicism or atheism. In the context of his time, though, Milton's view was a major attack on the stringent censorship that prevailed.

Perhaps Milton's most enduring contribution to the philosophy of freedom of expression was his statement that unrestricted debate would lead to the discovery of truth. Writing in England some 50 years later, John Locke retained some of this faith that truth would prevail. In "A Letter Concerning Toleration" (1689), he wrote:

> [T]ruth certainly would do well enough if she were once left to shift for herself. She seldom has received, and I fear never will receive, much assistance from the power of great men, to whom she is but rarely known and more rarely welcome. She is not taught by laws, nor has she any need of force to procure her entrance into the minds of men. Errors indeed prevail by the assistance of foreign and borrowed succors. But if truth makes not her way into the understanding by her own light, she will be but the weaker for any borrowed force violence can add to her.

Like Milton, Locke opposed prior restraints, and in 1694 he joined the opposition that finally obtained the abolition of the Licensing Order. Yet, also like Milton, Locke did not question the common law punishment for expression after publication, and advocated the suppression of "opinions contrary to human society or to those moral rules which are necessary to the preservation of civil society."

By 1776, the pendulum had swung still further away from government restriction of expression, on both sides of the Atlantic. In England Jeremy Bentham in his "Fragment on Government" was waging war against Blackstone. He wrote that one of the differences between a free and a despotic government was "the security with which malcontents may communicate their sentiments, concert their plans, and practise every mode of opposition short of actual revolt, before the executive power can be legally justified in disturbing them."

We can trace the regard for freedom of expression and skepticism about the wisdom of an absolute authority, be it church or state, back to Milton and perhaps earlier, but we must not ignore a concurrent strand of English thinking that condemned individual freedom and advocated an all-powerful authority that would wisely govern all civil affairs. This was represented in the mid-17th century by Thomas Hobbes, who, while Milton was squirming under the constraints of the Licensing Order, advocated in The Leviathan that a wise and absolute sovereign was essential: ". . . it is manifest that during the time men live without a common power to keep them all in awe, they are in that condition which is called war; and such a war as is of every man against every man." In the absence of such a power, there is no industry, no art, no knowledge; only fear, "and the life of man, solitary, poor, nasty, brutish and short."

Hobbes's major influence was felt on the continent, beginning a century later in the writing of Jean-Jacques Rousseau. Until Rousseau, individual freedom had been defined in terms of the absence of institutional restraint: "freedom from" externally imposed controls. Rousseau emphasized that freedom is not solely the lack of coercion; in fact, coercion may be required by the morality of the general will, freedom is positive and must be "freedom for" something.

The views of Hobbes and Rousseau remained conspicuous on the continent, while those of Milton and Locke and their adherents became part of the heritage of England that crossed the Atlantic Ocean.

English philosopher and economist John Stuart Mill, who wrote 200 years after Milton, believed in broader freedom of discussion than did Milton. Mill thought that society could function well only with such freedom. He saw freedom of thought, discussion, and investigation as "goods in their own right"; more importantly, though, society benefits from an exchange of ideas. People could replace their false notions with true ones, but only if they had access to true ones. Such open discussion would necessarily mean that false as well as true ideas would be expressed.

Mill, in On Liberty, contended that government could not "prescribe opinions" or "determine what doctrines or what arguments" people should hear. Not even if the government and the populace were at one on an issue should coercion regarding freedom of expression be allowed:

> The power itself is illegitimate. The best government has no more title to it than the worst. It is as noxious, or more noxious, when exerted in accordance with public opinion, than when in opposition to it. If all mankind minus one were of one opinion, and only one person were of the contrary opinion, mankind would be no more justified in silencing that one person, than he, if he had the power, would be justified in silencing mankind. . . . [T]he peculiar evil of silencing the expression of an opinion is, that it is robbing the human race: posterity as well as the existing generation; those who dissent from the opinion, still more than those who hold it. If the opinion is right, they are deprived of the opportunity of exchanging error for truth; if wrong, they lose what is almost as great a benefit, the clearer perception and livelier impression of truth, produced by its collision with error.
>
> . . .
>
> [T]he dictum that truth always triumphs over persecution is one of those pleasant falsehoods which men repeat after one another till they pass into common-places, but which all experience refutes. History teems with instances of truth put down by persecution. If not suppressed forever, it may be thrown back for centuries. . . . It is a piece of idle sentimentality that truth, merely as truth, has any inherent power denied to error of prevailing against the dungeon and the stake.

The marketplace of ideas, first envisioned by Milton and later developed by Mill, was recognized by Justice Holmes in Abrams v. United States, 250 U.S. 616 (1919). Abrams and others were accused of publishing pamphlets that criticized President Wilson's sending of troops to help counter the Russian revolution. The pamphlets also advocated a strike against munitions plants. A majority of the Supreme Court ruled that publishing such pamphlets during wartime was not protected by the First Amendment. In dissent, Justice Holmes, joined by Justice Brandeis, argued that the pamphlets did not attack the form of the United States government, and thus did not violate the sedition statute as charged. More generally, Holmes wrote:

> Persecution for the expression of opinions seems to me perfectly logical. If you have no doubt of your premises or your power and want a certain result with all your heart you naturally express your wishes in law and sweep away all opposition. To allow opposition by speech seems to indicate that you think the speech impotent, as when a man says that he has squared the circle, or that you do not care whole-heartedly for the result, or that you doubt either your power or your premises. But when men have realized that time has upset many fighting faiths, they may come to believe even more than they believe the very foundations of their own conduct that the ultimate good desired is better reached

by free trade in ideas—that the best test of truth is the power of the thought to get itself accepted in the competition of the market, and that truth is the only ground upon which their wishes safely can be carried out. That at any rate is the theory of our Constitution. It is an experiment, as all life is an experiment.

A similar sentiment was voiced by Judge Learned Hand in an antitrust case brought against the Associated Press. He observed that one of the most "vital of all general interests" was "the dissemination of news from as many different sources, and with as many different facets and colors as is possible. That interest is closely akin to, if indeed it is not the same as, the interest protected by the First Amendment; it presupposes that right conclusions are more likely to be gathered out of a multitude of tongues, than through any kind of authoritative selection. To many this is, and always will be, folly; but we have staked upon it our all." United States v. Associated Press, 52 F.Supp. 362 (S.D.N.Y.1943), affirmed 326 U.S. 1 (1944).

For an illuminating insight into the views of the First Amendment held by Justice Holmes, Judge Learned Hand, and Zechariah Chafee, see Gunther, Learned Hand and the Origins of Modern First Amendment Doctrine: Some Fragments of History, 27 Stan.L.Rev. 719 (1975).

The marketplace of ideas approach has been criticized from several sides as being based on inaccurate assumptions or having failed in its purpose. Other critics took quite a different approach. In the mid-1940s, the Commission on Freedom of the Press was organized to study the press in America. Funded primarily by Time, Inc., and Encyclopedia Britannica, Inc., and chaired by Robert M. Hutchins, the commission was composed of philosophers, historians, law professors, and others. No media professionals were included on the panel, but some were called to share their views with commission members. The commission concluded that press freedom was not seriously threatened in mid-20th century America, but that the press, despite the enforcement of antitrust laws, had become increasingly concentrated in the hands of fewer individuals. Media owners, in fact, were reasonably free from government interference, but the First Amendment had little direct application to most people.

The commission argued that publishers and broadcasters should be more socially responsible, treating each media outlet not as a personal soapbox, but as a means of disseminating a wide range of viewpoints. It suggested that the government finance new communications outlets and that an independent government agency oversee the press's performance. A Free and Responsible Press (1947).

Professor William Ernest Hocking, a philosopher and member of the commission, expanded on the group's work. He noted that protecting the press when it is composed of many units protects the consumer, who will have access to a wide range of offerings. But when the number of units shrinks, the consumer is helpless under traditional views of the First Amendment.

Hocking believed the public had a "right" as well as a need to have its news. Particularly since "the citizen's *political* duty is at stake, the right to have an adequate service of news becomes a *public responsibility* as well." The press thus becomes "clothed with a public interest" and must therefore be "adequate"—a term Hocking acknowledged to be "an indefinite standard." Adequacy, however, does imply giving the public a breadth of news coverage and viewpoints.

To accomplish this, Hocking suggested comparing the press with privately owned public utilities or private schools, which must meet certain government-established standards. Although the government should not intrude on press activities, it should "regulate the conditions under which those activities take place, so that the public interest is better served." He defined this to mean the "best service to the most people," to be accomplished by a "continuous survey of press performance" by an independent agency, with the government supplementing the private press by issuing information on its own. W. Hocking, Freedom of the Press 161–90 (1947).

Another commission member, Professor Chafee, stated that the press could not play its proper part in society in the "mere absence of governmental restrictions." Rather, "affirmative action by the government or others" would be needed. Chafee started with Justice Holmes's formulation: the "best test of truth is the power of the thought to get itself accepted in the competition of the market." But how, Chafee asked, could views compete in a market constricted by a lack of media outlets? He answered that "a free market requires regulation, just as a free market for goods needs law against monopoly. . . . The government can lay down the rules of the game which will promote rather than restrict free speech." Such laws might require "essential facilities accessible to all," methods to assure that communication channels remain open, and measures directed at particular communication industries "intended to promote freedom, improve content, or otherwise make them perform their proper function in a free society." Z. Chafee, 2 Government and Mass Communications 471 (1947).

More recently, Professor Jerome A. Barron adopted the same approach. He believes the marketplace is an antiquated concept because the media and society have changed so much since 1791. It is difficult for a person to begin a newspaper because of the prohibitive cost or to begin a broadcast service because of limits in spectrum allocation. Barron finds media the censors because they limit the views they disseminate and permit few new or unpopular ideas to be heard widely. Barron concluded that those who do not control media should be able to express their views through the mass media. "At the very minimum," Barron wrote, "the creation of two remedies is essential—(1) a nondiscriminating right to purchase editorial advertisements in daily newspapers, and (2) a right of reply for public figures and public officers defamed in newspapers." J. Barron, Freedom of the

Press for Whom? 6 (1973). See also, Barron, Access to the Press—A New First Amendment Right, 80 Harv.L.Rev. 1641 (1967).

The marketplace concept, as developed by Milton, Mill, and Holmes, holds that "truth" is most likely to emerge from competition with falsehood, and that the society will discover and accept the one over the other. Is "truth" so "objective" that it can be "discovered"? Are people sufficiently rational to select "truth" instead of falsehood? Is "truth" the same for all people regardless of their social, economic, geographical, or ethnic differences? The approach is criticized on these grounds in Baker, Scope of the First Amendment Freedom of Speech, 25 UCLA L.Rev. 964, 967–81 (1978) ("The assumptions on which the classic marketplace of ideas theory rests are almost universally rejected today.")

c. *Safety Valve*

Another of Professor Emerson's bases for freedom of expression was that it fosters stability and orderly change in society. For him, freedom of expression serves as a safety valve, allowing opposing views to be heard, some of which may be accepted by the majority. Justice Brandeis articulated this basis—and others—years ago, concurring in Whitney v. California, 274 U.S. 357, 375–77 (1927):

> Those who won our independence believed that the final end of the State was to make men free to develop their faculties; and that in its government the deliberative forces should prevail over the arbitrary. They valued liberty both as an end and as a means. They believed liberty to be the secret of happiness and courage to be the secret of liberty. They believed that freedom to think as you will and speak as you think are means indispensable to the discovery and spread of political truth; that without free speech and assembly discussion would be futile; that with them, discussion affords ordinarily adequate protection against the dissemination of noxious doctrine; that the greatest menace to freedom is an inert people; that public discussion is a political duty; and that this should be a fundamental principle of the American government. They recognized the risks to which all human institutions are subject. But they knew that order cannot be secured merely through fear of punishment for its infraction; that it is hazardous to discourage thought, hope and imagination; that fear breeds repression; that repression breeds hate; that hate menaces stable government; that the path of safety lies in the opportunity to discuss freely supposed grievances and proposed remedies; and that the fitting remedy for evil counsels is good ones. Believing in the power of reason as applied through public discussion, they eschewed silence coerced by law—the argument of force in its worst form. Recognizing the occasional tyrannies of governing majori-

ties, they amended the Constitution so that free speech and assembly should be guaranteed.

---

d. Self-Governance

FREEDOM OF EXPRESSION

Harry Wellington

88 Yale L.J. 1105, 1110–1116 (1979).

After [John Stuart] Mill, Alexander Meiklejohn may be the foremost philosopher of free expression. Unlike Mill, he addressed expression in the context of the American Constitution and was careful to distinguish between the protection that speech is afforded under the First Amendment and that which speech, as well as other conduct, receives under the due process clause of the Fifth.[23] The structure of American democracy in particular, and "the necessities of self-government by universal suffrage" in general, define the scope of the First Amendment. Its guarantee "is assured only to speech which bears, directly or indirectly, upon issues with which voters have to deal—only, therefore, to the consideration of matters of public interest." Other conduct, including speech that fails of Meiklejohn's definition, is protected by the substantially less rigorous requirement of the Fifth Amendment.

> Private speech, or private interest in speech . . . has no claim whatever to the protection of the First Amendment. If men are engaged, as we so commonly are, in argument, or inquiry, or advocacy, or incitement which is directed toward our private interests, private privileges, private possessions, we are, of course, entitled to "due process" protection of those activities.

One can take Meiklejohn to mean that private speech is protected in the same limited way by due process as is the vendor of eyeglasses or the user of drugs. The First Amendment, he says, "has no concern over such protection. That pronouncement remains forever confused and unintelligible unless we draw sharply and clearly the line which separates the public welfare of the community from the private goods of any individual citizen or group of citizens." [27]

23. A. Meiklejohn, Free Speech and Its Relation to Self-Government 27, at 37–39. In the case of the states, Meiklejohn drew a distinction between the First Amendment and the Fourteenth. Id. at 59.

27. [A. Meiklejohn at 94]. Although Meiklejohn, at least in his early work, did not designate specific categories of "public" and "private" expression, he did undertake to elaborate the conceptual basis of the distinction:

> On the one hand, each of us, as a citizen, has a part to play in the governing of the nation. In that capacity, we think and speak and plan and act for the general good. On the other hand, each of us, as an individual or as a member of some private group, is rightly pursuing his

What a wonderful faith Meiklejohn must have had in human abilities if he believed that any person could draw the public-private line sharply and clearly. And he was truly innocent if he thought that anyone's line was not determined in large part by the outcome desired rather than the other way around. "Private" and "public" are like blocks of clay that can be shaped as the potter desires. Thus, Meiklejohn himself was to find "novels and dramas and paintings and poems," [30] within "the freedom of speech," within "public speech," within "speech which bears . . . upon issues with which voters have to deal." [31] And he stated clearly that the First Amendment protected "novels which portray sexual experiences with a frankness that, to the prevailing conventions of our society, seems 'obscene.'" [32]

3.

Both Alexander Bickel and Robert Bork have acknowledged in their writings a debt to Meiklejohn. Bickel put it this way (and his reading of Bork seems correct):

> The social interest that the First Amendment vindicates is . . . , as Alexander Meiklejohn and Robert Bork have emphasized, the interest in the successful operation of the political process, so that the country may be better able to adopt the course of action that conforms to the wishes of the greatest number, whether or not it is wise or is founded in truth.[33]

Yet, in Meiklejohn's terms, Bickel drew the public-private line to exclude the obscene from "the freedom of speech," [34] and Bork's line banishes most *belles-lettres,* obscene or not.[35] Nor did either draw his line in a way that is inconsistent with Meiklejohn's main contention: Bickel and Bork disagree with their predecessor (and with each other) on what it takes to operate the political process successfully, including what a responsible voter needs to know. They do not disagree with Meiklejohn on the justification for the special place accorded freedom of expression in the American constitutional system. They also disagree—although this may just reflect their more fundamental differences—on the status given to expression by the language of the Amendment: Meiklejohn takes the linguistic formulation—the presumption it may be thought—to create—seriously; Bickel and Bork do not. But the

> own advantage, is seeking his own welfare. . . . [Each man's] private rights, including the right of "private" speech, are liable to such abridgments as the general welfare may require.

Id. at 95. Under this conceptual scheme, Meiklejohn asserted that both academic scholarship, see id. at 100, and broadcasting, see id. at 104, constitute "private" expression. But see p. 1112 infra (Meiklejohn's revised views).

30. Meiklejohn, The First Amendment is an Absolute, 1961 Sup.Ct.Rev. 245, 263.

31. *A. Meiklejohn,* supra note [23], at 93–94.

32. *Meiklejohn,* supra note 30, at 262.

33. A. Bickel, The Morality of Consent 62 (1975) (footnotes omitted).

34. Id. at 73–76.

35. *Bork,* supra note 13, at 27 ("If the dialectical progression is not to become an analogical stampede, the protection of the first amendment must be cut off when it reaches the outer limits of political speech.")

disagreement over the requirements of the political process is vastly more important. It has both empirical and normative dimensions. All three theorists make different assumptions about how legal rules affect human behavior, and these assumptions are influenced by each scholar's conception of American democracy. We know this in part because they tell us and in part because we know that there is so little information about the consequences of the legal rules with which we are concerned.

4.

If the "social interest that the First Amendment vindicates is . . . the interest in the successful operation of the political process," [40] a legal rule affecting expression might well be tested by asking the question: what are its consequences for the political process? For example, assume that there is no line of cases beginning with *New York Times Co. v. Sullivan,*[41] and that a state has a statute declaring it a tort for newspapers negligently to publish false information that injures the reputation of a candidate for political office. A newspaper publishes a story about a candidate for governor that asserts that he took a bribe when he was a congressman. After losing the election by less than a percentage point, the candidate sues. A jury determines that the story is false, that the newspaper was negligent (there was no showing of "actual malice"),[42] and that the candidate's reputation has been besmirched. It awards "compensatory" damages.[43]

Claiming that the statute violates the First Amendment, the newspaper appeals. It asks the court to consider the case "against the background of a profound national commitment to the principle that debate on public issues should be uninhibited, robust, and wide-open, and that it may well include vehement, caustic, and sometimes unpleasantly sharp attacks on government and public officials." It argues that the statute will make newspapers overly cautious, that they will be "deterred from voicing their criticism, even though it is believed to be true and even though it is in fact true, because of doubt whether it can be proved in court or fear of the expense of having to do so." And it insists that the statute "dampens the vigor and limits the variety of public debate."

The candidate, to the contrary, begs the court to recognize that the lies published about him misled the voters and thereby injured the political process. The statutory standard of due care, he insists, is the ideal standard for ensuring that the public is informed, rather than misled. Negligence is not to be encouraged in the reporting of political news any more than elsewhere, and if due care costs more than

40. *A. Bickel,* supra note 33, at 62.

41. 376 U.S. 254 (1964).

42. Id. at 280 ("actual malice" defined as knowing falsehood or "reckless disregard" of truth) . . . .

43. That is, the court awards only money damages sufficient to compensate the candidate for the injury to his reputation, but does not overturn the election or award damages for the loss of it. . . .

carelessness, the purpose of the First Amendment requires that newspapers rather than voters should bear that cost.[47] Moreover, if newspapers are free to lie, some of our most capable citizens will be deterred from running for office; the risk to reputation may outweigh the charm of public life.

It is doubtful that we can ascertain whether all or some of the newspaper's or the candidate's predictions about the impact of the statute on the political process are correct. Nor would we be able to evaluate the court's holding in consequentialist terms.[49] If we drop our assumption about the *Sullivan* case, we can be reasonably confident that the newspaper would win today and would have lost in the not-too-distant past. But who would have the temerity to say that the increased protection of defamatory speech can be shown to have contributed to a political process that functions better?

A consequentialist argument about the relationship between literature or obscenity and the functioning of the political process is also bound to founder on an absence of obtainable information. One learns much about political behavior from Anthony Trollope and about social behavior from Jane Austen. Does this knowledge help the voter discharge his obligation? The obscene teaches about the human condition. Is that not important to the voter as a voter?

Notes and Questions

1. As Wellington notes, disagreement over the requirements of the political process can be very important. In his 1948 book, as we have seen, Professor Meiklejohn drew a narrow boundary, leaving the protection of other speech to the due process clause. Professor Chafee criticized this in Book Review, 62 Harv.L.Rev. 891 (1949), on the grounds that the framers intended the First Amendment to give speech "all the protection they desired, and had no idea of supplementing it by the Fifth Amendment."

47. This may mean in practice that the class of newspaper owners, subscribers, and advertisers, many of whom are voters, will bear the cost.

49. In philosophical writing, "'consequentialism' . . . has come to mean the doctrine that one should judge the morality of an action by its consequences." Barry, Book Review, 88 Yale L.J. 629, 629–30 (1979). All that I mean by the sentence in the text, however, is that whatever the court holds, we will not know the effect of that holding on the successful operation of the political process. Recall that the successful operation of the political process is stipulated as the social interest vindicated by the First Amendment. [ ]

One way of resolving the problem of the court would be to say: when in doubt, prefer speech. This much at least, it might be thought, can be justified by the language of the First Amendment. But of course this approach represents a conclusion, not a reason. Why, after all, should some justices of the Supreme Court suddenly decide in the 1960s that defamatory utterances fit within the phrase "the freedom of speech?" Before this, few had had difficulty excluding defamation from the ambit of the protection provided by that phrase. See Chaplinsky v. New Hampshire, 315 U.S. 568, 572 (1942). A presumption in favor of speech, based on the language of the First Amendment, is apt to shift attention toward a definition of speech. For reasons that have been largely indicated to this point, I doubt on the whole that efforts to define speech will help very much in answering the questions addressed in this essay.

In his cited 1961 article, Meiklejohn acknowledged the lack of historical support but argued that the constitutional principle of self-government was capable of development and changing consequences as its implications became understood. It was also in this article that Meiklejohn extended his concept of what types of speech had to be protected to permit the political process to perform.

As suggested earlier by Wellington, if Meiklejohn found that particular speech came within the protection of the First Amendment, that protection was complete—and not to be undercut by the courts or the legislature.

2. In his cited article, Robert Bork argued that the only acceptable basis for protecting speech more than other activities was the importance of the "discovery and spread of political truth" facilitated by the unique ability of speech to deal "explicitly and specifically and directly with politics and government." But this difference "exists only with respect to one kind of speech: explicitly and predominantly political speech. This seems to me the only form of speech that a principled judge can prefer to other claimed freedoms. All other forms of speech raise only issues of human gratification."

Lillian BeVier agreed that constitutional protection existed only for "political" speech—"speech that participates in the process of representative democracy. . . . " But the need to "protect political speech fully in practice may justify the Court's extending first amendment protection to categories of speech other than the strictly political." This extra tier of protection was important because of the difficulty in predicting how the Court might later draw the line between political and other speech. Rather than sacrifice some of the political to exclude all nonpolitical, the Court should give more protection to the latter to ensure protection of the former. BeVier, The First Amendment and Political Speech: An Inquiry Into the Substance and Limits of Principle, 30 Stan.L.Rev. 299 (1978).

3. In his book The Morality of Consent, commenting on the range of speech to be protected, Alexander Bickel observed that some had justified protection of speech because of "its truth-seeking aspect." Bickel responded:

> Yet the First Amendment does not operate solely or even chiefly to foster the quest for truth, unless we take the view that truth is entirely a product of the marketplace and is definable as the perceptions of the majority of men, and not otherwise. The social interest that the First Amendment vindicates, is rather, as Alexander Meiklejohn and Robert Bork have emphasized, so that the country may better be able to adopt the course of action that conforms to the wishes of the greatest number, whether or not it is wise or is founded in truth.

Bickel concluded that open discussion was "crucial to our politics. . . . It would follow, then, that the First Amendment should protect and indeed encourage speech so long as it serves to make the political process work, seeking to achieve objectives through the political process by persuading a majority of voters; but *not* when it amounts to an effort to supplant, disrupt, or coerce the process, as by overthrowing the government, by rioting, or by other forms of violence, and also *not* when it constitutes a breach of an otherwise valid law, a violation of majority decisions embodied in law." (62–63) His book discussed these questions at length.

4. Meiklejohn's analogy to the model of the town meeting led him to assert that the First Amendment did "not require that, on every occasion, every citizen shall take part in public debate. Nor can it even give assurance that everyone shall have opportunity to do so. . . . What is essential is not that everyone shall speak, but that everything worth saying shall be said. . . ." Free Speech and Its Relation to Self-Government 65 (1948).

This view was challenged in Karst, Equality as a Central Principle in the First Amendment, 43 U.Chi.L.Rev. 20, 40 (1975):

> The state lacks "moderators" who can be trusted to know when "everything worth saying" has been said, and the legislature lacks the capacity to write laws that will tell a moderator when to make such a ruling. And even the repetition of speech conveys the distinctive message that an opinion is widely shared. The impression of a mounting consensus is of great importance in an "other-directed" society where opinion polls are self-fulfilling prophecies. A vital public forum requires a principle of equal liberty of expression that is broad, protecting speakers as well as ideas.

5. From a different direction, Professor Vince Blasi suggests that Meiklejohn's emphasis on self-governance may be unrealistic in light of our traditionally low participation in elections and political discussions. (Blasi notes that the framers did not intend that a large majority of the population would participate in political decisions.) Rather, Blasi would stress that the press needs extensive protection because it is the only continuing and well-funded organization in the private sector that can "check" official misbehavior by extensive investigation and reporting. Although in a democratic system of government, the general populace must be the ultimate judge of public officials' behavior, people need not be preoccupied with government and politics. Unlike Meiklejohn's focus on the daily participation of every citizen, the checking value does not emphasize the exchange of ideas on governmental matters, but the rights of citizens as listeners to learn about their government and public officials. Blasi is concerned more with the transmission of information concerning political behavior of public officials than with argumentation and persuasion. Government corruption is a serious problem, he says, and as government grows, the problem becomes more serious, as does the difficulty of discovering the misbehavior. The "central premise of the checking value is that abuse of government is an especially serious evil—more serious than the

abuse of private power, even by institutions such as large corporations which can affect the lives of millions of people."

The checking value allows citizens to follow their private pursuits while the press serves as "watchdog" over government. Most investigative reporting, he asserts, reflects the "checking value" more than the self-governance rationale. Blasi, The Checking Value in First Amendment Theory, 1977 Am.B.Found. Res.J. 521.

6. Although our primary focus will be on media, several Supreme Court decisions address the various rationales from broader perspectives. The following case is a good example.

FIRST NATIONAL BANK OF BOSTON v. BELLOTTI

Supreme Court of the United States, 1978.
435 U.S. 765, 98 S.Ct. 1407, 55 L.Ed.2d 707, 3 Med.L.Rptr. 2105.

MR. JUSTICE POWELL delivered the opinion of the Court.

In sustaining a state criminal statute that forbids certain expenditures by banks and business corporations for the purpose of influencing the vote on referendum proposals, the Massachusetts Supreme Judicial Court held that the First Amendment rights of a corporation are limited to issues that materially affect its business, property, or assets. The court rejected appellants' claim that the statute abridges freedom of speech in violation of the First and Fourteenth Amendments. The issue presented in this context is one of first impression in this Court. We postponed the question of jurisdiction to our consideration of the merits. . . . [ ] We now reverse.

I

The statute at issue, Mass.Gen.Laws Ann., ch. 55, § 8 (West Supp. 1977), prohibits appellants, two national banking associations and three business corporations, from making contributions or expenditures "for the purpose of . . . influencing or affecting the vote on any question submitted to the voters, other than one materially affecting any of the property, business or assets of the corporation." The statute further specifies that "[n]o question submitted to the voters solely concerning the taxation of the income, property or transactions of individuals shall be deemed materially to affect the property, business or assets of the corporation." A corporation that violates § 8 may receive a maximum fine of $50,000; a corporate officer, director, or agent who violates the section may receive a maximum fine of $10,000 or imprisonment for up to one year, or both.

Appellants wanted to spend money to publicize their views on a proposed constitutional amendment that was to be submitted to the voters as a ballot question at a general election on November 2, 1976. The amendment would have permitted the legislature to impose a graduated tax on the income of individuals. After appellee, the Attorney General of Massachusetts, informed appellants that he intended to enforce § 8 against them, they brought this action seeking to have the statute declared unconstitutional. . . .

. . .

. . . In addressing appellants' constitutional contentions, the court acknowledged that § 8 "operate[s] in an area of the most fundamental First Amendment activities," Buckley v. Valeo, 424 U.S. 1, 14 (1976), and viewed the principal question as "whether business corporations, such as [appellants], have First Amendment rights coextensive with those of natural persons or associations of natural persons." 371 Mass. 773, 783, 359 N.E.2d 1262, 1269. The court found its answer in the contours of a corporation's constitutional right, as a "person" under the Fourteenth Amendment, not to be deprived of property without due process of law. . . . Accordingly, the court held that "only when a general political issue materially affects a corporation's business, property or assets may that corporation claim First Amendment protection for its speech or other activities entitling it to communicate its position on that issue to the general public." . . .

. . .

. . . Adopting a narrowing construction of the statute,[7] the Supreme Judicial Court rejected the contention that § 8 is overbroad.

. . .

II

Because the 1976 referendum has been held, and the proposed constitutional amendment defeated, we face at the outset a question of mootness. As the case falls within the class of controversies "capable of repetition, yet evading review," [ ], we conclude that it is not moot. Present here are both elements identified in Weinstein v. Bradford, 423 U.S. 147, 149 (1975), as precluding a finding of mootness in the absence of a class action: "(1) the challenged action was in its duration too short to be fully litigated prior to its cessation or expiration, and (2) there [is] a reasonable expectation that the same complaining party [will] be subjected to the same action again."

. . .

III

The court below framed the principal question in this case as whether and to what extent corporations have First Amendment rights.

7. The court stated that § 8 would not prohibit the publication of "in-house" newspapers or communications to stockholders containing the corporation's view on a graduated personal income tax; the participation by corporate employees, at corporate expense, in discussions or legislative hearings on the issue; the participation of corporate officers, directors, stockholders, or employees in public discussion of the issue on radio or television, at news conferences, or through statements to the press or "similar means not involving contributions or expenditure of corporate funds"; or speeches or comments by employees or officers, on working hours, to the press or a chamber of commerce. [ ].

We believe that the court posed the wrong question. The Constitution often protects interests broader than those of the party seeking their vindication. The First Amendment, in particular, serves significant societal interests. The proper question therefore is not whether corporations "have" First Amendment rights and, if so, whether they are coextensive with those of natural persons. Instead, the question must be whether § 8 abridges expression that the First Amendment was meant to protect. We hold that it does.

A

The speech proposed by appellants is at the heart of the First Amendment's protection.

> "The freedom of speech and of the press guaranteed by the Constitution embraces at the least the liberty to discuss publicly and truthfully all matters of public concern without previous restraint or fear of subsequent punishment. . . . Freedom of discussion, if it would fulfill its historic function in this nation, must embrace all issues about which information is needed or appropriate to enable the members of society to cope with the exigencies of their period." Thornhill v. Alabama, 310 U.S. 88, 101–102 (1940).

The referendum issue that appellants wish to address falls squarely within this description. In appellants' view, the enactment of a graduated personal income tax, as proposed to be authorized by constitutional amendment, would have a seriously adverse effect on the economy of the State.

. . .

As the Court said in Mills v. Alabama, 384 U.S. 214, 218 (1966), "there is practically universal agreement that a major purpose of [the First] Amendment was to protect the free discussion of governmental affairs." If the speakers here were not corporations, no one would suggest that the State could silence their proposed speech. It is the type of speech indispensable to decisionmaking in a democracy,[11] and this is no less true because the speech comes from a corporation rather than an individual.[12] The inherent worth of the speech in terms of its

11. Freedom of expression has particular significance with respect to government because "[i]t is here that the state has a special incentive to repress opposition and often wields a more effective power of suppression." T. Emerson, Toward a General Theory of the First Amendment 9 (1966). See also A. Meiklejohn, Free Speech and Its Relation to Self-Government 24–26 (1948).

12. The individual's interest in self-expression is a concern of the First Amendment separate from the concern for open and informed discussion, although the two often converge. See G. Gunther, Cases and Materials on Constitutional Law 1044 (9th ed. 1975); T. Emerson, The System of Freedom of Expression 6 (1970). The Court has declared, however, that "speech concerning public affairs is more than self-expression; it is the essence of self-government." Garrison v. Louisiana, 379 U.S. 64, 74–75 (1964). And self-government suffers when those in power suppress competing views on public issues "from diverse and antagonistic sources." Associated Press v. United States, 326 U.S. 1, 20 (1945), quoted in New York Times Co. v. Sullivan, 376 U.S. 254, 266 (1964).

capacity for informing the public does not depend upon the identity of its source, whether corporation, association, union, or individual.

The court below nevertheless held that corporate speech is protected by the First Amendment only when it pertains directly to the corporation's business interests. In deciding whether this novel and restrictive gloss on the First Amendment comports with the Constitution and the precedents of this Court, we need not survey the outer boundaries of the Amendment's protection of corporate speech, or address the abstract question whether corporations have the full measure of rights that individuals enjoy under the First Amendment.[13] The question in this case, simply put, is whether the corporate identity of the speaker deprives this proposed speech of what otherwise would be its clear entitlement to protection. We turn now to that question.

B

The court below found confirmation of the legislature's definition of the scope of a corporation's First Amendment rights in the language of the Fourteenth Amendment. Noting that the First Amendment is applicable to the States through the Fourteenth, and seizing upon the observation that corporations "cannot claim for themselves the liberty which the Fourteenth Amendment guarantees," Pierce v. Society of Sisters, 268 U.S. 510, 535 (1925), the court concluded that a corporation's First Amendment rights must derive from its property rights under the Fourteenth.[14]

This is an artificial mode of analysis, untenable under decisions of this Court.

> "In a series of decisions beginning with Gitlow v. New York, 268 U.S. 652 (1925), this Court held that the liberty of speech and of the press which the First Amendment guarantees against abridgment by the federal government is within the *liberty* safeguarded by the Due Process Clause of the Fourteenth Amendment from invasion by state action. That principle has been followed and reaffirmed to the present day." Joseph Burstyn, Inc. v. Wilson, 343 U.S. 495, 500–501 (1952) (footnote omitted) (emphasis supplied).

13. Nor is there any occasion to consider in this case whether, under different circumstances, a justification for a restriction on speech that would be inadequate as applied to individuals might suffice to sustain the same restriction as applied to corporations, unions, or like entities.

14. . . .

In cases where corporate speech has been denied the shelter of the First Amendment, there is no suggestion that the reason was because a corporation rather than an individual or association was involved. . . . Certain "purely personal" guarantees, such as the privilege against compulsory self-incrimination, are unavailable to corporations and other organizations because the "historic function" of the particular guarantee has been limited to the protection of individuals. United States v. White, 322 U.S. 694, 698–701 (1944). Whether or not a particular guarantee is "purely personal" or is unavailable to corporations for some other reason depends on the nature, history, and purpose of the particular constitutional provision.

Freedom of speech and the other freedoms encompassed by the First Amendment always have been viewed as fundamental components of the liberty safeguarded by the Due Process Clause . . . . In Grosjean v. American Press Co., 297 U.S. 233, 244 (1936), the Court rejected the very reasoning adopted by the Supreme Judicial Court and did not rely on the corporation's property rights under the Fourteenth Amendment in sustaining its freedom of speech.

Yet appellee suggests that First Amendment rights generally have been afforded only to corporations engaged in the communications business or through which individuals express themselves, and the court below apparently accepted the "materially affecting" theory as the conceptual common denominator between appellee's position and the precedents of this Court. It is true that the "materially affecting" requirement would have been satisfied in the Court's decisions affording protection to the speech of media corporations and corporations otherwise in the business of communication or entertainment, and to the commercial speech of business corporations. See cases cited in n. 14, supra. In such cases, the speech would be connected to the corporation's business almost by definition. But the effect on the business of the corporation was not the governing rationale in any of these decisions. None of them mentions, let alone attributes significance to, the fact that the subject of the challenged communication materially affected the corporation's business.

The press cases emphasize the special and constitutionally recognized role of that institution in informing and educating the public, offering criticism, and providing a forum for discussion and debate. Mills v. Alabama, 384 U.S., at 219; see Saxbe v. Washington Post Co., 417 U.S. 843, 863–864 (1974) (Powell, J., dissenting). But the press does not have a monopoly on either the First Amendment or the ability to enlighten.[18] Cf. Buckley v. Valeo, 424 U.S., at 51 n. 56; Red Lion

18. If we were to adopt appellee's suggestion that communication by corporate members of the institutional press is entitled to greater constitutional protection than the same communication by appellants, the result would not be responsive to the informational purpose of the First Amendment. Certainly there are voters in Massachusetts, concerned with such economic issues as the tax rate, employment opportunities, and the ability to attract new business into the State and to prevent established businesses from leaving, who would be as interested in hearing appellants' views on a graduated tax as the views of media corporations that might be less knowledgeable on the subject. "[P]ublic debate must not only be unfettered; it must also be informed." Saxbe v. Washington Post Co., 417 U.S. 843, 862–863 (1974) (POWELL, J., dissenting).

MR. JUSTICE WHITE'S dissenting view would empower a State to restrict corporate speech far more narrowly than would the opinion of the Massachusetts court or the statute under consideration. This case involves speech in connection with a referendum. MR. JUSTICE WHITE'S rationale would allow a State to proscribe the expenditure of corporate funds at any time for the purpose of expressing views on "political [or] social questions" or in connection with undefined "ideological crusades," unless the expenditures were shown to be "integrally related to corporate business operations." [ ] Thus corporate activities that are widely viewed as educational and socially constructive could be prohibited. Corporations no longer would be able safely to support—by contributions or public service advertising—educational, charitable, cultural, or even human rights causes. . . .

Broadcasting Co. v. FCC, 395 U.S. 367, 389–390 (1969); New York Times Co. v. Sullivan, 376 U.S. 254, 266 (1964); Associated Press v. United States, 326 U.S. 1, 20 (1945). Similarly, the Court's decisions involving corporations in the business of communication or entertainment are based not only on the role of the First Amendment in fostering individual self-expression but also on its role in affording the public access to discussion, debate, and the dissemination of information and ideas.[19] See Red Lion Broadcasting Co. v. FCC, supra; Stanley v. Georgia, 394 U.S. 557, 564 (1969); Time, Inc. v. Hill, 385 U.S. 374, 389 (1967). Even decisions seemingly based exclusively on the individual's right to express himself acknowledge that the expression may contribute to society's edification. Winters v. New York, 333 U.S. 507, 510 (1948).

Nor do our recent commercial speech cases lend support to appellee's business interest theory. They illustrate that the First Amendment goes beyond protection of the press and the self-expression of individuals to prohibit government from limiting the stock of information from which members of the public may draw. A commercial advertisement is constitutionally protected not so much because it pertains to the seller's business as because it furthers the societal interest in the "free flow of commercial information." Virginia State Bd. of Pharmacy v. Virginia Citizens Consumer Council, 425 U.S. 748, 764 (1976); see Linmark Associates, Inc. v. Willingboro, 431 U.S. 85, 95 (1977).

C

. . .

In the realm of protected speech, the legislature is constitutionally disqualified from dictating the subjects about which persons may speak and the speakers who may address a public issue. Police Dept. of Chicago v. Mosley, 408 U.S. 92, 96 (1972). If a legislature may direct business corporations to "stick to business," it also may limit other corporations—religious, charitable, or civic—to their respective "business" when addressing the public. Such power in government to channel the expression of views is unacceptable under the First Amendment. Especially where, as here, the legislature's suppression of speech suggests an attempt to give one side of a debatable public question an advantage in expressing its views to the people,[22] the First Amendment

19. The suggestion in MR. JUSTICE WHITE'S dissent, [ ], that the First Amendment affords less protection to ideas that are not the product of "individual choice" would seem to apply to newspaper editorials and every other form of speech created under the auspices of a corporate body. No decision of this Court lends support to such a restrictive notion.

22. Cf. Madison School Dist. v. Wisconsin Employment Relations Comm'n, 429 U.S. 167, 175–176 (1976).

Our observation about the apparent purpose of the Massachusetts Legislature is not an endorsement of the legislature's factual assumptions about the views of corporations. We know of no documentation of the notion that corporations are likely to share a monolithic view on an issue such as the adoption of a graduated personal income tax. Corporations, like individuals or groups, are not homogeneous. They range from great multinational enterprises whose stock is publicly held and traded to

is plainly offended. Yet the State contends that its action is necessitated by governmental interests of the highest order. We next consider these asserted interests.

IV

The constitutionality of § 8's prohibition of the "exposition of ideas" by corporations turns on whether it can survive the exacting scrutiny necessitated by a state-imposed restriction of freedom of speech. Especially where, as here, a prohibition is directed at speech itself,[23] and the speech is intimately related to the process of governing, "the State may prevail only upon showing a subordinating interest which is compelling," Bates v. Little Rock, 361 U.S. 516, 524 (1960); see NAACP v. Button, 371 U.S. 415, 438–439 (1963); NAACP v. Alabama ex rel. Patterson, 357 U.S., at 463; Thomas v. Collins, 323 U.S. 516, 530 (1945), "and the burden is on the government to show the existence of such an interest." Elrod v. Burns, 427 U.S. 347, 362 (1976). Even then, the State must employ means "closely drawn to avoid unnecessary abridgment . . . ." Buckley v. Valeo, 424 U.S., at 25; see NAACP v. Button, supra, at 438; Shelton v. Tucker, 364 U.S. 479, 488 (1960).

The Supreme Judicial Court did not subject § 8 to "the critical scrutiny demanded under accepted First Amendment and equal protection principles," *Buckley,* supra, at 11, because of its view that the First Amendment does not apply to appellants' proposed speech. . . . Appellee nevertheless advances two principal justifications for the prohibition of corporate speech. The first is the State's interest in sustaining the active role of the individual citizen in the electoral process and thereby preventing diminution of the citizen's confidence in government. The second is the interest in protecting the rights of shareholders whose views differ from those expressed by management on behalf of the corporation. However weighty these interests may be in the context of partisan candidate elections,[26] they either are not

medium-size public companies and to those that are closely held and controlled by an individual or family. It is arguable that small or medium-size corporations might welcome imposition of a graduated personal income tax that might shift a greater share of the tax burden onto wealthy individuals. [ ]

23. It is too late to suggest "that the dependence of a communication on the expenditure of money itself operates to introduce a nonspeech element or to reduce the exacting scrutiny required by the First Amendment." Buckley v. Valeo, 424 U.S., at 16; see New York Times Co. v. Sullivan, 376 U.S., at 266. Furthermore, § 8 is an "attempt directly to control speech . . . rather [than] to protect, from an evil shown to be grave, some interest clearly within the sphere of governmental concern." Speiser v. Randall, 357 U.S., at 527. Cf. United States v. O'Brien, 391 U.S. 367 (1968).

26. . . .

The overriding concern behind the enactment of statutes such as the Federal Corrupt Practices Act was the problem of corruption of elected representatives through the creation of political debts. [ ] The importance of the governmental interest in preventing this occurrence has never been doubted. The case before us presents no comparable problem, and our consideration of a corporation's right to speak on issues of general public interest implies no comparable right in the quite different context of participation in a political campaign for election to public office. Congress might well be able to demonstrate the existence of a danger of real or apparent corruption in independent expenditures by corporations to influence candidate elections. [ ]

implicated in this case or are not served at all, or in other than a random manner, by the prohibition in § 8.

A

Preserving the integrity of the electoral process, preventing corruption, and "sustain[ing] the active, alert responsibility of the individual citizen in a democracy for the wise conduct of government" are interests of the highest importance. . . .

[ ] Preservation of the individual citizen's confidence in government is equally important. [ ] Appellee advances a number of arguments in support of his view that these interests are endangered by corporate participation in discussion of a referendum issue. They hinge upon the assumption that such participation would exert an undue influence on the outcome of a referendum vote, and—in the end—destroy the confidence of the people in the democratic process and the integrity of government. According to appellee, corporations are wealthy and powerful and their views may drown out other points of view. If appellee's arguments were supported by record or legislative findings that corporate advocacy threatened imminently to undermine democratic processes, thereby denigrating rather than serving First Amendment interests, these arguments would merit our consideration. Cf. Red Lion Broadcasting Co. v. FCC, 395 U.S. 367 (1969). But there has been no showing that the relative voice of corporations has been overwhelming or even significant in influencing referenda in Massachusetts,[28] or that there has been any threat to the confidence of the citizenry in government. [ ]

Nor are appellee's arguments inherently persuasive or supported by the precedents of this Court. Referenda are held on issues, not candidates for public office. . . .[29] To be sure, corporate advertising may influence the outcome of the vote; this would be its purpose. But the fact that advocacy may persuade the electorate is hardly a reason to suppress it: The Constitution "protects expression which is eloquent no less than that which is unconvincing." Kingsley Int'l Pictures Corp. v. Regents, 360 U.S., at 689. We noted only recently that "the concept that government may restrict the speech of some elements of our society in order to enhance the relative voice of others is wholly foreign to the First Amendment . . . ." *Buckley,* 424 U.S., at 48–49.[30] More-

28. In his dissenting opinion, MR. JUSTICE WHITE relies on incomplete facts with respect to expenditures in the 1972 referendum election, in support of his perception as to the "domination of the electroal process by corporate wealth." . . .

29. . . .

Appellee contends that the State's interest in sustaining the active role of the individual citizen is especially great with respect to referenda because they involve the direct participation of the people in the lawmaking process. But far from inviting greater restriction of speech, the direct participation of the people in a referendum, if anything, increases the need for " 'the widest possible dissemination of information from diverse and antagonistic sources.' " New York Times Co. v. Sullivan, 376 U.S., at 266 (quoting Associated Press v. United States, 326 U.S., at 20).

30. MR. JUSTICE WHITE argues, without support in the record, that because corporations are given certain privileges by law

over, the people in our democracy are entrusted with the responsibility for judging and evaluating the relative merits of conflicting arguments.[31] They may consider, in making their judgment, the source and credibility of the advocate.[32] But if there be any danger that the people cannot evaluate the information and arguments advanced by appellants, it is a danger contemplated by the Framers of the First Amendment. . . . [ ] In sum, "[a] restriction so destructive of the right of public discussion [as § 8], without greater or more imminent danger to the public interest than existed in this case, is incompatible with the freedoms secured by the First Amendment." [33]

B

[The Court rejected the argument "that § 8 protects corporate shareholders, an interest that is both legitimate and traditionally within the province of state law." Justice Powell found the provision under-inclusive because corporate activity was still permitted with regard to legislation and to public debate until an issue went to referendum—even though these activities occurred much more frequently than did referenda. The limitation to banks and business corporations was significant since the problem of dissenters could occur in other organized groups such a labor unions. The provision was over-inclusive because it provided no exception for cases in which the shareholders were unanimous. "Assuming, *arguendo,* that protection

they are able to "amass wealth" and then to "dominate" debate on an issue. [ ] He concludes from this generalization that the State has a subordinating interest in denying corporations access to debate and, correspondingly, in denying the public access to corporate views. The potential impact of this argument, especially on the news media, is unsettling. One might argue with comparable logic that the State may control the volume of expression by the wealthier, more powerful corporate members of the press in order to "enhance the relative voices" of smaller and less influential members.

Except in the special context of limited access to the channels of communication, see Red Lion Broadcasting Co. v. FCC, 395 U.S. 367 (1969), this concept contradicts basic tenets of First Amendment jurisprudence. We rejected a similar notion in Miami Herald Publishing Co. v. Tornillo, 418 U.S. 241 (1974). There we held that the First Amendment prohibits a State from requiring a newspaper to make space available at no cost for a reply from a candidate whom the newspaper has criticized. . . .

31. Government is forbidden to assume the task of ultimate judgment, lest the people lose their ability to govern themselves. . . .

The State's paternalism evidenced by this statute is illustrated by the fact that Massachusetts does not prohibit lobbying by corporations, which are free to exert as much influence on the people's representatives as their resources and inclinations permit. Presumably the legislature thought its members competent to resist the pressures and blandishments of lobbying, but had markedly less confidence in the electorate. If the First Amendment protects the right of corporations to petition legislative and administrative bodies, [ ] there hardly can be less reason for allowing corporate views to be presented openly to the people when they are to take action in their sovereign capacity.

32. Corporate advertising, unlike some methods of participation in political campaigns, is likely to be highly visible. Identification of the source of advertising may be required as a means of disclosure, so that the people will be able to evaluate the arguments to which they are being subjected. [ ] In addition, we emphasized in *Buckley* the prophylactic effect of requiring that the source of communication be disclosed. 424 U.S., at 67.

33. Thomas v. Collins, 323 U.S. 516, 537 (1945).

of shareholders is a 'compelling' interest under the circumstances of this case, we find 'no substantially relevant correlation between the governmental interest asserted and the State's effort' to prohibit appellants from speaking."]

V

Because that portion of § 8 challenged by appellants prohibits protected speech in a manner unjustified by a compelling state interest, it must be invalidated. The judgment of the Supreme Judicial Court is

Reversed.

MR. CHIEF JUSTICE BURGER, concurring.

I join the opinion and judgment of the Court but write separately to raise some questions likely to arise in this area in the future.

A disquieting aspect of Massachusetts' position is that it may carry the risk of impinging on the First Amendment rights of those who employ the corporate form—as most do—to carry on the business of mass communications, particularly the large media conglomerates. This is so because of the difficulty, and perhaps impossibility, of distinguishing, either as a matter of fact or constitutional law, media corporations from corporations such as the appellants in this case.

Making traditional use of the corporate form, some media enterprises have amassed vast wealth and power and conduct many activities, some directly related—and some not—to their publishing and broadcasting activities. See Miami Herald Publishing Co. v. Tornillo, 418 U.S. 241, 248–254 (1974). Today, a corporation might own the dominant newspaper in one or more large metropolitan centers, television and radio stations in those same centers and others, a newspaper chain, news magazines with nationwide circulation, national or worldwide wire news services, and substantial interests in book publishing and distribution enterprises. Corporate ownership may extend, vertically, to pulp mills and pulp timberlands to insure an adequate, continuing supply of newsprint and to trucking and steamship lines for the purpose of transporting the newsprint to the presses. Such activities would be logical economic auxiliaries to a publishing conglomerate. Ownership also may extend beyond to business activities unrelated to the task of publishing newspapers and magazines or broadcasting radio and television programs. Obviously, such far-reaching ownership would not be possible without the state-provided corporate form and its "special rules relating to such matters as limited liability, perpetual life, and the accumulation, distribution, and taxation of assets . . . ." (White, J., dissenting).

In terms of "unfair advantage in the political process" and "corporate domination of the electoral process," [ ], it could be argued that such media conglomerates as I describe pose a much more realistic threat to valid interests than do appellants and similar entities not regularly concerned with shaping popular opinion on public issues. [ ]

In *Tornillo,* for example, we noted the serious contentions advanced that a result of the growth of modern media empires "has been to place in a few hands the power to inform the American people and shape public opinion." 418 U.S., at 250.

. . .

[The remainder of Chief Justice Burger's opinion is reprinted at p. 62, infra.]

MR. JUSTICE WHITE, with whom MR. JUSTICE BRENNAN and MR. JUSTICE MARSHALL join, dissenting.

. . .

. . . The Court's fundamental error is its failure to realize that the state regulatory interests in terms of which the alleged curtailment of First Amendment rights accomplished by the statute must be evaluated are themselves derived from the First Amendment. The question posed by this case, as approached by the Court, is whether the State has struck the best possible balance, i.e., the one which it would have chosen, between competing First Amendment interests. Although in my view the choice made by the State would survive even the most exacting scrutiny, perhaps a rational argument might be made to the contrary. What is inexplicable, is for the Court to substitute its judgment as to the proper balance for that of Massachusetts where the State has passed legislation reasonably designed to further First Amendment interests in the context of the political arena where the expertise of legislators is at its peak and that of judges is at its very lowest. Moreover, the result reached today in critical respects marks a drastic departure from the Court's prior decisions which have protected against governmental infringement the very First Amendment interests which the Court now deems inadequate to justify the Massachusetts statute.

I

There is now little doubt that corporate communications come within the scope of the First Amendment. This, however, is merely the starting point of analysis, because an examination of the First Amendment values that corporate expression furthers and the threat to the functioning of a free society it is capable of posing reveals that it is not fungible with communications emanating from individuals and is subject to restrictions which individual expression is not. Indeed, what some have considered to be the principal function of the First Amendment, the use of communication as a means of self-expression, self-realization, and self-fulfillment, is not at all furthered by corporate speech.[3] It is clear that the communications of profitmaking corporations are not "an integral part of the development of ideas, of mental

3. See T. Emerson, Toward a General Theory of the First Amendment 4–7 (1966); Board of Education v. Barnette, 319 U.S. 624 (1943).

exploration and of the affirmation of self." [4] They do not represent a manifestation of individual freedom or choice. Undoubtedly, as this Court has recognized, see NAACP v. Button, 371 U.S. 415 (1963), there are some corporations formed for the express purpose of advancing certain ideological causes shared by all their members, or, as in the case of the press, of disseminating information and ideas. Under such circumstances, association in a corporate form may be viewed as merely a means of achieving effective self-expression. But this is hardly the case generally with corporations operated for the purpose of making profits. Shareholders in such entities do not share a common set of political or social views, and they certainly have not invested their money for the purpose of advancing political or social causes or in an enterprise engaged in the business of disseminating news and opinion. In fact, as discussed infra, the government has a strong interest in assuring that investment decisions are not predicated upon agreement or disagreement with the activities of corporations in the political arena.

Of course, it may be assumed that corporate investors are united by a desire to make money, for the value of their investment to increase. Since even communications which have no purpose other than that of enriching the communicator have some First Amendment protection, activities such as advertising and other communications integrally related to the operation of the corporation's business may be viewed as a means of furthering the desires of individual shareholders. This unanimity of purpose breaks down, however, when corporations make expenditures or undertake activities designed to influence the opinion or votes of the general public on political and social issues that have no material connection with or effect upon their business, property, or assets. . . .

The self-expression of the communicator is not the only value encompassed by the First Amendment. One of its functions, often referred to as the right to hear or receive information, is to protect the interchange of ideas. Any communication of ideas, and consequently any expenditure of funds which makes the communication of ideas possible, it can be argued, furthers the purposes of the First Amendment. This proposition does not establish, however, that the right of the general public to receive communications financed by means of corporate expenditures is of the same dimension as that to hear other forms of expression. In the first place, as discussed supra, corporate expenditures designed to further political causes lack the connection with individual self-expression which is one of the principal justifications for the constitutional protection of speech provided by the First Amendment. Ideas which are not a product of individual choice are entitled to less First Amendment protection. Secondly, the restriction of corporate speech concerned with political matters impinges much less severely upon the availability of ideas to the general public than do

4. *Emerson,* supra, at 5.

restrictions upon individual speech. Even the complete curtailment of corporate communications concerning political or ideological questions not integral to day-to-day business functions would leave individuals, including corporate shareholders, employees, and customers, free to communicate their thoughts. Moreover, it is unlikely that any significant communication would be lost by such a prohibition. These individuals would remain perfectly free to communicate any ideas which could be conveyed by means of the corporate form. Indeed, such individuals could even form associations for the very purpose of promoting political or ideological causes.

I recognize that there may be certain communications undertaken by corporations which could not be restricted without impinging seriously upon the right to receive information. In the absence of advertising and similar promotional activities, for example, the ability of consumers to obtain information relating to products manufactured by corporations would be significantly impeded. There is also a need for employees, customers, and shareholders of corporations to be able to receive communications about matters relating to the functioning of corporations. . . . It is for such reasons that the Court has extended a certain degree of First Amendment protection to activities of this kind.[8] None of these considerations, however, are implicated by a prohibition upon corporate expenditures relating to referenda concerning questions of general public concern having no connection with corporate business affairs.

. . .

The governmental interest in regulating corporate political communications, especially those relating to electoral matters, also raises considerations which differ significantly from those governing the regulation of individual speech. Corporations are artificial entities created by law for the purpose of furthering certain economic goals. In order to facilitate the achievement of such ends, special rules relating to such matters as limited liability, perpetual life, and the accumulation, distribution, and taxation of assets are normally applied to them. States have provided corporations with such attributes in order to increase their economic viability and thus strengthen the economy generally. It has long been recognized, however, that the special status of corporations has placed them in a position to control vast amounts of economic

8. In addition, newspapers and other forms of literature obviously do not lose their First Amendment protection simply because they are produced or distributed by corporations. It is, of course, impermissible to restrict any communication, corporate or otherwise, because of displeasure with its content. I need not decide whether newspapers have a First Amendment right to operate in a corporate form. It may be that for a State which generally permits businesses to operate as corporations to prohibit those engaged in the dissemination of information and opinion from taking advantage of the corporate form would constitute a departure from neutrality prohibited by the free press guarantee of the First Amendment. See Stewart, "Or of the Press," 26 Hastings L.J. 631 (1975); Bezanson, The New Free Press Guarantee, 63 Va.L.Rev. 731 (1977). There can be no doubt, however, that the First Amendment does not immunize media corporations any more than other types of corporations from restrictions upon electoral contributions and expenditures.

power which may, if not regulated, dominate not only the economy but also the very heart of our democracy, the electoral process. Although Buckley v. Valeo, 424 U.S. 1 (1976), provides support for the position that the desire to equalize the financial resources available to candidates does not justify the limitation upon the expression of support which a restriction upon individual contributions entails, the interest of Massachusetts and the many other States which have restricted corporate political activity is quite different. It is not one of equalizing the resources of opposing candidates or opposing positions, but rather of preventing institutions which have been permitted to amass wealth as a result of special advantages extended by the State for certain economic purposes from using that wealth to acquire an unfair advantage in the political process, especially where, as here, the issue involved has no material connection with the business of the corporation. The State need not permit its own creation to consume it. Massachusetts could permissibly conclude that not to impose limits upon the political activities of corporations would have placed it in a position of departing from neutrality and indirectly assisting the propagation of corporate views because of the advantages its laws give to the corporate acquisition of funds to finance such activities. Such expenditures may be viewed as seriously threatening the role of the First Amendment as a guarantor of a free marketplace of ideas. . . .

. . .

II

There is an additional overriding interest related to the prevention of corporate domination which is substantially advanced by Massachusetts' restrictions upon corporate contributions: assuring that shareholders are not compelled to support and financially further beliefs with which they disagree where, as is the case here, the issue involved does not materially affect the business, property, or other affairs of the corporation.[12] . . .

. . .

MR. JUSTICE REHNQUIST, dissenting.

. . .

The question presented today, whether business corporations have a constitutionally protected liberty to engage in political activities, has never been squarely addressed by any previous decision of this Court. However, the General Court of the Commonwealth of Massachusetts, the Congress of the United States, and the legislatures of 30 other States of this Republic have considered the matter, and have concluded that restrictions upon the political activity of business corporations are both politically desirable and constitutionally permissible. The judgment of such a broad consensus of governmental bodies expressed over

12. This, of course, is an interest that was not present in *Buckley v. Valeo*, supra, and would not justify limitations upon the activities of associations, corporate or otherwise, formed for the express purpose of advancing a political or social cause.

a period of many decades is entitled to considerable deference from this Court. I think it quite probable that their judgment may properly be reconciled with our controlling precedents, but I am certain that under my views of the limited application of the First Amendment to the States, which I share with the two immediately preceding occupants of my seat on the Court, but not with my present colleagues, the judgment of the Supreme Judicial Court of Massachusetts should be affirmed.

. . .

There can be little doubt that when a State creates a corporation with the power to acquire and utilize property, it necessarily and implicitly guarantees that the corporation will not be deprived of that property absent due process of law. Likewise, when a State charters a corporation for the purpose of publishing a newspaper, it necessarily assumes that the corporation is entitled to the liberty of the press essential to the conduct of its business. [ ][4] . . .

It cannot be so readily concluded that the right of political expression is equally necessary to carry out the functions of a corporation organized for commercial purposes. . . . So long as the Judicial Branches of the State and Federal Governments remain open to protect the corporation's interest in its property, it has no need, though it may have the desire, to petition the political branches for similar protection. Indeed, the States might reasonably fear that the corporation would use its economic power to obtain further benefits beyond those already bestowed. I would think that any particular form of organization upon which the State confers special privileges or immunities different from those of natural persons would be subject to like regulation, whether the organization is a labor union, a partnership, a trade association, or a corporation.

. . .

I can see no basis for concluding that the liberty of a corporation to engage in political activity with regard to matters having no material effect on its business is necessarily incidental to the purposes for which the Commonwealth permitted these corporations to be organized or admitted within its boundaries. Nor can I disagree with the Supreme Judicial Court's factual finding that no such effect has been shown by these appellants. Because the statute as construed provides at least as much protection as the Fourteenth Amendment requires, I believe it is constitutionally valid.

It is true, as the Court points out, [ ] that recent decisions of this Court have emphasized the interest of the public in receiving the information offered by the speaker seeking protection. The free flow of information is in no way diminished by the Commonwealth's decision to

4. It does not necessarily follow that such a corporation would be entitled to all the rights of free expression enjoyed by natural persons. Although a newspaper corporation must necessarily have the liberty to endorse a political candidate in its editorial columns, it need have no greater right than any other corporation to contribute money to that candidate's campaign. Such a right is no more "incidental to its very existence" than it is to any other business corporation.

permit the operation of business corporations with limited rights of political expression. All natural persons, who owe their existence to a higher sovereign than the Commonwealth, remain as free as before to engage in political activity. [ ]

I would affirm the judgment of the Supreme Judicial Court.

Notes and Questions

1. The mootness ruling is important in several media cases—those dealing with access to information as well as those involving elections.

2. What was wrong with the question posed by the state court? Do Justices Powell and White agree on the question?

3. How may media corporations be treated differently from banks?

4. How do the majority and dissenting opinions use the self-governance rationale? The role of the individual? The commercial speech doctrine?

5. Justice Rehnquist's reference to his two predecessors, Justices Jackson and Harlan, invoked a view of the First Amendment that the rest of the Court has rejected for half a century. The majority has assumed in all the cases we will read that whatever is forbidden to the federal government by the First Amendment is equally forbidden to the states by the Fourteenth Amendment. This would mean that whatever tests of validity are used in federal cases would be equally appropriate in state cases. Justice Rehnquist would apply a more relaxed review standard to restraints on speech and press by the state than to identical restraints imposed by the federal government.

He concluded that the state's interest in preventing corporations from using their wealth "to acquire an unfair advantage in the political process" provided a rational basis for sustaining the legislation in question. But he rejected any intimation that the state had in fact acted for that general purpose. "If inquiry into legislative motives were to determine the outcome of cases such as this, I think a very persuasive argument could be made that the General Court, desiring to impose a personal income tax but more than once defeated in that desire . . . simply decided to muzzle corporations on this sort of issue so that it could succeed in its desire."

This led Justice Rehnquist to observe that if Justice White believed that a function of the First Amendment was to protect the interchange of ideas "he cannot readily subscribe to the idea that, if the desire to muzzle corporations played a part in the enactment of this legislation, the General Court was simply engaged in deciding *which* First Amendment values to promote."

For Justice Rehnquist legislative motive was not controlling. What role did it appear to play in the two major opinions?

6. In *Bellotti,* the Court first determined that the speech in question was within the coverage of the First Amendment. It then rejected the contention that the identity of the speaker removed or reduced that

coverage. It then turned to the question of how much to protect the speech. Here, Justice Powell stated that "exacting scrutiny" was appropriate, which in turn required the state to show "a subordinating interest which is compelling" and that the means chosen were "drawn closely to avoid unnecessary abridgment." Are these balancing notions or do they erect thresholds that must be surmounted?

Justice White argued that the corporate identity of the speaker justified giving the ideas "less First Amendment protection." How might that "less" be translated into an operational standard? In an omitted part of his opinion, Justice White noted that the majority recognized that "fear of corporate domination of the electoral process would justify restrictions" upon corporate expenditures. He argued that the majority has failed to accord sufficient weight to past examples of such domination in Massachusetts.

Justice White also discussed at length state concern for the dissenting shareholders. Not only was this policy consistent with the First Amendment, it was "one which protected the very freedoms that this Court has held to be guaranteed by the First Amendment. In Board of Education v. Barnette, 319 U.S. 624 (1943), the Court struck down a West Virginia statute which compelled children enrolled in public school to salute the flag and pledge allegiance to it . . . ." Finally, Justice White rejected the majority's conclusion that the protection of shareholders was underinclusive and overinclusive.

If First Amendment concerns appear on both sides of the case, can something like the "exacting scrutiny" test be applied?

4. Current Analysis—An Introduction

---

a. The Literal Approach

As noted by Wellington, Justice Black, often joined by Justice Douglas, asserted that once the First Amendment was interpreted to cover a particular communication, there was no second question to be asked. But this does not give the full picture because on occasion they held certain conduct totally unprotected. In such cases, Justice Black was likely to say that speech was not involved; Justice Douglas was likely to call it "speech brigaded with action." As John Ely pointed out, these justices "do themselves no credit here, for 'answers' like this are simply not responsible. They refuse to display whatever reasoning in fact underlies the denial of protection, and by their transparent lack of principle substantially attenuate whatever hortatory value there was in the pronouncement that speech is always protected." J. Ely, Democracy and Distrust 109 (1980). Recall that Meiklejohn, too, believed in an absolute approach to the First Amendment—but only for "political speech."

b. The Two-Tiered Approach

From time to time, the Supreme Court has placed certain categories of words outside the First Amendment's protection.

In 1942, the Court indicated, in Chaplinsky v. New Hampshire, 315 U.S. 568 (1942), that certain classes of expression might be subject to legal sanctions after their utterance:

> There are certain well-defined and narrowly limited classes of speech, the prevention and punishment of which have never been thought to raise any Constitutional problem. These include the lewd and obscene, the profane, the libelous, and the insulting or "fighting" words—those which by their very utterance inflict injury or tend to incite an immediate breach of the peace. It has been well observed that such utterances are no essential part of any exposition of ideas, and are of such slight social value as a step to truth that any benefit that may be derived from them is clearly outweighed by the social interest in order and morality.

Chaplinsky was arrested for calling a town marshal a "God-damned racketeer and a damned Fascist." The Supreme Court characterized the expression as "fighting words . . . likely to cause violence." The expressive element was not protected because the words invited a violent response by the person to whom they were directed.

Note that protection hinges on the categories of expression and not on the point of view the speaker has expressed on a subject. Indeed, the Court frequently has asserted that government must not encourage or hinder speech based on whether officials like the views being expressed. For instance, a city cannot allow peaceful picketing by union members while prohibiting all other peaceful picketing. Such an ordinance in Chicago, which allowed demonstrations near school buildings only if labor matters were involved, was invalidated by the Court. Chicago Police Dept. v. Mosley, 408 U.S. 92, 96 (1972).

Whether some speech may be given less protection because of its content is still in dispute. Justice Stevens, in the plurality part of his opinion in Federal Communications Comm'n v. Pacifica Foundation, 438 U.S. 726, 744–45 (1978), contended that the Court in the past had approved governmental regulations that depended on the content of speech, citing *Chaplinsky* and other examples. Although he concurred in the judgment, Justice Powell disagreed with that view: "I do not subscribe to the theory that the Justices of this Court are free generally to decide on the basis of its content which speech protected by the First Amendment is most 'valuable' and hence deserving of the most protection, and which is less 'valuable' and hence deserving of less protection." Id. at 761. See Farber, Content Regulation and the First Amendment, 68 Geo.L.J. 727 (1980), arguing that Supreme Court decisions upholding content-related restrictions reveal a principled pattern. See also, Redish, The Content Distinction in First Amendment Analysis, 34 Stan.L.Rev. 113 (1981). *Pacifica* is considered in detail in Chapter XIV.

c. *Balancing*

Most frequently, the Supreme Court has used a balancing approach to determine the propriety of a restraint on freedom of expression. The test involves weighing two interests—the government's concern about protecting a particular interest, such as national security or individual reputation, against the speaker's or writer's and society's interests in expression.

Professor Chafee, an early advocate of balancing, expressed the virtues of that approach in his Free Speech in the United States 31 (1941):

> Or to put the matter another way, it is useless to define free speech by talk about rights. The agitator asserts his constitutional right to speak, the government asserts its constitutional right to wage war. The result is a deadlock. . . . To find the boundary line of any right, we must get behind rules of law to human facts. In our problem, we must regard the desires and needs of the individual human being who wants to speak and those of the great group of human beings among whom he speaks. That is, in technical language, there are individual interests and social interests, which must be balanced against each other, if they conflict, in order to determine which interest shall be sacrificed under the circumstances and which shall be protected and become the foundation of a legal right. It must never be forgotten that the balancing cannot be properly done unless all the interests involved are adequately ascertained, and the great evil of all this talk about rights is that each side is so busy denying the other's claim to rights that it entirely overlooks the human desires and needs behind that claim.

Balancing has had its champions and its detractors on the Court over the years, as we shall see.

Balancing on a case-by-case basis makes it difficult to predict whether a certain exercise of free speech will be protected in a later court test. Despite this and other criticisms, freedom of expression cases are frequently decided by balancing interests. Some will focus on the interests at stake in the individual case, commonly characterized as "ad hoc" balancing, where the specific interests applicable to the facts of the particular case are considered crucial. Others will use a more general process, called "definitional" balancing. Here the interests analyzed transcend the merits of a particular case. Rather than asking, for example, whether the value of speech in a particular case outweighed the arguments for proscribing it, the Court might generalize and consider the values of that category of speech, or that category of speaker, and develop a more general analysis. This approach makes it easier to predict outcomes because of the explicit generalized quality of the decision. See Nimmer, The Right to Speak from *Times* to *Time;* First Amendment Theory Applied to Libel and Misapplied to Privacy, 56 Calif.L.Rev. 935, 942–45 (1968), and Gunther, In Search of Judicial Quality on a Changing Court: The Case of Justice Powell, 24 Stan.L. Rev. 1001 (1972).

One important influence on the balancing test is the concept of "preferred position." Justice Stone, in United States v. Carolene Products Co., 304 U.S. 144 (1938), suggested in dictum in a famous footnote: "There may be narrower scope for operation of the presumption of constitutionality when legislation appears on its face to be within a specific prohibition of the Constitution, such as those of the first ten amendments, which are deemed equally specific when held to be embraced within the Fourteenth. . . . " Justice Frankfurter challenged this idea in his concurring opinion in Kovacs v. Cooper, 336 U.S. 77 (1949), and the phrase has largely fallen into disuse, but the idea of special consideration for freedom of communication still carries weight in the balancing process.

Was Justice Powell "balancing" in *Bellotti*?

Recall that in introducing the "exacting scrutiny" language, Justice Powell stressed that such a standard was appropriate "[e]specially where, as here, a prohibition is directed at speech itself . . . ." The implication that a different standard might apply where the prohibition was not directed at speech was made explicit in a footnote at that point that included "Compare United States v. O'Brien, 391 U.S. 367 (1968)."

In the O'Brien case, involving draft card burning, the Court declared that a government regulation was valid "if it furthers an important or substantial governmental interest; if the governmental interest is unrelated to the suppression of free expression; and if the incidental restriction on alleged First Amendment freedoms is no greater than is essential to the furtherance of that interest." The presence of the second requirement suggests one analysis if the government's interest is related to the content of the message and another if it is tied to a different goal. How does judicial review differ under the two situations? How easy is it to tell whether the government interest is related to content or to something else? For a defense of this two-track approach, see J. Ely, Democracy and Distrust 110–16 (1980). A unitary approach is defended in Redish, The Content Distinction in First Amendment Analysis, 34 Stan.L.Rev. 189 (1981). This dispute rarely comes into play in media cases because the government restriction on expression is usually framed directly in terms of content. See also Stone, Content Regulation and the First Amendment, 25 Wm. & Mary L.Rev. 189 (1983).

To the extent that government seeks to regulate speech for reasons totally unrelated to the content of the message, such as regulating activities of sound trucks, or preventing parades from tying up rush hour traffic, the standards of judicial review are much more relaxed. Although these "time, place, or manner" regulations form an important part of First Amendment law, they rarely involve the print or broadcast media. We will, therefore, not address this form of regulation in this general introduction.

d. Clear and Present Danger

During the nineteenth century the Supreme Court had few occasions to consider the First Amendment.* The beginning of serious awareness of First Amendment issues arose out of the litigation provoked by the Espionage Act of 1917 and related state statutes designed to unify the nation during and after World War I. The Espionage Act banned attempts to cause insubordination in the armed forces or to obstruct military recruiting or to conspire to achieve these results. Most of these cases, which confronted the Court from 1919 until the mid-1920s, involved radical speakers who opposed the war effort and criticized the political and economic structure of the country.

From these cases emerged the "clear and present danger" test, first proposed by Justice Holmes, in Schenck v. United States, 249 U.S. 47 (1919). Holmes said that expression could be punished when "the words used are used in such circumstances and are of such a nature as to create a clear and present danger that they will bring about the substantive evils that Congress has a right to prevent. It is a question of proximity and degree." The case involved a prosecution under the Espionage Act for publishing a leaflet that interfered with recruiting by urging young men to violate the draft law. Holmes, writing for the majority, upheld the conviction.

Abrams v. United States, 250 U.S. 616 (1919), involved pamphlets calling for a strike of munitions workers. The Supreme Court upheld the convictions. This time Justice Holmes, joined by Justice Brandeis, dissented and expanded his thesis:

> . . . I think that we should be eternally vigilant against attempts to check the expression of opinions that we loathe and believe to be fraught with death, unless they so imminently threaten immediate interference with the lawful and pressing purposes of the law that an immediate check is required to save the country. I wholly disagree with the argument of the Government that the First Amendment left the common law as to seditious libel in force. History seems to me against the notion. I had conceived that the United States through many years had shown its repentance for the Sedition Act of 1798 [ ], by repaying fines that it imposed. Only the emergency that makes it immediately dangerous to leave the correction of evil counsels to time warrants making any exception to the sweeping command, "Congress shall make no law . . . abridging the freedom of speech."

* Rabban, The First Amendment in Its Forgotten Years, 90 Yale L.J. 514 (1981), discusses free speech cases during that period in the Supreme Court, lower federal courts, and state courts. Generally, these decisions were antagonistic to free speech claims.

Gitlow v. New York, 268 U.S. 652 (1925), was a prosecution under a New York criminal statute that barred advocating overthrow of the government by violence. Although the majority accepted the view that the Fourteenth Amendment imposed on the states the same standards as the First Amendment, it upheld the conviction.

> . . . The State cannot reasonably be required to measure the danger from every such utterance in the nice balance of a jeweler's scale. A single revolutionary spark may kindle a fire that, smouldering for a time, may burst into a sweeping and destructive conflagration. It cannot be said that the State is acting arbitrarily or unreasonably when in the exercise of its judgment as to the measures necessary to protect the public peace and safety, it seeks to extinguish the spark without waiting until it has enkindled the flame or blazed into the conflagration. It cannot reasonably be required to defer the adoption of measures for its own peace and safety until the revolutionary utterances lead to actual disturbances of the public peace or imminent and immediate danger of its own destruction; but it may, in the exercise of its judgment, suppress the threatened danger in its incipiency. . . .
>
> . . .
>
> . . . In such cases it has been held that the general provisions of the statute may be constitutionally applied to the specific utterance of the defendant if its natural tendency and probable effect was to bring about the substantive evil which the legislative body might prevent. . . .

Justice Holmes, joined by Justice Brandeis, dissented:

> . . . I think that the criterion sanctioned by the full Court in Schenck v. United States, 249 U.S. 47, 52, applies. "The question in every case is whether the words used are used in such circumstances and are of such a nature as to create a clear and present danger that they will bring about the substantive evils that [the State] has a right to prevent." It is true that in my opinion this criterion was departed from in Abrams v. United States, 250 U.S. 616, but the convictions that I expressed in that case are too deep for it to be possible for me as yet to believe that it and Schaefer v. United States, 251 U.S. 466, have settled the law. If what I think the correct test is applied, it is manifest that there was no present danger of an attempt to overthrow the government by force on the part of the admittedly small minority who shared the defendant's views. It is said that this manifesto was more than a theory, that it was an incitement. Every idea is an incitement. It offers itself for belief and if believed it is acted on unless some other belief outweighs it or some failure of energy stifles the movement at its birth. The only difference between the expression of an opinion and an incitement in the narrower sense is the speaker's enthusiasm for the result. Eloquence may set fire to reason. But whatever may be thought of the redundant discourse before us it had no

chance of starting a present conflagration. If in the long run the beliefs expressed in proletarian dictatorship are destined to be accepted by the dominant forces of the community, the only meaning of free speech is that they should be given their chance and have their way.

Justice Brandeis, in a separate opinion joined by Justice Holmes, had occasion to expand upon their thinking two years later in Whitney v. California, 274 U.S. 357 (1927):

> Fear of serious injury cannot alone justify suppression of free speech and assembly. Men feared witches and burnt women. It is the function of speech to free men from the bondage of irrational fears. To justify suppression of free speech there must be reasonable ground to fear that serious evil will result if free speech is practiced. There must be reasonable ground to believe that the danger apprehended is imminent. There must be reasonable ground to believe that the evil to be prevented is a serious one. Every denunciation of existing law tends in some measure to increase the probability that there will be violation of it. . . . In order to support a finding of clear and present danger it must be shown either that immediate serious violence was to be expected or was advocated, or that the past conduct furnished reason to believe that such advocacy was then contemplated.
>
> . . . If there be time to expose through discussion the falsehood and fallacies, to avert the evil by the processes of education, the remedy to be applied is more speech, not enforced silence. Only an emergency can justify repression. Such must be the rule if authority is to be reconciled with freedom. Such, in my opinion, is the command of the Constitution. It is therefore always open to Americans to challenge a law abridging free speech and assembly by showing that there was no emergency justifying it.
>
> Moreover, even imminent danger cannot justify resort to prohibition of these functions essential to effective democracy, unless the evil apprehended is relatively serious. Prohibition of free speech and assembly is a measure so stringent that it would be inappropriate as the means for averting a relatively trivial harm to society. . . . [I]t is hardly conceivable that this Court would hold constitutional a statute which punished as a felony the mere voluntary assembly with a society formed to teach that pedestrians had the moral right to cross unenclosed, unposted, waste lands and to advocate their doing so, even if there was imminent danger that advocacy would lead to a trespass.

The Court did not resume these discussions until almost a quarter century later. The resumption occurred in a case in which the plurality of the Court recognized that the Holmes-Brandeis position had evolved to become a majority view—but the plurality then refused to apply it. Dennis v. United States, 341 U.S. 494 (1951), involved prosecution of 11 leading members of the Communist Party for conspiring to advocate the forcible overthrow of the government of the United States. The plurality observed that "Although no case subsequent to *Whitney* and *Gitlow* has expressly overruled the majority opinions in those cases, there is little doubt that subsequent opinions have inclined toward the Holmes-Brandeis rationale."

At the same time, however, the plurality noted that each case confronting Justices Holmes and Brandeis involved "a comparatively isolated event, bearing little relation in their minds to any substantial threat to the safety of the community. . . . They were not confronted with any situation comparable to the instant one—the development of an apparatus designed and dedicated to the overthrow of the Government, in the context of world crisis after crisis."

The plurality adopted the test framed by Judge Learned Hand in the lower court: "In each case [courts] must ask whether the gravity of the 'evil,' discounted by its improbability, justifies such invasion of free speech as is necessary to avoid the danger." That statement "takes into consideration those factors which we deem relevant, and relates their significances. More we cannot expect from words."

The plurality found that the requisite danger existed. The formation of a "highly organized conspiracy, with rigidly disciplined members subject to call when the leaders, these petitioners, felt the time had come for action, coupled with the inflammable nature of world conditions, similar uprisings in other countries, and the touch-and-go nature of our relations with countries with whom petitioners were in the very least ideologically attuned, convince us that their convictions were justified on this score . . . . If the ingredients of the reaction are present, we cannot bind the Government to wait until the catalyst is added."

The status of the clear and present danger test remained unclear until Brandenburg v. Ohio, 395 U.S. 444 (1969), involving prosecution of a Ku Klux Klan member for advocating racial and religious bigotry. The criminal syndicalism statute under which Ohio proceeded bore close similarities to the statute in *Whitney.* "But *Whitney* has been thoroughly discredited by later decisions. See [*Dennis*]. These later decisions have fashioned the principle that the constitutional guarantees of free speech and free press do not permit a State to forbid or proscribe advocacy of the use of force or of law violation except where such advocacy is directed to inciting or producing imminent lawless action and is likely to incite or produce such action."

Since the statute permitted punishment of advocacy without a showing that imminent lawless action was likely to follow, the convictions could not stand. *Whitney* was overruled.

Brandenburg was reinforced in Hess v. Indiana, 414 U.S. 105 (1973). The defendant was arrested during an antiwar demonstration on a college campus for shouting, "We'll take the fucking street later (or again)." His subsequent conviction for disorderly conduct was overturned by the Supreme Court. "At best, [the] statement could be taken as counsel for present moderation; at worst, it amounted to nothing more than advocacy of illegal action at some indefinite future time." Since there was no showing that the words "were intended to produce, and likely to produce, *imminent* disorder, those words could not be punished by the State on the ground that they had a 'tendency to lead to violence.' "

In *Dennis,* the Supreme Court had given great deference to the views of Congress. Recently, however, Chief Justice Burger stated in Landmark Communications, Inc. v. Virginia, 435 U.S. 829, 843–44 (1978), "Deference to a legislative finding cannot limit judicial inquiry when First Amendment rights are at stake. . . . A legislature appropriately inquires into and may declare the reasons impelling legislative action but the judicial function commands analysis of whether the specific conduct falls within reach of the statute and if so whether the legislation is consonant with the Constitution. Were it otherwise, the scope of freedom of speech and of the press would be subject to legislative definition and the function of the First Amendment as a check on legislative power would be nullified." We return to *Landmark* in Chapter III.

Although the clear and present danger test has been discussed over many years in the Supreme Court, its importance and utility must not be overstated.

Paul Freund has suggested that the classic example of falsely crying "Fire!" in a crowded theater, first formulated by Holmes in *Schenck,* is not a helpful example because it "is not the ordinary communication of information, or argument, or exhortation, or entertainment. It is in the nature of a preset signal to action, which could have been conveyed by lanterns in a belfry." Might the same analysis apply to a press report in wartime that a troop transport is sailing at a certain hour from a certain port?

Professor Freund also notes that several relevant factors are not explicitly part of the test. For example, the test "does not analyze the causal link between the speech and the danger: although the speech may be moderate and rational, the audience may be hostile and emotional."

Finally, and perhaps most importantly for our purposes, he notes that the clear and present danger test, although "it has its uses in the area of seditious speech where it arose, is not a broad-spectrum sovereign remedy for such other complaints as defamation, obscenity, and invasions of privacy, where the complex of interests at stake requires closer diagnosis and more refined treatment." Freund, The Great Disorder of Speech, 44 The American Scholar 541, 544–45 (1975). See also P. Freund, The Supreme Court of the United States 42–44 (1961): "No matter how rapidly we utter the phrase . . . or how closely we hyphenate the words, they are not a substitute for the weighing of values."

As the cases show, although the clear-and-present danger sounds rigorous except when converted into a balance in *Dennis,* even in its strong form the test has not prevented punishment for the content of political speech. John Ely asserted that the problem with this standard and, even more, the balancing approach, was that the First Amendment "simply cannot stand on the shifting foundation of ad hoc evaluations of specific threat." His response was to avoid such evaluations by proposing that whenever content is being regulated the First Amendment "immunizes all expression *save that which falls within a few clearly and narrowly defined categories.*" (Emphasis in original). For Ely, the advantage of this approach is that "the consideration of likely harm takes place at wholesale, in advance, outside the context of specific cases." Once the categories are fixed, "likely effect drops out of the calculation, and expression that does not fall within one of the categories is simply protected, irrespective of the identity of the speaker and the audience." J. Ely, Democracy and Distrust 109–10 (1985). Is it feasible to adopt an approach that always excludes consideration based on the perceived urgencies of the moment?

C. THE HISTORY OF THE FIRST AMENDMENT

1. The Framers' Intentions

The records of the 1787 Constitutional Convention reveal little about the framers' attitudes toward freedom of speech and press. Discussion of a bill of rights did not occur until the last few days of the convention and that brief debate was inconclusive. The Constitution itself was promulgated without a bill of rights.

Professor David Anderson argues that this is not significant because "[t]he federal Constitutional Convention of 1787 overwhelmingly accepted the Federalist view that a bill of rights would be superfluous; Congress simply had no power to do the things that would be prohibited by a bill of rights." Anderson, The Origins of the Press Clause, 30 UCLA L.Rev. 455, 466–67 (1983).

Alexander Hamilton, in The Federalist No. 84, went even further in suggesting that a declaration concerning freedom of the press was not only unnecessary, but would have been useless: "What signifies a declaration, that 'the liberty of the press shall be inviolably preserved'? What is the liberty of the press? Who can give it any definition which would not leave the utmost latitude for evasion? I hold it to be impracticable; and from this I infer, that its security, whatever fine declarations may be inserted in any constitution respecting it, must altogether depend on public opinion, and on the general spirit of the people and of the government." The Federalist No. 84, at 560 (A. Hamilton) (Modern Library edition, 1937).

The legislative history of the First Amendment does shed some light on the intentions of its framers. The Bill of Rights was the product of three Congressional committees, and was also amended several times on the floor by both Houses. The First Amendment itself went through five versions. The original language concerning freedom of the press was proposed in the House of Representatives by James Madison in two amendments. One was directed toward the states and was rejected by Congress. The other read: "The people shall not be deprived or abridged of their right to speak, to write, or to publish their sentiments; and the freedom of the press, as one of the great bulwarks of liberty, shall be inviolable." Anderson, supra, at 478. This amendment, along with Madison's others, was referred to the House select committee, where it was combined with Madison's right to assemble and petition amendment. The resulting language read: "The freedom of speech and of the press, and the right of the people to peaceably assemble and consult for their common good, and to apply to the Government for the redress of grievances, shall not be infringed." Anderson, supra, at 478.

The Amendment then went to the Senate for consideration. A proposal to insert language guaranteeing the right to instruct representatives was defeated. Then came a proposal to qualify freedom of the press by inserting the language "in as ample a manner as hath at any time been secured by the common law." Anderson, supra, at 480. The Senate's rejection of this language was perhaps the most significant event in the First Amendment's passage; had this language passed, "Blackstone's crabbed view of press freedom would have been frozen into our Constitution." Anderson, supra, at 481.

The Senate did alter the language from passive to active, specifying that "Congress shall make no law," and deleted the phrase "consult for their common good." The resulting text paralleled a House amendment guaranteeing freedom of religion, so the two were combined, to read:

> Congress shall make no law respecting an establishment of religion, or prohibiting the free exercise thereof; or abridging the freedom of speech, or of the press; or the right of the people peaceably to assemble, and to petition the Government for a redress of grievances.

U.S. Const. amend. I. This was the third of 12 amendments submitted to the states for ratification. When the first two—dealing with the election and compensation of Congressmen—failed, it became the First Amendment of the United States Constitution.

The reality of free speech and press was challenged soon after passage of the Bill of Rights by the Sedition Act of 1798. The Act made it a crime to "write, print, utter or publish . . . any false, scandalous and malicious writing or writings against the government of the United States, or either house of the Congress of the United States, or the President of the United States, with intent to defame." Professor Anderson (at 515–16) writes:

> [T]he Sedition Act was no idle threat. The Federalists brought fifteen indictments under the Act during the three years of its existence, and ten of those led to convictions. . . . The Act came perilously close to eliminating the entire opposition press in the United States. . . . A press whose editors could be imprisoned for urging citizens to join in opposition to the policies of government could scarcely be expected to function as "a fourth institution outside the Government [to serve] as an additional check on the three official branches." It is tempting to conclude that the Framers must have held some other view of the press clause, not inconsistent with the Sedition Act.

Anderson concludes, however, this interpretation is not necessarily supported by the evidence of the Act's passage. Although the Sedition Act was passed only nine years after the First Amendment was written, the framers of the two were different. Moreover, the political situation had changed dramatically: the excesses witnessed in the French Revolution had led many American leaders to conclude that the greatest danger faced by the United States was rampant democracy. Also, loose coalitions had formed into organized parties—Federalist and Republican—and perhaps the most marked feature of the Act was its partisan nature: the President and members of both houses of Congress were protected, but not Vice President Jefferson, who was a Republican. Finally, it seems clear that the Sedition Act was viewed by its own framers only as a stopgap measure, designed for the crisis of the moment, since its text included its own termination date, 1801. Anderson thinks it is unjustified to assign to the framers of the First Amendment what one may only speculate were the motivations of the framers of the Sedition Act nine years later.

---

2. A Special Role for the Press?

Our focus so far has been on expression generally. We turn now to the question of the relationship between the speech and press clauses. We consider first the historical evidence, as summarized by Professor Anderson.

THE ORIGINS OF THE PRESS CLAUSE

David Anderson

30 UCLA L.Rev. 455, 533–537 (1983).

Though scholars today may debate whether the press clause has any significance independent of the speech clause, historically there is no doubt that it did. Freedom of the press—not freedom of speech—was the primary concern of the generation that wrote the Declaration of Independence, the Constitution, and the Bill of Rights. Freedom of speech was a late addition to the pantheon of rights; freedom of the press occupied a central position from the very beginning.

By the time the press clause became part of our Constitution in 1791, it had a considerable legislative history. The revolutionary state constitutions, the ratifying conventions, and the First Congress produced numerous expressions of the idea. These expressions and the freedom-of-the-press literature from which they were drawn leave little doubt that press freedom was viewed as being closely related to the experiment of representative self-government. Freedom of the press in America was a product of revolutionary thought. The issue was born of the conflict with England, and its first expressions as a binding principle of law came in the state constitutions drafted contemporaneously with the Declaration of Independence. In these earliest expressions, the relation between freedom of the press and the idea of self-government was explicit. The press was a "bulwark of liberty," "essential to the security of freedom in a state." It had to be protected, not for its own sake, but because it provided a necessary restraint on what the patriots viewed as government's natural tendency toward tyranny and despotism.

In the minds of members of the First Congress, the press clause was part of the new plan of government, no less than if it had been in the original Constitution. To the Anti-Federalists, it was an essential modification of the original Constitution; to the Federalists, it expressed what was already implicit in the Constitution. Their quarrel was only over the necessity of specifically guaranteeing freedom of the press. Neither side doubted its utility. Its value lay, as Professor Blasi says, in "checking the inherent tendency of government officials to abuse the power entrusted to them." Because it plays this role, it is, in Justice Stewart's words, "a *structural* provision of the Constitution."

That the press clause has a distinct history does not mean, of course, that it must be given a meaning different from the speech clause today, or even that it had a different meaning in 1791. It is possible that checking government power was also the purpose of the speech clause. My own guess, however, is that the latter was more closely related to the incipient notion of individual autonomy that underlay the religion clauses. But in either event, most modern analysis, by focusing on the speech clause, gets the matter upside down. As a means of checking government power, speech was an afterthought, if it was viewed as serving that function at all; the press was expected to be the primary source of restraint.

. . .

I do not challenge [Leonard] Levy's conclusion that colonial America was a repressive society in which there was little meaningful freedom of speech or press. But I think the relevant experience, so far as the press clause is concerned, was the revolution, not the colonial period. And the press during the revolutionary period was free, in fact if not in law, to criticize the government seditiously and even licentiously. That the American patriots did not extend this freedom to the Tory press is beside the point. They may not have been sophisticated enough to realize that true freedom of expression must include freedom for even the most dangerous ideas, but they had seen the connection between press criticism and political change. Moreover, I accept Levy's conclusion that as legislators, judges, and executives, the Framers often behaved inconsistently with any expansive notion of freedom of expression; the Framers sometimes seemed as eager to silence dissent as George III had been. But in this I share George Anastaplo's view: they meant for us to do as they said, not as they did.[460] The behavior of our leaders was no more a reliable indicator of the meaning of the Constitution then than it is today. Our executive still seeks to impose prior restraints on publication; our Supreme Court denies full protection of the first amendment to our most popular medium of mass communication; Congress attempts to control mailing of political propaganda. If we do not accept these actions as definitive today, we should not assume that the actions of the Framers define the original understanding of the press clause.

The Sedition Act of 1798 is not definitive either. Its passage was indeed inconsistent with the view that the press clause was intended to protect the press as a critic of government. But the Sedition Act was also inconsistent with everything the Framers had said about the powers of the federal government. They had denied that the federal government had any power to control the press, even in the absence of a first amendment. The Sedition Act can best be understood as a lapse; those who passed it had to have known that it was unconstitutional, or at least that it was inconsistent with the original understanding of the constitution.

But whether they knew or not, the Sedition Act is hardly conclusive proof of the Framers' understanding of the press clause. The Federalist partisans who passed the Sedition Act were not the Framers, and the Federalists' views of the relationship between the people and their government were quite different from those upon which the Constitution and Bill of Rights were based.

I do not claim that the men who proposed, drafted, and ratified the first amendment had any comprehensive theory of freedom of the press. They undoubtedly held various views. Some may have viewed the press clause as a mere tactic to deprive the Anti-Federalists of one of the sticks with which they were beating the Constitution. But this cannot have been the dominant view; the stream of passionate rhetoric that flows through the legislative history of the press clause is too deep and too broad.

The sense one gets from that history is that most of the Framers perceived, however dimly, naively, or incompletely, that freedom of the

460. "In these matters, the sentiments of men are more important than their actions: for sentiments reflect principle, whereas actions are all too often the unfortunate products of passion." Anastaplo, Book Review, [39 N.Y.U.L.Rev. 735, 739 (1964)] (footnote omitted).

press was inextricably related to the new republican form of government and would have to be protected if their vision of government by the people was to succeed.

"OR OF THE PRESS" †

Potter Stewart *

26 Hastings L.J. 631 (1975).

I turn this morning to an inquiry into an aspect of constitutional law that has only recently begun to engage the attention of the Supreme Court. Specifically, I shall discuss the role of the organized press—of the daily newspapers and other established news media—in the system of government created by our Constitution.

It was less than a decade ago—during the Vietnam years—that the people of our country began to become aware of the twin phenomena on a national scale of so-called investigative reporting and an adversary press—that is, a press adversary to the Executive Branch of the Federal Government. And only in the two short years that culminated last summer in the resignation of a President did we fully realize the enormous power that an investigative and adversary press can exert.

The public opinion polls that I have seen indicate that some Americans firmly believe that the former Vice President and former President of the United States were hounded out of office by an arrogant and irresponsible press that had outrageously usurped dictatorial power. And it seems clear that many more Americans, while appreciating and even applauding the service performed by the press in exposing official wrongdoing at the highest levels of our national government, are nonetheless deeply disturbed by what they consider to be the illegitimate power of the organized press in the political structure of our society. It is my thesis this morning that, on the contrary, the established American press in the past ten years, and particularly in the past two years, has performed precisely the function it was intended to perform by those who wrote the First Amendment of our Constitution. I further submit that this thesis is supported by the relevant decisions of the Supreme Court.

Surprisingly, despite the importance of newspapers in the political and social life of our country the Supreme Court has not until very recently been called upon to delineate their constitutional role in our structure of government.

Our history is filled with struggles over the rights and prerogatives of the press, but these disputes rarely found their way to the Supreme

† Excerpted from an address on November 2, 1974, at the Yale Law School Sesquicentennial Convocation, New Haven, Connecticut. The Hastings Law Journal holds no copyright on this material.

* Associate Justice, United States Supreme Court.

Court. The early years of the Republic witnessed controversy over the constitutional validity of the short-lived Alien and Sedition Act, but the controversy never reached the Court. In the next half century there was nationwide turmoil over the right of the organized press to advocate the then subversive view that slavery should be abolished. In Illinois a publisher was killed for publishing abolitionist views. But none of this history made First Amendment law because the Court had earlier held that the Bill of Rights applied only against the Federal Government, not against the individual states.

With the passage of the Fourteenth Amendment, the constitutional framework was modified, and by the 1920's the Court had established that the protections of the First Amendment extend against all government—federal, state, and local.

The next fifty years witnessed a great outpouring of First Amendment litigation, all of which inspired books and articles beyond number. But, with few exceptions, neither these First Amendment cases nor their commentators squarely considered the Constitution's guarantee of a Free Press. Instead, the focus was on its guarantee of free speech. The Court's decisions dealt with the rights of isolated individuals, or of unpopular minority groups, to stand up against governmental power representing an angry or frightened majority. The cases that came to the Court during those years involved the rights of the soapbox orator, the nonconformist pamphleteer, the religious evangelist. The Court was seldom asked to define the rights and privileges, or the responsibilities, of the organized press.

In very recent years cases involving the established press finally have begun to reach the Supreme Court, and they have presented a variety of problems, sometimes arising in complicated factual settings.

In a series of cases, the Court has been called upon to consider the limits imposed by the free press guarantee upon a state's common or statutory law of libel. As a result of those cases, a public figure cannot successfully sue a publisher for libel unless he can show that the publisher maliciously printed a damaging untruth.[1]

The Court has also been called upon to decide whether a newspaper reporter has a First Amendment privilege to refuse to disclose his confidential sources to a grand jury. By a divided vote, the Court found no such privilege to exist in the circumstances of the cases before it.[2]

In another noteworthy case, the Court was asked by the Justice Department to restrain publication by the *New York Times* and other newspapers of the so-called Pentagon Papers. The Court declined to do so.[3]

In yet another case, the question to be decided was whether political groups have a First Amendment or statutory right of access to

1. See Rosenbloom v. Metromedia, Inc., 403 U.S. 29 (1971); Curtis Publ. Co. v. Butts, 388 U.S. 130 (1967); New York Times Co. v. Sullivan, 376 U.S. 254 (1964).

2. Branzburg v. Hayes, 408 U.S. 665 (1972).

3. New York Times Co. v. United States, 403 U.S. 713 (1971).

the federally regulated broadcast channels of radio and television. The Court held there was no such right of access.[4]

Last Term the Court confronted a Florida statute that required newspapers to grant a "right of reply" to political candidates they had criticized. The Court unanimously held this statute to be inconsistent with the guarantees of a free press.[5]

It seems to me that the Court's approach to all these cases has uniformly reflected its understanding that the Free Press guarantee is, in essence, a *structural* provision of the Constitution. Most of the other provisions in the Bill of Rights protect specific liberties or specific rights of individuals: freedom of speech, freedom of worship, the right to counsel, the privilege against compulsory self-incrimination, to name a few. In contrast, the Free Press Clause extends protection to an institution. The publishing business is, in short, the only organized private business that is given explicit constitutional protection.

This basic understanding is essential, I think, to avoid an elementary error of constitutional law. It is tempting to suggest that freedom of the press means only that newspaper publishers are guaranteed freedom of expression. They *are* guaranteed that freedom, to be sure, but so are we all, because of the Free Speech Clause. If the Free Press guarantee meant no more than freedom of expression, it would be a constitutional redundancy. Between 1776 and the drafting of our Constitution, many of the state constitutions contained clauses protecting freedom of the press while at the same time recognizing no general freedom of speech. By including both guarantees in the First Amendment, the Founders quite clearly recognized the distinction between the two.

It is also a mistake to suppose that the only purpose of the constitutional guarantee of a free press is to insure that a newspaper will serve as a neutral forum for debate, a "market place for ideas," a kind of Hyde Park corner for the community. A related theory sees the press as a neutral conduit of information between the people and their elected leaders. These theories, in my view, again give insufficient weight to the institutional autonomy of the press that it was the purpose of the Constitution to guarantee.

In setting up the three branches of the Federal Government, the Founders deliberately created an internally competitive system. As Mr. Justice Brandeis once wrote:[6]

> The [Founders'] purpose was, not to avoid friction, but, by means of the inevitable friction incident to the distribution of the governmental powers among three departments, to save the people from autocracy.

4. Columbia Broadcasting Sys., Inc. v. Democratic Nat'l Comm., 412 U.S. 94 (1973).

5. Miami Herald Publ. Co. v. Tornillo, [418 U.S. 241] (1974).

6. Myers v. United States, 272 U.S. 52, 293 (1926) (dissenting opinion).

The primary purpose of the constitutional guarantee of a free press was a similar one: to create a fourth institution outside the Government as an additional check on the three official branches. Consider the opening words of the Free Press Clause of the Massachusetts Constitution, drafted by John Adams:

> The liberty of the press is essential to the security of the state.

The relevant metaphor, I think, is the metaphor of the Fourth Estate. What Thomas Carlyle wrote about the British Government a century ago has a curiously contemporary ring:

> Burke said there were Three Estates in Parliament; but, in the Reporters' Gallery yonder, there sat a Fourth Estate more important far than they all. It is not a figure of speech or witty saying; it is a literal fact—very momentous to us in these times.

For centuries before our Revolution, the press in England had been licensed, censored, and bedeviled by prosecutions for seditious libel. The British Crown knew that a free press was not just a neutral vehicle for the balanced discussion of diverse ideas. Instead, the free press meant organized, expert scrutiny of government. The press was a conspiracy of the intellect, with the courage of numbers. This formidable check on official power was what the British Crown had feared—and what the American Founders decided to risk.

It is this constitutional understanding, I think, that provides the unifying principle underlying the Supreme Court's recent decisions dealing with the organized press.

Consider first the libel cases. Officials within the three governmental branches are, for all practical purposes, immune from libel and slander suits for statements that they make in the line of duty.[7] This immunity, which has both constitutional and common law origins, aims to insure bold and vigorous prosecution of the public's business. The same basic reasoning applies to the press. By contrast, the Court has never suggested that the constitutional right of free *speech* gives an *individual* any immunity from liability for either libel or slander.

In the cases involving the newspaper reporters' claims that they had a constitutional privilege not to disclose their confidential news sources to a grand jury, the Court rejected the claims by a vote of five to four, or, considering Mr. Justice Powell's concurring opinion, perhaps by a vote of four and a half to four and a half. But if freedom of the press means simply freedom of speech for reporters, this question of a reporter's asserted right to withhold information would have answered itself. None of us—as individuals—has a "free speech" right to refuse to tell a grand jury the identity of someone who has given us information relevant to the grand jury's legitimate inquiry. Only if a reporter is a representative of a protected *institution* does the question become a

7. See Barr v. Matteo, 360 U.S. 564 (1959).

different one. The members of the Court disagreed in answering the question, but the question did not answer itself.

The cases involving the so-called "right of access" to the press raised the issue whether the First Amendment allows government, or indeed *requires* government, to regulate the press so as to make it a genuinely fair and open "market place for ideas." The Court's answer was "no" to both questions. If a newspaper wants to serve as a neutral market place for debate, that is an objective which it is free to choose. And, within limits, that choice is probably necessary to commercially successful journalism. But it is a choice that government cannot constitutionally impose.

Finally the Pentagon Papers case involved the line between secrecy and openness in the affairs of Government. The question, or at least one question, was whether that line is drawn by the Constitution itself. The Justice Department asked the Court to find in the Constitution a basis for prohibiting the publication of allegedly stolen government documents. The Court could find no such prohibition. So far as the Constitution goes, the autonomous press may publish what it knows, and may seek to learn what it can.

But this autonomy cuts both ways. The press is free to do battle against secrecy and deception in government. But the press cannot expect from the Constitution any guarantee that it will succeed. There is no constitutional right to have access to particular government information, or to require openness from the bureaucracy.[8] The public's interest in knowing about its government is protected by the guarantee of a Free Press, but the protection is indirect. The Constitution itself is neither a Freedom of Information Act nor an Official Secrets Act.

The Constitution, in other words, establishes the context, not its resolution. Congress may provide a resolution, at least in some instances, through carefully drawn legislation. For the rest, we must rely, as so often in our system we must, on the tug and pull of the political forces in American society.

Newspapers, television networks, and magazines have sometimes been outrageously abusive, untruthful, arrogant, and hypocritical. But it hardly follows that elimination of a strong and independent press is the way to eliminate abusiveness, untruth, arrogance, or hypocrisy from government itself.

It is quite possible to conceive of the survival of our Republic without an autonomous press. For openness and honesty in government, for an adequate flow of information between the people and their representatives, for a sufficient check on autocracy and despotism, the traditional competition between the three branches of government, supplemented by vigorous political activity, might be enough.

8. Cf. Pell v. Procunier, [417 U.S. 817] (1974); Saxbe v. Washington Post Co., [417 U.S. 843] (1974).

The press could be relegated to the status of a public utility. The guarantee of free speech would presumably put some limitation on the regulation to which the press could be subjected. But if there were no guarantee of a free press, government could convert the communications media into a neutral "market place of ideas." Newspapers and television networks could then be required to promote contemporary government policy or current notions of social justice.[9]

Such a constitution is possible; it might work reasonably well. But it is not the Constitution the Founders wrote. It is not the Constitution that has carried us through nearly two centuries of national life. Perhaps our liberties might survive without an independent established press. But the Founders doubted it, and, in the year 1974, I think we can all be thankful for their doubts.

FIRST NATIONAL BANK OF BOSTON V. BELLOTTI. The following excerpt from Chief Justice Burger's concurring opinion in *Bellotti,* p. 37, supra, responds to Justice Stewart's approach:

Despite these factual similarities between media and nonmedia corporations, those who view the Press Clause as somehow conferring special and extraordinary privileges or status on the "institutional press"—which are not extended to those who wish to express ideas other than by publishing a newspaper—might perceive no danger to institutional media corporations flowing from the position asserted by Massachusetts. Under this narrow reading of the Press Clause, government could perhaps impose on nonmedia corporations restrictions not permissible with respect to "media" enterprises. [ ] The Court has not yet squarely resolved whether the Press Clause confers upon the "institutional press" any freedom from government restraint not enjoyed by all others.

I perceive two fundamental difficulties with a narrow reading of the Press Clause. First, although certainty on this point is not possible, the history of the Clause does not suggest that the authors contemplated a "special" or "institutional" privilege. [ ] The common 18th century understanding of freedom of the press is suggested by Andrew Bradford, a colonial American newspaperman. In defining the nature of the liberty, he did not limit it to a particular group:

> "But, by the *Freedom of the Press,* I mean a Liberty, within the Bounds of Law, for any Man to communicate to the Public, his Sentiments on the Important Points of *Religion* and *Government;* of proposing any Laws, which he apprehends may be for the Good of his Countrey, and of applying for the Repeal of such, as he Judges pernicious. . . .

9. Cf. Pittsburgh Press Co. v. Pittsburgh Comm'n on Human Relations, 413 U.S. 376 (1973).

> "This is the *Liberty of the Press,* the great *Palladium* of all our other *Liberties,* which I hope the good People of this Province, will forever enjoy . . . ." A. Bradford, *Sentiments on the Liberty of the Press,* in L. Levy, *Freedom of the Press from Zenger to Jefferson* 41–42 (1966) (emphasis deleted) (first published in Bradford's The American Weekly Mercury, a Philadelphia newspaper, Apr. 25, 1734).

. . .

Those interpreting the Press Clause as extending protection only to, or creating a special role for, the "institutional press" must either (a) assert such an intention on the part of the Framers for which no supporting evidence is available, [ ]; (b) argue that events after 1791 somehow operated to "constitutionalize" this interpretation, [ ]; or (c) candidly acknowledging the absence of historical support, suggest that the intent of the Framers is not important today. [ ]

To conclude that the Framers did not intend to limit the freedom of the press to one select group is not necessarily to suggest that the Press Clause is redundant. The Speech Clause standing alone may be viewed as a protection of the liberty to express ideas and beliefs,[4] while the Press Clause focuses specifically on the liberty to disseminate expression broadly and "comprehends every sort of publication which affords a vehicle of information and opinion." Lovell v. Griffin, 303 U.S. 444, 452 (1938).[5] Yet there is no fundamental distinction between expression and dissemination. The liberty encompassed by the Press Clause, although complementary to and a natural extension of Speech Clause liberty, merited special mention simply because it had been more often the object of official restraints. Soon after the invention of the printing press, English and continental monarchs, fearful of the power implicit in its use and the threat to Establishment thought and order—political and religious—devised restraints, such as licensing, censors, indices of prohibited books, and prosecutions for seditious libel, which generally

4. The simplest explanation of the Speech and Press Clauses might be that the former protects oral communications; the latter, written. But the historical evidence does not strongly support this explanation. The first draft of what became the free expression provisions of the First Amendment, one proposed by Madison on June 8, 1789, as an addition to Art. 1, § 9, read:

> "The people shall not be deprived or abridged of their right to speak, to write, or to publish their sentiments; and the freedom of the press, as one of the great bulwarks of liberty, shall be inviolable." 1 Annals of Cong. 434 (1789).

The language was changed to its current form, "freedom of speech, or of the press," by the Committee of Eleven to which Madison's amendments were referred. (There is no explanation for the change and the language was not altered thereafter.) It seems likely that the Committee shortened Madison's language preceding the semicolon in his draft to "freedom of speech" without intending to diminish the scope of protection contemplated by Madison's phrase; in short, it was a stylistic change.

5. It is not strange that "press," the word for what was then the sole means of broad dissemination of ideas and news, would be used to describe the freedom to communicate with a large, unseen audience.

Changes wrought by 20th century technology, of course, have rendered the printing press as it existed in 1791 as obsolete as Watt's copying or letter press. It is the core meaning of "press" as used in the constitutional text which must govern.

were unknown in the preprinting press era. Official restrictions were the official response to the new, disquieting idea that this invention would provide a means for mass communication.

The second fundamental difficulty with interpreting the Press Clause as conferring special status on a limited group is one of definition. [ ] The very task of including some entities within the "institutional press" while excluding others, whether undertaken by legislature, court, or administrative agency, is reminiscent of the abhorred licensing system of Tudor and Stuart England—a system the First Amendment was intended to ban from this country. Lovell v. Griffin, supra, at 451–452. Further, the officials undertaking that task would be required to distinguish the protected from the unprotected on the basis of such variables as content of expression, frequency or fervor of expression, or ownership of the technological means of dissemination. Yet nothing in this Court's opinions supports such a confining approach to the scope of Press Clause protection.[6] . . .

. . .

Because the First Amendment was meant to guarantee freedom to express and communicate ideas, I can see no difference between the right of those who seek to disseminate ideas by way of a newspaper and those who give lectures or speeches and seek to enlarge the audience by publication and wide dissemination. "[T]he purpose of the Constitution was not to erect the press into a privileged institution but to protect all persons in their right to print what they will as well as to utter it. '. . . the liberty of the press is no greater and no less . . . ' than the liberty of every citizen of the Republic." Pennekamp v. Florida, 328 U.S. 331, 364 (1946) (Frankfurter, J., concurring).

In short, the First Amendment does not "belong" to any definable category of persons or entities: It belongs to all who exercise its freedoms.

Notes and Questions

1. Professor Nimmer, in Introduction—Is Freedom of the Press a Redundancy: What Does It Add to Freedom of Speech? 26 Hastings L.J. 639, 641 (1975), argued that in the post-Revolutionary period "freedom of speech and of the press were thought of as interchangeable." He continued: "But as we have seen in other constitutional contexts, the original understanding of the Founders is not necessarily controlling. It is what they said, and not necessarily what they meant, that in the last analysis may be determinative."

Thus, with the historical roots of Justice Stewart's "institutional" press unclear or not controlling, the question shifted to whether, history aside, the present role of the press demands special First Amendment protection. Consider this passage from Abrams, The Press

6. Near v. Minnesota ex rel. Olson, 283 U.S. 697 (1931), which examined the meaning of freedom of the press, did not involve a traditional institutionalized newspaper but rather an occasional publication (nine issues) more nearly approximating the product of a pamphleteer than the traditional newspaper.

Is Different: Reflections on Justice Stewart and the Autonomous Press, 7 Hofstra L.Rev. 563, 591–92 (1979):

> The press is often likened to a watchdog guarding against abuse of government power. [ ]. . . . If, as I would urge, these metaphors are apt, it is hardly because the press invariably serves as a vigilant protector of the public from its government; few paper readers would recognize such a magical transformation of the too often bland products thrust upon their doorsteps. On the contrary, it is because the press is the *only* institution that can serve on a continuing basis as an open eye of the public—and because, now and again, the press plays precisely this role.

2. It might be argued that the speech clause of the First Amendment protects just that—speech—while the press clause protects written communication. Although the Chief Justice rejects that view, the answer is not that simple, according to Nimmer, at 651–52:

> Such a definition of "the press" would be odd because it is both too narrow and too broad. It is too narrow in that it would exclude from "the press" those components of the media which deal in spoken rather than written expression. . . .
>
> But to regard "the press" as relating to all written expression would also constitute an unduly broad definition. It is true that the Supreme Court has said that "[t]he liberty of the press is not confined to newspapers and periodicals. It necessarily embraces pamphlets and leaflets. . . . The press in its historic connotation comprehends every sort of publication which affords a vehicle of information and opinion,"[66] and, further, that it includes "the right of the lonely pamphleteer who uses carbon paper or a mimeograph as much as of the large metropolitan publisher who utilizes the latest photocomposition methods."[67] Flexible as this concept may be in terms of sophistication of equipment and production cost, it would seem that something more is called for than the mere act of applying words to paper, even if followed by a transfer of the paper to a given individual. As the above quoted passage suggests, at the very least in order to qualify as a part of "the press" there must be a "publication." That is, there must be an act of publishing in the copyright sense, i.e., copies of the work must be made available to members of the public. . . . Whether the distinction is to turn on the copyright definition of publication or on some other standard, it is clear that accepted usage already distinguishes between visual materials which comprise a part of press activities and those which are speech but not press.

In the following excerpt Professor Lange argues that separate treatment for speech and press is justified only if "enduring distinctions between them" can be recognized.

---

66. Lovell v. City of Griffin, 303 U.S. 444, 452 (1938).

67. Branzburg v. Hayes, 408 U.S. 665, 704 (1972).

THE SPEECH AND PRESS CLAUSES

David Lange

23 UCLA L.Rev. 77, 99 (1975).

Professor Nimmer suggests that the distinction between speech and press can be expressed in terms of publication or acts leading toward general dissemination.[113] That seems at least partially satisfactory. Historically, the first function of the press has been to amplify speech. Dissemination, then, not only reflects the difference between the two terms but expresses their relationship as well. The difficulty, however, is that Justice Stewart and Professor Nimmer are not prepared to rely on a distinction as highly conceptual as this. Instead they appear to fall back upon two other means of distinguishing "speech" from "press." The first employs a "structural" definition; "freedom of the press" is seen as protecting the social institution which has come to be known as the "mass media." An alternative, "functional" definition emphasizes the supposed differences between the social functions served by free speech and a free press.

At first reading, Justice Stewart seems explicit. He thinks of the organized press, of the business, the institution. He refers in his speech to "the publishing business," but it seems clear that he would include broadcasters and perhaps other representatives of the mass media as well. . . . It is not clear, however, who might be excluded from the press as he views it. Is "the lonely pamphleteer" protected by the press clause? What of the novelist and the film maker? The "underground press?" The traditional, if perhaps unthinking, answer of the Court would appear to be that they are included. And Justice Stewart's own opinions have not suggested clear disagreement with that response. Yet none of these is necessarily a part of the mass media and some, by definition, have virtually no institutional identification. Is it a misreading, after all, to suppose that Justice Stewart means to define the institutional press in terms of structure? Would he define it in terms of role or function instead? . . . If it is function, rather than structure, which defines the press, the definition again is at least approximately compatible with the conceptual relationship between speech and press. But a definition expressed in terms of function seems equally at odds with Justice Stewart's emphatic references to the organized mass media . . . . With misgivings, then, one is forced to conclude either that the Justice does not know himself what he means by "the press" or, more probably, that he has not yet had the occasion to express himself fully.

Perhaps the contemporary press must be defined by both structure and function. That seems to be Professor Nimmer's view. He describes the chief function of the press as the pursuit of the democratic

113. [ ] He suggests, however, that this may be a minimum standard and that others could be employed. [ ]

dialogue. And he expresses, if he does not quite define, his view of structure in his repeated use of the term "media" as a synonym for "the press." . . .

. . .

. . . It is not altogether impossible to define "the press." We do so every day for many general purposes and, less frequently, for the purpose of defining legal consequences as well. But it is still unlikely, in my opinion, that we will succeed in defining the press in ways which will prove satisfactory in recognizing separate rights under the press clause. The problem comes to this: If the press is defined broadly enough to include the pamphleteer and the underground, the definition also will have to approach speech so closely that the exclusion of speech will often seem arbitrary and unjustified. We will have, in Justice Stewart's words, "a structural provision," but with no distinct structure. If, on the other hand, the pamphleteer and the underground are excluded, the result is perverse; these are two elements in the contemporary press which the Framers themselves would have recognized. Alternatively, I suppose, each element in the speech-press spectrum might be examined individually, sometimes gaining the protection of the press clause and sometimes not. That may make sense as a general approach to the first amendment, but it is not clear that distinctions between speech and the press should be advanced that way. In fact, to make a system like that work—that is, to recognize overriding differences between speech and the press without particular regard for structure—it would be necessary to emphasize functions and, more important, to assign them values or weight. And that is just where the real uncertainties began.

Notes and Questions

1. If the above issues were resolved, what might the media gain from a substantive press clause? The press at various times has claimed immunity from "gag" orders and prior restraints; a privilege not to respond in civil suits to questions about reporters' and editors' states of mind; special protection against searches and seizures, at least when the press is not suspected of criminal activity; and general freedom from government regulations, such as those designed to promote fairness, diversity of press ownership, or other economic or social policy. The cases are collected and discussed by Baker, Press Rights and Government Power to Structure the Press, 34 U.Miami L.Rev. 838–39 (1980), who argues that the press is entitled only to what he terms "defensive rights": testimonial privileges, protection against searches and seizures, and some protections against regulation.

2. What might the press lose? If the media gain special rights because of their status as the public's eyes and ears, might special responsibilities follow? Anthony Lewis, a columnist for the New York Times, has expressed that fear:

> The whole idea of treating the press as an "institution" arouses uneasy feelings. In the American system, institutions are usually subject to external check. The press has operated as a freebooter, outside the system. The more formally it is treated as a fourth branch of government, the more pressing will be demands that it be made formally accountable.

Lewis, A Preferred Position for Journalism?, 7 Hofstra L.Rev. 595, 605 (1979). Further, he fears that special protection "may . . . encourage hubris, the excessive pride that goes before a fall":

> Powerful newspapers and networks are not universally beloved as it is; there is talk about the arrogance of the media. Ordinary citizens may find it hard to understand why the press should have rights denied to them. And in the long run, rights depend on public understanding and support.

In his cited article, Abrams responds at 574:

> . . . Lewis' position is . . . troubling. Not necessarily so in its assessment of the current public mood. For whatever else is true, the press will surely make no long-term friends by being unwilling to defend its own constitutional role in reporting the news to the public; and it will deceive no one except itself by acting as if it believes that the public interest in news reporting is no different from—or not more significant than—the public interest in many other aspects of American life.

See the horror story spun by Van Alstyne, The Hazards to the Press of Claiming a "Preferred Position," 28 Hastings L.J. 761 (1977).

Justice Stewart's speech suggests a middle ground in which the First Amendment would not grant the press special access to government-controlled information. Abrams apparently agrees: "A press that continually applies to the courts for vindication of its right to gather information cannot credibly be the same press that tells the same courts that what the press prints and why it prints it are not matters that the courts may even consider." (p. 591).

3. Lange and Lewis also argue that free *speech* rights may be impaired by a separate constitutional role for the press. Without the "distinct institutional identification" supplied by the press, Lange says, individual interests in speech "may find it more difficult to stand up against the constraints which a mass society inevitably finds it convenient to impose." Lange argues further that

> [I]f public issues are to be debated, it is not sensible to treat two speakers differently merely on the ground that one proposes to speak privately while another intends to use the media. No presupposition can justify that; we have no way of knowing how far the private communication will carry or which of the two will prove to be the more enduring. Today, the private letters of Madison, Jefferson and Adams are among our public treasures. . . .

Of course, it does not necessarily follow that separate first amendment status for the press will affect the interests of private speech adversely in these cases. It is even possible that a formal separation would force the Court to take a new and beneficial look at speech. Against this possibility, however, I think another is more likely. In the context of the libel cases alone, there is already evidence that the interests of nonmedia speech are apt to be degraded when they are set at odds with media speech. Mr. Justice Stewart is much too ready to point out that the "right of free speech" gives individuals no immunity. The statement would be significant if it were no more than an observation of fact. But his purpose, clearly, was to demonstrate the superior claim of the media to the immunity which speech is not to have.

4. Steven Shiffrin has argued forcefully against giving the media more First Amendment protection than that given to others:

> . . . The idea that first amendment protections should be consciously divvied out in more generous doses to those with knowledge, wealth, and capacity to cause damage is indefensible. . . .
>
> Affording non-media defendants less first amendment protection than media defendants would deter non-media contributions to the democratic dialogue (and thus would weaken the media's contribution), would favor those with greater capacity to cause damage and with greater ability to compensate for that damage (by spreading the risk), would require difficult determinations as to which communications would and would not merit the label "press" or "media," would strain basic principles of first amendment equality, and would diminish respect for the democratic process.

Shiffrin, Defamatory Non-Media Speech and First Amendment Methodology 25 UCLA L.Rev. 915, 934–35 (1978).

D. THE FIRST AMENDMENT APPLIED

1. Prior Restraint and Subsequent Sanctions

Blackstone's view of press freedom had support into this century. In one case, Justice Holmes observed that the First Amendment prevents all "previous restraints upon publications," but allows "the subsequent punishment of such as may be deemed contrary to the public welfare. . . . The preliminary freedom extends to the false as to the true; the subsequent punishment may extend as well to the true as to the false." Patterson v. Colorado, 205 U.S. 454, 462 (1907).

NEAR v. MINNESOTA

Supreme Court of the United States, 1931.
283 U.S. 697, 51 S.Ct. 625, 75 L.Ed. 1357.
Noted, 31 Colum.L.Rev. 1148, 30 Mich.L.Rev. 279, 80 U.Pa.L.Rev. 130, 41 Yale L.J. 262.

[A Minnesota law authorized abatement, as a public nuisance, of a "malicious, scandalous and defamatory newspaper, or other periodical." In that action the defendant had available the defense "that the truth was published with good motives and for justifiable ends." Pursuant to that law, a local prosecutor sought to abate publication of "The Saturday Press." The "Press" had published articles charging in substance "that a Jewish gangster was in control of gambling, bootlegging and racketeering in Minneapolis, and that law enforcing officers and agencies were not energetically performing their duties." After summarizing the nature of the charges, the Court concluded that "There is no question but that the articles made serious accusations against the public officials named and others in connection with the prevalence of crimes and the failure to expose and punish them." After the prosecutor presented his evidence the defendant rested without offering evidence. A state court order "abated" the "Press" and perpetually enjoined the defendants from publishing or circulating "any publication whatsoever which is a malicious, scandalous or defamatory newspaper." The state supreme court affirmed, adding that it saw no reason for "defendants to construe the judgment as restraining them from operating a newspaper in harmony with the public welfare, to which all must yield" and that defendants had not indicated a desire "to conduct their business in the usual and legitimate manner."]

MR. CHIEF JUSTICE HUGHES delivered the opinion of the Court.

. . .

This statute, for the suppression as a public nuisance of a newspaper or periodical, is unusual, if not unique, and raises questions of grave importance transcending the local interests involved in the particular action. It is no longer open to doubt that the liberty of the press, and of speech, is within the liberty safeguarded by the due process clause of the Fourteenth Amendment from invasion by state action. . . . Liberty of speech, and of the press, is also not an absolute right, and the State may punish its abuse. Whitney v. California, [ ]. Liberty, in each of its phases, has its history and connotation and, in the present instance, the inquiry is as to the historic conception of the liberty of the press and whether the statute under review violates the essential attributes of that liberty.

. . .

If we cut through mere details of procedure, the operation and effect of the statute in substance is that public authorities may bring the owner or publisher of a newspaper or periodical before a judge upon a charge of conducting a business of publishing scandalous and defamatory matter—in particular that the matter consists of charges against public officers of official dereliction—and unless the owner or publisher is able and disposed to bring competent evidence to satisfy the judge that the charges are true and are published with good motives and for justifiable ends, his newspaper or periodical is suppressed and further publication is made punishable as a contempt. This is of the essence of censorship.

The question is whether a statute authorizing such proceedings in restraint of publication is consistent with the conception of the liberty of the press as historically conceived and guaranteed. In determining the extent of the constitutional protection, it has been generally, if not universally, considered that it is the chief purpose of the guaranty to prevent previous restraints upon publication. The struggle in England, directed against the legislative power of the licenser, resulted in renunciation of the censorship of the press. The liberty deemed to be established was thus described by Blackstone: "The liberty of the press is indeed essential to the nature of a free state; but this consists in laying no *previous* restraints upon publications, and not in freedom from censure for criminal matter when published. Every freeman has an undoubted right to lay what sentiments he pleases before the public; to forbid this, is to destroy the freedom of the press; but if he publishes what is improper, mischievous or illegal, he must take the consequence of his own temerity." 4 Bl.Com. 151, 152; see Story on the Constitution, §§ 1884, 1889. The distinction was early pointed out between the extent of the freedom with respect to censorship under our constitutional system and that enjoyed in England. Here, as Madison said, "the great and essential rights of the people are secured against legislative as well as against executive ambition. They are secured, not by laws paramount to prerogative, but by constitutions paramount to laws. This security of the freedom of the press requires that it should be exempt not only from previous restraints by the Executive, as in Great Britain, but from legislative restraint also." Report on the Virginia Resolutions, Madison's Works, vol. IV, p. 543. . . .

The criticism upon Blackstone's statement has not been because immunity from previous restraint upon publication has not been regarded as deserving of special emphasis, but chiefly because that immunity cannot be deemed to exhaust the conception of the liberty guaranteed by state and federal constitutions. The point of criticism has been "that the mere exemption from previous restraint cannot be all that is secured by the constitutional provisions"; and that "the liberty of the press might be rendered a mockery and a delusion, and the phrase itself a by-word, if, while every man was at liberty to publish what he pleased, the public authorities might nevertheless punish him for harmless publications." 2 Cooley, Const.Lim., 8th ed., p. 885. But it is recognized that punishment for the abuse of the liberty accorded to the press is essential to the protection of the public, and that the common law rules that subject the libeler to responsibility for the public offense, as well as for the private injury, are not abolished by the protection extended in our constitutions. id. pp. 883, 884. The law of criminal libel rests upon that secure foundation. . . .

The objection has also been made that the principle as to immunity from previous restraint is stated too broadly, if every such restraint is deemed to be prohibited. That is undoubtedly true; the protection even as to previous restraint is not absolutely unlimited. But the limitation has been recognized only in exceptional cases: "When a nation is at war many things that might be said in time of peace are such a hindrance to its effort that their utterance will not be endured so long as men fight and that no Court could regard them as protected by any constitutional right." Schenck v. United States, 249 U.S. 47, 52. No one would question but that a government might prevent actual obstruction to its recruiting service or the publication of the sailing dates of transports or the number and location of troops. On similar grounds, the primary requirements of decency may be enforced against obscene publications. The security of the community life may be protected against incitements to acts of violence and the overthrow by force of orderly government. The constitutional guaranty of free speech does not "protect a man from an injunction against uttering words that may have all the effect of force. Gompers v. Buck Stove & Range Co., 221 U.S. 418, 439." Schenck v. United States, supra. These limitations are not applicable here. Nor are we now concerned with questions as to the extent of authority to prevent publications in order to protect private rights according to the principles governing the exercise of the jurisdiction of courts of equity.

The exceptional nature of its limitations places in a strong light the general conception that liberty of the press, historically considered and taken up by the Federal Constitution, has meant, principally although not exclusively, immunity from previous restraints or censorship. The conception of the liberty of the press in this country had broadened with the exigencies of the colonial period and with the efforts to secure freedom from oppressive administration. That liberty was especially cherished for the immunity it afforded from previous restraint of the publication of censure of public officers and charges of official misconduct. . . . Madison, who was the leading spirit in the preparation of the First Amendment of the Federal Constitution, thus described the practice and sentiment which led to the guaranties of liberty of the press in state constitutions: [10]

> "In every State, probably, in the Union, the press has exerted a freedom in canvassing the merits and measures of public men of every description which has not been confined to the strict limits of the common law. On this footing the freedom of the press has stood; on this footing it yet stands. . . . Some degree of abuse is inseparable from the proper use of everything, and in no instance is this more true than in that of the press. It has according-

10. Report on the Virginia Resolutions, Madison's Works, vol. iv, 544.

ly been decided by the practice of the States, that it is better to leave a few of its noxious branches to their luxuriant growth, than, by pruning them away, to injure the vigour of those yielding the proper fruits. . . . "

The fact that for approximately one hundred and fifty years there has been almost an entire absence of attempts to impose previous restraints upon publications relating to the malfeasance of public officers is significant of the deep-seated conviction that such restraints would violate constitutional right. . . .

The importance of this immunity has not lessened. . . . [T]he administration of government has become more complex, the opportunities for malfeasance and corruption have multiplied, crime has grown to most serious proportions, and the danger of its protection by unfaithful officials and of the impairment of the fundamental security of life and property by criminal alliances and official neglect, emphasizes the primary need of a vigilant and courageous press, especially in great cities. The fact that the liberty of the press may be abused by miscreant purveyors of scandal does not make any the less necessary the immunity of the press from previous restraint in dealing with official misconduct. Subsequent punishment for such abuses as may exist is the appropriate remedy, consistent with constitutional privilege.

In attempted justification of the statute, it is said that it deals not with publication *per se,* but with the "business" of publishing defamation. If, however, the publisher has a constitutional right to publish, without previous restraint, an edition of his newspaper charging official derelictions, it cannot be denied that he may publish subsequent editions for the same purpose. He does not lose his right by exercising it. . . .

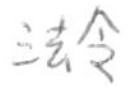

Nor can it be said that the constitutional freedom from previous restraint is lost because charges are made of derelictions which constitute crimes. . . . Historically, there is no such limitation; it is inconsistent with the reason which underlies the privilege, as the privilege so limited would be of slight value for the purposes for which it came to be established.

The statute in question cannot be justified by reason of the fact that the publisher is permitted to show, before injunction issues, that the matter published is true and is published with good motives and for justifiable ends. If such a statute, authorizing suppression and injunction on such a basis, is constitutionally valid, it would be equally permissible for the legislature to provide that at any time the publisher of any newspaper could be brought before a court, or even an administrative officer (as the constitutional protection may not be regarded as resting on mere procedural details) and required to produce proof of the truth of his publication, or of what he intended to publish, and of his motives, or stand enjoined. If this can be done, the legislature may provide machinery for determining in the complete exercise of its discretion what are justifiable ends and restrain publication accordingly. And it would be but a step to a complete system of censorship. . . .

. . .

For these reasons we hold the statute, so far as it authorized the proceedings in this action . . . to be an infringement of the liberty of the press guaranteed by the Fourteenth Amendment. . . .

MR. JUSTICE BUTLER, dissenting. . . .

The Minnesota statute does not operate as a *previous* restraint on publication within the proper meaning of that phrase. It does not authorize administrative control in advance such as was formerly exercised by the licensers and censors but prescribes a remedy to be enforced by a suit in equity. In this case there was previous publication made in the course of the business of regularly producing malicious, scandalous and defamatory periodicals. The business and publications unquestionably constitute an abuse of the right of free press. The statute denounces the things done as a nuisance on the ground, as stated by the state supreme court, that they threaten morals, peace and good order. . . . It is fanciful to suggest similarity between the granting or enforcement of the decree authorized by this statute to prevent *further* publication of malicious, scandalous and defamatory articles and the *previous restraint* upon the press by licensers as referred to by Blackstone and described in the history of the times to which he alludes. . . .

. . .

MR. JUSTICE VAN DEVANTER, MR. JUSTICE MCREYNOLDS, and MR. JUSTICE SUTHERLAND concur in this opinion.

Prior restraints are considered in a different context in the next case.

NEW YORK TIMES CO. v. UNITED STATES

Supreme Court of the United States, 1971.
403 U.S. 713, 91 S.Ct. 2140, 29 L.Ed.2d 822.
Noted, 85 Harv.L.Rev. 199, 18 Loyola L.Rev. 151, 47 Notre Dame Law. 927.

PER CURIAM.

We granted certiorari in these cases in which the United States seeks to enjoin the New York Times and the Washington Post from publishing the contents of a classified study entitled "History of U.S. Decision-Making Process on Viet Nam Policy." [ ]

"Any system of prior restraints of expression comes to this Court bearing a heavy presumption against its constitutional validity." Bantam Books, Inc. v. Sullivan, 372 U.S. 58, 70 (1963); see also Near v. Minnesota, 283 U.S. 697 (1931). The Government "thus carries a heavy burden of showing justification for the imposition of such a restraint." Organization for a Better Austin v. Keefe, 402 U.S. 415, 419 (1971). The District Court for the Southern District of New York in the *New York Times* case and the District Court for the District of Columbia and the Court of Appeals for the District of Columbia Circuit in the *Washington Post* case held that the Government had not met that burden. We agree.

The judgment of the Court of Appeals for the District of Columbia Circuit is therefore affirmed. The order of the Court of Appeals for the Second Circuit is reversed and the case is remanded with directions to enter a judgment affirming the judgment of the District Court for the Southern District of New York. The stays entered June 25, 1971, by the Court are vacated. The judgments shall issue forthwith.

So ordered.

MR. JUSTICE BLACK, with whom MR. JUSTICE DOUGLAS joins, concurring.

I adhere to the view that the Government's case against the Washington Post should have been dismissed and that the injunction against the New York Times should have been vacated without oral argument when the cases were first presented to this Court. I believe that every moment's continuance of the injunction against these newspapers amounts to a flagrant, indefensible, and continuing violation of the First Amendment. . . .

. . .

. . . The Government does not even attempt to rely on any act of Congress. Instead it makes the bold and dangerously far-reaching contention that the courts should take it upon themselves to "make" a law abridging freedom of the press in the name of equity, presidential power and national security, even when the representatives of the people in Congress have adhered to the command of the First Amendment and refused to make such a law. . . . To find that the President has "inherent power" to halt the publication of news by resort to the courts would wipe out the First Amendment and destroy the fundamental liberty and security of the very people the Government hopes to make "secure." No one can read the history of the adoption of the First Amendment without being convinced beyond any doubt that it was injunctions like those sought here that Madison and his collaborators intended to outlaw in this Nation for all time.

The word "security" is a broad, vague generality whose contours should not be invoked to abrogate the fundamental law embodied in the First Amendment. The guarding of military and diplomatic secrets at the expense of informed representative government provides no real security for our Republic. . . .

MR. JUSTICE DOUGLAS, with whom MR. JUSTICE BLACK joins, concurring.

While I join the opinion of the Court I believe it necessary to express my views more fully.

It should be noted at the outset that the First Amendment provides that "Congress shall make no law . . . abridging the freedom of speech, or of the press." That leaves, in my view, no room for governmental restraint on the press.

There is, moreover, no statute barring the publication by the press of the material which the Times and the Post seek to use. . . .

. . .

So any power that the Government possesses must come from its "inherent power."

The power to wage war is "the power to wage war successfully." See Hirabayashi v. United States, 320 U.S. 81, 93 (1943). But the war power stems from a declaration of war. The Constitution by Art. I, § 8, gives Congress, not the President, power "[t]o declare War." Nowhere are presidential wars authorized. We need not decide therefore what leveling effect the war power of Congress might have.

These disclosures [3] may have a serious impact. But that is no basis for sanctioning a previous restraint on the press. . . .

. . .

The Government says that it has inherent powers to go into court and obtain an injunction to protect the national interest, which in this case is alleged to be national security. Near v. Minnesota, [ ], repudiated that expansive doctrine in no uncertain terms.

The dominant purpose of the First Amendment was to prohibit the widespread practice of governmental suppression of embarrassing information. It is common knowledge that the First Amendment was adopted against the widespread use of the common law of seditious libel to punish the dissemination of material that is embarrassing to the powers-that-be. [ ] The present cases will, I think, go down in history as the most dramatic illustration of that principle. A debate of large proportions goes on in the Nation over our posture in Vietnam. That debate antedated the disclosure of the contents of the present documents. The latter are highly relevant to the debate in progress.

Secrecy in government is fundamentally anti-democratic, perpetuating bureaucratic errors. Open debate and discussion of public issues are vital to our national health. On public questions there should be "uninhibited, robust, and wide-open" debate. [ ]

. . .

MR. JUSTICE BRENNAN, concurring.

. . .

3. There are numerous sets of this material in existence and they apparently are not under any controlled custody. Moreover, the President has sent a set to the Congress. We start then with a case where there already is rather wide distribution of the material that is destined for publicity, not secrecy. I have gone over the material listed in the *in camera* brief of the United States. It is all history, not future events. None of it is more recent than 1968.

The error that has pervaded these cases from the outset was the granting of any injunctive relief whatsoever, interim or otherwise. The entire thrust of the Government's claim throughout these cases has been that publication of the material sought to be enjoined "could," or "might," or "may" prejudice the national interest in various ways. But the First Amendment tolerates absolutely no prior judicial restraints of the press predicated upon surmise or conjecture that untoward consequences may result.* Our cases, it is true, have indicated that there is a single, extremely narrow class of cases in which the First Amendment's ban on prior judicial restraint may be overridden. Our cases have thus far indicated that such cases may arise only when the Nation "is at war," Schenck v. United States, [ ], during which times "[n]o one would question but that a government might prevent actual obstruction to its recruiting service or the publication of the sailing dates of transports or the number and location of troops." Near v. Minnesota, [ ]. Even if the present world situation were assumed to be tantamount to a time of war, or if the power of presently available armaments would justify even in peacetime the suppression of information that would set in motion a nuclear holocaust, in neither of these actions has the Government presented or even alleged that publication of items from or based upon the material at issue would cause the happening of an event of that nature. . . .

MR. JUSTICE STEWART, with whom MR. JUSTICE WHITE joins, concurring.

. . .

In the absence of the governmental checks and balances present in other areas of our national life, the only effective restraint upon executive policy and power in the areas of our national life, the only effective restraint upon executive policy and power in the areas of national defense and international affairs may lie in an enlightened citizenry—in an informed and critical public opinion which alone can here protect the values of democratic government. For this reason it is perhaps here that a press that is alert, aware, and free most vitally serves the basic purpose of the First Amendment. For without an informed and free press there cannot be an enlightened people.

Yet it is elementary that the successful conduct of international diplomacy and the maintenance of an effective national defense require both confidentiality and secrecy. . . .

I think there can be but one answer to this dilemma, if dilemma it be. The responsibility must be where the power is. If the Constitution

* Freedman v. Maryland, 380 U.S. 51 (1965), and similar cases regarding temporary restraints of allegedly obscene materials are not in point. For those cases rest upon the proposition that "obscenity is not protected by the freedoms of speech and press." Roth v. United States, 354 U.S. 476, 481 (1957). Here there is no question but that the material sought to be suppressed is within the protection of the First Amendment; the only question is whether, notwithstanding that fact, its publication may be enjoined for a time because of the presence of an overwhelming national interest. . . .

gives the Executive a large degree of unshared power in the conduct of foreign affairs and the maintenance of our national defense, then under the Constitution the Executive must have the largely unshared duty to determine and preserve the degree of internal security necessary to exercise that power successfully. . . .

This is not to say that Congress and the courts have no role to play. Undoubtedly Congress has the power to enact specific and appropriate criminal laws to protect government property and preserve government secrets. Congress has passed such laws, and several of them are of very colorable relevance to the apparent circumstances of these cases. And if a criminal prosecution is instituted, it will be the responsibility of the courts to decide the applicability of the criminal law under which the charge is brought. Moreover, if Congress should pass a specific law authorizing civil proceedings in this field, the courts would likewise have the duty to decide the constitutionality of such a law as well as its applicability to the facts proved.

But in the cases before us we are asked neither to construe specific regulations nor to apply specific laws. We are asked, instead, to perform a function that the Constitution gave to the Executive, not the Judiciary. We are asked, quite simply, to prevent the publication by two newspapers of material that the Executive Branch insists should not, in the national interest, be published. I am convinced that the Executive is correct with respect to some of the documents involved. But I cannot say that disclosure of any of them will surely result in direct, immediate, and irreparable damage to our Nation or its people. That being so, there can under the First Amendment be but one judicial resolution of the issues before us. I join the judgments of the Court.

MR. JUSTICE WHITE, with whom MR. JUSTICE STEWART joins, concurring.

I concur in today's judgments, but only because of the concededly extraordinary protection against prior restraints enjoyed by the press under our constitutional system. I do not say that in no circumstances would the First Amendment permit an injunction against publishing information about government plans or operations.[1] Nor, after examin-

1. The Congress has authorized a strain of prior restraints against private parties in certain instances. The National Labor Relations Board routinely issues cease-and-desist orders against employers who it finds have threatened or coerced employees in the exercise of protected rights. See 29 U.S.C. § 160(c). Similarly, the Federal Trade Commission is empowered to impose a cease-and-desist orders against unfair methods of competition. 15 U.S.C. § 45(b). Such orders can, and quite often do, restrict what may be spoken or written under certain circumstances. See, e.g., NLRB v. Gissel Packing Co., 395 U.S. 575, 616–620 (1969). Article I, § 8, of the Constitution authorizes Congress to secure the "exclusive right" of authors to their writings, and no one denies that a newspaper can properly be enjoined from publishing the copyrighted works of another. See Westermann Co. v. Dispatch Printing Co., 249 U.S. 100 (1919). Newspapers do themselves rely from time to time on the copyright as a means of protecting their accounts of important events. However, those enjoined under the statutes relating to the National Labor Relations Board and the Federal Trade Commission are private parties, not the press; and when the press is enjoined under the copyright laws the complainant is a private copyright holder

ing the materials the Government characterizes as the most sensitive and destructive, can I deny that revelation of these documents will do substantial damage to public interests. Indeed, I am confident that their disclosure will have that result. But I nevertheless agree that the United States has not satisfied the very heavy burden that it must meet to warrant an injunction against publication in these cases, at least in the absence of express and appropriately limited congressional authorization for prior restraints in circumstances such as these.

. . .

At least in the absence of legislation by Congress, based on its own investigations and findings, I am quite unable to agree that the inherent powers of the Executive and the courts reach so far as to authorize remedies having such sweeping potential for inhibiting publications by the press. Much of the difficulty inheres in the "grave and irreparable danger" standard suggested by the United States. If the United States were to have judgment under such a standard in these cases, our decision would be of little guidance to other courts in other cases, for the material at issue here would not be available from the Court's opinion or from public records, nor would it be published by the press.

. . .

It is not easy to reject the proposition urged by the United States and to deny relief on its good-faith claims in these cases that publication will work serious damage to the country. But that discomfiture is considerably dispelled by the infrequency of prior-restraint cases. Normally, publication will occur and the damage be done before the Government has either opportunity or grounds for suppression. So here, publication has already begun and a substantial part of the threatened damage has already occurred. The fact of a massive breakdown in security is known, access to the documents by many unauthorized people is undeniable, and the efficacy of equitable relief against these or other newspapers to avert anticipated damage is doubtful at best.

. . .

The Criminal Code contains numerous provisions potentially relevant to these cases. Section 797 [5] makes it a crime to publish certain photographs of drawings of military installations. Section 798, also in precise language, proscribes knowing and willful publication of any classified information concerning the cryptographic systems or communication intelligence activities of the United States as well as any information obtained from communication intelligence operations. If any of the material here at issue is of this nature, the newspapers are presumably now in full notice of the position of the United States and must face the consequences if they publish. I would have no difficulty

enforcing a private right. These situations are quite distinct from the Government's request for an injunction against publishing information about the affairs of government, a request admittedly not based on any statute.

5. Title 18 U.S.C. § 797. . . .

in sustaining convictions under these sections on facts that would not justify the intervention of equity and the imposition of a prior restraint.

The same would be true under those sections of the Criminal Code casting a wider net to protect the national defense. . . .

It is thus clear that Congress has addressed itself to the problems of protecting the security of the country and the national defense from unauthorized disclosure of potentially damaging information. [ ] It has not, however, authorized the injunctive remedy against threatened publication. It has apparently been satisfied to rely on criminal sanctions and their deterrent effect on the responsible as well as the irresponsible press. I am not, of course, saying that either of these newspapers has yet committed a crime or that either would commit a crime if it published all the material now in its possession. That matter must await resolution in the context of a criminal proceeding if one is instituted by the United States. In that event, the issue of guilt or innocence would be determined by procedures and standards quite different from those that have purported to govern these injunctive proceedings.

MR. JUSTICE MARSHALL, concurring.

. . .

In these cases there is no problem concerning the President's power to classify information as "secret" or "top secret." Congress has specifically recognized Presidential authority, which has been formally exercised in Exec.Order 10501 (1953), to classify documents and information. See, e.g., 18 U.S.C. § 798; 50 U.S.C. § 783. Nor is there any issue here regarding the President's power as Chief Executive and Commander in Chief to protect national security by disciplining employees who disclose information and by taking precautions to prevent leaks.

. . .

It would, however, be utterly inconsistent with the concept of separation of powers for this Court to use its power of contempt to prevent behavior that Congress has specifically declined to prohibit. There would be a similar damage to the basic concept of these co-equal branches of Government if when the Executive Branch has adequate authority granted by Congress to protect "national security" it can choose instead to invoke the contempt power of a court to enjoin the threatened conduct. The Constitution provides that Congress shall make laws, the President execute laws, and courts interpret laws. Youngstown Sheet & Tube Co. v. Sawyer, 343 U.S. 579 (1952). It did not provide for government by injunction in which the courts and the Executive Branch can "make law" without regard to the action of Congress. It may be more convenient for the Executive Branch if it need only convince a judge to prohibit conduct rather than ask the Congress to pass a law, and it may be more convenient to enforce a contempt order than to seek a criminal conviction in a jury trial. Moreover, it may be considered politically wise to get a court to share the responsibility for arresting those who the Executive Branch has probable cause to believe are violating the law. But convenience and political considerations of the moment do not justify a basic departure from the principles of our system of government.

. . .

MR. CHIEF JUSTICE BURGER, dissenting.

. . .

It is not disputed that the Times has had unauthorized possession of the documents for three to four months, during which it has had its expert analysts studying them, presumably digesting them and preparing the material for publication. During all of this time, the Times, presumably in its capacity as trustee of the public's "right to know," has held up publication for purposes it considered proper and thus public knowledge was delayed. No doubt this was for a good reason; the analysis of 7,000 pages of complex material drawn from a vastly greater volume of material would inevitably take time and the writing of good news stories takes time. But why should the United States Government, from whom this information was illegally acquired by someone, along with all the counsel, trial judges, and appellate judges be placed under needless pressure? After these months of deferral, the alleged "right to know" has somehow and suddenly become a right that must be vindicated instanter.

. . .

The consequence of all this melancholy series of events is that we literally do not know what we are acting on. As I see it, we have been forced to deal with litigation concerning rights of great magnitude without an adequate record, and surely without time for adequate treatment either in the prior proceedings or in this Court. It is interesting to note that counsel on both sides, in oral argument before this Court, were frequently unable to respond to questions on factual points. Not surprisingly they pointed out that they had been working literally "around the clock" and simply were unable to review the documents that give rise to these cases and were not familiar with them. This Court is in no better posture. I agree generally with Mr. Justice Harlan and Mr. Justice Blackmun but I am not prepared to reach the merits.[3]

I would affirm the Court of Appeals for the Second Circuit and allow the District Court to complete the trial aborted by our grant of certiorari, meanwhile preserving the status quo in the *Post* case. I would direct that the District Court on remand give priority to the

3. With respect to the question of inherent power of the Executive to classify papers, records, and documents as secret, or otherwise unavailable for public exposure, and to secure aid of the courts for enforcement, there may be an analogy with respect to this Court. No statute gives this Court express power to establish and enforce the utmost security measures for the secrecy of our deliberations and records. Yet I have little doubt as to the inherent power of the Court to protect the confidentiality of its internal operations by whatever judicial measures may be required.

Times case to the exclusion of all other business of that court but I would not set arbitrary deadlines.

I should add that I am in general agreement with much of what Mr. Justice White has expressed with respect to penal sanctions concerning communication or retention of documents or information relating to the national defense.

We all crave speedier judicial processes but when judges are pressured as in these cases the result is a parody of the judicial function.

MR. JUSTICE HARLAN, with whom THE CHIEF JUSTICE and MR. JUSTICE BLACKMUN join, dissenting.

These cases forcefully call to mind the wise admonition of Mr. Justice Holmes, dissenting in Northern Securities Co. v. United States, 193 U.S. 197, 400–401 (1904):

> "Great cases like hard cases make bad law. For great cases are called great, not by reason of their real importance in shaping the law of the future, but because of some accident of immediate overwhelming interest which appeals to the feelings and distorts the judgment. These immediate interests exercise a kind of hydraulic pressure which makes what previously was clear seem doubtful, and before which even well settled principles of law will bend."

With all respect, I consider that the Court has been almost irresponsibly feverish in dealing with these cases.

Both the Court of Appeals for the Second Circuit and the Court of Appeals for the District of Columbia Circuit rendered judgment on June 23. The New York Times' petition for certiorari, its motion for accelerated consideration thereof, and its application for interim relief were filed in this Court on June 24 at about 11 a.m. The application of the United States for interim relief in the *Post* case was also filed here on June 24 at about 7:15 p.m. This Court's order setting a hearing before us on June 26 at 11 a.m., a course which I joined only to avoid the possibility of even more peremptory action by the Court, was issued less than 24 hours before. The record in the *Post* case was filed with the Clerk shortly before 1 p.m. on June 25; the record in the *Times* case did not arrive until 7 or 8 o'clock that same night. The briefs of the parties were received less than two hours before argument on June 26.

This frenzied train of events took place in the name of the presumption against prior restraints created by the First Amendment. Due regard for the extraordinarily important and difficult questions involved in these litigations should have led the Court to shun such a precipitate timetable. In order to decide the merits of these cases properly, some or all of the following questions should have been faced:

1. Whether the Attorney General is authorized to bring these suits in the name of the United States. . . .

2. Whether the First Amendment permits the federal courts to enjoin publication of stories which would present a serious threat to national security. See Near v. Minnesota, [ ], (dictum).

3. Whether the threat to publish highly secret documents is of itself a sufficient implication of national security to justify an injunction on the theory that regardless of the contents of the documents harm enough results simply from the demonstration of such a breach of secrecy.

4. Whether the unauthorized disclosure of any of these particular documents would seriously impair the national security.

5. What weight should be given to the opinion of high officers in the Executive Branch of the Government with respect to questions 3 and 4.

6. Whether the newspapers are entitled to retain and use the documents notwithstanding the seemingly uncontested facts that the documents, or the originals of which they are duplicates, were purloined from the Government's possession and that the newspapers received them with knowledge that they had been feloniously acquired. Cf. Liberty Lobby, Inc. v. Pearson, 129 U.S.App.D.C. 74, 390 F.2d 489 (1967, amended 1968).

7. Whether the threatened harm to the national security or the Government's possessory interest in the documents justifies the issuance of an injunction against publication in light of—

a. The strong First Amendment policy against prior restraints on publication;

b. The doctrine against enjoining conduct in violation of criminal statutes; and

c. The extent to which the materials at issue have apparently already been otherwise disseminated.

These are difficult questions of fact, of law, and of judgment; the potential consequences of erroneous decision are enormous. The time which has been available to us, to the lower courts, and to the parties has been wholly inadequate for giving these cases the kind of consideration they deserve. It is a reflection on the stability of the judicial process that these great issues—as important as any that have arisen during my time on the Court—should have been decided under the pressures engendered by the torrent of publicity that has attended these litigations from their inception.

Forced as I am to reach the merits of these cases, I dissent from the opinion and judgments of the Court. Within the severe limitations imposed by the time constraints under which I have been required to operate, I can only state my reasons in telescoped form, even though in different circumstances I would have felt constrained to deal with the cases in the fuller sweep indicated above.

. . .

. . . It is plain to me that the scope of the judicial function in passing upon the activities of the Executive Branch of the Government in the field of foreign affairs is very narrowly restricted. This view is, I think, dictated by the concept of separation of powers upon which our constitutional system rests.

. . .

The power to evaluate the "pernicious influence" of premature disclosure is not, however, lodged in the Executive alone. I agree that, in performance of its duty to protect the values of the First Amendment against political pressures, the judiciary must review the initial Executive determination to the point of satisfying itself that the subject matter of the dispute does lie within the proper compass of the President's foreign relations power. Constitutional considerations forbid "a complete abandonment of judicial control." Cf. United States v. Reynolds, 345 U.S. 1, 8 (1953). Moreover, the judiciary may properly insist that the determination that disclosure of the subject matter would irreparably impair the national security be made by the head of the Executive Department concerned—here the Secretary of State or the Secretary of Defense—after actual personal consideration by that officer. This safeguard is required in the analogous area of executive claims of privilege for secrets of state. [ ]

But in my judgment the judiciary may not properly go beyond these two inquiries and redetermine for itself the probable impact of disclosure on the national security. . . .

Even if there is some room for the judiciary to override the executive determination, it is plain that the scope of review must be exceedingly narrow. I can see no indication in the opinions of either the District Court or the Court of Appeals in the *Post* litigation that the conclusions of the Executive were given even the deference owing to an administrative agency, much less that owing to a co-equal branch of the Government operating within the field of its constitutional prerogative.

. . .

MR. JUSTICE BLACKMUN, dissenting.

I join MR. JUSTICE HARLAN in his dissent. I also am in substantial accord with much that MR. JUSTICE WHITE says, by way of admonition, in the latter part of his opinion.

. . .

With such respect as may be due to the contrary view, this, in my opinion, is not the way to try a lawsuit of this magnitude and asserted importance. . . .

The First Amendment, after all, is only one part of an entire Constitution. Article II of the great document vests in the Executive Branch primary power over the conduct of foreign affairs and places in that branch the responsibility for the Nation's safety. Each provision of the Constitution is important, and I cannot subscribe to a doctrine of unlimited absolutism for the First Amendment at the cost of downgrading other provisions. First Amendment absolutism has never commanded a majority of this Court. See for example, Near v. Minnesota, [ ], and Schenck v. United States, [ ]. What is needed here is a weighing, upon properly developed standards, of the broad right of the press to print and of the very narrow right of the Government to prevent. Such standards are not yet developed. The parties here are in disagreement as to what those standards should be. But even the newspapers concede that there are situations where restraint is in order and is constitutional. . . .

. . .

. . . I hope that damage has not already been done. If, however, damage has been done, and if, with the Court's action today, these newspapers proceed to publish the critical documents and there results therefrom "the death of soldiers, the destruction of alliances, the greatly increased difficulty of negotiation with our enemies, the inability of our diplomats to negotiate," to which list I might add the factors of prolongation of the war and of further delay in the freeing of United States prisoners, then the Nation's people will know where the responsibility for these said consequences rests.

Notes and Questions

1. How many votes might have shifted had Congress enacted a statute explicitly authorizing the government to seek an injunction to bar release of information once the Attorney General determined that release would pose "grave and immediate danger" to national security?

2. How many votes might have shifted if a criminal statute explicitly covering the behavior of the newspapers in this case rendered them subject to criminal prosecution? Would prosecution under such a statute have raised other constitutional questions?

3. Justice Brennan's reference to Freedman v. Maryland introduced the subject of censorship of motion pictures. From the invention of motion pictures, the Court permitted states to require that films be cleared by a government official or board before being shown. Failure to submit the film was an offense, even if the board would have had no choice but to approve the film. An effort to declare such a scheme unconstitutional on its face failed in Times Film Corp. v. Chicago, 365 U.S. 43 (1961).

But in the Freedman case, the Court noted the dangers in this type of prior restraint and required certain procedural safeguards. First, the censor bore the burden of proving that the film was unprotected expression. Second, because "only a judicial determination in an adversary proceeding ensures the necessary sensitivity to freedom of expression, only a procedure requiring a judicial determination suffices to impose a valid final restraint." This led the Court to require that the state "within a brief period, either issue a license or go to court to restrain showing the film." Any restraint had to be for "the shortest fixed period compatible with sound judicial resolution." Finally, the state had to assure a "prompt final judicial decision, to minimize the deterrent effect of an interim and possibly erroneous denial of a license."

On the role of procedural protections that support freedom of expression, see Monaghan, First Amendment "Due Process," 83 Harv.L. Rev. 518 (1970).

4. Is the Chief Justice correct in suggesting an analogy between the Pentagon Papers case and the Supreme Court's power to protect the confidentiality of its internal operations?

5. Alexander Bickel, who argued for the New York Times, discussed the significance of the case in A. Bickel, The Morality of Consent 79–88 (1976).

6. Although the government never sought to invoke criminal sanctions against the media in the Pentagon Papers episode, it did file charges against Daniel Ellsberg and Anthony Russo. The case is discussed in Nimmer, National Security Secrets v. Free Speech: The Issues Left Undecided in the Ellsberg Case, 26 Stan.L.Rev. 311 (1974).

7. The Progressive's H-Bomb Case. In March 1979, a federal district judge in Wisconsin issued a preliminary injunction, apparently the first of its kind, restraining a magazine from printing an article on national security grounds. The article by Howard Morland, entitled "The H Bomb Secret: How We Got It, Why We're Telling It," was to have appeared in The Progressive, a monthly magazine of political and social commentary with a circulation of 40,000.

The government relied on statutory authorization in the Atomic Energy Act, 42 U.S.C. § 2011 et seq., to seek the injunction. Section 2274 provides in part:

> Whoever, lawfully or unlawfully, having possession of, access to, control over, or being entrusted with any document, writing, sketch, photograph, plan, model, instrument, appliance, note, or information involving or incorporating Restricted Data—
>
> . . .
>
> (b) communicates, transmits, or discloses the same to any individual or person, or attempts or conspires to do any of the foregoing, with reason to believe such data will be utilized to injure the United States or to secure an advantage to any foreign nation, shall, upon conviction, be punished by a fine of not more than $10,000 or imprisonment for not more than ten years, or both.

"Restricted Data" was defined in § 2014(y) to include "all data concerning (1) design, manufacture or utilization of atomic weapons; (2) the production of special nuclear material; or (3) the use of special nuclear fuels in the production of energy . . . ." In § 2014(aa), "special nuclear material" includes "plutonium, uranium enriched in the isotope 233 or in the isotope 235," and other materials that may be designated.

The specific authority for an injunction is found in § 2280 of the Act:

> Whenever in the judgment of the Commission any person has engaged or is about to engage in any acts or practices which constitute or will constitute a violation of any provision of this chapter, or any regulation or order issued thereunder, the Attorney General on behalf of the United States may make application to the appropriate court for an order enjoining such acts or practices, or for an order enforcing compliance with such provision, and upon a showing by the Commission that such person has engaged or is about to engage in any such acts or practices, a permanent or temporary injunction, restraining order, or other order may be granted.

The judge ruled that the government had met its burden under § 2274 of the statute, which he held was not vague or overbroad. The word "communicates," which had disturbed some justices in *New York Times,* was easily resolved here: "The Court is convinced that the terms used in the statute—'communicates, transmits or discloses'—include publishing in a magazine." The judge found that the government had "met the test enunciated by two Justices in the *New York Times* case, namely, grave, direct, immediate and irreparable harm to the United States."

The Pentagon Papers case was distinguishable because the information at issue there was historical data. The only cogent national security reason for restraining its publication was embarrassment to the United States. The information in The Progressive article concerned "the most destructive weapon in the history of mankind, information of sufficient destructive potential to nullify the right to free speech and to endanger the right to life itself."

> The Secretary of State states that publication would increase thermonuclear proliferation and that this would "irreparably impair the national security of the United States." The Secretary of Defense says that dissemination of the Morland article will mean a substantial increase in the risk of thermonuclear proliferation and lead to use or threats that could "adversely affect the national security of the United States."

The judge recognized that a "mistake in ruling against The Progressive will seriously infringe cherished First Amendment rights." But "a mistake in ruling against the United States could pave the way for thermonuclear annihilation for us all. In that event, our right to life is extinguished and the right to publish becomes moot." He found the dictum of Near v. Minnesota applicable because "war by foot soldiers has been replaced in large part by war by machines and bombs." The "publication of the technical information on the hydrogen bomb contained in the article is analogous to publication of troop movements or locations in time of war and falls within the extremely narrow exception of the rule against prior restraint." The judge was also influenced by his belief that the purpose of the Morland article, to stimulate debate on nuclear non-proliferation, could be achieved without revealing the method of making such arms.

The reporter and the magazine argued that the information had been obtained from public sources, such as articles in encyclopedias. The judge responded that an affidavit from Dr. Hans Bethe asserted that "the design and operational concepts described in the manuscript are not expressed or revealed in the public literature nor do I believe they are known to scientists not associated with the government weapons program."

After study, the judge found "concepts within the article that [he did] not find in the public realm—concepts that are vital to the operation of the bomb." Although it has been asserted that the "secret" is nothing more than a few insights drawn from other scientific areas, the judge noted that sometimes what is obvious in one context may not be so obvious in another context. He cited a report that in the 1930s French scientists trying to develop a nuclear chain reaction were stymied for a year by their failure to grasp an "elementary" idea.

Although the judge recognized that it might only be a matter of time before other countries acquired their own hydrogen bombs, and that a "large, sophisticated industrial capacity" was required together with imaginative scientists, the article "could accelerate the membership of a candidate nation in the thermonuclear club." Moreover, "there are times in the course of human history when time itself may be very important." He mentioned the importance of Hitler's failure "to get his V–1 and V–2 bombs operational quickly enough to materially affect the outcome of World War II."

The Progressive appealed the granting of the preliminary injunction. After refusing a government request to bar the public from the argument, the court of appeals heard oral argument on September 13, 1979. The magazine asserted that the government had to prove that the publication would "surely result in direct, immediate and irreparable damage to our nation or its people," but had proven only that "in some unspecified time, some nations might acquire the capability to build a hydrogen bomb."

Just after the argument, the Madison Press Connection published a letter containing information that The Progressive had been enjoined from publishing. The Chicago Tribune then announced that it planned to publish the same letter. Once the information had been made public, any justification for enjoining its publication collapsed. The government then announced that it was withdrawing its complaint and the case was dismissed. Although the government reserved its right to bring criminal charges, no such case was brought.

See United States v. Progressive, Inc., 467 F.Supp. 990 (W.D.Wis.), motion to reconsider and to vacate preliminary injunction denied 486 F.Supp. 5 (W.D.Wis.), writ of mandamus for expedited appeal denied sub nom. Morland v. Sprecher, 443 U.S. 709, dismissed as moot 610 F.2d 819 (7th Cir.1979).

8. In May, 1980, Public Broadcasting Service broadcast a "documentary drama" portraying a love affair between a Saudi princess and a commoner and their subsequent execution. The program also dwelt on some aspects of Saudi Arabian life that the Saudi government asserted were totally misrepresented. The program was patterned on a true story.

If the Saudi government had made a credible threat to cut off all oil shipments to the United States immediately upon the presentation of the program, and if the best evidence had been that such a cutoff would cripple the American economy, would the government have been able to obtain an injunction against the showing of the program?

Is it crucial that no "secret" is involved? Lawsuits arising from refusals to show the Saudi program are discussed in Chapter XIV.

9. In Snepp v. United States, 444 U.S. 507 (1980), the Court reviewed a case in which a former CIA agent published a book without submitting it to the CIA for approval. The government sued the agent for breach of his employment contract, which barred publication, without prepublication approval, of information learned while working at the CIA.

The Supreme Court rejected Snepp's claim that the CIA contract amounted to prior restraint, stressing that Snepp voluntarily signed the contract when he joined the CIA and affirmed it when he left the agency. The Court also observed that "even in the absence of an express agreement—the CIA could have acted to protect substantial governmental interests by imposing reasonable restrictions on employee activities that in other contexts might be protected by the First Amendment." The government had a "compelling interest" in protecting the secrecy of information important to national security and "the appearance of confidentiality so essential to the effective operation of our foreign intelligence service."

10. The possibility of renewed action on the national security front is looming in mid–1986 as the result of efforts by C.I.A. Director William Casey to have the Justice Department move against newspapers and broadcasters who are accused of having revealed classified information about communications intelligence. Engelberg, Administration Debates Prosecution of the Press, N.Y.Times, May 8, 1986, at 16; Engelberg, C.I.A. Chief Seeking Possible Prosecution of NBC Over Broadcast, N.Y.Times, May 20, 1986, at 14; McDowell, C.I.A. Said to Warn Publisher on Book, N.Y.Times, June 25, 1986, at 18. See also National Security and the Press: An Interview with C.I.A. Chief William Casey, Wash.Journ.Rev., July, 1986, at 14.

RETHINKING PRIOR RESTRAINT

John Jeffries, Jr.

92 Yale L.J. 409, 422–33 (1983).

. . . The administrative apparatus erected to effect preclearance may screen a range of expression far broader than that which otherwise would be brought to official attention. The relative ease and economy of an administrative decision to suppress may make suppression more likely than it would be without a preclearance requirement. Under a system of administrative preclearance, suppression is accomplished "by a single stroke of the pen." At that point the burden falls on the would-be speaker to vindicate his right. Without administrative preclearance, the government's decision to suppress may be constrained by the time and money required to demonstrate in court an appropriate basis for such action. And the fact that those exercising the authority of preclearance operate in the relative informality of administrative action may tend to shield their decisions from effective public scrutiny. Most important, administrative preclearance requires a bureaucracy of censorship. Persons who choose to fill this role may well have psychological tendencies to overstate the need for suppression. Whether or not this is so, there are powerful institutional pressures to justify one's job, and ultimately one's own importance, by exaggerating the evils which suppression seeks to avoid. As [Thomas] Emerson put it: "The function of the censor is to censor. He has a professional interest in finding things to suppress." And finally, it may well be that a system of administrative preclearance would be enforced more energetically and efficiently than a system of subsequent punishment. Ultimately, both depend on criminal prosecution, but the issues presented for proof under a preclearance requirement may be significantly more manageable.

These and similar arguments have been detailed by Professor Emerson. They deal with matters of timing, process, and institutional structure rather than with the substantive content of speech, and in my view, they fully justify an attitude of special hostility toward preclearance requirements. All of these concerns, however, are linked to a single factor, a factor ordinarily determinative of the constitutional fate of preclearance requirements. That factor is discretion. Where broad discretion is left in the hands of executive officials—as in a statute authorizing denial of a permit for very general reasons—the vices described above loom very large indeed. Where, on the other hand, executive discretion is tightly controlled—as in a statute requiring issuance of a permit on specified showings—the problems of preclearance seem relatively less troublesome.

. . .

. . . The evil of broad preclearance requirements is not limited to the occasional case where the illegality of suppression is fully litigated.

It also extends to cases that never reach the courts. The operation of the preclearance requirement will suppress or inhibit speech in situations that judges never see. Laws that create a pervasive risk of unconstitutional suppression of protected speech should therefore be invalidated, even where the risk is not immediately realized, as a prophylaxis against the harm that will be done elsewhere.

This, of course, is a familiar argument. It goes under the name of the overbreadth doctrine. People disagree about details, but few would doubt that the overbreadth doctrine states a centrally important proposition for judicial administration of freedom of speech. In my view, it provides a more informative frame of reference for examining preclearance requirements than does the invocation of prior restraint.

Simply put, the doctrine asserts that an overbroad regulation of speech or publication may be subject to facial review and invalidation, even though its application in the instant case is constitutionally unobjectionable. Thus, a person whose activity could validly be suppressed under a more narrowly drawn law is allowed to challenge an overbroad law because of its application to others. The bare possibility of unconstitutional application is not enough; the law is unconstitutionally overbroad only if it reaches *substantially* beyond the permissible scope of legislative regulation. Thus, the issue under the overbreadth doctrine is whether a government restriction of speech that is arguably valid as applied to the case at hand should nevertheless be invalidated to avoid the substantial prospect of unconstitutional application elsewhere.

A rule of special hostility to administrative preclearance is just another way of saying that determinations under the overbreadth doctrine should take account not only of the substance of the law but also of the structure of its administration. The reason that the various features of timing, process, and institutional structure noted earlier are thought to render administrative preclearance requirements especially objectionable is precisely that they increase the prospect of unconstitutional application. . . .

The second major type of prior restraint is the injunction. Ever since *Near,* injunctions have been classed as prior restraints and subjected to the independent presumption of unconstitutionality for which that doctrine calls. In fact, despite its original reference to official licensing, the doctrine of prior restraint today is understood by many people to mean chiefly a rule of special hostility to injunctions. Of course, to the extent that the speech in question is constitutionally protected against suppression by subsequent punishment, it is also secured against suppression by injunction. This result in no way depends on an independent rule against prior restraint. That doctrine has functional significance only where it bars an injunction against speech that constitutionally could be proscribed by the penal law. The issue, therefore, is whether injunctions should be constitutionally disfavored even where they are directed against speech not otherwise protected under the First Amendment.

In this connection, it is instructive to note how different from administrative preclearance injunctions really are. Under a regime of injunctions, there is no routine screening of speech and no administrative shortcut to suppression. The government has to shoulder the entire burden of identifying the case for suppression and of demonstrating in court a constitutionally acceptable basis for such action. Moreover, because an injunction must be sought in open court, the character of the government's claims remains subject to public scrutiny and debate. Most important, the decision to suppress is made by a court, not a censor. Of course, judges are not perfect; sometimes they may err on the side of suppression and enjoin speech without sufficient justification. But the fact remains that judges, unlike professional censors, have no vested interest in the suppression of speech. The institution of the judiciary is peculiarly well suited—in personnel, training, ideology, and institutional structure—to implement the ideals of the First Amendment.[57] . . .

Not only are injunctions unlike administrative preclearance, they are also far more like subsequent punishments than the conventional rhetoric would suggest. In both cases the *threat* of punishment comes before publication; in both cases the *fact* of punishment comes after. The apparent distinction in timing is actually only a shift in the focus of attention. The procedures in an action for criminal contempt—the

57. Distrust of judges is a central and recurring theme in the writings of those who endorse the conventional doctrine of prior restraint. An articulate and sophisticated rendition of this sentiment appears in Blasi, [Toward a Theory of Prior Restraint: The Central Linkage, 66 Minn.L. Rev. 11, 52–53 (1981)]. Professor Blasi advances the notion that "judges tend to be unduly risk averse in ruling upon the claims of speakers" and notes the role of that idea in the works of Chafee, Kalven, and Emerson and in the opinions of Justices Holmes and Brandeis. Id. at 52. From this, Blasi concludes that "a preference for the dynamics of subsequent punishment"—in particular, adjudication of the dangers of speech only after the harm has been realized—"makes sense" as a counterweight to chronic judicial risk-aversion in the regulation of controversial speech. Id.

There is something to this point, but it is not, I think, a persuasive justification for maintaining the doctrine of prior restraint. Two considerations seem to me to support a different view. The first I hesitate to state, as it is both impressionistic and sure to elicit disagreement, but I confess to some doubt that the judiciary of today should be characterized as chronically or pervasively insensitive to First Amendment interests. . . .

The second point is more fundamental. To the extent that the judges of today can be thought, by whatever lights, chronically and pervasively insensitive to First Amendment interests, there is clearly a serious problem. But it is less clear that this problem can sensibly be addressed through a particularized hostility to injunctive relief. After all, the same judges will adjudicate the substantive content of First Amendment freedoms no matter what the form of government regulation. A generally inhospitable attitude would seem likely to affect actions to impose subsequent punishment as well as proceedings for injunctive relief. In order to make a case for a rule of special hostility to injunctions, one must go further and argue, as Professor Blasi suggests, that judges are *differentially* insensitive to First Amendment interests depending on the form of enforcement sought. On this crucial point the argument is quite speculative. In sum, therefore, it seems to me unlikely that a sharp distinction between injunctions and subsequent punishment can be supported by plausible assumptions about judicial behavior.

enforcement phase of the injunctive process—are generally the same as those used in ordinary criminal prosecutions. Proof must be had beyond a reasonable doubt, and the right to trial by jury is guaranteed where the sentence exceeds imprisonment for six months.[60]

On examination, the chief difference between the two schemes turns out to be this: Under a system of injunctions, the adjudication of illegality precedes publication; under a system of criminal prosecution, it comes later. This is a difference, and perhaps for some purposes it matters, but why the timing of the adjudication should affect the scope of First Amendment freedoms is not at all clear. Three related reasons are most frequently advanced.

The first and most common is that an injunction deters speech more effectively than does the threat of criminal prosecution and for that reason should be specially disfavored. Arguments to this effect are found in the opinions of the Supreme Court and in the writings of leading commentators. The idea has been variously expressed but never so pithily as in Alexander Bickel's remark that, "A criminal statute chills, prior restraint freezes." Yet, with all respect to such authority, it is very hard to credit this point. It may be true, as many have asserted, that an injunction, because it is particularized, immediate, and concrete, may impinge more forcefully on the consciousness of the individual enjoined than would a more generalized and impersonal threat of criminal prosecution. But that tells only half the story, and the wrong half at that. An injunction may be more effective at stopping the activity at which it is aimed, but it is also more narrowly confined. There is less risk of deterring activities beyond the adjudicated target of suppression—activities plainly outside the injunctive ban but arguably within the necessarily more general prohibition of a penal law. And many find even an uncertain prospect of criminal conviction and punishment sufficient incentive to steer well clear of arguably proscribed activities. In terms, therefore, of the system of free expression and of the aggregate of arguably protected First Amendment activity that might be inhibited under these regimes, it is anything but clear that injunctions are more costly. As Professor Barnett put it: "[T]he pinpointed freeze of a narrowly drawn [judicial] . . . order might produce less refrigeration overall than the broader chill of threatened subsequent punishment . . . ."

That point is strongly reinforced when one remembers that it is only the possibility of *erroneous* deterrence that should be the subject of concern. To the extent that the activity suppressed, whether by injunction or by criminal prosecution, is outside the protection of the First Amendment and within a legitimate sphere of legislative action, efficient inhibition is a good thing. . . .

60. Bloom v. Illinois, 391 U.S. 194 (1968). The absence of a jury trial where only petty penalties are imposed is a difference, but not, I think, one that counts for much under the First Amendment. Whatever may have been true in the days of John Peter Zenger, the essentially popular institution of the modern American jury seems unlikely to serve as a bulwark of protection for unpopular speech. . . .

Two additional reasons for regarding injunctions as especially deleterious to speech are really only variations on the theme of efficient deterrence. One is that suppression by criminal prosecution is preferable to suppression by injunction because the latter characteristically delays publication, at least for several days, even if the ban ultimately is lifted. The result is a loss in the immediacy of speech, and in some cases an accompanying loss in its value. The other contention is that criminal prosecution is preferable because it allows the disputed material to be published at least once and thus to enter the marketplace of ideas. An injunction, by contrast, is said to prevent the information from ever being made public.

Both of these contentions enjoy wide currency, but neither withstands scrutiny. Both are based on the implicit assumption that the deterrent impact of penal statutes is felt in those cases in which prosecution is brought. Of course, the opposite is true. Every violation of the penal law is, by hypothesis, a case of failed deterrence. Effective deterrence occurs when the violation never takes place. And in some cases, deterrence will be effective. Thus, while an injunction may delay publication for several days, the prospect of penal sanctions may delay publication forever. And while those publications that become subjects of criminal prosecution do become part of the marketplace of ideas, those that are deterred by the threat of penal sanctions never do. There is, in short, no necessary or dependable relation between the form of suppression and any identifiable measure of violence to First Amendment interests.[67]

67. Arguments of a different sort are advanced in Blasi, supra note [57]. Professor Blasi examines licensing and injunctions in an effort to assess whether the two modes of regulation are sufficiently similar to warrant lumping them together under the rubric of "prior restraint." He concludes that they are and accordingly pronounces the concept "coherent at the core." Id. at 93. Blasi, however, does not base his conclusion on the usual contention that licensing and injunctions are alike in producing significantly more self-censorship of speech than do schemes of subsequent punishment. In fact, he specifically disavows that view. Id. at 47. Instead, he suggests that a rule of special hostility to injunctions is justified by the common tendencies of licensing and injunctions to allow speculative assessments of the dangers of speech (the problem of "adjudication in the abstract"), to invite overuse by enforcement authorities, and to dilute the impact of speech on the audience to whom it is addressed.

Professor Blasi's analysis of these factors is both thoughtful and thought-provoking. It is also far too elaborate and detailed for point-by-point response. In my view, the strongest of these arguments goes under the heading of "adjudication in the abstract." See id. at 49–54. The crux of this discussion is an assumption of chronic judicial risk-aversion, and I have suggested elsewhere why that seems to me an unconvincing justification for the doctrine of prior restraint. See supra note 57.

Blasi's arguments on overuse, Blasi, supra note 13, at 54–63, and impact on audience reception, id. at 63–69, are developed with great care and subtlety. They also reflect the inevitable difficulties of drawing very specific inferences about relative impact from necessarily abstract speculations about the differences among legal regimes. Thus, for example, a key to Blasi's analysis of overuse as a ground for disfavoring prior restraints is the observation that injunctions are easier to obtain than penal statutes. See id. at 58. This may be true, but it is equally true that a criminal statute, once enacted, is likely to have a vastly greater longevity and breadth of potential application. It may be, therefore, that the better comparison is not between the relative ease of obtaining an injunction and the greater difficulty of enacting legislation but rather between the streamlined procedures for obtaining an injunction and the even more expeditious and informal

In my view, there is only one respect in which injunctions plausibly can be claimed to have a First Amendment impact significantly greater than the threat of subsequent punishment. That argument is based on the traditional rule that the legality of an injunction may not be challenged by disobeying its terms. In its most uncompromising form, the traditional approach would declare that the invalidity or even unconstitutionality of a court order would be no defense in a contempt proceeding based on violation of that order. An especially rigorous application of this rule is found in *Walker v. City of Birmingham*,[69] where the Supreme Court upheld contempt convictions for violating a court order against parading without a permit, despite the fact that the injunction tracked the language of a city ordinance later found to have been an unconstitutional restraint on free expression.[70] The right course, said *Walker*, was for the demonstrators to challenge the validity of the injunction in court before violating it on the streets. "[R]espect for judicial process," said Justice Stewart, "is a small price to pay for the civilizing hand of law . . . ."

Today, the continued vitality of *Walker v. City of Birmingham* is far from clear. The Supreme Court has declined to follow that course in analogous situations, and the lower courts have tended to curtail its reach. Nevertheless, the rule probably survives—at least one cannot confidently say otherwise—and thus must be taken into account. For

procedures by which a prosecutor may threaten or initiate criminal prosecution. My point here is not to suggest that an inquiry into potential for overuse would actually *favor* injunctive regulation over criminal prosecution, or even that the contrary perception is necessarily in error. My only point is to express doubt that any inference of this sort can reliably be drawn.

In many ways the most interesting aspect of Blasi's argument is the suggestion that injunctions and subsequent punishments are differentially incompatible with the underlying premises of the American constitutional scheme. This is not an argument based on predictions of behavioral consequences. It deals rather with matters of symbolism and tone. Much of this argument seems to me properly reflective of a generalized predisposition against governmental suppression of speech by whatever means, and, so understood, I agree with it wholeheartedly. I am less sure, however, that the fundamental concerns that argue against the suppression of speech generally—concerns that Blasi develops with elegance and insight—justify a sharp differentiation between injunctions and subsequent punishments.

Consider, for example, Blasi's analysis of "the premise of distrust." He summarizes his discussion of this point as follows: "[T]he widespread use of licensing or enjoining implies a premise of comparative distrust, a belief that it is more dangerous to trust audiences with controversial communications than it is to trust the legal process with the power to suppress speech." Id. at 85. This observation is both right and important, and I agree with it completely. It seems to me, however, that widespread use of criminal prosecution and punishment would be equally objectionable and for the same reason. Blasi distinguishes the two cases on the ground that "[t]he point of prior regulation is to suppress, not to sanction," id. at 72, and that its use is therefore specially incompatible with a system of freedom of speech. But the point of subsequent punishment is equally to suppress and not to sanction. In neither regime is the penalty an end in itself; in both it is imposed as a means to control primary conduct—specifically to suppress speech. The case for a sharp doctrinal differentiation between injunctions and subsequent punishment—as distinct from the more general (and more important) proposition of a healthy skepticism toward suppression by any means—seems to me unpersuasive.

69. 388 U.S. 307 (1967).

70. Shuttlesworth v. City of Birmingham, 394 U.S. 147 (1969).

whatever uncertainty may attend the current health of the collateral bar doctrine, its relevance to prior restraint is plain. If *Walker* were strictly followed *and* if immediate appellate review of judicial orders were not provided, the government might be able temporarily to suppress by injunction speech that could not be suppressed by threat of penal sanctions. . . . Of course, it is an important safeguard against such abuse that the order must be issued by a judge, not a bureaucrat, but the possibility of judicial error or insensitivity to First Amendment freedoms is not so trivial that it may safely be ignored.

Other writers—notably Professors Fiss and Barnett—have examined the rule of *Walker v. City of Birmingham* and noted its centrality to any convincing rationalization of the doctrine of prior restraint. They have argued that a policy of special hostility to injunctions is at least unjustified where the collateral bar rule is not in force. As should be clear from what has already been said, I agree with this view. Indeed, I would go further, for it seems to me that a properly limited collateral bar rule would not be destructive of our system of freedom of expression.

The reasons for the collateral bar rule are obvious and not unimportant. They include the preservation of judicial authority and the orderly settlement of disputes—values evoked by Justice Stewart's reference to "the civilizing hand of law." But it is also clear that, at least in the context of injunctions against speech, the collateral bar rule must be carefully circumscribed. The Supreme Court has recognized the point and limited the rule accordingly. Indeed, in *Walker* itself the Court acknowledged that a different situation would be presented if an injunction were "transparently invalid" or if delay or frustration were encountered in the effort to contest its validity.

The first of these exceptions covers the case of an injunction so palpably contrary to authority that it falls under a kind of "plain error" rule. The limitation is not trivial, for existing First Amendment precedents would render "transparently invalid" a vast range of injunctions against speech. Nevertheless, this formulation does not address the truly close case, however occasionally it may arise. The second exception may be more to the point, for it speaks directly to the central problem of the collateral bar rule—the risk that an injunction against speech, even though ultimately invalidated, will so delay publication as to make the speech untimely and hence valueless for its purpose. The worst case would be an election-eve attempt by the party in power to enjoin publication of politically damaging information. In such circumstances, even the few days necessary to obtain expedited appellate review might prove seriously prejudicial to that system of representative government which the First Amendment, above all else, should be thought to undergird. In my view, therefore, the normal operation of the collateral bar rule can be sustained only so long as expedited appellate review allows an immediate opportunity to test the validity of an injunction against speech and only so long as that opportunity is genuinely effective to allow timely publication should the injunction ultimately be adjudged invalid. In any event, this is, as Professor Blasi put it, only a "controversy over the validity and scope of the collateral bar rule." It should be addressed in those terms and not, in my view, as a remote and usually unarticulated premise underlying a broad and uncritical acceptance of the conventional rhetoric of prior restraint.

The conclusion that I draw from all this is embarrassingly modest. It is not that injunctions are preferable to subsequent punishment as a mechanism for suppression of speech, though that may be true in some cases. Nor would I assert that there is never a case in which injunctive relief should be specially disfavored. In some situations (the election-eve gambit comes to mind) an injunction may be differentially destructive of First Amendment values, just as in others (perhaps regulation of obscenity) it may prove differentially protective. My only point is to question the broad and categorical condemnation of injunctions as a form of "prior restraint."

In my view, a rule of special hostility to administrative preclearance is fully justified, but a rule of special hostility to injunctive relief is not. Lumping both together under the name of "prior restraint" obscures rather than clarifies what is at stake in these cases.

. . .

Notes and Questions

1. How central to the controversy is the doctrine of collateral bar? In states that do not follow the doctrine and allow challenges to the validity of the injunction after its violation, what are the major arguments in favor of retaining a prior restraint doctrine?

2. In an omitted section, Jeffries discusses the Pentagon Papers case. He concludes that the case should not have turned on the form of relief requested. Whether the proceeding was an effort to obtain an injunction or a criminal prosecution, it posed a "fundamental conflict between the ideals of the First Amendment and the demands of national security." He agreed with Justice Blackmun's conclusion that the case required "a weighing, upon properly developed standards, of the broad right of the press to print and of the very narrow right of the Government to prevent." Jeffries concluded that the "difficult process of weighing is, in my view, entirely unaided by reference to the doctrine of prior restraint." (p. 437) Does the application to this case make the Jeffries analysis more, or less, attractive?

3. The first important collateral bar case involving media was United States v. Dickinson, 465 F.2d 496 (5th Cir.1972), in which a federal judge, concerned about possible prejudice in a forthcoming trial, ordered reporters not to report any testimony being offered at that open session of court. Two reporters violated the order and were held in contempt and fined $300 each.

The court of appeals, relying on *Walker,* concluded that the order had been invalid but that it still had to be obeyed. Absent a showing of "transparent invalidity" or "patent frivolity surrounding the order, *it must be obeyed* until reversed" or vacated. The court did recognize the special problems of media:

> Timeliness of publication is the hallmark of 'news' and the difference between 'news' and 'history' is merely a matter of hours. Thus, where publishing of news is sought to be restrained, the incontestable inviolability of the order may depend on the immediate accessibility of orderly review. But in the absence of strong indications that the appellate process was being deliberately stalled—certainly not so in this record—violation with impunity does not occur simply because immediate decision is not forthcoming, even though the communication enjoined is 'news.' Of course the nature of the expression sought to be exercised is a factor to be considered in determining whether First Amendment rights can be effectively protected by orderly review so as to render disobedience to otherwise unconstitutional mandates nevertheless contemptuous. But newsmen are citizens, too. [ ] They too may sometimes have to wait. They are not yet wrapped in an immunity or given the absolute right to decide with impunity whether a Judge's order is to be obeyed or whether an appellate court is acting promptly enough.

The court noted that both it and the district court were available "and could have been contacted that very day, thereby affording speedy and effective but *orderly* review of the injunction in question swiftly enough to protect the right to publish news while it was still 'news.'"

The court remanded the case so that the trial judge might reconsider his sentence in light of the ruling that his order was invalid. The judge reaffirmed his sentence because it had been based on willful disobedience of the order rather than on any harm that had occurred. 349 F.Supp. 227 (M.D.La.1972), affirmed 476 F.2d 373 (5th Cir.1973), certiorari denied 414 U.S. 979 (1973) Douglas, J., dissenting.

In jurisdictions that follow the collateral bar rule, the "patent invalidity" and "frivolity" become central. What are the critical questions in states that do not follow the rule?

4. In In re Providence Journal, 630 F.Supp. 993, 12 Med.L.Rptr. 1881 (D.R.I. 1986), the court held the newspaper in contempt of court for publishing truthful information obtained under the Freedom of Information Act while it was under a temporary restraining order not to do so. The TRO was sought by a person who claimed that the government had obtained the information in the first place by means that violated the person's constitutional right to privacy—and that its release was improper. The judge offered to decide the merits in the next day or two after the TRO was entered. The newspaper asked the judge to defer for another day, during which it published the information.

Although the judge later denied the preliminary injunction, he found the newspaper in contempt. The basis for requiring obedience to the TRO was that a court "ought to have time to determine legal issues presented to it, and has the right in the meantime to preserve the *status quo*." The judge rejected the newspaper's argument that the plaintiff's claim was frivolous.

The judge sentenced the newspaper to a fine of $100,000 and the executive editor to 18 months probation and 200 hours of public service. 12 Med.L.Rptr. 1943 (D.R.I. 1986).

In June, 1986, the newspaper and its editor filed appeals.

5. In Smith v. Daily Mail Publishing Co., 443 U.S. 97 (1979), a West Virginia statute made it a crime for a newspaper to publish the name of a juvenile in connection with juvenile proceedings without a written order of the court. In the Supreme Court, the newspapers recognized that the statute was "not in the classic mold of a prior restraint" because there was no prior injunction against publication. Nonetheless, the newspapers argued that the statute should be analyzed as a prior restraint because it required prior court approval before a juvenile's name could be lawfully published. The Court refused to decide the question. After observing that "First Amendment protection has gone beyond prior restraints," the Court continued:

> Whether we view the statute as a prior restraint or as a penal sanction for publishing lawfully obtained, truthful information is not dispositive because even the latter action requires the highest form of state interest to sustain its validity. Prior restraints have been accorded the most exacting scrutiny in previous cases. [ ] However, even when a state attempts to punish publication after the event it must nevertheless demonstrate that its punitive action was necessary to further the state interest asserted. [ ] Since we conclude that this statute cannot satisfy the constitutional standards defined in *Landmark Communications, Inc.*, we need not decide whether . . . it operated as a prior restraint.

Does this suggest that the Court is receptive to arguments of the sort Jeffries is making? We return to the substance of *Daily Mail* and *Landmark* in Chapter III.

6. In the early 1980s, several commentators were rethinking the role of prior restraint. Along with Jeffries and Blasi, see Linde, Courts and Censorship, 66 Minn.L.Rev. 171 (1981); Mayton, Toward a Theory of First Amendment Process: Injunctions of Speech, Subsequent Punishment and the Costs of the Prior Restraint Doctrine, 67 Cornell L.Rev. 245 (1982); and Redish, The Proper Role of the Prior Restraint Doctrine in First Amendment Theory, 70 Va.L.Rev. 53 (1984).

2. The Role of the Framers' Views

MINNEAPOLIS STAR AND TRIBUNE COMPANY v. MINNESOTA COMMISSIONER OF REVENUE

Supreme Court of the United States, 1983.
460 U.S. 575, 103 S.Ct. 1365, 75 L.Ed.2d 295, 9 Med.L.Rptr. 1369.
Noted, 89 Dick.L.Rev. 261, 69 Iowa L.Rev. 1103, 58 Tul.L.Rev. 1073.

JUSTICE O'CONNOR delivered the opinion of the Court.*

This case presents the question of a State's power to impose a special tax on the press and, by enacting exemptions, to limit its effect to only a few newspapers.

I

Since 1967, Minnesota has imposed a sales tax on most sales of goods for a price in excess of a nominal sum. [ ] In general, the tax applies only to retail sales. An exemption for industrial and agricultural users shields from the tax sales of components to be used in the production of goods that will themselves be sold at retail. As part of this general system of taxation and in support of the sales tax, Minnesota also enacted a tax on the "privilege of using, storing or consuming in Minnesota tangible personal property." This use tax applies to any nonexempt tangible personal property unless the sales tax was paid on the sales price. Like the classic use tax, this use tax protects the State's sales tax by eliminating the residents' incentive to travel to States with lower sales taxes to buy goods rather than buying them in Minnesota.

The appellant, Minneapolis Star and Tribune Company ("Star Tribune"), is the publisher of a morning newspaper and an evening newspaper in Minneapolis. From 1967 until 1971, it enjoyed an exemption from the sales and use tax provided by Minnesota for periodic publications. In 1971, however, while leaving the exemption from the sales tax in place, the legislature amended the scheme to impose a "use tax" on the cost of paper and ink products consumed in the production of a publication. Ink and paper used in publications became the only items subject to the use tax that were components of goods to be sold at retail. In 1974, the legislature again amended the statute, this time to exempt the first $100,000 worth of ink and paper consumed by a publication in any calendar year, in effect giving each publication an annual tax credit of $4,000. Publications remained exempt from the sales tax.

After the enactment of the $100,000 exemption, 11 publishers, producing 14 of the 388 paid circulation newspapers in the State,

* JUSTICE BLACKMUN joins this opinion except footnote 12.

incurred a tax liability in 1974. Star Tribune was one of the 11, and, of the $893,355 collected, it paid $608,634, or roughly two-thirds of the total revenue raised by the tax.

Star Tribune instituted this action to seek a refund of the use taxes it paid from January 1, 1974 to May 31, 1975. The Minnesota Supreme Court upheld the tax.

II

Star Tribune argues that we must strike this tax on the authority of Grosjean v. American Press Co., Inc., 297 U.S. 233 (1936). Although there are similarities between the two cases, we agree with the State that *Grosjean* is not controlling.

In *Grosjean,* the State of Louisiana imposed a license tax of 2% of the gross receipts from the sale of advertising on all newspapers with a weekly circulation above 20,000. Out of at least 124 publishers in the State, only 13 were subject to the tax. After noting that the tax was "single in kind" and that keying the tax to circulation curtailed the flow of information, this Court held the tax invalid as an abridgment of the freedom of the press. Both the brief and the argument of the publishers in this Court emphasized the events leading up to the tax and the contemporary political climate in Louisiana. All but one of the large papers subject to the tax had "ganged up" on Senator Huey Long, and a circular distributed by Long and the governor to each member of the state legislature described "lying newspapers" as conducting "a vicious campaign" and the tax as "a tax on lying, 2c [*sic*] a lie." Although the Court's opinion did not describe this history, it stated, "[The tax] is bad because, in the light of its history and of its present setting, it is seen to be a deliberate and calculated device in the guise of a tax to limit the circulation of information," [ ], an explanation that suggests that the motivation of the legislature may have been significant.

Our subsequent cases have not been consistent in their reading of *Grosjean* on this point. Compare United States v. O'Brien, 391 U.S. 367, 384–385 (1968) (stating that legislative purpose was irrelevant in *Grosjean*) with Houchins v. KQED, Inc., 438 U.S. 1, 9–10 (1978) (plurality opinion) (suggesting that purpose was relevant in *Grosjean*); Pittsburgh Press Co. v. Pittsburgh Commission on Human Relations, 413 U.S. 376, 383 (1973) (same). Commentators have generally viewed *Grosjean* as dependent on the improper censorial goals of the legislature. [ ]. We think that the result in *Grosjean* may have been attributable in part to the perception on the part of the Court that the state imposed the tax with an intent to penalize a selected group of newspapers. In the case currently before us, however, there is no legislative history and no indication, apart from the structure of the tax itself, of any impermissible or censorial motive on the part of the legislature. We cannot resolve the case by simple citation to *Grosjean.*

Instead, we must analyze the problem anew under the general principles of the First Amendment.

III

Clearly, the First Amendment does not prohibit all regulation of the press. It is beyond dispute that the States and the Federal Government can subject newspapers to generally applicable economic regulations without creating constitutional problems. See, e.g., Citizens Publishing Co. v. United States, 394 U.S. 131, 139 (1969) (antitrust laws); Lorain Journal Co. v. United States, 342 U.S. 143, 155–156 (1951) (same); Breard v. Alexandria, 341 U.S. 622 (1951) (prohibition of door-to-door solicitation); Oklahoma Press Publishing Co. v. Walling, 327 U.S. 186, 192–193 (1946) (Fair Labor Standards Act); Mabee v. White Plains Publishing Co., 327 U.S. 178 (1946) (same); Associated Press v. United States, 326 U.S. 1, 6–7, 19–20 (1945) (antitrust laws); Associated Press v. NLRB, 301 U.S. 103, 132–133 (1937) (NLRA); see also Branzburg v. Hayes, 408 U.S. 665 (1972) (enforcement of subpoenas). Minnesota, however, has not chosen to apply its general sales and use tax to newspapers. Instead, it has created a special tax that applies only to certain publications protected by the First Amendment. Although the State argues now that the tax on paper and ink is part of the general scheme of taxation, the use tax provision is facially discriminatory, singling out publications for treatment that is, to our knowledge, unique in Minnesota tax law.

Minnesota's treatment of publications differs from that of other enterprises in at least two important respects: [4] it imposes a use tax that does not serve the function of protecting the sales tax, and it taxes an intermediate transaction rather than the ultimate retail sale. . . .

. . .

By creating this special use tax, which, to our knowledge, is without parallel in the State's tax scheme, Minnesota has singled out the press for special treatment. We then must determine whether the First Amendment permits such special taxation. A tax that burdens rights protected by the First Amendment cannot stand unless the burden is necessary to achieve an overriding governmental interest. See, e.g., United States v. Lee, 455 U.S. 252 (1982). Any tax that the press must pay, of course, imposes some "burden." But, as we have observed, [ ], this Court has long upheld economic regulation of the press. The cases approving such economic regulation, however, emphasized the general applicability of the challenged regulation to all businesses, [ ], suggesting that a regulation that singled out the press might place a heavier burden of justification on the State, and we now

4. A third difference is worth noting, though it may have little economic effect. The use tax is not visible to consumers, while the sales tax must, by law, be stated separately as an addition to the price.

conclude that the special problems created by differential treatment do indeed impose such a burden.

There is substantial evidence that differential taxation of the press would have troubled the Framers of the First Amendment.[6] The role of the press in mobilizing sentiment in favor of independence was critical to the Revolution. When the Constitution was proposed without an explicit guarantee of freedom of the press, the Antifederalists objected. Proponents of the Constitution, relying on the principle of enumerated powers, responded that such a guarantee was unnecessary because the Constitution granted Congress no power to control the press. . . .

The fears of the Antifederalists were well-founded. A power to tax differentially, as opposed to a power to tax generally, gives a government a powerful weapon against the taxpayer selected. When the State imposes a generally applicable tax, there is little cause for concern. We need not fear that a government will destroy a selected group of taxpayers by burdensome taxation if it must impose the same burden on the rest of its constituency. See Railway Express Agency v. New York, 336 U.S. 106, 112–113 (1949) (Jackson, J., concurring). When the State singles out the press, though, the political constraints that prevent a legislature from passing crippling taxes of general applicability are weakened, and the threat of burdensome taxes becomes acute. That threat can operate as effectively as a censor to check critical comment by the press, undercutting the basic assumption of our political system that the press will often serve as an important restraint on government.

Further, differential treatment, unless justified by some special characteristic of the press, suggests that the goal of the regulation is not unrelated to suppression of expression, and such a goal is presumptively unconstitutional. See, e.g., Police Department of the City of Chicago v. Mosley, 408 U.S. 92, 95–96 (1972); cf. Brown v. Hartlage, 456 U.S. 45 (1982) (First Amendment has its "fullest and most urgent" application in the case of regulation of the content of political speech). Differential taxation of the press, then, places such a burden on the interests protected by the First Amendment that we cannot counte-

6. It is true that our opinions rarely speculate on precisely how the Framers would have analyzed a given regulation of expression. In general, though, we have only limited evidence of exactly how the Framers intended the First Amendment to apply. There are no recorded debates in the Senate or in the States, and the discussion in the House of Representatives was couched in general terms, perhaps in response to Madison's suggestion that the representatives not stray from simple acknowledged principles. [ ] Consequently, we ordinarily simply apply those general principles, requiring the government to justify any burdens on First Amendment rights by showing that they are necessary to achieve a legitimate overriding governmental interest, see note 7, infra. But when we do have evidence that a particular law would have offended the Framers, we have not hesitated to invalidate it on that ground alone. Prior restraints, for instance, clearly strike to the core of the Framers' concerns, leading this Court to treat them as particularly suspect. Near v. Minnesota, 283 U.S. 697, 713, 716–718 (1931); cf. Grosjean v. American Press Co., Inc., 297 U.S. 233 (1936) (relying on the role of the "taxes on knowledge" in inspiring the First Amendment to strike down a contemporary tax on knowledge).

nance such treatment unless the State asserts a counterbalancing interest of compelling importance that it cannot achieve without differential taxation.[7]

IV

The main interest asserted by Minnesota in this case is the raising of revenue. Of course that interest is critical to any government. Standing alone, however, it cannot justify the special treatment of the press, for an alternative means of achieving the same interest without raising concerns under the First Amendment is clearly available: the State could raise the revenue by taxing businesses generally, avoiding the censorial threat implicit in a tax that singles out the press.

Addressing the concern with differential treatment, Minnesota invites us to look beyond the form of the tax to its substance. The tax is, according to the State, merely a substitute for the sales tax, which, as a generally applicable tax, would be constitutional as applied to the press.[9] There are two fatal flaws in this reasoning. First, the State has offered no explanation of why it chose to use a substitute for the sales tax rather than the sales tax itself. The court below speculated that the State might have been concerned that collection of a tax on such small transactions would be impractical. That suggestion is

7. JUSTICE REHNQUIST'S dissent analyzes this case solely as a problem of equal protection, applying the familiar tiers of scrutiny. We, however, view the problem as one arising directly under the First Amendment, for, as our discussion shows, the Framers perceived singling out the press for taxation as a means of abridging the freedom of the press, see note 6, supra. The appropriate method of analysis thus is to balance the burden implicit in singling out the press against the interest asserted by the State. Under a long line of precedent, the regulation can survive only if the governmental interest outweighs the burden and cannot be achieved by means that do not infringe First Amendment rights as significantly. [ ]

9. Star Tribune insists that the premise of the State's argument—that a generally applicable sales tax would be constitutional—is incorrect, citing Follett v. McCormick, 321 U.S. 573 (1944), Murdock v. Pennsylvania, 319 U.S. 105 (1943), and Jones v. Opelika, 319 U.S. 103 (1943). We think that Breard v. Alexandria, 341 U.S. 622 (1951), is more relevant and rebuts Star Tribune's argument. There, we upheld an ordinance prohibiting door-to-door solicitation, even though it applied to prevent the door-to-door sale of subscriptions to magazines, an activity covered by the First Amendment. Although Martin v. Struthers, 319 U.S. 141 (1943), had struck down a similar ordinance as applied to the distribution of free religious literature, the *Breard* Court explained that case as emphasizing that the information distributed was religious in nature and that the distribution was noncommercial. 341 U.S., at 642–643. As the dissent in *Breard* recognized, the majority opinion substantially undercut both *Martin* and the cases now relied upon by Star Tribune, in which the Court had invalidated ordinances imposing a flat license tax on the sale of religious literature. [ ] Whatever the value of those cases as authority after *Breard,* we think them distinguishable from a generally applicable sales tax. In each of those cases, the local government imposed a flat tax, unrelated to the receipts or income of the speaker or to the expenses of administering a valid regulatory scheme, as a *condition* of the right to speak. By imposing the tax as a condition of engaging in protected activity, the defendants in those cases imposed a form of prior restraint on speech, rendering the tax highly susceptible to constitutional challenge. [ ] In that regard, the cases cited by Star Tribune do not resemble a generally applicable sales tax. Indeed, our cases have consistently recognized that nondiscriminatory taxes on the receipts or income of newspapers would be permissible, Branzburg v. Hayes, 408 U.S. 665, 683 (dictum) [ ].

unpersuasive, for sales of other low-priced goods are not exempt. . . .[10] If the real goal of this tax is to duplicate the sales tax, it is difficult to see why the State did not achieve that goal by the obvious and effective expedient of applying the sales tax.

Further, even assuming that the legislature did have valid reasons for substituting another tax for the sales tax, we are not persuaded that this tax does serve as a substitute. The State asserts that this scheme actually *favors* the press over other businesses, because the same rate of tax is applied, but, for the press, the rate applies to the cost of components rather than to the sales price. We would be hesitant to fashion a rule that automatically allowed the State to single out the press for a different method of taxation as long as the effective burden was no different from that on other taxpayers or the burden on the press was lighter than that on other businesses. One reason for this reluctance is that the very selection of the press for special treatment threatens the press not only with the current *differential* treatment, but with the possibility of subsequent differentially *more burdensome* treatment. . . .

A second reason to avoid the proposed rule is that courts as institutions are poorly equipped to evaluate with precision the relative burdens of various methods of taxation.[12] The complexities of factual economic proof always present a certain potential for error, and courts have little familiarity with the process of evaluating the relative economic burden of taxes. In sum, the possibility of error inherent in the proposed rule poses too great a threat to concerns at the heart of the First Amendment, and we cannot tolerate that possibility. Minnesota, therefore, has offered no adequate justification for the special treatment of newspapers.[14]

10. JUSTICE REHNQUIST'S dissent explains that collecting sales taxes on newspapers entails special problems because of the unusual marketing practices for newspapers—sales from vending machines and at newsstands, for instance. [ ] The dissent does not, however, explain why the State cannot resolve these problems by using the same methods used for items like chewing gum and candy, marketed in these same unusual ways and subject to the sales tax. . . .

12. We have not always avoided evaluating the relative burdens of different methods of taxation in certain cases involving state taxation of the Federal Government and those with whom it does business. . . .

JUSTICE WHITE insists that the Court regularly inquires into the economic effect of taxes, relying on a number of cases arising under the Due Process Clause and the Commerce Clause. . . . In these cases, the Court required the taxpayer to show "gross overreaching," recognizing "the vastness of the State's taxing power and the latitude that the exercise of that power must be given before it encounters constitutional restraints." [ ] When delicate and cherished First Amendment rights are at stake, however, the constitutional tolerance for error diminishes drastically, and the risk increases that courts will prove unable to apply accurately the more finely tuned standards.

14. Disparaging our concern with the complexities of economic proof, JUSTICE REHNQUIST'S dissent undertakes to calculate a hypothetical sales tax liability for Star Tribune for the years 1974 and 1975. That undertaking, we think, illustrates some of the problems that inhere in any such inquiry. . . . Since newspapers receive a substantial portion of their revenues from advertising, [ ], it is not necessarily true even for profitable newspapers that the price of the finished product will exceed the cost of inputs. Consequently, it is not necessary that a tax imposed on components is less burdensome than a tax

V

Minnesota's ink and paper tax violates the First Amendment not only because it singles out the press, but also because it targets a small group of newspapers. The effect of the $100,000 exemption enacted in 1974 is that only a handful of publishers pay any tax at all, and even fewer pay any significant amount of tax. . . . Even if we were willing to accept the premise that large businesses are more profitable and therefore better able to bear the burden of the tax, the State's commitment to this "equity" is questionable, for the concern has not led the State to grant benefits to small businesses in general. And when the exemption selects such a narrowly defined group to bear the full burden of the tax, the tax begins to resemble more a penalty for a few of the largest newspapers than an attempt to favor struggling smaller enterprises.

VI

We need not and do not impugn the motives of the Minnesota legislature in passing the ink and paper tax. Illicit legislative intent is not the *sine qua non* of a violation of the First Amendment. . . . A tax that singles out the press, or that targets individual publications within the press, places a heavy burden on the State to justify its action. Since Minnesota has offered no satisfactory justification for its tax on the use of ink and paper, the tax violates the First Amendment, and the judgment below is reversed.

Reversed.

[Justice White agreed with Part V concerning the singling out of large newspapers. Although this led him to concur in the judgment, he disagreed with the rest of the Court's opinion—all of which he thought could have been left to another day in light of Part V.

He thought it "most questionable" that a state could threaten the press by imposing a different method of taxation that produced a lower tax than the uniform method. He also rejected the Court's argument that it was "poorly equipped" to evaluate alternative methods of taxation.

Justice Rehnquist dissented. He thought it "safe to assume that in 1791 'abridge' meant the same thing it means today: to diminish or curtail. Not until the Court's decision in this case, nearly two centuries after adoption of the First Amendment, has it been read to prohibit activities which in no way diminish or curtail the freedoms it protects."

After doing some elementary arithmetic, Justice Rehnquist observed that "We need no expert testimony from modern day Euclids or Einsteins to determine that the $1,224,747 paid in use taxes is significantly less burdensome than the $3,685,092 that could have been levied

at the same rate imposed on the price of the product. . . .

. . .

by a sales tax." Since the state's approach was "rational," he would have upheld it.

As to the $4,000 credit for each paper, there was no reason to conclude that the state had "acted other than reasonably and rationally to fit its sales and use tax scheme to its own local needs and usages."

He concluded that to "collect from newspapers their fair share of taxes under the sales and use tax scheme and at the same time avoid abridging the freedoms of the speech and press, the Court holds today that Minnesota must subject newspapers to millions of additional dollars in sales tax liability. Certainly this is a hollow victory for the newspapers and I seriously doubt the Court's conclusion that this result would have been intended by the 'Framers of the First Amendment.' "]

Notes and Questions

1. In *Grosjean,* the circular explaining the "tax on lying" also explained why the tax was being levied on a supporter of the Long machine: the framers could not think of a way to avoid it "but we would have done it if we could." As Justice O'Connor explains, the Court in *Grosjean* did not explicitly address the question of legislative motivation. The matter is discussed in J. Ely, Democracy and Distrust 143–45 (1980).

2. In Chicago Tribune Co. v. Johnson, 106 Ill.2d 63, 477 N.E.2d 482, 87 Ill.Dec. 505 (1985), the newspaper sought to come within an exemption to a general use tax. The paper had recently purchased several new printing presses. The Illinois Supreme Court upheld the appellate court's conclusion that the machinery did not come within an exemption for "machinery and equipment primarily [used] in the process of the manufacturing or assembling of tangible personal property. . . ."

The newspaper then argued that this interpretation violated the Constitution on two grounds. First, the newspaper alleged that "the State may not tax its machinery differently from that of other 'manufacturers.' " To do so, the Tribune argued, would violate the equal protection clause of the Fourteenth Amendment. The court rejected this argument, finding that there was "a rational relationship between the scope of the manufacturing-machinery exemption and the purpose for which it was enacted."

The newspaper's second constitutional argument was that the tax violated the First Amendment. The paper relied heavily on the part of the Minnesota case in which the Court expressed concern about special treatment for the press. The court distinguished the Minnesota case by the fact that the Minnesota tax applied only to publications; "the use tax here applies to all tangible personal property, including printing presses."

The Supreme Court dismissed the newspaper's appeal for want of substantial federal question. Justices White, Stevens, and O'Connor wanted to hear oral argument. 106 S.Ct. 241 (1985).

3. Ragland v. Arkansas Writers' Project, 287 Ark. 155, 697 S.W.2d 94, 698 S.W.2d 802 (1985), construed a state sales tax statute to cover the Arkansas Times Magazine, a "monthly magazine devoted to matters of general interest" that is sold mainly by mail subscription. The magazine did not come within a statute that exempted "religious, professional, trade and sports . . . publications printed and published within this State . . . when sold through regular subscriptions."

In denying rehearing, the court explicitly rejected two constitutional challenges. First, the magazine argued that the statute's exemptions denied the magazine equal protection. The court refused to address this because it would not help the magazine. If the exemption of another is invalid, "it is the exemption that would fall, not the tax against the *Times*. The courts cannot create a tax exemption; that must be done by the legislature."

Second, the magazine relied on the Star & Tribune and Grosjean cases to make a direct First Amendment challenge. The court responded that these cases did not establish immunity from any of the "ordinary forms of taxation" that support government. There is nothing suspect about a sales tax as opposed to property or income taxes.

The Supreme Court has noted probable jurisdiction, 106 S.Ct. 1966 (1986).

Part Two

LIMITS ON PUBLISHING

Chapter II

PROTECTING REPUTATION—DEFAMATION

A. COMMON LAW BACKGROUND

1. WHAT IS DEFAMATORY?

Defamation, perhaps the most pervasive legal nightmare for the media, is a concept that has come down through several centuries of English common law. In recent years, the Supreme Court has become involved in a continuing effort to determine the respective domains of freedom of communication and the protection of reputation.

Before we can appreciate the significance of the constitutional developments, we must understand the common law world of defamation. The constitutional developments have not created a totally new legal area; rather, they have altered some of the pre-existing state rules and left others in place. As a result, state law retains great significance in suits for defamation. It is often possible for a defendant to win a defamation case under the traditional state rules without ever having to rely on the First Amendment.

Defamation has a venerable and still influential history. Early in the sixteenth century the common law courts began to recognize a claim for defamation that had previously been within the exclusive jurisdiction of the ecclesiastical courts. Since the common law remedy was framed as an action on the case, with its traditional focus on damages rather than ecclesiastical sanctions, the common law action became extremely popular. In another development during this same period, the Star Chamber assumed jurisdiction over all aspects of the press, and printed defamations came to be treated as crimes. Attacks on officials were seditious libels, and libels against private persons contributed to breaches of the peace. After the Restoration both concepts were preserved: the Star Chamber's view of libel as a crime, and the antecedent common law view of slander as a tort. Each has exerted influence on the other ever since.

Although the English defamation law crossed the Atlantic, it seems never to have been enforced as vigorously in the United States as it was in England. This was true long before any constitutional questions were raised explicitly. In Government and Mass Communications 106–07 (1947), Professor Chafee speculated:

> [The difference] is probably due to the fact that English jurymen and judges live in a different intellectual climate from the fluid and migratory society of the United States. The Englishman is born into a definite status where he tends to stick for life. What he *is* has at least as much importance as what he *does* in an active career. A slur on his reputation, if not challenged, may cause him to drop several rungs down the social ladder. A man moves within a circle of friends and associates and feels bound to preserve his standing in their eyes. Consequently, *not* to sue for libel is taken as an admission of truth.
>
> An able American has too much else to do to waste time on an expensive libel suit. Most strangers will not read the article, most of his friends will not believe it, and his enemies, who will believe it of course, were against him before. Anyway, it is just one more blow in the rough-and-tumble of politics or business. Even if his reputation is lowered for a while, he can make a fresh start at his home or in a new region and accomplish enough to overwhelm old scandals. A libeled American prefers to vindicate himself by steadily pushing forward his career and not by hiring a lawyer to talk in a courtroom.

Even in the United States, however, certain slurs cannot be ignored, and justify legal recourse. Since the notion of reputation is at the core of the defamation action, we will begin our consideration with a look at that concept. In our discussion of the common law, the fact that the defendant is a publisher or broadcaster rather than an individual will not generally be central.

CIANCI v. NEW TIMES PUBLISHING CO.

United States Court of Appeals, Second Circuit, 1980.
639 F.2d 54, 6 Med.L.Rptr. 1625.

Noted, 69 Geo.L.J. 1495.

[The cover of the July 23, 1978 issue of New Times magazine bore a photograph captioned, "Vincent 'Buddy' Cianci Mayor of Providence, R.I." and a legend reading, "Was this man accused of raping a woman at gunpoint 12 years ago?" The seven-page article inside was titled "Buddy We Hardly Knew Ya." Two bold-face, boxed "inner headlines" asserted, "Redick [the rape victim's assumed name] took the lie detector test and passed; Cianci took it three times and failed each time," and "Redick has confirmed her account, and says that she did receive a $3,000 payoff." The article stated that the reporter had had access to police records; in addition, it "quoted liberally from a statement allegedly made by Redick to the article's author in 1978." The magazine's account began: "Twelve years ago, in a suburb of Milwaukee, a law student was accused of raping a woman at gunpoint. After receiving a $3,000 settlement, she dropped the charges and the incident was nearly forgotten. That student, Vincent 'Buddy' Cianci, Jr., is now the mayor of Providence, Rhode Island." The article stated that Redick said Cianci had invited her to his office one night in 1966 to do some of his law school work. The office turned out to be located in a house, and he raped her there after threatening her with a gun, she said. She went to the police the next morning. The article detailed the official investigation that followed. Results of some of the tests performed were inconclusive, but, as the court put it:

> The article continued to state as a fact that Redick took the lie detector test and passed, whereas Cianci took it three times and failed each time. This was followed by a quotation from a report by Harold Block, a River Hills police lieutenant in 1966: ". . . According to State Crime Lab expert, Joe Wilamovsky, the report on the polygraph test showed this to be one of the most clear cut cases of rape he had ever processed in his years with the State Crime Lab. In his opinion, Gayle Redick passed the test beyond a shadow of doubt while Cianci failed completely on three separate testings. . . . " The article proceeded with a statement by Redick that her attorney did not think she was well enough to go on with the case and told her "to drop the charges and settle out of court." It quoted her as saying she had received a settlement of $3,000 and went on to state that she withdrew her complaint. . . . Assistant District Attorney Boyle was stated to have explained recently that the lack of evidence stemmed from the fact that "[t]he victim, presumably the star witness, settled out of court, and would therefore probably not be willing to testify. . . . "

Contacted by a reporter 12 years after the alleged incident, Redick "confirmed her rape charge against Cianci and discussed the $3,000 settlement," the story stated. But she later relayed through her attorney the information that she had no complaint with the way the case had been handled, and that the reporter had obtained information from her by "threat and intimidation." The article continued, "for the nominal sum of $3,000, Cianci had managed to buy his way out of a possible felony charge. . . . Unlike tryst-and-tell heroines Judith Exner and Elizabeth Ray, Redick hasn't attempted to capitalize on her experience. . . . [She] has been reluctant to talk about the alleged rape."

Cianci, who was seeking re-election at the time the article was published, sued for defamation. During discovery, the defendants—the magazine publishing company and the publisher, editor, and author of the article—moved to dismiss the complaint. They alleged that the facts in the article were true or "protected as the neutral reportage of facts from an independent source clearly identified as such." They also alleged that to the extent that the article expressed the opinion that

Cianci was guilty of the alleged rape, the opinion was protected by the Constitution because all of the facts on which it was based were set forth in the article and because "the article does not state or imply that the defendants are privy to other facts not known to the general reader."

The district court granted the motion to dismiss, stating that the article was not defamatory, since it "carefully refrains from stating that Cianci was indicted, officially charged, or guilty of the crime of rape as claimed by Redick. Nor does the article ever state that Cianci paid Redick $3,000 as part of an agreement to drop criminal charges." To the extent the article implied that Cianci was guilty of rape or illegal payoffs, the lower court found, "such implications are constitutionally protected as expressions of opinion." Other parts of the opinion are set forth later in this section.]

Before FRIENDLY and MESKILL, CIRCUIT JUDGES, and THOMSEN, DISTRICT JUDGE.

FRIENDLY, CIRCUIT JUDGE.

. . .

I. THE ARTICLE WAS REASONABLY SUSCEPTIBLE OF A DEFAMATORY CONNOTATION

The initial question is whether the article is "reasonably susceptible of a defamatory connotation," [ ] so as to warrant its submission to a jury to determine if in fact the defamatory connotation was conveyed. Restatement, Second, Torts § 614. The allegedly defamatory passages must be considered in the context of the entire article and the words taken as they are commonly understood. Id. § 563. The article was capable of bearing a defamatory meaning for two reasons: it contained explicit statements and fair implications *by the writer* which could be considered defamatory, and it also republished defamatory statements made by others, for which a defendant, unless protected by a privilege, is as liable as if he had made the statements himself.

Our summary of the article has revealed many instances where defendants could be found to have made charges of criminal conduct on their own responsibility. We start with the words of the headline:

BUDDY WE HARDLY KNEW YA

A jury, considering this in light of the article as a whole, could surely conclude that New Times was saying that Mayor Cianci, instead of being the man of character he represented himself to be, was in fact a rapist and an obstructor of justice—not simply a person who had been accused of being such.[9] The statement in the inner headline about the lie detector test was clearly a statement of fact, although perhaps

9. The sarcastic comparison with the book by O'Donnell and Powers with the similar title could be found to have reinforced the defamatory implication. [This note is a reference to K. O'Donnell and D. Powers, Johnny, We Hardly Knew Ye (1970)—a book of memoirs of John F. Kennedy—by two very close friends.—ed.]

protected by privilege, as we shall see. The statement in the concluding portion of the article that "[f]or the nominal sum of $3,000, Cianci had managed to buy his way out of a possible felony charge" was a direct statement of fact by the New Times, not just the repetition of a statement by another. Later the article says that "Redick hasn't tried to capitalize on her experience . . . ." The "experience" was being the victim of rape at gunpoint, not of having accused Cianci of it.

Beyond this the organization of the section of the article relating the circumstances of the decision not to prosecute Cianci and the $3,000 payment is also reasonably susceptible of a defamatory connotation. According to the complaint and evidence developed by the plaintiff, the defendants knew that the decision not to prosecute Cianci was made prior to and independent of any settlement between Cianci and Redick. Yet the organization of the article, for which the defendants alone are responsible, strongly implies that the payment was prior to and was the primary reason for the decision not to prosecute. The section begins by surveying the items of evidence in the police file, and moves on to quote Lieutenant Block as saying "When you think you have enough, you send it up to the D.A. Then you hope for justice." This clearly refers to a possible criminal prosecution. The article then immediately moves to discuss the $3,000 settlement, never suggesting that it was made *after* the withdrawal of the criminal complaint and *after* the decision not to prosecute had been reached. Then the article returns to discuss the decision not to prosecute Cianci *criminally*. The clear implication, or at least one which a jury could find, was that the $3,000 payment was made prior to the withdrawal of the complaint and the decision not to prosecute and, particularly when read in connection with the rest of the article, that it was a payoff designed to affect these decisions.

The second point is even plainer. A federal court has recently referred to the "black-letter rule that one who republishes a libel is subject to liability just as if he had published it originally, even though he attributes the libelous statement to the original publisher, and even though he expressly disavows the truth of the statement." Hoover v. Peerless Publications, Inc., 461 F.Supp. 1206, 1209 (E.D.Pa.1978). This rule has been widely recognized. See, e.g., Restatement, Second, Torts § 578 (1977) ("one who repeats or otherwise republishes defamatory matter is subject to liability as if he had originally published it"); 1 Harper & James, [The Law of Torts § 5.20 at 417 (1956)]; Prosser, Torts § 113 at 768 (4th ed. 1971). A good example of the application of this rule is Olinger v. American Savings and Loan Assoc., 409 F.2d 142, 144 (D.C.Cir.1969). Defendant had sent a letter to plaintiff Olinger's military superiors containing the statements "Mrs. Olinger reports that Col. Olinger is unwilling to permit her to sell the property and he will not keep the payments current on the first and second trust." As the court noted, this statement "was 'true' only because it was prefaced by 'Mrs. Olinger reports that . . . ' " Id. at 144. Stating that "[t]he law affords no protection to those who couch their libel in the form of reports or repetition" and that "the repeater cannot defend on the ground of truth simply by proving that the source named did, in fact, utter the statement," the court reversed a grant of summary judgment for the defendant. The republication rule applies to the press, as it does to others, although the press may derive particular benefit from certain privileges discussed below. [ ] Any different rule would permit the expansion of a defamatory private statement, actionable but without serious consequences, into an article reaching thousands of readers, without liability on the part of the republisher. See [ ]; Metcalf v. Times Pub. Co., 20 R.I. 674, 40 A. 864, 865 (1898) ("If a man has not the right to go around and tell of charges made by one against another, much less should a newspaper have the right to spread it broadcast and in enduring form."). The New Times article is replete with defamatory statements of fact repeated from others—Redick's detailed description of the bedroom scene, the statement attributed to the State Crime Lab expert that the polygraph report "showed this to be one of the most clear cut cases of rape he had ever processed . . . ", Redick's statement that she had dropped the charges in return for a $3,000 payment, and so on.

II. THE ARTICLE IS NOT PROTECTED AS A STATEMENT OF OPINION

Despite this the judgment should stand if the district court was right in holding that the article was protected as an expression of opinion. [This part of the case is considered at p. 245, infra.]

Our holding that the article was not within the constitutional protection for false ideas requires us to consider whether it may nevertheless have been protected by the common law privilege of fair comment. . . .

The common law privilege of fair comment applied only if the disclosed facts were true or privileged. Restatement, First, Torts § 606; Gatley, Libel and Slander 325–31 (6th ed. 1967). Here plaintiff alleges that the article is replete with misstatements of fact. The issue of truth is surely not ripe for summary judgment, and we hold below, in Part III of this opinion, that not all the reported facts were protected by a constitutional privilege of neutral reportage or the common law privilege of fair report. The privilege of fair comment was also lost if the comments were made with malice, in the common law sense of spite or ill-will. Restatement, First, Torts § 606, comment d. Although such ill-will is not directly implicated [by constitutional concerns,] it would remain pertinent to this distinct common law issue, and plaintiff's complaint alleges it more than adequately.

Moreover it is unlikely that an expression in the form of "I think Cianci raped Redick at gunpoint" would be considered a "comment" so as to come within the fair comment privilege. It is far from the usual sort of evaluative judgment with which the privilege has traditionally been concerned. Contrast Restatement, First, Torts § 607, illustration 1 (police chief unfit for office); illustration 2 (magistrate criticized for fixing high bail); illustration 3 (quality of work by contractor on public streets criticized); illustration 4 (European dictator criticized for acts which impair world peace). The problems with an extension of the privilege of fair comment to include specific allegations of fact were articulated long ago and have not lost their validity:

> Were such an objection to be sustained to an action for slanderous words, it would be easy for one who designed to injure the character of another to effect his malicious purpose without incurring any responsibility. By circulating the slander, clothed in expressions of opinion or belief, he might destroy the fairest reputation with impunity. But the law will not permit an injury to character to be without remedy by such an artifice as this. Whatever may be the mode of expression used, if an assertion of guilt is implied or intended, the words will be actionable. Logan v. Steele, 1 Bibb. 593, 595 (Ky.1809).

In Professional & Business Men's Life Ins. Co. v. Bankers Life Co., 163 F.Supp. 274 (D.Mont.1958), the court sustained an action based on a notice which warned those approached by insurance salesmen making seven specified representations to contact the state insurance commissioner. The notice implied the opinion of dishonest business practices, and "a suspicion, belief, or opinion is as effectively a libel as though the charge were positively made," even though the basis for the opinion, the seven representations, was disclosed. Id. at 287 (quoting Woolston v. Montana Free Press, 90 Mont. 299, 2 P.2d 1020, 1022 (1931)). In Venn v. Tennessean Newspapers Inc., [201 F.Supp. 47, 56 (M.D.Tenn. 1962)], defendant newspaper published the comments of others linking plaintiff with underworld figures. The defense of fair comment was not allowed. "The libellous imputations and statements . . . are unadulterated imputations [or statements] of fact and by no stretch of the imagination could they be classified as comments or expressions of views or opinions. . . . " As indicated by . . . the more recent cases, . . . charges of specific criminal misconduct are not protected as "opinions." See also P. Keeton, Defamation and Freedom of the Press, 54 Tex.L.Rev. 1221, 1254 (1976) (arguing that when fault with respect to the truth or falsity of the defamatory matter published is a prerequisite to recovery "[a]ny charge of specific misconduct or defamatory fact should be treated as a statement of fact regardless of whether the publisher conveys his deductive opinion alone or with the information to support it.").

Further, the common law privilege of fair comment does not here apply because the disclosed facts and any implied opinion are inextricably intertwined in the accused article. The reader is not presented with facts and a separate inference therefrom; rather the opinion is conveyed as part and parcel of the factual disclosures. See Gatley, supra, at 324; Luster v. Retail Credit Co., 575 F.2d 609, 616–17 (8 Cir. 1978) (credit report detailing certain facts could be read as charging the plaintiff with arson and is actionable). In such a case it is meaningless to say that the opinion is protected, when the facts are not.

III. THE ARTICLE IS NOT PROTECTED BY A CONSTITUTIONAL PRIVILEGE OF NEUTRAL REPORTAGE OR THE COMMON LAW PRIVILEGE OF FAIR REPORT

[This part of the case is considered at p. 282, infra.]

. . .

The judgment dismissing the complaint is therefore reversed and the cause remanded for further proceedings consistent with this opinion.

. . .

Notes and Questions

1. Historically, some states required a defamatory communication to expose the plaintiff to hatred, ridicule, contempt, scorn, or shame. The modern view is reflected in the Restatement, Second, Torts § 559: "A communication is defamatory if it tends so to harm the reputation of another as to lower him in the estimation of the community or to deter third persons from associating or dealing with him."

Because defamation hinges on reputation, the defamatory statement must be communicated to someone other than the plaintiff. Although communication to even a single third party will satisfy the requirement that the defamatory statement be "published," the content of the statement must be of the sort that would prejudice the plaintiff "in the eyes of a substantial and respectable minority" of the community. Restatement, Second, Torts § 559, Comment e. What comprises a "substantial and respectable minority"? What "community"? In Ben-Oliel v. Press Publishing Co., 251 N.Y. 250, 167 N.E. 432 (1929), the plaintiff, an expert on Palestinian art and customs, was falsely stated to have written an article on that subject that appeared in the Sunday newspaper. The article would have impressed virtually all the newspaper's regular readers. Unfortunately, the article had several errors that would embarrass the author among fellow experts. The court ruled that the relevant community in that case was the small group of experts on the subject—and that a jury could find that those experts would have thought less of plaintiff as a scholar after hearing that she had written such an article.

But when a particular statement draws varying reactions from broad segments of the general community, a more difficult question is posed. In Grant v. Reader's Digest Ass'n, 151 F.2d 733 (2d Cir.1945), certiorari denied 326 U.S. 797 (1946), defendant published an article calling the plaintiff lawyer "a legislative representative for the Massachusetts Communist Party." Judge L. Hand stated the question to be "whether it is libellous . . . to write of a lawyer that he has acted as agent of the Communist Party and is a believer in its aims and methods." His analysis follows:

> The interest at stake in all defamation is concededly the reputation of the person assailed; and any moral obliquity of the opinions of those in whose minds the words might lessen that reputation, would normally be relevant only in mitigation of damages. A man may value his reputation even among those who do not embrace the prevailing moral standards; and it would seem that the jury should be allowed to appraise how far he should be indemnified for the disesteem of such persons. That is the usual rule. [ ] The New York . . . opinions at times seem to make it a condition that to be actionable the words must be such as would so affect "right-thinking" people. . . . The same limitation has apparently been recognized in England [ ]; and it is fairly plain that there must come a point where that is true. As was said in Mawe v. Piggott, Irish Rep. 4 Comm.Law, 54, 62, among those "who were themselves criminal or sympathized with crime," it would expose one "to great odium to represent him as an informer or prosecutor or otherwise aiding in the detection of crime"; yet certainly the words would not be actionable. Be that as it may, in New York if the exception covers more than such a case, it does not go far enough to excuse the utterance at bar. Katapodis v. Brooklyn Spectator, Inc., (287 N.Y. 17, 38 N.E.2d 112 (1941)) . . . held that the imputation of extreme poverty might be actionable; although certainly "right-thinking" people ought not shun, or despise, or otherwise condemn one because he is poor. . . . We do not believe, therefore, that we need say whether "right-thinking" people would harbor similar feelings toward a lawyer, because he had been an agent for the Communist Party, or was a sympathizer with its aims and means. It is enough if there be some, as there certainly are, who would feel so, even though they would be "wrong-thinking" people if they did. . . .

But how wrong-thinking? What about a story erroneously accusing a mobster of being a poor shot? See Note, The Community Segment in Defamation Actions: A Dissenting Essay, 58 Yale L.J. 1387 (1949).

2. Recall that *Cianci* pointed out that the New Times could be liable for quoting defamatory statements by others. This liability by "republication" was originally premised on the notion that by repeating a defamatory statement, the publisher "adopted" it. When that republication occurs in the media, it probably causes more injury than when spoken in ordinary conversation. Whatever the reason, however, liability by republication means that the common law might hold a newspaper liable, for example, for publishing a defamatory letter to the editor. Republication is discussed at p. 276, infra.

3. The New Times article never stated explicitly that Cianci was a rapist, but the court had no trouble finding that meaning in the article's words. How should a publication be interpreted when its meaning is not explicitly stated? In Cooper v. Greeley, 1 Denio 347 (N.Y.1845), Horace Greeley had written in the New York Tribune that

he was not worried about a suit filed against him by James Fenimore Cooper because "Mr. Cooper will have to bring his action to trial somewhere. He will not like to bring it in New York, for we are known here, nor in Otsego for he is known there." Cooper sued again—for defamation. Greeley contended that the statement meant only "that a prophet has no honor in his own country. The point of the article is the intimation that the plaintiff would prefer a trial where the prejudice and rivalries which assail every man at home could not reach him." Cooper alleged that the statement meant to suggest that he was in bad repute in Otsego. What is the judge's role in interpreting this statement? What is the jury's role?

See also Rovira v. Boget, 240 N.Y. 314, 148 N.E. 534 (1925) in which a member of the ship's crew called plaintiff, a stewardess on the same ship, a "cocotte," while both were eating at the crew's mess. A French interpreter testified that to some men the word "cocotte" means prostitute. "In other associations it may mean a poached egg."

Consider this passage from R. Sack, Libel, Slander, and Related Problems 74–75 (1980):

> The same word or expression may vary with context, jurisdiction and time. Thus, for example, the word "murderer" would appear to be quintessentially libelous. Yet, in the context of an attack on President Johnson's Vietnam war policy, it would certainly have been treated as non-defamatory, derogatory political opinion. To say that someone is a "bastard" is probably still defamatory if, in context, it means that the plaintiff was born out of wedlock. If it is merely an epithet directed at the same plaintiff, it would not be. . . . And times change. Imputing unchastity to a woman is a classic example of defamation. . . . But does it still have the same impact on "respectable" members of the community that it once had?

Would it be wise to provide that if there are two reasonable ways to interpret a statement, one defamatory and another non-defamatory, as a matter of law the non-defamatory meaning must be accepted as the only permissible reading? Illinois follows this "innocent construction" rule. Action Repair, Inc. v. American Broadcasting Cos., 776 F.2d 143, 12 Med.L.Rptr. 1398 (7th Cir.1985).

4. Verbal ambiguities aside, the meaning of a statement may be altered by punctuation, paragraphing, or typography. Thus, in Wildstein v. New York Post Corp., 40 Misc.2d 586, 243 N.Y.S.2d 386, affirmed without opinion 24 App.Div.2d 559, 261 N.Y.S.2d 254 (1965), the defendant wrote that the plaintiff was one of "several women described as 'associated' with" a slain executive. The judge observed that if the word "associated" had not been in quotation marks the statement would not have been defamatory; the quotation marks implied a euphemistic use of the word, suggesting an illicit relationship between plaintiff and the deceased. See also Heaphy v. Westchester Rockland Newspapers, Inc., 47 App.Div.2d 922, 367 N.Y.S.2d 52 (1975),

involving the use of "friend" without quotation marks. The actual paragraphing of the story may also be crucial in construing the meaning. See Vandenburg v. Newsweek, Inc., 507 F.2d 1024 (5th Cir.1975), and Swartz v. World Pub. Co., 57 Wash.2d 213, 356 P.2d 97 (1960).

5. Another problem arises when part of an article has a defamatory impact but another part of the article negates that impact. The headline may be defamatory although the article is not; the lead paragraph alone may be defamatory but the article as a whole may be harmless; and one sentence may be defamatory but the whole paragraph may be harmless. Gambuzza v. Time, Inc., 18 App.Div.2d 351, 239 N.Y.S.2d 466 (1963), involved a two-page spread of 12 photographs in a magazine article, each with a three-line legend beneath it. The story involved reports of the activities of a convicted spy. One photograph of plaintiff was captioned "HIS ADMIRER. Frank Gambuzza, a radio dealer who sold Abel some parts for a wireless receiver, praised the Russian for his electronic know-how." Plaintiff alleged that the first two words suggested sympathy for Abel and his cause. The majority noted that sometimes headlines might be read separately from the article and judged by their own words because "a person passing a newsstand . . . may be able to catch a glimpse of a headline without the opportunity or desire to read the accompanying article or may skim through the paper jumping from headline to headline." But this was not such a case because the caption was so close to the text that they had to be read together: "the article must be considered as a whole and its meaning gleaned not from isolated portions thereof but rather from the entire article. . . . " Two dissenters emphasized that the critical words in the caption were in bold capital letters and thus should be considered separately from the rest of the article.

In Kunst v. New York World Telegram Corp., 28 App.Div.2d 662, 280 N.Y.S.2d 798 (1967), the lead paragraph and a photograph caption conveyed a defamatory implication that was negated by a statement that a "persistent and careful reader would discover near the end of the reasonably lengthy article." The majority upheld the complaint, stressing that the writing must be "construed, not with the high degree of precision expected of and used by lawyers and judges, but as it would be read and understood by an ordinary member of the public to whom it is directed." A dissenter responded, "It is true this appears near the end of the article, but the article is to be taken as a whole and read in its entirety." He relied on *Gambuzza*.

6. The judge in a defamation case decides first whether, as a matter of law, a reasonable reader could have found the statement at issue to be defamatory. If so, the actual interpretation of the statement is left to the jury. Consider the following examples.

a. A statement that plaintiff was seduced by Rasputin. Raped by him. Youssoupoff v. Metro-Goldwyn-Mayer Pictures, Ltd., 50 T.L.R. 581 (1934). Would it be different if the man named had been an American movie idol instead of the infamous "mad monk"?

b. A statement that the plaintiff is of illegitimate birth. Shelby v. Sun Printing & Publishing Ass'n, 38 Hun 474 (1886), affirmed on the opinion below, 109 N.Y. 611, 15 N.E. 895 (1888). Can it ever be defamatory to say that someone is of legitimate birth?

c. A statement that the plaintiffs' child will have to be buried in Potters' Field because his parents are in "dire financial straits" and cannot afford a private burial. Katapodis v. Brooklyn Spectator, Inc., 287 N.Y. 17, 38 N.E.2d 112 (1941). Suppose the statement had been that the child would be buried in a wooden casket because the parents could not afford a silver casket. Can it ever be defamatory to say that someone is wealthy?

d. A statement that plaintiff endorses the tonic effects of a specific whiskey. Peck v. Tribune Co., 214 U.S. 185 (1909).

e. A statement that the plaintiff, who owns a service station and truck stop, reports to the Interstate Commerce Commission the names of truckers who violate I.C.C. rules limiting the number of consecutive hours they may work. Connelly v. McKay, 176 Misc. 685, 28 N.Y.S.2d 327 (1941). Might it be defamatory to say that he did not report such violators?

f. A statement that a reputable physician illegally terminated life support services on a terminally ill patient who was in great pain and stated that he wished to die. Might it be defamatory to say he refused the patient's request to do so?

g. A statement that the plaintiff has died. Cardiff v. Brooklyn Eagle, 190 Misc. 730, 75 N.Y.S.2d 222 (1947).

h. A statement by a candidate for the Democratic nomination for United States Senator from Florida to his backwoods audiences: "Are you aware that Claude Pepper is known all over Washington as a shameless extrovert? Not only that, but this man is reliably reported to practice nepotism with his sister-in-law, and he has a sister, who was once a thespian in wicked New York. Worst of all, it is an established fact that Mr. Pepper, before his marriage, practiced celibacy." See R. Sherrill, Gothic Politics in the Deep South 150 (1968), attributing the passage to George Smathers, who defeated Pepper, the incumbent, in that campaign. Smathers denied making the statement. N.Y.Times, Feb. 24, 1983 at 10.

i. In Burton v. Crowell Pub. Co., 82 F.2d 154 (2d Cir.1936), the plaintiff, a widely known gentleman steeplechaser, posed outside the paddock for an advertisement for Camel cigarettes. The position of the pommel, stirrup, and girth in front of plaintiff made the photograph "grotesque, monstrous, and obscene." Part of the text quoted the plaintiff as saying that Camel cigarettes restored him after "a crowded business day" and another passage said "Get a lift with a Camel." Plaintiff claimed that he had been subjected to much ridicule. Although the court observed that "it is patently an optical illusion, and carries its correction on its face as much as though it were a verbal utterance which expressly declared that it was false," it held the photograph prima facie actionable. The "mortification . . . was a very substantial grievance."

7. Suppose an article states only that the plaintiff had often been seen at "123 Hay Road." What if some in the community knew that there was a brothel at that address? Plaintiff need not show that the defamation was contained solely in the published words. When the words do not clearly convey any defamatory thrust, the plaintiff must plead extrinsic facts that would permit a defamatory meaning to be applied to the words used. This allegation of extrinsic facts—for example, that 123 Hay Road is a brothel—is called the "inducement." Where the statement and extrinsic facts are not clearly defamatory, plaintiff pleads that the "innuendo"—the meaning—of the passage is defamatory. Here, it is that the plaintiff patronized a house of prostitution. The innuendo is not a fact but is the plaintiff's assertion of how the passage would be understood by those who heard the defendant's words and knew the additional extrinsic facts.

Traditionally, the terms inducement and innuendo have been relevant solely to the problems of pleading. Courts require that the plaintiff allege the precise words claimed to be defamatory—but when this does not suffice, plaintiff must usually make further allegations. This kind of elaboration is often necessary. Consider, for example, Smith v. Smith, 236 N.Y. 581, 142 N.E. 292 (1923), concerning what may be the shortest defamation on record. Plaintiff alleged that the defendant, her former husband, long after their divorce, when filling out a marriage license application to marry another woman, answered "1" when asked "number of marriage" and "No" when asked "Is applicant a divorced person?" What added allegations might be necessary to spell out a defamation?

8. In one case, plaintiff alleged that the defendant magazine had asserted facts that imputed to him the crime of raping a 15-year-old girl. He claimed that the defamation resulted from the omission of several facts that would have put him in a better light, such as that he had passed a lie detector test in which he denied the rape; that a medical examination showed no evidence of rape; and that several federal inquiries had called the charge "unfounded." On this point, the court said:

> We note that the law does not recognize libel by omission as a tort. Libel, by definition, consists of the publication of a false and unprivileged fact. Thus, liability may be imposed in a libel case only for an assertion or implication of fact that is false and unprivileged, and not for mere omission of a relevant fact.

The court thought its view was supported by Miami Herald Publishing Co. v. Tornillo, 418 U.S. 241 (1974), p. 433, infra, in which the Court struck down a statute that punished as a misdemeanor the newspaper's failure to publish a reply from a candidate who had been attacked in its columns. "While newspapers have long been liable for that which they publish, they have never been liable solely for that which was omitted. . . . We believe the law is clear that for a recovery to lie, there must be a showing that what has been omitted has made a material assertion of fact untrue." Janklow v. Newsweek, Inc., 759 F.2d 644, 11 Med.L.Rptr. 1995 (8th Cir.1985). (This holding remains in effect after the en banc decision at 788 F.2d 1300, 12 Med.L. Rptr. 1961 (8th Cir.1986)). As we shall see, omission may be relevant at other points in the analysis.

9. May a refusal to discuss a subject lead to a defamatory inference? Plaintiff, former editor of defendant's newspaper, was fired. Another paper reported the purported reason. A concerned reader wrote defendant publisher, who responded that "Mr. Perry's termination was based on several factors and not the incident mentioned in the [other paper]. Rather than embarrass Mr. Perry further on the matter, we decided not to issue a statement."

The court held that reasonable triers of fact could find that this letter conveyed the sense that Perry had "conducted himself in a shameful manner, or in a manner inconsistent with the proper exercise of his profession." Perry v. Cosgrove, 464 So.2d 664, 11 Med.L.Rptr. 1931 (Fla.App.1985).

2. Of and Concerning Plaintiff

Identification. In addition to showing the defamatory nature of the publication, the plaintiff must show that the statement was understood to refer to, if not aimed at, the plaintiff. This is not difficult if the plaintiff is named or clearly identified in the publication, but sometimes the requirement can raise serious questions.

Thus, in the Smith case involving the man who claimed never to have been married before, the plaintiff would have to show that she was the person who was hurt in the eyes of others. This element is often called "colloquium" and performs the function of identifying the defamed person to the court.

A fairly common problem arises from the use of stock photographs to illustrate a story. The question is whether reasonable readers could understand that the persons pictured are alleged to have done the defamatory acts discussed in the accompanying article. See Morrell v. Forbes, Inc., 603 F.Supp. 1305, 11 Med.L.Rptr. 1869 (D.Mass.1985), in which plaintiff fisherman was shown in one of two photographs with recognizable persons in an article about organized crime on the Boston waterfront. The caption was "The Boston Fish Pier: smaller fry in a fishy business." The other photograph with a recognizable person bore the caption, "[f]ish market mobster Socks Lanza." Since the trier could find that plaintiff was being accused of being involved with organized crime, summary judgment was denied.

A similar result was reached in Clark v. American Broadcasting Cos., Inc., 684 F.2d 1208, 8 Med.L.Rptr. 2049 (6th Cir.1982), involving a program about prostitution. The plaintiff, who had been photographed without her knowledge while walking on a city street, was shown on the screen while the narrator was saying something that the court thought a jury might understand as suggesting that the plaintiff was engaged in prostitution.

For the special problems of identification of plaintiffs in works of fiction, see Symposium, Defamation in Fiction, 51 Brooklyn L.Rev. 223 (1985).

Corporations. It seems clear that corporations may be defamation plaintiffs. Section 561 of the Second Restatement states that a corporation for profit may sue if "the matter tends to prejudice it in the conduct of its business or to deter others from dealing with it." A corporation that is not for profit may sue if it "depends upon financial support from the public, and the matter tends to interfere with its activities by prejudicing it in public estimation."

A separate question involves the relationship between a corporation and its shareholders. If the corporation is large and its stock widely held, courts generally conclude that stockholders may not sue for the libel of the corporation. But in closely held corporations, courts have held that a libel of the corporation may be understood by the reasonable audience to be addressed as well to the controlling individuals, even if they are not mentioned in the story. This result is even clearer if the individual and the corporation have the same name. These matters are discussed in Schiavone Construction Co. v. Time, Inc., 619 F.Supp. 684, 12 Med.L.Rptr. 1153 (D.N.J.1985).

Group libel. Different problems arise when the statement is about one or more members of a group of individuals. In such cases might one member be able to claim that the statement hurt his or her personal reputation? At the extreme, an attack on all lawyers in the United States or on all clergymen would be held to be such a general broadside that no individual lawyer or clergyman could sue. The same would be true of broadside attacks on racial, religious, or ethnic groups.

At the other extreme, it is generally accepted that a charge made against a small group may defame all members of that group. For example, a newspaper article may assert that "the officers" of a corporation have embezzled funds. There are only four officers of the corporation. Each of them may be found to have been defamed, even though the statement was that "one of the officers of the corporation" had embezzled funds. The group is small enough so that all four officials are put under a shadow, and most states would permit all four to sue.

As the group grows larger the impact of the statement may depend on the number accused as well as the size of the total group. In a recent case, a defamatory charge was made against one unidentified member of a 21-member police force. All 21 sued. The trial court's dismissal was affirmed. It was feared that allowing the action would permit a suit by an entire baseball team over a report that one member was disciplined for brawling. Such a result "would chill communication to the marrow." The court explained, "By no stretch of imagination can it be thought to suggest that the conduct of the one [described in the article] is typical of all. Noting the individual's membership in the group does not suggest a common determinant of character so much as simply a practical reference point." But suppose the charge had been against "all but one" of the members of that police force? Such a statement may reflect on each member of the force. Arcand v. Evening Call Pub. Co., 567 F.2d 1163, 3 Med.L.Rptr. 1748 (1st Cir.1977).

One case presented three aspects of this problem. Two authors, in a book about Dallas, stated that "some" department store models were "call girls . . . . The salesgirls are good, too—pretty and often much cheaper . . . ." And "most of the [male] sales staff are fairies, too."

Suits were filed by all nine models, 15 of the 25 salesmen, and 30 of the 382 saleswomen. The defendants did not challenge the right of the nine models to sue. The other two groups were challenged as being too large.

The claim of "the salesgirls" was dismissed. The result would be the same even if the authors had explicitly referred to "all"—and even if all 382 had sued. The judge could find no case allowing a group of 382 to sue. He cited cases rejecting suits when the statements attacked all officials of a statewide union or all the taxicab drivers in Washington, D.C.

On the other hand, the salesmen's case was not dismissed. It was close to others involving members of a posse, or the 12 doctors on a hospital's residential staff. Would the result have been the same if the authors had referred to "some" or "a few" of the men? Neiman-Marcus v. Lait, 13 F.R.D. 311 (S.D.N.Y.1952).

Would the legal system find it administratively difficult to handle a damage action brought by 382 plaintiffs, even though they might deserve some compensation? Is the development of class actions relevant here?

In Michigan United Conservation Clubs v. CBS News, 485 F.Supp. 893, 5 Med.L.Rptr. 2566 (W.D.Mich.1980), plaintiffs claimed to represent over one million Michigan sport hunters who had been defamed by defendant's telecast on the ethics of hunters. After reviewing group libel cases, the judge dismissed the case:

> If plaintiffs were allowed to proceed with this claim, it could invite any number of vexatious lawsuits and seriously interfere with public discussion of issues, or groups, which are in the public eye. Statements about a religious, ethnic, or political group could invite thousands of lawsuits from disgruntled members of these groups claiming that the portrayal was inaccurate and thus libelous.

The dismissal was affirmed, 665 F.2d 110, 7 Med.L.Rptr. 2331 (6th Cir. 1981). See also Talal v. Fanning, 506 F.Supp. 186 (N.D.Cal.1980), dismissing a claim brought on behalf of 600 million Muslims.

One court has rejected the emphasis on the absolute size of the group; it considered the defined nature of the group, and its prominence, and is prepared to consider the role of the individual in the group. Using these criteria, the court concluded that 53 members of the 71-member police force of Newburgh, N.Y., in 1972, could sue for a statement in 1979 suggesting that, although they were not indicted for misdeeds along with 18 colleagues, the other 53 must have known what was going on. Brady v. Ottaway Newspapers, Inc., 84 App.Div.2d 226, 445 N.Y.S.2d 786 (1981).

Although defamation of large groups—ethnic, religious, professional—does not result in a cause of action in any state, some states have sought to develop criminal sanctions against certain group defamations. When a defamatory statement attacks a racial, religious, or ethnic group, the state's interest is not in individual or even group reputation, but the social hazards that unrestricted hate propaganda can cause. As early as 1917, some states enacted criminal group libel laws designed to restrict communication that arouses such hatred.

The systematic and effective Nazi defamation of minority groups and the increasingly apparent racial tensions in the United States brought renewed attention to group libel laws in the 1940s. David Riesman's Democracy and Defamation: The Control of Group Libel, 42 Colum.L.Rev. 727 (1942), saw group libel laws as a means of reducing group hatred and preventing the spread of socially disruptive attitudes. See Pemberton, Can the Law Provide a Remedy for Race Defamation in the United States?, 14 N.Y.L.F. 33 (1968).

The most common method of confronting group libel has been the enactment of criminal laws prohibiting communications that are abusive or offensive toward a group or that tend to arouse hatred, contempt, or ridicule of the group. Penalties have ranged from a fine of $50 or 30 days imprisonment, to $10,000 or two years in prison.

Beauharnais v. Illinois, 343 U.S. 250 (1952), is the only Supreme Court decision to review the constitutionality of group libel legislation. The Court, 5–4, affirmed a conviction under Illinois's 1917 group libel statute. The law prohibited publications portraying "depravity, criminality, unchastity, or lack of virtue of a class of citizens, of any race, color, creed, or religion" that subjected those described to "contempt, derision, or obloquy or which is productive of breach of the peace or riots." Beauharnais, the president of an organization called the "White Circle League," had distributed leaflets calling on the Mayor and City Council to halt the "further encroachment, harassment and invasion of white people, their property, neighborhoods and persons, by the Negro." The flyer also included an application for membership in the League and a call for a million white people to unite, adding that: "If persuasion and the need to prevent the white race from becoming mongrelized by the negro will not unite us, then the aggressions . . . rapes, robberies, knives, guns and marijuana of the negro, surely will."

Justice Frankfurter's opinion for the Court treated the statute as "a form of criminal libel law" and accepted the dictum of Chaplinsky v. New Hampshire, 315 U.S. 568 (1942), that libel was one of those "well-defined and narrowly limited classes of speech, the prevention and punishment of which have never been thought to raise any constitutional problem." The "precise question" for decision was thus:

> whether the protection of "liberty" in the Due Process Clause of the Fourteenth Amendment prevents a State from punishing such libels—as criminal libel has been defined, limited and constitutionally recognized time out of mind—directed at designated collectivities and flagrantly disseminated. . . . [I]f an utterance directed at an individual may be the object of criminal sanctions, we cannot deny to a State power to punish the same utterance directed at a defined group, unless we can say that this is a wilful and purposeless restriction unrelated to the peace and well-being of the State.

Justice Frankfurter traced the history of violent and destructive racial tension in Illinois and concluded that it would "deny experience" to say that the statute was without reason. In addition, since a person's opportunities are affected by attitudes toward his race and religion as well as by his own merits, "we are precluded from saying that speech concededly punishable when immediately directed at individuals cannot be outlawed if directed at groups with whose position and esteem in society the affiliated individual may be inextricably involved."

As for the problem of vagueness, the limitations imposed by construction and usage in the field of criminal libel sustained the statute. Justice Frankfurter disposed of the First Amendment in a single paragraph near the end of his opinion:

> Libelous utterances not being within the area of constitutionally protected speech, it is unnecessary, either for us or for the State courts, to consider the issue behind the phrase "clear and present danger." Certainly no one would contend that obscene speech, for example, may be punished only upon a showing of such circumstances. Libel, as we have seen, is in the same class.

Of the four dissenters, only Justices Black and Douglas addressed the First Amendment problems that the majority had cast aside by excluding the whole area of libel from First Amendment protection. Justice Black argued that the majority opinion "degrades First Amendment freedoms to the 'rational basis' level." He noted that Beauharnais had been petitioning the government for changes in the law, and analyzed the decision as an extension of the scope of the law of criminal libel from "the narrowest of areas" involving "purely private feuds" to "discussions of matters of public concern." This was an invasion of the First Amendment's absolute prohibition of laws infringing the freedom of public discussion. Justice Douglas concurred in Justice Black's opinion and wrote separately to emphasize that he would have required a demonstration that the "peril of speech" was "clear and present." He agreed with Justice Black that allowing a legislature to regulate "within reasonable limits" the right of free speech was "an ominous and alarming trend."

See Note, Group Vilification Reconsidered, 89 Yale L.J. 308 (1979), arguing that the First Amendment permits the criminal punishment of group vilifications involving false statements of fact that bypass the conscious faculties of recipients.

Only a half-dozen states retain group defamation statutes. The entire law of criminal libel has become increasingly vulnerable to constitutional and political attack, and is gradually being discarded. Perhaps Justice Brennan interred it in Garrison v. Louisiana, 379 U.S. 64 (1964), when he observed that the "virtual disappearance of criminal libel prosecutions" reflected the modern consensus that such laws were no longer justified by any danger of breach of the peace. More practically, such statutes tend to be vague, often provide the speakers another platform to air their views, and make them martyrs who can claim that their civil liberties have been violated when they are convicted. Z. Chafee, Government and Mass Communication 116–30 (1947); Comment, Race Defamation and the First Amendment, 34 Ford. L.Rev. 653 (1966); Note, Group Libel Laws: Abortive Efforts to Combat Hate Propaganda, 61 Yale L.J. 252 (1952). But see Arkes, Civility and the Restriction of Speech: Rediscovering the Defamation of Groups, 1974 Sup.Ct.Rev. 281.

3. Strict Liability and Damages

The common law often held a publisher strictly liable for defamatory statements. Thus, the case was established even if the offending statement appeared to be either neutral or positive, but, when supplemented by other facts, unknown to defendant, turned out to be defamatory. For example, a newspaper might, based on reliable information, incorrectly report a baby's birth. If some readers knew that its parents had been married only three months, the newspaper would be held to have committed defamation because in the eyes of those readers who knew the additional fact the newspaper story suggested unchastity. If a magazine carries what it believes to be fiction but readers reasonably think the words refer to an identifiable plaintiff, a defamation may be found. This subject is discussed at length in Smith, Jones v. Hulton: Three Conflicting Views as to Defamation, 60 U.Pa.L.Rev. 365, 461 (1912); Holdsworth, A Chapter of Accidents in the Law of Libel, 57 L.Q. Rev. 74 (1941).

Offsetting the rigor of strict liability, the common law requires some plaintiffs to prove "special damages." This burden depends in part on whether the allegedly defamatory statement is slander or libel. Historically, slanders were oral defamations and were handled by the common law courts; libels were written defamations that, because of the development of printing, became a major concern of the crown. After the days of the Star Chamber, oral and written defamation were redressed by the common law courts. Those courts, however, preserved some distinctions between the two that have survived to our day, mainly in relation to damages.

Two types of damages are central to this discussion. "Special damages" are specific identifiable losses that the plaintiff can prove he or she has sustained and can trace to the defendant's defamatory statement. "General damages" are damages to reputation that the plaintiff is presumed, without any proof, to have sustained as a result of the defendant's statement. The jury is permitted to speculate on the extent of injury based on the words used, the medium used, and the predicted response of the community.

The common law courts have treated libel as substantially more serious than slander. The distinction arose when relatively few people could read and the written word was awesome and thus more credible. A writing still may be given more weight because it requires more thought and planning than a spontaneous oral utterance. Furthermore, the writing is more lasting and is likely to reach a larger audience than most, if not all, slanders. Thus, libels as a class were more likely to cause harm than slanders, and the courts declared that plaintiffs in libel cases were able to recover general damages without any showing of special damages. Therefore a plaintiff proceeding under libel has always been at least as well off as, and often better off than, a plaintiff suing for slander for precisely the same words.

If an action is for slander, plaintiff must prove "special damages" unless the defamatory thrust fits into at least one of four categories. These categories are: the imputation of a serious crime punishable by imprisonment or involving moral turpitude; imputation of an existing venereal or loathsome disease; a charge that attacks the plaintiff's competence or honesty in his business, trade, or profession; or a charge of unchastity in a woman or, in some states, serious sexual misconduct by any person.

Such a spoken charge is called "slander per se" and permits an action enabling plaintiff to claim general damages to his or her reputation without proving actual pecuniary harm. Here the jury may conclude that publication of the charge caused substantial harm in the community, and can measure damages according to the number and identity of those who learned of the charge, and their presumed reaction based on the seriousness and credibility of the charge. If a plaintiff can also establish "special" damages, these may be recovered in addition to the general damages presumed.

If the slander is not within the four categories, then an action must be supported by proof of "special" damages. These must be pecuniary in nature—such as the loss of employment, the collapse of an advantageous business deal, or some other identifiable economic harm. Special damages have proven remarkably difficult to establish in many cases.

If they are required and established, the plaintiff may also recover his general reputational damages.

Consider these examples of damages, from the Restatement, Second, Torts § 575:

a. A, a Catholic priest, says to others that B, a merchant, has been excommunicated. It is proved that in consequence of this statement, B has lost Catholic customers. B has suffered special damages.

b. A says to B, a businessman contemplating employing C as a sales clerk, that C is a person of questionable moral character. It is proved that this statement induces B to break off employment negotiations with C. C has incurred special damages.

c. A says to B, who is C's uncle, that C has very crude manners. It is proved that this statement induces B to withdraw an invitation that he has previously extended to C to accompany him, at B's expense, on an extended voyage. C has incurred special damages.

d. A says to B that C is a vulgar and persistent gossip. It is proved that this statement induces B, who has previously been a friend of C, thereafter to refuse to speak to him. C has not incurred special damages.

e. The same facts as in d, except that B is induced to withdraw an invitation extended to C to spend his vacation at B's country place. C has incurred special damages.

So far as libel is concerned, the original rule was that special damages were never required. Then the courts began to distinguish between two types of libels: those clear on their face, called libel *per se,* to which courts applied the traditional general damage rules, and others, called libel *per quod,* in which the reader had to know one or more unstated facts in order to understand the defamatory thrust of the writing. In cases of the latter, the plaintiff had to allege inducement. Some courts, however, began to give the distinction substantive implications. Thus, a large number of state courts came to follow the rule that a plaintiff must prove special damages, unless the written defamation is either libel *per se,* or the libel *per quod* fits into one of the four slander *per se* subject-matter categories, previously discussed.

The distinction is somewhat confused because "per se" means different things, depending on whether it is applied to slander or libel. As explained by R. Sack, in Libel, Slander, and Related Problems 99–100 (1980):

> As a practical matter, words that, uttered orally, are slanderous *per se,* are *usually* also libelous *per se* when written. But the reason they are slanderous *per se* normally has little to do with the reason that they are libelous *per se.* To say of a woman that she is a whore or of a man that he robs his business associates blind is slanderous *per se* because it falls within one of the four categories.

The same words when written are libelous *per se,* not because they fit within a slander category, but because they tend on their face to disgrace the person about whom they are written. Extrinsic facts are unnecessary to explain their defamatory meaning. But the converse is not true. Statements which are libelous *per se* when written often are not slanderous *per se* when spoken. However degrading a statement, however injurious to reputation, however outrageous, however plain the defamatory meaning on the face of the statement and therefore however clear that the statement when written is libelous *per se,* unless the defamatory charge falls within one of the four specific slander categories, it is not slanderous *per se* when merely spoken, and "special damages" must be pleaded and proved.

The resulting libel-slander rules have sometimes permitted a plaintiff to recover enormous amounts in general damages and have at other times barred a plaintiff from recovering anything whatever because special damages were required but could not be proven, although serious general harm seemed likely.

In addition to general and special damages, two other classifications loom large in defamation law: nominal damages and punitive damages. Although nominal damages are unimportant in most tort actions, they may be central in defamation cases. The award of a symbolic amount such as six cents usually shows that the jury found the attack to be false but also found the words not to have hurt, either because the speaker was not credible or the plaintiff's strong reputation blunted the harm (or his reputation was so low nothing could really hurt it). For an example, see the suit by Quentin Reynolds against the Hearst Corporation and one of its columnists, upholding a jury award of $1 in compensatory damages and $175,000 in punitive damages against the various defendants. Reynolds v. Pegler, 223 F.2d 429 (2d Cir.), certiorari denied 350 U.S. 846 (1955) (Black, J. dissenting).

MATHERSON v. MARCHELLO

New York Appellate Division, Second Department, 1984.
100 A.D.2d 233, 473 N.Y.S.2d 998.

TITONE, J.P.

. . .

On October 28, 1980, radio station WBAB conducted an interview with the members of a singing group called "The Good Rats". Following a commercial which advertised a Halloween party at an establishment known as "OBI", a discussion ensued in which various members of the group explained that they are no longer permitted to play at OBI South because:

"Good Rat # 1: Well, you know, we had that law suit with Mr. Matherson.

"A Good Rat:	And we used to fool around with his wife.
"Good Rat # 1:	And we won.
"A Good Rat:	One of us used to fool around with his wife. He wasn't into that too much.
"D.J.:	Oh yea.
"Good Rat # 1: (interrupted and joined by another Good Rat)	We used to start off our gigs over there with the National Anthem, and he was very upset about that, now all of a sudden he's very patriotic and he's using it in his commercials.
"A Good Rat:	I don't think it was his wife that he got so upset about, I think it was when somebody started messing around with his boyfriend that he really freaked out. Really.
	(Laughter)
	That did it man."

Plaintiffs, who are husband and wife, subsequently commenced this action against "The Good Rats" (as individuals and against their record company), alleging that the words "we used to fool around with his wife" and "I don't think it was his wife that he got upset about, I think it was when somebody started messing around with his boyfriend that he really freaked out", were defamatory. They seek compensatory and punitive damages for humiliation, mental anguish, loss of reputation and injury to their marital relationship as well as for the loss of customers, business opportunities and good will allegedly suffered by Mr. Matherson. Special Term granted defendants' motion to dismiss, finding that the complaint failed to adequately allege special damages. However, it gave plaintiffs leave to replead. Plaintiffs declined the opportunity and have appealed.

Preliminarily, we observe that if special damages are a necessary ingredient of plaintiffs' cause of action, Special Term properly found the allegations of the complaint to be deficient.

Special damages consist of "the loss of something having economic or pecuniary value" (Restatement, Torts 2d, § 575, Comment b) which "must flow directly from the injury to reputation caused by the defamation; not from the effects of defamation" [Sack] and it is settled law that they must be fully and accurately identified "with sufficient particularity to identify actual losses" [ ]. When loss of business is claimed, the persons who ceased to be customers must be named and the losses itemized [ ]. "Round figures" or a general allegation of a dollar amount as special damages do not suffice [ ]. Consequently, plaintiffs' nonspecific conclusory allegations do not meet the stringent requirements imposed for pleading special damages [ ].

We must, therefore, determine whether an allegation of special damages is necessary. In large measure, this turns on which branch of the law of defamation is involved. As a result of historical accident, which, though not sensibly defensible today, is so well settled as to be beyond our ability to uproot it [ ], there is a schism between the law governing slander and the law governing libel [ ].

A plaintiff suing in slander must plead special damages unless the defamation falls into any one of four per se categories . . . .[2] The exceptions were established apparently for no other reason than a recognition that by their nature the accusations encompassed therein would be likely to cause material damage [ ].

On the other hand, a plaintiff suing in libel need not plead or prove special damages if the defamatory statement " 'tends to expose the plaintiff to public contempt, ridicule, aversion or disgrace, or induce an evil opinion of him in the minds of right-thinking persons, and to deprive him of their friendly intercourse in society' " [ ].[3] Thus, unlike the law of slander, in the law of libel the existence of damage is conclusively presumed from the publication itself and a plaintiff may rely on general damages (compare Restatement, Torts 2d, § 569 with § 570; but see Excessiveness or Inadequacy of Damages for Defamation, Ann., 35 A.L.R.2d 218, which suggests, by its scheme of classification, how relatively few cases of libel actually do arise which are not more or less easily referable to the categories of slander per se).

. . .

With the advent of mass communication, the differential was blurred. Motion pictures were held to be libel [ ]. No set rule

2. The first three categories were established relatively early. The fourth is of more recent vintage, having first been put into effect in England by the Slander of Women Act of 1891. . . . We do not view these categories as fixed or rigid and, in appropriate circumstances, a new category may be judicially established [ ].

3. We have avoided the use of the terms libel per se and libel per quod because, as explained in this footnote, the cases and commentators are divided on the question of whether any meaningful distinction exists between the two.

It is clear that when the defamatory import is apparent from the face of the publication itself without resort to any other source, the libel, often referred to as libel per se, is actionable without proof of special harm [ ]. Libel per quod, on the other hand, has been traditionally defined as an encompassing libel in which the defamatory import can only be ascertained by reference to facts not set forth in the publication [ ].

In the view of some writers, libel per quod does not exist in New York. Under their reasoning, special harm is a necessary component only under the so-called "single instance" rule, i.e., where the statement charges the plaintiff with a single dereliction in connection with his or her trade or profession [ ]. They read Hinsdale v. Orange County Pub., 17 N.Y.2d 284, 270 N.Y.S.2d 592, 217 N.E.2d 650 as establishing that all other libel, whether defamatory on its face or by extrinsic fact, is actionable without proof of special harm [ ].

Other commentators decline to interpret *Hinsdale* (supra) as obliterating the special harm requirements in extrinsic fact cases, viewing the pleading and proof of special damages as necessary both under the "single instance" rule and in extrinsic fact cases unless, with respect to extrinsic fact cases, it is "reasonably likely" that the plaintiff's reputation will be impaired among readers who are aware of the extrinsic facts [ ].

The cases simply state that if a libel is not per se, a plaintiff must plead and prove special damages as part of the prima facie case, without drawing a line of demarcation between them [ ]. Since neither the single instance rule nor extrinsic fact libel is involved, we have an opportunity to resolve the conflict.

developed with respect to radio and television [ ]. In some cases, distinction was drawn between contemporaneous speech, which was classified as slander, and words read from a script, which were classified as libel [ ]. This distinction was the subject of considerable criticism.

We today hold that defamation which is broadcast by means of radio or television should be classified as libel. As we have noted, one of the primary reasons assigned to justify the imposition of broader liability for libel than for slander has been the greater capacity for harm that a writing is assumed to have because of the wide range of dissemination consequent upon its permanence in form. Given the vast and far-flung audiences reached by the broadcasting media today, it is self-evident that the potential harm to a defamed person is far greater than that involved in a single writing (see Hartmann v. Winchell, 296 N.Y. 296, 304, 73 N.E.2d 30, supra [Fuld, J., concurring]). Section 568A of the Restatement of Torts, Second, and the more recent decisions in sister States (Defamation by Radio or Television, Ann., 50 A.L.R.3d 1311, §§ 3–5, pp. 1325–1329) opt for holding such defamation to be libel and we perceive no basis for perpetuating a meaningless, outmoded, distinction.

On the question of whether the allegedly defamatory statements are actionable, our scope of review is limited. . . . Unless we can say, as a matter of law, that the statements could not have had a defamatory connotation, it is for the jury to decide whether or not they did [ ].

Taken in the context of a rock and roll station's interview with musicians, and taking note of contemporary usage, we have no difficulty in concluding that the words "fooling around with his wife" could have been interpreted by listeners to mean that Mrs. Matherson was having an affair with one of the defendants. Such charges are clearly libelous on their face, thus obviating any need to allege and prove special damages. . . .

The second comment—"I don't think it was his wife that he got upset about, I think it was when somebody started messing around with his boyfriend that he really freaked out"—presents a far more subtle and difficult question (see Imputation of Homosexuality as Defamation, Ann., 3 A.L.R.4th 752). It is plaintiffs' contention that this statement constitutes an imputation of homosexuality which should be recognized as defamatory. Defendants, on the other hand, basically do not deny that such reading is plausible. Rather, they claim that many public officials have acknowledged their homosexuality and, therefore, no social stigma may be attached to such an allegation. We are constrained to reject defendants' position at this point in time.

It cannot be said that social opprobrium of homosexuality does not remain with us today. Rightly or wrongly, many individuals still view homosexuality as immoral (see *Newsweek,* Aug. 8, 1983, p. 33, containing the results of a Gallup poll; [ ]). Legal sanctions imposed upon homosexuals in areas ranging from immigration (Matter of Longstaff,

716 F.2d 1439) to military service (Watkins v. United States Army, 721 F.2d 687) have recently been reaffirmed despite the concurring Judge's observation in *Watkins* (p. 691) that it "demonstrates a callous disregard for the progress American law and society have made toward acknowledging that an individual's choice of life style is not the concern of government, but a fundamental aspect of personal liberty" [ ].

In short, despite the fact that an increasing number of homosexuals are publicly expressing satisfaction and even pride in their status, the potential and probable harm of a false charge of homosexuality, in terms of social and economic impact, cannot be ignored. Thus, on the facts of this case, where the plaintiffs are husband and wife, we find, given the narrow scope of review, that the imputation of homosexuality is "reasonably susceptible of a defamatory connotation" [ ], and is actionable without proof of special damages [ ].

For these reasons, the order should be reversed insofar as appealed from, with costs, the defendants' motion to dismiss should be denied and the complaint should be reinstated.

THOMPSON, BRACKEN, and RUBIN, JJ., concur.

Notes and Questions

1. What are the justifications for distinguishing libel from slander in this type of case? Does the court do a good job of alignment?

2. A few jurisdictions have resolved the broadcasting question by statute. California has called broadcasting slander; England has called it libel. (Do not confuse the libel-slander question in broadcasting with the different common law issue of whether broadcasters should be held strictly liable for utterances made over the station by non-employees. Several states have long had statutes based on a proposal of the National Association of Broadcasters providing that broadcasters are liable for the statements of non-employees only if the station knew or had reason to know that a defamation would be uttered and failed to exercise due care to avoid the danger. See Leflar, Radio and TV Defamation: "Fault" or Strict Liability?, 15 Ohio St.L.J. 252 (1954).)

3. In most states, whether slander is per se or per quod depends solely on whether the words—when fleshed out—fall into one of the four categories. New York has recently announced a much narrower position. In Aronson v. Wiersma, 65 N.Y.2d 592, 483 N.E.2d 1138, 493 N.Y.S.2d 1006, 12 Med.L.Rptr. 1150 (1985), plaintiff was a professional linguist who was working as a legislative assistant to the city council to make ends meet while she finished her studies. Without alleging special damages, plaintiff sued over the following oral statement allegedly made by the council president while he was having his hair cut in a barber shop:

> I've got to fire a person . . . one of my workers . . . I can't get her to hand in time sheets . . . I can't get her to do anything . . . The person is neglectful in their job . . . The person isn't doing their job . . . I've got to let her go . . . That's it . . . .

The court concluded that the language on its face did not hurt plaintiff in her trade or business. It was at worst, a "general reflection upon the plaintiff's character or qualities." Whether or not plaintiff "fails to 'hand in time sheets' or 'is neglectful' is no reflection upon her performance as a linguist or her ability to be a good writer or researcher."

Finally, the claim that "extrinsic facts could . . . render the statement defamatory with respect to plaintiff's trade, business or profession, is irrelevant. In this State, statements cannot be slanderous per se if reference to extrinsic facts is necessary to give them a defamatory import."

4. *Libel-Proof Plaintiffs.* A few libel cases have been brought by convicts. The claims are based on errors in other stories about their actions. The courts have developed a doctrine that "a libel-proof plaintiff is not entitled to burden a defendant with a trial in which the most favorable result the plaintiff could achieve is an award of nominal damages." Jackson v. Longcope, 394 Mass. 577, 476 N.E.2d 617, 11 Med.L.Rptr. 2282 (1985). The court insisted, though, that each case be investigated to be sure that the plaintiff's reputation was in fact so poor that it could have suffered no harm from errors in the defendant's article. Here there was no question since a convicted multiple murderer was challenging a statement that he had raped and strangled all of his victims.

An effort to apply the doctrine against Ariel Sharon failed. Sharon v. Time, Inc., 575 F.Supp. 1162, 10 Med.L.Rptr. 1146 (S.D.N.Y.1983). The fact that an Israeli commission had found him to have made a "grave mistake" in failing to anticipate violence at a refugee camp "cannot be said to have so severely harmed Sharon's formidable reputation as to render him libel proof to suggestions in the article that he anticipated but did not act to prevent the massacre or that he actually instigated such acts, or that he lied to the Commission, or that the Commission found that he lied but attempted to cover up his complicity in the massacre."

5. A plaintiff who previously had a good reputation may be found libel-proof if the unchallenged or true parts of an article have been so damaging that it is implausible that the actionable part of the article did any further damage to plaintiff's reputation. This aspect of the doctrine was applied in Simmons Ford, Inc. v. Consumers Union, 516 F.Supp. 742, 7 Med.L.Rptr. 1776 (S.D.N.Y.1981) ("Given the abysmal performance and safety evaluations detailed in the article, plaintiffs could not expect to gain more than nominal damages based on the addition to the article of the misstatement relating to federal safety standards.")

The doctrine was rejected in Gannett Co. v. Re, 496 A.2d 553, 11 Med.L.Rptr. 2327 (Del.1985), in which an experimental car, after failing to start on several tries, did finally start and ran a quarter-mile at 10 miles per hour. Two years later, the plaintiff-inventor was indicted on 19 felony and misdemeanor counts involving another invention. In reporting that story and giving background, the defendant's story asserted that the car "failed to start." The appellate court rejected the defense. See generally Note, The Libel-Proof Plaintiff Doctrine, 98 Harv.L.Rev. 1909 (1985).

6. Several states at common law have rejected the concept of punitive damages in all tort cases. As we shall see shortly, recent federal and state constitutional developments have also affected the availability of such damages.

7. In the cases of large awards, the distribution between compensatory and punitive damages may be significant from a tax perspective. See the extended discussion in Roemer v. Commissioner of Internal Revenue, 716 F.2d 693, 9 Med.L.Rptr. 2407 (9th Cir.1983). See also IRS Tech.Advice Memo 8601001, 86 Tax Notes Today 4–42 (1986).

Traditionally, the prima facie case in defamation has been easy to establish. The plaintiff had to prove the publication to a third person of a statement of and concerning plaintiff that injured plaintiff's reputation, and then had to meet whatever damage showing was required under the relevant libel-slander rules. These elements shown, (plus, in some states, an allegation of falsity, discussed infra), the prima facie case was complete. We turn now to defenses.

4. Defenses

---

a. *Truth*

The most obvious defense, but one little used, is to prove the essential truth of the defamatory statement. Historically, it was thought that in cases of alleged criminal libel, truth only aggravated the harm of the statement. Now that criminal libel has faded, truth is recognized as a complete defense to civil libel. Because the action is intended to compensate those whose reputations are damaged falsely, if the defendant has spoken the truth, the reputational harm is deemed to provide no basis for an action. A minority of states purport to require the truth to have been spoken with "good motives" or for "justifiable ends" or both.

The defendant need not prove literal truth but must establish the "sting" of his charge. Thus, if the defendant has charged the plaintiff with stealing $25,000 from a bank, truth will be established even if the actual amount was only $12,000. If the defendant cannot prove any theft whatever but can prove that the plaintiff is a bigamist, this information will not support his defense of truth. It *may* help mitigate damages to show that the plaintiff's reputation was already in low esteem for other reasons and thus he has suffered less harm than might otherwise have occurred.

These matters can raise troublesome questions. In Hovey v. Iowa State Daily Publication Board, 372 N.W.2d 253, 12 Med.L.Rptr. 1035 (Iowa 1985), the defendant newspaper reported on a violent episode that took place while plaintiff woman was serving as a bartender at an American Legion Hall. One customer knocked the only other customer unconscious and forced plaintiff to perform oral sex upon him. The man was charged with "sexual abuse." The paper, however, reported that the man had been charged with "raping a bartender." Another paragraph reported that he had been charged with "second degree sexual abuse, willful injury, and first degree robbery." The article also stated that bond for the "rape" and robbery charges had been set at $50,000.

The court rejected plaintiff's claim that "rape" referred only to "forcible genital sexual intercourse." It agreed with defendant that "rape" was broad enough to include "any forced sex act, including oral sex." The court referred to general dictionaries and to recent revisions in the Iowa criminal code that had subsumed rape into the crime of sexual abuse in 1978.

Finally, after adopting the substantial truth test, the court concluded that the "difference between the truth and the reported truth was not material enough for the inaccuracy to be actionable."

Truth is little used as a defense, though it would enable a decisive confrontation, because it may be very expensive to establish. A defendant relying on truth almost always bears the legal costs of a full-dress trial as well as the sometimes major expense of investigating the matter and gathering enough evidence to ensure the outcome. Particularly when the charge involved is vague and does not allege specific events, the defense of truth may be very costly—and risky.

Recent constitutional developments have sharply altered the role of truth. See p. 199, infra.

b. Privileges and Fair Comment

Not only were there disadvantages to the defense of truth, there were attractive alternatives. Over the centuries the law of defamation has developed several privileges to protect those who utter defamations. Some privileges are "absolute" in the sense that if the occasion gives rise to an absolute privilege, there will be no liability even if the speaker deliberately lied about the plaintiff. The most significant example is the federal and state constitutional privilege afforded legislators, who may not be sued for defamation for any statement made during debate. High executive officials, judges, and participants in judicial proceedings also have an absolute privilege to speak freely on matters relevant to their obligations. No matter how such a speaker abuses the privilege by lying, no tort liability will flow. See Barr v. Matteo, 360 U.S. 564 (1959).

The only absolute privilege granted the media occurs when broadcasters are required to grant equal opportunity on the air to all candidates for the same office. If a candidate commits defamation, the broadcaster is not liable. See Farmers Educational & Cooperative Union of America v. WDAY, Inc., 360 U.S. 525 (1959), discussed at p. 791, infra.

The much more common type of privilege is "conditional" or "qualified." The defendant who has such a privilege will prevail in an action for defamation unless the plaintiff can show that the speaker "abused" the privilege. The plaintiff shows abuse by proving that the defendant did not honestly believe what he said or that defendant published more information or published it more widely than was justified by the occasion that provided the privilege. Most courts have defined abuse in terms of the defendant's using the occasion for purposes other than what was intended by the creation of the privilege. For example, the common law gives a conditional privilege to communication between persons having a mutual commercial interest. One may malign a third party to one's partner if the speaker honestly believes his words, and if they relate to a contemplated business deal, but one may not lie or gratuitously discuss the third party's personal affairs with that partner or discuss even appropriate matters with the partner if others are present.

An auto repair shop sued over a local television news report that accused it of fraud. The defendant television station had claimed immunity under the state's fair comment privilege, Cal.Civ.Code § 47(3), protecting communications made without malice by one interested in a matter to another interested party. Plaintiff's appeal from a judgment notwithstanding the verdict was affirmed on appeal in Rollenhagen v. County of Orange, 116 Cal.App.3d 414, 172 Cal.Rptr. 49, 6 Med.L.Rptr. 2561 (1981).

The court of appeal noted that Rancho La Costa, Inc. v. Superior Court, 106 Cal.App.3d 646, 165 Cal.Rptr. 347, 6 Med.L.Rptr. 1351 (1980), had held that since the term "interested" in the statute required a "direct and immediate concern," an article about a California resort published in a national magazine with a large readership could not come under § 47(3). Without disputing that interpretation, the *Rollenhagen* court simply noted that it agreed that the privilege required a weighing of the relationship between the publisher and reader, as well as the legitimacy of the public interest in the report. Here, the court said, because plaintiff was a local shop and auto repair fraud had been a subject of recent legislative concern, sufficient direct interest was present even under the *LaCosta* standard. In a second (unreported) opinion, the *Rancho La Costa* court rejected the *Rollenhagen* analysis. Dalitz v. Penthouse Intl, Ltd., 11 Med.L.Rptr. 2153 (Cal.App.1985).

Most common law privileges apply to non-media individuals. Employers, for example, are conditionally privileged to comment to other employers about prospective employees. Credit reporting agencies often are similarly privileged. Family relationships create other conditional privileges. For the media, the major conditional privilege is that of fair comment upon matters of public interest, discussed in detail in *Cianci.*

Apparently this privilege entered English law in 1808 in Carr v. Hood, 1 Camp. 355, 170 Eng.Rep. 983. The defendant was charged with ridiculing the plaintiff author's talent so severely that sales of his book were discouraged and his reputation was destroyed. The plaintiff's attorney conceded that his client had exposed himself to literary criticism by making the book public, but insisted that the criticism should be "fair and liberal" and seek to enlighten the public about the book rather than to injure the author. The judge noted that ridicule may be an appropriate tool of criticism, but that criticism unrelated to the author as such would not be privileged. He urged that any "attempt against free and liberal criticism" should be resisted "at the threshold." The result was a rule that criticism, regardless of its merit, was privileged if it was made honestly, with honesty measured by the accuracy of the critic's descriptive observations. If a critic describing a literary, musical, or artistic endeavor gave the "facts" accurately and fairly, his honest conclusions would be privileged as "fair comment."

American law recognized this privilege, and as long as it was applied in cases of literary and artistic criticism it caused little confusion. Problems caused by such comment are discussed in Triggs v. Sun Printing & Pub. Co., 179 N.Y. 144, 71 N.E. 739 (1904), Adolf Philipp Co. v. New Yorker Staats-Zeitung, 165 App.Div. 377, 150 N.Y.Supp. 1044 (1914), and in the classic Cherry v. Des Moines Leader, 114 Iowa 298, 86 N.W. 323 (1901). But at the turn of the century, cases arose in which the privilege of fair comment was claimed with regard to other matters of public interest, including the conduct of politicians. This was not the privilege of reporting what certain public officials were doing in their official capacity. Rather the privilege claimed would permit citizens to criticize and argue about the conduct of their officials, and these cases presented the problem of distinguishing between facts and opinion. In the literary criticism area the application of the privilege could depend upon the accuracy of the "facts" because they were usually readily apparent. When dealing with politics, however, the "facts" were often elusive. This new problem created a judicial split.

In Post Publishing Co. v. Hallam, 59 F. 530 (6th Cir.1893), Judge Taft ruled that in order for criticism of officials to be privileged, it must be based upon true underlying facts. The newspaper asserted that it should be judged under the accepted rule that a former master responding to a request for information about a former servant would be privileged if the master stated some "facts" about the servant honestly but mistakenly. Judge Taft refused to apply this rule because in the servant case only the prospective master learned of the defamation, while here the entire public would hear of it. He continued:

The existence and extent of privilege in communications are determined by balancing the needs and good of society against the right of an individual to enjoy a good reputation when he has done nothing which ought to injure it. The privilege should always cease where the sacrifice of the individual right becomes so great that the public good to be derived from it is outweighed. . . . But, if the privilege is to extend to cases like that at bar, then a man who offers himself as a candidate must submit uncomplainingly to the loss of his reputation, not with a single person or a small class of persons, but with every member of the public, whenever an untrue charge of disgraceful conduct is made against him, if only his accuser honestly believes the charge upon reasonable ground. We think that not only is such a sacrifice not required of every one who consents to become a candidate for office, but that to sanction such a doctrine would do the public more harm than good.

We are aware that public officers and candidates for public office are often corrupt, when it is impossible to make legal proof thereof, and of course it would be well if the public could be given to know, in such a case, what lies hidden by concealment and perjury from judicial investigation. But the danger that honorable and worthy men may be driven from politics and public service by allowing too great latitude in attacks upon their characters outweighs any benefit that might occasionally accrue to the public from charges of corruption that are true in fact, but are incapable of legal proof. The freedom of the press is not in danger from the enforcement of the rule we uphold. No one reading the newspaper of the present day can be impressed with the idea that statements of fact concerning public men, and charges against them, are unduly guarded or restricted; and yet the rule complained of is the law in many of the states of the Union and in England.

The privilege became more inaccessible as those courts following the *Hallam* view came to treat questions of motive—why the politician or official acted as he did—as "facts" that had to be true in order for subsequent comment to be privileged.

A contrasting position was taken in Coleman v. MacLennan, 78 Kan. 711, 98 P. 281 (1908), in which the court noted that "men of unimpeachable character from all political parties continually present themselves as candidates in sufficient numbers to fill the public offices and manage the public institutions" even though Kansas had long held that facts relating to matters of public interest are themselves privileged if they are honestly believed to be true; and, if the facts are privileged even if wrong, the comments based upon those facts are also privileged if they are honestly believed. *Coleman* adhered to the state's rejection of the *Hallam* distinction between fact and comment or opinion.

Cianci reflects the majority view today that a statement is privileged as fair comment only if it is based on true or privileged facts about a matter of public interest. Privileged facts will be discussed below, but it is important to keep in mind that the fair comment privilege applies only where the comment expressed is honestly believed.

The fair comment privilege parallels a general principle that only expressions of fact, not opinion, may be defamatory. Thus, for example, epithets alone are not actionable. As pointed out in *Cianci,* however, often it is not so easy to distinguish between fact and opinion. As explained in R. Sack, Libel, Slander, and Related Problems 157 (1980):

> The determination . . . is made on the basis of the effect which the communication may reasonably be expected to have on its recipient. Although difficult to state in abstract terms, as a practical matter, the crucial difference between statement of fact and opinion depends on whether ordinary persons hearing or reading the matter complained of would be likely to understand it as an expression of the speaker's or writer's opinion or as a statement of existing fact. The opinion may ostensibly be in the form of a factual statement if it is clear from the context that the maker did not intend to assert another objective fact but only his personal comment upon the facts he had stated—and vice versa.

In *Cianci,* the New Times article was unprotected by the fair comment privilege because the facts on which the opinions were based were not yet shown to be true or privileged.

In a portion omitted from the *Cianci* excerpt above, the court considered a constitutional privilege for opinion. That privilege is discussed at p. 245 infra.

c. *Fair and Accurate Report*

MEDICO v. TIME, INC.

United States Court of Appeals for the Third Circuit, 1981.
643 F.2d 134, 6 Med.L.Rptr. 2529.
Certiorari denied, 454 U.S. 836, 102 S.Ct. 139, 70 L.Ed.2d 116 (1981).
Noted, 43 U.Pitt.L.Rev. 1143.

Before ADAMS, GARTH and SLOVITER, CIRCUIT JUDGES.

ADAMS, CIRCUIT JUDGE.

This appeal from a summary judgment in favor of the defendant presents an important question concerning the law of defamation. We must review the district court's determination that a news magazine enjoys a privilege, under the common law of Pennsylvania, to publish a summary of FBI documents identifying the plaintiff as a member of an organized crime "family." We affirm.

I.

In its March 6, 1978 issue, Time magazine published an article describing suspected criminal activities of then-Congressman Daniel J. Flood. The article stated that Stephen Elko, a former Flood aide, had characterized the Congressman as a "muscler"—an official who used his considerable influence to direct federal contracts to individuals and companies that responded with cash. The article further stated that at least eight separate United States Attorneys' offices had undertaken investigations of Flood's activities.

As an example of suspected misconduct, the Time article listed the following:

> Among the matters under scrutiny: Ties between Flood and Pennsylvania Rackets Boss Russell Bufalino. The suspected link: the Wilkes-Barre firm of Medico Industries, controlled by President Philip Medico and his brothers. The FBI discovered more than a decade ago that Flood steered Government business to the Medicos and traveled often on their company jet. Investigators say Bufalino frequently visited the Medico offices; agents tape-recorded Bufalino's description of Philip as a capo (chief) in his Mafia family. Elko's testimony has sparked new investigative interest in the Flood-Medico-Bufalino triangle.
>
> . . .

. . .

In January 1980, Time again moved for summary judgment based on the substantial truth of its publication. Time resubmitted the two FBI documents it had proffered to support its initial motion, supplemented with affidavits of two FBI agents. . . .

On this occasion the district court granted Time's motion for summary judgment, but not on the basis of the truth defense. . . .

After declining to hold for Time on the truth theory, the district court considered whether the Time article fell within the common law privilege accorded the press to report on official proceedings. The judge seemed troubled because Pennsylvania courts apparently had so far extended the privilege only to reports of proceedings open to the public, whereas Time had summarized reports which the FBI had kept secret and whose release to Time evidently had been unauthorized. But after an exhaustive analysis of Pennsylvania precedents, the court concluded that Pennsylvania courts, if presented with the question, would find summaries of non-public government reports within the privilege. The district judge then ascertained that the Time article represented a fair and accurate account of the FBI documents. Accordingly he held that the publication was privileged, and awarded summary judgment in favor of Time.

On appeal, Medico argues that the district court incorrectly determined that Time's publication was privileged under Pennsylvania law.

Time counters that the district judge accurately construed the applicable state law on privilege, and contends further that the defense of truth applies and affords an alternate basis for affirming the district court. . . .

II.

The fair report privilege on which the district court relied developed as an exception to the common law rule that the republisher of a defamation was subject to liability similar to that risked by the original defamer. Pennsylvania had adopted the republication rule by the turn of the century, and no case brought to our attention suggests that Pennsylvania has abandoned it. With this rule, the law indulged the fiction that the republisher of a defamatory statement "adopted" the statement as his own. The common law regime created special problems for the press. When a newspaper published a newsworthy account of one person's defamation of another, it was, by virtue of the republication rule, charged with publication of the underlying defamation. Thus, although the common law exonerated one who published a defamation as long as the statement was true, a newspaper in these circumstances traditionally could avail itself of the truth defense only if the truth of the underlying defamation were established.

To ameliorate the chilling effect on the reporting of newsworthy events occasioned by the combined effect of the republication rule and the truth defense, the law has long recognized a privilege for the press [9] to publish accounts of official proceedings or reports even when these contain defamatory statements. So long as the account presents a fair and accurate summary of the proceedings, the law abandons the assumption that the reporter adopts the defamatory remarks as his own.[11] The privilege thus permits a newspaper or other press defendant to relieve itself of liability without establishing the truth of the substance of the statement reported. The fair report privilege has a somewhat more limited scope than the truth defense, however. So long as the speaker establishes the truth of his statement, he is shielded from liability, regardless of his motives; the fair report privilege, on the

9. There is some dispute whether the privilege is available to non-press defendants. The *Restatement* suggests that "any person who makes an oral, written or printed report" on an official proceeding should have access to the defense. Restatement (Second) of Torts § 611, Comment c (1977). While some states adhere to this approach, [ ] other states grant the privilege only to specified press defendants, [ ]. . . .

11. See R. Sack, supra note 6, § VI.3.7, at 316 & n.213. Analytically, the fair report privilege is similar to the truth defense. Both make verity the issue, although requiring that a report be fair and accurate may allow the press a somewhat greater margin of error than requiring that its report be true. In those cases where a plaintiff claims that republication of an official report defamed him *not* by conveying the underlying defamation, but by leading the reading public to believe that a government agency had leveled defamatory charges against him, the two defenses are effectively "merged." The common law defense of truth would turn on whether the government actors had in fact so charged the plaintiff, and the fair report privilege would focus on the same inquiry. See Sowle, Defamation and the First Amendment: The Case for A Constitutional Privilege of Fair Report, 54 N.Y.U.L. Rev. 469, 506–07 (1979).

other hand, can be defeated in most jurisdictions by a showing that the publisher acted for the sole purpose of harming the person defamed.

Unlike many states, Pennsylvania has never codified the fair report privilege. In addition, while Pennsylvania follows the Restatement (Second) of Torts on most matters, the Pennsylvania Supreme Court evidently has not yet had occasion to comment on the Restatement's version of the fair report privilege. Earlier, however, the state courts had endorsed the privilege as set forth in the original *Restatement,* and this edition was similar in most respects to the more recent one. We believe it appropriate to accept as the law of Pennsylvania the version of the fair report privilege embodied in the current *Restatement.*

Section 611 of Restatement (Second) provides:

> Report of Official Proceeding or Public Meeting
>
> The publication of defamatory matter concerning another in a report of an official action or proceeding or of a meeting open to the public that deals with a matter of public concern is privileged if the report is accurate and complete or a fair abridgement of the occurrence reported.

With respect to the present controversy, the basic inquiry is whether Time's summary of FBI documents concerning Philip Medico is "a report of an official action or proceeding." [17]

The district court examined and rejected the possibility that the FBI reports in question are not "official" because they are not generally available to the public. Medico does not challenge this reasoning on appeal, and we perceive no need to rehearse arguments that the district court has already canvassed. Medico contends before this Court that the FBI documents should not be deemed "official" because they express only tentative and preliminary conclusions that the FBI has never adopted as accurate. He points out that the title page to the FBI report on La Cosa Nostra bears the following legend: "This document contains neither recommendations nor conclusions of the FBI. It is the property of the FBI and is loaned to your agency; it and its contents are not to be distributed outside your agency."

Neither the text of Section 611 nor the accompanying comments dispose of the issue Medico raises. Section 611 itself speaks only of "official" action or proceedings, without elaborating on when a statement is made in an official capacity. Comment d provides some support for locating the FBI documents concerning Medico within the scope of the privilege. That comment states: "The filing of a report by

17. Although the Time article did not explicitly credit the FBI Report on La Cosa Nostra or the FBI personal file card on Medico as the Magazine's sources of information, the statements about Medico, taken in context, may reasonably be understood to inform the reader that the story was based on FBI materials. The article should accordingly be regarded as a summary of a purportedly "official" government report. [ ] cf. R. Sack, [ ] at 325 (if the publication does not inform the reader of the identity or nature of the government proceeding, it probably is not a fair and accurate report).

an officer or agency of the government is an action bringing a reporting of the governmental report within the scope of the privilege." In the present case, the FBI included its information on Medico in a report on the Philadelphia activities of the Mafia, and forwarded it for inclusion in a report on nationwide organized crime.

But another comment casts doubt on the applicability of the fair report privilege to the FBI materials. Comment h indicates that, while a report of an arrest or of the charge of crime falls within the privilege, "statements made by the police or by the complainant or other witnesses or by the prosecuting attorney as to the facts of the case or the evidence expected to be given are not yet part of [a] judicial proceeding or of the arrest itself and are not privileged." Because the FBI's information concerning Medico never led to an arrest or prosecution, the FBI materials may be thought to stem from such an early stage of official proceedings that the Section 611 privilege does not attach.

Pennsylvania cases predating the publication of Restatement (Second) also fail to resolve definitively whether summaries of criminal investigatory files fall within the privilege. The two cases most nearly on point, however, strongly support Time's defense. In Sciandra v. Lynett, 409 Pa. 595, 187 A.2d 586 (1963), the defendant newspaper had published three articles based on the "Reuter Report," a study, commissioned by then-Governor of New York, Averell Harriman, of the activities and associations of individuals who had attended a meeting of alleged organized crime figures. The Pennsylvania Supreme Court held the newspaper's publication protected, announcing the fair report privilege in broad terms: "Upon the theory that it is in the public interest that information be made available as to what takes place in public affairs, a newspaper has the privilege to report the acts of the executive or administrative officials of government." Id. at 600, 187 A.2d at 588. As in the present case, there is no indication that the Reuter Report had led to the arrest or criminal prosecution of any suspected wrongdoer. The Reuter Report, however, bore stronger indicia of representing an "official" act than the FBI materials here: it was filed with the Governor and then released to the public, it evidently did not bear a legend indicating that it reached only tentative conclusions, and it resulted from an inquiry into the history and habits of organized crime figures that occupied New York State officials for several months. While *Sciandra* affords some basis for predicting that Pennsylvania would extend the fair report privilege to the publication challenged in this case, we doubt whether, standing alone, *Sciandra* disposes of this issue.

A decision by a federal district court construing Pennsylvania law also supports application of the privilege to Time's publication. In Hanish v. Westinghouse Broadcasting Co., 487 F.Supp. 397 (E.D.Pa. 1980), the court held that the privilege applied to a news report summarizing a civil complaint that contained defamatory accusations and that had formed the basis for a temporary restraining order. The court approvingly quoted Justice Holmes' statement in Cowley v. Pulsifer, 137 Mass. 392 (1884), that "[i]f pleadings and other documents can be published to the world by anyone who gets access to them, no more effectual way of doing malicious mischief with impunity could be devised than filing papers containing false and scurrilous charges, and getting those printed as news"; the district court concluded nonetheless that, at least when some judicial action has been taken on a complaint, the fair report privilege applies.[21]

Assuming the court in *Hanish* correctly predicted Pennsylvania law, we think that decision supports application of the Section 611 privilege to the present case. FBI files seem at least as "official" as the pleadings in civil cases. Although civil complaints are instituted, for the most part, by private parties, the FBI documents concerning Medico were compiled by government agents acting in their official capacities. Moreover, the danger that a civil litigant will willfully insert defamatory assertions in his complaint generally would appear at least as great as the risk that a criminal investigatory agency will knowingly include false or malicious statements in its files. If Pennsylvania courts would grant the privilege to newspaper accounts of civil complaints on which a court has acted ex parte, we think it likely that they would grant the privilege to republication of defamatory items from the FBI materials on Medico.

III.

Three policies underlie the fair report privilege, and an examination of them provides further guidance for our decision today. Initially, an agency theory was offered to rationalize a privilege of fair report: one who reports what happens in a public, official proceeding acts as an agent for persons who had a right to attend, and informs them of what they might have seen for themselves. The agency rationale, however, cannot explain application of the privilege to proceedings or reports not open to public inspection.

A theory of public supervision also informs the fair report privilege. Justice Holmes, applying the privilege to accounts of courtroom proceedings, gave the classic formulation of this principle:

> [The privilege is justified by] the security which publicity gives for the proper administration of justice. . . . It is desirable that the trial of causes should take place under the public eye, not because the controversies of one citizen with another are of public concern, but because it is of the highest moment that those who administer justice should always act under the sense of public responsibility

21. Considerable controversy surrounds republication of defamations contained in pleadings on which no official action has been taken. Although Comment e to Section 611 of the Restatement excludes such pleadings from the scope of the privilege. Professor Eldredge writes that "the weight of authority is contrary to the [Restatement] rule, and is that the report of pleadings filed in court which have not yet come before a judicial officer and upon which no judicial action has been taken comes within the privilege." L. Eldredge, The Law of Defamation § 79(b)(1), at 430 (1978). [ ]

> and that every citizen should be able to satisfy himself with his own eyes as to the mode in which a public duty is performed.

Cowley v. Pulsifer, 137 Mass. 392, 394 (1884). The supervisory rationale has been invoked in the context of executive action as well.

We believe the public supervision rationale applies to the present case. As public inspection of courtroom proceedings may further the just administration of the laws, public scrutiny of the proceedings and records of criminal investigatory agencies may often have the equally salutary effect of fostering among those who enforce the laws "the sense of public responsibility." For example, exposing the content of agency records may, in some cases, help ensure impartial enforcement of the laws.

[We need not] decide, however, whether the supervisory rationale is relevant to every republication of documents found in FBI files. For any general supervisory concern with respect to the FBI is heightened in the present case by the public's interest in examining the conduct of individuals it elects to positions of civic trust. Elected officials derive their authority from, and are answerable to, the public. If the citizenry is effectively and responsibly to discharge its obligation to monitor the conduct of its government, there can be no penalty for exposing to general view the possible wrongdoing of government officials. Because the alleged defamation of Medico occurred in an article analyzing the conduct of former Congressman Flood, we believe it implicates this aspect of the supervisory rationale. Moreover, even though Time's publication arguably may have tarnished the reputation of Medico, a private individual, as well as that of Representative Flood, the public has a lively interest in considering the relationships formed by elected officials.

A third rationale for the fair report privilege rests, somewhat tautologically, on the public's interest in learning of important matters.[27] While "mere curiosity in the private affairs of others is of insufficient importance to warrant granting the privilege," the present case does not involve such idle probing. The Time article discussed two topics of legitimate public interest. First, for the same reasons that support the supervisory rationale, examination of the affairs of elected officials is obviously a matter of legitimate public concern. In addition, as various federal courts have already recognized, there is significant public importance to reports on investigations of organized criminal activities, whether or not these implicate government officials.

Because the Time article focused on organized crime, we think the informational rationale is especially relevant. The district court in the case at hand commented on the difficulty of gathering information pertaining to organized criminal activity: "Due to the size, sophistica-

27. . . .

Some jurisdictions rely on the informational rationale to extend the privilege to accounts of the proceedings of public meetings of private, nongovernmental organizations, as long as the meeting deals with matters of concern to the public. . . .

tion and secrecy of most organized criminal endeavors, only the largest and most sophisticated intelligence-gathering entities can monitor them effectively. In practice this task has been taken up primarily by the Justice Department of the federal government and, in particular, by the FBI." Indeed, the documents that Time summarized had been compiled by a government agency. In light of the difficulty in obtaining independent corroboration of FBI information, the press may often have to rely on materials the government acquires if it is to report on organized crime at all. We believe Time's publication of FBI materials mentioning Medico served a legitimate public interest in learning about organized crime.

Care must be taken, of course, to ensure that the supervisory and informational rationales not expand into justifications for reporting any defamatory matter maintained in any government file. Personal interests in privacy are not to be taken lightly, and are not to be overborne by mere invocation of a public need to know.[30] But we believe that the public interest is involved when, as here, information compiled by an enforcement agency may help shed light on a Congressman's alleged criminal or unethical behavior.

. . .

V.

Once the libel defendant establishes the existence of a "privileged occasion" for the publication of a defamatory article, the burden returns to the plaintiff to prove that the defendant abused its privilege. [ ] Pennsylvania recognizes two forms of "abuse": the account of an official report may fail to be fair and accurate,[40] as when the publisher overly embellishes the account, [ ] or the defamatory material may be published for the sole purpose of causing harm to the person defamed, [ ]. Inasmuch as Medico does not allege that Time published its article for the purpose of harming him, the sole issue with respect to abuse of privilege is whether the district court erred in concluding that there was no genuine question whether Time's publication fairly and accurately summarized the FBI materials concerning Medico. .

We agree with the district court that nothing in the record suggests that the Time article unfairly or inaccurately reported on the FBI materials. . . .

30. The excesses of the McCarthy era, for example, prompted some commentators to point out the reputational injury the republication of official defamation can cause, and to advocate restricting the fair report privilege. See Pedrick, Senator McCarthy and the Law of Libel: A Study of Two Campaign Speeches, 48 Nw.U.L.Rev. 135 (1953); 13 Rutgers L.Rev. 723, 727 (1959). See also Coleman v. Newark Morning Ledger Co., 29 N.J. 357, 149 A.2d 193 (1959) (serviceman previously unknown to public defamed by Senator McCarthy's summary of secret Congressional hearings; newspaper account held privileged.)

40. Placement on the plaintiff of the burden of demonstrating that a privileged report was not fair and accurate traditionally distinguished the fair report privilege from the truth defense, in which defendant bore the burden of proving truth . . . .

. . . Time has accurately portrayed the FBI records as indicating that Medico has been identified as part of the Bufalino crime family.

VI.

Medico further contends that Time can avail itself of the fair report privilege only if it actually based its article on the FBI materials; if the report reflects the contents of the official materials merely by coincidence, the privilege does not attach. Medico maintains there is a genuine issue of fact whether Time employees worked with the FBI materials in preparing the article.

Pennsylvania law squarely contradicts this argument. . . .

VII.

We conclude that Time's publication of an allegedly defamatory article concerning Philip Medico falls within the scope of the Pennsylvania common law privilege of fair report, and that Medico has failed to establish a genuine issue of fact concerning a possible abuse of the privilege. . . .[42]

The judgment of the district court granting Time's motion for summary judgment will be affirmed.

Notes and Questions

1. In Bufalino v. Associated Press, 692 F.2d 266, 8 Med.L.Rptr. 2385 (2d Cir.1982), certiorari denied 462 U.S. 1111 (1983), the court rejected the Third Circuit's reading of Pennsylvania law on the question of whether the publisher must rely on the official report or proceeding. It refused defendant the benefit of official documents that it uncovered after publication while it was preparing for litigation. The privilege could not be "divorced from its underlying policy of encouraging the broad dissemination of public records." Protecting AP's reports here "does nothing to encourage the initial reporting of public records and proceedings. Certainly § 611 should not be interpreted to protect unattributed, defamatory statements supported only after-the-fact through a frantic search of official records."

42. The possible interpretations of Time's publication about Medico may be used to illustrate the different approaches to the truth defense. The Time article is subject to at least three constructions:

A. Medico is a Mafia *capo.*

B. Government agents overheard Bufalino describe Medico as a Mafia *capo.*

C. FBI records indicate that government agents overheard Bufalino describe Medico as a Mafia *capo.*

Under the fair report privilege, the accuracy of C relieves Time of liability. If the privilege did not apply, however, we would have to ascertain whether Pennsylvania law would exonerate Time on the basis of the truth defense if Time established the truth of B, or whether Time would have to prove A. In light of our holding that Time's publication comes under the fair report privilege, we need not dispose of this question. In addition, we need not review the district court's determination that Time has failed to demonstrate the truth of either A or B.

In a footnote, the Second Circuit observed that "even where the reporter has actually relied on official records, the privilege can be lost through failure to make proper attribution." Why?

2. Courts have not required precise use of legal language in testing the accuracy of these reports. In Gurda v. Orange County Publications, 56 N.Y.2d 705, 436 N.E.2d 1326, 451 N.Y.S.2d 724, 9 Med.L.Rptr. 1120 (1982), the court upheld a privilege for a newspaper that used "fraud" and "fine" to describe what had happened in a civil case in which the judge found that plaintiff had defrauded someone, and awarded damages and attorney's fees.

3. How accurate must the report be? See Holy Spirit Ass'n for the Unification of World Christianity v. New York Times Co., 49 N.Y.2d 63, 399 N.E.2d 1185, 424 N.Y.S.2d 165 (1979):

> [N]ewspaper accounts of legislative or other official proceedings must be accorded some degree of liberality. When determining whether an article constitutes a "fair and true" report, the language used therein should not be dissected and analyzed with a lexicographer's precision. This is so because a newspaper article is, by its very nature, a condensed report of events which must, of necessity, reflect to some degree the subjective view of its author. Nor should a fair report which is not misleading, composed and phrased in good faith under the exigencies of a publication deadline, be thereafter parsed and dissected on the basis of precise denotative meanings which may literally, although not contextually, be ascribed to the words used.

The Times articles had said that legislative intelligence reports had "stated as fact" allegations that had been previously reported as unverified:

> Here, there is no showing that defendant misquoted any material contained in the intelligence reports. While the use of the phrases "stated as fact" and "confirmed and elaborated" may denote, to some degree, a sense of legitimacy which, in hindsight, could be characterized as imprudent given the unverified nature of the reports, this observation does not, in and of itself, render the newspaper articles unfair.

4. In some states, as suggested in *Medico,* the privilege extends to the fact of an arrest and the charges but not to details of the alleged crime that an arresting officer provides.

5. As noted in *Medico,* most states have adopted legislation to codify this privilege. One typical version is New York's Civil Rights Law § 74, which provides:

> A civil action cannot be maintained against [any defendant] for the publication of a fair and true report of any judicial proceeding, legislative proceeding or other official proceeding. . . .
>
> This section does not apply to a libel contained in any other matter added by any person concerned in the publication; or in the

report of anything said or done at the time and place of such a proceeding which was not a part thereof.

Notice that this does not protect reports of public meetings held by nongovernmental organizations, such as medical associations or publicly held corporations, or remarks made by political, sports, or entertainment figures. Should it? How should a New York court approach the *Medico* situation?

Does the statute protect repetition of comments shouted out by a member of the audience at a city council meeting? Should it?

6. Questions of fairness usually arise in connection with the condensation or summary of a report. Comment f to § 611 states that "although it is unnecessary that the report be exhaustive and complete, it is necessary that nothing be omitted or misplaced in such a manner as to convey an erroneous impression to those who hear or read it, as for example a report of the discreditable testimony in a judicial proceeding and a failure to publish the exculpatory evidence." The matter is discussed in Schiavone Construction Co. v. Time, Inc., 735 F.2d 94, 10 Med.L.Rptr. 1831 (3d Cir.1984), in which the magazine reported that an individual's name appeared several times in FBI reports concerning the disappearance of Jimmy Hoffa, but failed to quote the passage in the report that said that none of the references "suggested any criminality or organized crime associations" on plaintiffs' parts. This raised a fact question about fairness that barred summary judgment.

7. The states are split over whether malice in the sense of spite or ill will deprives the defendant of the privilege. Why should the defendant's desire to cause harm be relevant?

8. Reporters of judicial opinions, official as well as unofficial, appear to be protected under this privilege. Beary v. West Publishing Co., 763 F.2d 66, 11 Med.L.Rptr. 2114 (2d Cir.1985), certiorari denied 106 S.Ct. 232 (1985).

d. Partial and Procedural Defenses

---

i. Retraction

State law has also provided some partial defenses that might reduce damages but not eliminate liability. One involves a showing that the plaintiff's reputation was already low either because of earlier publication of the charge in question or for other reasons. This might induce the jury to lower its estimate of the compensatory damage defendant's defamation had caused plaintiff.

A second partial defense revolves around the publication of a retraction. A prompt voluntary retraction might reduce the harm caused and might also show that the defendant had not acted maliciously in the first place. Some states have enacted retraction statutes that grant further protection to some media defendants. These vary in whether they apply to those who defame innocently, carelessly, or maliciously. What they have in common is a requirement that the prospective plaintiff must demand a retraction shortly after the defamation. If the publisher complies within a similar period of time, then the plaintiff may recover special damages but not general damages. If the retraction is not published within the time limit, the plaintiff may recover whatever damages the state law allows.

In California, for example, under Civil Code § 48a, the plaintiff must demand a retraction within 20 days after learning of the publication claimed to be libelous. If the retraction is not published within 21 days "in substantially as conspicuous a manner . . . as were the statements claimed to be libelous," plaintiff may recover general, special, and, in appropriate cases, exemplary damages. If the retraction is published or if no retraction is demanded, then, apparently, presumed general damages are not recoverable. The statute was upheld even when applied to deliberately false stories. Werner v. Southern California Associated Newspapers, 35 Cal.2d 121, 216 P.2d 825 (1950). Plaintiff's appeal to the Supreme Court was dismissed after the case was settled.

Oregon's statute, which applies unless plaintiff can prove that the defendant "actually intended to defame the plaintiff," was upheld in Holden v. Pioneer Broadcasting Co., 228 Or. 405, 365 P.2d 845 (1961), appeal dismissed and certiorari denied 370 U.S. 157 (1962).

But see Madison v. Yunker, 180 Mont. 54, 589 P.2d 126, 4 Med.L. Rptr. 1337 (1978), holding that Montana's retraction statute violates the state constitution's requirement that the courts be "open to every person, and speedy remedy afforded for every injury of person, property, or character." This was combined with the state's free expression provision that stated that speakers were "responsible for all abuse of that liberty" and which explicitly contemplated libel and slander actions.

Surely the most interesting retraction controversy in recent years was Burnett v. National Enquirer, Inc., 144 Cal.App.3d 991, 193 Cal. Rptr. 206, 9 Med.L.Rptr. 1921 (1983), appeal dismissed for want of jurisdiction, 465 U.S. 1014 (1984). The original article stated:

> Carol Burnett and Henry K. in Row
>
> In a Washington restaurant, a boisterous Carol Burnett had a loud argument with another diner, Henry Kissinger. Then she traipsed around the place offering everyone a bite of her dessert. But Carol really raised eyebrows when she accidentally knocked a glass of wine over one diner and started giggling instead of apologizing. The guy wasn't amused and "accidentally" spilled a glass of water over Carol's dress.

In fact, Burnett and her husband exchanged desserts with two other couples. As Burnett was leaving, a friend introduced her to Henry

Kissinger, and they had a "brief conversation." In response to Burnett's demand for a retraction, the Enquirer published the following:

> An item in this column on March 2 erroneously reported that Carol Burnett had an argument with Henry Kissinger at a Washington restaurant and became boisterous, disturbing other guests. We understand those events did not occur and we are sorry for any embarrassment our report may have caused Miss Burnett.

Is this an adequate correction? The court never reached that question because it upheld the trial judge's ruling that the Enquirer was not eligible to take advantage of the statute because it was not a "newspaper." The Enquirer's masthead claimed the "Largest Circulation Of Any Paper in America." It belonged to the American Newspaper Publishers Association; subscribed to Reuters News Service; called itself a newspaper in its filings with the tax authorities; and was granted state sales and use tax exemptions. On the other hand, eight mass media directories called it a magazine and, on its request in 1960, it was reclassified as a magazine by the Audit Bureau of Circulation. Also:

> According to a statement by its Senior Editor it is not a newspaper and its content is based on a consistent formula of "how to" stories, celebrity or medical or personal improvement stories, gossip items and TV column items, together with material from certain other subjects. It provides little or no current coverage of subjects such as politics, sports or crime, does not attribute content to wire services, and in general does not make reference to time. Normal "lead time" for its subject matter is one to three weeks. Its owner allowed it did not generate stories "day to day as a daily newspaper does."

After considering a cluster of conflicting cases, the court concluded that "the better view" was to limit the protection of the statute "to those who engage in the immediate dissemination of news on the ground that the Legislature could reasonably conclude that such enterprises . . . cannot always check their sources for accuracy and their stories for inadvertent publication error."

It was thus proper to extend protection "in those instances, and those only, where the constraints of time as a function of the requirements associated with production of the publication dictate the result." The Enquirer did not qualify. (Is this rationale consistent with the statute's clear protection for a daily newspaper's investigative story that was prepared over two months?)

Defamation is one of the few torts in which something other than money may help redress the initial injury. It is also, however, a tort that cannot be prevented. Injunctions have never been available to prevent personal defamation. See Pound, Equitable Relief Against Defamation and Injuries to Personality, 29 Harv.L.Rev. 640 (1916); Leflar, Legal Remedies for Defamation, 6 Ark.L.Rev. 423 (1952); Sedler, Injunctive Relief and Personal Integrity, 9 St. Louis L.J. 147 (1964).

The possibility of granting the plaintiff a right of reply is discussed at p. 433, infra.

ii. *Single Publication*

Consider the difficulties in treating each individual copy of a publication as a separate cause of action. Most states, either by case law or by adoption of the Uniform Single Publication Act, 13 U.L.A. 517, have developed the rule that the entire edition of a printed work is to be treated as a single publication and that all damages for this publication must be recovered in a single action. At first this was limited to one action in each state, but now it is recognized that all damages for the nationwide single publication may, and in some cases, must, be resolved in a single action that takes into account the substantive rules of the relevant states. See Hartmann v. Time, Inc., 166 F.2d 127 (3d Cir.1947), certiorari denied 334 U.S. 838 (1948); Waskow v. Associated Press, 462 F.2d 1173 (D.C.Cir.1972); Sorge v. Parade Publications, Inc., 20 A.D.2d 338, 247 N.Y.S.2d 317 (1964). The basic problems are addressed in Prosser, Interstate Publication, 51 Mich.L.Rev. 959 (1953).

If a new edition of the work is published, however, such as a new edition of a book or a soft-cover version of a hardback book, it is considered a new and separate publication for which a separate cause of action arises. R. Sack, Libel, Slander and Related Problems 91 (1980). This rule may soften the press protection provided by the relatively short Statute of Limitations for defamation in most states. In the majority of states, the Statute is only one or two years. R. Sack, Libel, Slander and Related Problems 587 (1980). But the statute begins anew for each new "single publication." See Rinaldi v. Viking Penguin, 52 N.Y.2d 422, 438 N.Y.S.2d 496, 420 N.E.2d 377, 7 Med.L.Rptr. 1202 (1981), where a printer re-bound unsold hardcover copies of a book in soft cover a year after the initial hard-cover printing. New York's Statute of Limitations is one year, and a cause of action for defamation was brought two months after the soft-cover printing, 14 months after the hard-cover printing. The court, noting that the soft-cover edition had a new publication date printed inside, held it was a separate publication and rejected the limitations defense. "By no means was this to be but a delayed circulation of the original edition."

iii. *Statute of Limitations*

On what date does the statute of limitations begin to run? The majority rule is that the publication date on the cover of a newspaper or magazine is irrelevant. In some states the critical date is the one on which the publication becomes available to the readers. See Fleury v. Harper & Row, 698 F.2d 1022, 9 Med.L.Rptr. 1200 (9th Cir.1983). Other states hold that the proper date is when the publication is placed in the hands of common carriers for shipment. The defendant in Williams v. RHG Publishing, 7 Med.L.Rptr. 1372 (N.Y.Sup.1981), argued that 5,122 copies of the publication, True Detective, had been mailed to subscribers before the publication date on the face of the magazine. The court stated the rule that plaintiff's cause of action accrues when the libel is effectively placed within the reach of the ultimate buying public. But the subscription list represented only two percent of total circulation. It would be unfair to hold that the statute began to run upon that mailing, before plaintiff had received a "reasonable opportunity to learn about" the alleged defamation. The defendant's motion to dismiss was denied, with leave to renew upon a showing that retailers also sold the magazine before the publication date on the cover.

iv. Jurisdiction

In two cases in 1984, the Supreme Court unanimously denied special jurisdictional protections to media defendants. In Calder v. Jones, 465 U.S. 783, 10 Med.L.Rptr. 1401 (1984), the Court held that individual writers and editors who lived in Florida and worked on a national publication could be required to defend a libel action in California by a California plaintiff.

The individual defendants worked on the article knowing that it "would have a potentially devastating impact upon respondent." Plaintiff "need not go to Florida to seek redress from persons who, though remaining in Florida, knowingly cause the injury in California." The defendants were entitled to the substantive protections of the First Amendment, to be developed shortly. "To reintroduce those concerns at the jurisdictional stage would be a form of double counting."

In the second case decided, Keeton v. Hustler Magazine, Inc., 465 U.S. 770, 10 Med.L.Rptr. 1405 (1984), a New York plaintiff sued an Ohio corporation in New Hampshire—the only state in which the statute of limitations had not yet run on her claim. Defendant circulated some 10,000 to 15,000 copies in the state each month.

The state was found to have a "substantial interest" in cooperating with other states in providing a single forum for efficiently litigating this type of case. Moreover, it had a "significant interest in redressing injuries that actually occur within the State," which extended to libel actions brought by nonresidents. "False statements of fact harm both the subject of the falsehood *and* the readers of the statement. New Hampshire may rightly employ its libel laws to discourage the deception of its citizens." Also, a libel plaintiff may suffer harm "even in a state in which he has hitherto been anonymous. The communication of the libel may create a negative reputation among the residents of a jurisdiction where the plaintiff's previous reputation was, however small, at least unblemished."

Plaintiff's lack of residence in the state does not defeat jurisdiction that is established on the basis of defendant's contacts with that state. Plaintiff is not limited to her own state. There was no unfairness in calling upon Hustler to answer for the contents of its magazine "wherever a substantial number of copies are regularly sold and distributed."

The Court did, however, leave open the question of whether if New Hampshire sought to apply its own statute of limitations to claims in other states "any arguable unfairness [would rise] to the level of a due process violation."

B. CONSTITUTIONAL PRIVILEGE

In Near v. Minnesota, p. 70, supra, the majority observed, "But it is recognized that punishment for the abuse of the liberty accorded to the press is essential to the protection of the public, and that the common-law rules that subject the libeler to responsibility for the public offense, as well as for the private injury, are not abolished by the protection extended in our Constitution." In the late 1930s a syndicated columnist asserted that Congressman Sweeney was blocking the appointment of a federal judge because the prospective appointee was Jewish. Sweeney sued several newspapers, with varying results. Compare Sweeney v. Patterson, 76 U.S.App.D.C. 23, 128 F.2d 457, certiorari denied 317 U.S. 678 (1942), holding the column privileged, with Sweeney v. Schenectady Union Pub. Co., 122 F.2d 288 (2d Cir.1941) affirmed by an equally divided Court 316 U.S. 642 (1942), in which the lower court had found no privilege. This Supreme Court split might have suggested the presence of a difficult constitutional question.

In Chaplinsky v. New Hampshire, 315 U.S. 568 (1942), however, the Supreme Court unanimously upheld the conviction of a Jehovah's Witness who had been prosecuted under a "fighting words" statute after having called a policeman a "God damned racketeer" and a "Damned fascist," and gotten into a fight as a result. In the course of his opinion for the court, Justice Murphy observed:

> There are certain well-defined and narrowly limited classes of speech, the prevention and punishment of which have never been thought to raise any Constitutional problem. These include the lewd and obscene, the profane, the libelous, and the insulting or "fighting" words—those which by their very utterance inflict injury or tend to incite an immediate breach of the peace. It has been well observed that such utterances are no essential part of any exposition of ideas, and are of such slight social value as a step to truth that any benefit that may be derived from them is clearly outweighed by the social interest in order and morality.

This language was often quoted approvingly. Justice Frankfurter, writing for a 5–4 majority in Beauharnais v. Illinois, 343 U.S. 250 (1952), to sustain a state criminal libel law, relied on *Chaplinsky* for the proposition that libelous utterances were not "within the area of constitutionally protected speech."

This sequence set the stage for the following case from Alabama, a state that had long followed the narrow *Hallam* view, p. 139, supra, for criticism of public officials. In considering constitutional protections, it may be useful to think of several different functions engaged in by the press. Three major ones come to mind. Perhaps the one we think most about is the situation in which the press behaves as an investigator or originator of a story, as in *Cianci*. A second function is that of explicit repeater of what others are saying. The Medico case suggests this role, as does the letter-to-the-editor column. The third function is that of criticism or editorializing on public matters—this comes close to the "fair comment" privilege at common law. Although these roles overlap, they may provide an organizing principle. (That having been said, it must be noted that the next case treats an advertisement the same way that it treats an investigative story published on the authority of the newspaper itself. As we shall see, it is still not clear that constitutional law recognizes sharp differences between originating and repeating information.)

1. The Press as Originator

a. *Public Officials*

NEW YORK TIMES CO. v. SULLIVAN

(Together with Abernathy v. Sullivan)

Supreme Court of the United States, 1964.
376 U.S. 254, 84 S.Ct. 710, 11 L.Ed.2d 686.
Noted, 52 Cornell L.Q. 419, 78 Harv.L.Rev. 201, 42 Texas L.Rev. 1080, 113 U.Pa.L.Rev. 284.

[This action was based on a full-page advertisement in The New York Times on behalf of several individuals and groups protesting a "wave of terror" against blacks involved in non-violent demonstrations in the South. Plaintiff, one of three elected commissioners of Montgomery, the capital of Alabama, was in charge of the police department. When he demanded a retraction, as state law required, The Times instead responded that it failed to see how he was defamed. He then filed suit against The Times and four clergymen whose names appeared—although they deny having authorized this—in the ad. Plaintiff alleged that the third and the sixth paragraphs of the advertisement libelled him:

> "In Montgomery, Alabama, after students sang 'My Country, 'Tis of Thee' on the State Capitol steps, their leaders were expelled from school, and truckloads of police armed with shotguns and tear-gas ringed the Alabama State College Campus. When the entire student body protested to state authorities by refusing to re-register, their dining hall was padlocked in an attempt to starve them into submission."
>
> . . .
>
> "Again and again the Southern violators have answered Dr. King's peaceful protests with intimidation and violence. They

> have bombed his home almost killing his wife and child. They have assaulted his person. They have arrested him seven times—for 'speeding,' 'loitering' and similar 'offenses.' And now they have charged him with 'perjury'—a *felony* under which they could imprison him for *ten years.* . . . "

Plaintiff claimed that he was libelled in the third paragraph by the reference to the police, since his responsibilities included supervision of the Montgomery police. He asserted that the paragraph could be read as charging the police with ringing the campus and seeking to starve the students by padlocking the dining hall. As to the sixth paragraph, he contended that the word "they" referred to his department since arrests are usually made by the police and the paragraph could be read as accusing him of committing the acts charged. Several witnesses testified that they read the statements as referring to plaintiff in his capacity as commissioner.

The defendants admitted several inaccuracies in these two paragraphs: the students sang The Star Spangled Banner, not My Country, 'Tis of Thee; nine students were expelled, not for leading the demonstration, but for demanding service at a lunch counter in the county courthouse; the dining hall was never padlocked; police at no time ringed the campus though they were deployed nearby in large numbers; they were not called to the campus in connection with the demonstration; Dr. King had been arrested only four times; and officers disputed his account of the alleged assault. Plaintiff proved that he had not been commissioner when three of the four arrests occurred and that he had nothing to do with procuring the perjury indictment.

The trial judge charged that the statements were libel per se, that the jury should decide whether they were made "of and concerning" the plaintiff and, if so, general damages were to be presumed. Although noting that punitive damages required more than carelessness, he refused to charge that they required a finding of actual intent to harm or "gross negligence and recklessness." He also refused to order the jury to separate its award of general and punitive damages. The jury returned a verdict for $500,000—the full amount demanded. The Alabama Supreme Court affirmed, holding that malice could be found in several aspects of The Times' conduct.]

MR. JUSTICE BRENNAN delivered the opinion of the Court.

. . .

I.

We may dispose at the outset of two grounds asserted to insulate the judgment of the Alabama courts from constitutional scrutiny. The first is the proposition relied on by the State Supreme Court—that "The Fourteenth Amendment is directed against State action and not private action." That proposition has no application to this case. Although this is a civil lawsuit between private parties, the Alabama courts have applied a state rule of law which petitioners claim to impose invalid restrictions on their constitutional freedoms of speech and press. It matters not that that law has been applied in a civil action and that it is common law only, though supplemented by statute. [ ] The test is not the form in which state power has been applied but, whatever the form, whether such power has in fact been exercised. [ ]

The second contention is that the constitutional guarantees of freedom of speech and of the press are inapplicable here, at least so far as the Times is concerned, because the allegedly libelous statements were published as part of a paid, "commercial" advertisement. [The argument was rejected. See p. 501, infra.]

II.

Under Alabama law as applied in this case, a publication is "libelous per se" if the words "tend to injure a person . . . in his reputation" or to "bring [him] into public contempt"; the trial court stated that the standard was met if the words are such as to "injure him in his public office, or impute misconduct to him in his office, or want of official integrity, or want of fidelity to a public trust. . . . " The jury must find that the words were published "of and concerning" the plaintiff, but where the plaintiff is a public official his place in the governmental hierarchy is sufficient evidence to support a finding that his reputation has been affected by statements that reflect upon the agency of which he is in charge. Once "libel per se" has been established, the defendant has no defense as to stated facts unless he can persuade the jury that they were true in all their particulars. [ ] His privilege of "fair comment" for expressions of opinion depends on the truth of the facts upon which the comment is based. [ ] Unless he can discharge the burden of proving truth, general damages are presumed, and may be awarded without proof of pecuniary injury. A showing of actual malice is apparently a prerequisite to recovery of punitive damages, and the defendant may in any event forestall a punitive award by a retraction meeting the statutory requirements. Good motives and belief in truth do not negate an inference of malice, but are relevant only in mitigation of punitive damages if the jury chooses to accord them weight. [ ]

The question before us is whether this rule of liability, as applied to an action brought by a public official against critics of his official conduct, abridges the freedom of speech and of the press that is guaranteed by the First and Fourteenth Amendments.

Respondent relies heavily, as did the Alabama courts, on statements of this Court to the effect that the Constitution does not protect libelous publications. Those statements do not foreclose our inquiry here. None of the cases sustained the use of libel laws to impose sanctions upon expression critical of the official conduct of public officials. . . . In deciding the question now, we are compelled by neither precedent nor policy to give any more weight to the epithet "libel" than we have to other "mere labels" of state law. NAACP v. Button, 371 U.S. 415, 429 (1963). Like insurrection, contempt, advocacy of unlawful acts, breach of the peace, obscenity, solicitation of legal business, and the various other formulae for the repression of expression that have been challenged in this Court, libel can claim no talismanic immunity from constitutional limitations. It must be measured by standards that satisfy the First Amendment.

The general proposition that freedom of expression upon public questions is secured by the First Amendment has long been settled by our decisions. . . . Mr. Justice Brandeis, in his concurring opinion in Whitney v. California, 274 U.S. 357, 375–376 (1927), gave the principle its classic formulation:

> "Those who won our independence believed . . . that public discussion is a political duty; and that this should be a fundamental principle of the American government. . . . Believing in the power of reason as applied through public discussion, they eschewed silence coerced by law—the argument of force in its worst form. Recognizing the occasional tyrannies of governing majorities, they amended the Constitution so that free speech and assembly should be guaranteed."

Thus we consider this case against the background of a profound national commitment to the principle that debate on public issues should be uninhibited, robust, and wide-open, and that it may well include vehement, caustic, and sometimes unpleasantly sharp attacks on government and public officials. See Terminiello v. Chicago, 337 U.S. 1, 4 (1949); De Jonge v. Oregon, 299 U.S. 353, 365 (1937). The present advertisement, as an expression of grievance and protest on one of the major public issues of our time, would seem clearly to qualify for the constitutional protection. The question is whether it forfeits that protection by the falsity of some of its factual statements and by its alleged defamation of respondent.

Authoritative interpretations of the First Amendment guarantees have consistently refused to recognize an exception for any test of truth—whether administered by judges, juries, or administrative officials—and especially one that puts the burden of proving truth on the speaker. Cf. Speiser v. Randall, 357 U.S. 513, 525–526 (1958). The constitutional protection does not turn upon "the truth, popularity, or social utility of the ideas and beliefs which are offered." NAACP v. Button, 371 U.S. 415, 445 (1963). As Madison said, "Some degree of abuse is inseparable from the proper use of every thing; and in no instance is this more true than in that of the press." 4 Elliot's Debates on the Federal Constitution (1876), p. 571. In Cantwell v. Connecticut, 310 U.S. 296, 310 (1940), the Court declared:

> "In the realm of religious faith, and in that of political belief, sharp differences arise. In both fields the tenets of one man may seem the rankest error to his neighbor. To persuade others to his own point of view, the pleader, as we know, at times, resorts to

exaggeration, to vilification of men who have been, or are, prominent in church or state, and even to false statement. But the people of this nation have ordained in the light of history, that, in spite of the probability of excesses and abuses, these liberties are, in the long view, essential to enlightened opinion and right conduct on the part of the citizens of a democracy."

That erroneous statement is inevitable in free debate, and that it must be protected if the freedoms of expression are to have the "breathing space" that they "need . . . to survive," NAACP v. Button, 371 U.S. 415, 433 (1963), was also recognized by the Court of Appeals for the District of Columbia Circuit in Sweeney v. Patterson, 76 U.S.App.D.C. 23, 24, 128 F.2d 457, 458, certiorari denied, 317 U.S. 678 (1942). Judge Edgerton spoke for a unanimous court which affirmed the dismissal of a Congressman's libel suit based upon a newspaper article charging him with anti-Semitism in opposing a judicial appointment. He said:

"Cases which impose liability for erroneous reports of the political conduct of officials reflect the obsolete doctrine that the governed must not criticize their governors. . . . The interest of the public here outweighs the interest of appellant or any other individual. The protection of the public requires not merely discussion, but information. Political conduct and views which some respectable people approve, and others condemn, are constantly imputed to Congressmen. Errors of fact, particularly in regard to a man's mental states and processes, are inevitable. . . . Whatever is added to the field of libel is taken from the field of free debate." [13]

Injury to official reputation affords no more warrant for repressing speech that would otherwise be free than does factual error. Where judicial officers are involved, this Court has held that concern for the dignity and reputation of the courts does not justify the punishment as criminal contempt of criticism of the judge or his decision. Bridges v. California, 314 U.S. 252 (1941). This is true even though the utterance contains "half-truths" and "misinformation." Pennekamp v. Florida, 328 U.S. 331, 342, 343, n. 5, 345 (1946). . . . Criticism of their official conduct does not lose its constitutional protection merely because it is effective criticism and hence diminishes their official reputations.

If neither factual error nor defamatory content suffices to remove the constitutional shield from criticism of official conduct, the combination of the two elements is no less inadequate. This is the lesson to be drawn from the great controversy over the Sedition Act of 1798, 1 Stat.

13. See also Mill, On Liberty (Oxford: Blackwell, 1947), at 47:

". . . [T]o argue sophistically, to suppress facts or arguments, to misstate the elements of the case, or misrepresent the opposite opinion . . . all this, even to the most aggravated degree, is so continually done in perfect good faith, by persons who are not considered, and in many other respects may not deserve to be considered, ignorant or incompetent, that it is rarely possible, on adequate grounds, conscientiously to stamp the misrepresentation as morally culpable; and still less could law presume to interfere with this kind of controversial misconduct."

§ 596, which first crystallized a national awareness of the central meaning of the First Amendment. . . .

Although the Sedition Act was never tested in this Court,[16] the attack upon its validity has carried the day in the court of history. Fines levied in its prosecution were repaid by Act of Congress on the ground that it was unconstitutional. . . . The invalidity of the Act has also been assumed by Justices of this Court. [ ] These views reflect a broad consensus that the Act, because of the restraint it imposed upon criticism of government and public officials, was inconsistent with the First Amendment.

There is no force in respondent's argument that the constitutional limitations implicit in the history of the Sedition Act apply only to Congress and not to the States. It is true that the First Amendment was originally addressed only to action by the Federal Government, and that Jefferson, for one, while denying the power of Congress "to controul the freedom of the press," recognized such a power in the States. [ ] But this distinction was eliminated with the adoption of the Fourteenth Amendment and the application to the States of the First Amendment's restrictions. [ ]

What a State may not constitutionally bring about by means of a criminal statute is likewise beyond the reach of its civil law of libel. The fear of damage awards under a rule such as that invoked by the Alabama courts here may be markedly more inhibiting than the fear of prosecution under a criminal statute. [ ] Alabama, for example, has a criminal libel law which subjects to prosecution "any person who speaks, writes, or prints of and concerning another any accusation falsely and maliciously importing the commission by such person of a felony, or any other indictable offense involving moral turpitude," and which allows as punishment upon conviction a fine not exceeding $500 and a prison sentence of six months. [ ] Presumably a person charged with violation of this statute enjoys ordinary criminal-law safeguards such as the requirements of an indictment and of proof beyond a reasonable doubt. These safeguards are not available to the defendant in a civil action. . . . And since there is no double-jeopardy limitation applicable to civil lawsuits, this is not the only judgment that may be awarded against petitioners for the same publication.[18] Whether or not a newspaper can survive a succession of such judgments, the pall of fear and timidity imposed upon those who would give voice to public criticism is an atmosphere in which the First Amendment freedoms cannot survive. Plainly the Alabama law of civil libel is "a form of regulation that creates hazards to protected freedoms markedly greater

16. The Act expired by its terms in 1801.

18. The Times states that four other libel suits based on the advertisement have been filed against it by others who have served as Montgomery City Commissioners and by the Governor of Alabama; that another $500,000 verdict has been awarded in the only one of these cases that has yet gone to trial; and that the damages sought in the other three total $2,000,000.

than those that attend reliance upon the criminal law." Bantam Books, Inc. v. Sullivan, 372 U.S. 58, 70 (1963).

The state rule of law is not saved by its allowance of the defense of truth. . . . Allowance of the defense of truth, with the burden of proving it on the defendant, does not mean that only false speech will be deterred.[19] Even courts accepting this defense as an adequate safeguard have recognized the difficulties of adducing legal proofs that the alleged libel was true in all its factual particulars. See, e.g., Post Publishing Co. v. Hallam, 59 F. 530, 540 (C.A. 6th Cir.1893); see also Noel, Defamation of Public Officers and Candidates, 49 Col.L.Rev. 875, 892 (1949). Under such a rule, would-be critics of official conduct may be deterred from voicing their criticism, even though it is believed to be true and even though it is in fact true, because of doubt whether it can be proved in court or fear of the expense of having to do so. They tend to make only statements which "steer far wider of the unlawful zone." Speiser v. Randall, supra, 357 U.S., at 526. The rule thus dampens the vigor and limits the variety of public debate. It is inconsistent with the First and Fourteenth Amendments.

The constitutional guarantees require, we think, a federal rule that prohibits a public official from recovering damages for a defamatory falsehood relating to his official conduct unless he proves that the statement was made with "actual malice"—that is, with knowledge that it was false or with reckless disregard of whether it was false or not. An oft-cited statement of a like rule, which has been adopted by a number of state courts, is found in the Kansas case of Coleman v. MacLennan, 78 Kan. 711, 98 P. 281 (1908). . . .

Such a privilege for criticism of official conduct is appropriately analogous to the protection accorded a public official when *he* is sued for libel by a private citizen. In Barr v. Matteo, 360 U.S. 564, 575 (1959), this Court held the utterance of a federal official to be absolutely privileged if made "within the outer perimeter" of his duties. The States accord the same immunity to statements of their highest officers, although some differentiate their lesser officials and qualify the privilege they enjoy. But all hold that all officials are protected unless actual malice can be proved. The reason for the official privilege is said to be that the threat of damage suits would otherwise "inhibit the fearless, vigorous, and effective administration of policies of government" and "dampen the ardor of all but the most resolute, or the most irresponsible, in the unflinching discharge of their duties." Barr v. Matteo, supra, 360 U.S., at 571. Analogous considerations support the privilege for the citizen-critic of government. It is as much his duty to criticize as it is the official's duty to administer. . . . As Madison said, [ ], "the censorial power is in the people over the Government, and not in the Government over the people." It would give public

19. Even a false statement may be deemed to make a valuable contribution to public debate, since it brings about "the clearer perception and livelier impression of truth, produced by its collision with error." Mill, On Liberty (Oxford: Blackwell, 1947), at 15; see also Milton, Areopagitica, in Prose Works (Yale, 1959), Vol. II, at 561.

servants an unjustified preference over the public they serve, if critics of official conduct did not have a fair equivalent of the immunity granted to the officials themselves.

We conclude that such a privilege is required by the First and Fourteenth Amendments.

III.

We hold today that the Constitution delimits a State's power to award damages for libel in actions brought by public officials against critics of their official conduct. Since this is such an action, the rule requiring proof of actual malice is applicable. While Alabama law apparently requires proof of actual malice for an award of punitive damages, where general damages are concerned malice is "presumed." Such a presumption is inconsistent with the federal rule. . . . Since the trial judge did not instruct the jury to differentiate between general and punitive damages, it may be that the verdict was wholly an award of one or the other. But it is impossible to know, in view of the general verdict returned. Because of this uncertainty, the judgment must be reversed and the case remanded.

Since respondent may seek a new trial, we deem that considerations of effective judicial administration require us to review the evidence in the present record to determine whether it could constitutionally support a judgment for respondent. . . .

Applying these standards, we consider that the proof presented to show actual malice, lacks the convincing clarity which the constitutional standard demands, and hence that it would not constitutionally sustain the judgment for respondent under the proper rule of law. The case of the individual petitioners requires little discussion. Even assuming that they could constitutionally be found to have authorized the use of their names on the advertisement, there was no evidence whatever that they were aware of any erroneous statements or were in any way reckless in that regard. The judgment against them is thus without constitutional support.

As to the Times, we similarly conclude that the facts do not support a finding of actual malice. . . .

. . .

We also think the evidence was constitutionally defective in another respect: it was incapable of supporting the jury's finding that the allegedly libelous statements were made "of and concerning" respondent. Respondent relies on the words of the advertisement and the testimony of six witnesses to establish a connection between it and himself. . . . There was no reference to respondent in the advertisement, either by name or official position. A number of the allegedly libelous statements—the charges that the dining hall was padlocked and that Dr. King's home was bombed, his person assaulted, and a perjury prosecution instituted against him—did not even concern the police; despite the ingenuity of the arguments which would attach this significance to the word "They," it is plain that these statements could not reasonably be read as accusing respondent of personal involvement in the acts in question. The statements upon which respondent principally relies as referring to him are the two allegations that did concern the police or police functions: that "truckloads of police . . . ringed the Alabama State College Campus" after the demonstration on the State Capitol steps, and that Dr. King had been "arrested . . . seven times." These statements were false only in that the police had been "deployed near" the campus but had not actually "ringed" it and had not gone there in connection with the State Capitol demonstration, and in that Dr. King had been arrested only four times. The ruling that these discrepancies between what was true and what was asserted were sufficient to injure respondent's reputation may itself raise constitutional problems, but we need not consider them here. Although the statements may be taken as referring to the police, they did not on their face make even an oblique reference to respondent as an individual. Support for the asserted reference must, therefore, be sought in the testimony of respondent's witnesses. But none of them suggested any basis for the belief that respondent himself was attacked in the advertisement beyond the bare fact that he was in overall charge of the Police Department and thus bore official responsibility for police conduct; to the extent that some of the witnesses thought respondent to have been charged with ordering or approving the conduct or otherwise being personally involved in it, they based this notion not on any statements in the advertisement, and not on any evidence that he had in fact been so involved, but solely on the unsupported assumption that, because of his official position, he must have been. This reliance on the bare fact of respondent's official position was made explicit by the Supreme Court of Alabama. . . .

This proposition has disquieting implications for criticism of governmental conduct. For good reason, "no court of last resort in this country has ever held, or even suggested, that prosecutions for libel on government have any place in the American system of jurisprudence." City of Chicago v. Tribune Co., 307 Ill. 595, 601, 139 N.E. 86, 88 (1923). The present proposition would sidestep this obstacle by transmuting criticism of government, however impersonal it may seem on its face, into personal criticism, and hence potential libel, of the officials of whom the government is composed. There is no legal alchemy by which a State may thus create the cause of action that would otherwise be denied for a publication which, as respondent himself said of the advertisement, "reflects not only on me but on the other Commissioners and the community." Raising as it does the possibility that a good-faith critic of government will be penalized for his criticism, the proposition relied on by the Alabama courts strikes at the very center of the constitutionally protected area of free expression.[30] We hold that

30. Insofar as the proposition means only that the statements about police conduct libeled respondent by implicitly criticizing his ability to run the Police Depart-

such a proposition may not constitutionally be utilized to establish that an otherwise impersonal attack on governmental operations was a libel of an official responsible for those operations. Since it was relied on exclusively here, and there was no other evidence to connect the statements with respondent, the evidence was constitutionally insufficient to support a finding that the statements referred to respondent.

The judgment of the Supreme Court of Alabama is reversed and the case is remanded to that court for further proceedings not inconsistent with this opinion.

Reversed and remanded.

MR. JUSTICE BLACK, with whom MR. JUSTICE DOUGLAS joins, concurring.

I concur in reversing this half-million-dollar judgment against the New York Times Company and the four individual defendants. In reversing the Court holds that "the Constitution delimits a State's power to award damages for libel in actions brought by public officials against critics of their official conduct." I base my vote to reverse on the belief that the First and Fourteenth Amendments not merely "delimit" a State's power to award damages to "public officials against critics of their official conduct" but completely prohibit a State from exercising such a power. The Court goes on to hold that a State can subject such critics to damages if "actual malice" can be proved against them. "Malice," even as defined by the Court, is an elusive, abstract concept, hard to prove and hard to disprove. The requirement that malice be proved provides at best an evanescent protection for the right critically to discuss public affairs and certainly does not measure up to the sturdy safeguard embodied in the First Amendment. Unlike the Court, therefore, I vote to reverse exclusively on the ground that the Times and the individual defendants had an absolute unconditional constitutional right to publish in the Times advertisement their criticisms of the Montgomery agencies and officials. . . .

The half-million-dollar verdict does give dramatic proof, however, that state libel laws threaten the very existence of an American press virile enough to publish unpopular views on public affairs and bold enough to criticize the conduct of public officials. . . . In fact, briefs before us show that in Alabama there are now pending eleven libel suits by local and state officials against the Times seeking $5,600,000 and five such suits against the Columbia Broadcasting System seeking $1,700,000. Moreover, this technique for harassing and punishing a free press—now that it has been shown to be possible—is by no means limited to cases with racial overtones; it can be used in other fields

ment, recovery is also precluded in this case by the doctrine of fair comment. See American Law Institute, Restatement of Torts (1938), § 607. Since the Fourteenth Amendment requires recognition of the conditional privilege for honest misstatements of fact, it follows that a defense of fair comment must be afforded for honest expression of opinion based upon privileged, as well as true, statements of fact. Both defenses are of course defeasible if the public official proves actual malice, as was not done here.

where public feelings may make local as well as out-of-state newspapers easy prey for libel verdict seekers. . . . This record certainly does not indicate that any different verdict would have been rendered here whatever the Court had charged the jury about "malice," "truth," "good motives," "justifiable ends," or any other legal formulas which in theory would protect the press. Nor does the record indicate that any of these legalistic words would have caused the courts below to set aside or to reduce the half-million-dollar verdict in any amount.

. . .

. . . An unconditional right to say what one pleases about public affairs is what I consider to be the minimum guarantee of the First Amendment.[6]

I regret that the Court has stopped short of this holding indispensable to preserve our free press from destruction.

MR. JUSTICE GOLDBERG, with whom MR. JUSTICE DOUGLAS joins, concurring in the result.

. . .

In my view, the First and Fourteenth Amendments to the Constitution afford to the citizen and to the press an absolute, unconditional privilege to criticize official conduct despite the harm which may flow from excesses and abuses. . . .

. . .

. . . It may be urged that deliberately and maliciously false statements have no conceivable value as free speech. That argument, however, is not responsive to the real issue presented by this case, which is whether that freedom of speech which all agree is constitutionally protected can be effectively safeguarded by a rule allowing the imposition of liability upon a jury's evaluation of the speaker's state of mind. If individual citizens may be held liable in damages for strong words, which a jury finds false and maliciously motivated, there can be little doubt that public debate and advocacy will be constrained. And if newspapers, publishing advertisements dealing with public issues, thereby risk liability, there can also be little doubt that the ability of minority groups to secure publication of their views on public affairs and to seek support for their causes will be greatly diminished. . . .

. . .

This is not to say that the Constitution protects defamatory statements directed against the private conduct of a public official or private citizen. Freedom of press and of speech insures that government will respond to the will of the people and that changes may be obtained by peaceful means. Purely private defamation has little to do with the political ends of a self-governing society. The imposition of liability for

6. Cf. Meiklejohn, Free Speech and Its Relation to Self-Government (1948).

private defamation does not abridge the freedom of public speech or any other freedom protected by the First Amendment.[4] . . .

. . .

Notes and Questions

1. Why does the majority reject strict liability? Absolute privilege? Is the test for abuse of this privilege different from that applied in the usual qualified privilege case?

2. Do you consider either of the concurring opinions preferable to the majority approach?

3. Toward the end of the opinion the Court discusses whether the libel was of and concerning the plaintiff. Why isn't that a jury question? For a discussion of how the Times's argument that the article was not about the plaintiff expanded during the oral argument, see Miller and Barron, The Supreme Court, The Adversary System, and the Flow of Information to the Justices: A Preliminary Inquiry, 61 Va.L.Rev. 1187 (1975). See generally, Lewis, Annals of Law, The Sullivan Case, The New Yorker, Nov. 5, 1984 at 52.

4. Commenting after the Times case, Professor Kalven speculated on the case's future:

> The closing question, of course, is whether the treatment of seditious libel as the key concept for development of appropriate constitutional doctrine will prove germinal. It is not easy to predict what the Court will see in the *Times* opinion as the years roll by. It may regard the opinion as covering simply one pocket of cases, those dealing with libel of public officials, and not destructive of the earlier notions that are inconsistent only with the larger reading of the Court's action. But the invitation to follow a dialectic progression from public official to government policy to public policy to matters in the public domain, like art, seems to me to be overwhelming. If the Court accepts the invitation, it will slowly work out for itself the theory of free speech that Alexander Meiklejohn has been offering us for some fifteen years now.

Kalven, The New York Times Case: A Note on "The Central Meaning of the First Amendment," 1964 Sup.Ct.Rev. 191, 221. Does his prediction seem sound? Keep it in mind as we proceed.

5. The majority in the New York Times case did not explicitly condemn the concurring approaches. A few months later, in Garrison v. Louisiana, 379 U.S. 64 (1964), the Court, in an opinion by Justice Brennan, extended the *Times* rule to cases of criminal libel and also

4. In most cases, as in the case at bar, there will be little difficulty in distinguishing defamatory speech relating to private conduct from that relating to official conduct. I recognize, of course, that there will be a gray area. The difficulties of applying a public-private standard are, however, certainly of a different genre from those attending the differentiation between a malicious and nonmalicious state of mind. . . .

held that truth must be a defense in cases brought by public officials. The majority explained its refusal to protect deliberate falsity:

> Although honest utterance, even if inaccurate, may further the fruitful exercise of the right of free speech, it does not follow that the lie, knowingly and deliberately published about a public official, should enjoy a like immunity. At the time the First Amendment was adopted, as today, there were those unscrupulous enough and skillful enough to use the deliberate or reckless falsehood as an effective political tool to unseat the public servant or even topple an administration. [ ] That speech is used as a tool for political ends does not automatically bring it under the protective mantle of the Constitution. For the use of the known lie as a tool is at once at odds with the premises of democratic government and with the orderly manner in which economic, social, or political change is to be effected. Calculated falsehood falls into that class of utterances which "are no essential part of any exposition of ideas, and are of such slight social value as a step to truth that any benefit that may be derived from them is clearly outweighed by the social interest in order and morality. . . . " Chaplinsky v. New Hampshire, 315 U.S. 568, 572 (1942). Hence the knowingly false statement and the false statement made with reckless disregard of the truth, do not enjoy constitutional protection.

In an explicit, but unsuccessful, effort to avoid confusion between the different uses of malice, the Court observed that

> Debate on public issues will not be uninhibited if the speaker must run the risk that it will be proved in court that he spoke out of hatred; even if he did speak out of hatred, utterances honestly believed contribute to the free interchange of ideas and the ascertainment of the truth.

6. The next case was Rosenblatt v. Baer, 383 U.S. 75 (1966). Plaintiff Baer had been hired by the three elected county commissioners to be supervisor of a public recreation facility owned by Belknap County, New Hampshire. Defendant columnist attacked the management of the facility. In reversing plaintiff's state court judgment, Justice Brennan's majority opinion held that Baer might be a "public official" under the *Times* rule and that the trial judge's charge did not give the jury the correct "malice" standard. Justice Brennan noted that the *Times* decision was based on the importance of debate about public issues and about the public officials who work to resolve these issues. He then noted:

> Criticism of government is at the very center of the constitutionally protected area of free discussion . . . . It is clear . . . that the "public official" designation applies at the very least to those among the hierarchy of government employees who have, or appear to the public to have, substantial responsibility for or control over the conduct of government affairs.

> . . . Where a position in government has such apparent importance that the public has an independent interest in the qualifications and performance of the person who holds it, beyond the general public interest in the qualifications and performance of all government employees, both elements we identified in *New York Times* are present and the *New York Times* malice standards apply.[13]

Justice Douglas, concurring, thought that although the *Times* rule was too limited, at least it should apply to all public officials including night watchmen and file clerks. Further, he thought the privilege should apply to influential private citizens as well, such as industrial and labor leaders:

> If the term "public official" were a constitutional term, we would be stuck with it and have to give it content. But the term is our own; and so long as we are fashioning a rule of free discussion of public issues, I cannot relate it only to those who, by the Court's standard, are deemed to hold public office.

Finally, he asked why these rules should be limited to political matters and not extended to "speech at the lower levels of science, the humanities, the professions, agriculture, and the like?"

Justice Stewart's separate concurrence in *Rosenblatt* sought to express the affirmative values to be found in a libel action:

> The right of a man to the protection of his own reputation from unjustified invasion and wrongful hurt reflects no more than our basic concept of the essential dignity and worth of every human being—a concept at the root of any decent system of ordered liberty.

From the social perspective, he warned of dangers associated with Senator Joseph McCarthy:

> Moreover, the preventive effect of liability for defamation serves an important public purpose. For the rights and values of private personality far transcend mere personal interests. Surely if the 1950's taught us anything, they taught us that the poisonous atmosphere of the easy lie can infect and degrade a whole society.

7. In a pair of cases involving false charges made about a candidate for office, the Court unanimously extended the *Times* rationale to candidates because "it can hardly be doubted that the constitutional guarantee has its fullest and most urgent application precisely to the conduct of campaigns for political office." Monitor Patriot Co. v. Roy, 401 U.S. 265 (1971), and Ocala Star-Banner Co. v. Damron, 401 U.S. 295

13. It is suggested that this test might apply to a night watchman accused of stealing state secrets. But a conclusion that the *New York Times* malice standards apply could not be reached merely because a statement defamatory of some person in government employ catches the public's interest: that conclusion would virtually disregard society's interest in protecting reputation. The employee's position must be one which would invite public scrutiny and discussion of the person holding it, entirely apart from the scrutiny and discussion occasioned by the particular charges in controversy.

(1971). In *Roy,* the charge related to criminal activity that allegedly took place many years earlier. The Court decided that the *Times* rule should include "anything which might touch on an official's fitness for office" when a candidate's behavior is being discussed:

> The principal activity of a candidate in our political system . . . consists in putting before the voters every conceivable aspect of his public and private life that he thinks may lead the electorate to gain a good impression of him. A candidate who, for example, seeks to further his cause through the prominent display of his wife and children can hardly argue that his qualities as a husband or father remain of "purely private" concern. And the candidate who vaunts his spotless record and sterling integrity cannot convincingly cry "Foul!" when an opponent or an industrious reporter attempts to demonstrate the contrary. Any test adequate to safeguard First Amendment guarantees in this area must go far beyond the customary meaning of the phrase "official conduct."
>
> Given the realities of our political life, it is by no means easy to see what statements about a candidate might be altogether without relevance to his fitness for the office he seeks. The clash of reputations is the staple of election campaigns, and damage to reputation is, of course, the essence of libel. But whether there remains some exiguous area of defamation against which a candidate may have full recourse is a question we need not decide in this case.

The Court concluded that a "charge of criminal conduct, no matter how remote in time or place, can never be irrelevant to an official's or a candidate's fitness for office" for purposes of applying the *Times* rule.

In *Damron,* the candidate was said to have been charged with a crime, when in fact his brother was the one charged. Again, the *Times* rule applied.

8. There is still substantial disagreement over the lower levels of public officialdom. Public school teachers and coaches are one area of dispute. Cf. Milkovich v. The News-Herald, 15 Ohio St.3d 292, 473 N.E.2d 1191, 11 Med.L.Rptr. 1598 (1984), certiorari denied 106 S.Ct. 322, 12 Med.L.Rptr. 1366 (1985), (high school wrestling coach not a public official) with Johnston v. Corinthian Television Corp., 583 P.2d 1101, 3 Med.L.Rptr. 2518 (Okl.1978) (grade school wrestling coach is a public official). In their dissent from the denial of certiorari in *Milkovich,* Justices Brennan and Marshall argued that "school teachers should be included because the Court repeatedly has upheld their importance in preparing students for later life."

For an illuminating extended discussion of how the lower courts have undertaken to identify public officials, see Elder, Defamation, Public Officialdom, and the *Rosenblatt v. Baer* Criteria—A Proposal for Revivification Two Decades After New York Times Co. v. Sullivan, 33 Buffalo L.Rev. 579 (1985).

b. Public Figures

Shortly after *New York Times* and *Rosenblatt,* the Court considered two cases together: Curtis Publishing Co. v. Butts, and Associated Press v. Walker, 388 U.S. 130 (1967).

In *Butts* the defendant magazine had accused the plaintiff athletic director of disclosing his game plan to an opposing coach before their game. Although he was on the staff of a state university, Butts was paid by a private alumni organization. In *Walker,* the defendant news service reported that the plaintiff, a former United States Army general who resigned to engage in political activity, had personally led students in an attack on federal marshals who were enforcing a desegregation order at the University of Mississippi.

In both cases, lower courts had affirmed substantial jury awards against the defendants and had refused to apply the *Times* doctrine on the ground that public officials were not involved. The Supreme Court divided several ways on several issues, affirming *Butts,* 5–4, and reversing *Walker,* 9–0. Chief Justice Warren wrote the pivotal opinion in which he concluded that both men were "public figures" and that the standard developed in *New York Times* should apply to "public figures" as well:

> To me, differentiation between "public figures" and "public officials" and adoption of separate standards of proof for each has no basis in law, logic, or First Amendment policy. Increasingly in this country, the distinctions between governmental and private sectors are blurred. Since the depression of the 1930's and World War II there has been a rapid fusion of economic and political power, a merging of science, industry, and government, and a high degree of interaction between the intellectual, governmental, and business worlds. Depression, war, international tensions, national and international markets, and the surging growth of science and technology have precipitated national and international problems that demand national and international solutions. While these trends and events have occasioned a consolidation of governmental power, power has also become much more organized in what we have commonly considered to be the private sector. In many situations, policy determinations which traditionally were channeled through formal political institutions are now originated and implemented through a complex array of boards, committees, commissions, corporations, and associations, some only loosely connected with the Government. This blending of positions and power has also occurred in the case of individuals so that many who do not hold public office at the moment are nevertheless intimately involved in the resolution of important public questions or, by reason of their fame, shape events in areas of concern to society at large.
>
> Viewed in this context then, it is plain that although they are not subject to the restraints of the political process, "public

> figures," like "public officials," often play an influential role in ordering society. And surely as a class these "public figures" have as ready access as "public officials" to mass media of communication, both to influence policy and to counter criticism of their views and activities. Our citizenry has a legitimate and substantial interest in the conduct of such persons, and freedom of the press to engage in uninhibited debate about their involvement in public issues and events is as crucial as it is in the case of "public officials." The fact that they are not amenable to the restraints of the political process only underscores the legitimate and substantial nature of the interest, since it means that public opinion may be the only instrument by which society can attempt to influence their conduct.

He found that on the merits the standard had not been met in *Walker*. In *Butts* he found that defendant's counsel had deliberately waived the *Times* doctrine and he also found evidence establishing reckless behavior. He thus voted to reverse *Walker* and affirm *Butts*.

Justice Harlan, joined by Justices Clark, Stewart, and Fortas, argued that the *Times* standard should not apply to public figures because criticism of government was not involved:

> We consider and would hold that a "public figure" who is not a public official may also recover damages for a defamatory falsehood whose substance makes substantial danger to reputation apparent, on a showing of highly unreasonable conduct constituting an extreme departure from the standards of investigation and reporting ordinarily adhered to by responsible publishers. . . .

Applying that standard, Justice Harlan concluded that Walker had failed to establish a case, but that Butts had shown that the Saturday Evening Post ignored elementary precautions in preparing a potentially damaging story. Together with the Chief Justice's vote, there were five votes to affirm *Butts*.

Justices Brennan and White agreed with the Chief Justice in *Walker* but found no waiver in *Butts* and would have reversed both cases. They agreed with the Chief Justice that Butts had presented enough evidence to come within the *Times* standard but thought that errors in the charge required a new trial.

Justices Black and Douglas adhered to their position, urged that the *Times* rule be abandoned, and voted to reverse both cases.

Although some courts seemed to regard Justice Harlan's opinion as the prevailing opinion, in part because it came first in the reports, it should have been clear that the same "actual malice" standard that applied in "public official" cases also applied in "public figure" cases.

Proving Actual Malice. The distinction between public and private plaintiffs is relevant only to the question of whether the First Amendment requires that "actual malice" be shown. The Court has twice had occasion to consider aspects of the *Times* standard.

In St. Amant v. Thompson, 390 U.S. 727 (1968), the defendant, a candidate for public office, read on television a series of statements he had received from Mr. Albin, a member of a Teamsters' Union local. The statements, made under oath, falsely implied that the plaintiff, a deputy sheriff, had taken bribes. The defendant had not checked the facts stated by Albin, nor had he investigated Albin's reputation for veracity. The state court ruled that these failures to inquire further sufficed to meet the required standard of reckless disregard for the truth. The Supreme Court reversed and concluded that the standard of "reckless disregard" had not been met. It recognized that the term could receive no single "infallible definition" and that its outer limits would have to be developed in "case-to-case adjudication, as is true with so many legal standards for judging concrete cases, whether the standard is provided by the Constitution, statutes or case law." There "must be sufficient evidence to permit the conclusion that the defendant in fact entertained serious doubts as to the truth of his publication" in order for recklessness to be found. Anticipating the charge that this position would encourage publishers not to verify their assertions, Justice White, for the Court, stated:

> The defendant in a defamation action brought by a public official cannot, however, automatically insure a favorable verdict by testifying that he published with a belief that the statements were true. The finder of fact must determine whether the publication was indeed made in good faith. Professions of good faith will be unlikely to prove persuasive, for example, where a story is fabricated by the defendant, is a product of his imagination, or is based wholly on an unverified anonymous telephone call. Nor will they be likely to prevail when the publisher's allegations are so inherently improbable that only a reckless man would have put them in circulation. Likewise, recklessness may be found where there are obvious reasons to doubt the veracity of the informant or the accuracy of his reports.

Justice Fortas dissented on the ground that the failure to make "a good-faith check" of the statement was sufficient to establish "reckless disregard." How would the Court's test apply to an extreme partisan who would readily believe anything derogatory about his opponent?

In Herbert v. Lando, 441 U.S. 153 (1979), the plaintiff, an admitted public figure, sued the producer and reporter of the television program "60 Minutes" and the CBS network for remarks on the program about his behavior while in military service in Vietnam. During his deposition, Lando, the producer, generally responded but he refused to answer some questions about why he made certain investigations and not others; what he concluded about the honesty of certain people he interviewed for the program; and about conversations he had with Mike Wallace, the reporter, in the preparation of the program segment. Lando contended that these thought processes and internal editorial discussions were protected from disclosure by the First Amendment. The Supreme Court disagreed.

Justice White, for the Court, began by observing that liability for defamation was "well established in the common law when the First Amendment was adopted" and the framers showed no intention of abolishing it. During the period before *New York Times,* mental processes and attitudes were often relevant on questions of conditional privilege and defendants often testified to their good faith in writing a story. "Courts have traditionally admitted any direct or indirect evidence relevant to the state of mind of the defendant and necessary to defeat a privilege" or to justify punitive damages in egregious cases.

Justice White understood the defendants to be arguing that "the defendant's reckless disregard of truth, a critical element, could not be shown by direct evidence through inquiry into the thoughts, opinions and conclusions of the publisher but could be proved only by objective evidence from which the ultimate fact could be inferred." This was a barrier of some substance, "particularly when defendants themselves are prone to assert their good-faith belief in the truth of their publications, and libel plaintiffs are required to prove knowing or reckless falsehood with 'convincing clarity.' "

Justice White concluded that permitting plaintiffs "to prove their cases by direct as well as indirect evidence is consistent with the balance struck by our prior decisions." He "found it difficult to believe that error-avoiding procedures will be terminated or stifled simply because there is liability for culpable error and because the editorial process will itself be examined in the tiny percentage of instances in which error is claimed and litigation ensues."

Justice White did note that pretrial discovery techniques had led to "mushrooming litigation costs," but noted that this was happening in all areas of litigation. Until major changes in pretrial procedures were developed for all cases, the Court would rely on "what in fact and in law are ample powers of the district judge to prevent abuse." (In this case, Lando's deposition had continued intermittently for over a year and filled nearly 3,000 pages.) Trial judges were reminded that discovery should be allowed only for "relevant" evidence.

Justice Powell concurred in the opinion of the Court but wrote separately to emphasize that trial judges must consider First Amendment interests as well as the private interests of plaintiffs in deciding how much pretrial discovery to allow.

Three justices dissented in separate opinions. Justice Stewart asserted that when the issue involves "actual malice" the only concern is what "was in fact published. What was *not* published has nothing to do with the case."

Justice Brennan agreed with the Court that questions about a reporter's mental processes in preparing a story were unlikely to be "chilled in the very processes of thought" if his mind could be explored in litigation. The "exceedingly generous standards" of the New York Times case were sufficient protection. He disagreed, however, with allowing discovery of editorial discussions because he feared this would hinder useful exchanges. He would have required revelation of such discussions only after the plaintiff had first proven that he had been defamed by a false statement.

Justice Marshall agreed with the Court and with Justice Brennan as to the mental processes. He would have granted editorial discussions absolute protection from ever having to be disclosed. He also wanted trial judges to control discovery more rigorously. In defamation cases, "some plaintiffs are animated by something more than a rational calculus of their chances of recovery."

After remand from the Supreme Court, the trial judge granted summary judgment for the defense as to nine of eleven specific statements. On appeal from that ruling, the court of appeals affirmed as to the nine statements and then granted summary judgment on the two remaining statements. Herbert v. Lando, 781 F.2d 298, 12 Med.L.Rptr. 1593 (2d Cir.), certiorari denied, 106 S.Ct. 2916 (1986).

One of the two statements in question involved a witness that Herbert told CBS was not candid with the Army because he still had two sons in the service. CBS falsely reported on the program that the man told them he had no sons at all.

The second statement involved the CBS statement that "to a man" people they spoke to said that Herbert never once said to them that he had been relieved of his command because he had tried to press war crimes charges. The trial judge found that one man had indeed told CBS the opposite.

The court of appeals refused to send the two statements to trial because they raised essentially the same issue—Herbert's credibility—on which summary judgment had already been granted as to nine other statements. The rest of the material gave CBS "ample grounds" to believe that that Herbert had not reported war crimes to his superiors and was relieved of command for other reasons. The two remaining statements were "subsidiary to these larger views." The court suggested limits to this view:

> We do not mean to imply . . . that [CBS] could have published with impunity a vast collection of false statements so extensive as to portray Herbert as a liar in every respect. . . . Rather, we hold that if [CBS's] published view that Herbert lied about reporting war crimes was not actionable, other statements—even those that might be found to have been published with actual malice—should not be actionable if they merely imply the same view, and are simply an outgrowth of and subsidiary to those claims upon which it has been held there can be no recovery. . . . Our holding is thus limited to those cases in which statements allegedly made with knowing falsity or reckless disregard give rise to defamatory inferences that are only supportive of

> inferences that are not actionable. For Herbert to base his defamation action on subsidiary statements whose ultimate defamatory implications are themselves not actionable, we believe, would be a classic case of the tail wagging the dog.

In a footnote, the court asserted that the case would be very different "if a statement, otherwise actionable, implied that Herbert was generally a liar or even that he had lied on some significant matter unrelated to the truth of statements determined not to be actionable."

In addition, it held that the trial judge had correctly held that the "overall impact" of the broadcast did not state a separate basis for libel over and above the eleven specific statements. The thrust of the specific charges was identical to that claimed overall thrust—that Herbert was not being candid about the reasons he was relieved from command.

The court also concluded that the Atlantic Monthly's conduct in running an article by Lando did not amount to actual malice on the part of the magazine.

Herbert indirectly suggests problems when a reporter is asked to identify the source of a story. That subject is discussed at length at p. 581, infra.

After a jury finding for the public-figure plaintiff, the trial court granted the defendant newspaper a judgment notwithstanding the verdict. The trial court's ruling was affirmed. Long v. Arcell, 618 F.2d 1145, 6 Med.L.Rptr. 1430 (5th Cir.1980), certiorari denied, 449 U.S. 1083 (1981). The only evidence for the jury involved conflicting accounts of conversations:

> If the applicable burden of proof had been a preponderance of the evidence, a jury verdict either way would have to stand. Similarly, if liability could be imposed on a clear and convincing showing of negligence, we would be hard pressed to disregard the jury's verdict. . . . This record simply does not contain clear and convincing evidence that the defendants knew that their information was incorrect or had a "high degree of awareness of . . . [its] probable falsity." [*Garrison*].

In the Westmoreland case, after having ordered CBS to give plaintiff a copy of an in-house report on the production of the program, Judge Leval later ruled that the report was inadmissible at trial because it dealt only with the fairness of the CBS program:

> The fairness of the broadcast is not at issue in the libel suit. Publishers and reporters do not commit a libel in a public figure case by publishing unfair one-sided attacks. . . . The fact that a commentary is one sided and sets forth categorical accusations has no tendency to prove that the publisher believed it to be false. The libel law does not require the publisher to grant his accused equal time or a fair reply. . . . A publisher who honestly believes in the truth of his accusations . . . is under no obligation under the

libel law to treat the subject of his accusations fairly or evenhandedly.

Westmoreland v. CBS, Inc., 601 F.Supp. 66, 11 Med.L.Rptr. 1703 (S.D. N.Y.1985).

The Bose case. The requirement of clear and convincing evidence has been bolstered by a further explicit requirement that appellate courts must exercise "independent review" to assure that the required proof has been presented with the required clarity. In Bose Corp. v. Consumers Union, 466 U.S. 485, 10 Med.L.Rptr. 1625 (1984), a federal judge sitting as trier found actual malice and entered judgment against defendant magazine. The court of appeals exercised a review more rigorous than that authorized by Rule 52(a) of the Federal Rules of Civil Procedure—and reversed. It asserted that it was required to "independently examin[e] the record to ensure that the district court has applied properly the governing constitutional law and that the plaintiff has indeed satisfied its burden of proof."

The Supreme Court, 6–3, upheld the court of appeals. It analogized libel cases to those involving fighting words, child pornography, clear and present danger, and obscenity, in which the unprotected character of particular communications depends upon "judicial evaluation of special facts that have been deemed to have constitutional significance."

> The rule of independent appellate review . . . emerged from the exigency of deciding concrete cases; it is law in its purest form under our common law heritage. It reflects a deeply held conviction that judges—and particularly members of this Court—must exercise such review in order to preserve the precious liberties established and ordained by the Constitution. The question whether the evidence in the record in a defamation case is of the convincing clarity required to strip the utterance of First Amendment protection is not merely a question for the trier of fact. Judges, as expositors of the Constitution, must independently decide whether the evidence in the record is sufficient to cross the constitutional threshold that bars the entry of any judgment that is not supported by clear and convincing proof of "actual malice."

Should this type of review be conducted with respect to credibility and demeanor?

In a footnote, the Court stated that Rule 52(a) applied to the many findings of fact in defamation cases that do not involve the constitutional standard.

In Levine v. CMP Publications, Inc., 738 F.2d 660, 10 Med.L.Rptr. 2337 (5th Cir.1984) rehearing and rehearing en banc denied, 753 F.2d 1341 (5th Cir.1985), the majority concluded that *Bose* did not apply to private plaintiff cases. *Bose* is criticized in Monaghan, Constitutional Fact Review, 85 Colum.L.Rev. 229 (1985). See also, Bezanson, Fault,

Falsity and Reputation in Public Defamation Law: An Essay on Bose Corporation v. Consumers Union, 8 Hamline L.Rev. 105 (1985).

Summary Judgment Standard. In Anderson v. Liberty Lobby, Inc., 106 S.Ct. 2505, 12 Med.L.Rptr. 2297 (1986), the Court held, 6–3, that the standard for considering summary judgment motions under Federal Rule 56 must take into account the burden plaintiff will have to meet at trial. Since the plaintiff in the case was held to be public, the Court held that on the summary judgment motion, the judge must decide "whether the evidence in the record could support a reasonable jury finding either that the plaintiff has shown actual malice by clear and convincing evidence or that the plaintiff has not." In response to the argument that at the summary judgment stage plaintiff need show only enough to prevail on a "preponderance" standard, the Court responded that it "makes no sense to say that a jury could reasonably find for either party without some benchmark as to what standards govern its deliberations and within what boundaries its ultimate decision must fall, and these standards and boundaries are in fact provided by the applicable evidentiary standards."

The Court denied that its holding denigrated the role of the jury. "Credibility determinations, the weighing of the evidence, and the drawing of legitimate inferences from the facts are jury functions, not those of a judge, whether he is ruling on a motion for summary judgment or for a directed verdict."

In a footnote, the Court addressed footnote 9 in the Hutchinson v. Proxmire, p. 206, infra in which the Court had suggested that proof of actual malice "does not readily lend itself to summary disposition." That sentence "was simply an acknowledgment of our general reluctance" to grant special procedural protections to the media in addition to the substantive standards announced in cases like *Times* and *Gertz*. This was not relevant here since the Court in *Liberty Lobby* was announcing a general approach for all civil cases—that the summary judgment standard was to be the same as the one that the plaintiff must meet at the trial itself.

Justice Brennan dissented out of concern that the majority's decision "may erode the constitutionally enshrined role of the jury, and also undermine the usefulness of summary judgment procedure." On the latter point, he was concerned that the decision would confuse the lower courts.

Justice Rehnquist, joined by Chief Justice Burger, also dissented. He offered some examples that he thought showed that the majority's decision would have no effect on a large class of cases. His examples follow:

(1) On a summary judgment motion, "the plaintiff concedes that his only proof of malice is the testimony of witness A. Witness A testifies at his deposition that the reporter who wrote the story in question told him that she, the reporter, had done absolutely no checking on the story and had real doubts about whether or not it was

correct as to the plaintiff. The defendant's examination of witness A brings out that he has a prior convicion for perjury." Justice Rehnquist says that summary judgment must be denied if the majority means what it says about the jury judging credibility.

(2) At trial, after plaintiff's case the defendant moves for a directed verdict. The trial testimony repeats the deposition testimony except that now the trial judge has seen A's demeanor—"and noticed that he fidgets when answering critical questions, his eyes shift from the floor to the ceiling, and he manifests all other indicia traditionally attributed to perjurers." Justice Rehnquist asserts that no directed verdict may be entered.

(3) The defense puts on its case which includes three disinterested witnesses who were present at the alleged conversation. Each "categorically denies that the reporter made the claimed statement" to A. Justice Rehnquist asserts that a directed verdict must be denied to the defendant.

The lesson he drew was that the standard does not matter in a credibility case. Even in cases based on documentary evidence he asserted that inferences from the documents are "as much the prerogative of the finder of fact as inferences as to the credibility of witnesses." He thought that although at times it might be practicable to distinguish between "evidence which should satisfy reasonable men, and the evidence which should satisfy reasonable men beyond a reasonable doubt, . . . in the long run the line between them is too thin for day to day use" (quoting Judge Learned Hand). If that was true, it was even more true where the standard was convincing clarity.

c. *Private Persons*

Soon after deciding its first "public figure" cases, the Court confronted Rosenbloom v. Metromedia, Inc., 403 U.S. 29 (1971), involving a broadcaster's charge that a magazine distributor sold obscene material and was arrested in a police raid. Justice Brennan, joined by Chief Justice Burger and Justice Blackmun, held that the *Times* standards should be extended to "all discussion and communication involving matters of public or general concern, without regard to whether the persons involved are famous or anonymous." The arrest and the distributor's subsequent claims against the police were thought to fit this category and the *Times* standard was applied. In reaching that position Justice Brennan concluded that the focus on the plaintiff's status begun in the *Times* case bore "little relationship either to the values protected by the First Amendment or to the nature of our society. . . . Thus, the idea that certain 'public' figures have voluntarily exposed their entire lives to public inspection, while private individuals have kept theirs carefully shrouded from public view is, at best, a legal fiction." Discussion of a matter of public concern must be protected even when it involves an unknown person. If the states fear that private citizens will be unable to respond to adverse publicity, "the solution lies in the direction of ensuring their ability to respond, rather than in stifling public discussion of matters of public concern," a reference to possible use of the right of reply.

Justice White concurred on the narrow ground that the press is privileged to report "upon the official actions of public servants in full detail." Justice Black provided the fifth vote against liability for the reasons stated in his earlier opinions. Justices Harlan, Stewart and Marshall dissented on various grounds but they agreed that the private plaintiff should be required to prove no more than negligence in this case. Justice Marshall feared that Justice Brennan's standard might apply to every case because "all human events are arguably within the area of 'public or general concern.'" The dissenters also agreed that some limitations on damages should exist. Yet the dissenters disagreed with each other as well as with the plurality on major points. Justice Douglas did not participate in the case. The area was ripe for rethinking.

GERTZ v. ROBERT WELCH, INC.

Supreme Court of the United States, 1974.
418 U.S. 323, 94 S.Ct. 2997, 41 L.Ed.2d 789.
Noted 41 Brooklyn L.Rev. 389, 88 Harv.L.Rev. 139, 69 Nw.U.L.Rev. 960, 1974 Wis.L.Rev. 1167.

[Plaintiff, an attorney, was retained to represent the family of a youth killed by Nuccio, a Chicago policeman. In that capacity, plaintiff attended the coroner's inquest and filed an action for damages but played no part in a criminal proceeding in which Nuccio was convicted of second degree murder. Respondent published American Opinion, a monthly outlet for the views of the John Birch Society. As part of its efforts to alert the public to an alleged nationwide conspiracy to discredit local police, the magazine's editor engaged a regular contributor to write about the Nuccio episode. The article that appeared charged a frame-up against Nuccio and portrayed plaintiff as a "major architect" of the plot. It also falsely asserted that he had a long police record, was an official of the Marxist League for Industrial Democracy, and was a "Leninist" and a "Communist-fronter." The editor had no reason to doubt the charges and made no effort to verify them.

Gertz filed an action for libel in District Court because of diversity of citizenship. The trial judge first ruled that Gertz was not a public official or public figure and that under Illinois law there was no defense. The jury awarded $50,000. On further reflection, the judge decided that since a matter of public concern was being discussed, the *Times* rule should apply and he granted the defendant judgment notwithstanding the jury's verdict. He thus anticipated the plurality's approach in Rosenbloom v. Metromedia, Inc. The court of appeals, relying on the intervening decision in *Rosenbloom,* affirmed because of the absence of "clear and convincing" evidence of "actual malice."

According to St. Amant v. Thompson, p. 174, supra, failure to investigate, without more, could not establish reckless disregard for truth. Gertz appealed.]

MR. JUSTICE POWELL delivered the opinion of the Court.

. . .

II.

The principal issue in this case is whether a newspaper or broadcaster that publishes defamatory falsehoods about an individual who is neither a public official nor a public figure may claim a constitutional privilege against liability for the injury inflicted by those statements. The Court considered this question on the rather different set of facts presented in Rosenbloom v. Metromedia, Inc., 403 U.S. 29 (1971). Rosenbloom, a distributor of nudist magazines, was arrested for selling allegedly obscene material while making a delivery to a retail dealer. The police obtained a warrant and seized his entire inventory of 3,000 books and magazines. He sought and obtained an injunction prohibiting further police interference with his business. He then sued a local radio station for failing to note in two of its newscasts that the 3,000 items seized were only "reportedly" or "allegedly" obscene and for broadcasting references to "the smut literature racket" and to "girlie-book peddlers" in its coverage of the court proceeding for injunctive relief. He obtained a judgment against the radio station, but the Court of Appeals for the Third Circuit held the *New York Times* privilege applicable to the broadcast and reversed. 415 F.2d 892 (1969).

This Court affirmed the decision below, but no majority could agree on a controlling rationale. The eight Justices who participated in *Rosenbloom* announced their views in five separate opinions, none of which commanded more than three votes. The several statements not only reveal disagreement about the appropriate result in that case; they also reflect divergent traditions of thought about the general problem of reconciling the law of defamation with the First Amendment. One approach has been to extend the *New York Times* test to an expanding variety of situations. Another has been to vary the level of constitutional privilege for defamatory falsehood with the status of the person defamed. And a third view would grant to the press and broadcast media absolute immunity from liability for defamation. To place our holding in the proper context, we preface our discussion of this case with a review of the several *Rosenbloom* opinions and their antecedents.

. . .

In his opinion for the plurality in Rosenbloom v. Metromedia, Inc., 403 U.S. 29 (1971), Mr. Justice Brennan took the *New York Times* privilege one step further. He concluded that its protection should extend to defamatory falsehoods relating to private persons if the statements concerned matters of general or public interest. . . .

. . .

In *Rosenbloom* Mr. Justice Harlan . . . acquiesced in the application of the privilege to defamation of public figures but argued that a different rule should obtain where defamatory falsehood harmed a private individual. He noted that a private person has less likelihood "of securing access to channels of communication sufficient to rebut falsehoods concerning him" than do public officials and public figures, 403 U.S., at 70, and has not voluntarily placed himself in the public spotlight. Mr. Justice Harlan concluded that the States could constitutionally allow private individuals to recover damages for defamation on the basis of any standard of care except liability without fault.

. . . The principal point of disagreement among the three dissenters concerned punitive damages. Whereas Mr. Justice Harlan thought that the States could allow punitive damages in amounts bearing "a reasonable and purposeful relationship to the actual harm done . . . ," id., at 75, Mr. Justice Marshall concluded that the size and unpredictability of jury awards of exemplary damages unnecessarily exacerbated the problems of media self-censorship and that such damages should therefore be forbidden.

III.

We begin with the common ground. Under the First Amendment there is no such thing as a false idea. However pernicious an opinion may seem, we depend for its correction not on the conscience of judges and juries but on the competition of other ideas. But there is no constitutional value in false statements of fact. Neither the intentional lie nor the careless error materially advances society's interest in "uninhibited, robust, and wide-open" debate on public issues. . . .

Although the erroneous statement of fact is not worthy of constitutional protection, it is nevertheless inevitable in free debate. . . . And punishment of error runs the risk of inducing a cautious and restrictive exercise of the constitutionally guaranteed freedoms of speech and press. Our decisions recognize that a rule of strict liability that compels a publisher or broadcaster to guarantee the accuracy of his factual assertions may lead to intolerable self-censorship. Allowing the media to avoid liability only by proving the truth of all injurious statements does not accord adequate protection to First Amendment liberties. . . . The First Amendment requires that we protect some falsehood in order to protect speech that matters.

The need to avoid self-censorship by the news media is, however, not the only societal value at issue. If it were, this Court would have embraced long ago the view that publishers and broadcasters enjoy an unconditional and indefeasible immunity from liability for defamation. . . .

The legitimate state interest underlying the law of libel is the compensation of individuals for the harm inflicted on them by defamatory falsehood. We would not lightly require the State to abandon this purpose, for, as Mr. Justice Stewart has reminded us, the individual's right to the protection of his own good name

> "reflects no more than our basic concept of the essential dignity and worth of every human being—a concept at the root of any decent system of ordered liberty. The protection of private personality, like the protection of life itself, is left primarily to the individual States under the Ninth and Tenth Amendments. But this does not mean that the right is entitled to any less recognition by this Court as a basic of our constitutional system." Rosenblatt v. Baer, 383 U.S. 75, 92 (1966) (concurring opinion).

Some tension necessarily exists between the need for a vigorous and uninhibited press and the legitimate interest in redressing wrongful injury. . . .

The *New York Times* standard defines the level of constitutional protection appropriate to the context of defamation of a public person. Those who, by reason of the notoriety of their achievements or the vigor and success with which they seek the public's attention, are properly classed as public figures and those who hold governmental office may recover for injury to reputation only on clear and convincing proof that the defamatory falsehood was made with knowledge of its falsity or with reckless disregard for the truth. This standard administers an extremely powerful antidote to the inducement to media self-censorship of the common-law rule of strict liability for libel and slander. And it exacts a correspondingly high price from the victims of defamatory falsehood. Plainly many deserving plaintiffs, including some intentionally subjected to injury, will be unable to surmount the barrier of the *New York Times* test. Despite this substantial abridgment of the state law right to compensation for wrongful hurt to one's reputation, the Court has concluded that the protection of the *New York Times* privilege should be available to publishers and broadcasters of defamatory falsehood concerning public officials and public figures. [ ] We think that these decisions are correct, but we do not find their holdings justified solely by reference to the interest of the press and broadcast media in immunity from liability. Rather, we believe that the *New York Times* rule states an accommodation between this concern and the limited state interest present in the context of libel actions brought by public persons. For the reasons stated below, we conclude that the state interest in compensating injury to the reputation of private individuals requires that a different rule should obtain with respect to them.

Theoretically, of course, the balance between the needs of the press and the individual's claim to compensation for wrongful injury might be struck on a case-by-case basis. As Mr. Justice Harlan hypothesized, "it might seem, purely as an abstract matter, that the most utilitarian approach would be to scrutinize carefully every jury verdict in every libel case, in order to ascertain whether the final judgment leaves fully protected whatever First Amendment values transcend the legitimate state interest in protecting the particular plaintiff who prevailed." Rosenbloom v. Metromedia, Inc., 403 U.S., at 63 (footnote omitted). But this approach would lead to unpredictable results and uncertain expectations, and it could render our duty to supervise the lower courts unmanageable. Because an *ad hoc* resolution of the competing interests at stake in each particular case is not feasible, we must lay down broad rules of general application. Such rules necessarily treat alike various cases involving differences as well as similarities. Thus it is often true that not all of the considerations which justify adoption of a given rule will obtain in each particular case decided under its authority.

With that caveat we have no difficulty in distinguishing among defamation plaintiffs. The first remedy of any victim of defamation is self-help—using available opportunities to contradict the lie or correct the error and thereby to minimize its adverse impact on reputation. Public officials and public figures usually enjoy significantly greater access to the channels of effective communication and hence have a more realistic opportunity to counteract false statements than private individuals normally enjoy.[9] Private individuals are therefore more vulnerable to injury, and the state interest in protecting them is correspondingly greater.

More important than the likelihood that private individuals will lack effective opportunities for rebuttal, there is a compelling normative consideration underlying the distinction between public and private defamation plaintiffs. An individual who decides to seek governmental office must accept certain necessary consequences of that involvement in public affairs. He runs the risk of closer public scrutiny than might otherwise be the case. And society's interest in the officers of government is not strictly limited to the formal discharge of official duties. As the Court pointed out in Garrison v. Louisiana, 379 U.S., at 77, the public's interest extends to "anything which might touch on an official's fitness for office . . . . Few personal attributes are more germane to fitness for office than dishonesty, malfeasance, or improper motivation, even though these characteristics may also affect the official's private character."

Those classed as public figures stand in a similar position. Hypothetically, it may be possible for someone to become a public figure through no purposeful action of his own, but the instances of truly involuntary public figures must be exceedingly rare. For the most part those who attain this status have assumed roles of especial prominence in the affairs of society. Some occupy positions of such persuasive power and influence that they are deemed public figures for all purposes. More commonly, those classed as public figures have thrust

9. Of course, an opportunity for rebuttal seldom suffices to undo harm of defamatory falsehood. Indeed, the law of defamation is rooted in our experience that the truth rarely catches up with a lie. But the fact that the self-help remedy of rebuttal, standing alone, is inadequate to its task does not mean that it is irrelevant to our inquiry.

themselves to the forefront of particular public controversies in order to influence the resolution of the issues involved. In either event, they invite attention and comment.

Even if the foregoing generalities do not obtain in every instance, the communications media are entitled to act on the assumption that public officials and public figures have voluntarily exposed themselves to increased risk of injury from defamatory falsehood concerning them. No such assumption is justified with respect to a private individual. He has not accepted public office or assumed an "influential role in ordering society." Curtis Publishing Co. v. Butts, supra, at 164 (Warren, C.J., concurring in result). He has relinquished no part of his interest in the protection of his own good name, and consequently he has a more compelling call on the courts for redress of injury inflicted by defamatory falsehood. Thus, private individuals are not only more vulnerable to injury than public officials and public figures; they are also more deserving of recovery.

For these reasons we conclude that the States should retain substantial latitude in their efforts to enforce a legal remedy for defamatory falsehood injurious to the reputation of a private individual. The extension of the *New York Times* test proposed by the *Rosenbloom* plurality would abridge this legitimate state interest to a degree that we find unacceptable. And it would occasion the additional difficulty of forcing state and federal judges to decide on an *ad hoc* basis which publications address issues of "general or public interest" and which do not—to determine, in the words of Mr. Justice Marshall, "what information is relevant to self-government." Rosenbloom v. Metromedia, Inc., 403 U.S., at 79. We doubt the wisdom of committing this task to the conscience of judges. Nor does the Constitution require us to draw so thin a line between the drastic alternatives of the *New York Times* privilege and the common law of strict liability for defamatory error. The "public or general interest" test for determining the applicability of the *New York Times* standard to private defamation actions inadequately serves both of the competing values at stake. On the one hand, a private individual whose reputation is injured by defamatory falsehood that does concern an issue of public or general interest has no recourse unless he can meet the rigorous requirements of *New York Times.* This is true despite the factors that distinguish the state interest in compensating private individuals from the analogous interest involved in the context of public persons. On the other hand, a publisher or broadcaster of a defamatory error which a court deems unrelated to an issue of public or general interest may be held liable in damages even if it took every reasonable precaution to ensure the accuracy of its assertions. And liability may far exceed compensation for any actual injury to the plaintiff, for the jury may be permitted to presume damages without proof of loss and even to award punitive damages.

We hold that, so long as they do not impose liability without fault, the States may define for themselves the appropriate standard of liability for a publisher or broadcaster of defamatory falsehood injurious to a private individual. This approach provides a more equitable boundary between the competing concerns involved here. It recognizes the strength of the legitimate state interest in compensating private individuals for wrongful injury to reputation, yet shields the press and broadcast media from the rigors of strict liability for defamation. At least this conclusion obtains where, as here, the substance of the defamatory statement "makes substantial danger to reputation apparent." [11] This phrase places in perspective the conclusion we announce today. Our inquiry would involve considerations somewhat different from those discussed above if a State purported to condition civil liability on a factual misstatement whose content did not warn a reasonably prudent editor or broadcaster of its defamatory potential. Cf. Time, Inc. v. Hill, 385 U.S. 374 (1967). Such a case is not now before us, and we intimate no view as to its proper resolution.

IV

Our accommodation of the competing values at stake in defamation suits by private individuals allows the States to impose liability on the publisher or broadcaster of defamatory falsehood on a less demanding showing than that required by *New York Times*. This conclusion is not based on a belief that the considerations which prompted the adoption of the *New York Times* privilege for defamation of public officials and its extension to public figures are wholly inapplicable to the context of private individuals. Rather, we endorse this approach in recognition of the strong and legitimate state interest in compensating private individuals for injury to reputation. But this countervailing state interest extends no further than compensation for actual injury. For the reasons stated below, we hold that the States may not permit recovery of presumed or punitive damages, at least when liability is not based on a showing of knowledge of falsity or reckless disregard for the truth.

The common law of defamation is an oddity of tort law, for it allows recovery of purportedly compensatory damages without evidence of actual loss. Under the traditional rules pertaining to actions for libel, the existence of injury is presumed from the fact of publication. Juries may award substantial sums as compensation for supposed damage to reputation without any proof that such harm actually occurred. The largely uncontrolled discretion of juries to award damages where there is no loss unnecessarily compounds the potential of any system of liability for defamatory falsehood to inhibit the vigorous exercise of First Amendment freedoms. Additionally, the doctrine of presumed damages invites juries to punish unpopular opinion rather than to compensate individuals for injury sustained by the publication of a false fact. More to the point, the States have no substantial

11. Curtis Publishing Co. v. Butts, supra, at 155.

interest in securing for plaintiffs such as this petitioner gratuitous awards of money damages far in excess of any actual injury.

We would not, of course, invalidate state law simply because we doubt its wisdom, but here we are attempting to reconcile state law with a competing interest grounded in the constitutional command of the First Amendment. It is therefore appropriate to require that state remedies for defamatory falsehood reach no farther than is necessary to protect the legitimate interest involved. It is necessary to restrict defamation plaintiffs who do not prove knowledge of falsity or reckless disregard for the truth to compensation for actual injury. We need not define "actual injury," as trial courts have wide experience in framing appropriate jury instructions in tort actions. Suffice it to say that actual injury is not limited to out-of-pocket loss. Indeed, the more customary types of actual harm inflicted by defamatory falsehood include impairment of reputation and standing in the community, personal humiliation, and mental anguish and suffering. Of course, juries must be limited by appropriate instructions, and all awards must be supported by competent evidence concerning the injury, although there need be no evidence which assigns an actual dollar value to the injury.

We also find no justification for allowing awards of punitive damages against publishers and broadcasters held liable under state-defined standards of liability for defamation. In most jurisdictions jury discretion over the amounts awarded is limited only by the gentle rule that they not be excessive. Consequently, juries assess punitive damages in wholly unpredictable amounts bearing no necessary relation to the actual harm caused. And they remain free to use their discretion selectively to punish expressions of unpopular views. Like the doctrine of presumed damages, jury discretion to award punitive damages unnecessarily exacerbates the danger of media self-censorship, but, unlike the former rule, punitive damages are wholly irrelevant to the state interest that justifies a negligence standard for private defamation actions. They are not compensation for injury. Instead, they are private fines levied by civil juries to punish reprehensible conduct and to deter its future occurrence. In short, the private defamation plaintiff who establishes liability under a less demanding standard than that stated by *New York Times* may recover only such damages as are sufficient to compensate him for actual injury.

V.

Notwithstanding our refusal to extend the *New York Times* privilege to defamation of private individuals, respondent contends that we should affirm the judgment below on the ground that petitioner is either a public official or a public figure. There is little basis for the former assertion. Several years prior to the present incident, petitioner had served briefly on housing committees appointed by the mayor of Chicago, but at the time of publication he had never held any remunerative governmental position. Respondent admits this but argues that petitioner's appearance at the coroner's inquest rendered him a "de facto public official." Our cases recognize no such concept. Respondent's suggestion would sweep all lawyers under the *New York Times* rule as officers of the court and distort the plain meaning of the "public official" category beyond all recognition. We decline to follow it.

Respondent's characterization of petitioner as a public figure raises a different question. That designation may rest on either of two alternative bases. In some instances an individual may achieve such pervasive fame or notoriety that he becomes a public figure for all purposes and in all contexts. More commonly, an individual voluntarily injects himself or is drawn into a particular public controversy and thereby becomes a public figure for a limited range of issues. In either case such persons assume special prominence in the resolution of public questions.

Petitioner has long been active in community and professional affairs. He has served as an officer of local civic groups and of various professional organizations, and he has published several books and articles on legal subjects. Although petitioner was consequently well known in some circles, he had achieved no general fame or notoriety in the community. None of the prospective jurors called at the trial had ever heard of petitioner prior to this litigation, and respondent offered no proof that this response was atypical of the local population. We would not lightly assume that a citizen's participation in community and professional affairs rendered him a public figure for all purposes. Absent clear evidence of general fame or notoriety in the community, and pervasive involvement in the affairs of society, an individual should not be deemed a public personality for all aspects of his life. It is preferable to reduce the public-figure question to a more meaningful context by looking to the nature and extent of an individual's participation in the particular controversy giving rise to the defamation.

In this context it is plain that petitioner was not a public figure. He played a minimal role at the coroner's inquest, and his participation related solely to his representation of a private client. He took no part in the criminal prosecution of Officer Nuccio. Moreover, he never discussed either the criminal or civil litigation with the press and was never quoted as having done so. He plainly did not thrust himself into the vortex of this public issue, nor did he engage the public's attention in an attempt to influence its outcome. We are persuaded that the trial court did not err in refusing to characterize petitioner as a public figure for the purpose of this litigation.

We therefore conclude that the *New York Times* standard is inapplicable to this case and that the trial court erred in entering judgment for respondent. Because the jury was allowed to impose liability without fault and was permitted to presume damages without proof of injury, a new trial is necessary. We reverse and remand for further proceedings in accord with this opinion.

It is so ordered.

MR. JUSTICE BLACKMUN, concurring.

[Although I joined the *Rosenbloom* plurality opinion,] I am willing to join, and do join, the Court's opinion and its judgment for two reasons:

1. By removing the specters of presumed and punitive damages in the absence of *New York Times* malice, the Court eliminates significant and powerful motives for self-censorship that otherwise are present in the traditional libel action. By so doing, the Court leaves what should prove to be sufficient and adequate breathing space for a vigorous press. What the Court has done, I believe, will have little, if any, practical effect on the functioning of responsible journalism.

2. The Court was sadly fractionated in *Rosenbloom.* A result of that kind inevitably leads to uncertainty. I feel that it is of profound importance for the Court to come to rest in the defamation area and to have a clearly defined majority position that eliminates the unsureness engendered by *Rosenbloom's* diversity. If my vote were not needed to create a majority, I would adhere to my prior view. A definitive ruling, however, is paramount. [ ]

For these reasons, I join the opinion and the judgment of the Court.

MR. CHIEF JUSTICE BURGER, dissenting.

The doctrines of the law of defamation have had a gradual evolution primarily in the state courts. In New York Times Co. v. Sullivan, 376 U.S. 254 (1964), and its progeny this Court entered this field.

Agreement or disagreement with the law as it has evolved to this time does not alter the fact that it has been orderly development with a consistent basic rationale. In today's opinion the Court abandons the traditional thread so far as the ordinary private citizen is concerned and introduces the concept that the media will be liable for negligence in publishing defamatory statements with respect to such persons. Although I agree with much of what Mr. Justice White states, I do not read the Court's new doctrinal approach in quite the way he does. I am frank to say I do not know the parameters of a "negligence" doctrine as applied to the news media. Conceivably this new doctrine could inhibit some editors, as the dissents of Mr. Justice Douglas and Mr. Justice Brennan suggest. But I would prefer to allow this area of law to continue to evolve as it has up to now with respect to private citizens rather than embark on a new doctrinal theory which has no jurisprudential ancestry.

The petitioner here was performing a professional representative role as an advocate in the highest tradition of the law, and under that tradition the advocate is not to be invidiously identified with his client. The important public policy which underlies this tradition—the right to counsel—would be gravely jeopardized if every lawyer who takes an "unpopular" case, civil or criminal, would automatically become fair game for irresponsible reporters and editors who might, for example, describe the lawyer as a "mob mouthpiece" for representing a client with a serious prior criminal record, or as an "ambulance chaser" for representing a claimant in a personal injury action.

I would reverse the judgment of the Court of Appeals and remand for reinstatement of the verdict of the jury and the entry of an appropriate judgment on that verdict.

MR. JUSTICE DOUGLAS, dissenting.

. . .

. . . The standard announced today leaves the States free to "define for themselves the appropriate standard of liability for a publisher or broadcaster" in the circumstances of this case. This of course leaves the simple negligence standard as an option with the jury free to impose damages upon a finding that the publisher failed to act as "a reasonable man." With such continued erosion of First Amendment protection, I fear that it may well be the reasonable man who refrains from speaking.

Since in my view the First and Fourteenth Amendments prohibit the imposition of damages upon respondent for this discussion of public affairs, I would affirm the judgment below.

MR. JUSTICE BRENNAN, dissenting.

I agree with the conclusion, expressed in Part V of the Court's opinion, that, at the time of publication of respondent's article, petitioner could not properly have been viewed as either a "public official" or "public figure"; instead, respondent's article, dealing with an alleged conspiracy to discredit local police forces, concerned petitioner's purported involvement in "an event of public or general interest." . . .

. . .

Although acknowledging that First Amendment values are of no less significance when media reports concern private persons' involvement in matters of public concern, the Court refuses to provide, in such cases, the same level of constitutional protection that has been afforded the media in the context of defamation of public persons. The accommodation that this Court has established between free speech and libel laws in cases involving public officials and public figures—that defamatory falsehood be shown by clear and convincing evidence to have been published with knowledge of falsity or with reckless disregard of truth—is not apt, the Court holds, because the private individual does not have the same degree of access to the media to rebut defamatory comments as does the public person and he has not voluntarily exposed himself to public scrutiny.

While these arguments are forcefully and eloquently presented, I cannot accept them, for the reasons I stated in *Rosenbloom:*

> "The *New York Times* standard was applied to libel of a public official or public figure to give effect to the [First] Amendment's function to encourage ventilation of public issues, not because the public official has any less interest in protecting his reputation

than an individual in private life. While the argument that public figures need less protection because they can command media attention to counter criticism may be true for some very prominent people, even then it is the rare case where the denial overtakes the original charge. Denials, retractions, and corrections are not 'hot' news, and rarely receive the prominence of the original story. When the public official or public figure is a minor functionary, or has left the position that put him in the public eye . . . , the argument loses all of its force. In the vast majority of libels involving public officials or public figures, the ability to respond through the media will depend on the same complex factor on which the ability of a private individual depends: the unpredictable event of the media's continuing interest in the story. Thus the unproved, and highly improbable, generalization that an as yet [not fully defined] class of 'public figures' involved in matters of public concern will be better able to respond through the media than private individuals also involved in such matters seems too insubstantial a reed on which to rest a constitutional distinction." [ ]

. . .

. . . Under a reasonable-care regime, publishers and broadcasters will have to make pre-publication judgments about juror assessment of such diverse considerations as the size, operating procedures, and financial condition of the newsgathering system, as well as the relative costs and benefits of instituting less frequent and more costly reporting at a higher level of accuracy. [ ] Moreover, in contrast to proof by clear and convincing evidence required under the *Times* test, the burden of proof for reasonable care will doubtless be the preponderance of the evidence. . . .

The Court does not discount altogether the danger that jurors will punish for the expression of unpopular opinions. This probability accounts for the Court's limitation that "the States may not permit recovery of presumed or punitive damages, at least when liability is not based on a showing of knowledge of falsity or reckless disregard for the truth." [ ] But plainly a jury's latitude to impose liability for want of due care poses a far greater threat of suppressing unpopular views than does a possible recovery of presumed or punitive damages. Moreover, the Court's broad-ranging examples of "actual injury," including impairment of reputation and standing in the community, as well as personal humiliation, and mental anguish and suffering, inevitably allow a jury bent on punishing expression of unpopular views a formidable weapon for doing so. Finally, even a limitation of recovery to "actual injury"—however much it reduces the size or frequency of recoveries—will not provide the necessary elbowroom for First Amendment expression. . . .

On the other hand, the uncertainties which the media face under today's decision are largely avoided by the *Times* standard. I reject the argument that my *Rosenbloom* view improperly commits to judges the task of determining what is and what is not an issue of "general or public interest." [3] I noted in *Rosenbloom* that performance of this task would not always be easy. Id., at 49 n. 17. But surely the courts, the ultimate arbiters of all disputes concerning clashes of constitutional values, would only be performing one of their traditional functions in undertaking this duty. . . .

MR. JUSTICE WHITE, dissenting.

. . .

The impact of today's decision on the traditional law of libel is immediately obvious and indisputable. No longer will the plaintiff be able to rest his case with proof of a libel defamatory on its face or proof of a slander historically actionable *per se*. In addition, he must prove some further degree of culpable conduct on the part of the publisher, such as intentional or reckless falsehood or negligence. And if he succeeds in this respect, he faces still another obstacle: recovery for loss of reputation will be conditioned upon "competent" proof of actual injury to his standing in the community. This will be true regardless of the nature of the defamation and even though it is one of those particularly reprehensible statements that have traditionally made slanderous words actionable without proof of fault by the publisher or of the damaging impact of his publication. The Court rejects the judgment of experience that some publications are so inherently capable of injury, and actual injury so difficult to prove, that the risk of falsehood should be borne by the publisher, not the victim. . . .

So too, the requirement of proving special injury to reputation before general damages may be awarded will clearly eliminate the prevailing rule, worked out over a very long period of time, that, in the case of defamations not actionable *per se*, the recovery of general damages for injury to reputation may also be had if some form of material or pecuniary loss is proved. Finally, an inflexible federal

3. The Court, taking a novel step, would not limit application of First Amendment protection to private libels involving issues of general or public interest, but would forbid the States from imposing liability without fault in any case where the substance of the defamatory statement made substantial danger to reputation apparent. As in Rosenbloom v. Metromedia, Inc., 403 U.S. 29, 44 n. 12, 48–49, n. 17 (1971), I would leave open the question of what constitutional standard, if any, applies when defamatory falsehoods are published or broadcast concerning either a private or public person's activities not within the scope of the general or public interest.

Parenthetically, my Brother White argues that the Court's view and mine will prevent a plaintiff—unable to demonstrate some degree of fault—from vindicating his reputation by securing a judgment that the publication was false. This argument overlooks the possible enactment of statutes, not requiring proof of fault, which provide for an action for retraction or for publication of a court's determination of falsity if the plaintiff is able to demonstrate that false statements have been published concerning his activities. Cf. Note, Vindication of the Reputation of a Public Official, 80 Harv.L.Rev. 1730, 1739–1747 (1967). Although it may be that questions could be raised concerning the constitutionality of such statutes, certainly nothing I have said today (and, as I read the Court's opinion, nothing said there) should be read to imply that a private plaintiff, unable to prove fault, must inevitably be denied the opportunity to secure a judgment upon the truth or falsity of statements published about him. [ ]

standard is imposed for the award of punitive damages. No longer will it be enough to prove ill will and an attempt to injure.

These are radical changes in the law and severe invasions of the prerogatives of the States. . . .

. . .

The central meaning of *New York Times,* and for me the First Amendment as it relates to libel laws, is that seditious libel—criticism of government and public officials—falls beyond the police power of the State. . . .

. . .

The Court evinces a deep-seated antipathy to "liability without fault." But this catch-phrase has no talismanic significance and is almost meaningless in this context where the Court appears to be addressing those libels and slanders that are defamatory on their face and where the publisher is no doubt aware from the nature of the material that it would be inherently damaging to reputation. He publishes notwithstanding, knowing that he will inflict injury. With this knowledge, he must intend to inflict that injury, his excuse being that he is privileged to do so—that he has published the truth. But as it turns out, what he has circulated to the public is a very damaging falsehood. Is he nevertheless "faultless"? Perhaps it can be said that the mistake about his defense was made in good faith, but the fact remains that it is he who launched the publication knowing that it could ruin a reputation.

In these circumstances, the law has heretofore put the risk of falsehood on the publisher where the victim is a private citizen and no grounds of special privilege are invoked. The Court would now shift this risk to the victim, even though he has done nothing to invite the calumny, is wholly innocent of fault, and is helpless to avoid his injury. I doubt that jurisprudential resistance to liability without fault is sufficient ground for employing the First Amendment to revolutionize the law of libel, and in my view, that body of legal rules poses no realistic threat to the press and its service to the public. The press today is vigorous and robust. To me, it is quite incredible to suggest that threats of libel suits from private citizens are causing the press to refrain from publishing the truth. I know of no hard facts to support that proposition, and the Court furnishes none.

The communications industry has increasingly become concentrated in a few powerful hands operating very lucrative businesses reaching across the Nation and into almost every home. Neither the industry as a whole nor its individual components are easily intimidated, and we are fortunate that they are not. Requiring them to pay for the occasional damage they do to private reputation will play no substantial part in their future performance or their existence.

In any event, if the Court's principal concern is to protect the communications industry from large libel judgments, it would appear that its new requirements with respect to general and punitive damages would be ample protection. . . .

It is difficult for me to understand why the ordinary citizen should himself carry the risk of damage and suffer the injury in order to vindicate First Amendment values by protecting the press and others from liability for circulating false information. This is particularly true because such statements serve no purpose whatsoever in furthering the public interest or the search for truth but, on the contrary, may frustrate that search and at the same time inflict great injury on the defenseless individual. The owners of the press and the stockholders of the communications enterprises can much better bear the burden. And if they cannot, the public at large should somehow pay for what is essentially a public benefit derived at private expense.

. . .

. . . Whether or not the course followed by the majority is wise, and I have indicated my doubts that it is, our constitutional scheme compels a proper respect for the role of the States in acquitting their duty to obey the Constitution. Finding no evidence that they have shirked this responsibility, particularly when the law of defamation is even now in transition, I would await some demonstration of the diminution of freedom of expression before acting.

For the foregoing reasons, I would reverse the judgment of the Court of Appeals and reinstate the jury's verdict.

Notes and Questions

1. Why did the majority adhere to the *Times* rule for public officials? Public figures? Some have argued that Gertz was a public figure and that the case should have been analyzed along the lines of *Butts* and *Walker.* See Pember and Teeter, Privacy and the Press Since Time, Inc. v. Hill, 50 Wash.L.Rev. 57, 75 (1974): "Gertz was a member of numerous boards and commissions in Illinois, had published several books on civil rights matters, had frequently been honored by civil rights groups and had represented some rather famous clients. . . . His publishing record belies the notion that he was a poor, helpless, private individual who could not gain access to the press." Would that suffice to meet the standard?

2. Why does the majority in *Gertz* prefer its approach to the plurality's approach in *Rosenbloom?*

3. What do you think of Justice Blackmun's position? The third member of the *Rosenbloom* plurality, along with Justices Brennan and Blackmun, was Chief Justice Burger. In view of that, what do you think of his opinion in *Gertz,* which is reproduced in its entirety?

4. Justice White is particularly concerned about having private citizens bear the burden of defamation. If the media cannot bear the expense of the harm they do, the public should "somehow pay for what is essentially a public benefit derived at private expense." It has been widely observed that defamation law has been running counter to the

great trends sweeping other areas of tort law. Thus, personal injury law is moving toward greater imposition of liability, through techniques that increase chances of recovery in negligence cases and through development of new doctrines that increase the imposition of strict liability, as in the law of defective products. Meanwhile, defamation law has been moving the other way—from strict liability to denying liability in many cases unless something substantially greater than negligence can be shown. Is this an even stronger situation for strict liability than the defective products area? These cross currents have drawn comments from several sources.

For an extensive discussion of the crosscurrents in strict liability see Weiler, Defamation, Enterprise Liability, and Freedom of Speech, 17 U.Toronto L.J. 278 (1967). See also Kalven, The Reasonable Man and the First Amendment: Hill, Butts, and Walker, 1967 Sup.Ct.Rev. 267, 301–03. One commentator argues that the analogy is flawed because the other enterprises "have no choice but to accept the additional risk of liability if they are to continue their profit-making activities, while most broadcasters and publishers can avoid liability, without discontinuing their activities or reducing their profits, by ceasing to carry material that creates the risk of liability—i.e., by increasing their self-censorship." Anderson, Libel and Press Self-Censorship, 53 Texas L.Rev. 422, 432 n. 52 (1975). Can a sound argument be made for strict liability in this area?

5. *The Role of Negligence.* Justice Powell phrased the permissible standard in private citizen cases negatively: states may use whatever standard they wish "so long as they do not impose liability without fault." Even if it were theoretically possible to develop a standard more protective than strict liability but less rigorous than negligence, states have not made the attempt. Note that at the end of part IV, Justice Powell himself used "negligence" in a way that suggests that he thinks that it is the next level above strict liability: ". . . punitive damages are wholly irrelevant to the state interest that justifies a negligence standard for private defamation actions."

Almost all the states that have ruled on this question have set the state standard of care at negligence. A few have adopted some version of the *Rosenbloom* plurality's approach. The most important aberrational state, New York, has developed its own standard for private figure cases. In Chapadeau v. Utica Observer-Dispatch, Inc., 38 N.Y.2d 196, 341 N.E.2d 569, 379 N.Y.S.2d 61 (1975), New York's highest court held that "where the content of the article is arguably within the sphere of legitimate public concern, which is reasonably related to matters warranting public exposition, the party may recover; however, to warrant such recovery he must first establish, by a preponderance of the evidence, that the publisher acted in a grossly irresponsible manner without due consideration for the standards of information gathering and dissemination ordinarily followed by responsible parties." Is this closer to *Gertz* or *Rosenbloom?*

New York has since strengthened the defendant's position under *Chapadeau.* In Gaeta v. New York News, Inc., 62 N.Y.2d 340, 465 N.E.2d 802, 477 N.Y.S.2d 82, 10 Med.L.Rptr. 1966 (1984), defendant wrote a story about the impact of a state program transferring patients from mental hospitals to nursing homes. The story used "the familiar journalistic technique of featuring the experience of a single individual, as exemplifying in human terms the plight of many." The patient's mother sued on the ground that the article, in explaining how the patient's mental condition developed, libelously described the mother's conduct. The lower courts both concluded that the discussion of the mother was not "arguably within the sphere of legitimate public concern" and that the *Chapadeau* protection did not apply. This led them to rule that ordinary negligence principles would apply.

The court of appeals reversed on the ground that references to the mother did indeed come within *Chapadeau:*

> [*Chapadeau*] recognizes the need for judgment and discretion to be exercised by journalists, subject only to review by the courts to protect against clear abuses. Determining what editorial content is of legitimate public interest and concern is a function for editors. . . . The press, acting responsibly, and not the courts must make the *ad hoc* decisions as to what are matters of public concern, and while subject to review, editorial judgments as to news content will not be second-guessed so long as they are sustainable.

The standard developed by the court bears a striking resemblance to that used by the Federal Communications Commission in reviewing determinations made by licensees about whether the fairness doctrine applies to something they have broadcast.

6. The general reliance on negligence as the standard raises several important issues. The first is presented by Justice Powell's statement that his standard applies where "the substance of the defamatory statement 'makes substantial danger to reputation apparent.' . . . Our inquiry would involve considerations somewhat different from those discussed above if a State purported to condition civil liability on a factual misstatement whose content did not warn a reasonably prudent editor or broadcaster of its defamatory potential." Does this apply to articles using fictitious names? Does it apply to an article announcing the birth of a child or the marriage of two people? Although the text may be flattering, or at least not defamatory, the editor must know that some combination of extrinsic facts can render almost any passage defamatory. Might Justice Powell mean that there is no duty to investigate the surrounding circumstances or the truth of charges that on their face do not appear defamatory?

A second problem is suggested by Justice Powell's use of the phrase "reasonably prudent editor or broadcaster." The phrase "reasonably prudent" makes sense when applied to automobile drivers or airplane pilots or even physicians. But how is that phrase to be applied to a field in which the media vary from sedate, if not stodgy, journals at one extreme to racy tabloids and scandal sheets at the other; from those that treat public relations releases as news to those that disbelieve every statement made by government officials and engage in extensive investigative reporting? What about differences between editors at very well financed and profitable publications or broadcast stations and those at marginal media with small, or nonexistent, research staffs and budgets too tight to pay for a resident libel lawyer?

The Restatement, Second, Torts § 580B, comment (h), suggests that the thoroughness of the investigation varies with the following factors: 1. "The time element"—investigations may be shorter for topical news than for a story that has no time pressure. 2. "The nature of the interest promoted by publication"—a story informing the public of matters important in a democracy may warrant quicker publication than a story involving "mere gossip." 3. "Potential damage to plaintiff if the communication proves to be false"—is the statement defamatory on its face; how many readers will understand the defamation; how harmful is the charge.

One court has added two somewhat overlapping factors: the nature and reliability of the source of the information and the "reasonableness in checking the veracity of the information, considering its cost in terms of money, time, personnel, urgency of the publication, nature of the news and any other pertinent element." Torres-Silva v. El Mundo, 3 Med.L.Rptr. 1508 (P.R.1977). Are these likely to be useful in a negligence case? Might others be added? See Bloom, Proof of Fault in Media Defamation Litigation, 38 Vand.L.Rev. 247 (1985).

Some have questioned the emphasis on time pressure. In "Defamation and the First Amendment," 52 Colo.L.Rev. 1 (1980), the former Chief Justice of Illinois, Walter Schaefer, said:

> It has been suggested that the press, television, and radio all operate under severe time constraints and that this consideration should excuse or justify defamatory statements. It should not be forgotten, however, that these time constraints are entirely self-imposed. Apparently the media people believe that for competitive reasons it is desirable to be first with a particular news story. My own impression is that the public is massively unconcerned about that question. But if my impression is wrong, deadline pressures afford no more justification for harm caused by negligent attacks upon reputation than for harm caused by a reporter's negligent driving in his haste to cover a story. Both negligent acts are and have been insurable.

Another question is whether the standard should be stated in terms of professional negligence or ordinary due care. This may be significant both in formulating the standard and in requiring expert testimony to show the standard and the deviation. The few states that have addressed this question have split. In Gobin v. Globe Pub. Co., 216 Kan. 223, 531 P.2d 76 (1975), the court stated the standard to be "the conduct of the reasonably careful publisher or broadcaster in the community or in similar communities under the existing circumstances." Troman v. Wood, 62 Ill.2d 184, 340 N.E.2d 292 (1975), rejected the professional negligence approach because "it would make the prevailing newspaper practices in a community controlling. In a community having only a single newspaper, the approach suggested would permit that paper to establish its own standards. And in any community it might tend, in 'Gresham's law' fashion, toward a progressive depreciation of the standard of care." Has this been a problem in medical malpractice?

The Restatement, Second § 580B, comment (g), states that a professional disseminator of news "is held to the skill and experience normally possessed by members of that profession. Customs and practices within the profession are relevant in applying the negligence standard, which is, to a substantial degree, set by the profession itself, though a custom is not controlling." Is this a compromise solution?

7. *Plaintiffs Must Prove Falsity.* Although the Court's focus was on the fault requirement, questions still lingered about who had the burden of proof on the question of truth or falsity. In Philadelphia Newspapers, Inc. v. Hepps, 106 S.Ct. 1558, 12 Med.L.Rptr. 1977 (1986), the Court, 5–4, held that the plaintiff had the burden of proving falsity in cases brought by private plaintiffs at least where the speech was of public concern. For the majority, Justice O'Connor concluded that to "ensure that true speech on matters of public concern is not deterred, we hold that the common-law presumption that defamatory speech is false cannot stand when a plaintiff seeks damages against a media defendant for speech of public concern." (Two of the five joining the majority opinion rejected the limitation to "media" defendants.) Even though this burden would "insulate from liability some speech that is false, but unprovably so," that result is essential to avoid the "chilling" effect that would otherwise accompany true speech on matters of public concern.

The majority asserted that its conclusion added "only marginally to the burdens" on libel plaintiffs because a jury is more likely to accept a "contention that the defendant was at fault in publishing the statements at issue if convinced that the relevant statements were false. As a practical matter, then, evidence offered by plaintiffs on the publisher's fault . . . will generally encompass evidence of the falsity of the matters asserted." The majority reserved the question of the quantity of proof of falsity that a plaintiff must present.

Justice Stevens, for the dissenters, thought the majority result "pernicious." He posited a situation in which a defendant, knowing that the plaintiff could not prove the statement false, deliberately lied about the plaintiff. This situation might occur due to the passage of time, the loss of critical records, or the absence of an eyewitness. The majority's analysis was an "obvious blueprint for character assassination." In his view, as long as publishers are protected by the fault requirement, "there can be little, if any, basis for a concern that a significant amount of true speech will be deterred unless the private person victimized by a malicious libel can also carry the burden of proving falsity."

In a footnote, Justice Stevens asserted that if the issue were before the Court, he "would be inclined to the view that public figures should not bear the burden of disproving the veracity of accusations made against them with 'actual malice' as the *New York Times* Court used that term." The contrary remarks in several cases were not necessary to the decisions in those cases, and the actual malice rule is enough protection.

Some of the nuances about "public concern" and "media" will become clearer after the Greenmoss case, p. 226, infra.

8. The *Gertz* retrial, which did not occur for several years, produced a jury verdict for plaintiff for $100,000 compensatory damages and $300,000 punitive damages. On appeal, the court affirmed. It concluded that the jury could find "actual malice" on the editor of the magazine who solicited a person with a "known and unreasonable propensity to label persons or organizations as Communist, to write the article; and after the article was submitted, made virtually no effort to check the validity of statements that were defamatory *per se* of Gertz, and in fact added further defamatory material based on [the writer's] 'facts.' "

In addition, the court concluded that the writer's conduct could be imputed to the magazine because of an agency relationship between them. The writer "was solicited to write this specific article, was given the story line and background material, was reimbursed for his expenses, and kept in contact with [the editor] during the preparation of the article. These facts, particularly the significant control exercised by [the editor] over the content and focus of the article, are sufficient to establish an agency relationship." Gertz v. Robert Welch, Inc., 680 F.2d 527, 8 Med.L.Rptr. 1769 (7th Cir.1982), certiorari denied 459 U.S. 1226 (1983).

Apparently, the defendant was uninsured and had to sell property to meet the judgment.

9. For a similar discussion see Herbert v. Lando, 596 F.Supp. 1178, 11 Med.L.Rptr. 1233 (S.D.N.Y.1984). One aspect of that case involved Atlantic Monthly's motion for summary judgment.

> The case against Atlantic Monthly is that it published an unsolicited, inherently plausible article authored by Lando, an apparently responsible journalist, who responded satisfactorily to whatever questions Atlantic's editors and attorneys raised about the article's contents. Atlantic conducted no independent inquiry into the facts because that is not its practice. It maintains no research department.

The judge held that Atlantic was under no obligation to investigate on these facts. Lando was "not a wild-eyed unknown, mouthing an improbable yarn about a prominent person. Rather, he was known to Atlantic's editors to be a former reporter with *Time* magazine and present producer of a respected (by many, at least) national news program." Lando's previous article for defendant had impressed the staff. This article "while unfavorable to Herbert, cannot be regarded as inherently implausible." It quoted at length from the transcript of the 60 Minutes program. "The fact that much of the article's substance had previously been broadcast by a respected news program was a factor the Atlantic editors were entitled to consider." The fact that others were expressing doubt about Herbert at the same time was also something the editors could consider.

Nothing in the *St. Amant* test imposed any duty to investigate in this situation. Finally, nothing in the editing process—the use of headlines or the suggestion that Lando add an attributed unfavorable quote about Herbert—suggested actual malice:

> I regard Atlantic's "contribution" to the article as nothing more than editorial techniques intended to attract and retain the reader's eye, and summarize the contents of the article. As such, I do not regard them as constituting Atlantic's "endorsement" of the article, in the sense of proclaiming an independent *imprimatur* of its truth. However, even if these editorial contributions should be so regarded, there is no proof that Atlantic's editors know of the actual or probable falsity of anything in the article."

An appeal of this decision went off on other grounds. Herbert v. Lando, 781 F.2d 298, 12 Med.L.Rptr. 1593 (2d Cir.), certiorari denied, 106 S.Ct. 2916 (1986). See also Hotchner v. Castillo-Puche, 551 F.2d 910, 2 Med.L.Rptr. 1545 (2d Cir.1977).

Would it raise First Amendment problems if a state were to conclude that actual malice on the part of an employee in the print shop or a dishonest reporter could subject the publisher to compensatory and punitive damages?

d. *The Public-Private Distinction*

The Firestone Case. The first significant application of *Gertz* occurred in Time, Inc. v. Firestone, 424 U.S. 448 (1976), in which a magazine reported, perhaps incorrectly, that a member of "one of America's wealthier industrial families" had received a divorce because of his wife's adultery. The divorce decree was probably based on either "extreme cruelty" or "lack of domestication," but the judge was not explicit. The state court upheld the wife's defamation award of $100,000. Time argued that the "actual malice" standard should apply for two reasons. First, it asserted that the plaintiff was a public figure, but the majority disagreed: "Respondent did not assume any role of especial prominence in the affairs of society, other than perhaps Palm Beach society, and she did not thrust herself to the forefront of any particular public controversy in order to influence the resolution of the issues involved in it." The Court rejected the argument that because the case was of great public interest, the respondent must have been a public figure: "Dissolution of a marriage through judicial proceedings is not the sort of 'public controversy' referred to in *Gertz,* even though the marital difficulties of extremely wealthy individuals may be of interest to some portion of the reading public." Moreover, the Court observed, plaintiff was compelled to go to court to seek relief in a marital dispute and her involvement was not voluntary. The fact that she held "a few" press conferences during the case did not change her otherwise private status. She did not attempt to use them to influence the outcome of the trial or to thrust herself into an unrelated dispute.

The second claim was that reporting of judicial proceedings should never lead to liability for negligence. Justice Rehnquist's opinion for the Court rejected the contention:

> It may be that all reports of judicial proceedings contain some informational value implicating the First Amendment, but recognizing this is little different from labeling all judicial proceedings matters of "public or general interest," as that phrase was used by the plurality in *Rosenbloom.* Whatever their general validity, use of such subject matter classifications to determine the extent of constitutional protection afforded defamatory falsehoods may too often result in an improper balance between the competing interests in this area. It was our recognition and rejection of this weakness in the *Rosenbloom* test which led us in *Gertz* to eschew a subject matter test for one focusing upon the character of the defamation plaintiff. [ ] By confining inquiry to whether a plaintiff is a public officer or a public figure who might be assumed to "have voluntarily exposed themselves to increased risk of injury from defamatory falsehood," we sought a more appropriate accommodation between the public's interest in an uninhibited press and its equally compelling need for judicial redress of libelous utterances. Cf. Chaplinsky v. New Hampshire, 315 U.S. 568 (1942).
>
> Presumptively erecting the *New York Times* barrier against all plaintiffs seeking to recover for injuries from defamatory falsehoods published in what are alleged to be reports of judicial proceedings would effect substantial depreciation of the individual's interest in protection from such harm, without any convincing assurance that such a sacrifice is required under the First Amendment. And in some instances such an undiscriminating approach might achieve results directly at odds with the constitutional balance intended. Indeed, the article upon which the *Gertz* libel action was based purported to be a report on the murder trial of a Chicago police officer. [ ] Our decision in that case should make it clear that no such blanket privilege for reports of judicial proceedings is to be found in the Constitution.
>
> It may be argued that there is still room for application of the *New York Times* protections to more narrowly focused reports of what actually transpires in the courtroom. But even so narrowed,

the suggested privilege is simply too broad. Imposing upon the law of private defamation the rather drastic limitations worked by *New York Times* cannot be justified by generalized references to the public interest in reports of judicial proceedings. The details of many, if not most, courtroom battles would add almost nothing towards advancing the uninhibited debate on public issues thought to provide principal support for the decision in *New York Times.* [ ] And while participants in some litigation may be legitimate "public figures," either generally or for the limited purpose of that litigation, the majority will more likely resemble respondent, drawn into a public forum largely against their will in order to attempt to obtain the only redress available to them or to defend themselves against actions brought by the State or by others. There appears little reason why these individuals should substantially forfeit that degree of protection which the law of defamation would otherwise afford them simply by virtue of their being drawn into a courtroom. The public interest in accurate reports of judicial proceedings is substantially protected by *Cox Broadcasting Co.* [Chap. III]. As to inaccurate and defamatory reports of facts, matters deserving no First Amendment protection, [ ], we think *Gertz* provides an adequate safeguard for the constitutionally protected interests of the press and affords it a tolerable margin for error by requiring some type of fault.

The Court vacated the judgment for lack of consideration of fault by either the jury or any of the state courts. Justices Powell and Stewart, though joining the majority, asserted that the grounds of divorce were so unclear in this "bizarre case" that there was "substantial evidence" that Time was not negligent. Justice White, believing that the state courts had found negligence, would have affirmed the award. In addition, since the article had been written before *Rosenbloom* and *Gertz,* he saw no reason to require any showing of fault. Justice Brennan dissented on the ground that reports of judicial proceedings should not lead to liability unless the errors are deliberate or reckless. He observed that even those who would confine the central meaning of the First Amendment to "explicitly political speech" would extend protection to speech concerned with governmental behavior. Justice Marshall, dissenting, thought that plaintiff was a public figure; he also doubted the existence of negligence. Justice Stevens took no part.

Mrs. Firestone, claiming vindication on the point of the inaccuracy of the report, dropped the case before retrial.

The Wolston Case. In Wolston v. Reader's Digest Ass'n, 443 U.S. 157, 5 Med.L.Rptr. 1273 (1979), defendant published a book in 1974 that included plaintiff's name on a list of "Soviet agents identified in the United States." A footnote said that the list consisted of agents "who were convicted of espionage or falsifying information or perjury and/or contempt charges following espionage indictments or who fled to the Soviet bloc to avoid prosecution."

Plaintiff had been convicted of contempt of court in 1958 for failing to appear before a grand jury investigating Soviet espionage. He was never indicted for any of the other offenses. At the time, plaintiff did not attempt to debate the propriety of his behavior. During the six weeks between his failure to appear and his sentencing, plaintiff's case was the subject of 15 stories in Washington and New York newspapers. "This flurry of publicity subsided" following the sentencing, and plaintiff "succeeded for the most part in returning to the private life he had led" prior to the subpoena.

When plaintiff sued for libel, the lower courts held that in both 1958 and 1974 he was a public figure and that summary judgment was properly granted against him because he had presented no evidence of actual malice. (In the Supreme Court, plaintiff abandoned the argument that even if he was a public figure in 1958, he was no longer in 1974.)

The Supreme Court reversed. For the majority, Justice Rehnquist reviewed the "self-help" and the "assumption of risk" explanations developed in *Gertz* to support the public-private distinction, and concluded that the second was the more important. He then quoted the passage from *Gertz* stating that some persons may be public figures because they "occupy positions of such persuasive power and influence that they are deemed public figures for all purposes. More commonly, those classed as public figures have thrust themselves to the forefront of particular public controversies in order to influence the resolution of the issues involved."

Justice Rehnquist concluded that plaintiff had neither "voluntarily thrust" nor "injected" himself into the forefront of the controversy surrounding the investigation of Soviet espionage in the United States. (He also noted that it was difficult to determine the relevant "public controversy" into which plaintiff was alleged to have thrust himself.)

> It would be more accurate to say that petitioner was dragged unwillingly into the controversy. The government pursued him in its investigation. Petitioner did fail to respond to a grand jury subpoena, and this failure, as well as his subsequent citation for contempt, did attract media attention. But the mere fact that petitioner voluntarily chose not to appear before the grand jury, knowing that his action might be attended by publicity, is not decisive on the question of public figure status. In *Gertz,* we held that an attorney was not a public figure even though he voluntarily associated himself with a case that was certain to receive extensive media exposure. 418 U.S., at 352. We emphasized that a court must focus on the "nature and extent of an individual's participation in the particular controversy giving rise to the defamation." Ibid. In *Gertz,* the attorney took no part in the criminal prosecution, never discussed the litigation with the press and limited his

participation in the civil litigation solely to his representation of a private client. Ibid. Similarly, petitioner never discussed this matter with the press and limited his involvement to that necessary to defend himself against the contempt charge. It is clear that petitioner played only a minor role in whatever public controversy there may have been concerning the investigation of Soviet espionage. We decline to hold that his mere citation for contempt rendered him a public figure for purposes of comment on the investigation of Soviet espionage.

Petitioner's failure to appear before the grand jury and citation for contempt no doubt were "newsworthy," but the simple fact that these events attracted media attention also is not conclusive of the public figure issue. A private individual is not automatically transformed into a public figure just by becoming involved in or associated with a matter that attracts public attention. To accept such reasoning would in effect reestablish the doctrine advanced by the plurality opinion in Rosenbloom v. Metromedia, Inc., [ ], which concluded that the *New York Times* standard should extend to defamatory falsehoods relating to private persons if the statements involved matters of public or general concern. We repudiated this proposition in *Gertz* and in *Firestone,* however, and we reject it again today. A libel defendant must show more than mere newsworthiness to justify application of the demanding burden of *New York Times.* [ ]

Nor do we think that petitioner engaged the attention of the public in an attempt to influence the resolution of the issues involved. . . . He did not in any way seek to arouse public sentiment in his favor and against the investigation. Thus, this is not a case where a defendant invites a citation for contempt in order to use the contempt citation as a fulcrum to create public discussion about the methods being used in connection with an investigation or prosecution. . . . In short, we find no basis whatsoever for concluding that petitioner relinquished, to any degree, his interest in the protection of his own name.

This reasoning leads us to reject the further contention of respondents that any person who engages in criminal conduct automatically becomes a public figure for purposes of comment on a limited range of issues relating to his conviction. [ ] We declined to accept a similar argument in Time, Inc. v. Firestone.

Here Justice Rehnquist quoted the passage from *Firestone* about protecting those drawn into a courtroom. He concluded, "We think that these observations remain sound, and that they control the disposition of this case. To hold otherwise would create an 'open season' for all who sought to defame persons convicted of a crime."

Justice Blackmun, joined by Justice Marshall, concurred in the result. He thought that the majority "seems to hold . . . that a person becomes a limited-issue public figure only if he literally or figuratively 'mounts a rostrum' to advocate a particular view. I see no need to adopt so restrictive a definition . . . on the facts before us." He would hold that even if plaintiff had acquired public figure status in 1958, "he clearly had lost that distinction" by 1974. Although plaintiff had not pressed that argument in the Supreme Court, Justice Blackmun, noting that the lower courts had decided the point, thought it still open as a basis for decision.

He quoted the passage from *Gertz* indicating that a person may become a public figure for a limited range of issues if he "voluntarily injects himself or is drawn into a particular public controversy." (Justice Rehnquist did not refer to that passage.) Even if, in 1958, plaintiff had access to the press to rebut the charge that he was a Soviet spy, it "would strain credulity" to suggest that he could command such media interest in 1974. Also, his "conscious efforts to regain anonymity" removed any assumption of risk justification for calling him a public figure in 1974.

Justice Blackmun recognized that his view put a more difficult burden on historians than on contemporary commentators. But this did "no violence to First Amendment values. While historical analysis is no less vital to the market place of ideas than reporting current events, historians work under different conditions than do their media counterparts." The reporter must move quickly, while the historian "has both the time for reflection and the opportunity to investigate the veracity of the pronouncements he makes."

Justice Brennan dissented. He thought plaintiff a public figure for the limited purpose of comment on his connection with espionage in the 1940s and 1950s. He remained a public figure in 1974 because the issue of Soviet espionage "continues to be a legitimate topic of debate today . . . ." But he found enough evidence of "actual malice" to warrant a trial under the *Times* standard.

The Hutchinson Case. In the Hutchinson case, decided the same day as *Wolston,* a research scientist had applied for, and received, grants amounting to more than $500,000 from various federal organizations to fund his efforts to develop an "objective measure of aggression, concentrating upon the behavior patterns of certain animals, such as the clenching of jaws when they were exposed to various aggravating stressful stimuli." The research reports were published in scientific journals.

In March, 1975, Senator Proxmire initiated his Golden Fleece Award of the Month to publicize what he considered wasteful government spending. His second award went to the agencies that had sponsored plaintiff's research. The Senator and an assistant prepared a speech for the Senate, issued a press release and newsletters, and phoned federal agencies. Plaintiff sued the Senator and his aide for defamation, claiming that they had distorted the substance of his research. The court of appeals held both defendants immune under the speech or debate clause except as to the phone calls and the Senator's comments on a television show. As to these, the court ruled that Hutchinson was a public figure who must show "actual malice."

The Supreme Court reversed. Hutchinson v. Proxmire, 443 U.S. 111, 5 Med.L.Rptr. 1279 (1979). For the majority, Chief Justice Burger first ruled that the speech or debate clause did not apply to the press release or newsletter because neither was "essential to the deliberations of the Senate" and "neither was part of the deliberative process." Nor did the clause cover telephone calls to federal agencies to persuade them to stop funding plaintiff, or the television show. Not everything "related" to the legislative process is protected by the clause. (Sen. Proxmire could not recall whether his Senate speech had actually been delivered on the floor or simply entered into the Congressional Record. The Court noted that it had never decided whether the clause protected a speech that had not actually been delivered, and need not decide that here.)

Turning to the First Amendment questions, Chief Justice Burger began with the same *Gertz* passage that Justice Rehnquist had built upon in *Wolston.* Neither the fact that plaintiff had successfully applied for federal funds nor that he had access to media to respond to Sen. Proxmire's charges, "demonstrates that Hutchinson was a public figure prior to the controversy . . . ."

> On this record Hutchinson's activities and public profile are much like those of countless members of his profession. His published writings reach a relatively small category of professionals concerned with research in human behavior. To the extent the subject of his published writings became a matter of controversy it was a consequence of the Golden Fleece Award. Clearly those charged with defamation cannot, by their own conduct, create their own defense by making the claimant a public figure. See Wolston v. Reader's Digest, Inc., [ ].
>
> Hutchinson did not thrust himself or his views into public controversy to influence others. Respondents have not identified such a particular controversy; at most, they point to concern about general public expenditures. But that concern is shared by most and relates to most public expenditures; it is not sufficient to make Hutchinson a public figure. If it were, everyone who received or benefited from the myriad public grants for research could be classified as a public figure—a conclusion that our previous opinions have rejected. The "use of such subject-matter classifications to determine the extent of constitutional protection afforded defamatory falsehoods may too often result in an improper balance between the competing interests in this area." Time, Inc. v. Firestone, [ ].
>
> Moreover, Hutchinson at no time assumed any role of public prominence in the broad question of concern about expenditures. Neither his applications for federal grants nor his publications in professional journals can be said to have invited that degree of

public attention and comment on his receipt of federal grants essential to meet the public figure level. The petitioner in Gertz v. Robert Welch, Inc., had published books and articles on legal issues; he had been active in local community affairs. Nevertheless, the Court concluded that his activities did not make him a public figure.

Finally, we cannot agree that Hutchinson had such access to the media that he should be classified as a public figure. Hutchinson's access was limited to responding to the announcement of the Golden Fleece Award. He did not have the regular and continuing access to the media that is one of the accoutrements of having become a public figure.

At the time of the award, plaintiff was director of a state mental hospital and an adjunct professor at a state university. Building on these facts, the district court had held plaintiff a "public official." In note 8, Chief Justice Burger observed that since the court of appeals had not reached the point, the Court expressed no opinion on the issue. "The Court has not provided precise boundaries for the category of 'public official'; it cannot be thought to include all public employees, however."

Justice Brennan was the sole dissenter. He believed that "public criticism by legislators of unnecessary governmental expenditures, whatever its form, is a legislative act shielded by the Speech or Debate Clause." He did not reach the public figure question.*

In the years following *Gertz,* the lower federal courts and the state courts have frequently had to work with the public-private distinction. The following case provides an extensive attempt to discern and apply the pattern developing from the Supreme Court cases.

WALDBAUM v. FAIRCHILD PUBLICATIONS, INC.

United States Court of Appeals, District of Columbia Circuit, 1980.
627 F.2d 1287, 5 Med.L.Rptr. 2629.
Certiorari denied 449 U.S. 898 (1980).
Noted, 30 Cath.U.L.Rev. 307, 12 U.Tol.L.Rev. 1027.

Before TAMM and MACKINNON, CIRCUIT JUDGES, and HAROLD H. GREENE, UNITED STATES JUDGE FOR THE DISTRICT OF COLUMBIA.

TAMM, CIRCUIT JUDGE. In this action we must determine when an individual not a public official has left the relatively safe harbor that the law of defamation provides for private persons and has become a

* In another footnote, n. 16, Chief Justice Burger observed that the lower courts had not considered whether the *New York Times* rule "can apply to an individual defendant rather than to a media defendant. . . . This Court has never decided the question; our conclusion that Hutchinson is not a public figure makes it unnecessary to do so in this case." Doesn't the same question lurk in cases brought by non-public figures? Recall the exchange in Chapter I between Justice Stewart and Chief Justice Burger over different treatment for press and speech.

public figure within the meaning of the Supreme Court's decision in Gertz v. Robert Welch, Inc., [ ]. After examining affidavits and exhibits submitted by the parties, Judge Howard F. Corcoran of the United States District Court for the District of Columbia concluded that the plaintiff was a limited public figure under *Gertz.* Because the plaintiff admitted that he could not prove "actual malice" on the part of the defendant, which *Gertz* requires public figures to do, Judge Corcoran entered summary judgment for the defendant. Having reviewed the facts in light of the criteria that govern the status of a defamation plaintiff, we agree with Judge Corcoran's decision and affirm.

I.

Although the parties in this case differ over how to classify the plaintiff, they fundamentally agree on the underlying facts. Eric Waldbaum, the plaintiff, became president and chief executive officer of Greenbelt Consumer Services, Inc. (Greenbelt) in January of 1971. Greenbelt is a diversified consumer cooperative that, during Waldbaum's tenure, ranked as the second largest cooperative in the country.

While serving as Greenbelt's president, Waldbaum played an active role not only in the management of the cooperative but also in setting policies and standards within the supermarket industry. He battled the traditional practices in the industry and fought particularly hard for the introduction of unit pricing and open dating in supermarkets. He held several meetings, to which press and public were invited, on topics varying from supermarket practices to energy legislation and fuel allocation. He pursued a vigorous policy of consolidating Greenbelt's operations to eliminate unprofitable outlets. These actions generated considerable comment on both Greenbelt and Waldbaum in trade journals and general-interest publications.

On March 16, 1976, Greenbelt's board of directors dismissed Waldbaum as the cooperative's president and chief executive officer. *Supermarket News,* a trade publication owned by the defendant, Fairchild Publications, Inc. (Fairchild), ran an item on Waldbaum's ouster on page 35 of its March 22 issue. The five-sentence article stated at one point that Greenbelt "has been losing money the last year and retrenching." Supplemental Appendix (Supp.App.) at 328.[5]

5. The story in its entirety read:

GREENBELT OUSTS ERIC WALDBAUM WASHINGTON (FNS). Eric Waldbaum has been replaced as president of Greenbelt Consumer Services.

Rowland Burnstan will serve as acting chief executive office[r] until a new president is named. Burnstan, an independent management consultant and economist, has worked for various Government agencies and businesses.

Greenbelt said part of his interim job will be to locate a new president for the co-op, which has been losing money the past year and retrenching.

Waldbaum had served as president since 1971. His plans are not known.

Supp.App. at 328.

On September 27, 1976, Waldbaum filed a libel action in the district court based upon this comment in the article. He contended that in fact Greenbelt had not been losing money or retrenching and that this allegedly false report damaged his reputation as a businessman. Waldbaum sought actual and exemplary damages totalling $75,000.

After discovery, Fairchild moved for summary judgment. It argued that Waldbaum was a public figure and, because he had admitted the absence of "actual malice," he could not recover damages for defamation. Waldbaum countered that he was not a public figure and thus would have to prove only negligence on the part of Fairchild in researching and publishing the article. On February 15, 1979, Judge Corcoran granted Faichild's motion. He concluded that although Waldbaum could not be considered a public figure for all purposes, he was a public figure for the limited range of issues concerning "Greenbelt's unique position within the supermarket industry and Waldbaum's efforts to advance that position." [ ]

Waldbaum now appeals.[7]

II.

[Here the court reviewed the reasoning of *New York Times* and *Gertz.*]

III.

Unfortunately, the Supreme Court has not yet fleshed out the skeletal descriptions of public figures and private persons enunciated in *Gertz.* The very purpose of the rule announced in *New York Times,* however, requires courts to articulate clear standards that can guide both the press and the public. From analyzing *Gertz* and more recent defamation cases, we believe that a person can be a general public figure only if he is a "celebrity"—his name a "household word"—whose ideas and actions the public in fact follows with great interest. We also conclude that a person has become a public figure for limited purposes if he is attempting to have, or realistically can be expected to have, a major impact on the resolution of a specific public dispute that has foreseeable and substantial ramifications for persons beyond its immediate participants. In undertaking this examination, a court must look through the eyes of a reasonable person at the facts taken as a whole.

A.

The Supreme Court acknowledged in *Gertz* that the peculiar circumstances of each case affect the balance between freedom of the

7. Fairchild concedes that Judge Corcoran was correct in ruling that Waldbaum was not a public figure for all purposes. It argues before us that Waldbaum was a public figure for limited purposes that include the statements made in the March 22, 1976, article.

press and an individual's interest in his reputation. [ ] The Justices nevertheless eschewed analyzing a person's status as a public figure case by case: a purely ad hoc approach, though perhaps more accurate in its final outcome, "would lead to unpredictable results and uncertain expectations . . . ." [ ]. Instead, courts should formulate "broad rules of general application" that accommodate the competing interests of press and personal reputation. [ ] Of course, litmus tests that define what is and is not protected and that the press, the public, and the courts could apply with perfect consistency and accuracy would reduce the need for the "breathing space" that *New York Times* creates. Unfortunately, we do not have such tests. Until we find them, we must search for more precise articulations of all aspects of the *New York Times* rules, realizing that the more certain our determinations become the less need there is to extend first amendment safeguards to matters that do not merit those safeguards on their own account.

Clear guidelines are important, first, for the press. As noted above, the entire scheme of "strategic protection" for certain defamatory statements rests not on the inherent value of those statements but instead on the need to avoid chilling the dissemination of information and ideas that are constitutionally protected for their own sake. [ ] Because the outcome of future litigation is never certain, members of the press might choose to err on the side of suppression when trying to predict how a court would analyze a news story's first amendment status. Questionable areas thus receive prophylactic protection to ensure that the press will not refrain from publishing material that has value under the first amendment due to its own content.

Precision also is important to members of the public generally, any one of whom might become the subject of a press defamation. Our society always has encouraged citizen involvement in public affairs. The fear of no redress for injury to reputation may deter an individual from engaging in some course of conduct that a court later might find to have altered his status.[11] Similarly, a person desiring to voice his views on public issues may not wish to have some aspects of his private life exposed and therefore may refrain from entering the public arena. To guard against these possibilities, society must provide the individual with clear rules that govern the potential consequences of his participation in public life. Clarity allows him to calculate correctly, and not overestimate or underestimate, the effect that undertaking some activity will have on the legal recourse available to him should he suffer injury due to defamation by the press.

11. As the Supreme Court observed in *Gertz*, "We should not lightly assume that a citizen's participation in community and professional affairs rendered him a public figure for all purposes." [ ]. Democracies should avoid deterring citizen involvement in public affairs. *Gertz* implicitly furthers this policy by making public figures only those who are extraordinarily prominent and pervasively involved in public matters or who, in particular instances, have become integrally involved in the disposition of particular public controversies—and then only for purposes related to those controversies. [ ]

B.

Given these considerations, a court [12] analyzing whether a given plaintiff is a public figure must look at the facts, taken as a whole, through the eyes of a reasonable person. This objective approach should enable both the press and the individual in question to assess the individual's status, in advance, against the same yardstick. Focusing on what a reporter, editor, or publisher actually knew or believed could introduce subjective elements that are difficult to prove and even more difficult to predict. Such a perspective would give the individual little opportunity to alter his conduct or lifestyle to preserve his anonymity. Similarly, looking only to what the individual thought would charge the press with discovering and evaluating the inner beliefs and peculiarities of particular individuals and thus would deprive the media of the very "breathing space" that *New York Times* sought to create and protect. Resolving these questions based upon what a reasonable person, looking at the entire situation, would conclude allows the press and the individual to evaluate public-figure status against a single, discoverable norm and from there to act as they see fit, understanding the consequences of their conduct under *New York Times.*

C.

With this background, we turn to the standards themselves for determining when a person is a public figure. A court first must ask whether the plaintiff is a public figure for all purposes. *Gertz,* as noted above, held that a plaintiff could be found to be a general public figure only after a clear showing "of general fame or notoriety in the community, and pervasive involvement in the affairs of society . . . ." [ ] He must have assumed a "role of especial prominence in the affairs of society . . . ." Time, Inc. v. Firestone, [ ]. Accord, Wolston v. Reader's Digest Association, [ ]. In other words, a general public figure is a well-known "celebrity," his name a "household word." [14] The public recognizes him and follows his words and deeds, either because it regards his ideas, conduct, or judgment as worthy of its attention or because he actively pursues that consideration.[15]

12. Whether the plaintiff is a public figure is a question of law for the court to resolve. Wolston v. Reader's Digest Ass'n, 578 F.2d 427, 429 (D.C.Cir.1978), rev'd on other grounds. [ ]. See Rosenblatt v. Baer, [ ].

14. See Robertson, Defamation and the First Amendment: In Praise of Gertz v. Robert Welch, Inc., 54 Tex.L.Rev. 199, 222–23 (1976); [ ].

15. In many instances, of course, the public may accord a person a degree of respect that a reasonable person—or judge—might believe is undeserved. This assessment, however, is not material to the issue before the court. Instead, the proper question is whether a reasonable person would conclude that, in fact, the public pays him heed.

In this vein, we note that many well-known athletes, entertainers, and other personages endorse commercial products, publicly support political candidates, or take open stands on public issues. This phenomenon, regardless of whether it is justified, indicates that famous persons may be able to transfer their recognition and influence from one field to another.

As a general rule, a person who meets this test has access to the media if defamed. The public's proven preoccupation with him indicates that the media would cover such an individual's response to statements he believes are inaccurate or unsupported. In general, too, the person has assumed the risk that public exposure might lead to misstatements about him. Famous persons may not have submitted voluntarily to a loss of reputation as such. Nevertheless, their renouncement of anonymity or tolerance of publicity unavoidably carries with it the possibility that the press, in fulfilling its role of reporting and critiquing matters of public concern, may investigate their talents, character, and motives. The media serve as a check on the power of the famous, and that check must be strongest when the subject's influence is strongest. Fame often brings power, money, respect, adulation, and self-gratification. It also may bring close scrutiny that can lead to adverse as well as favorable comment. When someone steps into the public spotlight, or when he remains there once cast into it, he must take the bad with the good.[18]

In determining whether a plaintiff has achieved the degree of notoriety and influence necessary to become a public figure in all contexts, a court may look to several factors.[19] The judge can examine statistical surveys, if presented, that concern the plaintiff's name recognition.[20] Previous coverage of the plaintiff in the press also is relevant.

At the very least, businessmen and politicians are willing to stake substantial funds on the effectiveness of this form of advertising. A person's power to capitalize on his general fame by lending his name to products, candidates, and causes indicates the broad influence he has. The ability to affect a variety of areas makes close scrutiny in the press especially appropriate, in particular to educate the public on the famous person's actual expertise with reference to whom or what he is promoting.

18. In rare instances, a celebrity may decide to abandon his prominent position in society to return to anonymity, but persistent press attention, most likely fueled by continuing public interest, may thwart his quest for privacy. In such a case, he still may be a public figure. Although he no longer is accepting the risk of defamation voluntarily, he remains able to reply to attacks through the press, which is continuing to cover him. Because he irretrievably has lost his anonymity, potential damage to reputation poses a small incremental danger. [ ] Moreover, his power and influence, due to his prominence, may continue despite his efforts to renounce publicity. Thus, his actions still, as *Gertz* put it, "invite attention and comment." 418 U.S. at 345. Media scrutiny remains appropriate and necessary to balance his undesired but nonetheless real impact on the affairs of society. *Gertz* itself acknowledged that such a situation might arise. See id. (recognizing the existence, at least in theory, of "involuntary public figures").

19. The court must examine these factors as they existed before the defamation was published. Otherwise, the press could convert a private individual into a general public figure simply by publicizing the defamation itself and creating a controversy surrounding it and, perhaps, litigation arising out of it. See Hutchinson v. Proxmire, [ ] ("those charged with defamation cannot, by their own conduct, create their own defense by making the claimant a public figure"). This perspective also ensures that the press and the individual can analyze the latter's status before the defamation, thereby enabling them to take steps they deem appropriate to investigate further (in the case of the media) or to renounce public involvement (in the case of the individual). [ ]

20. E.g., Robertson, supra note 14, at 224. We do not believe that the Supreme Court, in employing the phrase "*general* fame or notoriety" in *Gertz*, 418 U.S. at 352 (emphasis added), necessarily meant that a majority or more of the public must know of the plaintiff. Rather, we conclude that "general" fame means being known to a large percentage of the well-informed citizenry.

The judge can check whether others in fact alter or reevaluate their conduct or ideas in light of the plaintiff's actions. He also can see if the plaintiff has shunned the attention that the public has given him and determine if those efforts have been successful.[21] At all times, the judge should keep in mind the voluntariness of the plaintiff's prominence and the availability of self-help through press coverage of responses—in other words, whether the plaintiff has assumed the risk of reputational injury and whether he has access to the media. No one parameter is dispositive; the decision still involves an element of judgment. Nevertheless, the weighing of these and other relevant factors can lead to a more accurate—and a more predictable—assessment of a person's overall fame and notoriety in the community.[22]

D.

Few people, of course, attain the general notoriety that would make them public figures for all purposes. Nevertheless, many persons "have thrust themselves to the forefront of particular public controversies in order to influence the resolution of the issues involved." Gertz v. Robert Welch, Inc., 418 U.S. at 345. Thus, even if a court finds that a plaintiff is not a general public figure, it still must examine "the nature and extent of an individual's participation in the particular controversy giving rise to the defamation." Id. at 352.

As the first step in its inquiry, the court must isolate the public controversy. A public controversy is not simply a matter of interest to the public; it must be a real dispute, the outcome of which affects the

In *Gertz* the Court remarked, "None of the prospective jurors called at the trial had ever heard of petitioner prior to this litigation, and respondent offered no proof that this response was atypical of the local population." Id. We do not believe that this passing observation was intended to encourage polling jurors or veniremen to gauge a plaintiff's general fame or anonymity. Because of its small size and the non-random elements that go into its selection, we doubt that in most cases a jury would be a statistically reliable sample representative of the general population. The question is whether such a poll would be relevant—i.e., probative—evidence admissible on this issue.

21. Simply announcing that one no longer desires press coverage and then refusing to grant interviews may not be enough. A person who takes these steps may be continuing in a career that captivates the public, be it in politics, business, the arts, sports, or entertainment. Because public interest in him persists and because he has chosen to occupy a position that places him in the spotlight and thereby may make him influential, he retains his access to the media and has invited continued attention and comment. [ ]

22. In examining the status of the plaintiff in *Gertz,* the Court noted that he had "no general fame and notoriety *in the community*" and that he was not generally known to "the *local* population." 418 U.S. at 351–52 (emphasis added). We therefore conclude that nationwide fame is not required. Rather, the question is whether the individual had achieved the necessary degree of notoriety where he was defamed—i.e., where the defamation was published.

Dissemination to a wide audience creates special problems. For example, an individual may be well known in a small community, but the publication covers a larger area. In such a situation, it might be appropriate to treat the plaintiff as a public figure for the segment of the audience to which he is well known and as a private individual for the rest. In any event, the defamation's audience may be relevant in assessing damages, for injury may be less if the audience does not know of the victim and will have no occasion to interact with him in the future.

general public or some segment of it in an appreciable way. The Supreme Court has made clear that essentially private concerns or disagreements do not become public controversies simply because they attract attention. Time, Inc. v. Firestone, [ ].[23] Rather, a public controversy is a dispute that in fact has received public attention because its ramifications will be felt by persons who are not direct participants.

Courts must exercise care in deciding what is a public controversy. Newsworthiness alone will not suffice, for the alleged defamation itself indicates that someone in the press believed the matter deserved media coverage. Moreover, a court may not question the legitimacy of the public's concern; such an approach would turn courts into censors of " 'what information is relevant to self-government.' " [ ].[25] A vital

23. *Firestone* involved a national newsmagazine's allegedly defamatory report of divorce proceedings between the heir to the Firestone tire fortune and his socially prominent wife. The Court first rejected the contention that Mrs. Firestone was a general public figure. 424 U.S. at 453. It then stated:

> Dissolution of a marriage through judicial proceedings is not the sort of "public controversy" referred to in *Gertz,* even though the marital difficulties of extremely wealthy individuals may be of interest to some portion of the reading public. Nor did [Mrs. Firestone] freely choose to publicize issues as to the propriety of her married life.

Id. at 454. We read these remarks as meaning that matters essentially of a private nature do not become public controversies solely because members of the public find them appealing to their "morbid or prurient curiosity." Eaton, The American Law of Defamation Through Gertz v. Robert Welch, Inc. and Beyond: An Analytical Primer, 61 Va.L.Rev. 1349, 1446 (1975). Disputes of this nature, in addition, generally do not have appreciable consequences for non-participants. [ ]

Likewise, publicity surrounding litigation does not by itself elevate the parties to public figures, even if they could anticipate the publicity, unless they are using the court as a forum for espousing their views in other controversies. [*Wolston* and *Firestone*].

Nevertheless, litigation itself can become controversial. For example, the public might debate the prosecutor's use of his discretion in bringing particular criminal charges or the judge's conduct of the proceedings. In these instances, however, the controversy is not the matter being litigated. Parties to the original court action could become embroiled in the public controversy so much that they become public figures for that controversy; it is also possible that they will take no part in that debate. Refusing to make participation in publicized litigation a sufficient condition for becoming a public figure has salutary policy effects, for it avoids deterring either resort to the courts to settle disputes when one believes he has been wronged or active defense when he believes he has been accused of some civil or criminal misconduct unjustifiably.

25. As the Supreme Court wrote 40 years ago, "Freedom of discussion, if it would fulfill its historic function in this nation, must embrace all issues about which information is needed or appropriate to enable the members of society to cope with the exigencies of their period." Thornhill v. Alabama, 310 U.S. 88, 102 (1940). The controversy need not concern political matters. In a case that involved a defamation action brought by a professional athlete, one court observed:

> We obviously cannot say that the public's interest in professional football is important to the commonweal or to the operation of a democratic society in the same sense as are political and ideological matters. However, the fabric of our society is rich and variegated . . . . [I]nterest in professional football must be deemed an important incident among many incidents, of a society founded upon a high regard for free expression.

Chuy v. Philadelphia Eagles Football Club, 431 F.Supp. 254, 267 (E.D.Pa.1977), aff'd 595 F.2d 1265 (3d Cir.1979) (en banc). Cf. Ingber, Defamation: A Contest Between Reason and Decency, 65 Va.L.Rev. 785, 841–42 (1979) (fearing that *Gertz* leaves little room for debate of matters other than "mainstream issues").

part of open public debate is deciding what should be debated. No arm of the government, including the judiciary, should be able to set society's agenda. Thus, courts must look to what already were disputes. See Hutchinson v. Proxmire, [ ].

To determine whether a controversy indeed existed and, if so, to define its contours, the judge must examine whether persons actually were discussing some specific question.[27] A general concern or interest will not suffice. Id. The court can see if the press was covering the debate, reporting what people were saying and uncovering facts and theories to help the public formulate some judgment.[28] It should ask whether a reasonable person would have expected persons beyond the immediate participants in the dispute to feel the impact of its resolution. If the issue was being debated publicly and if it had foreseeable and substantial ramifications for nonparticipants, it was a public controversy.

Once the court has defined the controversy, it must analyze the plaintiff's role in it. Trivial or tangential participation is not enough. The language of *Gertz* is clear that plaintiffs must have "thrust themselves to the forefront" of the controversies so as to become factors in their ultimate resolution. 418 U.S. at 345. They must have achieved a "special prominence" in the debate. Id. at 351. The plaintiff either must have been purposely trying to influence the outcome or could realistically have been expected, because of his position in the controversy, to have an impact on its resolution. In undertaking this analysis, a court can look to the plaintiff's past conduct, the extent of press coverage, and the public reaction to his conduct and statements. [ ].[31] [ ].[32]

27. We do not believe it necessary to state that a court should define the controversy "narrowly" or "broadly." A narrow controversy will have fewer participants overall and thus fewer who meet the required level of involvement. A broad controversy will have more participants, but few can have the necessary impact. Indeed, a narrow controversy may be a phase of another, broader one, and a person playing a major role in the "subcontroversy" may have little influence on the larger questions or on other subcontroversies. In such an instance, the plaintiff would be a public figure if the defamation pertains to the subcontroversy in which he is involved but would remain a private person for the overall controversy and its other phases.

28. The public need not be the immediate decisionmaker, for in a democracy the people should be well informed on issues to be decided, at least directly, by their representatives. [ ]

31. Responding to press inquiries or attempting to reply to comments on oneself through the media does not necessarily mean that a person is attempting to play a significant role in resolving a controversy. See Time, Inc. v. Firestone, 424 U.S. 448, 454 n. 3 (1976).

32. At first glance, it may seem anomalous that a person who falls slightly short of the general fame required to be a general public figure but who is not involved in any particular public controversy is a private person, while a citizen who becomes influential in a single issue is a limited-purpose public figure. We believe that this result is correct and consistent with the principles underlying *New York Times* and *Gertz.* The limited public figure by definition is playing or attempting to play a major role in influencing one aspect of society. A well-known celebrity becomes a public figure because the press must be entitled to presume that persons to whom the general public pays close attention have substantial influence over a multitude of areas, see note 15 supra, and thus may play some role in their outcome. The person who lacks the level of recognition to be classified as a general public figure no

Finally, the alleged defamation must have been germane to the plaintiff's participation in the controversy. His talents, education, experience, and motives could have been relevant to the public's decision whether to listen to him.[33] Misstatements wholly unrelated to the controversy, however, do not receive the *New York Times* protection.

Those who attempt to affect the result of a particular controversy have assumed the risk that the press, in covering the controversy, will examine the major participants with a critical eye. Occasionally, someone is caught up in the controversy involuntarily and, against his will, assumes a prominent position in its outcome. Unless he rejects any role in the debate, he, too, has "invited comment" relating to the issue at hand. In any event, media coverage of the controversy can be expected to include reports on a major participant's reply to misstatements made about him.[34] In short, the court must ask whether a reasonable person would have concluded that this individual would play or was seeking to play a major role in determining the outcome of the controversy and whether the alleged defamation related to that controversy.

IV.

With the foregoing analysis in mind, we now must determine whether Judge Corcoran correctly concluded that Waldbaum was a public figure. . . .

Evidence submitted with Fairchild's motion for summary judgment indicates clearly that Greenbelt was an innovative company often the subject of news reports. As the second largest cooperative in the nation it attracted attention, and its pathbreaking marketing policies—e.g., unit pricing, open dating, and highly competitive advertising—became the subject of public debate within the supermarket industry and beyond, debate that would affect consumers and retailers in the Washington area and, perhaps, elsewhere. We therefore believe that, before *Supermarket News* published its story about Waldbaum's dismissal, public controversies existed over the viability of cooperatives as a form

longer can be assumed to have pervasive influence in society. Thus, we must return to a more particularized inquiry into the circumstances of his case. If in fact he is shaping or is trying to shape the outcome of a specific public controversy, he is a public figure for that controversy; if not, he remains a private individual.

33. See Restatement, Second, Torts § 580A (1977) (public figure's "conduct, fitness or role"). In Garrison v. Louisiana, 379 U.S. 64 (1964), decided shortly after *New York Times,* the Supreme Court remarked:

> The public-official rule protects the paramount public interest in a free flow of information to the people concerning public officials, their servants. To this end, anything which might touch on an official's fitness for office is relevant. Few personal attributes are more germane to fitness for office than dishonesty, malfeasance, or improper motivation, even though these characteristics may also affect the official's private character.

Id. at 77, quoted in part in Gertz v. Robert Welch, Inc., 418 U.S. at 344–45.

34. [ ]. Correcting inaccurate media reports about oneself does not by itself prove access or public-figure status. See note 31 supra.

of commercial enterprise and over the wisdom of various policies that Greenbelt in particular was pioneering.

With some admittedly overlapping controversies identified, we now must examine Waldbaum's role in them. Waldbaum was known as a leading advocate of certain precedent-breaking policies before coming to Greenbelt. [ ] He has admitted that as president and chief executive officer, he pursued these policies and other consumer-oriented activities. [ ] He felt that educating the community at large was one function of a cooperative such as Greenbelt. [ ] Greenbelt published its own monthly newspaper, *Co-op Consumer,* and Waldbaum "insisted" that he, as president, approve all information placed in it for the shareholders.

Being an executive within a prominent and influential company does not by itself make one a public figure. In many cases, a corporate official is simply a conduit for announcing and administering company policies made by others. Similarly, many executives who do make corporate policy do not thereby take stands in public controversies.[36] These descriptions, however, do not fit Eric Waldbaum at Greenbelt. His own deposition indicates that he was the mover and shaper of many of the co-operative's controversial actions. He made it a leader in unit pricing and open dating. He supervised, or at least approved, the consumer-oriented views that appeared in *Co-op Consumer.* In short, as Judge Corcoran so aptly put it, "he did not become merely a boardroom president whose vision was limited to the balance sheet. He became an activist, projecting his own image and that of the cooperative far beyond the dollars and cents aspects of marketing." [ ] Given Greenbelt's prominence, his activities certainly extended beyond those of a profit-maximizing manager of a single firm.

Thus, it would appear to a reasonable person that Waldbaum had thrust himself into the public controversies concerning unit pricing, open dating, the cooperative form of business, and other issues. He did so in an attempt to influence the policies of firms in the supermarket industry and merchandising generally. In the process, he assumed the risk that comment in the press might turn to the successfulness or profitability of enterprises under his management, for the commercial success or failure of the actions he was advocating certainly is strong evidence in the public debate over whether other firms should adopt them. Furthermore, Waldbaum had prior dealings with the media. Although he personally was not frequently the subject of articles, he was somewhat familiar with press operations and had held press

36. Sometimes position alone can make one a public figure. [ ] The position itself may be so prominent that any occupant unavoidably enters the limelight and thus becomes generally known in the community—a general public figure. Similarly, the responsibilities of a position may include decisionmaking that affects significantly one or more public controversies, in which case the occupant becomes a limited public figure for those controversies. Courts should avoid generalizing, however, for labelling certain positions as always being public is tantamount to making subject-matter classifications, forbidden under the case law. See [*Hutchinson* and *Firestone*]. Courts therefore must undertake the analysis outlined above in each case.

conferences to discuss Greenbelt's policies and operations. Looking at the overall picture, we conclude that Waldbaum was a public figure for the limited purpose of comment on Greenbelt's—and his own—innovation policies and that the article giving rise to this action was within the protected sphere of reporting. Because Fairchild concededly did not act with "actual malice," it was entitled to summary judgment.

V.

Not everyone who participates in activities that affect the public becomes a public figure. Nevertheless, when one assumes a position of great influence within a specific area and uses that influence to advocate and practice controversial policies that substantially affect others, he becomes a public figure for that debate. Waldbaum was such a person, and comment on his termination as president and chief executive officer of Greenbelt falls within the range of reports protected under *New York Times.* Therefore, the judgment of the district court is

Affirmed.

Notes and Questions

1. What does *Waldbaum* have to say about the role of the subject matter in these cases? Has *Gertz* successfully eliminated the question of whether a subject is of "general or public" interest or concern, which was developed in *Rosenbloom?* How should "public controversy" be analyzed?

2. General public figures have been few and far between since *Gertz.* See Buckley v. Littell, 539 F.2d 882 (2d Cir.1976), certiorari denied 429 U.S. 1062 (1977) (William F. Buckley, Jr.), Carson v. Allied News Co., 529 F.2d 206 (7th Cir.1976) (Johnny Carson); see also the *en banc* decision in Chuy v. Philadelphia Eagles Football Club, 595 F.2d 1265, 4 Med.L.Rptr. 2537 (3d Cir.1979) (a professional football player who is alleged to have a career-ending disease is a public figure). All were decided before *Hutchinson* and *Wolston.*

3. Involuntary public figures have been even harder to find. Among the few cases that have identified some so far are Meeropol v. Nizer, 560 F.2d 1061, 2 Med.L.Rptr. 2269 (2d Cir.1977), certiorari denied 434 U.S. 1013 (1978) (children of Julius and Ethel Rosenberg); Carson v. Allied News Co., 529 F.2d 206 (7th Cir.1976) (Johnny Carson's wife—unless "voluntary" through marriage to a famous person); Rosanova v. Playboy Enterprises, 580 F.2d 859, 4 Med.L.Rptr. 1550 (5th Cir.1978) (an accused mobster who did nothing to court publicity).

4. In Street v. National Broadcasting Co., 645 F.2d 1227, 7 Med.L.Rptr. 1001 (6th Cir.1981), the plaintiff was the main witness in the famous Scottsboro case of 1931, in which nine black youths in Alabama were accused of raping plaintiff and another white woman. The case itself engaged the attention of the nation at the time and has since been the subject of books and studies. Forty years later, NBC prepared a television dramatization based on a chapter of a book by a historian

that in turn relied heavily on the views of the one trial judge who found facts favorable to the nine defendants. The dramatization diverged from the record sufficiently so that it was not protected by the state's fair report privilege.

The court of appeals, 2–1, first held that plaintiff had been defamed. It then held her a public figure. During the criminal trial, much was written about plaintiff and she gave some interviews to the press. The trial and surrounding events were the kind of "public controversy" discussed in *Gertz* because it produced debate on whether equal justice was possible in the South and involved such issues as right to counsel and exclusion of blacks from serving on juries.

Plaintiff played a prominent role in the controversy. She clearly had access to media and was able to present her views. The critical issue was whether her role was "voluntary." Plaintiff "gave press interviews and aggressively promoted her version of the case outside of her actual courtroom testimony." She was a public figure "because she played a major role, had effective access to the media and encouraged public interest in herself."

The majority then concluded that plaintiff remained a public figure "for purposes of later commentary or treatment of *that controversy*" even though she had disappeared so completely from view that NBC thought she was dead. The public still discusses the Scottsboro case and its implications, even though it is now history rather than current events. "The mere passage of time does not automatically diminish the significance of events or the public's need for information." Plaintiff "was the pivotal character in the most famous rape case of the twentieth century. It became a political controversy as well as a legal dispute." As long as questions of equal justice persist, the Scottsboro case "will not be relegated to the dusty pages of the scholarly treatise. It will remain a living controversy."

Since the majority found that the evidence was insufficient to establish "actual malice," it dismissed the case.

The dissenter stressed that the passage of time had removed the plaintiff from the category of public figure. He would permit the states to impose liability for negligence "where the pressures of contemporaneous reporting are totally absent." Historical writing should not get the same protection.

The Supreme Court granted certiorari, 454 U.S. 815 (1981), but then dismissed the case when the parties settled it.

5. In some cases, persons accused of connections with organized crime have been held to be public figures. One case involved an attorney who represented persons alleged to have criminal connections and who was said to have "contributed down payments of up to $25,000 on grass transactions. Charges against him were dismissed because he cooperated with further investigations." Although recognizing that "mere newsworthiness" is not sufficient, the court first concluded that the

issue of "drug trafficking" was "a real dispute, the outcome of which affects the general public or some segment of it." As to plaintiff's part in it, the court noted that sometimes one can be a public figure without voluntary actions. "For example, sports figures are generally considered public figures because of their positions as athletes or coaches. [ ] If a position itself is so prominent that its occupant unavoidably enters the limelight, then a person who voluntarily assumes such a position may be presumed to have accepted public figure status." Marcone v. Penthouse International, Ltd., 754 F.2d 1072, 11 Med.L. Rptr. 1577 (3d Cir.), certiorari denied 106 S.Ct. 182 (1985).

The so-called "involuntary" public figure was not a separate category, but "merely one way an individual may come to be considered a general or limited purpose public figure. Thus, to the extent a person attains public figure status by position, status, or notorious act he might be considered an involuntary public figure." The court's examples are family members and those accused of connections with organized crime.

See also Rosanova v. Playboy Enterprises, Inc., 580 F.2d 859 (5th Cir.1978):

> Comment upon people and activities of legitimate public concern often illuminates that which yearns for shadow. It is no answer to the assertion that one is a public figure to say, truthfully, that one doesn't choose to be. It is sufficient, as the district court found, that "Mr. Rosanova voluntarily engaged in a course that was bound to invite attention and comment."

Although this decision predates *Wolston,* it is quoted with approval in *Marcone.* Can it be squared with *Wolston?* (It was the district judge in *Rosanova* who said that "Defining public figures is much like trying to nail a jellyfish to the wall." 411 F.Supp. at 443.)

6. In Dameron v. Washington Magazine, Inc., 779 F.2d 736, 12 Med.L. Rptr. 1508 (D.C.Cir.1985), certiorari denied, 106 S.Ct. 2247 (1986), plaintiff had been the only air traffic controller on duty in 1974 when a plane approaching Dulles crashed into Mt. Weather. The episode received much attention; plaintiff testified in hearings and a claim under the Federal Tort Claims Act was litigated. In that case the court dismissed claims based on controller negligence. In 1982 a plane crashed into the Potomac River. Part of the story on the 1982 crash in defendant's city magazine was a sidebar on earlier plane crashes and their causes. In that list the 1974 crash was attributed to "controller" failure. Plaintiff sued for libel. The district judge granted the magazine summary judgment.

The court held that although plaintiff had not injected himself into any controversy, persons "can become involved in public controversies and affairs without their consent or will. Air-controller Dameron, who had the misfortune to have a tragedy occur on his watch, is such a person. We conclude that Dameron did become an involuntary public figure for the limited purpose of discussions of the Mt. Weather crash."

In *Waldbaum* this court set out a three-part framework for analyzing whether someone has become a limited-purpose public figure. Under this test the court must determine that there is a public controversy; ascertain that the plaintiff played a sufficiently central role in that controversy; and find that the alleged defamation was germane to the plaintiff's involvement in the controversy. [ ] Central to the second prong of the *Waldbaum* analysis is an inquiry into the plaintiff's voluntary actions that have caused him to become embroiled in a public controversy. [ ] This analysis clearly must be modified somewhat to accommodate the possibility of a potentially involuntary limited-purpose public figure that is presented here. We think, however, that the facts here satisfy the Supreme Court's definition of a public figure and an appropriately modified *Waldbaum* inquiry. There was indisputably a public controversy here. Nor can it be doubted that the alleged defamation was germane to the question of controller responsibility for air safety in general and the Mt. Weather crash in particular. There is no question that Dameron played a central, albeit involuntary, role in this controversy. Thus, it only remains to inquire whether Dameron's relatively passive involvement in this controversy suffices to anyway qualify him as a public figure.

Although the Supreme Court had said that "the instances of truly involuntary public figures must be exceedingly rare," the court thought that "within the very narrow framework represented by the facts of this case, such has been Dameron's fate":

By sheer bad luck, Dameron happened to be the controller on duty at the time of the Mt. Weather crash. As in *Gertz,* Dameron "assume[d a] special prominence in the resolution of [a] public question [ ]." He became embroiled, through no desire of his own, in the ensuing controversy over the causes of the accident. He thereby became well known to the public in this one very limited connection. The numerous press reports on the Mt. Weather crash introduced by the defendants in their motion for summary judgment amply demonstrate this. . . . Paradoxically, the magazine article never mentions Dameron's name or other identifying characteristics. If Dameron had not been previously linked with accounts of the tragedy, no magazine reader could tie the alleged defamation to Dameron. Indeed, it was partly because of the defendant's public notoriety that he was identifiable at all from the oblique reference in The Washingtonian.

. . . Dameron's situation . . . is far removed from that of Mrs. Firestone. Dameron was at the center of a controversy involving the loss of many lives in a mishap involving a public carrier. At issue was the management of a program administered by the FAA, an arm of the government. Another governmental agency—the NTSB—conducted an extensive, public investigation into the events surrounding the Mt. Weather Crash. Dameron

> appeared at these hearings and testified for many hours about his role in the crash. The hearings, and Dameron's role in them, were widely publicized. We think that, like it or not, Dameron was embroiled in a public controversy.

The case was distinguishable from *Wolston* because Dameron was "a central figure, however involuntarily, in the discrete and specific public controversy with respect to which he was allegedly defamed—the controversy over the cause of the Mt. Weather crash." In *Wolston,* the plaintiff was defamed only with respect "to a controversy in which he played a role that was at most tangential—the investigation of Soviet espionage in general."

The court sought to limit its holding by asserting that the instances of involuntary public figures "will, we are confident, continue to be few and far between."

Finally, because plaintiff alleged that he would be "immediately recognized as the target" of the story, though unnamed in it, the court concluded that it "need not consider the question whether mere lapse of time would free plaintiff from his involuntary public figure status."

7. *The Milkovich case.* In Milkovich v. The News-Herald, 15 Ohio St. 3d 292, 473 N.E.2d 1191, 11 Med.L.Rptr. 1598 (1984), the plaintiff had been the head wrestling coach at a public high school. A fight had broken out at a meet after the referee had disqualified a wrestler on the coach's team. The state high school athletic association had held a hearing and imposed sanctions on the high school and a censure on plaintiff. The sanctions were relieved in court. Defendant's paper carried a story asserting that plaintiff had lied in public. The court held, 4–3, that plaintiff was not a public figure. (The part of the case involving the claim that plaintiff was a public official was considered at p. 171 supra.)

The reasoning on "public figure" was that although plaintiff was a nationally prominent wrestling coach and may have been "admired in his community for his coaching achievements, he does not occupy a position of persuasive power and influence by virtue of those achievements. By the same token, appellant's position in his community does not put him at the forefront of public controversies where he would attempt to exert influence over the resolution of those controversies." Nor did he assume the risk of comment by advertising his wrestling clinics. "If this were the case, then any widespread advertisements for purely business purposes could result in the classification of an individual as a public figure." The plaintiff, said the court, was more like Mrs. Firestone than like Mr. Butts.

One of the dissenters stressed that by plaintiff's own admission, he "is one of America's outstanding coaches and a nationally acclaimed sports figure. His coaching record is unparalleled in Ohio and throughout the country, and he has been honored by civil groups, legislative bodies and numerous sports organizations." This "unquestionably" made him a public figure.

The Supreme Court denied certiorari, 106 S.Ct. 322, 12 Med.L.Rptr. 1366 (1985), over a dissent by Justices Brennan and Marshall. They argued that the state court's holding on the public figure aspect of the case was "simply nonsense."

8. *Corporations as Public Figures.* The overwhelming majority of courts have concluded that the fact of incorporation alone does not make the plaintiff a public figure. See Schiavone Construction Co. v. Time, Inc., 619 F.Supp. 684, 12 Med.L.Rptr. 1153 (D.N.J.1985); Bank of Oregon v. Independent News, Inc., 298 Or. 434, 693 P.2d 35, 11 Med.L. Rptr. 1313, 1903, certiorari denied 106 S.Ct. 84 (1985). Contra, Jadwin v. Minneapolis Star and Tribune Co., 367 N.W.2d 476, 11 Med.L.Rptr. 1905 (Minn.1985):

> We hold . . . that corporate plaintiffs in defamation actions must prove actual malice by media defendants when the defendants establish that the defamatory material concerns matters of legitimate public interest in the geographic area in which the defamatory material is published, either because of the nature of the business conducted or because the public has an especially strong interest in the investigation or disclosure of the commercial information at issue. Such a rule will encourage the media to probe the business world to the depth which is necessary to permit the kind of business reporting vital to an informed public.

In Steaks Unlimited, Inc. v. Deaner, 623 F.2d 264, 6 Med.L.Rptr. 1129 (3d Cir.1980), plaintiff was a seller of inspected but ungraded frozen beef. To promote its four-day sale of meat at a chain of department stores in the Pittsburgh area, plaintiff "engaged in a widespread advertising campaign" costing $16,000. Defendants were the consumer affairs reporter of a local television station and the station. The reporter began investigating plaintiff when she noticed newspaper advertisements that did not indicate the grade of the meat. During the next four days she received telephone complaints about the quality of the meat and the plaintiff's sale practices. She then did a critical story on the quality of the meat.

The court concluded that plaintiff was a public figure for the purposes of the controversy giving rise to the case. It had conducted an intensive advertising campaign. "In short, through its advertising blitz, Steaks invited public attention, comment, and criticism." Plaintiff also possessed "regular and continuing access to channels of communication." There was no suggestion that any media had refused to air plaintiff's side after the defendant's report was aired.

In Arctic Co., Ltd. v. Loudoun Times Mirror, 624 F.2d 518, 6 Med.L. Rptr. 1433 (4th Cir.1980), certiorari denied 449 U.S. 1102 (1981), Fairfax County wished to expand its water supply. To get a permit from the Army Corps of Engineers it had to provide an inventory and evaluation of all known archaeological and historical resources in the area to be affected by the new facilities. The county contracted with plaintiff, a firm engaged in such research, to do the inventory. Plaintiff filed a report with the county. The changes the construction project would require were controversial. Defendant local paper ran a story that reflected adversely on the quality of the work plaintiff had done.

The court of appeals held that plaintiff was not a public figure: "It was not generally known in the community . . . . It merely performed a narrowly-defined professional service in a highly technical field." Neither was plaintiff a public official by virtue of being a government consultant. *Rosenblatt* indicated that the position of the government employee "must be one which would invite public scrutiny and discussion of the person holding it, entirely apart from the scrutiny and discussion occasioned by the particular charges in controversy."

In Bruno & Stillman, Inc. v. Globe Newspaper Co., 633 F.2d 583, 6 Med.L.Rptr. 2057 (1st Cir.1980), plaintiff was engaged in the manufacture and sale of fishing boats. From its beginning in 1971, when it sold eight boats, it had become the largest builder of fishing boats in New England by 1977. In that year, defendant newspaper published a series of stories listing defects observed in one or more of the defendant's boats and quoting various sources that were critical of the boats.

The court rejected the idea that corporations as a class had any particular advantage over private individuals in gaining access to media. Taking a particularized approach, the court held that defendant had not borne its burden of showing plaintiff to be a public figure. The record showed no public controversy antedating the Globe's story. The article reported dissatisfaction and "unhappy—or worse—experiences but we know little or nothing of ongoing private controversies, not to mention public ones." *Steaks Unlimited* was distinguished on the ground that the defendants and the Bureau of Consumer Affairs in that case had received "numerous" complaints before the critical broadcast.

Nor was there any suggestion of a "thrusting into the vortex . . . . We know absolutely nothing of its promotional efforts, either in scale or nature." This was in contrast to the concentrated "advertising blitz" of *Steaks Unlimited:*

> Based on the record before us, what we appear to face in the case at bar is the paradigm middle echelon, successful manufacturer-merchant. While the company is recognized in its field and in its area, if such activity and success were alone sufficient to make it a public figure, virtually every entrepreneur, however parochial, who has avoided bankruptcy might also qualify.

The court rejected the suggestion that companies dominant in their fields or markets should be called public figures. If plaintiff were a public figure on this record, the result might apply to equally successful individuals and sellers of services as well as goods. Finally, the court rejected defendant's argument that since issues of product safety and quality "may well be just as important to the continued operation of a sound capitalistic democracy as issues concerning the fitness of an individual to hold office," "all reasonably successful manufacturers" should be public figures.

9. Other federal appellate courts have faced the public figure problem since *Waldbaum*. Their approaches are summarized as follows in Schiavone Construction Co. v. Time, Inc., 619 F.Supp. 684, 12 Med.L. Rptr. 1153 (D.N.J.1985).

10. It is not clear who decides whether plaintiff is or is not public for this purpose. See Schiavone Construction Co. v. Time, Inc., 619 F.Supp. 684, 12 Med.L.Rptr. 1153 (D.N.J.1985) ("The question of whether one is a public figure is a question of law, to be determined by the court."); Maule v. NYM Corporation, 54 N.Y.2d 880, 429 N.E.2d 416, 444 N.Y.S.2d 909, 7 Med.L.Rptr. 2092 (1981) (refusing to decide whether the question was for the court, the jury, or both); and Nash v. Keene Publishing Corp., 214 N.H. 127, 498 A.2d 348, 12 Med.L.Rptr. 1025 (1985) (when the criteria point in different directions, the jury decides the factual as well as the normative issues).

11. The states disagree over whether private plaintiffs who prevail on a negligence theory may recover damages for emotional distress without showing actual harm to reputation. Compare Hearst Corp. v. Hughes, 297 Md. 112, 466 A.2d 486, 9 Med.L.Rptr. 2504 (1983) (affirmative) with Gobin v. Globe Publishing Co., 232 Kan. 1, 649 P.2d 1239, 8 Med.L.Rptr. 2191 (1982) (negative). The Maryland court asserted that the Kansas view failed to "respect the centuries of human experience which led to a presumption of harm flowing from words actionable per se. One reason for that common law position was the difficulty a defamation plaintiff has in proving harm to reputation." Since victims of defamation "can reasonably become genuinely upset as a result of the publication," the court saw "no social purpose to be served by requiring the plaintiff additionally to prove actual impairment of reputation."

e. *The Media-Nonmedia Question*

DUN & BRADSTREET, INC. v. GREENMOSS BUILDERS, INC.

Supreme Court of the United States, 1985.
472 U.S. ___, 105 S.Ct. 2939, 86 L.Ed.2d 593, 11 Med.L.Rptr. 2417.
Noted, 60 St. Johns L.Rev. 144.

[Dun & Bradstreet, a credit reporting agency, provides confidential information to subscribers about financial conditions of businesses. Under these agreements, the subscriber may not reveal the information to anyone else. D & B sent a report to five subscribers stating that respondent construction contractor had filed a voluntary petition for bankruptcy. The report was incorrect. In fact, a high school student employed by D & B to review Vermont bankruptcy proceedings had inadvertently attributed to Greenmoss a bankruptcy petition filed by one of its former employees. Respondent's bank told respondent's president that it had received the report. He immediately called D & B, explained the error, asked for a correction, and asked the names of those who had received the false report. A week later, D & B wrote the five subscribers that the filing had been by a former employee and that Greenmoss "continued in business as usual." D & B refused to identify the five subscribers.

A jury in state court returned a judgment for $50,000 in compensatory damages and $300,000 in punitive damages. D & B argued that *Gertz* required a finding of "actual malice" before presumed or punitive damages could be awarded and that the trial judge had not charged the jury in those terms. The trial judge expressed doubt about whether *Gertz* applied to "non-media cases" but granted the new trial in the "interests of justice." The Vermont Supreme Court reversed. It concluded that credit agencies were not the "type of media worthy of First Amendment protection as contemplated by" the Times case "and its progeny." As a "matter of federal constitutional law, the media protections outlined in *Gertz* are inapplicable to nonmedia defamation actions."

The Supreme Court granted certiorari to resolve the disagreement among lower courts about when the protections of *Gertz* applied. After argument, the Court ordered the parties to reargue the case and asked them to address the role of the "commercial speech" doctrine, p. 500, infra, in libel law.]

JUSTICE POWELL announced the judgment of the Court and delivered an opinion, in which JUSTICE REHNQUIST and JUSTICE O'CONNOR joined.

In [*Gertz*] we held that the First Amendment restricted the damages that a private individual could obtain from a publisher for a libel that involved a matter of public concern. More specifically, we held that in these circumstances the First Amendment prohibited awards of presumed and punitive damages for false and defamatory statements unless the plaintiff shows "actual malice," that is, knowledge of falsity or reckless disregard for the truth. The question presented in this case is whether this rule of *Gertz* applies when the false and defamatory statements do not involve matters of public concern.

. . .

. . . We now affirm, although for reasons different from those relied upon by the Vermont Supreme Court.

. . .

III

In *New York Times Co. v. Sullivan,* [ ], the Court for the first time held that the First Amendment limits the reach of state defamation laws. That case concerned a public official's recovery of damages for the publication of an advertisement criticizing police conduct in a civil rights demonstration. As the Court noted, the advertisement concerned "one of the major public issues of our time." [ ] Noting that "freedom of expression *upon public questions* is secured by the First Amendment," [ ] (emphasis added), and that "debate *on public issues* should be uninhibited, robust, and wide-open," [ ] (emphasis added), the Court held that a public official cannot recover damages for defamatory falsehood unless he proves that the false statement was made with " 'actual malice'—that is, with knowledge that it was false or with reckless disregard of whether it was false or not," [ ]. In later cases, all involving public issues, the Court extended this same constitutional protection to libels of public figures, e.g., *Butts,* and in one case suggested in a plurality opinion that this constitutional rule should extend to libels of any individual so long as the defamatory statements involved a "matter of public or general interest," [*Rosenbloom*].

In [*Gertz*], we held that the protections of *New York Times* did not extend as far as *Rosenbloom* suggested. . . . Like every other case in which this Court has found constitutional limits to state defamation laws, *Gertz* involved expression on a matter of undoubted public concern.

In *Gertz,* we held that the fact that expression concerned a public issue did not by itself entitle the libel defendant to the constitutional protections of *New York Times.* . . . Largely because private persons have not voluntarily exposed themselves to increased risk of injury from defamatory statements and because they generally lack effective opportunities for rebutting such statements, [ ] we found that the State possessed a "strong and legitimate . . . interest in compensating private individuals for injury to reputation." [ ] Balancing this stronger state interest against the same First Amendment interest at stake in *New York Times,* we held that a State could not allow recovery of presumed and punitive damages absent a showing of "actual malice." Nothing in our opinion, however, indicated that this same balance would be struck regardless of the type of speech involved.[4]

4. The dissent states that "[a]t several points the Court in *Gertz* makes perfectly clear [that] the restrictions of presumed and punitive damages were to apply in all cases." [ ] Given the context of *Gertz,* however, the Court could have made "perfectly clear" only that these restrictions applied in cases involving public speech. . . .

The dissent also incorrectly states that *Gertz* "specifically held," [ ] both "that the award of presumed and punitive damages on less than a showing of actual malice is not a narrowly tailored means to achieve the legitimate state purpose of protecting the reputation of private persons . . . ," [ ] and that "unrestrained presumed and punitive damages were 'unnecessarily' broad . . . in relation to the legitimate state interests," [ ]. Although the Court made both statements, it did so only within the context of public speech. Neither statement controls here. What was "not . . . narrowly tailored" or was " 'unnecessarily' broad" with respect to public speech is not necessarily so with respect to the speech now at issue. Properly understood, *Gertz* is consistent with the result we reach today.

Other areas of the law provide further examples [citing the exchange of information about securities, corporate proxy statements, the exchange of price and production information among competitors, and employers' threats of retaliation for the labor activities of employees]. . . . [T]he power of the State to license lawyers, psychiatrists, and public school teachers—all of whom speak for a living—is unquestioned . . . .

IV

We have never considered whether the *Gertz* balance obtains when the defamatory statements involve no issue of public concern. To make this determination, we must employ the approach approved in *Gertz* and balance the State's interest in compensating private individuals for injury to their reputation against the First Amendment interest in protecting this type of expression. This state interest is identical to the one weighed in *Gertz.* There we found that it was "strong and legitimate." . . .

The First Amendment interest, on the other hand, is less important than the one weighed in *Gertz.* We have long recognized that not all speech is of equal First Amendment importance.[5] It is speech on " 'matters of public concern' " that is "at the heart of the First Amendment's protection." [*Bellotti*] As we stated in Connick v. Myers, 461 U.S. 138, 145 (1983), this "special concern [for speech on public issues] . . . is no mystery":

> "The First Amendment 'was fashioned to assure unfettered interchange of ideas for the bringing about of political and social changes desired by the people.' [*Roth*]. '[S]peech concerning public affairs is more than self-expression; it is the essence of self-government.' [*Garrison*] Accordingly, the Court has frequently reaffirmed that speech on public issues occupies the " 'highest rung of the hierarchy of First Amendment values,' " and is entitled to special protection. NAACP v. Claiborne Hardware Co., 458 U.S. 886, 913 (1982); Carey v. Brown, 447 U.S. 455, 467 (1980)."

5. This Court on many occasions has recognized that certain kinds of speech are less central to the interests of the First Amendment than others. Obscene speech and "fighting words" long have been accorded no protection. [ ]; [Near] (publication of troop ship sailings during war time may be enjoined). In the area of protected speech, the most prominent example of reduced protection for certain kinds of speech concerns commercial speech. Such speech, we have noted, occupies a "subordinate position in the scale of First Amendment values." Ohralik v. Ohio State Bar Assn., 436 U.S. 447, 456 (1978). It also is more easily verifiable and less likely to be deterred by proper regulation. [ ] Accordingly, it may be regulated in ways that might be impermissible in the realm of noncommercial expression. [*Ohralik*]; Central Hudson Gas & Elec. v. Public Serv. Comm'n, 447 U.S. 557, 562–563 (1980).

Other areas of the law provide further examples. In *Ohralik* we noted that there are "[n]umerous examples . . . of communications that are regulated without offending the First Amendment, such as the exchange of information about securities, . . . corporate proxy statements, . . . the exchange of price and production information among competitors, . . . and employers' threats of retaliation for the labor activities of employees." 436 U.S., at 456 (citations omitted). Yet similar regulation of political speech is subject to the most rigorous scrutiny. See Brown v. Hartlage, 456 U.S. 45, 52–53 (1982); New York Times Co. v. Sullivan, 376 U.S. 254, 279, n.19 (1964); Buckley v. Valeo, 424 U.S. 1, 14 (1976). Likewise, while the power of the State to license lawyers, psychiatrists, and public school teachers—all of whom speak for a living—is unquestioned, this Court has held that a law requiring licensing of union organizers is unconstitutional under the First Amendment. Thomas v. Collins, 323 U.S. 516 (1945); see also Rosenbloom v. Metromedia, 403 U.S. 29, 44 (1971) (opinion of Brennan, J.) ("the determinant whether the First Amendment applies to state libel actions is whether the utterance involved concerns an issue of public or general concern").

In contrast, speech on matters of purely private concern is of less First Amendment concern. 461 U.S., at 146–147. As a number of state courts, including the court below, have recognized, the role of the Constitution in regulating state libel law is far more limited when the concerns that activated *New York Times* and *Gertz* are absent.[6] In such a case,

> "[t]here is no threat to the free and robust debate of public issues; there is no potential interference with a meaningful dialogue of ideas concerning self-government; and there is no threat of liability causing a reaction of self-censorship by the press. The facts of the present case are wholly without the First Amendment concerns with which the Supreme Court of the United States has been struggling." Harley-Davidson Motorsports, Inc. v. Markley, 279 Or. 361, 366, 568 P.2d 1359, 1363 (1977).

Accord [ ].

While such speech is not totally unprotected by the First Amendment, see [*Connick* at 147], its protections are less stringent. In *Gertz,* we found that the state interest in awarding presumed and punitive damages was not "substantial" in view of their effect on speech at the core of First Amendment concern. [ ] This interest, however, *is* "substantial" relative to the incidental effect these remedies may have on speech of significantly less constitutional interest. The rationale of the common law rules has been the experience and judgment of history that "proof of actual damage will be impossible in a great many cases where, from the character of the defamatory words and the circumstances of publication, it is all but certain that serious harm has resulted in fact." [ ] As a result, courts for centuries have allowed juries to presume that some damage occurred from many defamatory utterances and publications. [ ] This rule furthers the state interest in providing remedies for defamation by ensuring that those remedies are effective. In light of the reduced constitutional value of speech involving no matters of public concern, we hold that the state interest adequately supports awards of presumed and punitive damages—even absent a showing of "actual malice."[7]

6. As one commentator has remarked with respect to "the case of a commercial supplier of credit information that defames a person applying for credit"—the case before us today—"If the first amendment requirements outlined in *Gertz* apply, there is something clearly wrong with the first amendment or with *Gertz.*" Shiffrin, The First Amendment and Economic Regulation: Away From a General Theory of the First Amendment, 78 Nw.L.Rev. 1212, 1268 (1983).

7. The dissent, purporting to apply the same balancing test that we do today, concludes that even speech on purely private matters is entitled to the protections of *Gertz.* . . . *Gertz* however, did not say that the state interest was "irrelevant" in absolute terms. Indeed, such a statement is belied by *Gertz* itself, for it held that presumed and punitive damages were available under some circumstances. Rather, what the *Gertz* language indicates is that the State's interest is not substantial relative to the First Amendment interest in *public speech.* This language is thus irrelevant to today's decision.

The dissent's "balance," moreover, would lead to the protection of all libels—no matter how attenuated their constitutional interest. If the dissent were the law, a woman of impeccable character who was branded a "whore" by a jealous neighbor would have no effective recourse unless she

V

The only remaining issue is whether petitioner's credit report involved a matter of public concern. In a related context, we have held that "[w]hether . . . speech addresses a matter of public concern must be determined by [the expression's] content, form, and context . . . as revealed by the whole record." *Connick v. Myers,* [ ] These factors indicate that petitioner's credit report concerns no public issue.[8] It was speech solely in the individual interest of the speaker and its specific business audience. [ ] This particular interest warrants no special protection when—as in this case—the speech is wholly false and clearly damaging to the victim's business reputation. [ ] Moreover, since the credit report was made available to only five subscribers, who, under the terms of the subscription agreement, could not disseminate it further, it cannot be said that the report involves any "strong interest in the free flow of commercial information." [ ] There is simply no credible argument that this type of credit reporting requires special protection to ensure that "debate on public issues [will] be uninhibited, robust, and wide-open." [ ]

In addition, the speech here, like advertising, is hardy and unlikely to be deterred by incidental state regulation. See [*Virginia Pharmacy*]. It is solely motivated by the desire for profit, which, we have noted, is a force less likely to be deterred than others. [ ] Arguably, the reporting here was also more objectively verifiable than speech deserving of greater protection. [ ] In any case, the market provides a powerful incentive to a credit reporting agency to be accurate, since false credit reporting is of no use to creditors. Thus, any incremental "chilling" effect of libel suits would be of decreased significance.[9]

VI

We conclude that permitting recovery of presumed and punitive damages in defamation cases absent a showing of "actual malice" does not violate the First Amendment when the defamatory statements do not involve matters of public concern. Accordingly, we affirm the judgment of the Vermont Supreme Court.

could prove "actual malice" by clear and convincing evidence. This is not malice in the ordinary sense, but in the more demanding sense of *New York Times.* The dissent would, in effect, constitutionalize the entire common law of libel.

8. The dissent suggests that our holding today leaves all credit reporting subject to reduced First Amendment protection. This is incorrect. The protection to be accorded a particular credit report depends on whether the report's "content, form, and context" indicate that it concerns a public matter. We also do not hold, as the dissent suggests we do, [ ] that the report is subject to reduced constitutional protection because it constitutes economic or commercial speech. We discuss such speech, along with advertising, only to show how many of the same concerns that argue in favor of reduced constitutional protection in those areas apply here as well.

9. The Fifth Circuit Court of Appeals has noted that, while most States provide a qualified privilege against libel suits for commercial credit reporting agencies, in those States that do not there is a thriving credit reporting business and commercial credit transactions are not inhibited.

. . .

CHIEF JUSTICE BURGER, concurring in the judgment.

. . .

I dissented in *Gertz*. . . . *Gertz,* however, is now the law of the land, and until it is overruled, it must, under the principle of stare decisis, be applied by this Court.

. . . I agree [with the plurality opinion] that *Gertz* is limited to circumstances in which the alleged defamatory expression concerns a matter of general public importance, and that the expression in question here relates to a matter of essentially private concern. I therefore agree with the plurality opinion to the extent that it holds that *Gertz* is inapplicable in this case for the two reasons indicated. No more is needed to dispose of the present case.

I continue to believe, however, that *Gertz* was ill-conceived, and therefore agree with JUSTICE WHITE that *Gertz* should be overruled. I also agree generally with JUSTICE WHITE's observations concerning *New York Times v. Sullivan. New York Times,* however, equates "reckless disregard of the truth" with malice; this should permit a jury instruction that malice may be found if the defendant is shown to have published defamatory material which, in the exercise of reasonable care, would have been revealed as untrue. But since the Court has not applied the literal language of *New York Times* in this way, I agree with JUSTICE WHITE that it should be reexamined. The great rights guaranteed by the First Amendment carry with them certain responsibilities as well.

Consideration of these issues inevitably recalls the aphorism of journalism attributed to the late Roy Howard that, "too much checking on the facts has ruined many a good news story."

JUSTICE WHITE, concurring in the judgment.

. . .

I joined the judgment and opinion in *New York Times.* I also joined later decisions extending the *New York Times* standard to other situations. But I came to have increasing doubts about the soundness of the Court's approach and about some of the assumptions underlying it. I could not join the plurality opinion in *Rosenbloom,* and I dissented in *Gertz,* asserting that the common-law remedies should be retained for private plaintiffs. I remain convinced that *Gertz* was erroneously decided. I have also become convinced that the Court struck an improvident balance in the *New York Times* case between the public's interest in being fully informed about public officials and public affairs and the competing interest of those who have been defamed in vindicating their reputation.

In a country like ours, where the people purport to be able to govern themselves through their elected representatives, adequate information about their government is of transcendent importance. That flow of intelligence deserves full First Amendment protection. Criticism and assessment of the performance of public officials and of government in general are not subject to penalties imposed by law. But these First Amendment values are not at all served by circulating false statements of fact about public officials. On the contrary, erroneous information frustrates these values. They are even more disserved when the statements falsely impugn the honesty of those men and women and hence lessen the confidence in government. As the Court said in *Gertz,* "there is no constitutional value in false statements of fact. Neither the intentional lie nor the careless error materially advances society's interest in 'uninhibited, robust, and wide-open' debate on public issues." [ ] Yet in *New York Times* cases, the public official's complaint will be dismissed unless he alleges and makes out a jury case of a knowing or reckless falsehood. Absent such proof, there will be no jury verdict or judgment of any kind in his favor, even if the challenged publication is admittedly false. The lie will stand, and the public continue to be misinformed about public matters. This will recurringly happen because the putative plaintiff's burden is so exceedingly difficult to satisfy and can be discharged only by expensive litigation. . . .[2] . . .

. . .

The *New York Times* rule thus countenances two evils: first, the stream of information about public officials and public affairs is polluted and often remains polluted by false information; and second, the reputation and professional life of the defeated plaintiff may be destroyed by falsehoods that might have been avoided with a reasonable effort to investigate the facts. In terms of the First Amendment and reputational interests at stake, these seem grossly perverse results.

. . .

Although there was much talk in *Gertz* about liability without fault and the unfairness of presuming damages, all of this, as was the case in *New York Times,* was done in the name of the First Amendment, purportedly to shield the press and others writing about public affairs from possibly intimidating damages liability. But if protecting the press from intimidating damages liability that might lead to excessive timidity was the driving force behind *New York Times* and *Gertz,* it is evident that the Court engaged in severe overkill in both cases.

2. If the plaintiff succeeds in proving a jury case of malice, it may be that the jury will be asked to bring in separate verdicts on falsity and malice. In that event, there could be a verdict in favor of the plaintiff on falsity, but against him on malice. There would be no judgment in his favor, but the verdict on falsity would be a public one and would tend to set the record right and clear the plaintiff's name.

It might be suggested that courts, as organs of the government, cannot be trusted to discern what the truth is. But the logical consequence of that view is that the First Amendment forbids all libel and slander suits . . . . We entrust to juries and the courts the responsibility of decisions affecting the life and liberty of persons. It is perverse indeed to say that these bodies are incompetent to inquire into the truth of a statement of fact in a defamation case. I can therefore discern nothing in the Constitution which forbids a plaintiff from obtaining a judicial decree that a statement is false—a decree he can then use in the community to clear his name and to prevent further damage from a defamation already published.

In *New York Times,* instead of escalating the plaintiff's burden of proof to an almost impossible level, we could have achieved our stated goal by limiting the recoverable damages to a level that would not unduly threaten the press. Punitive damages might have been scrutinized as Justice Harlan suggested in *Rosenbloom,* [ ], or perhaps even entirely forbidden. Presumed damages to reputation might have been prohibited, or limited, as in *Gertz.* Had that course been taken and the common-law standard of liability been retained, the defamed public official, upon proving falsity, could at least have had a judgment to that effect. His reputation would then be vindicated; and to the extent possible, the misinformation circulated would have been countered. He might have also recovered a modest amount, enough perhaps to pay his litigation expenses. At the very least, the public official should not have been required to satisfy the actual malice standard where he sought no damages but only to clear his name. In this way, both First Amendment and reputational interests would have been far better served.

. . . It could be suggested that even without the threat of large presumed and punitive damage awards, press defendants' communication will be unduly chilled by having to pay for the actual damages caused to those they defame. But other commercial enterprises in this country not in the business of disseminating information must pay for the damage they cause as a cost of doing business, and it is difficult to argue that the United States did not have a free and vigorous press before the rule in *New York Times* was announced. In any event, the *New York Times* standard was formulated to protect the press from the chilling danger of numerous large damage awards. Nothing in the central rationale behind *New York Times* demands an absolute immunity from suits to establish the falsity of a defamatory misstatement about a public figure where the plaintiff cannot make out a jury case of actual malice.

I still believe the common-law rules should have been retained where plaintiff is not a public official or public figure. As I see it, the Court undervalued the reputational interest at stake in such cases. I have also come to doubt the easy assumption that the common-law rules would muzzle the press. . . .

It is interesting that JUSTICE POWELL declines to follow the *Gertz* approach in this case. I had thought that the decision in *Gertz* was intended to reach cases that involve any false statements of fact injurious to reputation, whether the statement is made privately or publicly and whether or not it implicates a matter of public importance. JUSTICE POWELL, however, distinguishes *Gertz* as a case that involved a matter of public concern, an element absent here. Wisely, in my view, JUSTICE POWELL does not rest his application of a different rule here on a distinction drawn between media and non-media defendants. On that issue, I agree with JUSTICE BRENNAN that the First Amendment gives no more protection to the press in defamation suits than it does to others exercising their freedom of speech. None of our cases affords such a distinction; to the contrary, the Court has rejected it at every turn.[4] It should be rejected again, particularly in this context, since it makes no sense to give the most protection to those publishers who reach the most readers and therefore pollute the channels of communication with the most misinformation and do the most damage to private reputation. If *Gertz* is to be distinguished from this case, on the ground that it applies only where the allegedly false publication deals with a matter of general or public importance, then where the false publication does not deal with such a matter, the common-law rules would apply whether the defendant is a member of the media or other public disseminator or a non-media individual publishing privately. Although JUSTICE POWELL speaks only of the inapplicability of the *Gertz* rule with respect to presumed and punitive damages, it must be that the *Gertz* requirement of some kind of fault on the part of the defendant is also inapplicable in cases such as this.

[I doubt that *Gertz*] has made any measurable contribution to First Amendment or reputational values since its announcement. Nor am I sure that it has saved the press a great deal of money. Like the *New York Times* decision, the burden that plaintiffs must meet invites long and complicated discovery involving detailed investigation of the workings of the press, how a news story is developed, and the state of mind of the reporter and publisher. See Herbert v. Lando, [ ] That kind of litigation is very expensive. I suspect that the press would be no worse off financially if the common-law rules were to apply and if the judiciary was careful to insist that damages awards be kept within bounds. A legislative solution to the damages problem would also be appropriate. Moreover, since libel plaintiffs are very likely more interested in clearing their names than in damages, I doubt that limiting recoveries would deter or be unfair to them. In any event, I cannot assume that the press, as successful and powerful as it is, will be intimidated into withholding news that by decent journalistic standards it believes to be true.

The question before us is whether *Gertz* is to be applied in this case. For either of two reasons, I believe that it should not. First, I am unreconciled to the *Gertz* holding and believe that it should be overruled. Second, as JUSTICE POWELL indicates, the defamatory publication in this case does not deal with a matter of public importance. Consequently, I concur in the Court's judgment.

JUSTICE BRENNAN, with whom JUSTICE MARSHALL, JUSTICE BLACKMUN and JUSTICE STEVENS join, dissenting.

This case involves a difficult question of the proper application of [*Gertz*] to credit reporting—a type of speech at some remove from that which first gave rise to explicit First Amendment restrictions on state

4. We explained in Branzburg v. Hayes, 408 U.S. 665 (1972) that "the informative function asserted by representatives of the organized press" to justify greater privileges under the First Amendment was also "performed by lecturers, political pollsters, novelists, academic researchers, and dramatists." . . .

defamation law—and has produced a diversity of considered opinions, none of which speaks for the Court. . . . The four who join this opinion would reverse the judgment of the Vermont Supreme Court. We believe that, although protection of the type of expression at issue is admittedly not the "central meaning of the First Amendment," [ ] [*Gertz*] makes clear that the First Amendment nonetheless requires restraints on presumed and punitive damage awards for this expression. The lack of consensus in approach to these idiosyncratic facts should not, however, obscure the solid allegiance the principles of New York Times v. Sullivan continue to command in the jurisprudence of this Court. [ ]

. . .

Our cases since New York Times v. Sullivan have proceeded from the general premise that all libel law implicates First Amendment values to the extent it deters true speech that would otherwise be protected by the First Amendment. . . .

In libel law, no less than any other governmental effort to regulate speech, states must therefore use finer instruments to ensure adequate space for protected expression. [ ] The ready availability and unconstrained application of presumed and punitive damages in libel actions is too blunt a regulatory instrument to satisfy this First Amendment principle, even when the alleged libel does not implicate directly the type of speech at issue in New York Times v. Sullivan. Justice Harlan made precisely this point in *Rosenbloom:*

> "At a minimum, *even in the purely private libel area,* I think the First Amendment should be construed to limit the imposition of punitive damages to those situations in which actual malice is proved. This is the typical standard employed in assessing anyone's liability for punitive damages where the underlying aim of the law is to compensate for harm actually caused, . . . and no conceivable state interest could justify imposing a harsher standard on the exercise of *those freedoms that are given explicit protection by the First Amendment.*" 403 U.S., at 73 (dissenting opinion) (emphasis added).

[ ]

. . .

II

The question presented here is narrow. . . . The only question presented is whether a jury award of presumed and punitive damages based on less than a showing of actual malice is constitutionally permissible. *Gertz* provides a forthright negative answer. To preserve the jury verdict in this case, therefore, the opinions of JUSTICE POWELL and JUSTICE WHITE have cut away the protective mantle of *Gertz.*

A

Relying on the analysis of the Vermont Supreme Court, Respondent urged that this pruning be accomplished by restricting the applicability of *Gertz* to cases in which the defendant is a "media" entity. Such a distinction is irreconcilable with the fundamental First Amendment principle that "[t]he inherent worth of . . . speech in terms of its capacity for informing the public does not depend upon the identity of its source, whether corporation, association, union, or individual." [Bellotti] First Amendment difficulties lurk in the definitional questions such an approach would generate.[6] And the distinction would likely be born an anachronism.[7] Perhaps most importantly, the argument that *Gertz* should be limited to the media misapprehends our cases. We protect the press to ensure the vitality of First Amendment guarantees. This solicitude implies no endorsement of the principle that speakers other than the press deserve lesser First Amendment protection. "In the realm of protected speech, the legislature is constitutionally disqualified from dictating . . . the speakers who may address a public issue." [*Bellotti*]

The free speech guarantee gives each citizen an equal right to self-expression and to participation in self-government. . . .[9] Accordingly, at least six Members of this Court (the four who join this opinion and JUSTICE WHITE and THE CHIEF JUSTICE) agree today that, in the context of defamation law, the rights of the institutional media are no greater and no less than those enjoyed by other individuals or organizations engaged in the same activities. [ ][10]

6. An attempt to characterize petitioner Dun & Bradstreet illustrates the point. Like an account of judicial proceedings in a newspaper, magazine or news broadcast, a statement in petitioner's reports that a particular company has filed for bankruptcy is a report of a timely news event conveyed to members of the public by a business organized to collect and disseminate such information. Thus it is not obvious why petitioner should find less protection in the First Amendment than do established print or electronic media. . . .

. . . That petitioner's information is "specialized" or that its subscribers pay "substantial fees" hardly distinguishes these reports from articles in many publications that would surely fall on the "media" side of the line . . . . Few published statements are of universal interest and few publications are distributed without charge. Much fare of any metropolitan daily is specialized information for which a selective, finite audience pays a fee. Nor is there any reason to treat petitioner differently than a more widely circulated publication because it has "a limited number of subscribers." Indeed, it would be paradoxical to increase protection to statements injurious to reputation as the size of their audience, and hence their potential to injure, grows. [ ]

7. Owing to transformations in the technological and economic structure of the communications industry, there has been an increasing convergence of what might be labeled "media" and "nonmedia." [ ]

9. In light of the "increasingly prominent role of mass media in our society, and the awesome power it has placed in the hands of a select few," [*Gertz,*] (WHITE, J., dissenting), protection for the speech of nonmedia defendants is essential to ensure a diversity of perspectives. . . .

10. JUSTICE POWELL's opinion does not expressly reject the media/nonmedia distinction, but does expressly decline to apply that distinction to resolve this case.

B

Eschewing the media/nonmedia distinction, the opinions of both JUSTICE WHITE and JUSTICE POWELL focus primarily on the content of the credit report as a reason for restricting the applicability of *Gertz.* Arguing that at most *Gertz* should protect speech that "deals with a matter of public or general importance," [ ] JUSTICE WHITE, without analysis or explanation, decides that the credit report at issue here falls outside this protected category. The plurality opinion of JUSTICE POWELL offers virtually the same conclusion with at least a garnish of substantive analysis.

Purporting to "employ the approach approved in *Gertz,*" [ ] JUSTICE POWELL balances the state interest in protecting private reputation against the First Amendment interest in protecting expression on matters not of public concern. The state interest is found to be identical to that at stake in *Gertz.* The First Amendment interest is, however, found to be significantly weaker because speech on public issues, such as that involved in *Gertz,* receives greater constitutional protection than speech that is not a matter of public concern. [ ] JUSTICE POWELL is willing to concede that such speech receives some First Amendment protection, but on balance finds that such protection does not reach so far as to restrain the state interest in protecting reputation through presumed and punitive damage awards in state defamation actions. [ ] Without explaining what *is* a "matter of public concern," the plurality opinion proceeds to serve up a smorgasbord of reasons why the speech at issue here is not, [ ], and on this basis affirms the Vermont courts' award of presumed and punitive damages.

In professing allegiance to *Gertz,* the plurality opinion protests too much. As JUSTICE WHITE correctly observes, JUSTICE POWELL departs completely from the analytic framework and result of that case . . . .[11] Even accepting the notion that a distinction can and should be drawn between matters of public concern and matters of purely private concern, however, the analyses presented by both JUSTICE POWELL and JUSTICE WHITE fail on their own terms. Both, by virtue of what they hold in this case, propose an impoverished definition of "matters of

11. One searches *Gertz* in vain for a single word to support the proposition that limits on presumed and punitive damages obtained only when speech involved matters of public concern. *Gertz* could not have been grounded in such a premise. Distrust of placing in the courts the power to decide what speech was of public concern was precisely the rationale *Gertz* offered for rejecting the *Rosenbloom* plurality approach. [ ] It would have been incongruous for the Court to go on to circumscribe the protection against presumed and punitive damages by reference to a judicial judgment as to whether the speech at issue involved matters of public concern. At several points the Court in *Gertz* makes perfectly clear the restrictions of presumed and punitive damages were to apply in all cases. [ ]

Indeed, JUSTICE POWELL's opinion today is fairly read as embracing the approach of the *Rosenbloom* plurality to deciding when the Constitution should limit state defamation law. The limits imposed, however, are less stringent than those suggested by the *Rosenbloom* plurality. Under the approach of today's plurality. . . .

public concern" that is irreconcilable with First Amendment principles. The credit reporting at issue here surely involves a subject matter of sufficient public concern to require the comprehensive protections of *Gertz.* Were this speech appropriately characterized as a matter of only private concern, moreover, the elimination of the *Gertz* restrictions on presumed and punitive damages would still violate basic First Amendment requirements.

(1)

The five Members of the Court voting to affirm the damage award in this case have provided almost no guidance as to what constitutes a protected "matter of public concern." . . .

In evaluating the subject matter of expression, this Court has consistently rejected the argument that speech is entitled to diminished First Amendment protection simply because it concerns economic matters or is in the economic interest of the speaker or the audience. [ ] See also Abood v. Detroit Bd. of Education, 431 U.S. 209, 231–232, and n. 28. "[O]ur cases have never suggested that expression about philosophical, social, artistic, economic, literary, or ethical matters—to take a nonexhaustive list of labels—is not entitled to full First Amendment protection." Id., at 231. The breadth of this protection evinces recognition that freedom of expression is not only essential to check tyranny and foster self-government but also intrinsic to individual liberty and dignity and instrumental in society's search for truth. See [Bose Corp. v. Consumers Union p. 178, supra, and *Whitney* (Brandeis, J., concurring)].

Speech about commercial or economic matters, even if not directly implicating "the central meaning of the First Amendment," [ ] is an important part of our public discourse. . . .

The credit reporting of Dun & Bradstreet falls within any reasonable definition of "public concern" consistent with our precedents. JUSTICE POWELL'S reliance on the fact that Dun & Bradstreet publishes credit reports "for profit," [ ] is wholly unwarranted. Time and again we have made clear that speech loses none of its constitutional protection "even though it is carried in a form that is 'sold' for profit." [ ] More importantly, an announcement of the bankruptcy of a local company is information of potentially great concern to residents of the community where the company is located; like the labor dispute at issue in *Thornhill,* such a bankruptcy "in a single factory may have economic repercussions for a whole region." . . .

. . .[14]

14. JUSTICE POWELL purports to draw from [*Connick*] a test for distinguishing matters of public concern from matters of private concern. This reliance perpetuates a definition of "public concern" wholly out of accord with our consistent precedents and with the common law understanding of the concept. [ ] Moreover, *Connick* explicitly limited its distinction between public and private concern to the "context" of a government employment situation. [ ]

(2)

Even if the subject matter of credit reporting were properly considered—in the terms of JUSTICE WHITE and JUSTICE POWELL—as purely a matter of private discourse, this speech would fall well within the range of valuable expression for which the First Amendment demands protection.

Our economic system is predicated on the assumption that human welfare will be improved through informed decisionmaking. In this respect, ensuring broad distribution of accurate financial information comports with the fundamental First Amendment premise that "the widest possible dissemination of information from diverse and antagonistic sources is essential to the welfare of the public." Associated Press v. United States, 326 U.S. 1, 20. The economic information Dun & Bradstreet disseminates in its credit reports makes an undoubted contribution to this private discourse essential to our well-being. . . .

The credit reports of Dun & Bradstreet bear few of the earmarks of commercial speech that might be entitled to somewhat less rigorous protection. In *every* case in which we have permitted more extensive state regulation on the basis of a commercial speech rationale the speech being regulated was pure advertising—an offer to buy or sell goods and services or encouraging such buying and selling. . . .

It is worth noting in this regard that the common law of most states, although apparently not of Vermont, [ ] recognizes a qualified privilege for reports like that at issue here. See Maurer, Common Law Defamation and the Fair Credit Reporting Act, 72 Geo.L.Rev. 95, 99–105 (1983). The privilege typically precludes recovery for false and defamatory credit information without a showing of bad faith or malice, a standard of proof which is often defined according to the *New York Times* formulation. [ ] The common law thus recognizes that credit reporting is quite susceptible to libel's chill; this accumulated learning is worthy of respect.

Even if JUSTICE POWELL's characterization of the credit reporting at issue here were accepted in its entirety, his opinion would have done no more than demonstrate that this speech is the equivalent of commercial speech. The opinion, after all, relies on analogy to advertising. Credit reporting is said to be hardy, motivated by desire for profit, and relatively verifiable. [ ] But this does not justify the elimination of restrictions on presumed and punitive damages. State efforts to regulate commercial speech in the form of advertising must abide by the requirement that the regulatory means chosen be narrowly tailored so as to avoid any unnecessary chilling of protected expression. [ ]

The Court in *Gertz* specifically held that unrestrained presumed and punitive damages were "unnecessarily" broad, [ ] in relation to the legitimate state interests. Indeed, *Gertz* held that in a defamation action punitive damages, designed to chill and not to compensate, were "*wholly irrelevant*" to furtherance of any valid state interest. . . .

What was "irrelevant" in *Gertz* must still be irrelevant and the requirement that the regulatory means be no broader than necessary is no less applicable even if the speech is simply the equivalent of commercial speech. Thus, unrestrained presumed and punitive damages for this type of speech must run afoul of First Amendment guarantees.[17]

(3)

Even if not at "the essence of self-government," *Garrison v. Louisiana,* [ ] the expression at issue in this case is important to both our public discourse and our private welfare. That its motivation might be the economic interest of the speaker or listeners does not diminish its First Amendment value. [ ] Whether or not such speech is sufficiently central to First Amendment values to require actual malice as a standard of liability, this speech certainly falls within the range of speech that *Gertz* sought to protect from the chill of unrestrained presumed and punitive damage awards.[18]

. . . The special harms caused by inaccurate credit reports, the lack of public sophistication about or access to such reports, and the fact that such reports by and large contain statements that are fairly readily susceptible of verification, all may justify appropriate regulation designed to prevent the social losses caused by false credit reports. And in the libel context, the states' regulatory interest in protecting reputation is served by rules permitting recovery for actual compensatory damages upon a showing of fault. Any further interest in deterring potential defamation through case-by-case judicial imposition of presumed and punitive damage awards on less than a showing of actual malice simply exacts too high a toll on First Amendment values. Accordingly, Greenmoss Builders should be permitted to recover for any actual damage it can show resulted from Dun & Bradstreet's

17. JUSTICE POWELL's analysis fails to apply the requirement that regulation be narrowly tailored. At one point the opinion reads: "This particular interest [in credit reporting] warrants no special protection when . . . the speech is wholly false and clearly damaging to the victim's business reputation." [ ] The point, of course, is not that false speech intrinsically deserves protection, see *Gertz,* [ ] but that the burdening of unintentional false speech potentially chills truthful speech. Thus, the state interest in compensating injury resulting from false speech must be vindicated by means that are narrowly tailored to avoid this deleterious result.

18. JUSTICE POWELL also relies in part on the fact that the expression had a limited circulation and was expressly kept confidential by those who received it. Because the subject matter of the expression at issue in this case would clearly receive the comprehensive protections of *Gertz* were the speech publicly disseminated, this factor of confidential circulation to a limited number of subscribers is perhaps properly understood as the linchpin of JUSTICE POWELL's analysis.

This argument does not save the analysis. The assertion that the limited and confidential circulation might make the expression less a matter of public concern is dubious on its own terms and flatly inconsistent with our decision in Givhan v. Western Line Consolidated School Dist., 439 U.S. 410 (1979). Perhaps more importantly, Dun & Bradstreet doubtless provides thousands of credit reports to thousands of subscribers who receive the information pursuant to the same strictures imposed on the recipients in this case. As a systemic matter, therefore, today's decision diminishes the free flow of information because Dun & Bradstreet will generally be made more reticent in providing information to all its subscribers.

negligently false credit report, but should be required to show actual malice to receive presumed or punitive damages. Because the jury was not instructed in accordance with these principles, we would reverse and remand for further proceedings not inconsistent with this opinion.

Notes and Questions

1. In the cited case of Connick v. Myers, plaintiff was employed as an assistant district attorney at the pleasure of the district attorney. Over her protests, she was ordered transferred. She prepared and distributed a questionnaire soliciting the views of fellow staff members about office transfer policy, office morale, the need for a grievance committee, the level of confidence in supervisors, and whether employees felt political pressure. The DA fired plaintiff on the ground of her refusal to accept transfer.

The Court upheld the firing, 5–4. It first reviewed its decisions in the area of protecting public employees from being fired because of their political views. The most important was Pickering v. Board of Education, 391 U.S. 563 (1968), which protected the right of a public employee "as a citizen, in commenting upon matters of public concern." That line of cases led the majority to conclude in *Connick* that if plaintiff's questionnaire "cannot be fairly characterized as constituting speech on a matter of public concern, it is unnecessary for us to scrutinize the reasons for her discharge":

> When employee expression cannot be fairly considered as relating to any matter of political, social, or other concern to the community, government officials should enjoy wide latitude in managing their offices, without intrusive oversight by the judiciary in the name of the First Amendment.
>
> . . . We hold only that when a public employee speaks not as a citizen upon matters of public concern, but instead as an employee upon matters only of personal interest, absent the most unusual circumstances, a federal court is not the appropriate forum in which to review the wisdom of a personnel decision taken by a public agency allegedly in reaction to the employee's behavior.

Then the Court turned to the question of whether the speech in question addressed a "matter of public concern." This "must be determined by the content, form, and context of a given statement, as revealed by the whole record. In this case, with but one exception, the questions posed by Myers to her coworkers do not fall under the rubric of matters of 'public concern.'" The exception was whether employees felt pressured to work in political campaigns on behalf of office-supported candidates.

The other questions did not address public concerns because Myers did not seek to inform the public that the office was not discharging its governmental responsibilities or seek to inform about actual or potential wrongdoing. "Indeed, the questionnaire, if released to the public, would convey no information at all other than the fact that a single employee is upset with the status quo." To consider all matters within a public office as matters of public concern would "mean that virtually every remark—and certainly every criticism directed at a public official—would plant the seed of a constitutional case. While as a matter of good judgment, public officials should be receptive to constructive criticism offered by their employees, the First Amendment does not require a public office to be run as a roundtable for employee complaints over internal office affairs."

Since one item was protected, the majority had to consider whether the firing was justified. It concluded that it was.

2. In Part IV, Justice Powell observed that speech on "matters of purely private concern" is "not totally unprotected by the First Amendment" and cited *Connick* for that proposition. In *Connick,* at the cited page (147), the Court stated:

> We do not suggest, however, that Myers' speech, even if not touching upon a matter of public concern, is totally beyond the protection of the First Amendment. "[T]he First Amendment does not protect speech and assembly only to the extent it can be characterized as political. 'Great secular causes, with smaller ones, are guarded.' " [ ] We in no sense suggest that speech on private matters falls into one of the narrow and well-defined classes of expression which carries so little social value, such as obscenity, that the State can prohibit and punish such expression by all persons in its jurisdiction. [ ] For example, an employee's false criticism of his employer on grounds not of public concern may be cause for his discharge but would be entitled to the same protection in a libel action accorded an identical statement made by a man on the street. . . .

How is Connick v. Myers relevant to the Greenmoss case?

3. What factors are relevant to Justice Powell in Part V? What is the significance of the last two sentences in that part? What are Justice Brennan's objections to each? When all is said and done, has part of *Gertz* been overruled?

4. What analysis in *Greenmoss* if the local newspaper had published the report in question? What if it had been a regional business newspaper? What if it had been a national construction industry newsletter? What if it had been a national magazine in an article on people and companies with funny names in the news that week? What if the high school employee's mother wrote a letter to a relative reporting the "bankruptcy"?

5. When certiorari was originally granted in the Greenmoss case, the petition asserted that the case raised the question whether a distinction should be drawn between protection of media and nonmedia defendants. The parties argued it that way. The Court then ordered the case reargued and asked the parties to address the significance of the

"commercial speech" doctrine. Do the opinions offer insights on these questions?

6. Justice Brennan asserts that Justice Powell "is willing to concede that [speech that is not a matter of public concern] receives some First Amendment protection . . . ." Does Justice Powell concede that? What might be the nature of that protection?

7. On what basis does Justice White assert that "it must be that the *Gertz* requirement of some kind of fault on the part of the defendant is also inapplicable in cases such as this"?

8. In Great Coastal Express, Inc. v. Ellington, 230 Va. 142, 334 S.E.2d 846, 12 Med.L.Rptr. 1100 (1985), a nonmedia slander case, plaintiff's employer told a group of employees that plaintiff had been discharged because he "tried to bribe one of my mechanics" to alter the engine on plaintiff's truck. Under its reading of *Greenmoss,* the court decided that it would not, under "state law, apply to speech actionable *per se,* involving no matters of public concern, the *Gertz* rule inhibiting presumed compensatory damages." It did, however, adhere as a matter of state law to the rule that "actual malice" must be shown before punitive damages can be awarded in any defamation case.

The court observed that the adoption of a rule that made words actionable per se did not mean that the court was imposing liability without fault. It then decided that a private plaintiff "must still prove negligence as a predicate for recovery, even if the words published are actionable *per se.* A plaintiff who proves the publication of words actionable *per se* is simply relieved of the necessity of proving the quantum of his damages for injury to reputation, humiliation, and embarrassment."

9. In New England Tractor-Trailer Training of Connecticut, Inc. v. Globe Newspaper Co., 395 Mass. 471, 480 N.E.2d 1005 (1985), plaintiff driver-training school claimed that a story in defendant's paper critical of a different driving school could be read as being "of and concerning" plaintiff. The court noted in passing that *Greenmoss* might be read as holding that the fault requirement of *Gertz* did not apply to "private parties suing on matters of private concern." The court refused to decide whether its case "touched on matters of public concern. We view the fault requirement of *Gertz* to be intact regardless whether the private parties are suing on matters of public or private concern. In any case, we base our holding in the present case—that a private plaintiff must prove that the defendant was negligent in publishing defamatory words which reasonably could be interpreted to refer to the plaintiff—on our own common law. . . . The failure to take care when there is a reasonable opportunity to do so—i.e., fault—is the cornerstone of much of our tort law."

10. If actual malice and the state prerequisites to punitive damages are proven, it may be possible to recover punitive damages in a case in which the jury finds that no actual harm has occurred. See Newsom v. Henry, 443 So.2d 817, 10 Med.L.Rptr. 1421 (Miss.1983) (approving an

award of $2500 punitive damages where the jury awarded nothing for actual damages).

Other courts insist that a "reasonable relationship" exist between the actual damages and the punitive damages. See, e.g., Marcone v. Penthouse International, Ltd, 577 F.Supp. 318, 10 Med.L.Rptr. 1193 (E.D.Pa.1983), holding that an award of $30,000 compensatory damages could not support a punitive award of $537,000 and ordering a remittitur of $337,000. Plaintiff accepted the remittitur. The court of appeals reversed and dismissed for lack of liability. 754 F.2d 1072, 11 Med.L.Rptr. 1577 (3d Cir.1985). Does *Greenmoss* affect these cases?

11. Justice White suggests several alternative ways the Court might have proceeded in this area. Do any of them seem more attractive constitutional approaches than what the Court has done? What leads him to describe the press as "successful and powerful"? In constitutional cases is it appropriate to think of the press as monolithic or to ask whether some elements might be "chilled"?

12. Justice Brennan from his perspective has suggested that nonmonetary remedies would be permissible. Justice White, from his constitutional perspective suggests the same thing. How can two justices so far apart on constitutional libel law be so close on this point?

13. Questions of legislative change within current constitutional doctrine are discussed at p. 290, infra.

2. The Press as Commentator

In two sentences early in his *Gertz* opinion, Justice Powell asserted in dictum a proposition that has led to much litigation:

> Under the First Amendment there is no such thing as a false idea. However pernicious an opinion may seem, we depend for its correction not on the conscience of judges and juries but on the competition of other ideas.

The background and the subsequent history of that passage are discussed below. This is another portion of the Cianci case, whose main part was reprinted at p. 110, supra. Quoting the two sentences, the trial judge had held that the article in New Times was opinion.

CIANCI v. NEW TIMES PUBLISHING CO.

United States Court of Appeals, Second Circuit, 1980.
639 F.2d 54, 6 Med.L.Rptr. 1625.

FRIENDLY, J.

. . .

. . . JUSTICE POWELL'S very next sentence, however, was that "there is no constitutional value in false statements of fact." The alleged libels in *Gertz,* which were deemed sufficiently "factual" to support an action for defamation, included an "implication that petitioner had a criminal record" and charges that he was a "Leninist" or "Communist-fronter". Id. at 326. The sort of idea which can never be false was illustrated by reference to Thomas Jefferson's Inaugural Address, where the President argued for freedom for those "who would wish to dissolve this Union or change its republican form." Id. at 340 n. 8.[10] A statement that Cianci raped Redick at gunpoint twelve years ago and then paid her in an effort to obstruct justice falls within the Court's explication of false statements of fact rather than its illustrations of false ideas where public debate is the best solvent.

The other Supreme Court cases cited as creating a constitutional exception for statements of opinion, Greenbelt Cooperative Publishing Ass'n v. Bresler, 398 U.S. 6 (1970), and Letter Carriers v. Austin, 418 U.S. 264 (1974), are equally inapplicable to this case. In *Greenbelt* a newspaper was sued for republishing a speaker's comment at a city council meeting that plaintiff was "blackmailing" the city in connection with pending negotiations. Justice Stewart wrote for the Court that no libel had been committed because no one who read the account would have considered that the plaintiff was being charged with the crime of blackmail. The word was "no more than rhetorical hyperbole, a vigorous epithet used by those who considered Bresler's negotiating position extremely unreasonable." [ ] The clear implication is that if an accusation of actual criminal wrongdoing had been conveyed, e.g., a statement that Bresler had threatened a councilman with exposure of an extramarital episode unless he voted Bresler's way, it would have been held actionable, unless within a privilege of fair reportage of public proceedings. . . .

In Letter Carriers v. Austin, supra, the Court relied on *Greenbelt* in holding that no one could reasonably understand publication of a well-known definition of a "scab", attributed to Jack London, as a "traitor to his God, his country, his family and his class", as charging the crime of treason. The words were protected because defendants were using them "in a loose, figurative sense . . . merely rhetorical hyperbole, a lusty and imaginative expression of the contempt felt by union members to those who refuse to join." [ ]

This court's first relevant post-*Gertz* discussion of the distinction between statements of fact and of opinion was in Buckley v. Littell, 539 F.2d 882 (1976), cert. denied, 429 U.S. 1062 (1977). The court there examined three alleged libels which the district court had found to have been perpetrated on William F. Buckley, Jr., admittedly a "public figure." The first was that Buckley was a fellow traveler of the fascists, as Buckley interpreted the term, or a fellow traveler of the radical right or the right wing. This court held that the use of such

10. Mr. Justice Powell's reference to "the competition of other ideas" doubtless stemmed, consciously or subconsciously, from Mr. Justice Holmes' eloquent observation in Abrams v. United States, 250 U.S. 616, 630 (1919) (dissenting opinion) "that the best test of truth is the power of the thought to get itself accepted in the competition of the market." This origin also points strongly to the view that the "opinions" held to be constitutionally protected were the sort of thing that could be corrected by discussion.

expressions "cannot be regarded as having been proved to be statements of fact, among other reasons, because of the tremendous imprecision of the meaning and usage of these terms in the realm of political debate, an imprecision which is simply echoed in the book." [ ] The second asserted libel was what the district court had characterized as accusing Buckley of "deliberately acting as a deceiver in the purveying of fascist material", [ ], and of printing news items and interpretations picked up from openly fascist journals. The court reversed the holding below on this alleged libel as well, reasoning as to the first accusation that it rested on one interpretation of the accused book when another could be supported as readily, and as to the second accusation that the issue of what constituted "openly fascist journals" was as much a matter of debate as what constituted "fascism" itself.

In sharp contrast to these rulings with regard to "loosely definable, variously interpretable statements of opinion . . . made inextricably in the contest of political, social, or philosophical debate", [ ], was the court's treatment of the statement:

> Like Westbrook Pegler, who lied day after day in his column about Quentin Reynolds and goaded him into a lawsuit, Buckley could be taken to court by any one of several people who had enough money to hire competent legal counsel and nothing else to do.

This was considered to be a defamatory assertion of fact, namely, that Buckley had made false and libelous statements. After repeating the contrast drawn in *Gertz* between expressions of "pure opinion" and "false statements of fact", the court held the statement was actionable because "the clear meaning to be inferred was that *he considered* Buckley to be a libeler like Pegler." [ ] (emphasis supplied). Since surely this was a statement of Littell's opinion, our decision must mean that when an "opinion" is something more than a generally derogatory remark but is laden with factual content, such as charging the commission of serious crimes, the First Amendment confers no absolute immunity, as distinguished from the qualified protection accorded by *Sullivan* in the case of public figures. And the court did not rest its decision at all on the basis that Littell implied he had reasons for believing Buckley to have been a libeller and defamer other than those disclosed in his articles.

No departure from this ruling was made by Hotchner v. Castillo-Puche, 551 F.2d 910 (2 Cir.1976), cert. denied, 434 U.S. 834 (1977). The uncomplimentary references to Hotchner there at issue, such as that of being a "toady" and a "hypocrite", were of a most general and imprecise sort, see id. at 912. It was in this context that the court said, citing *Gertz* and *Buckley,* id. at 913: "A writer cannot be sued for simply expressing his opinion of another person, however unreasonable the opinion or vituperous the expressing of it may be."

The highest courts of our two largest states have reached conclusions in accord with this court's analysis in *Buckley.* In Rinaldi v. Holt, Rinehart & Winston, Inc., 42 N.Y.2d 369, 397 N.Y.S.2d 943, cert. denied,

434 U.S. 969 (1977), plaintiff, a state court judge, charged defendants with libel in writing and publishing a book which charged the judge with being corrupt and incompetent and advocated his removal from office. The court ruled that the charge of incompetence and the advocacy of the judge's removal were protected as statements of opinion, but the charge of corruption was not:

> Accusations of criminal activity, *even in the form of opinion,* are not constitutionally protected. . . . While inquiry into motivation is within the scope of absolute privilege, outright charges of illegal conduct, if false, are protected solely by the actual malice test. As noted by the Supreme Court of California, there is a critical distinction between opinions which attribute improper motives to a public officer and accusations, *in whatever form,* that an individual has committed a crime or is personally dishonest. No First Amendment protection enfolds false charges of criminal behavior. Gregory v. McDonnell Douglas Corp. [17 Cal.3d 596, 604, 131 Cal.Rptr. 641, 646 (1976).] [ ] (emphasis supplied).

Almost any charge of crime, unless made by an observer and sometimes even by him, [ ] is by necessity a statement of opinion. It would be destructive of the law of libel if a writer could escape liability for accusations of crime simply by using, explicitly or implicitly, the words "I think".

The principle of the *Greenbelt-Letter Carriers-Gertz* trilogy, of our own *Buckley* decision, and of the New York Court of Appeals decision in *Rinaldi* is (1) that a pejorative statement of opinion concerning a public figure generally is constitutionally protected, quite apart from *Sullivan,* no matter how vigorously expressed; (2) that this principle applies even when the statement includes a term which could refer to criminal conduct if the term could not reasonably be so understood in context; but (3) that the principle does not cover a charge which could reasonably be understood as imputing specific criminal or other wrongful acts.

It is clear from the foregoing that even if the article were to be read as only expressing the "opinion" that Cianci committed the crimes of rape and obstruction of justice, it is not absolutely protected as distinguished from the protection afforded by *Sullivan.* The charges of rape and obstruction of justice were not employed in a "loose, figurative sense" or as "rhetorical hyperbole". A jury could find that the effect of the article was not simply to convey the idea that Cianci was a bad man unworthy of the confidence of the voters of Providence but rather to produce a specific image of depraved conduct—committing rape with the aid of trickery, drugs and threats of death or serious injury, and the scuttling of a well-founded criminal charge by buying off the victim. Such serious charges have not yet become "undefined slogans that are part of the conventional give-and-take in our economic and political controversies." . . .

Defendants also argue that any implied opinion conveyed by the article is protected because it set forth the facts which, in their view at least, supported this opinion. Restatement, Second, Torts § 566 states:

> A defamatory communication may consist of a statement in the form of an opinion, but a statement of this nature is actionable only if it implies the allegation of undisclosed defamatory facts as the basis for the opinion.

As acknowledged by the reporter, § 566 is the result of combining the limited constitutional protection of opinions and ideas surveyed above and the common law privilege of fair comment. See Wade, The Communicative Torts and the First Amendment, 48 Miss.L.J. 671, 694–95 (1977). Our analysis has shown that . . . opinions may support a defamation action when they convey false representations of defamatory fact, even though there is no implication that the writer is relying on facts not disclosed, [ ]. While the disclosure of factual background may indicate whether a particular word constituted a direct charge of crime or a looser protected opinion, as with "blackmail" in *Greenbelt* or "traitor" in *Letter Carriers,* nothing in those cases nor in our own *Buckley* and *Hotchner* decisions suggests that such disclosure would protect as opinion a direct accusation of criminal misconduct.

. . .

Notes and Questions

1. Is there something special about accusations of crime? To what other kinds of charges might this rationale apply?

2. In *Greenbelt,* the Court refused to leave the question of meaning to state law. It asserted that "as a matter of constitutional law, the word 'blackmail' in these circumstances was not slander when spoken, and not libel when reported." It was "simply impossible to believe that a reader . . . would not have understood exactly what was meant." Justice White concurred only on the inadequacy of the judge's charge. It was for the jury to decide how an ambiguous word was used. He could not join the majority's claim "of superior insight" as to how readers in Greenbelt would have understood the term.

3. Are the lines drawn in *Buckley* and *Rinaldi* drawn soundly?

OLLMAN v. EVANS

United States Court of Appeals, District of Columbia Circuit, en banc, 1984.
750 F.2d 970, 11 Med.L.Rptr. 1433.
Certiorari denied, 471 U.S. ___, 105 S.Ct. 2662, 86 L.Ed.2d 278 (1985).

Noted, 71 Iowa L.Rev. 913, 34 U.Kan.L.Rev. 367.

[A departmental search committee nominated Bertell Ollman, a Marxist political science professor at New York University, to head the Department of Government and Politics at the University of Maryland. The ensuing public debate centered largely on the propriety of appointing a Marxist to the University of Maryland position. In a syndicated column on the controversy, Evans and Novak called the public debate "wrong-headed"; the "crucial question" was "not Ollman's beliefs, but his intentions." Complaining that Ollman's pending appointment seemed to trouble only a "minority" of "professors throughout the country," the column charged that Ollman's "candid writings avow his desire to use the classroom as an instrument for preparing what he calls 'the revolution' "—possibly "a form of indoctrination that could transform the real function of a university." The column claimed that, although described in news accounts as a "respected Marxist scholar," Ollman was "an outspoken proponent of 'political Marxism' " and was "widely viewed in his profession as a political activist." The column then discussed Ollman's unsuccessful campaigns for election to the Council of the American Political Science Association, in which Ollman pledged that, if elected, he would "use every means at my disposal to promote the study of Marxism and Marxist approaches to politics." Next, the column reviewed an article entitled "On Teaching Marxism and Building the Movement," in which Ollman had argued that "a correct understanding of Marxism . . . leads automatically to its acceptance" and claimed that, indeed, most students taking his political science course ended with a "Marxist outlook." Finally, Evans and Novak quoted a "political scientist in a major eastern university" who, although refusing to be identified, claimed that "Ollman has no status within the profession, but is a pure and simple activist."

Soon after the column's appearance, the president of the University of Maryland rejected Ollman's appointment. The district court dismissed Ollman's libel suit, holding the Evans-Novak column absolutely protected by the First Amendment. A three-judge appellate panel reversed. This rehearing en banc is being heard by 11 judges.]

STARR, CIRCUIT JUDGE:

. . .

. . . In *Gertz,* the Supreme Court in *dicta* seemed to provide absolute immunity from defamation actions for all opinions and to discern the basis for this immunity in the First Amendment. . . . [H]owever, the Supreme Court provided little guidance in *Gertz* itself as to the manner in which the distinction between fact and opinion is to be discerned. . . .

Indeed, *Gertz* did not focus on this distinction at all. Rather, assuming without lengthy discussion that the statements in that case could be construed as statements of fact, the Court held that the plaintiff, who was a private rather than public figure, could prove that the statements at issue there were libelous upon demonstrating that they were negligently made. The distinction in our law between public and private figures, however, does not directly bear on the distinction between fact and opinion. . . . In a word, *Gertz*'s reasoning immunizes an opinion, not because the opinion is asserted about a public figure, but because there is no such thing as a "false" opinion. . . .

. . .

B

. . .

In formulating a test to distinguish between fact and opinion, courts are admittedly faced with a dilemma. Because of the richness and diversity of language, as evidenced by the capacity of the same words to convey different meanings in different contexts, it is quite impossible to lay down a bright-line or mechanical distinction. . . .

C

. . .

First, we will analyze the common usage or meaning of the specific language of the challenged statement itself. Our analysis of the specific language under scrutiny will be aimed at determining whether the statement has a precise core of meaning for which a consensus of understanding exists or, conversely, whether the statement is indefinite and ambiguous. [ ] Readers are, in our judgment, considerably less likely to infer facts from an indefinite or ambiguous statement than one with a commonly understood meaning. Second, we will consider the statement's verifiability—is the statement capable of being objectively characterized as true or false? [ ] Insofar as a statement lacks a plausible method of verification, a reasonable reader will not believe that the statement has specific factual content. And, in the setting of litigation, the trier of fact obliged in a defamation action to assess the truth of an unverifiable statement will have considerable difficulty returning a verdict based upon anything but speculation. Third, moving from the challenged language itself, we will consider the full context of the statement—the entire article or column, for example—inasmuch as other, unchallenged language surrounding the allegedly defamatory statement will influence the average reader's readiness to infer that a particular statement has factual content. [ ] Finally, we will consider the broader context or setting in which the statement appears. Different types of writing have . . . widely varying social conventions which signal to the reader the likelihood of a statement's being either fact or opinion. . . .

. . .

D

After deciding that a particular statement is opinion rather than fact, courts often undertake a second mode of analysis before wrapping the statement in the mantle of the First Amendment's opinion privilege. Relying upon the Restatement (Second) of Torts § 566, the court's consider whether the opinion implies the existence of undisclosed facts as the basis for the opinion.[28] If the opinion implied factual assertions, courts have held that it should not receive the benefit of First Amendment protection as an opinion.

We have no quarrel with the purpose of section 566. . . . In our view, however, the tests already articulated are a sufficient aid in determining whether a statement implies the existence of undisclosed facts. . . . A separate inquiry into whether a statement, already classified in this painstaking way as opinion, implies allegedly defamatory facts would, in our view, be superfluous. . . .

We are fortified in this respect by section 566's potential, on occasion, to mislead. Comments to that section may be taken to imply that only the disclosure of facts which form the basis of the statement will signal to the reader that the author is not employing an opinion to imply undisclosed facts.[30] To be sure, we fully agree that in some contexts statements should be submitted to the trier of fact, unless the presence of facts surrounding the statement suggests that it is merely a characterization of those facts and thus is best classified, like the characterization in *Greenbelt Publishing,* supra, as an opinion. For instance, in the context of a front page news story or magazine article, the presence of such facts may be the only factor that would prevent the allegedly defamatory statement from being submitted to the jury.

However, in other contexts, as we have shown above, factors besides the disclosure of facts are relevant in determining whether a statement implies factual allegations to the reasonable reader. Here, for instance, as we shall discuss more fully, that the statements challenged by Professor Ollman were found in a column on the Op-Ed page suggests, among other factors, that the statements would be understood by the reasonable reader as opinion—even in the absence of full disclosure of facts signalling to the reader that the allegedly defamatory statement was a characterization. In a word, disclosure of facts in the surrounding text is not the *only* signal that hard facts cannot reasonably be inferred from a statement. We think that our four-factor test takes account of the insights provided by section 566, while not rejecting the other factors that may signal that a statement is to be read as opinion.[31]

28. The Restatement (Second) of Torts § 566 provides:

> A defamatory communication may consist of a statement in the form of an opinion, but a statement of this nature is actionable only if it implies the allegation of undisclosed defamatory facts as the basis for the opinion.

This section lies at the basis of Chief Judge Robinson's dissent. It is our difficulty with the Restatement position, as expressed throughout this opinion, that leads to our disagreement with his position.

30. See Restatement (Second) of Torts § 566, comment c(4) (stating that "[i]f the defendant expresses a derogatory opinion without disclosing the facts on which it is based, he is subject to liability, if the comment creates the reasonable inference that the opinion is justified by the existence of unexpressed defamatory facts").

31. Judge Bork would reach the same result in this case by employing a methodology which he calls a "totality of the circumstances" approach, informed by First Amendment values. Suffice it to say that many, although not all, of the considerations that guide him are in fact taken into account by the methodological approach

III

. . .

The reasonable reader who peruses an Evans and Novak column on the editorial or Op-Ed page is fully aware that the statements found there are not "hard" news like those printed on the front page or elsewhere in the news sections of the newspaper. Readers expect that columnists will make strong statements, sometimes phrased in a polemical manner that would hardly be considered balanced or fair elsewhere in the newspaper. . . . That proposition is inherent in the very notion of an "Op-Ed page." Because of obvious space limitations, it is also manifest that columnists or commentators will express themselves in condensed fashion without providing what might be considered the full picture. Columnists are, after all, writing a column, not a full-length scholarly article or a book. This broad understanding of the traditional function of a column like Evans and Novak will therefore predispose the average reader to regard what is found there to be opinion.[33]

A reader of this particular Evans and Novak column would also have been influenced by the column's express purpose. . . . Evans and Novak made it clear that they were not purporting to set forth definitive conclusions, but instead meant to ventilate what in their view constituted the central questions raised by Mr. Ollman's prospective appointment. In the penultimate paragraph of the column, . . . the authors expressly posed the following "questions:"

> What is the true measurement of Ollman's scholarship? Does he intend to use the classroom for indoctrination? Will he indeed be

agreed to by the majority of the members of the court.

We also note that application of our four-factor analysis will arrive at the same result as that reached in the section 566 examples. For instance, example 3 of section 566 states: "A writes to B about his neighbor C: 'I think he must be an alcoholic.' " Section 566 indicates that this remark should be submitted to the jury as a statement that may imply that "A knew undisclosed facts that would justify his opinion."

Under our analysis, we would first examine the definiteness-ambiguity of the term "alcoholic." It is clear that, even outside of medical usage, this term has a fairly well-defined meaning. Moving to the verifiability branch of our analysis, the statement would appear to be eminently verifiable. Whether A is an "alcoholic," as the term is commonly understood, is capable of being proven true or false through the submission to a trier of fact of evidence of A's actions and conditions at various times in A's life, coupled presumably with expert testimony. Examining the linguistic context, we would note that the prefatory words "I think" qualify as language of "apparency," which in some contexts favors treating the statement that follows as an expression of opinion. Here, however, the statement . . . is so well defined and verifiable that the language of apparency would be given relatively little weight on the opinion side of the scale. [ ] Finally, the social context does not militate in favor of treating the statement as one of opinion because a neighbor would generally be thought likely to be in a position to report facts, namely that he has been in a position to make first-hand observations of A's conduct and demeanor. Thus, the statement provided by example 3 of section 566 would, under this approach, appear to be factual in nature and thus appropriate to treat as fact and to submit to the jury.

33. Of course, we do not hold that any statement on an editorial or Op-Ed page is constitutionally privileged opinion.

. . .

followed by other Marxist professors? Could the department in time become closed to non-Marxists, following the tendency at several English universities?

Prominently displayed in the Evans and Novak column, therefore, is interrogatory or cautionary language that militates in favor of treating statements as opinion.

A

Having reviewed the context of the challenged statements, we turn next to the alleged defamation that, in our view, is most clearly opinion, namely that "[Ollman] is an outspoken proponent of political Marxism." This kind of characterization is much akin to the characterization, "fascist," found absolutely protected in *Buckley v. Littell,* [ ]. This is unmistakably a "loosely definable, variously interpretable statement[ ] of opinion . . . made inextricably in the contest of political, social or philosophical debate . . . ." 539 F.2d at 895. It is obviously unverifiable. Since Mr. Ollman concedes that he is a Marxist, [ ] the trier of fact in assessing the statement would have the dubious task of trying to distinguish "political Marxism" from "nonpolitical Marxism," whatever that may be.

Nor is the statement that "[Mr. Ollman] is widely viewed in his profession as a political activist" a representation or assertion of fact. "Political activist" is a term, like "political Marxism," that is hopelessly imprecise and indefinite. It is difficult to imagine, much less construct, a means of deciding the quantum of political activity justifying the label "activist." While Mr. Ollman argues that this assertion is defamatory since it *implies* that he has no reputation as a scholar, we are rather skeptical of the strength of that implication, particularly in the context of this column. It does not appear the least bit evident that "scholarship" and "political activism" are generally understood to be incompatible. Moreover, Evans and Novak set out facts which signalled to the reader that this statement represents a characterization arising from the columnists' view of the facts. . . . A reasonable reader would conclude that the authors' judgment that Mr. Ollman was "widely viewed as a political activist" was a characterization based upon the latter's unsuccessful electoral endeavors within his profession.

B

Next we turn to Mr. Ollman's complaints about the column's quotations from and remarks about his writings, and specifically his article, "On Teaching Marxism and Building the Movement." We note in this respect that even before the appearance of the constitutionally based opinion privilege in *Gertz,* commentary on another's writing was considered a privileged occasion at common law and therefore received the benefit of the fair comment doctrine. When a critic is commenting about a book, the reader is on notice that the critic is engaging in interpretation, an inherently subjective enterprise, and therefore realizes that others, including the author, may utterly disagree with the critic's interpretation. The average reader further understands that because of limitations of space, not to mention those limitations imposed by the patience of the prospective audience, the critic as a practical matter will be able to support his opinion only by rather truncated quotations from the book or work under scrutiny. The reader is thus predisposed to view what the critic writes as opinion. In this context, courts have rightly been wary of finding statements to be defamatory, unless the statements misquote the author, put words into the author's mouth or otherwise clearly go beyond the realm of interpretation.

Evans and Novak's statements about Mr. Ollman's article clearly do not fall into the category of misquotation or misrepresentation. . . . To be sure, the quotation has not been printed in its complete context. But that is neither here nor there; the quotation of remarks without the complete context in which the remarks appeared is entirely commonplace when summarizing a written work in a brief space. We are fully aware that this practice can be highly irritating when the context does not seem fully and fairly stated. The balm for the irritation, however, cannot be a libel suit, unless triers of fact are to sit in editorial judgment.[38]

Professor Ollman also objects to the column's posing the question, prompted in Evans' and Novak's view by Mr. Ollman's article, of whether he intended to use the classroom for indoctrination. As we noted previously, the column in no wise affirmatively stated that Mr. Ollman was indoctrinating his students. Moreover, indoctrination is not, at least as used here in the setting of academia, a word with a well-defined meaning. To paraphrase Justice Harlan in another context, see Cohen v. California, 403 U.S. 15, 25 (1971), what is indoctrination to one person is merely the vigorous exposition of ideas to another. We therefore conclude that the column's statements concerning "indoctrination" constitute protected opinion.

Mr. Ollman also complains of the statement: "His candid writings avow his desire to use the classroom as an instrument for preparing what he calls the 'revolution'." This statement, unlike the column's remarks about indoctrination, is stated without any interrogatory language to allow the reader to discount it as opinion. However, it is clear from the context that the statement represents Evans' and Novak's interpretation of Mr. Ollman's writing. And, like the charge of indoctrination, this statement does not have a well-defined meaning or admit of a method of proof or disproof. What to one person is a patently

38. We note that in this case Mr. Ollman took advantage of another recourse. *The Washington Post* published Mr. Ollman's letter to set his statements in his article in a fuller context. [ ]

Of course, at some point the deletion or omission of proper context can be so egregious as to amount to misquotation. Omitting a negative word from a sentence with the result that that sentence has a meaning opposite to that which the author intended is a rather clear cut example of a misquotation.

improper use of the classroom for political purposes may represent to another no more than the imparting of ideas, in the faith that ideas have consequences.

C

Finally, we turn to the most troublesome statement in the column.* In the third-to-last paragraph, an anonymous political science professor is quoted as saying: "Ollman has no status within the profession but is a pure and simple activist." . . .

We are of the view . . . that under the constitutionally based opinion privilege announced in *Gertz,* this quotation, under the circumstances before us, is protected. A confluence of factors leads us to this conclusion. First, as we have stated, inasmuch as the column appears on the Op-Ed page, the average reader will be influenced by the general understanding of the functions of such columns and read the remark to be opinion. The identical quotation in a newspaper article purporting to publish facts or in an academic publication which purported to rate status within a given discipline would, of course, be quite another matter. But here we deal with statements by well-known, nationally syndicated columnists on the Op-Ed page of a newspaper, the well-recognized home of opinion and comment. In addition, the thrust of the column, taken as a whole, is to raise questions about Mr. Ollman's scholarship and intentions, not to state conclusively from Evans' and Novak's first-hand knowledge that Professor Ollman is not a scholar or that his colleagues do not regard him as such.

Moreover, the anonymous professor's unflattering comment appears only after the columnists expressly state that Mr. Ollman is a professor at New York University, a highly respected academic institution, a fact which provides objective evidence of Mr. Ollman's "status." So too, the controversy itself was occasioned by Professor Ollman's nomination by the departmental search committee as chairman of an academic department at the University of Maryland, a fact stated in the column's opening paragraph which also plainly suggested to the average reader that Professor Ollman did in fact enjoy some considerable status in academia. Finally in this regard, the column expressly states that Professor Ollman's imminent ascension to the departmental chairmanship at Maryland was troubling only to a clear minority of academics. Thus, the charge of "no status" in this context would plainly appear to the average reader to be "rhetorical hyperbole" within the meaning of *Greenbelt,* and which in turn would lead the reader to treat the statement as one of opinion.[42]

* The analysis in this portion of the opinion is concurred in only by Circuit Judges Tamm and Wilkey and Senior Circuit Judge MacKinnon. [footnote by the court]

42. While generally agreeing with the methodological approach employed here, the dissent goes to some considerable length to argue that the statement is verifiable, such as by conducting a poll of all members of the American Political Science Association. That, however, is most assuredly an extraordinarily burdensome and utterly impracticable procedure in a field

We note especially in this respect that the anonymous academician quoted in the column goes on to say that he would not repeat his charge publicly, stating that: "[o]ur academic culture does not permit the raising of such questions." Thus, while Mr. Ollman's critic is asserting a proposition about Mr. Ollman, he is simultaneously implying that, in the contemporary academic environment, no evidence can publicly be adduced to support it. Whether right or wrong, this admission by the anonymous political scientist would clearly tend to make the reader treat this proposition as opinion.

But most fundamentally, we are reminded that in the accommodation of the conflicting concerns reflected in the First Amendment and the law of defamation, the deep-seated constitutional values embodied in the Bill of Rights require that we not engage, without bearing clearly in mind the context before us, in a Talmudic parsing of a single sentence or two, as if we were occupied with a philosophical enterprise or linguistic analysis. Ours is a practical task, with elemental constitutional values of freedom looming large as we go about our work. And in that undertaking, we are reminded by *Gertz* itself of our duty "to assure to the freedoms of speech and press that 'breathing space' essential to their fruitful exercise." [ ] The provision of breathing space counsels strongly against straining to squeeze factual content from a single sentence in a column that is otherwise clearly opinion. . . .[45]

IV

The judgment of the District Court is therefore

Affirmed.

BORK, CIRCUIT JUDGE, with whom WILKEY and GINSBURG, CIRCUIT JUDGES, and MACKINNON, SENIOR CIRCUIT JUDGE, join, concurring:

. . . .

. . . [I]n the past few years a remarkable upsurge in libel actions, accompanied by a startling inflation of damage awards, has threatened to impose a self-censorship on the press which can as effectively inhibit debate and criticism as would overt governmental regulation that the first amendment most certainly would not permit. . . .

. . .

as huge and disparate as political science. . . .

The dissent refuses to accept the real-world, common-sense conclusion that the statement was, in context, rhetorical hyperbole, concluding that the article "could as well be understood to portray Ollman's prominence *as due solely to his vociferousness* . . . ." [ ] (emphasis added). Surely this contention is itself utterly hyberbolic. An understanding derived from the article, fairly read as a whole, that Mr. Ollman is a mere vociferous organ of political Marxism and nothing more is at the least, entirely fanciful. . . .

45. We emphasize, however, that we are by no means holding that in other circumstances a charge that a person lacks status within his or her profession could not solidly provide the basis for a defamation action. We conclude only that the statement here is opinion under the totality of circumstances in which it appeared and in light of our analysis under the factors previously set forth.

The only solution to the problem libel actions pose would appear to be close judicial scrutiny to ensure that cases about types of speech and writing essential to a vigorous first amendment do not reach the jury. See Bose Corp. v. Consumers Union of United States, Inc., 466 U.S. 485 (1984). This requires a consideration of the totality of the circumstances that provide the context in which the statement occurs and which determine both its meaning and the extent to which making it actionable would burden freedom of speech or press. . . .

. . .

I.

It is plain, I think, that the opinion-fact dichotomy is not as rigid as the various dissents suppose. . . .

. . .

A comparison of *Gertz,* on the one hand, with *Bresler* and *Letter Carriers,* on the other, indicates the actual state of the law. The fact that the epithets "Leninist" and "Communist-fronter" were deemed actionable, while the epithets "blackmail," "scab," and "traitor" were not, demonstrates that, when it comes to first amendment analysis, the Supreme Court does not employ a simplistic opinion-fact dichotomy. A statement that, on its face and standing alone, sounds like an assertion of fact may not be actionable. Context is crucial and can turn what, out of context, appears to be a statement of fact into "rhetorical hyperbole," which is not actionable. Thus, it is clear that the Supreme Court, in the service of the first amendment, employs a test which requires consideration of the totality of the circumstances in which a statement appears. . . .[6]

. . .

II.

There are several factors that convince me Ollman cannot maintain this action. . . . The factors . . . are: Ollman, by his own actions, entered a political arena in which heated discourse was to be expected and must be protected; the "fact" proposed to be tried is in truth wholly unsuitable for trial, which further imperils free discussion; the statement is not of the kind that would usually be accepted as one of hard fact and appeared in a context that further indicated it was rhetorical hyperbole.

6. It should be noted that a number of scholars have sharply criticized the utility of the opinion-fact dichotomy both at common law and in various lower court opinions applying *Gertz.* . . .

Scholarly criticism of the opinion/fact distinction is not surprising since even at common law a significant minority of jurisdictions rejected the opinion-fact dichotomy as unworkable and gave more weight to the question whether the public interest in free discussion was implicated. . . .

A.

. . .

. . . [I]n order to protect a vigorous marketplace in political ideas and contentions, we ought to accept the proposition that those who place themselves in a political arena must accept a degree of derogation that others need not. . . .

. . .

. . . Professor Ollman was an active proponent not just of Marxist scholarship but of Marxist politics. . . . It was plain that Ollman was a political activist and that he saw his academic post as, among other things, a means of advancing his political goals. This is controversial behavior for an academic, no matter what political creed he espoused, and was bound to raise for debate the question whether he used his position as a teacher to indoctrinate the young with his political beliefs. . . .

. . .

The important point about all of this is that Ollman was not simply a scholar who was suddenly singled out by the press or by Evans and Novak. Whatever the merits of his scholarship, he was also a political man who publicly tried to forward his political goals. . . .

. . .

B.

Particularly troubling in a first amendment context is the kind of fact that is proposed for trial and, on either side's demand, jury determination. Here it is well to recur to one of the functions of the rough division between opinions and facts. It is relatively easy to litigate a false statement of fact; it may be impossible to prove or disprove an opinion. Courts of law may reasonably limit their dockets to questions which they are competent to resolve. . . .

The evidence is mounting that juries do not give adequate attention to limits imposed by the first amendment and are much more likely than judges to find for the plaintiff in a defamation case. It is appropriate for judges, therefore, to . . . decide when allowing a case to go to a jury would, in the totality of the circumstances, endanger first amendment freedoms. That danger is overwhelming when the issue is of the sort presented here.

The issue the dissents would have tried—the political science academic community's opinion of Professor Ollman's stature as a political scientist—is inherently incapable of being adjudicated with any expectation of accuracy. . . .

. . . Perhaps both the plaintiff and defendants [c]ould devise and send out questionnaires so that the jury, weighing scientific arguments about which experts cannot agree, would have to decide which poll was the more methodologically sound. I do not think the results of a trial on issues like these could be anything but random and, whatever we might be willing of necessity to allow in a different kind of trial, I would be utterly unwilling to let first amendment freedoms ride upon an outcome determined by chance.

. . .

Let us suppose, however, that the jury chooses one poll as methodologically more acceptable than the other. And let us suppose that the results show that most of the scores awarded Ollman range between 2 and 7, with a scattering of 1's and 10's, and a mean of 3.5 and a median of 4. What on earth is a jury to make of that? That Ollman has high status?, that he has low status but not "no status"? If low status, is that close enough to "no status" to afford the statement of "no status" protection as permissible hyperbole? It is not at all clear what the term "no status" connotes. The term is so vague as to suggest little more than general, but not necessarily universal, disapproval. Thus, if the profession were sharply divided so that a fifth of those responding ranked Ollman at 8 and the remainder ranked him at 1, would the jury be permitted to find [that] that, in effect, showed "no status" or would it be instructed that any favorable opinion showed "some status" so that the column's statement was one of false fact?

How is the jury, or an appellate court, to know whether knowledge that the poll was for use in a lawsuit skewed the results? . . . Indeed, must not the ideological coloration of the entire political science academic profession become an issue for the jury in evaluating the poll? . . .

Matters are really worse than this, however. . . . [W]e are not talking about opinions concerning the professional credentials of a faculty member in the school of engineering or medicine, fields in which ideology plays little or no part in estimations of status. We are talking about an academic specialty which, as anyone remotely familiar with it knows, is politically highly charged and riven. Political outlook may color professional estimation. In this field there are varieties of liberals, conservatives, libertarians, Marxists, and Straussians. Suppose, to put a not wholly unreasonable hypothetical, that on the questionnaire the dissent proposes, Ollman received 9's and 10's from Marxists and 1's and 2's from Straussians. It may be doubted that either set of numbers has any significance that a jury should be entitled to consider. . . .

The suggestion that reputation could be verified by the testimony of prominent political scientists cures none of this. If prominent political scientists could be induced to testify, and if those who could be induced represented a fair cross-section of the academic community, both heroic assumptions, the jury would be left with contradictory opinions about opinions. I do not know how the jury could reach any informed judgment unless it were told that any opinion favorable to Ollman meant that the allegation of "no status" was false.

. . .[9]

C.

The statement of "no status" is very unlikely to be read as a flat statement of fact. Rather, it strikes the reader primarily as an exaggerated expression of the anonymous professor's own view of Ollman's academic credentials. It is wrong to speak as though there is always a sharp distinction between opinion and fact. There certainly is at the extremes an obvious difference in kind. The assertion that "Jones stole $100 from the church poor box last Friday night," cannot be tortured into an opinion, just as the assertion that "I think Jones is the kind of man who would steal from the church poor box" is obviously only a statement of the speaker's opinion of Jones' character. But the statement that "Half the people in this town think Jones is the kind of man who would steal from the poor box" is not quite like either of the first two. It is less harmful than the first and perhaps more damaging than the second. I say "perhaps" because the assertion of what others think always has a ring of hyperbole about it. The hearer knows that what he is being told is, in fact, one man's opinion about others' opinions. It can be called an assertion of fact, which in a sense it is, but it is also the kind of criticism that we are used to hearing and about which we regularly suspend judgment. Told by Smith that Jones actually stole the money, we think that Smith would not dare say such a thing if it were not so. There is a hard quality to the statement: it is capable of proof or disproof and it describes a physical action that did or did not take place. Told by Smith that half the town thinks Jones is the kind of fellow who would steal the money, we instantly discount it as an expression of Smith's antipathy to Jones. We think it may or may not be so and we realize that there is very little chance of verifying the truth of the assertion as made.

So it is here with the statement that Ollman has no status within the profession of political scientists.

. . .

When we come to the context in which this statement occurred, it becomes even more apparent that few people were likely to perceive it as a direct assertion of fact, to be taken at face value. That context was one of controversy and opinion, and it is known to be such by readers. It is significant, in the first place, that the column appeared on the Op-Ed pages of newspapers. . . . More than this, before the

9. Judge Scalia suggests there is not much danger to press freedom here since Ollman would have to prove his case by "clear and convincing evidence." That is next to no protection. If Ollman put three knowledgeable political scientists on the stand to testify that his academic standing was in fact high, and if Evans and Novak put three equally credible witnesses on the stand to testify that Ollman's reputation was low, I fail to see on what theory the trial judge could take the case from the jury. . . .

reader comes to the passage in question, he will have discovered many times over that Evans and Novak are, to say the least of it, suspicious of Ollman's intentions and that they regard him as a remarkably wayward academic. All of that impression is conveyed in language and expressions of opinion that no one on this court finds actionable. By the time the reader comes to the assertion of an anonymous professor's statement of academic opinion about Ollman, he is, I think, likely to read the remark as more of the same. He is most unlikely to regard that assertion as to be trusted automatically. It is an assertion of a kind of fact, it is true, but a hyperbolic "fact" so thoroughly embedded in opinion and tendentiousness that it takes on their qualities.

. . .

MACKINNON, SENIOR CIRCUIT JUDGE (concurring):

. . .

. . . [A] claim that someone has little or no "status" is unverifiable in a politically controversial context. It is unverifiable because whatever method one chooses to measure "status" and other "quantities" of its ilk, one must commit oneself to some politically controversial view about what that so-called quantity really consists of. Choosing a method, a survey for example, settles nothing; it merely shifts the political debate from whether a person has "status," or some other such quality, to how best to measure it. . . .

. . .

ROBINSON, CHIEF JUDGE, with whom WRIGHT, CIRCUIT JUDGE, joins, dissenting in part: . . . I think there may well be material issues of fact affecting the availability of the opinion privilege for several of the statements.

I

The First Amendment embodies a special solicitude for unfettered expression of opinion. . . .

. . .

II

. . .

. . . [Y]et the universe of statements cannot be neatly divided, by some logically discernible equator, into hemispheres of fact and opinion. Fact is the germ of opinion, and the transition from assertion of fact to expression of opinion is a progression along a continuum. . . .

At one end of the continuum are statements that may appropriately be called "pure" opinion. These are expressions which commonly are regarded as incapable of being adjudged true or false in any objective sense of those terms. Matters of personal taste, aesthetics, literary criticism, religious beliefs, moral convictions, political views and social theories would fall within this category. These are statements which by nature "could be corrected by discussion," and accordingly statements whose survival in our society's discourse should be committed to "the competition of the market" in ideas.

Also near the pure-opinion end of the continuum, I think, are those "loosely definable, variously interpretable" derogatory remarks that frequently are flung about in colloquial argument and debate. The hallmark of these statements is not that they are innocuous or impotent, but rather that they are so far in the realm of vernacular epithet as to become expressions of generalized criticism or dislike, without any specific factual moorings. Evaluating such statements as true or false is problematic largely because of the difficulty of arriving at a consensus on precisely what evidence would be relevant and sufficient to justify their use.

Finally, metaphorical language is also allied to pure opinion. When context makes it apparent that a word is being used figuratively or imaginatively without any intention to rely on its literal meaning, the labels "true" and "false" are inapposite.

. . .

Expressions at or near the pure-opinion end of the continuum probably constitute only a relatively small portion of the statements that become subjects of defamation lawsuits. Perhaps far more common, and certainly more perplexing, are statements that reflect the author's deductions or evaluations but are "laden with factual content." The apparent proportions of opinion and fact in these "hybrid" statement varies considerably. For example, a statement that "Jones is incompetent to handle that job" suggests some factual underpinning but, on the whole, imports a fairly high degree of subjective judgment. By contrast, a statement that "Smith is a murderer" appears much closer to an assertion of objective fact. Analytically, however, the accusation of murder could be regarded as an opinion, for it, like the charge of incompetence, reflects a conclusion ultimately reached by the author on the basis of an amalgamation and interpretation of underlying facts.

Hybrid statements differ from pure opinion in that most people would regard them as capable of denomination as true or false, depending upon what the background facts are revealed to be. At the same time, they generally are not propositions that a scientist or logician would regard as provable facts. . . .

When the proponent of a hybrid statement discloses to the reader the pertinent background facts with reasonable completeness and accuracy, there is a strong argument for including the statement within the realm of absolute privilege.[66] In these circumstances, the reader can easily recognize the statement as the author's synthesis and, placing it beside the predicate facts, can make up his own mind about how much weight and credence to give to the author's conclusion. . . .

66. The argument would apply equally to the case where the reader already knows, from personal observations or other source, the same degree of knowledge of the pertinent background facts.

In these circumstances, hybrid statements would seem to pose little or no threat to the reputation interest safeguarded by defamation law because they could be subjected to rigorous and fair evaluation by fully-informed readers.[67] At the same time, their claim to First Amendment protection would be great because they would share the primary immunizing characteristic of pure opinion, for the presence of the background data would ensure that the only really active element of the statement is its judgmental or interpretive component.

This balancing of First Amendment and defamation implications of hybrid statements works flawlessly where the critical background facts are accurately set forth. A significant imbalance results, however, when a hybrid statement appears without any recitation of the underlying facts, or when those facts are stated incompletely or erroneously. When that is the case, the reader is unable to place the author's judgment in perspective, because he either is completely unaware of the predicate facts or is in some degree misled as to what they are. False hybrid statements obviously can wreak considerable damage to reputation. A reader supplied with no background at all may well assume that there are facts which support the derogatory conclusion, particularly if it is announced by the author with apparent assurance.[70] A reader given materially incorrect or incomplete facts, mistakenly supposing that the pertinent data are accurately assembled before him, might give even more credence to the author's conclusion.[71] Hybrid

67. This point can be neatly illustrated hypothetically. The author is a person who takes the extreme view that the killing of one human by another is murder irrespective of the circumstances. The author makes the following communication:

> One evening, Smith went to White's house. She had with her a small gun which she customarily carried in her purse for protection. She and White began a discussion which escalated into a heated argument. White became enraged, grabbed a butcher knife and lunged across the room toward Smith with the weapon raised. Smith drew out her gun, aimed it at White's heart, and pulled the trigger. White died from the wound. Smith is a murderer.

Most readers would likely consider the hybrid "Smith is a murderer" to be an irrational and thus a false conclusion. Presumably their view of Smith would not be adversely affected by what commonly would be regarded as an unwarranted application of the charge by the author. Because the readers possess the relevant background data, they would not be misled by the innuendo of the word "murderer."

70. Consider, for example, a variation on the illustration given in note 67 supra. This time the author states, without elaboration, that "Smith is a murderer" to persons with no knowledge of the circumstances. The average reader is unlikely to even consider the possibility that the author entertains a bizarre conception of murder which fails to distinguish between unjustified intentional killing and self-defense. Readers are thus apt to assume the existence of some factual predicate which, by common understanding, would warrant use of the charge "murderer"—particularly if the author were someone who appeared to be in a position to know about the incident to which the statement ostensibly refers.

71. In one more variation on the illustration, note 67 supra, consider the case where the author recites the story of Smith's encounter with White except that he omits the sentence describing how White came at Smith with a knife. In this event, the statement "Smith is a murderer" is probably both the most damaging to Smith's reputation, and the most deceptive of all the hypothetical hybrids, because it is seemingly accompanied by a complete set of facts which, on their face, justify its use. Neither the damage nor the deception would likely be significantly lessened if the author had said instead "I think Smith is a murderer." The problem is not with the reader's ability to recognize that this is the author's conclusion, but rather

statements unaccompanied by any predicate facts, or attended by defective recitals of the underlying facts, thus should occupy a very different position in the concerns of libel law, for their claim to First Amendment protection is far less compelling. If the background data reaching the reader are deficient, the hybrid statement is as much a representation of the facts it implies as it is a judgment or interpretation of the communicated data.

. . .

I would hold that a hybrid statement is absolutely privileged as opinion when it is accompanied by a *reasonably* full and accurate narration of the facts pertinent to the author's conclusion. I would further hold that hybrid statements not so accompanied are not entitled to that degree of protection unless those facts are already known to the author's listeners or readers. . . .

. . .

. . . [I]f critical background data are omitted or are erroneous, the absolute opinion privilege is still available when the infirmity is not traceable, in the case of a public official or public figure, to actual malice or reckless disregard of truth or falsity, or, in the case of a private figure, to culpability great enough to incur liability under relevant state defamation law.

. . .

III

I now turn my attention to the passages of the syndicated column which are subjects of complaint in the case at bar. I agree with the District Court that Evans' and Novak's characterization of Ollman as an "outspoken proponent of 'political Marxism'" is absolutely privileged. It falls well within the class of "loosely definable, variously interpretable statements of opinion . . . made inextricably in the contest of political, social or philosophical debate. . . ." . . .

. . .

A statement that Ollman's peers do not respect him as a scholar stands, I submit, on quite different footing from a statement that Evans and Novak do not themselves rank him as one. The latter might well fall into the category of pure opinion, as a subjective appraisal of the value of Ollman's writings. The former, however, if not actually a representation of fact, certainly rises no higher than a hybrid statement.[115] It may convey the authors' ultimate assessment of what the

the reader's inability to separate out, and dismiss as erroneously suggested, the factual component of the charge "murderer" in these circumstances.

115. There is some reason for treating the statement as a factual representation. It purports uncategorically to announce what a finite set of people—political scientists—think about a given subject—Ollman's scholarship. In theory at least, the truth or falsity of this representation could be established empirically by polling each member of the group and tabulating the results. That each of the answers is in itself the respondent's opinion does not make the summary of how many people gave which answer any less a statement of fact. . . .

political science profession thinks of Ollman, but it also implies the existence of facts inducing that conclusion, such as evaluations of Ollman's work by a sampling of academicians, critical reviews of his articles, or a poll taken of members of the profession. Our attention is directed to a passage describing how Ollman came in last in two American Political Science Association elections, but just what this fact has to do with Ollman's scholarly reputation in the profession is not immediately apparent; indeed, the article itself professes some uncertainty about "[w]hether or not [the election results] represent[ ] a professional judgment by his colleagues." Ollman, on the other hand, points to a 1978 published survey in which, so he claims, "a poll of 317 leading and representative political scientists" ranked him "10th in the entire field of all political scientists in terms of occupational prestige." I thus think that, although the matter is not wholly free from doubt, the paucity of supporting facts in the column, coupled with the survey Ollman proffers, raises a genuine issue as to whether there was a culpable error or omission in the background facts presented to the reader.

I come finally to a set of statements relating to Ollman's writings and to what assertedly they reveal about his objectives as an instructor [in his "candid writings" and his "On Teaching."]

I would note initially that these excerpts do not represent literary, scholarly or ideological criticism. . . . A jury reasonably could read these passages as saying that Ollman, in his writings, openly admits that he wishes to use the classroom to indoctrinate his students and transform them into Marxists. To be sure, whenever an author undertakes to encapsulate and describe the contents of another's lengthy work, the product is apt to reflect some amount of the author's own interpretation and judgment. Here, however, a significant component of factual representation also comes through, particularly in such strong and apparently unequivocal phrases as "[h]is candid writings avow," "Ollman's intentions become explicit" and "Ollman concedes." I therefore think these passages should properly be regarded as hybrid statements of what Ollman's writings say about his intentions in the classroom.

A fair amount of background material on this point is provided in the column under attack, largely in the form of direct quotations from Ollman's writings. There is some question, however, as to the completeness and accuracy with which these predicate facts are set out. The District Court, after review of the article, found that "[w]hile [Evans and Novak] refer to [Ollman's] writings and speeches, Ollman's statements are selected to reflect [their] opinion. Portions contrary to Evan's [sic] and Novak's viewpoint are carefully omitted." The court also suggested that "this may be thought of as biased journalism," and an examination of the full text of the sources quoted could lead one to believe that this appellation may not be undeserved.

I conclude, then, that these passages also present a genuine issue whether the absolute privilege for opinion has been forfeited by culpable omissions or errors in the supporting facts which the article offered its readers.

WALD, CIRCUIT JUDGE, with whom CIRCUIT JUDGES EDWARDS and SCALIA join, dissenting in part: I basically agree with the majority's outline of the appropriate strategy for identifying absolutely privileged opinion . . . .

. . .

[However,] I believe that the challenged statement is properly characterized as a factual assertion rather than a rhetorical hyperbole under either the majority's or the concurrence's approach. The statement that Ollman has no status within his profession undoubtedly admits of a sufficiently ascertainable and stable core of meaning: a decisive majority of his fellow political scientists do not regard him as a good scholar. That one might find a wide diversity of views among political scientists about Ollman's work and about what constitutes scholarly excellence in no way undermines the commonly understood meaning of a statement like this about reputation. The statement says to the ordinary reader that, however each individual scholar evaluates excellence, there is an overwhelming consensus that Ollman does not have it.

Furthermore, Ollman's scholarly reputation is adequately verifiable. One could, for instance, devise a poll of American Political Science Association members as to their opinion, on a scale of one to ten, of the scholarly value of Ollman's work. Testimony of prominent political scientists or other measures of reputation would also serve to verify or refute the statement about Ollman's reputation without sending the jury into a sea of speculation.

As both Judge Bork and Judge MacKinnon point out, neither a poll nor the testimony of his peers will, in all likelihood, *conclusively* establish Ollman's professional reputation in the eyes of the jury. Nonetheless, juries traditionally are called on to resolve conflicting opinions in libel cases, and the uncertainties endemic to determining a person's reputation do not, in themselves, render the issue "inherently unsusceptible to accurate resolution by a jury." [1]

. . . [2] . . .

1. After the war of words has ended, I am left with the simple fact that, in assessing or mitigating damages, juries have historically been required to determine what a plaintiff's reputation was before the libel in order to determine how much the plaintiff has been injured by the libel. . . .

2. Judge Bork's concurrence would apply the fact-opinion distinction differently to statements made in the context of public political controversy than to those made in other contexts. . . . By transforming arguably factual assertions into privileged statements of opinion or rhetorical hyperbole merely because they appear in a charged political context, Judge Bork's wholly novel approach would deprive the plaintiff of an opportunity even to prove that Evans and Novak acted with actual malice or reckless disregard of the truth. In my view, the first amendment does not require such an egregious result, and *New York Times*, by giving quite a different

. . . Our decision today . . . means that, even assuming that the statement was utterly false, that it was made with knowledge of its falsity, and that it precipitated Ollman's loss of an important academic position and a decline in his professional standing, the statement's authors cannot be made to answer in a suit for libel. I do not believe that the first amendment requires this result, and I therefore respectfully dissent.

EDWARDS, CIRCUIT JUDGE, concurring in part and dissenting in part: . . .

. . . [A]s a former member of the academic community, I am somewhat taken aback by the notion that one's reputation within the profession (which is *easily* verifiable) may be so freely and glibly libelled. I can find no meaningful case authority to convince me that the First Amendment is designed to condone such loose muckraking. . . .

. . .

SCALIA, CIRCUIT JUDGE, dissenting, with whom WALD and EDWARDS, CIRCUIT JUDGES, join: . . .

. . . Existing doctrine provides ample protection against the entire list of horribles supposedly confronting the defenseless modern publicist:

—The need to give special scope to political rhetoric is already met by recognition that hyperbole is an expected form of expression in that context. If Evans and Novak had chosen to call Ollman a traitor to our nation, fair enough. No reasonable person would believe, in that context, that they really *meant* a violation of 18 U.S.C. § 2381 (1982). [ ] The concurrence correctly claims the defense of this doctrine for the "no status" assertion. Surely it did not mean that Ollman had *no* status—only that his regard in the profession was not *high*. But to say, as the concurrence does, that hyperbole excuses not merely the exaggeration but *the fact sought to be vividly conveyed by the exaggeration* is to mistake a freedom to enliven discourse for a freedom to destroy reputation. The libel that "Smith is an incompetent carpenter" is not converted into harmless and nonactionable word-play by merely embellishing it into the statement that "Smith is the worst carpenter this side of the Mississippi."

—The expectation that one who enters the "public, political arena," [ ], must be prepared to take a certain amount of "public bumping," [ ], is already fulsomely assured by the *New York Times Co. v. Sullivan,* [ ], requirement of actual malice in the defamation of public figures. . . . This is a formidable task, and in the present case

effect to the "political context" factor, implicitly forbids it.

. . . Under Judge Bork's approach, if an editorialist makes identical, maliciously false statements concerning the professional reputation of a retiring scholar and that of an activist academic, only the former could bring a defamation action. In effect, trial judges would be required to distinguish politics from scholarship as a condition of allowing a defamation suit to proceed at all. . . .

it is likely that the defendants would have to do no more to defeat it than to establish that a "political scientist in a major eastern university, whose scholarship and reputation as a liberal are well known" did indeed tell them what they printed. See *St. Amant v. Thompson,* [ ].

—The difficulty of proving academic reputation, which the concurrence dwells upon at some length, [ ], is fully accounted for under current law by the fact that any failure of proof harms the *plaintiff's* rather than the *defendant's* case—and harms it in particularly devastating fashion when the "clear and convincing evidence" standard applicable to public figures governs. If the statistical evidence were indeed as inconclusive as the concurrence portrays, the result would be precisely what the concurrence desires, a dismissal of the suit.

—The problem that "juries . . . are much more likely than judges to find for the plaintiff in a defamation case," . . . , has been met by the Supreme Court's holding that "[j]udges . . . must independently decide whether the evidence in the record is sufficient to cross the constitutional threshold that bars the entry of any judgment that is not supported by clear and convincing proof of 'actual malice.'" *Bose Corp. v. Consumers Union, Inc.,* [ ].

It is difficult to see what valid concern remains that has not already been addressed by first amendment doctrine and that therefore requires some constitutional evolving—unless it be, quite plainly, the concern that political publicists, even with full knowledge of the falsity or recklessness of what they say, should be able to destroy private reputations at will.

When its lengthy "balancing" of the "totality of the circumstances" is complete, the concurrence ends up straddling two propositions: First, that the reasonable meaning of this statement is *not* that Ollman is poorly regarded within his profession. Second, that such an unquestionable libel is permitted in the course of political polemics. The first of these propositions distorts reality. . . . [T]hey did *not* say he was incompetent. They said that his *professional peers* regarded him as incompetent—and there is no way *that* conclusion can be understood to be a product of their econo-political opinions. In fact, they went even further out of their way to dissociate this factual statement from their opinions: they put it in the mouth of one whom they describe as (1) an expert on the subject of status in the political science profession, and (2) a political *liberal,* i.e., one whose view of Ollman would *not* be distorted on the basis of greatly differing political opinion. They were saying, in effect, "This is not merely our prejudiced view; it is the conclusion of an impartial and indeed sympathetic expert." Try as they may, however, to convey to the world the *fact* that Ollman is poorly regarded in his profession, the concurrence insists upon calling it an opinion. It will not do.

Hence the second thread of argument which is subtly woven through the concurring opinion: In the field of political polemics, even statements that *are* fact rather than opinion must be excused because the reader "is most unlikely to regard [them] as to be *trusted* automatically." [ ] (emphasis added). . . . And since he would be a fool to *believe* them, they are not actionable. I am not prepared to accept this novel view that since political debate is always discounted, a decent amount of defamation in that context is protected by the first amendment. . . .

. . .

. . . For the foregoing reasons, I join Judge Wald's dissent on the professional status point.

Notes and Questions

1. What are the major disagreements between Judge Starr and Judge Bork?

2. What are the major disagreements between Judges Starr and Bork on the one hand and the various dissenters on the other? Is it helpful to consider how each of the judges would have decided the examples offered by the other judges?

Judge Starr: (a) "A writes to B about his neighbor C: 'I think he must be an alcoholic.' "

Judge Bork: (a) "Jones stole $100 from the church poor box last Friday night." (b) "I think Jones is the kind of man who would steal from the church poor box." (c) "Half the people in this town think Jones is the kind of man who would steal from the poor box."

Chief Judge Robinson: (a) "Jones is incompetent to handle that job." (b) "Smith is a murderer." (c) The extended Smith-White murder sequence.

Judge Scalia: (a) "Smith is an incompetent carpenter." (b) "Smith is the worst carpenter this side of the Mississippi." (c) "The conclusion of an impartial and indeed sympathetic expert" is that Ollman (the carpenter?) "has no status in the profession" (is incompetent).

3. The plaintiff's petition for a writ of certiorari was denied, 105 S.Ct. 2662, 11 Med.L.Rptr. 2015 (1985), over a dissent by Justice Rehnquist, joined by Chief Justice Burger, that said in part:

> . . . I think that the result reached by the Court of Appeals in this case is nothing less than extraordinary. At the heart of the common law of defamation were a few areas of expression which even when spoken rather than written were regarded as so damaging as to be classified as "slander per se" and therefore not to require the proof of any special damages in order to allow recovery. One of these categories consists of statements which defame the plaintiff in connection with his business or occupation. [ ]
>
> Much of the extended treatment of this question in the Court of Appeals was devoted to the question of whether or not this statement was one of "fact" or of "opinion," the implication being that if the statement were one of "opinion" it could not be actionable under any circumstances. But for nationally syndicated colum-

nists to quote an unnamed political scientist as saying that petitioner has "no status within the profession" is far more than the mere statement of opinion traditionally protected by qualified privilege under the common law of libel. Doctors who are disapproved of by other doctors may find solace in the fees paid by their patients; lawyers disapproved of by other lawyers may comfort themselves by the retainers paid by their clients. But the academic who is disapproved of by his peers has no such healthy recourse outside of the profession. There, if ever, the opinion of one's peers is virtually the sole component of one's professional reputation.

. . .

At the time I joined the opinion in [*Gertz*], I regarded [the two sentences about opinion] as an exposition of the classical views of Thomas Jefferson and Oliver Wendell Holmes that there was no such thing as a false "idea" in the political sense, and that the test of truth for political ideas is indeed the market place and not the courtroom. I continue to believe that is the correct meaning of the quoted passage. But it is apparent from the cases cited by petitioner that lower courts have seized upon the word "opinion" in the second sentence to solve with a meat axe a very subtle and difficult question . . . .

. . .

I would grant the petition for certiorari in this case.

4. In Janklow v. Newsweek, Inc., 788 F.2d 1300, 12 Med.L.Rptr. 1961 (8th Cir.1986), the court en banc generally followed the *Ollman* approach. Certiorari was denied on Oct. 14, 1986.

5. Consider the following cases in light of the tests offered by Judge Friendly and the various opinions in *Ollman*:

a. Those who represent banks say of a lawyer who has sued some banks that he is "in a time warp," and that he "is not known for his research, and probably doesn't even know the difference between state and federally chartered S & L associations." Belli v. Berryhill, 11 Med. L.Rptr. 1221 (Cal.App., not officially reported, 1984).

b. A talk show host and restaurant critic says during a discussion of restaurants that "the people who own the place are unconscionably rude and vulgar people. And the attitude that they communicate is awful. But the food is fine. And it kills me to say this because I would like to be able to dump on their restaurant. I keep going there hoping it will decline and it doesn't. The food is fine, the people who run it are PIGS."

When plaintiffs asserted that listeners could have understood the comments to imply the existence of undisclosed defamatory facts, the court responded with a quotation from another case: "In the present case, it is not clear that any undisclosed facts are implied, or if any are implied, it is unclear what they are. Finally, it is entirely unclear (even assuming that facts are implied) that they are defamatory facts."

Pritsker v. Brudnoy, 389 Mass. 776, 452 N.E.2d 227, 9 Med.L.Rptr. 2028 (1983).

c. Defendant's restaurant guide, published in book form, carried a quite negative review of plaintiff's Chinese restaurant, including the following passages: (1) the "sweet and sour pork contained more dough . . . than meat"; (2) the "green peppers . . . remained still frozen on the plate"; and (3) pancakes with the Peking duck were the thickness of a finger." At trial, the plaintiff presented video tapes of the staff's preparation of these dishes. In addition, the flour chef gave a live demonstration of his method of making Chinese pancakes. The defense presented the reviewer, his wife who corroborated the story, and another reviewer who testified to the reputation of defendant's restaurant guide and to a "negative dining experience he had had" at plaintiff's restaurant.

One statement was that the Peking duck dish "was made up of only one dish (instead of the three traditional ones). . . . " The trial judge entered judgment on a jury's general verdict for plaintiff for $20,000 in compensatory damages and $5 in punitive damages. What result on appeal? See Mr. Chow of New York v. Ste. Jour Azur S.A., 759 F.2d 219, 11 Med.L.Rptr. 1713 (2d Cir.1985).

d. Political opponents in a town write a letter asserting "There are many of us who recognize [plaintiff's] service to the village in the past, and who have supported him in the past. But we also recognize that 'power tends to corrupt, and absolute power corrupts absolutely.' There is no longer any question about the corruptness of [plaintiff's] administration of the affairs of the Village of Ocean Beach." Silsdorf v. Levine, 59 N.Y.2d 8, 449 N.E.2d 716, 462 N.Y.S.2d 822, 9 Med.L.Rptr. 1815 (1983).

6. In his opinion, Judge Bork suggests that if each side presented three experts, the jury's verdict would have to stand on that point. Is this different from a case under New York Times v. Sullivan, in which the plaintiff and a defendant reporter testify to diametrically opposing views of their interview? See LaRue, Living with *Gertz*: A Procedural Look at Constitutional Libel Standards, 67 Va.L.Rev. 287 (1981). Recall the Bose case, p. 178, supra.

7. As we have seen, Judges Wald and Scalia rejected Judge Bork's suggestion that the political aspect of the Ollman case was relevant to the question before the court. Judge Bork responded to their comments in the following excerpt from his opinion:

> Two of the dissenting opinions [ ] maintain that commentary about public figures is already adequately protected by the actual malice requirement of New York Times v. Sullivan. According to this view, there is no reason to go beyond *Sullivan* and accord greater first amendment protection to some false political statements made knowingly and with actual malice. But the Supreme Court has already placed the law in precisely the posture to which the dissent objects. *Gertz,* of course, means that a statement

characterized as an opinion cannot be actionable even if made with actual malice and even if it severely damages the person discussed. In such circumstances, society must depend upon the competition of ideas to correct pernicious opinions rather than on "the conscience of judges and juries."

Bresler and *Letter Carriers* make the point even clearer. In both, apparent factual assertions—in *Bresler* that plaintiff engaged in "blackmail"; in *Letter Carriers* that plaintiffs were "scabs" and "traitors"—were held not actionable because, in context, the reader would take them not as assertions of fact but as vigorous hyperbole. In neither case did the Court inquire about actual malice. It assumed that even if these statements were made with actual malice, they were protected because the context in which they appeared alerted the reader that the statements were not to be read as factual allegations.

Recall Judge Scalia's assertion that Judge Bork was saying that in the field of "political polemics, even statements that *are* fact rather than opinion must be excused because the reader is 'most unlikely to regard [them] as to be *trusted* automatically.' " Is there a difference between saying (1) that statements made in some political contexts should not be actionable because they are not taken literally and (2) that some statements that readers are likely to take literally and that can sensibly be understood as assertions of disprovable propositions should not be actionable because the political arena should be free from judicial control?

See Desert Sun Publishing Co. v. Superior Court, 97 Cal.App.3d 49, 158 Cal.Rptr. 519 (1979), denying an action for the following charges made against a candidate:

> The portions of the letter to which Block objects accused him of "contrived public opinion polls, unfounded statements, emphatic denials, committees no one ever heard of, attacks on straw men and a lot of slick, big-time, expensive political public relations." It also charged Block with an "amateurish job of chicanery." It refers to Block as being a "Desert Dirty Trickster," says he used "touched-up photographs," and presented the "same ol' formula politics-as-usual techniques of the L.A. research and political packaging agency crowd" and refers to his "fancy L.A. political counsellor-pollster-manipulator."
>
> . . .
>
> A reader of this letter could come to no other conclusion but that the writer has accused Block of being a city slicker who is trying to bamboozle the good citizens of Palm Springs with the old snake-oil routine. That is the content of the letter—the opinion of the writer that Block is a political huckster. As such, it is a statement of opinion, not fact.

See generally, Franklin and Bussel, The Plaintiff's Burden in Defamation: Awareness and Falsity, 25 Wm. & Mary L.Rev. 825, 875 (1984).

8. Judge Bork's passage about the surge of libel awards provoked a side debate between Judges Bork and Scalia. Judge Bork suggested that judges properly consider constitutional values as new problems arise. He discussed this in the context of electronic surveillance and the "intricate interdependence of today's economic activities." Then:

> The first amendment's guarantee of freedom of the press was written by men who had not the remotest idea of modern forms of communication. But that does not make it wrong for a judge to find the values of the first amendment relevant to radio and television broadcasting.
>
> So it is with defamation actions. We know very little of the precise intentions of the framers and ratifiers of the speech and press clauses of the first amendment. But we do know that they gave into our keeping the value of preserving free expression and, in particular, the preservation of political expressions, which is commonly conceded to be the value at the core of those clauses. Perhaps the framers did not envision libel actions as a major threat to that freedom. I may grant that, for the sake of the point to be made. But if, over time, the libel action becomes a threat to the central meaning of the first amendment, why should not judges adapt their doctrines? Why is it different to refine and evolve doctrine here, so long as one is faithful to the basic meaning of the amendment, than it is to adapt the fourth amendment to take account of electronic surveillance, the commerce clause to adjust to interstate motor carriage, or the first amendment to encompass the electronic media? I do not believe there is a difference. To say that such matters must be left to the legislature is to say that changes in circumstances must be permitted to render constitutional guarantees meaningless. It is to say that not merely the particular rules but the entire enterprise of the Supreme Court in New York Times v. Sullivan was illegitimate.
>
> . . . The important thing, the ultimate consideration, is the constitutional freedom that is given into our keeping. A judge who refuses to see new threats to an established constitutional value, and hence provides a crabbed interpretation that robs a provision of its full, fair and reasonable meaning, fails in his judicial duty. That duty, I repeat, is to ensure that the powers and freedoms the framers specified are made effective in today's circumstances. The evolution of doctrine to accomplish that end contravenes no postulate of judicial restraint. . . .

Judge Scalia responded:

> It seems to me that the identification of "modern problems" to be remedied is quintessentially legislative rather than judicial business—largely because it is such a subjective judgment; and that the remedies are to be sought through democratic change rather than through judicial pronouncement that the Constitution now prohibits what it did not prohibit before. The concurrence

perceives a "modern problem" consisting of "the freshening stream of libel actions, which . . . may threaten the public and constitutional interest in free, and frequently rough, discussion," [ ] and of claims for damages that are "quite capable of silencing political commentators forever," [ ]. Perhaps that perception is correct, though it is hard to square with the explosion of communications in general, and political commentary in particular, in this "Media Age." But then again, perhaps those are right who discern a distressing tendency for our political commentary to descend from discussion of public issues to destruction of private reputations; who believe that, by putting some brake upon that tendency, defamation liability under existing standards not only does not impair but fosters the type of discussion the first amendment is most concerned to protect; and who view high libel judgments as no more than an accurate reflection of the vastly expanded damage that can be caused by media that are capable of holding individuals up to public obloquy from coast to coast and that reap financial rewards commensurate with that power. I do not know the answers to these questions, but I do know that it is frightening to think that the existence or nonexistence of a constitutional rule (the willfully false disparagement of professional reputation in the context of political commentary cannot be actionable) is to depend upon our ongoing personal assessments of such sociological factors. And not only is our cloistered capacity to identify "modern problems" suspect, but our ability to provide condign solutions through the rude means of constitutional prohibition is nonexistent. What a strange notion that the problem of excessive libel awards should be solved by permitting, in political debate, intentional destruction of reputation—rather than by placing a legislative limit upon the amount of libel recovery. It has not often been thought, by the way, that the press is among the least effective of legislative lobbyists.

In a footnote Judge Scalia responded to other aspects of Judge Bork's comments:

In opposing such unguided "evolution" I am not in need of the concurrence's reminder that the fourth amendment must be applied to modern electronic surveillance, the commerce clause to trucks and the first amendment to broadcasting. [ ] The application of existing principles to new phenomena—either new because they have not existed before or new because they have never been presented to a court before, see New York Times Co. v. Sullivan, [ ]—is what I would call not "evolution" but merely routine elaboration of the law. What is under discussion here is not application of preexisting principles to new phenomena, but rather alteration of preexisting principles in their application to preexisting phenomena on the basis of judicial perception of changed social circumstances. The principle that the first amendment does not protect the deliberate impugning of character or reputation, in its

> application to the preexisting phenomenon of political controversy, is to be revised to permit "bumping" of some imprecisable degree because we perceive that libel suits are now too common and too successful.

The full opinions in Ollman v. Evans are certainly worth reading.

3. The Press as Repeater

As noted earlier, the common law developed a special rule protecting those who repeated certain kinds of statements. To the extent that the original speech had to have emanated from government, the basis for the privilege could be found in the self-governance rationale. But when it was extended to public meetings held by nongovernmental organizations, the rationale became less sharp. Some have urged expanding the common law protection to other situations.

The argument for the development of some constitutional privilege in this area is set out in K. Sowle, Defamation and the First Amendment: The Case for a Constitutional Privilege of Fair Report, 54 N.Y. U.L.Rev. 469, 520 (1979):

> If the first amendment was enacted in large measure to facilitate the people's capacity for self-government, then logically it must protect not only "robust debate" about persons who shape events of public concern, but also the supervisory function of the public over government. . . . A right to engage in robust debate about those possessing the stewardship of government would be meaningless if the public lacked access to information about the operations of government itself.

Note that the first privilege to emerge from that thinking would apply to reports of government proceedings. But a second one, following the thrust of Chief Justice Warren's opinion in *Butts* and *Walker,* might rely on the public's need to learn about important nongovernmental proceedings or events. Only then might the "robust debate" rationale come to center stage. (Although Professor Sowle observed that the reluctance to focus on content in *Gertz* suggested that the Court would reject a constitutional privilege applied to reports of non-governmental proceedings, she saw some room for such a privilege. Has *Greenmoss* changed this?)

As we already know, the law did not develop this way. The early emergence of the *New York Times* rule led lawyers and judges to shape analyses in its terms. Thus, Professor Sowle shows that in the Firestone case, p. 201, supra, when the magazine argued that its report of the judicial proceeding should be protected, it did so in terms of *New York Times,* rather than trying to create a totally new constitutional privilege that might cover accurate, or slightly inaccurate, reports of judicial proceedings.

In Greenbelt Cooperative Publishing Ass'n v. Bresler, 398 U.S. 6 (1970), a newspaper accurately reported a speaker's comment at a city

council meeting. The speaker said plaintiff was "blackmailing" the city in connection with pending land negotiations. The Court considered whether the word used could, in context, be understood to impute a crime. As a "matter of constitutional law," the Court concluded that the word could not have that meaning: "It is simply impossible to believe that a reader . . . would not understand exactly what was meant. . . . " Might the case have been analyzed in terms of a constitutional privilege to report accurately what transpires at a government proceeding, even though the words quoted were not used by government officials?

In Time, Inc. v. Pape, 401 U.S. 279 (1971), a report by the Civil Rights Commission included some unverified complaints of police brutality as examples of the types of complaints being received. Time reported the release of the volume and quoted one of the complaints without indicating that it had not been verified. The police officers named in that complaint sued Time. The *Times* rule admittedly applied and the question was whether the facts would permit a jury to find the requisite malice. The Court chose a very narrow ground that stressed the difficulties of reporting what someone has said as opposed to what someone has done. Here the Commission's own words might have been read to suggest that the complaints were probably valid and thus Time may have accurately captured the sense of the Commission's report, even though it excluded the word "alleged." Even if the story was inaccurate, the Court held as a matter of law that there was no basis for finding deliberate or reckless falsity. Again, no attention was given to the possibility of creating a totally new constitutional privilege.

That question did not arise until 1977. When it did arise, it was in the context of a nongovernmental controversy rather than in the more congenial context of a report of some governmental proceeding.

EDWARDS v. NATIONAL AUDUBON SOCIETY, INC.

United States Court of Appeals, Second Circuit, 1977.
556 F.2d 113, 2 Med.L.Rptr. 1849.
Certiorari denied 434 U.S. 1002, 98 S.Ct. 647, 54 L.Ed.2d 498.
Noted, 77 Colum.L.Rev. 1266, 1978 Utah L.Rev. 347,
1979 U.Ill.L.F. 943, 69 Va.L.Rev. 853.

[The National Audubon Society has been in the forefront of groups opposing the use of pesticides, such as DDT, because of their effect on the environment. Proponents of pesticides argued that without DDT millions of human beings would die of disease and starvation. The Society conducted an annual count of birds, which showed a steady increase in sightings despite increased use of pesticides. Some scientists cited these counts to show that pesticides were not harming animal life. The Society believed that the increased sightings were due to more watchers using more skill and better observation areas. Upset by what he thought was misuse of the annual counts, Arbib, editor of the Society's publication, *American Birds* wrote an attack in the foreword to one issue. He concluded that whenever members hear a "scientist" make such an argument, "you are in the presence of someone who is being paid to lie, or is parroting something he knows little about." Arbib apparently had no "factual basis" for the charge.

Devlin, a nature reporter for the New York Times, read the article and called Arbib to find out who he was attacking. After Devlin's "persistent urging that many eminent persons associated with the pesticide industry might be hurt unnecessarily by the Society's indiscriminate attack," Arbib promised to furnish some names. Arbib turned to Clement, a Society vice-president, who told Arbib that he could not call any specific person a paid liar. Clement did, however, identify for Arbib those who Clement thought had most persistently "misused" the bird count.

Arbib then gave Devlin the names of five scientists. Arbib testified that he told Devlin that these five were misusers but not necessarily "paid liars." Devlin "flatly denied" that Arbib had said this. Devlin sought responses from the five. He reached three, who all denied the charges. Devlin then wrote a story saying that although the article in *American Birds* did not identify its objects, "Mr. Arbib said in an interview that they included" the five scientists.

Three of the five scientists sued the Society and the Times for libel. At the trial, the judge charged, among other things, that the jury could find that Devlin had "actual malice" if he had serious doubts about the accuracy of Arbib's statements in the interview—even if he was sure he was accurately reporting Arbib's comments. The jury exonerated Arbib, but held the Times and Clement liable. The trial judge upheld the verdict against the Times on the ground that the jury could have found Devlin reckless in publishing without investigating further after the strong denials.

On appeal, the court exonerated Clement. The portion relating to the New York Times follows.]

Before KAUFMAN, CHIEF JUDGE, CLARK, ASSOCIATE JUSTICE and JAMESON, DISTRICT JUDGE.

IRVING R. KAUFMAN, CHIEF JUDGE.

In a society which takes seriously the principle that government rests upon the consent of the governed, freedom of the press must be the most cherished tenet. It is elementary that a democracy cannot long survive unless the people are provided the information needed to form judgments on issues that affect their ability to intelligently govern themselves. As we said in James v. Board of Education, 461 F.2d 566, 572, "To preserve the 'marketplace of ideas' so essential to our system of democracy, we must be willing to assume the risk of argument and lawful disagreement." In the thirteen years since New York Times v. Sullivan, [ ], the federal courts have steadfastly sought to afford broad protection to expression by the media, without unduly sacrificing the individual's right to be free of unjust damage to his reputation. [ ] This important case requires us to return again to this task.

We are invited today to affirm a libel judgment against the *New York Times* for accurately reporting dramatic statements of the National Audubon Society attacking the good faith of prominent scientists supporting continued use of the insecticide DDT. There can be little doubt that the *Times* reasonably considered these accusations of a leading environmentalist organization to be newsworthy. . . . We are convinced that the First Amendment requires us to decline [this invitation]. Accordingly we will reverse and order the complaint dismissed.

I.

A brief summary of the facts is indispensable to understanding the difficult legal issues presented by this appeal.

. . .

II.

Implicit in the jury's verdict . . . is the finding, which we must accept, that the *Times* accurately reported the five scientists whose names were furnished by Arbib were the "paid liars" referred to in the *American Birds* Foreword. We believe that a libel judgment against the *Times*, in the face of this finding of fact, is constitutionally impermissible.

At stake in this case is a fundamental principle. Succinctly stated, when a responsible, prominent organization like the National Audubon Society makes serious charges against a public figure, the First Amendment protects the accurate and disinterested reporting of those charges, regardless of the reporter's private views regarding their validity. See Time, Inc. v. Pape, [ ]; Medina v. Time, Inc., 439 F.2d 1129 (1st Cir. 1971). What is newsworthy about such accusations is that they were made. We do not believe that the press may be required under the First Amendment to suppress newsworthy statements merely because it has serious doubts regarding their truth. Nor must the press take up cudgels against dubious charges in order to publish them without fear of liability for defamation. Cf. Miami Herald Publishing Co. v. Tornillo, 418 U.S. 241 (1974). The public interest in being fully informed about controversies that often rage around sensitive issues demands that the press be afforded the freedom to report such charges without assuming responsibility for them.

The contours of the press's right of neutral reportage are, of course, defined by the principle that gives life to it. Literal accuracy is not a prerequisite: if we are to enjoy the blessings of a robust and unintimidated press, we must provide immunity from defamation suits where the journalist believes, reasonably and in good faith, that his report accurately conveys the charges made. Time, Inc. v. Pape, supra. It is equally clear, however, that a publisher who in fact espouses or concurs in the charges made by others, or who deliberately distorts these statements to launch a personal attack of his own on a public figure, cannot rely on a privilege of neutral reportage. In such instances he assumes responsibility for the underlying accusations. [ ]

It is clear here, that Devlin reported Audubon's charges fairly and accurately. He did not in any way espouse the Society's accusations: indeed, Devlin published the maligned scientists' outraged reactions in the same article that contained the Society's attack. The *Times* article, in short, was the exemplar of fair and dispassionate reporting of an unfortunate but newsworthy contretemps. Accordingly, we hold that it was privileged under the First Amendment.

III.

Even absent the special protection afforded to neutral reportage, see *Time, Inc. v. Pape,* supra, the evidence adduced at trial was manifestly insufficient to demonstrate "actual malice" on the part of the *Times.* It is uncontested that Devlin was unaware of the baselessness of the Audubon Society's dramatic allegations. Nor was there a shred of evidence from which the jury might have found that Devlin entertained serious doubts concerning the truth of Arbib's charge that the appellees were "paid liars."

It is conceded that the *Times* might have published the Audubon Society's accusations without fear of liability had Devlin but refrained from eliciting the views of the Society's victims. The appellees would punish the *Times* for its effort to confirm the story, apparently maintaining that a little prudence is a dangerous thing. They assert that once Devlin heard the scientists' denials and received materials explaining their general stand in the DDT controversy, he became charged with the duty to publish absolutely nothing until he conducted a full-scale investigation plumbing to the bottom of the matter.

We do not believe, however, that the scientists' responses to Devlin's inquiries could be found sufficient to warn Devlin of the probable falsity of the Society's charges. Surely liability under the "clear and convincing proof" standard of New York Times v. Sullivan cannot be predicated on mere denials, however vehement; such denials are so commonplace in the world of potential charge and countercharge that, in themselves, they hardly alert the conscientious reporter to the likelihood of error. . . .

. . .

V.

We do not underestimate the pain and distress which the publication of the Audubon Society's thoughtless charges has caused the appellees. And we are fully aware that, in Professor Emerson's words,

> A member of a civilized society should have some measure of protection against unwarranted attack upon his honor, his dignity and his standing in the community.

Our holding today does not in any way condone the mischievous and unwarranted assault on the good name of the appellees, who appear from their writings to have entered the lists in favor of DDT in good faith and from humanitarian motives that ought to be beyond reproach.

Nevertheless, we believe that the interest of a public figure in the purity of his reputation cannot be allowed to obstruct that vital pulse of ideas and intelligence on which an informed and self-governing people depend. It is unfortunate that the exercise of liberties so precious as freedom of speech and of the press may sometimes do harm that the state is powerless to recompense; but this is the price that must be paid for the blessings of a democratic way of life.

We believe that the *New York Times* cannot, consistently with the First Amendment, be afflicted with a libel judgment for the accurate reporting of newsworthy accusations made by a responsible and well-noted organization like the National Audubon Society. . . .

Notes and Questions

1. In Note, The Privilege of Neutral Reportage, 1978 Utah L.Rev. 347, the author argues that the *Edwards* privilege "is too lenient in merely requiring neutrality" because, in most situations, readers cannot judge the credibility of the sources being quoted. "Where the reporter has knowledge of falsity or serious doubts about the truth of a charge, meeting the 'actual malice' test, the reporter should be under a duty to report that information. Where there is reason to know the falsity of a statement, the reporter must also do more than merely print a refutation." The obligation would be greater when "hot news" is not involved. Are there arguments the other way?

2. What are the limits of the *Edwards* principle? It has been distinguished in Dixson v. Newsweek, Inc., 562 F.2d 626 (10th Cir.1977), on the ground that *Edwards* involved public figures whereas Mr. Dixon was a private citizen. Are there times when the public should be informed of charges that are not made by a "responsible, prominent organization"? What is the test for whether a report of a particular charge is "newsworthy"? What level of error in the report, if any, should deprive the reporter of the privilege? These problems are discussed in Comment, Constitutional Privilege to Republish Defamation, 77 Colum.L.Rev. 1266 (1977).

3. The *Edwards* privilege of neutral reportage was rejected in Dickey v. CBS, Inc., 583 F.2d 1221 (3d Cir.1978), as inconsistent with *St. Amant,* since *Edwards* would allow one who reports a story that he knows to be false or has serious doubts about, to be protected from liability. Since *Edwards* allowed such a privilege where the subject was newsworthy, the Third Circuit thought *Edwards* also violated the *Gertz* rationale, which had rejected the newsworthiness focus of *Rosen-*

bloom. The court ultimately affirmed the CBS judgment because plaintiff had failed to satisfy the *St. Amant* burden of proving recklessness.

In Medico v. Time, Inc., p. 141, supra, the same court asserted that Dickey's rejection of neutral reportage was "irrelevant" to the decision because *Dickey* went off on a failure to show "actual malice." The *Medico* court cited *Edwards* with approval in determining that Pennsylvania would extend its common law privilege to an accurate summary of an investigative file of the FBI.

4. In the home of the neutral reportage doctrine, the Second Circuit may have limited its potential sweep. In *Cianci,* the court said:

> While the Supreme Court has not yet addressed the question of the existence of a constitutional privilege of neutral reportage, going beyond that generally recognized at common law,[15] this circuit is on record that the media enjoy such a privilege with respect to public officials or figures. That step was taken in Edwards v. National Audubon Society, . . .
>
> . . .
>
> The New Times article fulfills almost none of the conditions laid down in *Edwards.* While, as indicated above, the precise bounds of the privilege remain to be delineated, it is enough for decision in this case that a jury could well find that the New Times did not simply report the charges but espoused or concurred in them; indeed, despite the ingenious construction of the article, more naivete than ought to be demanded even of judges is needed to consider the article as doing anything else. In addition to the instances cited [earlier], the New Times made no mention of Cianci's claim of innocence of the charge of rape, [ ] save in the backhanded form of quoting Eisenberg's remark that he had called the charge a "shakedown". It said nothing of Cianci's position, [ ] that the $3,000 was paid in settlement of Redick's contemplated civil suit rather than to induce her to withdraw the criminal charge. Indeed the New Times did not obtain Cianci's version of the facts, although it allowed a lawyer for him to meet with some of its representatives and submit certain papers to them.[18] The

15. The Sowle article, supra, at 501–08, demonstrates that when Time, Inc. v. Pape, [ ], is closely analyzed, it does not mandate a constitutional report privilege when plaintiff is a public official or figure, as asserted in Prosser, [ ].

18. Professor Sowle, a strong advocate of a constitutional privilege for neutral reportage, including non-official statements, states at 539–40:

> A special problem arises with the fairness requirement as it pertains to reports of non-governmental statements and proceedings. If a report privilege is to extend to statements made to the press on matters of legitimate public concern, fairness requires that the publisher, to be protected, present a balanced report, not just of the statement itself, but of the debate on the controversy to which the statement is addressed. Thus, the report of a statement besmirching an individual—public or private—would fall within the privilege only if it is fair to the individual involved in the public issue, presenting his or her side of the story as well as the other. This requirement merely follows the common law fair report privilege, which, for example, allows the publisher to make an ongoing,

article made no mention of the statement by Redick's own attorney to the author that "a crime did not occur. That's my—that's our position." The article conveys the impression that Boyle decided not to prosecute largely because Redick dropped the charges and polygraph results were inadmissible, but in the interview with the author Boyle stated "I have no idea in fact as to what the lawyers or the parties themselves decided. That's immaterial to me. What is material to me is the analysis of evidence from the standpoint of proof beyond a reasonable doubt." What the article described as the "hard-nosed techniques" employed by the first reporters who attempted to revive the story were described by Redick herself as "pressuring me and threatening me and harassing me and trying to get me to talk . . . that if I didn't tell them that they would have the story printed with my name, identify my family and take pictures of my home and my children." Plaintiff cites numerous other examples which would undermine a claim of "fair" and "neutral" reporting, such as the failure to reveal facts undermining the credibility of such critical figures as Eisenberg and Redick.

The need for the careful limitation of a constitutional privilege for fair reportage is demonstrated by the breadth of that defense, which confers immunity even for publishing statements believed to be untrue. Absent the qualifications set forth by Chief Judge Kaufman in *Edwards,* all elements of the media would have absolute immunity to espouse and concur in the most unwarranted attacks, at least upon any public official or figure, based on episodes long in the past and made by persons known to be of scant reliability. . . .

5. A motion was made to rehear *Cianci* en banc. Originally, four judges, led by Judge Kaufman, voted to rehear the case on the grounds that it appeared to undermine *Edwards.* Since no majority voted to rehear *Cianci,* "Apparently, my colleagues do not read the opinion here as inconsistent with *Edwards.* . . . Thus, although the panel does not always discuss *Edwards* in the terms I would have chosen, *Edwards* survives *Cianci* unscathed." The four concurred in the denial of rehearing en banc. 639 F.2d at 71, 6 Med.L.Rptr. 2145 (Kaufman, J., concurring).

6. Professor Sowle's proposal would protect a publisher from liability for defamation for

(a)(1) reports of public proceedings of all branches and all levels of government, including reports concerning pleadings filed with a court and available for public inspection, whether or not they have been the object of official action, and including reports of public, official pronouncements about non-public governmental activities; *and*

balanced report of the day-to-day events at a public trial, but would not protect a partial report, which, for example, reported only the prosecution's evidence in a criminal case and omitted the defendant's.

(2) reports of public nongovernmental statements and proceedings dealing with matters of legitimate public concern;

(b) if the reports are fair and accurate, or published with due care to ensure fairness and accuracy;

(c) whether or not defamatory statements reported are republished with knowledge of their falsity or reckless disregard of their truth, or with any other form of common law malice;

(d) provided that the publication purports to be an account of a public statement or proceeding encompassed within the privilege.

7. How important is it that the protagonists be identified? What about a neutral report of a rumor? In Martin v. Wilson Publishing Co., 497 A.2d 322, 12 Med.L.Rptr. 1049 (R.I.1985), the defendant paper reported about the reactions of a very small community whose residents were very concerned that plaintiff was acquiring a vast percentage of the property in the community. Despite his announced good intentions for the community, plaintiff's actions made many residents apprehensive. The article then continued:

> Some residents stretch available facts when they imagine Mr. Martin is connected with the 1974 rash of fires in the village (the abandoned depot, the back of the Shannock Spa, and even that old barn he loved). Local fire officials feel that certain local kids did it for kicks. The same imaginations note that the fire at the old Shannock mill before he bought it made it cheaper (but less valuable), or that the fire there since he bought it might have been profitable (though derelict buildings, such as it was, are customarily uninsurable).

Defendant's effort to analogize the situation to fair report was rejected because at governmental proceedings, identified and identifiable persons participate. In public proceedings those who are attacked may attend and defend themselves against attacks. But the "spreading of rumors does not give the person defamed by them the opportunity to rebut the underlying allegation of the rumor. To attempt to defend against a rumor is not unlike attempting to joust with a cloud. Publication of a rumor further fuels the continued repetition and does so in an especially egregious way by enshrining it in print."

Even if the court were inclined to apply *Edwards,* it would not do so here because no "prominent responsible organization" made the charges.

8. The most famous rumor episode involved an assertion in a gossip column in the Washington Post that a rumor was making the rounds in Washington that in the days before leaving office, President Carter bugged Blair House where President-elect Reagan was staying. Carter threatened suit unless the report was retracted. The Post first responded with an editorial asserting that it might have been foolish for the paper to expect readers "to sift out the fair from the unfair or the justified from the unjustified inferences." The editorial asserted that

the editors found the "rumor utterly impossible to believe." (What were the pros and cons of running that editorial?)

Carter treated the editorial as a refusal to retract and continued exploring the possibility of suit. About ten days after the editorial, the publisher of the Post sent a letter to the Carters apologizing for the story and retracting it. A news report on page 1 of the Post reported fully on the letter. See Taylor, Post Apologizes to Carter for Gossip Column Item, Washington Post, Oct. 23, 1981, at 1. For a story tracing the rumor and its demise, see Gailey, The Trail of the Rumor on Blair House's "Bug," N.Y.Times, Nov. 18, 1981, at 10. See also Note, Libel and the Reporting of Rumor, 92 Yale L.J. 85 (1982), suggesting a framework of protection adapted from the *Edwards* approach.

9. In a profile on Congressman Jack Kemp, prominently mentioned as a possible Republican candidate for President, Newsweek states:

> Kemp aides know they must also deal—publicly—with a more delicate personal matter: a persistent rumor, for which no evidence has ever surfaced, that Kemp is or was homosexual. The rumor was printed—and knocked down—by conservative columnists Rowland Evans and Robert Novak in 1978. It resurfaced recently in veiled press reports and has been drifting around Washington ever since Kemp expressed an interest in the nomination.

If the magazine had been told that Kemp's aides had decided not to discuss the matter publicly and to try to keep the matter out of the press, might Newsweek have run a risk in reporting the existence of the rumor? Is this like the Martin case? See Fineman, Kemp, New Ideas, Old Questions, Newsweek, Dec. 2, 1985, at 54.

10. Among the important states to have rejected the *Edwards* privilege are New York and Illinois. New York's rejection, in Hogan v. The Herald Co., 58 N.Y.2d 630, 444 N.E.2d 1002, 458 N.Y.S.2d 538, 8 Med.L. Rptr. 2567 (1982), may lead to a situation in which the state courts and the federal courts sitting in diversity cases in New York will use different law in libel cases.

PACELLA v. MILFORD RADIO CORPORATION

Appeals Court of Massachusetts, 1984.
18 Mass.App.Ct. 6, 462 N.E.2d 355.

DREBEN, JUSTICE.

In 1975 Nicholas P. Pacella was a candidate for the Milford board of selectmen. On the day before the election, an anonymous caller telephoned the corporate defendant's radio station and made certain defamatory remarks directed against Pacella on a talk show devoted to the election. Although an electronic delay system gave the defendant Joseph G. Hyder, the talk show's host, a seven-second preview of the caller's question and an opportunity to prevent its broadcast, he did not use the abort button. Pacella lost the election and, in this libel action, sued Hyder and the corporate defendant, the former employer of Hyder. A Superior Court jury assessed $15,000 damages against the defendants, but the trial judge allowed the defendants' motion for judgment notwithstanding the verdict. We affirm on the ground that Pacella, a public figure, did not meet his burden of proving by clear and convincing evidence that the defendants published the caller's statement "with knowledge that it was false or with reckless disregard of whether it was false or not." [ ]

. . . Hyder explained the proposed format to Pacella—statements by the candidates were to be followed by a question and answer session with the station's call-in audience. Pacella, a school teacher with inflexible hours, decided not to appear in person but to submit a taped statement. He expressed uneasiness about the question and answer format but was assured by Hyder that there would be no problems, Hyder stating, "How can they ask you questions if you are not here?"

Nevertheless, at the time of the actual broadcast, Hyder and an anonymous caller to "Counterpoint" had the following interchange during the question period following the candidates' statements:

> CALLER: "I have a question for Mr. Pacella."
>
> HYDER: "Mr. Fernandez is here. Mr. Pacella was on tape recording earlier. He was not present."
>
> CALLER: "So I can't ask a question of him?"
>
> HYDER: "He's not here to answer. How can you possibly do that, dear? [sic] If you can tell me how, I'll be happy to relay the question."
>
> CALLER: "Well, could I ask the question and you can relay it to him?"
>
> HYDER: "Well, ah, by the time we get an answer the elections will be over. Rhetorically, if you want to ask it, go ahead."
>
> CALLER: "Pardon?"
>
> HYDER: "Go ahead."
>
> FERNANDEZ: "Maybe I could answer for him."
>
> HYDER: "Yeah. Go ahead, ask the question."
>
> CALLER: "All right. He is represented by the Concerned Citizens, and their motto is, 'The people have a right to know,' which I agree with. Especially when the integrity of a candidate is in doubt. My question is: Did you, Mr. Pacella, during the construction of your home, ever take without authority certain building materials from the construction site? And were you brought in for questioning by the Milford Police and let go because the owner wouldn't press charges? That is my question."

At this point, Hyder decided to terminate the call and stated: "Uh huh? Well I suggest you contact Mr. Pacella tonight when he comes home from his job, alright?" Later in the program, Pacella's wife and one of his supporters responded, calling the charge vicious, upsetting, and untrue. Hyder concluded his conversation by thanking Mrs. Pacella as set forth in the [footnote].[4]

Although the defendants at trial introduced evidence as to the truth of the construction site story, referred to as the "Grant Street rumor," the jury found otherwise. There was also evidence that the rumor had persistence and had been heard by several persons. Pacella testified that he had heard the story several times, first in 1962 or 1963, again in 1974 and once again in 1975 prior to the broadcast. He had discussed it with some of his campaign workers and his campaign manager. Although concerned about the rumor, Pacella never alerted Hyder to the possibility that it might surface. . . .

Hyder testified that he had heard the Grant Street story some five or six years before the broadcast in a "social context" and that at that time he had no personal knowledge whether the rumor was true. [A witness testified that some time before the program Hyder had called Pacella a "crook." Hyder denied the episode.] Hyder testified that he did not use the abort button on May 6, 1975, and that he intentionally allowed the call to be broadcast because he believed that the public has the right to know about a candidate. He also testified that the seven seconds were sufficient time for him to exercise that judgment.

. . .

Our review of the record indicates that there was no evidence that Hyder had actual knowledge that the rumor was false. Thus, the crucial question is whether Hyder acted "with reckless disregard of whether it is false or not." . . .

Of particular importance here is "the medium by which the statement is disseminated and the audience to which it is published." Cole v. Westinghouse Bdcst. Co., 386 Mass. at 309, 453 N.E.2d 1021, quoting from Information Control Corp. v. Genesis One Computer Corp., 611 F.2d 781, 784 (9th Cir.1980). The defendants organized a program concerning an upcoming election, asked the candidates to present statements, and afforded the public the opportunity to question the candidates freely. Neither Hyder nor the station had any power to restrict or censor the material presented by the candidates. This is because the United States Supreme Court, relying on the public interest in "full and unrestricted" political discussion, has held in unmistakable terms that 47 U.S.C. § 315(a) prevents a broadcaster from deleting libelous statements of candidates and that radio stations are immune from liability for broadcasting such statements. Farmers Educational & Co-op. Union v. WDAY, Inc., 360 U.S. 525, 530–531 (1959). See also G.L. c. 231, § 91A.

It is readily apparent that caution must be exercised before imposing liability on Hyder for insufficient use of the abort button lest the

4. "Mrs. Pacella, thank you so much for calling. I'm glad that you were able to clarify it for us, and I think that somebody has taken advantage of the opportunity, the fact that your husband was not here to reply, and I think that you've handled it very nicely."

"robust and wide-open debate" protected by *New York Times* be inhibited in a substantial way. This consideration was emphasized in Adams v. Frontier Bdcst. Co., 555 P.2d 556 (Wyo.1976), where the Supreme Court of Wyoming ruled that the decision of a radio station not to use an electronic delay system in connection with a talk show did not constitute "reckless disregard" under the *New York Times* rule. The station was held not liable for broadcasting a defamatory falsehood made by an anonymous caller. [ ]

The court in *Adams* also noted, "The impact of the censorship would not fall upon the broadcaster's words and ideas; instead, it would be applied to the opinions and ideas of those members of the public who elected to participate in this kind of public forum." [ ] See also [*New York Times*] where the Supreme Court pointed out the dangers of shutting off "an important outlet for the promulgation of information and ideas by persons who do not themselves have access to publishing facilities—who wish to exercise their freedom of speech even though they are not members of the press."

Unlike the commercial advertisement in *New York Times* which can be checked for accuracy prior to publication, a statement called into a talk show can not be verified within the seven seconds afforded by electronic equipment. . . .

Moreover, the role of a talk-show host differs from that of a reporter or newscaster. His function is not to discover the news but to moderate the public debate. "It is one thing to require a newspaper to check the accuracy of an interview. But it may be another matter to hold a TV newsperson responsible for the spontaneous live utterance of an interviewee." Jones v. Taibbi, 508 F.Supp. 1069, 1074–1075 n. 12 (D.Mass.), cert. denied 454 U.S. 1085 (1981). To impose on the talk-show host a duty of private censorship [13] whenever he has an insufficient basis for assessing the truth of a statement would surely result in the extinction of the public talk show.

We now return to Pacella's claims that there is here sufficient evidence to prove with convincing clarity that Hyder published the statement with "reckless disregard" of its truth. Pacella is correct that an anonymous call carries less reliability than one from an identified source. A story "based wholly on an unverified anonymous telephone call" is one of the instances in St. Amant v. Thompson, 390 U.S. at 732, where the Supreme Court indicated "[p]rofessions of good faith will be unlikely to prove persuasive." However, sole reliance on an anonymous telephone tip in a context where there is time to check it out is quite different from receiving a call on a talk show where there is no such time. Even if the talk-show host were to require identification, a caller on a talk show (unlike the tipster whose identity could later be verified) could easily adopt an assumed name and the host would be

13. The term "censorship" connotes "all factors which would inhibit the freedom and spontaneity of the public dialogue." Adams v. Frontier Bdcst. Co., 555 P.2d at 565. See New York Times, 376 U.S. at 277 (fear of damage awards "may be markedly more inhibiting than the fear of prosecution under a criminal statute").

none the wiser. We think the lack of identification, although undesirable, is not enough.

[The fact that a supporter of Pacella denied the truth of the accusation before the program was not dispositive: The court quoted *Edwards* to the effect that denials are so commonplace that they do not alert reporters to the likelihood of error.]

There was no evidence that Hyder knew Pacella personally. [ ] He had met him once, knew that he was a teacher and a family man, and that he had held town offices. Certainly such knowledge did not make the allegation "inherently improbable." St. Amant, 390 U.S. at 732.

Hyder's own statement that he had enough time to decide to publish based on his view that the public had the right to know does not, in any way, indicate recklessness, but only intentional publication. See St. Amant v. Thompson, 390 U.S. at 733. His other alleged statement that he published the call "for effect" does not approach a showing of malice in the constitutional sense. Bad motive or hostility is not what is meant by malice in the *New York Times* sense.

In sum, we conclude that there has been no showing by "clear and convincing proof," that Hyder permitted the statement to be broadcast "with reckless disregard of whether it was false or not," a standard which, in this context, requires at least that Hyder be aware of the "probable falsity" of the caller's remarks. [ ] The trial judge was correct in allowing the defendants' motion.

Judgment affirmed.

Notes and Questions

1. Without opinion, the Supreme Judicial Court of Massachusetts affirmed by an equally divided court. 394 Mass. 1051, 476 N.E.2d 595, certiorari denied 106 S.Ct. 133 (1985).

2. Could the caller be held liable if identified?

3. What role does "actual malice" play in the court's analysis? Does it go to the failure to use the abort system? Could a claim be based on a station's failure to buy an abort system?

4. What is the purpose of the seven second delay system?

5. The citation to § 315 and to the WDAY case involves the so-called "equal opportunities" rule (sometimes mistakenly called the "equal time" rule), discussed in detail in Chapter XV.

In the WDAY case, the Court unanimously decided that the statute barred the licensee from censoring the comments of one who was exercising rights under § 315. By a vote of 5–4, the Court also decided that the section preempted state defamation law and created an absolute privilege for the licensee.

How is the statute or the WDAY case relevant to *Pacella*?

6. At one point the court suggests that the "role of a talk-show host differs from that of a reporter or newscaster." Is the court suggesting that the two functions warrant different rules? Or is it that radio (and broadcasting generally) have certain capacities that print media lack?

7. How different might the situation be if a person wrote a letter to the editor attacking a candidate for local office or a public official? Should the editor be able to run that letter even if the editor has doubts about its accuracy? What are the differences between a radio call-in show and a letters page in a newspaper?

8. In Heitkemper v. Fox, 11 Med.L.Rptr. 2246 (Wis.App., publication not recommended, 1985), the defendant published a letter to the editor from a criminal attacking a public official. The court granted summary judgment on the ground that actual malice was lacking. Might some other analysis be appropriate?

9. How does a letter to the editor differ from neutral reportage? What analysis if the Audubon Society had written a letter to the New York Times accusing five scientists of being paid liars—and the Times had printed the letter? Is that a stronger, or weaker, case for protecting the Times than the actual Edwards case? What if the Times doubts the accuracy of the letter?

10. Might the nature of the letters page be relevant? In Nash v. Keene Publishing Corp., 127 N.H. 214, 498 A.2d 348, 12 Med.L.Rptr. 1025 (1985), the defendant's letters page contained the following statement: "Letters Policy: The readers' column is for your opinions. . . . [W]e do not publish letters we feel to be libelous . . . or that make allegations we are unable to verify independently."

Consider the implications if the letters page had said: "This page is a forum for readers. We take no steps to verify the content of any letters (though we do verify signatures and will not print an anonymous letter). We do not stand behind any statements made in any letter. Readers should judge the source of the letter in deciding how much credence to give it." (Can a call-in show be run this way?)

11. What about a newspaper that carries a wire service story that it disbelieves or doubts? Is that different from a letter? The role of wire services is discussed in Appleby v. Daily Hampshire Gazette, 395 Mass. 32, 478 N.E.2d 721 (1985).

C. REFORM PROPOSALS

1. NEED FOR REFORM?

The current state of libel law has been deplored by almost everyone affected by it.

Plaintiffs. As the sections on doctrine suggest, plaintiffs have had a most difficult time winning cases under the "actual malice" rule. Their success rate, leaving aside a relatively small number of settlements, runs under 10 percent. Plaintiffs whose primary interest was in showing the falsity of the story rather than in obtaining dollars, might have been satisfied if the system had offered them a chance to prove that falsity. But, as noted, over 75 percent of the cases resulted in summary judgments for the defendant, so the issue of truth or falsity was never decided. A case like Sharon v. Time, Inc., which produced a jury verdict of falsity but without actual malice, is a rarity. That outcome was made possible only because the trial judge denied the motion for summary judgment, believing Sharon had a plausible chance to prove actual malice.

Plaintiffs who can get past summary judgment have a success rate with juries in the range of 80 percent. But defendants appeal virtually all jury losses and obtain reversals in some 70 percent of the cases. Most of these lead to dismissals; a few lead to new trials or reduced awards.

Private plaintiffs fare somewhat better because they get to juries more often, win before juries at least as often, and are not likely to lose their awards on appeal for failure to prove negligence.

Defendants. As a group, defendants obviously cannot complain about their overall success rate in these cases. But they are unhappy that the constitutional protections do not operate earlier in the litigation process; that pretrial discovery is so expensive; and that appeals are necessary in virtually every case in which summary judgment is denied.

Larger media stress these high costs of successful defense and suggest that they are being diverted from the investigative reporting that should be going on by the preparation for litigation. They are not yet worried about damage awards because although claims have been filed for hundreds of millions of dollars, the largest judgment against media finally upheld on appeal has not exceeded $500,000 (as of July, 1986).

Smaller media are concerned about the very fact of being sued and having to spend money for legal defense. They are also concerned that a judgment of tens of thousands of dollars, much less millions, might bankrupt them. Insurance is becoming increasingly expensive in this area because of the large defense costs. Insurance is not much protection to smaller media for several reasons. First, all libel insurance is written with a "deductible" or retained exposure under which the insured bears the first several thousand dollars of expenses in the case. This amount, which can vary from as little as $1,500 to as much as $100,000, is intended to cause the management to consider carefully the material it is about to run and whether it wants to engage in investigative reporting at all. Second, in 1986, one of the few major libel insurers began requiring that in addition to the "deductible," insureds bear 20 percent of the legal expenses throughout the case, whatever the outcome. The problem with both these limits on coverage is that the publication may suffer uncovered losses whenever it is sued, even if it ultimately wins the case. Thus, smaller media may be more likely to stop doing any investigative reporting or to avoid running stories that may antagonize litigious persons or groups in the community.

Public. If the defendants are likely to perceive the situation as "chilling" and to respond by reducing their coverage of important activities, it may be that the public will lose by learning less true information about how our government is functioning. Although occasional stories purport to document the "chilling effect," it is something that major media figures do not like to talk about and deny exists. Smaller media, on the other hand, do assert that this is affecting their coverage.

2. Proposed Reforms

In recent years, attacks have been mounted on the *Times* rule from several directions. Some argue that the Court engaged in overkill and that a negligence standard would be quite protective enough. Others argue that the *Times* rule is appropriate for public officials (however defined) but that public figures should not have to face the same hurdles. Still others argue that the *Times* rule has not protected the media as it was intended to do, because of the high costs that have become associated with even successful defense. These critics would erect absolute privilege at least to bar suits by public officials. The argument is premised on a desirable symmetry of giving those who attack public officials the same protection of absolute privilege that the officials themselves have.

In the absence of constitutional change, some have proposed a series of interstitial changes that might reduce the expenses involved in these cases. These include such steps as channeling discovery into the single topic, such as falsity, that appears to be the weakest link in plaintiff's case; or making routine the sequential step-verdict used in the Sharon case.

A few courts have begun to assess costs against plaintiffs in cases that have been begun or continued after it became clear that there was little hope of success. See, e.g., Beary v. West Publishing Co., 763 F.2d 66, 11 Med.L.Rptr. 2114 (2d Cir.1985), certiorari denied 106 S.Ct. 232 (1985) (awarding double costs and $1,000 damages for frivolous appeal).

See also Daily Gazette Co., Inc. v. Canady, 332 S.E.2d 262, 11 Med. L.Rptr. 2243 (W.Va.1985), in which the court concluded that it had inherent power to assess the winner's attorney's fees against the losing attorney in cases involving "vexatious, wanton, or oppressive assertion of a claim or defense that cannot be supported by a good faith argument for the application, extension, modification, or reversal of existing law." The court "firmly" rejected the newspaper's argument that "frivolity" alone should suffice: sometimes frivolity was simply a function of "sheer incompetence." The case discusses at length the power to shift legal fees.

These interstitial moves have given plaintiffs no help in clearing their names, and defendants little help in avoiding the gigantic damage claims.

Proposed major reforms have taken two directions. One focuses on the retraction technique. The other uses a declaratory judgment approach. Consider the short draft proposals that follow. In each case consider whether the legislation should be at the state or federal level.

---

a. *Defamation Correction Statute*

Proposed in CENDALI, OF THINGS TO COME—THE ACTUAL IMPACT OF HERBERT v. LANDO AND A PROPOSED NATIONAL CORRECTION STATUTE

22 Harvard J. Legislation 441, 500–02 (1985).

SECTION 1.

In any action against a media organization for damages for the publication of a defamatory statement through any medium, the plaintiff shall recover no more than special damages unless the plaintiff shall allege and prove that the plaintiff made a timely sufficient request for correction and that the media organization failed to make conspicuous and timely publication of the correction.

SECTION 2.

A "media organization" shall be interpreted broadly to include all publishers and broadcasters that have continued access to a medium of expression.

SECTION 3.

A "sufficient request for correction" is a good faith request for correction that is in writing; that is signed by the plaintiff or his or her duly authorized attorney or agent; that specifies the statement or statements claimed to be false and defamatory, states how they are false, sets forth the true facts, is accompanied with substantially the same evidence as to truth that would be presented at trial, including the identity of sources or references, such that the media organization can reasonably assess the truth; and that is delivered to the defendant within a timely period.

SECTION 4.

A "timely" request for correction is a request made within twenty (20) days of publication or twenty (20) days after the publication was widely circulated, whichever is later.

SECTION 5.

A "correction" is either (a) the good faith publication of the true facts, or (b) the good faith publication of the plaintiff's statement of the true facts in a reply written by the plaintiff but exclusive of any portions that are defamatory of another, obscene, or otherwise improper for publication. If the request for correction has specified two or more statements as false and defamatory, the correction may deal with some of such statements pursuant to (a) above and with other of such statements pursuant to (b) above. The defendant has the option to using either (a) or (b); however, if the plaintiff declines to make a reply under (b) the defendant must still make a correction pursuant to (a) in order to fulfill the requirements of the statute.

SECTION 6.

A "conspicuous" publication in a visual or sound television or radio broadcast is a good faith publication that is broadcast at substantially the same time of day, and with the same sending power, as the statement(s) specified to be false and defamatory in the request for correction. A "conspicuous" publication for a print publisher is a good faith publication that is printed in substantially the same manner as the statement(s) specified to be false and defamatory in the request for correction. A publication in a particular manner that is agreeable to the plaintiff shall in any event be deemed "conspicuous."

SECTION 7.

A "timely" publication for a media publication published with a frequency of less than thirty (30) days is within twenty (20) days of receipt of the request for correction. A "timely" publication for a media publication published with a frequency of thirty (30) days or greater is either within twenty (20) days of receipt of the request for correction or in the next edition of the publication, whichever is later, provided that publication is within six (6) months of the request for correction. A publication on a particular day that is agreeable to the plaintiff shall in any event be deemed "timely."

SECTION 8.

A correction of a statement(s) that is (are) false and defamatory about a candidate for public office is presumed not to be "timely" unless it is published at three (3) days before the election or on a particular day agreeable to the plaintiff.

SECTION 9.

A good faith conspicuous correction published by the defendant before the plaintiff makes a request for correction shall have the same force and effect as though such correction had been published in a timely manner after a request by the plaintiff.

SECTION 10.

There is a privilege for discovery into the investigative and editorial process of all materials, communications, and thoughts of the defendant or any of its employees from the time the request for correction is delivered [until] the decision whether to publish the correction is made.

SECTION 11.

A book publisher, media organization that publishes with a frequency of greater than six (6) months, or any person or organization which publishes a statement(s) that is (are) false and defamatory, and then makes a good faith publication of the true facts in some medium of expression, shall have that publication deemed to mitigate damages.

SECTION 12.

"Special damages" are pecuniary damages that the plaintiff alleges and proves that the plaintiff has suffered with respect to the plaintiff's property, business, trade, profession, or occupation (including such amounts of money as the plaintiff alleges and proves he has expended, exclusive of attorneys' fees, as a proximate result of the alleged defamation), and no other.

SECTION 13.

The media organization and the plaintiff shall make a good faith effort to settle a claim for special damages out of court.

SECTION 14.

This statute is enacted through Congress's power under the Commerce Clause and is preemptive of state law.

---

b. H.R. 2846, Introduced in 1985 by Congressman Charles Schumer

A BILL

To protect the constitutional right to freedom of speech by establishing a new cause of action for defamation, and for other purposes.

Be it enacted by the Senate and House of Representatives of the United States of America in Congress assembled,

SECTION 1. Action for Declaratory Judgment That Statement Is False and Defamatory.

(a) Cause of Action

(1) A public official or public figure who is the subject of a publication or broadcast which is published or broadcast in the print or electronic media may bring an action in any court of competent jurisdiction for a declaratory judgment that such publication or broadcast was false and defamatory.

(2) Paragraph (1) shall not be construed to require proof of the state of mind of the defendant.

(3) No damages shall be awarded in such an action.

(b) Burden of Proof. The plaintiff seeking a declaratory judgment under subsection (a) shall bear the burden of proving by clear and convincing evidence each element of the cause of action described in subsection (a).

(c) Bar To Certain Claims. A plaintiff who brings an action for a declaratory judgment under subsection (a) shall be forever barred from asserting any other claim or cause of action arising out a publication or broadcast which is the subject of such action.

(d) Election by Defendant.

(1) A defendant in an action brought by a public official or public figure arising out of a publication or broadcast in the print or electronic media which is alleged to be false and defamatory shall have the right, at the time of filing its answer or within 90 days from the commencement of the action, whichever comes first, to designate the action as an action for a declaratory judgment pursuant to subsection (a).

(2) Any action designated as an action for a declaratory judgment pursuant to paragraph (1) shall be treated for all purposes as if it had been filed originally as an action for a declaratory judgment under subsection (a), and the plaintiff shall be forever barred from asserting or recovering for any other claim or cause of action arising out of a publication or broadcast which is the subject of such action.

SECTION 2. Limitation on Action.

Any action arising out of a publication or broadcast which is alleged to be false and defamatory must be commenced not later than one year after the first date of such publication or broadcast.

SECTION 3. Punitive Damages Prohibited.

Punitive damages may not be awarded in any action arising out of a publication or broadcast which is alleged to be false and defamatory.

SECTION 4. Attorney's Fees.

In any action arising out of a publication or broadcast which is alleged to be false and defamatory, the court shall award the prevailing party reasonable attorney's fees, except that—

(1) the court may reduce or disallow the award of attorney's fees if it determines that there is an overriding reason to do so; and

(2) the court shall not award attorney's fees against a defendant which proves that it exercised reasonable efforts to ascertain that the publication or broadcast was not false and defamatory or

that it published or broadcast a retraction not later than 10 days after the action was filed.

SECTION 5. Effective Date.

This Act shall apply to any cause of action which arises on or after the date of the enactment of this Act.

---

c. *The Plaintiff's Option Libel Reform Act*

Proposed in FRANKLIN, A DECLARATORY-JUDGMENT ALTERNATIVE TO CURRENT LIBEL LAW

74 Calif.L.Rev. ___ (1986).

SECTION 1. Action for Declaratory Judgment That Statement Is False and Defamatory

(a) Cause of Action

(1) Any person who is the subject of any defamation may bring an action in any court of competent jurisdiction for a declaratory judgment that such publication or broadcast was false and defamatory.

(2) Paragraph (1) shall not be construed to require proof of the state of mind of the defendant.

(3) No damages shall be awarded in such an action.

(b) Burden of Proof. The plaintiff seeking a declaratory judgment under subsection (a) shall bear the burden of proving by clear and convincing evidence each element of the cause of action described in subsection (a). In an action under subsection (a), a report of a statement made by an identified source not associated with the defendant shall not be deemed false if it is accurately reported.

(c) Defenses. Privileges that already exist at common law or by statute, including but not limited to the privilege of fair and accurate report, shall apply to actions brought under this section.

(d) Bar to Certain Claims. A plaintiff who brings an action for a declaratory judgment under subsection (a) shall be forever barred from asserting any other claim or cause of action arising out of a publication or broadcast which is the subject of such action.

SECTION 2. Limitation on Action

(a) Any action arising out of a publication or broadcast which is alleged to be false and defamatory must be commenced not later than one year after the first date of such publication or broadcast.

(b) It shall be a defense to an action brought under Section 1 that the defendant published or broadcast an appropriate retraction before the action was filed.

(c) No pretrial discovery of any sort shall be allowed in any action brought under Section 1.

(d) When setting trial dates, courts shall give actions brought under Section 1 priority over other civil actions.

SECTION 3. Proof and Recovery in Damage Actions

(a) In any action for damages for libel or slander or false-light invasion of privacy, the plaintiff may recover no damages unless plaintiff proves falsity and actual malice by clear and convincing evidence.

(b) Punitive damages may not be awarded in any action for libel or slander or false-light invasion of privacy.

(c) A plaintiff who brings an action for damages for libel or slander or false-light invasion of privacy shall be forever barred from asserting any other claim or cause of action arising out of a publication or broadcast which is the subject of such action.

SECTION 4. Attorney's Fees

(a) General Rule. Except as provided in subsection (b), in any action arising out of a publication or broadcast which is alleged to be false and defamatory, the court shall award the prevailing party reasonable attorney's fees.

(b) Exceptions.

(1) In an action for damages, a prevailing defendant shall not be awarded attorney's fees if the plaintiff sustained special damages and the action is found to have been brought or maintained with a reasonable chance of success.

(2) In an action brought under Section 1, a prevailing defendant shall not be awarded attorney's fees if the plaintiff has brought or maintained the action with a reasonable chance of success and presented, or formally tried to present, to the defendant evidence that the statement was false and defamatory before the action was filed.

(3) In an action under Section 1, a prevailing plaintiff shall not be awarded attorney's fees if the plaintiff has prevailed on the basis of evidence that the plaintiff did not present, or formally try to present, to the defendant before the action was filed.

(4) In any action brought under Section 1 in which the defendant has made an appropriate retraction after the filing of suit, the plaintiff shall be treated as the prevailing party up to that point and the defendant shall be treated as the prevailing party after that point.

SECTION 5. Effective Date

This Act shall apply to any cause of action that arises on or after the date of the enactment of this Act.

Notes and Questions

1. The merits of these proposals are debated in Franklin, A Declaratory-Judgment Alternative to Current Libel Law, 74 Calif.L.Rev. ___ (1986) and Barrett, Libel Reform: A Better Alternative, 74 Calif.L.Rev. ___ (1986).

2. What are the strengths of each approach? The weaknesses?

3. What empirical questions are central to your analysis of these proposed reforms?

4. Do any of these proposals conflict with the current Supreme Court view of libel law?

5. Consider the following proposal, which does require changes in constitutional law, proposed in Ingber, Defamation: A Conflict Between Reason and Decency, 65 Va.L.Rev. 785 (1979):

> § 1. *Fault-Free Defamation.* Only the defamatory nature of the publication is proved by the plaintiff.
>
> Regardless of the status of the plaintiff—whether a public or private figure—damages should be awarded only for actual pecuniary loss. If the plaintiff cannot prove such loss, the court should allow a simple action for a declaratory judgment affirming the false and defamatory nature of the statement. The defendant must choose between publishing a retraction or financing the reasonable costs of a reply elsewhere. Compensation for reply costs is contingent upon the plaintiff making a good faith effort to obtain media reply time or space without cost. No award for plaintiff attorney fees should be authorized.
>
> § 2. *Negligent Defamation.* In addition to proving defamation, the plaintiff also demonstrates that the defendant acted negligently in preparing or publishing the defamatory statement.
>
> Remedies would include, in addition to those existing for fault-free defamation, awards by the court for reasonable attorney fees.
>
> § 3. *Defamation with Scienter.* In addition to proving defamation and falsity, plaintiff also demonstrates that defendant knew of the falsity of his statement or recklessly disregarded personally held suspicions of such falsity.
>
> Remedies would include, in addition to those existing for negligent defamation, awards for actual but nonpecuniary injuries. No punitive damages would be allowed.

For a more elaborate proposal along the same lines, see Ingber, Rethinking Intangible Injuries: A Focus on Remedy, 73 Calif.L.Rev. 772, 832–39 (1985).

6. For a preliminary report on a large empirical study of libel law, see Bezanson, Cranberg, and Soloski, Libel Law and the Press: Setting the Record Straight, 71 Iowa L.Rev. 215 (1985).

Chapter III

PROTECTING PRIVACY

Privacy is a relatively new legal concept with many facets. We focus first on disclosure by the press of true statements that an individual would rather not have publicly disseminated, sometimes called the tort of "public disclosure." We then turn to statements that present the plaintiff in a "false light," and to those that involve the right of publicity. Finally, we turn to related aspects of state secrets. In Chapter XI, we will look at the "intrusion" aspect of privacy in connection with how far reporters may go to obtain information from unwilling sources.

A. PUBLIC DISCLOSURE OF TRUTH

1. State Developments

The idea that this interest should be legally protected can be traced to a law review article by Louis D. Brandeis and his law partner, Samuel D. Warren, The Right to Privacy, 4 Harv.L.Rev. 193 (1890). The authors, reacting to the editorial practices of Boston newspapers, particularly a report about a family gathering the Warrens had thought was private, made clear their concerns:

> The press is overstepping in every direction the obvious bounds of propriety and of decency. Gossip is no longer the resource of the idle and of the vicious, but has become a trade, which is pursued with industry as well as effrontery. To satisfy a prurient taste the details of sexual relations are spread broadcast in the columns of the daily papers. To occupy the indolent, column upon column is filled with idle gossip, which can only be procured by intrusion upon the domestic circle. . . . When personal gossip attains the dignity of print, and crowds the space available for matters of real interest to the community, what wonder that the ignorant and thoughtless mistake its relative importance. Easy of comprehension, appealing to that weak side of human nature which is never wholly cast down by the misfortunes and frailties of our neighbors, no one can be surprised that it usurps the place of interest in brains capable of other things. Triviality destroys at once robustness of thought and delicacy of feelings. No enthusiasm can flourish, no generous impulse can survive under its blighting influence.

Working with a variety of rather remote precedents from other areas of law, the authors developed an argument that courts should recognize an action for invasion of privacy by media publication.

The theory was rejected in the first major case to consider it. In Roberson v. Rochester Folding Box Co., 171 N.Y. 538, 64 N.E. 442 (1902), the defendants, a flour company and a box company, obtained a good likeness of the plaintiff, a very pretty girl, and reproduced it on their advertising posters. Plaintiff said she was humiliated and suffered great distress. The court, 4–3, rejected a common law privacy action on grounds that suggested concern about innovating after so many centuries; an inability to see how the doctrine, once accepted, could be judicially limited to appropriate situations; and skepticism about finding liability for an action that might actually please some potential "victims." The Warren and Brandeis article was discussed at length, but the court concluded that the precedents relied upon were too remote to sustain the proposed right.

The outcry was immediate. At its next session, the New York legislature created a statutory right of privacy (New York Civil Rights Law, §§ 50 and 51). The basic provision was that "a person, firm or corporation that uses for advertising purposes, or the purposes of trade, the name, portrait or picture of any living person without having first obtained the written consent of such person, or if a minor of his or her parent or guardian, is guilty of a misdemeanor." The other section provided for an injunction and created an action for compensatory and punitive damages.

Other states, perhaps learning from the New York experience, slowly began to develop a common law right to privacy that was not influenced by statutory language and not limited to advertising invasions. In addition to an action for commercial use of one's name, the courts also developed an action for truthful use of plaintiff's name that was thought to be outside the areas of legitimate public concern. The action for invasion of privacy by publication of true editorial material began to take hold during the 1920s and early 1930s. See, e.g., Melvin v. Reid, 112 Cal.App. 285, 297 P. 91 (1931), in which the plaintiff, a reformed prostitute who had been tried for murder in 1918 and acquitted, was permitted to recover from a motion picture producer who had used her true name in a movie about her past.

Courts in the late 1930s became more attentive to the Supreme Court's expanding protection of expression. Operating on a common law level, they tended to broaden protection for the media by taking a narrow view of what were legitimately private areas.

The newsworthiness defense expanded because courts were reluctant to impose normative standards of what should be newsworthy. Instead, they leaned toward a descriptive definition that protected whatever an editor had decided would interest his readers. See, Comment, The Right of Privacy: Normative-Descriptive Confusion in the Defense of Newsworthiness, 30 U.Chi.L.Rev. 722 (1963). By the 1960s, it was unclear whether the action for invasion of privacy had any remaining vitality. See, Kalven, Privacy in Tort Law—Were Warren and Brandeis Wrong? 31 Law and Contemporary Problems 326 (1966);

Bloustein, Privacy, Tort Law, and the Constitution: Is Warren and Brandeis' Tort Petty and Unconstitutional As Well?, 46 Texas L.Rev. 611 (1968).

It was precisely during the last part of the 1960s and the beginning of the 1970s, however, that society began sensing that privacy as a general social value was threatened in different ways by the encroachment of computers, data banks, and electronic devices, as well as the media. The concept of privacy was also expanded in Supreme Court cases dealing with birth control, abortion, and other personal issues.

The new thinking broadened the area of privacy protection and reduced the area once covered by common law notions of newsworthiness. At the same time, however, the defamation cases, beginning with New York Times Co. v. Sullivan, were signalling a countertrend of press protection.

Since we are dealing, in the first instance at least, with a state tort action, it is appropriate to begin our consideration with a sampling of recent state cases to see what types of situations give rise to "public disclosure" cases.

a. Some Illustrations

The New York Situation. As noted, the New York experience has been substantially different from those of states that developed a common law jurisprudence. New York's highest court still adheres to the rule that actions for truthful revelations must be based on the statute. For example, in Freihofer v. Hearst Corp., 65 N.Y.2d 135, 480 N.E.2d 349, 490 N.Y.S.2d 735, 12 Med.L.Rptr. 1056 (1985), plaintiff husband in a divorce action sued defendant newspaper for stories relating to the action. The stories were based upon the reporter's having read some court documents that, by statute, are to be kept confidential by court officials. Since the reporter did not violate the confidentiality statute, the court held that the only basis for liability would be the privacy statute. The articles were not published for "advertising purposes" and were not for "purposes of trade" even though they were published to help the paper make a profit. The critical factor under the statute "is the content of the published article in terms of whether it is newsworthy, which is a question of law, and not the defendant's motive to increase circulation."

See also Stephano v. News Group Publications, Inc., 64 N.Y.2d 174, 474 N.E.2d 580, 485 N.Y.S.2d 220, 11 Med.L.Rptr. 1303 (1984), asserting that the newsworthiness exception in the statute "applies not only to reports of political happenings and social trends [ ], but also to news stories and articles of consumer interest including developments in the fashion world." In that case, the court rejected an action by a male model whose photograph in a "bomber jacket" was used in a magazine's "Best Bets" column. The text included the approximate price of the jacket, the name of the designer, and the names of three stores where the jacket could be bought. The court concluded that the use was not for advertising purposes nor was it an advertisement in disguise. Similar information is used in reviews or in news announcements of new products or new books or movies. "In short, the plaintiff has not presented any facts which would set this particular article apart from the numerous other legitimate news items concerning new products."

To avoid confusing the common law and the New York situations, the following illustrations will be drawn exclusively from states that do not rely on statutes.

Sexual Matters

1. In a study of official misconduct at a county home, a newspaper reported the involuntary sterilization of a named 18-year-old young woman seven years earlier. Howard v. Des Moines Register and Tribune Co., 283 N.W.2d 289, 5 Med.L.Rptr. 1667 (Iowa 1979), certiorari denied 445 U.S. 904 (1980) (case dismissed).

2. A newspaper columnist included the following item: "More education stuff: The students at the College of Alameda will be surprised to learn that their student body president, Toni Diaz, is no lady, but is in fact a man whose real name is Antonio.

"Now I realize, that in these times, such a matter is no big deal, but I suspect his female classmates in P.E. 97 may wish to make other showering arrangements." A $775,000 judgment for plaintiff, who had had sex-change surgery, was reversed on appeal. A new trial was ordered. Diaz v. Oakland Tribune, Inc., 139 Cal.App.3d 118, 188 Cal. Rptr. 762, 9 Med.L.Rptr. 1121 (1983).

3. During an assassination attempt on President Ford in San Francisco, Oliver Sipple knocked the arm of the assailant, Sara Jane Moore, as she sought to aim a second shot at the President. Sipple was the object of extensive media attention, including stories that disclosed his homosexuality. Sipple, asserting that relatives who lived in the Midwest did not know of his sexual preference, sued the San Francisco Chronicle. The newspaper defended in part on the argument that privacy was not involved because Sipple had marched in gay parades and had acknowledged that at least 100 to 500 people in San Francisco knew he was a homosexual.

Summary judgment was affirmed on appeal. First, the facts were not private. Second, they were newsworthy. It was prompted by "legitimate political considerations, i.e., to dispel the false public opinion that gays were timid, weak and unheroic figures and to raise the equally important political question whether the President of the United States entertained a discriminatory attitude or bias against a minority group such as homosexuals." Sipple v. Chronicle Publishing Co., 154 Cal.App.3d 1040, 201 Cal.Rptr. 665, 10 Med.L.Rptr. 1690 (1984).

4. Television cameras went to the scene of a report that a man was threatening harm to his housekeeper's sister. The crew arrived and began filming as police led the stark-naked man from the house. In a news report the following evening, plaintiff's "buttocks and geni-

tals were visible to television viewers for a time period of approximately eight-to-nine-tenths of one second." Taylor v. K.T.V.B. Inc., 96 Idaho 202, 525 P.2d 984 (1974) (case remanded to determine defendant's reasons for using the film).

5. Plaintiff was kidnapped by her estranged husband and taken to an apartment. He forced her to disrobe and then beat her. Police came. After the husband committed suicide, police hurried plaintiff from the apartment nude "save for a mere towel." Defendant's photographer's picture of the partially covered woman appeared in the paper.

On appeal, plaintiff's judgment for $1,000 compensatory and $9,000 punitive damages was reversed and the case was dismissed. Cape Publications, Inc. v. Bridges, 423 So.2d 426, 8 Med.L.Rptr. 2535 (Fla. App.1982), certiorari denied 464 U.S. 893 (1983).

6. A group of Pittsburgh Steelers fans urged a photographer from Sports Illustrated to take pictures of them. The photographer did so. From among many photographs available for use, the editors chose one that showed the plaintiff with his fly open. Neff v. Time, Inc., 406 F.Supp. 858 (W.D.Pa.1976) (case dismissed).

7. A newspaper reported the identity of a deceased rape victim. Cox Broadcasting Corp. v. Cohn, 420 U.S. 469 (1975) (case is reported at p. 320, infra).

Criminal Behavior

8. A magazine article, to prove that truck hijacking was a chancy venture, reported that 11 years earlier the plaintiff and another had hijacked a truck in Kentucky, only to find that it contained four bowling pin spotting machines. The article was published in 1967, by which time plaintiff alleged that he had served his time, had become rehabilitated, and was living in California with family and friends who did not know about his past. Briscoe v. Reader's Digest Ass'n, 4 Cal.3d 529, 93 Cal.Rptr. 866, 483 P.2d 34 (1971) (case remanded to determine whether the defendant published with "reckless disregard" for the article's offensiveness).

9. A newspaper that regularly reproduced pages from editions of 20 years earlier, published two old editions that accurately reported the conviction of the three plaintiff brothers for cattle theft. Judgments of $35,000 for each plaintiff were reversed and the cases dismissed. Roshto v. Hebert, 439 So.2d 428, 9 Med.L.Rptr. 2417 (La.1983).

10. Plaintiff was arrested for drunk driving. At the police station, he was "hitting and banging on his cell door, hollering and cursing from the time of his arrest" until five hours later. A local broadcaster taped some of the noise and played excerpts on the radio. Holman v. Central Arkansas Broadcasting Co., 610 F.2d 542, 4 Med.L.Rptr. 2300 (8th Cir.1979) (case dismissed).

Poverty

11. A newspaper article included a front-page photograph of the plaintiff's home. The photograph was one of a series on the newspaper's hometown and its environs. The caption read, "one of Crowley's stately homes, a bit weatherworn and unkempt, stands in the shadow of a spreading oak." Jaubert v. Crowley Post-Signal, Inc., 375 So.2d 1386, 5 Med.L.Rptr. 2084 (La.1979) (case dismissed).

Idiosyncrasies

12. The New Yorker magazine did one of its extensive profiles on a man who, 27 years earlier, had been an 11-year-old child prodigy who had lectured to mathematicians. For the last 20 years, however, he had lived as unobtrusively as possible. The profile reported that the plaintiff was living in a hall bedroom on Boston's "shabby south end," that his room was untidy, that he had a curious laugh, that he collected streetcar transfers, and that he was interested at the moment in the lore of the Okamakammessett Indians. The article was judged to be "merciless in its dissection of intimate details of its subject's personal life" and a "ruthless exposure of a once public character who has since sought and has now been deprived of the seclusion of private life." Sidis v. F–R Pub. Corp., 113 F.2d 806 (2d Cir.), certiorari denied 311 U.S. 711 (1940) (case dismissed).

13. Sports Illustrated planned an article about a California beach reputed to be the world's most dangerous site for body surfing. Plaintiff, known as the most daring surfer at the site, was interviewed and was referred to in the story as one who extinguished cigarettes in his mouth, ate various insects, dove head first down a flight of stairs, had never learned to read, and was perceived by other surfers as "abnormal." Virgil v. Time, Inc., 527 F.2d 1122 (9th Cir.1975), certiorari denied 425 U.S. 998 (1976) (affirming denial of defense motion for summary judgment). (Although plaintiff had once consented to be interviewed, he withdrew the consent when he learned the shape the story would take. The court rejected the defense of consent.)

Embarrassment or Ridicule

14. The defendant newspaper ran a feature about a public school class for mentally retarded children. A photograph accompanying the article showed several members of the class and identified four children of one family. Deaton v. Delta Democrat Pub. Co., 326 So.2d 471 (Miss. 1976) (case remanded for trial).

15. A newspaper article reported that the basketball team at the state university was in trouble because four named players, of the eight who were returning, "are on academic probation and in danger of flunking." Bilney v. Evening Star Newspaper Co., 43 Md.App. 560, 406 A.2d 652, 4 Med.L.Rptr. 1924 (1979) (case dismissed).

16. Plaintiff was a janitor who found $240,000 that had fallen from an armored car. He returned it (and received a reward of

$10,000), to the scorn of his neighbors and his children's friends. When their hostile reaction was reported, he received many congratulatory letters and messages, including one from President Kennedy. The full story was reported in a periodical and reprinted in a college English textbook. Johnson v. Harcourt, Brace, Jovanovich, Inc., 43 Cal.App.3d 880, 118 Cal.Rptr. 370 (1974) (case dismissed).

b. Legal Analysis

As the common law has been developing, the plaintiff must show that the information made public was in fact "private," that the disclosure would be "highly offensive to a reasonable person, and that the subject matter was not "newsworthy." We look at each element in turn.

Private Information. The courts have not been very attentive to this aspect of the matter—perhaps because in most cases the information is clearly something that the plaintiff had held closely and did not want bandied about. Our examples ranged from one extreme to the other. The plaintiff in the sex-change case had not publicized the surgery. On the other hand, facts are unlikely to be private when the exterior of a home is shabby, when someone at a football game with his fly open poses for a professional photographer, or when someone at a police station shouts so loudly that others cannot help but hear him.

Between these extremes we have cases like that of Oliver Sipple, whose sexual preference was not a secret among his friends and his immediate community, and who was willing to march in gay parades but wanted the information kept inside San Francisco. Although some cases should be eliminated on the ground that the information published had not been "private" at the time of the publication, many do seem to involve matters that most people would attempt to keep secret.

As with defamation, most states consider an action for public disclosure of private facts to be personal. In Hendrickson v. California Newspapers, Inc., 48 Cal.App.3d 59, 121 Cal.Rptr. 429 (1975), defendant published an obituary revealing that the deceased had had a criminal record. The obituary also named his survivors. The widow and children sued, claiming that the defendant had revealed a "family secret." The court held that no action could be brought by the estate. Nor did an action accrue to the survivors, because reference to them was "purely relational."

The same results were reached in Fry v. Ionia Sentinel-Standard, 101 Mich.App. 725, 300 N.W.2d 687, 6 Med.L.Rptr. 2497 (1980), in which a news story reported that plaintiff's husband and a woman had been killed in an accidental fire in a rural cottage. The story identified the dead man's wife and children as his survivors.

"Highly Offensive to a Reasonable Person." This element of the action receives much more attention. Although the specific language is taken from the Restatement, Second, Torts § 652D, similar expressions have been used in the cases during this tort's development. The single

most important consideration appears to be the substance of the statement. In some cases it appears difficult to argue that the revelation would be highly offensive to a reasonable person—as in the case of the janitor who returned the money he found, even though some members of plaintiff's community criticized his behavior. This would also apply to the "weatherworn and unkempt" house. Perhaps a similar analysis would apply to the cases involving idiosyncrasies—the body surfer and the child prodigy. Even though the article about the prodigy was described as "merciless in its dissection of intimate details of its subject's personal life," perhaps what was revealed would not be highly offensive to a reasonable person. That some people may wish to keep private some of their quirks does not mean that reasonable people would find the revelation of that information highly offensive.

"Newsworthiness" or "Legitimate Concern." In addition to requiring that the publicized matter be private and "highly offensive to a reasonable person," the courts demand that the matter be "not of legitimate concern to the public." Most litigation has revolved around this or similar phrases, such as claims that the article in question was "newsworthy" or that it was of "general or public concern."

There was a period in which the courts seemed to treat "newsworthy" or "of legitimate concern" as descriptive terms. Any article appearing in a newspaper would meet that requirement because if an editor chose to include it, it must be newsworthy. Such an approach, of course, would eliminate the privacy action. More recently, the courts have shifted and are now attempting to develop normative guidelines to determine when the information might be of "legitimate concern to the public."

The main distinction here is between voluntary and involuntary public figures. It should not be surprising that those who seek the public limelight should be thought to have a lesser claim to privacy protection than those brought into the glare of publicity simply because they are either the unfortunate victims of an accident or crime or are otherwise swept up in an event. But even involuntary subjects are not immune. As comment (f) to § 652D puts it:

> These persons are regarded as properly subject to the public interest, and publishers are permitted to satisfy the curiosity of the public as to its heroes, leaders, villains and victims, and those who are closely associated with them. As in the case of the voluntary public figure, the authorized publicity is not limited to the event that itself arouses the public interest, and to some extent includes publicity given to facts about the individual that would otherwise be purely private.

Our examples include a variety of plaintiffs. The body surfer has voluntarily brought himself into the public eye by his prowess, his continued attendance at a particular beach, and his engaging in a particular type of activity. Sidis, who may have been a voluntary public figure at age 11 and in his teens, later sought obscurity—but the public has a legitimate concern with what happens to prodigies in later life. Is there a similar concern as to criminals? Others "voluntarily" become public figures on the spur of the moment—as when Sipple knocked the arm of the President's assailant or when Johnson returned the money he found in the street. Most of our examples, however, involved involuntary public figures—those who wished to keep their sterilization or mental retardation private and had in no other way been voluntarily in the public spotlight.

Although courts sometimes suggest that the distinction is relevant to the decision, the difference is at most a matter of degree and more often may control the question of whether the editor will choose to name the person in the story. As a practical matter, an already voluntary public figure who is involved in an accident or other misfortune is much more likely to be named in any story that results from the episode than is a previously anonymous person. Those who seek the limelight risk having their names used in unwanted contexts. But this does not mean that every aspect of their lives may be revealed. The Restatement seeks to draw a line in comment (h):

> Permissible publicity to information concerning either voluntary or involuntary public figures is not limited to the particular events that arouse the interest of the public. That interest, once aroused by the event, may legitimately extend, to some reasonable degree, to further information concerning the individual and to facts about him, which are not public and which, in the case of one who had not become a public figure, would be regarded as an invasion of his purely private life. Thus the life history of one accused of murder, together with such heretofore private facts as may throw some light upon what kind of person he is, his possible guilt or innocence, or his reasons for committing the crime, are a matter of legitimate public interest. . . . On the same basis the home life and daily habits of a motion picture actress may be of legitimate and reasonable interest to the public that sees her on the screen.
>
> The extent of the authority to make public private facts is not, however, unlimited. There may be some intimate details of her life, such as sexual relations, which even the actress is entitled to keep to herself. In determining what is a matter of legitimate public interest, account must be taken of the customs and conventions of the community; and in the last analysis what is proper becomes a matter of the community mores. The line is to be drawn when the publicity ceases to be the giving of information to which the public is entitled, and becomes a morbid and sensational prying into private lives for its own sake, with which a reasonable member of the public, with decent standards, would say that he had no concern. The limitations, in other words, are those of common decency, having due regard to the freedom of the press and its reasonable leeway to choose what it will tell the public, but also

due regard to the feelings of the individual and the harm that will be done to him by the exposure. Some reasonable proportion is also to be maintained between the event or activity that makes the individual a public figure and the private facts to which publicity is given. Revelations that may properly be made concerning a murderer or the President of the United States would not be privileged if they were to be made concerning one who is merely injured in an automobile accident.

In Virgil v. Time, Inc., p. 305, supra, plaintiff had been interviewed and photographed at the beach. To verify the accuracy of the article, a checker for the magazine called plaintiff's home. Plaintiff claims that he learned then for the first time that the article would deal not only with his prominence as a surfer but also with "some rather bizarre incidents in his life that were not directly related to surfing." These included diving head first down a flight of stairs and eating "spiders and other insects." The events, and the facts that he had never learned to read and that other surfers thought him "abnormal," were thought to have some bearing on plaintiff's "reckless disregard for his own safety" in body surfing. When plaintiff learned of the scope of the proposed article, he "revoked his consent" to any mention of his name or use of his photograph in the article. When the article appeared with the information about plaintiff and photographs of him, he sued for invasion of privacy.

The trial court's denial of summary judgment to the magazine was affirmed on interlocutory appeal. The court first ruled that plaintiff's participation in the interviews did not make the information public. Selective discussion with others was not the same as broadcasting information to the public. A person speaking with a member of the press, however, should anticipate that the material will become public at a later time and speaking will be taken as consent—unless, as alleged here, the consent is withdrawn before the publication.

The court adopted the view of the Restatement, Second, Torts, that liability may be imposed if the matter published is "not of legitimate concern to the public." Then the court quoted from what later became § 652D comment (h):

> In determining what is a matter of legitimate public interest, account must be taken of the customs and conventions of the community; and in the last analysis what is proper becomes a matter of the community mores. The line is to be drawn when the publicity ceases to be the giving of information to which the public is entitled, and becomes a morbid and sensational prying into private lives for its own sake, with which a reasonable member of the public, with decent standards, would say that he had no concern. . . .

On remand in *Virgil,* the trial judge granted the magazine summary judgment. First, he concluded that the facts were "generally unflattering and perhaps embarrassing, but they are simply not offensive to the degree of morbidity or sensationalism. In fact, they connote nearly as strong a positive image as they do a negative one. On the one hand Mr. Virgil can be seen as a juvenile exhibitionist, but on the other hand he also comes across as the tough, aggressive maverick, an archetypal character occupying a respected place in the American consciousness. Given this ambiguity . . . no reasonable juror could conclude that [the facts] were highly offensive."

"Even if" offensiveness were found, the magazine was entitled to summary judgment because the parties "agree that body surfing at the Wedge is a matter of legitimate public interest, and it cannot be doubted that Mike Virgil's unique prowess at the same is also of legitimate public interest. Any reasonable person . . . would have to conclude that the personal facts concerning Mike Virgil were included as a legitimate journalistic attempt to explain Virgil's extremely daring and dangerous style of body surfing at the Wedge. There is no possibility that a juror could conclude that the personal facts were included for any inherent morbid, sensational, or curiosity appeal they might have." Virgil v. Sports Illustrated, 424 F.Supp. 1286 (S.D.Cal. 1976).

The magazine Medical Economics carried an article entitled, "Who Let This Doctor In The O.R.? The Story Of A Fatal Breakdown In Medical Policing." The article outlined two cases in which the plaintiff, an anesthesiologist, had allegedly committed malpractice that led to fatal or severely disabling injuries to patients. The article detailed the plaintiff's asserted history of psychiatric and related personal problems and suggested a causal connection between these problems and the malpractice, suggested that the causal connection was known or should have been known to policing agents of the medical profession, and concluded that better policing was needed.

A summary judgment for defendants was affirmed on appeal. Gilbert v. Medical Economics Co., 665 F.2d 305, 7 Med.L.Rptr. 2373 (10th Cir.1981). The court sought to limit liability to the "extreme case, thereby providing the breathing space needed by the press." The required balancing was to be achieved by requiring that "every private fact disclosed in an otherwise truthful, newsworthy publication must have some substantial relevance to a matter of legitimate public concern."

In response to plaintiff's claim that her name and photograph should not have been used, the court responded that "they strengthen the impact and credibility of the article." Their use provided "an aura of immediacy and even urgency that might not" have existed otherwise.

Plaintiff also claimed that the article should not have discussed her personal problems "until a public tribunal had made . . . a causal connection [between those problems and the alleged malpractice]."

The court thought this "far too restrictive" because the press must be able to draw inferences. Here, since the inferences drawn "are not, as a matter of law, so purely conjectural that no reasonable editor could draw them other than through guesswork and speculation, we hold that defendants did not abuse their editorial discretion in this case."

Note also that sometimes a court may find all three elements wanting. In *Bridges,* p. 304, supra, for example, the court noted that although plaintiff was "clutching a dish towel to her body in order to conceal her nudity," the photograph "revealed little more than could be seen had [plaintiff] been wearing a bikini and somewhat less than some bathing suits seen on the beaches. There were other more revealing photographs taken which were not published."

The court concluded that although the photo, "which won industry awards, could be considered by some to be in bad taste," state law was settled that one involved in an occurrence of public interest has no claim against those who publish a photo of the event. The fact that the event is painful to the plaintiff does not mean that the newspaper "cannot publish what is otherwise newsworthy."

We conclude the beginning section on what the plaintiff must show by noting that no complex damage rules, such as exist in defamation, have emerged in privacy. The plaintiff who can successfully demonstrate an invasion of privacy will recover damages measured by the emotional harm suffered. Obviously, damages here cannot rehabilitate the plaintiff in the way that damages in defamation might pay for the reputational harm caused by the false statement.

The plaintiff's case is so challenging that formal defenses have little place.

Before concluding the common law section, we turn to a recent case that takes an atypical view of the tort.

ANDERSON v. FISHER BROADCASTING COMPANIES, INC.

Supreme Court of Oregon, 1986.
300 Or. 452, 712 P.2d 803, 12 Med.L.Rptr. 1604.

LINDE, JUSTICE.

A television cameraman for defendant broadcasting company photographed the scene of an automobile accident in which plaintiff was injured. Plaintiff was recognizable and was shown bleeding and in pain while receiving emergency medical treatment. Defendant did not use the video taped pictures or report the accident on its regular news program. Some time later, without seeking plaintiff's consent, defendant used a brief excerpt showing plaintiff to illustrate promotional spots advertising a special news report about a new system for dispatching emergency medical help.

Plaintiff sued for general damages for mental anguish, alleging that defendant "violated plaintiff's right to privacy" by "appropriating to defendant's own use and advantage" the pictures its photographer had taken of plaintiff and by "publicizing" his picture in a condition "offensive to a reasonable person" and not of legitimate public concern. In defense, the broadcaster asserted that its use of plaintiff's picture occurred in advertising another news program, that this use was constitutionally privileged and that the undisputed facts gave rise to no common-law claim. The trial court gave summary judgment for defendant, holding that the pictures were "newsworthy," that they remained so despite not being promptly published, and that they did not lose their newsworthiness when used only to advertise another newsworthy broadcast.

The Court of Appeals [reversed]. . . .

. . .

We shall not decide this case on constitutional grounds when it is unnecessary to do so, and when a premature decision would foreclose legislative consideration. In the present case, we hold that the undisputed facts do not give rise to a claim for damages. We therefore reverse the Court of Appeals and reinstate the judgment of the circuit court.

I. Invasion of Privacy in Oregon Tort Law

Plaintiff asserts two grounds to hold the broadcasting company liable for causing him mental anguish. One is that the publicity defendant gave to plaintiff's injuries and pain concerned plaintiff's private life and would be offensive to a reasonable person. The other is that defendant appropriated plaintiff's recorded image without his consent to its own commercial purpose.

The question whether truthfully publicizing a fact about a private individual that the individual reasonably prefers to keep private is, without more, a tort has not yet been squarely decided by this court.

We recently had occasion, in Humphers v. First Interstate Bank, 298 Or. 706, 696 P.2d 527 (1985), to review Oregon cases on "privacy" since Hinish v. Meier & Frank Co., 166 Or. 482, 113 P.2d 438 (1941). In *Hinish,* plaintiff's name had been signed without his consent to a telegram urging the governor to veto a bill. In *Humphers,* [ ] we noted:

> "An essential element in *Hinish* was the allegation that plaintiff's name was used without his consent and against his will, in other words, that using his name on the telegram was fraudulent. The case does not hold that it would be an actionable invasion of privacy to write the governor that 'Mr. Hinish, too, opposes this bill,' if Hinish had made such a statement to the writer. The false appropriation, not the potential public exposure of Hinish's actual views, constituted the tort."

. . .

Generally, Oregon decisions have not allowed recovery for injury to a stranger's feelings as such, unless the infliction of psychic distress was the object of defendant's conduct or the conduct violated some legal duty apart from causing the distress. [ ] In the absence of some other duty or relationship of the defendant to plaintiff, it does not suffice for tort liability that defendant's offensive conduct is an intentional act. The conduct must be designed to cause severe mental or emotional distress, whether for its own sake or as a means to some other end, and it must qualify as extraordinary conduct that a reasonable jury could find to be beyond the farthest reach of socially tolerable behavior. . . .

II. Nature of "Privacy" Interests

"Privacy" denotes a personal or cultural value placed on seclusion or personal control over access to places or things, thoughts or acts. "Privacy" also can be used to label one or more legally recognized interests, and this court has so used the term in several cases since *Hinish*. But like the older word "property," which it partially overlaps, "privacy" has been a difficult legal concept to delimit. Lawyers and theorists debate the nature of the interests that privacy law means to protect, the criteria of wrongful invasions of those interests, and the matching of remedies to the identified interests. These questions confront us in the present case.

. . . The second Restatement of Torts, following the work of its original Reporter, Dean Prosser, noted that "invasion of the right of privacy" mixed four distinct wrongs, related not by similarity of defendants' acts but only by "the interest of the individual in leading, to some reasonable extent, a secluded and private life, free from the prying eyes, ears and publications of others." Restatement, Second, Torts § 652A, comment b (1977). The Restatement defined these distinct wrongs as "intrusion upon seclusion" (§ 652B), "appropriation of name or likeness" (§ 652C), "publicity given to private life" (§ 652D), and "publicity placing person in false light" (§ 652E). . . . [A]ccepting the classification for convenience, plaintiff makes no claim that the broadcaster's cameraman intruded on a scene of seclusion or that the pictures broadcast by defendant placed plaintiff in a false light. . . .

The common-law tort claim based solely on publicizing private facts that are true but not newsworthy has met critical response. . . . Criticism has not implied a lack of sympathy with the feelings of persons whose past or present lives are brought to public attention against their own wishes; but the obstacles to defining when publicity as such is tortious, without more, are formidable.

What is "private" so as to make its publication offensive likely differs among communities, between generations, and among ethnic, religious, or other social groups, as well as among individuals. Likewise, one reader's or viewer's "news" is another's tedium or trivia. The editorial judgment of what is "newsworthy" is not so readily submitted to the ad hoc review of a jury as the Court of Appeals believed. It is not properly a community standard. Even when some editors themselves vie to tailor "news" to satisfy popular tastes,[9] others may believe that the community should see or hear facts or ideas that the majority finds uninteresting or offensive.

If the tort is defined to protect a plaintiff's interest in nondisclosure only against widespread publicity, as in the Restatement's § 652D, it singles out the print, film, and broadcast media for legal restraints that will not be applied to gossip-mongers in neighborhood taverns or card parties, to letter writers or telephone tattlers. [ ] Finally, a successful tort action may serve to rectify a defamatory, appropriative, or "false light" publication, but in the pure "private facts" tort even success sacrifices rather than protects the plaintiff's interest in the privacy of the wrongfully publicized facts, for litigation only breeds renewed and often wider publicity, this time unquestionably privileged. Writing in 1979, Professor Dorsey D. Ellis, Jr., found that there had been no reported case in which a plaintiff successfully recovered damages for truthful disclosure by the press since the United States Supreme Court reversed a New York judgment in Time, Inc. v. Hill, 385 U.S. 374 (1967), and he concluded that the tort's "very existence is in doubt, at least outside the law reviews." Ellis, Damages and the Privacy Tort: Sketching a Legal Profile, 64 Iowa L.Rev. 1111, 1133 (1979).

III. Pictorial Representation

Discussion of the tort often assumes that what the plaintiff objects to is the reporting of past or present "facts" or "information" by traditional forms of written publication. The classic illustration is [*Sidis*] . . . . Arguably, the widespread dissemination of a person's picture, which television has made the essence of much otherwise unremarkable as well as of traditional "news," sacrifices the pictured person's privacy in a sense distinct from disclosure of factual information.

Claims to a right to prevent unconsented use of one's likeness in fact long antedate the advent of television. The first decisions respec-

9. Bezanson, Public Disclosure as News: Injunctive Relief and Newsworthiness in Privacy Actions Involving the Press, 64 Iowa L.Rev. 1061, 1066–76 (1979), distinguishes "news" from "history" by factors of immediacy in time or locale and proposes to test the "newsworthiness" of a disclosure of private facts by the contribution it makes to the substance or to the impact of reporting some "public" event. The test fails when the primary interest of large segments of the public is "news" of the private lives of known personalities and of dramatic events in the lives of otherwise anonymous persons.

. . .

Brandeis and Warren believed, and Judge Posner does not, that the press creates the demand for shocking, scandalous, pathetic, or titillating "human interest" news by providing a supply. See Warren and Brandeis, The Right to Privacy, 4 Harv.L.Rev. 193, 196 (1890); Posner, The Right of Privacy, 12 Ga.L.Rev. 393, 396 (1978). Whatever fowl first laid this egg or first was hatched from it, the editors of newsmagazines and news broadcasts unquestionably have felt driven to compete for the audience for such material.

tively rejecting and accepting a "privacy" basis for such claims, [*Roberson*] and Pavesich v. New England Life Ins. Co., 122 Ga. 190, 50 S.E. 68 (1905), involved commercial use of plaintiffs' pictures. Sensitivity about reproduction of one's likeness is not a 19th century refinement of western civilization, as is sometimes supposed; many cultures have feared the magical power conferred by possession of a person's image. . . . Civil law systems derive limits on the unconsented publication of photographs by subsuming a right to one's own likeness under a "right of personality."

Doubtless in many instances a picture not only is worth a thousand words to a publisher but words would be worth nothing at all. The respective editors would not likely have thought it worthwhile to publish a written report that Mrs. Graham had her dress blown by air jets at an amusement park, see Daily Times Democrat v. Graham, 276 Ala. 380, 162 So.2d 474 (1964), or that Mr. and Mrs. Gill showed affection characteristic of "love at first sight," see Gill v. Curtis Pub. Co., 38 Cal.2d 273, 239 P.2d 630 (1952). Some filmed or broadcast scenes compare to verbal reports in dramatic impact about as hearing music compares to reading a score, and the emotional reaction of the person who is depicted rather than described may likewise be greater.

. . .

Nonetheless, the difference between undesired publicity by word or by picture seems to concern only the degree of the subject's psychic discomfort rather than the nature of the interest claimed to be invaded. Perhaps the present plaintiff would not have felt offended if KATU–TV had verbally described his bloodied and disheveled condition rather than showing it. But neither the courts nor the commentators have made a distinction in principle between one woman's objections to a book based on her experiences, [ ] and another's to a motion picture, [ ] and we perceive none.

A distinction has been perceived, however, between publicizing a person's name, image, or other identifying facts for some intrinsic interest or for purposes of advertising someone's products or services.

. . .

Plaintiff in the present case concedes that KATU–TV would not be liable to him if it had included his picture in the ordinary news coverage of a traffic accident. He contends that the broadcaster became liable because instead it used the footage to draw audience attention to a later broadcast concerning emergency medical services, in which plaintiff's picture was not included. Does the distinction between "commercial" and "noncommercial" use of a person's name, likeness, or life history rest on a difference in the interest invaded by the publication or in the character of the publisher's motives and purposes? The reason should bear on the remedy.

When actors, athletes or other performers object, not to a loss of anonymity, but to unauthorized exploitation of their valuable public identities, the remedy should reflect the wrongful appropriation of a "right to publicity" that has economic value to the plaintiff as well as to the defendant, rather than damages for psychic distress at a loss of "privacy." [ ] When a person who neither has nor wants a marketable public identity demands damages for unauthorized publicity, such a person may claim injury to a noneconomic rather than an economic interest in his or her privacy; but it is not always obvious, as it is not in this case, why the loss of privacy is different when it occurs in a "commercial" rather than a "noncommercial" form of publication. . . .

Our system relies for freedom of information, ideas, and entertainment, high or low, primarily on privately owned media of communication, operating at private cost and seeking private profit. Books, newspapers, films, and broadcasts are produced and distributed at private cost and for private profit, that is to say, "commercially," and the use of materials from the lives of living persons in such publications can enrich authors, photographers, and publishers just as their use in advertisements . . . . This predictably causes problems in applying a test such as New York's "advertising" or "purposes of trade," . . . . Publication of an accident victim's photograph is not appropriation for commercial use simply because the medium itself is operated for profit. Leverton v. Curtis Publishing Co., 192 F.2d 974 (3rd Cir.1951) (applying Pennsylvania law).

There is another reason why an unauthorized use of a person's name or image to sell goods or services can be a tortious appropriation when the same use in the content of material published to be sold is not. The use may make it appear that the person has consented to endorse the advertised product, with or without being paid to do so. When that impression is in fact false, the appropriation of the person's identity places the person in a false light much as the unauthorized use of Mr. Hinish's name in the political telegram did in Hinish v. Meier & Frank Co., supra. Such an inference is most likely to be drawn about professional performers, who are widely known to be paid for endorsing products in print and television advertisements and even for using their sponsors' sports clothes and equipment in their work. They have been allowed to prevent the exploitation of their public identities even to promote the publication in which they are depicted. See Cher v. Forum International, Ltd., 692 F.2d 634 (9th Cir.1982), cert. den. 462 U.S. 1120 (1983) (applying California law). The right is not limited to professionals; in an early New Jersey case, the inventor Thomas Edison won an injunction against the use of his image and a fictitious endorsement on medicine labels. [ ]

This theory is not available, however, to a person whose image, with no established public familiarity, appears in a commercial context only incidentally, perhaps as one of several persons in a public scene, or otherwise under circumstances that plainly are not presented so as to convey any endorsement by that person. . . .

. . . Without a showing that plaintiff's picture was either obtained or broadcast in a manner or for a purpose wrongful beyond the unconsented publication itself, that claim fails.

IV. Conclusion

To summarize, we conclude that in Oregon the truthful presentation of facts concerning a person, even facts that a reasonable person would wish to keep private and that are not "newsworthy," does not give rise to common-law tort liability for damages for mental or emotional distress, unless the manner or purpose of defendant's conduct is wrongful in some respect apart from causing the plaintiff's hurt feelings. For instance, a defendant might incur liability for purposely inflicting emotional distress by publishing private information in a socially intolerable way, [ ] or the publicized information might be wrongfully obtained by conversion, bribery, false pretenses, or trespassory intrusion, [ ] or published by a photographer who has been paid for what the subject reasonably expects to be the exclusive use of a picture; or when a defendant disregards a duty of confidentiality or other statutory duty, [ ] or exploits a distinctive economic value of an individual's identity or image beyond that of other similar persons for purposes of associating it with a commercial product or service, although this court has not decided all such issues. And, of course, the distressing report or presentation of a person's private affairs might not be truthful, [ ]. Because plaintiff has shown no such wrongful element in defendants' conduct, we have no occasion to anticipate constitutional questions in the event the legislature were to enter this field of tort law.

The decision of the Court of Appeals is reversed, and the judgment of the circuit court is reinstated.

Notes and Questions

1. Would the case be different if the station had used the tape on a news program before using it as it did?

2. Are there situations in which differences between verbal and photographic format might involve more than "only the degree of the subject's psychic discomfort"?

3. What role does newsworthiness play in the case?

4. In Creel v. Crown Publishers, Inc., 115 App.Div.2d 414, 496 N.Y.S.2d 219, 12 Med.L.Rptr. 1558 (1985), plaintiffs alleged that their pictures were used without their consent in defendant's "World Guide to Nude Beaches and Recreation." The photographer's affidavit stated that he met the plaintiffs at a beach and took 100 photographs of them for the publication with their oral consent. The trial judge granted plaintiff summary judgment on liability on the ground that the primary purpose of the book was to print 200 photographs of nude persons and not to disseminate information. (If the photograph was within the New

York statute, the oral consent was insufficient to bar liability though it might reduce damages.)

The appellate court reversed and dismissed the case. A picture illustrating an article or book was not for purposes of trade unless it had no real relationship to the article, or the article was an advertisement in disguise. "A guide to beaches where nude bathing is permitted is a matter of some public interest . . . . The focus of inquiry . . . is not only upon the particular photograph but also upon the article or book within which the photograph appears. Here, the photograph was utilized to illustrate a guide book which disseminated information concerning a matter of public interest and not, therefore, utilized for purposes of 'trade' within" the statute.

5. Elsewhere in his article cited in note 9, Richard Posner suggested that a person who seeks to withhold some part of his or her past is trying to present a misrepresentation to the public. Although the individual is free to try to hide this information, Posner argued that the law should not impose sanctions on those who tell the public the truth about such a person.

A 67-year-old man who had lived in the community for 25 years and run a successful locksmith and security business, decided to run for the local school board. A local newspaper investigated his background and discovered that he had concealed his past under a different name as a forger who served time in both state and federal prisons.

Reactions varied. "In every way I respect the man still as I did before," said a past president of the chamber of commerce. A member of his party's executive committee said, "I don't feel embarrassed or betrayed. These weren't violent crimes like armed robbery." Some disagreed. The president of a civic association said, "Others might be able to close their eyes and say forget it, he's paid his debt. I don't buy it. To me he's still living a lie." N.Y.Times, Sept. 3, 1985, at 11.

6. Who has the better of the dispute between Brandeis and Warren on the one hand and Posner on the other, set out in note 9 of the court's opinion?

7. In its conclusion, the court suggests that liability might be permitted if the defendant sought to inflict "emotional distress by publicizing private information in a socially intolerable way, cf. [Hall v. The May Dept. Stores, 292 Or. 131, 637 P.2d 126 (1981)]." In *Hall,* liability was imposed for intentional infliction of emotional distress in a case in which the jury could have found that a store detective, suspecting a young employee of theft, browbeat her in a coercive environment in an attempt to obtain a confession. How might this be relevant to a newspaper or broadcaster situation?

8. The specific problems of famous plaintiffs and their assertion of a "right of publicity" is discussed at p. 338, infra.

9. *Enjoining Invasions of Privacy.* The court in *Fisher* observes that a damage action for this type of invasion of privacy "sacrifices rather

than protects the plaintiff's interest in the privacy . . . for litigation only breeds renewed and often wider publicity." This has led plaintiffs who have obtained advance warning of a possible invasion to seek injunctive relief. Although injunctions in defamation cases have long been impermissible on nonconstitutional grounds, the situation in privacy is not so clear.

The Supreme Court has had a curious record with regard to injunctions barring invasions of privacy by the media. Although three significant cases have presented the issue, the Court has yet to come to grips with it. In the first, a famous baseball player persuaded the New York courts to enjoin the publication of an unauthorized biography that contained false dialogue. Spahn v. Julian Messner, Inc., 21 N.Y.2d 124, 286 N.Y.S.2d 832, 233 N.E.2d 840 (1967). The defendants' appeal to the Supreme Court raised questions only about the merits of the decision. The Supreme Court noted probable jurisdiction of the appeal and asked the parties to brief and argue the question of whether the injunctive relief granted plaintiff might constitute an unconstitutional restraint upon publication. 393 U.S. 818 (1968). At that point the case was settled and removed from the docket by stipulation of the parties. 393 U.S. 1046 (1969).

The second chance involved a motion picture, "Titticut Follies," about conditions inside a Massachusetts institution for the criminally insane. The state court barred showing of the picture except to professional groups because of the producer's invasion of the privacy of the inmates, assertedly in violation of an agreement he signed in order to get permission to make the film. Commonwealth v. Wiseman, 356 Mass. 251, 249 N.E.2d 610 (1969). The Supreme Court denied certiorari to Wiseman, the producer, 398 U.S. 960 (1969), over a lengthy dissent by Justice Harlan, joined by Justices Douglas and Brennan:

> . . . [The movie's] stark portrayal of patient-routine and treatment of the inmates is at once a scathing indictment of the inhumane conditions that prevailed at the time of the film and an undeniable infringement of the privacy of the inmates filmed, who are shown nude and engaged in acts that would unquestionably embarrass an individual of normal sensitivity. . . .
>
> . . . It is important that conditions in public institutions should not be cloaked in secrecy, lest citizens may disclaim responsibility for the treatment that their representative government affords those in its care. At the same time it must be recognized that the individual's concern with privacy is the key to the dignity which is the promise of civilized society.

Wiseman's petition for rehearing was denied. Justices Harlan, Brennan, and Blackmun dissented. "Mr. Justice Douglas took no part in the consideration or decision of this motion and petition." 400 U.S. 860, 954 (1970). The issue central to *Wiseman* reappeared in a state court case in New York in 1976, when a television crew entered an institution for care of neglected children and filmed some of the children. See Quinn v. Johnson, 51 App.Div.2d 391, 381 N.Y.S.2d 875 (1976).

The third Supreme Court case involved a different claim of privacy raised by a former patient trying to enjoin her analyst from publishing a book the analyst had written about her treatment. Although names and other facts were changed in the book, the plaintiff alleged that she and her family were easily identifiable. The trial court granted a preliminary injunction only as to such distributions "as were not reasonably calculated to reach the scientific reader." The Appellate Division modified by enjoining all distribution until the litigation concluded. Doe v. Roe, 42 App.Div.2d 559, 345 N.Y.S.2d 560 (1973) affirmed mem. 33 N.Y.2d 902, 352 N.Y.S.2d 626, 307 N.E.2d 823 (1973). Defendants, including the book's publisher, sought certiorari, objecting to the restraint on concededly true statements that concerned matters of medical and scientific importance. The Court granted certiorari, 417 U.S. 907 (1974), heard arguments, and then dismissed the writ as having been "improvidently granted." 420 U.S. 307 (1975). The fact that this case had a murky record and the complication of the confidential relationship might have dissuaded the Court from deciding it.

After the Supreme Court's refusal to decide Doe v. Roe, the case was remanded for trial, at which the judge found that plaintiff was entitled to recover for the defendants' violation of their implied covenant to treat the plaintiff in confidence. He rejected the view that the book was a "major contribution to scientific knowledge." He then found that as a result of the distribution of 220 copies before the injunction was imposed, the plaintiff sustained $1,500 in lost earnings and spent $1,500 for psychiatric help. In addition, plaintiff "had insomnia and nightmares. She became reclusive as a consequence of the shame and humiliation induced by the book's publication and her well-being and emotional health were significantly impaired for three years." He awarded damages of $20,000 and permanently enjoined distribution of the book. By subsequent order, the remaining volumes were destroyed. Doe v. Roe, 93 Misc.2d 201, 400 N.Y.S.2d 668 (1977).

2. CONSTITUTIONAL PRIVILEGE

In 1975, the Supreme Court decided its first "true-facts" privacy case.

COX BROADCASTING CORP. v. COHN

Supreme Court of the United States, 1975.
420 U.S. 469, 95 S.Ct. 1029, 43 L.Ed.2d 328.
Noted, 24 Emory L.J. 1205, 9 Ga.L.Rev. 963, 15 Washburn L.J. 163.

[Mr. Cohn's 17-year-old daughter was raped in Georgia and did not survive the occurrence. In Georgia it is a misdemeanor for "any news media or any other person to print and publish, broadcast, televise or disseminate through any other medium of public dissemination . . . the name or identity of any female who may have been raped. . . . " Ga.Code Ann. § 26–9901. Similar statutes exist in a few other states. The girl was not identified at the time. Eight months later, appellant's reporter, Wassell, also an appellant, attended a hearing for the six youths charged with the rape and learned the girl's name by inspecting the indictment in the courtroom. His report naming the girl was telecast.

The Georgia Supreme Court held that the complaint stated a common law action for damages for invasion of the father's own privacy. Defendant's First Amendment argument was rejected on the ground that the statute was an authoritative declaration that Georgia considered a rape victim's name not to be a matter of public concern. The court could discern "no public interest or general concern about the identity of the victim of such a crime as will make the right to disclose the identity of the victim rise to the level of First Amendment protection."

On appeal, the Supreme Court first decided that the decision below was a "final" judgment so as to give the Court jurisdiction even though damages had not yet been assessed. The Court then turned to the First Amendment issue.]

MR. JUSTICE WHITE delivered the opinion of the Court.

. . .

Georgia stoutly defends both § 26–9901 and the State's common-law privacy action challenged here. Her claims are not without force, for powerful arguments can be made and have been made, that however it may be ultimately defined, there *is* a zone of privacy surrounding every individual, a zone within which the State may protect him from intrusion by the press, with all its attendant publicity. Indeed, the central thesis of the root article by Warren and Brandeis, The Right to Privacy, 4 Harv.L.Rev. 193, 196 (1890), was that the press was overstepping its prerogatives by publishing essentially private information and that there should be a remedy for the alleged abuses.

More compellingly, the century has experienced a strong tide running in favor of the so-called right of privacy. . . .

. . . Because the gravamen of the claimed injury is the publication of information, whether true or not, the dissemination of which is embarrassing or otherwise painful to an individual, it is here that claims of privacy most directly confront the constitutional freedoms of speech and press. The face-off is apparent, and the appellants urge upon us the broad holding that the press may not be made criminally or civilly liable for publishing information that is neither false nor misleading but absolutely accurate, however damaging it may be to reputation or individual sensibilities.

It is true that in defamation actions, where the protected interest is personal reputation, the prevailing view is that truth is a defense; and the message of [*Times; Garrison; Butts*], and like cases is that the defense of truth is constitutionally required where the subject of the publication is a public official or public figure. What is more, the defamed public official or public figure must prove not only that the publication is false but that it was knowingly so or was circulated with reckless disregard for its truth or falsity. Similarly, where the interest at issue is privacy rather than reputation and the right claimed is to be free from the publication of false or misleading information about one's affairs, the target of the publication must prove knowing or reckless falsehood where the materials published, although assertedly private, are "matters of public interest." Time, Inc. v. Hill, supra, at 387–388.

The Court has nevertheless carefully left open the question whether the First and Fourteenth Amendments require that truth be recognized as a defense in a defamation action brought by a private person as distinguished from a public official or public figure. *Garrison* held that where criticism is of a public official and his conduct of public business, "the interest in private reputation is overborne by the larger public interest, secured by the Constitution, in the dissemination of truth," [ ] (footnote omitted), but recognized that "different interests may be involved where purely private libels, totally unrelated to public affairs, are concerned; therefore, nothing we say today is to be taken as intimating any views as to the impact of the constitutional guarantees in the discrete area of purely private libels." [ ] In similar fashion, Time, Inc. v. Hill, supra, expressly saved the question whether truthful publication of very private matters unrelated to public affairs could be constitutionally proscribed. [ ]

Those precedents, as well as other considerations, counsel similar caution here. In this sphere of collision between claims of privacy and those of the free press, the interests on both sides are plainly rooted in the traditions and significant concerns of our society. Rather than address the broader question whether truthful publications may ever be subjected to civil or criminal liability consistently with the First and Fourteenth Amendments, or to put it another way, whether the State may ever define and protect an area of privacy free from unwanted publicity in the press, it is appropriate to focus on the narrower interface between press and privacy that this case presents, namely, whether the State may impose sanctions on the accurate publication of the name of a rape victim obtained from public records—more specifically, from judicial records which are maintained in connection with a public prosecution and which themselves are open to public inspection. We are convinced that the State may not do so.

In the first place, in a society in which each individual has but limited time and resources with which to observe at first hand the operations of his government, he relies necessarily upon the press to bring to him in convenient form the facts of those operations. Great responsibility is accordingly placed upon the news media to report fully and accurately the proceedings of government, and official records and documents open to the public are the basic data of governmental operations. Without the information provided by the press most of us and many of our representatives would be unable to vote intelligently or to register opinions on the administration of government generally. With respect to judicial proceedings in particular, the function of the press serves to guarantee the fairness of trials and to bring to bear the beneficial effects of public scrutiny upon the administration of justice. See Sheppard v. Maxwell, 384 U.S. 333, 350 (1966).

Appellee has claimed in this litigation that the efforts of the press have infringed his right to privacy by broadcasting to the world the fact that his daughter was a rape victim. The commission of crime, prosecutions resulting from it, and judicial proceedings arising from the prosecutions, however, are without question events of legitimate concern to the public and consequently fall within the responsibility of the press to report the operations of government.

The special protected nature of accurate reports of judicial proceedings has repeatedly been recognized. This Court, in an opinion written by Mr. Justice Douglas, has said:

> "A trial is a public event. What transpires in the court room is public property. If a transcript of the court proceedings had been published, we suppose none would claim that the judge could punish the publisher for contempt. And we can see no difference though the conduct of the attorneys, of the jury, or even of the judge himself, may have reflected on the court. *Those who see and hear what transpired can report it with impunity.* There is no special perquisite of the judiciary which enables it, as distinguished from other institutions of democratic government, to suppress, edit, or censor events which transpire in proceedings before it." Craig v. Harney, 331 U.S. 367, 374 (1947) (emphasis added).

See also [ ].

The developing law surrounding the tort of invasion of privacy recognizes a privilege in the press to report the events of judicial proceedings. The Warren and Brandeis article, supra, noted that the proposed new right would be limited in the same manner as actions for libel and slander where such a publication was a privileged communication: "the right to privacy is not invaded by any publication made in a court of justice . . . and (at least in many jurisdictions) reports of any such proceedings would in some measure be accorded a like privilege."

. . .

Thus even the prevailing law of invasion of privacy generally recognizes that the interests in privacy fade when the information involved already appears on the public record. The conclusion is compelling when viewed in terms of the First and Fourteenth Amendments and in light of the public interest in a vigorous press. The Georgia cause of action for invasion of privacy through public disclosure of the name of a rape victim imposes sanctions on pure expression—the content of a publication—and not conduct or a combination of speech and nonspeech elements that might otherwise be open to regulation or prohibition. See United States v. O'Brien, 391 U.S. 367, 376–377 (1968). The publication of truthful information available on the public record contains none of the indicia of those limited categories of expression, such as "fighting" words, which "are no essential part of any exposition of ideas, and are of such slight social value as a step to truth that any benefit that may be derived from them is clearly outweighed by the social interest in order and morality." Chaplinsky v. New Hampshire, [ ].

By placing the information in the public domain on official court records, the State must be presumed to have concluded that the public interest was thereby being served. Public records by their very nature are of interest to those concerned with the administration of government, and a public benefit is performed by the reporting of the true contents of the records by the media. The freedom of the press to publish that information appears to us to be of critical importance to our type of government in which the citizenry is the final judge of the proper conduct of public business. In preserving that form of government the First and Fourteenth Amendments command nothing less than that the States may not impose sanctions on the publication of truthful information contained in official court records open to public inspection.

We are reluctant to embark on a course that would make public records generally available to the media but forbid their publication if offensive to the sensibilities of the supposed reasonable man. Such a rule would make it very difficult for the media to inform citizens about the public business and yet stay within the law. The rule would invite timidity and self-censorship and very likely lead to the suppression of many items that would otherwise be published and that should be made available to the public. At the very least, the First and Fourteenth Amendments will not allow exposing the press to liability for truthfully publishing information released to the public in official court records. If there are privacy interests to be protected in judicial proceedings, the States must respond by means which avoid public documentation or other exposure of private information. Their political institutions must weigh the interests in privacy with the interests of the public to know and of the press to publish.[26] Once true information is disclosed in public court documents open to public inspection, the press cannot be sanctioned for publishing it. In this instance as in others reliance must rest upon the judgment of those who decide what to publish or broadcast. See Miami Herald Pub. Co. v. Tornillo, 418 U.S., at 258.

Appellant Wassell based his televised report upon notes taken during the court proceedings and obtained the name of the victim from the indictments handed to him at his request during a recess in the hearing. Appellee has not contended that the name was obtained in an

26. We mean to imply nothing about any constitutional questions which might arise from a state policy not allowing access by the public and press to various kinds of official records, such as records of juvenile court proceedings.

improper fashion or that it was not on an official court document open to public inspection. Under these circumstances, the protection of freedom of the press provided by the First and Fourteenth Amendments bars the State of Georgia from making appellants' broadcast the basis of civil liability.[27]

Reversed.

MR. CHIEF JUSTICE BURGER concurs in the judgment.

MR. JUSTICE POWELL, concurring.

. . .

I am in entire accord with the Court's determination that the First Amendment proscribes imposition of civil liability in a privacy action predicated on the truthful publication of matters contained in open judicial records. But my impression of the role of truth in defamation actions brought by private citizens differs from the Court's. . . .

MR. JUSTICE DOUGLAS, concurring in the judgment.

I agree that the state judgment is "final," and I also agree in the reversal of the Georgia court.* On the merits, the case for me is on all fours with New Jersey State Lottery Comm'n v. United States, 491 F.2d 219 (CA3d 1974), vacated and remanded [420 U.S. 371]. For the reasons I stated in my dissent from our disposition of that case, there is no power on the part of government to suppress or penalize the publication of "news of the day."

MR. JUSTICE REHNQUIST, dissenting [for lack of a final judgment.]

Notes and Questions

1. What issues does Justice White avoid by his narrow statement of the question in the case?

2. Would Justice White's emphasis on the public's reliance on the media to report "the proceedings of government" warrant greater protection for the press than the public?

27. Appellants have contended that whether they derived the information in question from public records or instead through their own investigation, the First and Fourteenth Amendments bar any sanctions from being imposed by the State because of the publication. Because appellants have prevailed on more limited grounds, we need not address this broader challenge to the validity of § 26–9901 and of Georgia's right of action for public disclosure.

* While I join in the narrow result reached by the Court, I write separately to emphasize that I would ground that result upon a far broader proposition, namely, that the First Amendment, made applicable to the States through the Fourteenth, prohibits the use of state law "to impose damages for merely discussing public affairs . . . ." [ ] In this context, of course, "public affairs" must be broadly construed—indeed, the term may be said to embrace "any matter of sufficient general interest to prompt media coverage . . . ." Gertz v. Robert Welch, Inc., [ ] (Douglas, J. dissenting). By its now-familiar process of balancing and accommodating First Amendment freedoms with state or individual interests, the Court raises a specter of liability which must inevitably induce self-censorship by the media, thereby inhibiting the rough-and-tumble discourse which the First Amendment so clearly protects.

3. In Briscoe v. Reader's Digest Ass'n, involving the allegedly rehabilitated hijacker, the court stated that "Ideally, his neighbors should recognize his present worth and forget his past life of shame. But men are not so divine as to forgive the past trespasses of others, and plaintiff therefore endeavored to reveal as little as possible of his past life." The court concluded that it was for the trier of fact to decide whether plaintiff had been rehabilitated, whether "identifying him as a former criminal would be highly offensive and injurious to the reasonable man," whether defendant published the information "with a reckless disregard for its offensiveness," and whether any independent justification existed for printing plaintiff's identity. How is each determination to be made? How much of *Briscoe* remains after *Cox?*

4. In *Roshto,* p. 304, supra, involving the republication of an old front page, the court asserted that "To the extent that the *Cox Broadcasting* opinion dealt with a current prosecution, that decision is not controlling in the present case."

The court distinguished *Briscoe* on the ground that there the defendant had "deliberately included plaintiff's name as a convicted hijacker although plaintiff had since reformed and taken a place in respectable society." Here, however, the fact of the convictions "was publicized inadvertently as part of the publication of a randomly selected front page, which contained a number of articles. No one deliberately pointed the finger of blame at plaintiffs. There was no attempt to highlight the matter or to relate plaintiffs' past history to their present life and place of residence." The cases were dismissed.

Does the court correctly read *Cox Broadcasting?* Does the court satisfactorily distinguish *Briscoe?* What if plaintiffs can prove that the editor's choice of old front pages was not random, but was motivated by an effort to embarrass the Roshto brothers?

5. In Doe v. Sarasota-Bradenton Florida Television Co., Inc., 436 So.2d 328, 9 Med.L.Rptr. 2074 (Fla.App.1983), plaintiff agreed to testify at the trial of her accused rapist after being assured by the state her name and photograph would not be published or displayed. During her testimony, defendant's television news team was in the courtroom. That night, during the evening news the station ran a videotape of the trial featuring plaintiff's testimony. As the tape ran, the newscaster identified plaintiff by name.

The court dismissed plaintiff's case as indistinguishable from *Cox Broadcasting.* The court then launched into an attack on the station's conduct because the plaintiff's name and photograph were "completely unnecessary" to the story. She was not famous or otherwise newsworthy. The court also took the opportunity "to chastise the state somewhat for not having sought a protective order regarding cameras in the courtroom or other proper steps to support its alleged assurance" to plaintiff. The court concluded that the Cox case barred it from balancing in this situation between the harm to plaintiff and the importance of information to the public. But this did not bar the media from engaging in their own balancing.

The matter of closing the courtroom in this type of case is discussed in Chapter XII.

Problems of expungement are discussed at p. 357, infra.

6. Does the First Amendment protect a newspaper that identifies a rape victim in a case in which a man arrested on a rape charge claims that the warden beat him up? (The alleged rape victim is the warden's daughter.)

What analysis in a case in which the rape victim is the daughter of a man who is a strong proponent of rehabilitation and early paroles? What if the rapist had been recently paroled after serving time for rape?

What analysis in a case in which a statute provides that an accused rapist is not to be identified unless and until he is brought to trial?

7. In *Virgil,* the publisher, citing *Cox,* argued that the First Amendment protected all true statements from liability. The court disagreed:

> To hold that privilege extends to all true statements would seem to deny the existence of "private" facts, for if facts be facts—that is, if they be true—they would not (at least to the press) be private, and the press would be free to publicize them to the extent it sees fit. The extent to which areas of privacy continue to exist, then, would appear to be based not on rights bestowed by law but on the taste and discretion of the press. We cannot accept this result.

Defendant then made a different argument:

> A press which must depend upon a governmental determination as to what facts are of "public interest" in order to avoid liability for their truthful publication is not free at all. . . . A constitutional rule can be fashioned which protects all the interests involved. This goal is achieved by providing a privilege for truthful publications which is defeasible only when the court concludes as a matter of law that the truthful publication complained of constitutes a clear abuse of the editor's constitutional discretion to publish and discuss subjects and facts which in his judgment are matters of public interest.

Again the court disagreed. In libel and obscenity cases juries utilize community standards, and the court thought they should do so here, too, "subject to close judicial scrutiny to ensure that the jury resolutions comport with First Amendment principles." What is the difference between Time's position and that adopted by the court? Is the court's view consistent with *Cox?* Over the dissents of Justices Brennan and Stewart, the Supreme Court denied certiorari in *Virgil.* 425 U.S. 998 (1976). *Virgil* is noted in 29 Vand.L.Rev. 870 (1976).

8. The courts have tended to take this area case by case, and editors complain that such an approach breeds intolerable uncertainty. An editor must decide today what might happen in court in several years—and the standards are said to be vague. Who can predict what will be found "highly offensive to a reasonable person" or to violate "community standards and mores"? Juries given these questions may punish unpopular publishers or broadcasters.

Compare this situation with that confronting an editor in the defamation area. There the editor, with advice from lawyers, must decide whether the *Times* or *Gertz* rule applies and then decide whether the publication's conduct meets that standard. And truth is always a defense. Do you see a sharp difference between the editor's position there and where the case involves privacy? See Ingber, Rethinking Intangible Injuries: A Focus on Remedy, 73 Calif.L.Rev. 772, 849–56 (1985).

9. The most important recent case has been *Diaz,* p. 303, supra, involving the story about the plaintiff's sex change surgery. Until *Diaz,* no damage award in a privacy case had ever approached those in libel cases. Although it reversed the plaintiff's judgment, the *Diaz* court went out of its way to say that the size of the award ($250,000 compensatory and $525,000 punitive) might not be a problem. The author knew the result would be "devastating" but never sought to contact plaintiff beforehand. His attempt to be "flip" and what the jury could find to be his "callous and conscious disregard for Diaz's privacy interests" justified the punitive award. The court expressed its concern about the potentially inhibiting effect of large punitive awards and cautioned the trial judge on retrial "to scrutinize strictly any award of punitive damages to make sure it is not used to silence unpopular persons or speech and that it does not exceed the proper level necessary to punish and deter similar behavior."

As to compensatory damages, the court noted that plaintiff's actual injury was much greater than her $800 out-of-pocket loss. Although the amount of the award was "high, it cannot be said that it is so grossly disproportionate, considering the past and future pain and humiliation, as to be excessive as a matter of law." Shortly after this decision, the parties settled the case by a substantial payment.

10. A rare successful privacy case has resulted in an award of $1,500 actual and $25,000 punitive damages. Hawkins v. Multimedia, Inc., 288 S.C. 569, 344 S.E.2d 145, 12 Med.L.Rptr. 1878 (1986). In a sidebar article to a story on teenage pregnancies, defendant's newspaper identified plaintiff as the teenage father of an illegitimate child. The majority of the article focused on the teenage mother. After the mother identified plaintiff as the father, the reporter called plaintiff twice to obtain comments. The first time she spoke with plaintiff's mother. The second time she spoke with the reluctant plaintiff for three or four minutes. "In neither call did the reporter request permission to identify or quote [plaintiff]."

Over defendant's objection, the trial judge charged that a minor cannot consent to an invasion of privacy. The appellate court did not reach the issue because it found that defendant had failed to establish consent in the first place. Although plaintiff did not hang up immediately, he was "very shy." He never agreed to the use of his name.

The court rejected defense arguments that the article was of "general interest" because that defense requires "legitimate" public interest. "Public or general interest does not mean mere curiosity, and newsworthiness is not necessarily the test." This issue was properly submitted to the jury.

Finally, the trial judge refused the defendant's charge that "malice must be shown by clear and convincing evidence." The appellate court concluded that malice "need not be shown to recover for invasion of privacy." It is relevant only for punitive damages. The proper burden for punitive damages was not raised at trial and could not be raised on appeal.

The defendant has filed a petition for certiorari.

11. The press itself has been notably timid in this area, perhaps uncertain about the degree to which it is protected because the courts have been generous, but vague. In an article in the April, 1975, issue of [MORE], Washington columnist Brit Hume condemned the reluctance of editors to publish stories about lawmakers who seemed senile at Committee hearings, extramarital activities of Presidents, public drunkenness of high officials, and similar matters.

In 1976, the Detroit News broke a story that the Democratic candidate for United States Senator from Michigan had had an extramarital affair seven years earlier with a member of his congressional staff. Chicago columnist Mike Royko argued that unless the affair could be tied to the candidate's performance as a representative, it should not have been printed. He suggested that it had been printed only because the newspaper was supporting the candidate's opponent.

Compare a 1981 article reporting that 50 years earlier the current head of the National Rifle Association, then 17, had shot and killed a 15-year-old youth. His conviction was overturned for error in the jury charge, and the case was subsequently dismissed. He is quoted as saying that "The motivation behind any story which reaches back 50 years is truly outrageous." N.Y. Times, May 7, 1981, at 9.

B. FALSE-LIGHT PRIVACY

The conventional idea of invasion of privacy as conceived by Warren and Brandeis involved true statements about aspects of plaintiff's life that others had no business knowing. But along the way, a few cases involved false charges that placed the plaintiff in a false light but did not harm his "reputation" so as to permit an action for defamation. As one example, a group used the plaintiff's name without authorization on a petition to the governor to veto a bill. Although falsely stating that plaintiff had signed the petition would not have been defamatory, the court found the situation actionable because it cast plaintiff in a false light. Hinish v. Meier & Frank Co., 166 Or. 482, 113 P.2d 438 (1941).

The line between defamation and privacy was obviously being tested by this type of case. But the line between this and the "true" privacy case also became blurred after Time, Inc. v. Hill, 385 U.S. 374 (1967). In September, 1952, James Hill and his family were held hostage in their home for 19 hours by three escaped convicts who apparently treated them decently. The incident received extensive nationwide coverage. Thereafter the Hills moved to another state, sought seclusion and refused to make public appearances. A novel modeled in general on the event was published the following year. In 1955, Life magazine in a very short article announced that a play and a motion picture were being made from the novel, which they said was "inspired" by the Hill episode. The play, "a heartstopping account of how a family rose to heroism in a crisis," would enable the public to see the Hill story "re-enacted." Photographs in the magazine showed actors performing scenes from the play at the house at which the original events had occurred. The Hills claimed that the story was inaccurate because the novel and the play showed the convicts committing violence on the father and uttering a "verbal sexual insult" at the daughter.

Suit was brought under the New York statute that required plaintiff to show that the article was being used for advertising purposes or for purposes of trade. A truthful article, no matter how unpleasant for the Hills, would not have been actionable. The state courts had previously indicated that falsity would show that the article was really for purposes of trade and not for public enlightenment. The state courts allowed recovery after lengthy litigation.

The Supreme Court by a very fragile majority decided that the privilege to comment on matters of public interest had constitutional protection and could not be lost by the introduction of falsity unless the falsity was either deliberate or reckless. The Court used the defamation analogy that was then being developed in the wake of the Times case and applied it to this privacy case that involved falsity, ignoring the fact that the falsity was relatively trivial. Was the false report any more harmful than an absolutely true one would have been? If not, why does the falsity matter? The Court had not yet considered defamation actions by private citizens. (The preliminary vote of the Court in Time, Inc. v. Hill favored the Hills. For the story and the opinions in that first stage, see B. Schwartz, The Unpublished Opinions of the Warren Court 240–303 (1985).)

For contemporary comment, see Kalven, The Reasonable Man and the First Amendment: Hill, Butts, and Walker, 1967 Sup.Ct.Rev. 267.

CANTRELL v. FOREST CITY PUBLISHING CO.

Supreme Court of the United States, 1974.
419 U.S. 245, 95 S.Ct. 465, 42 L.Ed.2d 419.

MR. JUSTICE STEWART delivered the opinion of the Court.

Margaret Cantrell and four of her minor children brought this diversity action in a Federal District Court for invasion of privacy against the Forest City Publishing Co., publisher of a Cleveland newspaper, the Plain Dealer, and against Joseph Eszterhas, a reporter formerly employed by the Plain Dealer, and Richard Conway, a Plain Dealer photographer. The Cantrells alleged that an article published in the Plain Dealer Sunday Magazine unreasonably placed their family in a false light before the public through its many inaccuracies and untruths. The District Judge struck the claims relating to punitive damages as to all the plaintiffs and dismissed the actions of three of the Cantrell children in their entirety, but allowed the case to go to the jury as to Mrs. Cantrell and her oldest son, William. The jury returned a verdict * against all three of the respondents for compensatory money damages in favor of these two plaintiffs.

The Court of Appeals for the Sixth Circuit reversed, holding that, in the light of the First and Fourteenth Amendments, the District Judge should have granted the respondents' motion for a directed verdict as to all the Cantrells' claims. . . .

I.

On December 1967, Margaret Cantrell's husband Melvin was killed along with 43 other people when the Silver Bridge across the Ohio River at Point Pleasant, West Virginia, collapsed. The respondent Eszterhas was assigned by the Plain Dealer to cover the story of the disaster. He wrote a "news feature" story focusing on the funeral of Melvin Cantrell and the impact of his death on the Cantrell family.

Five months later, after conferring with the Sunday Magazine editor of the Plain Dealer, Eszterhas and photographer Conway returned to the Point Pleasant area to write a follow-up feature. The two men went to the Cantrell residence, where Eszterhas talked with the children and Conway took 50 pictures. Mrs. Cantrell was not at home at any time during the 60 to 90 minutes that the men were at the Cantrell residence.

Eszterhas' story appeared as the lead feature in the August 4, 1968, edition of the Plain Dealer Sunday Magazine. The article stressed the family's abject poverty; the children's old, ill-fitting clothes and the

* The verdict was for $60,000—ed.

deteriorating condition of their home were detailed in both the text and accompanying photographs. As he had done in his original, prize-winning article on the Silver Bridge disaster, Eszterhas used the Cantrell family to illustrate the impact of the bridge collapse on the lives of the people in the Point Pleasant area.

It is conceded that the story contained a number of inaccuracies and false statements. Most conspicuously, although Mrs. Cantrell was not present at any time during the reporter's visit to her home, Eszterhas wrote, "Margaret Cantrell will talk neither about what happened nor about how they are doing. She wears the same mask of non-expression she wore at the funeral. She is a proud woman. Her world has changed. She says that after it happened, the people in town offered to help them out with money and they refused to take it." Other significant misrepresentations were contained in details of Eszterhas' descriptions of the poverty in which the Cantrells were living and the dirty and dilapidated conditions of the Cantrell home.

The case went to the jury on a so-called "false light" theory of invasion of privacy. In essence, the theory of the case was that by publishing the false feature story about the Cantrells and thereby making them the objects of pity and ridicule, the respondents damaged Mrs. Cantrell and her son William by causing them to suffer outrage, mental distress, shame, and humiliation.[2]

II.

In [*Hill*], the Court considered a similar false-light, invasion-of-privacy action. The New York Court of Appeals had interpreted New York Civil Rights Law §§ 50–51 to give a "newsworthy person" a right of action when his or her name, picture or portrait was the subject of a "fictitious" report or article. Material and substantial falsification was the test for recovery. [ ], Under this doctrine the New York courts awarded the plaintiff James Hill compensatory damages based on his complaint that Life Magazine had falsely reported that a new Broadway play portrayed the Hill family's experience in being held hostage by three escaped convicts. This Court, guided by its decision in New York Times Co. v. Sullivan, [ ], which recognized constitutional limits on a State's power to award damages for libel in actions brought by public officials, held that the constitutional protections for speech and press precluded the application of the New York statute to allow recovery for "false reports of matters of public interest in the absence of proof that the defendant published the report with knowledge of its falsity or in reckless disregard of the truth." [ ] Although the jury

2. Although this is a diversity action based on state tort law, there is remarkably little discussion of the relevant Ohio or West Virginia law by the District Court, the Court of Appeals, and counsel for the parties. It is clear, however, that both Ohio and West Virginia recognize a legally protected interest in privacy. [ ] Publicity that places the plaintiff in a false light in the public eye is generally recognized as one of the several distinct kinds of invasions actionable under the privacy rubric. [ ]

could have reasonably concluded from the evidence in the Hill case that Life had engaged in knowing falsehood or had recklessly disregarded the truth in stating in the article that "the story re-enacted" the Hill family's experience, the Court concluded that the trial judge's instructions had not confined the jury to such a finding as a predicate for liability as required by the Constitution. [ ].

The District Judge in the case before us, in contrast to the trial judge in Time, Inc. v. Hill, did instruct the jury that liability could be imposed only if it concluded that the false statements in the Sunday Magazine feature article on the Cantrells had been made with knowledge of their falsity or in reckless disregard of the truth. No objection was made by any of the parties to this knowing-or-reckless-falsehood instruction. Consequently, this case presents no occasion to consider whether a State may constitutionally apply a more relaxed standard of liability for a publisher or broadcaster of false statements injurious to a private individual under a false-light theory of invasion of privacy, or whether the constitutional standard announced in Time, Inc. v. Hill applies to all false-light cases. Cf. [*Gertz*]. Rather, the sole question that we need decide is whether the Court of Appeals erred in setting aside the jury's verdict.

III.

At the close of the petitioners' case-in-chief, the District Judge struck the demand for punitive damages. He found that Mrs. Cantrell had failed to present any evidence to support the charges that the invasion of privacy "was done maliciously within the legal definition of that term." The Court of Appeals interpreted this finding to be a determination by the District Judge that there was no evidence of knowing falsity or reckless disregard of the truth introduced at the trial. Having made such a determination, the Court of Appeals held that the District Judge should have granted the motion for a directed verdict for respondents as to all the Cantrells' claims. [ ]

. . .

Although the verbal record of the District Court proceedings is not entirely unambiguous, the conclusion is inescapable that the District Judge was referring to the common-law standard of malice rather than to the *New York Times* "actual malice" standard when he dismissed the punitive damages claims. . . .

Moreover, the District Judge was clearly correct in believing that the evidence introduced at trial was sufficient to support a jury finding that the respondents Joseph Eszterhas and Forest City Publishing Co. had published knowing or reckless falsehoods about the Cantrells.[5] There was no dispute during the trial that Eszterhas, who did not

5. Although we conclude that the jury verdicts should have been sustained as to Eszterhas and Forest City Publishing Co., we agree with the Court of Appeals' conclusion that there was insufficient evidence to support the jury's verdict against the photographer Conway. . . .

testify, must have known that a number of the statements in the feature story were untrue. In particular, his article plainly implied that Mrs. Cantrell had been present during his visit to her home and that Eszterhas had observed her "wear[ing] the same mask of non-expression she wore [at her husband's] funeral." These were "calculated falsehoods," and the jury was plainly justified in finding that Eszterhas had portrayed the Cantrells in a false light through knowing or reckless untruth.

The Court of Appeals concluded that there was no evidence that Forest City Publishing Co. had knowledge of any of the inaccuracies contained in Eszterhas' article. However, there was sufficient evidence for the jury to find that Eszterhas' writing of the feature was within the scope of his employment at the Plain Dealer and that Forest City Publishing Co. was therefore liable under traditional doctrines of *respondeat superior*. . . .

For the foregoing reasons, the judgment of the Court of Appeals is reversed and the case is remanded to that court with directions to enter a judgment affirming the judgment of the District Court as to the respondents Forest City Publishing Co. and Joseph Eszterhas.

It is so ordered.

MR. JUSTICE DOUGLAS, dissenting.

. . .

A bridge accident catapulted the Cantrells into the public eye and their disaster became newsworthy. To make the First Amendment freedom to report the news turn on subtle differences between common-law malice and actual malice is to stand the Amendment on its head. Those who write the current news seldom have the objective, dispassionate point of view—or the time—of scientific analysts. They deal in fast-moving events and the need for "spot" reporting. The jury under today's formula sits as a censor with broad powers—not to impose a prior restraint, but to lay heavy damages on the press. The press is "free" only if the jury is sufficiently disenchanted with the Cantrells to let the press be free of this damages claim. That regime is thought by some to be a way of supervising the press which is better than not supervising it at all. But the installation of the Court's regime would require a constitutional amendment. Whatever might be the ultimate reach of the doctrine Mr. Justice Black and I have embraced, it seems clear that in matters of public import such as the present news reporting, there must be freedom from damages lest the press be frightened into playing a more ignoble role than the Framers visualized.

I would affirm the judgment of the Court of Appeals.

Notes and Questions

1. Justice Stewart readily analyzes this case as involving the "false-light" category of privacy. Might it also be analyzed as a public disclosure privacy case in which the media claimed the defense of

newsworthiness, but the Court held that the defense is not available when the material reported is deliberately or recklessly false? What are the differences between the two analyses?

A few years after *Cantrell,* in Zacchini v. Scripps-Howard Broadcasting Co., reprinted at p. 411, infra, the Court approvingly quoted Dean Prosser's statement that the interest protected in false-light actions "is clearly that of reputation, with the same overtones of mental distress as in defamation." Under this view, why should errors that do not harm reputation be permitted to give rise to liability?

2. In a footnote to his concurring opinion in *Cox Broadcasting,* p. 320, supra, Justice Powell observed:

> . . . The Court's abandonment of the "matter of general or public interest" standard as the determinative factor for deciding whether to apply the *New York Times* malice standard to defamation litigation brought by private individuals, [ ], calls into question the conceptual basis of Time, Inc. v. Hill. In neither *Gertz* nor our more recent decision in Cantrell v. Forest City Pub. Co., [ ], however, have we been called upon to determine whether a State may constitutionally apply a more relaxed standard of liability under a false-light theory of invasion of privacy. [ ]

How might *Time, Inc.* have been compromised?

3. What is the nature of the *respondeat superior* problem in *Cantrell*? Might this point be significant in future defamation cases in determining whose behavior to evaluate in considering liability?

4. Why did plaintiffs fail to recover punitive damages?

5. How are compensatory damages to be measured in this case? Is the falsity relevant in that calculation?

6. How would you analyze a defamation action brought by the Cantrells?

7. In Machleder v. Diaz, 618 F.Supp. 1367, 12 Med.L.Rptr. 1193 (S.D. N.Y.1985), the jury found a television station and its reporter liable for presenting the plaintiff in a false light as the result of an interview. (In an earlier ruling, summary judgment was denied. 538 F.Supp. 1364 (S.D.N.Y.1982)). The reporter went, with a camera crew, to a place where chemicals had been dumped. He encountered the plaintiff, a 71-year-old man, and the following dialogue occurred, which was presented on the evening news:

> P: Get that damn camera out of here.
>
> D: Sir . . . Sir . . .
>
> P: I don't want to be involved with you people . . .
>
> D: Just tell me why—why are those chemicals dumped in the back . . .
>
> P: I don't want . . . I don't need . . . I don't need any publicity . . .

D: Why are those chemicals dumped in the back?

P: We don't . . . we didn't dump 'em.

In fact, plaintiff had reported the presence of the chemicals to the authorities two years earlier, as the program noted. Further, the chemicals were on land that did not belong to plaintiff. An hour before the program, the plaintiff called to complain and to say that he had been "improperly implicated" in the dumping. The attorney who spoke with him at that time testified that he appeared agitated.

The jury rejected plaintiff's claims for libel, slander, trespass, and assault, but awarded plaintiff $250,000 in compensatory damages and $1,000,000 in punitive damages on the false light claim. The trial judge refused to reduce either amount. He concluded:

> The evidence before the Court supports a substantial award of punitive damages. Defendant's conduct was shown to be callous and indifferent to the rights of plaintiff. CBS employees deliberately decided to broadcast the film of Mr. Machleder, despite a lack of evidence that he was responsible for the abandoned drums and despite knowledge that he had in fact reported their presence to local government agencies two years earlier. The evidence suggests the film was used in order to lend some excitement to an otherwise uneventful story. Serious questions existed whether plaintiff's reaction to the reporter and film crew was newsworthy.
>
> One purpose of a punitive damages award is to deter future conduct of a similar nature. [ ] The evidence presented about the attitude of CBS employees toward the handling of the broadcast indicates there is a likelihood that such activity will be repeated as part of a business policy. [ ]

Those commenting on the case have disagreed about whether this should be called an "ambush" interview. The CBS attorney is quoted as saying that an ambush interview is "a pursuit of a 'recalcitrant' subject who is known not to want to talk." He called this a "a hot story." He said further that the report did not involve any "characterization," and was merely "cinema verite." Broadcasting, June 10, 1985 at 36–37.

In an editorial, Broadcasting noted that although CBS denied that an ambush interview had occurred, "the jury obviously thought otherwise. Its members saw an elderly man cornered by a camera." The size of the verdict "showed that people don't want to see other people pushed around on television news." Broadcasting, June 10, 1985 at 138. The court of appeals reversed and dismissed in September, 1986.

For an extended discussion of television interviews based on the summary judgment ruling in the the Machleder case, see Note, The Ambush Interview: A False Light Invasion of Privacy?, 34 Case Western Res.L.Rev. 72 (1983). The note argues that "actual malice" is present in every unscheduled interview because the "news crew has made a deliberate decision to catch the victim unprepared and show him at his worst. No one is more sensitive or knowledgeable about on-the-air credibility than the broadcaster. Thus, a television news crew that waits for and deliberately startles a subject with unsettling accusations shows a reckless, if not intentional, disregard for creating a fair, accurate portrayal." Id. at 89.

The note concludes that the ambush interview is "incompatible with the purposes of constitutional protection of freedom of the press, because it forecloses rather than promotes discussion; obscures rather than illuminates the facts; and, by involving the reporter as a *participant* and removing him from an objective role, diminishes the chances for accurate reporting." Id. at 101.

8. Although the false-light privacy action has been rejected in a handful of states, see Renwick v. The News and Observer Publishing Co., 310 N.C. 312, 312 S.E.2d 405, 10 Med.L.Rptr. 1443 (1984), certiorari denied 105 S.Ct. 187 (1984), (action not sufficiently different from defamation to warrant its introduction), the overwhelming majority of states have adopted the action. We have seen that this raises such substantive questions as identifying its relation to defamation in close cases. Beyond that, it requires considering whether the array of common-law and statutory limitations on defamation, such as retraction statutes, special damage requirements, and statutes of limitations, apply as well to false-light privacy. *Renwick* is noted in 63 N.C.L.Rev. 767 (1985).

9. In Fellows v. National Enquirer, Inc., 211 Cal.Rptr. 809 (Cal.App. 1985), defendant's article asserted that "Gorgeous Angie Dickinson's all smiles about the new man in her life—TV producer Arthur Fellows. Angie's steady-dating Fellows all over TinselTown, and happily posed for photographers with him as they exited the swanky Spago restaurant in Beverly Hills." Accompanying the article was a photograph of Dickinson and Fellows over the caption stating that Dickinson was "Dating a Producer."

Fellows demanded a retraction under Calif. Civil Code § 48a, asserting that plaintiff "has never dated Miss Dickinson, is not 'the new man in her life,' and has been married to Phyllis Fellows for the last 18 years." Defendant refused retraction and plaintiff sued for libel and false-light privacy. After substantial jockeying at the complaint stage, plaintiff withdrew his libel claim and proceeded solely on a false-light claim with no allegation of special damages.

Under California law, libel that relied on extrinsic facts had to be supported by special damages. Civil Code § 45a. Plaintiff's privacy claim asserted that he had been falsely portrayed as the "new man" in Dickinson's life and as "steady-dating" her. The trial judge dismissed the privacy claim for lack of special damages.

The court of appeal reversed on the ground that the two actions were sufficiently different in the harms they redressed so that there was no reason to apply § 45a to a false-light action.

The court concluded that the requirement of special damages made sense only in the context of reputation but not of peace of mind and injured feelings, which were direct injuries. This differentiated it from § 48a, the retraction section, which has been applied to both types of actions.

The court concluded that although both libel and false light actions were subject to the retraction statute, the defense of truth, the one-year statute of limitations, and the single publication rule, they were under different rules as to special damages.

The supreme court reversed. 42 Cal.3d 234, 228 Cal.Rptr. 215, 721 P.2d 97 (1986). The clear purpose of § 45a was to provide additional protection to libel defendants. Since "virtually every published defamation would support an action for false light invasion of privacy, exempting such actions from the requirement of proving special damages would render the statute a nullity." Under this rationale is there any state requirement that protects libel defendants that would not also be applied to plaintiffs who sue on a false-light theory? What should happen if a false-light claim is based on language that does not rise to the level of being defamatory? The court went out of its way to announce that its ruling did not apply to false-light claims "that would be actionable as a public disclosure of private facts had the representation made in the publication been true."

10. Some courts have concluded that a plaintiff who has agreed to be photographed for one purpose may complain that the photos later appeared in another magazine—in which the plaintiff would rather not have appeared. Douglass v. Hustler Magazine, Inc., 769 F.2d 1128, 11 Med. L. Rptr. 2264 (7th Cir. 1985), certiorari denied 106 S.Ct. 1489 (1986); Braun v. Flynt, 726 F.2d 245, 10 Med. L.Rptr. 1497 (5th Cir. 1984), certiorari denied 105 S.Ct. 252 (1984). Compare Brewer v. Hustler Magazine, Inc., 749 F.2d 527 (9th Cir. 1984) (rejecting copyright approach to issue) and Martin v. Penthouse International, Ltd., 12 Med. L. Rptr. 2058 (Cal. App. 1986) (plaintiffs cannot complain that a photograph documenting their public appearance has appeared in a magazine they consider "pornographic").

C. THE RIGHT OF PUBLICITY

The right of publicity involves the right of celebrities to control the exploitation of their names, likenesses, and fame and any pecuniary value resulting therefrom. In much the same way that Warren and Brandeis's law review article helped create a right of privacy, Melville Nimmer's 1954 article *The Right of Publicity,* 19 Law & Contemp.Prob. 203 (1954), was instrumental in establishing a publicity right in the American legal system. The right of publicity had been recognized explicitly for the first time a year earlier in Haelan Laboratories v. Topps Chewing Gum, Inc., 202 F.2d 866 (2d Cir.), certiorari denied 346 U.S. 816 (1953), in which the court spoke to the need to protect the proprietary interest of celebrities in their names and likenesses. *Haelan* involved a famous baseball player who assigned the right to the use of his name and likeness to a bubblegum manufacturer for the promotion of its products. A competing manufacturer subsequently induced the ballplayer to enter into a similar contract with full knowledge of the preexisting agreement. The court recognized the right of publicity as a method through which such misappropriation could be prevented.

Since *Haelan,* and largely as a result of the Nimmer article, the right of publicity has been recognized by most states. Although some states have adopted the right of publicity as a separate common law remedy, most have adopted the right as an offshoot of either the common law right of privacy or of a privacy statute.

Is the right of publicity a type of privacy, or should it be properly conceptualized as a distinct tort? One inherent difference between the right of publicity and the more traditional privacy rights is that privacy protects against undesired public intrusion into one's personal life, while the right of publicity is designed to protect against *unauthorized* publication of one's celebrity status. For example, the famous person does not generally wish to prevent commercial exploitation of his publicity value but does want to be compensated for it.

Whether or not the right of publicity is considered as a subset of privacy rights has important implications for its judicial development. For example, it is unclear whether a right of publicity survives the death of the celebrity in whom the right is based; that is, whether a celebrity's heirs or assigns can profit from any such right after the famous person has died. Courts that have found the right to be descendible have analogized the right of publicity to an ordinary property right or a copyright, both of which are inheritable. Courts that have found no descendible right have emphasized the personal nature of the right of publicity, the analogy to rights of privacy, which are not inheritable, and the line-drawing difficulties inherent in any development of a right of publicity that survives the death of the celebrity.

Although the courts are still in conflict over the descendible nature of the right of publicity, legislation is beginning to answer the question. California adopted legislation in 1984 that was split between a new Civil Code § 990 and amendments to § 3344. The broad effect was to create a descendible right that lasts 50 years after the death of the person and is freely transferable to prevent uses of the deceased person's "name, voice, signature, photograph, or likeness, in any manner, on or in products, merchandise, or goods, or for the purposes of advertising or selling, or soliciting purchases of, products, merchandise, goods, or services, without prior consent from the person or persons" specified in the statute.

Section 990 dealt with deceased personalities; section 3344 dealt with living persons.

A "deceased personality" is defined to include a natural person any of whose enumerated aspects, such as name or voice, "has commercial value at the time of his or her death, whether or not during the lifetime of that natural person the person used his or her name, . . . on or in products, merchandise or goods, or for purposes of advertising or selling, or solicitation of purchase of, products, merchandise, goods or service."

The use of an enumerated aspect does not constitute a use "solely because the material containing such use is commercially sponsored or contains paid advertising. Rather it shall be a question of fact whether or not the use of the deceased personality's [name, etc.] was so directly connected with the commercial sponsorship or with the paid advertising as to constitute a use for which consent is required . . . ."

Both sections state that the use of any enumerated aspect "in connection with any news, public affairs, or sports broadcast or account, or any political campaign," is not a "use" and thus does not require consent.

Both sections state that they do not apply to "the owners or employees of any medium used for advertising, including, but not limited to, [print and broadcast media] by whom any advertisement or solicitation in violation of [the sections] is published or disseminated, unless it is established that such owners or employees had knowledge of the unauthorized use of the person's name . . . ."

Finally, § 990(m) provides that § 990 "shall not apply to the use of a deceased personality's name . . . " in any of the following instances (there is nothing comparable in § 3344):

(1) A play, book, magazine, newspaper, musical composition, film, radio or television program, other than an advertisement or commercial announcement not exempt under paragraph (4).

(2) Material that is of political or newsworthy value.

(3) Single and original works of fine art.

(4) An advertisement or commercial announcement for a use permitted by paragraph (1), (2), or (3).

Is there a difference under the statute between mass marketing of plastic busts of a decedent and making a marble bust? Plastic busts were at issue in Martin Luther King Center for Social Change, Inc. v. American Heritage Products, Inc., 250 Ga. 135, 296 S.E.2d 697, 8 Med.L. Rptr. 2377 (1982).

Consider whether the California statute would affect the Cher and Eastwood cases that follow. Both were decided before the effective date of the statute. Consider also whether the statute addresses the docudrama question that is raised shortly in the context of Elizabeth Taylor.

a. *The Cher Case.* In Cher v. Forum International, Ltd., 7 Med.L. Rptr. 2593 (C.D.Cal.1982), the judge, after a nonjury trial, awarded an entertainer $763,000 for loss of her right of publicity. Cher had agreed to give an interview to one magazine, reserving the right to bar publication if she did not like the results. She exercised that right.

The interviewer, however, then sold the interview to the two defendant magazines, each of which published excerpts. One defendant's cover asserted that it was an exclusive interview. Cher alleged that she would not have given either of the defendants an interview because she did not approve of them.

On the appeal in Cher's case, the court reversed as to one magazine but affirmed as to the other. Cher v. Forum International, Ltd., 692 F.2d 634, 8 Med.L.Rptr. 2484 (9th Cir.1982), certiorari denied 462 U.S. 1120 (1983). Star had put on its cover "Exclusive Series" followed by "Cher: My life, my husbands and my many, many men." The court concluded that star "was entitled to inform its readers that the issue contained an article about Cher, that the article was based on an interview with Cher herself, and that the article had not previously appeared elsewhere." The words used to convey that information "cannot support a finding of the knowing or reckless falsity required under Time, Inc. v. Hill." Nor did the words convey the false claim that Cher endorsed the magazine. The earlier California "right of publicity" statute, Civil Code § 3344, contains an express exception for news accounts. That exception covered this case.

Forum magazine changed the text to make it appear that Forum was posing the questions to Cher in the interview—"apparently a common practice in the industry." The cover said "Exclusive: Cher Talks Straight." Forum also used Cher's name on a subscription pull-out card that asserted that things Cher would not tell Us (magazine) she was telling Forum. The card also stated "So join Cher and Forum's hundreds of thousands of other adventurous readers today." The First Amendment does not protect advertising that falsely claims that a public figure endorses the publication. The claim that Cher was telling Forum readers things she would not tell Us was "patently false. This kind of mendacity is not protected by the First Amendment . . . ." The falsity was particularly clear here because Us was the first magazine, to which Cher *was* willing to give an interview.

The trial court also found liability for the "join Cher" language on the card. Although the court of appeals thought the language somewhat ambiguous, it was willing to accept the trial court's reading that this was an implied endorsement of Forum and its conclusion that the falsity of that reading showed a reckless disregard for the truth. The court of appeals concluded that "no matter how carefully the editorial staff of Forum may have trod the border between the actionable and the protected, the advertising staff engaged in the kind of knowing falsity that strips away the protection of the First Amendment."

b. *The Eastwood Case.* Eastwood v. Superior Court, 149 Cal.App. 3d 409, 198 Cal.Rptr. 342, 10 Med.L.Rptr. 1073 (1983), involved a claim by Clint Eastwood against the National Enquirer for the unauthorized use of his likeness on the cover and in related television advertisements about a false nondefamatory story inside the issue. The story involved allegations that Eastwood was romantically involved with two other celebrities. The court concluded that the use was commercial exploitation and was not privileged under state or federal law. The trial court had improperly sustained a demurrer to the complaint. The court of appeal saw no reason why Eastwood should have to show that he was being falsely said to be endorsing the National Enquirer. This was one way to impose liability but was not essential. The court also concluded that the article was not necessarily protected as a news account because of an allegation that the story was a calculated falsehood. The court discussed at length the emerging right of publicity.

Consider this series of hypotheticals from Shiffrin, The First Amendment and Economic Regulation: Away from a General Theory of the First Amendment, 78 Nw.U.L.Rev. 1212, 1257 n. 275 (1983):

> A magazine may have a profit motive in taking a particular position on a particular subject, but the courts will ordinarily not count that motivation as significant. In thinking about profit motive and the dissemination of truth consider these examples: (1) Without his consent, Mercedes Benz *truthfully* advertises that Frank Sinatra drives a Mercedes. Sinatra sues for misappropriation. Does it make a difference if Mercedes in its ad says, "We didn't ask Sinatra's permission to tell you this" or "Sinatra doesn't want us to tell you this but . . . "? (2) Suppose *Time* magazine writes a story on Mercedes Benz and puts Sinatra on the cover with a picture of his Mercedes. Suppose they put Sinatra on the cover purely for reasons of profit. (3) Suppose Time, Inc. advertises: "Get the recent issue of *Time* with Frank Sinatra on the cover with his Mercedes." (4) Suppose *Time* truthfully advertises: "Sinatra doesn't want us to tell you this, but he is one of our regular readers."

A new problem has arisen in which advertisers use in their ads unknown persons who closely resemble famous stars. For two approaches to the look-alike problem, see Onassis v. Christian Dior—N.Y., 122 Misc.2d 603, 472 N.Y.S.2d 254 (1984), and Allen v. National Video, Inc., 610 F.Supp. 612 (S.D.N.Y.1985).

What if the book or movie admits to being a fictional account of a celebrity's life? In Hicks v. Casablanca Records, 464 F.Supp. 426, 4 Med.L.Rptr. 1497 (S.D.N.Y.1978), a novel was based on a fictionalized explanation of Agatha Christie's mysterious 11-day disappearance in 1926.

The court engrafted upon the right of publicity a protection for "matters of news, history, biography, and other factual subjects of public interest, despite the necessary references to" the names of living persons. That protection did not apply here, however, because the 11-day episode discussed in the book was fictional and did not purport to be biographical.

But the book was entitled to constitutional protection. Although fiction, the book did not contain deliberate falsehood and did not falsely purport to be biographical. The reader would know by the word "novel" that the work was fictitious. The "protection usually accorded novels and movies outweighs whatever publicity rights plaintiffs may possess."

Courts are less willing to grant First Amendment protection, however, when the vehicle of dissemination is not a book or movie. For example, in Factors Etc., Inc. v. Pro Arts, Inc., 579 F.2d 215, 4 Med.L. Rptr. 1144 (2d Cir.1978), certiorari denied 440 U.S. 908 (1979), defendants produced a posthumous poster of Elvis Presley, composed of a photograph and the words "In Memory" and the dates "1935–1977." Defendant claimed that the poster was a commentary on a newsworthy event. The court rejected the claim. The case was brought under the New York statute that barred using a person's name or picture "for advertising purposes or for purposes of trade" without consent.

The court distinguished Paulsen v. Personality Posters, Inc., 59 Misc.2d 444, 299 N.Y.S.2d 501 (1968), in which defendants had distributed a poster of comedian Pat Paulsen during his mock presidential campaign in 1968 with a banner "FOR PRESIDENT" draped across Paulsen's chest. The *Paulsen* court held that such a poster was constitutionally protected because, even though the poster was being sold for profit, its distribution was also viewed as a political comment. Paulsen's choice of the political arena for satire made the comedian's presidential campaign newsworthy. In distinguishing *Paulsen,* the *Presley* court simply said it could not accept "defendant's effort to place its poster" in the same category as one picturing a presidential candidate, albeit a mock candidate.*

New York has decided that a medium's use of an earlier story to advertise its own product does not come within "advertising purposes" under the statute. In Booth v. Curtis Publishing Co., 15 App.Div.2d 343, 223 N.Y.S.2d 737 (1962), aff'd without opinion 11 N.Y.2d 907, 182 N.E.2d 812, 228 N.Y.S.2d 468 (1962), Holiday magazine published a photograph of actress Shirley Booth in a story about a prominent resort. The color photograph was "a very striking one, show[ing] Miss Booth in the water up to her neck, but wearing a brimmed, high-crowned street hat of straw." Several months after the story appeared, Holiday took out full-page advertisements in the New Yorker and Advertising Age magazines. Both expressly presented the Booth photograph as a sample of the content of Holiday magazine. "Because of the photograph's striking qualities it would be quite effective in drawing attention to the advertisements; but it was also a sample of magazine content."

* The *Presley* court reached this position only after finding that the plaintiffs had a descendible property right. It later receded from that position. 652 F.2d 278, 7 Med.L.Rptr. 1617 (2d Cir.1981). Certiorari was denied, 456 U.S. 927 (1982).

The court found the use of the photograph to be an "incidental" mentioning of plaintiff in the course of advertising itself. "It stands to reason that a publication can best prove its worth and illustrate its content by submission of complete copies of or extraction from past editions. . . . And, of course, it is true that the publisher must advertise in other public media, just as it must by poster, circular, cover, or soliciting letter. This is a practical necessity which the law may not ignore in giving effect to the purposes of the statute."

Although the court recognized that "realistically" the use of the photograph attracted the attention of the reader, that use was outweighed by the magazine's need to demonstrate its content. Finally, nothing in the advertisement suggested that plaintiff endorsed defendant's magazine.

The court in Namath v. Sports Illustrated, 48 App.Div.2d 487, 371 N.Y.S.2d 10 (1975), affirmed 39 N.Y.2d 897, 352 N.E.2d 584, 386 N.Y.S. 2d 397 (1976), quoted *Booth* in recognizing that the republication "was in motivation, sheer advertising and solicitation. This alone is not determinative of the question so long as the law accords an exempt status to incidental advertising of the news medium itself."

Since the court reaches this result when the plaintiff is a prominent figure who could have sold his or her endorsement to others, does it follow that the same analysis applies when the subject is an ordinary citizen?

c. *Elizabeth Taylor and Docudramas.* How should one analyze the relatively new technique of the "docudrama," in which the program mixes truth and fiction? When ABC announced in 1982 that it was planning a docudrama on the life of Elizabeth Taylor, the actress responded by seeking an injunction. Her first theory was that "I am my own commodity. I am my own industry." Someday "I will write my autobiography, and perhaps film it, but that will be my choice. By doing this, ABC is taking away from my income."

Media lawyers responded that no one had been able to draw a legal line between "news" and "entertainment," and that any decision in the case would necessarily affect both. Floyd Abrams is quoted as saying "Docudramas may be troublesome in their relationship, or non-relationship to news, but on balance, a docudrama, if done fairly, serves a useful function of informing in an entertaining manner."

Taylor's second theory was false-light invasion of privacy. "They plan to use my name throughout the show, to hire an actress who supposedly resembles me and to have her speak lines which they want the public to believe I used in numerous personal and private conversations."

Taylor's lawyer contended: "The docudrama is a fairly new form of expression. It's not biography, it's not a documentary and it's not her story. It's a drama. We're talking about a live actress who is entitled not to have lies told about her. When you mix fact and fiction and say this is a life story, no matter how flattering you are, you're showing the subject in a false light, and creating a wrong image."

In May, 1983, ABC announced that it had dropped its plans, for "creative reasons." The account of this dispute is taken mainly from Lewin, Whose Life Is It Anyway? Legally, It's Hard to Tell, N.Y. Times, Nov. 21, 1982, § II, at 1. See Manson, The Television Docudrama and the Right of Publicity, 7 Comm. & the Law 41 (Feb. 1985), concluding that since the docudrama is "neither fiction nor straight documentary" it does not fall within the protection accorded "biographies and documentaries; it does not provide a dissemination of information. Furthermore, the docudrama does not come under the first amendment protection of drama; it is not evident to the public that the events depicted in the docudrama are fictitious." By its "very nature, the docudrama tends to confuse the viewer, making it difficult to discern when true events in the life of the public figure portrayed merge and blend with purely fanciful fabrications. To confuse the viewer is a disservice to the public—to society. Further, confusion also diminishes and thereby damages the value of the public figure's 'name, likeness and persona.'"

D. OTHER SECRETS

The Administration of Justice, "Clear and Present Danger," and the Contempt Power. Although Craig v. Harney, discussed in *Cox Broadcasting,* set the pattern for protecting reports of what occurred in open courtrooms, the case primarily concerned the power of the press and public to comment on how judges should decide pending cases. (Questions of pretrial publicity, which may affect jurors rather than judges, and are discussed in Chapter IX.)

Until recently, state courts, acting under their asserted inherent power, held editors and publishers in criminal contempt for trying to influence pending judicial decisions. In one part of Bridges v. California, 314 U.S. 252 (1941), the Los Angeles Times had been held in contempt for asserting that a judge in a pending case would make "a serious mistake if he granted probation to" two Teamsters accused of assaulting non-union truck drivers. The Court, 5–4, held that the contempt power could be used against comments uttered outside the courtroom only when they presented a "clear and present danger" of obstructing justice.

The majority found that given the newspaper's well-known hostility toward unions, "it is inconceivable that any judge in Los Angeles would expect anything but adverse criticism from it in the event probation were granted. Yet such criticism after final disposition of the proceedings would clearly have been privileged." The four dissenters stressed that the judge was facing reelection in a year and that the editorial "was hardly an exercise in futility." Can it be that a newspaper whose editorial views are well known is more protected in this situation than a newspaper whose views are less predictable?

Is there a clear and present danger that the citizenry will think that a judge has been influenced by an editorial if the judge's decision reaches the same conclusion? How clearly can the judge himself tell whether he has been influenced by the editorial—either to follow it or to lean over backwards to avoid following it or appearing to follow it?

In Pennekamp v. Florida, 328 U.S. 331 (1946), a newspaper was held in contempt for its criticism of judges based on misstatements of fact. The Supreme Court found the errors inconsequential and found no clear and present danger.

The new view was followed in Craig v. Harney, which involved a lay judge. The Supreme Court, over three strong dissents, found no clear and present danger of obstruction. The "law of contempt is not made for the protection of judges who may be sensitive to the winds of public opinion. Judges are supposed to be men of fortitude, able to thrive in a hardy climate. . . . Judges who stand for reelection run on their records. . . . Discussion of their conduct is appropriate, if not necessary. The fact that the discussion at this particular point of time was not in good taste falls far short of meeting the clear and present danger test."

See also Wood v. Georgia, 370 U.S. 375 (1962), finding no clear and present danger in a sheriff's criticism of a charge to a grand jury to investigate questions of racial bloc-voting. The claim of clear and present danger was unsubstantiated. When the grand jury "is performing its investigatory function into a general problem area, . . . society's interest is best served by a thorough and extensive investigation, and a greater degree of disinterestedness and impartiality is assured by allowing free expression of contrary opinion. [In] the absence of any showing of an actual interference with the undertakings of the grand jury, this record lacks persuasion in illustrating the serious degree of harm to the administration of law necessary to justify exercise of the contempt power."

The Supreme Court has not upheld a use of the criminal contempt power in this type of situation since *Bridges.*

In the following case the state court, relying on this line of cases, used the clear and present danger test. Why does the Supreme Court "question the relevance of that standard"?

LANDMARK COMMUNICATIONS, INC. v. VIRGINIA

Supreme Court of the United States, 1978.
435 U.S. 829, 98 S.Ct. 1535, 56 L.Ed.2d 1, 3 Med.L.Rptr. 2153.
Noted, 64 A.B.A.J. 892, 2 COMM/ENT L.J. 707, 31 Fed.Com.L.J. 85.

[The Virginia constitution directed the legislature to create a commission to investigate charges against judges—and decreed that proceedings before the commission "shall be confidential." A statute creating the commission declared that the proceedings were confidential "and shall not be divulged by any person to anyone except the Commission, except that the record of any proceeding filed with the Supreme Court shall lose its confidential character." A proceeding is filed with the Supreme Court only when the commission finds grounds for filing a formal complaint.

Landmark's newspaper, the Virginian Pilot, accurately reported that a named judge was under investigation by the Commission. Landmark was found guilty of a misdemeanor and fined $500 plus costs of prosecution. The Supreme Court of Virginia affirmed. It rejected Landmark's argument that the statute applied only to the participants in the proceedings or to initial disclosure of confidential information. Instead, it concluded that the paper's actions "clearly . . . violated" the statute.

On appeal, the Supreme Court of the United States noted that virtually every state had such a commission, and that all provided for confidentiality. The accepted reasons for confidentiality were (1) it is thought to encourage the filing of complaints and willing participation of witnesses; (2) judges are protected from injury by publication of unexamined complaints until the meritorious can be separated from the unjustified; and (3) confidence in the judiciary is maintained by avoiding announcement of groundless claims. In addition, when removal is justified judges are more likely to resign voluntarily or retire if publicity can be avoided.

But even accepting the value of confidentiality, the Court considered this "only the beginning of the inquiry." Landmark was not attacking the confidentiality requirement. It was objecting to making it a crime to divulge or publish the information—a step taken by only Virginia and Hawaii.]

MR. CHIEF JUSTICE BURGER delivered the opinion of the Court.

. . .

III.

The narrow and limited question presented, then, is whether the First Amendment permits the criminal punishment of third persons who are strangers to the inquiry, including the news media, for divulging or publishing truthful information regarding confidential proceedings of the Judicial Inquiry and Review Commission. We are not here concerned with the possible applicability of the statute to one who secures the information by illegal means and thereafter divulges it. We do not have before us any constitutional challenge to a State's power to keep the Commission's proceedings confidential or to punish participants for breach of this mandate.[10] Cf. Nebraska Press Assn. v. Stuart, 427 U.S. 539, 564 (1976); id., at 601 n. 27 (Brennan, J.,

10. At least two categories of "participants" come to mind: Commission members and staff employees, and witnesses or putative witnesses not officers or employees of the Commonwealth. No issue as to either of these categories is presented by this case.

concurring); Wood v. Georgia, 370 U.S. 375, 393–394 (1962). Nor does Landmark argue for any constitutionally compelled right of access for the press to those proceedings. Cf. Saxbe v. Washington Post Co., 417 U.S. 843 (1974); Pell v. Procunier, 417 U.S. 817 (1974). Finally, as the Supreme Court of Virginia held, and appellant does not dispute, the challenged statute does not constitute a prior restraint or attempt by the State to censor the news media.

Landmark urges as the dispositive answer to the question presented that truthful reporting about public officials in connection with their public duties is always insulated from the imposition of criminal sanctions by the First Amendment. It points to the solicitude accorded even untruthful speech when public officials are its subjects, see, e.g., New York Times Co. v. Sullivan, [ ], and the extension of First Amendment protection to the dissemination of truthful commercial information, see, e.g., Virginia State Board of Pharmacy v. Virginia Citizens Consumer Council, 425 U.S. 748 (1976); Linmark Associates, Inc. v. Willingboro, 431 U.S. 85 (1977), to support its contention. We find it unnecessary to adopt this categorical approach to resolve the issue before us. We conclude that the publication Virginia seeks to punish under its statute lies near the core of the First Amendment, and the Commonwealth's interests advanced by the imposition of criminal sanctions are insufficient to justify the actual and potential encroachments on freedom of speech and of the press which follow therefrom. [ ]

A.

In Mills v. Alabama, 384 U.S. 214, 218 (1966), this Court observed: "Whatever differences may exist about interpretations of the First Amendment, there is practically universal agreement that a major purpose of that Amendment was to protect the free discussion of governmental affairs." . . .

The operations of the courts and the judicial conduct of judges are matters of utmost public concern. . . .

The operation of the Virginia Commission, no less than the operation of the judicial system itself, is a matter of public interest, necessarily engaging the attention of the news media. The article published by Landmark provided accurate factual information about a legislatively authorized inquiry pending before the Judicial Review and Inquiry Commission, and in so doing clearly served those interests in public scrutiny and discussion of governmental affairs which the First Amendment was adopted to protect. See [*Times*].

B.

. . .

The Commonwealth . . . focuses on what it perceives to be the pernicious effects of public discussion of Commission proceedings to support its argument. It contends that the public interest is not served by discussion of unfounded allegations of misconduct which defames honest judges and serves only to demean the administration of justice. The functioning of the Commission itself is also claimed to be impeded by premature disclosure of the complainant, witnesses, and the judge under investigation. Criminal sanctions minimize these harmful consequences, according to the Commonwealth, by ensuring that the guarantee of confidentiality is more than an empty promise.

It can be assumed for purposes of decision that confidentiality of Commission proceedings serves legitimate state interests. The question, however, is whether these interests are sufficient to justify the encroachment on First Amendment guarantees which the imposition of criminal sanctions entails with respect to nonparticipants such as Landmark. The Commonwealth has offered little more than assertion and conjecture to support its claim that without criminal sanctions the objectives of the statutory scheme would be seriously undermined. While not dispositive, we note that more than 40 States having similar commissions have not found it necessary to enforce confidentiality by use of criminal sanctions against nonparticipants.

Moreover, neither the Commonwealth's interest in protecting the reputation of its judges, nor its interest in maintaining the institutional integrity of its courts is sufficient to justify the subsequent punishment of speech at issue here, even on the assumption that criminal sanctions do in fact enhance the guarantee of confidentiality. Admittedly, the Commonwealth has an interest in protecting the good repute of its judges, like that of all other public officials. Our prior cases have firmly established, however, that injury to official reputation is an insufficient reason "for repressing speech that would otherwise be free." New York Times Co. v. Sullivan, [ ]. See also Garrison v. Louisiana, [ ]. The remaining interest sought to be protected, the institutional reputation of the courts, is entitled to no greater weight in the constitutional scales. . . . Mr. Justice Frankfurter, in his dissent in *Bridges,* [314 U.S. 252 (1941)] agreed that speech cannot be punished when the purpose is simply "to protect the court as a mystical entity or the judges as individuals or as anointed priests set apart from the community and spared the criticism to which in a democracy other public servants are exposed." [ ]

The Commonwealth has provided no sufficient reason for disregarding these well-established principles. We find them controlling and, on this record, dispositive.

IV.

The Supreme Court of Virginia relied on the clear-and-present-danger test in rejecting Landmark's claim. We question the relevance of that standard here; moreover we cannot accept the mechanical application of the test which led that court to its conclusion. Mr. Justice Holmes' test was never intended "to express a technical legal doctrine or to convey a formula for adjudicating cases." Pennekamp v.

Florida, 328 U.S. 331, 353 (1946) (Frankfurter, J., concurring). Properly applied, the test requires a court to make its own inquiry into the imminence and magnitude of the danger said to flow from the particular utterance and then to balance the character of the evil, as well as its likelihood, against the need for free and unfettered expression. The possibility that other measures will serve the State's interests should also be weighed.

Landmark argued in the Supreme Court of Virginia that "before a state may punish expression, it must prove by 'actual facts' the existence of a clear and present danger to the orderly administration of justice." [ ] The court acknowledged that the record before it was devoid of such "actual facts," but went on to hold that such proof was not required when the legislature itself had made the requisite finding "that a clear and present danger to the orderly administration of justice would be created by divulgence of the confidential proceedings of the Commission." [ ] This legislative declaration coupled with the stipulated fact that Landmark published the disputed article was regarded by the court as sufficient to justify imposition of criminal sanctions.

Deference to a legislative finding cannot limit judicial inquiry when First Amendment rights are at stake. . . . A legislature appropriately inquires into and may declare the reasons impelling legislative action but the judicial function commands analysis of whether the specific conduct charged falls within the reach of the statute and if so whether the legislation is consonant with the Constitution. Were it otherwise, the scope of freedom of speech and of the press would be subject to legislative definition and the function of the First Amendment as a check on legislative power would be nullified.

It was thus incumbent upon the Supreme Court of Virginia to go behind the legislative determination and examine for itself "the particular utteranc[e] here in question and the circumstances of [its] publication to determine to what extent the substantive evil of unfair administration of justice was a likely consequence, and whether the degree of likelihood was sufficient to justify [subsequent] punishment." Bridges v. California, 314 U.S., at 271. Our precedents leave little doubt as to the proper outcome of such an inquiry.

In a series of cases raising the question of whether the contempt power could be used to punish out-of-court comments concerning pending cases or grand jury investigations, this Court has consistently rejected the argument that such commentary constituted a clear and present danger to the administration of justice. . . .

The efforts of the Supreme Court of Virginia to distinguish those cases from this case are unpersuasive. The threat to the administration of justice posed by the speech and publications in *Bridges, Pennekamp, Craig,* and *Wood* was, if anything, more direct and substantial than the threat posed by Landmark's article. If the clear-and-present-danger test could not be satisfied in the more extreme circumstances of those cases, it would seem to follow that the test cannot be met here. It is true that some risk of injury to the judge under inquiry, to the system of justice, or to the operation of the Judicial Review and Inquiry Commission may be posed by premature disclosure, but the test requires that the danger be "clear and present" and in our view the risk here falls far short of that requirement. Moreover, much of the risk can be eliminated through careful internal procedures to protect the confidentiality of Commission proceedings. Cf. Nebraska Press Assn. v. Stuart, 427 U.S., at 564; id., at 601 n. 27 (Brennan, J., concurring in judgment). In any event, we must conclude as we did in Wood v. Georgia, that "[t]he type of 'danger' evidenced by the record is precisely one of the types of activity envisioned by the Founders in presenting the First Amendment for ratification." 370 U.S., at 388.

Accordingly, the judgment of the Supreme Court of Virginia is reversed, and the case remanded for further proceedings not inconsistent with this opinion.

MR. JUSTICE BRENNAN and MR. JUSTICE POWELL took no part in the consideration or decision of this case.

MR. JUSTICE STEWART, concurring in the judgment.

Virginia has enacted a law making it a criminal offense for "any person" to divulge confidential information about proceedings before its Judicial Inquiry and Review Commission. I cannot agree with the Court that this Virginia law violates the Constitution.

There could hardly be a higher governmental interest than a State's interest in the quality of its judiciary. Virginia's derivative interest in maintaining the confidentiality of the proceedings of its Judicial Inquiry and Review Commission seems equally clear. Only such confidentiality, the State has determined, will protect upright judges from unjustified harm and at the same time insure the full and fearless airing in Commission proceedings of every complaint of judicial misconduct. I find nothing in the Constitution to prevent Virginia from punishing those who violate this confidentiality. [ ]

But in this case Virginia has extended its law to punish a newspaper, and that it cannot constitutionally do. If the constitutional protection of a free press means anything, it means that government cannot take it upon itself to decide what a newspaper may and may not publish. Though government may deny access to information and punish its theft, government may not prohibit or punish the publication of that information once it falls into the hands of the press, unless the need for secrecy is manifestly overwhelming.*

It is on this ground that I concur in the judgment of the Court.

* National defense is the most obvious justification for government restrictions on publication. Even then, distinctions must be drawn between prior restraints and subsequent penalties. See, e.g., [*Times* and *Near*].

Notes and Questions

1. What was the "categorical" approach that the majority rejected? Why did it reject it?

2. Under the majority's approach, who can be punished for revealing the judge's name? Under Justice Stewart's approach, who can be punished for revealing the judge's name? Is his position required by his 1974 speech, reprinted at p. 57, supra?

3. Why does the Chief Justice "question the relevance of that standard" in this case? Assuming its applicability, what was Virginia's error in applying it?

4. How might the Court have analyzed a claim by the judge for invasion of privacy?

5. The Chief Justice appears to think it significant that the information was not gathered by "illegal means." This theme recurs in the next case and also in Justice Stevens's opinion in Nebraska Press Ass'n v. Stuart, in Chapter IX. Why might the legality of the gathering process affect the outcome of a claim based on the content of what is published?

SMITH v. DAILY MAIL PUBLISHING CO.

Supreme Court of the United States, 1979.
443 U.S. 97, 99 S.Ct. 2667, 61 L.Ed.2d 399, 5 Med.L.Rptr. 1305.
Noted, 7 Hastings Const.L.Q. 352, 65 Iowa L.Rev. 1471, 56 N.D.L.Rev. 279, 7 Ohio N.U.L.Rev. 148.

[A West Virginia statute made it a crime for a "newspaper" to publish the names of juveniles in connection with juvenile proceedings without a written order of the court. The respondent newspapers learned over a police radio about a killing at a junior high school. Reporters went to the scene and obtained the name of the suspect by asking witnesses, the police, and a prosecuting attorney. The name was revealed thereafter in the newspapers and over several broadcasting stations.

After being indicted, the newspapers obtained an order from the state supreme court barring any prosecution on the ground that the statute was unconstitutional.]

MR. CHIEF JUSTICE BURGER delivered the opinion of the Court.

We granted certiorari to consider whether a West Virginia statute violates the First and Fourteenth Amendments of the United States Constitution by making it a crime for a newspaper to publish, without the written approval of the juvenile court, the name of any youth charged as a juvenile offender.

. . .

(2)

Respondents urge this Court to hold that because § 49–7–3 requires court approval prior to publication of the juvenile's name it operates as a "prior restraint" on speech.[1] [ ] Respondents concede that this statute is not in the classic mold of prior restraint, there being no prior injunction against publication. Nonetheless, they contend that the prior-approval requirement acts in "operation and effect" like a licensing scheme and thus is another form of prior restraint. See Near v. Minnesota [ ]. As such, respondents argue, the statute bears "a 'heavy presumption' against its constitutional validity." [ ] They claim that the State's interest in the anonymity of a juvenile offender is not sufficient to overcome that presumption.

Petitioners do not dispute that the statute amounts to a prior restraint on speech. Rather, they take the view that even if it is a prior restraint the statute is constitutional because of the significance of the State's interest in protecting the identity of juveniles.

(3)

The resolution of this case does not turn on whether the statutory grant of authority to the juvenile judge to permit publication of the juvenile's name is, in and of itself, a prior restraint. First Amendment protection reaches beyond prior restraints, [*Landmark* and *Cox Broadcasting*], and respondents acknowledge that the statutory provision for court approval of disclosure actually may have a less oppressive effect on freedom of the press than a total ban on the publication of the child's name.

Whether we view the statute as a prior restraint or as a penal sanction for publishing lawfully obtained, truthful information is not dispositive because even the latter action requires the highest form of state interest to sustain its validity. Prior restraints have been accorded the most exacting scrutiny in previous cases. [ ]. However, even when a state attempts to punish publication after the event it must nevertheless demonstrate that its punitive action was necessary to further the state interests asserted. [*Landmark*]. Since we conclude that this statute cannot satisfy the constitutional standards defined in *Landmark Communications, Inc.,* we need not decide whether, as argued by respondents, it operated as a prior restraint.

Our recent decisions demonstrate that state action to punish the publication of truthful information seldom can satisfy constitutional standards. In *Landmark Communications* we declared unconstitutional a Virginia statute making it a crime to publish information regard-

1. Respondents do not argue that the statute is a prior restraint because it imposes a criminal sanction for certain types of publication. At page 11 of their brief they state: "The statute in question is, to be sure, not a prior restraint because it subjects newspapers to criminal punishments for what they print" after the event.

. . .

ing confidential proceedings before a state judicial review commission that heard complaints about alleged disabilities and misconduct of state-court judges. In declaring that statute unconstitutional, we concluded:

> "[T]he publication Virginia seeks to punish under its statute lies near the core of the First Amendment, and the Commonwealth's interests advanced by the imposition of criminal sanctions are insufficient to justify the actual and potential encroachments on freedom of speech and of the press which follow therefrom." 435 U.S., at 838.

In [*Cox Broadcasting*], we held that damages could not be recovered against a newspaper for publishing the name of a rape victim. The suit had been based on a state statute that made it a crime to publish the name of the victim; the purpose of the statute was to protect the privacy right of the individual and the family. The name of the victim had become known to the public through official court records dealing with the trial of the rapist. In declaring the statute unconstitutional, the Court, speaking through Mr. Justice White, reasoned:

> "By placing the information in the public domain on official court records, the State must be presumed to have concluded that the public interest was thereby being served. . . . States may not impose sanctions on the publication of truthful information contained in official court records open to public inspection." 420 U.S., at 495.

One case that involved a classic prior restraint is particularly relevant to our inquiry. In Oklahoma Publishing Co. v. District Court, 430 U.S. 308 (1977), we struck down a state-court injunction prohibiting the news media from publishing the name or photograph of an 11-year-old boy who was being tried before a juvenile court. The juvenile judge had permitted reporters and other members of the public to attend a hearing in the case, notwithstanding a state statute closing such trials to the public. The court then attempted to halt publication of the information obtained from that hearing. We held that once the truthful information was "publicly revealed" or "in the public domain" the court could not constitutionally restrain its dissemination.

None of these opinions directly controls this case; however, all suggest strongly that if a newspaper lawfully obtains truthful information about a matter of public significance then state officials may not constitutionally punish publication of the information, absent a need to further a state interest of the highest order. These cases involved situations where the government itself provided or made possible press access to the information. That factor is not controlling. Here respondents relied upon routine newspaper reporting techniques to ascertain the identity of the alleged assailant. A free press cannot be made to rely solely upon the sufferance of government to supply it with information. See Houchins v. KQED, Inc., 438 U.S. 1, 11 (1978) (plurality opinion); Branzburg v. Hayes, 408 U.S. 665, 681 (1972). If the information is lawfully obtained, as it was here, the state may not punish its publication except when necessary to further an interest more substantial than is present here.

(4)

The sole interest advanced by the State to justify its criminal statute is to protect the anonymity of the juvenile offender. It is asserted that confidentiality will further his rehabilitation because publication of the name may encourage further antisocial conduct and also may cause the juvenile to lose future employment or suffer other consequences for this single offense. In Davis v. Alaska, 415 U.S. 308 (1974), similar arguments were advanced by the State to justify not permitting a criminal defendant to impeach a prosecution witness on the basis of his juvenile record. We said there that "[w]e do not and need not challenge the State's interest as a matter of its own policy in the administration of criminal justice to seek to preserve the anonymity of a juvenile offender." [ ] However, we concluded that the State's policy must be subordinated to the defendant's Sixth Amendment right of confrontation. Ibid. The important rights created by the First Amendment must be considered along with the rights of defendants guaranteed by the Sixth Amendment. See Nebraska Press Assn. v. Stuart, [ ]. Therefore, the reasoning of *Davis* that the constitutional right must prevail over the state's interest in protecting juveniles applies with equal force here.

The magnitude of the State's interest in this statute is not sufficient to justify application of a criminal penalty to respondents. Moreover, the statute's approach does not satisfy constitutional requirements. The statute does not restrict the electronic media or any form of publication, except "newspapers," from printing the names of youths charged in a juvenile proceeding. In this very case, three radio stations announced the alleged assailant's name before the Daily Mail decided to publish it. Thus, even assuming the statute served a state interest of the highest order, it does not accomplish its stated purpose.

In addition, there is no evidence to demonstrate that the imposition of criminal penalties is necessary to protect the confidentiality of juvenile proceedings. . . . [A]ll 50 states have statutes that provide in some way for confidentiality, but only five, including West Virginia, impose criminal penalties on nonparties for publication of the identity of the juvenile. Although every state has asserted a similar interest, all but a handful have found other ways of accomplishing the objective. See [*Landmark*].[3]

3. The approach advocated by the National Council of Juvenile Court Judges is based on cooperation between juvenile court personnel and newspaper editors. It is suggested that if the courts make clear their purpose and methods then the press will exercise discretion and generally decline to publish the juvenile's name without some prior consultation with the juvenile court judge.

(5)

Our holding in this case is narrow. There is no issue before us of unlawful press access to confidential judicial proceedings, see [*Cox Broadcasting*]; there is no issue here of privacy or prejudicial pretrial publicity. At issue is simply the power of a state to punish the truthful publication of an alleged juvenile delinquent's name lawfully obtained by a newspaper.[4] The asserted state interest cannot justify the statute's imposition of criminal sanctions on this type of publication. Accordingly, the judgment of the West Virginia Supreme Court of Appeals is

Affirmed.

MR. JUSTICE POWELL took no part in the consideration or decision of this case.

[Justice Rehnquist, who concurred in the judgment, filed the only separate opinion. He believed that protecting juveniles in this type of case was an interest of the "highest order" and "far outweighs any minimal interference with freedom of the press . . . ." He also noted that the Court's decision "renders nugatory" state expungement laws, because a potential employer may now obtain information on juvenile offenses by visiting the morgue of the local newspaper. Also, in future cases the "press will still be able to obtain the child's name in the same manner as it was acquired in this case. [ ] Thus, the Court's reference to effective alternatives [other than criminal punishment] for accomplishing the State's goal is a mere chimera."

He did concur, however, because the state's statute did not accomplish its stated purpose. Since broadcasters could, and did, identify the juvenile, it was "difficult to take very seriously West Virginia's asserted need to preserve the anonymity of its youthful offenders when it permits other, equally, if not more, effective means of mass communication to distribute this information without fear of punishment."]

Notes and Questions

1. How does this case differ from *Landmark*? From *Cox Broadcasting*? From *Oklahoma Publishing*?

2. What is the significance of the statute's failure to bar broadcasts of this information?

3. How might the Court's analysis have differed if the juvenile had sued for invasion of privacy? Would the existence of the statute matter?

4. Compare Justice Rehnquist's view of the importance of this statute with Justice Stewart's opinion in *Landmark* about the importance of that statute.

4. In light of our disposition of the First and Fourteenth Amendment issue, we need not reach respondents' claim that the statute violates equal protection by being applicable only to newspapers but not other forms of journalistic expression.

5. Chief Justice Burger ends by stressing the "narrow" nature of the holding. What makes the decision narrow?

6. Again, note the same stress on legal acquisition of the material that we saw in *Landmark.* Why might legality of acquisition matter here?

7. In Kansas v. Stauffer Communications, Inc., 225 Kan. 540, 592 P.2d 891, 5 Med.L.Rptr. 1081 (1979), defendant newspaper was prosecuted for violating a statute that barred reporting the issuance of search or arrest warrants before they had been executed. The court held that the statute could not constitutionally be applied in a case in which the information published was obtained from a public record. It relied primarily on *Cox Broadcasting* and *Oklahoma Publishing.*

8. *Expungement.* Many states do have expungement statutes of one type or another. Some apply only to juveniles; others apply to adults who were arrested but not convicted, or to adults who were convicted of certain offenses. The theory behind the statutes is that, at least in the case of adult offenders, once rehabilitated, they deserve a chance to be free of their past. Records may be sealed, segregated, or withheld from the public eye in other ways. In a sense the state seeks to declare what had been previously public—the conviction or arrest—to have become a state secret.

Is Justice Rehnquist correct in observing that the Daily Mail case renders expungement statutes ineffective? Could they withstand direct constitutional attack in a prosecution for publishing a previous conviction when the state makes such publication a crime?

See Shifflet v. Thomson Newspapers, Inc., 69 Ohio St.2d 179, 431 N.E.2d 1014, 8 Med.L.Rptr. 1199 (1982), in which the plaintiff's 1965 conviction for indecent exposure was expunged in open court in 1978. A reporter in the courtroom wrote a story identifying the plaintiff with home address and reporting the expungement. The plaintiff, who claimed that he was not guilty of the original charge, sued for libel and for invasion of privacy. The libel claim fell because the report said only that he had been convicted in 1965, not that he was guilty of the charge. The privacy claim fell because of the First Amendment protection that came from the *Cox-Landmark* cluster: the First and Fourteenth Amendments "would not permit exposing the press to liability for truthfully publishing information released to the public in court proceedings and from court records."

The court rejected plaintiff's claim that the courtroom should be deemed closed for expungement proceedings. The goal of these statutes is to prevent public officials from further dissemination of certain records except under special circumstances. To permit the statute to be used to allow denial of what had occurred, would turn it "from the limited shield it may be for the offender, into a sword for the confounding of the public which has a right, except perhaps in special circumstances not here applicable or apparent, to attend criminal proceedings and a right to speak the truth." Is this consistent with the Briscoe and Roshto cases, p. 304 supra?

9. *The Credit Call Code.* In State v. Northwest Passage, Inc., 90 Wash.2d 741, 585 P.2d 794 (1978), defendant newspaper published an article telling its readers how the telephone company established credit card numbers for its subscribers, how to make calls with false card numbers, and how to avoid detection. "A fair reading of the article is that its sole purpose was to tell readers how to defraud the telephone company and how to avoid being caught." The defendant was prosecuted under a criminal provision punishing one who "publishes . . . the numbering or coding which is employed in the issuance of telephone company credit cards, with the intent that it be used or with knowledge or reason to believe that it will be used to avoid the payment of any lawful charge . . . ."

Defendant's conviction was upheld. The court considered this a narrow restriction on speech that was justified by the goal of preventing fraud against the phone company and its customers. Defendant argued that a less restrictive alternative existed because another provision punished the use of false credit card numbers. The court responded that this was an acceptable alternative only so long as the code remained secret. Defendant's publication of the code destroyed its own argument. Considering all the factors, the court concluded that the provision was not overbroad.

Notice that this case involves using the legal system to protect a product or service developed through the research efforts of the telephone company. If the publication were permitted, the result would be either higher rates on credit card calls to cover those made by persons who successfully avoided identification or, if that loss were too great, the termination of credit card calls or the development of a new and "unbreakable" coding system.

On the other hand, the newspaper published only available information and engaged in no criminal conduct to discover the coding system—and the story is apparently accurate. Should the publisher's intent matter? What if this article were published in newspapers or magazines whose readers were unlikely to use the information to the detriment of the telephone company?

10. In the late 1970s some publications began identifying CIA agents on duty in foreign countries. Congress responded with the Intelligence Identities Protection Act of 1982, 50 U.S.C. § 421. The statute punishes two groups of persons. The first covers those who have had authorized access to classified information and who then disclose it without authorization. The second covers those who "in the course of a pattern of activities intended to identify and expose covert agents and with reason to believe that such activities would impair or impede the foreign intelligence activities of the United States" disclose information that identifies covert agents, knowing that the government is trying to conceal those persons' identity. "The term 'pattern of activities' requires a series of acts with a common purpose or objective."

It was much debated whether a reporter who wrote a story about the CIA would violate the statute if that story contained information that identified a covert agent. Language in the conference committee report suggests that routine news reporting is beyond the statute. See Notes, 49 Brooklyn L.Rev. 479 and 83 Colum.L.Rev. 727.

Chapter IV

PROTECTING PHYSICAL AND EMOTIONAL SECURITY

Recent lawsuits have asserted that mass media are liable for personal injuries traceable in one way or another to a publication or broadcast. These cases raise some of the most hotly disputed questions in all of media liability. The examples that follow suggest the range of situations that might rise to controversy.

HYDE v. CITY OF COLUMBIA

Missouri Court of Appeals, 1982.
637 S.W.2d 251.
Certiorari denied, 459 U.S. 1226, 103 S.Ct. 1233, 75 L.Ed.2d 467 (1983).

SHANGLER, P.J.

The plaintiff Hyde sued the City of Columbia for the negligent disclosure of her name and address by the city police to reporter Brown of the Columbia Daily Tribune and to reporter Potter of the Columbia Missourian and for the negligent publication of that information subsequently by the newspapers. The petition alleges that on August 20, 1980, after midnight, the plaintiff was abducted and kidnapped by an unknown male assailant but escaped from his car; that she made a full report of that incident to the City of Columbia Police Department; that on that date, the police, without knowledge or authority of the plaintiff, released her name and address to the reporters for publication when the police knew the assailant was still at large; that on that very day the Columbia Daily Tribune published that information and on the next day, August 21, 1980, the Columbia Missourian published that information with the knowledge that the assailant was not in custody. The petition then alleges that the release and publication of her name and address identified the plaintiff to the unknown assailant who thereafter terrorized her on seven different occasions. . . . The prayer was for actual damages.

[The trial judge dismissed the petition. On appeal, the court first concluded that the only claim was one of negligence.]

. . .

The pleadings enlarged by the interrogatory evidence, understood in legal effect, posit that the plaintiff reported the kidnapping and assault to the police as an official account of a crime and not for publication, and that the municipality owed the victim a duty not to disclose her identity and address to the reporter for publication without prior consent—and so protect her from the foreseeable risk of intentional harm by the assailant . . . . The pleadings . . . posit also that the defendants reporter and newspaper owed a duty to the victim not to publish her identity and address and so protect her from the foreseeable risk of intentional harm by the assailant, when they knew the assailant was still at large and the practice of publication was otherwise forbidden by internal policy,[4] but that reporter Brown and newspaper Columbia Daily Tribune breached the duty and the plaintiff suffered emotional harm from the intentional threats of imminent death and injury proximately caused by the negligent conduct of the reporter and newspaper.

[The defendants assert that no tort duty is owed; that if a tort duty is found, the First Amendment would not permit such a duty to be imposed; and that a crime against persons report is a public record under the Sunshine Law and publishing such a record can engender no liability.]

In negligence jurisprudence, whether a duty exists presents a question of law. . . . The judicial determination of the existence of a duty rests on sound public policy as derived from a calculus of factors: among them, the social consensus that the interest is worthy of protection; the foreseeability of harm and the degree of certainty that the protected person suffered injury; moral blame society attaches to the conduct; the prevention of future harm; considerations of cost and ability to spread the risk of loss; the economic burden upon the actor and the community—and others. . . .

Our law imposes the duty on an actor in some circumstances to foresee that the misconduct of a third person will result in injury to another [the plaintiff] and imposes liability for failure to protect against that risk of harm. [ ] [This principle] has scope even where the misconduct of the third person is intentional or criminal. . . . In certain situations, the law expects a reasonable actor to anticipate and protect the plaintiff against the intentional or criminal misconduct of a third person whom the actor has given occasion for association with the plaintiff, when the actor knows or should know that the third person is "peculiarly likely to commit intentional misconduct, under circumstances which afford a peculiar opportunity for temptation for such misconduct." Restatement (Second) of Torts § 302B, comment e, note D (1965). . . .

The averments of the petition given the most favorable intendment as a negligence cause of action fall within these statements of principle . . . and so plead a prima facie breach of duty—unless, as the municipality and newspaper contend, the information was a public record under the Sunshine Law and otherwise protected by the First Amendment. The press enjoys no constitutional right to police records. The right of the press for access to governmental records, rather, is no greater than by the public generally. Pell v. Procunier, 417 U.S. 817,

4. The responses to interrogatories by the defendants reporter and newspaper disclose an unwritten policy in effect on August 20, 1980, that the Columbia Daily Tribune would not print the name of a female victim of an attempted or actual sexual offense. The responses explain that those practices "are based on the police department's classification of the crime." . . .

850 (1974). The right of the defendant news medium to have the name and address of the victim from the municipal police, therefore, depends upon whether that information was a public record.

The common law gave access to public records only where the citizen could show that the purpose of inspection was to vindicate a private or public right. [ ] The legislature then enacted §§ 109.180 and 109.190 to open all state, county and municipal records kept under statute or ordinance to personal inspection "by any citizen of Missouri"—a privilege not to be refused "to any citizen." Whatever vestige of a common law interest to enable inspection lingered . . . was swept away by the enactment of the Sunshine Law [ ]. That chapter defines a public record as any record retained by or of any public governmental body [ ] and then directs that the public records shall be open to the public for inspection and duplication [ ]—subject only to the enumerated exceptions of § 610.025.

. . .

To construe the Sunshine Law to open all criminal investigation information to anyone with a request subserves neither the public safety policy of our state nor the personal security of a victim—but rather, courts constitutional violations of the right of privacy of a witness or other citizen unwittingly drawn into the criminal investigation process as well as the right of an accused to a fair trial. Such a construction leads to the absurdity . . . that an assailant unknown as such to the authorities, from whom the victim has escaped, need simply walk into the police station, demand name and address or other personal information—without possibility of lawful refusal, so as to intimidate the victim as a witness or commit other injury. Statute as written, we determine that the name and address of a victim of crime who can identify an assailant not yet in custody is not a public record under the Sunshine Law.

. . .

The defendants reporter and newspaper contend that the report of the abduction by the victim to the police—facts pleaded in the petition—was her consent to the preparation of the formal crime report and its subsequent publication by the news medium. That argument disregards altogether the duty of citizenship to report criminal conduct—to raise a "hue and cry" of felony to the authorities. Roberts v. United States, 445 U.S. 552 (1980).

That the victim-name-and-address information kept by the municipal police department was by law confidential does not mean that once disclosed to a newspaper it retained its confidential character. Nor do allegations which suffice to plead a cause of action against the official keeper for the negligent release of that confidential record ipso facto suffice as a tort cause of action against a news medium for publication of that information. The difference reposes in the favor the free speech and free press components of the First Amendment display for the autonomy of the institutional press. New York Times Company v.

United States, 403 U.S. 713 (1971) "So far as the Constitution goes, the autonomous press may publish what it knows, and may seek to learn what it can." Potter Stewart, "Or of the Press," 26 Hastings L.J. 631, 636 (1975).

The defendants reporter and newspaper contend that the report of crime was a matter of legitimate public concern and interest so that the adjudication of tort liability for the publication of that information were an impermissible interference with the exercise of free speech and of a free press in violation of the First Amendment.[19] The defendants develop the argument in terms of newsworthiness of the publication and the status of the victim-plaintiff as a subject of public interest. They apply these considerations and commingle them with the invasion of privacy, outrageous conduct and defamation torts. The petition, however, pleads negligence—a tort which protects an interest distinctive from the other torts. . . . The First Amendment protects a news medium from tortious publication to the extent that the interest in free speech and free press overbalances the governmental interest the tort protects. . . .

. . .

Gertz repudiated the public interest-newsworthy test . . . in actions for defamation and balanced, rather, the free speech free press values against the cogent state interests in the compensation of private injury to reputation. . . .

. . .

. . . The events the petition describes are of a private person become unwilling victim of a crime—not of one who has injected her person into a public controversy. The damages she pleads are for actual loss. In sum, the petition comes validly within the culminated constitutional balance struck by Gertz which allows a private redress against a newspaper for a negligent publication of information on a theory of fault free from the proof constraints of New York Times. The question remains then whether under the negligence law of our state the petition pleads a cause of action.

The [defendants'] . . . constitutional, as well as local law, arguments recite principles apt to defamation and privacy, but not negligence cases. The defendants assume that each of those remedies protects the same private interest. They do not. The defamation

19. That brief argues also that the dismissal of the petition was proper because the news medium defendants merely gave further publicity to information already public. We have determined that the name and address of the victim under the circumstances pleaded was not public information under the Sunshine Law. Nor was that information a component of an arrest report—and so a public record under §§ 610.100 and 610.105, nor a judicial record—and so open to the public and news media alike. [*Cox*]

. . .

We should note, since the several defendants argue the term public interest without differentiation as to its constitutional as distinct from its common law content, that the privilege of a police officer to communicate official information to another appertains only as to statements made in the proper exercise of the official duty—such as to allay a public danger. . . .

remedy protects reputation. [ ] The right of privacy remedy protects personal sensibility from public disclosure of private facts and from the appropriation of the likeness or name. [ ] The outrageous conduct remedy protects against intentional or reckless infliction of emotional distress. [ ] The negligence remedy extends to protect against invasion of bodily security even to life itself. . . .

. . .

We have determined that the name and address of the victim-plaintiff prior to the arrest of the assailant was not an official report under the Sunshine Law and so was not a privileged publication under the tenor of that statute or the rules of the common law. . . . We determine also that the name and address of an abduction witness who can identify an assailant still at large before arrest is a matter of such trivial public concern compared with the high probability of risk to the victim by their publication, that a news medium owes a duty in such circumstances to use reasonable care not to give likely occasion for a third party [assailant still at large] to do injury to the plaintiff by the publication. That duty derives as an "expression of the sum total of those considerations of policy which lead the law to say that the particular plaintiff is entitled to protection." Prosser, The Law of Torts, 325–6 (4th ed. 1971). It derives from a balance of interests between the public right to know and the individual right to personal security—between the social value of the right the press advances and the social value of the right of the individual at risk. [ ] It derives from the social consensus that common decency considers such information of insignificant public importance compared to the injury likely to be done by the exposure.[25] Restatement Second of Torts 652D, comments g and h (1977). It derives from "the known character, past conduct and tendencies of the person [assailant] whose intentional conduct causes the harm, the temptation or opportunity which the situation [publication] may afford him for such misconduct, the gravity of the harm which may result." . . . The petition does not contest the truth of the publication nor assail an unpopular opinion. It does not tend the medium to that course of self-censorship which offends a free press, but engenders an attitude of due care for the safety of one likely to be harmed from the reportage of trivial information. To delete the name and address of the abduction victim from the news

25. The "unwritten policy" [the news medium defendant concedes in the answers to interrogatories] not to print the name and address of a female victim of a reported male attempted or actual sexual assault is nothing more than a usual news medium practice in conformance with precepts of "common decency" and the discerned "mores of the community." . . .

. . . *Cox*, as we noted, dealt with judicial records, not with any official action before arrest. . . . *Cox* holds no more than that publication of rape victim name information in a [judicial] record already open to the public does not give a basis for an invasion of privacy suit. That is because [ ] "interests in privacy fade when the information involved already appears on the public record." Information already open to the public, of course, is also open to the press for publication. *Cox* has nothing to do with extra-judicial reports, such as a report of crime to the police . . . .

. . .

medium publication would impair no significant news function nor public interest in the reportage of crime and apprehension of criminals. To report that information when the assailant can be identified—as the news publication clearly informs—rather, encourages not only a likelihood of injury but of additional crime.

. . .

[The court held that state tort law permitted recovery in this situation for emotional distress absent physical injury.]

. . .

The judgment of dismissal is reversed and remanded with directions to the trial court to reinstate the petition against the defendants on appeal.

All concur.

Notes and Questions

1. What is the significance of the newspaper's internal policy? Media lawyers debate, usually in the context of negligence in libel cases, whether an internal policy is more a help or a hindrance. What would you advise?

2. What is the significance of the *Gertz* opinion in this case? Are the two kinds of negligence equivalent?

3. Is *Hyde* consistent with Cox Broadcasting v. Cohn? With *Oklahoma Publishing*?

4. Is there a difference between emotional distress caused by the fear of personal injury or death and emotional distress that arises from other concerns, such as humiliation?

5. Is the case any different if, in fact, plaintiff had been stalked and killed or injured by the assailant who learned her address from the newspaper?

6. In June, 1980, some 17 PBS stations chose not to show a documentary about a 62-year-old woman with breast cancer who committed suicide with the advance knowledge of her family and friends. The program manager of one of the stations explained the decision by saying that the program had the "potential for encouraging others to commit suicide." If that was so, should such a result produce legal consequences for stations that show the program? N.Y. Times, June 4, 1980, at C30. Would the case be different if the stimulus to attempting suicide had come from reading a book that presented suicide in a favorable light?

7. The National Enquirer published a poem by John W. Hinckley, Jr., entitled "Bloody Love," depicting Hinckley's fantasy of killing actress Jodie Foster with a knife. A front-page headline ran "Hinckley Reveals Details of His Plan to Kill Jodie Foster." Foster's lawyers told the Justice Department that the Enquirer had violated a federal criminal statute punishing "whoever transmits in interstate commerce

any communication containing any threat to kidnap any person or any threat to injure the person of another." 18 U.S.C. § 875(c).

The Enquirer's lawyer responded that this was not a threat because Hinckley was "fantasizing." He added that "Even if it were an outright threat, with the personalities involved and the historical context, the First Amendment protects the Enquirer's right to print it." The Justice Department took no action. N.Y. Times, Aug. 25, 1982 at 15.

8. The Hyde case was settled for a payment of $6,000 from the city and nothing from the newspaper. News Media & Law, Sept.-Oct. 1983, at 41.

9. *Hyde* is discussed in Dreschel, Negligent Infliction of Emotional Distress: New Tort Problem for the Mass Media, 12 Pepperdine L.Rev. 889 (1985); Linder, When Names Are Not News, They're Negligence: Media Liability for Personal Injuries Resulting from the Publication of Accurate Information, 52 UMKC L.Rev. 421 (1984); Note, Identifying the Rape Victim: A Constitutional Clash Between the First Amendment and the Right to Privacy, 18 John Marshall L.Rev. 987 (1985).

10. A newspaper learns that an apparently ordinary citizen has been a double agent who has eluded the foreign government for which he once worked. The paper checks with the citizen who confirms it but credibly says he will commit suicide if the story is published. The story is published and the citizen commits suicide. Any liability?

11. Assume that the source who tells the paper about the double agent also tells the paper that if the name is published the foreign government will kill the man within hours. The paper prints the name without first checking with the man. Within hours he is killed. Any liability?

12. Might there be liability for a detailed news story that accurately reported how an assassination was carried out if another group learns the technique from the article and carries out its own successful assassination?

13. What role should the defendant's motivation play in this type of case? What about the defendant's awareness of the nature of the risk it is creating? Should it be enough that the risk is measured by court or jury after the fact as being unreasonable? Extremely unreasonable? Outrageous?

14. *The Daily Pantagraph Case.* Two girls, 12 and 14, were charged in juvenile proceedings with having sexually abused three young children they were babysitting overnight. In addition, they were alleged to have deliberately dropped one of them on the floor several times, causing a fractured skull. The juvenile court placed them in a detention center.

The girls' names and whereabouts had been released during early stages of the investigation, apparently in connection with charges being filed against an adult in another case. The girls' attorneys told Juvenile Court Judge Baner that as a result of the release, the girls had been the subject of bomb threats and concern for their safety. They asked the judge to order the press not to report the girls' identities or their present locations. The judge issued such an order against a group of local media, some of which sought to upset the order on appeal.

The Illinois Supreme Court, 4–3, refused requests that it hear and decide the case. The media organizations then sought to persuade Justice Stevens, sitting as Circuit Justice, to stay the order of the juvenile court while the organizations prepared to ask the full Supreme Court to review the case. Instead, he distributed the papers to all the justices.

The press argued that a prior restraint could be issued only if "there were an immediate threat of irreparable harm to others which could not be alleviated by means other than a prior restraint." They also argued that since the names and original addresses were already public knowledge and could be disseminated by anyone not subject to Judge Baner's order, the order "cannot protect the juveniles from potential threats to their safety or privacy." The lawyers for the two girls argued that lifting the restraint could result in the death or serious injury of the girls.

The Court, 6–3, without opinion, denied the press organizations' motion to stay Judge Baner's order. The Daily Pantagraph v. Baner, 105 S.Ct. 376 (1984). Justice Brennan, joined by Justices Marshall and Blackmun, dissented: "The trial court found that the names of these individuals, as well as their former location while in custody, had been lawfully released to the public. I would grant the stay with respect to that information. I would also grant the application with respect to any other information that the trial court, after a hearing, finds to have been made public." He cited Near v. Minnesota and his opinion in the Pentagon Papers case.

Why does the fact that the information was once made public absolutely guarantee the right to continue publishing it—even in the face of a claim of physical danger? Does it matter how it was made public? In this case, it appears that on the night in question a 20-year-old man came to the house and had sexual intercourse with the 14-year-old girl. The man was indicted for having intercourse with a minor in an open indictment that named the 14-year-old. Presumably it was not difficult for the press to put two and two together. Is any of this relevant? What if a juvenile judge under statutory authority to make a juvenile's name public in grievous cases, used that discretion here—and then changed his mind after the juveniles, much to the judge's surprise, received death threats?

No formal petition was filed and the case went back to Illinois. In In re M.B. et al., 137 Ill.App.3d 992, 484 N.E.2d 1154, 12 Med.L.Rptr. 1551 (1985), the court upheld the part of the order that barred the media "from revealing directly or indirectly the identity of the minor or the minor victim."

15. In Tumminello v. Bergen Evening Record, Inc., 454 F.Supp. 1156, 3 Med.L.Rptr. 2547 (D.N.J.1978), a reporter understood a judge to say at a meeting that his court would soon render a decision holding that the five-year statute of limitations applied in murder cases. Plaintiff, who was under indictment for murder, read this and became elated. The next day the court held that the statute did *not* apply in murder cases.

The plaintiff alleged that he was rendered "despondent and depressed, suffered in his health, both physically and mentally" and was unable to sleep. He claimed both intentional and negligent infliction of emotional distress. The court held that the intentional tort claim should be dismissed in the absence of an allegation that the defendants knew they were publishing an untrue story and that it was substantially likely to hurt this plaintiff. The judge also doubted that the state's negligence law allowed recovery for these damages. Even if the judge assumed that failure to confirm a story before printing it amounted to recklessness, so as to come within Time, Inc. v. Hill, plaintiff "was not one to whom the defendants owed any particular duty of care." See also Gutter v. Dow Jones, Inc., 22 Ohio St.3d 286, 490 N.E.2d 898, 12 Med.L.Rptr. 1999 (1986), finding no duty to plaintiff who bought bonds after reading false information in the Wall Street Journal. The paper had omitted an "f" in its listings that would have shown that the bonds were trading "flat"—without interest.

16. In Rubinstein v. New York Post, Corp., 128 Misc.2d 1, 488 N.Y.S. 2d 331, 11 Med.L.Rptr. 1329 (1985), the newspaper erroneously reported the plaintiff's death. A negligence action was brought by plaintiff and his wife for emotional distress and loss of consortium. Plaintiff's father sued for emotional distress. A motion to dismiss the claim was granted on the ground that no duty was owed to specific persons in this situation. Even if a duty were to be found, it would not involve checking the accuracy of submitted obituaries before publication. The likelihood of error or, as appears to have been the case here, practical jokes, is so remote that the burden of checking and the delay involved outweigh the potential harm.

WALT DISNEY PRODUCTIONS, INC. v. SHANNON

Supreme Court of Georgia, 1981.
247 Ga. 402, 276 S.E.2d 580, 7 Med.L.Rptr. 1209.
Noted, 33 Mercer L.Rev. 423.

MARSHALL, JUSTICE. In this rather novel lawsuit, a child plaintiff is seeking to subject to tort liability various companies responsible for the broadcast of a children's television program. The plaintiff's complaint is that statements made during the course of the program constituted an invitation, accepted by the plaintiff, to do something posing a foreseeable risk of injury to children of tender years.

The facts giving rise to this case occurred on February 28, 1978, when plaintiff Craig Shannon was watching the "Mickey Mouse Club" on television. It was stated during the course of the program: "Our special feature on today's show is all about the magic you can create with sound effects." One of the participants in this feature proceeded to show the audience how to reproduce the sound of a tire coming off an automobile by putting a BB pellet inside a "large, round balloon," filling the balloon with air, and rotating the BB inside the balloon. Craig, who was 11 years old, undertook to repeat what he had seen on television. He put a piece of lead almost twice the size of a BB into a "large, skinny balloon." He blew up the balloon and the balloon burst, impelling the lead into Craig's eye and partially blinding him. He then brought this tort suit against the producer, syndicator, and broadcaster of the Mickey Mouse Club Show: Walt Disney Productions, Inc., SFM Media Services, and Turner Communications, Inc., respectively.

The trial judge granted the defendants' motions for summary judgment under general tort principles and on First Amendment grounds. The Court of Appeals reversed, refusing to hold as a matter of law that the defendants cannot be held liable in tort for the plaintiff's injuries. . . .

1. The defendants argue that this suit is barred by the First Amendment; and, in so arguing, they rely on New York Times v. Sullivan. . . .

. . .

As was stated in the New York Times decision itself, that case must be considered "against the background of a profound national commitment to the principle that debate on public issues should be uninhibited, robust, and wide-open . . ." 376 U.S. at page 270. There is nothing in the content of what was broadcast in this television program that would bring it within the scope of New York Times. Therefore, we hold that New York Times and its progeny are inapposite here.

2. However, the plaintiff in this case is seeking to hold the defendants liable in tort for statements communicated to the plaintiff through the medium of television. This highlights the fact that this case does involve questions concerning freedom of speech or expression. Therefore, before the defendants can be subjected to liability for the statements uttered during this program, it must be determined whether these statements constitute protected speech within the meaning of the First Amendment.

In determining whether a given form of expression is entitled to protection under the First Amendment, there have evolved various defined categories of speech or communicative conduct which have been held not to be entitled to constitutional protection. [Quoting *Chaplinsky.*] An utterance can be suppressed or penalized on the ground that it tends to incite an immediate breach of peace, if "the words used are used in such circumstances and are of such a nature as to create a clear and present danger that they will bring about the substantive evils that Congress has a right to prevent." Schenck v. United States, 249 U.S. 47, 52 (1919).[2]

We conclude that the Schenck formulation of the "clear and present danger" doctrine provides the appropriate analytical framework for resolving this case. The substantive evil which the tort law seeks to redress is the infliction of personal injury. For reasons which follow, we hold that the defendants' motions for summary judgment were correctly granted by the trial judge, because it cannot be said that the statements uttered during the course of this television program gave rise to a clear and present danger of personal injury to the plaintiff.

3. Here, a child plaintiff is seeking to hold adult defendants liable on the ground that they invited him to do something posing a foreseeable risk of injury. The only arguable precedent for an action such as this is found in a line of so-called "pied piper" cases. "And when children are in the vicinity, much is necessarily to be expected of them which would not be looked for on the part of an adult. It may be anticipated that a child will dash into the street in the path of a car, or meddle with a turntable. It may be clear negligence to entrust him with a gun, or to allow him to drive an automobile, or to throw candy where a crowd of boys will scramble for it. There have been a number of 'pied piper' cases, in which street vendors of ice cream, and the like, which attract children into the street, have been held liable for failure to protect them against traffic." (Footnotes omitted.) Prosser, Law of Torts, 172, 173, § 33 (4th Ed.1971).

As we read the pied piper cases, they contain two basic elements: (1) there must be an express or implied invitation extended to the child to do something posing a foreseeable risk of injury; and (2) the defendant must be chargeable with maintaining or providing the child with the instrumentality causing the injury. In this case, the first element is arguably present, but the second element is undisputably absent.

We can, nonetheless, envision situations in which an adult could be held liable in tort solely on the ground that statements uttered by him constituted an invitation to a child to do something causing the child injury. However, under First Amendment jurisprudence, the adult should not be subjected to liability under such a theory unless what the

2. In the language of Brandenburg v. Ohio, 395 U.S. 444 (1969), the utterance is not protected if it "is directed to inciting or producing imminent lawless action and is likely to incite or produce such action."

In our opinion, [Weirum v. RKO General, Inc., 15 Cal.3d 40, 539 P.2d 36, 123 Cal. Rptr. 468 (1975), and the first appeal in Olivia N. v. National Broadcasting Co., p. 373, infra.] constitute authority for the proposition that a tort defendant can be held liable if the defendant incited, within the meaning of Brandenburg, a third party to commit a crime against the plaintiff. There is nothing in what the plaintiff was allegedly invited to do here that was "imminently lawless." Therefore, even assuming the correctness of the holdings in RKO and Olivia N. under the facts present there, we hold that these decisions are inapposite under the facts here.

adult invited the child to do presented a clear and present danger that injury would in fact result. Although it can be said that what the defendants allegedly invited the child to do in this case posed a foreseeable risk of injury, it cannot be said that it posed a clear and present danger of injury.[4]

Thus, although we conclude in Division 1, supra, that the New York Times line of decisions is not applicable here as such, we do hold that this case is governed by a constitutionally mandated standard of care that is essentially the same as the New York Times "limited immunity" rule. Therefore, we agree with the trial judge that this suit is barred by the First Amendment. To hold otherwise would, as the saying goes, open the Pandora's box; and it would, in our opinion, have a seriously chilling effect on the flow of protected speech through society's mediums of communication.

Judgment reversed.

All the Justices concur, except JORDAN, C.J., concurs in the judgment only.

SMITH, J., disqualified.

Notes and Questions

1. How does *Shannon* differ from *Hyde*? What standard (if any) is appropriate in each case? What role does the First Amendment play in each case?

2. In Walter v. Bauer, 109 Misc.2d 189, 439 N.Y.S.2d 821 (1981), a fourth-grade student claimed that he had suffered an eye injury while performing a science experiment with a ruler and rubber band. The experiment was in a book published by defendant. Plaintiff claimed that strict liability applied because the experiment contained an unreasonable risk of harm for young children. The court disagreed. Strict liability was intended "to protect the customer from defectively produced merchandise." The "plaintiff was not injured by use of the book for the purpose for which it was designed, i.e., to be read." More important was the chilling effect strict liability would have on publishers and authors. "Would any author wish to be exposed to liability for writing on a topic which might result in physical injury? e.g. How to cut trees; how to keep bees?" *Walter* was affirmed, 88 App.Div.2d 787, 451 N.Y.S.2d 533 (1982).

3. In 1980, a jury returned a verdict in what was said to be the first case in which a textbook publisher was held liable for what the jury found confusing and misleading language that led to personal injury. Two experiments in a section of a science book called for methyl alcohol; a third, calibrating an alcohol thermometer by heating and then cooling, did not call for methyl alcohol but did not warn against its use either. Students used methyl alcohol for the thermometer experi-

4. In this connection, it is relevant that the evidence shows that of an estimated 16 million children watching this program, only the plaintiff in this case reported an injury.

ment and two were badly burned when it exploded. The defendant argued that although 390,000 copies of the book had been distributed, this was the first complaint. The awards totalled $825,000. No appeal was taken. Bertrand v. Rand McNally & Co. (D.Mass.1980) reported in National Law Journal, Sept. 22, 1980 at 3.

4. In Alm v. Van Nostrand Reinhold Co., Inc., 134 Ill.App.3d 716, 480 N.E.2d 1263, 89 Ill.Dec. 520 (1985), plaintiff alleged that he was injured while following instructions in a book published by defendant entitled "The Making of Tools." The dismissal of plaintiff's action based on a negligent failure to warn was affirmed on appeal, using state law. If plaintiff's theory were adopted, it "would place upon publishers the duty of scrutinizing and even testing all procedures contained in any of their publications. The scope of liability would extend to an undeterminable number of potential readers."

The court adhered to an earlier case, MacKown v. Illinois Publishing & Printing Co., 289 Ill.App. 59, 6 N.E.2d 526 (1937), which refused to impose liability on a newspaper for physical injuries the reader suffered from using a dandruff remedy recommended in an article. Are newspapers comparable to publishers of books? Is there a difference between harm from following an advertisement in the paper and harm from following something in a column?

Plaintiff in *Alm* sought to distinguish "bad advice in a 'How To' book from 'a treatise on politics, religion, philosophy, interpersonal relationships, or the like.'" The court thought such an effort would lead to impermissible content-based discriminations. "More important . . . is the chilling effect which liability would have upon publishers . . . . Even if liability could be imposed consistently with the Constitution, we believe that the adverse effect of such liability upon the public's free access to ideas would be too high a price to pay."

What about a suit against the author?

5. In DeFilippo v. Nat'l Broadcasting Co., Inc., 446 A.2d 1036, 8 Med.L. Rptr. 1872 (R.I. 1982), plaintiffs' 13-year-old son was watching the Tonight show with Johnny Carson and his guest, a professional stuntman named Robinson. Carson announced that after the commercial break he would attempt a stunt that involved dropping through a trapdoor with a noose around his neck. Robinson then said "Believe me, it's not something that you want to go and try. This is a stunt. . . ." The audience began to laugh, producing the following dialogue:

Robinson: I've got to laugh—you know, you're all laughing . . . .

Carson: Explain that to me.

Robinson: I've seen people try things like this. I really have. I happen to know somebody who did something similar to it, just fooling around, and almost broke his neck . . . .

The commercial break followed. After the break, Carson did the stunt accompanied by comic dialogue. Carson came through unscathed. Several hours after the broadcast, plaintiffs' son was found hanging from a noose in front of the television set which was still on and tuned to the station that had presented the Tonight show.

The plaintiffs asserted a variety of theories, including defective products, negligence, failure to warn, and intentional tort-trespass. The court upheld the trial judge's summary judgment on the ground that the First Amendment barred all actions. It identified four classes of speech that states may proscribe: obscenity, fighting words, defamation, and "words likely to produce imminent lawless action (incitement)." Only the incitement theory was possible here and that failed because the son was apparently the only person who is alleged to have "emulated the action portrayed" on the show. Moreover, the quoted dialogue indicated that those on the show tried to prevent emulation—and certainly did not invite it. To permit recovery here "on the basis of one minor's action would invariably lead to self-censorship by broadcasters in order to remove any matter that may be emulated and lead to a law suit."

Which is more central—that the participants sought to discourage emulation or that only one person tried to emulate? The case is noted in 6 W.New Eng.L.Rev. 897 (1984).

6. It is generally held, often as the result of so-called Printer's Ink statutes, that publishers are not liable for harm caused readers by advertisements unless the publisher knew of the danger created by the advertised product, or of the dishonesty of the ad. See Yuhas v. Mudge, 129 N.J.Super. 207, 332 A.2d 824 (1974) (Popular Mechanics not liable for injury that reader suffered when he bought defective fireworks that had been advertised in the magazine).

7. See also Herceg v. Hustler Magazine, Inc., 565 F.Supp. 802, 9 Med. L.Rptr. 1959 (S.D.Tex.1983), rejecting a claim that sought to tie decedent's death to his reading of an article on the practice of "autoerotic asphyxiation," entitled "Orgasm of Death." The claim was that the article was an attractive nuisance or a dangerous instrumentality.

8. See Note, Media Liability for Injuries that Result from Television Broadcasts to Immature Audiences, 22 San Diego L.Rev. 377 (1985).

OLIVIA N. v. NATIONAL BROADCASTING CO.

Court of Appeal of California, 1981.
126 Cal.App.3d 488, 178 Cal.Rptr. 888, 7 Med.L.Rptr. 2359.
Certiorari denied, 458 U.S. 1108 (1982).

CHRISTIAN, J. Olivia N. appeals from a judgment of nonsuit terminating her action against the National Broadcasting Company and the Chronicle Broadcasting Company. Appellant sought damages for physical and emotional injury inflicted by assailants who had seen a television broadcast of a film drama.

A defense motion for summary judgment was denied, and the case was set for trial by jury. Before impanelment of a jury the trial court viewed the film and determined for itself that the film did not serve to incite violent and depraved conduct such as the crimes committed against the plaintiff and on that basis rendered judgment for defendants.

On appeal from the judgment this court recognized that certain narrowly limited classes of speech may be prevented or punished by the state consistent with the principles of the First Amendment and held that "the trial court's action in viewing the film, and thereupon making fact findings and rendering judgment for respondents, was a violation of appellant's constitutional right to trial by jury." (Olivia N. v. National Broadcasting Co. (1977) 74 Cal.App.3d 383, 389 [141 Cal.Rptr. 511].) Therefore, the judgment was reversed with directions to impanel a jury and proceed to trial of the action. [Certiorari was denied, 435 U.S. 1000 (1978)].

On remand, appellant's counsel in his opening statement to the jury indicated that the evidence would establish negligence and recklessness on respondents' part, rather than incitement.[1] At the conclusion of appellant's opening statement, respondents moved for a judgment of nonsuit [ ] on the grounds that appellant admittedly could not meet the test for incitement. (Brandenburg v. Ohio (1969) 395 U.S. 444, 447.) Appellant's counsel again acknowledged his inability to meet the incitement test; the trial court granted respondents' motion and rendered judgment dismissing the action. Plaintiff again appealed.

. . . Where a nonsuit is granted on the opening statement, factual recitals in the opening statement must be accepted as true. [ ]

At 8 p.m. on September 10, 1974, NBC telecast nationwide, and Chronicle Broadcasting Company broadcast locally, a film entitled "Born Innocent." "The subject matter of the television film was the harmful effect of a state-run home upon an adolescent girl who had become a ward of the state. In one scene of the film, the young girl enters the community bathroom of the facility to take a shower. She is then shown taking off her clothes and stepping into the shower, where she bathes for a few moments. Suddenly, the water stops and a look of fear comes across her face. Four adolescent girls are standing across from her in the shower room. One of the girls is carrying a 'plumber's

1. Appellant's counsel stated that: "The plaintiffs in this case at no time in this trial are going to prove what is known as 'incitement.'

"At no time in this trial are we going to prove that either through negligence or recklessness there was incitement, which incitement is telling someone to go out encouraging them, directing them, advising them; that there will be no evidence that NBC ever told anybody or incited anyone to go out and rape a girl with an artificial instrument or in any other way.

"So at all times during this trial, I want you to have in mind, ladies and gentlemen, that all of our proof will not be based on any type of incitement, but will be based on stimulation, foreseeability, negligence, proximate cause."

helper,' waving it suggestively by her side. The four girls violently attack the younger girl, wrestling her to the floor. The young girl is shown naked from the waist up, struggling as the older girls force her legs apart. Then, the television film shows the girl with the plumber's helper making intense thrusting motions with the handle of the plunger until one of the four says, 'That's enough.' The young girl is left sobbing and naked on the floor." [quoted from earlier appeal] It is alleged that on September 14, 1974, appellant, aged 9, was attacked and forcibly "artificially raped" with a bottle by minors at a San Francisco beach. [ ] The assailants had viewed and discussed the "artificial rape" scene in "Born Innocent," and the film allegedly caused the assailants to decide to commit a similar act on appellant. Appellant offered to show that NBC had knowledge of studies on child violence and should have known that susceptible persons might imitate the crime enacted in the film. Appellant alleged that "Born Innocent" was particularly likely to cause imitation and that NBC televised the film without proper warning in an effort to obtain the largest possible viewing audience. Appellant alleged that as a proximate result of respondents' telecast, she suffered physical and psychological damage.

Appellant contends that where there is negligence, liability could constitutionally be imposed despite the absence of proof of incitement as defined in Brandenburg v. Ohio, [ ]. Appellant argues in the alternative that a different definition of "incitement" should be applied to the present circumstances.

"Analysis of this appeal commences with recognition of the overriding constitutional principle that material communicated by the public media, including fictional material such as the television drama here at issue, is generally to be accorded protection under the First Amendment to the Constitution of the United States. (Joseph Burstyn, Inc. v. Wilson (1952) 343 U.S. 495, 501 [ ]; Winters v. New York (1948) 333 U.S. 507, 510 [ ].)" (*Olivia N. v. National Broadcasting Co.,* supra). First Amendment rights are accorded a preferred place in our democratic society. [ ] First Amendment protection extends to a communication, to its source and to its recipients. (Va. Pharmacy Bd. v. Va. Consumer Council (1976) 425 U.S. 748, 756.) "[A]bove all else, the First Amendment means that government has no power to restrict expression because of its message, its ideas, its subject matter, or its content." (Police Department of Chicago v. Mosley (1972) 408 U.S. 92, 95; [ ])

. . .

Motion pictures are accorded First Amendment protections. (Joseph Burstyn, Inc. v. Wilson, [ ]. "[T]he central concern of the First Amendment in this area is that there be a free flow from creator to audience of whatever message a film or a book might convey . . . . [T]he central First Amendment concern remains the need to maintain free access of the public to the expression." (Young v. American Mini Theatres (1976) 427 U.S. 50, 77 [conc. opn. of Powell, J.]) Freedom of speech is not limited to political expression or comment on public affairs. [*Hill*], Free speech must "embrace all issues about which information is needed or appropriate to enable the members of society to cope with the exigencies of their period." (Thornhill v. Alabama (1940) 310 U.S. 88, 102.) The commercial nature of an enterprise does not introduce a nonspeech element or relax the scrutiny required by the First Amendment. [ ]

The electronic media are also entitled to First Amendment protection. . . .

Appellant does not seek to impose a prior restraint on speech, rather, she asserts civil liability premised on traditional negligence concepts. But the chilling effect of permitting negligence actions for a television broadcast is obvious. "The fear of damage awards . . . may be markedly more inhibiting than the fear of prosecution under a criminal statute." (New York Times Co. v. Sullivan, [ ].) Realistically, television networks would become significantly more inhibited in the selection of controversial materials if liability were to be imposed on a simple negligence theory. "[T]he pall of fear and timidity imposed upon those who would give voice to public criticism is an atmosphere in which the First Amendment freedoms cannot survive." [Id. at 278] The deterrent effect of subjecting the television networks to negligence liability because of their programming choices would lead to self-censorship which would dampen the vigor and limit the variety of public debate. (Id., at p. 279.)

Although the First Amendment is not absolute, the television broadcast of "Born Innocent" does not, on the basis of the opening statement of appellant's attorney, fall within the scope of unprotected speech. Appellant concedes that the film did not advocate or encourage violent acts and did not constitute an "incitement" within the meaning of [*Brandenburg*]. Notwithstanding the pervasive effect of the broadcasting media (see FCC v. Pacifica Foundation (1978) 438 U.S. 726, 748; Note, The Future of Content Regulation in Broadcasting (1981) 69 Cal.L.Rev. 555, 580–581) and the unique access afforded children [*Pacifica Foundation*], the effect of the imposition of liability could reduce the U.S. adult population to viewing only what is fit for children. (See Butler v. Michigan (1957) 352 U.S. 380, 383.) Incitement is the proper test here. (See Kingsley Pictures Corp. v. Regents (1959) 360 U.S. 684, 688.) In areas outside of obscenity the United States Supreme Court has "consistently held that the fact that protected speech may be offensive to some does not justify its suppression. See, e.g., Cohen v. California, 403 U.S. 15 (1971)." (Carey v. Population Services International (1977) 431 U.S. 678, 701.) Just as the advertising in *Carey,* supra, was not "directed to inciting or producing imminent lawless action and . . . likely to incite or produce such action" [ ] the television broadcast which is the subject of this action concededly did not fulfill the incitement requirements of *Brandenburg.* Thus it is constitutionally protected.

Appellant would distinguish between the fictional presentation of "Born Innocent" and news programs and documentaries. But that distinction is too blurred to protect adequately First Amendment values. "Everyone is familiar with instances of propaganda through fiction. What is one man's amusement, teaches another's doctrine." [Winters v. New York] If a negligence theory is recognized, a television network or local station could be liable when a child imitates activities portrayed in a news program or documentary. Thus, the distinction urged by appellant cannot be accepted. (See Krattenmaker and Powe, Jr., Televised Violence: First Amendment Principles and Social Science Theory (1978) 64 Va.L.Rev. 1123, 1169 fn. 253. For a similar conclusion regarding content regulation, see Note, Regulation of Programming Content to Protect Children After Pacifica (1979) 32 Vand.L.Rev. 1377, 1410–1411.) "Among free men, the deterrents ordinarily to be applied to prevent crime are education and punishment for violations of the law, not abridgment of the rights of free speech . . . ." (*Whitney* [Brandeis, J., concurring] overruled by [*Brandenburg*]; [ ]). The trial court's determination that the First Amendment bars appellant's claim where no incitement is alleged must be upheld.

Appellant argues from Weirum v. RKO General, Inc. (1975) 15 Cal. 3d 40 [123 Cal.Rptr. 468, 539 P.2d 36], that the First Amendment should not bar a negligence action. In *Weirum,* the California Supreme Court upheld a jury finding that a Los Angeles rock radio station was liable for the wrongful death of a motorist killed by two teenagers participating in a contest sponsored by the station. The court emphasized that the youthful contestants' reckless conduct was stimulated by the radio station's broadcast. (Id., at p. 47.) Limiting its ruling, the court indicated that "[t]he giveaway contest was no commonplace invitation to an attraction available on a limited basis. It was a competitive scramble in which the thrill of the chase to be the one and only victor was intensified by the live broadcasts which accompanied the pursuit. . . . In [other] situations there [was] no attempt, as here, to generate a competitive pursuit on public streets, accelerated by *repeated importuning* by radio to be the very first to arrive at a particular destination." (Id., at p. 48; italics added.) Disposing of the radio station's First Amendment claim, the court said: "Defendant's contention that the giveaway contest must be afforded the deference due society's interest in the First Amendment is clearly without merit. The issue here is civil accountability for the foreseeable results of a broadcast which created an undue risk of harm to decedent. The First Amendment does not sanction the infliction of physical injury merely because achieved by word, rather than act." (Id.) Although the language utilized by the Supreme Court was broad, it must be understood in light of the particular facts of that case. The radio station's broadcast was designed to encourage its youthful listeners to be the first to arrive at a particular location in order to win a prize and gain momentary glory. The *Weirum* broadcasts actively and repeatedly encouraged listeners to speed to announced locations. Liability was imposed on the broadcaster for urging listeners to act in an inherently dangerous manner. No such urging can be imputed to respondents here. Appellant only alleges that the teenage viewers of "Born Innocent" acted on the stimulus of the broadcast rather than in response to encouragement of such conduct. *Weirum* does not control the present case.

Appellant also relies on [*Pacifica*]. But the narrowness of the *Pacifica* decision precludes its application here. "We simply hold that when the Commission finds that a pig has entered the parlor, the exercise of its *regulatory* power does not depend on proof that the pig is obscene." ([ ]; italics added.) Furthermore, Justice Powell in his concurrence emphasized that the court is not free "to decide on the basis of its content which speech protected by the First Amendment is most 'valuable' and hence deserving of the most protection, and which is less 'valuable' and hence deserving of less protection." [ ] As the United States District Court indicated in Zamora v. Columbia Broadcasting System, supra, 480 F.Supp. 199, 206, reliance on FCC v. Pacifica Foundation "is misplaced because of both the factual and legal bases for that decision." Other methods of controlling violence on television must be found. *Pacifica* deals with regulation of indecency, not the imposition of general tort liability. Imposing liability on a simple negligence theory here would frustrate vital freedom of speech guarantees. Gertz v. Robert Welch, Inc. (1974) 418 U.S. 323, is also to be distinguished: There the United States Supreme Court recognized the power of the states to impose civil liability for defamation "so long as the States [do] not impose liability without fault." The holding does not extend more broadly to tort liability for speech in areas outside the law of defamation.

The judgment is affirmed.

CALDECOTT, P.J., and POCHÉ, J., concurred.

[The California Supreme Court denied a hearing, 5–2.]

Notes and Questions

1. Is there any possible showing that should entitle plaintiff to a judgment against NBC? What if the plaintiff can show that NBC officials had been warned by psychologists that the program was likely to provoke imitation? Is it significant that there was only one reported case of imitation? What if plaintiff can show only that the attackers heard about the program from friends but that none of them saw it? Is it relevant that the show was presented at 8:00 p.m.?

2. Is there a difference between the "Born Innocent" program and a news story (or broadcast) that reports the details of a recent case of torture in the city—which is then imitated? What about live coverage of a hostage situation that leads to imitations?

3. Is the Weirum case adequately distinguished?

4. Is the defamation area adequately distinguished?

5. In Bill v. Superior Court, 137 Cal.App.3d 1002, 187 Cal.Rptr. 625 (1982), a person was shot by someone who had seen "Boulevard Nights." The claim against the movie theater was that it knew or should have known that the violent movie would attract persons prone to violence who were likely to cause bodily harm to persons at or near the movie. The court thought that essentially the same concerns as in *Olivia N* were involved here, though perhaps less directly because this plaintiff did not rely on the content of the film as the basis of liability. Relying on common law analysis, the court dismissed the case.

The challenged activity—producing and distributing a motion picture—was "socially unobjectionable" even if it had the tendency to attract violence-prone individuals. The proper analysis was in the tort "duty to warn" area. Here the court concluded we live "regrettably, in a violence-prone society. . . . The nature of the warnings that would be required . . . would of necessity be general in nature, and addressed to the public at large. And, there is nothing that the public could effectively do in response to such a warning" except to stay away from the area of the theater. "It seems unlikely that a volume of such warnings would contribute measurably to the effective protection of the public."

6. How does *Olivia N.* differ from *Shannon*? From *Hyde*?

7. *The Zamora Case.* In Florida, 15-year-old Ronald Zamora was convicted of murdering his 83-year-old neighbor and was sentenced to a long prison term. He sued all three networks claiming that between the ages of 5 and 15 he had become involuntarily addicted to, and "completely subliminally intoxicated" by, extensive viewing of television violence. He claimed that the networks had "impermissibly stimulated, incited and instigated" him to duplicate the atrocities he viewed on television. He alleged further that he had developed a sociopathic personality, had become desensitized to violent behavior, and had become a danger to himself and others. The trial judge dismissed the complaint. Zamora v. Columbia Broadcasting System, 480 F.Supp. 199, 5 Med.L.Rptr. 2109 (S.D.Fla.1979).

The judge refused to impose any tort obligation on the networks because he concluded that courts lack "the legal and institutional capacity to identify isolated depictions of violence, let alone the ability to set the standard for media dissemination of items containing 'violence' in one form or the other. Airway dissemination is, and to some extent, should be regulated, but not on the basis or by the [tort] procedure suggested by the plaintiffs." The judge was alluding to regulatory controls on broadcasting of the sort that we will discuss in Chapter XV. Why have radio and television been so prominent in this area?

To the extent plaintiff was arguing for the regulation of programming that would adversely affect "susceptible" viewers, the judge indicated that the "imposition of such a generally undefined and undefinable duty would be an unconstitutional exercise by this Court in any event." Plaintiffs "would place broadcasters in jeopardy for televising Hamlet, Julius Caesar, Grimm's Fairy Tales; more contemporary offerings such as All Quiet On The Western Front, and even The Holocaust; and indeed would render John Wayne a risk not acceptable by any but the boldest broadcasters."

The judge observed, however, that "One day, medical or other sciences with or without the cooperation of programmers may convince the F.C.C. or the Courts that the delicate balance of First Amendment rights should be altered to permit some additional limitations in programming." But this case did not present such an occasion.

The judge implied that the plaintiff's approach in the Born Innocent case was stronger because of its claim that a specific program stimulated the harmful conduct. Is that a sound distinction?

Intentional Emotional Distress. A few cases proceed on the theory of intentional infliction of emotional distress.

In one case an undercover narcotics agent, Burns, was on his way to the courthouse to testify at a preliminary hearing. Ross and Wreford, reporters for an Ann Arbor newspaper, began to photograph him. A photograph of Burns appeared in the newspaper above the caption "Know Your Enemies," accompanying an article decrying the activities of undercover narcotics agents in the Ann Arbor area. One issue in Ross v. Burns, 612 F.2d 271, 5 Med.L.Rptr. 2277 (6th Cir.1980), was a jury award of $5,000 compensatory and $35,000 punitive damages against the reporters for intentional infliction of emotional distress.

On appeal, the court held that an essential element of that tort—extreme and outrageous conduct—had not been shown. Photographing an undercover agent in a public place and identifying him in conjunction with a news article expressing strong views on a current controversy could not amount to the requisite conduct. "The actor's motivation, however deplorable, is a separate question which must not be allowed to infect the objective assessment of his conduct." Having disposed of the case on state grounds, the court did not reach the constitutional claims of the reporters. Why did Burns press no privacy claim?

See the cases discussed in Dreschel, Intentional Infliction of Emotional Distress: New Tort Liability for Mass Media, 89 Dick.L.Rev. 339 (1985).

More recently, Hustler Magazine carried an "Ad Parody—Not to Be Taken Seriously" that included a fake interview with the Reverend Jerry Falwell that implied that he was a "hypocritical incestuous drunkard." Falwell sued for libel and for intentional infliction of emotional distress. Hustler publisher Larry Flynt testified that he intended to cause Falwell emotional distress. The jury found that the material was so clearly parody that no reader could reasonably have taken it as fact. But the jury awarded Falwell $200,000 for emotional distress.

The trial judge entered judgment on the verdict. Flynt's intention removed whatever protection the First Amendment might have offered. Falwell v. Flynt (W.D.Va.1985). The unreported case is discussed in Hustler Magazine, Inc. v. Moral Majority, Inc., 606 F.Supp. 1526 (C.D.Cal. 1985) and in Note, 85 Colum.L.Rev. 1749 (1985).

The court of appeals affirmed. Falwell v. Flynt, 797 F.2d 1270, 13 Med.L.Rptr. 1145 (4th Cir. 1986). The court noted that during his deposition Flynt gave himself several other names and said the parody had been written by Yoko Ono and Billy Idol. Flynt testified that he wanted to upset Falwell. When asked if he knew that his publication had portrayed Falwell as a liar, Flynt replied "A. He's a glutton. Q. How about a hypocrite? A. Yeah. . . . Q. And, wasn't one of your objectives to destroy [Falwell's] integrity, or harm it, if you could? A. To assassinate it."

Although the court agreed that the defendants were "entitled to the same level of first amendment protection in the claim for intentional infliction of emotional distress that they received in Falwell's claim for libel," this did not mean "literal application of the actual malice standard." The court held "that when the first amendment requires application of the actual malice standard, the standard is met when the jury finds that the defendant's intentional or reckless misconduct has proximately caused the injury complained of."

The court also rejected Flynt's contention that since the jury found that the parody could not be taken literally, it must be opinion and be constitutionally protected. The tort is concerned with outrageous conduct and not with "statements per se." The issue was whether the publication "was sufficiently outrageous to constitute intentional infliction of emotional distress."

The intentional element could be found from Flynt's deposition testimony. The outrageousness "is quite obvious from the language in the parody and in the fact that Flynt republished the parody after this lawsuit was filed." The final elements, showing that the conduct caused serious emotional distress, were established by Falwell's testimony that he had never had a personal experience as intense as the feeling he had when he first saw the parody. "Since I have been a Christian I don't think I have ever intentionally hurt anyone. . . . I really think that at that moment if Larry Flynt had been nearby I might have physically reacted." A colleague testified that Falwell's "enthusiasm and optimism visibly suffered" as a result of the parody; and that his "ability to concentrate on the myriad details of running his extensive ministry was diminished." That was enough to permit recovery. (See Godbout v. Cousens, 396 Mass. 254, 485 N.E.2d 940 (1985)).

Chapter V

PROTECTING CREATIVE ACTIVITY

In this Chapter we explore situations in which the legal system seeks to protect and encourage the creativity of its citizens. This may be achieved by a statute—such as the copyright law, which uses damage actions to discourage copying another's creation—or by common law tort actions. Occasionally the criminal law may be involved. In previous chapters, it has been easy to predict that the media would be on a particular side of a controversy. In this Chapter, we will sometimes find media as plaintiffs and sometimes as defendants—and sometimes suing each other.

Although many problems in copyright law involve fiction, we will stress plaintiffs' attempts to protect material in the nonfiction sector—or in which defendants justify their invasion of plaintiffs' otherwise protected domain on the ground that the public should have the information obtained.

Historically, this protection was first achieved through copyright law. Since later developments have been shaped by analogy to copyright, it is an appropriate starting point.

A. COPYRIGHT PROTECTION

The laws of copyright are among the most conspicuous but least condemned restraints on freedom of expression. Article I, § 8, of the Constitution gives Congress the power "to promote the progress of science and useful arts by securing for limited times to authors and inventors the exclusive right to their respective writings and discoveries . . . ." The first Congress used that authority to adopt copyright legislation, and it has been with us in some form ever since.

The origins of copyright are interwoven with the licensing procedures discussed in Chapter I. One technique for controlling the printing press was to organize printers into a group that became known as the Stationers Company. The Crown granted to that company a monopoly on all printing, with the power to seek out and suppress material published by non-members who violated the monopoly. The Crown's goal was to deter seditious libel and other objectionable material. The printers, for their part, seized on the monopoly situation to control reproduction of whatever they printed. The result was the licensed printers' right to control copies based on the censorship of the 16th and 17th centuries. When licensing was discontinued in 1695, the rights of the printers were undermined. They petitioned Parliament to adopt protections resembling what they had had under the licensing schemes. In 1709 Parliament responded with the Statute of Anne, which has set the pattern for copyright legislation both in England and in this country. The Stationers Company remained, but its new role was to register printed material to protect that material against unauthorized copying.

The first Congress adopted a similar procedure: printed matter could be protected if a copy was filed with the newly established copyright office, headed by the "Register of Copyrights." The types of writings protected and the period of protection have been expanded since the 1790 statute, which protected only books, maps, and charts for a period of 14 years plus renewal for a second 14-year term.

In 1976, the copyright statute enacted in 1909 was replaced with new legislation that preserves the basic philosophical strands of copyright law, including the denial of copyright for federal government documents. Changes have been made in legal technicalities as well as to accommodate media that emerged after 1909 and did not easily fit within the old framework.*

Section 102 of the new legislation sets out the basic pattern of protection when it states that copyright protection subsists in "original works of authorship fixed in any tangible medium of expression, now known or later developed, from which they can be perceived, reproduced, or otherwise communicated, either directly or with the aid of a machine or device." The statute lists such categories as literary works, musical works, dramatic works, motion pictures, and sound recordings as coming within "works of authorship." The section then states the other side of the coin: "In no case does copyright protection for an original work of authorship extend to any idea, procedure, process, system, method of operation, concept, principle, or discovery, regardless of the form in which it is described, explained, illustrated, or embodied in such work." (17 U.S.C. § 102)

1. Section 106 states the nature of the protection extended to the copyright owner:

   Subject to sections 107 through 118, the owner of copyright under this title has the exclusive right to do and to authorize any of the following:

   (1) to reproduce the copyrighted work in copies or phonorecords;

   (2) to prepare derivative works based upon the copyrighted work;

* Under the 1909 statute, published works were protected by federal law while unpublished works were protected under state law. Under the new legislation, all protection is to be found in a single national framework. Copyright protection used to last for 28 years with the opportunity to renew for another 28 years. Under the new statute, copyrights last for the author's life plus 50 years—as in most other countries. Copyright notices must still be affixed to published works but omission or error in placing the notice will no longer result in automatic forfeiture of the copyright.

(3) to distribute copies or phonorecords of the copyrighted work to the public by sale or other transfer of ownership, or by rental, lease, or lending;

(4) in the case of literary, musical, dramatic, and choreographic works, pantomimes, and motion pictures and other audiovisual works, to perform the copyrighted work publicly; and

(5) in the case of literary, musical, dramatic, and choreographic works, pantomimes, and pictorial, graphic, or sculptural works, including the individual images of a motion picture or other audiovisual work, to display the copyrighted work publicly.

The significance of § 106 is suggested in a case in which the Court, 5–4, held that the use of videotape recorders did not infringe the copyrights of the producers of the programs that were copied. Sony Corp. of America v. Universal City Studios, 464 U.S. 417 (1984). The majority began by noting that the "monopoly privileges that Congress may authorize are neither unlimited nor primarily designed to provide a special private benefit. Rather, the limited grant is a means by which an important public purpose may be achieved. It is intended to motivate the creative activity of authors and inventors by the provision of a special reward, and to allow the public access to the products of their genius after the limited period of exclusive control has expired."

The Court also observed that the clause assigned Congress the primary responsibility for defining the scope of protection. "Because the task involves a difficult balance between the interests of authors and inventors in the control and exploitation of their writings and discoveries on the one hand, and society's competing interest in the free flow of ideas, information, and commerce on the other hand, our patent and copyright statutes have been amended repeatedly."

In this case, dealing with new technology, the majority stressed that the "judiciary's reluctance to expand the protections afforded by the copyright without explicit legislative guidance is a recurring theme. [ ] Sound policy, as well as history, supports our consistent deference to Congress when major technological innovations alter the market for copyrighted materials."

The only protections accorded copyright are statutory and are listed in § 106. An "unlicensed use of the copyright is not an infringement unless it conflicts with one of the specific exclusive rights conferred by the copyright statute." Beyond that, § 106 is explicitly made subject to a cluster of following sections, including the central § 107, dealing with fair use.

Fair Use. As noted, the grant of rights to the owner of the copyright is conditioned on a series of limitations expressed in §§ 107–118. These include permitting libraries to make one photocopy of an article and permitting persons to make phonograph records of music without permission upon payment of certain royalties. Section 111 deals with the cable television problem. Probably the most important of these limitations is found in § 107, dealing with the problem of fair use. Until the 1976 statute, fair use had been left to develop as a judicially created exception to the rights of the copyright owner. There was great controversy over whether to recognize the defense explicitly and, if so, how to do it. The result is § 107:

> Notwithstanding the provisions of section 106, the fair use of a copyrighted work, including such use by reproduction in copies or phonorecords or by any other means specified by that section, for purposes such as criticism, comment, news reporting, teaching (including multiple copies for classroom use), scholarship, or research, is not an infringement of copyright. In determining whether the use made of a work in any particular case is a fair use the factors to be considered shall include—
>
> (1) the purpose and character of the use, including whether such use is of a commercial nature or is for nonprofit educational purposes;
>
> (2) the nature of the copyrighted work;
>
> (3) the amount and substantiality of the portion used in relation to the copyrighted work as a whole; and
>
> (4) the effect of the use upon the potential market for or value of the copyrighted work.

HARPER & ROW, PUBLISHERS, INC. v. NATION ENTERPRISES

Supreme Court of the United States, 1985.
471 U.S. ___, 105 S.Ct. 2218, 85 L.Ed.2d 588, 11 Med.L.Rptr. 1969.
Noted, 99 Harv.L.Rev. 292.

JUSTICE O'CONNOR delivered the opinion of the Court.

This case requires us to consider to what extent the "fair use" provision of the Copyright Revision Act of 1976, 17 U.S.C. § 107 (hereinafter the Copyright Act), sanctions the unauthorized use of quotations from a public figure's unpublished manuscript. In March 1979, an undisclosed source provided The Nation magazine with the unpublished manuscript of "A Time to Heal: The Autobiography of Gerald R. Ford." Working directly from the purloined manuscript, an editor of The Nation produced a short piece entitled "The Ford Memoirs—Behind the Nixon Pardon." The piece was timed to "scoop" an article scheduled shortly to appear in Time magazine. Time had agreed to purchase the exclusive right to print prepublication excerpts from the copyright holders, Harper & Row Publishers, Inc. (hereinafter Harper & Row) and Reader's Digest Association, Inc. (hereinafter Reader's Digest). As a result of The Nation article, Time canceled its agreement. Petitioners brought a successful copyright action [for

$12,500] against The Nation. On appeal, the Second Circuit reversed the lower court's finding of infringement, holding that The Nation's act was sanctioned as a "fair use" of the copyrighted material. We granted certiorari, [ ], and we now reverse.

. . .

II

We agree with the Court of Appeals that copyright is intended to increase and not to impede the harvest of knowledge. But we believe the Second Circuit gave insufficient deference to the scheme established by the Copyright Act for fostering the original works that provide the seed and substance of this harvest. The rights conferred by copyright are designed to assure contributors to the store of knowledge a fair return for their labors.

Article I, § 8, of the Constitution provides that:

> "The Congress shall have Power . . . to Promote the Progress of Science and useful Arts, by securing for limited Times to Authors and Inventors the exclusive Right to their respective Writings and Discoveries."

As we noted last Term, "[this] limited grant is a means by which an important public purpose may be achieved. It is intended to motivate the creative activity of authors and inventors by the provision of a special reward, and to allow the public access to the products of their genius after the limited period of exclusive control has expired." [*Sony*] "The monopoly created by copyright thus rewards the individual author in order to benefit the public." Id., at 477 (dissenting opinion). This principle applies equally to works of fiction and nonfiction. The book at issue here, for example, was two years in the making, and began with a contract giving the author's copyright to the publishers in exchange for their services in producing and marketing the work. In preparing the book, Mr. Ford drafted essays and word portraits of public figures and participated in hundreds of taped interviews that were later distilled to chronicle his personal viewpoint. It is evident that the monopoly granted by copyright actively served its intended purpose of inducing the creation of new material of potential historical value.

Section 106 of the Copyright Act confers a bundle of exclusive rights to the owner of the copyright. Under the Copyright Act, these rights—to publish, copy, and distribute the author's work—vest in the author of an original work from the time of its creation. In practice, the author commonly sells his rights to publishers who offer royalties in exchange for their services in producing and marketing the author's work. The copyright owner's rights, however, are subject to certain statutory exceptions. Among these is § 107 which codifies the traditional privilege of other authors to make "fair use" of an earlier writer's work. In addition, no author may copyright facts or ideas.

The copyright is limited to those aspects of the work—termed "expression"—that display the stamp of the author's originality.

Creation of a nonfiction work, even a compilation of pure fact, entails originality. . . . The copyright holders of "A Time to Heal" complied with the relevant statutory notice and registration procedures. Thus there is no dispute that the unpublished manuscript of "A Time to Heal," as a whole, was protected by § 106 from unauthorized reproduction. Nor do respondents dispute that verbatim copying of excerpts of the manuscript's original form of expression would constitute infringement unless excused as fair use. [ ] Yet copyright does not prevent subsequent users from copying from a prior author's work those constituent elements that are not original—for example, quotations borrowed under the rubric of fair use from other copyrighted works, facts, or materials in the public domain—as long as such use does not unfairly appropriate the author's original contributions. [ ] Perhaps the controversy between the lower courts in this case over copyrightability is more aptly styled a dispute over whether The Nation's appropriation of unoriginal and uncopyrightable elements encroached on the originality embodied in the work as a whole. Especially in the realm of factual narrative, the law is currently unsettled regarding the ways in which uncopyrightable elements combine with the author's original contributions to form protected expression. . . .

We need not reach these issues, however, as The Nation has admitted to lifting verbatim quotes of the author's original language totalling between 300 and 400 words and constituting some 13% of [the 2,250 words in] The Nation article. In using generous verbatim excerpts of Mr. Ford's unpublished manuscript to lend authenticity to its account of the forthcoming memoirs, The Nation effectively arrogated to itself the right of first publication, an important marketable subsidiary right. For the reasons set forth below, we find that this use of the copyrighted manuscript, even stripped to the verbatim quotes conceded by the Nation to be copyrightable expression, was not a fair use within the meaning of the Copyright Act.

III

A

Fair use was traditionally defined as "a privilege in others than the owner of the copyright to use the copyrighted material in a reasonable manner without his consent." [ ] The statutory formulation of the defense of fair use in the Copyright Act of 1976 reflects the intent of Congress to codify the common-law doctrine. Section 107 requires a case-by-case determination whether a particular use is fair, and the statute notes four nonexclusive factors to be considered. This approach was "intended to restate the [pre-existing] judicial doctrine of fair use, not to change, narrow, or enlarge it in any way." H.R.Rep. No. 94–1476, p. 66 (1976) (hereinafter House Report).

"[T]he author's consent to a reasonable use of his copyrighted works ha[d] always been implied by the courts as a necessary incident of the constitutional policy of promoting the progress of science and the useful arts, since a prohibition of such use would inhibit subsequent writers from attempting to improve upon prior works and thus . . . frustrate the very ends sought to be attained." . . .

. . .

Perhaps because the fair use doctrine was predicated on the author's implied consent to "reasonable and customary" use when he released his work for public consumption, fair use traditionally was not recognized as a defense to charges of copying from an author's as yet unpublished works. Under common-law copyright, "the property of the author . . . in his intellectual creation [was] absolute until he voluntarily part[ed] with the same." [ ] This absolute rule, however, was tempered in practice by the equitable nature of the fair use doctrine. In a given case, factors such as implied consent through *de facto* publication or performance or dissemination of a work may tip the balance of equities in favor of prepublication use. [ ] But it has never been seriously disputed that "the fact that the plaintiff's work is unpublished . . . is a factor tending to negate the defense of fair use."

. . .

The Copyright Revision Act of 1976 represents the culmination of a major legislative reexamination of copyright doctrine. Among its other innovations, it eliminated publication "as a dividing line between common law and statutory protection," [ ], extending statutory protection to all works from the time of their creation. It also recognized for the first time a distinct statutory right of first publication, which had previously been an element of the common-law protections afforded unpublished works. The Report of the House Committee on the Judiciary confirms that "Clause (3) of section 106, establishes the exclusive right of publication . . . . Under this provision the copyright owner would have the right to control the first public distribution of an authorized copy . . . of his work."

Though the right of first publication, like the other rights enumerated in § 106, is expressly made subject to the fair use provision of § 107, fair use analysis must always be tailored to the individual case. The nature of the interest at stake is highly relevant to whether a given use is fair. From the beginning, those entrusted with the task of revision recognized the "overbalancing reasons to preserve the common law protection of undisseminated works until the author or his successor chooses to disclose them." [ ] The right of first publication implicates a threshold decision by the author whether and in what form to release his work. First publication is inherently different from other § 106 rights in that only one person can be the first publisher; as the contract with Time illustrates, the commercial value of the right lies primarily in exclusivity. Because the potential damage to the author from judicially enforced "sharing" of the first publication right with unauthorized users of his manuscript is substantial, the balance of equities in evaluating such a claim of fair use inevitably shifts.

. . .

. . . The author's control of first public distribution implicates not only his personal interest in creative control but his property interest in exploitation of prepublication rights, which are valuable in themselves and serve as a valuable adjunct to publicity and marketing. See Belushi v. Woodward, 598 F.Supp. 36 (DC 1984) (successful marketing depends on coordination of serialization and release to public); Marks, Subsidiary Rights and Permissions, in What Happens in Book Publishing, 230 (C. Grannis ed. 1967) (exploitation of subsidiary rights is necessary to financial success of new books). Under ordinary circumstances, the author's right to control the first public appearance of his undisseminated expression will outweigh a claim of fair use.

B

Respondents, however, contend that First Amendment values require a different rule under the circumstances of this case. The thrust of the decision below is that "[t]he scope of [fair use] is undoubtedly wider when the information conveyed relates to matters of high public concern." . . . Respondents explain their copying of Mr. Ford's expression as essential to reporting the news story it claims the book itself represents. In respondents' view, not only the facts contained in Mr. Ford's memoirs, but "the precise manner in which [he] expressed himself was as newsworthy as what he had to say." Respondents argue that the public's interest in learning this news as fast as possible outweighs the right of the author to control its first publication.

The Second Circuit noted, correctly, that copyright's idea/expression dichotomy "strike[s] a definitional balance between the First Amendment and the Copyright Act by permitting free communication of facts while still protecting an author's expression." 723 F.2d, at 203. No author may copyright his ideas or the facts he narrates. . . . As this Court long ago observed: "[T]he news element—the information respecting current events contained in the literary production—is not the creation of the writer, but is a report of matters that ordinarily are *publici juris;* it is the history of the day." International News Service v. Associated Press, 248 U.S. 215, 234 (1918). But copyright assures those who write and publish factual narratives such as "A Time to Heal" that they may at least enjoy the right to market the original expression contained therein as just compensation for their investment.

. . . The promise of copyright would be an empty one if it could be avoided merely by dubbing the infringement a fair use "news report" of the book.

Nor do respondents assert any actual necessity for circumventing the copyright scheme with respect to the types of works and users at issue here.[6] Where an author and publisher have invested extensive resources in creating an original work and are poised to release it to the public, no legitimate aim is served by preempting the right of first publication. . . .

. . .

It is fundamentally at odds with the scheme of copyright to accord lesser rights in those works that are of greatest importance to the public. Such a notion ignores the major premise of copyright and injures author and public alike. "[T]o propose that fair use be imposed whenever the 'social value [of dissemination] . . . outweighs any detriment to the artist,' would be to propose depriving copyright owners of their right in the property precisely when they encounter those users who could afford to pay for it." . . .

. . .

IV

Fair use is a mixed question of law and fact. Pacific and Southern Co. v. Duncan, 744 F.2d 1490, 1495, n. 8 (CA11 1984). Where the District Court has found facts sufficient to evaluate each of the statutory factors, an appellate court "need not remand for further factfinding . . . [but] may conclude as a matter of law that [the challenged use] do[es] not qualify as a fair use of the copyrighted work." Id., at 1495. Thus whether The Nation article constitutes fair use under § 107 must be reviewed in light of the principles discussed above. The factors enumerated in the section are not meant to be exclusive: "[S]ince the doctrine is an equitable rule of reason, no generally applicable definition is possible, and each case raising the question must be decided on its own facts." [ ] The four factors identified by Congress as especially relevant in determining whether the use was fair are: (1) the purpose and character of the use; (2) the nature of the copyrighted work; (3) the substantiality of the portion used in relation to the copyrighted work as a whole; (4) the effect on the potential market for or value of the copyrighted work. We address each one separately.

Purpose of the Use. The Second Circuit correctly identified news reporting as the general purpose of The Nation's use. News reporting is one of the examples enumerated in § 107 to "give some idea of the sort of activities the courts might regard as fair use under the circumstances." . . . The fact that an article arguably is "news" and therefore a productive use is simply one factor in a fair use analysis.

. . . The Nation has every right to seek to be the first to publish information. But The Nation went beyond simply reporting uncopyrightable information and actively sought to exploit the headline

6. It bears noting that Congress in the Copyright Act recognized a public interest warranting specific exemptions in a number of areas not within traditional fair use, see, e.g., 17 U.S.C. § 115 (compulsory license for records); § 105 (no copyright in government works). No such exemption limits copyright in personal narratives written by public servants after they leave government service.

value of its infringement, making a "news event" out of its unauthorized first publication of a noted figure's copyrighted expression.

The fact that a publication was commercial as opposed to non-profit is a separate factor that tends to weigh against a finding of fair use. "[E]very commercial use of copyrighted material is presumptively an unfair exploitation of the monopoly privilege that belongs to the owner of the copyright." [*Sony*] In arguing that the purpose of news reporting is not purely commercial, The Nation misses the point entirely. The crux of the profit/nonprofit distinction is not whether the sole motive of the use is monetary gain but whether the user stands to profit from exploitation of the copyrighted material without paying the customary price.

In evaluating character and purpose we cannot ignore The Nation's stated purpose of scooping the forthcoming hardcover and Time abstracts. The Nation's use had not merely the incidental effect but the *intended purpose* of supplanting the copyright holder's commercially valuable right of first publication. Also relevant to the "character" of the use is "the propriety of the defendant's conduct." [ ] The trial court found that The Nation knowingly exploited a purloined manuscript. Unlike the typical claim of fair use, The Nation cannot offer up even the fiction of consent as justification. Like its competitor newsweekly, it was free to bid for the right of abstracting excerpts from "A Time to Heal." . . .

Nature of the Copyrighted Work. Second, the Act directs attention to the nature of the copyrighted work. "A Time to Heal" may be characterized as an unpublished historical narrative or autobiography. The law generally recognizes a greater need to disseminate factual works than works of fiction or fantasy. . . . Some of the briefer quotes from the memoir are arguably necessary adequately to convey the facts; for example, Mr. Ford's characterization of the White House tapes as the "smoking gun" is perhaps so integral to the idea expressed as to be inseparable from it. But The Nation did not stop at isolated phrases and instead excerpted subjective descriptions and portraits of public figures whose power lies in the author's individualized expression. Such use, focusing on the most expressive elements of the work, exceeds that necessary to disseminate the facts.

The fact that a work is unpublished is a critical element of its "nature." Our prior discussion establishes that the scope of fair use is narrower with respect to unpublished works. . . .

In the case of Mr. Ford's manuscript, the copyrightholders' interest in confidentiality is irrefutable; the copyrightholders had entered into a contractual undertaking to "keep the manuscript confidential" and required that all those to whom the manuscript was shown also "sign an agreement to keep the manuscript confidential." While the copyrightholders' contract with Time required Time to submit its proposed article seven days before publication, The Nation's clandestine publication afforded no such opportunity for creative or quality control.

It was hastily patched together and contained "a number of inaccuracies." A use that so clearly infringes the copyrightholder's interests in confidentiality and creative control is difficult to characterize as "fair."

Amount and Substantiality of the Portion Used. Next, the Act directs us to examine the amount and substantiality of the portion used in relation to the copyrighted work as a whole. In absolute terms, the words actually quoted were an insubstantial portion of "A Time to Heal." The district court, however, found that "[T]he Nation took what was essentially the heart of the book." [ ] We believe the Court of Appeals erred in overruling the district judge's evaluation of the qualitative nature of the taking. See, e.g., *Roy Export Co. Establishment v. Columbia Broadcasting System, Inc.,* [p. 409, infra] (taking of 55 seconds out of one hour and twenty-nine minute film deemed qualitatively substantial). A Time editor described the chapters on the pardon as "the most interesting and moving parts of the entire manuscript." . . .

As the statutory language indicates, a taking may not be excused merely because it is insubstantial with respect to the *infringing* work. As Judge Learned Hand cogently remarked, "[N]o plagiarist can excuse the wrong by showing how much of his work he did not pirate." Sheldon v. Metro-Goldwyn Pictures Corp., 81 F.2d 49, 56 (CA2), cert. denied, 298 U.S. 669 (1936). Conversely, the fact that a substantial portion of the infringing work was copied verbatim is evidence of the qualitative value of the copied material, both to the originator and to the plagiarist who seeks to profit from marketing someone else's copyrighted expression.

Stripped to the verbatim quotes,[8] the direct takings from the unpublished manuscript constitute at least 13% of the infringing article. See Meeropol v. Nizer, 560 F.2d 1061, 1071 (CA2 1977) (copyrighted letters constituted less than 1% of infringing work but were prominently featured). The Nation article is structured around the quoted excerpts which serve as its dramatic focal points. In view of the expressive value of the excerpts and their key role in the infringing work, we cannot agree with the Second Circuit that the "magazine took a meager, indeed an infinitesimal amount of Ford's original language." [ ]

Effect on the Market. Finally, the Act focuses on "the effect of the use upon the potential market for or value of the copyrighted work."

8. See Appendix [ ]. The Court of Appeals found that only "approximately 300 words" were copyrightable but did not specify which words. The court's discussion, however, indicates it excluded from consideration those portions of The Nation's piece that, although copied verbatim from Ford's manuscript, were quotes attributed by Ford to third persons and quotations from government documents. At oral argument, counsel for The Nation did not dispute that verbatim quotes and very close paraphrase could constitute infringement. Thus the Appendix identifies as potentially infringing only verbatim quotes or very close paraphrase and excludes from consideration government documents and words attributed to third persons. The Appendix is not intended to endorse any particular rule of copyrightability but is intended merely as an aid to facilitate our discussion.

This last factor is undoubtedly the single most important element of fair use. . . . [O]nce a copyrightholder establishes with reasonable probability the existence of a causal connection between the infringement and a loss of revenue, the burden properly shifts to the infringer to show that this damage would have occurred had there been no taking of copyrighted expression. Petitioners established a prima facie case of actual damage that respondent failed to rebut. The trial court properly awarded actual damages and accounting of profits.

. . .

It is undisputed that the factual material in the balance of The Nation's article, besides the verbatim quotes at issue here, was drawn exclusively from the chapters on the pardon. The excerpts were employed as featured episodes in a story about the Nixon pardon—precisely the use petitioners had licensed to Time. The borrowing of these verbatim quotes from the unpublished manuscript lent The Nation's piece a special air of authenticity—as Navasky [The Nation's editor] expressed it, the reader would know it was Ford speaking and not The Nation. Thus it directly competed for a share of the market for prepublication excerpts. . . .

V

. . . In sum, the traditional doctrine of fair use, as embodied in the Copyright Act, does not sanction the use made by The Nation of these copyrighted materials. Any copyright infringer may claim to benefit the public by increasing public access to the copyrighted work. But Congress has not designed, and we see no warrant for judicially imposing, a "compulsory license" permitting unfettered access to the unpublished copyrighted expression of public figures.

The Nation conceded that its verbatim copying of some 300 words of direct quotation from the Ford manuscript would constitute an infringement unless excused as a fair use. Because we find that The Nation's use of these verbatim excerpts from the unpublished manuscript was not a fair use, the judgment of the Court of Appeals is reversed and remanded for further proceedings consistent with this opinion.

It is so ordered.

APPENDIX TO OPINION OF THE COURT

The portions of The Nation article which were copied verbatim from "A Time to Heal," excepting quotes from government documents and quotes attributed by Ford to third persons, are identified in bold face in the text. The corresponding passages in the Ford manuscript are footnoted.

THE FORD MEMOIRS BEHIND THE NIXON PARDON

In his memoirs, *A Time To Heal,* which Harper & Row will publish in late May or early June, former President Gerald R. Ford says that the idea of giving a blanket pardon to Richard M. Nixon was raised before Nixon resigned from the Presidency by Gen. Alexander Haig, who was then the White House chief of staff.

Ford also writes that, but for a misunderstanding, he might have selected Ronald Reagan as his 1976 running mate, that Washington lawyer Edward Bennett Williams, a Democrat, was his choice for head of the Central Intelligence Agency, that Nixon was the one who first proposed Rockefeller for Vice President, and that he regretted his **"cowardice"** [1] in allowing Rockefeller to remove himself from Vice Presidential contention. Ford also describes his often prickly relations with Henry Kissinger.

The Nation obtained the 655-page typescript before publication. Advance excerpts from the book will appear in *Time* in mid-April and in *The Reader's Digest* thereafter. Although the initial print order has not been decided, the figure is tentatively set at 50,000; it could change, depending upon the public reaction to the serialization.

Ford's account of the Nixon pardon contains significant new detail on the negotiations and considerations that surrounded it. According to Ford's version, the subject was first broached to him by General Haig on August 1, 1974, a week before Nixon resigned. General Haig revealed that the newly transcribed White House tapes were the equivalent of the **"smoking gun"** [2] and that Ford should prepare himself to become President.

Ford was deeply hurt by Haig's revelation: **"Over the past several months Nixon had repeatedly assured me that he was not involved in Watergate, that the evidence would prove his innocence, that the matter would fade from view."** [3] Ford had believed him, but he let Haig explain the President's alternatives.

He could **"ride it out"** [4] or he could resign, Haig said. He then listed the different ways Nixon might resign and concluded by pointing out that **Nixon could agree to leave in return for an agreement that the new President, Ford, would pardon him.**[5] Although Ford said it would be improper for him to make any recommendation, he basically agreed with Haig's assessment and adds, **"Because of his**

1. I was angry at myself for showing cowardice in not saying to the ultraconservatives, "It's going to be Ford and Rockefeller, whatever the consequences." p. 496.

2. [I]t contained the so-called smoking gun. p. 3.

3. [O]ver the past several months Nixon had repeatedly assured me that he was not involved in Watergate, that the evidence would prove his innocence, that the matter would fade from view. p. 7.

4. The first [option] was that he could try to "ride it out" by letting impeachment take its natural course through the House and the Senate trial, fighting against conviction all the way. p. 4.

5. Finally, Haig said that according to some on Nixon's White House staff, Nixon could agree to leave in return for an agreement that the new President—Gerald Ford—would pardon him. p. 5.

references to the pardon authority, I did ask Haig about the extent of a President's pardon power." [6]

"It's my understanding from a White House lawyer," Haig replied, "that a President does have authority to grant a pardon even before criminal action has been taken against an individual."

But because Ford had neglected to tell Haig he thought the idea of a resignation conditioned on a pardon was improper, his press aide, Bob Hartmann, suggested that Haig might well have returned to the White House and told President Nixon that he had mentioned the idea and Ford seemed comfortable with it. "Silence implies assent."

Ford then consulted with White House special counsel James St. Clair, who had no advice one way or the other on the matter more than pointing out that he was not the lawyer who had given Haig the opinion on the pardon. Ford also discussed the matter with Jack Marsh, who felt that the mention of a pardon in this context was a "time bomb," and with Bryce Harlow, who had served six Presidents and who agreed that **the mere mention of a pardon "could cause a lot of trouble."** [7]

As a result of these various conversations, Vice President Ford called Haig and read him a written statement: "I want you to understand that I have no intention of recommending what the President should do about resigning or not resigning and that nothing we talked about yesterday afternoon should be given any consideration in whatever decision the President may wish to make."

Despite what Haig had told him about the "smoking gun" tapes, Ford told a Jackson, Mich., luncheon audience later in the day that **the President was not guilty of an impeachable offense. "Had I said otherwise at that moment,"** he writes, **"the whole house of cards might have collapsed."** [8]

In justifying the pardon, Ford goes out of his way to assure the reader that **"compassion for Nixon as an individual hadn't prompted my decision at all."** [9] Rather, he did it because he had **"to get the monkey off my back one way or the other."** [10]

The precipitating factor in his decision was a series of secret meetings his general counsel, Phil Buchen, held with Watergate Special Prosecutor Leon Jaworski in the Jefferson Hotel, where they were both staying at the time. Ford attributes Jaworski with providing some

6. Because of his references to pardon authority, I did ask Haig about the extent of a President's pardon power. pp. 5–6.

7. Only after I had finished did [Bryce Harlow] let me know in no uncertain terms that he agreed with Bob and Jack, that the mere mention of the pardon option could cause a lot of trouble in the days ahead. p. 18.

8. During the luncheon I repeated my assertion that the President was not guilty of an impeachable offense. Had I said otherwise at that moment, the whole house of cards might have collapsed. p. 21.

9. But compassion for Nixon as an individual hadn't prompted my decision at all. p. 266.

10. I had to get the monkey off my back one way or another. p. 236.

"crucial" information [11]—i.e., that Nixon was under investigation in ten separate areas, and that **the court process could "take years."** [12] Ford cites a memorandum from Jaworski's assistant, Henry S. Ruth Jr., as being especially persuasive. Ruth had written:

"If you decide to recommend indictment I think it is fair and proper to notify Jack Miller and the White House sufficiently in advance so that pardon action could be taken before the indictment." He went on to say: "One can make a strong argument for leniency and if President Ford is so inclined, I think he ought to do it early rather than late."

Ford decided that court proceedings against Nixon might take six years, that **Nixon "would not spend time quietly in San Clemente,"** [13] and **"it would be virtually impossible for me to direct public attention on anything else."** [14]

Buchen, Haig and Henry Kissinger agreed with him. Hartmann was not so sure.

Buchen wanted to condition the pardon on Nixon agreeing to settle the question of who would retain custody and control over the tapes and Presidential papers that might be relevant to various Watergate proceedings, but Ford was reluctant to do that.

At one point a plan was considered whereby the Presidential materials would be kept in a vault at a Federal facility near San Clemente, but the vault would require two keys to open it. One would be retained by the General Services Administration, the other by Richard Nixon.

The White House did, however, want Nixon to make a full confession on the occasion of his pardon or, at a minimum, express true contrition. Ford tells of the negotiation with Jack Miller, Nixon's lawyer, over the wording of Nixon's statement. But as Ford reports Miller's response, Nixon was not likely to yield. **"His few meetings with his client had shown him that the former President's ability to discuss Watergate objectively was almost nonexistent."** [15]

The statement they really wanted was never forthcoming. As soon as Ford's emissary arrived in San Clemente, he was confronted with an ultimatum by Ron Zeigler, Nixon's former press secretary. "Let's get one thing straight immediately," Zeigler said, "President Nixon is not issuing any statement whatsoever regarding Watergate, whether Jerry Ford pardons him or not." Zeigler proposed a draft, which was turned down on the ground that **"no statement would be better than**

11. Jaworski gave Phil several crucial pieces of information. p. 246.

12. And if the verdict was Guilty, one had to assume that Nixon would appeal. That process would take years. p. 248.

13. The entire process would no doubt require years: a minimum of two, a maximum of six. And Nixon would not spend time quietly in San Clemente. p. 238.

14. It would be virtually impossible for me to direct public attention on anything else. p. 239.

15. But [Miller] wasn't optimistic about getting such a statement. His few meetings with his client had shown him that the former President's ability to discuss Watergate objectively was almost nonexistent. p. 246.

that." [16] They went through three more drafts before they agreed on the statement Nixon finally made, which stopped far short of a full confession.

When Ford aide Benton Becker tried to explain to Nixon that acceptance of a pardon was an admission of guilt, he felt the President wasn't really listening. Instead, Nixon wanted to talk about the Washington Redskins. And when Becker left, Nixon pressed on him some cuff links and a tiepin "out of my own jewelry box."

Ultimately, Ford sums up the philosophy underlying his decision as one he picked up as a student at Yale Law School many years before. **"I learned that public policy often took precedence over a rule of law. Although I respected the tenet that no man should be above the law, public policy demanded that I put Nixon—and Watergate—behind us as quickly as possible."** [17]

Later, when Ford learned that Nixon's phlebitis had acted up and his health was seriously impaired, he debated whether to pay the ailing former President a visit. **"If I made the trip it would remind everybody of Watergate and the pardon. If I didn't, people would say I lacked compassion."** [18] Ford went:

> **He was stretched out flat on his back. There were tubes in his nose and mouth, and wires led from his arms, chest and legs to machines with orange lights that blinked on and off. His face was ashen, and I thought I had never seen anyone closer to death.**[19]

The manuscript made available to The Nation includes many references to Henry Kissinger and other personalities who played a major role during the Ford years.

On Kissinger. Immediately after being informed by Nixon of his intention to resign, Ford returned to the Executive Office Building and phoned Henry Kissinger to let him know how he felt. **"Henry,"** he said, **"I need you. The country needs you. I want you to stay. I'll do everything I can to work with you."** [20]

"Sir," Kissinger replied, "it is my job to get along with you and not yours to get along with me."

16. When Zeigler asked Becker what he thought of it, Becker replied that *no* statement would be better than that. p. 251.

17. Years before, at Yale Law School, I'd learned that public policy often took precedence over a rule of law. Although I respected the tenet that no man should be above the law, public policy demanded that I put Nixon—and Watergate—behind us as quickly as possible. p. 256.

18. My staff debated whether or not I ought to visit Nixon at the Long Beach Hospital, only half an hour away. If I made the trip, it would remind everyone of Watergate and the pardon. If I didn't, people would say I lacked compassion. I ended their debate as soon as I found out it had begun. Of course I would go. p. 298.

19. He was stretched out flat on his back. There were tubes in his nose and mouth, and wires led from his arms, chest and legs to machines with orange lights that blinked on and off. His face was ashen, and I thought I had never seen anyone closer to death. p. 299.

20. "Henry," I said when he came on the line, "I need you. The country needs you. I want you to stay. I'll do everything I can to work with you." p. 46.

"We'll get along," Ford said. **"I know we'll get along."** Referring to Kissinger's joint jobs as Secretary of State and National Security Adviser to the President, Ford said, **"I don't want to make any change. I think it's worked out well, so let's keep it that way."** [21]

Later Ford did make the change and relieved Kissinger of his responsibilities as National Security Adviser at the same time that he fired James Schlesinger as Secretary of Defense. Shortly thereafter, he reports, Kissinger presented him with a "draft" letter of resignation, which he said Ford could call upon at will if he felt he needed it to quiet dissent from conservatives who objected to Kissinger's role in the firing of Schlesinger.

On John Connally. When Ford was informed that Nixon wanted him to replace Agnew, he told the President he had **"no ambition to hold office after January 1977."** [22] Nixon replied that that was good since his own choice for his running mate in 1976 was John Connally. "He'd be excellent," observed Nixon. Ford says he had "no problem with that."

On the Decision to Run Again. Ford was, he tells us, so sincere in his intention not to run again that he thought he would announce it and enhance his credibility in the country and the Congress, as well as keep the promise he had made to his wife, Betty.

Kissinger talked him out of it. "You can't do that. It would be disastrous from a foreign policy point of view. For the next two and a half years foreign governments would know that they were dealing with a lame-duck President. All our initiatives would be dead in the water, and I wouldn't be able to implement your foreign policy. It would probably have the same consequences in dealing with the Congress on domestic issues. You can't reassert the authority of the Presidency if you leave yourself hanging out on a dead limb. You've got to be an affirmative President."

On David Kennerly, the White House photographer. Schlesinger was arguing with Kissinger and Ford over the appropriate response to the seizure of the *Mayaguez.* At issue was whether airstrikes against the Cambodians were desirable; Schlesinger was opposed to bombings. Following a lull in the conversation, Ford reports, up spoke the 30-year-old White House photographer David Kennerly who had been taking pictures for the last hour.

"Has anyone considered," Kennerly asked, "that this might be the act of a local Cambodian commander who has just taken it into his own hands to stop any ship that comes by?" Nobody, apparently, had considered it, but following several seconds of silence, Ford tells us, the view carried the day. **"Massive airstrikes would constitute**

21. "We'll get along," I said. "I know we can get along." We talked about the two hats he wore, as Secretary of State and National Security Adviser to the President. "I don't want to make any change," I said, "I think it's worked out well, so let's keep it that way." p. 46.

22. I told him about my promise to Betty and said that I had no ambitions to hold office after January 1977. p. 155.

overkill," Ford decided. **"It would be far better to have Navy jets from the Coral Sea make surgical strikes against specific targets."** [23]

On Nixon's Character. **Nixon's flaw,** according to Ford **was "pride." "A terribly proud man,"** writes Ford, **"he detested weakness in other people. I'd often heard him speak disparagingly of those whom he felt to be soft and expedient. (Curiously, he didn't feel that the press was weak. Reporters, he sensed, were his adversaries. He knew they didn't like him, and he responded with reciprocal disdain.)"** [24]

Nixon felt disdain for the Democratic leadership of the House, whom he also regarded as weak. According to Ford, **"His pride and personal contempt for weakness had overcome his ability to tell the difference between right and wrong,"** [25] all of which leads Ford to wonder whether Nixon had known in advance about Watergate.

On hearing Nixon's resignation speech, which Ford felt lacked an adequate plea for forgiveness, he was persuaded that **"Nixon was out of touch with reality."** [26]

In February of last year, when *The Washington Post* obtained and printed advance excerpts from H.R. Haldeman's memoir, *The Ends of Power,* on the eve of its publication by Times Books, *The New York Times* called *The Post's* feat "a second-rate burglary."

The Post disagreed, claiming that its coup represented "first-rate enterprise" and arguing that it had burglarized nothing, that publication of the Haldeman memoir came under the Fair Comment doctrine long recognized by the courts, and that "There is a fundamental journalistic principle here—a First Amendment principle that was central to the Pentagon Papers case."

In the issue of *The Nation* dated May 5, 1979, our special Spring Books number, we will discuss some of the ethical problems raised by the issue of disclosure.

JUSTICE BRENNAN, with whom JUSTICE WHITE and JUSTICE MARSHALL join, dissenting.

The Court holds that The Nation's quotation of 300 words from the unpublished 200,000-word manuscript of President Gerald R. Ford

23. Subjectively, I felt that what Kennerly had said made a lot of sense. Massive airstrikes would constitute overkill. It would be far better to have Navy jets from the *Coral Sea* make surgical strikes against specific targets in the vicinity of Kompong Som. p. 416.

24. In Nixon's case, that flaw was pride. A terribly proud man, he detested weakness in other people. I'd often heard him speak disparagingly of those whom he felt to be soft and expedient. (Curiously, he didn't feel that the press was weak. Reporters, he sensed, were his adversaries. He knew they didn't like him, and he responded with reciprocal disdain.) p. 53.

25. His pride and personal contempt for weakness had overcome his ability to tell the difference between right and wrong. p. 54.

26. The speech lasted fifteen minutes, and at the end I was convinced Nixon was out of touch with reality. p. 57.

infringed the copyright in that manuscript, even though the quotations related to a historical event of undoubted significance—the resignation and pardon of President Richard M. Nixon. Although the Court pursues the laudable goal of protecting "the economic incentive to create and disseminate ideas," this zealous defense of the copyright owner's prerogative will, I fear, stifle the broad dissemination of ideas and information copyright is intended to nurture. Protection of the copyright owner's economic interest is achieved in this case through an exceedingly narrow definition of the scope of fair use. The progress of arts and sciences and the robust public debate essential to an enlightened citizenry are ill served by this constructed reading of the fair use doctrine. I therefore respectfully dissent.

I

A

This case presents two issues. First, did The Nation's use of material from the Ford manuscript in forms other than direct quotation from that manuscript infringe Harper & Row's copyright. Second, did the quotation of approximately 300 words from the manuscript infringe the copyright because this quotation did not constitute "fair use" within the meaning of § 107 of the Copyright Act. The Court finds no need to resolve the threshold copyrightability issue. The use of 300 words of quotation was, the Court finds, beyond the scope of fair use and thus a copyright infringement. Because I disagree with the Court's fair use holding, it is necessary for me to decide the threshold copyrightability question.

. . .

The "originality" requirement now embodied in § 102 of the Copyright Act is crucial to maintenance of the appropriate balance between these competing interests. Properly interpreted in the light of the legislative history, this section extends copyright protection to an author's literary form but permits free use by others of the ideas and information the author communicates. . . .

The "promotion of science and the useful arts" requires this limit on the scope of an author's control. Were an author able to prevent subsequent authors from using concepts, ideas, or facts contained in his or her work, the creative process would wither and scholars would be forced into unproductive replication of the research of their predecessors. This limitation on copyright also ensures consonance with our most important First Amendment values. . . .

It follows that infringement of copyright must be based on a taking of literary form, as opposed to the ideas or information contained in a copyrighted work. Deciding whether an infringing appropriation of literary form has occurred is difficult for at least two reasons. First, the distinction between literary form and information or ideas is often elusive in practice. Second, infringement must be based on a *substan-*

tial appropriation of literary form. This determination is equally challenging. Not surprisingly, the test for infringement has defied precise formulation. In general, though, the inquiry proceeds along two axes: *how closely* has the second author tracked the first author's particular language and structure of presentation; and *how much* of the first author's language and structure has the second author appropriated.

. . .

The Language. Much of the information The Nation conveyed was not in the form of paraphrase at all, but took the form of synopsis of lengthy discussions in the Ford manuscript. In the course of this summary presentation, The Nation did use occasional sentences that closely resembled language in the original Ford manuscript. But these linguistic similarities are insufficient to constitute an infringement . . . .

At most The Nation paraphrased disparate isolated sentences from the original. A finding of infringement based on paraphrase generally requires far more close and substantial a tracking of the original language than occurred in this case.

The Structure of Presentation. The article does not mimic Mr. Ford's structure. The information The Nation presents is drawn from scattered sections of the Ford work and does not appear in the sequence in which Mr. Ford presented it. . . . Also, it is difficult to suggest that a 2000-word article could bodily appropriate the structure of a 200,000-word book. Most of what Mr. Ford created, and most of the history he recounted, was simply not represented in The Nation's article.

When The Nation was not quoting Mr. Ford, therefore, its efforts to convey the historical information in the Ford manuscript did not so closely and substantially track Mr. Ford's language and structure as to constitute an appropriation of literary form.

II

The Nation is thus liable in copyright only if the quotation of 300 words infringed any of Harper & Row's exclusive rights under § 106 of the Act. . . . The question here is whether The Nation's quotation was a noninfringing fair use within the meaning of § 107.

. . .

With respect to a work of history, particularly the memoirs of a public official, the statutorily-prescribed analysis cannot properly be conducted without constant attention to copyright's crucial distinction between protected literary form and unprotected information or ideas. The question must always be: was the subsequent author's use of *literary form* a fair use within the meaning of § 107, in light of the purpose for the use, the nature of the copyrighted work, the amount of literary form used, and the effect of this use of literary form on the value of or market for the original.

Limiting the inquiry to the propriety of a subsequent author's use of the copyright owner's literary form is not easy in the case of a work of history. Protection against only substantial appropriation of literary form does not ensure historians a return commensurate with the full value of their labors. . . . Copyright thus does not protect that which is often of most value in a work of history and courts must resist the tendency to reject the fair use defense on the basis of their feeling that an author of history has been deprived of the full value of his or her labor. A subsequent author's taking of information and ideas is in no sense piratical because copyright law simply does not create any property interest in information and ideas.

The urge to compensate for subsequent use of information and ideas is perhaps understandable. An inequity seems to lurk in the idea that much of the fruit of the historian's labor may be used without compensation. This, however, is not some unforeseen by-product of a statutory scheme intended primarily to ensure a return for works of the imagination. Congress made the affirmative choice that the copyright laws should apply in this way . . . .

. . . Application of the statutorily prescribed analysis with attention to the distinction between information and literary form leads to a straightforward finding of fair use within the meaning of § 107.

The Purpose of the Use. The Nation's purpose in quoting 300 words of the Ford manuscript was, as the Court acknowledges, news reporting. . . .

. . .

The Court concedes the validity of the news reporting purpose but then quickly offsets it against three purportedly countervailing considerations. First, the Court asserts that because The Nation publishes for profit, its publication of the Ford quotes is a presumptively unfair commercial use. Second, the Court claims that The Nation's stated desire to create a "news event" signalled an illegitimate purpose of supplanting the copyright owner's right of first publication. Third, The Nation acted in bad faith, the Court claims, because its editor "knowingly exploited a purloined manuscript."

The Court's reliance on the commercial nature of The Nation's use as "a separate factor that tends to weigh against a finding of fair use," is inappropriate in the present context. Many uses § 107 lists as paradigmatic examples of fair use, including criticism, comment and *news reporting,* are generally conducted for profit in this country, a fact of which Congress was obviously aware when it enacted § 107. To negate any argument favoring fair use based on news reporting or criticism because that reporting or criticism was published for profit is to render meaningless the congressional imprimatur placed on such uses.

Nor should The Nation's intent to create a "news event" weigh against a finding of fair use. Such a rule, like the Court's automatic presumption against news reporting for profit, would undermine the congressional validation of the news reporting purpose. . . . The record suggests only that The Nation sought to be the first to reveal the information in the Ford manuscript. The Nation's stated purpose of scooping the competition should under those circumstances have no negative bearing on the claim of fair use. Indeed the Court's reliance on this factor would seem to amount to little more than distaste for the standard journalistic practice of seeking to be the first to publish news.

The Court's reliance on The Nation's putative bad faith is equally unwarranted. No court has found that The Nation possessed the Ford manuscript illegally or in violation of any common law interest of Harper & Row; all common law causes of action have been abandoned or dismissed in this case. Even if the manuscript had been "purloined" by someone, nothing in this record imputes culpability to The Nation. On the basis of the record in this case, the most that can be said is that The Nation made use of the contents of the manuscript knowing the copyright owner would not sanction the use.

. . .

The Nature of the Copyrighted Work. . . .

The Court acknowledges that "[t]he law generally recognizes a greater need to disseminate factual works than works of fiction or fantasy," and that "some of the briefer quotations from the memoir are arguably necessary to convey the facts," ibid. But the Court discounts the force of this consideration, primarily on the ground that "the fact that a work is unpublished is a crucial element of its 'nature.' " At this point the Court introduces into analysis of this case a categorical presumption against prepublication fair use. ("Under ordinary circumstances, the author's right to control the first public appearance of his undisseminated expression will outweigh a claim of fair use").

This categorical presumption is unwarranted on its own terms and unfaithful to congressional intent. Whether a particular prepublication use will impair any interest the Court identifies as encompassed within the right of first publication, will depend on the nature of the copyrighted work, the timing of prepublication use, the amount of expression used and the medium in which the second author communicates. Also, certain uses might be tolerable for some purposes but not for others. . . .

. . .

The Amount and Substantiality of the Portion Used. More difficult questions arise with respect to judgments about the importance to this case of the amount and substantiality of the quotations used. . . .

. . .

At least with respect to the six particular quotes of Mr. Ford's observations and reflections about President Nixon, I agree with the

Court's conclusion that The Nation appropriated some literary form of substantial quality. I do not agree, however, that the substantiality of the expression taken was clearly excessive or inappropriate to The Nation's news reporting purpose.

Had these quotations been used in the context of a critical book review of the Ford work, there is little question that such a use would be fair use within the meaning of § 107 of the Act. The amount and substantiality of the use—in both quantitative and qualitative terms—would have certainly been appropriate to the purpose of such a use. It is difficult to see how the use of these quoted words in a news report is less appropriate. . . .

. . .

The Effect on the Market. The Court correctly notes that the effect on the market "is undoubtedly the single most important element of fair use," and the Court properly focuses on whether The Nation's use adversely affected Harper & Row's serialization potential and not merely the market for sales of the Ford work itself. Unfortunately, the Court's failure to distinguish between the use of information and the appropriation of literary form badly skews its analysis of this factor.

. . .

The Nation's publication indisputably precipitated Time's eventual cancellation. But that does not mean that The Nation's use of the 300 quoted words caused this injury to Harper & Row. Wholly apart from these quoted words, The Nation published significant information and ideas from the Ford manuscript. If it was this publication of information, and not the publication of the few quotations, that caused Time to abrogate its serialization agreement, then whatever the negative effect on the serialization market, that effect was the product of wholly legitimate activity.

. . .

Balancing the Interests. Once the distinction between information and literary form is made clear, the statutorily prescribed process of weighing the four statutory fair use factors discussed above leads naturally to a conclusion that The Nation's limited use of literary form was not an infringement. . . .

III

The Court's exceedingly narrow approach to fair use permits Harper & Row to monopolize information. This holding "effect[s] an important extension of property rights and a corresponding curtailment in the free use of knowledge and of ideas." International News Service v. Associated Press, 248 U.S., at 263 (Brandeis, J., dissenting). The Court has perhaps advanced the ability of the historian—or at least the public official who has recently left office—to capture the full economic value of information in his or her possession. But the Court does so only by risking the robust debate of public issues that is the "essence of self-government." Garrison v. Louisiana, 379 U.S., at 74–75. The Nation was providing the grist for that robust debate. The Court imposes liability upon The Nation for no other reason than that The Nation succeeded in being the first to provide certain information to the public. I dissent.

Notes and Questions

1. How does the analysis change if the Nation's article had appeared a week after the book was published? A week after the Time publication?

2. During the oral argument, counsel for the Nation asserted that "There are two words to describe what the Nation was doing: news reporting." Does the majority accept that view?

3. Although most commentators have concluded that the 1976 statute does not change the prior law of fair use, it seems safer to consider cases decided since then. A sampling of recent fair use cases follows.

a. In the Sony case, the Court observed that "although every commercial use of copyrighted material is presumptively an unfair exploitation of the monopoly privilege," a different rule applied for noncommercial uses. Here, plaintiff must show "either that the particular use is harmful, or that if it should become widespread, it would adversely affect the potential market for the copyrighted work. Actual present harm need not be shown . . . . Nor is it necessary to show with certainty that future harm will result. What is necessary is a showing by a preponderance of the evidence that *some* meaningful likelihood of future harm exists. If the intended use is for commercial gain, that likelihood may be presumed. But if it is for a noncommercial purpose, the likelihood must be demonstrated."

Two critical findings of the trial court led the majority to deny protection. "First, Sony demonstrated a significant likelihood that substantial numbers of copyright holders who license their works for broadcast on free television would not object to having their broadcasts time-shifted by private viewers. And second, respondents failed to demonstrate that time-shifting would cause any likelihood of nonminimal harm to the potential market for, or the value of, their copyrighted works." These led the Court to conclude that time-shifting, by far the most common use of the recorders, was fair use.

b. In Pacific and Southern Co. v. Duncan, 744 F.2d 1490, 11 Med. L.Rptr. 1135, 56 R.R.2d 1620 (11th Cir.1984), certiorari denied 105 S.Ct. 1867 (1985), plaintiff television station WXIA–TV presented four copyrighted local news programs daily. It audiotaped and videotaped each program. It retained the audio tape and the written transcript of the program for an indefinite time; it erased the videotape after seven days. WXIA did not market clips of its own stories, though it honored requests for tapes when made.

Defendant, doing business as TV News Clips, taped the news programs of television stations and tried to sell copies of the clips to those persons or groups covered by the news reports. The copies are not copyrighted and state "for personal use only not for rebroadcast." Defendant erases tapes after one month.

The court of appeals found a valid copyright even though the only fixed copy was defendant's. The plaintiff's tapes satisfied the requirement that the work be fixed for a period of "more than transitory duration." On the fair use question, the court turned to the four factors. The commercial nature of defendant's practices "militates quite strongly against a finding of fair use." Moreover, defendant's use "is neither productive nor creative in any way. It does not analyze the broadcast or improve it at all. . . . TV New Clips only copies and sells." Since the court treated each story on the news as a "coherent narrative," it found that the defendant had taken the entire work. The fourth factor also cut against defendant since it "uses the broadcasts for a purpose that WXIA might use for its own benefit." The potential market is undermined.

The second factor might be seen to favor defendant because of the importance to society of access to the news. "But the courts should also take care not to discourage authors from addressing important topics for fear of losing their copyright protections."

Defendant argued that as a government licensee, plaintiff was obligated to "provide public access to newscasts" and should not be allowed to use the copyright laws to restrict that access. The court, relying on arguments developed at p. 739, infra, rejected the existence of such a duty.

Defendant then asserted two constitutional defenses to statutory liability. First, it argued that WXIA's destruction of videotapes eliminated evidence that might be of possible use in defamation cases brought against it. The court responded that an "effort to discourage defamation suits might be an abuse of the copyright laws and a violation of the First Amendment, but that possibility is entirely imaginary in this case."

The second claim was the denial of public access to broadcast material. The court responded that the public interest in "making television broadcasting more available" (an interest that justified the use of tape recorders in the Sony case), might be threatened "if WXIA absolutely refused to allow the public to view recordings or scripts of its broadcasts." But that public interest "does not protect every activity that exposes more viewers to a broadcast. Furthermore, TV News Clips only increases access in a limited way by selling to a small group of customers, some of whom would buy a tape from WXIA anyway." Thus, the public already has access to the material and defendant does not offer anything more than WXIA can provide, and defendant's activities "fall well beyond whatever protections might be available to further this public access interest."

Finally, defendant argued that every copyright must further the ends of the copyright clause and that this one does not because of WXIA's systematic destruction of videotapes. (Although the defendant treated this as a First Amendment argument, the court thought it should be addressed under fair use.) Not every copyright holder "must offer benefits to society, for the copyright is an incentive rather than a command. And, a fortiori, a copyright holder need not provide the most complete public access possible. WXIA provides complete access for seven days and permanent access to everything except the visual images broadcast live from within the studio. The public benefits from this creative work; therefore, enforcing the copyright statute in this case does not violate the Copyright Clause."

The court held that the district court had abused its discretion by refusing to issue an injunction after finding an infringement.

c. In Diamond v. Am-Law Publishing Corp., 745 F.2d 142 (2d Cir. 1984), defendant American Lawyer published a story reporting that a formal grievance had been filed against plaintiff lawyer. He wrote defendant demanding an apology and a retraction. The editor invited the plaintiff to write a letter stating that no grievance had been filed. Plaintiff then sent a long letter making that point and also attacking the reporting practices of the defendant. The letter stated that "You are authorized to publish this letter but only it its entirety." Defendant published excerpts from the letter that made the point about the grievance but omitted, without showing any deletions, the parts attacking the defendant.

Plaintiff obtained a copyright on the letter and sued for infringement. The trial court's grant of summary judgment for defendant and its award of $15,000 in attorney's fees and costs were affirmed on appeal.

Fair use was established as a matter of law. The nonuse or editing of the letter did not put the copyrighted work in an unfair or distorted light. The omissions involved an unrelated matter and did not mislead the public about the contents of the entire letter. (Even if it did, it was not clear that this made it a copyright violation.) In any event, the use here was for comment or news reporting, uses protected under § 107. The claim that too little was used differs from the usual claim and did not help the plaintiff. Finally, plaintiff could show no present or future use of the letter that had been adversely affected by defendant's use.

d. Plaintiff specialized in preparing copyrighted "in-depth analytical reports on approximately 275 industrial, financial, utility and railroad corporations." The reports, up to 40 pages long and involving months of an analyst's time, were used by 900 clients of plaintiff, including banks, insurance companies, and mutual funds. Defendant, a weekly financial newspaper, featured a column called "Wall Street Roundup" that consisted almost exclusively of abstracts of institutional research reports. Defendant's advertising promised readers "a fast-reading, pinpointed account of heavyweight reports from the top institutional research firms."

Plaintiff sued for infringement and sought a preliminary injunction. The trial judge granted it and was upheld on appeal. Defendant argued that it was simply covering the financial news. The court disagreed. Although a news event cannot be copyrighted, the expression used by the author may be protected. Here, defendant was found to have copied the manner of expression used by plaintiff's analysts. The court noted that, unlike traditional news coverage, defendant's column provided no independent analysis or research; it carried no industry comments on the reports and included no criticism or praise of the reports. "Rather, the Transcript appropriated almost verbatim the most creative and original aspects of the reports, the financial analyses and predictions, which represent a substantial investment of time, money and labor." Wainwright Securities, Inc. v. Wall Street Transcript Corp., 558 F.2d 91, 2 Med.L.Rptr. 2153 (2d Cir.1977), certiorari denied 434 U.S. 1014 (1978).

e. Defendant wrote a book about Julius and Ethel Rosenberg: their trial, conviction, and execution for conspiring to transmit national defense information to the Soviet Union. The book quoted verbatim from 28 copyrighted letters written by the Rosenbergs while in prison—a total of 1,957 words. The plaintiffs, sons of the Rosenbergs, claimed the copyright in the letters, which had been published as the book Death House Letters. The trial judge dismissed the claim but was reversed on appeal.

The court noted that although the letters represented less than one percent of the defendant's book, they were featured prominently in promotional literature for the book. Several questions of fact had to be resolved before the fair use question could be answered: the purpose for which the letters were used in the defendant's book; the need for verbatim copying of the letters; and the effect of their use on the future market for Death House Letters. The fact that Death House Letters had been out of print for 20 years did not necessarily mean that the letters had no future market. The possibilities of republication, and sale of motion picture rights, might have been affected by their use in defendant's book. Meeropol v. Nizer, 560 F.2d 1061, 2 Med.L.Rptr. 2269 (2d Cir.1977), certiorari denied 434 U.S. 1013 (1978).

f. In 1977, after an arrest in the famous "Son of Sam" murder case, five sequences of "Doonesbury" were devoted to commentary on the way a columnist for the New York Daily News behaved during the search for the killer. The News, which held the New York City rights to the comic strip, decided not to use the sequences. The New York Post reported the action of the News and, since "censorship is news," the Post reprinted the five sequences to show its readers what the News had refused to carry. No suit resulted. Might the copyright owner have successfully sued the Post?

g. When a network televised a parade during which music copyrighted by plaintiff was being played, the court held that the fair use doctrine protected the network. Italian Book Corp. v. American Broadcasting Companies, Inc., 458 F.Supp. 65, 4 Med.L.Rptr. 1762 (S.D.N.Y. 1978).

h. In Roy Export Co. v. Columbia Broadcasting System, Inc., 672 F.2d 1095, 8 Med.L.Rptr. 1637 (2d Cir.), certiorari denied 459 U.S. 826 (1982), CBS presented excerpts from plaintiff's copyrighted films of Charlie Chaplin in a special program reporting on his death. Among its defenses to an infringement action was a First Amendment claim that Chaplin's fame was based on his films and that this gave CBS a limited right to use "gems" of Chaplin's films "in order adequately to memorialize him at his death." The court was unpersuaded and observed that no court of appeals "has ever held that the First Amendment provides a privilege in the copyright field distinct from the accommodation embodied in the 'fair use' doctrine." Even if the court were inclined to create such an exception, this would not be the case for it. "The showing of copyrighted films was not essential to CBS's news report of Charlie Chaplin's death or to its assessment of his place in history; public domain films were available for the purpose, and the public is already generally familiar with his work."

i. Consumer Reports magazine has long had a policy that its product ratings could not be used in advertising or for any commercial purposes. This was successfully challenged by the manufacturer of a lightweight vacuum cleaner in Consumers Union of United States, Inc. v. General Signal Corp., 724 F.2d 1044 (2d Cir.1983), rehearing and rehearing en banc denied 730 F.2d 47 (2d Cir.), certiorari denied 105 S.Ct. 100 (1984). The court, in denying a preliminary injunction, stressed that the defendant's commercials, reporting that plaintiff had given its cleaner a high rating, did not suggest that plaintiff was endorsing the product. Fair use was likely to be a successful defense to any copyright claim. Claims of false and misleading advertising were likely to fail since the defendant explicitly disclaimed plaintiff's endorsement.

Does anything prevent plaintiff from not testing defendant's products in the future?

4. The reason why First Amendment concerns have not played a great part in copyright cases to date is suggested in Note, Copyright Infringement and the First Amendment, 79 Colum.L.Rev. 320, 328 (1979):

> The four limitations on the copyright holder's monopoly—duration, authorship, the idea-expression distinction, and fair use—effectively accommodate many first amendment claims that might otherwise arise in actions for copyright infringement. Most importantly, the idea-expression distinction will often justify a finding of infringement when an infringer's first amendment rights are not damaged, and the fair use doctrine will often sanction an unauthorized use when a first amendment right might otherwise be claimed. However, when the idea-expression distinction is not applicable because the idea sought to be expressed is "wedded" to the copyright holder's expression of it (as in the case of a graphic

work), and unauthorized use cannot be sanctioned as fair use because of damage to the copyright holder's economic interests, there is a narrow, but nevertheless real conflict between copyright and the first amendment that cannot be resolved by the internal structure of the Copyright Act.

Such a conflict is suggested by Time, Inc. v. Bernard Geis Associates, 293 F.Supp. 130 (S.D.N.Y.1968), involving the Zapruder film of the assassination of President Kennedy. Plaintiff bought and copyrighted Zapruder's film. Defendant wanted to produce a study of the assassination but could not come to terms with plaintiff on getting a license to use the photographs. Instead, defendant prepared sketches that were admittedly copied very closely from published copies of the Zapruder film. The court found the need for copying the expression very strong here because of the difficulty of paraphrasing photographs and the central importance of the film. The court found fair use after concluding that the defendant's book would not be likely to hurt the sales of plaintiff's magazine.

If it were shown that the book had indeed seriously hurt plaintiff's sales of the copyrighted material, then fair use might not have been available. In such a case the copyright statute would permit Time, Inc. to seek an injunction against defendant or, if too late for injunctive relief, perhaps punitive damages. Would the First Amendment have permitted these remedies? Would it permit plaintiff to recover compensatory damages or the defendant's profits for the infringement?

The note suggests that if a First Amendment privilege is necessary above and beyond fair use, the constitutional interest would be met by barring injunctions and punitive damages against the copier. In such a case, the copier would in effect be given a compulsory license, but the owner would receive compensatory damages for that use of the copyrighted material.

6. In 1982, Susan Sontag made a speech in New York's Town Hall equating communism and fascism. The Soho News republished nearly the entire text of the speech because of the "political importance" of Sontag's remarks. The meeting was a public event to which the press had been invited. Can Sontag win a claim of copyright infringement? Can a reporter attending an event at which a poet reads his own poetry make a transcript and publish the poet's work?

7. See, generally, Francione, Facing *The Nation*: The Standards for Copyright, Infringement, and Fair Use of Factual Works, 134 U.Pa.L.Rev. 519 (1986).

B. COMMON-LAW PROTECTION

ZACCHINI v. SCRIPPS-HOWARD BROADCASTING CO.

Supreme Court of the United States, 1977.
433 U.S. 562, 97 S.Ct. 2849, 53 L.Ed.2d 965.
Noted, 1978 Duke L.J. 1198, 91 Harv.L.Rev. 208, 30 Stan.L.Rev. 1185, 1977 Utah L.Rev. 817.

MR. JUSTICE WHITE delivered the opinion of the Court.

Petitioner, Hugo Zacchini, is an entertainer. He performs a "human cannonball" act in which he is shot from a cannon into a net some 200 feet away. Each performance occupies some 15 seconds. In August and September 1972, petitioner was engaged to perform his act on a regular basis at the Geauga County Fair in Burton, Ohio. He performed in a fenced area, surrounded by grandstands, at the fair grounds. Members of the public attending the fair were not charged a separate admission fee to observe his act.

On August 30, a freelance reporter for Scripps-Howard Broadcasting Co., the operator of a television broadcasting station and respondent in this case, attended the fair. He carried a small movie camera. Petitioner noticed the reporter and asked him not to film the performance. The reporter did not do so on that day; but on the instructions of the producer of respondent's daily newscast, he returned the following day and videotaped the entire act. This film clip, approximately 15 seconds in length, was shown on the 11 o'clock news program that night, together with favorable commentary.[1]

Petitioner then brought this action for damages, alleging that he is "engaged in the entertainment business," that the act he performs is one "invented by his father and . . . performed only by his family for the last fifty years," that respondent "showed and commercialized the film of his act without his consent," and that such conduct was an "unlawful appropriation of plaintiff's professional property." App. 4–5. Respondent answered and moved for summary judgment, which was granted by the trial court.

. . .

. . . Insofar as the Ohio Supreme Court held that the First and Fourteenth Amendments of the United States Constitution required judgment for respondent, we reverse the judgment of that court.

. . .

1. The script of the commentary accompanying the film clip read as follows:

> "This . . . now . . . is the story of a *true spectator* sport . . . the sport of human cannonballing . . . in fact, the great *Zacchini* is about the only human cannonball around, these days . . . just happens that, *where* he is, is the Great Geauga County Fair, in Burton . . . and believe me, although it's not a *long* act, it's a thriller . . . and you really need to see it *in person* . . . to appreciate it. . . . " (Emphasis in original.)

Even if the judgment in favor of respondent must nevertheless be understood as ultimately resting on Ohio law, it appears that at the very least the Ohio court felt compelled by what it understood to be federal constitutional considerations to construe and apply its own law in the manner it did. In this event, we have jurisdiction and should decide the federal issue; for if the state court erred in its understanding of our cases and of the First and Fourteenth Amendments we should so declare, leaving the state court free to decide the privilege issue solely as a matter of Ohio law. [ ] If the Supreme Court of Ohio "held as it did because it felt under compulsion of federal law as enunciated by this Court so to hold, it should be relieved of that compulsion. It should be freed to decide . . . these suits according to its own local law." [ ]

. . .

The Ohio Supreme Court relied heavily on Time, Inc. v. Hill, [ ], but that case does not mandate a media privilege to televise a performer's entire act without his consent. Involved in Time, Inc. v. Hill was a claim under the New York "Right of Privacy" statute that Life Magazine, in the course of reviewing a new play, had connected the play with a long-past incident involving petitioner and his family and had falsely described their experience and conduct at that time. The complaint sought damages for humiliation and suffering flowing from these non-defamatory falsehoods that allegedly invaded Hill's privacy. The Court held, however, that the opening of a new play linked to an actual incident was a matter of public interest and that Hill could not recover without showing that the Life report was knowingly false or was published with reckless disregard for the truth—the same rigorous standard that had been applied in New York Times Co. v. Sullivan [ ].

Time, Inc. v. Hill, which was hotly contested and decided by a divided Court, involved an entirely different tort from the "right of publicity" recognized by the Ohio Supreme Court. . . .

The differences between these two torts are important. First, the State's interests in providing a cause of action in each instance are different. "The interest protected" in permitting recovery for placing the plaintiff in a false light "is clearly that of reputation, with the same overtones of mental distress as in defamation." Prosser, [Privacy, 48 Calif.L.Rev. 383, 400 (1960)]. By contrast, the State's interest in permitting a "right of publicity" is in protecting the proprietary interest of the individual in his act in part to encourage such entertainment. As we later note, the State's interest is closely analogous to the goals of patent and copyright law, focusing on the right of the individual to reap the reward of his endeavors and having little to do with protecting feelings or reputation. Second, the two torts differ in the degree to which they intrude on dissemination of information to the public. In "false light" cases the only way to protect the interests involved is to attempt to minimize publication of the damaging matter, while in "right of publicity" cases the only question is who gets to do the publishing. An entertainer such as petitioner usually has no objection to the widespread publication of his act as long as he gets the commercial benefit of such publication. Indeed, in the present case petitioner did not seek to enjoin the broadcast of his act; he simply sought compensation for the broadcast in the form of damages.

Nor does it appear that our later cases such as [*Rosenbloom; Gertz;* and *Firestone*] require or furnish substantial support for the Ohio court's privilege ruling. These cases, like *New York Times,* emphasize the protection extended to the press by the First Amendment in defamation cases, particularly when suit is brought by a public official or a public figure. None of them involve an alleged appropriation by the press of a right of publicity existing under state law.

Moreover, Time, Inc. v. Hill, New York Times, [*Rosenbloom*], *Gertz,* and *Firestone* all involved the reporting of events; in none of them was there an attempt to broadcast or publish an entire act for which the performer ordinarily gets paid. It is evident, and there is no claim here to the contrary, that petitioner's state-law right of publicity would not serve to prevent respondent from reporting the newsworthy facts about petitioner's act. Wherever the line in particular situations is to be drawn between media reports that are protected and those that are not, we are quite sure that the First and Fourteenth Amendments do not immunize the media when they broadcast a performer's entire act without his consent. The Constitution no more prevents a State from requiring respondent to compensate petitioner for broadcasting his act on television than it would privilege respondent to film and broadcast a copyrighted dramatic work without liability to the copyright owner, [ ], or to film and broadcast a prize fight, [ ], or a baseball game, [ ], where the promoters or the participants had other plans for publicizing the event. There are ample reasons for reaching this conclusion.

The broadcast of a film of petitioner's entire act poses a substantial threat to the economic value of that performance. As the Ohio court recognized, this act is the product of petitioner's own talents and energy, the end result of much time, effort, and expense. Much of its economic value lies in the "right of exclusive control over the publicity given to his performance"; if the public can see the act free on television, it will be less willing to pay to see it at the fair.[12] The effect of a public broadcast of the performance is similar to preventing petitioner from charging an admission fee. . . . Moreover, the broadcast of petitioner's entire performance, unlike the unauthorized use of another's name for purposes of trade or the incidental use of a name or picture by the press, goes to the heart of petitioner's ability to earn a living as an entertainer. Thus, in this case, Ohio has recognized what

12. It is possible, of course, that respondent's news broadcast increased the value of petitioner's performance by stimulating the public's interest in seeing the act live. In these circumstances, petitioner would not be able to prove damages and thus would not recover. But petitioner has alleged that the broadcast injured him to the extent of $25,000. App. 5, and we think the State should be allowed to authorize compensation of this injury if proved.

may be the strongest case for a "right of publicity"—involving, not the appropriation of an entertainer's reputation to enhance the attractiveness of a commercial product, but the appropriation of the very activity by which the entertainer acquired his reputation in the first place.

Of course, Ohio's decision to protect petitioner's right of publicity here rests on more than a desire to compensate the performer for the time and effort invested in his act; the protection provides an economic incentive for him to make the investment required to produce a performance of interest to the public. This same consideration underlies the patent and copyright laws long enforced by this Court. . . .

There is no doubt that entertainment, as well as news, enjoys First Amendment protection. It is also true that entertainment itself can be important news. Time, Inc., v. Hill. But it is important to note that neither the public nor respondent will be deprived of the benefit of petitioner's performance as long as his commercial stake in his act is appropriately recognized. Petitioner does not seek to enjoin the broadcast of his performance; he simply wants to be paid for it. Nor do we think that a state-law damages remedy against respondent would represent a species of liability without fault contrary to the letter or spirit of Gertz v. Robert Welch, Inc., [ ]. Respondent knew exactly that petitioner objected to televising his act but nevertheless displayed the entire film.

We conclude that although the State of Ohio may as a matter of its own law privilege the press in the circumstances of this case, the First and Fourteenth Amendments do not require it to do so.

Reversed.

MR. JUSTICE POWELL, with whom MR. JUSTICE BRENNAN and MR. JUSTICE MARSHALL join, dissenting.

Disclaiming any attempt to do more than decide the narrow case before us, the Court reverses the decision of the Supreme Court of Ohio based on repeated incantation of a single formula: "a performer's entire act." The holding today is summed up in one sentence:

> "Wherever the line in particular situations is to be drawn between media reports that are protected and those that are not, we are quite sure that the First and Fourteenth Amendments do not immunize the media when they broadcast a performer's entire act without his consent."

I doubt that this formula provides a standard clear enough even for resolution of this case.[1] In any event, I am not persuaded that the

1. Although the record is not explicit, it is unlikely that the "act" commenced abruptly with the explosion that launched petitioner on his way, ending with the landing in the net a few seconds later. One may assume that the actual firing was preceded by some fanfare, possibly stretching over several minutes, to heighten the audience's anticipation: introduction of the performer, description of the uniqueness and danger, last-minute checking of the apparatus, and entry into the cannon, all accompanied by suitably ominous commentary from the master of ceremonies. If this is found to be the case on remand, then respondent could not be said to have appropriated the "entire act" in its 15-second news-clip—and the Court's opinion

Court's opinion is appropriately sensitive to the First Amendment values at stake, and I therefore dissent.

Although the Court would draw no distinction, [ ] I do not view respondent's action as comparable to unauthorized commercial broadcasts of sporting events, theatrical performances, and the like where the broadcaster keeps the profits. There is no suggestion here that respondent made any such use of the film. Instead, it simply reported on what petitioner concedes to be a newsworthy event, in a way hardly surprising for a television station—by means of film coverage. The report was part of an ordinary daily news program, consuming a total of 15 seconds. It is a routine example of the press fulfilling the informing function so vital to our system.

The Court's holding that the station's ordinary news report may give rise to substantial liability has disturbing implications, for the decision could lead to a degree of media self-censorship. [ ] Hereafter whenever a television news editor is unsure whether certain film footage received from a camera crew might be held to portray an "entire act," he may decline coverage—even of clearly newsworthy events—or confine the broadcast to watered-down verbal reporting, perhaps with an occasional still picture. The public is then the loser. This is hardly the kind of news reportage that the First Amendment is meant to foster. [ ]

In my view the First Amendment commands a different analytical starting point from the one selected by the Court. Rather than begin with a quantitative analysis of the performer's behavior—is this or is this not his entire act?—we should direct initial attention to the actions of the news media: what use did the station make of the film footage? When a film is used, as here, for a routine portion of a regular news program, I would hold that the First Amendment protects the station from a "right of publicity" or "appropriation" suit, absent a strong showing by the plaintiff that the news broadcast was a subterfuge or cover for private or commercial exploitation.[4]

. . . In a suit like the one before us, however, the plaintiff does not complain about the fact of exposure to the public, but rather about its timing or manner. He welcomes some publicity, but seeks to retain control over means and manner as a way to maximize for himself the monetary benefits that flow from such publication. But having made the matter public—having chosen, in essence, to make it newsworthy—he cannot, consistent with the First Amendment, complain of routine news reportage. Cf. Gertz v. Robert Welch, Inc., [ ] (clarifying the

then would afford no guidance for resolution of the case. Moreover, in future cases involving different performances, similar difficulties in determining just what constitutes the "entire act" are inevitable.

4. This case requires no detailed specification of the standards for identifying a subterfuge, since there is no claim here that respondent's news use was anything but bona fide. [ ] I would point out, however, that selling time during a news broadcast to advertisers in the customary fashion does not make for "commercial exploitation" in the sense intended here. [ ]

different liability standards appropriate in defamation suits, depending on whether or not the plaintiff is a public figure).

Since the film clip here was undeniably treated as news and since there is no claim that the use was subterfuge, respondent's actions were constitutionally privileged. I would affirm.

[Mr. Justice Stevens dissented on the ground that he could not tell whether the Ohio Supreme Court had relied on federal constitutional issues in deciding the case. He would have remanded the case to that court "for clarification of its holding before deciding the federal constitutional issue."]

On remand, the Ohio Supreme Court took advantage of the opportunity afforded by the majority opinion and decided that nothing in the Ohio Constitution protected the behavior of the media defendant. The case was remanded for trial and for assessment of damages if liability was established. Zacchini v. Scripps-Howard Broadcasting Co., 54 Ohio St.2d 286, 376 N.E.2d 582 (1978).

Notes and Questions

1. How important is it that the majority treats the 15 seconds as the "entire act"? In a case involving the televising of a figure skating championship, a telecaster argued that a short newscast drawn from hours of film would not be an "entire" act under *Zacchini.* The judge, however, said it was "conceivable that a two-minute broadcast, focused solely on the top performer of the day, would embody the essence of the commercially valuable performance, and thus could possibly be a broadcast of the entire act." The case went off on other issues. Post Newsweek Stations-Connecticut, Inc. v. Travelers Insurance Co., 510 F.Supp. 81, 6 Med.L.Rptr. 2540 (D.Conn.1981).

2. Does *Zacchini* involve an aspect of "privacy"? Does it resemble the Cox Broadcasting case in that both involved lawfully obtained information of interest or concern to the public? Can you explain why the defendant in *Cox Broadcasting* did not have to pay while the defendant in *Zacchini* may have to pay?

3. Earlier in this section, in discussing copyright, it was suggested that defendants might be able to assert the First Amendment as a defense even if they have overstepped the bounds of fair use. The Zacchini case seems to suggest that the Court would not be sympathetic to such a defense. At the very least, however, the First Amendment would seem to bar injunctions in this type of case.

4. After *Zacchini,* what would happen in a case in which a street artist who survives on contributions from passersby—a mime, an accordionist, a dancer—is photographed by the local television station and shown in a story about summer diversions on the streets of the city? Is the street artist's claim as strong as Zacchini's?

5. Another important question—one requiring a balancing of property rights and First Amendment rights—is to what extent a news organization can make unauthorized use of the research and labor of a competitor either by directly copying its work or by "appropriating" the facts contained in its news release. Although the substance of news cannot be protected by common law or statutory copyright, the doctrine of unfair competition has been used to protect the gatherer of news from the direct, unauthorized reproduction of its material for commercial use. In International News Service v. Associated Press, 248 U.S. 215 (1918), I.N.S. was enjoined from copying news from A.P. bulletin boards and early editions of A.P. member newspapers until "the commercial value" of the news to the complainant and all of its members had passed. The Court found unfair competition in the taking of material acquired through the expenditure of skill, labor, and money by A.P., for the purpose of diverting "a material portion of the profit" to I.N.S. Although the Court condemned the "habitual failure" of I.N.S. to give credit to A.P. as the source of its news, the misrepresentation was not considered essential to a finding of unfair competition: "It is something more than the advantage of celebrity of which complainant is being deprived."

This doctrine of misappropriation was extended in Veatch v. Wagner, 14 Alaska 470, 116 F.Supp. 904 (1953), to protect a newspaper publisher from a radio station's verbatim broadcast of news from the plaintiff's newspaper. Similarly, in Pottstown Daily News Pub. Co. v. Pottstown Broadcasting Co., 411 Pa. 383, 192 A.2d 657 (1963), the plaintiff stated a cause of action based on a violation of property rights and a claim of unfair competition in pleading that the defendant had taken news items from plaintiff's newspaper for broadcast over defendant's radio station.

The following year, however, in two cases dealing with product imitations, the Supreme Court held that an action for unfair competition based upon the copying of an unpatentable article cannot be maintained unless the copier misrepresents its goods to be originals. Sears Roebuck & Co. v. Stiffel Co., 376 U.S. 225 (1964); Compco Corp. v. Day-Brite Lighting, Inc., 376 U.S. 234 (1964). In a broad dictum, Justice Black stated that "when an article is unprotected by a patent or a copyright, state law may not forbid others to copy that article."

State courts, however, have been reluctant to abandon the misappropriation doctrine. Two years after the *Sears* case, a New York publisher of a financial newsletter was enjoined from using information about government and municipal bonds gathered by a competitor. Bond Buyer v. Dealers Digest Pub. Co., 25 App.Div.2d 158, 267 N.Y.S.2d 944 (1966). Federal courts have also been reluctant to apply the *Sears* and *Compco* decisions to the media. In a suit seeking to prohibit defendant from reproducing plaintiff's edition of an uncopyrightable book through the use of less expensive photographic processes, Grove Press, Inc. v. Collectors' Publication, Inc., 264 F.Supp. 603 (C.D.Cal.

1967), the court, in granting the preliminary injunction, said that "unfair appropriation of the property of a competitor is unfair competition and redressable in a situation of this kind despite the holdings in *Sears* . . . and *Compco.*" These lower courts correctly anticipated that the Court would retreat from the *Sears* dictum. See Goldstein v. California, 412 U.S. 546 (1973) (states may forbid unauthorized re-recordings) and Kewanee Oil Co. v. Bicron Corp., 416 U.S. 470 (1974) (federal patent laws do not preempt state trade secret law).

One commentator has found the misappropriation doctrine to be necessary in a very limited context: when the refusal of the court to provide protection against competitors would destroy the commercial value of the product or service to the originator. Rahl, The Right to "Appropriate" Trade Values, 23 Ohio St.L.J. 56 (1962). According to Rahl, such situations are encountered where "appropriation at the initial stage" may frustrate the opportunity of the plaintiff to market his product or service. With respect to news, for example, so long as news is "hot," allowing competitors to make unauthorized use of others' stories without some sort of right of initial release could destroy the commercial incentive that rewards prompt news gathering and dissemination. Rahl suggests plaintiffs may need judicial aid in reaching the marketplace "with values so fragile that they otherwise cannot make it."

After a law firm mistakenly forgot to put exhibits in a trade secret case under seal, portions of the documents appeared in an industry newsletter. The report apparently included seven of the client's important trade secrets. The law firm then obtained an order from the judge in the underlying case requiring the editor who published the original story to return his copy and directing the newsletter's 2,000 subscribers to return their copies, and enjoining them from using or disclosing the information contained in the story.

To achieve the return of the copies, the court ordered the editor to turn over his subscription list. He returned his own copy but refused to provide his list. In a compromise, he agreed to include a copy of the order with each copy of his next issue. The largest newspaper in the region returned the copy it had obtained—but only after the plaintiff went back to court and got the paper exempted from the return order. Rashi, Firm's Disclosure of Trade Secrets Creates Turmoil, Nat'l L.J. Oct. 29, 1984 at 3; Sanger, Silicon Valley Secrecy Drama, N.Y. Times, Oct. 18, 1984, § IV, at 1.

Chapter VI

THE PRESS AND THE POLITICAL PROCESS

So far we have been considering particular common law or statutory notions that have produced important litigation testing the boundaries of protection for the press when sued, usually in civil cases. In this Chapter, we turn to broader questions about the role of the press generally in the political process. This includes the electoral process itself as well as the political climate between elections and political discussion generally.

This Chapter will emphasize the print media. Some broadcasting activities will be considered because the problems they present arise from the speed with which these media can transmit information, rather than from the special limited-spectrum aspects of broadcasting that have been used to justify most regulation. Most special regulation of broadcasting in the electoral and political arenas will be considered at length in Chapter XV.

A. PROTECTING ELECTORAL INTEGRITY

The Supreme Court and many state courts have long recognized a legitimate and often compelling state interest in safeguarding the integrity of the electoral process and individual citizens' ability to participate in it. As Justice Frankfurter described them, these issues are "not less than basic to a democratic society." United States v. United Automobile Workers, 352 U.S. 567 (1957).

The First Amendment, however, may constrain statutes that regulate mechanisms of political discussion as a means of ensuring electoral integrity. The importance of freedom of expression rests at least in part on its role in effective self-government. Full and free discussion may be so fundamental to the political process that attempts to regulate expression to purify the process ultimately may undermine it instead. On the other hand, some cleansing measures may be necessary, despite their First Amendment implications. It could be that some limitations on free expression that would be unconstitutional in other contexts should be upheld if they contribute to the integrity of elections.

1. PREVENTING DISHONESTY

MILLS v. ALABAMA

Supreme Court of the United States, 1966.
384 U.S. 214, 86 S.Ct. 1434, 16 L.Ed.2d 484.
Noted, 52 A.B.A.J. 675, 19 Okla.L.Rev. 440.

MR. JUSTICE BLACK delivered the opinion of the Court.

The question squarely presented here is whether a State, consistently with the United States Constitution, can make it a crime for the editor of a daily newspaper to write and publish an editorial *on election day* urging people to vote a certain way on issues submitted to them.

On November 6, 1962, Birmingham, Alabama, held an election for the people to decide whether they preferred to keep their existing city commission form of government or replace it with a mayor-council government. On election day the Birmingham Post-Herald, a daily newspaper, carried an editorial written by its editor, appellant, James E. Mills, which strongly urged the people to adopt the mayor-council form of government. Mills was later arrested on a complaint charging that by publishing the editorial *on election day* he had violated § 285 of the Alabama Corrupt Practices Act, Ala. Code, 1940, Tit. 17, §§ 268–286, which makes it a crime "to do any electioneering or to solicit any votes . . . in support of or in opposition to any proposition that is being voted on on the day on which the election affecting such candidates or propositions is being held." The trial court sustained demurrers to the complaint on the grounds that the state statute abridged freedom of speech and press in violation of the Alabama Constitution and the First and Fourteenth Amendments to the United States Constitution. On appeal by the State, the Alabama Supreme Court held that publication of the editorial on election day undoubtedly violated the state law and then went on to reverse the trial court by holding that the state statute as applied did not unconstitutionally abridge freedom of speech or press. Recognizing that the state law did limit and restrict both speech and press, the State Supreme Court nevertheless sustained it as a valid exercise of the State's police power. . . .

[The state judgment was held to be an appealable "final judgment," despite the fact that it remanded the case to the trial court for further proceedings. If the case were to return there, "the trial, so far as this record shows, would be no more than a few formal gestures leading inexorably towards a conviction, and then another appeal . . . ."]

II.

We come now to the merits. The First Amendment, which applies to the States through the Fourteenth, prohibits laws "abridging the freedom of speech, or of the press." The question here is whether it abridges freedom of the press for a State to punish a newspaper editor for doing no more than publishing an editorial on election day urging people to vote a particular way in the election. We should point out at once that this question in no way involves the extent of a State's power to regulate conduct in and around the polls in order to maintain peace, order and decorum there. The sole reason for the charge that Mills violated the law is that he wrote and published an editorial on election day urging Birmingham voters to cast their votes in favor of changing their form of government.

Whatever differences may exist about interpretations of the First Amendment, there is practically universal agreement that a major purpose of that Amendment was to protect the free discussion of governmental affairs. This of course includes discussions of candidates, structures and forms of government, the manner in which government is operated or should be operated, and all such matters relating to the political process. . . . It is difficult to conceive of a more obvious and flagrant abridgment of the constitutionally guaranteed freedom of the press.

Admitting that the state law restricted a newspaper editor's freedom to publish editorials on election day, the Alabama Supreme Court nevertheless sustained the constitutionality of the law on the ground that the restrictions on the press were only "reasonable restrictions" or at least "within the field of reasonableness." The court reached this conclusion because it thought the law imposed only a minor limitation on the press—restricting it only on election days—and because the court thought the law served a good purpose. It said:

> "It is a salutary legislative enactment that protects the public from confusive last-minute charges and countercharges and the distribution of propaganda in an effort to influence voters on an election day; when as a practical matter, because of lack of time, such matters cannot be answered or their truth determined until after the election is over." [ ]

This argument, even if it were relevant to the constitutionality of the law, has a fatal flaw. The state statute leaves people free to hurl their campaign charges up to the last minute of the day before election. The law held valid by the Alabama Supreme Court then goes on to make it a crime to answer those "last-minute" charges on election day, the only time they can be effectively answered. Because the law prevents any adequate reply to these charges, it is wholly ineffective in protecting the electorate "from confusive last-minute charges and countercharges." We hold that no test of reasonableness can save a state law from invalidation as a violation of the First Amendment when that law makes it a crime for a newspaper editor to do no more than urge people to vote one way or another in a publicly held election.

The judgment of the Supreme Court of Alabama is reversed and the case is remanded for further proceedings not inconsistent with this opinion.

It is so ordered.

[Justice Douglas wrote a separate concurrence, joined by Justice Brennan, focusing on the special light thrown on the jurisdictional issue by the First Amendment.

Justice Harlan wrote separately to disagree with the Court's assertion of jurisdiction in the case. Because the appellant still faced a trial in the state court, where an acquittal was possible, the judgment was not final. He added, however, that had the issue properly been before the Court, he would reverse on the ground that the relevant provision—to do any electioneering or to solicit any votes on election day—"did not give the appellant . . . fair warning that the publication of an editorial of this kind was reached."]

Notes and Questions

1. It is a crime in several states to make certain false statements affecting an election campaign. The details of the offense vary, as these examples suggest:

> Wis.Stat.Ann. § 12.05 (Supp.1981). No person may knowingly make or publish, or cause to be made or published, a false representation pertaining to a candidate which is intended or tends to affect voting at an election.
>
> Miss.Code Ann. § 23–3–33 (1972). No person, including a candidate, shall publicly or privately make, in a campaign then in progress, any charge or charges reflecting upon the honesty, integrity or moral character of any candidate, so far as his private life is concerned, unless the charge be in fact true and actually capable of proof; and any person who makes any such charge shall have the burden of proof to show the truth thereof when called to account therefor under any affidavit or indictment against him for a violation of this section. And any language deliberately uttered or published which, when fairly and reasonably construed and as commonly understood, would clearly and unmistakably imply any such charge, shall be deemed and held to be the equivalent of a direct charge. And in no event shall any such charge, whether true or untrue, be made on the day of the primary, or within the last five days immediately preceding the date of the primary.

2. Are these statutes within the standards for punishment of criticism of public figures set down in New York Times Co. v. Sullivan and its progeny, especially *Garrison, Roy, Hepps,* and *Keeton?* Does the public interest in the honesty of elections add a new ingredient here?

3. In Brown v. Hartlage, 456 U.S. 45 (1982), Kentucky courts had ordered a new election after a candidate promised the electorate that he would reduce his salary—an illegal promise—if elected. There was no showing the candidate knew the promise was illegal—and he retracted it as soon as he became aware of the problem. The Supreme Court held that nullifying the victory violated the First Amendment, in part because there was no showing that Brown knew he was promising something illegal.

The candidate's "promise to confer some ultimate benefit on the voter, qua taxpayer, citizen, or member of the general public, does not [lie] beyond the pale of First Amendment protection." If the statute was designed to keep wealthy, but inept, candidates from prevailing in elections, the means chosen was impermissible. The First Amendment "embodies our trust in the free exchange of ideas as the means by which the people are to choose between good ideas and bad, and between candidates for political office. The State's fear that voters might make an ill-advised choice does not provide the State with a compelling justification for limiting speech. It is simply not the function of government to 'select which issues are worth discussing or debating' in the course of a political campaign."

To the extent the state wanted to avoid distortions in the political process due to inaccurate speech, the purpose was "somewhat different" from the rationale for protecting defamatory speech about public officials. Nonetheless, the same principles should apply: "In a political campaign, a candidate's factual blunder is unlikely to escape the notice of, and correction by, the erring candidate's political opponent. The preferred First Amendment remedy" was "more speech, not enforced silence." The Kentucky remedy had imposed a form of absolute liability for error. "The chilling effect of such absolute accountability for factual misstatements in the course of political debate is incompatible with the atmosphere of free discussion contemplated by the First Amendment in the context of political campaigns."

4. In 1984, California adopted a constitutional amendment that provides for upsetting an election if the winner is found liable in a civil action for defamation against an opponent and it is further found that the defamation "was a major contributing cause in the defeat of an opposing candidate." Cal.Const. Art. 7, Sec. 10. If a defamation is not protected under Times v. Sullivan, is there any reason why the state cannot add this sanction to the existing array?

Would the California amendment violate the First Amendment if it were to provide for a new election if a losing candidate could prove an actionable libel committed by a publisher or broadcaster and could show that it was "a major contributing cause" in that candidate's defeat?

Does Brown v. Hartlage prevent the state from ordering a new election where there is a clear showing that the public was swayed by a last-minute defamation from an opponent that the speaker honestly believed to be true? What if it came from the dominant newspaper in the electoral district?

5. New York Election Law § 472(a) provided for the adoption of a "fair campaign code" that would prohibit, among other things, attacks based on racial, religious, or ethnic background and deliberate misrepresentation of a candidate's qualifications, positions on political issues, party affiliation, or party endorsement. The statute specifically excluded "any person, association, or corporation engaged in the publication or

distribution of any newspaper or other publication issued at regular intervals." Why exclude an editorial or article that deliberately misstated facts about a candidate? Could the press have been covered?

A three-judge court invalidated the code adopted by the administrators. At the outset, the court agreed with the state's argument, based on *Garrison,* "that calculated falsehoods are of such slight social value that no matter what the context in which they are made, they are not constitutionally protected." This was true even though freedom of speech "has its fullest and most urgent applications" in political campaigns. Monitor Patriot Co. v. Roy, p. 170, supra. This approach, however, did not save the provisions of the code that barred "misrepresentations" of a candidate's position, party affiliation, or qualifications because the regulations failed to require that the misrepresentations be "deliberately" or "recklessly" false.

The court also rejected the "blanket prohibition" on attacks on a candidate's race, sex, religion, or ethnic background. The state had defended these prohibitions on the ground that such statements were "completely unrelated to any candidate's 'fitness for office.'" Calling this an "exercise in self-delusion," the court stated that it "would be a retreat from reality to hold that voters do not consider race, religion, sex or ethnic background when choosing political candidates." The court relied on Monitor Patriot Co. v. Roy, in which the Court had held "as a matter of constitutional law that a charge of criminal conduct, no matter how remote in time or place, can never be irrelevant to an official's or a candidate's fitness for office" for purposes of applying the "knowing falsehood or reckless disregard" rule of *New York Times.* The court also noted that given the "realities of our political life, it is by no means easy to see what statements about a candidate might be altogether without relevance to his fitness for the office he seeks." Vanasco v. Schwartz, 401 F.Supp. 87 (E.D.N.Y.1975). The Supreme Court affirmed without opinion, 423 U.S. 1041 (1976). These provisions have been repealed in their entirety.

6. In Wilson v. Superior Court, 13 Cal.3d 652, 532 P.2d 116, 119 Cal. Rptr. 468 (1975), the California Supreme Court reviewed a preliminary injunction issued by a trial court requiring a candidate's campaign newsletter to be "fair and balanced . . . with a full presentation of the facts" in its discussion of the opponent. The newsletter reproduced newspaper articles stating that the opponent had been indicted for bribery, without showing that the indictment had occurred seven years earlier and that an acquittal had resulted. The trial court held that the petitioner could bring his opponent's history before the public, but only "in such a manner that the average voter, looking at that will understand that they are not current articles." A narrow view of the truth "may well be a falsehood" in this context.

The California Supreme Court held the injunction invalid under both the First Amendment and the state constitution: "The concept that a statement on a public issue may be suppressed because it is believed by a court to be untrue is entirely inconsistent with constitutional guarantees and raises the spectre of censorship in a most pernicious form." The court relied on *Pentagon Papers* in asserting that "any prior restraint on expression bears a heavy presumption against its constitutional validity." Moreover, "the truth or falsity of a statement on a public issue is irrelevant to the question whether it should be repressed in advance of publication." Efforts to defend the injunction on the grounds that it protected against a "clear and present danger" of misleading charges against a candidate, and that it affected conduct, not speech, were rejected.

2. Evaluating Arguments—Anonymity

Even if false campaign statements are prevented and the views of the candidates are conveyed to the voters, the electorate may still lack a complete basis for judging all it hears. Some campaign literature may be anonymous, and voters may not know how much credence to give it—except that they may consider the fact of anonymity itself. Carefully drafted prohibitions against false statements could handle the related problem of misattributed literature. But the problem of anonymity has received special treatment. In Talley v. California, 362 U.S. 60 (1960), the Court overturned an ordinance barring distribution of "any hand-bill in any place under any circumstances, which does not have printed on the cover, or the face thereof, the name and address" of the person who "printed, wrote, compiled or manufactured" it and the person "who caused the same to be distributed." The state sought to defend it on the ground that the ordinance helped identify those responsible for fraud, false advertising, and libel. But the majority responded that the ordinance swept much more broadly than that in covering all handbills under all circumstances. The Court noted the great importance of anonymous pamphlets through history: "Persecuted groups and sects from time to time throughout history have been able to criticize oppressive practices and laws either anonymously or not at all. The obnoxious press licensing law of England . . . was due in part to the knowledge that exposure of the names of printers, writers and distributors would lessen the circulation of literature critical of the government." After discussing the role of anonymous literature in England, the opinion recalls that "Even the Federalist Papers, written in favor of the adoption of our Constitution, were published under fictitious names. It is plain that anonymity has sometimes been assumed for the most constructive purposes."

For the three dissenters, Justice Clark argued that Talley failed to present "any claim, much less proof, that he will suffer any injury whatever by identifying the handbill with his name," and thus failed to show how the ordinance was restraining his speech. Justice Clark stated he stood "second to none in supporting Talley's right of free speech—but not his freedom of anonymity. The Constitution says nothing about freedom of anonymous speech." An additional concern was that 36 states had similar statutes relating to election campaign literature.

In People v. Duryea, 76 Misc.2d 948, 351 N.Y.S.2d 978, affirmed without opinion 44 App.Div.2d 663, 354 N.Y.S.2d 129 (1974), the judge dismissed an indictment for violation of a general statute banning anonymous election literature. The trial judge observed:

> Of course, the identity of the source is helpful in evaluating ideas. But "the best test of truth is the power of the thought to get itself accepted in the competition of the market" (Abrams v. United States, 250 U.S. 616, 630 (1919) [HOLMES, J.]). Do not underestimate the common man. People are intelligent enough to evaluate the source of an anonymous writing. They can see it is anonymous. They know it is anonymous. They can evaluate its anonymity along with its message, as long as they are permitted, as they must be, to read that message. And then, once they have done so, it is for them to decide what is "responsible", what is valuable, and what is truth.

Compare Canon v. Justice Court, 61 Cal.2d 446, 393 P.2d 428, 39 Cal. Rptr. 228 (1964), involving a statute banning anonymous literature attacking the "personal character" of a candidate for office. Although later voiding the statute on unrelated grounds, the court unanimously agreed that this provision did not violate freedom of speech. The statute's purposes—to facilitate public evaluation of campaign material, to deter irresponsible attacks, and to facilitate rebuttals by candidates—helped assure that "elections will be the expression of the will of an undeceived, well-informed public." The statute was limited to personal attacks on candidates, excluded general political writings, and applied only during election periods. The court observed that "Adequate dissemination of rebuttal or refutation is virtually impossible in the situation of preelection attacks. The heat of an election campaign and limitations of time work against the effective use of 'counterargument and education.'" Although recognizing the value of anonymity, the court concluded that too often it led to irresponsible attacks on candidates with resultant deceit of the electorate.

Recall Wilson v. Superior Court, p. 424, supra, in which the same court 11 years later barred injunctions against unfair or misleading campaign literature. The court stressed the commitment to "uninhibited, robust, and wide-open" debate and stressed the danger of the court's assuming the role of government censor in approving certain versions of proposed literature but not others. The court also observed that "The judiciary has been ever mindful of Thomas Jefferson's aphorism that 'error of opinion may be tolerated when reason is free to combat it.'"

A less difficult question is presented by statutes that would require authors to sign newspaper editorials. The Supreme Judicial Court of Maine invalidated such a statute in a short opinion citing *Talley.* Opinion of the Justices, 306 A.2d 18 (Me.1973). Is the newspaper case distinguishable from that of handbills? According to the Delaware Supreme Court, the signed-editorial statute presents a stronger case for invalidation, since a newspaper publisher, unlike a pamphleteer, is not anonymous, and "adopts the unsigned editorial as its own, regardless of the identity of the penman." In re Opinion of the Justices, 324 A.2d 211 (Del.1974).

3. Affecting Behavior During Polling Times

On the election day itself, voters may be influenced as they are approaching or at the polls, or may be influenced not to vote. Traditional bans on electioneering within a certain distance of the polls have addressed the problem of influence near the voting booth.

The concern about media influence on whether eligible voters actually turn out to vote is a relatively new one. Two issues must be separated here. One arises when broadcasters report the actual vote counts after the polls in a state have closed. Using this information the broadcaster may go one step further and project the winner statewide or districtwide. This practice cannot affect voters when all of the polls in a district or state close at the same time, as is true in most states. The concern arises in presidential elections, when the polls in the eastern states may close hours before those in the West.

In 1980, for example, projections from counted votes in the East led networks to project Ronald Reagan the winner over Jimmy Carter nationwide when the voters in the Pacific states still had two or three hours to vote. (Jimmy Carter may have compounded the problem by conceding shortly after the network projections). Voters were said to have left voter lines after learning of these facts. In addition, voting officials in western states asserted that the expected after-work vote did not materialize because of these reports. Assuming the accuracy of the network projections, these voting officials were especially concerned about the impact of these missing voters on statewide and local issues. Is there any reason to think that more Reagan supporters than Carter supporters stayed home? If not, is there any reason to think that the outcome of any state or local race or ballot proposition was affected by whatever lower turnout occurred? Might western voters think that their votes "count less" than those of eastern voters?

Consider the following suggestions for minimizing or avoiding early projections in presidential elections:

(1) punishing media organizations that report vote counts anywhere until all polls in that election have closed;

(2) punishing media organizations that send reports of vote counts from states whose polls have closed into areas in which the same election is still being conducted;

(3) forbidding the counting of any ballots in an election until all the polls participating in that election have closed;

(4) requiring uniform poll closing.

In early 1986, by a vote of 204–171, the House passed H.R. 3525, providing for a uniform poll closing of 9 p.m. (E.S.T.) in presidential elections. Alaska and Hawaii were excluded—and a special provision for New Hampshire would permit state law to supersede the closing hour at any polling place when all eligible voters have voted. (Before passage, the networks agreed not to use data from exit polls to predict presidential winners in a state until all the polls in that state have closed.)

The second new development in election reporting has been the practice of "exit polling," in which surveys are taken among those who have actually voted in an election as they leave the polling stations. Although media have long taken pre-election polls to determine the attitudes of prospective voters, exit polling causes greater concern. Is this because it is likelier to be accurate?

The State of Washington sought to address exit polling by amending its legislation regulating behavior around polling stations to state that no person within 300 feet of any polling place may "conduct any exit poll or public opinion poll with voters." RCW 29.51.020. A district court judgment upholding the statute was vacated in Daily Herald Co. v. Munro, 758 F.2d 350, 11 Med.L.Rptr. 1033 (9th Cir.1984). The majority remanded the case for further proceedings on such questions of "material fact" as whether the statute was necessary to protect order, peace, and decorum around the polls. Judge Norris, concurring in part and dissenting in part, would have invalidated the statute on the ground that it "is not a regulation aimed primarily at disruptive behavior, but rather is one aimed at the use to which information is put":

> This makes defense of the statute difficult because the end use of the polling data bears no relationship to the disruptive potential of the physical act of surveying the voters as they leave the polling place. The Washington statute is thus both too restrictive—reaching exit polling that is not disruptive—and, at the same time, underinclusive—failing to reach voter interviewing not part of a scientifically reliable polling process.

Judge Norris thought the same danger of influencing voters inhered here as in Mills v. Alabama, and that the answer in both was the same: if voters are going to misuse information there is nothing the law can do about it. Rehearing en banc was denied.

On remand, after a short trial, the judge concluded that the sole purpose of the statute had been to thwart exit polling and that no case of disruption caused by such polling had been presented. The statute was declared unconstitutional because its bar was too broad. The judge was clear that exit polling could be prevented in the actual voting area. The ruling did not disturb other parts of the statute directly addressing electioneering and disruption around the polls. N.Y.Times, Dec. 19, 1985, at 10. See generally, Note, Exit Polls and the First Amendment, 98 Harv.L.Rev. 1927 (1985). Another appeal has been taken.

Again, is there a difference between making conduct criminal and saying that if the voters are misled by an erroneous fact (here a false projection), a new election may be ordered? For a broad view of the situation, see Symposium, Early Calls of Election Results and Exit Polls: Pros, Cons, and Constitutional Considerations, 49 Pub.Op.Q. 1 (1985).

Later in this Chapter we consider whether voters may lie to the media to discourage this practice.

4. POLITICAL ADVOCATES' ACCESS TO THE PUBLIC

The role of the press in informing the public about government, issues, and candidates is at the root of the First Amendment. Does this imply a corresponding duty to inform the public about these matters? Florida Stat. § 104.38 provided a "right of reply" for a candidate "in any election" whose personal character or official record was assailed in a newspaper. Upon such an attack, the candidate had the right to demand that the newspaper print, free of charge, any reply he might make, "in as conspicuous a place and in the same kind of type as the matter that calls for such reply, provided such reply does not take up more space than the matter replied to." Violators were guilty of a first degree misdemeanor.

In the fall of 1972, the Miami Herald ran two editorials criticizing Pat Tornillo, a candidate for the Florida House of Representatives. When he demanded that the newspaper print his replies verbatim, it refused. He sued, seeking declaratory and injunctive relief, and actual and punitive damages. The trial court refused the injunction, holding that the statute violated the First Amendment because ordering what a newspaper must print was comparable to ordering what not to print. On direct appeal, the Florida Supreme Court reversed, 287 So.2d 78 (Fla.1973):

> The election of leaders of our government by a majority of the qualified electors is the fundamental precept upon which our system of government is based, and is an integral part of our nation's history. Recognizing that there is a right to publish without prior governmental restraint, we also emphasize that there is a correlative responsibility that the public be fully informed.
>
> The entire concept of freedom of expression as seen by our founding fathers rests upon the necessity for a fully informed electorate. James Madison wrote that "A popular government without popular information or the means of acquiring it is but a prologue to a farce or tragedy; or, perhaps both. Knowledge will forever govern ignorance; and a people who mean to be their own governors, must arm themselves with the power which knowledge gives." (To W.T. Barry, August 4, 1822).
>
> The public "*need to know*" is most critical during an election campaign. By enactment of the first comprehensive corrupt prac-

> tices act relating to primary elections in 1909 our legislature responded to the need for insuring free and fair elections. . . . The statutory provision . . . was enacted not to punish, coerce or censor the press but rather as a part of a centuries old legislative task of *maintaining conditions conducive to free and fair elections.* The Legislature in 1913 decided that owners of the printing press had already achieved such political clout that when they engaged in character assailings, the victim's electoral chances were unduly and improperly diminished. To assure fairness in campaigns, the assailed candidate had to be provided an equivalent opportunity to respond; otherwise not only the candidate would be hurt *but also* the people would be deprived of both sides of the controversy.
>
> What some segments of the press seem to lose sight of is that the First Amendment guarantee is "not for the benefit of the press so much as for the benefit of us all." [10] Speech concerning public affairs is more than self expression. It is the essence of self government.[11]
>
> . . .
>
> In conclusion, we do not find that the operation of the statute would interfere with freedom of the press as guaranteed by the Florida Constitution and the Constitution of the United States. Indeed it strengthens the concept in that it presents both views leaving the reader the freedom to reach his own conclusion. This decision will encourage rather than impede the wide open and robust dissemination of ideas and counterthought which the concept of free press both fosters and protects and which is essential to intelligent self government.

For the legislative history of the Florida statute, including the odd fact that it was sponsored by an editor and that seven of the eight journalists in the legislature supported it, see Hoffer and Butterfield, The Right to Reply: A Florida First Amendment Aberration, 53 Journ.Q. 111 (1976). Would such a right of access to the public via the press be equally valid outside of the electoral arena?

The Federal Election Campaign Act Amendments of 1974 sought to limit the amount that individual supporters could contribute and also set total spending limits. In Buckley v. Valeo, 424 U.S. 1 (1976), the Court upheld a $1,000 limitation on individual contributions to any candidate, but invalidated provisions limiting overall campaign spending, personal expenditures by candidates, and spending by individuals or groups in support of a candidate.

In Federal Election Commission v. National Conservative Political Action Committee, 105 S.Ct. 1459 (1984), the Court held unconstitutional a Congressional statute that barred political action committees (PACs) from spending more than $1,000 in support of the election of any candidate. The Court adhered to its view in *Buckley* that "prevent-

10. Time, Inc. v. Hill, [ ].

11. Garrison v. Louisiana, [ ].

ing corruption or the appearance of corruption are the only legitimate and compelling government interests thus far identified for restricting campaign finances." Since these were not found here, the restriction fell.

The Federal Election Campaign Act's filing and registration requirements are implicated when an individual, corporation, or other entity makes expenditures that expressly advocate the election or defeat of a clearly identified candidate. 2 U.S.C. § 434(e). The Act defines expenditures to exclude "any news story, commentary, or editorial distributed through the facilities of any broadcasting station, newspaper, magazine, or other periodical publication, unless such facilities are owned or controlled by any political party, political committee, or candidate." 2 U.S.C. § 431(9)(B)(i). Litigation has resulted from complaints that some media organizations were using their exempt status for purposes other than the publication of news and editorial materials.

In Reader's Digest Ass'n v. Federal Election Commission, 509 F.Supp. 1210, 7 Med.L.Rptr. 1053 (S.D.N.Y.1981), for example, the FEC suspected that the magazine's corporate owner had made an illegal campaign contribution when it distributed videotapes of a computer reenactment of Sen. Edward Kennedy's accident at Chappaquidick to publicize a major investigative article on the subject. The judge denied Reader's Digest's request for an injunction to halt the FEC's investigation because, although it was clear that the magazine was not owned or controlled by a political party, a fact question remained: whether the distribution of the tapes was sufficiently related to a press function, namely, that of publicizing the issue containing the Chappaquidick piece. The judge would not, however, allow the FEC to investigate the substance of its complaint until the press exemption was shown to be inapplicable:

> [That] seems to me to be the necessary accommodation between, on the one hand, the Commission's duty to investigate possible violations and, on the other, the statutory exemption for the press combined with a First Amendment distaste for government investigation of press functions.

In Federal Election Commission v. Phillips Publishing, Inc., 517 F.Supp. 1308, 7 Med.L.Rptr. 1825 (D.D.C.1981), the commission sought to compel discovery of information about a bi-weekly newsletter called The Pink Sheet on the Left, whose publisher had criticized Edward Kennedy in a mailing to regular and potential subscribers soliciting subscriptions. The court first noted that legislative history indicated that the press exemption was intended to be "broad." Because the FEC had offered no evidence in opposition to Phillips's statement that the Pink Sheet and its publisher "are not political committees, do not solicit or receive any political contributions, or make any contributions to any candidate," the court held the commission had no need for the information it sought in discovery. Furthermore:

> [I]t is clear that the respondent was acting in its capacity as the publisher of a newsletter in printing and distributing the solicitation letter for The Pink Sheet. The court takes judicial notice of the fact that newsletters and other publications solicit subscriptions, and in their advertising doing so, they publicize content and editorial positions . . . . Because the purpose of the solicitation letter was to publicize The Pink Sheet and obtain new subscribers, both of which are normal, legitimate press functions, the press exemption applies. . . .
>
> This opinion should not be read to imply that FEC enforcement requests should always be denied where a press entity is the subject of a "reason to believe" finding and the FEC seeks further information. Clearly further investigation would be warranted if The Pink Sheet had not been in existence for over 10 years but rather had been established for the sole purpose of supporting or opposing a candidate, or if the FEC had some evidence linking The Pink Sheet with a political organization or candidate. However, . . . the district court need not permit further investigation by the FEC if additional factual information is not needed. . . .

Relying on the Reader's Digest case, the FEC argued that the determination of what was a normal function of a magazine was a fact question. The judge disagreed. Although "circulation of a video tape to publicize a magazine article may well be a normal press function, it is certainly more unusual and thus subject to greater scrutiny than a routine mailing soliciting new subscribers for a publication."

In Federal Election Commission v. Massachusetts Citizens for Life, 769 F.2d 13, 12 Med.L.Rptr. 1041 (1st Cir.1985), the FEC sued a nonprofit citizens group for publishing in its regular newsletter the voting records of members of Congress on abortion and related issues. The number of issues printed far exceeded both the number usually run and the number of members of the organization. The court found that the statute covered, and proscribed, this behavior. It then held the statute unconstitutional. It was a content-based restriction that would be justified only by showing a "substantial government interest." The reasons for the fears in the Buckley case, corruption or its appearance, did not apply here. Moreover, the government "has less interest in regulating independent expenditures than in regulating direct campaign contributions." It was no answer that the group could have set up a separate organization to publish the newsletter. Some nonprofit groups may not be able to do this and, in any event, that course would require making public the names of the contributors. The Supreme Court has noted probable jurisdiction of the FEC's appeal, 106 S.Ct. 783 (1986).

B. PUBLIC ACCESS TO THE PRESS

MIAMI HERALD PUBLISHING CO. v. TORNILLO

Supreme Court of the United States, 1974.
418 U.S. 241, 94 S.Ct. 2831, 41 L.Ed.2d 730.
Noted, 43 Ford.L.Rev. 223, 88 Harv.L.Rev. 174, 73 Mich.L.Rev. 186, 35 Ohio St.L.J. 954.

MR. CHIEF JUSTICE BURGER delivered the opinion of the Court.

The issue in this case is whether a state statute granting a political candidate a right to equal space to reply to criticism and attacks on his record by a newspaper, violates the guarantees of a free press.

I.

In the fall of 1972, appellee, Executive Director of the Classroom Teachers Association, apparently a teachers' collective-bargaining agent, was a candidate for the Florida House of Representatives. On September 20, 1972, and again on September 29, 1972, appellant printed editorials critical of appellee's candidacy.* In response to these editorials appellee demanded that appellant print verbatim his replies, defending the role of the Classroom Teachers Association and the organization's accomplishments for the citizens of Dade County. Appellant declined to print the appellee's replies, and appellee brought suit in Circuit Court, Dade County, seeking declaratory and injunctive relief and actual and punitive damages in excess of $5,000. The action was premised on Florida Statute § 104.38 (1973), a "right of reply" statute which provides that if a candidate for nomination or election is assailed regarding his personal character or official record by any newspaper, the candidate has the right to demand that the newspaper print, free of cost to the candidate, any reply the candidate may make to the newspaper's charges. The reply must appear in as conspicuous a place and in the same kind of type as the charges which prompted the reply, provided it does not take up more space than the charges. Failure to comply with the statute constitutes a first-degree misdemeanor.[2]

Appellant sought a declaration that § 104.38 was unconstitutional. After an emergency hearing requested by appellee, the Circuit Court denied injunctive relief because, absent special circumstances, no in-

* [The editorials are reprinted in the opinion. The proposed replies are printed in Lange, The Role of the Access Doctrine in the Regulation of the Mass Media: A Critical Review and Assessment, 52 N.C.L. Rev. 1, 60 n. 272 (1973)—ed.]

2. "104.38 *Newspaper Assailing Candidate in an Election; Space for Reply.* If any newspaper in its columns assails the personal character of any candidate for nomination or for election in any election, or charges said candidate with malfeasance or misfeasance in office, or otherwise attacks his official record, or gives to another free space for such purpose, such newspaper shall upon request of such candidate immediately publish free of cost any reply he may make thereto in as conspicuous a place and in the same kind of type as the matter that calls for such reply, provided such reply does not take up more space than the matter replied to. Any person or firm failing to comply with the provisions of this section shall be guilty of a misdemeanor of the first degree, punishable as provided in § 775.082 or § 775.083."

junction could properly issue against the commission of a crime, and held that § 104.38 was unconstitutional as an infringement on the freedom of the press under the First and Fourteenth Amendments to the Constitution. 38 Fla.Supp. 80 (1972). The Circuit Court concluded that dictating what a newspaper must print was no different from dictating what it must not print. The Circuit Judge viewed the statute's vagueness as serving "to restrict and stifle protected expression." Id., at 83. Appellee's cause was dismissed with prejudice.

On direct appeal, the Florida Supreme Court reversed, holding that § 104.38 did not violate constitutional guarantees. 287 So.2d 78 (1973). It held that free speech was enhanced and not abridged by the Florida right-of-reply statute, which in that court's view, furthered the "broad societal interest in the free flow of information to the public." Id., at 82. It also held that the statute is not impermissibly vague; the statute informs "those who are subject to it as to what conduct on their part will render them liable to its penalties." Id., at 85.[4] Civil remedies, including damages, were held to be available under this statute; the case was remanded to the trial court for further proceedings not inconsistent with the Florida Supreme Court's opinion.

. . .

III.

A.

The challenged statute creates a right to reply to press criticism of a candidate for nomination or election. The statute was enacted in 1913 and this is only the second recorded case decided under its provisions.

Appellant contends the statute is void on its face because it purports to regulate the content of a newspaper in violation of the First Amendment. Alternatively it is urged that the statute is void for vagueness since no editor could know exactly what words would call the statute into operation. It is also contended that the statute fails to distinguish between critical comment which is and which is not defamatory.

B.

The appellee and supporting advocates of an enforceable right of access to the press vigorously argue that government has an obligation to ensure that a wide variety of views reach the public.[8] The conten-

4. The Supreme Court placed the following limiting construction on the statute:

"[W]e hold that the mandate of the statute refers to 'any reply' which is wholly responsive to the charge made in the editorial or other article in a newspaper being replied to and further that such reply will be neither libelous nor slanderous of the publication nor anyone else, nor vulgar nor profane." Id., at 86.

8. See generally Barron, Access to the Press—A New First Amendment Right, 80 Harv.L.Rev. 1641 (1967).

tions of access proponents will be set out in some detail.[9] It is urged that at the time the First Amendment to the Constitution was enacted in 1791 as part of our Bill of Rights the press was broadly representative of the people it was serving. While many of the newspapers were intensely partisan and narrow in their views, the press collectively presented a broad range of opinions to readers. Entry into publishing was inexpensive; pamphlets and books provided meaningful alternatives to the organized press for the expression of unpopular ideas and often treated events and expressed views not covered by conventional newspapers. A true marketplace of ideas existed in which there was relatively easy access to the channels of communication.

Access advocates submit that although newspapers of the present are superficially similar to those of 1791 the press of today is in reality very different from that known in the early years of our national existence. In the past half century a communications revolution has seen the introduction of radio and television into our lives, the promise of a global community through the use of communications satellites, and the specter of a "wired" nation by means of an expanding cable television network with two-way capabilities. The printed press, it is said, has not escaped the effects of this revolution. Newspapers have become big business and there are far fewer of them to serve a larger literate population. Chains of newspapers, national newspapers, national wire and news services, and one-newspaper towns,[13] are the dominant features of a press that has become noncompetitive and enormously powerful and influential in its capacity to manipulate popular opinion and change the course of events. Major metropolitan newspapers have collaborated to establish news services national in scope. Such national news organizations provide syndicated "interpretive reporting" as well as syndicated features and commentary, all of which can serve as part of the new school of "advocacy journalism."

The elimination of competing newspapers in most of our large cities, and the concentration of control of media that results from the only newspaper's being owned by the same interests which own a television station and a radio station, are important components of this trend toward concentration of control of outlets to inform the public.

The result of these vast changes has been to place in a few hands the power to inform the American people and shape public opinion.[15]

9. For a good overview of the position of access advocates see Lange, The Role of the Access Doctrine in the Regulation of the Mass Media: A Critical Review and Assessment, 52 N.C.L.Rev. 1, 8–9 (1973) (hereinafter Lange).

13. "Nearly half of U.S. daily newspapers, representing some three-fifths of daily and Sunday circulation, are owned by newspaper groups and chains, including diversified business conglomerates. One-newspaper towns have become the rule with effective competition operating in only 4 percent of our large cities." Background Paper by Alfred Balk in Twentieth Century Fund Task Force Report for a National News Council, A Free and Responsive Press 18 (1973).

15. "Local monopoly in printed news raises serious questions of diversity of information and opinion. What a local newspaper does not print about local affairs does not see general print at all. And, having the power to take initiative in reporting and enunciation of opinions, it has extraordinary power to set the atmos-

Much of the editorial opinion and commentary that is printed is that of syndicated columnists distributed nationwide and, as a result, we are told, on national and world issues there tends to be a homogeneity of editorial opinion, commentary, and interpretive analysis. The abuses of bias and manipulative reportage are, likewise, said to be the result of the vast accumulations of unreviewable power in the modern media empires. In effect, it is claimed, the public has lost any ability to respond or to contribute in a meaningful way to the debate on issues. The monopoly of the means of communication allows for little or no critical analysis of the media except in professional journals of very limited readership. . . .

The obvious solution, which was available to dissidents at an earlier time when entry into publishing was relatively inexpensive, today would be to have additional newspapers. But the same economic factors which have caused the disappearance of vast numbers of metropolitan newspapers,[16] have made entry into the marketplace of ideas served by the print media almost impossible. It is urged that the claim of newspapers to be "surrogates for the public" carries with it a concomitant fiduciary obligation to account for that stewardship. From this premise it is reasoned that the only effective way to insure fairness and accuracy and to provide for some accountability is for government to take affirmative action. The First Amendment interest of the public in being informed is said to be in peril because the "marketplace of ideas" is today a monopoly controlled by the owners of the market.

Proponents of enforced access to the press take comfort from language in several of this Court's decisions which suggests that the First Amendment acts as a sword as well as a shield, that it imposes obligations on the owners of the press in addition to protecting the press from government regulation. In Associated Press v. United States, [ ], the Court, in rejecting the argument that the press is immune from the antitrust laws by virtue of the First Amendment, stated:

> "The First Amendment, far from providing an argument against application of the Sherman Act, here provides powerful reasons to the contrary. That Amendment rests on the assumption that the widest possible dissemination of information from diverse and antagonistic sources is essential to the welfare of the public, that a free press is a condition of a free society. Surely a command that the government itself shall not impede the free flow of ideas does not afford non-governmental combinations a refuge if they impose restraints upon that constitutionally guaranteed freedom. Freedom to publish means freedom for all and not for some. Freedom

phere and determine the terms of local consideration of public issues." B. Bagdikian, *The Information Machines* 127 (1971).

16. The newspapers have persuaded Congress to grant them immunity from the antitrust laws in the case of "failing" newspapers for joint operations. 84 Stat. 466, 15 U.S.C. § 1801 et seq.

> to publish is guaranteed by the Constitution, but freedom to combine to keep others from publishing is not. Freedom of the press from governmental interference under the First Amendment does not sanction repression of that freedom by private interests." (Footnote omitted.)

In New York Times Co. v. Sullivan, [ ], the Court spoke of "a profound national commitment to the principle that debate on public issues should be uninhibited, robust, and wide-open." It is argued that the "uninhibited, robust" debate is not "wide-open" but open only to a monopoly in control of the press. Appellee cites the plurality opinion in Rosenbloom v. Metromedia, Inc., 403 U.S. 29, 47, and n. 15 (1971), which he suggests seemed to invite experimentation by the States in right-to-access regulation of the press.[18]

Access advocates note that Mr. Justice Douglas a decade ago expressed his deep concern regarding the effects of newspaper monopolies:

> "Where one paper has a monopoly in an area, it seldom presents two sides of an issue. It too often hammers away on one ideological or political line using its monopoly position not to educate people, not to promote debate, but to inculcate in its readers one philosophy, one attitude—and to make money." "The newspapers that give a variety of views and news that is not slanted or contrived are few indeed. And the problem promises to get worse . . . ." The Great Rights 124–125, 127 (E. Cahn ed. 1963).

They also claim the qualified support of Professor Thomas I. Emerson, who has written that "[a] limited right of access to the press can be safely enforced," although he believes that "[g]overnment measures to encourage a multiplicity of outlets, rather than compelling a few outlets to represent everybody, seems a preferable course of action." T. Emerson, The System of Freedom of Expression 671 (1970).

18. "If the States fear that private citizens will not be able to respond adequately to publicity involving them, the solution lies in the direction of ensuring their ability to respond, rather than in stifling public discussion of matters of public concern.*

"[*] Some states have adopted retraction statutes or right-of-reply statutes . . . .

"One writer, in arguing that the First Amendment itself should be read to guarantee a right of access to the media not limited to a right to respond to defamatory falsehoods, has suggested several ways the law might encourage public discussion. Barron, Access to the Press—A New First Amendment Right, 80 Harv.L.Rev. 1641, 1666–1678 (1967). It is important to recognize that the private individual often desires press exposure either for himself, his ideas, or his causes. Constitutional adjudication must take into account the individual's interest in access to the press as well as the individual's interest in preserving his reputation, even though libel actions by their nature encourage a narrow view of the individual's interest since they focus only on situations where the individual has been harmed by undesired press attention. A constitutional rule that deters the press from covering the ideas or activities of the private individual thus conceives the individual's interest too narrowly."

IV.

However much validity may be found in these arguments, at each point the implementation of a remedy such as an enforceable right of access necessarily calls for some mechanism, either governmental or consensual. If it is governmental coercion, this at once brings about a confrontation with the express provisions of the First Amendment and the judicial gloss on that Amendment developed over the years.[20]

The Court foresaw the problems relating to government-enforced access as early as its decision in Associated Press v. United States, supra. There it carefully contrasted the private "compulsion to print" called for by the Association's bylaws with the provisions of the District Court decree against appellants which "does not compel AP or its members to permit publication of anything which their 'reason' tells them should not be published." 326 U.S., at 20 n. 18. In Branzburg v. Hayes, [ ], we emphasized that the cases then before us "involve no intrusions upon speech or assembly, no prior restraint or restriction on what the press may publish, and no express or implied command that the press publish what it prefers to withhold." In Columbia Broadcasting System, Inc. v. Democratic National Committee, 412 U.S. 94, 117 (1973), the plurality opinion as to Part III noted:

> "The power of a privately owned newspaper to advance its own political, social, and economic views is bounded by only two factors: first, the acceptance of a sufficient number of readers—and hence advertisers—to assure financial success; and, second, the journalistic integrity of its editors and publishers."

An attitude strongly adverse to any attempt to extend a right of access to newspapers was echoed by several Members of this Court in their separate opinions in that case. Id., at 145 (Stewart, J., concurring); id., at 182 n. 12 (Brennan, J., dissenting). Recently, while approving a bar against employment advertising specifying "male" or "female" preference, the Court's opinion in Pittsburgh Press Co. v. Human Relations Comm'n, 413 U.S. 376, 391 (1973), took pains to limit its holding within narrow bounds:

> "Nor, *a fortiori,* does our decision authorize any restriction whatever, whether of content or layout, on stories or commentary originated by Pittsburgh Press, its columnists, or its contributors. On the contrary, we reaffirm unequivocally the protection afforded to editorial judgment and to the free expression of views on these and other issues, however controversial."

Dissenting in *Pittsburgh Press,* Mr. Justice Stewart, joined by Mr. Justice Douglas, expressed the view that no "government agency—local, state, or federal—can tell a newspaper in advance what it can print and what it cannot." [ ]

20. Because we hold that § 104.38 violates the First Amendment's guarantee of a free press we have no occasion to consider appellant's further argument that the statute is unconstitutionally vague.

We see that beginning with *Associated Press,* supra, the Court has expressed sensitivity as to whether a restriction or requirement constituted the compulsion exerted by government on a newspaper to print that which it would not otherwise print. The clear implication has been that any such a compulsion to publish that which " 'reason' tells them should not be published" is unconstitutional. A responsible press is an undoubtedly desirable goal, but press responsibility is not mandated by the Constitution and like many other virtues it cannot be legislated.

Appellee's argument that the Florida statute does not amount to a restriction of appellant's right to speak because "the statute in question here has not prevented the *Miami Herald* from saying anything it wished" begs the core question. Compelling editors or publishers to publish that which " 'reason' tells them should not be published" is what is at issue in this case. The Florida statute operates as a command in the same sense as a statute or regulation forbidding appellant to publish specified matter. Governmental restraint on publishing need not fall into familiar or traditional patterns to be subject to constitutional limitations on governmental powers. Grosjean v. American Press Co., [ ]. The Florida statute exacts a penalty on the basis of the content of a newspaper. The first phase of the penalty resulting from the compelled printing of a reply is exacted in terms of the cost in printing and composing time and materials and in taking up space that could be devoted to other material the newspaper may have preferred to print. It is correct, as appellee contends, that a newspaper is not subject to the finite technological limitations of time that confront a broadcaster but it is not correct to say that, as an economic reality, a newspaper can proceed to infinite expansion of its column space to accommodate the replies that a government agency determines or a statute commands the readers should have available.[22]

Faced with the penalties that would accrue to any newspaper that published news or commentary arguably within the reach of the right-of-access statute, editors might well conclude that the safe course is to avoid controversy. Therefore, under the operation of the Florida statute, political and electoral coverage would be blunted or reduced. Government-enforced right of access inescapably "dampens the vigor and limits the variety of public debate," New York Times Co. v. Sullivan, [ ]. The Court, in Mills v. Alabama, [ ], stated that

> "there is practically universal agreement that a major purpose of [the First] Amendment was to protect the free discussion of govern-

22. "However since the amount of space a newspaper can devote to 'live news' is finite,* if a newspaper is forced to publish a particular item, it must as a practical matter, omit something else.

"[*] The number of column inches available for news is predetermined by a number of financial and physical factors, including circulation, the amount of advertising, and increasingly, the availability of newsprint. . . . " Note, 48 Tulane L.Rev. 433, 438 (1974) (one footnote omitted).

Another factor operating against the "solution" of adding more pages to accommodate the access matter is that "increasingly subscribers complain of bulky, unwieldly papers." Bagdikian, Fat Newspapers and Slim Coverage, Columbia Journalism Review 19 (Sept./Oct.1973).

mental affairs. This of course includes discussions of candidates . . . ."

Even if a newspaper would face no additional costs to comply with a compulsory access law and would not be forced to forego publication of news or opinion by the inclusion of a reply, the Florida statute fails to clear the barriers of the First Amendment because of its intrusion into the function of editors. A newspaper is more than a passive receptacle or conduit for news, comment, and advertising. The choice of material to go into a newspaper, and the decisions made as to limitations on the size and content of the paper, and treatment of public issues and public officials—whether fair or unfair—constitute the exercise of editorial control and judgment. It has yet to be demonstrated how governmental regulation of this crucial process can be exercised consistent with First Amendment guarantees of a free press as they have evolved to this time. Accordingly, the judgment of the Supreme Court of Florida is reversed.

It is so ordered.

MR. JUSTICE BRENNAN, with whom MR. JUSTICE REHNQUIST joins, concurring.

I join the Court's opinion which, as I understand it, addresses only "right of reply" statutes and implies no view upon the constitutionality of "retraction" statutes affording plaintiffs able to prove defamatory falsehoods a statutory action to require publication of a retraction. See generally Note, Vindication of the Reputation of a Public Official, 80 Harv.L.Rev. 1730, 1739–1747 (1967).

MR. JUSTICE WHITE, concurring.

The Court today holds that the First Amendment bars a State from requiring a newspaper to print the reply of a candidate for public office whose personal character has been criticized by that newspaper's editorials. According to our accepted jurisprudence, the First Amendment erects a virtually insurmountable barrier between government and the print media so far as government tampering, in advance of publication, with news and editorial content is concerned. New York Times Co. v. United States, [ ]. A newspaper or magazine is not a public utility subject to "reasonable" governmental regulation in matters affecting the exercise of journalistic judgment as to what shall be printed. Cf. Mills v. Alabama, [ ]. We have learned, and continue to learn, from what we view as the unhappy experiences of other nations where government has been allowed to meddle in the internal editorial affairs of newspapers. Regardless of how beneficent-sounding the purposes of controlling the press might be, we prefer "the power of reason as applied through public discussion" and remain intensely skeptical about those measures that would allow government to insinuate itself into the editorial rooms of this Nation's press. . . .

. . .

To justify this statute, Florida advances a concededly important interest of ensuring free and fair elections by means of an electorate informed about the issues. But prior compulsion by government in matters going to the very nerve center of a newspaper—the decision as to what copy will or will not be included in any given edition—collides with the First Amendment. Woven into the fabric of the First Amendment is the unexceptionable, but nonetheless timeless, sentiment that "liberty of the press is in peril as soon as the government tries to compel what is to go into a newspaper." 2 Z. Chafee, Government and Mass Communications 633 (1947).

The constitutionally obnoxious feature of § 104.38 is not that the Florida Legislature may also have placed a high premium on the protection of individual reputational interests; for government certainly has "a pervasive and strong interest in preventing and redressing attacks upon reputation." Rosenblatt v. Baer, 383 U.S. 75, 86 (1966). Quite the contrary, this law runs afoul of the elementary First Amendment proposition that government may not force a newspaper to print copy which, in its journalistic discretion, it chooses to leave on the newsroom floor. . . .

. . .

Reaffirming the rule that the press cannot be forced to print an answer to a personal attack made by it, however, throws into stark relief the consequences of the new balance forged by the Court in the companion case also announced today. Gertz v. Robert Welch, Inc., [ ], goes far toward eviscerating the effectiveness of the ordinary libel action, which has long been the only potent response available to the private citizen libeled by the press. Under *Gertz,* the burden of proving liability is immeasurably increased, proving damages is made exceedingly more difficult, and vindicating reputation by merely proving falsehood and winning a judgment to that effect are wholly foreclosed. Needlessly, in my view, the Court trivializes and denigrates the interest in reputation by removing virtually all the protection the law has always afforded.

Of course, these two decisions do not mean that because government may not dictate what the press is to print, neither can it afford a remedy for libel in any form. *Gertz* itself leaves a putative remedy for libel intact, albeit in severely emaciated form; and the press certainly remains liable for knowing or reckless falsehoods under New York Times Co. v. Sullivan, [ ], and its progeny, however improper an injunction against publication might be.

One need not think less of the First Amendment to sustain reasonable methods for allowing the average citizen to redeem a falsely tarnished reputation. . . . To me it is a near absurdity to so deprecate individual dignity, as the Court does in *Gertz,* and to leave the people at the complete mercy of the press, at least in this stage of our history when the press, as the majority in this case so well documents, is steadily becoming more powerful and much less likely to be deterred by threats of libel suits.

Notes and Questions

1. The fact that the statute covered only elections was relied upon by the Florida Supreme Court in upholding it. How does the Chief Justice treat that limitation? How might the Court have reacted to a statute that required access to those attacked in the columns of the newspaper *except* for candidates?

2. Jerome A. Barron, whose 1967 article in the Harvard Law Review is cited in *Tornillo,* was the first modern proponent of access to the press as a First Amendment right. Barron also represented Mr. Tornillo in the Supreme Court. His views place great weight on changes in the media between 1791 and today. Some of these are traced in the following notes.

3. *The Role of Antitrust.* Although, as the Court noted, the antitrust laws apply to the newspaper industry, they have had little effect in stemming the demise of local competition. The number of cities in which dailies competed has dropped from 502 in 1923 to 109 in 1948 and to 23 by 1982. Of course, since these are likely to be the largest cities, the percentage of persons having access to competing papers is far larger than the percentage of cities in which papers compete.

Some potential demises were prevented when the competitors entered into joint operating agreements by which the papers integrated their business operations, including printing, acquisition of advertising, and distribution, but kept their editorial operations as separate as they always had been. Profits are generally shared in a predetermined ratio. The government challenged such an arrangement entered into by the papers in Tucson, Arizona, as an antitrust violation.

The Supreme Court affirmed the trial court's finding of violations of section 1 of the Sherman Act and section 7 of the Clayton Act. Citizen Publishing Co. v. United States, 394 U.S. 131 (1969). The Court relied on the finding that "there was no serious probability that the Citizen was on the verge of going out of business or that, even had the Citizen been contemplating liquidation, the Star was the only available purchaser."

4. *The Newspaper Preservation Act.* Congressional reaction was swift, largely because the decision raised doubt about the validity of similar agreements in 22 other cities. The result was the passage, in 1970, of the Newspaper Preservation Act, 15 U.S.C. § 1801 et seq. Congress declared its purpose to maintain "a newspaper press editorially and reportorially independent and competitive in all parts of the United States." Joint newspaper operating agreements were authorized to link virtually all mechanical and commercial aspects of the newspaper but there was to be no combination of editorial or reportorial staffs. A "failing newspaper" was defined as one that "regardless of its ownership or affiliation, is in probable danger of financial failure." The Act

provided that joint agreements previously entered into are valid if when started, "not more than one of the newspaper publications involved . . . was likely to remain or become a financially sound publication." Future joint operating agreements required the approval of the Attorney General, who must first "determine that not more than one of the newspaper publications involved in the arrangement is a publication other than a failing newspaper" and that approval of the agreement would advance the policy of the Act. Predatory practices that would be unlawful if engaged in by a single entity may not be engaged in by the members of the joint operating agreement.

For an extensive review of the Act and its operation, see Committee for an Independent P–I v. Hearst Corp., 704 F.2d 467, 9 Med.L.Rptr. 1489 (9th Cir.), certiorari denied 464 U.S. 892 (1983), involving the operating agreement between the Seattle Post-Intelligencer and the Seattle Times. The court upheld the Attorney General's determination that the case met the requirements for the approval of the agreement.

The court then rejected two claims that the Act violated the First Amendment. The first was that the agreement would impair the rights of smaller newspapers in the market. The court rejected this because the Act does not affect content of speech. "The Act is an economic regulation which has the intent of promoting and aiding the press. At most, the Act *may* affect the number of 'readers' a newspaper has. But that the Act may have such an [effect] is not different, in our view, than any other economic regulation of the newspaper industry [citing cases holding that newspapers must comply with general labor relations legislation]."

Whether or not the exemption from the antitrust laws should be considered a "license," as the challengers argued, was not controlling. The antitrust laws are "the creation of Congress. They are not mandated by the first amendment or anywhere else in the Constitution. What Congress has passed, it may repeal." The challengers' unhappiness that certain papers are given preferential treatment is irrelevant because any "newspapers in the Seattle area, large or small, may participate in a joint operating agreement if they qualify."

The second constitutional claim was that the statutory delegation to the Attorney General was vague and overbroad. Here, as earlier, the court saw no "clearly defined first amendment injury." Moreover, the court did not think the delegation overly broad.

5. In a related matter, group ownership of newspapers has grown rapidly. In 1960, some 109 groups owned a total of 552 daily papers. By 1980, 155 groups owned 1136 of the 1750 dailies.

Consider the comments of a former assistant attorney general in charge of the antitrust division: "Control of all daily newspapers by five chains, for example, would cause me as an American citizen far greater concern than would control of a similarly sized manufacturing industry by five business entities." Shenefield, Ownership Concentration in Newspapers, 65 A.B.A.J. 1332, 1335 (1979).

We consider questions of broadcast concentration and of newspaper-broadcast combinations in Chapter XVI.

6. Is it relevant to Barron's position that today's newspapers average about 60 to 65 percent advertising and 35 to 40 percent editorial content?

7. Access proponents argued that such a right can be judicially created under First Amendment analysis. In *Tornillo,* the legislature had enacted such a provision—and the judiciary was being asked to uphold the statute rather than to create a new right at the constitutional level. Are these two situations distinguishable?

8. How does the Chief Justice deal with the Florida Supreme Court's argument that "free speech was enhanced and not abridged" by the statute?

9. Can *Tornillo* be seen as a conflict between "freedom from" and "freedom to"? Or a conflict between "press" and "speech"?

10. Might the statute in *Tornillo* have withstood attack if it had required a demonstration of "falsity"—or deliberate falsity—in the newspaper coverage before making access available?

11. Is there a basis for Justice Brennan's assertion that the Court's opinion does not bring into question a statute that would give defamation plaintiffs who prove falsity the right to a mandatory retraction? Consider the differences among statutes that required the paper to say "We were wrong," or "A court has ordered us to state that it has found that we were in error," or "A court has ordered us to retract our statement. . . . "

12. What about a statute that gave the publisher a choice between paying damages and issuing a retraction? Can the publisher object so long as the amount of damages does not depend on whether a retraction is issued?

13. In a book devoted almost exclusively to the access question, it is claimed that the *Tornillo* ruling is "almost devoid of reasoned support, its use of precedent is disingenuous, and the constitutional principle announced is not consistent with other rules grounded in the First Amendment." B. Schmidt, Jr., Freedom of the Press vs. Public Access 13 (1976). Since unreasoned opinions are fragile, "the sweeping and conclusive fashion in which the Court rejected the constitutionality of access statutes may prove less durable than less categorical arguments against broad access requirements." Later, at p. 234, the author suggests that the Court may have written sweepingly to counter the broad claims of the Florida opinions and the academic supporters of access. Although the case does recognize "autonomy of the press" as a "guarantee of constitutional dimension," later cases may impose some limit on the broad proposition, as in other First Amendment areas. For a similar suggestion that the case may be less sweeping than its language, see The Supreme Court, 1973 Term, 88 Harv.L.Rev. 43, 177–78 (1974).

Schmidt's analysis is rejected in Abrams, In Defense of Tornillo, 86 Yale L.J. 361 (1976), a review of Schmidt's book. Abrams argues that although the Court's opinion leaves much to be desired, its basic points are sound. Of the broad language used by the Court, Abrams says:

> Equally unpersuasive is Schmidt's suggestion that *Tornillo* is flawed because it "betrays no hint of relativity."[41] The absolute "constitutional principle announced" by *Tornillo,* Schmidt concludes, "is not consistent with other rules grounded in the First Amendment." But it is. The Court's rulings in *Tornillo* and other recent cases indicate that the degree of First Amendment protection afforded the press depends on the extent to which the alleged intrusion on press freedom impinges on the editorial decisionmaking process. The cases fall into three categories, each of which involves a different degree of protection. First, the press enjoys virtually absolute protection when the state, through the judiciary or otherwise, attempts to determine either what must not be printed (i.e., prior restraint) or what must be printed (i.e., access). Second, when the state seeks to punish the press after publication, the First Amendment requires an extremely high, although by no means absolute, degree of protection. Third, and least protected, is the right of the press to gather information. Here there is extensive First Amendment protection, but it is based upon a balancing test that often provides the press with less protection than that afforded under the other two categories. So viewed, *Tornillo* is hardly absolutist; rather, it is representative of the vast freedom afforded the press at the apex of its First Amendment protection.
>
> Ultimately, *Tornillo* demanded a choice of First Amendment philosophies—a choice between the possibility of more expression reaching more people, but decreed and enforced by the machinery of the State, and the principle that "[f]or better or worse, editing is what editors are for." In *Tornillo* the Court concluded that any "intrusion into the function of editors" would pose too grave a threat to the freedom of the press.

14. One response to the *Tornillo* problem has been increased discussion of unofficial "press councils" to pass upon complaints brought against media by members of the public. The subject is explored in Ritter and Leibowitz, Press Councils: The Answer to Our First Amendment Dilemma, 1974 Duke L.J. 845.

15. *Tornillo* has been discussed in several Supreme Court cases.

Recall Buckley v. Valeo, 424 U.S. 1 (1976), in which the Court, among other things, invalidated a provision, 18 U.S.C. § 608(e)(1), limiting to $1,000 the amount a citizen could spend "relative to a clearly identified candidate":

41. P. 13. Schmidt is not alone in his qualms about the breadth of the Court's language. See Karst, Equality as a Central Principle in the First Amendment, 43 U.Chi.L.Rev. 20, 50 (1975) (*Tornillo* "is so sweeping that it is hard to believe the Court could possibly mean what it said.")

While the independent expenditure ceiling thus fails to serve any substantial governmental interest in stemming the reality or appearance of corruption in the electoral process, it heavily burdens core First Amendment expression. For the First Amendment right to " 'speak one's mind . . . on all public institutions' " includes the right to engage in " 'vigorous advocacy' no less than 'abstract discussion.' " [New York Times Co. v. Sullivan]. Advocacy of the election or defeat of candidates for federal office is no less entitled to protection under the First Amendment than the discussion of political policy generally or advocacy of the passage or defeat of legislation.

It is argued, however, that the ancillary governmental interest in equalizing the relative ability of individuals and groups to influence the outcome of elections serves to justify the limitation on express advocacy of the election or defeat of candidates imposed by § 608(e)(1)'s expenditure ceiling. But the concept that government may restrict the speech of some elements of our society in order to enhance the relative voice of others is wholly foreign to the First Amendment, which was designed "to secure 'the widest possible dissemination of information from diverse and antagonistic sources,' " and " 'to assure unfettered interchange of ideas for the bringing about of political and social changes desired by the people.' " [New York Times Co. v. Sullivan]. The First Amendment's protection against governmental abridgment of free expression cannot properly be made to depend on a person's financial ability to engage in public discussion. [ ]

The Court's decisions in Mills v. Alabama, [ ], and Miami Herald Publishing Co. v. Tornillo, [ ], held that legislative restrictions on advocacy of the election or defeat of political candidates are wholly at odds with the guarantees of the First Amendment. . . . [T]he prohibition of election-day editorials invalidated in *Mills* is clearly a lesser intrusion on constitutional freedom than a $1,000 limitation on the amount of money any person or association can spend *during an entire election year* in advocating the election or defeat of a candidate for public office. More recently in *Tornillo,* the Court held that Florida could not constitutionally require a newspaper to make space available for a political candidate to reply to its criticism. Yet under the Florida statute, every newspaper was free to criticize any candidate as much as it pleased so long as it undertook the modest burden of printing his reply. [ ] The legislative restraint involved in *Tornillo* thus also pales in comparison to the limitations imposed by § 608(e)(1).

In Wooley v. Maynard, 430 U.S. 705 (1977), New Hampshire prosecuted a motorist who covered the motto on his license plate, "Live Free or Die", because he found it "morally, ethically, religiously and politically abhorrent." The Court held that the state could not require the motorist to display an abhorrent motto:

> A system which secures the right to proselytize religious, political, and ideological causes must also guarantee the concomitant right to decline to foster such concepts. The right to speak and the right to refrain from speaking are complementary components of the broader concept of "individual freedom of mind." This is illustrated by the recent case of Miami Herald Publishing Co. v. Tornillo, [ ], where we held unconstitutional a Florida statute placing an affirmative duty upon newspapers to publish the replies of political candidates whom they had criticized.

In PruneYard Shopping Center v. Robins, 447 U.S. 74 (1980), the Court upheld a California ruling permitting persons to set up a card table at the shopping center to gather signatures for a petition to the United Nations. The shopping center argued that, under *Tornillo,* its own First Amendment rights barred the state from requiring it to allow others to use its facilities to take positions on political issues. For the majority, Justice Rehnquist responded:

> [*Tornillo*] rests on the principle that the State cannot tell a newspaper what it must print. The Florida statute contravened this principle in that it "exact[ed] a penalty on the basis of the content of a newspaper." [ ] There also was a danger in *Tornillo* that the statute would "dampe[n] the vigor and limi[t] the variety of public debate" by deterring editors from publishing controversial political statements that might trigger the application of the statute. [ ] Thus, the statute was found to be an "intrusion into the function of editors." [ ] These concerns obviously are not present here.

Justices Powell and White, though concurring, suggested that if the shopping center had a strong view on an issue, its First Amendment rights might be infringed if persons with an opposing view were permitted to espouse that view on the premises of the shopping center. Although *Wooley* involved speech whose content was mandated by the state, the First Amendment is involved even when the content is left to persons the property owner is forced to admit to his land. "In many situations, a right of access is no less intrusive than speech compelled by the State itself." They cited *Tornillo* and likened the situation to "compelled affirmation," which was "presumptively unconstitutional." In the actual case, however, the shopping center had not alleged that it disagreed with the messages at issue.

In Pacific Gas & Electric v. Public Utilities Commission, 106 S.Ct. 903 (1986), the Court overturned a California ruling that required utilities that had distributed newsletters in their billing envelopes to permit organizations with opposing views to insert their messages in the envelopes several times a year. The plurality concluded that access to the envelope was not content-neutral because groups with views consistent with those of PG&E were not eligible to use the envelope. This resembled *Tornillo* in two ways. Access was triggered by a particular category of newspaper speech, and was awarded only to those who disagreed with the newspaper's views. In the PG&E case, the first point was different because access did not depend on any "particular" expression by PG&E. Nonetheless, the utility had to "contend with the fact that whenever it speaks out on a given issue, it may be forced—at [the opponent's] discretion—to help disseminate hostile views." This might well lead PG&E to avoid controversy. This was not a permissible subsidy for speech because it favored one side of the debate.

The state had argued that PG&E did not own the "extra space" in the envelope—the space not taken up by the bill itself and legal notices—that was usable without causing an increase in the postal rate. The plurality thought the ownership question irrelevant:

> A different conclusion would necessarily imply that our decision in *Tornillo* rested on the Miami Herald's ownership of the space that would have been used to print candidate replies. Nothing in *Tornillo* suggests that the result would have been different had the Florida Supreme Court decided that the newspaper space needed to print candidates' replies was the property of the newspaper's readers, or had the court ordered the Miami Herald to distribute inserts owned and prepared by the candidates together with its newspapers. The constitutional difficulty with the right-of-reply statute was that it required the newspaper to disseminate a message with which the newspaper disagreed. This difficulty did not depend on whether the particular paper on which the replies were printed belonged to the newspaper or to the candidate.

No sufficient state justification was found. Even if the state's interest in "fair and effective utility regulation" was a compelling one, it could be met by less intrusive devices such as awarding costs and fees. The PUC also argued that the order furthered the state's interest in "promoting speech by making a variety of views available to [PG&E's] customers." The problem here was that the order was not content-neutral. Moreover, the means chosen impermissibly tend to inhibit PG&E's expression. "It follows that the Commission's order is not a narrowly tailored means of furthering this interest."

16. *Paid Advertisements.* The statute in *Tornillo* applied to newspaper "columns" generally. Would a different question of access be raised if Tornillo wanted to purchase space for political advertising?

In Home Placement Service, Inc. v. The Providence Journal Co., 682 F.2d 274, 8 Med.L.Rptr. 1881 (1st Cir.1982), certiorari denied 460 U.S. 1028 (1983), the paper rejected classified advertisements submitted by a rental service that charged fees to those seeking housing but nothing to landlords who listed with the service. This service conflicted with the paper's interests in selling classified ads to landlords. The paper could not show the ads were deceptive (as it had in an earlier case). Nor, said the court, could it justify refusal to accept the ads by the "paternal judgment that the public should not have to pay a fee to find housing." That decision was for the market. Although the paper could refuse ads on policy grounds, it could not do so when it was "using its dominance in the newspaper advertising market to foreclose competition in the housing vacancy information market."

In the absence of a legitimate business reason, the use of monopoly power to destroy a potential competitor violated section 2 of the Sherman Act. The case was remanded for further proceedings, including the "appropriate form of injunctive relief, if any is needed."

See also Knox County Local v. National Rural Letter Carriers' Ass'n, 720 F.2d 936, 10 Med.L.Rptr. 1350 (6th Cir.1984), interpreting the "Bill of Rights" section of the Landrum-Griffin Act, 29 U.S.C. § 411, as requiring union publications to refrain from content-based decisions in accepting ads.

Exceptions to Editorial Freedom. Although there is a general protection for editorial decisionmaking, we have already seen that in the antitrust situation, the remedial aspect may permit such a requirement. In a nonmedia case, the Supreme Court addressed a related question. In United States v. National Society of Professional Engineers, 555 F.2d 978 (D.C.Cir.1977), the lower court found the defendant had violated the antitrust law because its Code of Ethics prohibited competitive bids on engineering projects. As part of the remedy the judge ordered the defendant to state affirmatively that it did not consider competitive bidding to be unethical. The court of appeals rejected that part of the decree as more intrusive than necessary to satisfy the government's interest. "To force an association of individuals to express as its own opinion judicially dictated ideas is to encroach on that sphere of free thought and expression protected by the First Amendment." The government's goals could be met by an order that barred the Society from "future expression that the price practice is unethical, and requiring it to publish an advice that its prior ruling has been rescinded in light of the court's decree. . . . "

The Supreme Court affirmed the decree over the objection that the Society was constitutionally entitled to state or imply that it considered competitive bidding unethical. The lower court may consider "the fact that its injunction may impinge upon rights that would otherwise be constitutionally protected, but those protections do not prevent it from remedying the antitrust violation."

Chief Justice Burger dissented: "The First Amendment guarantees the right to express such a position and that right cannot be impaired under the cloak of remedial judicial action." National Society of Professional Engineers v. United States, 435 U.S. 679 (1978).

A comparable remedial issue arose in a labor relations case in which the NLRB had found that a reporter was improperly discriminated against because of union activity. The discrimination included dropping his weekly column. The court upheld the Board's power to investigate such claims involving newspapers and its finding of an unfair labor practice. Passaic Daily News v. Nat'l Labor Relations Board, 736 F.2d 1543, 10 Med.L.Rptr. 1905 (D.C.Cir.1984).

The original order had required the employer to restore the reporter "to his former position as weekly columnist, and resume publication of [the reporter's] weekly column, subject to the same lawful standards and requirements that [the Company] imposes or may impose on its employees." The court, relying on *Miami Herald,* thought this order injected the Board into the paper's "editorial decision-making process on an ongoing basis." The Board's goals "must yield to the Company's First Amendment interest in retaining control over prospective editorial decisions."

On remand, the Board changed its order to require that the employer restore the reporter "to the column-writing duties he enjoyed prior to his demotion, and decide whether to publish his submissions based upon any factors other than his union or protected activity; provided that nothing in this Order shall be interpreted as a requirement that the [Company] publish any of the columns submitted by [the reporter]. 276 NLRB No. 78 (1985). Does this solve the court's problem?

Contract. In Herald Telephone v. Fatouros, 431 N.E.2d 171 (Ind. App.1982), Fatouros was a candidate for county school board. She discussed with a member of the advertising department of the local paper an advertisement for the day before the election. She paid in advance for the ad. After the paper received the copy, the advertising director told Fatouros that her ad violated the paper's "Policy Considerations Covering Political Advertisements" because it was inflammatory and contained derogatory statements. The paper would either run the unobjectionable parts or refund the candidate's money. Instead, Fatouros obtained a court order enjoining the paper from breaching its contract with Fatouros. That order was affirmed on appeal after the court found that a contract had been shown.

The paper argued that the trial court had erred in failing to treat the guidelines as part of the contract. It argued that the "exercise of editorial discretion is a part of every newspaper contract regardless of whether the policy guidelines are shown to a customer." The court disagreed:

> We agree that a newspaper is a private business which can do business with whomever it wishes and refuse to do business with whomever it wishes. [ ] While a newspaper has a right to reject any ad it wishes, this right exists only until a contract is formed. [ ] Once the contract is entered into, the newspaper stands in the same position as any other business entity and may reject an ad only if it reserved the right to do so or has an equitable defense to specific performance. [The court found no such defenses here.] Furthermore, it did not make known its policy to Ms. Fatouros and therefore the policy could not possibly be part of the contract.

Finally, the court rejected a First Amendment claim based on the right to publish or reject advertising as its judgment dictates. This was true only until a contract was entered into. The paper may still "choose to publish or not publish any material it wishes, as long as the decision is made before a binding contract is formed."

Is there any basis for arguing that although liability for damages would not violate the First Amendment in this case, the use of an injunction was impermissible?

In Evenson v. Ortega, 605 F.Supp. 1115, 11 Med.L.Rptr. 1886 (D.Ariz.1985), plaintiff, publisher of a newspaper entitled "Bachelor's World News Beat," sought to enjoin the defendant sheriff from using undercover means to place ads in the paper as part of an investigation of prostitution. Plaintiff's first response had been to require all prospective advertisers to sign affidavits that the ads were being placed solely for the purposes stated in the ads. The undercover deputy sheriff's affidavit "was, of course, false."

The court agreed that the plaintiff had an absolute right under *Tornillo* to reject any ads, but the court also refused to help the plaintiff exercise that right by enjoining the sheriff's use of undercover means to place ads. The court discussed at length the cases that permit government to use decoys and deception in the investigation of crime.

C. FIGHTING BACK

As we have seen, the print media are generally able to control editorial content and advertising content with a minimum of government interference. This in turn raises the important question of how those adversely affected by these rules can respond. Although most persons tend to imagine private individuals as the angry or frustrated group, government, too, may be frustrated. For example, one state had a policy that when a child was adjudicated a delinquent for the second time, "his name and the name of his parents or the persons in whose custody he lives shall thereupon be published in a newspaper having a general circulation" in the county along with the fact of adjudication. This Mississippi statute was repealed in 1979. State policy will be frustrated if no newspaper will print such material.

See also Del. Code Ann. 6541, adopted in 1983, providing that upon placing an inmate in supervised custody or work release, a state department "shall publish the name of that inmate and the crimes for which he is incarcerated. Said information shall be published in each of the 3 counties of this State in a newspaper located in that county and having a general circulation throughout the county. No inmate shall be placed on supervised custody or work release until the notice provided for herein has been released for publication to the newspaper." What if the last words had instead said that release could occur only upon the publication?

Usually, newspapers are eager to be specified as the official outlet for the publication of government notices—such items as the agenda for city council meetings, and the like. Cases are often brought by the loser in such a contest, asserting that the winner was not eligible for the contract.

Occasionally, cases may be brought over the withdrawal of such advertising. See Frissel v. Rizzo, 597 F.2d 840, 3 Med.L.Rptr. 2249 (3d Cir.1979), certiorari denied 444 U.S. 841 (1979), in which the Mayor of Philadelphia withdrew advertising from a newspaper after it reported on some activity of the mayor. The annual loss in revenue was $280,000. The case was brought by a resident and taxpayer, but not by the paper. The court dismissed the case for lack of standing. The court noted that there might be conflicts between the plaintiff and the paper, such as the paper's desire to appear to be a crusading paper independent of the city's hierarchy.

On the other hand, some governments have set up their own newspapers when they have become dissatisfied with the existing papers. Claiming that the Staten Island Advance was reporting unfairly on plans to construct a generating plant in the area, the Power Authority of the State of New York started its own eight-page newspaper, The Record, that offered its own version of the dispute. The Record was distributed free by use of an existing shopper. The Advance, which claims to reach nine out of ten homes on Staten Island, asserted that the authority was upset because of the paper's editorial policy rather than its news coverage. The authority responded that the newspaper had run "editorials disguised as news stories," and had buried positive rulings by environmental agencies, had denied the authority the opportunity to respond to editorials, and had refused to correct errors in their stories. In one case in which the Advance carried an op-ed piece by the authority, the Advance took exception to the piece in an editorial published the same day. Editor & Publisher, March 20, 1982, at 40a.

See P.A.M. News Corp. v. Butz, 514 F.2d 272 (D.C.Cir.1975), in which a disseminator of agricultural information sued to enjoin the Department of Agriculture from engaging in a similar venture. Plaintiff, relying on *Grosjean,* argued that "government activity which curtails the press' income and inhibits circulation" was invalid. The court agreed that the plaintiff's wire service was entitled to constitutional protection but found nothing impermissible in the government's behavior. "The government is increasing, not limiting, the flow of information. The first amendment profits from this sort of governmental activity."

For exploration of issues raised by government publications, see M. Yudof, When Government Speaks: Politics, Law and Government Expression in America (1983); Schauer, Is Government Speech a Problem?, 35 Stan.L.Rev. 373 (1983) (reviewing Yudof's book); Shiffrin, Government Speech 27 UCLA L.Rev. 565 (1980).

We turn now to the alternatives of aggrieved private parties.

ENVIRONMENTAL PLANNING AND INFORMATION COUNCIL OF WESTERN EL DORADO COUNTY, INC. v. SUPERIOR COURT

Supreme Court of California, 1984.
36 Cal.3d 188, 680 P.2d 1086, 203 Cal.Rptr. 127.

[The Environmental Planning and Information Council (EPIC), a nonprofit corporation with approximately 100 members, disagreed with editorial positions of the Foothill Times, published by Detmold Publishing Co. and distributed in the region without charge. In a newsletter, EPIC sharply criticized the Times, accusing it of ignoring established facts, printing errors, and blatantly editorializing in its news articles. The basic substantive disagreement was that the four directors of the local irrigation district, who had been backed by the paper, had taken over the district for the benefit of a "very limited development group."

The newsletter then suggested three courses of action. First, citizens should inform themselves. "An adequately informed citizenry is the only hope for curing bad government." Second, the readers of the newsletter were encouraged to write letters to the editor of the Times. Third, the newsletter asked "What about *contacting businesses advertising in the Foothill Times* and requesting that they discontinue that advertising? Freedom of speech is one thing; vicious, irresponsible journalism is another, and perhaps you would prefer not to patronize businesses that advertise in such a publication." The newsletter concluded by proposing a recall of the four district directors.

Attached to the two-page newsletter was a list of eighty newspaper advertisers. The top of the list stated: "This is not a black list! No condemnation of these businesses is implied! This list is merely for your convenience should you wish to contact *Foothill Times* advertisers."

Two weeks later Detmold (real party in interest) sued EPIC for libel and intentional interference with economic relationships. The trial judge dismissed the libel action but denied EPIC summary judgment on the intentional interference claim. EPIC sought a writ of mandate to require the trial judge to dismiss the interference claim.

On appeal, the court assumed that the newsletter could be understood as "intended and likely to be viewed as affirmatively advocating and encouraging" a boycott of the Times's advertisers. The court also assumed that some readers withheld patronage from some advertisers. The court then turned to the question whether these were "material" issues of fact.]

GRODIN, J.

. . .

We begin with the common law. The courts of this state have recognized that an unjustified, or unprivileged, intentional interference with the prospective economic advantage of another may subject the actor to liability in tort, even when that interference does not take the form of inducing a breach of contract. [ ] The tort of interference with contract, we have observed, "is merely a species of the broader tort of interference with prospective economic advantage." [ ]

The contours of justification, or privilege, are not precisely defined. In relation to the tort of interference with contract, we have said: "Whether an intentional interference by a third party is justifiable depends upon a balancing of the importance, social and private, of the objective advanced by the interference against the importance of the interest interfered with, considering all circumstances including the nature of the actor's conduct and the relationship between the parties." (Herron v. State Farm Mutual Ins. Co. (1961) 56 Cal.2d 202, 206, 14 Cal. Rptr. 294, 363 P.2d 310.)[3] When the defendant's action does not interfere with the performance of existing contracts, the range of acceptable justification is broader; for example, a competitor's stake in advancing his own economic interest will not justify the intentional inducement of a contract breach [ ], whereas such interests will suffice where contractual relations are merely contemplated or potential. [ ]

Most of the cases in which claims of tortious interference have been considered have involved either pure commercial relationships or union-management relationships.[4] There is a paucity of authority in the application of common law principles to a situation such as this, in which a group organized for political purposes allegedly undertakes a consumer boycott to achieve its ends. What authority does exist in this arena strongly suggests, even apart from constitutional doctrine, that such action will not give rise to liability. Certainly the defendants' objective—to change the editorial policies of the Foothill Times in relation to public issues affecting the environment[5]—is a lawful one, and the means used—a peaceful secondary boycott—have likewise been held to be lawful under the common law of this state. [ ] And, in somewhat analogous context, the Supreme Court of Pennsylvania has held that no cause of action exists against church leaders who threatened to lead a boycott of church members against a department store in order to influence the broadcasting policies of a radio station which was under the same ownership (Watch Tower Bible & Tract Soc. v. Dougher-

3. The factors enumerated by this court in *Herron* were patterned closely after those listed in the original Restatement of Torts (1939) section 767. The Restatement Second of the Law of Torts (1977) abandons use of the term "privilege" or "justification" in favor of the term "improperly interferes," so as to avoid questions of burden of pleading or proof [ ] but the factors to be used in determining whether interference is "improper" (§ 767) are essentially the same.

4. [ ] Labor disputes, insofar as they are subject to state common law, have come to be governed by special rules which recognize the right of workers to pursue their economic self-interest by lawful means.

5. While Detmold's complaint alleged that defendants acted "with the intent of injuring plaintiff's business and goodwill and in so doing acted maliciously and oppressively towards plaintiff," Detmold does not dispute that the defendants' objective was anything other than that reflected in the newsletter and in the declarations submitted by defendants in support of the motion for summary judgment. In this context, "malice" means simply "without justification." (Rest.2d Torts, p. 5.)

ty (1940) 337 Pa. 286, 11 A.2d 147, 148; see also, Kuryer Pub. Co. v. Messmer (1916) 162 Wis. 565, 156 N.W. 948 [Catholic boycott of newspaper gave rise to no cause of action].)[7]

This case cannot realistically be viewed from an exclusively common law perspective, however, since the very nature of the activities complained of invites constitutional analysis as well. In a case of this sort, constitutional principles impose outer limits upon the category of conduct that may be subject to liability on the basis of common law doctrine, and thus serve to shape the doctrine itself. Moreover, it is precisely the constitutional aspect of this case that warrants appellate intervention through extraordinary writ.

The United States Supreme Court recently had occasion to consider First Amendment limitations upon the power of a state to regulate secondary consumer boycotts directed at political objectives. NAACP v. Claiborne Hardware Co., supra, 458 U.S. 886, 102 S.Ct. 3409, involved a boycott by black citizens in Port Gibson, Mississippi, against white merchants in that city, aimed at putting pressure on white elected officials to accede to the citizens' demands for racial equality and integration. The Mississippi Supreme Court upheld, on common law tort grounds, a judgment for injunctive relief and damages against certain civil rights organizations, their leaders, and their members responsible for the boycott. The basis for the state court holding was that the boycott was accompanied by some acts and threats of violence. In reversing that holding, the high court declared: "The right of the States to regulate economic activity could not justify a complete prohibition against a nonviolent, politically motivated boycott designed to force governmental and economic change and to effectuate rights guaranteed by the Constitution itself." [ ] Accordingly, the court held that the nonviolent elements of the petitioners' activities were entitled to First Amendment protection. [ ]

Claiborne Hardware draws a crucial distinction between solely economic boycott activity which can be and has been regulated, i.e., by antitrust laws, and political boycotts. The same distinction is present in this case. Justice Stevens pointed out for a unanimous court in *Claiborne Hardware:* "While States have broad power to regulate economic activity, we do not find a comparable right to prohibit peaceful political activity such as that found in the boycott in this case. This Court has recognized that expression on public issues 'has always rested on the highest rung of the hierarchy of First Amendment values.' " ([ ] quoting from Carey v. Brown (1980) 447 U.S. 455, 467,

7. Our research discloses one case which provides apparent support to plaintiff, holding that a trial court erred in granting summary judgment for defendant humane society in a suit brought by plaintiff business owners who alleged that the society had intentionally interfered with their economic advantage by urging a tourist boycott of a county in which their businesses were located, in order to pressure local officials into improving conditions at a local dog pound. (Searle v. Johnson (Utah 1982) 646 P.2d 682.) A careful reading of the opinion reveals, however, that the court did not pass upon the merits of plaintiff's theory. . . .

100 S.Ct. 2286, 2293, 65 L.Ed.2d 263.)[8] The court observed that even in the antitrust area, it has been held that the Sherman Act does not proscribe a publicity campaign designed to influence legislation, even if the campaign is undertaken with an anticompetitive purpose. (Ibid., citing Eastern R. Conf. v. Noerr Motors (1961) 365 U.S. 127, 81 S.Ct. 523, 5 L.Ed.2d 464; see State of Mo. v. Nat. Organization for Women (8th Cir.1980) 620 F.2d 1301, cert. den. (1980) 449 U.S. 842, 100 S.Ct. 122, 66 L.Ed.2d 49 [boycott of states which did not ratify Equal Rights Amendment protected by First Amendment]; but see Council of Defense v. International Magazine Co. (8th Cir.1920) 267 F. 390 [boycott of International protesting William Randolph Hearst's alleged pro-German policies held to state an antitrust cause of action; distinguished in *State of Mo.,* supra, 620 F.2d at p. 1304, fn. 4].)

Detmold would have us distinguish *Claiborne Hardware* on the basis of the objective sought by the boycott in that case. The activities of those defendants, Detmold suggests, were "clearly entitled to full First Amendment protections as the objective of their boycott was to vindicate rights of equality and freedom that lie at the heart of the Fourteenth Amendment," whereas these defendants—an "irresponsible few," according to Detmold—are seeking to further merely their private views on environmental matters, and at the expense of Detmold's own rights of free expression.

Detmold's argument might have merit if this were an ordinary case of interference with advantageous economic relationships in the commercial context; for there, as we have observed, courts may be called upon to balance the social and private importance of the defendant's objective against the substantiality of the interest which plaintiff asserts. As in *Claiborne Hardware,* however, defendants' activities constitute a "politically motivated boycott designed to force governmental and economic change" [ ] and the fact that the change which they seek bears upon environmental quality rather than racial equality, can hardly support a different result. On the contrary, we are precluded by the First Amendment itself from gauging the degree of constitutional protection by the content or subject matter of the speech: "[T]here is an 'equality of status' in the field of ideas" (Police Department of Chicago v. Mosley (1972) 408 U.S. 92, 95–96, 92 S.Ct. 2286, 2290, 33 L.Ed.2d 212).

Nor is a different result dictated by the fact that the boycott in this case is aimed at changing the editorial policies of a newspaper. The freedom of a newspaper to formulate editorial policies is obviously of great value in our society, and the spectacle of different groups seeking to influence those policies through the use of economic boycott is troublesome to contemplate. Yet, the newspaper is not in a position to claim infringement of its own constitutional rights by such conduct, since no governmental action is implicated, and the degree of economic coercion which exists may be no greater than that which might lawful-

8. Similar expressions of our own abound. . . .

ly be exerted by an advertiser who, on his own, seeks to influence editorial policy by withdrawing or threatening to withdraw its patronage. The market place of ideas contemplated by the First Amendment [ ] cannot be so insulated. Moreover, this case is not distinguishable from *Claiborne Hardware* on that basis, since in that case, as well, the boycott sought to influence political expression and behavior by private citizens. [ ]

Applying common law principles, and construing them in light of the First Amendment and article I, section 2 of the state Constitution [ ][9] we conclude that petitioners are entitled to summary judgment as a matter of law.

Let a writ of mandate issue commanding respondent court to vacate its order denying petitioners' motion for summary judgment and directing it to enter a new and different order granting said motion and dismissing this action. Costs to petitioners.

BIRD, C.J., and MOSK, KAUS, BROUSSARD and REYNOSO, JJ., concur.

Notes and Questions

1. Is it relevant that the Foothill Times is distributed without charge?

2. Why does the court find it "troublesome to contemplate" an economic boycott aimed at a newspaper? What is the socially preferred response when citizens in a community, whether or not readers or viewers of the particular medium, become disenchanted with the policies of that medium? Is there a difference between those who normally read the newspaper in question and other members of the community?

3. Is the case any different if it appears that EPIC has hopes of destroying the Foothill Times and turning its newsletter into the district's newspaper? Does it matter whether the motive is to have greater influence on the district's environmental development, or to make money for EPIC's treasury, or simply that the editor of the newsletter would like to run a general newspaper?

4. In Beardsley v. Kilmer, 236 N.Y. 80, 140 N.E. 203 (1923), plaintiff newspaper owner in Binghamton attacked the patent medicine "Swamp Root" manufactured by defendant. Defendant retaliated by starting a competing newspaper in the city. The evidence at trial showed that defendant had mixed motives in starting the paper: to force plaintiff out of business, to defend themselves against what they thought were unfair charges, and to "give Binghamton the best paper in the state." The court unanimously concluded that "if the defendant honestly believed that they were being persecuted under whatever guise and

9. Certain of the distinctions made by the United States Supreme Court in *Claiborne,* between "political" boycotts on the one hand and "economic" or "labor" boycotts on the other, have been criticized by some commentators as artificial (e.g., Harper, The Consumer's Emerging Right to Boycott: NAACP v. Claiborne Hardware and its Implications for American Labor Law (1984) 93 Yale L.J. 409, 440–442). For purposes of this opinion it is unnecessary for us to decide, and we do not decide, whether or to what extent such distinctions are appropriate under the California Constitution.

that the only way to stop that persecution was by establishing a paper and driving the other paper out of existence such a purpose of self-protection was not malicious and unlawful but quite the contrary."

Beyond that, justification "ought not to rest entirely upon selfishness. Altruism ought to have some place in the consideration of enabling motives, and if one of the purposes is to perform an act or establish a business which will be of benefit to others and give them service not before enjoyed we think such an act ought to confer the same protections as one which looks only to personal and selfish gains."

Have any of the constitutional developments since 1923 altered the analysis of the Beardsley case? Which way do they cut?

5. In the cited Watch Tower case, a department store owned a radio station. For ten years, plaintiff had conducted a series of programs. Defendants, the Roman Catholic Archbishop of Philadelphia and a priest, began objecting that plaintiff "attacks the Catholic Church, misrepresents her teachings and foments religious hatred and bigotry." The priest threatened to cancel his charge account at the department store if it renewed the plaintiff's contract to broadcast—and allegedly urged parishioners to do the same. The store refused to renew the plaintiff's contract. Plaintiff's case was dismissed.

6. Why might critics reject a line drawn between economic and labor boycotts on the one hand and political boycotts on the other?

7. The press sometimes engages in the same conduct. In the Consumer Reports case, p. 409, supra, the magazine urged its readers to write to General Signal to express their unhappiness with the manufacturer's use of the product report.

8. On the subject of exit polling, some have suggested that the public can stop the activity by lying to the pollsters so that their surveys will be unreliable. Broadcasting, Oct. 10, 1983, at 93. From a theoretical perspective, is there a tort theory on which the networks could sue an identified voter if they could prove that he lied to a pollster? What about deceit?

On the same subject, Representative Al Swift warned pollsters that some group, such as the League of Women Voters, might start a campaign to tell citizens that a vote is secret and not to be shared with anyone. He speculated that enough refusals to answer would destroy statistical validity. Swift, The Congressional Concern About Early Calls, 49 Pub.Op.Q. 1, 4 (1985).

Chapter VII

PROTECTING COMMUNITY MORALS—OBSCENITY

We turn in this Chapter and the next to government efforts to protect the community at large from exposure to material deemed harmful to an important aspect of community life. In this Chapter we deal with concerns about public and private morality. In Chapter VIII we deal with concern about market morality and commercial honesty.

Government concern with morality stretches far beyond the question of obscenity. State and local governments have sought for many years to protect the citizenry from exposure to events or reports that might threaten the desired social fabric. The State of Washington, for example, until 1982, made it a misdemeanor for any person to publish "in any book, newspaper, magazine or other printed publication" any "detailed account" of the commission or attempted commission of crimes of a sexual nature, or of the trial of such a charge. Among the other bans was one on any "detailed account of the execution of any person convicted of crime." (RCW § 9.68.020, repealed Laws 1982 ch. 184 § 11).

Another example from outside the field of obscenity involved an effort by the state of New York to apply its power to censor motion pictures to prevent showing of "The Miracle" on the ground that it was "sacrilegious," which the state defined as treating religion with "contempt, mockery, scorn, and ridicule." The Supreme Court invalidated the ban, observing that the breadth of this definition permitted regulation "upon a boundless sea amid a myriad of conflicting currents of religious views." Beyond that, the state had "no legitimate interest in protecting all or any religions from views distasteful to them which is sufficient to justify prior restraints upon the expression of those views." Joseph Burstyn, Inc. v. Wilson, 343 U.S. 495 (1952).

New York next tried to ban the film of "Lady Chatterley's Lover" on the ground that it was "immoral" because it presented acts of adultery as "desirable, acceptable, or proper patterns of behavior." The Court rejected the attempt on the ground that the First Amendment's protection "is not confined to the expression of ideas that are conventional or shared by a majority. It protects advocacy of the opinion that adultery may sometimes be proper, no less than advocacy of socialism or the single tax." Kingsley International Pictures Corp. v. Regents, 360 U.S. 684 (1959).

Despite the generally negative attitude toward prior restraint, the Supreme Court has not invalidated legislation that requires motion picture distributors to present their films for approval before distribution. Failure to follow the procedure is a crime even if the film, if presented, could not lawfully have been denied approval. As recently as 1961, the Court, 5–4, refused to invalidate pre-screening clearance procedures. Times Film Corp. v. Chicago, 365 U.S. 43 (1961). Later cases have tightened the procedures the government must follow to ensure speedy judicial review of any adverse administrative determinations. E.g., Freedman v. Maryland, 380 U.S. 51 (1965). Although the Court has upheld these special restrictions on motion pictures, only a handful of governments are still taking advantage of the available opportunity.

In another case involving a claim of obscenity, the Court validated a different type of procedure and suggested that in this context prior restraint might offer more protection to free expression than criminal prosecution could offer. In Kingsley Books, Inc. v. Brown, 354 U.S. 436 (1957), the Court, 5–4, upheld a New York procedure that sought to prevent the sale and distribution of obscene printed matter by using an ex parte injunction to ban sales, followed by a trial on the merits in a day and a decision two days after that. If the material was found obscene, an order for seizure and destruction could follow.

The majority concluded that "One would be bold to assert that the in terrorem effect" of criminal prosecution was less restraining than the injunctive procedure. Under the statute the dealer was subject to penalty only for ignoring a court order setting the process in motion. "Until then, he may keep the book for sale and sell it on his own judgment rather than steer 'nervously among the treacherous shoals' " of a possible criminal prosecution.

State and local governments that pursue efforts to limit the presence of obscene activities in their communities, may take advantage of such other techniques as abating public nuisances. See Avenue Book Store v. City of Tallmadge, 459 U.S. 997, 8 Med.L.Rptr. 2452 (1982) in which three justices dissented, with opinion, from the denial of certiorari in a case in which state courts had ordered permanently closed the part of a bookstore in which obscene books were found to have been displayed and sold. See also Cooper v. Mitchell Brothers' Santa Ana Theater, 454 U.S. 90, 7 Med.L.Rptr. 2273 (1981) (proof beyond a reasonable doubt not required in a public nuisance abatement action).

In the material that follows, we deal with fiction and with books and movies rather than newspapers and broadcasters. Nonetheless, the limited disgression is important because it permits us to try to identify why the Court puts certain material beyond the protection of the First Amendment.

A. THE NATURE OF OBSCENITY 猥亵

In 1942, in the famous dictum in *Chaplinsky v. New Hampshire,* p. 44, supra, Justice Murphy stated that "lewd and obscene" words were among those "certain well-defined and narrowly limited classes of speech, the prevention and punishment of which have never been thought to raise any Constitutional problem." That may explain why, even though laws against obscenity had been in effect in this country for many years, it was not until 1957 that the Supreme Court confronted the question of the impact of the First Amendment on the law of obscenity. In Roth v. United States, 354 U.S. 476 (1957), the Court held that even though it was "expression," obscenity was outside the protection of the First and Fourteenth Amendments. Yet, "sex and obscenity are not synonymous." Sex, "a great and mysterious motive force in human life, has indisputably been a subject of absorbing interest to mankind through the ages; it is one of the vital problems of human interest and public concern." Basically, the majority decided that obscenity could be determined by asking "whether to the average person, applying contemporary community standards, the dominant theme of the material taken as a whole appeals to prurient interest." In a footnote, the Court defined "prurient interest":

> I.e., material having a tendency to excite lustful thoughts. Webster's New International Dictionary (Unabridged, 2d ed., 1949) defines *prurient,* in pertinent part, as follows:
>
> > ". . . Itching; longing; uneasy with desire or longing; of persons, having itching, morbid, or lascivious longings; of desire, curiosity, or propensity, lewd . . . ."
>
> *Pruriency* is defined, in pertinent part, as follows:
>
> > ". . . Quality of being prurient; lascivious desire or thought . . . ."
>
> See also Mutual Film Corp. v. Industrial Comm'n, 236 U.S. 230, 242, where this Court said as to motion pictures: ". . . They take their attraction from the general interest, eager and wholesome it may be, in their subjects, but a *prurient interest may be excited and appealed to* . . . ." (Emphasis added.)
>
> We perceive no significant difference between the meaning of obscenity developed in the case law and the definition of the A.L.I., Model Penal Code, § 207.10(2) (Tent. Draft No. 6, 1957), viz.:
>
> > ". . . A thing is obscene if, considered as a whole, its predominant appeal is to prurient interest, i.e., a shameful or morbid interest in nudity, sex, or excretion, and if it goes substantially beyond customary limits of candor in description or representation of such matters."

Shortly thereafter, the majority consensus began to collapse as justices began probing for the line between the protected and the unprotected. For example, Justice Stewart, concurring in Jacobellis v. Ohio, 378 U.S. 184, 197 (1964), asserted that "hardcore pornography" was the only type of material that could be prohibited. He continued, "I shall not today attempt further to define the kinds of material I understand to be embraced within that shorthand description; and perhaps I could never succeed in intelligibly doing so. But I know it when I see it, and the motion picture involved in this case is not that."

By 1967, the Court had been reduced to reversing convictions for obscenity without hearing oral argument or rendering written opinions whenever five members of the Court, using their own tests, concluded that the material in the case was not obscene. See Redrup v. New York, 386 U.S. 767 (1967). The only prosecutions with strong likelihood of success were cases in which the defendants pandered to the public by advertising that the material was titillating, Ginzburg v. United States, 383 U.S. 463 (1966), or sought out minors as buyers, Ginsberg v. New York, 390 U.S. 629 (1968).

In Kois v. Wisconsin, 408 U.S. 229 (1972), one count of defendant publisher's conviction was based on the fact that his underground newspaper ran two "relatively small pictures showing a nude man and nude woman embracing in a sitting position." The photographs accompanied an article about the arrest of one of the newspaper's photographers on a charge of possessing obscene material. The article said that the two photographs were "similar" to those taken from the photographer.

The Supreme Court summarily reversed the conviction. Relying on *Roth,* the Court concluded that it could not "fairly be said, either considering the article as it appears or the record before the state court, that the article was a mere vehicle for the publication of the pictures. A quotation from Voltaire in the flyleaf of a book will not constitutionally redeem an otherwise obscene publication," but these photographs were "rationally related to an article that itself was clearly" protected. There was no need to decide whether the dissemination of the photographs by themselves could be prohibited.

MILLER v. CALIFORNIA

Supreme Court of the United States, 1973.
413 U.S. 15, 93 S.Ct. 2607, 37 L.Ed.2d 419.

MR. CHIEF JUSTICE BURGER delivered the opinion of the Court.

This is one of a group of "obscenity-pornography" cases being reviewed by the Court in a re-examination of standards enunciated in earlier cases involving what Mr. Justice Harlan called "the intractable obscenity problem." Interstate Circuit, Inc. v. Dallas, 390 U.S. 676, 704 (1968) (concurring and dissenting).

Appellant conducted a mass mailing campaign to advertise the sale of illustrated books, euphemistically called "adult" material. After a jury trial, he was convicted of violating California Penal Code § 311.2(a), a misdemeanor, by knowingly distributing obscene matter,[1]

1. At the time of the commission of the alleged offense, which was prior to June 25, 1969, § 311.2(a) and § 311 of the California Penal Code read in relevant part:

"§ 311.2 Sending or bringing into state for sale or distribution; printing, exhibiting, distributing or possessing within state

"(a) Every person who knowingly: sends or causes to be sent, or brings or causes to be brought, into this state for sale or distribution, or in this state

and the Appellate Department, Superior Court of California, County of Orange, summarily affirmed the judgment without opinion. Appellant's conviction was specifically based on his conduct in causing five unsolicited advertising brochures to be sent through the mail in an envelope addressed to a restaurant in Newport Beach, California. The envelope was opened by the manager of the restaurant and his mother. They had not requested the brochures; they complained to the police.

The brochures advertise four books entitled "Intercourse," "Man-Woman," "Sex Orgies Illustrated," and "An Illustrated History of Pornography," and a film entitled "Marital Intercourse." While the brochures contain some descriptive printed material, primarily they consist of pictures and drawings very explicitly depicting men and women in groups of two or more engaging in a variety of sexual activities, with genitals often prominently displayed.

I

This case involves the application of a State's criminal obscenity statute to a situation in which sexually explicit materials have been thrust by aggressive sales action upon unwilling recipients who had in no way indicated any desire to receive such materials. This Court has recognized that the States have a legitimate interest in prohibiting dissemination or exhibition of obscene material [2] when the mode of

prepares, publishes, prints, exhibits, distributes, or offers to distribute, or has in his possession with intent to distribute or to exhibit or offer to distribute, any obscene matter is guilty of a misdemeanor. . . . "

"§ 311. Definitions

"As used in this chapter:

"(a) 'Obscene' means that to the average person, applying contemporary standards, the predominant appeal of the matter, taken as a whole, is to prurient interest, i.e., a shameful or morbid interest in nudity, sex, or excretion, which goes substantially beyond customary limits of candor in description or representation of such matters and is matter which is utterly without redeeming social importance.

. . .

"(e) 'Knowingly' means having knowledge that the matter is obscene."

2. This Court has defined "obscene material" as "material which deals with sex in a manner appealing to prurient interest," Roth v. United States, supra, at 487, but the *Roth* definition does not reflect the precise meaning of "obscene" as traditionally used in the English language. Derived from the Latin *obscaenus, ob,* to, plus *caenum,* filth, "obscene" is defined in the Webster's Third New International Dictionary (Unabridged 1969) as "1a: disgusting to the senses . . . b: grossly repugnant to the generally accepted notions of what is appropriate . . . 2: offensive or revolting as countering or violating some ideal or principle." The Oxford English Dictionary (1933 ed.) gives a similar definition, "[o]ffensive to the senses, or to taste or refinement; disgusting, repulsive, filthy, foul, abominable, loathsome."

The material we are discussing in this case is more accurately defined as "pornography" or "pornographic material." "Pornography" derives from the Greek (*pornè*, harlot, and *graphos,* writing). The word now means "1: a description of prostitutes or prostitution 2: a depiction (as in writing or painting) of licentiousness or lewdness: a portrayal of erotic behavior designed to cause sexual excitement." Webster's Third New International Dictionary, supra. Pornographic material which is obscene forms a sub-group of all "obscene" expression, but not the whole, at least as the word "obscene" is now used in our language. We note, therefore, that the words "obscene material" as used in this case, have a specific judicial meaning which derives from the *Roth* case, i.e., obscene material "which deals with sex." *Roth,* supra, at 487. See also ALI Model

dissemination carries with it a significant danger of offending the sensibilities of unwilling recipients or of exposure to juveniles. [ ] It is in this context that we are called on to define the standards which must be used to identify obscene material that a State may regulate without infringing on the First Amendment as applicable to the States through the Fourteenth Amendment.

The dissent of Mr. Justice Brennan reviews the background of the obscenity problem, but since the Court now undertakes to formulate standards more concrete than those in the past, it is useful for us to focus on two of the landmark cases in the somewhat tortured history of the Court's obscenity decisions. In Roth v. United States, 354 U.S. 476 (1957), the Court sustained a conviction under a federal statute punishing the mailing of "obscene, lewd, lascivious or filthy . . . " materials. The key to that holding was the Court's rejection of the claim that obscene materials were protected by the First Amendment. Five Justices joined in the opinion stating:

> "All ideas having even the slightest redeeming social importance—unorthodox ideas, controversial ideas, even ideas hateful to the prevailing climate of opinion—have the full protection of the [First Amendment] guaranties, unless excludable because they encroach upon the limited area of more important interests. But implicit in the history of the First Amendment is the rejection of obscenity as utterly without redeeming social importance. . . .
> "We hold that obscenity is not within the area of constitutionally protected speech or press." 354 U.S., at 484–485 (footnotes omitted).

Nine years later, in Memoirs v. Massachusetts, 383 U.S. 413 (1966), the Court veered sharply away from the *Roth* concept and, with only three Justices in the plurality opinion, articulated a new test of obscenity. The plurality held that under the *Roth* definition

> "as elaborated in subsequent cases, three elements must coalesce: it must be established that (a) the dominant theme of the material taken as a whole appeals to a prurient interest in sex; (b) the material is patently offensive because it affronts contemporary community standards relating to the description or representation of sexual matters; and (c) the material is utterly without redeeming social value." Id., at 418.

. . .

While *Roth* presumed "obscenity" to be "utterly without redeeming social importance," *Memoirs* required that to prove obscenity it must be affirmatively established that the material is "*utterly* without redeeming social value." Thus, even as they repeated the words of *Roth,* the *Memoirs* plurality produced a drastically altered test that called on the prosecution to prove a negative, i.e., that the material was "*utterly* without redeeming social value"—a burden virtually impossible to discharge under our criminal standards of proof. Such considerations caused Mr. Justice Harlan to wonder if the "*utterly* without redeeming social value" test had any meaning at all. [ ]

Apart from the initial formulation in the Roth case, no majority of the Court has at any given time been able to agree on a standard to determine what constitutes obscene, pornographic material subject to regulation under the States' police power. [ ] We have seen "a variety of views among the members of the Court unmatched in any other course of constitutional adjudication." Interstate Circuit, Inc. v. Dallas, 390 U.S., at 704–705 (Harlan, J., concurring and dissenting).[3] This is not remarkable, for in the area of freedom of speech and press the courts must always remain sensitive to any infringement on genuinely serious literary, artistic, political, or scientific expression. This is an area in which there are few eternal verities.

The case we now review was tried on the theory that the California Penal Code § 311 approximately incorporates the three-stage *Memoirs* test, supra. But now the *Memoirs* test has been abandoned as unworkable by its author,[4] and no Member of the Court today supports the *Memoirs* formulation.

II

. . .

The basic guidelines for the trier of fact must be: (a) whether "the average person, applying contemporary community standards" would find that the work, taken as a whole, appeals to the prurient interest, [ ]; (b) whether the work depicts or describes, in a patently offensive way, sexual conduct specifically defined by the applicable state law; and (c) whether the work, taken as a whole, lacks serious literary, artistic, political, or scientific value. We do not adopt as a constitutional standard the "*utterly* without redeeming social value" test of Memoirs v. Massachusetts, 383 U.S., at 419; that concept has never commanded the adherence of more than three Justices at one time.

. . .

We emphasize that it is not our function to propose regulatory schemes for the States: That must await their concrete legislative efforts. It is possible, however, to give a few plain examples of what a state statute could define for regulation under part (b) of the standard announced in this opinion, supra:

3. In the absence of a majority view, this Court was compelled to embark on the practice of summarily reversing convictions for the dissemination of materials that at least five members of the Court, applying their separate tests, found to be protected by the First Amendment. Redrup v. New York, 386 U.S. 767 (1967). Thirty-one cases have been decided in this manner. Beyond the necessity of circumstances, however, no justification has ever been offered in support of the *Redrup* "policy." [ ] The *Redrup* procedure has cast us in the role of an unreviewable board of censorship for the 50 States, subjectively judging each piece of material brought before us.

4. See the dissenting opinion of Mr. Justice Brennan in Paris Adult Theatre I v. Slaton, [ ].

(a) Patently offensive representations or descriptions of ultimate sexual acts, normal or perverted, actual or simulated.

(b) Patently offensive representations or descriptions of masturbation, excretory functions, and lewd exhibition of the genitals.

Sex and nudity may not be exploited without limit by films or pictures exhibited or sold in places of public accommodation any more than live sex and nudity can be exhibited or sold without limit in such public places. At a minimum, prurient, patently offensive depiction or description of sexual conduct must have serious literary, artistic, political, or scientific value to merit First Amendment protection. [ ] For example, medical books for the education of physicians and related personnel necessarily use graphic illustrations and descriptions of human anatomy. In resolving the inevitably sensitive questions of fact and law, we must continue to rely on the jury system, accompanied by the safeguards that judges, rules of evidence, presumption of innocence, and other protective features provide, as we do with rape, murder, and a host of other offenses against society and its individual members.

Mr. Justice Brennan, [ ] [abandoning his former position], now maintains that no formulation of this Court, the Congress, or the States can adequately distinguish obscene material unprotected by the First Amendment from protected expression, [ ]. Paradoxically, Mr. Justice Brennan indicates that suppression of unprotected obscene material is permissible to avoid exposure to unconsenting adults, as in this case, and to juveniles, although he gives no indication of how the division between protected and nonprotected materials may be drawn with greater precision for these purposes than for regulation of commercial exposure to consenting adults only. Nor does he indicate where in the Constitution he finds the authority to distinguish between a willing "adult" one month past the state law age of majority and a willing "juvenile" one month younger.

Under the holdings announced today, no one will be subject to prosecution for the sale or exposure of obscene materials unless these materials depict or describe patently offensive "hard core" sexual conduct specifically defined by the regulating state law, as written or construed. We are satisfied that these specific prerequisites will provide fair notice to a dealer in such materials that his public and commercial activities may bring prosecution. . . .

. . .

III

Under a national Constitution, fundamental First Amendment limitations on the powers of the States do not vary from community to community, but this does not mean that there are, or should or can be, fixed, uniform national standards of precisely what appeals to the "prurient interest" or is "patently offensive." These are essentially questions of fact, and our nation is simply too big and too diverse for this Court to reasonably expect that such standards could be articulated for all 50 States in a single formulation, even assuming the prerequisite consensus exists. When triers of fact are asked to decide whether "the average person, applying contemporary community standards" would consider certain materials "prurient," it would be unrealistic to require that the answer be based on some abstract formulation. The adversary system, with lay jurors as the usual ultimate factfinders in criminal prosecutions, has historically permitted triers of fact to draw on the standards of their community, guided always by limiting instructions on the law. To require a State to structure obscenity proceedings around evidence of a *national* "community standard" would be an exercise in futility.

. . .

It is neither realistic nor constitutionally sound to read the First Amendment as requiring that the people of Maine or Mississippi accept public depiction of conduct found tolerable in Las Vegas, or New York City. [ ] People in different States vary in their tastes and attitudes, and this diversity is not to be strangled by the absolutism of imposed uniformity. As the Court made clear in Mishkin v. New York, 383 U.S., at 508–509, the primary concern with requiring a jury to apply the standard of "the average person, applying contemporary community standards" is to be certain that, so far as material is not aimed at a deviant group, it will be judged by its impact on an average person, rather than a particularly susceptible or sensitive person—or indeed a totally insensitive one. [ ] We hold that the requirement that the jury evaluate the materials with reference to "contemporary standards of the State of California" serves this protective purpose and is constitutionally adequate.

IV

The dissenting Justices sound the alarm of repression. But, in our view, to equate the free and robust exchange of ideas and political debate with commercial exploitation of obscene material demeans the grand conception of the First Amendment and its high purposes in the historic struggle for freedom. It is a "misuse of the great guarantees of free speech and free press. . . . " Breard v. Alexandria, 341 U.S., at 645. The First Amendment protects works which, taken as a whole, have serious literary, artistic, political, or scientific value, regardless of whether the government or a majority of the people approve of the ideas these works represent. "The protection given speech and press was fashioned to assure unfettered interchange of *ideas* for the bringing about of political and social changes desired by the people," Roth v. United States, supra, at 484 (emphasis added). [ ] But the public portrayal of hard core sexual conduct for its own sake, and for the ensuing commercial gain, is a different matter.

There is no evidence, empirical or historical, that the stern 19th century American censorship of public distribution and display of material relating to sex, [ ] in any way limited or affected expression of serious literary, artistic, political, or scientific ideas. . . .

Mr. Justice Brennan finds "it is hard to see how state-ordered regimentation of our minds can ever be forestalled." Paris Adult Theatre I v. Slaton (Brennan, J., dissenting). These doleful anticipations assume that courts cannot distinguish commerce in ideas, protected by the First Amendment, from commercial exploitation of obscene material. Moreover, state regulation of hard core pornography so as to make it unavailable to nonadults, a regulation which Mr. Justice Brennan finds constitutionally permissible, has all the elements of "censorship" for adults; indeed even more rigid enforcement techniques may be called for with such dichotomy of regulation. . . .

In sum, we (a) reaffirm the *Roth* holding that obscene material is not protected by the First Amendment; (b) hold that such material can be regulated by the States, subject to the specific safeguards enunciated above, without a showing that the material is "*utterly* without redeeming social value"; and (c) hold that obscenity is to be determined by applying "contemporary community standards," [ ] not "national standards." The judgment of the Appellate Department of the Superior Court, Orange County, California, is vacated and the case remanded to that court for further proceedings not inconsistent with the First Amendment standards established by this opinion. [ ]

MR. JUSTICE DOUGLAS, dissenting.

. . .

Today the Court retreats from the earlier formulations of the constitutional test and undertakes to make new definitions. This effort, like the earlier ones, is earnest and well intentioned. The difficulty is that we do not deal with constitutional terms, since "obscenity" is not mentioned in the Constitution or Bill of Rights. And the First Amendment makes no such exception from "the press" which it undertakes to protect nor, as I have said on other occasions, is an exception necessarily implied, for there was no recognized exception to the free press at the time the Bill of Rights was adopted which treated "obscene" publications differently from other types of papers, magazines, and books. So there are no constitutional guidelines for deciding what is and what is not "obscene." The Court is at large because we deal with tastes and standards of literature. What shocks me may be sustenance for my neighbor. What causes one person to boil up in rage over one pamphlet or movie may reflect only his neurosis, not shared by others. We deal here with a regime of censorship which, if adopted, should be done by constitutional amendment after full debate by the people.

. . .

My contention is that until a civil proceeding has placed a tract beyond the pale, no criminal prosecution should be sustained. For no more vivid illustration of vague and uncertain laws could be designed than those we have fashioned. . . .

While the right to know is the corollary of the right to speak or publish, no one can be forced by government to listen to disclosure that he finds offensive. That was the basis of my dissent in Public Utilities Comm'n v. Pollak, 343 U.S. 451, 467 (1952), where I protested against making a streetcar audience a "captive" audience. There is no "captive audience" problem in these obscenity cases. No one is being compelled to look or to listen. Those who enter news stands or bookstalls may be offended by what they see. But they are not compelled by the State to frequent those places; and it is only state or governmental action against which the First Amendment, applicable to the States by virtue of the Fourteenth, raises a ban.

. . .

MR. JUSTICE BRENNAN, with whom MR. JUSTICE STEWART and MR. JUSTICE MARSHALL join, dissenting.

In my dissent in Paris Adult Theatre I v. Slaton, decided this date, I noted that I had no occasion to consider the extent of state power to regulate the distribution of sexually oriented material to juveniles or the offensive exposure of such material to unconsenting adults. In the case before us, appellant was convicted of distributing obscene matter in violation of California Penal Code § 311.2, on the basis of evidence that he had caused to be mailed unsolicited brochures advertising various books and a movie. I need not now decide whether a statute might be drawn to impose, within the requirements of the First Amendment, criminal penalties for the precise conduct at issue here. For it is clear that under my dissent in *Paris Adult Theatre I*, the statute under which the prosecution was brought is unconstitutionally overbroad, and therefore invalid on its face. "[T]he transcendent value to all society of constitutionally protected expression is deemed to justify allowing 'attacks on overly broad statutes with no requirement that the person making the attack demonstrate that his own conduct could not be regulated by a statute drawn with the requisite narrow specificity.' "

. . .

PARIS ADULT THEATRE I v. SLATON

Supreme Court of the United States, 1973.
413 U.S. 49, 93 S.Ct. 2628, 37 L.Ed.2d 446.

[Respondents, a district attorney and a local court solicitor, filed civil complaints seeking injunctions against petitioners, two Atlanta movie theatres, on the ground they were exhibiting obscene motion pictures. Signs outside the theatres identified them as showing "mature feature films" and stated that entrants must be "21 and able to prove it. If viewing the nude body offends you, Please Do Not Enter." Nothing outside indicated the full nature of what was being shown. "In particular, nothing indicated that the films depicted as they did—scenes of simulated fellatio, cunnilingus, and group sex intercourse. There was no evidence that minors had ever entered the theatres."

The trial court denied the injunction on the ground that the exclusion of minors and the general notice of content made the showing constitutionally permissible. The Georgia Supreme Court unanimously reversed on the grounds that the movies were "hard core pornography" and their exhibition was not protected by the First Amendment.]

MR. CHIEF JUSTICE BURGER delivered the opinion of the Court.

. . .

II

We categorically disapprove the theory, apparently adopted by the trial judge, that obscene, pornographic films acquire constitutional immunity from state regulation simply because they are exhibited for consenting adults only. This holding was properly rejected by the Georgia Supreme Court. Although we have often pointedly recognized the high importance of the state interest in regulating the exposure of obscene materials to juveniles and unconsenting adults, [ ] this Court has never declared these to be the only legitimate state interests permitting regulation of obscene material. The States have a long-recognized legitimate interest in regulating the use of obscene material in local commerce and in all places of public accommodation, as long as these regulations do not run afoul of specific constitutional prohibitions. . . .

In particular, we hold that there are legitimate state interests at stake in stemming the tide of commercialized obscenity, even assuming it is feasible to enforce effective safeguards against exposure to juveniles and to passersby. [7] Rights and interests "other than those of the advocates are involved." Breard v. Alexandria, 341 U.S. 622, 642 (1951). These include the interest of the public in the quality of life and the total community environment, the tone of commerce in the great city centers, and, possibly, the public safety itself. The Hill-Link Minority Report of the Commission on Obscenity and Pornography indicates that there is at least an arguable correlation between obscene material and crime. Quite apart from sex crimes, however, there remains one problem of large proportions aptly described by Professor Bickel:

"It concerns the tone of the society, the mode, or to use terms that have perhaps greater currency, the style and quality of life, now

7. It is conceivable that an "adult" theater can—if it really insists—prevent the exposure of its obscene wares to juveniles. An "adult" bookstore, dealing in obscene books, magazines, and pictures, cannot realistically make this claim. The Hill-Link Minority Report of the Commission on Obscenity and Pornography emphasizes evidence (the Abelson National Survey of Youth and Adults) that, although most pornography may be bought by elders, "the heavy users and most highly exposed people to pornography are adolescent females (among women) and adolescent and young adult males (among men)." The Report of the Commission on Obscenity and Pornography 401 (1970). The legitimate interest in preventing exposure of juveniles to obscene material cannot be fully served by simply barring juveniles from the immediate physical premises of "adult" bookstores, when there is a flourishing "outside business" in these materials.

and in the future. A man may be entitled to read an obscene book in his room, or expose himself indecently there. . . . We should protect his privacy. But if he demands a right to obtain the books and pictures he wants in the market, and to foregather in public places—discreet, if you will, but accessible to all—with others who share his tastes, *then to grant him his right is to affect the world about the rest of us, and to impinge on other privacies.* Even supposing that each of us can, if he wishes, effectively avert the eye and stop the ear (which, in truth, we cannot), what is commonly read and seen and heard and done intrudes upon us all, want it or not." 22 The Public Interest 25–26 (Winter 1971). (Emphasis added.)

. . .

But, it is argued, there are no scientific data which conclusively demonstrate that exposure to obscene material adversely affects men and women or their society. It is urged on behalf of the petitioners that, absent such a demonstration, any kind of state regulation is "impermissible." We reject this argument. It is not for us to resolve empirical uncertainties underlying state legislation, save in the exceptional case where that legislation plainly impinges upon rights protected by the Constitution itself. . . . Although there is no conclusive proof of a connection between antisocial behavior and obscene material, the legislature of Georgia could quite reasonably determine that such a connection does or might exist. . . .

From the beginning of civilized societies, legislators and judges have acted on various unprovable assumptions. Such assumptions underlie much lawful state regulation of commercial and business affairs. [ ] The same is true of the federal securities and antitrust laws and a host of federal regulations. [ ] On the basis of these assumptions both Congress and state legislatures have, for example, drastically restricted associational rights by adopting antitrust laws, and have strictly regulated public expression by issuers of and dealers in securities, profit sharing "coupons," and "trading stamps," commanding what they must and must not publish and announce. [ ] Understandably those who entertain an absolutist view of the First Amendment find it uncomfortable to explain why rights of association, speech, and press should be severely restrained in the marketplace of goods and money, but not in the marketplace of pornography.

Likewise, when legislatures and administrators act to protect the physical environment from pollution and to preserve our resources of forests, streams, and parks, they must act on such imponderables as the impact of a new highway near or through an existing park or wilderness area. . . . The fact that a congressional directive reflects unprovable assumptions about what is good for the people, including imponderable aesthetic assumptions, is not a sufficient reason to find that statute unconstitutional.

If we accept the unprovable assumption that a complete education requires certain books, see Board of Education v. Allen, 392 U.S. 236, 245 (1968) [ ], and the well nigh universal belief that good books, plays, and art lift the spirit, improve the mind, enrich the human personality, and develop character, can we then say that a state legislature may not act on the corollary assumption that commerce in obscene books, or public exhibitions focused on obscene conduct, have a tendency to exert a corrupting and debasing impact leading to antisocial behavior? . . . The sum of experience, including that of the past two decades, affords an ample basis for legislatures to conclude that a sensitive, key relationship of human existence, central to family life, community welfare, and the development of human personality, can be debased and distorted by crass commercial exploitation of sex. Nothing in the Constitution prohibits a State from reaching such a conclusion and acting on it legislatively simply because there is no conclusive evidence or empirical data.

It is argued that individual "free will" must govern, even in activities beyond the protection of the First Amendment and other constitutional guarantees of privacy, and that government cannot legitimately impede an individual's desire to see or acquire obscene plays, movies, and books. We do indeed base our society on certain assumptions that people have the capacity for free choice. Most exercises of individual free choice—those in politics, religion, and expression of ideas—are explicitly protected by the Constitution. Totally unlimited play for free will, however, is not allowed in our or any other society. We have just noted, for example, that neither the First Amendment nor "free will" precludes States from having "blue sky" laws to regulate what sellers of securities may write or publish about their wares. [ ] Such laws are to protect the weak, the uninformed, the unsuspecting, and the gullible from the exercise of their own volition. Nor do modern societies leave disposal of garbage and sewage up to the individual "free will," but impose regulation to protect both public health and the appearance of public places. States are told by some that they must await a "laissez faire" market solution to the obscenity-pornography problem, paradoxically "by people who have never otherwise had a kind word to say for laissez faire," particularly in solving urban, commercial, and environmental pollution problems. [ ]

The States, of course, may follow such a "laissez faire" policy and drop all controls on commercialized obscenity, if that is what they prefer, just as they can ignore consumer protection in the marketplace, but nothing in the Constitution *compels* the States to do so with regard to matters falling within state jurisdiction. . . .

It is asserted, however, that standards for evaluating state commercial regulations are inapposite in the present context, as state regulation of access by consenting adults to obscene material violates the constitutionally protected right to privacy enjoyed by petitioners' customers. Even assuming that petitioners have vicarious standing to assert potential customers' rights, it is unavailing to compare a theater open to the public for a fee, with the private home of Stanley v. Georgia, 394 U.S., at 568, and the marital bedroom of Griswold v. Connecticut, [381 U.S.] at 485–486. This Court, has, on numerous occasions, refused to hold that commercial ventures such as a motion-picture house are "private" for the purpose of civil rights litigation and civil rights statutes. [ ] The Civil Rights Act of 1964 specifically defines motion-picture houses and theaters as places of "public accommodation" covered by the Act as operations affecting commerce. [ ]

Our prior decisions recognizing a right to privacy guaranteed by the Fourteenth Amendment included "only personal rights that can be deemed 'fundamental' or 'implicit in the concept of ordered liberty.' [ ]." [ ] This privacy right encompasses and protects the personal intimacies of the home, the family, marriage, motherhood, procreation, and child rearing. [ ] Nothing, however, in this Court's decisions intimates that there is any "fundamental" privacy right "implicit in the concept of ordered liberty" to watch obscene movies in places of public accommodation.

If obscene material unprotected by the First Amendment in itself carried with it a "penumbra" of constitutionally protected privacy, this Court would not have found it necessary to decide *Stanley* on the narrow basis of the "privacy of the home," which was hardly more than a reaffirmation that "a man's home is his castle" Cf. Stanley v. Georgia, supra, at 564.[13] Moreover, we have declined to equate the privacy of the home relied on in *Stanley* with a "zone" of "privacy" that follows a distributor or a consumer of obscene materials wherever he goes. [ ] The idea of a "privacy" right and a place of public accommodation are, in this context, mutually exclusive. Conduct or depictions of conduct that the state police power can prohibit on a public street do not become automatically protected by the Constitution merely because the conduct is moved to a bar or a "live" theater stage, any more than a "live" performance of a man and woman locked in a sexual embrace at high noon in Times Square is protected by the Constitution because they simultaneously engage in a valid political dialogue.

. . .

Finally, petitioners argue that conduct which directly involves "consenting adults" only has for that sole reason, a special claim to constitutional protection. Our Constitution establishes a broad range of conditions on the exercise of power by the States, but for us to say that our Constitution incorporates the proposition that conduct involving consenting adults only is always beyond state regulation, is a step

13. The protection afforded by Stanley v. Georgia, 394 U.S. 557 (1969), is restricted to a place, the home. In contrast, the constitutionally protected privacy of family, marriage, motherhood, procreation, and child rearing is not just concerned with a particular place, but with a protected intimate relationship. Such protected privacy extends to the doctor's office, the hospital, the hotel room, or as otherwise required to safeguard the right to intimacy involved. [ ] Obviously, there is no necessary or legitimate expectation of privacy which would extend to marital intercourse on a street corner or a theater stage.

we are unable to take.[15] Commercial exploitation of depictions, descriptions, or exhibitions of obscene conduct on commercial premises open to the adult public falls within a State's broad power to regulate commerce and protect the public environment. The issue in this context goes beyond whether someone, or even the majority, considers the conduct depicted as "wrong" or "sinful." The States have the power to make a morally neutral judgment that public exhibition of obscene material, or commerce in such material, has a tendency to injure the community as a whole, to endanger the public safety, or to jeopardize, in Mr. Chief Justice Warren's words, the States' "right . . . to maintain a decent society." Jacobellis v. Ohio, 378 U.S., at 199 (dissenting opinion).

To summarize, we have today reaffirmed the basic holding of *Roth v. United States,* supra, that obscene material has no protection under the First Amendment. See Miller v. California. . . . In this case we hold that the States have a legitimate interest in regulating commerce in obscene material and in regulating exhibition of obscene material in places of public accommodation, including so-called "adult" theaters from which minors are excluded. In light of these holdings, nothing precludes the State of Georgia from the regulation of the allegedly obscene material exhibited in Paris Adult Theatre I or II, provided that the applicable Georgia law, as written or authoritatively interpreted by the Georgia courts, meets the First Amendment standards set forth in Miller v. California, [ ]. The judgment is vacated and the case remanded to the Georgia Supreme Court for further proceedings not inconsistent with this opinion and Miller v. California, supra. [ ].

Vacated and remanded.

MR. JUSTICE DOUGLAS, dissenting.

My Brother Brennan is to be commended for seeking a new path through the thicket which the Court entered when it undertook to sustain the constitutionality of obscenity laws and to place limits on their application. I have expressed on numerous occasions my disagreement with the basic decision that held that "obscenity" was not protected by the First Amendment. I disagreed also with the definitions that evolved. Art and literature reflect tastes; and tastes, like musical appreciation, are hardly reducible to precise definitions. That is one reason I have always felt that "obscenity" was not an exception to the First Amendment. . . .

. . .

15. The state statute books are replete with constitutionally unchallenged laws against prostitution, suicide, voluntary self-mutilation, brutalizing "bare fist" prize fights, and duels, although these crimes may only directly involve "consenting adults." . . .

As Professor Irving Kristol has observed: "Bearbaiting and cockfighting are prohibited only in part out of compassion for the suffering animals; the main reason they were abolished was because it was felt that they debased and brutalized the citizenry who flocked to witness such spectacles." On the Democratic Idea in America 33 (1972).

MR. JUSTICE BRENNAN, with whom MR. JUSTICE STEWART and MR. JUSTICE MARSHALL join, dissenting.

This case requires the Court to confront once again the vexing problem of reconciling state efforts to suppress sexually oriented expression with the protections of the First Amendment, as applied to the States through the Fourteenth Amendment. No other aspect of the First Amendment has, in recent years, demanded so substantial a commitment of our time, generated such disharmony of views, and remained so resistant to the formulation of stable and manageable standards. I am convinced that the approach initiated 16 years ago in Roth v. United States, 354 U.S. 476 (1957), and culminating in the Court's decision today, cannot bring stability to this area of the law without jeopardizing fundamental First Amendment values, and I have concluded that the time has come to make a significant departure from that approach.

. . .

. . . The essence of our problem in the obscenity area is that we have been unable to provide "sensitive tools" to separate obscenity from other sexually oriented but constitutionally protected speech, so that efforts to suppress the former do not spill over into the suppression of the latter. . . .

. . .

Of course, the vagueness problem would be largely of our own creation if it stemmed primarily from our failure to reach a consensus on any one standard. But after 16 years of experimentation and debate I am reluctantly forced to the conclusion that none of the available formulas, including the one announced today, can reduce the vagueness to a tolerable level while at the same time striking an acceptable balance between the protections of the First and Fourteenth Amendments, on the one hand, and on the other the asserted state interest in regulating the dissemination of certain sexually oriented materials. Any effort to draw a constitutionally acceptable boundary on state power must resort to such indefinite concepts as "prurient interest," "patent offensiveness," "serious literary value," and the like. The meaning of these concepts necessarily varies with the experience, outlook, and even idiosyncrasies of the person defining them. Although we have assumed that obscenity does exist and that we "know it when [we] see it," Jacobellis v. Ohio, supra, at 197 (Stewart, J., concurring), we are manifestly unable to describe it in advance except by reference to concepts so elusive that they fail to distinguish clearly between protected and unprotected speech.

. . . These considerations suggest that no one definition, no matter how precisely or narrowly drawn, can possibly suffice for all situations, or carve out fully suppressible expression from all media without also creating a substantial risk of encroachment upon the guarantees of the Due Process Clause and the First Amendment.[9]

The vagueness of the standards in the obscenity area produces a number of separate problems, and any improvement must rest on an understanding that the problems are to some extent distinct. First, a vague statute fails to provide adequate notice to persons who are engaged in the type of conduct that the statute could be thought to proscribe. . . .

In addition to problems that arise when any criminal statute fails to afford fair notice of what it forbids, a vague statute in the areas of speech and press creates a second level of difficulty. We have indicated that "stricter standards of permissible statutory vagueness may be applied to a statute having a potentially inhibiting effect on speech; a man may the less be required to act at his peril here, because the free dissemination of ideas may be the loser." Smith v. California, 361 U.S. 147, 151 (1959). . . .

. . .

The problems of fair notice and chilling protected speech are very grave standing alone. But it does not detract from their importance to recognize that a vague statute in this area creates a third, although admittedly more subtle, set of problems. These problems concern the institutional stress that inevitably results where the line separating protected from unprotected speech is excessively vague. In *Roth* we conceded that "there may be marginal cases in which it is difficult to determine the side of the line on which a particular fact situation falls. . . ." 354 U.S., at 491–492. Our subsequent experience demonstrates that almost every case is "marginal." And since the "margin" marks the point of separation between protected and unprotected speech, we are left with a system in which almost every obscenity case presents a constitutional question of exceptional difficulty. . . .

. . .

. . . In addition, the uncertainty of the standards creates a continuing source of tension between state and federal courts, since the need for an independent determination by this Court seems to render superfluous even the most conscientious analysis by state tribunals. And our inability to justify our decisions with a persuasive rationale—or indeed, any rationale at all—necessarily creates the impression that we are merely second-guessing state court judges.

The severe problems arising from the lack of fair notice, from the chill on protected expression, and from the stress imposed on the state

9. Although I did not join the opinion of the Court in Stanley v. Georgia, 394 U.S. 557 (1969), I am now inclined to agree that "the Constitution protects the right to receive information and ideas," and that "[t]his right to receive information and ideas, regardless of their social worth . . . is fundamental to our free society." . . . Whether or not a class of "obscene" and thus entirely unprotected speech does exist, I am forced to conclude that the class is incapable of definition with sufficient clarity to withstand attack on vagueness grounds. Accordingly, it is on principles of the void-for-vagueness doctrine that this opinion exclusively relies.

and federal judicial machinery persuade me that a significant change in direction is urgently required. I turn, therefore, to the alternatives that are now open.

IV

1. The approach requiring the smallest deviation from our present course would be to draw a new line between protected and unprotected speech, still permitting the States to suppress all material on the unprotected side of the line. In my view, clarity cannot be obtained pursuant to this approach except by drawing a line that resolves all doubt in favor of state power and against the guarantees of the First Amendment. We could hold, for example, that any depiction or description of human sexual organs, irrespective of the manner or purpose of the portrayal, is outside the protection of the First Amendment and therefore open to suppression by the States. That formula would, no doubt, offer much fairer notice of the reach of any state statute drawn at the boundary of the State's constitutional power. And it would also, in all likelihood, give rise to a substantial probability of regularity in most judicial determinations under the standard. But such a standard would be appallingly overbroad, permitting the suppression of a vast range of literary, scientific, and artistic masterpieces. Neither the First Amendment nor any free community could possibly tolerate such a standard. Yet short of that extreme it is hard to see how any choice of words could reduce the vagueness problem to tolerable proportions, so long as we remain committed to the view that some class of materials is subject to outright suppression by the State.

2. The alternative adopted by the Court today recognizes that a prohibition against any depiction or description of human sexual organs could not be reconciled with the guarantees of the First Amendment. But the Court does retain the view that certain sexually oriented material can be considered obscene and therefore unprotected by the First and Fourteenth Amendment. To describe that unprotected class of expression, the Court adopts a restatement of the *Roth-Memoirs* definition of obscenity. . . .

. . .

Although the Court's restatement substantially tracks the three-part test announced in Memoirs v. Massachusetts, supra, it does purport to modify the "social value" component of the test. Instead of requiring, as did *Roth* and *Memoirs,* that state suppression be limited to materials utterly lacking in social value, the Court today permits suppression if the government can prove that the materials lack "*serious* literary, artistic, political or scientific value." But the definition of "obscenity" as expression utterly lacking in social importance is the key to the conceptual basis of *Roth* and our subsequent opinions. In *Roth* we held that certain expression is obscene, and thus outside the protection of the First Amendment, precisely *because* it lacks even the slightest redeeming social value. [ ] The Court's approach necessarily assumes that some works will be deemed obscene—even though they clearly have *some* social value—because the State was able to prove that the value, measured by some unspecified standard, was not sufficiently "serious" to warrant constitutional protection. That result is not merely inconsistent with our holding in *Roth;* it is nothing less than a rejection of the fundamental First Amendment premises and rationale of the *Roth* opinion and an invitation to widespread suppression of sexually oriented speech. Before today, the protections of the First Amendment have never been thought limited to expressions of *serious* literary or political value. [ ]

. . .

4. Finally, I have considered the view, urged so forcefully since 1957 by our Brothers Black and Douglas, that the First Amendment bars the suppression of any sexually oriented expression. That position would effect a sharp reduction, although perhaps not a total elimination, of the uncertainty that surrounds our current approach. Nevertheless, I am convinced that it would achieve that desirable goal only by stripping the States of power to an extent that cannot be justified by the commands of the Constitution, at least so long as there is available an alternative approach that strikes a better balance between the guarantee of free expression and the States' legitimate interests.

V

Our experience since *Roth* requires us not only to abandon the effort to pick out obscene materials on a case-by-case basis, but also to reconsider a fundamental postulate of *Roth:* that there exists a definable class of sexually oriented expression that may be totally suppressed by the Federal and State Governments. Assuming that such a class of expression does in fact exist, I am forced to conclude that the concept of "obscenity" cannot be defined with sufficient specificity and clarity to provide fair notice to persons who create and distribute sexually oriented materials, to prevent substantial erosion of protected speech as a byproduct of the attempt to suppress unprotected speech, and to avoid very costly institutional harms. Given these inevitable side effects of state efforts to suppress what is assumed to be *unprotected* speech, we must scrutinize with care the state interest that is asserted to justify the suppression. For in the absence of some very substantial interest in suppressing such speech, we can hardly condone the ill effects that seem to flow inevitably from the effort.

Obscenity laws have a long history in this country. . . .

This history caused us to conclude in *Roth* "that the unconditional phrasing of the First Amendment [that "Congress shall make no law . . . abridging the freedom of speech, or of the press . . . "] was not intended to protect every utterance." . . .

Because we assumed—incorrectly, as experience has proved—that obscenity could be separated from other sexually oriented expression without significant costs either to the First Amendment or to the judicial machinery charged with the task of safeguarding First Amendment freedoms, we had no occasion in *Roth* to probe the asserted state interest in curtailing unprotected, sexually oriented speech. Yet, as we have increasingly come to appreciate the vagueness of the concept of obscenity, we have begun to recognize and articulate the state interests at stake. . . .

The opinions in *Redrup* and Stanley v. Georgia reflected our emerging view that the state interest in protecting children and in protecting unconsenting adults may stand on a different footing from the other asserted state interests. . . . Similarly, if children are "not possessed of that full capacity for individual choice which is the presupposition of the First Amendment guarantees," Ginsberg v. New York, 390 U.S., at 649–650 (Stewart, J., concurring), then the State may have a substantial interest in precluding the flow of obscene materials even to consenting juveniles. [ ]

But, whatever the strength of the state interests in protecting juveniles and unconsenting adults from exposure to sexually oriented materials, those interests cannot be asserted in defense of the holding of the Georgia Supreme Court in this case. . . .

At the outset it should be noted that virtually all of the interests that might be asserted in defense of suppression, laying aside the special interests associated with distribution to juveniles and unconsenting adults, were also posited in Stanley v. Georgia, supra, where we held that the State could not make the "mere private possession of obscene material a crime." Id., at 568. That decision presages the conclusions I reach here today.

In *Stanley* we pointed out that "[t]here appears to be little empirical basis for" the assertion that "exposure to obscene materials may lead to deviant sexual behavior or crimes of sexual violence." Id., at 566 and n. 9.[26] In any event, we added that "if the State is only concerned about printed or filmed materials inducing antisocial conduct, we believe that in the context of private consumption of ideas and information we should adhere to the view that '[a]mong free men, the deterrents ordinarily to be applied to prevent crime are education and punishment for violations of the law. . . .' Whitney v. California, 274 U.S. 357, 378 (1927) (Brandeis, J., concurring)." Id., at 566–567.

26. Indeed, since *Stanley* was decided, the President's Commission on Obscenity and Pornography has concluded:

> "In sum, empirical research designed to clarify the question has found no evidence to date that exposure to explicit sexual materials plays a significant role in the causation of delinquent or criminal behavior among youth or adults. The Commission cannot conclude that exposure to erotic materials is a factor in the causation of sex crime or sex delinquency." Report of the Commission on Obscenity and Pornography 27 (1970) (footnote omitted).

To the contrary, the Commission found that "[o]n the positive side, explicit sexual materials are sought as a source of entertainment and information by substantial numbers of American adults. At times, these materials also appear to serve to increase and facilitate constructive communication about sexual matters within marriage." Id., at 53.

Moreover, in *Stanley* we rejected as "wholly inconsistent with the philosophy of the First Amendment," id., at 566, the notion that there is a legitimate state concern in the "control [of] the moral content of a person's thoughts," id., at 565, and we held that a State "cannot constitutionally premise legislation on the desirability of controlling a person's private thoughts." Id., at 566. That is not to say, of course, that a State must remain utterly indifferent to—and take no action bearing on—the morality of the community. . . .

. . .

If, as the Court today assumes, "a state legislature may . . . act on the . . . assumption that commerce in obscene books, or public exhibitions focused on obscene conduct, have a tendency to exert a corrupting and debasing impact leading to antisocial behavior," then it is hard to see how state-ordered regimentation of our minds can ever be forestalled. For if a State may, in an effort to maintain or create a particular moral tone, prescribe what its citizens cannot read or cannot see, then it would seem to follow that in pursuit of that same objective a State could decree that its citizens must read certain books or must view certain films. . . .

Recognizing these principles, we have held that so-called thematic obscenity—obscenity which might persuade the viewer or reader to engage in "obscene" conduct—is not outside the protection of the First Amendment:

> "It is contended that the State's action was justified because the motion picture attractively portrays a relationship which is contrary to the moral standards, the religious precepts, and the legal code of its citizenry. This argument misconceives what it is that the Constitution protects. Its guarantee is not confined to the expression of ideas that are conventional or shared by a majority. It protects advocacy of the opinion that adultery may sometimes be proper, no less than advocacy of socialism or the single tax. And in the realm of ideas it protects expression which is eloquent no less than that which is unconvincing." Kingsley International Pictures Corp. v. Regents, 360 U.S. 684, 688–689 (1959).

Even a legitimate, sharply focused state concern for the morality of the community cannot, in other words, justify an assault on the protections of the First Amendment. [ ] Where the state interest in regulation of morality is vague and ill defined, interference with the guarantees of the First Amendment is even more difficult to justify.

In short, while I cannot say that the interests of the State—apart from the question of juveniles and unconsenting adults—are trivial or nonexistent, I am compelled to conclude that these interests cannot justify the substantial damage to constitutional rights and to this Nation's judicial machinery that inevitably results from state efforts to bar the distribution even of unprotected material to consenting adults. [ ] I would hold, therefore, that at least in the absence of distribution to juveniles or obtrusive exposure to unconsenting adults, the First and

Fourteenth Amendments prohibit the State and Federal Governments from attempting wholly to suppress sexually oriented materials on the basis of their allegedly "obscene" contents. Nothing in this approach precludes those governments from taking action to serve what may be strong and legitimate interests through regulation of the manner of distribution of sexually oriented material.

. . . Difficult questions must still be faced, notably in the areas of distribution to juveniles and offensive exposure to unconsenting adults. Whatever the extent of state power to regulate in those areas,[29] it should be clear that the view I espouse today would introduce a large measure of clarity to this troubled area, would reduce the institutional pressure on this Court and the rest of the State and Federal Judiciary, and would guarantee fuller freedom of expression while leaving room for the protection of legitimate governmental interests. . . .

Notes and Questions

1. What changes are wrought by *Miller?* How are they justified?

2. What different question is raised in *Paris?* What motivates the majority's answer to that question?

3. What underlies Justice Douglas's argument that no prosecution for obscenity should be possible until after a particular tract has been declared "beyond the pale" in a civil proceeding? What would still be subject to sanction under Justice Brennan's new approach to obscenity?

4. In Jenkins v. Georgia, 418 U.S. 153 (1974), Jenkins had been convicted for showing the film "Carnal Knowledge." The state courts had relied on the jury's finding, but the Court reversed on the ground that the standards set in *Miller* did not justify the jury's verdict. Although "ultimate sexual acts" took place "the camera does not focus on the bodies of the actors at such times. There is no exhibition whatever of the actors' genitals, lewd or otherwise, during these scenes. There are occasional scenes of nudity, but nudity alone is not enough to make material legally obscene" under *Miller.* Was the Supreme Court back in the business of reviewing individual books and movies?

5. In *Miller,* California had chosen to use a statewide community standard and the Court had observed that a national standard was "hypothetical and unascertainable." In *Jenkins,* the majority had said that a state was not required to define the phrase "contemporary community standards" in more precise geographical terms. In Hamling v. United States, 418 U.S. 87 (1974), the Court interpreted a federal statute barring the mailing of obscene materials as making the relevant community the one from which the jury was drawn.

29. The Court erroneously states, Miller v. California, ante, [ ], that the author of this opinion "indicates that suppression of unprotected obscene material is permissible to avoid exposure to unconsenting adults . . . and to juveniles. . . . " I defer expression of my views as to the scope of state power in these areas until cases squarely presenting these questions are before the Court. See n. 9, supra; Miller v. California, supra (dissenting opinion).

6. In Erznoznik v. Jacksonville, 422 U.S. 205 (1975), the Court struck down an ordinance forbidding the showing of nudity on drive-in theatre screens visible from public streets. After its captive audience justification failed, the city asserted that the ordinance was justified as a protection of children. This also failed because the restriction was "broader than permissible. The ordinance is not directed against sexually explicit nudity, nor is it otherwise limited. Rather, it sweepingly forbids display of films containing any uncovered buttocks or breasts, irrespective of contexts or pervasiveness. Thus, it would bar a film containing a picture of a baby's buttocks, the nude body of a war victim, or scenes from a culture in which nudity is indigenous . . .. Clearly all nudity cannot be deemed obscene even as to minors." In appropriately drafted statutes, it is possible to protect minors from obscenity even though such a statute could not apply to the general public. See Ginsberg v. New York, 390 U.S. 629 (1968), for a discussion of the states' power to regulate minors' access to obscene material.

7. In Ward v. Illinois, 431 U.S. 767 (1977), the Court, 5–4, rejected a claim that the state's obscenity statute could not be invoked against petitioner because it did not explicitly ban sado-masochistic material, which was at issue here, and such material was not mentioned in *Miller.* First, the majority concluded that the state courts had given sufficient prior guidance. Second, the specifics in *Miller* were "examples" and "were not intended to be exhaustive." The dissenters asserted that the state had not "specifically defined" what was prohibited.

8. When evaluating allegedly obscene material, the jury may look for guidance beyond the material itself to the circumstances of its sale and distribution. Citing *Hamling* and *Ginzburg,* Justice Rehnquist, for the majority, in Splawn v. California, 431 U.S. 595 (1977), concluded that as "a matter of First Amendment law, evidence of pandering to prurient interests in the creation, promotion or dissemination of material is relevant in determining whether the material is obscene."

Justice Stevens, in a dissent joined by Justices Brennan, Stewart, and Marshall, declared that the majority decision allowed non-obscene material to be classified as obscene solely because of truthful advertising that emphasized its sexually provocative nature. In a footnote, he asserted that *Virginia Pharmacy,* p. 503, infra, granted constitutional protection to truthful advertisements.

9. In a federal prosecution for the mailing of obscene materials, a state statute is not conclusive evidence of community standards, although it may be relevant to the jury's determination. In Smith v. United States, 431 U.S. 291 (1977), the Court, 5–4, held that mailing obscene materials from one part of Iowa to another violated federal law, even though Iowa did not then bar the distribution of such materials to adults.

For the majority, Justice Blackmun asserted the question to be "whether the jury is entitled to rely on its own knowledge of community standards, or whether a state legislature (or a smaller legislative body) may declare what the community standards shall be, and, if such a declaration has been made, whether it is binding in a federal prosecution under § 1461." He concluded that a permissive state could not force the federal government to allow its mails to be used for obscene materials. He also suggested that the Iowa statute might not show community standards at all, but indicate only "that the resources of its prosecutors' offices should be devoted to matters deemed to have greater priority than the enforcement of obscenity statutes."

Justice Brennan, joined by Justices Stewart and Marshall, dissented on the ground that the statute was "clearly overbroad and unconstitutional on its face."

Justice Stevens, who joined the Court after *Miller,* used his dissent in *Smith* to point out "the need for a principled re-examination of the premises" on which *Miller* rests, and his belief that "criminal prosecutions are an unacceptable method of abating a public nuisance which is entitled to at least a modicum of First Amendment protection."

He seriously questioned the ability of jurors to determine community standards of offensiveness with "even-handed" consistency. He saw no reason why a standard for a metropolitan area was any less "hypothetical and unascertainable" than the national standard the Court had previously questioned. He feared subtle but powerful peer pressure in the jury room since "it is much more popular to be against sin than to be tolerant of it," and suggested that "a juror might well find certain materials appealing and yet be unwilling to say so."

The problem with the categorical approach of the majority was that it assumed that "all communications within the protected area are equally immune from governmental restraint, whereas those outside that area are utterly without social value and, hence, deserving of no protection. . . . The fact that speech is protected by the First Amendment does not mean that it is wholly immune from state regulation. Although offensive or misleading statements in a political oration cannot be censored, offensive language in a courtroom or misleading representations in a securities prospectus may surely be regulated. Nuisances such as sound trucks and erotic displays in a residential area may be abated under appropriately flexible civil standards even though the First Amendment provides a shield against criminal prosecution."

For Justice Stevens, it was "ridiculous to assume that no regulation of the display of sexually oriented material is permissible unless the same regulation could be applied to political comment. On the other hand, I am not prepared to rely on either the average citizen's understanding of an amorphous community standard or on my fellow judges' appraisal of what has serious artistic merit as a basis for deciding what one citizen may communicate to another by appropriate means."

He also observed that it was not clear what role "erotic" appeal played in the majority's analysis in view of its use of the term "patent offensiveness" in the analysis. He alluded to the majority's use of "excretory functions" as an example of what was beyond protection. He did not know whether the material at issue had "any beneficial value," citing conflicting views of experts. "In the end, I believe we must rely on the capacity of the free marketplace of ideas to distinguish that which is useful or beautiful from that which is ugly or worthless."

Offensive Words. The relationship between obscenity and offensive speech is developed in Cohen v. California, 403 U.S. 15 (1971), in which the Supreme Court overturned the conviction of a person who wore a jacket on which the words "Fuck the Draft" were plainly visible. The state courts had upheld the defendant's conviction for disturbing the peace because he wore the jacket in a courthouse corridor in which women and children were present. The Court reversed, 5–4.

Justice Harlan concluded that the controlling point was whether "the States, acting as guardians of public morality, may properly remove this offensive word from the public vocabulary." He began consideration of that question by reemphasizing the values of free expression "in a society as diverse and populous as ours," citing Justice Brandeis's concurrence in *Whitney,* p. 20, supra. He then turned to the specific facts of the case:

> Against this perception of the constitutional policies involved, we discern certain more particularized considerations that peculiarly call for reversal of this conviction. First, the principle contended for by the State seems inherently boundless. How is one to distinguish this from any other offensive word? Surely the State has no right to cleanse public debate to the point where it is grammatically palatable to the most squeamish among us. Yet no readily ascertainable general principle exists for stopping short of that result were we to affirm the judgment below. For, while the particular four-letter word being litigated here is perhaps more distasteful than most others of its genre, it is nevertheless often true that one man's vulgarity is another's lyric. Indeed, we think it is largely because governmental officials cannot make principled distinctions in this area that the Constitution leaves matters of taste and style so largely to the individual.
>
> Additionally, we cannot overlook the fact, because it is well illustrated by the episode involved here, that much linguistic expression serves a dual communicative function: it conveys not only ideas capable of relatively precise, detached explication, but otherwise inexpressible emotions as well. In fact, words are often chosen as much for their emotive as their cognitive force. We cannot sanction the view that the Constitution, while solicitous of the cognitive content of individual speech, has little or no regard for that emotive function which, practically speaking, may often be the more important element of the overall message sought to be communicated. . . .

Some have pressed the importance of the Cohen case as one involving political speech—and the recognition that limits on political expression are particularly dangerous, as well as the difficulty government will have in deciding what words to bar. In addition, the use of offensive speech often reveals important information to the rest of society—sometimes the ugliness of the speaker's cause; sometimes the deep extent of the speaker's frustration; and sometimes the ugliness of the situation being challenged. On this analysis, efforts to prevent group libels and to purify political speech (except perhaps for captive audiences) would be impermissible. Compare Farber, Civilizing Public Discourse: An Essay on Professor Bickel, Justice Harlan, and the Enduring Significance of Cohen v. California, 1980 Duke L.J. 283 (rejecting limits on such speech), with Arkes, Civility and the Restriction of Speech: Rediscovering the Defamation of Groups, 1974 Sup.Ct. Rev. 281 (supporting statutes proscribing certain types of attacks on racial and religious groups).

The special problem of the use of four-letter words in broadcasting is explored in Chapter XIV.

B. SPECIAL ASPECTS OF OBSCENITY

Apart from the general subject of obscenity addressed in the first section, specialized situations raise more specific questions. One example is Pinkus v. United States, 436 U.S. 293, 3 Med.L.Reptr. 2329 (1978), involving the validity of jury instructions dealing with the response to defendant's materials among children, sensitive persons, and "deviant groups." We turn now to what has become known as "child pornography."

NEW YORK v. FERBER

Supreme Court of the United States, 1982.
458 U.S. 747, 102 S.Ct. 3348, 73 L.Ed.2d 1113, 8 Med.L.Rptr. 1809.

Noted, 10 Fla.St.U.L.Rev. 684, 13 Golden Gate U.L.Rev. 675, 96 Harv.L.Rev. 141, 23 Santa Clara L.Rev. 675.

[Ferber, the owner of a Manhattan bookstore, was arrested for selling two sexually explicit films to an undercover policeman. He was acquitted on charges of promoting an obscene sexual performance under § 263.10 of the New York Penal Law, but convicted under § 263.15 for promoting a sexual performance by a child. The conviction was overturned by the N.Y. Court of Appeals, which held that § 263.15 violated the First Amendment.]

JUSTICE WHITE delivered the opinion of the Court.

At issue in this case is the constitutionality of a New York criminal statute which prohibits a person from knowingly promoting sexual performances by children under the age of 16 by distributing material which depicts such performances.

. . .

II

The Court of Appeals proceeded on the assumption that the standard of obscenity incorporated in § 263.10, which follows the guidelines enunciated in Miller v. California [ ], constitutes the appropriate line dividing protected from unprotected expression by which to measure a regulation directed at child pornography. . . .

The Court of Appeals' assumption was not unreasonable in light of our decisions. This case, however, constitutes our first examination of a statute directed at and limited to depictions of sexual activity involving children. We believe our inquiry should begin with the question of whether a State has somewhat more freedom in proscribing works which portray sexual acts or lewd exhibitions of genitalia by children.

. . .

B

The *Miller* standard, like its predecessors, was an accommodation between the state's interests in protecting the "sensibilities of unwilling recipients" from exposure to pornographic material and the dangers of censorship inherent in unabashedly content-based laws. Like obscenity statutes, laws directed at the dissemination of child pornography run the risk of suppressing protected expression by allowing the hand of the censor to become unduly heavy. For the following reasons, however, we are persuaded that the States are entitled to greater leeway in the regulation of pornographic depictions of children.

First. It is evident beyond the need for elaboration that a state's interest in "safeguarding the physical and psychological well being of a minor" is "compelling." [ ] "A democratic society rests, for its continuance, upon the healthy well-rounded growth of young people into full maturity as citizens. Prince v. Massachusetts, 321 U.S. 158, 168 (1944). Accordingly, we have sustained legislation aimed at protecting the physical and emotional well-being of youth even when the laws have operated in the sensitive area of constitutionally protected rights. In *Prince v. Massachusetts,* supra, the Court held that a statute prohibiting use of a child to distribute literature on the street was valid notwithstanding the statute's effect on a First Amendment activity. In Ginsberg v. New York [ ] we sustained a New York law protecting children from exposure to non-obscene literature. Most recently, we held that the government's interest in the "well-being of its youth" justified special treatment of indecent broadcasting received by adults as well as children. FCC v. Pacifica Foundation, 438 U.S. 726 (1978).

The prevention of sexual exploitation and abuse of children constitutes a government objective of surpassing importance. . . . The legislative judgment, as well as the judgment found in the relevant literature, is that the use of children as subjects of pornographic materials is harmful to the physiological, emotional, and mental health of the child. That judgment, we think, easily passes muster under the First Amendment.

Second. The distribution of photographs and films depicting sexual activity by juveniles is intrinsically related to the sexual abuse of children in at least two ways. First, the materials produced are a permanent record of the children's participation and the harm to the child is exacerbated by their circulation. Second, the distribution network for child pornography must be closed if the production of material which requires the sexual exploitation of children is to be effectively controlled.

Respondent does not contend that the State is unjustified in pursuing those who distribute child pornography. Rather, he argues that it is enough for the State to prohibit the distribution of materials that are legally obscene under the *Miller* test. While some States may find that this approach properly accommodates its interests, it does not follow that the First Amendment prohibits a State from going further. The *Miller* standard, like all general definitions of what may be banned as obscene, does not reflect the State's particular and more compelling interest in prosecuting those who promote the sexual exploitation of children. Thus, the question under the *Miller* test of whether a work, taken as a whole, appeals to the prurient interest of the average person bears no connection to the issue of whether a child has been physically or psychologically harmed in the production of the work. Similarly, a sexually explicit depiction need not be "patently offensive" in order to have required the sexual exploitation of a child for its production. In addition, a work which, taken as a whole, contains serious literary, artistic, political, or scientific value may nevertheless embody the hardest core of child pornography. "It is irrelevant to the child [who has been abused] whether or not the material . . . has a literary, artistic, political, or social value." [ ] We therefore cannot conclude that the *Miller* standard is a satisfactory solution to the child pornography problem.

Third. The advertising and selling of child pornography provides an economic motive for and is thus an integral part of the production of such materials, an activity illegal throughout the nation. "It rarely has been suggested that the constitutional freedom for speech and press extends its immunity to speech or writing used as an integral part of conduct in violation of a valid criminal statute." [ ] . . .

Fourth. The value of permitting live performances and photographic reproductions of children engaged in lewd sexual conduct is exceedingly modest, if not *de minimis.* We consider it unlikely that visual depictions of children performing sexual acts or lewdly exhibiting their genitals would often constitute an important and necessary part of a literary performance or scientific or educational work. . . .

Fifth. Recognizing and classifying child pornography as a category of material outside the protection of the First Amendment is not incompatible with our earlier decisions. "The question whether speech is, or is not protected by the First Amendment often depends on the content of the speech." [ ] . . . Thus, it is not rare that a content-based classification of speech has been accepted because it may be appropriately generalized that within the confines of the given classification, the evil to be restricted so overwhelmingly outweighs the expressive interests, if any, at stake, that no process of case-by-case adjudication is required. When a definable class of material, such as that covered by § 263.15, bears so heavily and pervasively on the welfare of children engaged in its production, we think the balance of competing interests is clearly struck and that it is permissible to consider these materials as without the protection of the First Amendment.

C

There are, of course, limits on the category of child pornography which, like obscenity, is unprotected by the First Amendment. As with all legislation in this sensitive area, the conduct to be prohibited must be adequately defined by the applicable state law, as written or authoritatively construed. Here the nature of the harm to be combatted requires that the state offense be limited to works that *visually* depict sexual conduct by children below a specified age. The category of "sexual conduct" proscribed must also be suitably limited and described.

The test for child pornography is separate from the obscenity standard enunciated in *Miller,* but may be compared to it for purpose of clarity. The *Miller* formulation is adjusted in the following respects: A trier of fact need not find that the material appeals to the prurient interest of the average person; it is not required that sexual conduct portrayed be done so in a patently offensive manner; and the material at issue need not be considered as a whole. We note that the distribution of descriptions or other depictions of sexual conduct, not otherwise obscene, which do not involve live performance or photographic or other visual reproduction of live performances, retains First Amendment protection. . . .

. . .

III

It remains to address the claim that the New York statute is unconstitutionally overbroad because it would forbid the distribution of material with serious literary, scientific or educational value or material which does not threaten the harms sought to be combatted by the State. Respondent prevailed on that ground below, and it is to that issue we now turn.

The New York Court of Appeals recognized that overbreadth scrutiny has been limited with respect to conduct-related regulation [ ], but it did not apply [that] test because the challenged statute, in its view, was directed at "pure speech." The Court went on to find that

§ 263.15 was fatally overbroad: "[T]he statute would prohibit the showing of any play or movie in which a child portrays a defined sexual act, real or simulated, in a nonobscene manner. It would also prohibit the sale, showing, or distributing of medical or educational materials containing photographs of such acts. Indeed, by its terms, the statute would prohibit those who oppose such portrayals from providing illustrations of what they oppose."

A

The traditional rule is that a person to whom a statute may constitutionally be applied may not challenge that statute on the ground that it may conceivably be applied unconstitutionally to others in situations not before the Court. [ ] . . .

What has come to be known as the First Amendment overbreadth doctrine is one of the few exceptions to this principle and must be justified by "weighty countervailing policies." [ ] The doctrine is predicated on the sensitive nature of protected expression: "persons whose expression is constitutionally protected may well refrain from exercising their rights for fear of criminal sanctions by a statute susceptible of application to protected expression." [ ] It is for this reason that we have allowed persons to attack overly broad statutes even though the conduct of the person making the attack is clearly unprotected and could be proscribed by a law drawn with the requisite specificity. [ ]

The scope of the First Amendment overbreadth doctrine, like most exceptions to established principles, must be carefully tied to the circumstances in which facial invalidation of a statute is truly warranted. Because of the wide-reaching effects of striking a statute down on its face at the request of one whose own conduct may be punished despite the First Amendment, we have recognized that the overbreadth doctrine is "strong medicine" and have employed it with hesitation, and then "only as a last resort." Broadrick v. Oklahoma, 413 U.S. 601 (1973). We have, in consequence, insisted that the overbreadth involved be "substantial" before the statute involved will be invalidated on its face.

. . .

Broadrick was a regulation involving restrictions on political campaign activity, an area not considered "pure speech," and thus it was unnecessary to consider the proper overbreadth test when a law arguably reaches traditional forms of expression such as books and films. As we intimated in *Broadrick,* the requirement of substantial overbreadth extended "at the very least," to cases involving conduct plus speech. This case, which poses the question squarely, convinces us that the rationale of *Broadrick* is sound and should be applied in the present context involving the harmful employment of children to make sexually explicit materials for distribution.

. . . The requirement of substantial overbreadth is directly derived from the purpose and nature of the doctrine. While a sweeping statute, or one incapable of limitation, has the potential to repeatedly chill the exercise of expressive activity by many individuals, the extent of deterrence of protected speech can be expected to decrease with the declining reach of the regulation. This observation appears equally applicable to the publication of books and films as it is to activities, such as picketing or participation in election campaigns, which have previously been categorized as involving conduct plus speech. . . .

. . .

IV

Because § 263.15 is not substantially overbroad, it is unnecessary to consider its application to material that does not depict sexual conduct of a type that New York may restrict consistent with the First Amendment. As applied to Paul Ferber and to others who distribute similar material, the statute does not violate the First Amendment as applied to the States through the Fourteenth. The decision of the New York Court of Appeals is reversed and the case is remanded to that Court for further proceedings not inconsistent with this opinion.

So ordered.

JUSTICE BLACKMUN concurs in the result.

[Justice O'Connor concurred separately to emphasize the narrowness of the Court's decision. In her view the case held only that even if the New York statute made some constitutionally protected speech illegal, it was not sufficiently overbroad to justify facial invalidation. She then indicated that the compelling state interest in protecting minors might be sufficient to justify banning the works in question even if they had serious literary, artistic, political or scientific value.]

[Justice Brennan, joined by Justice Marshall, concurred in the judgment, but argued that application of the statute to materials with serious literary, artistic, political or scientific value would violate the First Amendment.]

[Justice Stevens concurred in the judgment on the ground that the category of speech covered by the statute was of lesser importance than other speech. Since such "marginal" speech falls near the bottom of the First Amendment hierarchy, according to Justice Stevens, the extraordinary protection of the overbreadth doctrine was not justified.]

Notes and Questions

1. In what ways is *Miller* modified?

2. What is the justification for the changes?

3. After *Ferber,* Congress and several states adopted similar legislation. For the Congressional version, see the Child Protection Act of 1984, P.L. 98–292, deleting the provision in 18 U.S.C. § 2252 that had

required sexually explicit material to be obscene before child pornography could be controlled.

4. *Pornography and Violence Toward Women.* In the early 1980s, groups perceiving a correlation between pornography and violence toward women sought the adoption of local ordinances that defined pornography in terms of material that presented women as sexual objects or in positions of sexual subordination. Such material would then be prohibited. The focus was on specific content—the presentation of women in certain ways—and there was no room for a defense that the work taken as a whole had substantial artistic, literary, or social value. After the city of Indianapolis adopted such an ordinance, it was challenged, and overturned, in American Booksellers Association, Inc. v. Hudnut, 771 F.2d 323, 11 Med.L.Rptr. 2465 (7th Cir.1985).

The court accepted the premises of the city that the materials barred "tend to perpetuate subordination," which in turn leads to violence against women:

> There is much to this perspective. Beliefs are also facts. People often act in accordance with the images and patterns they find around them. People raised in a religion tend to accept the tenets of that religion, often without independent examination. . . . Words and images act at the level of the subconscious before they persuade at the level of the conscious. Even the truth has little chance unless a statement fits within the framework of beliefs that may never have been subjected to rational study.

Yet this simply confirmed the power of pornography as speech. "All of these unhappy effects depend on mental intermediation":

> Pornography affects how people see the world, their fellows, and social relations. If pornography is what pornography does, so is other speech. Hitler's orations affected how some Germans saw Jews. Communism is a world view, not simply a Manifesto by Marx and Engels or a set of speeches. Efforts to suppress communist speech in the United States were based on the belief that the public acceptability of such ideas would increase the likelihood of totalitarian government. Religions affect socialization in the most pervasive way.
>
> Racial bigotry, anti-semitism, violence on television, reporters' biases—these and many more influence the culture and shape our socialization. None is directly answerable by more speech, unless that speech too finds its place in the popular culture. Yet all is protected as speech, however insidious. Any other answer leaves the government in control of all of the institutions of our culture, the great censor and director of which thoughts are good for us.
>
> Sexual responses often are unthinking responses, and the association of sexual arousal with the subordination of women therefore may have a substantial effect. But almost all cultural stimuli provoke unconscious responses. Religious ceremonies condition

their participants. Teachers convey messages by selecting what not to cover; the implicit message about what is off limits or unthinkable may be more powerful than the messages for which they present rational argument. Television scripts contain unarticulated assumptions. People may be conditioned in subtle ways. If the fact that speech plays a role in a process of conditioning were enough to permit governmental regulation, that would be the end of freedom of speech.

. . .

Much of Indianapolis's argument rests on the belief that when speech is "unanswerable," and the metaphor that there is a "marketplace of ideas" does not apply, the First Amendment does not apply either. The metaphor is honored; Milton's Areopagitica and John Stuart Mill's On Liberty defend freedom of speech on the ground that the truth will prevail, and many of the most important cases under the First Amendment recite this position. The Framers undoubtedly believed it. As a general matter it is true. But the Constitution does not make the dominance of truth a necessary condition of freedom of speech. To say that it does would be to confuse an outcome of free speech with a necessary condition for the application of the amendment.

A power to limit speech on the ground that truth has not yet prevailed and is not likely to prevail implies the power to declare truth. At some point the government must be able to say (as Indianapolis has said): "We know what the truth is, yet a free exchange of speech has not driven out falsity, so that we must now prohibit falsity." If the government may declare the truth, why wait for the failure of speech? Under the First Amendment, however, there is no such thing as a false idea, Gertz v. Robert Welch, Inc., 418 U.S. 323, 339 (1974), so the government may not restrict speech on the ground that in a free exchange truth is not yet dominant.

At any time, some speech is ahead in the game; the more numerous speakers prevail. Supporters of minority candidates may be forever "excluded" from the political process because their candidates never win, because few people believe their positions. This does not mean that freedom of speech has failed.

The Supreme Court has rejected the position that speech must be "effectively answerable" to be protected by the Constitution. . . .

Finally, the city argued that this was "low value" speech far from the political core, which could be regulated more readily than other speech. The court disagreed:

At all events, "pornography" is not low value speech within the meaning of these cases. Indianapolis seeks to prohibit certain speech because it believes this speech influences social relations and politics on a grand scale, that it controls attitudes at home and in the legislature. This precludes a characterization of the speech as low value. True, pornography and obscenity have sex in common. But Indianapolis left out of its definition any reference to literary, artistic, political, or scientific value. The ordinance applies to graphic sexually explicit subordination in works great and small. The Court sometimes balances the value of speech against the costs of its restriction, but it does this by category of speech and not by the content of particular works. [ ] Indianapolis has created an approved point of view and so loses the support of these cases.

In the absence of any element comparable to the lack of serious value in obscenity, the court was concerned that books such as Homer's Iliad and James Joyce's Ulysses might be covered by the ordinance because "both depict women as submissive objects for conquest and domination."

In response to the appellate ruling, proponents of the ordinance filed an appeal in the Supreme Court. Based on the briefs alone, without hearing oral argument, the Court affirmed without opinion, 6–3. 106 S.Ct. 1172 (1986). Chief Justice Burger and Justices Rehnquist and O'Connor voted to note probable jurisdiction of the appeal and to set the case for oral argument.

In July, 1986, the Attorney General's Commission on Pornography submitted its final report. The Commission concluded that sexually violent materials had been shown to have negative effects. Material that showed "sexual activity without violence but with degradation, submission, domination or humiliation" was also found to have negative effects. All Commissioners found that "some" materials concerning sexual activity that did not fit into either category "may be harmful." Some Commissioners "agreed that not all materials in this classification are not harmful." This third category was found to make up a "very small percentage of the total universe of pornographic materials." Finally, as to materials that featured "nudity without force, coercion, sexual activity or degradation," all Commissioners agreed that "some materials . . . may be harmful." Again, some Commissioners agreed that "not all materials in this classification are not harmful." The Commission majority proposed a total of 92 recommendations collected at pages 433–58 of the report.

Some of the Commission's actions have already drawn legal attention. See Playboy Enterprises, Inc. v. Meese, 639 F.Supp. 581, 13 Med.L.Rptr. 1101 (D.D.C.1986) (preliminary injunction issued to prevent the Commission from listing retailers of magazines that one witness had called pornographic).

Chapter VIII

PROTECTING THE MARKETPLACE

In this Chapter we address questions concerning the power of government to regulate or prohibit speech that evolves from attempts to influence economic behavior, whether or not the defendant is speaking as an advertiser. Most aspects of this topic, involving questions of regulation of advertising, are beyond our focus on the journalistic aspects of mass media. Nonetheless, some questions are close enough to warrant attention.

A. MEDIA RESPONSIBILITY IN THE MARKETPLACE

A newspaper that carries a false or misleading advertisement is generally protected in the absence of knowledge of falsity so long as it will identify the source of the advertisement. The FTC Act provides, for example, that "No publisher, radio-broadcast licensee, or agency or medium for the dissemination of advertising . . . shall be liable under this section by reason of the dissemination by him of any false advertisement, unless he has refused" to identify the source. 15 U.S.C. § 54. State law provides comparable kinds of protection. See, e.g., Cal.Bus. & Prof.Code § 17502 protecting media at least where the advertisement was published "in good faith, without knowledge of its false, deceptive, or misleading character."

Of course, the law aside, media generally make serious efforts to avoid carrying false or deceptive advertising in order to avoid alienating their readers or audience.

The second question, the responsibility of media for editorial content, is much less clear. Some actual examples will suggest the breadth of the inquiry.

1. *Lowe v. SEC.* Lowe was an investment adviser registered under the Investment Advisers Act of 1940. After Lowe's third conviction for "serious misconduct in connection with his investment advisory business," the Securities and Exchange Commission revoked his registration. Lowe continued to publish his newsletters containing investment advice even though, because he was not registered, this violated the 1940 Act. The SEC sought to enjoin these publications. The trial judge concluded that the statute could not be construed to permit the SEC to bar Lowe's newsletters. He concluded that commercial speech referred only to advertising and then construed the Act to avoid reaching the constitutional question concerning the newsletter.

On appeal, the court of appeals reversed. First, the court concluded that the Act could not be read to avoid the constitutional question. The statute does exempt from the definition of "investment adviser" the "publisher of any bona fide newspaper, news magazine or business or financial publication of general and regular circulation." In an earlier case, the second circuit had denied that this exemption covered a weekly tabloid that sold for $5 per issue and consisted primarily of reports on specific securities, each of which was identified with the name and address of a broker or dealer. [SEC v. Wall Street Transcript Corp., 422 F.2d 1371 (2d Cir.), certiorari denied 398 U.S. 958 (1970)]. His constitutional arguments were rejected, 2–1.

The Supreme Court granted certiorari and reversed. Lowe v. Securities and Exchange Comm'n, 105 S.Ct. 2557 (1985). After extended analysis, the five-member majority construed the "bona fide" exception in the statute broadly and concluded that it exempted Lowe. "Bona fide" covered the publication and not the publisher. Lowe's newsletters were not "personal communications masquerading in the clothing of newspapers, news magazines, or financial publications. Moreover, there is no suggestion that they contained any false or misleading information, or that they were designed to tout any security in which petitioners had an interest. Further, petitioners' publications are 'of general and regular circulation' ":

> The dangers of fraud, deception, or overreaching that motivated the enactment of the statute are present in personalized communications but are not replicated in publications that are advertised and sold in an open market. . . . As long as the communications between petitioners and their subscribers remain entirely impersonal and do not develop into the kind of fiduciary, person-to-person relationships that were discussed at length in the legislative history of the Act and that are characteristic of investment adviser-client relationships, we believe the publications are, at least presumptively, within the exclusion and thus not subject to registration under the Act.

Justice White, joined by the Chief Justice and Justice Rehnquist, concurred on the ground that Lowe was covered by the statute but that the First Amendment protected his right to publish. The government's justification was that it was regulating a "speaking profession" and that "it may require that investment advisers, like lawyers, evince the qualities of truth-seeking, honor, discretion, and fiduciary responsibility." Justice White responded that this principle of restricting entry to a profession had "never been extended to encompass the licensing of speech per se or of the press. [ ] At some point, a measure is no longer a regulation of a profession but a regulation of speech or of the press; beyond that point, the statute must survive the level of scrutiny demanded by the First Amendment."

Justice White rejected the government's claim that locating that point should be left to the legislature. Quoting Marbury v. Madison, Justice White responded that "It is emphatically the province and duty of the judicial department to say what the law is." He continued that, although Congressional enactments came to the Court with a presumption in favor of their validity, Congressional "characterization of its legislation cannot be decisive of the question of its constitutionality where individual rights are at issue. [ ] Surely it cannot be said, for example, that if Congress were to declare editorial writers fiduciaries for their readers and establish a licensing scheme under which 'unqualified' writers were forbidden to publish, this Court would be powerless to hold that the legislation violated the First Amendment. It is for us, then, to find some principle by which to answer the question whether the Investment Advisers Act as applied to petitioner operated as a regulation of speech or of professional conduct."

Justice White concluded that "Where the personal nexus between professional and client does not exist, and a speaker does not purport to be exercising judgment on behalf of any particular individual with whose circumstances he is directly acquainted, government regulation ceases to function as legitimate regulation of professional practice with only incidental impact on speech; it becomes regulation of speaking or publishing as such," subject to the First Amendment.

Turning finally to what regulation might be permissible here under the First Amendment, Justice White found it unnecessary to decide whether Lowe's speech was "fully protected" or "commercial." Even if the speech was considered commercial, the means chosen to prevent investors from falling into the hands of "scoundrels and swindlers" was "extreme." It cannot "be plausibly maintained that investment advice from a person whose background indicates that he is unreliable is *inherently* misleading or deceptive," nor was it clear that less drastic remedies than outright suppression were inadequate.

See Aman, SEC v. Lowe: Professional Regulation and the First Amendment, 1985 Sup.Ct.Rev. 93; Lively, Securities Regulation and Freedom of the Press: Toward a Marketplace of Ideas in the Marketplace of Investment, 60 Wash.L.Rev. 843 (1985).

2. *The Winans case.* In 1984, it was revealed that Winans, one of the two main writers of the "Heard on the Street" column in the Wall Street Journal, had leaked items from forthcoming columns to investors and friends who used the tips to make quick profits. He was prosecuted under the "insider trading" section of the Securities Act of 1934, on the ground that he owed a duty to the Journal and to his readers to inform them that he was profiting by what he printed in the column. Section 10b–5 makes it "unlawful for any person to employ any device, scheme or artifice to defraud or to engage in any act, practice or course of business which operates as a fraud or deceit upon any person." The defense argued that, although he might have violated his publisher's policies and rules, he was an "outsider" who gathered public information and did not defraud his employer or readers.

The judge asserted that Winans was subject to the Act because he dealt with "market-sensitive material," and found him guilty. The misappropriation of information theory can be used only where the employer has a policy treating the revealed information as confidential. United States v. Winans, 612 F.Supp. 827 (S.D.N.Y.1985), affirmed on all but one count, sub nom. United States v. Carpenter, 791 F.2d 1024, 12 Med.L.Rptr. 2169 (2d Cir. 1986). The majority stressed that the confidentiality restrictions came from the newspaper and not from the government.

3. *Reducing the Likelihood of Counterfeit Bills.* In the mid-19th century, Congress, pursuant to its power to establish currency and to punish infringers, adopted what is now 18 U.S.C. § 474, which creates criminal liability for anyone who "prints, photographs or in any other manner makes or executes any engraving, photograph, print, or impression in the likeness" of any currency. The Treasury Department began granting exemptions for certain illustrations. In 1958, Congress added to 18 U.S.C. § 504 provisions that codified these exemptions by permitting the "printing, publishing, or importation . . . of illustrations of . . . any [currency] for philatelic, numismatic, educational, historical or newsworthy purposes in articles, books, journals, newspapers, or albums. . . ." At the same time, Congress required these illustrations to be in black-and-white and either less than three-fourths or more than one and one-half times the size of the original; also, negatives and plates used had to be destroyed after their authorized use. Thus, a proper publication reproducing the illustration for a proper purpose, was protected so long as the illustration was not in color, was the proper size, and the plates or negatives used were destroyed after use.

Over 20 years, Time, Inc. was warned by the Secret Service on several occasions that illustrations for its magazines had violated the provisions of §§ 474 and 504. After one of these episodes, Time sought a declaratory judgment that the two sections were unconstitutional on their face and as applied to Time, as well as an injunction. On cross-motions for summary judgment, the trial court granted Time's motion. It found Time's use of the illustrations protected by the First Amendment; that § 474 was overbroad; and that § 504 could not save it because its "purpose" and "publication" requirements were unconstitutionally vague. The government took a direct appeal to the Supreme Court, which affirmed in part and reversed in part in Regan v. Time, Inc., 468 U.S. 641 (1984).

Four justices, in a plurality opinion by Justice White, found the "purpose" requirement of § 504 to be unconstitutional because determinations of the "newsworthiness" and "educational value" of a photograph "cannot help but be based on the content of the photograph and the message it delivers." "Regulations which permit the Government to discriminate on the basis of the content of the message cannot be tolerated under the First Amendment [citing Carey v. Brown and Police Dept. v. Mosley]."

The plurality refused to address the "publication" restriction because Time had no standing to raise it. The plurality then concluded that even if the publication requirement was unconstitutional, the restrictions on use of color and on size were severable and were constitutional as "time, place and manner" restrictions. They were not based on "either the content or subject matter of speech;" They served a "significant governmental interest;" and they left ample alternative channels for the communication of the information.

The critical fifth vote to reverse part of the trial court ruling came from Justice Stevens. On the "purpose" part of § 504 he disagreed with all the other justices. He thought that Time was asking the Court to adopt the most confusing construction of the statute so that the statute would appear unconstitutional. He thought that the section should be read broadly and that it would cover Time.

In response to Time's claim that "Congress can do a much better job in preventing counterfeiting than the present § 474 and § 504," Justice Stevens observed that the question was "whether the job [Congress] did violates Time's right to free expression. It does not: Time is free to publish the symbol it wishes to publish and to express the messages it wishes to convey by use of that symbol; it merely must comply with restrictions on the manner of printing that symbol which are reasonably related to the strong governmental interests in preventing counterfeiting and deceptive uses of likenesses of the currency."

The other four justices agreed with Justice White that the "purpose" requirement of § 504 was unconstitutional. But they rejected the rest of the plurality opinion.

4. New York City Consumer Protection Law Regulation 18 (1972) provides:

> It is a deceptive practice in connection with the sale or offering for sale of consumer goods and services for any person . . . to place in an advertisement or on a billboard or marquee any word or phrase from a critical review or comment, which word or phrase is restricted in said review or comment to a limited aspect of the work unless the advertisement clearly discloses or indicates that such word or phrase refers only to such aspect.

Each offense is punishable by a fine of up to $500. The regulation gives examples to show that "beautiful scenery" is permitted but that "beautiful" taken from the phrase "the scenery is beautiful" is not. The City Record, Jan. 29, 1972, at 331.

In 1984, the producers of a Broadway play paid fines to settle a complaint under this section. The advertisements quoted the drama critic of the New York Times as saying that the show was "the kind of play we hardly see on Broadway anymore." In the same review the critic had called the play "quite awful." N.Y.Times, Nov. 1, 1984, at 29; Nov. 11, 1984, at 14.

5. In Blatty v. New York Times Co., 221 Cal.Rptr. 236 (Cal.App.1985), plaintiff, the author of a work of fiction entitled "Legion," sued the defendant newspaper for failing to include his book in the list of best sellers that the newspaper regularly published. Plaintiff claimed,

among other things, that defendant advertised its list as being an "objective, unbiased, and accurate compilation of actual sales of books each week by 2,000 book stores in every region of the United States;" that the defendant knew this was false because it did not use actual sales but instead used an "undisclosed method of 'weighting' certain sales more than others." Plaintiff alleged that his figures showed that his book qualified for the list, but that it was included only one week—and then in last position.

The trial judge dismissed all claims. On appeal, the court affirmed dismissal of claims for negligence or negligent interference with prospective advantage:

> The complaint fails to allege how it was determined that enough copies of the book were sold to warrant its inclusion, or what other criteria were met and by whom they were established. For all that appears, defendant, for reasons of its own and employing criteria different from those which plaintiff considered to be conclusive, deemed the book unqualified for inclusion in the list. Public policy also weighs against imposition of such a duty. The list is a means of informing the public of the relative popularity of current works of fiction and nonfiction. If defendant were held to owe a duty to plaintiff to include his book in its list, other authors could assert a like duty owed to them. Faced with such a situation defendant might well cease compilation and publication of the list, thereby depriving the public of a valuable service.

A claim for trade libel was also rejected on the ground that "silence is not libel." A claim labeled "breach of public duty and trust to report the news fairly and honestly without bias or prejudice" was dismissed on the basis of the Tornillo case.

Finally, the court upheld the claim for intentional interference with prospective economic advantage by misleading prospective buyers and bookstores that stock and discount the most popular sellers. The claim that defendant knew of the falsity of its representations about the list was sufficient to state a tort claim. The court then turned to the constitutional defense:

> Defendant further argues that inasmuch as the list was compiled in the exercise of its editorial judgment and represented its opinion of which books were best sellers, the First Amendment shields defendant from liability for interference with plaintiff's prospective advantage by refusing to include his book in the list. [ ] This contention ignores the amended complaint's allegation that defendant falsely represented with knowledge of falsity . . . . The list was not held out as the product of defendant's editorial judgment or an expression of its opinion, but was falsely represented to be in

> fact a compilation of best sellers based on objective criteria. Under these circumstances the First Amendment does not foreclose plaintiff's cause of action [citing *Gertz* on the lack of constitutional value in false statements of fact].

The California Supreme Court granted a hearing in 1986.

B. COMMERCIAL SPEECH

Commercial advertising had little First Amendment protection until the 1970s. Although the Supreme Court has now brought such speech within the First Amendment, the extent of the protection is not yet clear.

The Court's exposure to these cases began with bans on distribution of leaflets without prior consent of a city official. In Lovell v. Griffin, 303 U.S. 444 (1938), such a ban on distributing "literature of any kind" was held invalid on its face as an example of the type of general licensing requirement that had precipitated the "struggle for the freedom of the press." In Schneider v. State, 308 U.S. 147 (1939), the municipalities, to circumvent *Griffin,* argued that their restraints on distribution were aimed at preventing fraud, disorder, and littering. The Court concluded that the proper response was to punish the acts of fraud and littering themselves. Concern for littering could not justify prohibiting "a person rightfully on a public street from handing literature to one willing to receive it."

The protection was not extended to leaflets used for advertising. A man who had bought a used Navy submarine passed out handbills urging the people to tour the ship for a fee. Police told him that a city ordinance barred distribution of commercial handbills on the streets; only handbills containing "information or public protest" were permitted. He then printed a protest against the city's refusal to rent him a particular pier on one side of the sheet and an advertisement for his submarine tours on the other side. When police stopped him again, he obtained an injunction against the city's interference with his distribution of the handbill. The Supreme Court unanimously upheld the regulation in Valentine v. Chrestensen, 316 U.S. 52 (1942):

> This court has unequivocally held that the streets are proper places for the exercise of the freedom of communicating information and disseminating opinion and that though the states and municipalities may appropriately regulate the privilege in the public interest, they may not unduly burden or proscribe its employment in these public thoroughfares. We are equally clear that the Constitution imposes no such restraint on government as respects purely commercial advertising. Whether, and to what extent, one may promote or pursue a gainful occupation in the streets, to what extent such activity shall be adjudged a derogation of the public right of user, are matters for legislative judgment.

This attitude toward commercial speech may partially explain Breard v. City of Alexandria, 341 U.S. 622 (1951), in which the Court upheld an ordinance banning door-to-door solicitation for purposes of sales—as applied to solicitors of magazine subscriptions. (In Martin v. City of Struthers, 319 U.S. 141 (1943), the Court had invalidated the application of an ordinance against uninvited solicitors—as applied to members of a religious group.)

For 22 years courts followed the *Chrestensen* approach. But in 1964, the Court gave protection to editorial advertisements, ads that promote ideas and causes rather than products or services. In *New York Times Co. v. Sullivan,* p. 157, supra, the Court said the publication "was not a 'commercial' advertisement in the sense in which the word was used in *Chrestensen.* It communicated information, expressed opinion, recited grievances, protested claimed abuses, and sought financial support on behalf of a movement whose existence and objectives are matters of the highest public interest and concern."

Pittsburgh Press Co. v. Pittsburgh Comm'n on Human Relations, 413 U.S. 376 (1973), was a step back toward *Chrestensen.* An ordinance barred employers from discriminating in employment and also barred others from aiding in such discrimination. The Pittsburgh Press carried Help Wanted advertisements in columns captioned "Jobs—Male Interest," "Jobs—Female Interest," and "Male—Female," according to the wishes of the advertiser. The Commission ordered the Press to stop using such captions except where the ordinance provided that "the employer or advertiser is free to make hiring or employment referral decisions on the basis of sex." The Supreme Court upheld the order, 5–4:

> In the crucial respects, the advertisements in the present record resemble the *Chrestensen* rather than the *Sullivan* advertisement. None expresses a position on whether, as a matter of social policy, certain positions ought to be filled by members of one or the other sex, nor does any of them criticize the Ordinance or the Commission's enforcement practices. Each is no more than a proposal of possible employment. The advertisements are thus classic examples of commercial speech.

The newspaper argued that the case involved an editorial judgment concerning the placement of such advertisements. Although the newspaper always acceded to the advertisers' requests, Justice Powell, for the majority, acknowledged that some editorial judgment was involved. He concluded, however, that in this case the newspaper was entitled to no greater protection than the advertiser itself:

> Discrimination in employment is not only commercial activity, it is *illegal* commercial activity under the Ordinance. We have no doubt that a newspaper constitutionally could be forbidden to publish a want ad proposing a sale of narcotics or soliciting prostitutes. Nor would the result be different if the nature of the transaction were indicated by placement under columns captioned "Narcotics for Sale" and "Prostitutes Wanted" rather than stated within the four corners of the advertisement.

> The illegality in this case may be less overt, but we see no difference in principle here. . . .

The Court emphasized that nothing in the holding allowed government to forbid the newspaper to "publish and distribute advertisements commenting on the Ordinance, the enforcement practices of the Commission, or the propriety of sex preferences in employment."

Chief Justice Burger dissented on the ground that the order functioned as a prior restraint on publication. Justice Stewart dissented on the ground that the government had no power to tell a newspaper in advance "what it can print and what it cannot." He thought this the first case "in this or any other American court that permits a government agency to enter a composing room of a newspaper and dictate to the publisher the layout and makeup of the newspaper's pages." If government can do this with classified advertising "what is there to prevent it from dictating the layout of the news pages tomorrow?"

Two years after *Pittsburgh Press,* the Court gave a measure of First Amendment protection to commercial speech. Bigelow v. Virginia, 421 U.S. 809 (1975), involved the publication in a Virginia newspaper of a New York group's advertisement stating that abortions were legal in New York with no residency requirement and offering to provide information and to arrange abortions in accredited hospitals at low cost. An address and telephone numbers were listed. Bigelow, the manager of the newspaper, was prosecuted under a statute making it a misdemeanor for "any person, by publication . . . or by the sale or circulation of any publication . . . [to] encourage or prompt the procuring of" an abortion. The state courts upheld the conviction and relied on the state's interest that women come to decisions about abortions "without the commercial advertising pressure usually incidental to the sale of a box of soap powder."

The Supreme Court reversed, 7–2. In his opinion for the Court, Justice Blackmun placed the advertisement closer to that in the New York Times case than to those of the other cases because it conveyed "information of potential interest and value to a diverse audience." The opinion also stressed that the activities advertised were legal in New York and that, although Virginia might be concerned about the health and welfare of its citizens, it could not keep from them information about legal activities in other states. Virginia had erred in assuming that "advertising, as such, was entitled to no First Amendment protection. . . . " At the same time advertising, "like all public expression, may be subject to reasonable regulation that serves a legitimate public interest. [ ] To the extent that commercial activity is subject to regulation, the relationship of speech to that activity may be one factor, among others, to be considered in weighing the First Amendment interest against the governmental interest alleged." In performing that balancing, the Court concluded that the advertisement was protected by the First Amendment. Justice Rehnquist, joined by Justice White, dissented on the grounds that the speech should be

treated as unprotected commercial speech and that, even if given some First Amendment protection, the speech interest was outweighed by the state's interest in "preventing commercial exploitation of the health needs of its citizens."

Virginia Pharmacy. Finally, in 1976, the Court repudiated the notion that commercial speech was outside the First Amendment. A Virginia statute declared any pharmacist who "advertises . . . any . . . price . . . for any drugs which may be dispensed only by prescription" guilty of "unprofessional conduct" punishable by penalties ranging from fines to revocation of license. The parties stipulated that "about 95% of all prescriptions are now filled with dosage forms prepared by the pharmaceutical manufacturer." They also stipulated that prices for the same drug in the same city varied greatly. The statute was challenged by consumer groups and an individual on the ground that the First Amendment entitled them to receive information that pharmacists wished to communicate to them. A three-judge district court agreed and invalidated the statute. The Supreme Court affirmed. Virginia State Board of Pharmacy v. Virginia Citizens Consumer Council, Inc., 425 U.S. 748 (1976). For the majority, Justice Blackmun said:

> Here, . . . the question whether there is a First Amendment exception for "commercial speech" is squarely before us. Our pharmacist does not wish to editorialize on any subject, cultural, philosophical, or political. He does not wish to report any particularly newsworthy fact, or to make generalized observations even about commercial matters. The "idea" he wishes to communicate is simply this: "I will sell you the X prescription drug at the Y price." Our question, then, is whether this communication is wholly outside the protection of the First Amendment.

He answered that it was "settled . . . that speech does not lose its First Amendment protection because money is spent to project it, as in a paid advertisement. . . . Speech likewise is protected even though it is carried in a form that is 'sold' for profit, . . . and even though it may involve a solicitation to purchase or otherwise pay or contribute money." He said that "speech which does 'no more than propose a commercial transaction'" is not "so removed from any 'exposition of ideas'" that it lacks protection. This regulation hit hardest at the poor, the sick, and the elderly. Cheaper drugs could mean "alleviation of physical pain or the enjoyment of basic necessities." This type of person may have a keener interest in the free flow of commercial information than in the "day's most urgent political debate." Moreover, "[a]dvertising, however tasteless and excessive . . . is nonetheless dissemination of information as to who is producing and selling what product, for what reason, and at what price."

The Court did not free advertising completely: "Some forms of commercial speech regulation are surely permissible." For instance, false and misleading advertising and advertisements for illegal activi-

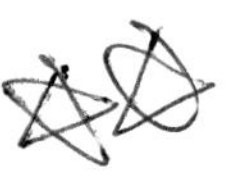

ties or products may be regulated. In what has become the famous footnote 24, Justice Blackmun said:

> In concluding that commercial speech enjoys First Amendment protection, we have not held that it is wholly undifferentiable from other forms. There are commonsense differences between speech that does "no more than propose a commercial transaction," [*Pittsburgh Press*] and other varieties. Even if the differences do not justify the conclusion that commercial speech is valueless, and thus subject to complete suppression by the State, they nonetheless suggest that a different degree of protection is necessary to insure that the flow of truthful and legitimate commercial information is unimpaired. The truth of commercial speech, for example, may be more easily verifiable by its disseminator than, let us say, news reporting or political commentary, in that ordinarily the advertiser seeks to disseminate information about a specific product or service that he himself provides and presumably knows more about than anyone else. Also, commercial speech may be more durable than other kinds. Since advertising is the *sine qua non* of commercial profits there is little likelihood of its being chilled by proper regulation and forgone entirely.
>
> Attributes such as these, the greater objectivity and hardiness of commercial speech, may make it less necessary to tolerate inaccurate statements for fear of silencing the speaker. [ ] They may also make it appropriate to require that a commercial message appear in such a form, or include such additional information, warnings, and disclaimers, as are necessary to prevent its being deceptive. [ ] They may also make inapplicable the prohibition against prior restraints. [ ]

Justice Stewart concurred separately to explain why the decision did not destroy the "constitutional legitimacy of every state and federal law regulating false or deceptive advertising." He emphasized that such laws generally are aimed at commercial advertisers who know the product they are advertising and can more easily verify the accuracy of representations made, than can "the press, which must often attempt to assemble the true facts from sketchy and sometimes conflicting sources under the pressure of publication deadlines. . . . " There was little likelihood of chilling accurate advertising by proscribing false advertising. "Indeed, the elimination of false and deceptive claims serves to promote the one facet of commercial price and product advertising that warrants First Amendment protection—its contribution to the flow of accurate and reliable information relevant to public and private decisionmaking."

Justice Rehnquist dissented, saying the Constitution did not require "the Virginia Legislature to hew to the teachings of Adam Smith." Recognizing the difficulty of drawing the line between protected speech and commercial speech in previous cases, he nevertheless thought the majority had been unwise in drawing a new line between truthful commercial speech and false and misleading commercial speech. The Court's view that the First Amendment was "primarily an instrument to enlighten public decisionmaking in a democracy" referred to "political, social, and other public issues, rather than the decision of a particular individual as to whether to purchase one or another kind of shampoo. It is undoubtedly arguable that many people in the country regard the choice of shampoo as just as important as who may be elected to local, state, or national political office, but that does not automatically bring information about competing shampoos within the protection of the First Amendment." He was also concerned that pharmacists might use this opportunity to promote the use of drugs by such advertisements as "Don't spend another sleepless night. Ask your doctor to prescribe Seconal without delay."

Chief Justice Burger concurred separately to emphasize that "the Court wisely leaves" the question of medical and legal services advertising "to another day." Because 95 percent of prescriptions are already in dosage units, he thought the pharmacist "no more renders a true professional service than does a clerk who sells lawbooks." He suggested that advertising of price by professionals might be inherently misleading since "what the professional must do will vary greatly in individual cases."

When a case involving the advertising of legal services did arise, the Court granted protection. Bates v. State Bar of Arizona, 433 U.S. 350 (1977); but see Ohralik v. Ohio State Bar Ass'n, 436 U.S. 447 (1978) (distinguishing in-person solicitation from advertising). In Zauderer v. Office of Disciplinary Counsel, 105 S.Ct. 2265 (1984), the Court upheld the constitutional right of lawyers to use printed advertising to seek clients for specific cases: here, Dalkon shield litigation. The state argued that it was too difficult in these cases for regulators to distinguish accurate advertising from false or misleading ads. The Court responded that the protections "afforded commercial speech would mean little indeed if such arguments were allowed to prevail." Although the Court upheld the basic advertisement and the use of an illustration that violated state bar rules, it did find one aspect of the lawyer's ad misleading: the part in which he said that if the case was not successful "no legal fees are owed by our clients." That part was misleading because it did not reveal that clients might be liable for various court costs in case of failure.

Central Hudson. In Central Hudson Gas v. Public Service Comm'n, 447 U.S. 557, 6 Med.L.Rptr. 1497 (1980), in which the New York Public Service Commission was not allowed to ban all promotional advertising by an electric utility, Justice Powell's majority opinion summarized the Court's current method of analyzing commercial speech cases:

> The First Amendment's concern for commercial speech is based on the informational function of advertising. [ ] Consequently, there can be no constitutional objection to the suppression

of commercial messages that do not accurately inform the public about lawful activity. The government may ban forms of communication more likely to deceive the public than to inform it, [ ], or commercial speech related to illegal activity, [*Pittsburgh Press*].

If the communication is neither misleading nor related to unlawful activity, the government's power is more circumscribed. The State must assert a substantial interest to be achieved by restrictions on commercial speech. Moreover, the regulatory technique must be in proportion to that interest. The limitation on expression must be designed carefully to achieve the State's goal. Compliance with this requirement may be measured by two criteria. First, the restriction must directly advance the state interest involved; the regulation may not be sustained if it provides only ineffective or remote support for the government's purpose. Second, if the governmental interest could be served as well by a more limited restriction on commercial speech, the excessive restrictions cannot survive.

Under the first criterion, the Court has declined to uphold regulations that only indirectly advance the state interest involved. [*Bates; Virginia Pharmacy*]. . . .

The second criterion recognizes that the First Amendment mandates that speech restrictions be "narrowly drawn." [ ] The regulatory technique may extend only as far as the interest it serves. The State cannot regulate speech that poses no danger to the asserted state interest, nor can it completely suppress information when narrower restrictions on expression would serve its interest as well. . . .

In commercial speech cases, then, a four-part analysis has developed. At the outset, we must determine whether the expression is protected by the First Amendment. For commercial speech to come within that provision, it at least must concern lawful activity and not be misleading. Next, we ask whether the asserted governmental interest is substantial. If both inquiries yield positive answers, we must determine whether the regulation directly advances the governmental interest asserted, and whether it is not more extensive than is necessary to serve that interest.

In his concurrence, Justice Stevens expressed concern about identifying "commercial speech":

In my judgment one of the two definitions the Court uses in addressing that issue is too broad and the other may be somewhat too narrow. The Court first describes commercial speech as "expression related solely to the economic interest of the speaker and its audience." Although it is not entirely clear whether this definition uses the subject matter of the speech or the motivation of the speaker as the limiting factor, it seems clear to me that it encompasses speech that is entitled to the maximum protection afforded by the First Amendment. Neither a labor leader's exhortation to strike, nor an economist's dissertation on the money supply should receive any lesser protection because the subject matter concerns only the economic interests of the audience. Nor should the economic motivation of a speaker qualify his constitutional protection; even Shakespeare may have been motivated by the prospect of pecuniary reward. Thus, the Court's first definition of commercial speech is unquestionably too broad.

The Court's second definition refers to "speech proposing a commercial transaction." A salesman's solicitation, a broker's offer, and a manufacturer's publication of a price list or the terms of his standard warranty would unquestionably fit within this concept. Presumably, the definition is intended to encompass advertising that advises possible buyers of the availability of specific products at specific prices and describes the advantages of purchasing such items. Perhaps it also extends to other communications that do little more than make the name of a product or a service more familiar to the general public. Whatever the precise contours of the concept, and perhaps it is too early to enunciate an exact formulation, I am persuaded that it should not include the entire range of communication that is embraced within the term "promotional advertising."

. . .

In sum, I concur in the result because I do not consider this to be a "commercial speech" case.

Shortly after *Central Hudson,* and based in part on it, the Court struck down an ordinance forbidding, with certain limited exceptions, all outdoor or billboard advertising. Metromedia, Inc. v. San Diego, 453 U.S. 490 (1981). There was no majority opinion, and Justice Rehnquist, in dissent, referred to the five opinions as "a virtual Tower of Babel." In his concurrence, Justice Brennan suggested a continuum from commercial to noncommercial speech: (1) Visit Joe's Ice Cream Shoppe; (2) Joe's Ice Cream Shoppe uses only the highest quality dairy products; (3) Because Joe thinks that dairy products are good for you, please shop at Joe's Shoppe; (4) Joe says to support dairy price supports; they mean lower prices for you at his Shoppe.

The Puerto Rico case. In 1948, Puerto Rico legalized certain forms of casino gambling in an effort to encourage tourism. Although local residents were not banned from using the casinos, the legislature provided that casinos were not to advertise to the local public. Over the years, the focus of the regulation became one of identifying the primary audience of the advertisement in question. This meant that casinos might advertise within Puerto Rico if their primary audience was tourists rather than residents. In Posadas de Puerto Rico Associates v. Tourism Co. of Puerto Rico, 106 S.Ct. 2968 (1986), the Court, 5–4, rejected a casino's facial challenge to the statute and regulations.

For the majority, Justice Rehnquist began by noting that the case involved "pure commercial speech which does 'no more than propose a commercial transaction.'" He then applied the four-part test of *Central Hudson.* First, the regulation concerned a lawful activity and was not misleading or fraudulent. Second, the "reduction of demand for casino gambling by the residents of Puerto Rico" was a "substantial" government interest. Third, the regulation "directly advanced" the government's asserted interest:

> The Puerto Rico Legislature obviously believed . . . that advertising of casino gambling aimed at the residents of Puerto Rico would serve to increase the demand for the product advertised. We think the legislature's belief is a reasonable one . . ..

The Court rejected the casino's argument that the regulation was underinclusive because other types of gambling could be advertised to residents. First, the restrictions do in fact directly advance the government's interest in this case. Second, the legislature's concern might have been casino gambling rather than horse racing, cockfighting, and the lottery, which "have been traditionally part of the Puerto Rican's roots."

Fourth, the restrictions were "no more extensive than necessary to serve the government's interest." The casino argued that the First Amendment required the government to reduce demand for casino gambling "not by suppressing commercial speech that might *encourage* such gambling, but by promulgating additional speech designed to *discourage* it." The Court disagreed:

> We think it is up to the legislature to decide whether or not such a "counterspeech" policy would be as effective in reducing the demand for casino gambling as a restriction on advertising. The legislature could conclude, as it apparently did here, that residents of Puerto Rico are already aware of the risks of casino gambling, yet would nevertheless be induced by widespread advertising to engage in such potentially harmful conduct. Cf. Capital Broadcasting Co. v. Mitchell, 333 F.Supp. 582, 585 (D.C.1971) (three-judge court) ("Congress had convincing evidence that the Labeling Act of 1965 had not materially reduced the incidence of smoking") aff'd 405 U.S. 1000 (1972); Dunagin v. City of Oxford, Miss., 718 F.2d 738, 751 (5th Cir.1983) (en banc) (". . . The state's concern is not that the public is unaware of the dangers of alcohol. . . . The concern instead is that advertising will unduly promote alcohol consumption despite known dangers"), cert. denied, 467 U.S. 1259 (1984).

This led the Court to conclude that the *Central Hudson* test had been met and that the lower courts had properly rejected the First Amendment claim. In passing, the Court added that the casino would fare no better under an equal protection claim because the Court had found a sufficient "fit" between the legislature's means and ends to satisfy the First Amendment. This "fit" was "surely adequate under the applicable 'rational basis' equal protection analysis."

The casino argued that cases like Bigelow v. Virginia dictated protection here. The Court disagreed. In *Bigelow,* the underlying activity itself was protected. Here, though, the legislature "surely could have prohibited casino gambling" by residents altogether.

Finally, the casino argued that once the government chose to legalize casino gambling for residents, the First Amendment barred it from using restrictions on advertising to reduce demand for the activity. The Court disagreed:

> In our view, [the casino] has the argument backwards. . . . [I]t is precisely *because* the government could have enacted a wholesale prohibition of the underlying conduct that it is permissible for the government to take the less intrusive step of allowing the conduct, but reducing the demand through restrictions on advertising. It would surely be a Pyrrhic victory for casino owners . . . to gain recognition of a First Amendment right . . . only to thereby force the legislature into banning casino gambling by residents altogether. It would just as surely be a strange constitutional doctrine which would concede to the legislature the authority to totally ban a product or activity, but deny to the legislature the authority to forbid the stimulation of demand for the product or activity through advertising . . .. Legislative regulation of products or activities deemed harmful, such as cigarettes, alcoholic beverages, and prostitution, has varied from outright prohibition on the one hand, [ ], to legalization of the product or activity with restrictions on stimulation of its demand on the other hand, [ ]. To rule out the latter intermediate kind of response would require more than we find in the First Amendment.

Justice Brennan, joined by Justices Marshall and Blackmun, dissented. None of the differences between commercial and other speech "justify protecting commercial speech less extensively where, as here, the government seeks to manipulate behavior by depriving citizens of truthful information concerning lawful activities." Regulation of speech based on "fear that recipients will act on the information provided, . . . should be subject to strict judicial scrutiny." The majority improperly used the "relaxed standards" normally applied to commercial speech in its First Amendment analysis and improperly used the "rational basis" standard in its equal protection analysis. It was incumbent on the government to "*prove* that the interests it seeks to further are real and substantial." Here there was no showing that "serious harmful effects" will result if local residents gambled in casinos.

Even if a substantial government interest had been shown, Justice Brennan found no showing that the advertising regulation would meet concerns about corruption or organized crime. Finally, he objected that Puerto Rico could "seek directly to address the specific harms" by monitoring casino operations to guard against the influences of crime, by vigorously enforcing its criminal laws to combat crime and prostitution, by putting limits on the size of bets, or by promulgating additional speech. Contrary to the majority's view, it is not "up to the legislature" to decide whether the government's interest can be met by less intrusive means:

> Rather, it is incumbent upon the government to *prove* that more limited means are not sufficient to protect its interests, and for a *court* to decide whether or not the government has sustained this burden. [ ] In this case, nothing suggests that the Puerto Rico Legislature ever considered the efficacy of measures other than suppressing protected expression. More importantly, there has been no showing that alternative measures would inadequately safeguard the Commonwealth's interest in controlling the harmful effects allegedly associated with casino gambling. Under these circumstances, Puerto Rico's ban on advertising clearly violates the First Amendment.

Justice Brennan also rejected the majority's argument that banning speech was "less intrusive" than banning the activity itself. Once Puerto Rico made it legal for residents to gamble in casinos, the decision to ban truthful speech about that activity raised "serious" First Amendment questions. "I do not agree that a ban on casino advertising is 'less intrusive' than an outright prohibition of such activity. . . . [t]he 'constitutional doctrine' which bans Puerto Rico from banning advertisements concerning lawful casino gambling is not so strange a restraint—it is called the First Amendment."

Justice Stevens also dissented, joined by Justices Marshall and Blackmun. His focus was on the operation of the Puerto Rico regulatory scheme which he found to discriminate between publications and to involve aspects of prior restraint.

What does this case suggest about future efforts to limit advertising of alcoholic beverages or of cigarettes or of legal prostitution? The lower court cases are cited in the majority opinion. What about banning advertising for motion pictures that could be banned as obscene, but which are permitted by the state? What about banning advertising for any spectator sport that charges more than $20 for a seat, on the ground that citizens should be discouraged from spending their money on such expensive events?

Chapter IX

PROTECTING THE RIGHT TO AN IMPARTIAL JURY

A. INTRODUCTION

In this Chapter and in related discussions in later Chapters, the main text is the first part of the Sixth Amendment to the United States Constitution: "In all criminal prosecutions, the accused shall enjoy the right to a speedy and public trial, by an impartial jury of the State and district wherein the crime shall have been committed . . . ." Although civil cases may occasionally raise concerns about fair trials, we will focus on criminal cases—usually those that involve either sensational crimes or prominent persons. Defendants in these cases have often feared that extensive press coverage, especially before trial, will make it impossible or difficult for them to obtain impartial juries when, and if, their cases reach trial. Attempts to avoid this danger have led defendants to seek judicial help of the following kinds:

1. Using one or more of the array of protections offered by criminal procedure, such as continuance, change of venue, or intense voir dire;
2. Preventing the press from making public any prejudicial information it has learned about the case, such as the results of a lie detector test, or plea bargaining;
3. Ordering those with access to potentially prejudicial information not to reveal it, especially to the press (those under such orders might include attorneys, court officials, and the police);
4. Barring the press (and perhaps the public as well) from access to judicial proceedings at which prejudicial information might emerge.

The underlying assumption of each of these approaches—and, of course, of the entire concern—is that members of the public who are later called as prospective jurors will be either unwilling or unable to set aside what they have learned earlier and be in fact "impartial" at the trial.

This assumption has been tested in some experimental settings and has been questioned by many journalists, but the judiciary has not been persuaded that jurors are able to eradicate what they have learned. For a review of the literature, see R.J. Simon, The Jury: Its Role in American Society (1980).

The situation, then, is that judges are concerned about the impact of prejudicial information on prospective jurors. (The timing of the matter means that the information is virtually always "pretrial." A separate concern exists in some cases over prejudicial information being revealed after the jury has been selected. This is generally thought to be a less serious problem because of the possibility of sequestering the jury if a case appears to have that potential. As we shall see, sequestration may not so easily eliminate that problem.)

The Supreme Court's concern in this area may be dated to an opinion by Justice Frankfurter, concurring in the denial of certiorari in Maryland v. Baltimore Radio Show, 338 U.S. 912 (1950). He abhorred the torrent of pretrial publicity in the case and noted that in the United Kingdom the law of contempt barred newspapers from virtually all reporting on pending cases.

The next year, the Court reversed a conviction because of improper selection of the grand jury. Justice Jackson, joined by Justice Frankfurter, concurred, emphasizing the mob violence and tensions that had surrounded the celebrated rape case: "prejudicial influences outside the courtroom, becoming all too typical of a highly publicized trial, were brought to bear on this jury with such force that the conclusion is inescapable that these defendants were prejudged as guilty and the trial was but a legal gesture to register a verdict already dictated by the press and the public opinion which it generated." Shepherd v. Florida, 341 U.S. 50 (1951).

In 1959, the Court for the first time reversed a federal conviction because, during a trial for illegally dispensing pills, seven jurors were exposed to one or two newspaper articles reporting that the defendant had been convicted of forgery and had practiced medicine without a license. This evidence had been inadmissible in the trial. Even though each juror denied being influenced by the episode, the Court ordered a new trial. "The prejudice to the defendant is almost certain to be as great when that evidence reaches the jury through news accounts as when it is a part of the prosecution's evidence. [ ] It may indeed be greater for it is then not tempered by protective procedures." The Court acted in the exercise of its "supervisory power to formulate and apply proper standards for enforcement of the criminal law in the federal courts." Justice Black dissented without opinion. Marshall v. United States, 360 U.S. 310 (1959).

In 1961, the Court for the first time reversed a state conviction for lack of an impartial jury. Irvin v. Dowd, 366 U.S. 717 (1961). Irvin had been charged with the murder of one person, tried, convicted, and sentenced to death. (The venue had been changed once in accordance with state law.) Before the trial, local newspapers and radio and television blanketed the rural Indiana area of the crime and trial with reports about the defendant's prior convictions for arson, for burglary, and for being AWOL during wartime. In addition:

> The headlines announced his police line-up identification, that he faced a lie detector test, had been placed at the scene of the crime and that the six murders were solved but [Irvin] refused to confess.

> Finally, they announced his confession to the six murders and the fact of his indictment for four of them in Indiana. They reported [Irvin's] offer to plead guilty if promised a 99-year sentence . . . . In many of the stories [Irvin] was described as the "confessed slayer of six," a parole violator and fraudulent-check artist. . . . On the day before the trial the newspapers carried the story that Irvin had orally admitted the murder of Kerr (the victim in this case) as well as [five other murders].

The Court reviewed efforts to get a jury in the case. The voir dire record, covering the examination of 430 prospective jurors, ran 2,783 pages. Almost 90 percent of those examined on the point "entertained some opinion as to guilt—ranging in intensity from mere suspicion to absolute certainty." Of the 430, 268 were excused for cause for having fixed opinions as to guilt; 103 were excused because of objection to the death penalty; 20 were peremptorily challenged by Irvin and 10 by the state; 12 plus 2 alternates were seated, and the rest were excused for such reasons as deafness and doctors' letters.

> Eight out of the 12 [seated jurors] thought Irvin was guilty. With such an opinion permeating their minds, it would be difficult to say that each could exclude this preconception of guilt from his deliberations. The influence that lurks in an opinion once formed is so persistent that it unconsciously fights detachment from the mental processes of the average man. [ ] Where one's life is at stake—and accounting for the frailties of human nature—we can only say that in light of the circumstances here the finding of impartiality does not meet constitutional standards. Two-thirds of the jurors had an opinion that petitioner was guilty and were familiar with the material facts and circumstances involved . . . . One said that he "could not . . . give the defendant the benefit of the doubt that he is innocent." . . . No doubt each juror was sincere when he said that he would be fair and impartial to petitioner, but the psychological impact requiring such a declaration before one's fellows is often its father. Where so many, so many times, admitted prejudice, such a statement of impartiality can be given little weight. As one of the jurors put it, "You can't forget what you hear and see."

Justice Frankfurter concurred separately to decry the "miscarriage of justice due to anticipatory trial by newspaper instead of trial in court before a jury." He observed that "More than one student of society has expressed the view that not the least significant test of the quality of a civilization is its treatment of those charged with crime, particularly with offenses which arouse the passions of a community. . . . How can fallible men and women reach a disinterested verdict based exclusively on what they heard in court when, before they entered the jury box, their minds were saturated by press and radio for months preceding by matter designed to establish the guilt of the accused."

In Rideau v. Louisiana, 373 U.S. 723 (1963), the morning after defendant's arrest, the sheriff conducted a filmed "interview" during which the defendant confessed to a capital crime. The interview was televised later that same day on a local station and seen by an estimated 24,000 viewers. The next day it was rebroadcast and seen by 53,000. The following day it was again shown and seen by 29,000. The parish had a population of 150,000.

A change of venue motion was denied and trial was held before a jury that included three who saw at least one showing and two jurors who were deputy sheriffs. After the defense had used all its peremptory challenges, it moved to challenge these jurors for cause. Those challenges were denied. At the trial, the film was not introduced. Defendant was convicted and sentenced to death. The Court reversed:

> [W]e hold that it was a denial of due process of law to refuse the request for a change of venue, after the people of [the parish] had been exposed repeatedly and in depth to the spectacle of Rideau personally confessing in detail to the crimes with which he was later to be charged. For anyone who has ever watched television the conclusion cannot be avoided that this spectacle, to the tens of thousands of people who saw and heard it, in a very real sense was Rideau's trial—at which he pleaded guilty to murder. Any subsequent court proceedings in a community so pervasively exposed to such a spectacle could be but a hollow formality.

The Court did "not hesitate to hold, without pausing to examine a particularized transcript of the *voir dire* examination of the members of the jury, that due process of law in this case required a trial before a jury drawn from a community of people who had not seen and heard Rideau's televised 'interview.'"

In Estes v. Texas, 381 U.S. 532 (1965), the Court held that the very act of televising parts of defendant's already-widely publicized trial over his objections violated defendant's right to a fair trial. The state argued that the objections to a televised trial were all speculative and that none had been established in the case. The Court thought the dangers real enough in an already notorious case to warrant reversal under *Rideau* despite any specific showing of prejudice in the trial. We return to this case in Chapter XII.

SHEPPARD v. MAXWELL

Supreme Court of the United States, 1966.
384 U.S. 333, 86 S.Ct. 1507, 16 L.Ed.2d 600.
Noted, 80 Harv.L.Rev. 180, 45 N.C.L.Rev. 183, 62 Nw.U.L.Rev. 89, 41 St. John's L.Rev. 438.

[In 1954, Sheppard was charged with murdering his wife. The case attracted great public attention and extensive media coverage beginning shortly after the murder, before any arrest had been made. The publicity continued through the pretrial and trial period. Sheppard was convicted of second-degree murder. After serving several years in prison, he sought habeas corpus in the federal courts. The district court granted the writ, but the court of appeals reversed. The Supreme Court reversed and ordered Sheppard released unless the state gave him a new trial. The Court's lengthy opinion traced the facts in great detail and placed the responsibility on the trial judge for failing to give Sheppard a fair trial:

> While we cannot say that Sheppard was denied due process by the judge's refusal to take precautions against the influence of pretrial publicity alone, the court's later rulings must be considered against the setting in which the trial was held. In light of this background, we believe that the arrangements made by the judge with the news media caused Sheppard to be deprived of that "judicial serenity and calm to which [he] was entitled" [quoting *Estes*]. The fact is that bedlam reigned at the courthouse during the trial and newsmen took over practically the entire courtroom, hounding most of the participants in the trial, especially Sheppard. . . . Having assigned almost all of the available seats in the courtroom to the news media the judge lost his ability to supervise the environment. The movement of the reporters in and out of the courtroom caused frequent confusion and disruption of the trial.

Beyond this concern with the judge's lack of control over the courtroom the Court was troubled by publicity during the trial.]

MR. JUSTICE CLARK delivered the opinion of the Court.

. . .

Much of the material printed or broadcast during the trial was never heard from the witness stand, such as the charges that Sheppard had purposely impeded the murder investigation and must be guilty since he had hired a prominent criminal lawyer; that Sheppard was a perjurer; that he had sexual relations with numerous women; that his slain wife had characterized him as a "Jekyll-Hyde"; that he was "a bare-faced liar" because of his testimony as to police treatment; and, finally, that a woman convict claimed Sheppard to be the father of her illegitimate child. As the trial progressed, the newspapers summarized and interpreted the evidence, devoting particular attention to the material that incriminated Sheppard, and often drew unwarranted inferences from testimony. At one point, a front-page picture of Mrs. Sheppard's blood-stained pillow was published after being "doctored" to show more clearly an alleged imprint of a surgical instrument.

Nor is there doubt that this deluge of publicity reached at least some of the jury. On the only occasion that the jury was queried, two jurors admitted in open court to hearing the highly inflammatory charge that a prison inmate claimed Sheppard as the father of her illegitimate child. Despite the extent and nature of the publicity to which the jury was exposed during trial, the judge refused defense counsel's other requests that the jurors be asked whether they had read or heard specific prejudicial comment about the case, including the incidents we have previously summarized. In these circumstances, we can assume that some of this material reached members of the jury. [ ]

VII.

The court's fundamental error is compounded by the holding that it lacked power to control the publicity about the trial. From the very inception of the proceedings the judge announced that neither he nor anyone else could restrict prejudicial news accounts. And he reiterated this view on numerous occasions. Since he viewed the news media as his target, the judge never considered other means that are often utilized to reduce the appearance of prejudicial material and to protect the jury from outside influence. We conclude that these procedures would have been sufficient to guarantee Sheppard a fair trial and so do not consider what sanctions might be available against a recalcitrant press nor the charges of bias now made against the state trial judge.

The carnival atmosphere at trial could easily have been avoided since the courtroom and courthouse premises are subject to the control of the court. . . .

Secondly, the court should have insulated the witnesses. All of the newspapers and radio stations apparently interviewed prospective witnesses at will, and in many instances disclosed their testimony. A typical example was the publication of numerous statements by Susan Hayes, before her appearance in court, regarding her love affair with Sheppard. Although the witnesses were barred from the courtroom during the trial the full verbatim testimony was available to them in the press. This completely nullified the judge's imposition of the rule. [ ]

Thirdly, the court should have made some effort to control the release of leads, information, and gossip to the press by police officers, witnesses, and the counsel for both sides. Much of the information thus disclosed was inaccurate, leading to groundless rumors and confusion. . . . Defense counsel immediately brought to the court's attention the tremendous amount of publicity in the Cleveland press that "misrepresented entirely the testimony" in the case. Under such circumstances, the judge should have at least warned the newspapers to check the accuracy of their accounts. And it is obvious that the judge should have further sought to alleviate this problem by imposing control over the statements made to the news media by counsel, witnesses, and especially the Coroner and police officers. The prosecution repeatedly made evidence available to the news media which was never offered in the trial. Much of the "evidence" disseminated in this fashion was clearly inadmissible. The exclusion of such evidence in court is rendered meaningless when news media make it available to the public. For example, the publicity about Sheppard's refusal to take a lie detector test came directly from police officers and the Coroner. The story that Sheppard had been called a "Jekyll-Hyde" personality by his wife was attributed to a prosecution witness. No such testimony was given. The further report that there was "a 'bombshell witness' on tap" who would testify as to Sheppard's "fiery temper" could only have emanated from the prosecution. Moreover, the newspapers described in detail clues that had been found by the police, but not put into the record.

The fact that many of the prejudicial news items can be traced to the prosecution, as well as the defense, aggravates the judge's failure to take any action. [ ] Effective control of these sources—concededly within the court's power—might well have prevented the divulgence of inaccurate information, rumors, and accusations that made up much of the inflammatory publicity, at least after Sheppard's indictment.

More specifically, the trial court might well have proscribed extrajudicial statements by any lawyer, party, witness, or court official which divulged prejudicial matters, such as the refusal of Sheppard to submit to interrogation or take any lie detector tests; any statement made by Sheppard to officials; the identity of prospective witnesses or their probable testimony; any belief in guilt or innocence; or like statements concerning the merits of the case. . . . Being advised of the great public interest in the case, the mass coverage of the press, and the potential prejudicial impact of publicity, the court could also have requested the appropriate city and county officials to promulgate a regulation with respect to dissemination of information about the case by their employees. . . . Had the judge, the other officers of the court, and the police placed the interest of justice first, the news media would have soon learned to be content with the task of reporting the case as it unfolded in the courtroom—not pieced together from extrajudicial statements.

From the cases coming here we note that unfair and prejudicial news comment on pending trials has become increasingly prevalent. Due process requires that the accused receive a trial by an impartial jury free from outside influences. Given the pervasiveness of modern communications and the difficulty of effacing prejudicial publicity from the minds of the jurors, the trial courts must take strong measures to ensure that the balance is never weighed against the accused. And appellate tribunals have the duty to make an independent evaluation of the circumstances. Of course, there is nothing that proscribes the press from reporting the events that transpire in the courtroom. But where there is a reasonable likelihood that prejudicial news prior to trial will prevent a fair trial, the judge should continue the case until the threat abates, or transfer it to another county not so permeated with publicity. In addition, sequestration of the jury was something the judge should have raised *sua sponte* with counsel. If publicity during the proceedings threatens the fairness of the trial, a new trial should be ordered. But we must remember that reversals are but palliatives; the cure lies in those remedial measures that will prevent the prejudice at its inception. The courts must take such steps by rule and regulation that will protect their processes from prejudicial outside interferences. Neither prosecutors, counsel for defense, the accused, witnesses, court staff nor enforcement officers coming under the jurisdiction of the court should be permitted to frustrate its function. Collaboration between counsel and the press as to information affecting the fairness of a criminal trial is not only subject to regulation, but is highly censurable and worthy of disciplinary measures.

Since the state trial judge did not fulfill his duty to protect Sheppard from the inherently prejudicial publicity which saturated the community and to control disruptive influences in the courtroom, we must reverse the denial of the habeas petition. The case is remanded to the District Court with instructions to issue the writ and order that Sheppard be released from custody unless the State puts him to its charges again within a reasonable time.

It is so ordered.

MR. JUSTICE BLACK dissents.

Notes and Questions

1. On Sheppard's retrial he was acquitted and released—after having served ten years in prison.

A recent study suggests that this problem affects very few cases. In the years 1976–80, of the 63,000 appeals in criminal cases to highest state appellate courts, 368 claimed that news coverage prejudiced the outcome of the trial. Of these 368, reversals based on the publicity were ordered in only 18, or 5 percent. This led the author to conclude that in the years since the Kennedy assassination in 1963, fewer than 100 cases have been reversed on this ground. The author concluded that the controversy was "in reality a red herring outside the courtroom, because the issue is rarely raised on appeal. The trial judges are doing their job." Spencer, The So-Called Problem of Prejudicial Publicity Is a Red Herring, 2 Comm. Lawyer 11 (Spring 1984). How might Justice Frankfurter respond?

2. The reason for using the Kennedy assassination as a benchmark is not that concerns about prejudicial publicity did not exist before then. Rather, it is that the assassination led to extensive reconsideration of court practices in this area.

In an omitted part of its opinion in Sheppard v. Maxwell, the Court referred to the Report of the President's Commission on the Assassination of President John F. Kennedy, in which the Commission, headed by Chief Justice Earl Warren, expressed grave doubts about whether Lee Harvey Oswald could possibly have gotten a fair trial after all the publicity. In response, the ABA created the Reardon Commission to explore the question. That group filed its first report in 1968 suggesting that some limits on the behavior of others might be needed in addition to the traditional criminal procedure techniques. These produced a flurry of activity that we consider here and in Chapter XII.

3. It is clear that jurors are not unacceptable simply because they have heard something about the case. In Murphy v. Florida, 421 U.S. 794 (1975), the jurors in defendant's robbery trial had learned through news stories about some or all of the defendant's earlier convictions for murder, securities theft, and for the 1964 theft of the Star of India sapphire from a New York museum. The majority stated that qualified jurors need not be totally ignorant of the facts surrounding the case. The Court found in the voir dire no showing of hostility to the defendant. Four of the six jurors had volunteered that defendant's past was irrelevant. Moreover, the defendant's attorney during voir dire informed several of the jurors of crimes they had not known about, leading the Court to observe, "We will not readily discount the assurances of a juror insofar as his exposure to a defendant's past crimes comes from the defendant or counsel." The indicia of impartiality "might be disregarded in a case where the general atmosphere in the community or courtroom is sufficiently inflammatory, but the circumstances surrounding petitioner's trial are not at all of that variety." Only 20 of the 78 persons examined were excused because of an opinion of guilt. "This may indeed be 20 more than would occur in the trial of a totally obscure person, but it by no means suggests a community with sentiment so poisoned against petitioner as to impeach the indifference of jurors who displayed no hostile animus of their own." Only Justice Brennan dissented.

4. As these cases suggest, certain types of information are thought particularly likely to breed the sort of prejudice that can undermine the impartiality of a jury. Three of these involve the revelation of information that may not be presented or admissible at the trial. The first of these is that the defendant has confessed to the crime. If the confession was not obtained in accordance with constitutional and statutory requirements it may not be admissible. The second is the result of an unreasonable search and seizure, which is not likely to be admissible if the defendant does not take the witness stand. The third is the report of defendant's prior convictions, which may not be admissible if the defendant does not testify. A fourth concern is the press preoccupation with a heavy-hitting campaign against a defendant of the sort that occurred in both *Irvin* and *Sheppard.* The name-calling and the constant attention might be thought especially conducive to an atmosphere in which jurors will feel a strong pull to conform to the expectations that the community has developed—even if no devastating adverse information is revealed.

5. Although *Sheppard* involved judicial conduct during the trial, the Court took the occasion to comment on pretrial practices as well. The Court suggests the array already set forth in this Chapter, starting with techniques in the criminal justice system to protect the defendant's fair trial interests without limiting the rights of other participants in the administration of justice or the press. In the following enumeration the goal is to suggest some reasons why the suggested device may not necessarily achieve its goal, and why the courts in some of the cases

that follow have resorted to rulings that *do* impinge upon interests of persons other than the parties to the criminal case. This survey is not an effort to settle upon the merits of each device.

a. *Continuance.* Most of the offenses that provoke intensive publicity are so serious that either bail is not available or the accused cannot raise the amount in question. If that is the case, then a continuance means incarceration for an extended period of time.

Whether the accused is kept in prison or not, the delay may infringe upon the provision of the Sixth Amendment that calls for a "speedy" trial. Finally, how sure can the judge be that when the case is readied for trial at a later date, the feared publicity will not begin again?

b. *Change of Venue.* This device may move the defendant from his home community to a distant place where he will lose the support system of family and friends. It may also change drastically the nature of the jury pool. This is evident in a change from a rural area to an urban area, or from an area with one set of moral values to another with a different set. These shifts are most likely in large states. But in small states, particularly those covered by one newspaper or by the same set of television stations, how much will a change of venue help? What about the additional financial costs imposed on the defense? In federal court this might be a major concern, since venue may be changed across state lines. See the discussion in United States v. Chagra, 701 F.2d 354, 9 Med.L.Rptr. 1409 (5th Cir.1983).

A defendant who seeks a change of venue, may not demand a specific new venue, though sometimes it is possible to predict the likeliest choices.

May the state request a change? Or may the defendant be "forced" to request one after other measures fail? Recall that the Sixth Amendment speaks of a right to be tried in the "State and district wherein the crime shall have been committed. . . ." Some state courts have strongly suggested that the trial judge must take into account the accused's right to a local trial. See Miami Herald Publishing Co. v. Lewis, 426 So.2d 1, 8 Med.L.Rptr. 2281 (Fla.1982), finding a state constitutional right to be tried "in the county where the crime was committed," and Matter of Westchester Rockland Newspapers, Inc. v. Leggett, 48 N.Y.2d 430, 399 N.E.2d 518, 423 N.Y.S.2d 630, 5 Med.L. Rptr. 2009 (1979), concluding that an accused "should not be placed in a position where he will have to submit to a continuance at the expense of his right to a speedy trial, or to a change of venue which would require a waiver of his fundamental right to a trial in the vicinage by a jury of his peers." See also the Chagra case, supra, in which a concurring judge asserted that the press had no constitutional right to obtain and print information that would "force" the defendant to request a change of venue.

c. *Change of Venire.* This involves bringing to the original venue a group of prospective jurors from another area. In what ways does this resemble the change of venue? What differences are critical?

d. *Voir Dire.* How might a penetrating voir dire help meet the concerns about an impartial jury? How might the defense attorney attempt to learn whether a prospective juror has heard about an alleged confession or the seizure of some vital evidence that will not be admitted in evidence, or about the defendant's prior activities?

e. *Waiver of Jury.* Although the judge cannot force this option upon the defendant, some defendants have felt the need to do this to avoid what they perceived to be the impossibility of getting an impartial jury. Of course, this option destroys the defendant's Sixth Amendment right to trial by jury.

f. *New Trial or Reversal.* As the Court in *Sheppard* noted, these are palliatives at best.

g. *Sequestration.* This technique is traditionally thought to become available only after the actual jurors are selected. Yet, in the Nebraska Press case that follows, the opinions discuss the use of sequestration in a case involving concerns about pretrial publicity. As you read that case consider the role of sequestration in meeting the Court's concerns.

6. Problems during the trial. The devices discussed in the preceding note might be of limited use in achieving the goal of selecting impartial jurors. When an impartial jury is selected, some problems may be encountered in keeping it impartial during the trial. The major concern here is the possible impact on the jurors of learning alleged facts about the case from the media or from friends rather than from the evidence. Two criminal procedure devices address this concern.

a. *Admonishing the Jury.* Under this procedure, the trial judge admonishes the jury after selection and, possibly, at the end of each trial session, to avoid discussing the case with anyone, including family and friends, and also to avoid reading about it in the press or exposing themselves to discussions of the case on radio or television. Sometimes they are instructed to avoid reading the paper or listening to radio or television for the course of the trial.

As in the Marshall case, supra, possible problems or violations may be brought to the judge's attention. The question of mistrial may depend on the nature of the material encountered and its likely impact on the jurors exposed to it.

b. *Sequestration.* If the judge or one of the parties expects massive media coverage of the trial with the danger of revelation of inadmissible evidence or perhaps fear of one-sided coverage, the issue of sequestration will arise. Keeping the jurors from all contact with the outside world for the entire length of the trial (as well as the for deliberations, when virtually all juries are sequestered), will surely skew the jury. It will most likely eliminate parents with very young children, and older people who need regular medical attention, and tend to produce jurors who have no family responsibilities. The longer the expected length of the trial, the more likely the skewing.

The actual impact of sequestration is not so clear. Since it is a great inconvenience neither party wants the jury to know that it has sought it. This need not be a problem if the trial judge can order it without indicating who has sought it—assuming the situation is not clear to the jury. But the more pressing question is what consequence flows from getting a skewed group of jurors. Apparently, most defense attorneys think it harmful. But one jury consultant who has aided defenses says that "generally the most authoritarian and punitive potential jurors" find ways to avoid being on sequestered panels and that "open, civic-minded people" tend to accept such service. See Friendly, Judge Sequesters Jurors for Retrial of von Bulow, N.Y.Times, Apr. 17, 1985, at 11.

The states vary greatly in their attitudes toward sequestration. Some stress the inconvenience to the jury and the added expense to the state; others the need to use the device to avoid more serious limits on the press and public. It also turns out to be a serious problem if the need for the sequestration arises only after the trial has begun in the normal fashion and prospective jurors have not been asked about whether they can handle sequestration.

In KUTV, Inc. v. Wilkinson, 686 P.2d 456, 10 Med.L.Rptr. 1749, 2276 (Utah 1984), Gatto was on trial for felony theft. After the first day, the jury was given the "usual admonitions . . . to insulate themselves from media reports concerning the trial." That evening a local television station reported that Gatto was tied closely to the Mafia. The next day a newspaper reported the connection. Four jurors had been approached by others during this period, including one who received a telephone call from a parent in Montana asking if she was "on the case with the two Mafia guys."

The next day, after notice and argument, the trial judge concluded that jury waiver was too great a price for Gatto to pay; that sequestration was not a reasonable alternative because the trial was expected to be long (four weeks) and because of the attendant high costs and hardship to the jurors, and also because sequestration at that stage might cause the jury "to question the procedure and thus prejudice them against Gatto;" and that strong and frequent admonitions might also result in prejudice against Gatto.

Given the inadequacy of these alternatives, the trial judge "permanently restrained and enjoined [the press] from broadcasting, publishing . . . any information concerning [Gatto's] direct connection and/or association with the Mafia and/or organized crime, until such time as the jurors have retired to deliberate in this case."

On appeal from the order, the court affirmed, 4–1, and expanded the order to include "indirect" as well as direct connections. The trial judge had followed proper procedural steps, including seeking voluntary compliance from the media. The order met the three-part test outlined in *Nebraska Press Association* (infra) in that (1) the prejudicial publicity was not only likely, it had occurred and would continue to occur; (2) other measures short of an injunction were not appropriate; and (3) the injunction would achieve the desired result.

The court then added a fourth criterion to meet the state constitutional protection for speech and press: "the degree of public interest in immediate access to the information that the proposed order would deny them for the duration of the trial." Here there was no public interest in immediate access to Gatto's alleged connections. The case did not, for example, involve a public official or charges of public misconduct or connections with organized crime. "In those types of cases legitimate public interest is at its highest peak and the right to know could well outweigh competing interests and justify the expense and risk of sequestering the jury."

The court concluded that "we emphasize that orders imposing any prior restraints on the media can rarely be justified." They must be accompanied by suitable written findings so that the media can seek immediate review.

An approach quite unlike Utah's was taken in Commonwealth v. Genovese, 337 Pa.Super. 485, 487 A.2d 364, 11 Med.L.Rptr. 1388 (1985), in which the trial judge denied a defense request for sequestration "because of the expense" it would entail. On appeal, the court asserted that "if it had been necessary to protect the jurors . . ., the most effective way to insulate them during the trial would have been sequestration. Neither the temporary inconvenience to the jurors and their families nor the cost of sequestration was an adequate reason to impose a prior restraint" on the press.

The Georgia Supreme Court has mandated the use of sequestration. In R.W. Page Corp. v. Lumpkin, 249 Ga. 576, 292 S.E.2d 815, 8 Med.L. Rptr. 1824 (1982), the defendant in a murder case, without prior notice or offering justification, moved to clear the court at trial. The trial court "summarily granted the motion." On appeal this was reversed: "While federal trial court judges are admonished to *consider* jury sequestration (or some other remedy) as an alternative to the closing of hearings to the public and the press, we now hold that a Georgia trial court judge shall *use* jury sequestration (or some other means) to exclude prejudicial matters from the jury's knowledge and consideration" unless the judge can fully articulate why they would not suffice.

As these excerpts suggest, courts' attitudes toward sequestration differ in the abstract. But another relevant factor is the perceived alternative. If the choice is between sequestration and ordering lawyers or others not to speak, or closing a judicial proceeding, the courts may reject sequestration. We will consider the possibility of limiting the ability of the press to acquire information in Chapter XII. If the choice is between sequestration and "prior restraint," courts may draw on the traditions discussed in Chapter I. We turn to that question now.

B. PREVENTING PUBLICATION

NEBRASKA PRESS ASSOCIATION v. STUART

Supreme Court of the United States, 1976.
427 U.S. 539, 96 S.Ct. 2791, 49 L.Ed.2d 683.
Noted, 90 Harv.L.Rev. 159, 25 Kan.L.Rev. 258, 29 Stan.L.Rev. 243, 87 Yale L.J. 342.

MR. CHIEF JUSTICE BURGER delivered the opinion of the Court.

The respondent State District Judge entered an order restraining the petitioners from publishing or broadcasting accounts of confessions or admissions made by the accused or facts "strongly implicative" of the accused in a widely reported murder of six persons. We granted certiorari to decide whether the entry of such an order on the showing made before the state court violated the constitutional guarantee of freedom of the press.

I.

On the evening of October 18, 1975, local police found the six members of the Henry Kellie family murdered in their home in Sutherland, Neb., a town of about 850 people. Police released the description of a suspect, Erwin Charles Simants, to the reporters who had hastened to the scene of the crime. Simants was arrested and arraigned in Lincoln County Court the following morning, ending a tense night for this small rural community.

The crime immediately attracted widespread news coverage, by local, regional, and national newspapers, radio and television stations. Three days after the crime, the County Attorney and Simants' attorney joined in asking the County Court to enter a restrictive order relating to "matters that may or may not be publicly reported or disclosed to the public," because of the "mass coverage by news media" and the "reasonable likelihood of prejudicial news which would make difficult, if not impossible, the impaneling of an impartial jury and tend to prevent a fair trial." The County Court heard oral argument but took no evidence; no attorney for members of the press appeared at this stage. The County Court granted the prosecutor's motion for a restrictive order and entered it the next day, October 22. The order prohibited everyone in attendance from "releas[ing] or authoriz[ing] for public dissemination in any form or manner whatsoever any testimony given or evidence adduced"; the order also required members of the press to observe the Nebraska Bar-Press Guidelines.[1]

1. The Nebraska Guidelines are voluntary standards adopted by members of the state bar and news media to deal with the reporting of crimes and criminal trials. They outline the matters of fact that may appropriately be reported, and also list what items are not generally appropriate for reporting, including: confessions, opin-

Simants' preliminary hearing was held the same day, open to the public but subject to the order. The County Court bound over the defendant for trial to the State District Court. The charges, as amended to reflect the autopsy findings, were that Simants had committed the murders in the course of a sexual assault.

Petitioners—several press and broadcast associations, publishers, and individual reporters—moved on October 23 for leave to intervene in the District Court, asking that the restrictive order imposed by the County Court be vacated. The District Court conducted a hearing, at which the County Judge testified and newspaper articles about the Simants case were admitted in evidence. The District Judge granted petitioners' motion to intervene and, on October 27, entered his own restrictive order. The judge found "because of the nature of the crimes charged in the complaint that there is a clear and present danger that pre-trial publicity could impinge upon the defendant's right to a fair trial." The order applied only until the jury was impaneled and specifically prohibited petitioners from reporting five subjects: (1) the existence or contents of a confession Simants had made to law enforcement officers, which had been introduced in open court at arraignment; (2) the fact or nature of statements Simants had made to other persons; (3) the contents of a note he had written the night of the crime; (4) certain aspects of the medical testimony at the preliminary hearing; (5) the identity of the victims of the alleged sexual assault and the nature of the assault. It also prohibited reporting the exact nature of the restrictive order itself. Like the County Court's order, this order incorporated the Nebraska Bar-Press Guidelines. Finally, the order set out a plan for attendance, seating and courthouse traffic control during the trial.

Four days later, on October 31, petitioners asked the District Court to stay its order. At the same time, they applied to the Nebraska Supreme Court for a writ of mandamus, a stay, and an expedited appeal from the order. The State of Nebraska and the defendant Simants intervened in these actions. The Nebraska Supreme Court heard oral argument on November 25, and issued its *per curiam* opinion December 2. [ ][2]

ions on guilt or innocence, statements that would influence the outcome of a trial, the results of tests or examinations, comments on the credibility of witnesses, and evidence presented in the jury's absence. The publication of an accused's criminal record should, under the Guidelines, be "considered very carefully." The Guidelines also set out standards for taking and publishing photographs, and set up a joint bar-press committee to foster cooperation in resolving particular problems that emerge.

2. In the interim, petitioners applied to Mr. Justice Blackmun as Circuit Justice for a stay of the State District Court's order. He postponed ruling on the application out of deference to the Nebraska Supreme Court, 423 U.S. 1319 (Nov. 13, 1975) (Blackmun, J., in Chambers); when he concluded that the delay before that court had "exceed[ed] tolerable limits," he entered an order. 423 U.S. 1327, 1329 (Nov. 20, 1975) (Blackmun, J., in Chambers). We need not set out in detail Mr. Justice Blackmun's careful decision on this difficult issue. In essence he stayed the order insofar as it incorporated the admonitory Bar-Press Guidelines and prohibited reporting of some other matters. But he declined "at least on application for a stay and at this distance, [to] impose a prohibition upon the Nebraska courts from placing any restric-

The Nebraska Supreme Court balanced the "heavy presumption against . . . constitutional validity" that an order restraining publications bears, [New York Times v. United States], against the importance of the defendant's right to trial by an impartial jury. Both society and the individual defendant, the court held, had a vital interest in assuring that Simants be tried by an impartial jury. Because of the publicity surrounding the crime, the court determined that this right was in jeopardy. The court noted that Nebraska statutes required the District Court to try Simants within six months of his arrest, and that a change of venue could move the trial only to adjoining counties, which had been subject to essentially the same publicity as Lincoln County. The Nebraska Supreme Court held, "Unless the absolutist position of the relators was constitutionally correct, it would appear that the District Court acted properly." [ ]

The Nebraska Supreme Court rejected that "absolutist position," but modified the District Court's order to accommodate the defendant's right to a fair trial and the petitioners' interest in reporting pretrial events. The order as modified prohibited reporting of only three matters: (a) the existence and nature of any confessions or admissions made by the defendant to law enforcement officers, (b) any confessions or admissions made to any third parties, except members of the press, and (c) other facts "strongly implicative" of the accused. The Nebraska Supreme Court did not rely on the Nebraska Bar-Press Guidelines. After construing Nebraska law to permit closure in certain circumstances, the court remanded the case to the District Judge for reconsideration of the issue whether pretrial hearings should be closed to the press and public.

We granted certiorari to address the important issues raised by the District Court order as modified by the Nebraska Supreme Court, but we denied the motion to expedite review or to stay entirely the order of the State District Court pending Simants' trial. [ ] We are informed by the parties that since we granted certiorari, Simants has been convicted of murder and sentenced to death. His appeal is pending in the Nebraska Supreme Court.

II.

[The Court concluded that the controversy was not moot because the dispute was "capable of repetition".]

tions at all upon what the media may report prior to trial." Id., at 1332. He therefore let stand that portion of the District Court's order that prohibited reporting the existence or nature of a confession, and declined to prohibit that court from restraining publication of facts that were so "highly prejudicial" to the accused or "strongly implicative" of him that they would "irreparably impair the ability of those exposed to them to reach an independent and impartial judgment as to guilt." Id., at 1333. Subsequently, petitioners applied for a more extensive stay; this was denied by the full Court. 423 U.S. 1027 (1975).

III.

The problems presented by this case are almost as old as the Republic. Neither in the Constitution nor in contemporaneous writings do we find that the conflict between these two important rights was anticipated, yet it is inconceivable that the authors of the Constitution were unaware of the potential conflicts between the right to an unbiased jury and the guarantee of freedom of the press. . . .

The trial of Aaron Burr in 1807 presented Chief Justice Marshall, presiding as a trial judge, with acute problems in selecting an unbiased jury. Few people in the area of Virginia from which jurors were drawn had not formed some opinions concerning Mr. Burr or the case, from newspaper accounts and heightened discussion both private and public. The Chief Justice conducted a searching *voir dire* of the two panels eventually called, and rendered a substantial opinion on the purposes of *voir dire* and the standards to be applied. [ ]. Burr was acquitted, so there was no occasion for appellate review to examine the problem of prejudicial pretrial publicity. Chief Justice Marshall's careful *voir dire* inquiry into the matter of possible bias makes clear that the problem is not a new one.

The speed of communication and the pervasiveness of the modern news media have exacerbated these problems, however, as numerous appeals demonstrate. The trial of Bruno Hauptmann in a small New Jersey community, for the abduction and murder of the Charles Lindberghs' infant child, probably was the most widely covered trial up to that time, and the nature of the coverage produced widespread public reaction. Criticism was directed at the "carnival" atmosphere that pervaded the community and the courtroom itself. Responsible leaders of press and the legal profession—including other judges—pointed out that much of this sorry performance could have been controlled by a vigilant trial judge and by other public officers subject to the control of the court. [ ].

The excesses of press and radio and lack of responsibility of those in authority in the Hauptmann case and others of that era led to efforts to develop voluntary guidelines for courts, lawyers, press and broadcasters. . . .

In practice, of course, even the most ideal guidelines are subjected to powerful strains when a case such as Simants' arises, with reporters from many parts of the country on the scene. Reporters from distant places are unlikely to consider themselves bound by local standards. They report to editors outside the area covered by the guidelines, and their editors are likely to be guided only by their own standards. To contemplate how a state court can control acts of a newspaper or broadcaster outside its jurisdiction, even though the newspapers and broadcasts reach the very community from which jurors are to be selected, suggests something of the practical difficulties of managing such guidelines.

The problems presented in this case have a substantial history outside the reported decisions of courts, in the efforts of many responsible people to accommodate the competing interests. We cannot resolve all of them, for it is not the function of this Court to write a code. We look instead to this particular case and the legal context in which it arises.

IV.

[The Court reviewed its cases touching this problem in which it upset convictions: Irvin v. Dowd, Rideau v. Louisiana, Estes v. Texas, and Sheppard v. Maxwell, quoting the passage from *Sheppard* requiring the trial judge to take "strong measures" to protect the defendant.]

Cases such as these are relatively rare, and we have held in other cases that trials have been fair in spite of widespread publicity. In Stroble v. California, 343 U.S. 181 (1951), for example, the Court affirmed a conviction and death sentence challenged on the ground that pretrial news accounts, including the prosecutor's release of the defendant's recorded confession, were allegedly so inflammatory as to amount to a denial of due process. The Court disapproved of the prosecutor's conduct, but noted that the publicity had receded some six weeks before trial, that the defendant had not moved for a change of venue, and that the confession had been found voluntary and admitted in evidence at trial. The Court also noted the thorough examination of jurors on *voir dire* and the careful review of the facts by the state courts, and held that petitioner had failed to demonstrate a denial of due process. See also Murphy v. Florida, [ ]; Beck v. Washington, 369 U.S. 541 (1962).

Taken together, these cases demonstrate that pretrial publicity—even pervasive, adverse publicity—does not inevitably lead to an unfair trial. The capacity of the jury eventually impaneled to decide the case fairly is influenced by the tone and extent of the publicity, which is in part and often in large part, shaped by what attorneys, police, and other officials do to precipitate news coverage. The trial judge has a major responsibility. What the judge says about a case, in or out of the courtroom, is likely to appear in newspapers and broadcasts. More important, the measures a judge takes or fails to take to mitigate the effects of pretrial publicity—the measures described in *Sheppard* —may well determine whether the defendant receives a trial consistent with the requirements of due process. That this responsibility has not always been properly discharged is apparent from the decisions just reviewed.

The costs of failure to afford a fair trial are high. In the most extreme cases, like *Sheppard* and *Estes,* the risk of injustice was avoided when the convictions were reversed. But a reversal means that justice has been delayed for both the defendant and the State; in some cases, because of lapse of time retrial is impossible or further prosecution is gravely handicapped. Moreover, in borderline cases in which the conviction is not reversed, there is some possibility of an injustice unredressed. The "strong measures" outlined in Sheppard v. Maxwell are means by which a trial judge can try to avoid exacting these costs from society or from the accused.

The state trial judge in the case before us acted responsibly, out of a legitimate concern, in an effort to protect the defendant's right to a fair trial.[4] What we must decide is not simply whether the Nebraska courts erred in seeing the possibility of real danger to the defendant's rights, but whether in the circumstances of this case the means employed were foreclosed by another provision of the Constitution.

V.

[The Court here reviewed its cases considering the imposition of a prior restraint against publishing certain material, primarily Near v. Minnesota and New York Times Co. v. United States. None of these cases dealt with problems of prejudicial publicity.]

The thread running through all these cases is that prior restraints on speech and publication are the most serious and the least tolerable infringement on First Amendment rights. A criminal penalty or a judgment in a defamation case is subject to the whole panoply of protections afforded by deferring the impact of the judgment until all avenues of appellate review have been exhausted. Only after judgment has become final, correct or otherwise, does the law's sanction become fully operative.

A prior restraint, by contrast and by definition, has an immediate and irreversible sanction. If it can be said that a threat of criminal or civil sanctions after publication "chills" speech, prior restraint "freezes" it at least for the time.

The damage can be particularly great when the prior restraint falls upon the communication of news and commentary on current events. Truthful reports of public judicial proceedings have been afforded special protection against subsequent punishment. See Cox Broadcasting Corp. v. Cohn, [ ]; see also, Craig v. Harney, [ ]. For the same reasons the protection against prior restraint should have particular force as applied to reporting of criminal proceedings, whether the crime in question is a single isolated act or a pattern of criminal conduct. . . . The extraordinary protections afforded by the First Amendment carry with them something in the nature of a fiduciary duty to exercise the protected rights responsibly—a duty widely acknowledged but not always observed by editors and publishers. It is not asking too much to suggest that those who exercise First Amendment rights in newspapers or broadcasting enterprises direct some effort to protect the rights of an accused to a fair trial by unbiased jurors.

4. The record also reveals that counsel for both sides acted responsibly in this case, and there is no suggestion that either sought to use pretrial news coverage for partisan advantage. . . .

Of course, the order at issue—like the order requested in *New York Times*—does not prohibit but only postpones publication. Some news can be delayed and most commentary can even more readily be delayed without serious injury, and there often is a self-imposed delay when responsible editors call for verification of information. But such delays are normally slight and they are self-imposed. Delays imposed by governmental authority are a different matter. . . . As a practical matter, moreover, the element of time is not unimportant if press coverage is to fulfill its traditional function of bringing news to the public promptly.

The authors of the Bill of Rights did not undertake to assign priorities as between First Amendment and Sixth Amendment rights, ranking one as superior to the other. In this case, the petitioners would have us declare the right of an accused subordinate to their right to publish in all circumstances. But if the authors of these guarantees, fully aware of the potential conflicts between them, were unwilling or unable to resolve the issue by assigning to one priority over the other, it is not for us to rewrite the Constitution by undertaking what they declined. It is unnecessary, after nearly two centuries, to establish a priority applicable in all circumstances. Yet it is nonetheless clear that the barriers to prior restraint remain high unless we are to abandon what the Court has said for nearly a quarter of our national existence and implied throughout all of it. . . .

. . .

VI.

We turn now to the record in this case to determine whether, as Learned Hand put it, "the gravity of the 'evil,' discounted by its improbability, justifies such invasion of free speech as is necessary to avoid the danger." Dennis v. United States, 183 F.2d 201, 212 (1950), aff'd, 341 U.S. 494 (1951); see also L. Hand, The Bill of Rights 58–61 (1958). To do so, we must examine the evidence before the trial judge when the order was entered to determine (a) the nature and extent of pretrial news coverage; (b) whether other measures would be likely to mitigate the effects of unrestrained pretrial publicity; (c) how effectively a restraining order would operate to prevent the threatened danger. The precise terms of the restraining order are also important. We must then consider whether the record supports the entry of a prior restraint on publication, one of the most extraordinary remedies known to our jurisprudence.

A.

In assessing the probable extent of publicity, the trial judge had before him newspapers demonstrating that the crime had already drawn intensive news coverage, and the testimony of the County Judge, who had entered the initial restraining order based on the local and national attention the case had attracted. The District Judge was required to assess the probable publicity that would be given these shocking crimes prior to the time a jury was selected and sequestered. He then had to examine the probable nature of the publicity and determine how it would affect prospective jurors.

Our review of the pretrial record persuades us that the trial judge was justified in concluding that there would be intense and pervasive pretrial publicity concerning this case. He could also reasonably conclude, based on common human experience, that publicity might impair the defendant's right to a fair trial. He did not purport to say more, for he found only "a clear and present danger that pretrial publicity *could* impinge upon the defendant's right to a fair trial." (Emphasis added.) His conclusion as to the impact of such publicity on prospective jurors was of necessity speculative, dealing as he was with factors unknown and unknowable.

B.

We find little in the record that goes to another aspect of our task, determining whether measures short of an order restraining all publication would have insured the defendant a fair trial. Although the entry of the order might be read as a judicial determination that other measures would not suffice, the trial court made no express findings to that effect; the Nebraska Supreme Court referred to the issue only by implication. [ ]

Most of the alternatives to prior restraint of publication in these circumstances were discussed with obvious approval in Sheppard v. Maxwell, [ ]: (a) change of trial venue to a place less exposed to the intense publicity that seemed imminent in Lincoln County; [7] (b) postponement of the trial to allow public attention to subside; (c) use of searching questioning of prospective jurors, as Chief Justice Marshall did in the *Burr* case, to screen out those with fixed opinions as to guilt or innocence; (d) the use of emphatic and clear instructions on the sworn duty of each juror to decide the issues only on evidence presented in open court. Sequestration of jurors is, of course, always available. Although that measure insulates jurors only after they are sworn, it also enhances the likelihood of dissipating the impact of pretrial publicity and emphasizes the elements of the jurors' oaths.

This Court has outlined other measures short of prior restraints on publication tending to blunt the impact of pretrial publicity. See Sheppard v. Maxwell, [ ]. Professional studies have filled out these suggestions, recommending that trial courts in appropriate cases limit what the contending lawyers, the police, and witnesses may say to

7. The respondent and intervenors argue here that a change of venue would not have helped, since Nebraska law permits a change only to adjacent counties, which had been as exposed to pretrial publicity in this case as Lincoln County. We have held that state laws restricting venue must on occasion yield to the constitutional requirement that the State afford a fair trial. Groppi v. Wisconsin, 400 U.S. 505 (1971). We note also that the combined population of Lincoln County and the adjacent counties is over 80,000, providing a substantial pool of prospective jurors.

anyone. See American Bar Association, Standards for Criminal Justice, Fair Trial and Free Press 2–15 (Approved Draft, 1968).[8]

We have noted earlier that pretrial publicity, even if pervasive and concentrated, cannot be regarded as leading automatically and in every kind of criminal case to an unfair trial. The decided cases "cannot be made to stand for the proposition that juror exposure to information about a state defendant's prior convictions or to news accounts of the crime with which he is charged alone presumptively deprives the defendant of due process." Murphy v. Florida, [ ]. Appellate evaluations as to the impact of publicity take into account what other measures were used to mitigate the adverse effects of publicity. The more difficult prospective or predictive assessment that a trial judge must make also calls for a judgment as to whether other precautionary steps will suffice.

We have therefore examined this record to determine the probable efficacy of the measures short of prior restraint on the press and speech. There is no finding that alternative measures would not have protected Simants' rights, and the Nebraska Supreme Court did no more than imply that such measures might not be adequate. Moreover, the record is lacking in evidence to support such a finding.

C.

We must also assess the probable efficacy of prior restraint on publication as a workable method of protecting Simants' right to a fair trial, and we cannot ignore the reality of the problems of managing and enforcing pretrial restraining orders. The territorial jurisdiction of the issuing court is limited by concepts of sovereignty [ ]. The need for *in personam* jurisdiction also presents an obstacle to a restraining order that applies to publication at-large as distinguished from restraining publication within a given jurisdiction. [ ]

The Nebraska Supreme Court narrowed the scope of the restrictive order, and its opinion reflects awareness of the tensions between the need to protect the accused as fully as possible and the need to restrict publication as little as possible. The dilemma posed underscores how difficult it is for trial judges to predict what information will in fact undermine the impartiality of jurors, and the difficulty of drafting an order that will effectively keep prejudicial information from prospective jurors. When a restrictive order is sought, a court can anticipate only part of what will develop that may injure the accused. But information

8. Closing of pretrial proceedings with the consent of the defendant when required is also recommended in guidelines that have emerged from various studies. At oral argument petitioners' counsel asserted that judicially imposed restraints on lawyers and others would be subject to challenge as interfering with press rights to news sources. [ ] We are not now confronted with such issues.

We note that in making its proposals, the American Bar Association recommended strongly against resort to direct restraints on the press to prohibit publication. ABA Standards, at 68–73. Other groups have reached similar conclusions. [ ]

not so obviously prejudicial may emerge, and what may properly be published in these "gray zone" circumstances may not violate the restrictive order and yet be prejudicial.

Finally, we note that the events disclosed by the record took place in a community of 850 people. It is reasonable to assume that, without any news accounts being printed or broadcast, rumors would travel swiftly by word of mouth. One can only speculate on the accuracy of such reports, given the generative propensities of rumors; they could well be more damaging than reasonably accurate news accounts. But plainly a whole community cannot be restrained from discussing a subject intimately affecting life within it.

Given these practical problems, it is far from clear that prior restraint on publication would have protected Simants' rights.

D.

Finally, another feature of this case leads us to conclude that the restrictive order entered here is not supportable. At the outset the County Court entered a very broad restrictive order, the terms of which are not before us; it then held a preliminary hearing open to the public and the press. There was testimony concerning at least two incriminating statements made by Simants to private persons; the statement—evidently a confession—that he gave to law enforcement officials was also introduced. The State District Court's later order was entered after this public hearing and, as modified by the Nebraska Supreme Court, enjoined reporting of (1) "[c]onfessions or admissions against interests made by the accused to law enforcement officials"; (2) "[c]onfessions or admissions against interest, oral or written, if any, made by the accused to third parties, excepting any statements, if any, made by the accused to representatives of the news media"; and (3) all "[o]ther information strongly implicative of the accused as the perpetrator of the slayings."

To the extent that this order prohibited the reporting of evidence adduced at the open preliminary hearing, it plainly violated settled principles: "there is nothing that proscribes the press from reporting events that transpire in the courtroom." Sheppard v. Maxwell, [ ]. See also *Cox Broadcasting Corp. v. Cohn,* supra; *Craig v. Harney,* supra. The County Court could not know that closure of the preliminary hearing was an alternative open to it until the Nebraska Supreme Court so construed state law; but once a public hearing had been held, what transpired there could not be subject to prior restraint.

The third prohibition of the order was defective in another respect as well. As part of a final order, entered after plenary review, this prohibition regarding "implicative" information is too vague and too broad to survive the scrutiny we have given to restraints on First Amendment rights. [ ] The third phase of the order entered falls outside permissible limits.

E.

The record demonstrates, as the Nebraska courts held, that there was indeed a risk that pretrial news accounts, true or false, would have some adverse impact on the attitudes of those who might be called as jurors. But on the record now before us it is not clear that further publicity, unchecked, would so distort the views of potential jurors that 12 could not be found who would, under proper instructions, fulfill their sworn duty to render a just verdict exclusively on the evidence presented in open court. We cannot say on this record that alternatives to a prior restraint on petitioners would not have sufficiently mitigated the adverse effects of pretrial publicity so as to make prior restraint unnecessary. Nor can we conclude that the restraining order actually entered would serve its intended purpose. Reasonable minds can have few doubts about the gravity of the evil pretrial publicity can work, but the probability that it would do so here was not demonstrated with the degree of certainty our cases on prior restraint require.

Of necessity our holding is confined to the record before us. But our conclusion is not simply a result of assessing the adequacy of the showing made in this case; it results in part from the problems inherent in meeting the heavy burden of demonstrating, in advance of trial, that without prior restraint a fair trial will be denied. The practical problems of managing and enforcing restrictive orders will always be present. In this sense, the record now before us is illustrative rather than exceptional. It is significant that when this Court has reversed a state conviction because of prejudicial publicity, it has carefully noted that some course of action short of prior restraint would have made a critical difference. [ ] However difficult it may be, we need not rule out the possibility of showing the kind of threat to fair trial rights that would possess the requisite degree of certainty to justify restraint. This Court has frequently denied that First Amendment rights are absolute and has consistently rejected the proposition that a prior restraint can never be employed. [ ]

Our analysis ends as it began, with a confrontation between prior restraint imposed to protect one vital constitutional guarantee and the explicit command of another that the freedom to speak and publish shall not be abridged. We reaffirm that the guarantees of freedom of expression are not an absolute prohibition under all circumstances, but the barriers to prior restraint remain high and the presumption against its use continues intact. We hold that, with respect to the order entered in this case prohibiting reporting or commentary on judicial proceedings held in public, the barriers have not been overcome; to the extent that this order restrained publication of such material, it is clearly invalid. To the extent that it prohibited publication based on information gained from other sources, we conclude that the heavy burden imposed as a condition to securing a prior restraint was not met and the judgment of the Nebraska Supreme Court is therefore

Reversed.

MR. JUSTICE BRENNAN, with whom MR. JUSTICE STEWART and MR. JUSTICE MARSHALL concur, concurring in the judgment.

. . . The right to a fair trial by a jury of one's peers is unquestionably one of the most precious and sacred safeguards enshrined in the Bill of Rights. I would hold, however, that resort to prior restraints on the freedom of the press is a constitutionally impermissible method for enforcing that right; judges have at their disposal a broad spectrum of devices for ensuring that fundamental fairness is accorded the accused without necessitating so drastic an incursion on the equally fundamental and salutary constitutional mandate that discussion of public affairs in a free society cannot depend on the preliminary grace of judicial censors.

[After a most extensive review of the facts, Justice Brennan turned to a consideration of the values protected by the Sixth and First Amendments.]

II.

A.

. . . So basic to our jurisprudence is the right to a fair trial that it has been called "the most fundamental of all freedoms." Estes v. Texas, [ ]. It is a right essential to the preservation and enjoyment of all other rights, providing a necessary means of safeguarding personal liberties against Government oppression. [ ]

The First Amendment to the United States Constitution, however, secures rights equally fundamental in our jurisprudence, and its ringing proclamation that "Congress shall make no law . . . abridging the freedom of speech or of the press . . ." has been both applied through the Fourteenth Amendment to invalidate restraints on freedom of the press imposed by the States, [ ]; and interpreted to interdict such restraints imposed by the courts [ ]. Indeed, it has been correctly perceived that a "responsible press has always been regarded as the handmaiden of effective judicial administration, especially in the criminal field. . . . The press does not simply publish information about trials but guards against the miscarriage of justice by subjecting the police, prosecutors, and judicial processes to extensive public scrutiny and criticism." Sheppard v. Maxwell, [ ]. See also, e.g., Cox Broadcasting Corp. v. Cohn, [ ]. Commentary and reporting on the criminal justice system is at the core of First Amendment values, for the operation and integrity of that system is of crucial import to citizens concerned with the administration of Government. Secrecy of judicial action can only breed ignorance and distrust of courts and suspicion concerning the competence and impartiality of judges; free and robust reporting, criticism, and debate can contribute to public understanding of the rule of law and to comprehension of the functioning of the entire criminal justice system, as well as improve the quality of that system by subjecting it to the cleansing effects of exposure and public accountability. [ ]

No one can seriously doubt, however, that unmediated prejudicial pretrial publicity may destroy the fairness of a criminal trial, see, e.g., *Sheppard v. Maxwell,* supra, and the past decade has witnessed substantial debate, colloquially known as the Free Press/Fair Trial controversy, concerning this interface of First and Sixth Amendment rights. In effect, we are now told by respondents that the two rights can no longer coexist when the press possesses and seeks to publish "confessions and admissions against interest" and other information "strongly implicative" of a criminal defendant as the perpetrator of a crime, and that one or the other right must therefore be subordinated. I disagree. Settled case law concerning the impropriety and constitutional invalidity of prior restraints on the press compels the conclusion that there can be no prohibition on the publication by the press of any information pertaining to pending judicial proceedings or the operation of the criminal justice system, no matter how shabby the means by which the information is obtained.[15] This does not imply, however, any subordination of Sixth Amendment rights, for an accused's right to a fair trial may be adequately assured through methods that do not infringe First Amendment values.

B.

. . . A commentator has cogently summarized many of the reasons for this deep-seated American hostility to prior restraints:

> "A system of prior restraints is in many ways more inhibiting than a system of subsequent punishment: It is likely to bring under government scrutiny a far wider range of expression; it shuts off communication before it takes place; suppression by a stroke of the pen is more likely to be applied than that suppression through criminal process; the procedures do not require attention to the safeguards of the criminal process; the system allows less opportunity for public appraisal and criticism; the dynamics of the system drive toward excesses, as the history of all censorship shows." T. Emerson, The System of Freedom of Expression 506 (1970).

Respondents correctly contend that "the [First Amendment] protection even as to prior restraint is not absolutely unlimited." Near v. Minnesota, [ ]. However, the exceptions to the rule have been confined to "exceptional cases." . . .

[Justice Brennan discussed these situations at length, particularly *Near* and *New York Times.*]

I would decline [an invitation to create a new category for the use of prior restraints]. In addition to the almost insuperable presumption

15. Of course, even if the press cannot be enjoined from reporting certain information, that does not necessarily immunize it from civil liability for libel or invasion of privacy or from criminal liability for transgressions of general criminal laws during the course of obtaining that information.

against the constitutionality of prior restraints even under a recognized exception, and however laudable the State's motivation for imposing restraints in this case, there are compelling reasons for not carving out a new exception to the rule against prior censorship of publication.

1.

Much of the information that the Nebraska courts enjoined petitioners from publishing was already in the public domain, having been revealed in open court proceedings or through public documents. Our prior cases have foreclosed any serious contention that further disclosure of such information can be suppressed before publication or even punished after publication. "A trial is a public event. What transpires in the court room is public property. . . . Those who see and hear what transpired can report it with impunity. There is no special perquisite of the judiciary which enables it, as distinguished from other institutions of democratic government, to suppress, edit, or censor events which transpire in proceedings before it." Craig v. Harney, [ ] . . . .

2.

The order of the Nebraska Supreme Court also applied, of course, to "confessions" and other information "strongly implicative" of the accused which was obtained from sources other than official records or open court proceedings. But for the reasons that follow—reasons equally applicable to information obtained by the press from official records of public court proceedings—I believe that the same rule against prior restraints governs *any* information pertaining to the criminal justice system, even if derived from nonpublic sources and regardless of the means employed by the press in its acquisition.

. . .

A judge importuned to issue a prior restraint in the pretrial context will be unable to predict the manner in which the potentially prejudicial information would be published, the frequency with which it would be repeated or the emphasis it would be given, the context in which or purpose for which it would be reported, the scope of the audience that would be exposed to the information,[22] or the impact, evaluated in terms of current standards for assessing juror impartiality, the information would have on that audience. These considerations would render speculative the prospective impact on a fair trial of reporting even an alleged confession or other information "strongly implicative" of the accused. Moreover, we can take judicial notice of the fact that given the prevalence of plea bargaining, few criminal

22. It is suggested that prior restraints are really only necessary in "small towns," since media saturation would be more likely and incriminating materials that are published would therefore probably come to the attention of all inhabitants. Of course, the smaller the community, the more likely such information would become available through rumors and gossip, whether or not the press is enjoined from publication. . . .

cases proceed to trial, and the judge would thus have to predict what the likelihood was that a jury would even have to be impaneled.[24] Indeed, even in cases that do proceed to trial, the material sought to be suppressed before trial will often be admissible and may be admitted in any event. And, more basically, there are adequate devices for screening from jury duty those individuals who have in fact been exposed to prejudicial pretrial publicity.

Initially, it is important to note that once the jury is impaneled, the techniques of sequestration of jurors and control over the courtroom and conduct of trial should prevent prejudicial publicity from infecting the fairness of judicial proceedings. Similarly, judges may stem much of the flow of prejudicial publicity at its source, before it is obtained by representatives of the press.[27] But even if the press nevertheless obtains potentially prejudicial information and decides to publish that information, the Sixth Amendment rights of the accused may still be adequately protected. In particular, the trial judge should employ the *voir dire* to probe fully into the effect of publicity. The judge should broadly explore such matters as the extent to which prospective jurors had read particular news accounts or whether they had heard about incriminating data such as an alleged confession or statements by purportedly reliable sources concerning the defendant's guilt. . . . Moreover, *voir dire* may indicate the need to grant a brief continuance[28] or to grant a change of venue,[29] techniques that can effectively mitigate any publicity at a particular time or in a particular locale. Finally, if the trial court fails or refuses to utilize these devices effectively, there are the "palliatives" of reversals on appeal and directions for a new trial. . . . Indeed, the traditional techniques approved in *Sheppard* for ensuring fair trials would have been adequate in every case in which we have found that a new trial was required due to lack of fundamental fairness to the accused.

24. Of course, judges accepting guilty pleas must guard against the danger that pretrial publicity has effectively coerced the defendant into pleading guilty.

27. A significant component of prejudicial pretrial publicity may be traced to public commentary on pending cases by court personnel, law enforcement officials, and the attorneys involved in the case. . . . As officers of the court, court personnel and attorneys have a fiduciary responsibility not to engage in public debate that will redound to the detriment of the accused or that will obstruct the fair administration of justice. It is very doubtful that the court would not have the power to control release of information by these individuals in appropriate cases, [ ], and to impose suitable limitations whose transgression could result in disciplinary proceedings. [ ] Similarly, in most cases courts would have ample power to control such actions by law enforcement personnel.

28. Excessive delay, of course, would be impermissible in light of the Sixth Amendment right to a speedy trial. [ ] However, even short continuances can be effective in attenuating the impact of publicity, especially as other news crowds past events off the front pages. And somewhat substantial delays designed to ensure fair proceedings need not transgress the speedy trial guarantee. See Groppi v. Wisconsin, 400 U.S. 505, 510 (1971); [ ].

29. In Rideau v. Louisiana, [ ], we held that it was a denial of due process to deny a request for a change of venue that was necessary to preserve the accused's Sixth Amendment rights. And state statutes may not restrict changes of venue if to do so would deny an accused a fair trial. Groppi v. Wisconsin, [ ].

For these reasons alone I would reject the contention that speculative deprivation of an accused's Sixth Amendment right to an impartial jury is comparable to the damage to the Nation or its people that *Near* and *New York Times* would have found sufficient to justify a prior restraint on reporting. Damage to that Sixth Amendment right could never be considered so direct, immediate and irreparable, and based on such proof rather than speculation, that prior restraints on the press could be justified on this basis.

C.

There are additional, practical reasons for not starting down the path urged by respondents.[32] . . .

. . .

. . . Recognition of any judicial authority to impose prior restraints on the basis of harm to the Sixth Amendment rights of particular defendants, especially since that harm must remain speculative, will thus inevitably interject judges at all levels into censorship roles that are simply inappropriate and impermissible under the First Amendment. Indeed, the potential for arbitrary and excessive judicial utilization of any such power would be exacerbated by the fact that judges and committing magistrates might in some cases be determining the propriety of publishing information that reflects on their competence, integrity or general performance on the bench.

There would be, in addition, almost intractable procedural difficulties associated with any attempt to impose prior restraints on publication of information relating to pending criminal proceedings, and the ramifications of these procedural difficulties would accentuate the burden on First Amendment rights. The incentives and dynamics of the system of prior restraints would inevitably lead to overemployment of the technique. In order to minimize pretrial publicity against his clients and pre-empt ineffective assistance of counsel claims, counsel for defendants might routinely seek such restrictive orders. Prosecutors would often acquiesce in such motions to avoid jeopardizing a conviction on appeal. And although judges could readily reject many such claims as frivolous, there would be a significant danger that judges would nevertheless be predisposed to grant the motions, both to ease their task of ensuring fair proceedings and to insulate their conduct in the criminal proceeding from reversal. We need not raise any spectre of floodgates of litigation or drain on judicial resources to note that the litigation with respect to these motions will substantially burden the media. . . .

32. I include these additional considerations, many of which apply generally to any system of prior restraints, only because of the fundamentality of the Sixth Amendment right invoked as the justification for imposition of the restraints in this case; the fact that there are such overwhelming reasons for precluding *any* prior restraints even to facilitate preservation of such a fundamental right reinforces the longstanding constitutional doctrine that there is effectively an absolute prohibition against prior restraints against publication of *any* material otherwise covered within the meaning of the free press guarantee of the First Amendment. [ ]

. . .

. . . And, as noted, given the significant financial disincentives, particularly on the smaller organs of the media, to challenge any restrictive orders once they are imposed by trial judges, there is the distinct possibility that many erroneous impositions would remain uncorrected.

III.

I unreservedly agree with Mr. Justice Black that "free speech and fair trials are two of the most cherished policies of our civilization, and it would be a trying task to choose between them." Bridges v. California, [ ]. But I would reject the notion that a choice is necessary, that there is an inherent conflict that cannot be resolved without essentially abrogating one right or the other. To hold that courts cannot impose any prior restraints on the reporting of or commentary upon information revealed in open court proceedings, disclosed in public documents, or divulged by other sources with respect to the criminal justice system is not, I must emphasize, to countenance the sacrifice of precious Sixth Amendment rights on the altar of the First Amendment. For although there may in some instances be tension between uninhibited and robust reporting by the press and fair trials for criminal defendants, judges possess adequate tools short of injunctions against reporting for relieving that tension. To be sure, these alternatives may require greater sensitivity and effort on the part of judges conducting criminal trials than would the stifling of publicity through the simple expedient of issuing a restrictive order on the press; but that sensitivity and effort is required in order to ensure the full enjoyment and proper accommodation of both First and Sixth Amendment rights.

There is, beyond peradventure, a clear and substantial damage to freedom of the press whenever even a temporary restraint is imposed on reporting of material concerning the operations of the criminal justice system, an institution of such pervasive influence in our constitutional scheme. And the necessary impact of reporting even confessions can never be so direct, immediate and irreparable that I would give credence to any notion that prior restraints may be imposed on that rationale. It may be that such incriminating material would be of such slight news value or so inflammatory in particular cases that responsible organs of the media, in an exercise of self-restraint, would choose not to publicize that material, and not make the judicial task of safeguarding precious rights of criminal defendants more difficult. Voluntary codes such as the Nebraska Bar-Press Guidelines are a commendable acknowledgement by the media that constitutional prerogatives bring enormous responsibilities, and I would encourage continuation of such voluntary cooperative efforts between the bar and the media. However, the press may be arrogant, tyrannical, abusive, and sensationalist, just as it may be incisive, probing, and informative. But at least in the context of prior restraints on publication, the decision of what, when, and how to publish is for editors, not judges. [ ] Every restrictive order imposed on the press in this case was accordingly an unconstitutional prior restraint on the freedom of the press, and I would therefore reverse the judgment of the Nebraska Supreme Court and remand for further proceedings not inconsistent with this opinion.

MR. JUSTICE WHITE, concurring.

Technically there is no need to go farther than the Court does to dispose of this case, and I join the Court's opinion. I should add, however, that for the reasons which the Court itself canvasses there is grave doubt in my mind whether orders with respect to the press such as were entered in this case would ever be justifiable. It may be the better part of discretion, however, not to announce such a rule in the first case in which the issue has been squarely presented here. Perhaps we should go no farther than absolutely necessary until the federal courts, and ourselves, have been exposed to a broader spectrum of cases presenting similar issues. If the recurring result, however, in case after case is to be similar to our judgment today, we should at some point announce a more general rule and avoid the interminable litigation that our failure to do so would necessarily entail.

MR. JUSTICE POWELL, concurring.

Although I join the opinion of the Court, in view of the importance of the case I write to emphasize the unique burden that rests upon the party, whether it be the state or a defendant, who undertakes to show the necessity for prior restraint on pretrial publicity.

In my judgment a prior restraint properly may issue only when it is shown to be necessary to prevent the dissemination of prejudicial publicity that otherwise poses a high likelihood of preventing, directly and irreparably, the impaneling of a jury meeting the Sixth Amendment requirement of impartiality. This requires a showing that (i) there is a clear threat to the fairness of trial, (ii) such a threat is posed by the actual publicity to be restrained, and (iii) no less restrictive alternatives are available. Notwithstanding such a showing, a restraint may not issue unless it also is shown that previous publicity or publicity from unrestrained sources will not render the restraint inefficacious. The threat to the fairness of the trial is to be evaluated in the context of Sixth Amendment law on impartiality, and any restraint must comply with the standards of specificity always required in the First Amendment context.

I believe these factors are sufficiently addressed in the Court's opinion to demonstrate beyond question that the prior restraint here was impermissible.

MR. JUSTICE STEVENS, concurring in the judgment.

For the reasons eloquently stated by Mr. Justice Brennan, I agree that the judiciary is capable of protecting the defendant's right to a fair trial without enjoining the press from publishing information in the public domain, and that it may not do so. Whether the same absolute protection would apply no matter how shabby or illegal the means by which the information is obtained, no matter how serious an intrusion on privacy might be involved, no matter how demonstrably false the information might be, no matter how prejudicial it might be to the interests of innocent persons, and no matter how perverse the motivation for publishing it, is a question I would not answer without further argument. [ ] I do, however, subscribe to most of what Mr. Justice Brennan says and, if ever required to face the issue squarely, may well accept his ultimate conclusion.

Notes and Questions

1. What is the essential difference between Chief Justice Burger's approach and Justice Brennan's approach? What is the effect of the other concurring opinions? Will any 12 impartial jurors do?

2. Note that Justice Stevens is concerned about cases in which the news is obtained by "shabby or illegal" means. How might that affect the outcome of this type of case?

3. What is the significance of the Nebraska statute that limits changes of venue to an adjoining county? What if a Nebraska judge concludes that a change of venue beyond the terms of the statute is necessary if the defendant is to have the requisite impartial jury?

4. The opinions discuss the role of sequestration, although this case raised only pretrial problems. How might sequestration aid in this type of case?

5. As the opinions note, the press, bench, and bar in Nebraska had collaborated on the promulgation of a set of voluntary guidelines. Such agreements exist in about half of the states, but this case is apparently the first in which a judge attempted to use the guidelines as mandatory provisions. Some members of the press have warned that such guidelines might be converted into mandatory statements, and have noted that guidelines have failed to deter judges from issuing restrictive orders.

In passing on the application for a stay, Justice Blackmun rejected this attempt out of hand, largely on the ground that the guidelines, since they were intended to be voluntary, used terms such as "consider carefully" that did not lend themselves to incorporation into a judicial order. (The Nebraska guidelines are reprinted as an appendix to Justice Brennan's opinion in the principal case.)

6. A priest in Michigan was charged with criminal sexual conduct. His attorney applied to the state judge for an order under Mich.Comp. Law Ann. § 750.520(k), which states in relevant part:

> Upon the request of the counsel or the victim or the actor in a prosecution under [specified sections dealing with sexual offenses] the magistrate before whom any person is brought on a charge of having committed [such an offense] shall order that the names of the victim and the actor and details of the alleged offense be

suppressed until such time as the actor is arraigned on the information, the charge is dismissed, or the case is otherwise concluded, whichever occurs first.

The judge immediately issued the order and met with press representatives to explain it and to warn that violators might be held in contempt of court. That night, despite the warning, WXYZ–TV broadcast an account of the incident, including the name of the priest. It then sued to prevent the judge from enforcing the suppression order and to have the statute declared unconstitutional.

The district court entered such an order and was affirmed on appeal. WXYZ, Inc. v. Hand, 658 F.2d 420, 7 Med.L.Rptr. 1817 (6th Cir.1981). The court agreed with the state that there were significant differences between the interests protected here and those in other cases in which prior restraints were involved, such as *Near* and New York Times Co. v. United States. Nonetheless, the interests were not sufficient to overcome the heavy presumption against the use of prior restraints.

Even if the statute had provided only criminal penalties for violation, *Smith v. Daily Mail*, p. 352, supra, indicated that "the highest form of state interest" must be shown to sustain its validity. Cases such as *Smith* and *Cox Broadcasting* seemed to dictate the result here.

Even if the court was wrong on that point, the statute was fatally defective because it required that the order issue upon application and did not even permit a hearing on the merits. "Deference to such legislative judgments is impossible when First Amendment interests are at stake. [citing *Landmark*]. . . . If a statute like this one is ever to pass constitutional muster, it must require the state court to go behind the legislative determination and examine for itself the likelihood that disclosure would result in an invasion of privacy, and whether the degree of likelihood is sufficient to justify a suppression order or criminal sanction."

Finally, the court said that even the desire to protect the parties would not justify the statute's ban on discussing the "details of the alleged offense."

7. In Goldblum v. National Broadcasting Co., 584 F.2d 904 (9th Cir. 1978), plaintiff, former executive officer of Equity Funding Corp., was serving a sentence for fraudulent activity in connection with the corporation's insolvency. NBC produced a "docudrama" based on the case, using the names of plaintiff and the corporation. Plaintiff, alleging that the program was inaccurate, sought an injunction against the showing of the program on the ground that it might inflame public opinion against him, jeopardize his release on parole, and adversely affect jury selection in any future criminal or civil cases arising out of the episode.

The district judge ordered NBC to produce the movie for review the day its presentation was scheduled. When NBC refused, the judge ordered counsel for the network imprisoned until the film was produced. A few hours later, a panel of the court of appeals granted a petition for mandamus and freed the attorney. In a subsequent opinion, the court said that it found "no authority which is even a remote justification" for issuing a prior restraint on the theory that parole officials might become inflamed. The order to produce and the imprisonment were invalid.

8. In Hays v. Marano, 114 App.Div.2d 387, 493 N.Y.S.2d 904 (1985), a reporter was granted access to a public court file in a case pending against a former well known athlete. In the file he found the grand jury testimony of a co-defendant, which had been inadvertently put in the file. Despite requests by the athlete's attorney and the judge, the reporter wrote an article about the testimony that appeared in the newspaper.

Among other fallout, defense counsel asked the judge to order the reporter not to write any more articles based upon his reading of the minutes. The judge complied but did not place other media persons under a similar order. Relying on *Cox, Smith,* and *Oklahoma Publishing,* in Chapter III, the appellate court held that since the testimony was in a public court file it was not obtained improperly. Nor was it disclosed unlawfully.

Even if the reporter knows more from the minutes than he has published, he should not be restrained "since it has not been demonstrated that other measures, such as a thorough voir dire, would not insure Pepitone a fair trial, [*Nebraska Press*]. In addition, since the 'gag' order was directed at [the reporter] alone, it would not have been an effective means to insure a fair trial because other members of the media were free to report on the proceedings based upon [the reporter's] research."

9. A similar episode occurred when a court-reporting firm, not realizing that a deposition had been sealed by the federal judge, released copies to three newspapers. The underlying case involved the widely-reported bankruptcy of J. David & Co. That evening, before publication was possible, the judge ordered the papers not to publish the names, locations, or account numbers of five foreign banks at which the bankrupt was reported to have accounts.

At a 30-minute hearing the next day, the bankruptcy trustee testified that he feared that revelation of the banks' names would lead investors to interfere with "delicate negotiations" that he was conducting. The judge withdrew his order at the end of the hearing on the ground that the trustee had not met the "extremely heavy burden" of justifying a prior restraint. Taylor, California Prior Restraint Sparks Furor, Nat'l L.J., April 23, 1984, at 3.

10. The assumption that the judicial branch has inherent power to issue orders against the press to preserve a defendant's right to a fair trial is considered and rejected in Note, Protective Orders Against the Press and the Inherent Powers of the Courts, 87 Yale L.J. 342 (1977).

The same point is made in Linde, Fair Trials and Press Freedom—Two Rights Against the State, 13 Willamette L.J. 211 (1977): "I find it striking that no one seems to ask what law authorized issuance of a gag order, before reaching the question of its constitutionality." Beyond that observation, Linde argued that *Sheppard* was "careful to avoid any suggestion that a court could take any action directed against publication of whatever information the media did obtain or whatever comments they might choose to publish." Nothing in *Sheppard* "said that the state could forbid a publication in order to assure itself of the ability to obtain a conviction. *Sheppard* was a decision protecting one constitutional right, under the sixth amendment, not infringing another one, under the first amendment."

He found no conflict between the two amendments. "The interests of individuals, for instance the interests of suspects and of newspaper reporters, can and often do conflict. But not their constitutional rights." The basic point was that the accused "has no constitutional right against the press. Sheppard's right . . . is to have the government refrain from acting unconstitutionally against him. His right is *not* to have the government act against the Cleveland press."

The existing view, Linde asserted, "transforms the defendant's fair trial claim against the state into a claim against the media. It lets the state turn two constitutional limitations on its powers into a classic example of 'let's you and him fight.' It asks defendants and reporters to trade off their rights between themselves or let a court do it for them. But this is not constitutional law."

What are the implications of accepting Linde's view?

11. In Columbia Broadcasting Systems, Inc. v. United States District Court, 729 F.2d 1174, 10 Med.L.Rptr. 1529 (9th Cir.1984), during the pretrial preparations for the trial of John DeLorean on drug charges, the trial judge issued an order restraining CBS from "disseminating and/or broadcasting any portion of any and all government surveillance tapes generated in the investigation and prosecution" of the case. CBS had obtained copies of tapes the government made during its investigation and arrest of DeLorean.

The order was issued on Saturday and vacated by a court of appeals panel on Sunday. In the opinion issued several months later, the court spoke of the need to "resolve the tension between two constitutional rights . . . ." The district court here had made the inquiry required by the Court in the Nebraska Press case and had found (1) that the case had generated "enormous, incessant and continually increasing publicity" and that the release of the tapes would have a "devastating effect"; (2) that there was no way to remove the taint from the minds of potential jurors; and (3) that the restraining order would be effective.

Subjecting that order to the de novo review required by *Nebraska Press,* the panel rejected the first two findings. Although it agreed that the publicity was enormous, it observed that "Widespread publicity, however, does not necessarily lead to an unfair trial." It was "not enough that publicity might prejudice one directly exposed to it. If it is to be restrained, the publicity must threaten to prejudice the entire community so that twelve unbiased jurors cannot be found." The district court here had failed to inquire into whether the publicity, beyond affecting viewers, also had the "capacity to inflame and prejudice the entire community."

Looking at the facts, the court concluded that the judge could not have answered the question affirmatively. The case was "neither lurid nor highly inflammatory. . . . It seems hardly a week passes in which there is not media coverage of a major narcotics arrest or trial. While Mr. DeLorean's prominence has certainly distinguished his case from the others . . . there is no evidence that his prominence will inflame public sentiment."

The final problem with the first finding was that in a large metropolitan district publicity is less likely to endanger the right to fair trial than it is in a small community. The "size and heterogeneity" of large cities "make it unlikely that even the most sensational case" will become a "*cause célèbre.*" Moreover, the "pool of potential jurors is so large that even in cases attracting extensive and inflammatory publicity, it is usually possible to find an adequate number of untainted jurors." The Central District of California was found to be the most populous district in the federal system, with nearly 12,000,000 people, and encompassed "one of the most heterogeneous metropolitan areas in the United States—Los Angeles."

Turning to the second finding, the court noted that the district judge had rejected the use of extensive voir dire because no matter how searching the questions, "certain matters are not detectable, especially those motives relative to bias and prejudice." This was found to be inconsistent with *Nebraska Press,* which treated voir dire as an important alternative. The district court also failed to consider the adequacy of "emphatic and clear instructions to the jury."

The court concluded that if a prior restraint is ever to be justified in a fair trial case, this is not the case.

Two judges concurred in the main opinion and also wrote separately. For them, a "judge's assignment to preside over a criminal trial carries with it no general commission to issue orders to persons not before the court whose conduct has not yet caused a disruption or impediment to the work of the court."

Finally, the concurrers adopted Justice Linde's view that there was no conflict between the two rights. "Both are limitations upon government, not upon citizens."

Part Three

LIMITS ON GATHERING

In Part II, covering Chapters II–IX, we considered the array of major government restrictions on the ability of the media to publish information it had acquired. In Part III, covering Chapters X–XII, we consider the legal barriers to gathering information. The information may be within the control of private sources or of government sources. The person or agency that controls the information may be either a willing source or an unwilling source. The unwilling sources' reasons for being unwilling will vary significantly—ranging from protecting the fair trial right of an accused, to protecting one's own privacy, to national security.

It might seem that at least one of the categories included in the previous paragraph should present no legal problems—the case of the willing private source. After all, if the reporter is seeking information and the private source is willing to provide that information, why might legal intervention occur? The answer is to be found in one of the most controversial areas of media law—the law of confidential sources. As we shall see, legal questions may arise in each of the four possible combinations suggested: the willing private source, the unwilling private source, the willing government source, and the unwilling government source. We will also see that each area may raise questions ranging from common law to statutory to constitutional issues.

We begin with the willing private source because that area has been simmering for some time and because it gave rise to the first Supreme Court decision affecting the gathering of information.

Chapter X

WILLING PRIVATE SOURCES

In this Chapter, we consider the power of the government to obtain two kinds of information from reporters and others in the media. The first is the identification of the source of the information that the reporter has obtained. The information in question has generally been published, which is what has brought it to the attention of government. The attribution in the article usually indicates that the report has been obtained from someone with firsthand knowledge of the facts and that the reporter does not have such knowledge. Why do reporters object to identifying sources who wished to remain confidential? Do any of these reasons extend to identifying sources who did not request or demand confidentiality?

The second kind of information that may be sought from a reporter is the content of unpublished information—material gathered by the reporter but not reported in the published story. This may include photographs or film footage shot but not used in the finished product. These materials are often called "outtakes" when visual material is involved, and "notes" when written information is being sought. In these cases no confidential source is being protected. Why might reporters object to providing this kind of information?

Both kinds of information may be sought by the government for use in pursuing a criminal investigation, for example, or sought by a party to a civil litigation who needs the information to help prove a case at trial. On occasion, the information is sought by the legislative branch or by a judge seeking to identify the source of a "leak."

The possible sanctions for refusal to comply raise another cluster of issues. The usual threat is civil contempt of court, in which the reporter is imprisoned until he or she complies with the order to disclose—a coercive imprisonment. Occasionally, the disobedience also produces a sentence for a definite term—criminal contempt of court. In the libel area, we shall see that the array of possible sanctions is still broader.

In the material that follows, keep in mind in each case which of the two kinds of information is being sought, for what reasons, and by whom.

A. REPORTER'S PRIVILEGE—INTRODUCTION

It has been generally accepted that persons thought to have relevant information may be subpoenaed to testify as witnesses at certain governmental proceedings. Nevertheless, some relationships have been held to give rise to "privileges" permitting a party to withhold information he has learned in a confidential relationship. The most venerable of these relationships have been those of physician and patient, lawyer and client, and priest and penitent. In each of these the recipient may be prevented by the source from testifying as to information learned in confidence in that professional capacity. A relatively new privilege has now emerged: that of the reporter not to divulge the source of certain information and, sometimes, the information itself. The assertion of this privilege at common law was generally rejected, but it has made headway as a statutory protection. Since the first reporter's privilege statute was enacted in Maryland in 1896, half the states have enacted such privileges. Journalists commonly refer to these statutes as "shield" laws.

In states without privilege statutes, reporters tried, with little success, to claim such a privilege under common law. Then in 1958 columnist Marie Torre tried a different approach. She had reported that a CBS executive had made certain disparaging remarks about Judy Garland. Garland sued CBS for defamation and sought by deposition to get Torre to identify the particular executive. Torre attacked the effort as a threat to freedom of the press, refused to answer the question, and asserted that the First Amendment protected her refusal. The court, though seeing some constitutional implications, held that even if the First Amendment were to provide some protection, the reporter must testify when the information sought goes to the "heart" of the plaintiff's claim. Garland v. Torre, 259 F.2d 545 (2d Cir.), certiorari denied 358 U.S. 910 (1958). Torre ultimately served ten days in jail for criminal contempt.

After *Garland,* reporters continued to assert First Amendment claims, still with little success. In the late 1960s the situation became more serious as the federal government began to serve subpoenas on reporters more frequently. The media asserted that this made previously willing sources of information unwilling because of fear that the courts would not protect the reporter or the source and reporters would violate confidences when pressed by the government.

BRANZBURG v. HAYES

(Together with In re Pappas and United States v. Caldwell)

Supreme Court of the United States, 1972.
408 U.S. 665, 92 S.Ct. 2646, 33 L.Ed.2d 626.
Noted, 8 Harv.Civ.Rights-Civ.Lib.L.Rev. 181, 86 Harv.L.Rev. 137, 51 N.C.L.Rev. 562, 82 Yale L.J. 709.

[This group of cases involved demands on three reporters by grand juries. In *Branzburg,* the reporter wrote a newspaper article about persons supposedly using a chemical process to change marijuana into hashish. He was called before a grand jury and directed to identify the two individuals. He refused and sought an order from the Kentucky Court of Appeals prohibiting the trial judge from insisting that he answer the questions. He based his claim on both the Kentucky privilege statute and the First Amendment. The Court of Appeals construed the statute to protect a reporter who refused to divulge the identity of an informant who supplied him with information but not to protect the silence of a reporter about his personal observations. Constitutional arguments were rejected.

In a second episode, Branzburg wrote a story after interviewing drug users and watching some of them smoking marijuana. He was again subpoenaed before a grand jury but before he was due to appear he again asked the Kentucky Court of Appeals to prevent the grand jury from forcing him to appear. Again the court denied his requested relief.

In *Pappas,* a Massachusetts television reporter recorded and photographed statements of local Black Panther Party officials during a period of racial turmoil. He was allowed to enter the Party's headquarters to cover an expected police raid in return for his promise to disclose nothing he observed within. He stayed three hours, no raid occurred, and he wrote no story. He was summoned before the county grand jury but refused to answer any questions about what had taken place while he was there. When he was recalled, he moved to quash the second summons. The motion was denied by the trial judge, who noted the absence of a statutory newsman's privilege in Massachusetts and denied the existence of a constitutional privilege. The Supreme Judicial Court of Massachusetts affirmed.

In the third case, Caldwell had been assigned by the New York Times to cover the Black Panther Party and other black militant groups. He was subpoenaed to appear before a federal grand jury and to bring with him notes and tape recordings of interviews given to him for publication by officers and spokesmen of the Black Panther Party concerning aims, purposes, and activities of the group. The court of appeals held that in the absence of a compelling showing of need by the prosecution, Caldwell need not even appear before the grand jury, much less answer its questions.]

Opinion of the Court by MR. JUSTICE WHITE, announced by the CHIEF JUSTICE [BURGER].

. . .

II.

. . . Although the newsmen in these cases do not claim an absolute privilege against official interrogation in all circumstances, they assert that the reporter should not be forced either to appear or to testify before a grand jury or at trial until and unless sufficient grounds are shown for believing that the reporter possesses information relevant to a crime the grand jury is investigating, that the information the reporter has is unavailable from other sources, and that the need for the information is sufficiently compelling to override the claimed invasion of First Amendment interests occasioned by the disclosure. Principally relied upon are prior cases emphasizing the importance of the First Amendment guarantees to individual development and to our system of representative government, decisions requiring that official action with adverse impact on First Amendment rights be justified by a public interest that is "compelling" or "paramount," and those precedents establishing the principle that justifiable governmental goals may not be achieved by unduly broad means having an unnecessary impact on protected rights of speech, press, or association. The heart of the claim is that the burden on news gathering resulting from compelling reporters to disclose confidential information outweighs any public interest in obtaining the information.

We do not question the significance of free speech, press, or assembly to the country's welfare. Nor is it suggested that news gathering does not qualify for First Amendment protection; without some protection for seeking out the news, freedom of the press could be eviscerated. But these cases involve no intrusions upon speech or assembly, no prior restraint or restriction on what the press may publish, and no express or implied command that the press publish what it prefers to withhold. No exaction or tax for the privilege of publishing, and no penalty, civil or criminal, related to the content of published material is at issue here. The use of confidential sources by the press is not forbidden or restricted; reporters remain free to seek news from any source by means within the law. No attempt is made to require the press to publish its sources of information or indiscriminately to disclose them on request.

The sole issue before us is the obligation of reporters to respond to grand jury subpoenas as other citizens do and to answer questions relevant to an investigation into the commission of crime. Citizens generally are not constitutionally immune from grand jury subpoenas; and neither the First Amendment nor any other constitutional provision protects the average citizen from disclosing to a grand jury information that he has received in confidence. . . .

It is clear that the First Amendment does not invalidate every incidental burdening of the press that may result from the enforcement of civil or criminal statutes of general applicability. Under prior cases, otherwise valid laws serving substantial public interests may be enforced against the press as against others, despite the possible burden that may be imposed. [The Court here referred to the taxation, labor, and antitrust cases.]

The prevailing view is that the press is not free to publish with impunity everything and anything it desires to publish. Although it may deter or regulate what is said or published, the press may not circulate knowing or reckless falsehoods damaging to private reputation without subjecting itself to liability for damages, including punitive damages, or even criminal prosecution. See New York Times Co. v. Sullivan, [ ]. A newspaper or a journalist may also be punished for contempt of court, in appropriate circumstances. Craig v. Harney, [ ].

It has generally been held that the First Amendment does not guarantee the press a constitutional right of special access to information not available to the public generally. Zemel v. Rusk, 381 U.S. 1, 16–17 (1965); [ ]. In *Zemel v. Rusk,* supra, for example, the Court sustained the Government's refusal to validate passports to Cuba even though that restriction "render[ed] less than wholly free the flow of information concerning that country." Id., at 16. The ban on travel was held constitutional, for "[t]he right to speak and publish does not carry with it the unrestrained right to gather information." Id., at 17.[22]

Despite the fact that news gathering may be hampered, the press is regularly excluded from grand jury proceedings, our own conferences, the meetings of other official bodies gathered in executive session, and the meetings of private organizations. Newsmen have no constitutional right of access to the scenes of crime or disaster when the general public is excluded, and they may be prohibited from attending or publishing information about trials if such restrictions are necessary to assure a defendant a fair trial before an impartial tribunal. In Sheppard v. Maxwell, [ ], for example, the Court reversed a state court conviction where the trial court failed to adopt "stricter rules governing the use of the courtroom by newsmen, as Sheppard's counsel requested," neglected to insulate witnesses from the press, and made no "effort to control the release of leads, information, and gossip to the press by police officers, witnesses, and the counsel for both sides." Id., at 358, 359. "[T]he trial court might well have proscribed extrajudicial statements by any lawyer, party, witness, or court official which divulged prejudicial matters." Id., at 361. See also Estes v. Texas, [ ].

It is thus not surprising that the great weight of authority is that newsmen are not exempt from the normal duty of appearing before a grand jury and answering questions relevant to a criminal investigation. At common law, courts consistently refused to recognize the existence of any privilege authorizing a newsman to refuse to reveal confidential information to a grand jury. . . .

The prevailing constitutional view of the newsman's privilege is very much rooted in the ancient role of the grand jury that has the dual function of determining if there is probable cause to believe that a crime has been committed and of protecting citizens against unfounded criminal prosecutions. Grand jury proceedings are constitutionally mandated for the institution of federal criminal prosecutions for capital or other serious crimes. . . . The Fifth Amendment provides that "[n]o person shall be held to answer for a capital, or otherwise infamous crime, unless on a presentment or indictment of a Grand Jury." . . .

22. "There are few restrictions on action which could not be clothed by ingenious argument in the garb of decreased data flow. For example, the prohibition of unauthorized entry into the White House diminishes the citizen's opportunities to gather information he might find relevant to his opinion of the way the country is being run, but that does not make entry into the White House a First Amendment right." 381 U.S., at 16–17.

Although state systems of criminal procedure differ greatly among themselves, the grand jury is similarly guaranteed by many state constitutions and plays an important role in fair and effective law enforcement in the overwhelming majority of the States. Because its task is to inquire into the existence of possible criminal conduct and to return only well-founded indictments, its investigative powers are necessarily broad. . . .

A number of States have provided newsmen a statutory privilege of varying breadth, but the majority have not done so, and none has been provided by federal statute. Until now the only testimonial privilege for unofficial witnesses that is rooted in the Federal Constitution is the Fifth Amendment privilege against compelled self-incrimination. We are asked to create another by interpreting the First Amendment to grant newsmen a testimonial privilege that other citizens do not enjoy. This we decline to do.[29] Fair and effective law enforcement aimed at providing security for the person and property of the individual is a fundamental function of government, and the grand jury plays an important, constitutionally mandated role in this process. On the records now before us, we perceive no basis for holding that the public interest in law enforcement and in ensuring effective grand jury proceedings is insufficient to override the consequential, but uncertain, burden on news gathering that is said to result from insisting that reporters, like other citizens, respond to relevant questions put to them in the course of a valid grand jury investigation or criminal trial.

This conclusion itself involves no restraint on what newspapers may publish or on the type or quality of information reporters may seek to acquire, nor does it threaten the vast bulk of confidential relationships between reporters and their sources. Grand juries address themselves to the issues of whether crimes have been committed and who committed them. Only where news sources themselves are implicated in crime or possess information relevant to the grand jury's task need they or the reporter be concerned about grand jury subpoenas. Nothing before us indicates that a large number or percentage of *all* confidential news sources falls into either category and would in any way be deterred by our holding that the Constitution does not, as it never has, exempt the newsman from performing the citizen's normal duty of appearing and furnishing information relevant to the grand jury's task.

The preference for anonymity of those confidential informants involved in actual criminal conduct is presumably a product of their desire to escape criminal prosecution, and this preference, while understandable, is hardly deserving of constitutional protection. It would be frivolous to assert—and no one does in these cases—that the First Amendment, in the interest of securing news or otherwise, confers a license on either the reporter or his news sources to violate valid

29. The creation of new testimonial privileges has been met with disfavor by commentators since such privileges obstruct the search for truth. . . .

criminal laws. Although stealing documents or private wiretapping could provide newsworthy information, neither reporter nor source is immune from conviction for such conduct, whatever the impact on the flow of news. Neither is immune, on First Amendment grounds, from testifying against the other, before the grand jury or at a criminal trial. The Amendment does not reach so far as to override the interest of the public in ensuring that neither reporter nor source is invading the rights of other citizens through reprehensible conduct forbidden to all other persons. . . .

Thus, we cannot seriously entertain the notion that the First Amendment protects a newsman's agreement to conceal the criminal conduct of his source, or evidence thereof, on the theory that it is better to write about crime than to do something about it. . . .

There remain those situations where a source is not engaged in criminal conduct but has information suggesting illegal conduct by others. Newsmen frequently receive information from such sources pursuant to a tacit or express agreement to withhold the source's name and suppress any information that the source wishes not published. Such informants presumably desire anonymity in order to avoid being entangled as a witness in a criminal trial or grand jury investigation. They may fear that disclosure will threaten their job security or personal safety or that it will simply result in dishonor or embarrassment.

The argument that the flow of news will be diminished by compelling reporters to aid the grand jury in a criminal investigation is not irrational, nor are the records before us silent on the matter. But we remain unclear how often and to what extent informers are actually deterred from furnishing information when newsmen are forced to testify before a grand jury. The available data indicate that some newsmen rely a great deal on confidential sources and that some informants are particularly sensitive to the threat of exposure and may be silenced if it is held by this Court that, ordinarily, newsmen must testify pursuant to subpoenas, but the evidence fails to demonstrate that there would be a significant constriction of the flow of news to the public if this Court reaffirms the prior common-law and constitutional rule regarding the testimonial obligations of newsmen. Estimates of the inhibiting effect of such subpoenas on the willingness of informants to make disclosures to newsmen are widely divergent and to a great extent speculative.[32] It would be difficult to canvass the views of the

32. Cf. e.g., the results of a study conducted by Guest & Stanzler, which appears as an appendix to their article, [64 Nw.U.L. Rev. 18]. A number of editors of daily newspapers of varying circulation were asked the question, "Excluding one- or two-sentence gossip items, on the average how many stories based on information received in confidence are published in your paper each year? Very rough estimate." Answers varied significantly, e.g., "Virtually innumerable," Tucson Daily Citizen (41,969 daily circ.), "Too many to remember," Los Angeles Herald-Examiner (718,221 daily circ.), "Occasionally," Denver Post (252,084 daily circ.), "Rarely," Cleveland Plain Dealer (370,499 daily circ.), "Very rare, some politics," Oregon Journal (146,403 daily circ.). This study did not purport to measure the extent of deterrence of informants caused by subpoenas to the press.

informants themselves; surveys of reporters on this topic are chiefly opinions of predicted informant behavior and must be viewed in the light of the professional self-interest of the interviewees.[33] Reliance by the press on confidential informants does not mean that all such sources will in fact dry up because of the later possible appearance of the newsman before a grand jury. The reporter may never be called and if he objects to testifying, the prosecution may not insist. . . . Moreover, grand juries characteristically conduct secret proceedings, and law enforcement officers are themselves experienced in dealing with informers, and have their own methods for protecting them without interference with the effective administration of justice. . . .

Accepting the fact, however, that an undetermined number of informants not themselves implicated in crime will nevertheless, for whatever reason, refuse to talk to newsmen if they fear identification by a reporter in an official investigation, we cannot accept the argument that the public interest in possible future news about crime from undisclosed, unverified sources must take precedence over the public interest in pursuing and prosecuting those crimes reported to the press by informants and in thus deterring the commission of such crimes in the future.

We note first that the privilege claimed is that of the reporter, not the informant, and that if the authorities independently identify the informant, neither his own reluctance to testify nor the objection of the newsman would shield him from grand jury inquiry, whatever the impact on the flow of news or on his future usefulness as a secret source of information. More important, it is obvious that agreements to conceal information relevant to commission of crime have very little to recommend them from the standpoint of public policy. . . . It is apparent from this statute, as well as from our history and that of England, that concealment of crime and agreements to do so are not looked upon with favor. Such conduct deserves no encomium, and we decline now to afford it First Amendment protection by denigrating the duty of a citizen, whether reporter or informer, to respond to grand jury subpoena and answer relevant questions put to him.

Of course, the press has the right to abide by its agreement not to publish all the information it has, but the right to withhold news is not equivalent to a First Amendment exemption from the ordinary duty of all other citizens to furnish relevant information to a grand jury performing an important public function. Private restraints on the flow of information are not so favored by the First Amendment that they override all other public interests. As Mr. Justice Black declared

33. In his Press Subpoenas: An Empirical and Legal Analysis, Study Report of the Reporters' Committee on Freedom of the Press 6–12, Prof. Vince Blasi discusses these methodological problems. Prof. Blasi's survey found that slightly more than half of the 975 reporters questioned said that they relied on regular confidential sources for at least 10% of their stories. Id., at 21. Of this group of reporters, only 8% were able to say with some certainty that their professional functioning had been adversely affected by the threat of subpoena; another 11% were not certain whether or not they had been adversely affected. Id., at 53.

in another context, "[f]reedom of the press from governmental interference under the First Amendment does not sanction repression of that freedom by private interests." Associated Press v. United States, 326 U.S., at 20.

Neither are we now convinced that a virtually impenetrable constitutional shield, beyond legislative or judicial control, should be forged to protect a private system of informers operated by the press to report on criminal conduct, a system that would be unaccountable to the public, would pose a threat to the citizen's justifiable expectations of privacy, and would equally protect well-intentioned informants and those who pay or otherwise betray their trust to their employer or associates. The public through its elected and appointed law enforcement officers regularly utilizes informers, and in proper circumstances may assert a privilege against disclosing the identity of these informers. . . . Such informers enjoy no constitutional protection. Their testimony is available to the public when desired by grand juries or at criminal trials; their identity cannot be concealed from the defendant when it is critical to his case. [ ] Clearly, this system is not impervious to control by the judiciary and the decision whether to unmask an informer or to continue to profit by his anonymity is in public, not private, hands. We think that it should remain there and that public authorities should retain the options of either insisting on the informer's testimony relevant to the prosecution of crime or of seeking the benefit of further information that his exposure might prevent.

We are admonished that refusal to provide a First Amendment reporter's privilege will undermine the freedom of the press to collect and disseminate news. But this is not the lesson history teaches us. As noted previously, the common law recognized no such privilege, and the constitutional argument was not even asserted until 1958. From the beginning of our country the press has operated without constitutional protection for press informants and the press has flourished. The existing constitutional rules have not been a serious obstacle to either the development or retention of confidential news sources by the press.

It is said that currently press subpoenas have multiplied, that mutual distrust and tension between press and officialdom have increased, that reporting styles have changed, and that there is now more need for confidential sources, particularly where the press seeks news about minority cultural and political groups or dissident organizations suspicious of the law and public officials. These developments, even if true, are treacherous grounds for a far-reaching interpretation of the First Amendment fastening a nationwide rule on courts, grand juries, and prosecuting officials everywhere. . . .

. . .

The privilege claimed here is conditional, not absolute; given the suggested preliminary showings and compelling need, the reporter would be required to testify. Presumably, such a rule would reduce the instances in which reporters could be required to appear, but predicting in advance when and in what circumstances they could be compelled to do so would be difficult. Such a rule would also have implications for the issuance of compulsory process to reporters at civil and criminal trials and at legislative hearings. If newsmen's confidential sources are as sensitive as they are claimed to be, the prospect of being unmasked whenever a judge determines the situation justifies it is hardly a satisfactory solution to the problem. For them it would appear that only an absolute privilege would suffice.

We are unwilling to embark the judiciary on a long and difficult journey to such an uncertain destination. The administration of a constitutional newsman's privilege would present practical and conceptual difficulties of a high order. Sooner or later, it would be necessary to define those categories of newsmen who qualified for the privilege, a questionable procedure in light of the traditional doctrine that liberty of the press is the right of the lonely pamphleteer who uses carbon paper or a mimeograph just as much as of the large metropolitan publisher who utilizes the latest photocomposition methods. . . . The informative function asserted by representatives of the organized press in the present cases is also performed by lecturers, political pollsters, novelists, academic researchers, and dramatists. Almost any author may quite accurately assert that he is contributing to the flow of information to the public, that he relies on confidential sources of information, and that these sources will be silenced if he is forced to make disclosures before a grand jury.

In each instance where a reporter is subpoenaed to testify, the courts would also be embroiled in preliminary factual and legal determinations with respect to whether the proper predicate had been laid for the reporter's appearance: Is there probable cause to believe a crime has been committed? Is it likely that the reporter has useful information gained in confidence? Could the grand jury obtain the information elsewhere? Is the official interest sufficient to outweigh the claimed privilege?

Thus, in the end, by considering whether enforcement of a particular law served a "compelling" governmental interest, the courts would be inextricably involved in distinguishing between the value of enforcing different criminal laws. By requiring testimony from a reporter in investigations involving some crimes but not in others, they would be making a value judgment that a legislature had declined to make since in each case the criminal law involved would represent a considered legislative judgment, not constitutionally suspect, of what conduct is liable to criminal prosecution. The task of judges, like other officials outside the legislative branch, is not to make the law but to uphold it in accordance with their oaths.

At the federal level, Congress has freedom to determine whether a statutory newsman's privilege is necessary and desirable and to fashion standards and rules as narrow or broad as deemed necessary to deal with the evil discerned and, equally important, to refashion those rules as experience from time to time may dictate. There is also merit in leaving state legislatures free, within First Amendment limits, to fashion their own standards in light of the conditions and problems with respect to the relations between law enforcement officials and press in their own areas. It goes without saying, of course, that we are powerless to bar state courts from responding in their own way and construing their own constitutions so as to recognize a newsman's privilege, either qualified or absolute.

In addition, there is much force in the pragmatic view that the press has at its disposal powerful mechanisms of communication and is far from helpless to protect itself from harassment or substantial harm. . . .

Finally, as we have earlier indicated, news gathering is not without its First Amendment protections, and grand jury investigations if instituted or conducted other than in good faith, would pose wholly different issues for resolution under the First Amendment. Official harassment of the press undertaken not for purposes of law enforcement but to disrupt a reporter's relationship with his news sources would have no justification. Grand juries are subject to judicial control and subpoenas to motions to quash. We do not expect courts will forget that grand juries must operate within the limits of the First Amendment as well as the Fifth.

III.

We turn, therefore, to the disposition of the cases before us. From what we have said, it necessarily follows that the decision in *United States v. Caldwell,* must be reversed. If there is no First Amendment privilege to refuse to answer the relevant and material questions asked during a good-faith grand jury investigation, then it is *a fortiori* true that there is no privilege to refuse to appear before such a grand jury until the Government demonstrates some "compelling need" for a newsman's testimony. . . .

The decisions in *Branzburg v. Hayes* and *Branzburg v. Meigs,* must be affirmed. . . . In both cases, if what petitioner wrote was true, he had direct information to provide the grand jury concerning the commission of serious crimes.

The only question presented at the present time in In re Pappas is whether petitioner Pappas must appear before the grand jury to testify pursuant to subpoena. . . . We affirm the decision of the Massachusetts Supreme Judicial Court and hold that petitioner must appear before the grand jury to answer the questions put to him, subject, of course, to the supervision of the presiding judge as to "the propriety, purposes, and scope of the grand jury inquiry and the pertinence of the probable testimony." [ ]

So ordered.

MR. JUSTICE POWELL, concurring.

I add this brief statement to emphasize what seems to me to be the limited nature of the Court's holding. The Court does not hold that newsmen, subpoenaed to testify before a grand jury, are without constitutional rights with respect to the gathering of news or in safeguarding their sources. Certainly, we do not hold, as suggested in Mr. Justice Stewart's dissenting opinion, that state and federal authorities are free to "annex" the news media as "an investigative arm of government." The solicitude repeatedly shown by this Court for First Amendment freedoms should be sufficient assurance against any such effort, even if one seriously believed that the media—properly free and untrammeled in the fullest sense of these terms—were not able to protect themselves.

As indicated in the concluding portion of the opinion, the Court states that no harassment of newsmen will be tolerated. If a newsman believes that the grand jury investigation is not being conducted in good faith he is not without remedy. Indeed, if the newsman is called upon to give information bearing only a remote and tenuous relationship to the subject of the investigation, or if he has some other reason to believe that his testimony implicates confidential source relationships without a legitimate need of law enforcement, he will have access to the court on a motion to quash and an appropriate protective order may be entered. The asserted claim to privilege should be judged on its facts by the striking of a proper balance between freedom of the press and the obligation of all citizens to give relevant testimony with respect to criminal conduct. The balance of these vital constitutional and societal interests on a case-by-case basis accords with the tried and traditional way of adjudicating such questions.*

In short, the courts will be available to newsmen under circumstances where legitimate First Amendment interests require protection.

MR. JUSTICE DOUGLAS, dissenting in United States v. Caldwell [and the other two cases].

. . .

It is my view that there is no "compelling need" that can be shown which qualifies the reporter's immunity from appearing or testifying before a grand jury, unless the reporter himself is implicated in a

* It is to be remembered that Caldwell asserts a constitutional privilege not even to appear before the grand jury unless a court decides that the Government has made a showing that meets the three preconditions specified in the dissenting opinion of Mr. Justice Stewart. To be sure, this would require a "balancing" of interests by the court, but under circumstances and constraints significantly different from the balancing that will be appropriate under the court's decision. The newsman witness, like all other witnesses, will have to appear; he will not be in a position to litigate at the threshold the State's very authority to subpoena him. Moreover, absent the constitutional pre-conditions that Caldwell and that dissenting opinion would impose as heavy burdens of proof to be carried by the State, the court—when called upon to protect a newsman from improper or prejudicial questioning—would be free to balance the competing interests on their merits in the particular case. The new constitutional rule endorsed by that dissenting opinion would, as a practical matter, defeat such a fair balancing and the essential societal interest in the detection and prosecution of crime would be heavily subordinated.

crime. His immunity in my view is therefore quite complete, for, absent his involvement in a crime, the First Amendment protects him against an appearance before a grand jury and if he is involved in a crime, the Fifth Amendment stands as a barrier. Since in my view there is no area of inquiry not protected by a privilege, the reporter need not appear for the futile purpose of invoking one to each question.

. . .

The starting point for decision pretty well marks the range within which the end result lies. The New York Times, whose reporting functions are at issue here, takes the amazing position that First Amendment rights are to be balanced against other needs or conveniences of government. My belief is that all of the "balancing" was done by those who wrote the Bill of Rights. By casting the First Amendment in absolute terms, they repudiated the timid, watered-down, emasculated versions of the First Amendment which both the Government and the New York Times advance in the case.

. . .

Sooner or later, any test which provides less than blanket protection to beliefs and associations will be twisted and relaxed so as to provide virtually no protection at all. As Justice Holmes noted in [*Abrams*] such was the fate of the "clear and present danger" test which he had coined in [*Schenck*]. Eventually, that formula was so watered down that the danger had to be neither clear nor present but merely "not improbable." [*Dennis*] See my concurring opinion in [*Brandenburg*]. A compelling-interest test may prove as pliable as did the clear-and-present-danger test. Perceptions of the worth of state objectives will change with the composition of the Court and with the intensity of the politics of the times. . . .

. . .

The press has a preferred position in our constitutional scheme, not to enable it to make money, not to set newsmen apart as a favored class, but to bring fulfillment to the public's right to know. The right to know is crucial to the governing powers of the people, to paraphrase Alexander Meiklejohn. Knowledge is essential to informed decisions.

. . .

The intrusion of government into this domain is symptomatic of the disease of this society. As the years pass the power of government becomes more and more pervasive. It is a power to suffocate both people and causes. Those in power, whatever their politics, want only to perpetuate it. Now that the fences of the law and the tradition that has protected the press are broken down, the people are the victims. The First Amendment, as I read it, was designed precisely to prevent that tragedy.

. . .

MR. JUSTICE STEWART, with whom MR. JUSTICE BRENNAN and MR. JUSTICE MARSHALL join, dissenting.

The Court's crabbed view of the First Amendment reflects a disturbing insensitivity to the critical role of an independent press in our society. The question whether a reporter has a constitutional right to a confidential relationship with his source is of first impression here, but the principles that should guide our decision are as basic as any to be found in the Constitution. While Mr. Justice Powell's enigmatic concurring opinion gives some hope of a more flexible view in the future, the Court in these cases holds that a newsman has no First Amendment right to protect his sources when called before a grand jury. The Court thus invites state and federal authorities to undermine the historic independence of the press by attempting to annex the journalistic profession as an investigative arm of government. Not only will this decision impair performance of the press' constitutionally protected functions, but it will, I am convinced, in the long run harm rather than help the administration of justice.

I respectfully dissent.

I.

The reporter's constitutional right to a confidential relationship with his source stems from the broad societal interest in a full and free flow of information to the public. . . .

Enlightened choice by an informed citizenry is the basic ideal upon which an open society is premised,[3] and a free press is thus indispensable to a free society. Not only does the press enhance personal self-fulfillment by providing the people with the widest possible range of fact and opinion, but it also is an incontestable precondition of self-government. . . . As private and public aggregations of power burgeon in size and the pressures for conformity necessarily mount, there is obviously a continuing need for an independent press to disseminate a robust variety of information and opinion through reportage, investigation, and criticism, if we are to preserve our constitutional tradition of maximizing freedom of choice by encouraging diversity of expression.

A.

In keeping with this tradition, we have held that the right to publish is central to the First Amendment and basic to the existence of constitutional democracy. [ ]

. . .

No less important to the news dissemination process is the gathering of information. News must not be unnecessarily cut off at its source, for without freedom to acquire information the right to publish would be impermissibly compromised. Accordingly, a right to gather news, of some dimensions, must exist. . . .

3. See generally Z. Chafee, *Free Speech in the United States* (1941); A. Meiklejohn, *Free Speech and Its Relation to Self-Government* (1948); T. Emerson, *Toward a General Theory of the First Amendment* (1963).

B.

The right to gather news implies, in turn, a right to a confidential relationship between a reporter and his source. This proposition follows as a matter of simple logic once three factual predicates are recognized: (1) newsmen require informants to gather news; (2) confidentiality—the promise or understanding that names or certain aspects of communications will be kept off the record—is essential to the creation and maintenance of a news-gathering relationship with informants; and (3) an unbridled subpoena power—the absence of a constitutional right protecting, in *any* way, a confidential relationship from compulsory process—will either deter sources from divulging information or deter reporters from gathering and publishing information.

It is obvious that informants are necessary to the news-gathering process as we know it today. If it is to perform its constitutional mission, the press must do far more than merely print public statements or publish prepared handouts. Familiarity with the people and circumstances involved in the myriad background activities that result in the final product called "news" is vital to complete and responsible journalism, unless the press is to be a captive mouthpiece of "newsmakers."

It is equally obvious that the promise of confidentiality may be a necessary prerequisite to a productive relationship between a newsman and his informants. An officeholder may fear his superior; a member of the bureaucracy, his associates; a dissident, the scorn of majority opinion. All may have information valuable to the public discourse, yet each may be willing to relate that information only in confidence to a reporter whom he trusts, either because of excessive caution or because of a reasonable fear of reprisals or censure for unorthodox views. The First Amendment concern must not be with the motives of any particular news source, but rather with the conditions in which informants of all shades of the spectrum may make information available through the press to the public. [ ]

In *Caldwell,* the District Court found that "confidential relationships . . . are commonly developed and maintained by professional journalists, and are indispensable to their work of gathering, analyzing and publishing the news." Commentators and individual reporters have repeatedly noted the importance of confidentiality. And surveys among reporters and editors indicate that the promise of nondisclosure is necessary for many types of news gathering.

Finally, and most important, when governmental officials possess an unchecked power to compel newsmen to disclose information received in confidence, sources will clearly be deterred from giving information, and reporters will clearly be deterred from publishing it, because uncertainty about exercise of the power will lead to "self-censorship." [ ] The uncertainty arises, of course, because the judiciary has traditionally imposed virtually no limitations on the grand jury's broad investigatory powers. [ ]

After today's decision, the potential informant can never be sure that his identity or off-the-record communications will not subsequently be revealed through the compelled testimony of a newsman. A public-spirited person inside government, who is not implicated in any crime, will now be fearful of revealing corruption or other governmental wrongdoing, because he will now know he can subsequently be identified by use of compulsory process. The potential source must, therefore, choose between risking exposure by giving information or avoiding the risk by remaining silent.

The reporter must speculate about whether contact with a controversial source or publication of controversial material will lead to a subpoena. In the event of a subpoena, under today's decision, the newsman will know that he must choose between being punished for contempt if he refuses to testify, or violating his profession's ethics [10] and impairing his resourcefulness as a reporter if he discloses confidential information.

. . .

The impairment of the flow of news cannot, of course, be proved with scientific precision, as the Court seems to demand. Obviously, not every news-gathering relationship requires confidentiality. And it is difficult to pinpoint precisely how many relationships do require a promise or understanding of nondisclosure. But we have never before demanded that First Amendment rights rest on elaborate empirical studies demonstrating beyond any conceivable doubt that deterrent effects exist; we have never before required proof of the exact number of people potentially affected by governmental action, who would actually be dissuaded from engaging in First Amendment activity.

. . .

To require any greater burden of proof is to shirk our duty to protect values securely embedded in the Constitution. We cannot await an unequivocal—and therefore unattainable—imprimatur from empirical studies.[19] We can and must accept the evidence developed in the record, and elsewhere, that overwhelmingly supports the premise

10. The American Newspaper Guild has adopted the following rule as part of the newsman's code of ethics: "[N]ewspapermen shall refuse to reveal confidences or disclose sources of confidential information in court or before other judicial or investigating bodies." G. Bird & F. Merwin, *The Press and Society* 592 (1971).

19. Empirical studies, after all, can only provide facts. It is the duty of courts to give legal significance to facts; and it is the special duty of this Court to understand the constitutional significance of facts. We must often proceed in a state of less than perfect knowledge, either because the facts are murky or the methodology used in obtaining the facts is open to question. It is then that we must look to the Constitution for the values that inform our presumptions. And the importance to our society of the full flow of information to the public has buttressed this Court's historic presumption in favor of First Amendment values.

that deterrence will occur with regularity in important types of news-gathering relationships.

Thus, we cannot escape the conclusion that when neither the reporter nor his source can rely on the shield of confidentiality against unrestrained use of the grand jury's subpoena power, valuable information will not be published and the public dialogue will inevitably be impoverished.

II.

Posed against the First Amendment's protection of the newsman's confidential relationships in these cases is society's interest in the use of the grand jury to administer justice fairly and effectively. The grand jury serves two important functions: "to examine into the commission of crimes" and "to stand between the prosecutor and the accused, and to determine whether the charge was founded upon credible testimony or was dictated by malice or personal ill will." Hale v. Henkel, 201 U.S. 43, 59. And to perform these functions the grand jury must have available to it every man's relevant evidence. [ ].

Yet the longstanding rule making every person's evidence available to the grand jury is not absolute. The rule has been limited by the Fifth Amendment, the Fourth Amendment, and the evidentiary privileges of the common law. . . . And in United States v. Bryan, 339 U.S. 323, the Court observed that any exemption from the duty to testify before the grand jury "presupposes a very real interest to be protected." Id., at 332.

Such an interest must surely be the First Amendment protection of a confidential relationship that I have discussed above in Part I. As noted there, this protection does not exist for the purely private interests of the newsman or his informant, nor even, at bottom, for the First Amendment interests of either partner in the news-gathering relationship. Rather, it functions to insure nothing less than democratic decisionmaking through the free flow of information to the public, and it serves, thereby, to honor the "profound national commitment to the principle that debate on public issues should be uninhibited, robust, and wide-open." New York Times Co. v. Sullivan, [ ].

In striking the proper balance between the public interest in the efficient administration of justice and the First Amendment guarantee of the fullest flow of information, we must begin with the basic proposition that because of their "delicate and vulnerable" nature, NAACP v. Button, 371 U.S., at 433, and their transcendent importance for the just functioning of our society, First Amendment rights require special safeguards.

A.

This Court has erected such safeguards when government, by legislative investigation or other investigative means, has attempted to pierce the shield of privacy inherent in freedom of association. In no previous case have we considered the extent to which the First Amendment limits the grand jury subpoena power. . . .

. . .

Thus, when an investigation impinges on First Amendment rights, the government must not only show that the inquiry is of "compelling and overriding importance" but it must also "convincingly" demonstrate that the investigation is "substantially related" to the information sought.

Governmental officials must, therefore, demonstrate that the information sought is *clearly* relevant to a *precisely* defined subject of governmental inquiry. [ ] They must demonstrate that it is reasonable to think the witness in question has that information. [ ] And they must show that there is not any means of obtaining the information less destructive of First Amendment liberties. [ ]

These requirements, which we have recognized in decisions involving legislative and executive investigations, serve established policies reflected in numerous First Amendment decisions arising in other contexts. . . .

I believe the safeguards developed in our decisions involving governmental investigations must apply to the grand jury inquiries in these cases. Surely the function of the grand jury to aid in the enforcement of the law is no more important than the function of the legislature, and its committees, to make the law. . . .

Accordingly, when a reporter is asked to appear before a grand jury and reveal confidences, I would hold that the government must (1) show that there is probable cause to believe that the newsman has information that is clearly relevant to a specific probable violation of law; (2) demonstrate that the information sought cannot be obtained by alternative means less destructive of First Amendment rights; and (3) demonstrate a compelling and overriding interest in the information.

This is not to say that a grand jury could not issue a subpoena until such a showing were made, and it is not to say that a newsman would be in any way privileged to ignore any subpoena that was issued. Obviously, before the government's burden to make such a showing were triggered, the reporter would have to move to quash the subpoena, asserting the basis on which he considered the particular relationship a confidential one.

B.

The crux of the Court's rejection of any newsman's privilege is its observation that only "where news sources themselves are implicated in crime or possess information *relevant* to the grand jury's task need they or the reporter be concerned about grand jury subpoenas." See ante, at 691 (emphasis supplied). But this is a most misleading construct. For it is obviously not true that the only persons about whom reporters will be forced to testify will be those "confidential informants involved in actual criminal conduct" and those having "information suggesting illegal conduct by others." See ante, at 691, 693. As noted above, given the grand jury's extraordinarily broad investigative powers and the weak standards of relevance and materiality that apply during such inquiries, reporters, if they have no testimonial privilege, will be called to give information about informants who have neither committed crimes nor have information about crime. It is to avoid deterrence of such sources and thus to prevent needless injury to First Amendment values that I think the government must be required to show probable cause that the newsman has information that is clearly relevant to a specific probable violation of criminal law.

. . .

Both the "probable cause" and "alternative means" requirements would thus serve the vital function of mediating between the public interest in the administration of justice and the constitutional protection of the full flow of information. . . . No doubt the courts would be required to make some delicate judgments in working out this accommodation. But that, after all, is the function of courts of law. Better such judgments, however difficult, than the simplistic and stultifying absolutism adopted by the Court in denying any force to the First Amendment in these cases.

The error in the Court's absolute rejection of First Amendment interests in these cases seems to me to be most profound. For in the name of advancing the administration of justice, the Court's decision, I think, will only impair the achievement of that goal. People entrusted with law enforcement responsibility, no less than private citizens, need general information relating to controversial social problems. Obviously, press reports have great value to government, even when the newsman cannot be compelled to testify before a grand jury. The said paradox of the Court's position is that when a grand jury may exercise an unbridled subpoena power, and sources involved in sensitive matters become fearful of disclosing information, the newsman will not only cease to be a useful grand jury witness; he will cease to investigate and publish information about issues of public import. I cannot subscribe to such an anomalous result, for, in my view, the interests protected by the First Amendment are not antagonistic to the administration of justice. Rather, they can, in the long run, only be complementary, and for that reason must be given great "breathing space." NAACP v. Button, 371 U.S., at 433.

Notes and Questions

1. Justice Powell suggests some grounds for protecting reporters from grand jury investigations. Does Justice White's opinion suggest the same protections?

2. Does Justice White's opinion support Justice Powell's call for "balancing of these vital constitutional and societal interests on a case-by-case basis"?

3. In what ways do Justices Powell and Stewart disagree?

4. Is Justice Stewart suggesting ad hoc balancing? Is his three-part formula subject to the criticism that the reporter will be unable to tell in advance when he will be required to testify?

5. Was the same kind of information being sought in each of the three cases that made up *Branzburg?* For the same reasons? By the same organ of government?

6. Justice Douglas notes with obvious dismay that the reporters did not seek "absolute" privilege. What would such a privilege have meant in this case? Why do you think such an argument was not made? Are sources more likely to place confidence in reporters if state or federal law provides "absolute" privilege for reporters than if it provides only qualified—or no—privilege? What controls the source's decision about whether to rely on the reporter's promise of confidentiality?

7. Justice White cites examples for the view that "The administration of a constitutional newsman's privilege would present practical and conceptual difficulties of a high order." How significant is that objection?

8. Although it does not involve the reporter's privilege, the Nixon tapes case shows the Supreme Court's skeptical attitude toward privileges in general. United States v. Nixon, 418 U.S. 683 (1974). The special prosecutor served a subpoena on President Nixon seeking certain tapes and documents that might be relevant to the Watergate cover-up trial. The President moved to quash on the grounds (1) that the separation of powers doctrine precluded judicial review of the President's decision that it would not be in the public interest to disclose the contents of confidential conversations between a President and his close advisers, and (2) that as a matter of constitutional law, executive privilege prevailed over the subpoena. Although granting that the need for "complete candor and objectivity from advisers calls for great deference from the courts," the Court decided that absent a claim of "need to protect military, diplomatic, or sensitive national security secrets," the Court must weigh the competing interests to determine which should prevail:

> We have elected to employ an adversary system of criminal justice in which the parties contest all issues before a court of law. The need to develop all relevant facts in the adversary system is both fundamental and comprehensive. The ends of criminal justice would be defeated if judgments were to be founded on a partial or speculative presentation of the facts. The very integrity of the judicial system and public confidence in the system depend on full disclosure of all the facts, within the framework of the rules of evidence. To ensure that justice is done, it is imperative to the

function of courts that compulsory process be available for the production of evidence needed either by the prosecution or by the defense.

Only recently the Court restated the ancient proposition of law, albeit in the context of a grand jury inquiry rather than a trial, "that 'the public . . . has a right to every man's evidence,' except for those persons protected by a constitutional, commonlaw, or statutory privilege, [ ]. . . ." *Branzburg v. Hayes,* [ ]. The privileges referred to by the Court are designed to protect weighty and legitimate competing interests. . . . Whatever their origins, these exceptions to the demand for every man's evidence are not lightly created nor expansively construed, for they are in derogation of the search for truth.

. . .

In this case we must weigh the importance of the general privilege of confidentiality of Presidential communications in performance of his responsibilities against the inroads of such a privilege on the fair administration of criminal justice. The interest in preserving confidentiality is weighty indeed and entitled to great respect. However, we cannot conclude that advisers will be moved to temper the candor of their remarks by the infrequent occasions of disclosure because of the possibility that such conversations will be called for in the context of a criminal prosecution.

On the other hand, the allowance of the privilege to withhold evidence that is demonstrably relevant in a criminal trial would cut deeply into the guarantee of due process of law and gravely impair the basic function of the courts. A President's acknowledged need for confidentiality in the communications of his office is general in nature, whereas the constitutional need for production of relevant evidence in a criminal proceeding is specific and central to the fair adjudication of a particular criminal case in the administration of justice. Without access to specific facts a criminal prosecution may be totally frustrated. The President's broad interest in confidentiality of communications will not be vitiated by disclosure of a limited number of conversations preliminarily shown to have some bearing on the pending criminal cases.

Is this discussion applicable to the reporters' situation?

9. In In re Special Grand Jury Investigation, 104 Ill.2d 419, 472 N.E.2d 450, 84 Ill.Dec. 490, 11 Med.L.Rptr. 1142 (1984), a reporter quoted statements made by a juvenile court judge during court proceedings. The reporter had apparently obtained the transcripts by a leak from a judicial inquiry board that was investigating the judge. A grand jury then began to seek the source of the leak. After three members of the board invoked their constitutional right not to testify, the state's attorney sought to remove the reporter's protection under the state shield law. That statute provided that the privilege may be divested when "all other available sources of information have been exhausted

and disclosure of the information sought is essential to the protection of the public interest involved."

The appellate court agreed with the lower court that the public interest was great, but did not agree that "all other available sources" had been tried. The court identified three other board members who had transcripts, as well as several staff members and other government offices. The record showed that several jurors wanted to call some of these other people but "were repeatedly dissuaded by the special prosecutor on the basis that their testimony would be unnecessary if [the reporter's] privilege could first be divested. . . . We think it clear that the statute requires more than a showing of inconvenience to the investigator before a reporter can be compelled to disclose his sources . . . ."

One concurring justice doubted that the public interest requirement had been met. The reporter revealed nothing more than one who had been in the open courtroom at the time could have learned and legally revealed. "My opinion is that the grand jury investigation served no useful purpose and should never have been instituted."

10. In State v. Korkala, 99 A.D.2d 161, 472 N.Y.S.2d 310, 10 Med.L. Rptr. 1355 (1984), the state sought outtakes from an interview that interviewers from CBS's "60 Minutes" had held with the defendant. CBS had broadcast 22 minutes from interviews that were said to have lasted several hours. CBS argued that the New York shield law gave reporters an "absolute privilege" against having to turn over such information. The court disagreed on the ground that the statute covered only cases in which the source had an expectation of confidentiality. Here the defendant had spoken openly with others on the subject.

On the First Amendment issue, the court balanced and concluded that although relevance was clear, it was not yet clear that the information would actually be needed in the prosecution. That would depend on the tack taken by defendant at the trial. The court ordered that the outtakes be shown to the trial judge in camera. If the defense takes a turn that makes delivery relevant, then the judge may order production of the relevant material.

CBS did not appeal further. It made the outtakes available to the judge, who viewed them in a CBS screening room. CBS asserted that if the judge were to order any material to be delivered to the prosecutor, CBS might again take legal action. N.Y. Times, Apr. 6, 1984, at 25.

A danger in this procedure is suggested by an episode involving a reporter on the Sacramento Union whose notes were demanded by a person accused of murder. "She refused, but allowed the judge to review a copy of them. . . . As it turned out, the judge ruled that the defense attorney was the only one capable of reviewing the notes. [Reporter] was ready to face contempt charges, but the judge avoided a showdown by turning over his copy of her notes to the defense." Feed/back, Winter 1985, at 28.

11. The manager of a Los Angeles radio station was found in contempt for refusing to comply with demands that he produce the original of a "communiqué" from an underground group that claimed responsibility for a bombing. Lewis v. United States, 517 F.2d 236 (9th Cir.1975). An earlier episode also led to a finding of contempt. In re Lewis, 501 F.2d 418 (9th Cir.1974), certiorari denied 420 U.S. 913 (1975). In each case, the communiqué had been delivered to the broadcaster apparently without any prior arrangement.

B. REPORTER'S PRIVILEGE—OTHER CONTEXTS

In this section, we consider situations in which some person or organization other than the grand jury is seeking information from the reporter. Before getting into specific situations, reflect upon Justice White's opinion in *Branzburg.* Can Justice White's analysis be applied if a criminal defendant seeks the information? A plaintiff in civil litigation?

In each context, identify the precise interest asserted to justify ordering the reporter to reveal the sought information. Note also that the role of statutory and common law protection may vary with the specific context involved, as well as with the text of the specific statute.

At the time of *Branzburg,* as the Court noted, a majority of states had not adopted "shield" statutes. But in the aftermath of *Branzburg,* with its statement about the possibility of state legislation, enough states did act so that 25 to 30 states had protective legislation of some sort within a few years. (Congress has not acted.) We will consider aspects of these state statutes shortly. In the meantime, consider whether state legislation can control the outcome in each of the following situations. (In all cases, note the gap where a state statute provides protection before, say, state grand juries, but the reporter is called before a federal grand jury in that state.)

1. CRIMINAL CASES—PROSECUTOR WANTS INFORMATION

Once the grand jury has indicted, or an information has been returned, the criminal case heads toward trial. If the prosecutor seeks to obtain information held by the reporter, are the considerations involved different from those raised when the grand jury seeks the information? Is there a difference between seeking facts to determine whether an indictment is warranted and seeking facts to determine guilt or innocence?

2. CRIMINAL CASES—DEFENDANT WANTS INFORMATION

This situation introduces the provision of the Sixth Amendment, also found in state constitutions, that the accused in a criminal case is to "have compulsory process for obtaining witnesses." Perhaps the most dramatic case raising this issue arose in a murder prosecution in New Jersey.

The Farber Case. Myron Farber, a reporter for the New York Times, began investigating general mysterious deaths that had occurred some years earlier at a hospital in New Jersey. His investigations led to a series of articles and to murder indictments against a physician. During the six-month murder trial, the defendant's attorney had subpoenas served on the reporter and the newspaper demanding that they produce certain documents relating to interviews with witnesses at the trial. Motions to quash the subpoenas were denied, but the trial judge did order that the documents be delivered to him for *in camera* inspection. Farber and the Times refused. Efforts to stay the order pending appeals were denied by the state appellate courts and by Justices White and Marshall.

Farber and the Times refused to comply and were held in civil and criminal contempt. The civil contempt involved a fine of $5,000 per day on the Times and a flat $1,000 on Farber, who was sentenced to jail until he complied. The criminal penalties were $100,000 on the newspaper, and $1,000 on Farber plus six months in jail. On review, the New Jersey Supreme Court affirmed, 5–2. Matter of Farber, 78 N.J. 259, 394 A.2d 330, 4 Med.L.Rptr. 1360 (1978).

The court rejected the argument that the First Amendment protected Farber's refusal in order to keep newsgathering and dissemination from being substantially impaired. It concluded that *Branzburg* "squarely held that no such First Amendment right exists." "Thus we do no weighing or balancing of societal interests in reaching our determination that the First Amendment does not afford appellants the privilege they claim." Moreover, "the obligation to appear at a criminal trial on behalf of a defendant who is enforcing his Sixth Amendment rights is at least as compelling as the duty to appear before a grand jury."

The court then turned to the state "shield law," which provided that persons employed by media are privileged to refuse to disclose "in any legal . . . proceeding . . . including, but not limited to, any court, grand jury, petit jury, . . . or elsewhere" the source of information acquired or "any news or information obtained in the course of pursuing his professional activities whether or not it is disseminated." The court found a legislative desire to protect sources and information obtained by reporters "to the greatest extent permitted" by the state and federal constitutions. Since Farber was clearly covered by the statute, the court turned to the constitutional question.

The criminal defendant argued that the right to have compulsory process for obtaining witnesses in his favor prevailed over the statute if there was a conflict. The court agreed, noting that in the Nixon tapes case, the Supreme Court ordered the President to deliver materials to the special prosecutor although the President claimed an executive privilege and the prosecutor had nothing like the Sixth Amendment to support his demand.

The court concluded that the state constitution afforded a criminal defendant the right to compel witnesses to attend and to compel the production of documents "for which he may have, or may believe he has, a legitimate need in preparing or undertaking his defense." Witnesses properly summoned must testify or produce material demanded by a properly phrased subpoena. The state constitutional provision "prevails over" the shield statute, "but in recognition of the strongly expressed legislative viewpoint favoring confidentiality, we prescribe the imposition" of some procedural safeguards.

The court directed that in similar cases in the future the reporter would be "entitled to a preliminary determination before being compelled to submit the subpoenaed materials to a trial judge." The court reiterated that this result was based on its obligation to give as much effect to the shield statute as possible, consistent with the conflicting constitutional provisions. The hearing was not mandated by the First Amendment.

In such a hearing, the defendant would have to show "by a fair preponderance of the evidence, including all reasonable inferences, that there was a reasonable probability or likelihood that the information sought by the subpoena was material and relevant to his defense, that it could not be secured from any less intrusive source, and that the defendant had a legitimate need to see and otherwise use it."

In Farber's case, the trial judge's failure to accord such a hearing was not error because "it is perfectly clear that on the record before him a conclusion of materiality, relevancy, unavailability of another source, as well as need was quite inescapable." The judge had been trying the case for eighteen weeks. "His knowledge of the factual background and of the part Farber had played was intimate and pervasive. Perhaps most significant is the trial court's thorough awareness of appellant Farber's close association with the Prosecutor's office since a time preceding the indictment." The court then listed the claims asserted by the defendant in the criminal case and considered the role of each witness and why the defendant might want Farber's files. These included some who admitted having spoken to Farber at various times, and one who refused to speak with the defense. Since there was enough to have persuaded a trial judge to order *in camera* submission of the materials had a hearing been held before such an order, and since Farber knew of all these facts, the court concluded that the requirements for an *in camera* order had been met.

The civil and criminal contempt convictions were upheld. (The majority did not mention the fact that Farber had signed a contract to write a book about the case. That issue emerged in a federal court hearing and did not enter into the state court proceeding.)

Justice Pashman dissented because at "no point prior to the rendition of the contempt judgments were appellants accorded an opportunity to marshal legal arguments against *in camera* production of the subpoenaed materials." On the merits, he concluded that the shield law barred forced disclosure *in camera* of confidential data. Therefore, he had no occasion to pass on First Amendment arguments against disclosure. To deal with the defendant's Sixth Amendment arguments, Justice Pashman urged a six-step process. (1) The person claiming protection under the shield law should make a prima facie showing of the essential elements. (2) The criminal defendant should then show need for the information, subject to rebuttal by the newsperson. (3) If the criminal defendant has prevailed, the documents must be produced for *in camera* inspection. At this stage the newsperson "should be permitted to delete the names of informants and any other identification indicia." (4) After inspection, the judge should decide what is "relevant, material and necessary" to the defense and whether such material will probably be admissible at trial. This material should be released to the defense. Counsel should be heard at this stage. (5) The judge must make findings of fact and conclusions of law at each stage. (6) Either party may seek leave to appeal decisions as to *in camera* inspection or release of the information after inspection. "Throughout all stages of the proceeding, the judge should constantly keep in mind the strong presumption against disclosure of protected materials. All doubts concerning disclosure should be resolved in favor of non-disclosure."

Finally, Justice Pashman argued that the state's highest court should not engage in original factfinding and that the majority's attempt to compensate for the "procedural infirmities by engaging in *ad hoc* factfinding is 'too little, too late.' "

Justice Handler also dissented, although he was "in substantial accord with much of the reasoning of the Court." He agreed that the First Amendment provided no privilege, that the shield law privilege was not absolute, and that *in camera* inspection may be necessary on a requisite showing. He dissented, however, because he thought that the shield law should not be overcome without a hearing devoted to the question "whether *in camera* inspection of contested information is appropriate in the face of a claim based on" the shield law.

The Supreme Court denied certiorari sub nom. New York Times Co. v. New Jersey, 439 U.S. 997 (1978). Justice Brennan took no part in the decision.

Mr. Farber spent several days in county jail for civil contempt before his own state court case just summarized. He was then released pending the outcome of that case. After the adverse decision, he returned to jail. He was released after the jury received the murder case since he could no longer effectively comply with the court's order to turn over the documents. He spent a total of forty days in jail. The Times paid civil and criminal fines totalling $285,000. After the criminal trial ended in the acquittal of the physician, several other pending citations for contempt of court against Farber were dismissed and the sentence for criminal contempt was suspended without probation.

After *Farber,* the New Jersey Legislature amended its shield law to provide more clearly that a showing of need must be made before the reporter can be required to reveal confidential information even to the trial judge in chambers, much less the litigants. The state's supreme court twice upheld and applied the statute shortly thereafter.

As noted, the majority in *Farber* recognized that the legislature intended to protect the confidentiality of the press "to the greatest extent permitted by the Constitution of the United States and that of the State of New Jersey." In that case, why isn't the proper course to discharge the defendant—at least when the defendant can show the likelihood of prejudice from the assertion of the privilege? Questions of the proper interpretation of privileges, whether defendants must show prejudice from the assertion of reporters' privileges, and how they might do this are discussed thoughtfully in Hill, Testimonial Privilege and Fair Trial, 80 Colum.L.Rev. 1173 (1980). Hill also comments on differences between privileges asserted by government prosecutors and those that are asserted by persons not connected with government.

The executive editor of the New York Times, A.M. Rosenthal, is quoted as having said in a speech that the First and Sixth Amendments need never "be in true conflict." Instead of limiting the flow of information, judges could "strengthen the Sixth Amendment—by control of the courthouse, by . . . change of venue, by sequestration of jurors and witnesses, by instructions to jurors and even by freeing defendants." N.Y. Times, Nov. 10, 1981, at 12.

Just before leaving office in early 1982, New Jersey Governor Brendan Byrne pardoned the New York Times and Myron Farber and ordered return of $101,000 collected in fines for criminal contempts. Another $185,000 imposed for civil contempts was not affected by the pardon. The Governor stated that the defendants had been "attempting to uphold a principle they believed in. They should not be burdened by a record of criminal contempt any longer." Editor & Publisher, Jan. 23, 1982, at 16.

What is the interplay of state and federal, and of statutory and constitutional, issues that emerges from the Farber case? Once the procedural confusions are resolved, how is a state court likely to analyze such a case in the future?

1. If the state court goes as far as to order the reporter to provide the sought information, but the reporter refuses to comply, what happens to the prosecution? Does it depend on how severely the state coerces the reporter? In Hammarley v. Superior Court, 89 Cal.App.3d 388, 153 Cal.Rptr. 608, 4 Med.L.Rptr. 2055 (1978), a criminal defendant sought information from a reporter who was claiming a privilege. The court ordered the information delivered. Although the court noted that it had no reason to anticipate that the reporter would not comply, it volunteered that although "the state must make available its process to insure to the extent possible the availability to defendants of needed witnesses and evidence," the state "has no unfailing mechanism for

behavior modification," and cannot force a reporter to comply with such an order. The reporter's refusal to comply, despite the state's efforts, "would not implicate defendants' constitutional right to a fair trial—a right inviolable through conduct that is strictly private and unofficial. Accordingly, it is clear that a contemnor may not by his resistance to legal process prevent the trial of underlying criminal charges in circumstances such as these." The state supreme court denied a hearing.

Recall the episode of the judge who obtained a copy of the reporter's notes for *in camera* inspection and turned them over to the defense attorney without further consultation with the reporter, p. 569, supra. If the reporter had demanded the notes back and accepted punishment for contempt of court, might the state's prosecution have been compromised if the judge had returned the notes to the reporter instead of delivering them to the defense? Is this a situation that should be avoided? If so, how can it be avoided?

2. C.B.S., Inc. v. Superior Court, 85 Cal.App.3d 241, 149 Cal.Rptr. 421, 4 Med.L.Rptr. 1568 (1978), involved an arrangement between CBS and the Santa Clara County sheriff's department under which CBS was permitted to photograph meetings between undercover agents and two men. The meetings led to the arrest of both men for selling controlled substances—and CBS showed the arrest sequence on its program "60 Minutes." Before the criminal trial, the attorney for one defendant sought the CBS "outtakes" and the trial judge ordered them turned over to the defense.

On appeal, the court concluded that under state law, "where a criminal defendant has demonstrated a *reasonable possibility* that evidence sought to be discovered might result in his exoneration, he is entitled to its discovery." The court ordered the judge to conduct a preliminary screening of the film and to consider whether delivery of voice clips alone would satisfy the defendant's needs.

On remand, the tapes were made available to the parties. As a result, the prosecutor dropped the charges against the defendant who had sought the film. That defendant's attorney is reported to have said that the film clips showed that although the defendant was present, "he didn't participate" in the transaction, contrary to the officers' version. S.F. Chronicle, Feb. 24, 1979, at 4.

3. In a federal criminal prosecution, the defense asked for statements that "60 Minutes" had obtained from various sources. In United States v. Cuthbertson, 630 F.2d 139, 6 Med.L.Rptr. 1545 (3d Cir.1980), certiorari denied 449 U.S. 1126 (1981), the court of appeals first ruled that under F.R.Cr.P. 17(c), the district judge's order was valid to the extent it required CBS to produce, for *in camera* inspection, statements from persons on the government's list of witnesses. CBS then argued that it had a qualified First Amendment privilege not to produce such documents.

The court had earlier, in a federal civil rights act case, developed a qualified federal common law privilege under Fed.R.Evid. 501 that permitted journalists to refuse to divulge confidential sources in a civil case. (See Riley v. City of Chester, 612 F.2d 708 (3d Cir.1979)). The criminal defendants in this case argued that the Sixth Amendment required a different result than in *Riley*. The court disagreed. *Riley* had been influenced by First Amendment values encouraging unfettered communication to the public of information and opinion. The interest of the press in preserving the confidentiality of sources did not change in value depending on whether the case that ensued happened to be civil or criminal. Moreover, the Sixth Amendment did not automatically override the First Amendment claim. Here, the court relied on the passage in *Nebraska Press Association,* p. 524, supra, that the "authors of the Bill of Rights did not undertake to assign priorities as between" the two amendments.

Turning to the precise facts of this case, the court noted that all the government witnesses had been identified and had authorized the disclosure of their prior statements. Thus, there could be no claim of preserving confidentiality of sources. CBS asserted, however, that the *Riley* privilege also protected unpublished material obtained from known sources. The court agreed, but it did observe that "the lack of a confidential source may be an important element in balancing the defendant's need for the material sought against the interest of the journalist in preventing production in a particular case."

The waivers by witnesses were not conclusive because the court concluded that the privilege "belongs to CBS, not the potential witnesses, and it may be waived only by its holder." The result of this part of the case was that CBS had a qualified privilege to refuse to produce previously unpublished statements from identified sources.

When it turned to the balancing process, the court first addressed the argument that CBS could not be required to submit the material even for *in camera* inspection unless the defendants had first made a showing that they could not obtain the materials elsewhere and that the materials were of central relevance to the case. The court agreed that a simple demand from the defendant could not be enough. It then considered whether there might be alternative sources of this material. Verbatim statements by "their very nature are not obtainable from any other source. They are unique bits of evidence that are frozen at a particular place and time." They might be uniquely useful for impeachment at trial.

CBS then argued that defendants had not shown that the materials were "centrally relevant" to the case. The court ruled that the standard of Rule 17(c)—relevant evidentiary material—was the proper standard to use in this balancing process. Since both unavailability and relevance were shown, the trial judge had properly ordered CBS to present the materials for an *in camera* inspection. "We need not decide, however, whether any additional showing must be made by the defendants to overcome the privilege and to compel production of these statements to them at trial."

The district judge's order on remand that the documents be turned over to the defendant was reversed because defendant had failed to exhaust other sources and the evidence did not qualify as obtainable exculpatory evidence. At best, it would be available only for impeachment as each witness testified. 651 F.2d 189 (3d Cir.1981).

3. CIVIL CASES—THE PRESS IS NOT A PARTY

When we turn to civil cases, we confront other justifications for insisting on a reporter's testimony. Since the case is not criminal, society's interest may be less direct and no one's freedom or life is at stake. Instead, a private person or group is suing for injury to person, property, privacy or reputation. What happens to the *Branzburg* rationale in this situation?

1. Shortly after *Branzburg,* an action was brought on behalf of "all Negroes in the City of Chicago who purchased homes from approximately 60 named defendants between 1952 and 1969." The claim was that the real estate brokers had engaged in "blockbusting," a discriminatory practice that involved buying homes from whites at low prices and reselling them to blacks at high prices. To help prove their case the plaintiffs asked a reporter, Balk, to identify the source of an article he wrote in 1962 about real estate practices in Chicago, entitled "Confessions of a Block-Buster." Although sympathetic to the plaintiffs' position, Balk refused to testify because he got the story in confidence. The trial judge's refusal to order Balk to testify was affirmed on appeal. Baker v. F & F Investment, 470 F.2d 778 (2d Cir. 1972), certiorari denied 411 U.S. 966 (1973).

The court read *Branzburg* as offering reporters some First Amendment protection and relied heavily on Justice Powell's statement that "these vital constitutional and societal interests" should be decided on a case-by-case basis. The court observed the great weight that Justice White gave to the role of the grand jury and to the "importance of combatting crime." Since Justice Powell suggested that for him (and also the four dissenters) situations existed in criminal cases in which the First Amendment might override the interest in disclosure of information about crime, "surely in civil cases, courts must recognize that the public interest in non-disclosure of journalists' confidential sources will often be weightier than the private interest in compelled disclosure." The court found no compelling interest in disclosure in the facts of the case because the identity of the source "simply did not go to the heart of" plaintiffs' case.

2. A qualified privilege also was found in Democratic National Committee v. McCord, 356 F.Supp. 1394 (D.D.C.1973). The Committee for the Re-election of the President (President Nixon's reelection committee) was defending several suits arising out of the Watergate break-in. To obtain evidence for use in the trials, the committee caused subpoe-

nas to be issued against a number of journalists. On motions to quash the subpoenas, a federal court held that since all other means had not been used to obtain the material before requesting it from reporters, and since the committee had not shown clearly that the material was relevant to the trials, the subpoenas should be quashed. In so ruling, the court discussed "the right of the press to gather and publish, and that of the public to receive, news from . . . ofttimes confidential sources." The court also noted that the suits in question were civil, not criminal, and that the media were not parties to the suits.

The court thus adapted to civil cases the thrust of Justice Stewart's dissent in *Branzburg*, in which he contended that three conditions be met before a journalist is forced to testify or submit material: "the government must (1) show that there is probable cause to believe that the newsman has information that is clearly relevant to a specific probable violation of law; (2) demonstrate that the information sought cannot be obtained by alternative means less destructive of First Amendment rights; and (3) demonstrate a compelling and overriding interest in the information." (See p. 565, supra.) A number of federal cases involving subpoenas to reporters in civil suits have followed the *McCord* approach.

3. See also Zerilli v. Smith, 656 F.2d 705, 7 Med.L.Rptr. 1121 (D.C.Cir. 1981), involving a claim against several government officials and agencies for leaking transcripts of wiretapped conversations in which plaintiffs were discussing various illegal activities. The leaks were published in the Detroit News. The Department of Justice gave plaintiffs the names of the four department employees who knew the most about the transcripts and a list—of unstated length—of all officials who had access to the information. Plaintiff did not attempt to depose any of these government employees on the ground that it would be time-consuming and costly and would probably not have been productive. Instead, they sought to depose the reporter who got the leaks and wrote the story. He refused to identify his sources.

The district court refused to compel the testimony. The court of appeals affirmed upon a determination that the trial court had not abused its discretion. Although a qualified privilege was held to exist and the testimony was clearly central to a showing that the leak originated in the Department of Justice, the plaintiffs had not exhausted other leads to learn the identities of the leakers. Although there are limits to the obligation to explore alternative sources, some cases suggest that as many as 60 persons might have to be deposed before a court found exhaustion. Here, at the very least, plaintiffs should have deposed the four employees who knew most about the logs. The court explicitly reserved the question of whether that would have sufficed.

4. In a damage action brought under § 1983 for the death of a man in police custody, the issue was whether the decedent had been subjected to a "choke hold." A reporter wrote several stories about the incident in the local paper, including one stating that a confidential source had

told him he saw the choke hold being applied by one of the defendants and saw the decedent fall to the floor. Plaintiff sought to depose the reporter to learn the identity of this witness because plaintiff had been unable to find such testimony. The reporter refused to identify the source but did admit that the source had identified a second witness to the event. The story did not reveal this second name because of an editorial decision, not because of any promise of confidentiality.

State and local investigations had failed to produce either witness. Nine persons at the jail the night in question all denied seeing a choke hold applied. The medical evidence indicated that a choke hold was one of three possible causes of death. All parties to the damage action joined in the motion to force the reporter to name both the source and information about the other witness.

The judge first ruled that in civil actions a qualified First Amendment privilege applied, requiring the party moving to compel the testimony to show a "compelling need" for the information and an inability to obtain it elsewhere. If no privilege covered "material received from confidential sources, litigants in a case of public notoriety could begin their discovery subpoenaing and deposing reporters covering the story so long as no confidential information is involved." In a privileged situation, "protection against disclosure of the *name* of a confidential source is stronger than the protection against disclosure of non-confidential *information* revealed by that source." Why?

Applying these principles to the case, the judge first concluded that the damage action was not frivolous and that the plaintiff had exhausted "every reasonable alternative source for the information sought." He also found that the "names of the confidential source and witness not only *go to* the heart of plaintiff's case, they very well may *be* the heart of the case." Despite the judge's great concern for the public's interest in the freedom of reporters to prepare stories without being forced to disclose confidential sources and information, the balance here favored the plaintiff.

Although the judge found that plaintiff had made a compelling showing as to the source and the identity of the witness, the judge ordered revelation of only the identity of the witness, which "would not force the reporter to break a promise of confidentiality." Miller v. Mecklenburg County, 606 F.Supp. 488, 11 Med.L.Rptr. 1566 (W.D.N.C. 1985).

After this order, the reporter identified the witness, who turned out to be a defendant in the case who had already denied seeing any choke hold. All parties returned to court to compel identification of the source. The judge agreed that the compelling need remained and justified compelling disclosure. But despite the court's "strong aversion to secret trials and sealed materials," and although the reporter's promise "will be compromised by compliance with the court order, the extent of the intrusion into the functions of the press can be limited somewhat by not requiring that the disclosure be made in open court, as requested by plaintiff."

The result was an order to identify the source to all counsel and under seal to the court. A protective order was entered barring any attorney from revealing the name "to anyone other than the court and other counsel. The attorneys specifically are prohibited from revealing the name of the source to their clients. Any additional pleading that may tend to identify the source, including a notice of deposition, shall be filed with the court under the seal and shall be served upon counsel in such a way that only counsel will see the document."

The court "will reconsider the protective order once the case is set for trial. The court does not anticipate that the protective order shall apply to trial proceedings." Miller v. Mecklenburg County, 606 F.Supp. 488, 11 Med.L.Rptr. 1836 (W.D.N.C.1985).

5. A state's shield law may provide absolute protection when the press is not a party to a civil case. A California court has construed that state's shield statute and identical constitutional provision to eliminate the need to balance the civil litigant's interests against those of the press in situations covered by the provisions. Playboy Enterprises, Inc. v. Superior Court, 154 Cal.App.3d 14, 201 Cal.Rptr. 207, 10 Med.L.Rptr. 1569 (1984). Civil litigants have only a statutory right to discovery. The shield statute and constitutional provision show the legislature's desire to favor press interests in confidentiality over more general discovery values. The court noted that discovery is also subject to other statutory limitations. The importance of the information sought to the underlying litigation was irrelevant.

4. Civil Cases—The Press as Plaintiff

What if the reporter is a party in the case? Syndicated columnist Jack Anderson sued several officials of the Nixon administration for conspiring to harass him. The defendants asserted that the statute of limitations had run and denied the merits of the claims. As part of their defense they asked plaintiff when and how he learned about the alleged harassment and also sought information on other aspects of his claims. Several of these questions required disclosure of confidential sources, but plaintiff refused to reveal them. The judge ordered Anderson to reveal the sources on the ground that they were central to the defenses being raised:

> Here the newsman is not being obliged to disclose his sources. Plaintiff's pledge of confidentiality would have remained unchallenged had he not invoked the aid of the Court seeking compensatory and punitive damages based on his claim of conspiracy. Plaintiff is attempting to use the First Amendment simultaneously as a sword and a shield. He believes he was wronged by a conspiracy that sought to retaliate against his sources and to undermine his reliability and professional standing before the public because what he said was unpopular with the conspirators. But when those he

accuses seek to defend by attempting to discover who his sources were, so that they may find out what the sources knew, their version of what they told him and how they were hurt, plaintiff says this is off limits—a forbidden area of inquiry. He cannot have it both ways. Plaintiff is not a bystander in the process but a principal. He cannot ask for justice and deny it to those he accuses.

The judge rejected plaintiff's assertion that the conflicting claims should be "balanced." This was "most unrealistic. Having chosen to become a litigant, the newsman is not exempt from those obligations imposed by the rule of law on all litigants. . . . " The choice was plaintiff's: reveal the sources or have the case dismissed. Anderson v. Nixon, 444 F.Supp. 1195, 3 Med.L.Rptr. 1687 (D.D.C.1978). The case was subsequently dismissed.

5. CIVIL CASES—THE PRESS AS DEFENDANT

One complex question that cuts across several areas we have discussed is whether media defendants in defamation cases are privileged to refuse to identify confidential sources who gave them the allegedly defamatory information. The philosophy of New York Times Co. v. Sullivan counsels that debate should be open and robust—but that the press should be liable for defamations that are deliberately or recklessly false. What if the public figure plaintiff must know the source of the story to prove that the falsehood was deliberate or reckless? On the other hand, if the plaintiff can expose confidential sources simply by the expedient of suing for libel, such sources may disappear. Is *Branzburg* relevant on this aspect of reporter's privileges?

Several courts struggled with this matter in the early and mid-1970s. (Recall that in the Judy Garland case, the media were not sued.) In 1979, Herbert v. Lando, p. 174, supra, shed some light on the question. Recall that the Supreme Court held that the First Amendment did not protect a journalist from having to testify about his thoughts, opinions and conclusions as he was researching and preparing a story, and about his intra-office communications with others working on the story. The Court stressed that a plaintiff operating under the *New York Times* standard had a difficult task and should be able to seek direct evidence of constitutional malice.

The Court's suggestion that relevant evidence should be available to the plaintiff would suggest that confidential sources not be protected. On the other hand, the Herbert case involved little or no potential for chilling information sources because it involved only the professional journalist's thoughts and communications. The compulsory identification of confidential sources would raise a different question.

These cases present two different issues. The first is when may courts order journalists to reveal confidential sources. It is highly unlikely that any court will allow a person to sue a newspaper for libel and then immediately learn all the confidential sources that were involved in the creation of the story. It is more likely, whether under state law or the First Amendment, that courts will require the plaintiff to show his need for the information. The role the source played in the story's development and in the article will be crucial.

The second question is what sanction should be imposed on a defendant who refuses to obey an order to disclose the identity of its confidential sources. Since Herbert v. Lando, a few state and lower federal courts have begun to address both questions.

1. In Miller v. Transamerican Press, Inc., 621 F.2d 721, rehearing denied, 628 F.2d 932, 6 Med.L.Rptr. 2252 (5th Cir.1980), the court read the *Times* sequence of cases, *Branzburg,* and *Herbert* to create a First Amendment privilege:

> *Herbert* held that the press had no First Amendment privilege against discovery of mental processes where the discovery was for the purpose of determining whether malice existed.
>
> The policies supporting a First Amendment privilege would appear to be stronger here, where a defamation plaintiff seeks to compel disclosure of the name of a confidential informant, than they were in either *Branzburg* or *Herbert.* In *Herbert,* the Supreme Court reasoned that requiring disclosure of journalists' thought processes would have no chilling effect on the editorial process; the only effect would be to deter recklessness. However, forced disclosure of journalists' sources might deter informants from giving their stories to newsmen, except anonymously. This might cause the press to face the unwelcome alternatives of not publishing because of the inherent unreliability of anonymous tips, or publishing anonymous tips and becoming vulnerable to charges of recklessness.
>
> Similarly, there is a more apparent interest in protecting the confidentiality of journalists' sources in libel cases than in grand jury proceedings. In *Branzburg,* the prosecutor had an interest in keeping the informant's identity secret in order to protect him from reprisal. The government and the press had a similar purpose, both were ferreting out wrongdoing and seeking to correct it. In a libel case, the plaintiff and the press are on opposite sides. And a defamed plaintiff might relish an opportunity to retaliate against the informant.
>
> . . .
>
> A final First Amendment consideration, in a case involving a public figure, is that it will often be possible to establish malice or lack of malice without disclosure of the identity of the informant. A plaintiff may be able to find other evidence of malice, or a defendant may be able to come forward with sufficient evidence of prudence in printing which would carry the burden in support of a motion for summary judgment.

The privilege, however, was not absolute. The court drew on a passage in *Herbert:* "Evidentiary privileges in litigation are not favored, and even those rooted in the Constitution must give way in proper circumstances." In *Miller,* the facts indicated that (1) the identity was relevant; (2) the plaintiff had exhausted other efforts to obtain the information; and (3) on balance, after considering other fact situations, the plaintiff's need to learn the identity was compelling. The source was central to the defendant's story and plaintiff could not prove the required type of falsity without knowing the source's identity. In addition, plaintiff must present "substantial evidence" that the statement "is both factually untrue and defamatory."

After ordering the defendant to reveal the source, the court observed that the judge "should protect the informant by restricting the information about the informant's identity to counsel and requiring that it be used strictly for the litigation." Is this likely to induce disclosure? Cross-petitions for certiorari were denied, 450 U.S. 1041 (1981).

2. In Downing v. Monitor Pub. Co., 120 N.H. 383, 415 A.2d 683, 6 Med. L.Rptr. 1193 (1980), the court refused to require the plaintiff to prove the statement false before the defendant had to disclose the source. Plaintiff need only "satisfy the trial court that he has evidence to establish that there is a genuine issue of fact regarding" falsity. Then the court anticipated the question of what should happen if the defendant refused to disclose the source:

> We come to the question of enforcement of the court's order. Of course, the trial court is free to exercise its contempt power to enforce its order. We are aware, however, that most media personnel have refused to obey court orders to disclose, electing to go to jail instead. Confining newsmen to jail in no way aids the plaintiff in proving his case. Although we do not say that the contempt power should not be exercised, we do say that something more is required to protect the rights of a libel plaintiff. Therefore, we hold that when a defendant in a libel action brought by a plaintiff who is required to prove actual malice under *New York Times,* refuses to declare his sources of information upon a valid order of the court, there shall arise a presumption that the defendant had no source. This presumption may be removed by a disclosure of the sources a reasonable time before trial. Because such a disclosure may, for the press, be similar to the disclosure of a "trade secret," there may be circumstances under which an appropriate order limiting outside access to the informant's name when disclosed would not be improper.

3. In one highly publicized case a trial judge, to punish the defendant for refusal to reveal the source, ordered all of the defendant's defenses to be struck—and awarded judgment for plaintiff. On appeal, the state's highest court reversed. First, it doubted the need for the identity of the source, which apparently told the newspaper only where

the relevant information could be found. But even if the order to disclose was valid, the appropriate remedy for disobedience was to tailor the sanction to those aspects of the case in which plaintiff was hampered by the defendant's refusal to disclose the essential information. Sierra Life Ins. Co. v. Magic Valley Newspapers, 101 Idaho 795, 623 P.2d 103, 6 Med.L.Rptr. 1769 (1980).

The results in these cases appear to permit the defendant who refuses to obey an order still to prevail on the truth-falsity issue, or to prove that the damages claimed were not caused by the defamation.

4. State shield laws may affect this question if they directly create a testimonial privilege for reporters that extends to cases where the reporter is a party. Otherwise, even the most elaborate shield statutes will not be used in libel cases. California's version states: "A . . . reporter . . . cannot be adjudged in contempt by a judicial . . . body . . . for refusing to disclose . . . the source of any information procured . . . ." A legislative report stated that although the purpose of the statute was to protect the reporter from being held in contempt, "it does not create a privilege. Thus, the section will not prevent the use of other sanctions for refusal of a newsman to make discovery when he is a party to a civil proceeding." The California statute was discussed in Miller v. Transamerican Press, supra. See also Rancho LaCosta v. Penthouse Int'l, Ltd., 6 Med.L.Rptr. 1249, 1540 (Cal. Super.Ct.1980), ordering the defendant to disclose its sources. If it failed to do so, the jury would be told it had no source. The appellate courts refused to review the case—even though just before the case the California shield law had been adopted verbatim as part of the state Constitution.

In Maressa v. New Jersey Monthly, 89 N.J. 176, 445 A.2d 376, 8 Med.L.Rptr. 1473, certiorari denied 459 U.S. 907 (1982), a state legislator sued the defendant magazine for libel. During discovery the reporters and editors refused to provide any information about their sources or editorial processes. The court upheld the refusals, 6–1, under the broad New Jersey statute. After the Farber case, p. 571, supra, the legislature had again amended the statute to broaden the protection. Now, in *Maressa,* the court concluded that "Absent any countervailing constitutional right, the newsperson's statutory privilege not to disclose confidential information is absolute." The court then concluded that the right to sue for defamation was not required by either the state or federal constitution.

The dissenter sought to establish a state constitutional right to sue for defamation from the sentence "Every person may freely speak, write and publish his sentiments on all subjects, being responsible for the abuse of that right." The majority responded that the second part meant only that the first part should not be read to preclude the availability of libel suits if the legislature thought them appropriate. "It would not be wise to construe our Constitution in a way that etches in stone any particular resolution of the difficult conflict between the right of the media to criticize public figures and the right of public figures to have redress for libel." The court's balance could always be changed by legislation.

The court concluded by observing that an absolute privilege was not the same as an absolute immunity; some public figures would be able to establish the requisite level of misconduct by inferential evidence.

In Coughlin v. Westinghouse Broadcasting & Cable, Inc., 780 F.2d 340, 12 Med.L.Rptr. 1529 (3d Cir.1985), certiorari denied, 106 S.Ct. 2927 (1986), the trial judge granted summary judgment against plaintiff police officer in his libel action for lack of evidence of actual malice. The central issue was the judge's refusal to order the delivery of outtakes or the revelation of the editorial process because of Pennsylvania's shield statute. On appeal, the court affirmed in a cryptic opinion that simply upheld the statute (which was interpreted to protect all the information) against state and federal constitutional challenges. Judge Becker wrote an extended concurring opinion that addressed a wide variety of underlying questions.

A California court construed its shield law otherwise. In KSDO v. Superior Court, 136 Cal.App.3d 375, 186 Cal.Rptr. 211, 8 Med.L.Rptr. 2360 (1982), police officers were suing radio station KSDO for defamation. The court construed the state statute as doing no more than protecting against being held in contempt in cases it covered. It cited much legislative history showing that the legislature "clearly rejected the concept of privilege." Putting the statute into the constitution did not change this.

The court then turned to KSDO's First Amendment argument. Here, it held that a balance was called for. The court finally concluded that plaintiff had not shown that the information sought was unavailable from other sources. Indeed, the reporter at his deposition had identified his sources. Plaintiffs had not shown that they needed the reporter's notes to test the reliability of the sources.

In New York, a newspaper was sued for libel because of a letter to the editor it had published anonymously. The court ruled that the state's shield law protected the paper from having to identify the source and it could not be held in contempt for refusing to do so. This prevented the plaintiff from suing the writer of the letter. But the court also held that in the suit against the paper, the paper's refusal to identify the source might hinder the plaintiff's efforts to prove some essential parts of its case. This would subject the paper to discovery sanctions, but these had to be properly assessed so as not to "create new obstacles to newsgathering or undermine the strong legislative policy expressed in the Shield Law." The lower court had struck the defendant's answer. This was excessive. Barring the paper from introducing evidence on the relevant points "should adequately protect the plaintiffs' interests without intolerably burdening the newspaper." Indeed, the paper had indicated that it would rely exclusively on its own investigation without placing any reliance on the source, and plaintiff had not claimed that this was inadequate. Oak Beach Inn Corp. v. Babylon Beacon, Inc., 62 N.Y.2d 158, 464 N.E.2d 967, 476 N.Y.S.2d 269, 10 Med.L.Rptr. 1761 (1984), certiorari denied 105 S.Ct. 907 (1985).

5. A curious but potentially important tort case emerged in 1983 involving the Phil Donahue show. During a program on parental child-napping, Donahue presented a father, disguised, talking about why he had taken his child. The mother, watching the program, recognized the father. She asked Donahue for help in locating the child. He refused, citing the promise of confidentiality he had given the father. The mother, Cramlet, sued Donahue and Multimedia Program Productions, Inc., his producer. In addition to claiming non-help, Cramlet was able to show that while the father was on the show, Donahue's staff babysat the child backstage. Cramlet's lawyer said that this was analogous to holding a bank robber's loot while interviewing him and then handing it back. The first jury hung. The second awarded Cramlet $1.7 million in compensatory damages and $4.2 million in punitive damages.

A few days after the verdict was announced, an anonymous source revealed the child's whereabouts and he was reunited with his mother. On motion, the trial judge decided that the return of the child had substantially changed the situation because the jury undoubtedly considered the child's future absence in its award. A new trial was granted solely on damages.

The judge found no error in his earlier refusal to permit the defense to introduce journalism experts "to stamp its conduct with the seal of ethical approval. Yet it submitted no written canons of journalism ethics that purport to justify its actions in this case. In effect, the experts were to be called to instruct the jury on the meaning of the First Amendment, a function of this court if applicable, and to tell 'war stories' about journalists' experiences in other cases."

A Colorado statute requires that liability for punitive damages must be established beyond a reasonable doubt. Plaintiff argued that this infringed unconstitutionally on the Colorado Supreme Court's inherent rulemaking powers, and that that court had adopted the preponderance of the evidence standard for all civil cases. The trial judge agreed to seek a declaratory ruling on the subject from the state supreme court. Cramlet v. Multimedia, Inc., 11 Med.L.Rptr. 1707 (D.Colo.1985).

6. Identifying Violators of Judicial Orders

Another issue of privilege arises when a judge or a grand jury wants to learn who gave a reporter information that was supposed to be secret. The problem is illustrated by the case of William Farr, a newspaper reporter covering the lurid Manson trial in Los Angeles. To reduce potentially prejudicial publicity in that case, the trial judge ordered the attorneys and certain others not to speak about specific phases of the case. Farr reported certain facts that he could have learned only from a person covered by the judge's order. The judge demanded that Farr identify his source despite the California privilege statute: "A publisher, editor, reporter . . . cannot be adjudged in contempt by a court . . . for refusing to disclose the source of any information procured for publication and published in a newspaper . . . ." Farr stated that the information had come from forbidden sources, including two of the six attorneys. Each attorney denied having been a source. The judge again asked Farr to identify the individuals. Farr refused and was held in contempt.

The statute was held inapplicable because the legislature had no power to prohibit the court from seeking to preserve the integrity of its own operations. The legislature's efforts to immunize persons from punishment for violation of court orders violated the separation of powers. To immunize Farr "would severely impair the trial court's discharge of a constitutionally compelled duty to control its own officers. The trial court was enjoined by controlling precedent of the United States Supreme Court to take reasonable action to protect the defendants in the Manson case from the effects of prejudicial publicity." Farr v. Superior Court, 22 Cal.App.3d 60, 99 Cal.Rptr. 342 (1971). The Supreme Court of California denied a hearing and the Supreme Court of the United States denied certiorari, 409 U.S. 1011 (1972).

In a later proceeding Farr argued that a contempt citation upon him was essentially a sentence of imprisonment for life because he clearly would not comply. The court noted that an order committing a person until he complies with a court order is "coercive and not penal in nature." The purpose of this sanction is not to punish but to obtain compliance with the order. Where an individual demonstrates conclusively that the coercion will fail, the contempt power becomes penal and comes within a five-day maximum sentence set by California statute. The case was remanded to determine whether coercion could be justified. In re Farr, 36 Cal.App.3d 577, 111 Cal.Rptr. 649 (1974).

Farr was followed by Rosato v. Superior Court, 51 Cal.App.3d 190, 124 Cal.Rptr. 427 (1975), in which four employees of the Fresno Bee were ordered to testify about how they obtained a copy of a grand jury report that had been ordered sealed. The reporters' privilege did not apply to questions directed at learning whether persons under the court's sealing order had violated it. Hearing was denied in the state supreme court, and a petition for certiorari was denied, 427 U.S. 912 (1976). Two reporters and two editors served fifteen days in jail. The judge then held a hearing and concluded that they would not testify. They were found in criminal contempt, sentenced to five-day terms, given credit for time served, and released.

Farr, Rosato, and other cases are discussed at length in Note, A Study in Governmental Separation of Powers: Judicial Response to State Shield Laws, 66 Geo.L.J. 1273 (1978) and in Day, Shield Laws and the Separation of Powers Doctrine, 2 Comm. and the Law 1 (1980).

7. Disclosing Information to Other Bodies

Not only courts ask journalists for information, so do legislatures and administrative agencies. In 1971, the House of Representatives Commerce Committee subpoenaed CBS president Frank Stanton, ordering him to produce portions of film shot for, but not shown on, the documentary "The Selling of the Pentagon." When Stanton refused to give the "outtakes" to the Committee, it voted 25–13 to recommend that Congress issue a contempt citation. The House refused to do so.

A few years later, Daniel Schorr, a former CBS journalist, obtained a copy of a "secret" report of the House Intelligence Committee concerning the Central Intelligence Agency. He gave the report to the Village Voice, which published it in 1976. When asked by the House Ethics Committee to name the person from whom he received the report, Schorr declined. The Committee did not vote to ask for a contempt citation.

8. Suing the Source

Sometimes the reporter is asked to identify the source so that the plaintiff may sue the source directly. In United Liquor Co. v. Gard, 88 F.R.D. 123, 6 Med.L.Rptr. 2197 (D.Ariz.1980), an IRS official illegally leaked information about plaintiff's tax return to a reporter, who published it. Plaintiff had a civil action against the IRS official under 26 U.S.C. §§ 7213 and 7217—if he could be identified. The reporter admitted that the information came from an IRS official but would not identify him.

The trial judge, utilizing a balancing process, ordered identification. At the same time, he noted that if the reporter is also liable for the disclosure of the tax information, he might be able to plead the privilege against self-incrimination to avoid identifying the source.

In another case, a newspaper published a letter to the editor attacking a public official. The paper, honoring the writer's request, published the letter signed as "name withheld." The public official, who wanted to sue the letter writer, sued the paper and "John Doe," and then demanded that the paper produce the letter. Apparently, the paper produced the letter and the plaintiff then dropped his action against the paper. The episode is reported in Editor & Publisher, Feb. 14, 1981, at 12. Is there any reason why a person who writes a letter to the editor for publication and demands anonymity cannot be a confidential source? Note the difficulties in suing the source that are suggested in the Oak Beach Inn case, p. 585, supra.

9. Suit by the Source

Does a paper that reveals a confidential source in violation of its agreement expose itself to legal liability? The answer might have been forthcoming in a case in which a former San Jose policeman sued a television station and its reporter for identifying him to high police officials as the source of leaks about the department. Plaintiff claimed he had to leave the police force as a result of the revelation. The station claimed that there may have been no promise of anonymity in the case and that the name was never broadcast. Should it matter that the name was never revealed in a story—only in a conversation? Might this amount to a breach of contract? What terms should be implied into this type of contract? Broadcasting, Aug. 25, 1980, at 106.

The jury deadlocked after a one-month trial. The only theory that went to the jury was that the reporter had acted with "malice" when she revealed plaintiff's name. The trial judge told the jury that malice included reckless disregard of the consequences for plaintiff. The jury asked to rehear the malice instruction "several times and twice indicated they were deadlocked before finally agreeing further debate would be fruitless." Nat'l L.J., Apr. 2, 1984, at 9. The case was then settled.

In some cases, after the media have fought unsuccessfully to protect the confidentiality, the source may permit identification. In Carey v. Hume, 492 F.2d 631 (D.C.Cir.), certiorari dismissed 417 U.S. 938 (1974), two columnists had relied on a confidential source in reporting that high officials of a union had removed files from union headquarters and had then called the police to report that the files had been stolen. The officials sued for libel. Before trial, the court ordered disclosure. After the appellate decision, the source permitted disclosure of her name and the case went to trial. N.Y. Times, Mar. 23, 1975, at 39. The jury decided for the defendants. N.Y. Times, Nov. 16, 1975, at 49.

To the extent the situation lends itself to a relatively formal agreement, might sources be willing to agree to release the reporter and publisher after they have fought the case as far as possible? Would this poison the atmosphere between reporter and source?

A random sample of 200 members of the American Society of Newspaper Editors estimated that 56 percent of all sources who sought anonymity would speak for the record if pressed hard enough. Editor & Publisher, Sept. 27, 1980, at 22.

See also Maynard v. City of Madison, 101 Wis.2d 273, 304 N.W.2d 163 (App.1981), upholding a tort action against a city whose officials negligently disclosed a confidential informant's identity after promising to protect that confidence. Recall also Hyde v. City of Columbia, p. 360, supra.

C. THE FUTURE OF SHIELD LAWS

There remains substantial disagreement about whether a statutory privilege is desirable, and, if so, the extent and nature of the privilege. Scholars of the law of evidence tend to oppose all privileges as obstacles to the search for truth. The legal profession has accepted some privileges but has refused to endorse a privilege for reporters. At its February 1974 meeting, the House of Delegates of the American Bar

Association voted 157–122 to reject the proposition that a reporter's privilege is essential "to protect the public interest . . . in the free dissemination of news and information to the American people on matters of public importance." 99 A.B.A.Ann.Rept. 162 (1974).

Privilege legislation has also been opposed by a few representatives of the media: in 1974 the Washington Post in an editorial argued that the "best shield is the First Amendment, without the supposed reinforcement of even the purest form of shield law." Editor & Publisher, Mar. 30, 1974, at 15. The justification for this position is the belief that Congress has no business legislating about the press, whether protectively or otherwise. If Congress is conceded power to help the press now it may later be assumed to have power to enact legislation hostile to the press. This concern was voiced during the debate over the Newspaper Preservation Act. Those espousing it would prefer to litigate each case in the courts solely in terms of the First Amendment.

This view is likely to produce more litigation than would a statutory protection—even if limited to certain types of cases. Some media representatives, particularly those from smaller newspapers and broadcasters, believe a limited statute would help avoid expensive litigation without creating new dangers.

After rejecting the case-by-case approach because of its legal cost and uncertainties, a media lawyer considered objections to legislation in Paul, Why a Shield Law?, 29 U.Miami L.Rev. 459 (1975):

> There is, however, the Graham-Knight argument which frets about compromising a basic constitutional right by allowing the legislature to tinker. This problem could be solved by adding two sentences to any shield legislation: "No provision of this act shall be construed to create or imply any limitations upon or otherwise affect any rights secured by the Constitution of the United States. The rights provided by this Act shall be in addition to any rights provided by the Constitution." . . .
>
> The Graham-Knight theorists are also worried about putting reporters in a special class. This ignores what the first amendment is all about. Gatherers and disseminators of information are already in a special class under the first amendment, as are people who insist on religious freedom. The founding fathers put them there. Of course it would be a terrible mistake to draw shield legislation so narrowly that it would apply only to reporters. A broad, one sentence shield law might serve the purpose:
>
>> No person shall be required in any federal or state proceeding to disclose either the source of any published or unpublished information obtained for any medium offering communication to the public, or any unpublished information obtained or prepared in gathering or processing information for any public medium of communication.

> A shield law should be short, simple, and absolute because it must be a badge which a reporter can carry and completely understand without having to hire a lawyer or go to court. Some individuals, however, have argued that other factors should be balanced against the first amendment to justify shield law exceptions when: (1) the only way to prove that the defendant is innocent is to have the reporter testify; (2) the reporter is the only source concerning a committed crime; or (3) national security is involved. I do not accept any of these exceptions. They would create loopholes which would destroy the privilege and bring us back to the case-by-case method. While this might result in some miscarriages of justice, so does the privilege against self-incrimination. The fact that a person is the only witness to a crime does not mean he is required to waive his privilege against self-incrimination.

Would you support an absolute statute? If not, in which of the situations we have been discussing should reporters be fully protected? Partially protected?

Congress has failed to enact federal shield laws in the years since *Branzburg* because of the lack of consensus.

As noted, just over half the states have some form of statute that protects reporters from having to reveal sources or other information in certain situations. These are collected in Matter of Roche, 411 N.E.2d 466, 6 Med.L.Rptr. 2121 (1980). In that case, the court affirmed a ruling holding a reporter in civil contempt. Massachusetts has no "shield" statute. The court rejected constitutional arguments that the reporter need not testify in an inquiry into misbehavior by state judges. If discernible harm to the flow of information were shown over a period of time, some constitutional relief might be required. But the First Amendment "does not define the limits of permissible concern for those values the amendment is designed to serve. In our view it is at the nonconstitutional level of statutory enactment and common law development that precise limitations on the protection to be afforded those persons such as Roche may be best defined." Roche had not properly preserved a state constitutional claim.

After rejecting Roche's other claims, the majority announced its "willingness to consider, in future cases, whether the central role a free discussion of public issues plays in a self-governing society requires, as a matter of Massachusetts practice, that persons addressing such issues be afforded more clearly defined protection against intrusive discovery than that provided by [the state version of Federal Rule 26(c)]. That courts should play an active role in defining these limits at a nonconstitutional level seems particularly appropriate in view of our traditional responsibility for fashioning rules of evidence. The incremental process of common law development would address the need to avoid overly broad generalizations that in some cases may result in depriving litigants of relevant evidence or inhibiting speech."

In 1985, the Supreme Judicial Court rejected petitions from a task force appointed by the Governor asking it to adopt rules creating a reporters' shield by court rule. Assuming that it had the power to adopt the rule, the court declined, preferring to proceed on a case-by-case basis. Petition for the Promulgation of Rules, 395 Mass. 164, 479 N.E.2d 154, 11 Med.L.Rptr. 2307 (1985).

One reason offered by the court was the lack of consensus among all the proponents as to whether it should be limited to organized media; whether it should be unqualified in scope; and, if qualified, when the privilege should be rejected. Another reason was the advantage of the common law approach, which "will result in less static and dogmatic principles than those enshrined in a rule." The court rejected arguments that the common law approach left the press and public with insufficient guidance.

In 1980, the voters of California decided to place their shield statute verbatim in the state constitution. Art. I, § 2(b). In what ways might this action change the judicial approach in California?

Any legislative enactment will have to define those who would be able to take advantage of the protection. This requirement troubled the majority in *Branzburg*. Is the same problem raised by legislation? How broadly would you write the legislation?

D. THE USE OF SEARCH WARRANTS

Search warrants for outtakes or information leading to the identification of confidential sources may avoid the types of litigation discussed in the previous section because the police conducting the search are thereby permitted to look for the items listed in the warrants.

Although all search warrants may present serious problems of privacy, the matter did not come to a head until a search of the offices of the Stanford Daily. Police believed that Daily photographers had taken photographs that would aid in identifying persons who had assaulted policemen during a violent demonstration. The police obtained a search warrant and served it on the Daily. The affidavits accompanying the request for the warrant indicated no reason why a subpoena might not have sufficed.

After the search, the Daily brought an action under 42 U.S.C. § 1983 against the chief of police and other local officials for a determination that the search had violated the Daily's First, Fourth, and Fourteenth Amendment rights. The district judge granted declaratory relief, concluding that no search warrant could issue against any person not suspected of a crime unless a subpoena was shown to be impracticable. Where the object of the search was a newspaper, the judge ruled that a warrant issue only "where there is a *clear showing* that (1) important materials will be destroyed or removed from the jurisdiction; *and* (2) a restraining order would be futile." The court of appeals adopted the trial judge's opinion and affirmed.

The Supreme Court reversed, 5–3. Zurcher v. Stanford Daily, 436 U.S. 547, 3 Med.L.Rptr. 2377 (1978). Justice White, for the majority, began by stating that "Under existing law, valid warrants may be issued to search *any* property, whether or not occupied by a third party, at which there is probable cause to believe that fruits, instrumentalities, or evidence of a crime will be found. Nothing on the face of the Amendment suggests that a third-party search warrant should not normally issue." Since the state's interest in obtaining evidence of crime is the same wherever the evidence is located, the validity of a warrant does not depend on whether the occupant of the property is suspected of crime, but whether there is reasonable cause to believe the evidence is on particular property.

Justice White also observed that "rational" prosecutors would use subpoenas when they could because they are easier to use and do not require formal affidavits or presentation to a magistrate.

He then turned to the First Amendment question:

> The District Court held, and respondents assert here, that, whatever may be true of third-party searches generally, where the third party is a newspaper, there are additional factors derived from the First Amendment that justify a nearly *per se* rule forbidding the search warrant and permitting only the subpoena *duces tecum.* The general submission is that searches of newspaper offices for evidence of crime reasonably believed to be on the premises will seriously threaten the ability of the press to gather, analyze, and disseminate news. This is said to be true for several reasons: First, searches will be physically disruptive to such an extent that timely publication will be impeded. Second, confidential sources of information will dry up, and the press will also lose opportunities to cover various events because of fears of the participants that press files will be readily available to the authorities. Third, reporters will be deterred from recording and preserving their recollections for future use if such information is subject to seizure. Fourth, the processing of news and its dissemination will be chilled by the prospects that searches will disclose internal editorial deliberations. Fifth, the press will resort to self-censorship to conceal its possession of information of potential interest to the police.

Justice White recognized that where the materials sought to be seized may be protected by the First Amendment, the requirements of the Fourth Amendment must be applied with "scrupulous exactitude." Also, seizures reasonable in one context may not be reasonable "in a different setting or with respect to another kind of material." Even so, nothing in the Fourth Amendment barred searches of newspaper offices. They were subject to the same procedures, including the approval of "neutral magistrates." Few searches of newspaper premises had occurred recently. "This reality hardly suggests abuse; and if abuse occurs, there will be time enough to deal with it. Furthermore, the press is not only an important, critical, and valuable asset to society, but it is not easily intimidated—nor should it be."

Finally, he noted that nothing in the Fourth Amendment barred "legislative or executive efforts to establish nonconstitutional protections against possible abuses of the search warrant procedure."

Justice Stewart dissented in an opinion joined by Justice Marshall. They relied on the First Amendment and feared a serious interference with the flow of information. Even the reporter's promise of confidentiality could no longer be relied upon. To guarantee confidentiality, the reporter would have to destroy notes or would have to take extreme steps to hide them.

The issue was not the existence of a privilege, as in *Branzburg,* but "only whether any significant societal interest would be impaired if the police were generally required to obtain evidence from the press by means of a subpoena rather than a search."

Here, the application for the warrant showed no emergency need to protect life or property. (Justice Powell, in a concurring opinion, had mentioned that the Daily had an announced policy of destroying materials that might help law enforcement groups—but the application for the warrant contained no such allegation.)

Justice Stevens dissented solely on the Fourth Amendment ground. He viewed the problem as an outgrowth of Warden v. Hayden, 387 U.S. 294 (1967), in which the Court extended the use of search warrants from "contraband, weapons, and plunder" to "mere evidence." He concluded that the only reason for an unannounced search of any innocent person was fear of concealment or destruction. With no such claim in the application for this warrant, and with no claim that the Daily was suspected of a crime, the Fourth Amendment's requirements had not been satisfied.

Justice Brennan did not participate in the case.

After the decision, a few states enacted bans on the issuance of search warrants against media. Most attention centered on Congress, however, where legislative efforts were complicated because the press did not want the bill to be addressed solely to the press, and the Justice Department would accept a bill limited to the press but not one that protected all innocent third parties. The result, the Privacy Protection Act of 1980, codified in 42 U.S.C. § 2000aa, was a compromise.

The basic provision makes it unlawful for an official of any government to search or seize "any work product material possessed by a person reasonably believed to have a purpose to disseminate to the public a newspaper, book, broadcast, or other similar form of public communication, in or affecting interstate or foreign commerce." This provision does not apply where there is probable cause to believe that the person possessing the materials has committed or is committing the offense to which the materials relate. This, in turn, has an exception: no search may occur where the charge involves "receipt, possession, or communication of information relating to the national defense, classified information, or restricted data" under specific espionage, atomic energy, or subversive activities control legislation.

A second ground for searching for work products is "reason to believe that the immediate seizure of such materials is necessary to prevent the death of, or serious bodily injury to, a human being."

"Work product" is defined to mean materials other than contraband prepared in anticipation of communication to the public, no matter who authored them, and may include "mental impressions, conclusions, opinions, or theories of the person who prepared, produced, authored, or created such material."

A second major provision deals with "documentary materials," which are defined as materials "upon which information is recorded, and includes, but is not limited to," written or printed materials, photographs, film, tapes, discs, and punch cards. The same two exceptions to the ban on searches and seizures that applied to work products apply to documentary materials possessed by "a person reasonably believed to have a purpose to disseminate . . . ." In addition, government officials may search for documentary materials (1) where there is reason to believe that giving notice of a subpoena would lead to destruction or concealment; and (2) where the material has not been delivered in response to an earlier subpoena and all appellate remedies have been exhausted.

Civil remedies are provided against governments or officials for violations of the statute.

Next, the statute directs the Attorney General to issue guidelines that federal employees are to use in obtaining documentary materials "in the private possession of a person when the person is not reasonably believed to be a suspect in such offense or related by blood or marriage to such a suspect." The guidelines are to incorporate recognition of the privacy interest of the person; recognition of special relationships such as those involving doctors, lawyers, and clergymen; a requirement that the least intrusive method be used to obtain the materials; and that applications for warrants be approved by a government attorney except in emergency situations. Violation of the guidelines would lead to appropriate administrative disciplinary action, but alleged failures to comply are not to be litigated and provide no basis for suppression of the evidence obtained. The final regulations were adopted in 46 Fed. Reg. 22362 (Apr. 17, 1981).

Telephone Records. The government may learn about reporters' sources and activities in ways that do not involve search warrants or subpoenas. Reporters Committee for Freedom of the Press v. American Tel. & Tel. Co., 593 F.2d 1030 (D.C.Cir.1978), involved government requests for records of long distance calls charged to (but perhaps not made to or from) telephone numbers. Reporters asserted that the First and Fourth Amendments required that subscribers be given notice before AT&T honored the government's request for toll-call records.

The court, 2–1, concluded that balancing was not appropriate because "Government access to third-party evidence in the course of a good faith felony investigation in no sense 'abridges' plaintiffs' information-gathering activities." The possibility of bad-faith investigations (to harass reporters) did not warrant prior judicial intervention unless the reporter could establish "a clear and imminent threat of such future misconduct." The dissenter would have afforded reporters the opportunity to have judicial decisions on such requests made in advance on a case-by-case basis. Certiorari was denied. 440 U.S. 949 (1979), Brennan, Marshall and Stewart, JJ., dissenting.

After the Department of Justice, in 1979, obtained records of a reporter's toll calls from the local telephone company, the press urged government attention to the problem. The result was the promulgation, in November 1980, of amendments to the subpoena guidelines to provide that discussions with the reporter should precede any subpoena to the telephone company where the appropriate Assistant Attorney General concludes that such disclosure would not jeopardize the investigation. Before any subpoena is issued, the "express authorization of the Attorney General" is required. Such authorization should not be requested from the Attorney General unless there is reason to believe a crime has been committed, the need is clear, and alternative investigative steps have been unsuccessfully explored. The reporter should be informed within forty-five days (though that may be delayed another forty-five days) and the information obtained shall be closely held to prevent unauthorized persons from learning what the records reveal. The amended guidelines are codified in 28 C.F.R. § 50.10, and are reprinted in 6 Media L.Rptr. 2153 (1980).

In drafting legislation involving search warrants or telephone records, how broadly would you define the group to be protected? Are these definitions of the same breadth as those you thought appropriate for the shield legislation?

Chapter XI

UNWILLING PRIVATE SOURCES

In Chapter X, we considered some of the possible ways in which government might interfere with communications between willing sources and eager gatherers. We also considered how government might cause some sources who otherwise might have been willing to discuss a situation, to cease to be willing to do so. In this Chapter, we consider the extents to which media may legally go to obtain information from private persons or organizations that have the information sought but do not wish to divulge it to the seeker.

PRAHL v. BROSAMLE

Court of Appeals of Wisconsin, 1980.
98 Wis.2d 130, 295 N.W.2d 768.

Before GARTZKE, P.J., and BABLITCH and DYKMAN, JJ.

GARTZKE, PRESIDING JUDGE.

This appeal arises out of the trial court's dismissal of the complaint at the close of the plaintiffs' case in a jury trial. The plaintiffs are Dr. Helmut Prahl, Dynatron Research Foundation and Dynatron Research Corporation.

Dr. Prahl, a biochemist, is the executive director of the foundation and the sole stockholder and president of the research corporation. His residence, the offices of the foundation and the laboratory of the research corporation are located in a single building on about six acres fronting on Struck Road in a township adjacent to Madison. Dr. Prahl owns the land and building. The Madison Police Department received a complaint June 18, 1975, that shots had been fired at four boys who were bicycling in the area. Dane County sheriff's deputies and the police investigated the report that night. Employees of Forward Communications, operators of television station WMTV, broadcast newscasts of the incident.

Dr. Prahl seeks damages for a claimed violation of his civil rights from Bryan Brosamle, a newscaster for WMTV, and from the deputies and police, and damages for defamation from Brosamle, two other WMTV newscasters and WMTV.[1] Dr. Prahl, the foundation and the research corporation seek damages for negligent performance of procedures from the deputies, the police, the City of Madison and Dane County, and damages for trespass from Brosamle, WMTV, the deputies and the police. Plaintiffs seek compensatory and punitive damages as

1. Dr. Prahl also sought damages for false imprisonment and battery but does not contest dismissal of the complaint as to those claims.

to all claims except the claim based upon negligence, as to which only compensatory damages are sought.

Before proceeding to a more detailed statement of the facts, we first note the appropriate standard of review. . . .

Accordingly, we state only those facts which are favorable to the plaintiffs and which are pertinent to the issues raised on appeal.

After the boys allegedly shot at were interviewed, the police assembled the city's Strategic Weapons and Tactics Squad (SWAT). About 9:30 p.m. officers from the squad positioned themselves behind, to the side and in front of the building. Other officers assembled in squad cars at the Struck Road entrance to the driveway. Lieutenant Kuenning of the sheriff's office took command because the Prahl property was not in Madison. No search or arrest warrant was procured or requested.

The police made a telephone call to Dr. Prahl, requesting that he step outside his residence. Fifteen minutes passed before Dr. Prahl emerged, and when he did so, the police charged the residence on foot and in squad cars. Dr. Prahl was frisked outside his house and the police searched the residence and laboratory. Plaintiffs concede that the search was made with probable cause. The police found a .22 caliber rifle containing seven rounds in the entrance hallway. They found Dr. Prahl's fourteen-year-old son in his bedroom. The youth surrendered a pellet gun to the police. Both guns were confiscated.

The police interviewed Dr. Prahl in an office in the building. He said that he often shot gophers on his property. He said that several boys had been playing with antique cars which he kept on the premises, that he asked the boys to leave, and that after a delay to allow them to do so he had shot at a gopher.

Dr. Prahl was not taken into custody. A deputy sheriff told Dr. Prahl that he would be charged with the crime of reckless use of a weapon and told him to report to the district attorney's office June 20.

Brosamle heard the call summoning the SWAT team while he was monitoring a police scanner at WMTV, grabbed a silent movie camera, and went to the scene. He introduced himself to the officers on Struck Road and made inquiries. Brosamle asked Lieutenant Kuenning for a ride to the Prahl residence and was told that he could come forward when the situation was under control. Brosamle filmed the squad cars as they charged up the driveway to the building and rode to the building with Lieutenant Kuenning. Brosamle went into the building, positioned himself in the entranceway or vestibule, and filmed officers confiscating the guns and part of the police interview with Dr. Prahl.

Brosamle did not request or receive Dr. Prahl's permission to go upon the premises, to enter the building, or to take pictures inside the building. "No trespassing" signs were located at points on the boundaries of the premises but not at the driveway entrance on Struck Road. There is no evidence that Brosamle, the officers or the deputies knew about the signs. Dr. Prahl saw Brosamle taking pictures but thought that he was an officer or a deputy and did not tell Brosamle to stop or to leave. Brosamle talked to Dr. Prahl's son in a laboratory. Lieutenant Kuenning testified that while on the premises he may have told Brosamle that Dr. Prahl would be charged with reckless use of a weapon.

Brosamle returned to WMTV where he drafted a news script and edited his film. The story was broadcast that evening and the next day. The story consisted of film shots showing police cars driving to the building, officers holding the confiscated guns and Dr. Prahl talking to officers in his office. The gist of the broadcasts was that Dr. Prahl had been charged with the crime of reckless use of a weapon.

Dr. Prahl reported as directed to the district attorney. No charge, however, was made against Dr. Prahl as a result of the June 18 incident.

1. VIOLATION OF CIVIL RIGHTS

. . .

The evidence, viewed most favorably as to Dr. Prahl, fails to show a violation of 42 U.S.C. § 1983. The circuit court therefore properly dismissed that part of the complaint which seeks damages on the basis of that statute.

2. DEFAMATION

Dr. Prahl claims that he was defamed by the television broadcasts.

. . .

This state has not announced a post-*Gertz* standard of liability applicable to defamation of private persons by the press. We need not, however, undertake that task because of the applicability of the *Gertz* limitations on damages to the facts of this case. Dr. Prahl has shown no basis to recover punitive damages and has not established actual damages arising out of the defamation.

The circuit court found, and we agree, that the record shows no malice or ill will, bad motive, knowledge of falseness or reckless disregard for the truth. A newscaster cannot be said to act with knowledge of falsity or with reckless disregard of the truth by broadcasting that a person has been or will be charged with a crime where that person was told by a deputy sheriff that he would be so charged. The difference between a charge in fact and a charge to be made, in this context, is inconsequential. Accordingly, *Gertz* prevents the recovery of punitive damages.

Evidence as to Dr. Prahl's damages was directed to the effect of the incident at his residence and its televised coverage, with no reference whatever to the effect of the defamatory statement. . . .

Consequently, regardless of the standard of liability for a publisher or broadcaster of defamatory falsehood injurious to a private individual, actual injury from the defamation has not been shown. The action for defamation therefore cannot survive under the *Gertz* limitations. The trial court properly dismissed this part of Dr. Prahl's claim.

3. TRESPASS

A. *Trespass By Brosamle Established*

The circuit court held that Brosamle was not a trespasser. We reject that conclusion.

The common-law rule of liability for intentional intrusion of land as set forth in Restatement (Second) of Torts sec. 158 at 277 (1965), so far as is material, is as follows:

> One is subject to liability to another for trespass, irrespective of whether he thereby causes harm to any legally protected interest of the other, if he intentionally
>
> (a) enters land in the possession of the other, or causes a thing or a third person to do so, ...

Comment e adds that conduct which would otherwise constitute a trespass is not a trespass if it is privileged by consent of the possessor or by law.

Proof of entry, without more, is insufficient to establish a claim for trespass. The plaintiff must also show thc plaintiff's right to possession. Failure to establish the element of possession is fatal to the claim. [ ]

There is evidence from which the jury could conclude that Dr. Prahl not only owned the six acres and the building but had a right to possession of that part of the building occupied by him as a residence, that the laboratory in the building was that of the research corporation and that the office in the building was that of the foundation. That evidence consists of Dr. Prahl's statement that the plaintiffs maintained those respective facilities in the building and that he owned the land and building. Brosamle at least positioned himself in the entranceway or vestibule of the building. All persons having a right to use the common way are parties to this action. Additionally, the research corporation may bring trespass for entry of its laboratory.

Consent to entry is a defense to an action for trespass. [ ] That consent may be given expressly or it may be implied from the conduct of the plaintiff, from the relationship of the parties or from custom. [ ]

Express consent was never given. Nothing in the conduct of Dr. Prahl on his own behalf or that of the corporations suggests a consent to entry by Brosamle. Acquiescence by a plaintiff in past intrusions by members of the same class as the defendant is conduct from which a consent to entry may be implied. [ ] There is no evidence of past conduct by the plaintiffs which could be interpreted as a consent to

Brosamle's entry. No relationship exists between the parties from which a consent may be implied.

Brosamle and WMTV argue that plaintiffs impliedly consented, by custom and usage, to the presence of newsmen on the premises. They do not assert that this record establishes such a custom or usage but rely upon Florida Pub. Co. v. Fletcher, 340 So.2d 914 (Fla.1977), cert. denied 431 U.S. 930 (1977).

The facts in the *Fletcher* case are that following a fire which killed plaintiffs' daughter in their home, a large group of firemen, news photographers and onlookers gathered at the scene. The fire marshal and a police sergeant invited news representatives to enter the house. The representatives entered through an open door without objection to gather news of the fire and death. The marshal requested defendant's photographer to take a picture of the "silhouette" left on the floor after removal of the body. The marshal and sergeant testified that it was common custom and usage to permit news media to enter under such circumstances. Affidavits to the same effect were filed by the sheriff, attorney general of the state and several newspapers and television stations.

Fletcher held that the plaintiffs could not recover for trespass because the entry was effected by an implied consent arising out of a longstanding custom to allow news representatives to enter private property where a disaster has occurred and the officers investigating the calamity invite the entry.

The authorities relied upon by *Fletcher* deal with the implied invitation by businessmen, tradesmen and professionals to the public to come to their shops and offices, the implied invitation by a householder to others to come to the home for business or information, and the implied consent of landowners to sportsmen to enter land if consent is customarily given. *Fletcher,* 340 So.2d at 916. The following quotations from two of the authorities relied upon by *Fletcher* are representative:

> Consent to enter on land in the possession of another may be derived from the relationship of the parties, as in the case of intimate friends or social or business visitors. Unless the possessor manifests otherwise, a general or local custom may confer a consent, as where a traveler enters another's land to make inquiry as to the road or where in a particular neighborhood it is customary to permit persons to wander, fish, shoot and camp at will on unenclosed land. Restatement of Torts sec. 167, comment d at 403 (1934).[5]

5. Restatement (Second) of Torts has modified the language of Restatement of Torts sec. 167, comment d. Restatement (Second) of Torts sec. 167 at 309, provides that the rules stated in secs. 892–892D as to the effect of consent to the actor's conduct apply to entry or remaining on land. Restatement (Second) of Torts sec. 892(2) at 362 provides, "If words or conduct are reasonably understood by another to be intended as consent, they constitute apparent consent and are as effective as consent in fact." Comment d to sec. 892(2) states:

So every man, by implication, invites others to come to his house as they may have proper occasion, either of business, of courtesy, for information, etc. Custom must determine in these cases what the limit is of the implied invitation. 2 Cooley on Torts sec. 248 at 238 (4th ed. 1932) (footnotes omitted).

Fletcher is distinguishable from the facts of this case. No official requested Brosamle's assistance in the investigation. Brosamle and WMTV do not rely upon record evidence of a custom of the type described in *Fletcher.*

We will not imply a consent as a matter of law. It is of course well known that news representatives want to enter a private building after or even during a newsworthy event within the building. That knowledge is no basis for an implied consent by the possessor of the building to the entry. Because of reasonable expectations, landowners commonly post their lands against trespassers. Businesses, professionals and homeowners are known to post their buildings against anticipated solicitations. Few private persons anticipate, however, that an unplanned newsworthy event will occur on their property. An advance objection to entry under remotely possible circumstances need not be made, and it is unreasonable to require an objection after entry under distracting circumstances, especially when the identity of the intruder is unknown.

We conclude that custom and usage have not been shown in fact or law to confer an implied consent upon news representatives to enter a building under the circumstances presented by this case.

The jury could have found at the conclusion of Dr. Prahl's case that Brosamle trespassed by entering the six acres from Struck Road as well as by entering the building.

A custom exists in this state from which a consent or invitation of the type described by 2 Cooley on Torts sec. 248, supra, is implied. That custom is the basis for the holding in Brabazon v. Joannes Brothers Co., 231 Wis. 426, 433, 286 N.W. 21, 25 (1939), that business visitors to a store are "impliedly licensed to enter and be there for the purpose of offering articles and demonstrating the nature or operation thereof in the usual and customary manner, as long as reasonably necessary to accomplish those purposes or the plaintiffs permitted them to remain."

An implied consent to enter the land of another for business or informational purposes creates a privilege to enter only for that purpose. *Brabazon,* [ ]. Brosamle did not enter Dr. Prahl's land to do

In determining whether conduct would be understood by a reasonable person as indicating consent, the customs of the community are to be taken into account. This is true particularly of silence or inaction. Thus if it is the custom in wooded or rural areas to permit the public to go hunting on private land or to fish in private lakes or streams, anyone who goes hunting or fishing may reasonably assume, in the absence of a posted notice or other manifestation to the contrary, that there is the customary consent to his entry upon private land to hunt or fish.

business with the plaintiffs or to obtain permission to gather news on the land or in the building. He did not seek information of the type covered by the custom, such as directions.[6]

Accordingly, a new trial must be had as to the claims of Dr. Prahl against Brosamle and his employer for trespass by entering the six acres from Struck Road without permission, unless entry was otherwise privileged.

Brosamle and WMTV argue that they should be accorded a privilege to trespass stemming from the first amendment to the United States Constitution. No case is cited to support that proposition. On the contrary, Branzburg v. Hayes, [ ], states in dictum, "Newsmen have no constitutional right of access to the scenes of crime or disaster when the general public is excluded, ..." Le Mistral, Inc. v. Columbia Broadcasting, 61 A.D.2d 491, 402 N.Y.S.2d 815 (1978), appeal dismissed 46 N.Y.2d 940 (1979), held that a television broadcast station was not entitled to immunity from damages for trespass by virtue of the first amendment. *Le Mistral* relied upon Dietemann v. Time, Inc., 449 F.2d 245, 249 (9th Cir.1971), in which the court of appeals observed in an action for invasion of privacy that "[t]he First Amendment has never been construed to accord newsmen immunity from torts or crimes committed during the course of newsgathering. The First Amendment is not a license to trespass, ..."

We conclude that the claimed constitutional privilege to trespass does not exist.

B. Damages Recoverable for Trespass by Brosamle

The circuit court also found that the plaintiffs had failed to show damages to the premises caused by Brosamle's entry and that the damage, if any, from the television broadcast was not caused by Brosamle's presence on the premises. The court concluded that the damages asserted in Dr. Prahl's claim for defamation could not support his claim in trespass.

The circuit court erred in not allowing the plaintiffs at least to recover nominal damages as determined by the jury. A trespasser who has not damaged the property or its possessor is nevertheless liable to the possessor for nominal damages.

Compensatory and punitive damages have been held recoverable from news representatives for trespass. Le Mistral, Inc. v. Columbia Broadcasting, [ ], Belluomo v. KAKE TV & Radio, Inc., 3 Kan.App.2d 461, 596 P.2d 832 (1979).

In *Le Mistral,* CBS directed an employee and a camera crew to visit restaurants which had been cited for health code violations in New

6. The "no trespassing" signs erected on Dr. Prahl's land bear upon his refusal to accede to the custom from which consent is implied to enter for business or information. However, there is no evidence that those signs were so located as to be brought to the attention of a person at the Struck Road entrance to the premises. See n. 5.

York City. The camera crew and the employee entered the plaintiff's restaurant with a camera "rolling." The court found that a trespass had occurred and allowed . . . compensatory damages and punitive damages.

In *Belluomo,* defendant's newsmen accompanied a food inspector to the plaintiffs' restaurant. One of the owners was fraudulently induced by the newsmen to grant permission to enter and photograph the nonpublic area of the restaurant. Defendant's television broadcast stated that unsanitary conditions existed in the restaurant and showed sections of the restaurant. The theory of the plaintiffs' claim was tortious conduct, trespass, in defendant's newsgathering, not defamatory falsehood. Plaintiffs sought compensatory damages based upon reduced customer patronage after the broadcast and punitive damages for the fraud. The court held that "a party is entitled to recover compensatory damages for injury resulting from publication of information acquired by tortious conduct," and, "Truth of what was broadcast was no defense to plaintiffs' claim." 3 Kan.App.2d at 471, 476, 596 P.2d at 842, 845. The court appears to have relied heavily upon *Dietemann,* 449 F.2d at 250, where it is said, "A rule forbidding the use of publication as an ingredient of damages would deny to the injured plaintiff recovery for real harm done to him without any countervailing benefit to the legitimate interest of the public in being informed."

Belluomo extends a trespasser's traditional liability to include nonphysical harm subsequent to the trespass. Restatement (Second) of Torts sec. 162 at 291–92 (1965), provides:

> A trespass on land subjects the trespasser to liability for physical harm to the possessor of the land at the time of the trespass, or to the land or to his things, or to members of his household or to their things, caused by any act done, activity carried on, or condition created by the trespasser, ...

The extension to include nonphysical harm from an intrusion of the type involved is reasonable. To allow only nominal damages under the circumstances presented because of lack of physical harm would permit the trespasser to enjoy the benefits of his tort without fully compensating a plaintiff for his loss.

A new trial must therefore be granted as to the plaintiffs' claims for trespass by Brosamle.

Establishing the effect of publication of the tortiously acquired information at the trial, as contrasted to the effect of publication of information lawfully acquired by Brosamle, may be difficult. It is only the film and information obtained during the trespass which were tortiously acquired. The damages recoverable from publication, insofar as mental distress is claimed, are further subject to the rule that, "In intentional torts, substantial other damages in addition to damages for emotional distress are required." Anderson v. Continental Ins. Co., 85 Wis.2d 675, 694, 271 N.W.2d 368, 378 (1978).

C. Trespass By Lieutenant Kuenning Established

A new trial must be had with respect to the plaintiffs' claims for trespass against Lieutenant Kuenning and Dane County but not as to the other deputies, officers and the City of Madison. The deputies and police were privileged under the circumstances of this case to enter the land and building. Restatement (Second) of Torts secs. 204–06 at 381–88 (1965).[7]

Lieutenant Kuenning's statement that Brosamle could come forward when the situation was under control may have been intended only to indicate no objection to Brosamle's presence. A jury could find that, however, it constituted a consent to Brosamle's entry upon the premises.

Lieutenant Kuenning had no authority to extend a consent to Brosamle to enter the land of another. Although entry by Lieutenant Kuenning was privileged, he committed a trespass by participating in the trespass by Brosamle. "All persons who cooperate, instigate, command, encourage, ratify, condone, aid, assist, or advise the commission of a trespass are liable as cotrespassers." Dooley, 3 Modern Tort Law sec. 40.11 at 165 (1977) (citations omitted).

There is no evidence that an officer or a deputy other than Lieutenant Kuenning told Brosamle that he could enter the premises or the building. . . .

. . .

The judgment is reversed insofar as it dismisses the fourth claim in the complaint against Bryan Brosamle, Forward Communications Corporation, Lieutenant Kuenning and Dane County for damages for trespass. A new trial is ordered, limited to that claim. The judgment is otherwise affirmed.

Notes and Questions

1. On remand, the trial judge dismissed the case. He found that it was "a common and accepted custom in the State of Wisconsin and nationally for reporters and photographers to accompany public officers and firemen onto private premises where newsworthy events of general public interest such as crime, shootings, fires or storms have or are occurring, provided that (1) such entry can be made peacefully, without force or physical destruction; (2) there is no objection to such entry; and (3) such entry is made for purposes of newsgathering or the taking of news photographs."

7. Restatement (Second) of Torts sec. 204 at 381 (1965), provides:

> The privilege to make an arrest for a criminal offense carries with it the privilege to enter land in the possession of another for the purpose of making such an arrest, if the person sought to be arrested is on the land or if the actor reasonably believes him to be there.

Section 206(1) provides that the privilege to enter land stated in sec. 204 carries with it the privilege to use force to enter a dwelling if the person sought to be taken into custody is in the dwelling but only after explanation and demand for admittance, unless the actor reasonably believes such demand to be impractical or useless.

Based on that finding he concluded that this custom "was an implied consent by the plaintiffs to such entry which is a defense to plaintiffs' cause of action for trespass." Prahl v. Brosamle, Case No. 152–062, Circuit Court, Dane County, Aug. 28, 1982 (Pekowsy, J.).

2. *No Express Consent.* The starkest issues arise when the entry has been without the express consent of the possessor. In *Fletcher,* involving the entry after a disastrous fire, the court stressed "custom and usage" but noted that these "do not rest upon the previous nonobjection to entry by the particular owner of the property in question but rest upon custom and practice generally." The court emphasized the total destruction of the premises. *Fletcher* is noted in 30 Fed.Com.L.J. 77 (1977).

3. Compare Green Valley School Inc. v. Cowles Florida Broadcasting, Inc., 327 So.2d 810 (Fla.App.1976). State officials planned a midnight raid, under a properly issued warrant, to search the premises of a controversial local boarding school. The head of the party of 50 raiders invited reporters and photographers from several local media organizations to accompany the party. The defendant television station presented an extensive report of the raid on the evening news the following night, suggesting that the raid had turned up evidence of mistreatment of the students and rampant sexual misbehavior and use of drugs. The school sued the station for defamation and for trespass.

The affidavits of students and faculty asserted that the raiders had strewn things around rooms and caused confusion among the students. One affidavit charged that defendant's reporter "helped those cops mess up things, and he only took pictures after cops called him over with some special goodie they had made up. He was ugly and obscene to the girls and made Cathy especially humiliated."

The trial judge granted summary judgment to the station on the trespass count. The court of appeal reversed, addressing the question entirely in the following passage:

> To uphold appellees' assertion that their entry upon appellant's property at the time, manner, and circumstances as reflected by this record was as a *matter of law* sanctioned by "the request of and with the consent of the State Attorney" and with the "common usage and custom in Florida" could well bring to the citizenry of this state the hobnail boots of a Nazi stormtrooper equipped with glaring lights invading a couple's bedroom at midnight with the wife hovering in her nightgown in an attempt to shield herself from the scanning TV camera. In this jurisdiction, a law enforcement officer is not as a *matter of law* endowed with the right or authority to invite people of his choosing to invade private property and participate in a midnight raid of the premises.

The Florida Supreme Court granted further review to Cowles. But on the same day it decided *Fletcher,* it dismissed the Cowles case after having heard arguments. 340 So.2d 1154 (Fla.1976). The court's jurisdiction in *Green Valley* depended on a conflict with other decisions—and it found no conflict between its own decision in *Fletcher* and the lower court decision in *Green Valley* to justify jurisdiction. There was no further explanation. How might the two cases be reconciled?

4. In Le Mistral v. Columbia Broadcasting System, cited in *Prahl,* CBS, as owner and operator of WCBS–TV in New York City, directed reporter Rich and a camera crew to visit restaurants that had been cited for health code violations. Plaintiff was on the list. The crew entered plaintiff's restaurant with cameras "rolling" and using bright lights that were necessary to get the pictures. The jury found CBS liable for trespass and awarded plaintiff $1,200 in compensatory damages and $250,000 in punitive damages. After verdict (in a passage approved on appeal), the trial judge stated:

> The instructions given to the crew, whether specific to this event or as standing operating procedure, were to avoid seeking an appointment or permission to enter any of the premises where a story was sought, but to enter unannounced catching the occupants by surprise; "with cameras rolling" in the words of CBS' principal witness, Rich. From the evidence the jury was entitled to conclude that following this procedure the defendant's employees burst into plaintiff's restaurant in noisy and obtrusive fashion and following the loud commands of the reporter, Rich, to photograph the patrons dining, turned their lights and camera upon the dining room. Consternation, the jury was informed, followed. Patrons waiting to be seated left the restaurant. Others who had finished eating, left without waiting for their checks. Still others hid their faces behind napkins or table cloths or hid themselves beneath tables. (The reluctance of the plaintiff's clientele to be video taped was never explained, and need not be. Patronizing a restaurant does not carry with it an obligation to appear on television). [The] president of the plaintiff and manager of its operations, refused to be interviewed, and as the camera continued to "roll" he pushed the protesting Miss Rich and her crew from the premises. All told, the CBS personnel were in the restaurant not more than ten minutes, perhaps as little as one minute, depending on the testimony the jury chose to credit. The jury by its verdict clearly found the defendant guilty of trespass and from the admissions of CBS' own employees they were guilty of trespass. The witness Rich sought to justify her crew's entry into the restaurant by calling it, on a number of occasions, a "place of public accommodation," but, as she acknowledges, they did not seek to avail themselves of the plaintiff's "accommodation"; they had no intention of purchasing food or drink.

The trial judge upheld the determination of liability but set aside both damage awards because he had erroneously barred a defense witness from testifying as to CBS's motive and purpose in entering the premises. On appeal, the court held that its review of the record "demonstrates an adequate basis to justify the compensatory damage award rendered by the jury and, accordingly, such award must stand." As to punitive damages, the court agreed that the judge had erred in excluding the testimony because all "circumstances immediately connected with the transaction tending to exhibit or explain the motive of the defendant are admissible." One judge thought it clear that the defendants were "not motivated by actual malice or such an intentional disregard of plaintiff's rights as would justify the imposition of punitive damages. [ ] The defendant was merely pursuing a newsworthy item in the overly aggressive but good faith manner that characterizes the operation of the news media today. . . . In this sensitive and evolving First Amendment area, I would permit this precedent-setting opinion to stand as a warning to all news gatherers that future trespasses may well be met with an award of punitive damages."

Further appeal was barred by the lack of a final judgment.

Would the analysis differ if a newspaper reporter had entered to get the story? Would he have been a trespasser from the moment of entry, or only after being asked to leave? Would the case be affected by a sign at the front door stating that reporters were not allowed to enter? Might state law be invoked to create a privilege for news reporters to enter certain kinds of property, even against the demonstrated wishes of the possessor?

5. Sometimes the intrusion occurs in a nontrespassory situation. In Galella v. Onassis, 487 F.2d 986 (2d Cir.1973), the widow and children of President John F. Kennedy sought to stop the behavior of Galella, who "fancies himself as a 'paparazzo' (literally a kind of annoying insect . . .). Paparazzi make themselves as visible to the public and obnoxious to their photographic subjects as possible to aid in the advertisement and wide sale of their works." Among his actions, Galella brought his power boat close to Mrs. Onassis as she was swimming; jumped out of bushes as she was walking past; jumped into a child's path to take a photograph of him riding his bicycle; and invaded the children's schools. In addition, he "followed a practice of bribing apartment house, restaurant and nightclub doormen as well as romancing a family servant to keep him advised of the movements of the family." After a trial, during which damage claims were dropped, Galella was enjoined from keeping the defendant or children under surveillance and was ordered to keep certain distances away from Onassis and the children.

On appeal, the court relied on Galella's violation of a New York criminal statute against "harassment" and concluded that it could be invoked in a civil case. In response to Galella's First Amendment claims, the court concluded that "Crimes and torts committed in news gathering are not protected. [*Branzburg* and *Dietemann.*] There is no threat to a free press in requiring its agents to act within the law."

Liability was upheld but the minimum distances were reduced from 100 yards to 25 or 30 feet. Galella was also enjoined from blocking movement in public places and from "any act foreseeably or reasonably calculated to place the life and safety" of Onassis in jeopardy or that could "reasonably be foreseen to harass, alarm or frighten" her. Similar injunctions were awarded in favor of the Secret Service so far as the children were concerned.

In 1982, Galella was found guilty of 12 violations of the earlier order for taking photographs within 25 feet of Mrs. Onassis. The judge suspended a fine of $120,000 when Galella agreed to pay the $10,000 in legal fees incurred by Onassis and never again to photograph her. The judge warned that if Galella should renege, the judge would revive the $10,000 fine or impose a six-month jail sentence for each violation, N.Y. L.J. Mar. 25, 1982, at 1.

6. In 1979, a TV camera crew trailed a man as he was trying to pay a ransom to persons who had kidnapped his wife. Despite his pleas, the crew followed the man, apparently along public ways. The episode attracted much press discussion after the FBI said the action had "put that woman's life in danger." An editorial in Editor & Publisher, July 28, 1979, at 6, asserted that although the TV crew might have considered its actions "enterprising reporting . . . it was more like sheer stupidity. . . . It is this sort of arrogance and brashness that gets media in trouble with the public."

Should the husband be able to sue for mental anguish he suffered as a result of the crew's actions? Criminal liability might be possible if it is shown that the crew learned of the man's movements by making unauthorized interceptions of messages on a nonbroadcast frequency in violation of § 605 (now § 705) of the Communications Act. Should the law impose a sanction against reporters whose gathering efforts in fact lead to harm because kidnappers panic or get angry that their instructions apparently are not being followed?

7. In 1975, it was disclosed that a reporter had been sifting through the contents of garbage cans outside the home of Secretary of State Henry Kissinger. If the cans were on the public sidewalk waiting to be emptied by the garbage collectors, has the reporter committed any tort? Crime?

In a very short editorial, Editor & Publisher, July 19, 1975, at 6, attacked the practice: "Pawing through someone else's garbage is a revolting exercise and doing it in the name of journalism makes it none the less so."

8. In a case treated as one involving a private plaintiff, a pueblo in New Mexico sued a newspaper that had sent a low-flying airplane over the pueblo to take photographs of a sacred ritual, and published them. Although the pueblo permits outsiders to view most ritual dances, it has a longstanding and well-known rule against photography, sketching, or recording the dances. Outsiders are barred from certain special rituals. After several abortive efforts, the dispute was finally settled. N.Y.Times, Feb. 4, 1985, at 7.

9. *Criminal Liability.* Trespass and other torts covered in this section may lead to criminal liability as well as civil liability. The significance of the criminal liability is seen in a trespass prosecution against reporters covering a demonstration at a construction site for a nuclear plant in Oklahoma. The utility, PSO, did not want extensive coverage of the marchers—as had occurred at an earlier demonstration. This time, PSO warned all reporters that they would be arrested if they entered the fenced property at any point not permitted by PSO. PSO then set up a viewing area that reporters might use on its otherwise closed property. It was not clear in advance whether the demonstration or any confrontation would be visible from that point.

Several reporters used the viewing area. Others followed the demonstrators and entered the land when the demonstrators went through the fence. These reporters were the ones convicted of trespass. The judge found that they knew or should have known of PSO's intent to prosecute this conduct. He ruled that newsmen had no constitutional right of access to scenes when the general public was excluded, but he also found a First Amendment right to reasonable access to the news such as is available to the public generally. (Since the property was closed, the origin of this right is not clear.) He then decided that some balancing was required. Against the interest in gathering the news, he arrayed PSO's right to be secure in its property and the police power of the state to maintain public order and enforce criminal statutes. In making his balance the judge also threw in the fact that PSO's purpose in hampering news coverage was "an ignoble one hardly compatible with the rights of a free people." He also gave some weight to the fact that when the marchers entered the land at a point not readily visible from the "viewing area," reporters in that area demanded, and were taken to, a better spot. (How could this have been known in time to the reporters who were with the marchers?)

The judge thought the balance favored the government because the restrictions did not deny access to "particularly significant news" since those in the viewing area could see almost everything. When several defendants claimed that they had to enter the land to meet "their professional obligation to report the news," the judge responded that although this might have been a matter of conscience, it was also "a deliberate violation of law." If a person commits an act of civil disobedience, he "may claim an exemption from an obligation to obey a particular law on moral or professional grounds, but that person may not claim immunity from application of sanction for committing that offense." Each was fined $25. Oklahoma v. Bernstein, 5 Media L.Rptr. 2313 (1980).

The reporters' convictions were affirmed, 2–1, in Stahl v. State, 665 P.2d 839, 9 Med.L.Rptr. 1945 (Okl.Crim.1983), certiorari denied 464 U.S. 1069 (1984). The majority relied on the lack of general public access to the site, and concluded that the site was not a traditional public forum. The dissenter found the prosecution violated the state constitutional protection of freedom of press. See also State v. McCormack, 101 N.M. 349, 682 P.2d 742 (App.1984).

In People v. Rewald, 65 Misc.2d 453, 318 N.Y.S.2d 40 (1971), a county court dismissed a criminal trespass charge against a reporter who had entered a migrant labor camp to speak with some of the residents. The camp was thought to resemble a company town more than "private property used solely for the owner's private purposes."

10. After the arrest of David Berkowitz in the "Son of Sam" case, police obtained a warrant to search his apartment. After the search, they left no guard, but closed the door and posted a sign on it stating "Do Not Enter, Crime Scene." Several reporters gained entrance to the apartment, were apprehended by the police, and were prosecuted for trespass. Because the police lacked a sufficient possessory interest to support the charge and the information also failed to allege that the reporters were there without the permission of the tenant, the information was dismissed. The judge went out of his way to suggest that some other crime might have been committed by the failure to obey a police directive, and also felt compelled to observe that the actions that admittedly took place here "can best be described as reprehensible and cannot be justified as legitimate in the pursuit of a news story." People v. Berliner, 3 Med.L.Rptr. 1942 (Yonkers, N.Y., City Court 1978).

11. Sometimes the questions of whether consent has been obtained or what was consented to become central. The problem is introduced by the Dietemann case, to which the court in *Prahl* alluded.

DIETEMANN v. TIME, INC.

United States Court of Appeals, Ninth Circuit, 1971.
449 F.2d 245.
Noted, 6 Loyola U.L.A.L.Rev. 200, 47 Notre Dame Law. 1067, 50 Tex.L.Rev. 514.

[Plaintiff, "a disabled veteran with little education, was engaged in the practice of healing with clay, minerals, and herbs." He had no listings and did not advertise; he did not own a telephone and made no charges for his diagnoses or his prescriptions. Two employees of defendant's Life Magazine, Mrs. Metcalf and Mr. Ray, arranged with the office of the District Attorney of Los Angeles County to go to plaintiff's home. On the day in question they rang the bell outside plaintiff's locked gate. When he appeared they falsely stated that they had been sent by a certain person. Plaintiff unlocked the gate, admitted them to his house and brought them to his den. After using some equipment and holding what appeared to be a wand, plaintiff told Metcalf that she had a lump in her breast from having eaten rancid butter 11 years, 9 months and 7 days earlier. While plaintiff was examining Metcalf, Ray took photographs with a hidden camera. A radio transmitter hidden in Metcalf's purse transmitted the entire conversation to another Life employee and two government officials parked in a nearby automobile. Life subsequently ran a story on plaintiff's activities, including a photograph and reference to the recorded conversation. Thereafter when plaintiff was arrested for his activities Life and newspaper photographers accompanied the police and took photographs. Plaintiff sued for damages on the ground that his privacy had been invaded by the intrusion. Suit was brought in federal court because of the diversity of citizenship. The district judge concluded that California would hold plaintiff entitled to damages and he awarded $1,000 general damages for injury to plaintiff's "feelings and peace of mind." Defendant appealed.]

Before CARTER and HUFSTEDLER, CIRCUIT JUDGES, and VON DER HEYDT, DISTRICT JUDGE.

HUFSTEDLER, CIRCUIT JUDGE.

. . .

The appeal presents three ultimate issues: (1) Under California law, is a cause of action for invasion of privacy established upon proof that defendant's employees, by subterfuge, gained entrance to the office portion of plaintiff's home wherein they photographed him and electronically recorded and transmitted to third persons his conversation without his consent as a result of which he suffered emotional distress? (2) Does the First Amendment insulate defendant from liability for invasion of privacy because defendant's employees did those acts for the purpose of gathering material for a magazine story and a story was thereafter published utilizing some of the material thus gathered? (3) Were the defendant's employees acting as special agents of the police and, if so, did their acts violate the First, Fourth, and Fourteenth Amendments of the Federal Constitution, thereby subjecting defendant to liability under the Civil Rights Act (42 U.S.C. § 1983)? Because we hold that plaintiff proved a cause of action under California law and that the First Amendment does not insulate the defendant from liability, we do not reach the third issue.

Were it necessary to reach the Civil Rights Act questions, we would be obliged to explore the relationship between the defendant's employees and the police for the purpose of ascertaining the existence of the "color of law" element of the Act. Because we do not reach the issue, we can and do accept the defendant's disclaimer that its employees were acting for or on behalf of the police.

In jurisdictions other than California in which a common law tort for invasion of privacy is recognized, it has been consistently held that surreptitious electronic recording of a plaintiff's conversation causing him emotional distress is actionable. Despite some variations in the description and the labels applied to the tort, there is agreement that publication is not a necessary element of the tort, that the existence of a technical trespass is immaterial, and that proof of special damages is not required. [ ]

Although the issue has not been squarely decided in California, we have little difficulty in concluding that clandestine photography of the plaintiff in his den and the recordation and transmission of his conversation without his consent resulting in his emotional distress warrants recovery for invasion of privacy in California. . . .

. . .

Concurrently with the development of privacy law, California had decided a series of cases according plaintiffs relief from unreasonable penetrations of their mental tranquility based upon the tort of intentional infliction of emotional distress. [ ] Although these cases are not direct authority in the privacy area, they are indicative of the trend of California law to protect interests analogous to those asserted by plaintiff in this case.

We are convinced that California will "approve the extension of the tort of invasion of privacy to instances of intrusion, whether by physical trespass or not, into spheres from which an ordinary man in plaintiff's position could reasonably expect that the particular defendant should be excluded." (Pearson v. Dodd, 410 F.2d at 704.)

Plaintiff's den was a sphere from which he could reasonably expect to exclude eavesdropping newsmen. He invited two of defendant's employees to the den. One who invites another to his home or office takes a risk that the visitor may not be what he seems, and that the visitor may repeat all he hears and observes when he leaves. But he does not and should not be required to take the risk that what is heard and seen will be transmitted by photograph or recording, or in our modern world, in full living color and hi-fi to the public at large or to any segment of it that the visitor may select. A different rule could have a most pernicious effect upon the dignity of man and it would surely lead to guarded conversations and conduct where candor is most valued, e.g., in the case of doctors and lawyers.

The defendant claims that the First Amendment immunizes it from liability for invading plaintiff's den with a hidden camera and its concealed electronic instruments because its employees were gathering news and its instrumentalities "are indispensable tools of investigative reporting." We agree that newsgathering is an integral part of news dissemination. We strongly disagree, however, that the hidden mechanical contrivances are "indispensable tools" of newsgathering. Investigative reporting is an ancient art; its successful practice long antecedes the invention of miniature cameras and electronic devices. The First Amendment has never been construed to accord newsmen immunity from torts or crimes committed during the course of newsgathering. The First Amendment is not a license to trespass, to steal, or to intrude by electronic means into the precincts of another's home or office.[2] It does not become such a license simply because the person

2. In this respect the facts of this case are different from those in Pearson v. Dodd, supra, 410 F.2d 701 (D.C.Cir.1969). In *Pearson,* the defendant received documents knowing that they had been removed by the donor without the plaintiff's consent. But the donor was not the defendant's agent, and the defendant did not participate in purloining the documents.

subjected to the intrusion is reasonably suspected of committing a crime.

Defendant relies upon the line of cases commencing with New York Times Co. v. Sullivan, [ ] . . . to sustain its contentions that (1) publication of news, however tortiously gathered, insulates defendant from liability for the antecedent tort, and (2) even if it is not thus shielded from liability, those cases prevent consideration of publication as an element in computing damages.

As we previously observed, publication is not an essential element of plaintiff's cause of action. Moreover, it is not the foundation for the invocation of a privilege. Privilege concepts developed in defamation cases and to some extent in privacy actions in which publication is an essential component are not relevant in determining liability for intrusion conduct antedating publication. [ ] Nothing in *New York Times* or its progeny suggests anything to the contrary. Indeed, the Court strongly indicates that there is no First Amendment interest in protecting news media from calculated misdeeds. [ ]

No interest protected by the First Amendment is adversely affected by permitting damages for intrusion to be enhanced by the fact of later publication of the information that the publisher improperly acquired. Assessing damages for the additional emotional distress suffered by a plaintiff when the wrongfully acquired data are purveyed to the multitude chills intrusive acts. It does not chill freedom of expression guaranteed by the First Amendment. A rule forbidding the use of publication as an ingredient of damages would deny to the injured plaintiff recovery for real harm done to him without any countervailing benefit to the legitimate interest of the public in being informed. The same rule would encourage conduct by news media that grossly offends ordinary men.

The judgment is affirmed.

JAMES M. CARTER, CIRCUIT JUDGE (concurring and dissenting).

I concur in all of the majority opinion except that portion refusing to meet the issue of the liability of defendants' agents, acting as agents of the police. . . .

. . .

Notes and Questions

1. Is the court correct in saying that one "who invites another to his home or office takes a risk that the visitor may not be what he seems, and that the visitor may repeat all he hears and observes when he leaves"? If the court is correct, how does the actual case differ from that situation? Is it relevant that Dietemann's premises were not open to the public?

2. Restatement, Second, of Torts § 892B provides that consent to conduct of another is effective "for all consequences of the conduct and

for the invasion of any interests resulting from it" unless within the limitation of subsection (2):

> If the person consenting to the conduct of another is induced to consent by a substantial mistake concerning the nature of the invasion of his interests or the extent of the harm to be expected from it and the mistake is known to the other or is induced by the other's misrepresentation, the consent is not effective for the unexpected invasion or harm.

Is this relevant to plaintiff's misunderstanding about who sent the reporters? Why they wanted to come into his home? His belief that the woman really did have a physical complaint?

3. Were any misrepresentations involved in connection with the tape recorder or camera parts of the case? Why does liability flow for these actions of the reporters?

4. Is there a difference between a tape recorder, which preserves the words actually spoken, and a camera, which creates and preserves visual images that the reporters could have described afterward only from memory?

5. Could this case be analyzed as a trespass, with the defendants claiming consent and the plaintiff arguing that the consent was obtained by fraud? How would the damages be measured? On the court's theory what damages would be recoverable if the article had never been published?

6. Does the court meet the First Amendment argument satisfactorily? Would the case be different if Dietemann had been a lay member of the state's board of medical examiners? Or a candidate for school board?

7. *Secret Recording.* Florida made it criminal for any "person not acting under color of law" to intercept a wire or oral communication unless all parties to the communication had given prior consent.

Reporters and others challenged the statute, claiming that the use of concealed recording equipment was essential to investigative reporting for three reasons: it aided accuracy of reporting; persons being interviewed would not be candid if they knew they were being recorded; and the recording provided corroboration in case of suit for defamation.

The Florida Supreme Court upheld the statute's constitutionality. The statute allows "each party to a conversation to have an expectation of privacy from interception by another party to the conversation. It does not exclude any source from the press, intrude upon the activities of the news media in contacting sources, prevent the parties to the communication from consenting to the recording, or restrict the publication of any information gained from the communication. First Amendment rights do not include a constitutional right to corroborate news gathering activities when the legislature has statutorily recognized the private rights of individuals."

The court followed *Dietemann* in holding that "a person should not take the risk that what is seen and heard will be transmitted by photograph or recording in full living color and hi-fi to the public at large. A different rule could have a most pernicious effect upon the dignity of man." In response to the argument that secret recording may be the only way to get credible information about crime, the court stated that protection against intrusion might protect even a person "reasonably suspected of committing a crime." Shevin v. Sunbeam Television Corp., 351 So.2d 723 (Fla.1977).

The Supreme Court dismissed the appeal by the press for want of a substantial federal question, 435 U.S. 920 (1978). Justices Brennan, White and Blackmun would have noted probable jurisdiction and set the case for oral argument. *Shevin* is noted in 30 U.Fla.L.Rev. 652 (1978).

8. In Ribas v. Clark, 38 Cal.3d 355, 696 P.2d 637, 212 Cal.Rptr. 143 (1985), a wife asked the defendant to listen in on an extension phone as she talked to her estranged husband. The husband learned about the episode when the defendant testified in an arbitration hearing about matters she overheard. He then sued for violation of Calif. Penal Code § 631(a), which provides in relevant part for punishment of any person "who . . . intentionally taps, or makes any unauthorized connection . . . with any . . . telephone wire, line, cable or instrument, . . . or who willfully and without the consent of all parties to the communication, or in any unauthorized manner, reads, or attempts to read, or to learn the contents or meaning of any message . . . while the same is in transit . . . , or is being sent from, or received at any place within this state . . . ."

Section 637.2 provided a civil action against violators for the greater of $3,000 or trebled actual damages. The court upheld the complaint. The statute was read broadly to bar "far more than illicit wiretapping," including the recording of a conversation without the other's consent:

> While one who imparts private information risks the betrayal of his confidence by the other party, a substantial distinction has been recognized between the secondhand repetition of the contents of a conversation and its simultaneous dissemination to an unannounced second auditor, whether that auditor be a person or mechanical device. [ ]
>
> As one commentator has noted, such secret monitoring denies the speaker an important aspect of privacy of communication—the right to control the nature and extent of the firsthand dissemination of his statement. [ ] Partly because of this factor, the Privacy Act has been read to require the assent of all parties to a communication before another may listen.

Although the majority and the concurrers disagreed about the availability of a defense under the statute based on the content of the existing tariff, all agreed that an action lay for $3,000. (The plaintiff was barred from proving and collecting actual damages because the revelation—and accompanying harm—had occurred in a privileged legal proceeding for which the defendant could not be held liable. But the violation itself had occurred at the time of the overhearing, and thus liability could follow.)

9. *Federal Restrictions.* A federal limitation on eavesdropping was enacted in 1968 in the Omnibus Crime Control and Safe Streets Act. 18 U.S.C. § 2510 et seq. Under the Act, interception of any conversation is banned if it (1) is carried over a wire, or (2) is a non-wire oral conversation that is conducted in a situation carrying with it an expectation of privacy.

The federal statute is less protective than some state provisions because it exempts from the ban any conversation in which one party records the contents or in which one party authorizes a third party to record it—so long as the recording is not "for the purpose of committing any criminal or tortious act . . . [or] committing any other injurious act." 18 U.S.C. § 2511(2)(d). On the other hand, one who knows that a conversation has been illegally recorded, commits a crime by disclosing that conversation—even if he had nothing to do with the original illegality. Finally, the statute authorizes civil damage actions for those harmed by the violations.

In Benford v. American Broadcasting Cos., 502 F.Supp. 1148, 6 Med.L.Rptr. 2489 (D.Md.1980), affirmed 661 F.2d 917 (4th Cir.), certiorari denied 454 U.S. 1060 (1981), a television crew was invited by Congressional investigators to secretly record a conversation between the investigators posing as prospective purchasers of cancer insurance and the plaintiff, a cancer insurance salesman. After excerpts were broadcast on a news program, plaintiff sued.

The court determined that Congress intended the "expectation of privacy" to be determined on a case-by-case basis. Here, the plaintiff was not engaging in criminal activity. "Rather, plaintiff was making a standard sales pitch. In addition, the conversation transpired in a private home [to] which plaintiff had been invited. Under these circumstances, it was reasonable for plaintiff to expect that his conversation would not be taped or overheard."

ABC's next defense was that it was recording the episode under "color of law" because it was acting in concert with the Congressional parties, and thus came within an exception. The court concluded that to establish that defense, ABC "would *at least* have to show that its only purpose in taping the meeting was to aid the congressional subcommittee." Since that was a disputed fact, summary judgment was denied. (Is it likely that ABC could show that this was its "only" purpose?)

ABC's final defense was that it was doing the recording with the consent of one of the parties. But this raised the question of whether the recording was done for the purpose of "committing any criminal or tortious act . . . or for the purpose of committing any other injurious act." The court concluded that "ABC's purpose in taping and broadcasting the meeting . . . clearly presents a genuine issue of material fact." If the televised excerpt showed the plaintiff in an embarrassing light as a high-pressure salesman does ABC lose its defense?

In Boddie v. American Broadcasting Cos., 731 F.2d 333, 55 R.R.2d 1145, 10 Med.L.Rptr. 1923 (6th Cir.1984), plaintiff was being interviewed for defendant's "20/20" television program. Although she consented to the interview, she refused to appear on camera. "Unbeknownst to Boddie, the journalists recorded the interview by using a hidden videotape camera and concealed microphones. The sound picked up by the microphones was transmitted to a receiver in a nearby van and there recorded." A segment of the interview, both audio and visual, was shown on the air. The trial court had dismissed plaintiff's damage action based on a violation of 18 U.S.C. § 2511(1)(a), (c), and (d). (Section 2520 authorizes private damage actions for violations of these sections.) The court of appeals reversed.

The court concluded that plaintiff had established a prima facie violation of the statute. Section 2511(2)(d) provided a privilege for private persons "unless such communication is intercepted . . . for the purpose of committing any other injurious act." ABC asserted that it acted to preserve evidence of wrongdoing based on what Boddie was saying about a judge who was the subject of the investigation. The court thought ABC's motivation was for the jury to decide. (Earlier cases had indicated that Boddie might have the required expectation of privacy if she was not expecting to be electronically recorded—and this again was for the jury.)

A concurring judge cited other circuit court cases indicating that a desire to make an accurate record of a conversation is a purpose that justifies the privilege, as is acting "out of a legitimate desire to protect himself." The term "injurious act" could not "embrace every act which disadvantages the other party to this communication."

Some assert that the federal statute pre-empts state laws on the subject and thus permits self-protective recording. See, Landau, Tape Record Important Interviews, Editor & Publisher, Jan. 21, 1984, at 22, in which the author encourages all reporters to tape record "all their important telephone and in-person interviews" whether or not the other person consents. A lawyer who represents journalists wrote a lengthy letter to the editor to "beg to differ." Editor & Publisher, Feb. 25, 1984, at 9. See generally Spellman, Tort Liability of the News Media for Surreptitious Recording, 62 Journ. Q. 289 (1985).

10. In Cassidy v. American Broadcasting Cos., 60 Ill.App.3d 831, 17 Ill. Dec. 936, 377 N.E.2d 126 (1978), plaintiff, an undercover policeman, was sent to a massage parlor. After paying $30 he was escorted to a room by a model to see " 'de-luxe' lingerie modeling." Upon entering he noticed camera lights and remarked that the lights made the room quite warm. He asked, "What are we on, TV?" The model replied "Yes, we're making a movie." As plaintiff reclined on the bed watching the model change her lingerie several times, he made suggestive remarks and advances. He then arrested the model for solicitation.

The entire scene was in fact being photographed from an adjacent room by a local television station through a two-way mirror, because the manager of the parlor had complained that police were harassing him.

Plaintiff sued the station for damages. One claim was based on a tort duty derived from an eavesdropping statute similar to Florida's. The court held the statute inapplicable because only pictures but no sounds were picked up from the room. In any event, the plaintiff apparently did not intend his remarks to be private because he knew that someone might be making a movie of his conduct. He testified his actions were in the line of duty as an officer and that if the model wished to sell him a completed film he would use it as evidence in his investigation. Plaintiff had no expectation of privacy.

The court rejected an intrusion claim on the ground that plaintiff was a "public official performing a laudable public service and discharging a public duty." In such cases, no privacy interest exists. *Dietemann* was distinguished on this basis.

Recipients of Tortiously Obtained Information. The cases so far have involved defendants who were alleged to have behaved tortiously in gathering information. But one of the early cases in this area involved the receipt of information obtained as a result of tortious behavior of others. In Pearson v. Dodd, 410 F.2d 701 (D.C.Cir.), certiorari denied 395 U.S. 947 (1969), aides to Senator Thomas Dodd secretly removed documents from his files, made copies of them, and then delivered them to columnists Drew Pearson and Jack Anderson, who published them.

Dodd claimed invasion of privacy and conversion. The court concluded that invasion of privacy should include "instances of intrusion, whether by physical trespass or not, into spheres from which an ordinary man in a plaintiff's position could reasonably expect that the particular defendant should be excluded." The court drew analogies to the Fourth Amendment's protection from government intrusions. Assuming that the Senator's aides committed tortious intrusions, the court nonetheless concluded that no liability attached to the defendant even though they received the documents "knowing" they "had been removed without authorization."

> If we were to hold appellants liable for invasion of privacy on these facts, we would establish the proposition that one who receives information from an intruder, knowing it has been obtained by improper intrusion, is guilty of a tort. In an untried and developing area of tort law, we are not prepared to go so far. A person approached by an eavesdropper with an offer to share in the information gathered through the eavesdropping would perhaps play the nobler part should he spurn the offer and shut his ears. However, it seems to us that at this point it would place too great a strain on human weakness to hold one liable in damages who merely succumbs to temptation and listens.

> Of course, appellants did more than receive and peruse the copies of the documents taken from appellee's files; they published excerpts from them in the national press. But in analyzing a claimed breach of privacy, injuries from intrusion and injuries from publication should be kept clearly separate. Where there is intrusion, the intruder should generally be liable whatever the content of what he learns. An eavesdropper to the marital bedroom may hear marital intimacies, or he may hear statements of fact or opinion of legitimate interest to the public; for purposes of liability that should make no difference. On the other hand, where the claim is that private information concerning plaintiff has been published, the question of whether that information is genuinely private or is of public interest should not turn on the manner in which it has been obtained. Of course, both forms of invasion may be combined in the same case.
>
> Here we have separately considered the nature of appellants' publications concerning appellee, and have found that the matter published was of obvious public interest. The publication was not itself an invasion of privacy. Since we have also concluded that appellants' role in obtaining the information did not make them liable to appellee for intrusion, their subsequent publication, itself no invasion of privacy, cannot reach back to render that role tortious.

The court then concluded that no action lay for conversion.

One author states that Anderson convinced one of Dodd's aides "to carry thousands of documents from Dodd's files to Anderson's home, where he and [the aide] went over them night after night, weekend after weekend, for nearly a year . . . ." L. Downie, Jr., The New Muckrakers 142 (1976).

For another Pearson-Anderson legal battle over "lifted" records, see Liberty Lobby, Inc. v. Pearson, 390 F.2d 489 (D.C.Cir.1968). For an extended discussion of the ethics of newsgathering, see T. Goldstein, The News at Any Cost (1985).

Recall that the Omnibus Crime Act makes it a crime to publish a conversation known to have been recorded illegally, and creates a damage action.

Measuring Damages. Several cases have involved the question whether the liability imposed for tortious conduct while gathering news extends to damages for the article that is subsequently published. Notice that it is one thing to say that the truth of the resulting publication or its social utility is not a defense to the initial tortious behavior. It is quite different to argue that the plaintiff may use the subsequent article to establish recoverable harm proximately flowing from the initial tort. Both *Prahl* and *Dietemann* suggest that harm from the improperly obtained publication may be included as part of the damages. *Dodd* disagrees.

In Costlow v. Cusimano, 34 App.Div.2d 196, 311 N.Y.S.2d 92 (1970), plaintiffs alleged that their two children suffocated in a refrigerator located at the family's residence; that defendant, employee of a local radio station, arrived at the scene and photographed the premises and the bodies of the children; and that the photographs were published, causing plaintiffs intense emotional distress. The court held that since the articles were newsworthy, no claim could be based on their publication. It then held that the only remedies for any trespass to the premises were nominal and punitive damages: "There is no support for plaintiffs' argument that damages for injury to reputation and for emotional disturbance are recoverable on the alleged facts as the natural consequence of the trespass. . . . [D]amages for trespass are limited to consequences flowing from the interference with possession and not for separable acts more properly allocated under other categories of liability."

See King and Muto, Compensatory Damages for Newsgatherer Torts: Toward a Workable Standard, 14 U.C.D.L.Rev. 919 (1981).

Chapter XII

ACCESS TO GOVERNMENT SOURCES

In Chapters X and XI we have considered direct and indirect limits on the press in gathering information from private sources. In this Chapter we shift our focus to efforts to gather information from government officials and agencies, ranging from revelation of material in files to access to premises controlled by government from which the gatherers may learn for themselves what is going on. Perhaps a logical starting point is the proposition that if no legal restraints apply, government officials may freely decide whether to disclose some information they have or to grant access to premises under their control. This means that if they are not required to disclose information or grant access and are not required to refuse disclosure or access, the officials and agencies are free to decide on their own.

The Chapter begins with statutory constraints on this presumptive official freedom—including both mandatory disclosure and access, and mandatory nondisclosure and nonaccess. We move then to the constitutional questions that arise when an official decides to reveal certain information or grant access, but wishes to do so only to certain seekers or to certain media. Finally, we consider situations in which statutory disclosure and access are not applicable, but the gatherer asserts that constitutional provisions mandate some minimum amount of access beyond what the government is willing to provide.

A. STATUTORY ACCESS

1. Freedom of Information Act

As long as legislatures were the preeminent lawmakers in the country, persons concerned with government actions could keep track of the process. With the New Deal, however, vast numbers of administrative agencies and organizations emerged. Congress empowered most to promulgate their own internal rules, to issue substantive regulations, to enforce laws, to adjudicate some controversies, and take other action of great importance to citizens. The sheer number of regulations and orders being promulgated made it difficult to keep track of the process. In addition, some of the agencies were not open about their operations.

In 1946, Congress passed the Administrative Procedure Act to require all administrative agencies to follow certain procedures in the adoption of regulations and in their adjudicative hearings. Congress also sought to make the internal rules and procedures of agencies more readily available to the public.

For a variety of reasons, this first effort at openness was not notably successful. In 1967, Congress responded to growing criticism by adopting the first version of the Freedom of Information Act. The scope of the FOIA was expanded in 1974, 5 U.S.C.A. § 552.

The FOIA applies to all federal government agencies except Congress, the courts, the government of the District of Columbia, and courts martial or the military during wartime. The Act requires each agency to publish in the Federal Register a description of its organization and a list of its personnel through whom the public can obtain information. Each agency must also explain the procedures by which it will furnish information. Each agency must make available to the public staff manuals and internal instructions that affect members of the public, final opinions in adjudicated cases, and current indexes.

Agencies may set reasonable fees for finding and copying material requested by the public. These fees are to be waived when the information will be of primary benefit to the general public.

Agencies must respond quickly to requests for information. Should an agency not comply with the FOIA, a member of the public may ask a federal district court to enforce the request. The court may review in private the material the agency wishes to withhold, but it is the agency that bears the burden of showing that the material may be withheld under one of the exemptions to the Act discussed below. If the court decides the information should be released, it can order the government to pay all costs associated with the court action. Additionally, the agency employee who authorized the improper withholding of the information may be punished.

The FOIA contains nine exemptions—categories of material that need not be made available to the public. Several exemptions were amended in 1974 to require more material to be given to the public. The current version provides:

> (b) This section does not apply to matters that are—
>
> (1)(A) specifically authorized under criteria established by an Executive order to be kept secret in the interest of national defense or foreign policy and (B) are in fact properly classified pursuant to such Executive order;
>
> (2) related solely to the internal personnel rules and practices of an agency;
>
> (3) specifically exempted from disclosure by statute (other than [the Sunshine Act]), provided that such statute (A) requires that the matters be withheld from the public in such a manner as to leave no discretion on the issue, or (B) establishes particular criteria for withholding or refers to particular types of matters to be withheld;
>
> (4) trade secrets and commercial or financial information obtained from a person and privileged or confidential;

(5) inter-agency or intra-agency memorandums or letters which would not be available by law to a party other than an agency in litigation with the agency;

(6) personnel and medical files and similar files the disclosure of which would constitute a clearly unwarranted invasion of personal privacy;

(7) investigatory records compiled for law enforcement purposes, but only to the extent that the production of such records would (A) interfere with enforcement proceedings, (B) deprive a person of a right to a fair trial or an impartial adjudication, (C) constitute an unwarranted invasion of personal privacy, (D) disclose the identity of a confidential source and, in the case of a record compiled by a criminal law enforcement authority in the course of a criminal investigation, or by an agency conducting a lawful national security intelligence investigation, confidential information furnished only by the confidential source, (E) disclose investigative techniques and procedures, or (F) endanger the life or physical safety of law enforcement personnel;

(8) contained in or related to examination, operating, or condition reports prepared by, on behalf of, or for the use of an agency responsible for the regulation or supervision of financial institutions; or

(9) geological and geophysical information and data, including maps, concerning wells.

Any reasonably segregable portion of a record shall be provided to any person requesting such record after deletion of the portions which are exempt under this subsection.

Notes and Questions

1. Notice that nothing in the Act gives any special rights to the press as opposed to the public generally. Is that surprising?

2. What appear to be the critical limitations of the Act?

3. Needless to say, each exemption has produced its share of litigation. Those causing the most difficulty appear to be the first, third, fifth, and seventh. In some cases amendments have already altered interpretations when Congress disagreed with judicial interpretations. The procedures under the Act can get quite complicated. Several organizations have prepared handbooks that provide guidance.

The Supreme Court has had occasion to pass on several cases interpreting the Act. These are often technical in nature and not particularly useful for our purposes. Suffice it to say that the courts are having difficulty with the Act.

4. According to a 1982 study, out of 276,327 agency denials between 1976 and 1979, 11,476 were appealed. Of these, 15 percent were totally reversed on appeal and 45 percent were partially reversed. The largest number of denials occurred in connection with the seventh exemption

(36,485), the second largest with the fifth exemption (17,424), and between 12,500 and 14,000 for each of the third, fourth, and sixth exemptions. Archibald, Use of the FOIA, (Freedom of Information Center Rep. No. 457, 1982).

5. Although they vary a great deal, state access to information statutes exist in every state, and they frequently parallel the federal statute by beginning with a premise that all government records should be publicly available and then listing a series of exceptions or exemptions.

2. The Privacy Act

The movement toward openness in government has been tempered by growing concern about the dangers to individual privacy resulting from the growing number of records and of federal agencies keeping records. In response, Congress passed the Privacy Act of 1974. 5 U.S.C. § 552a. One major part of the Act permits subjects of records to see their files, to obtain copies, and to correct inaccuracies. The individual is not required to give the agency any reason for wanting to see his or her file. Civil actions may be brought for improper refusals to provide the file and for improper refusals to make corrections.

The part of the Act of most interest to the press, however, is the part that restricts disclosure of the contents of records unless certain conditions are met:

> **(b) Conditions of disclosure.**—No agency shall disclose any record which is contained in a system of records by any means of communication to any person, or to another agency, except pursuant to a written request by, or with the prior written consent of, the individual to whom the record pertains, unless disclosure of the record would be—
>
> (1) to those officers and employees of the agency which maintains the record who have a need for the record in the performance of their duties;
>
> (2) required under section 552 of this title [FOIA];
>
> (3) for a routine use as defined . . . ;
>
> (4) to the Bureau of the Census for purposes of planning or carrying out a census or survey or related activity . . . ;
>
> (5) to a recipient who has provided the agency with advance adequate written assurance that the record will be used solely as a statistical research or reporting record, and the record is to be transferred in a form that is not individually identifiable;
>
> (6) to the National Archives and Records Administration as a record which has sufficient historical or other value to warrant its continued preservation by the United States Government, or for evaluation by the Archivist of the United

States or the designee of the Archivist to determine whether the record has such value;

(7) to another agency or to an instrumentality of any governmental jurisdiction within or under the control of the United States for a civil or criminal law enforcement activity if the activity is authorized by law, and if the head of the agency or instrumentality has made a written request to the agency which maintains the record specifying the particular portion desired and the law enforcement activity for which the record is sought;

(8) to a person pursuant to a showing of compelling circumstances affecting the health or safety of an individual if upon such disclosure notification is transmitted to the last known address of such individual;

(9) to either House of Congress, or, to the extent of matter within its jurisdiction, any committee or subcommittee thereof, any joint committee of Congress or subcommittee of any such joint committee;

(10) to the Comptroller General, or any of his authorized representatives, in the course of the performance of the duties of the General Accounting Office;

(11) pursuant to the order of a court of competent jurisdiction; or

(12) to a consumer reporting agency . . . .

Notes and Questions

1. Notice that the restrictions of the Privacy Act are framed as limits on what government officials may disclose. They do not provide punishment for media that publish information improperly made public by the government.

Attempts by the Reagan administration in the 1980s to reduce disclosure of information by the federal government under the Freedom of Information Act have also had an impact on use of the Privacy Act as a reason for non-disclosure.

2. Statutes providing for freedom of information have not been challenged on privacy grounds, even in states in which there may be no comparable privacy legislation. Such a challenge nearly occurred in 1984, as an outgrowth of David Kennedy's death in Florida. The media sought release of photographs and videotapes that police had made during their investigation of Kennedy's death. The media argued that the death was shrouded in mystery and the public had an interest in knowing the cause of death. Two of the deceased's siblings responded by bringing a lawsuit claiming that publication or broadcast of the photographs would invade the privacy of the family. They also challenged the constitutionality of the state public records law.

An agreement was reached whereby a lawyer trusted by both sides viewed the sixty-nine photographs and the videotape. Under the agreement, the material would not be disclosed to the press if the lawyer concluded that the death was drug-related. The lawyer was also sworn to secrecy. After viewing, the lawyer reported that the death was indeed drug-related—caused by an overdose of drugs—and the lawsuits of both sides were dropped. N.Y.Times, Nov. 23, 1984, at 10.

3. ACCESS TO PUBLIC MEETINGS

Guidelines for access to meetings of Congress or its committees and access to information about Congressional proceedings are prescribed initially in the Constitution. (Art. I, § 5):

> Each House may determine the Rules of its Proceedings. . . . Each House shall keep a Journal of its Proceedings, and from time to time publish the same, excepting such Parts as may in their Judgment require Secrecy; and the Yeas and Nays of the Members of either House on any question shall, at the Desire of one fifth of those Present, be entered on the Journal.

From the earliest days, sessions of the full House or Senate have usually been open to the public. Senate sessions were occasionally closed for discussion of treaties or nominations, and in the thirty years between 1945 and 1975, the Senate held seventeen closed sessions, devoted usually to foreign relations or defense questions. Guide to the Congress of the United States 73 (2d ed. 1976).

Although most sessions of the full House and Senate have been open, most committee meetings were closed unless hearings were being held. Since 1970, there has been a sharp increase in open committee meetings, extending first to mark-up sessions (in which a pending bill may be approved, amended, or rewritten), and later to conference committee meetings in which representatives of the two houses try to reconcile two different versions of proposed legislation. In 1975 the House and Senate voted to require open conferences unless a majority of conferees from either chamber vote in public to close a session. Can such negotiations be conducted effectively in open sessions? Should all meetings of all committees and subcommittees be open?

A different problem arises out of the conduct of Congressional investigations. The power to legislate implies the power to inquire into subjects that may require legislation and allows Congress to conduct investigations and hold hearings. Congress may compel the attendance of witnesses and the production of documents at these hearings under threat of citation for contempt. The arguments against open hearings do not involve national security or the inhibiting effect of publicity on legislative compromise. Rather they reflect a concern for the privacy of witnesses and those whose behavior is under scrutiny. The advent of television coverage of some Congressional hearings has made this concern more significant and has led to some restrictions on coverage.

The "Sunshine" Act

At the urging of Congressmen and Senators from Florida, which had had good experience with its "Sunshine" Law, Congress, in 1976, passed a federal "Government in the Sunshine Act." 5 U.S.C. § 552b. The statement of purpose accompanying the Act declares that "the public is entitled to the fullest practicable information regarding the decision-making processes of the Federal Government." The Act sought to "provide the public with such information while protecting the rights of individuals and the ability of the Government to carry out its responsibilities."

Essentially, the Act provides that all federal agencies headed by boards of two or more persons appointed by the President—approximately fifty agencies—must hold "every portion of every meeting" open to the public. Adequate advance notice must be given of each meeting. Even if a meeting is closed because it falls within one of the ten exemptions to be noted, the agency must make public a transcript or minutes of all parts of the meeting that do not contain exempt material. Meetings may be closed only after a publicly recorded vote of a majority of the full membership of the agency.

The exemptions apply where the agency "properly determines" that a portion of its meeting "is likely to" result in the disclosure of specified information. The exemptions include verbatim copies of several FOIA exemptions—(1) involving national defense or foreign policy; (2) involving internal rules and practices of the agency; (3) matters specifically exempted from disclosure by another statute; (4) trade secrets; (7) law enforcement investigatory records; and (8) involving financial institutions. In addition, another exemption tracks very closely the "clearly unwarranted invasion of personal privacy" language of the sixth exemption of the FOIA. Given the similar goals of the two statutes these similarities are not surprising.

In addition, the Sunshine Act contains the following summarized exemptions not found in the FOIA:

(5) disclosures that "involve accusing any person of a crime, or formally censuring any person;"

(9) "premature disclosure" involving agencies that regulate currencies, securities, commodities, or financial institutions, where the disclosure would be likely to (i) lead to "significant financial speculation" in these items or (ii) "significantly endanger the financial stability of any financial institution"; or, in the case of any agency, where the disclosure would be likely to "significantly frustrate implementation of a proposed agency action."

(10) information concerning an agency's issuance of a subpoena or its participation in a civil action or proceeding.

STATE OPEN MEETINGS STATUTES

Clearly, less governmental business is conducted by the state legislature than by the multitude of agencies created by the legislature or by the executive branch under legislative authorization. In an effort to bring these agencies and their decision-making processes under public scrutiny, many state legislatures have adopted "open meeting" or "sunshine" laws. These vary greatly and are summarized in "State Open Meeting Laws: An Overview" by Prof. John B. Adams (Freedom of Information Foundation Series No. 3, July, 1974).

B. SELECTIVE ACCESS

Clearly, a private person may decide whether or not to become a source of information and, if so, whether to grant an exclusive to one eager gatherer or to deal with more than one. Among the motivations that might enter into the prospective source's decisions are the personal relationships with the gatherers and the financial rewards offered by one or more of the gatherers. So-called "checkbook journalism" is a recurrent concern. For a suggestion of its role as reporters sought information about Bernhard Goetz, see Geist, About New York, N.Y. Times Jan 12, 1985, at 8. (That report also suggested that the carloads of reporters still staking out his apartment building three weeks after Goetz shot four people in the New York subways were there "because the reporters from the other papers were still there.")

Consider the situation that confronted a restaurant reviewer for the New York Times who reported that when she went to a new restaurant she and her guests were shown to a table but were not given menus. "After repeated requests for menus were ignored, a maitre d'hotel came to the table and whispered, 'We have reason to believe there are food critics at this table.'" The critic acknowledged that there was a restaurant critic at the table. The party left.

The manager, who had previously expressed dissatisfaction with a rating this critic had given an earlier venture of his, said that although his food was ready for the public, "he disapproved of critiques not only of restaurants, but also of plays and films." When asked if he would bar critics who gave him favorable reviews, he said, "The person I really do want to keep out is you, but to be legal about it, I guess I have to keep out any critic I recognize, at least for the foreseeable future." He identified two other reviewers that he recognized and would not serve.

The reviewer reported that lawyers had said that according to New York common law a restaurant could refuse service "only on fair, established and reasonable grounds (usually meaning improper dress, drunkenness, being obstreperous or obnoxious) and that under New York statutory law, a person can claim to have been refused illegally only if the refusal was for reasons of race, sex or religion." Sheraton, Restaurants, N.Y.Times, Jan. 7, 1983, at 16.

Does the legal advice seem sound? Does it matter whether the manager excludes all reviewers or practices selective exclusion? Would it be permissible for the courts to develop a common law or constitutional protection—or for the legislature to adopt a statute—that required restaurants to serve food critics unless they behaved improperly on the premises?

When the source is a government official or agency, however, it is clear that certain discriminations are impermissible. It would presumably be unthinkable for a government official to bar certain reporters from a press conference, for example, because of their religious views. In this section, assume that the official is under no constitutional obligation to reveal any information or to accord any access. The question, then, is once the decision has been reached to make something public, how far the constitution constrains the choices to be made. Several issues are explored in the following case.

1. Individual Discrimination

SHERRILL v. KNIGHT

United States Court of Appeals, District of Columbia Circuit, 1977.
569 F.2d 124, 3 Med.L.Rptr. 1514.

[Sherrill, Washington correspondent for the Nation, had credentials for the House and Senate press galleries, but was denied a White House press pass. After an applicant shows congressional credentials, residence in Washington, and an editor's verification of the reporter's need to report from the White House regularly, the pass is issued unless the Secret Service objects. Here, it was ultimately learned, the Secret Service had recommended against issuing the pass on the ground that Sherrill posed a security risk because he had assaulted the press secretary to the governor of Florida and also faced assault charges in Texas. In Sherrill's suit to obtain a press pass, the district court had ordered the Secret Service to formulate "narrow and specific" standards for judgment and to institute certain procedures for handling such requests. The Secret Service appealed.]

Before McGowan, Leventhal and Robb, Circuit Judges. McGowan, Circuit Judge.

. . .

The District Court based its requirement of a written decision upon its determination that denial of a White House press pass to a bona fide journalist violates the first amendment unless it furthers a compelling governmental interest identified by narrowly and specifically drawn standards. The Court felt it would be unable to undertake proper judicial review of the denial of the press pass to Sherrill unless the Secret Service first explained why application of such standards to Sherrill necessitated the denial. With respect to its requirement of notice and opportunity to rebut, the Court relied on its determination that denial of a White House press pass constitutes a deprivation of "liberty" without due process of law within the meaning of the fifth amendment because it interferes with the free exercise of the profession of journalism.

We agree with the District Court that both first and fifth amendment concerns are heavily implicated in this case.[14] We conclude, however, that neither of these concerns requires the articulation of detailed criteria upon which the granting or denial of White House press passes is to be based. We further conclude that notice, opportunity to rebut, and a written decision are required because the denial of a pass potentially infringes upon first amendment guarantees. Such impairment of this interest cannot be permitted to occur in the absence of adequate procedural due process.

III.

Appellants argue that because the public has no right of access to the White House, and because the right of access due the press generally is no greater than that due the general public, denial of a White House press pass is violative of the first amendment only if it is based upon the content of the journalist's speech or otherwise discriminates against a class of protected speech. While we agree with appellants that arbitrary or content-based criteria for press pass issuance are prohibited under the first amendment, there exist additional first amendment considerations ignored by appellants' argument.

These considerations can perhaps be best understood by first recognizing what this case does *not* involve. It is not contended that standards relating to the security of the President are the sole basis upon which members of the general public may be refused entry to the White House, or that members of the public must be afforded notice and hearing concerning such refusal. The first amendment's protection of a citizen's right to obtain information concerning "the way the country is being run" does not extend to every conceivable avenue a citizen may wish to employ in pursuing this right. Nor is the discretion of the President to grant interviews or briefings with selected journalists challenged. It would certainly be unreasonable to suggest that because the President allows interviews with some bona fide

14. We reject at the outset the contention of appellants that this case is nonjusticiable either because protection of the President is vested within the sole discretion of the Executive or because there are no judicially manageable standards for presidential protection. The former argument is wholly without force. Nothing in the Constitution suggests that courts are not to be final arbiters of the legality of the actions of those protecting the President. . . .

Appellant's second argument is precisely that made in A Quaker Action Group v. Hickel, 137 U.S.App.D.C. 176, 421 F.2d 1111 (1969). We reassert our conclusion in that case that

> We cannot agree with the Government's argument that mere mention of the President's safety must be allowed to trump any First Amendment issue.
>
> . . . [A]bsent a compelling showing . . . that courts cannot evaluate the questions of fact in estimating danger to the President, the final judgment must rest with the courts.
>
> . . .

journalists, he must give this opportunity to all. Finally, appellee's first amendment claim is not premised upon the assertion that the White House must open its doors to the press, conduct press conferences, or operate press facilities.

Rather, we are presented with a situation where the White House has voluntarily decided to establish press facilities for correspondents who need to report therefrom. These press facilities are perceived as being open to all bona fide Washington-based journalists, whereas most of the White House itself, and press facilities in particular, have not been made available to the general public. White House press facilities having been made publicly available as a source of information for newsmen, the protection afforded newsgathering under the first amendment guarantee of freedom of the press, see [*Branzburg* and *Pell*], requires that this access not be denied arbitrarily or for less than compelling reasons. [ ] Not only newsmen and the publications for which they write, but also the public at large have an interest protected by the first amendment in assuring that restrictions on newsgathering be no more arduous than necessary, and that individual newsmen not be arbitrarily excluded from sources of information. [ ]; United States v. Associated Press, 52 F.Supp. 362, 372 (S.D.N.Y.1943) ("right conclusions are more likely to be gathered out of a multitude of tongues, than through any kind of authoritative selection") (L. Hand, J.).

Given these important first amendment rights implicated by refusal to grant White House press passes to bona fide Washington journalists, such refusal must be based on a compelling governmental interest. Clearly, protection of the President is a compelling, "even an overwhelming," interest . . . . However, this standard for denial of a press pass has never been formally articulated or published. Merely informing individual rejected applicants that rejection was for "reasons of security" does not inform the public or other potential applicants of the basis for exclusion of journalists from White House press facilities. Moreover, we think that the phrase "reasons of security" is unnecessarily vague and subject to ambiguous interpretation.

Therefore, we are of the opinion that appellants must publish or otherwise make publicly known the actual standard employed in determining whether an otherwise eligible journalist will obtain a White House press pass. We do agree with appellants that the governmental interest here does not lend itself to detailed articulation of narrow and specific standards or precise identification of all the factors which may be taken into account in applying this standard. It is enough that the Secret Service be guided solely by the principle of whether the applicant presents a potential source of physical danger to the President and/or his immediate family so serious as to justify his exclusion. [ ] This standard is sufficiently circumspect so as to allow the Secret Service, exercising expert judgment which frequently must be subjective in nature, considerable leeway in denying press passes for security reasons. At the same time, the standard does specify in a meaningful way the basis upon which persons will be deemed security risks, and therefore will allow meaningful judicial review of decisions to deny press passes. We anticipate that reviewing courts will be appropriately deferential to the Secret Service's determination of what justifies the inference that an individual constitutes a potential risk to the physical security of the President or his family.

IV.

In our view, the procedural requirements of notice of the factual bases for denial, an opportunity for the applicant to respond to these, and a final written statement of the reasons for denial are compelled by the foregoing determination that the interest of a bona fide Washington correspondent in obtaining a White House press pass is protected by the first amendment. This first amendment interest undoubtedly qualifies as liberty which may not be denied without due process of law under the fifth amendment.[22] The only further determination which this court must make is "what process is due," Morrissey v. Brewer, 408 U.S. 471, 481 (1972). We think that notice to the unsuccessful applicant of the factual bases for denial with an opportunity to rebut is a minimum prerequisite for ensuring that the denial is indeed in furtherance of Presidential protection, rather than based on arbitrary or less than compelling reasons. [ ] The requirement of a final statement of denial and the reasons therefor is necessary in order to assure that the agency has neither taken additional, undisclosed information into account, nor responded irrationally to matters put forward by way of rebuttal or explanation. This requirement also will avoid situations such as occurred in the case before us, where an applicant does not receive official written notification of his status until more than five years after the status decision is made.

Having determined that appellants' failure to articulate and publish an explicit and meaningful standard governing denial of White House press passes for security reasons, and to afford procedural protections to those denied passes, violates the first and fifth amendments, we affirm that portion of the District Court's judgment requiring notice, opportunity to be heard, and a final written statement of the bases of denial. We remand that portion of the District Court's judgment requiring appellants to develop "narrow and specific stan-

22. A related and perhaps equally compelling *property* interest may also be said to require the procedural protections of the fifth amendment. . . . It could be argued, convincingly we believe, that in these circumstances, appellee has a justifiable expectation that the only basis for the government's refusal to grant a White House press pass is concern for the physical security of the President or his family. While appellee's entitlement is not created expressly by the Constitution or by positive federal law, it is created by the consistent, positive action of government officials. . . . However, because appellee's first amendment liberty interest independently requires the standards and procedural protections set forth in this opinion, we do not reach the question of whether appellee also has a property entitlement of constitutional magnitude.

dards" for press pass denials in order that this requirement may be modified in accordance with this opinion.

Notes and Questions

1. What are the First Amendment bases for the reporter's attack?

2. What are the Fifth Amendment bases for his attack?

3. If government is limited in its ability to discriminate among persons similarly situated, what justifies the court's passing observation upholding the President's discretion to grant interviews to selected journalists? Is this because the President is involved? Could the same rule be justified for the Attorney General? The local army base commander? The press officer at the Supreme Court?

4. Compare Borreca v. Fasi, 369 F.Supp. 906 (D.Hawaii 1974), in which the mayor of Honolulu ordered his aides to deny Borreca, a reporter for a local paper, access to press conferences. The complaint was that the reporter had been "irresponsible, inaccurate, biased, and malicious in reporting on the mayor and the city administration." The newspaper was encouraged to send any other reporter, but the paper refused and sued to gain admission for Borreca. In an action under 42 U.S.C. § 1983, the judge enjoined the mayor from preventing Borreca from attending press conferences "on the same basis and to the same extent that other news reporters attend" them.

If the mayor discontinues press conferences and instead invites all local reporters except Borreca to his office, can anything be done? Suppose two other reporters are also excluded? Is there a difference between inviting one reporter and excluding ten, and inviting ten and excluding one? Are political considerations likely to inhibit this kind of conduct?

5. Can physical limitations on the size of a meeting hall or office justify limited invitations to the press? Suppose that the mayor decided to hold a meeting in his small office with room for only three visitors. Does *Sherrill* suggest any limitations on who may be invited? Or on the mayor's power to decide to meet in his small office?

6. Several bases for discrimination have been litigated. Some of the more important issues are discussed in the notes below.

7. *Personal qualities. Sherrill* involved a restriction that was based on the person, rather than on what he wrote. What other kinds of personal qualities might justify the approach of the court in *Sherrill?*

8. In Watson v. Cronin, 384 F.Supp. 652 (D.Colo.1974), plaintiff was denied a press card because of a conviction for forgery and a pending trial for robbery. The court upheld the denial of the press card because that document could be used to go behind police lines and to other sensitive areas. The judge noted that plaintiff had not been able to show harm from the lack of a card.

9. *Sex Discrimination.* In a case against the New York Yankees for excluding women reporters from the locker rooms after a game, Yankee

Stadium was on property owned by the city and thus presented a case of state action amenable to § 1983. The judge ordered a woman reporter for Sports Illustrated admitted to the Yankees' dressing room when male reporters are admitted. Ludtke v. Kuhn, 461 F.Supp. 86, 4 Med.L.Rptr. 1625 (S.D.N.Y.1978).

On equal protection grounds, the judge found no justification for excluding women reporters. The players' privacy could be protected in other, less restrictive ways: "the total exclusion of women sports reporters . . . is not substantially related to the privacy protection objective and thus deprives" plaintiff of equal protection. On a due process point, the court concluded that privacy could be protected by means that did not interfere so greatly with plaintiff's liberty of pursuing her profession. "The other two interests asserted by defendants, maintaining the status of baseball as a family sport and conforming to traditional notions of decency and propriety, are clearly too insubstantial to merit serious consideration."

10. *Labor Disputes as a Basis for Different Treatment.* Public officials and candidates have been concerned about their public stances in labor disputes. This concern extends to labor disputes involving media. In Westinghouse Broadcasting Co. v. Dukakis, 409 F.Supp. 895 (D.Mass. 1976), a station involved in a dispute with a union began using non-union camera crews. The Boston City Council ordered that station's crew barred from the area normally used by all television crews in the council chamber. In a suit brought under 42 U.S.C. § 1983, the court issued a temporary restraining order barring the council members from denying equal access. The judge did not specify whether he found a First Amendment or an Equal Protection violation.

A claim against the governor for barring the crew from a press conference was rejected because it appeared that the crew had in fact attended the conference although the governor's assistant had told the station it was not welcome. At the press conference the governor announced that he had asked the crew not to attend and that his request "should have been honored."

Other claims against the state legislature and the governor were too complex for summary decision. One involved a scheduled appearance by the governor at Boston University. The union picketed the site and the governor announced he would not cross the lines. The pickets would not leave unless the non-union crew already inside agreed to leave. The chairman of the meeting persuaded the crew to leave the hall but it continued to film events outside from its truck. The chairman of the meeting then commandeered the truck and drove it down the street. The pickets then dispersed, the governor entered, and the meeting proceeded.

11. See also American Broadcasting Cos. v. Cuomo, 570 F.2d 1080 (2d Cir.1977), in which the local ABC station, which was being struck, sought to send management crews to cover the election-night activities of the two candidates in a runoff Democratic primary for mayor of New

York City. Previous efforts had led to one arrest and threats of further arrests for criminal trespass. The candidates asserted their concern that if ABC were allowed in, crews for the other two networks would leave. ABC sought, under § 1983, to enjoin the candidates and the police commissioner from preventing the crews' entry to the two headquarters.

The candidates asserted that their activities were private and that an invitation was needed to permit anyone, including the press, to enter and remain. The court held that "once the press is invited, . . . there is a dedication of those premises to public communications use. It is idle to speak of privacy when the affair is publicly transmitted by broadcast to millions of viewers. The issue is not whether the public is or is not generally excluded, but whether the members of the broadcast media are generally excluded." The court found First Amendment support for the station and its viewers—some of whom might receive only one channel and could not see what others might see.

The candidates asserted that they were not agents of the state and thus not amenable to liability under § 1983—though the police commissioner was. But the court noted that the commissioner had asserted that he would arrest for criminal trespass only if there was a complaint from the owner of the premises and the owner gave some assurance that he would follow up by being a complainant in a court action. This led the court to conclude that arrests in such actions resulted from combined activity of the police and the complainants—and rendered all defendants liable.

The court also stated that if CBS and NBC responded to this decision by deciding not to cover the election-night activities, ABC could not use this injunction to gain entry. The goal was to place the networks on a par, not to allow ABC to obtain a "scoop."

12. *Nature of the Publication.* In Los Angeles Free Press, Inc. v. City of Los Angeles, 9 Cal.App.3d 448, 88 Cal.Rptr. 605 (1970), the county sheriff issued 3,000 press cards annually. The city police issued some 1,800. Both refused to issue any passes whatever to specialized publications such as trade or financial papers, college newspapers, or to media "who perform functions other than those directly connected with the regular gathering and distribution of hard core news generated through police and fireman activities." The press cards were used to get behind police lines and to attend press conferences.

In the suit by the Free Press to get press cards, the trial judge found that the newspaper did not cover daily police or fire stories and dismissed the suit. On appeal, the judgment was affirmed. The court found a "reasonable basis" for the classification, though it did recognize that other bases might be used, such as first-come-first-served. The classification was not arbitrary. The Supreme Court denied certiorari over the dissents of Justices Black, Douglas, and Brennan. 401 U.S. 982 (1971).

13. See also Consumers' Union v. Periodical Correspondents' Ass'n, 365 F.Supp. 18 (D.D.C.1973), reversed 515 F.2d 1341 (D.C.Cir.1975), certiorari denied 423 U.S. 1051 (1976), involving the efforts of Consumer Reports to get membership in the defendant organization of correspondents and use its facilities to cover Congress. Of the four press galleries in Congress, only this one barred a publication that was not "owned and operated independently of any industry, business, association, or institution." The trial judge ordered the periodical admitted. The court of appeals reversed on the ground that the association was acting under express delegation from Congress and its actions were immune from attack because of the speech or debate clause.

14. *Substantive Disagreement with Publication.* An explicit claim that a newspaper deserves less favorable treatment than a competitor simply because the government official prefers the policies or style of the competitor is unlikely to be accepted. In addition to *Borreca,* see the cases collected in Southwestern Newspapers Corp. v. Curtis, 584 S.W.2d 362 (Tex.Civ.App.1979) finding no compelling state interest to justify forcing the plaintiff to make an appointment to gain access to news sources in the district attorney's office while its competitors could obtain the same information without appointments.

15. *Preferring the Public to the Press.* There seems virtually no reason for government to make information available to members of the public while making it more difficult, or impossible, for the press to obtain that same information.

State legislation or prison regulations determine who may attend executions. These usually list state officials, members of the clergy, physicians, and a certain number of reporters. If state law barred all reporters, could they mount a successful challenge? Could the condemned prisoner, who wanted press coverage of his execution, upset such a statute? Could a state insist that reporters be permitted to attend despite the prisoner's desire to exclude them?

See Kearns-Tribune Corp. v. Utah Bd. of Corrections, 2 Med.L.Rptr. 1353 (D.Utah 1977), rejecting a challenge by the press to a statute that limited attendance to those officially involved plus five "persons, relatives or friends" selected by the condemned prisoner.

In 1979, Utah amended its statute on witnesses to executions. The warden "shall cause" a physician to attend. At the "discretion of the warden," others may attend, including a prosecutor, an attorney general or a deputy, and "Religious representatives, friends or relatives designated by the defendant not exceeding a total of five in number." "The warden shall permit the attendance . . . of a total of nine members of the press and broadcast media named by the director of the division of corrections in accordance with rules and regulations of the division of corrections, provided that the selected news media members shall serve as a pool for other members of the news media as a condition of attendance."

"No photographic or recording equipment shall be permitted at the execution site" until the site "has been restored to an orderly condition." Utah Code Ann. § 77-36-18.

16. In 1979, the Massachusetts legislature asked the state supreme court whether an act would be constitutional if it required some public officials and "all representatives or employees of the news media regularly or ordinarily assigned to news coverage of the activities of the members and sessions" of the legislature to file financial statements that would be open to public inspection. The court advised that the statute would be unconstitutional as applied to the press. Opinion of the Justices, 378 Mass. 816, 392 N.E.2d 849 (1979).

The court started with the proposition that nothing in the state or federal constitutions protected the press from the operation of "general laws which relate to its business aspects." But this was not a general law because it applied only to certain press members. Although it would not deny access to non-compliers, the act would expose those who failed to comply to civil penalties. This might well discourage some from covering the legislature.

Although the court received no briefs in favor of the statute, it concluded that the goals were to allow the public to evaluate biased reporting and perhaps to protect the legislators from secret lobbying. "Neither goal can save the act. Impartial coverage of State House activities cannot be compelled by statute." The court cited the passage in *Tornillo* that responsibility and like virtues cannot be legislated. To the extent reporters engage in lobbying, they can be controlled as are other lobbyists. "We have grave doubts that any asserted governmental interest would support a law such as this, that places a special burden on the press not imposed on the general public."

17. Under Penal Code § 409.5(a), California permits law enforcement officials to close areas imperiled by natural disasters or mass accidents. Subsection (b) provides for closing areas around any "emergency field command post" established as the result of a calamity or "any riot or other civil disturbance." Subsection (d) provides that "nothing in this section shall prevent a duly authorized representative of any news service . . . from entering the areas closed pursuant to this section."

States generally have statutes requiring citizens to obey lawful orders of police officials. In State v. Lashinsky, 81 N.J. 1, 404 A.2d 1121, 5 Med.L.Rptr. 1418 (1979), the defendant news photographer came upon a fatal freeway crash and began taking photographs. By the time a state trooper arrived fifteen minutes later, forty to fifty people had gathered. The trooper saw that a young girl pinned in the car was going into shock. After calling for an ambulance he noticed that gas and oil were leaking and that the battery had cracked open. In addition, much personal property was strewn in the area. Fearing a fire and wanting to preserve the property, the trooper ordered everyone not involved in first aid to leave the area. Defendant refused. When the trooper persisted, defendant showed his press pass. The trooper responded, "I don't care at this point" and again asked him to leave. After another refusal, defendant was arrested and convicted under a statute punishing anyone who, in any place, public or private, "obstructs, molests or interferes with any person lawfully therein."

The conviction was affirmed, 4–3. The majority stressed that the dispute took time and kept the trooper from doing his duty at the scene. One dissenter said that the proper behavior of the trooper was to get non-press persons to retreat and to leave defendant alone. To the extent safety was a reason for the trooper's order, the dissent concluded that the defendant was "sufficiently mature to evaluate the safety risks posed by the overturned vehicle and to position himself so as to minimize those risks. This is not to say that newsmen must be allowed access to any site, no matter what the risk of harm might be. Where, however, as in the present case, the risk is not substantial, a media representative should be allowed to situate himself" near the scene.

2. Discrimination Among Media

On occasion, the government's position is that any and all members of the press (and public) may gain access to a place, but that certain types of equipment may not be brought in by anyone. The usual problem here involves efforts to keep television cameras (and tape recorders) from certain premises and proceedings.

When Bruno Hauptmann was brought to trial for kidnapping and slaying the son of Charles and Anne Morrow Lindbergh in 1932, journalists and photographers packed the courtroom. Hauptmann, found guilty and sentenced to death, may not have gotten a fair trial because of the adverse publicity. In response, the American Bar Association adopted Canon 35 in 1937. Together with amendments in 1952 and 1963, this ethical stricture bans radio and television broadcasting and still cameras from courtrooms. In 1979, an ABA committee proposed that Canon 3A(7), the successor to Canon 35, be amended to allow televising of trials at the judge's discretion. The ABA rejected the recommendation, but many states eventually adopted it.

In the first Supreme Court case, Estes v. Texas, 381 U.S. 532 (1965), defendant had been indicted in the Texas state courts for "swindling"—inducing farmers to buy nonexistent fertilizer tanks and then to deliver to him mortgages on the property. The nature of the charges, and the large sums of money involved, attracted nationwide interest. Texas was one of two states that then permitted televised trials. Over defendant's objection, the trial judge permitted televising of a two-day hearing before trial. Estes was convicted.

The Supreme Court reversed, 5–4, and upset the conviction. In his majority opinion Justice Clark concluded that the use of television involved "such a probability that prejudice will result that it is deemed inherently lacking in due process" even without any showing of specific prejudice. He was concerned about the impact on jurors, judges, parties, witnesses, and lawyers.

Justice Harlan, who provided the crucial fifth vote for reversal, joined the majority opinion only to the extent that it applied to televised coverage of "courtroom proceedings of a criminal trial of widespread public interest," "a criminal trial of great notoriety," and "a heavily publicized and highly sensational affair." In such cases he was worried about the impact on jurors.

In Chandler v. Florida, 449 U.S. 560 (1981), the Court unanimously rejected the view that televising a criminal trial over the objections of the defendant automatically rendered the trial unfair. (In Florida, only the consent of the trial judge is required to allow a trial to be televised.) The defendants had argued that the impact of television on the participants introduced potentially prejudicial but unidentifiable aspects into the trial. The majority, in an opinion by Chief Justice Burger, first concluded that *Estes* did not stand for the proposition that broadcasting was barred "in all cases and under all circumstances." Because of Justice Harlan's narrow views in that case, the ruling in *Estes* should apply only to cases of widespread interest. (On this point, two Justices insisted that *Chandler* overruled *Estes* and should say so.)

Then, Chief Justice Burger continued that the risk of prejudice from press coverage of a trial was not limited to broadcasting. "The risk of juror prejudice in some cases does not justify an absolute ban on news coverage of trials by the printed media; so also the risk of such prejudice does not warrant an absolute constitutional ban on all broadcast coverage." A case attracts attention because of its intrinsic interest to the public. The "appropriate safeguard" against prejudice in such cases "is the defendant's right to demonstrate that the media's coverage of his case—be it printed or broadcast—compromised the ability of the particular jury that heard the case to adjudicate fairly." The Court also observed that the changes in technology since *Estes* supported the state's argument that it now be permitted to allow television in the courtroom.

Since the defendants in *Chandler*—two former city policemen accused of burglarizing a restaurant—showed no adverse impact from the televising, the convictions were upheld.

Notice that this case involved criminal defendants attacking their convictions. The case did not involve a First Amendment claim by broadcasters claiming a right to bring their equipment into the courtroom in a state that barred such entry. The Court did not discuss First Amendment cases. As of the time *Chandler* was decided more than half the states were permitting television in the courtroom either on an experimental basis or on a permanent basis after a successful experiment. In many of these states, the consent of a criminal defendant was required. States that completely bar entry or require consent of a party before entry may continue their practices after *Chandler*.

As of 1986, over forty states permitted televising of criminal proceedings. In some, the defendant has to agree; in others, the trial judge must agree. The situation has been extensively considered in a series of Florida cases. See Petition of Post-Newsweek Stations, 370 So. 2d 764, 5 Med.L.Rptr. 1039 (Fla.1979); State v. Palm Beach Newspapers, Inc., 395 So.2d 544, 7 Med.L.Rptr. 1021 (Fla.1981); State v. Green, 395 So.2d 532, 7 Med.L.Rptr. 1025 (Fla.1981).

In the states in which cameras are banned, and in the federal courts, television news directors have resorted to having artists sketch in the courtroom. Sweeping bans against the practice have been rejected. United States v. Columbia Broadcasting System, Inc., 497 F.2d 102 (5th Cir.1974).

In one case, however, the ban was tied to jurors' fear of being identified. The judge assured them he would do what he could to prevent their pictures from being displayed. When the judge saw two sketchers in the courtroom, he ordered that all drawings must be reviewed by the court before being broadcast. Justice Rehnquist, sitting as Circuit Justice, refused to stay the order. KPNX Broadcasting Co. v. Superior Court, 459 U.S. 1302 (1982). He thought the order would have been easier to defend if the judge had "flatly banned courtroom sketching of the jurors, and if he had extended the ban to those who sketch for the print media as well as to those who sketch for television." Justice Rehnquist concluded that "of all conceivable reportorial messages that could be conveyed by reporters or artists watching such trials, one of the least necessary to appreciate the significance of the trial would be individual juror sketches."

On remand, the state court invalidated the sketch order on First Amendment grounds. KPNX Broadcasting Co. v. Superior Court, 139 Ariz. 246, 678 P.2d 431, 10 Med.L.Rptr. 1289 (1984). The record did not show sufficient support for a prior restraint. Of the 150 jurors questioned, "several" expressed fear—and none of these was on the final panel. Using the three-part approach of the Nebraska Press case, the court concluded that the danger was not significant or imminent enough to justify the censorship; less restrictive measures would have sufficed (voir dire); and the sketch order was likely to have very limited success in meeting the judge's concern.

Federal Courts. In the federal courts there is still a complete ban on all photography. Some recent cases suggest the arguments. In United States v. Kerley, 753 F.2d 617, 11 Med.L.Rptr. 1572 (7th Cir. 1985), the defendant, charged with failing to register for the draft, sought to videotape his own trial. The court read Rule 53 of the Federal Rules of Criminal Procedure as an absolute ban on the videotaping: "The taking of photographs in the court room during the progress of judicial proceedings . . . shall not be permitted."

On the constitutional level, the court agreed with the court in United States v. Hastings, 695 F.2d 1278, 8 Med.L.Rptr. 2617 (11th Cir. 1983), certiorari denied sub nom. Post-Newsweek Stations, Florida, Inc.

v. United States, 461 U.S. 931 (1983). In *Hastings,* a federal judge on trial for bribery wanted to allow videotaping.

On the First Amendment point, the *Kerley* court agreed with *Hastings* that Rule 53 was a "time, place, and manner" regulation that had to be upheld if "neutral and reasonable." In both, the defendants waived any claim to prejudice from the presence of cameras, but the *Kerley* court responded that "a criminal trial is not a game. Rather, the trial plays an important part in preserving order and liberty in our society. Although strategic decisions often result in the waiver of some of the safeguards of a trial, it would be anomalous for the court to close its eyes in advance to what some believe to be impending unfairness and for the government to participate in a plan to hold a trial that could be regarded as unfair. And as noted in *Hastings,* another interest advanced by Rule 53 is the court's interest in preserving the decorum of the courtroom."

Although acknowledging that many of Kerley's reasons for videotaping (providing broad public access to the criminal process, and ensuring that media reports of the trial are accurate) were "attractive," the court found "significant institutional interests" supporting the rule. The conflict was not between an open and a closed proceeding. In fact, the judge permitted Kerley to record the trial on audiotape.

Finally, although cameras had gotten smaller, it "was not unreasonable to conclude that cameras are qualitatively different from reporters' notetaking and sketching." The possibility that participants who know they are being televised might want to "star" was substantial enough to permit the courts to ask that " 'actors' concentrate on their roles in the trial rather than on their roles on television. No doubt the interest in decorum and concentration that Rule 53 serves would not be enough to justify a total ban on media reporting of trials, but it is enough to justify the narrow limitation on the reporting embodied in Rule 53."

Kerley's effort to rely on cases permitting the copying of exhibits was rejected on the ground that in those cases the copying "can be accomplished outside of the courtroom and would have no apparent effect on the proceedings themselves."

In civil proceedings in the federal courts, the barrier is the Judicial Conference of the United States. In Westmoreland v. CBS, the Cable News Network (CNN) wanted to televise the trial. Both parties concurred. Nonetheless, the trial judge barred the cameras under Rule 7 adopted by the Judges of the Southern District of New York pursuant to the Judicial Conference, and was upheld on appeal. Westmoreland v. CBS, Inc., 752 F.2d 16, 11 Med.L.Rptr. 1013 (2d Cir.1984), certiorari denied sub nom. CNN, Inc. v. United States District Court, 105 S.Ct. 3478 (1985).

The majority concluded that although the public might have a constitutional right to attend trials, this did not require the televising of that trial. The majority relied in part on a case that upheld a local court rule banning the use of tape recorders in court, discussed below.

Judge Winter concurred separately in the CNN case. Since "live television is one of the many ways in which such information may be conveyed, the First Amendment is implicated in a request to televise. However, I believe that Rule 7 is a legitimate time, place or manner restriction on otherwise protected speech." Answering a CNN attack on "per se" rules, Judge Winter responded that case-by-case analysis is unworkable and will "likely evolve into a presumption in favor of television. If the apprehensions about television are to be given weight, therefore, a per se rule can be justified."

Among other concerns, he noted that in this case both parties might "actually desire television. It is certain that neither would dare object. Finally, the fear of seeming to oppose television will likely induce parties to avoid making any of the arguments against it in a particular case." He stressed that television was not the only way to reach the public with information about a trial. It is easier to bar it if it is "thought to impinge on the adjudicatory process in an undesirable fashion."

In 1986, the Supreme Court, 6–3, voted to deny radio coverage of the oral arguments on the constitutionality of the Gramm-Rudman-Hollings Act. Justices Brennan, Marshall, and Stevens voted to permit the coverage. Taylor, High Court Rejects Radio Coverage, N.Y. Times, April 20, 1986, § I, at 18.

Non-courtroom Situations. Occasionally, television cameras have been barred from places other than the courtroom.

In Garrett v. Estelle, 556 F.2d 1274, 2 Med.L.Rptr. 2265 (5th Cir. 1977), certiorari denied 438 U.S. 914 (1978), the court upheld Texas's refusal to allow cameras or tape recorders into the execution chamber. The state was willing to allow press pool reporters into the chamber and to permit other reporters to view the events over simultaneous closed circuit television. The court held, following *Pell* and *Saxbe,* that "the first amendment does not accompany the press where the public may not go." There was no public right to entry or to film the event.

The reporter then argued that he was being denied equal protection of the law because "other members of the press are allowed free use of their usual reporting tools." The court disagreed because the regulation also denied "the print reporter use of his camera and the radio reporter use of his tape recorder. Garrett is free to make his report by means of anchor desk or stand-up delivery on the TV screen, or even by simulation."

The final argument was that Texas had already chosen to make executions public by televising them over a closed circuit. Texas responded that legislation closing executions had already been upheld, Holden v. Minnesota, 137 U.S. 483 (1890), and that the limited televising of an execution should not be equated with making the event public. The court agreed that the closed circuit television was for those allowed to be present and should not be used to justify opening the event to the public. *Garrett* is noted in 63 Iowa L.Rev. 724 (1978).

Tape Recorders. Some states have banned certain reportorial aids for all reporters. Thus, the heads of both houses of the Maryland legislature barred reporters from attending sessions with "tape-recording devices." This was challenged by reporters, who claimed that "speed and accuracy are essential attributes of media news services" and that recorders will ensure accuracy. Their claims were rejected in Sigma Delta Chi v. Speaker, Maryland House of Delegates, 270 Md. 1, 310 A.2d 156 (1973). Conceding that newsgathering was entitled to some First Amendment protection, the court unanimously denied that banning tape recorders infringed such a right—plaintiffs were not prevented from carrying out their usual duties and the recorders were usable anywhere in the State House except in the chambers. Greater accuracy, although desirable, did not merit constitutional protection.

The court also rejected a due process claim that the restriction interfered with reporters' opportunity to earn a livelihood by diminishing the value of their product, "oral news." The reporters relied on Nevens v. City of Chino, 233 Cal.App.2d 755, 44 Cal.Rptr. 50 (1965), in which a similar ban had been upset on the ground that since the recorders were silent and unobtrusive, their exclusion unreasonably deprived reporters of the means to make an accurate record of what transpired. The California court analogized the ban to an attempt to prohibit the use of "pen, or pencil and paper." The Maryland court thought the analogy inappropriate: while "the removal of pen and paper might frustrate *all* effective communication, the prohibition against tape recorders is a mere inconvenience." There was no due process violation in rules that "may tend to exalt the preservation of order and decorum in the legislative chambers over increased efficiency of the press."

Finally, the reporters claimed that they were being denied equal protection of the laws because press members were being singled out by the ban. The court countered that the rules barred everyone, public and press, from bringing tape recorders into the chambers. The ban was against the equipment, not a class of persons.

Other states have taken the opposite approach. See Feldman v. Town of Bethel, 106 App.Div.2d 695, 484 N.Y.S.2d 147 (3d Dept.1984), upholding the award of damages to a reporter who was arrested for using a tape recorder at a town board meeting. The use of the recorder in an unobtrusive manner was protected by state law.

In United States v. Yonkers Board of Education, 747 F.2d 111, 10 Med.L.Rptr. 2521 (2d Cir.1984), the court denied a print reporter's request to tape proceedings to be sure of getting them right. Despite his promises not to broadcast or distribute the tapes, the refusal was upheld on appeal. Among the court's concerns was that "witnesses would be inhibited by the mere knowledge that their words were being recorded by outside observers"; that other would-be users "might be less reliable in their expressions of innocent intent"; and that use of recorders would "detract from the dignity and decorum of the courtroom." A final concern was that the use of tape recorders "might undermine the official court reporter system."

If one were to find a limited First Amendment right to gather news using whatever tools or aids the reporter wishes, what considerations might overcome that incipient right other than those suggested here? What about the contention that tape recorders destroy the free give-and-take of the legislative debate by freezing the words and intonations used by the speakers? Is that good—or bad? Is this related to the trend toward greater openness in the legislative process? What about an argument that tape-recorded words will be accepted as accurate by those who hear them no matter how many witnesses testify that the speaker used different words—and that tapes may be altered so that false implications would be drawn? Are the arguments different when the recorder is being used openly in a public place?

C. MINIMUM ACCESS

We come now to the most basic claims for access to information and premises: the claim that even though no other argument is applicable, the would-be gatherer has a constitutional right to obtain the information or access sought. In considering the cases and arguments in this section, focus on what is being sought, and the reasons being offered by government to defeat the gatherer.

1. Access to Premises

The Supreme Court first confronted this issue when a citizen claimed a right to travel to Cuba, in violation of a travel ban, to learn first hand about "the effects abroad of our Government's policies, foreign and domestic, and . . . conditions abroad which might affect such policies." Zemel v. Rusk, 381 U.S. 1 (1965). Although the Court agreed that the travel ban rendered "less than wholly free the flow of information concerning" Cuba, it rejected the "contention that it is a First Amendment right which is involved. . . . There are few restrictions on action which could not be clothed by ingenious argument in the garb of decreased data flow. For example, the prohibition of unauthorized entry into the White House diminishes the citizen's opportunities to gather information he might find relevant to his opinion of the way the country is being run, but that does not make entry into the White House a First Amendment right. The right to speak and publish does not carry with it the unrestrained right to gather information." Furthermore, reporters are prohibited from following the President some places, and police keep unauthorized persons from the immediate area of a hostage situation.

In 1974, for example, President Ford excluded all reporters from mingling with guests at White House receptions. In 1975, he announced new rules under which a small pool of reporters, carrying only notebooks, might circulate at such events "with the understanding that the pool reporters will respect the privacy of personal communications between myself or Mrs. Ford and our guests." Editor & Publisher, Sept. 13, 1975, at 15.

When President Carter took a steamer trip down the Mississippi River, he set rules for reporters who wished to accompany him: that the White House must approve all photographs, that no photos be bought from tourists, and that national organizations not distribute photos taken by local photographers along the way. As a result, several organizations refused to send observers on the trip. N.Y. Times, Aug. 15, 1979, at A18. These conditions are enforced, if challenged, by White House security personnel or by physical barriers.

a. Access to Prisons

Almost a decade passed before the Court confronted a press claim for access. In 1974, the Court decided two companion cases in which the press sought to enter prisons after the warden had imposed limitations on that access. In Pell v. Procunier, 417 U.S. 817 (1974), a regulation of the California Department of Corrections provided that "media interviews with specific individual inmates will not be permitted." Saxbe v. Washington Post Co., 417 U.S. 843 (1974), involved a similar ban by the federal prison system. The Court concluded in *Pell* that the security and penological considerations of incarceration were sufficient to justify rejection of the inmates' claims that the interview ban violated their First Amendment rights.

Justice Stewart, writing for the Court in *Pell* and in *Saxbe,* then turned to the claims raised by the press. He noted that "this regulation is not part of an attempt by the State to conceal the conditions in its prisons or to frustrate the press' investigation and reporting of those conditions." Reporters could visit the institutions and "speak about any subject to any inmates whom they might encounter." Interviews with inmates selected at random were also permitted, and both the press and the public could take tours through the prisons. "In short, members of the press enjoy access to California prisons that is not available to other members of the public." Indeed, the only apparent restriction was the one being challenged.

The majority placed great weight on the passage from *Branzburg* that said:

> It has generally been held that the First Amendment does not guarantee the press a constitutional right of special access to information not available to the public generally . . . . Despite the fact that newsgathering may be hampered, the press is regularly excluded from grand jury proceedings, our own conferences, the meetings of other official bodies in executive session, and the meetings of private organizations. Newsmen have no constitution-

> al right of access to the scenes of crime or disaster when the general public is excluded.

This passage led Justice Stewart to add: "Similarly, newsmen have no constitutional right of access to prisons or their inmates beyond that afforded the general public." He reached this conclusion even though another part of *Branzburg* had observed that "without some protection for seeking out the news, freedom of the press could be eviscerated." Justice Stewart continued:

> The First and Fourteenth Amendments bar government from interfering in any way with a free press. The Constitution does not, however, require government to accord the press special access to information not shared by members of the public generally. It is one thing to say that a journalist is free to seek out sources of information not available to members of the general public, that he is entitled to some constitutional protection of the confidentiality of such sources, cf. Branzburg v. Hayes, supra, and that government cannot restrain the publication of news emanating from such sources. Cf. N.Y. Times v. United States, supra. It is quite another thing to suggest that the Constitution imposes upon government the affirmative duty to make available to journalists sources of information not available to members of the public generally. That proposition finds no support in the words of the Constitution or in any decision of this Court. Accordingly, since § 415.071 does not deny the press access to sources of information available to members of the general public, we hold that it does not abridge the protections that the First and Fourteenth Amendments guarantee.

Four Justices dissented on the press question. Justice Powell, joined by Justices Brennan and Marshall, writing in *Saxbe*, asserted that the government was not protecting privileged or confidential information. It "has no legitimate interest in preventing newsmen from obtaining the information . . . . Quite to the contrary, federal prisons are public institutions. The administration of these institutions, the effectiveness of their rehabilitative programs, the conditions of confinement that they maintain, and the experiences of the individuals incarcerated therein are all matters of legitimate societal interest and concern."

Citizens could not undertake to learn this information for themselves. "In seeking out the news the press therefore acts as an agent of the public at large." Justice Powell could not "follow the Court in concluding that *any* governmental restriction on press access to information, so long as it is nondiscriminatory, falls outside the purview of First Amendment concern." This did not mean that government must justify every regulation that might tangentially interfere with access to news. On the other hand, it was "equally impermissible" to conclude that governmental restrictions never warrant constitutional scrutiny. "At some point official restraints on access to news sources, even though not directed solely at the press, may so undermine the function of the First Amendment that it is both appropriate and necessary to require the Government to justify such regulations in terms more compelling than discretionary authority and administrative convenience."

Justice Powell concluded that the total ban on interviews impaired "a core value of the First Amendment." Although a total ban was impermissible, this did not mean that the government had to approach these matters on a case-by-case basis. It would be permissible to adopt rules that barred interviews with prisoners being disciplined or that limited the number of interviews that might be held with any one person. If the government wanted to limit such interviews to the "press," this could be accomplished by using a definition the prisons were already using for another purpose: "A newspaper entitled to second class mailing privileges; a magazine or periodical of general distribution; a national or international news service; a radio or television network or station." If too many qualified persons wanted interviews, Justice Powell suggested the use of pools.

Justice Douglas, joined by Justice Brennan and Marshall, also dissented.

As emerged in later cases, the majority opinions in *Pell* and *Saxbe* contained a serious ambiguity. If the First Amendment did not authorize a right of access in these cases, why did it matter that the prisons had generally operated quite openly? In other words, was the majority decision based on the fact that the prisons in these cases already were fairly generous in allowing outsiders to visit, or on the view that no right of access could be found in the Constitution? Subsequent cases reveal a second ambiguity—does the press lose these cases because it is asking for a special privilege that members of the general public do not have? If members of the public had sought entry to interview a specific named and willing prisoner, and the prison authorities had responded in the same fashion, would the Supreme Court majority have written its opinion any differently?

A few years later, the Supreme Court returned to the prison question in a slightly different context.

HOUCHINS v. KQED, INC.

Supreme Court of the United States, 1978.
438 U.S. 1, 98 S.Ct. 2588, 57 L.Ed.2d 553, 3 Med.L.Rptr. 2521.
Noted, 92 Harv.L.Rev. 174, 6 Hastings Const.L.Q. 933, 54 Notre Dame Law. 288, 33 U.Miami L.Rev. 680.

[A suicide occurred at the Alameda County Jail at Santa Rita, California. KQED, licensee of a television station in nearby San Francisco, reported the story and quoted a psychiatrist as saying that conditions at the Little Greystone building were responsible for the illnesses of his patient-prisoners at the jail. In an earlier proceeding, a federal judge had ruled that the conditions at Greystone constituted cruel and unusual punishment. Houchins, the county sheriff, refused to admit a camera crew KQED sent to get the story and to photograph the facilities, including Greystone. At the time, no public tours of the jail were permitted.

KQED and the NAACP filed suit under 42 U.S.C. § 1983 claiming violation of their First Amendment rights. The NAACP claimed that information about the jail was essential to permit public debate on jail conditions in Alameda County. The complaint requested preliminary and permanent injunctions to prevent the sheriff from "excluding KQED news personnel from the Greystone cells and Santa Rita facilities and generally preventing full and accurate news coverage of the conditions prevailing therein."

Shortly after suit was filed, the sheriff announced a program of monthly tours. The press received advance notice, and several reporters, including one from KQED, went on the first tour. Each tour was limited to 25 persons and did not include Little Greystone. Cameras and tape recorders were barred, though the sheriff did supply photographs of some parts of the jail. Tour members "were not permitted to interview inmates and inmates were generally removed from view."

KQED argued that the tours were unsatisfactory because advance scheduling prevented timely access and because photography and interviewing were barred. The sheriff defended his policy on grounds of "inmate privacy," the danger of creating "jail celebrities" who would "undermine jail security," and the concern that unscheduled tours would "disrupt jail operations."

The district judge issued a preliminary injunction barring the sheriff from denying access to "responsible representatives" of the news media "at reasonable times and hours" and "from preventing KQED news personnel and responsible representatives of the news media from utilizing photographic and sound equipment or from utilizing inmate interviews in providing full and accurate coverage of the Santa Rita facilities." He found that a more flexible policy was "both desirable and attainable" without danger to prison discipline. The court of appeals, in three separate opinions, rejected the sheriff's argument that *Pell* and *Saxbe* controlled, and affirmed the injunction.]

MR. CHIEF JUSTICE BURGER announced the judgment of the Court and delivered an opinion, in which MR. JUSTICE WHITE and MR. JUSTICE REHNQUIST joined.

The question presented is whether the news media have a constitutional right of access to a county jail, over and above that of other persons, to interview inmates and make sound recordings, films, and photographs for publication and broadcasting by newspapers, radio and television.

. . .

II.

Notwithstanding our holding in Pell v. Procunier, supra, respondents assert that the right recognized by the Court of Appeals flows logically from our decisions construing the First Amendment. They argue that there is a constitutionally guaranteed right to gather news under Pell v. Procunier, [ ], and Branzburg v. Hayes, [ ]. From the right to gather news and the right to receive information, they argue for an implied special right of access to government controlled sources of information. This right, they contend, compels access as a *constitutional* matter. . . .

III.

We can agree with many of the respondents' generalized assertions; conditions in jails and prisons are clearly matters "of great public importance." Pell v. Procunier, supra, at 830 n. 7. Penal facilities are public institutions which require large amounts of public funds, and their mission is crucial in our criminal justice system. Each person placed in prison becomes, in effect, a ward of the state for whom society assumes broad responsibility. It is equally true that with greater information, the public can more intelligently form opinions about prison conditions. Beyond question, the role of the media is important; acting as the "eyes and ears" of the public, they can be a powerful and constructive force, contributing to remedial action in the conduct of public business. They have served that function since the beginning of the Republic, but like all other components of our society media representatives are subject to limits.

The media are not a substitute for or an adjunct of government, and like the courts, they are "ill-equipped" to deal with problems of prison administration. Cf. Procunier v. Martinez, [ ]. We must not confuse the role of the media with that of government; each has special, crucial functions each complementing—and, sometimes conflicting with—the other.

The public importance of conditions in penal facilities and the media's role of providing information afford no basis for reading into the Constitution a right of the public or the media to enter these institutions, with camera equipment, and take moving and still pictures of inmates for broadcast purposes. This Court has never intimated a First Amendment guarantee of a right of access to all sources of information within government control. Nor does the rationale of the decisions upon which respondents rely lead to the implication of such a right.

. . .

Branzburg v. Hayes, supra, offers even less support for the respondents' position. Its observation, in dictum, that "news gathering is not without its First Amendment protections," 408 U.S., at 707, in no sense implied a constitutional right of access to news sources. That observation must be read in context; it was in response to the contention that forcing a reporter to disclose to a grand jury information received in confidence would violate the First Amendment by deterring news sources from communicating information. *Branzburg,* supra, at 680. There is an undoubted right to gather news "from any source by means within the law," id., at 681–682, but that affords no basis for the claim that the First Amendment compels others—private persons or governments—to supply information.

. . .

The right to *receive* ideas and information is not the issue in this case. [ ] The issue is a claimed special privilege of access which the Court rejected in *Pell* and *Saxbe,* a right which is not essential to guarantee the freedom to communicate or publish.

IV.

The respondents' argument is flawed, not only because it lacks precedential support and is contrary to statements in this Court's opinions, but also because it invites the Court to involve itself in what is clearly a legislative task which the Constitution has left to the political processes. Whether the government should open penal institutions in the manner sought by respondents is a question of policy which a legislative body might appropriately resolve one way or the other.

A number of alternatives are available to prevent problems in penal facilities from escaping public attention. The early penal reform movements in this country and England gained impetus as a result of reports from citizens and visiting committees who volunteered or received commissions to visit penal institutions and make reports. [ ] Citizen task forces and prison visitation committees continue to play an important role in keeping the public informed on deficiencies of prison systems and need for reforms. Grand juries, with the potent subpoena power—not available to the media—traditionally concern themselves with conditions in public institutions; a prosecutor or judge may initiate similar inquiries and the legislative power embraces an arsenal of weapons for inquiry relating to tax supported institutions. In each case, these public bodies are generally compelled to publish their findings, and if they default, the power of the media is always available to generate public pressure for disclosure. But the choice as to the most effective and appropriate method is a policy decision to be resolved by legislative decision. We must not confuse what is "good," "desirable" or "expedient" with what is constitutionally commanded by the First Amendment. To do so is to trivialize constitutional adjudication.

Unarticulated but implicit in the assertion that media access to the jail is essential for informed public debate on jail conditions is the assumption that media personnel are the best qualified persons for the task of discovering malfeasance in public institutions. But that assumption finds no support in the decisions of this Court or the First

Amendment. Editors and newsmen who inspect a jail may decide to publish or not to publish what information they acquire. [ ] Public bodies and public officers, on the other hand, may be coerced by public opinion to disclose what they might prefer to conceal. No comparable pressures are available to anyone to compel publication by the media of what they might prefer not to make known.

There is no discernible basis for a constitutional duty to disclose, or for standards governing disclosure of or access to information. Because the Constitution affords no guidelines, absent statutory standards, hundreds of judges would, under the Court of Appeals' approach, be at large to fashion ad hoc standards, in individual cases, according to their own ideas of what seems "desirable" or "expedient." We, therefore, reject the Court of Appeals' conclusory assertion that the public and the media have a First Amendment right to government information regarding the conditions of jails and their inmates and presumably all other public facilities such as hospitals and mental institutions.

> "There is no constitutional right to have access to particular government information, or to require openness from the bureaucracy. [Citing *Pell v. Procunier,* supra.] The public's interest in knowing about its government is protected by the guarantee of a Free Press, but the protection is indirect. The Constitution itself is neither a Freedom of Information Act nor an Official Secrets Act.
>
> "The Constitution, in other words, establishes the contest, not its resolution. Congress may provide a resolution, at least in some instances, through carefully drawn legislation. For the rest, we must rely, as so often in our system we must, on the tug and pull of the political forces in American society." Stewart, "Or of the Press," 26 Hastings L.J. 631, 636 (1975).

Petitioner cannot prevent respondents from learning about jail conditions in a variety of ways, albeit not as conveniently as they might prefer. Respondents have a First Amendment right to receive letters from inmates criticizing jail officials and reporting on conditions. See Procunier v. Martinez, [ ]. Respondents are free to interview those who render the legal assistance to which inmates are entitled. See id., at 419. They are also free to seek out former inmates, visitors to the prison, public officials, and institutional personnel, as they sought out the complaining psychiatrist here.

Moreover, California statutes currently provide for a prison Board of Corrections that has the authority to inspect jails and prisons and *must* provide a public report at regular intervals. . . .

Neither the First Amendment nor Fourteenth Amendment mandates a right of access to government information or sources of information within the government's control. Under our holdings in *Pell* [and *Saxbe*], until the political branches decree otherwise, as they are free to do, the media have no special right of access to the Alameda County Jail different from or greater than that accorded the public generally.

The judgment of the Court of Appeals is reversed and the case is remanded for further proceedings.

Reversed.

MR. JUSTICE MARSHALL and MR. JUSTICE BLACKMUN took no part in the consideration or decision of this case.

MR. JUSTICE STEWART, concurring in the judgment.

I agree that the preliminary injunction issued against the petitioner was unwarranted, and therefore concur in the judgment. In my view, however, KQED was entitled to injunctive relief of more limited scope.

The First and Fourteenth Amendments do not guarantee the public a right of access to information generated or controlled by government, nor do they guarantee the press any basic right of access superior to that of the public generally. The Constitution does no more than assure the public and the press equal access once government has opened its doors. Accordingly, I agree substantially with what the opinion of The Chief Justice has to say on that score.

We part company, however, in applying these abstractions to the facts of this case. Whereas he appears to view "equal access" as meaning access that is identical in all respects, I believe that the concept of equal access must be accorded more flexibility in order to accommodate the practical distinctions between the press and the general public.

When on assignment, a journalist does not tour a jail simply for his own edification. He is there to gather information to be passed on to others, and his mission is protected by the Constitution for very specific reasons. "Enlightened choice by an informed citizenry is the basic ideal upon which an open society is premised . . . ." Branzburg v. Hayes, 408 U.S. 665, 726 (dissenting opinion). Our society depends heavily on the press for that enlightenment. . . .

That the First Amendment speaks separately of freedom of speech and freedom of the press is no constitutional accident, but an acknowledgment of the critical role played by the press in American society. The Constitution requires sensitivity to that role, and to the special needs of the press in performing it effectively. A person touring Santa Rita Jail can grasp its reality with his own eyes and ears. But if a television reporter is to convey the jail's sights and sounds to those who cannot personally visit the place, he must use cameras and sound equipment. In short, terms of access that are reasonably imposed on individual members of the public may, if they impede effective reporting without sufficient justification, be unreasonable as applied to journalists who are there to convey to the general public what the visitors see.

Under these principles, KQED was clearly entitled to some form of preliminary injunctive relief. At the time of the District Court's decision, members of the public were permitted to visit most parts of the Santa Rita Jail, and the First and Fourteenth Amendments required the Sheriff to give members of the press *effective* access to the same areas. The Sheriff evidently assumed that he could fulfill this obligation simply by allowing reporters to sign up for tours on the same terms as the public. I think he was mistaken in this assumption, as a matter of constitutional law.

The District Court found that the press required access to the jail on a more flexible and frequent basis than scheduled monthly tours if it was to keep the public informed. By leaving the "specific methods of implementing such a policy . . . [to] Sheriff Houchins," the Court concluded that the press could be allowed access to the jail "at reasonable times and hours" without causing undue disruption. The District Court also found that the media required cameras and recording equipment for effective presentation to the viewing public of the conditions at the jail seen by individual visitors, and that their use could be kept consistent with institutional needs. These elements of the Court's order were both sanctioned by the Constitution and amply supported by the record.

In two respects, however, the District Court's preliminary injunction was overbroad. It ordered the Sheriff to permit reporters into the Little Greystone facility and it required him to let them interview randomly encountered inmates. In both these respects, the injunction gave the press access to areas and sources of information from which persons on the public tours had been excluded, and thus enlarged the scope of what the Sheriff and Supervisors had opened to public view. The District Court erred in concluding that the First and Fourteenth Amendments compelled this broader access for the press.

Because the preliminary injunction exceeded the requirements of the Constitution in these respects, I agree that the judgment of the Court of Appeals affirming the District Court's order must be reversed. But I would not foreclose the possibility of further relief for KQED on remand. In my view, the availability and scope of future permanent injunctive relief must depend upon the extent of access then permitted the public, and the decree must be framed to accommodate equitably the constitutional role of the press and the institutional requirements of the jail.

MR. JUSTICE STEVENS, with whom MR. JUSTICE BRENNAN and MR. JUSTICE POWELL join, dissenting.

The Court holds that the scope of press access to the Santa Rita jail required by the preliminary injunction issued against petitioner is inconsistent with the holding in Pell v. Procunier, [ ], that "newsmen have no constitutional right of access to prisons or their inmates beyond that afforded the general public" and therefore the injunction was an abuse of the District Court's discretion. I respectfully disagree.

. . .

For two reasons, which shall be discussed separately, the decisions in *Pell* and *Saxbe* do not control the propriety of the District Court's preliminary injunction. First, the unconstitutionality of petitioner's policies which gave rise to this litigation does not rest on the premise that the press has a greater right of access to information regarding prison conditions than do other members of the public. Second, relief tailored to the needs of the press may properly be awarded to a representative of the press which is successful in proving that it has been harmed by a constitutional violation and need not await the grant of relief to members of the general public who may also have been injured by petitioner's unconstitutional access policy but have not yet sought to vindicate their rights.

. . .

It is well settled that a defendant's corrective action in anticipation of litigation or following commencement of suit does not deprive the court of power to decide whether the previous course of conduct was unlawful. . . .

In Pell v. Procunier, [ ], the Court stated that "newsmen have no constitutional right of access to prisons or their inmates beyond that afforded the general public." But the Court has never intimated that a nondiscriminatory policy of excluding entirely both the public and the press from access to information about prison conditions would avoid constitutional scrutiny. Indeed, *Pell* itself strongly suggests the contrary.

. . .

The decision in *Pell,* therefore, does not imply that a state policy of concealing prison conditions from the press, or a policy denying the press any opportunity to observe those conditions, could have been justified simply by pointing to like concealment from, and denial to, the general public. If that were not true, there would have been no need to emphasize the substantial press and public access reflected in the record of that case. What *Pell* does indicate is that the question whether respondents established a probability of prevailing on their constitutional claim is inseparable from the question whether petitioner's policies unduly restricted the opportunities of the general public to learn about the conditions of confinement in Santa Rita jail. As in *Pell,* in assessing its adequacy, the total access of the public and the press must be considered.

Here, the broad restraints on access to information regarding operation of the jail that prevailed on the date this suit was instituted are plainly disclosed by the record. . . . Petitioner's no-access policy, modified only in the wake of respondents' resort to the courts, could survive constitutional scrutiny only if the Constitution affords no protection to the public's right to be informed about conditions within those public institutions where some of its members are confined because they have been charged with or found guilty of criminal offenses.

II.

The preservation of a full and free flow of information to the general public has long been recognized as a core objective of the First Amendment to the Constitution. It is for this reason that the First Amendment protects not only the dissemination but also the receipt of information and ideas. . . .

In addition to safeguarding the right of one individual to receive what another elects to communicate, the First Amendment serves an essential societal function. Our system of self-government assumes the existence of an informed citizenry.[21] . . . It is not sufficient, therefore, that the channels of communication be free of governmental restraints. Without some protection for the acquisition of information about the operation of public institutions such as prisons by the public at large, the process of self-governance contemplated by the Framers would be stripped of its substance.[22]

For that reason information-gathering is entitled to some measure of constitutional protection. See, e.g., Branzburg v. Hayes, [ ]; Pell v. Procunier, [ ]. As this Court's decisions clearly indicate, however, this protection is not for the private benefit of those who might qualify as representatives of the "press" but to insure that the citizens are fully informed regarding matters of public interest and importance.

A recognition that the "underlying right is the right of the public generally" is also implicit in the doctrine that "newsmen have no constitutional right of access to prisons or their inmates beyond that afforded the general public." Pell v. Procunier, [ ]. In *Pell*, it was unnecessary to consider the extent of the public's right of access to information regarding the prison and its inmates in order to adjudicate the press claim to a particular form of access, since the record demonstrated that the flow of information to thc public, both directly and through the press, was adequate to survive constitutional challenge; institutional considerations justified denying the single, additional mode of access sought by the press in that case.

Here, in contrast, the restrictions on access to the inner portions of the Santa Rita jail that existed on the date this litigation commenced concealed from the general public the conditions of confinement within the facility. The question is whether petitioner's policies, which cut off the flow of information at its source, abridged the public's right to be informed about those conditions.

21. See A. Meiklejohn . . . .

22. Admittedly, the right to receive or acquire information is not specifically mentioned in the Constitution. But "the protection of the Bill of Rights goes beyond the specific guarantees to protect from . . . abridgment those equally fundamental personal rights necessary to make the express guarantees fully meaningful. . . . The dissemination of ideas can accomplish nothing if otherwise willing adherents are not free to receive and consider them. It would be a barren marketplace of ideas that had only sellers and no buyers." Lamont v. Postmaster General, 381 U.S., at 308 (Brennan, J., concurring). It would be an even more barren marketplace that had willing buyers and sellers and no meaningful information to exchange.

The answer to that question does not depend upon the degree of public disclosure which should attend the operation of most governmental activity. Such matters involve questions of policy which generally must be resolved by the political branches of government.[25] Moreover, there are unquestionably occasions when governmental activity may properly be carried on in complete secrecy. For example, the public and the press are commonly excluded from "grand jury proceedings, our own conferences, [and] the meetings of other official bodies gathering in executive session . . . ." Branzburg v. Hayes [ ]. In addition, some functions of government—essential to the protection of the public and indeed our country's vital interests—necessarily require a large measure of secrecy, subject to appropriate legislative oversight. In such situations the reasons for withholding information from the public are both apparent and legitimate.

In this case, however, "[r]espondents do not assert a right to force disclosure of confidential information or to invade in any way the decisionmaking processes of governmental officials." [28] They simply seek an end to petitioner's policy of concealing prison conditions from the public. Those conditions are wholly without claim to confidentiality. While prison officials have an interest in the time and manner of public acquisition of information about the institutions they administer, there is no legitimate, penological justification for concealing from citizens the conditions in which their fellow citizens are being confined.

The reasons which militate in favor of providing special protection to the flow of information to the public about prisons relate to the unique function they perform in a democratic society. Not only are they public institutions, financed with public funds and administered by public servants; they are an integral component of the criminal justice system. The citizens confined therein are temporarily, and sometimes permanently, deprived of their liberty as a result of a trial which must conform to the dictates of the Constitution. By express command of the Sixth Amendment the proceeding must be a "public trial." It is important not only that the trial itself be fair, but also that the community at large have confidence in the integrity of the proceeding. That public interest survives the judgment of conviction and appropriately carries over to an interest in how the convicted person is treated during his period of punishment and hoped-for rehabilitation.

. . .

Some inmates—in Santa Rita, a substantial number—are pretrial detainees. Though confined pending trial, they have not been convicted of an offense against society and are entitled to the presumption of innocence. Certain penological objectives, i.e., punishment, deterrence and rehabilitation, which are legitimate in regard to convicted prisoners, are inapplicable to pretrial detainees. Society has a special inter-

25. In United States v. Nixon, 418 U.S. 683, 705 n. 15, we pointed out that the Founders themselves followed a policy of confidentiality . . . .

28. Saxbe v. Washington Post Co. [ ] (Powell, J. dissenting).

est in ensuring that unconvicted citizens are treated in accord with their status.

In this case, the record demonstrates that both the public and the press had been consistently denied any access to the inner portions of the Santa Rita jail, that there had been excessive censorship of inmate correspondence, and that there was no valid justification for these broad restraints on the flow of information. An affirmative answer to the question whether respondent established a likelihood of prevailing on the merits did not depend, in final analysis, on any right of the press to special treatment beyond that accorded the public at large. Rather, the probable existence of a constitutional violation rested upon the special importance of allowing a democratic community access to knowledge about how its servants were treating some of its members who have been committed to their custody. An official prison policy of concealing such knowledge from the public by arbitrarily cutting off the flow of information at its source abridges the freedom of speech and of the press protected by the First and Fourteenth Amendments to the Constitution.

III.

The preliminary injunction entered by the District Court granted relief to KQED without providing any specific remedy for other members of the public. Moreover, it imposed duties on petitioner that may not be required by the Constitution itself. The injunction was not an abuse of discretion for either of these reasons.

If a litigant can prove that he has suffered specific harm from the application of an unconstitutional policy, it is entirely proper for a court to grant relief tailored to his needs without attempting to redress all the mischief that the policy may have worked on others. . . . Accordingly, even though the Constitution provides the press with no greater right of access to information than that possessed by the public at large, a preliminary injunction is not invalid simply because it awards special relief to a successful litigant which is a representative of the press.[36]

Nor is there anything novel about injunctive relief which goes beyond a mere prohibition against repetition of previous unlawful conduct. In situations which are both numerous and varied the chancellor has required a wrongdoer to take affirmative steps to eliminate the effects of a violation of law even though the law itself imposes no duty to take the remedial action decreed by the court.[37] . . .

36. Moreover, the relief granted to KQED will redound to the benefit of members of the public interested in obtaining information about conditions in the Santa Rita jail. The press may have no greater constitutional right to information about prisons than that possessed by the general public. But when the press does acquire information and disseminate it to the public, it performs an important societal function. . . .

In the context of fashioning a remedy for a violation of rights protected by the First Amendment, consideration of the role of the press in our society is appropriate.

37. For an extensive discussion of this practice in the context of desegregation

The Court of Appeals found no reason to question the specific preliminary relief ordered by the District Court. Nor is it appropriate for this Court to review the scope of the order. The order was preliminary in character, and would have been subject to revision before the litigation reached a final conclusion.

I would affirm the judgment of the Court of Appeals.

Notes and Questions

1. Does this case cast light on the basis for the *Pell* and *Saxbe* decisions?

2. What does the Chief Justice see as the crucial question?

3. Why would Justice Stewart allow access at times other than those at which the public can enter the jail? What would he do if the sheriff were to stop the public tours?

4. Does the dissent add anything to the arguments of Justice Powell's dissent in *Saxbe?*

5. Do the several opinions indicate how they would handle a request from the NAACP to have its own representatives enter the jail, rather than having KQED be the one to enter?

6. Taking into account the limits that Justice Stevens imposes in his dissenting opinion, to what other kinds of public institutions might his analysis apply?

7. *Exclusive Contracts and Gathering.* Although it was not central to the Court's analysis, the Zacchini case, p. 411, supra, was triggered by the plaintiff's failure to exert effective control over the admission of photographers into the enclosure. That issue arose in connection with the week-long World Figure Skating Championships held in the Hartford Civic Center Coliseum in 1981. The event was awarded to the local sponsors in Hartford by the ISU, a Swiss-based group that controls amateur skating competitions. The ISU had previously granted to Candid exclusive television rights to the championship including "exclusivity against television news broadcasts of any length which would include video film or videotape coverage of any of the Championships prior to our telecasts." ABC Sports acquired Candid's rights and planned a nationwide presentation on ABC's Wide World of Sports the week after the event concluded.

Hartford's sponsors had bid for the event subject to the exclusive television rights. After winning the bid, the sponsors sent letters to television stations in the Hartford area informing them of the situation and enclosing a document to be signed by anyone who wished to bring a television camera into the Civic Center. The critical clause provided that "the permittee will not broadcast . . . any of the material or coverage obtained during the championships until after the conclusion of the entire telecast of the event by [ABC] whether such telecast occurs

decrees, see the Court's opinion last Term in Milliken v. Bradley, 433 U.S. 267.

live or at a later time or date." Each local station also had to agree to indemnify the sponsors for costs and attorney's fees they might incur if the station should violate any part of the agreement.

Plaintiff, owner of the local CBS affiliate, sought a preliminary injunction permitting entry to the arena without signing any agreement. Plaintiff insisted on a right to gather news and relied heavily on *Zacchini.* The judge found that *Zacchini* had "no application" because it did not involve the issue of gathering.

The ISU had a "legitimate commercial stake in this event" and, like Mr. Zacchini, it was "entitled to contract regarding the distribution of this entertainment product." Since the restrictions apply to anyone seeking to enter the arena with a television camera, "plaintiff is seeking access of a type which is denied to the public generally." Since the case law did not support special access, it was "clear" that the restrictions "would be given full effect if the Civic Center were privately operated."

Even though the Civic Center was owned and operated by the City of Hartford, so that state action was involved, the management was functioning in a proprietary manner and competing with private arenas for entertainment events. There was evidence that the City Council was concerned by reports that the Civic Center was incurring operating losses. Since a commercial venture was involved, the restrictions should be upheld unless they were arbitrary or capricious. No such showing was possible here. First, the judge stressed the entertainment quality of the event. Although *Zacchini* said that entertainment is news, this was an athletic event. "As such, it is on the periphery of protected speech (for purposes of balancing conflicting interests), as opposed, for example, to political speech, which is at the core of first amendment protection."

A second factor was the severity of the restriction imposed. Here the general public had ready access to the event, and it would be reported by newspaper and radio. Television itself could report it by using still photographs.

Third, the restrictions were not arbitrary. "Television broadcasting would have an unusual impact on the entertainment value of this event. That is, figure skating is a uniquely visual sport. Newspaper and radio coverage will not diminish its commercial value; television broadcasting could do so."

A more rigorous approach could jeopardize the revenue that cities receive for their arenas and shift future events to private arenas, where broadcast coverage could be more effectively restricted. Post Newsweek Stations-Connecticut, Inc. v. Travelers Insurance Co., 510 F.Supp. 81, 6 Med.L.Rptr. 2540 (D.Conn.1981).

In a later phase of the case, ABC, which had not been a party earlier, intervened to assert the commercial value of its contract rights—and to oppose the plaintiff's claimed right to gather news. 7

Med.L.Rptr. 1110 (D.Conn.1981). See Gunther, ABC Gets What It Pays For, Wash.Journ.Rev. 11 (May 1981) and N.Y. Times, Mar. 14, 1981, at 13.

b. Access to Judicial Proceedings

In the remarkably short span of seven years (1979–86), the Court has developed a First Amendment right of access. In all the cases that follow, the Court concluded that the matters should be addressed even though the cases had concluded. An exception to the mootness doctrine applies to situations that are "capable of repetition, yet evading review" because they occur and end so quickly.

1. The process began with confusion in Gannett Co. v. DePasquale, 443 U.S. 368, 5 Med.L.Rptr. 1337 (1979), involving closure of a pretrial suppression hearing in a New York criminal proceeding. The Court, 5-4, held that the Sixth Amendment right to a public trial was "personal to the accused" and could not be invoked by the media. Only two of the members of the majority reached the First Amendment question: Justice Powell, who found such a right, but who thought the trial judge had properly balanced in favor of the accused's right to a fair trial, and Justice Rehnquist, who denied a First Amendment right. Although four justices found a Sixth Amendment right in the press (and no sufficient reason for denying access in the case at bar) and Justice Powell found a First Amendment right of access in some cases, the majority upheld the state's denial of access.

2. The next year, the Court for the first time found a right of access under the First Amendment. In Richmond Newspapers, Inc. v. Virginia, 448 U.S. 555, 6 Med.L.Rptr. 1833 (1980), the trial judge, acting on the defendant's request and without objection from the prosecution, had ordered the courtroom closed during the defendant's fourth trial for the same murder. The judge never clearly indicated the reasons for his decision. The Court reversed the closure, 7–1, though without a majority opinion. For the plurality of three, Chief Justice Burger stressed that criminal trials had been open for hundreds of years, and for good reason.

Justice Brennan, joined by Justice Marshall, stressed both the history and a "structural" approach that relied upon the view that the First Amendment "embodies more than a commitment to free expression and communicative interchange for their own sakes; it has a *structural* role to play in securing and fostering our republican system of government."

Justice Stevens, although joining the plurality, wrote separately to observe that this was a "watershed case" because no prior case had "squarely held that the acquisition of newsworthy matter is entitled to any constitutional protection whatsoever." He also found it "ironic" that the Court should recognize the right here but not in the prison cases.

Justice Rehnquist, dissenting, could find nothing in the Constitution creating a public right to attend trials. He argued that the Court's effort to gather to itself "all of the ultimate decisionmaking power over how justice shall be administered, not merely in the federal system, but in each of 50 states, is a task that no Court consisting of nine persons, however gifted, is equal to." Later, he asserted that "it is basically unhealthy to have so much authority concentrated in a small group of lawyers who have been appointed to the Supreme Court and enjoy life tenure."

3. The next case involved a Massachusetts statute that had been interpreted to require that the courtroom be closed during the testimony of minor victims of sexual offenses. A majority concurred in an opinion by Justice Brennan striking the statute. Globe Newspaper Co. v. Superior Court, 457 U.S. 596, 8 Med.L.Rptr. 1689 (1982). The history of open criminal trials developed in *Richmond Newspapers* applied here even though trials involving sexual offenses or other sensational aspects had frequently been closed. The critical question was not the historical openness of a particular type of trial but rather the "state interests assertedly supporting the restriction."

In this case those reasons—to protect the victim from further trauma and to encourage such victims to come forward—did not suffice. Although safeguarding the physical and psychological well-being of minors is a compelling state interest, it did not justify mandatory closure. This is best done on a case-by-case basis in which the trial judge considers such matters as the age of the victim, the victim's maturity, the nature of the crime, the desires of the victim, and the interests of parents and relatives. In the case before the Court, for example, the victims were 16 and 17, and may have been willing to testify in public. In deciding whether to close the courtroom, the trial judge might explore the issues in an in camera proceeding.

The state's interest in encouraging victims to come forward did not suffice because the state had presented no support for the claim that automatic closure will achieve that result. The Court doubted the connection because the statute only barred public attendance in court—it did not bar press access to the transcript or other ways in which the press might learn and report what occurred in the closed courtroom. Even if the state's interest was effectively advanced by automatic closure, "it is doubtful that the interest would be sufficient to overcome the constitutional attack, for that same interest could be relied on to support an array of mandatory closure rules designed to encourage victims to come forward." To assert that closure would get more victims of all sorts to come forward and more candid testimony, would run contrary to "the very foundation of the right of access recognized in *Richmond Newspapers.*"

Chief Justice Burger, joined by Justice Rehnquist, dissented on the merits. They stressed the lack of historical openness in this type of case and that the statute need not be "precisely tailored so long as the state's interest overrides the law's impact on First Amendment rights and the restrictions imposed further that interest." Since the statute only barred access during the victim's testimony and rationally served the state's overriding interest in avoiding serious psychological damage, they would have upheld the statute. They also feared the effect on parents of learning that their child might have to undergo an in camera hearing before it could be known whether the trial would be closed during the child's testimony. The statute had a "relatively minor incidental impact on First Amendment rights and gives effect to the overriding state interest in protecting child rape victims. Paradoxically, the Court today denies the victims the kind of protection routinely given to juveniles who commit crimes."

Justice Stevens dissented on the ground that the order under review was too abstract for decision.

4. A black defendant was charged with the rape and murder of a white teenage girl. When a newspaper sought access to the voir dire, the state objected on the ground that juror responses would lack the candor needed in such a case. The trial judge closed all but three days of the six week voir dire. When the newspaper sought the transcript of the voir dire, both the state and the defense objected on the ground that this would violate the jurors' right to privacy because they had answered sensitive questions under an "implied promise of confidentiality." After the trial was over, the judge continued to refuse to release the transcript.

The Supreme Court unanimously reversed. Press-Enterprise Co. v. Superior Court, 464 U.S. 501, 10 Med.L.Rptr. 1161 (1984) (*Press-Enterprise I*). Chief Justice Burger observed that the "primacy of the accused's right is difficult to separate from the right of everyone in the community to attend the *voir dire* which promotes fairness." The standard created, building upon language from the Globe case, was that

> The presumption of openness may be overcome only by an overriding interest based on findings that closure is essential to preserve higher values and is narrowly tailored to serve that interest. The interest is to be articulated along with findings specific enough that a reviewing court can determine whether the closure order was properly entered.

The trial judge had made no findings and had not considered whether alternatives to closure might have worked. The Court did recognize that when interrogation touches on "deeply personal matters" a juror may have a compelling interest in privacy. Such concern might be met by informing jurors in advance that they may request a meeting in chambers with the judge and counsel and a court reporter if something potentially embarrassing comes up during voir dire. If necessary, that part of the transcript might be sealed, but the bulk would be open.

5. In Waller v. Georgia, 467 U.S. 39, 10 Med.L.Rptr. 1714 (1984), some criminal defendants moved to suppress certain wiretaps. The state then moved to close the proceedings to protect innocent parties and to

protect some evidence it wanted to use later in the trial. The judge closed the proceedings. After conviction, the defendants appealed on the ground that they had been denied their Sixth Amendment right to an open trial.

The Supreme Court unanimously reversed. The Sixth Amendment extended to suppression hearings, which often resembled a bench trial. The judge's findings were too general to permit review and he failed to consider alternatives to closure. Also, even if closure were justified for the playing of the tapes, that took only two or three hours out of the seven-day hearing. The case was remanded for a new suppression hearing. A new trial would be needed only if more material was suppressed now than had been suppressed at the first hearing.

6. This set the stage for the Court to return to the First Amendment aspects of the pretrial situation, which occurred in *Press-Enterprise II.*

PRESS–ENTERPRISE CO. v. SUPERIOR COURT (II)

Supreme Court of United States, 1986.
478 U.S. ___, 106 S.Ct. 2735, 92 L.Ed.2d 1, 13 Med.L.Rptr. 1001.

CHIEF JUSTICE BURGER delivered the opinion of the Court.

We granted certiorari to decide whether petitioner has a First Amendment right of access to transcripts of a preliminary hearing growing out of a criminal prosecution.

I

On December 23, 1981, the State of California filed a complaint in the Riverside County Municipal Court, charging Robert Diaz with 12 counts of murder and seeking the death penalty. The complaint alleged that Diaz, a nurse, murdered 12 patients by administering massive doses of the heart drug lidocaine. The preliminary hearing on the complaint commenced on July 6, 1982. Diaz moved to exclude the public from the proceedings under California Penal Code Ann. § 868 (West 1985), which requires such proceedings to be open unless "exclusion of the public is necessary in order to protect the defendant's right to a fair and impartial trial." [1] The Magistrate granted the unopposed motion, finding that closure was necessary because the case had attracted national publicity and "only one side may get reported in the media."

The preliminary hearing continued for 41 days. Most of the testimony and the evidence presented by the State was medical and

1. . . .

Before 1982, the statute gave the defendant the unqualified right to close the proceedings. After the California Supreme Court rejected a First Amendment attack on the old statute in San Jose Mercury-News v. Superior Court, 30 Cal.3d 498, 655 P.2d 655 (1982), the California Legislature amended the statute to include the present requirement that the hearing be closed only upon a finding by the Magistrate that closure is "necessary in order to protect the defendant's right to a fair trial."

scientific; the remainder consisted of testimony by personnel who worked with Diaz on the shifts when the 12 patients died. Diaz did not introduce any evidence, but his counsel subjected most of the witnesses to vigorous cross-examination. Diaz was held to answer on all charges. At the conclusion of the hearing, petitioner Press-Enterprise Company asked that the transcript of the proceedings be released. The Magistrate refused and sealed the record.

On January 21, 1983, the State moved in Superior Court to have the transcripts of the preliminary hearing released to the public; petitioner later joined in support of the motion. Diaz opposed the motion, contending that release of the transcripts would result in prejudicial pretrial publicity. The Superior Court found that the information in the transcript was "as factual as it could be," and that the facts were neither "inflammatory" nor "exciting" but there was, nonetheless, "a reasonable likelihood that release of all or any part of the transcript might prejudice defendant's right to a fair and impartial trial."

Petitioner then filed a peremptory writ of mandate with the Court of Appeal. That court originally denied the writ but, after being so ordered by the California Supreme Court, set the matter for a hearing. Meanwhile, Diaz waived his right to a jury trial and the Superior Court released the transcript. After holding that the controversy was not moot, the Court of Appeal denied the writ of mandate.

The California Supreme Court thereafter denied petitioner's peremptory writ of mandate, holding that there is no general First Amendment right of access to preliminary hearings. The court reasoned that the right of access to criminal proceedings recognized in [*Press-Enterprise I*] and [*Globe Newspaper*], extended only to actual criminal trials. [ ] Furthermore, the reasons that had been asserted for closing the proceedings in *Press-Enterprise I* and *Globe*—the interests of witnesses and other third parties—were not the same as the right asserted in this case—the defendant's right to a fair and impartial trial by a jury uninfluenced by news accounts.

Having found no general First Amendment right of access, the court then considered the circumstances in which the closure would be proper under the California access statute, Cal.Penal Code Ann. § 868 (West 1985). Under the statute, the court reasoned, if the defendant establishes a "reasonable likelihood of substantial prejudice" the burden shifts to the prosecution or the media to show by a preponderance of the evidence that there is no such reasonable probability of prejudice. [ ] We granted certiorari. [ ] We reverse.

II

[The Court held that the case was not moot.]

III

It is important to identify precisely what the California Supreme Court decided:

> "(W)e conclude that the magistrate shall close the preliminary hearing upon finding a reasonable likelihood of substantial prejudice which would impinge upon the right to a fair trial. Penal code section 868 makes clear that the primary right is the right to a fair trial and that the public's right of access must give way when there is conflict." [ ]

It is difficult to disagree in the abstract with that court's analysis balancing the defendant's right to a fair trial against the public right of access. It is also important to remember that these interests are not necessarily inconsistent. Plainly, the defendant has a right to a fair trial but, as we have repeatedly recognized, one of the important means of assuring a fair trial is that the process be open to neutral observers.

The right to an open public trial is a shared right of the accused and the public, the common concern being the assurance of fairness. Only recently, in Waller v. Georgia, [ ] for example, we considered whether the defendant's Sixth Amendment right to an open trial prevented the closure of a suppression hearing over the defendant's objection. We noted that the First Amendment right of access would in most instances attach to such proceedings and that "the explicit Sixth Amendment right of the accused is no less protective of a public trial than the implicit First Amendment right of the press and public." [ ] When the defendant objects to the closure of a suppression hearing, therefore, the hearing must be open unless the party seeking to close the hearing advances an overriding interest that is likely to be prejudiced.

Here, unlike *Waller,* the right asserted is not the defendant's Sixth Amendment right to a public trial since the defendant requested a closed preliminary hearing. Instead, the right asserted here is that of the public under the First Amendment. [ ] The California Supreme Court concluded that the First Amendment was not implicated because the proceeding was not a criminal trial, but a preliminary hearing. However, the First Amendment question cannot be resolved solely on the label we give the event, i.e., "trial" or otherwise, particularly where the preliminary hearing functions much like a full scale trial.

In cases dealing with the claim of a First Amendment right of access to criminal proceedings, our decisions have emphasized two complementary considerations. First, because a " 'tradition of accessibility implies the favorable judgment of experience' " [ ] we have considered whether the place and process has historically been open to the press and general public.

In *Press-Enterprise I,* for example, we observed "that, since the development of trial by jury, the process of selection of jurors has presumptively been a public process with exceptions only for good cause shown." [ ] In *Richmond Newspapers,* we reviewed some of the early history of England's open trials from the day when a trial was much like a "town meeting." In the days before the Norman Conquest, criminal cases were brought before "moots," a collection of the freemen in the community. The public trial, "one of the essential qualities of a court of justice" in England, was recognized early on in the colonies. There were risks, of course, inherent in such a "town meeting" trial—the risk that it might become a gathering moved by emotions or passions growing from the nature of a crime; a "lynch mob" ambience is hardly conducive to calm, reasoned decision-making based on evidence. Plainly the modern trial with jurors open to interrogation for possible bias is a far cry from the "town meeting trial" of ancient English practice. Yet even our modern procedural protections have their origin in the ancient common law principle which provided, not for closed proceedings, but rather for rules of conduct for those who attend trials. [ ]

Second, in this setting the Court has traditionally considered whether public access plays a significant positive role in the functioning of the particular process in question. [ ] Although many governmental processes operate best under public scrutiny, it takes little imagination to recognize that there are some kinds of government operations that would be totally frustrated if conducted openly. A classic example is that "the proper functioning of our grand jury system depends upon the secrecy of grand jury proceedings." Douglas Oil Co. v. Petrol Stops Northwest, 441 U.S. 211, 218 (1979). Other proceedings plainly require public access. In *Press-Enterprise I,* we summarized the holdings of prior cases, noting that openness in criminal trials, including the selection of jurors, "enhances both the basic fairness of the criminal trial and the appearance of fairness so essential to public confidence in the system." [ ]

These considerations of experience and logic are, of course, related, for history and experience shape the functioning of governmental processes. If the particular proceeding in question passes these tests of experience and logic, a qualified First Amendment right of public access attaches. But even when a right of access attaches, it is not absolute. [ ] While open criminal proceedings give assurances of fairness to both the public and the accused, there are some limited circumstances in which the right of the accused to a fair trial might be undermined by publicity.[2] In such cases, the trial court must determine whether the situation is such that the rights of the accused override the qualified First Amendment right of access. In *Press-Enterprise I* we stated:

> "the presumption may be overcome only by an overriding interest based on findings that closure is essential to preserve higher values

2. Similarly, the interests of those other than the accused may be implicated. The protection of victims of sex crimes from the trauma and embarrassment of public scrutiny may justify closing certain aspects of a criminal proceeding. [ ]

and is narrowly tailored to serve that interest. The interest is to be articulated along with findings specific enough that a reviewing court can determine whether the closure order was properly entered." [ ]

IV

A

The considerations that led the Court to apply the First Amendment right of access to criminal trials in *Richmond Newspapers* and *Globe* and the selection of jurors in *Press-Enterprise I* lead us to conclude that the right of access applies to preliminary hearings as conducted in California.

First, there has been a tradition of accessibility to preliminary hearings of the type conducted in California. Although grand jury proceedings have traditionally been closed to the public and the accused, preliminary hearings conducted before neutral and detached magistrates have been open to the public. Long ago in the celebrated trial of Aaron Burr for treason, for example, with Chief Justice Marshall sitting as trial judge, the probable cause hearing was held in the Hall of the House of Delegates in Virginia, the court room being too small to accommodate the crush of interested citizens. United States v. Burr, 25 F.Cas. 1 (CC Va.1807) (No. 14,692). From *Burr* until the present day, the near uniform practice of state and federal courts has been to conduct preliminary hearings in open court.[3] As we noted in *Gannett,* several states following the original New York Field Code of Criminal Procedure published in 1850 have allowed preliminary hearings to be closed on the motion of the accused. [ ] But even in these states the proceedings are presumptively open to the public and are closed only for cause shown. Open preliminary hearings, therefore, have been accorded " 'the favorable judgment of experience.' " [ ]

The second question is whether public access to preliminary hearings as they are conducted in California plays a particularly significant positive role in the actual functioning of the process. We have already determined in *Richmond Newspapers, Globe,* and *Press-Enterprise I* that public access to criminal trials and the selection of jurors is essential to the proper functioning of the criminal justice system. California preliminary hearings are sufficiently like a trial to justify the same conclusion.

In California, to bring a felon to trial, the prosecutor has a choice of securing a grand jury indictment or a finding of probable cause follow-

3. The vast majority of States considering the issue have concluded that the same tradition of accessibility that applies to criminal trials applies to preliminary proceedings. [ ]

Other courts have noted that some pretrial proceedings have no historical counterpart, but, given the importance of the pretrial proceeding to the criminal trial, the traditional right of access should still apply. [ ]

ing a preliminary hearing. Even when the accused has been indicted by a grand jury, however, he has an absolute right to an elaborate preliminary hearing before a neutral magistrate. [ ] The accused has the right to personally appear at the hearing, to be represented by counsel, to cross-examine hostile witnesses, to present exculpatory evidence, and to exclude illegally obtained evidence. [ ] If the magistrate determines that probable cause exists, the accused is bound over for trial; such a finding leads to a guilty plea in the majority of cases.

It is true that unlike a criminal trial, the California preliminary hearing cannot result in the conviction of the accused and the adjudication is before a magistrate or other judicial officer without a jury. But these features, standing alone, do not make public access any less essential to the proper functioning of the proceedings in the overall criminal justice process. Because of its extensive scope, the preliminary hearing is often the final and most important step in the criminal proceeding. [*Waller*]. As the California Supreme Court stated in San Jose Mercury-News v. Municipal Court, 30 Cal.3d 498, 511, 638 P.2d 655, 663 (1982), the preliminary hearing in many cases provides "the sole occasion for public observation of the criminal justice system." [ ]

Similarly, the absence of a jury, long recognized as "an inestimable safeguard against the corrupt or overzealous prosecutor and against the complaint, biased, or eccentric judge," Duncan v. Louisiana, 391 U.S. 145, 156 (1968), makes the importance of public access to a preliminary hearing even more significant. "People in an open society do not demand infallibility from their institutions, but it is difficult for them to accept what they are prohibited from observing." [*Richmond Newspapers*]

Denying the transcripts of a 41-day preliminary hearing would frustrate what we have characterized as the "community therapeutic value" of openness. [ ] Criminal acts, especially certain violent crimes, provoke public concern, outrage, and hostility. "When the public is aware that the law is being enforced and the criminal justice system is functioning, an outlet is provided for these understandable reactions and emotions." [ ] In sum,

> "The value of openness lies in the fact that people not actually attending trials can have confidence that standards of fairness are being observed; the sure knowledge that anyone is free to attend gives assurance that established procedures are being followed and that deviations will become known. Openness thus enhances both the basic fairness of the criminal trial and the appearance of fairness so essential to public confidence in the system." Press-Enterprise I, 464 U.S., at 508. (emphasis in original).

We therefore conclude that the qualified First Amendment right of access to criminal proceedings applies to preliminary hearings as they are conducted in California.

B

Since a qualified First Amendment right of access attaches to preliminary hearings in California under Cal.Penal Code Ann. §§ 858 et seq. (West 1985), the proceedings cannot be closed unless specific, on the record findings are made demonstrating that "closure is essential to preserve higher values and is narrowly tailored to serve that interest." [ ] If the interest asserted is the right of the accused to a fair trial, the preliminary hearing shall be closed only if specific findings are made demonstrating that first, there is a substantial probability that the defendant's right to a fair trial will be prejudiced by publicity that closure would prevent and, second, reasonable alternatives to closure cannot adequately protect the defendant's free trial rights. [ ]

The California Supreme Court, interpreting its access statute, concluded "that the magistrate shall close the preliminary hearing upon finding a reasonable likelihood of substantial prejudice." [ ] As the court itself acknowledged, the "reasonable likelihood" test places a lesser burden on the defendant than the "substantial probability" test which we hold is called for by the First Amendment. [ ] Moreover, the court failed to consider whether alternatives short of complete closure would have protected the interests of the accused.

In *Gannett* we observed that:

> "Publicity concerning pretrial suppression hearings such as the one involved in the present case poses special risks of unfairness. The whole purpose of such hearings is to screen out unreliable or illegally obtained evidence and insure that this evidence does not become known to the jury. Cf. Jackson v. Denno, 378 U.S. 368. Publicity concerning the proceedings at a pretrial hearing, however, could influence public opinion against a defendant and inform potential jurors of inculpatory information wholly inadmissible at the actual trial." [ ]

But this risk of prejudice does not automatically justify refusing public access to hearings on every motion to suppress. Through voir dire, cumbersome as it is in some circumstances, a court can identify those jurors whose prior knowledge of the case would disable them from rendering an impartial verdict. And even if closure were justified for the hearings on a motion to suppress, closure of an entire 41-day proceeding would rarely be warranted. The First Amendment right of access cannot be overcome by the conclusory assertion that publicity might deprive the defendant of [the right to a fair trial]. And any limitation " 'must be narrowly tailored to serve that interest.' " [ ]

The standard applied by the California Supreme Court failed to consider the First Amendment right of access to criminal proceedings. Accordingly, the judgment of the California Supreme Court is reversed.

JUSTICE STEVENS, with whom JUSTICE REHNQUIST joins as to Part II, dissenting.

The constitutional question presented by this case is whether members of the public have a First Amendment right to insist upon access to the transcript of a preliminary hearing during the period before the public trial, even though the accused, the prosecutor, and the trial judge have all agreed to the sealing of the transcript in order to assure a fair trial.

. . .

I

Although perhaps obvious, it bears emphasis that the First Amendment right asserted by petitioner is not a right to publish or otherwise communicate information lawfully or unlawfully acquired. That right, which lies at the core of the First Amendment and which erased the legacy of restraints on publication against which the drafters of that Amendment rebelled, see Grosjean v. American Press Co., 297 U.S. 233, 245–250 (1936), may be overcome only by a governmental objective of the highest order attainable in no less intrusive way. See, e.g., [*Smith, Landmark, Oklahoma Publishing, Nebraska Press Assn.,* and *Cox Broadcasting.*] The First Amendment right asserted by petitioner in this case, in contrast, is not the right to publicize information in its possession, but the right to acquire access thereto.

I have long believed that a proper construction of the First Amendment embraces a right of access to information about the conduct of public affairs [quoting from Justice Stevens's dissent in *Houchins*].

Neither our elected nor our appointed representatives may abridge the free flow of information simply to protect their own activities from public scrutiny. An official policy of secrecy must be supported by some legitimate justification that serves the interest of the public office.

. . .

But it has always been apparent that the freedom to obtain information that the Government has a legitimate interest in not disclosing, [ ], is far narrower than the freedom to disseminate information, which is "virtually absolute" in most contexts, [*Richmond Newspapers,* (STEVENS, J., concurring)]. In this case, the risk of prejudice to the defendant's right to a fair trial is perfectly obvious. For me, that risk is far more significant than the countervailing interest in publishing the transcript of the preliminary hearing sooner rather than later. Cf. [*Gannett*] (upholding closure of suppression hearing in part because "any denial of access in this case was not absolute but only temporary"). The interest in prompt publication—in my view—is no greater than the interest in prompt publication of grand jury transcripts. As explained more fully below, we have always recognized the legitimacy of the governmental interest in the secrecy of grand jury proceedings, and I am unpersuaded that the difference between such proceedings and the rather elaborate procedure for determining probable cause that California has adopted strengthens the First Amendment claim to access asserted in this case.

II

The Court nevertheless reaches the opposite conclusion by applying the "two complementary considerations," [ ], of "experience and logic," [ ]. In my view, neither the Court's reasoning nor the result it reaches is supported by our precedents.

The historical evidence proffered in this case is far less probative than the evidence adduced in prior cases granting public access to criminal proceedings. In those cases, a common law tradition of openness at the time the First Amendment was ratified suggested an intention and expectation on the part of the Framers and ratifiers that those proceedings would remain presumptively open. Thus, in [*Richmond Newspapers*] THE CHIEF JUSTICE explained that "(w)hat is significant for present purposes is that throughout its evolution, the trial has been open to all who cared to observe." "(T)he historical evidence demonstrates conclusively that *at the time when our organic laws were adopted,* criminal trials both here and in England had long been presumptively open." [ ] (emphasis added). . . .

In this case, however, it is uncontroverted that a common law right of access did not inhere in preliminary proceedings at the time the First Amendment was adopted, and that the Framers and ratifiers of that provision could not have intended such proceedings to remain open. As Justice Stewart wrote for the Court in [*Gannett*]:

> "(T)here exists no persuasive evidence that at common law members of the public had any right to attend pretrial proceedings; indeed, there is substantial evidence to the contrary. By the time of the adoption of the Constitution, . . . pretrial proceedings, precisely because of the . . . concern for a fair trial, were never characterized by the same degree of openness as were actual trials. . . ."

. . .

In the final analysis, the Court's lengthy historical disquisition demonstrates only that in many States preliminary proceedings are generally open to the public. . . . To paraphrase the Court's analysis in McMillan v. Pennsylvania, 106 S.Ct. 2411, 2419 (1986) (footnote omitted) "the fact that the States" have adopted different rules regarding the openness of preliminary proceedings "is merely a reflection of our federal system, which demands '(t)olerance for a spectrum of state procedures dealing with a common problem of law enforcement,' Spencer v. Texas, 385 U.S. 554, 566 (1967). That (California's) particular approach has been adopted in few other States does not render (its) choice unconstitutional." As Justice Stewart admonished: we must not "confus(e) the existence of a constitutional right with the common-law tradition of open . . . proceedings." [*Gannett*] The recent common law developments reported by the Court are relevant, if at all, only insofar as they suggest that preliminary proceedings merit the "beneficial effects of public scrutiny." [*Cox Broadcasting*] The Court's historical crutch cannot carry the weight of opening a preliminary proceeding that the State has ordered closed; that determination must stand or fall on whether it satisfies the second component of the Court's test.

If the Court's historical evidence proves too little, the "value of openness," [ ] on which it relies proves too much, for this measure would open to public scrutiny far more than preliminary hearings "as they are conducted in California" (a comforting phrase invoked by the Court in one form or another more than 8 times in its opinion).[7] In brief, the Court's rationale for opening the "California preliminary hearing" is that it "is often the final and most important step in the criminal proceeding"; that it provides " 'the sole occasion for public observation of the criminal justice system' "; that it lacks the protective presence of a jury; and that closure denies an outlet for community catharsis. [ ] The obvious defect in the Court's approach is that its reasoning applies to the traditionally secret grand jury with as much force as it applies to California preliminary hearings. A grand jury indictment is just as likely to be the "final step" in a criminal proceeding and the "sole occasion" for public scrutiny as is a preliminary hearing. Moreover, many critics of the grand jury maintain that the grand jury protects the accused less well than does a legally-knowledgable judge who personally presides over a preliminary hearing. See Hawkins v. Superior Court, 22 Cal.3d 584, 590, 586 P.2d 916, 919–920 (1978) (holding deprivation of preliminary hearing to constitute a denial of equal protection under State Constitution in part because " 'the grand jury is the total captive of the prosecutor who, if he is candid, will concede that he can indict anybody, at any time, for almost anything, before any grand jury' " (quoting Campbell, Eliminate the Grand Jury, 64 J.Crim.L. & C. 174 (1973)). Finally, closure of grand juries denies an outlet for community rage. When the Court's explanatory veneer is stripped away, what emerges is the reality that the California preliminary hearing is functionally identical to the traditional grand jury. . . .

The Court's reasoning—if carried to its logical outcome—thus contravenes the "long-established policy that maintains the secrecy of the grand jury proceedings in the federal courts" and in the courts of 19 States. . . .[8]

7. Given the Court's focus on the history of preliminary proceedings in general, and its reliance on the broad values served by openness, [ ], I do not see the relevance of the fact that preliminary proceedings in California bear an outward resemblance to criminal trials. To the extent that it matters that in California "(t)he accused has the right to personally appear at the hearing, to be represented by counsel, to cross-examine hostile witnesses, to present exculpatory evidence, and to exclude illegally obtained evidence," [ ] it bears mention that many other States have reformed their grand juries to include one or more of these procedural reforms, [ ]. After today's decision, one can only wonder whether the public enjoys a right of access to any or all of these proceedings as well.

8. Five reasons are commonly given for the policy of grand jury secrecy:

"(1) To prevent the escape of those whose indictment may be contemplated; (2) to insure the utmost freedom to the grand jury in its deliberations, and to prevent persons subject to indictment or their friends from importuning the grand jurors; (3) to prevent subornation of perjury or tampering with the wit-

In fact, the logic of the Court's access right extends even beyond the confines of the criminal justice system to encompass proceedings held on the civil side of the docket as well. As Justice Stewart explained:

> "If the existence of a common-law rule were the test for whether there is a Sixth Amendment public right to a public trial, therefore, there would be such a right in civil as well as criminal cases. . . . In short, there is no principled basis upon which a public right of access to judicial proceedings can be limited to criminal cases if the scope of the right is defined by the common law rather than the text and structure of the Constitution.
>
> "Indeed, many of the advantages of public criminal trials are equally applicable in the civil trial context. . . . Thus, in some civil cases the public interest in access, and the salutary effect of publicity, may be as strong as, or stronger than, in most criminal cases." [*Gannett*]

Cf. Seattle Times Co. v. Rhinehart, 467 U.S. 20, 29–37 (1984) (newspaper not allowed to publish information to which it was privy as a litigant in a civil action). Despite the Court's valiant attempt to limit the logic of its holding, the ratio decidendi of today's decision knows no bounds.

By abjuring strict reliance on history and emphasizing the broad value of openness, the Court tacitly recognizes the importance of public access to government proceedings generally. Regrettably, the Court has taken seriously the stated requirement that the sealing of a transcript be justified by a "compelling" or "overriding" governmental interest and that the closure order be "narrowly tailored to serve that interest." . . . The cases denying access have done so on a far lesser showing than that required by a compelling governmental interest/least restrictive-means analysis, [ ], and cases granting access have recognized as legitimate grounds for closure interests that fall far short of those traditionally thought to be "compelling," [ ].

A requirement of some legitimate reason for closure in this case requires an affirmance. The constitutionally-grounded fair trial interests of the accused if he is bound over for trial, and the reputational interests of the accused if he is not, provide a substantial reason for delaying access to the transcript for at least the short time before trial. By taking its own verbal formulation seriously, the Court reverses—without comment or explanation or any attempt at reconciliation—the holding in *Gannett* that a "reasonable probability of prejudice" is enough to overcome the First Amendment right of access to a preliminary proceeding. It is unfortunate that the Court neglects this opportunity to fit the result in this case into the body of precedent dealing

nesses who may testify before (the) grand jury and later appear at the trial of those indicted by it; (4) to encourage free and untrammeled disclosures by persons who have information with respect to the commission of crimes; (5) to protect an innocent accused who is exonerated from disclosure of the fact that he has been under investigation, and from the expense of standing trial where there was no probability of guilt." [ ]

with access rights generally. I fear that today's decision will simply further unsettle the law in this area.

I respectfully dissent.

Notes and Questions

1. What is the status of the Gannett case after this case?

2. Does this sequence concerning access to the courtroom suggest any doubt about the cases denying access to prisons and jails?

3. The decision in *Press-Enterprise II* suggests renewed attention to the administration of change of venue and voir dire. Some state courts have doubted the legitimacy of opening pretrial proceedings if that would mean "forcing" the defendant to seek a change of venue. See, e.g., Miami Herald Publishing Co. v. Lewis, 426 So.2d 1, 8 Med.L.Rptr. 2281 (Fla.1982) (the state constitution gives the accused the right "to have a . . . trial . . . in the county where the crime was committed").

4. Some have suggested that changes of venue are not as needed as some students of the problem suggest. In one case the trial judge excluded the press and the public from the voir dire in a criminal case. United States v. Peters, 754 F.2d 753, 11 Med.L.Rptr. 1513 (7th Cir. 1985). On appeal, the court inquired into whether the presumption of openness had been sufficiently rebutted. First, the court's review of the record "convinces us that the district court failed to identify with any specificity an 'overriding interest' which required closure to serve that interest's 'higher value.' The judge did not question any potential jurors about what they had read about the first day of voir dire or whether any exposure had impaired their ability to be jurors."

Second, the record showed that defense counsel, "who carried the burden of persuasion as the proponents of closure, failed to explain why [alternatives other than sequestration of the entire venire] were unavailable":

> The judge could have reiterated on a daily basis his instruction to the panel not to read newspapers, listen to radio, or watch television. The judge could have questioned the potential jurors the next day as to whether or not those instructions had been followed and, if they had not, whether contact with the media had rendered the potential juror unable to be impartial. The judge could have dismissed jurors unable to be impartial; if necessary the judge could have dismissed the entire venire and called another until twelve impartial jurors, unaffected by the media's stories on the trial, were found.
>
> There is, of course, a temptation to assume that the public at large devotes time and effort to reading and remembering news items on pending cases. The real fact is that people who read and write for a living—such as those in the legal or journalism field—tend to believe that everyone else reads news stories with devoted

attention. Considering that a voir dire interrogation of prospective jurors has about the same attention-grabbing excitement as a report on the annual rainfall in northern Tibet, an assumption that anyone read such a story is probably misplaced; at any rate, the admonition given by the court *not* to read such newspaper stories, and a questioning of the jurors after the story has been printed, would seem adequate to prevent any contamination. As to the fears expressed by defense counsel that jurors would not be honest in following the admonition or candid in admitting such a gaffe, the simple answer is that the entire voir dire relies on honest and candid answers to questions of court and counsel. There is no more reason to doubt the integrity of jurors in this regard than in any other area of inquiry.

The opinion cited a variety of studies suggesting that readers remember little of what they have read about crime. This suggested to the court that alternatives to closure are likely to be effective.

5. Some situations do not fall neatly into pretrial or trial stages. In Poughkeepsie Newspapers, Inc. v. Rosenblatt, 92 App.Div.2d 232, 459 N.Y.S.2d 857 (1983), aff'd 61 N.Y.2d 1005, 463 N.E.2d 1222, 475 N.Y.S.2d 370 (1984), the trial was already in progress when the defense asked that the court be closed while he objected to evidence that the prosecution sought to introduce. Because the jury had not been sequestered and because of the devastating effect of the submitted evidence, the judge closed the court for the motion. His action was upheld on appeal. The usual possibility of voir dire was no longer available. The case was getting extensive publicity and the judge would have had to interrogate the jury to ascertain whether anyone had learned of the evidence. This would lengthen an already lengthy trial—and might produce answers that would necessitate a mistrial. Taking everything into account, the judge acted properly. The court of appeals, in addition, volunteered that the trial court "properly considered the interests of the jurors in reaching his determination." Is this a response to the possibility of a surprise sequestration after a case has begun?

6. *Bail Hearings.* In United States v. Chagra, 701 F.2d 354, 9 Med.L. Rptr. 1409 (5th Cir.1983), defendant in a murder trial sought to close a hearing at which he was seeking to have his bond reduced. One issue involved the possible later introduction of a statement. The court held that the press and public have a First Amendment right to attend such hearings but that it was overridden here by the concerns about a later fair trial should the public learn about the details of the statement in question. The trial judge had carefully considered alternatives to closure and found them inadequate. The case involved the murder of a federal judge and the trial judge had concluded that the publicity would follow the defendant throughout Texas.

The court of appeals affirmed, but noted that the judge should have considered the possibility of changing venue outside of Texas. This would have meant considering whether the defendant would be adequately protected at such a great distance and whether he would have been willing to waive his rights to have the case tried in the state in which the crime was committed, [U.S. Const. art. III, § 2, cl. 3], and the right under the Criminal Rules to be tried in the district in which the crime was committed. The judge should also have considered the additional costs to the parties of such a change, the problems of conducting a defense at that distance, and whether the publicity would be likely to follow. For procedural reasons it was not necessary to remand.

One judge concurred specially to disagree with the suggestion about moving the case out of Texas. "The San Antonio press has no right to a change of venue so as to permit it to publish this information prior to trial. . . . [T]he judge should not be required to widen the distance between the place where the indictment was brought and the trial, so as to accommodate the desire of the local press to publicize highly prejudicial material shortly before trial."

In In re Globe Newspaper Co., 729 F.2d 47, 10 Med.L.Rptr. 1433 (1st Cir.1984), seven defendants had been indicted under an anti-racketeering statute. In their bail proceedings much of the evidence consisted of conversations obtained by authorized wiretaps. The legality of the taps had not yet been tested—and one who reveals information obtained in unlawful taps is criminally and civilly liable. The lower court had closed the hearing and impounded the transcript and some of the documents. The court of appeals thought the procedural posture such that defendants could not reasonably be expected to mount a challenge to their admissibility at this time:

> In sum, we find that the First Amendment right of access does extend to bail hearings and to documents filed in support of the parties' arguments at those hearings. We believe, however, that the interests of the press and the public weigh less heavily at this early point in the proceedings than they do later, both because the tradition of openness in bail hearing is not as strong and because the press and public will have later opportunities to examine the material admitted at those hearings. By contrast, the privacy and fair trial interests of the defendants are at their zenith during the bail hearings, since they have not yet had an opportunity to test the material admitted at the hearings. We can scarcely imagine a stronger case for closure than the one now before us, in which the defendants are accused of participation in organized crime, the pretrial publicity is intense, and the material to which the press seeks access is extremely prejudicial. If these bail proceedings must be open to the public, it is difficult for us to conceive of circumstances in which a pretrial proceeding could be closed.

The impounding was to continue "until defendants have had a fair opportunity to challenge the legality" of the taps. The trial court may close that hearing if it concludes that public disclosure of the taps cannot be avoided by any less restrictive means. If the lower court concludes that the taps are legal and admissible it "must consider whether the remaining danger of prejudicial pretrial publicity is sufficient to warrant continued closure of pretrial proceedings and impoundment of documents."

Are bail hearings covered by *Press-Enterprise II?*

7. *Rehabilitating Juvenile Offenders.* Judges and legislators have shown considerable ambivalence about protecting the privacy of juveniles accused of offenses or otherwise involved in juvenile proceedings. Some argue that confidentiality allows the youth to be rehabilitated—the purported purpose of the juvenile justice system. They believe that the stigma of publicity delays or prevents rehabilitation. Others think publicity will better achieve rehabilitation. Others may think privacy aids rehabilitation but believe that it is more important for the public to know how juvenile offenders are being treated.

Responses to this situation have ranged from substantially protecting juveniles' privacy to treating such persons as adults would be treated. Some middle positions have been developed. An Illinois statute, for example, specifically protects only press access: "The general public except the news media shall be excluded from any [juvenile] hearing. . . . " Ill.Rev.Stat. ch. 37, § 701–20(6).

Protection of access may be found in state constitutions. Oregon's constitution provides that "No court shall be secret, but justice shall be administered, openly and without purchase, completely and without delay." A statute barring the public from juvenile proceedings unless the judge finds that they "have a proper interest in the case or the work of the court" was held to violate the state constitution in State ex rel. Oregonian Pub. Co. v. Deiz, 289 Or. 277, 613 P.2d 23, 6 Med.L.Rptr. 1369 (1980). The court cautioned that its holding should not be interpreted to guarantee the right of public access to all judicial proceedings. The court cited jury deliberations and court conferences as examples of secrecy existing when the state's constitution was adopted that would still survive. Also, the court noted that it was not faced with a fair trial question or the issue of whether "certain persons can be excluded from certain court proceedings."

See Cohen, Reconciling Media Access with Confidentiality for the Individual in Juvenile Court, 20 Santa Clara L.Rev. 405 (1980), suggesting a contract between the judge of the juvenile court and the press calling for damages to be paid to the injured party if names, photographs, addresses, or other identifying information are published. Damages would not lie for "pain and suffering or loss of reputation in the community." The author recognizes that the contract could be valid only as long as no constitutional right exists to attend juvenile proceedings. For other views, see Humphrey, Privacy or Protection: The Juvenile Dilemma, 21 Santa Clara L.Rev. 499 (1981); McNulty, First Amendment versus Sixth Amendment: A Constitutional Battle in the Juvenile Courts, 10 N.M.L.Rev. 311 (1980); Comment, Freedom of the Press vs. Juvenile Anonymity: A Conflict Between Constitutional Priorities and Rehabilitation, 65 Iowa L.Rev. 1471 (1980); Note: The Press and Juvenile Delinquency Hearings: A Contextual Analysis of the Unrefined First Amendment Right of Access, 39 U.Pitt.L.Rev. 121 (1977).

Does *Press-Enterprise II* address juvenile hearings?

8. *Trade Secrets.* The protection of trade secrets has also been recognized by lower courts and by individual justices as justifying the closure of some judicial proceedings. See In re Iowa Freedom of Information Council, 724 F.2d 658 (8th Cir.1983), affirming the closure of a contempt hearing at which a trade secret was being discussed. The underlying case was a wrongful death claim against Procter & Gamble for toxic shock syndrome. During discovery, the plaintiff's attorney signed a non-disclosure agreement promising to keep confidential certain information he had acquired about defendant. This contempt proceeding resulted when defendant charged the attorney with a violation of the agreement. Although the judge closed the hearing, he later made available a transcript with deletions at critical points. The court concluded that although the First Amendment applied to such proceedings, the revelation of trade secrets justified the closure. The press argued that the court should weigh the First Amendment claim against the property rights involved. The court refused:

> We stress that this case involves private commercial conduct. If the material still under seal had some substantial relation to an important governmental or political question, an entirely different question would be presented, and we might be required to embark on the weighing process urged on us by petitioners. . . . As we have previously explained, trade secrets partake of the nature of property, the value of which is completely destroyed by disclosure. Where only private commercial interests or damage are involved, we think the law justifies the steps taken by the District Court to avoid the destruction of these property rights.

9. The lower federal courts have tended to find a constitutional right of access in civil cases. See Publicker Industries v. Cohen, 733 F.2d 1059, 10 Med.L.Rptr. 1777 (3d Cir.1984) (under common law and the First Amendment, civil proceedings are presumptively open to the public; any closure must be "essential to preserve higher values and . . . narrowly tailored to serve that interest"). Does *Press-Enterprise II* shed light on this question? See Seattle Times Co. v. Rhinehart, p. 690, infra.

10. It may be possible to avoid the public civil trial in some states through the device known as private judging. Under this system, the parties agree to have their case adjudicated without a jury, usually before a retired judge who is appointed by the presiding judge. Normal appellate review is possible from the trial decision. These cases are usually held in secret and no findings are rendered—solely a judgment. The constitutionality of this device is considered in Comment, Private

Means to Public Ends: Implications of the Private Judging Phenomenon in California, 17 U.C.Davis L.Rev. 611 (1984).

c. *War Fronts*

A variety of other attempts to gain access to premises have reached the courts. Perhaps the most noteworthy recent case arose from a military move.

On October 25, 1983, the United States began a military operation on the island nation of Grenada, in the Caribbean Sea. Press representatives were excluded from entry to the island until October 27, when a limited group of reporters was flown to the island by military aircraft. By November 7, all travel restrictions had been lifted and the press had unlimited access to the island. After conditions had returned to normal, plaintiff publisher of Hustler magazine sued the Secretary of Defense and others for declaratory and injunctive relief. Damages were not sought. The district judge granted a government motion to dismiss the case on ground of mootness.

On appeal, the court affirmed the dismissal and vacated the lower court's opinion. Flynt v. Weinberger, 762 F.2d 134, 11 Med.L.Reptr. 2118 (D.C.Cir.1985). The request for injunctive relief was clearly moot because the events had passed. The request for declaratory relief was also moot because the complaint was addressed solely to the constitutionality of the ban in Grenada. There was no "reasonable expectation" that the Grenada controversy would recur. Since the district court's opinion had also discussed the merits and had dismissed the complaint with prejudice, the court vacated that opinion and ordered the dismissal solely on the grounds of mootness.

Judge Edwards, concurring, asserted that the court had no occasion to consider "whether it is unconstitutional for the government to ban the press from covering military actions where the sole or principal justification offered by the government is the safety of the press (and especially where an allegation is made that the government's actual motivation is to prevent unfavorable press coverage which might influence public opinion)." Since that issue was not encompassed in the complaint, there was no need to "decide whether this issue, if properly raised, would be moot."

For an extended consideration of this question, see Cassell, Restrictions on Press Coverage of Military Operations: The Right of Access, Grenada, and "Off-the-Record Wars," 73 Geo.L.J. 931 (1985). Cassell concludes that access "would undoubtedly allow the press to witness events that might otherwise go unreported and could thereby increase the flow of information to the public. Yet, the possibility that wide press access may lead to the imposition of censorship should certainly give one pause before concluding that access is an unmitigated blessing. . . . The press should explicitly consider the implications of its demand for access in terms of the possibility of a censorship overreaction. To do otherwise is to risk confirming Senator Hiram Johnson's observation that '[t]he first casualty when war comes is truth.'"

After the outcry over the episode, the Defense Department created a panel under Major General Winant Sidle to consider alternatives. That panel proposed, and the Defense Department put into effect, a limited pool to cover the early stages of surprise military operations. The Defense Department picks the organizations to participate in the pool, but the organizations pick the specific reporters.

2. Access to Information

We have been considering the extent to which the press and the public may have a constitutional right of access to premises under the control of the government. If that access permits the would-be gatherer to acquire the information sought, the matter is at an end. But frequently, access to a place does not carry with it the opportunity to acquire what is sought. As we shall see, access to a courtroom in a large urban area may not permit the press or public to learn the identity of the jurors. Nor does such access necessarily permit the press to obtain copies of all the documentary evidence used in the case. Furthermore, sometimes government imposes limits on whether those who hold information may reveal it. Also, as we shall see, sometimes the holder of the information has obtained it with government assistance—and the government may feel some obligation to limit its further use. These questions have been litigated much less frequently at the constitutional level than have claims of access to premises—perhaps because of the presence of freedom of information legislation. As a final note of introduction, virtually all of the cases involve claims for information arising out of litigation, perhaps because the press has had greater success in seeking access to judicial premises.

NIXON v. WARNER COMMUNICATIONS, INC.

Supreme Court of the United States, 1978.
435 U.S. 589, 98 S.Ct. 1306, 55 L.Ed.2d 570, 3 Med.L.Rptr. 2074.
Noted, 64 A.B.A.J. 891.

[The third episode took shape during the Watergate trial. The tape reels obtained from the President were played in the judge's chambers before trial. Some conversations were declared irrelevant or privileged and were not reproduced. The other conversations were rerecorded on new tapes designated Copy A for the district court and Copy B for the special prosecutor. Some but not all of the conversations on Copy A were admitted into evidence. Some but not all of these were played to the jury. Some were played in full; others only in part. "Deletions were effected not by modifying the exhibit itself, but by skipping deleted portions on the tape or by interrupting the sound transmission to the jurors' headphones." Written transcripts of the conversations being played to the jurors were provided to the jurors and others in the court—all of whom heard the tapes over headphones.

After four defendants were convicted, the trial judge denied the broadcasters' motion to release the parts of Copy A played at trial because of the possibility of successful appeals and retrials. He also observed that immediate access to the tapes might "result in manufacture of permanent phonograph records and tape recordings, perhaps with commentary by journalists or entertainers; marketing of the tapes would probably involve mass merchandising techniques designed to generate excitement in an air of ridicule to stimulate sales." The court of appeals reversed and held the denial to be an abuse of discretion because of the importance of the common-law privilege to inspect and copy judicial records. The possibility of prejudice did not overcome the public's right to access to the evidence. It also noted that after release of the tapes the court's power to control uses and marketing techniques "is sharply limited by the First Amendment."]

MR. JUSTICE POWELL delivered the opinion of the Court.

. . .

II.

Both petitioner and respondents acknowledge the existence of a common-law right of access to judicial records, but they differ sharply over its scope and the circumstances warranting restrictions of it. An infrequent subject of litigation, its contours have not been delineated with any precision. Indeed, no case directly in point—that is, addressing the applicability of the common-law right to exhibits subpoenaed from third parties—has been cited or discovered.

A.

It is clear that the courts of this country recognize a general right to inspect and copy public records and documents, including judicial records and documents. In contrast to the English practice, [ ], American decisions generally do not condition enforcement of this right on a proprietary interest in the document or upon a need for it as evidence in a lawsuit. The interest necessary to support the issuance of a writ compelling access has been found, for example, in the citizen's desire to keep a watchful eye on the workings of public agencies, [ ], and in a newspaper publisher's intention to publish information concerning the operation of government [ ].

It is uncontested, however, that the right to inspect and copy judicial records is not absolute. Every court has supervisory power over its own records and files, and access has been denied where court files might have become a vehicle for improper purposes. For example, the common-law right of inspection has bowed before the power of a court to insure that its records are not "used to gratify private spite or promote public scandal" through the publication of "the painful and sometimes disgusting details of a divorce case." [ ]. Similarly, courts have refused to permit their files to serve as reservoirs of libelous statements for press consumption, [ ], or as sources of business information that might harm a litigant's competitive standing, [ ].

It is difficult to distill from the relatively few judicial decisions a comprehensive definition of what is referred to as the common-law right of access or to identify all the factors to be weighed in determining whether access is appropriate. The few cases that have recognized such a right do agree that the decision as to access is one best left to the sound discretion of the trial court, a discretion to be exercised in light of the relevant facts and circumstances of the particular case. In any event, we need not undertake to delineate precisely the contours of the common-law right, as we assume, *arguendo,* that it applies to the tapes at issue here.

B.

Petitioner advances several reasons supporting the exercise of discretion against release of the tapes.[11]

First, petitioner argues that he has a property interest in the sound of his own voice, an interest that respondents intend to appropriate unfairly. In respondents' view, our decision in Nixon v. Administrator of General Services, 433 U.S. 425 (1977), upholding the constitutionality of the Presidential Recordings Act, divested petitioner of any property rights in the tapes that could be asserted against the general public. Petitioner insists, however, that respondents' point is not fully responsive to his argument. Petitioner is not asserting a proprietary right to the tapes themselves. He likens his interest to that of a third party whose voice is recorded in the course of a lawful wiretap by police officers and introduced into evidence on tape. In petitioner's view, use of one's voice as evidence in a criminal trial does not give rise to a license for commercial exploitation.

Petitioner also maintains that his privacy would be infringed if aural copies of the tapes were distributed to the public. The Court of Appeals rejected this contention. It reasoned that with the playing of the tapes in the courtroom, the publication of their contents in the form of written transcripts, and the passage of the Presidential Recordings Act—in which Congress contemplated ultimate public distribution of aural copies—any realistic expectation of privacy disappeared. [ ]. Furthermore, the court ruled that as Presidential documents the tapes were "impressed with the 'public trust'" and not subject to ordinary

11. Petitioner also contends that the District Court was totally without discretion to consider release of the tapes at all. He offers three principal arguments in support of that position: (i) exhibit materials subpoenaed from third parties are not "court records" in terms of the common-law right of access; (ii) recorded materials, as opposed to written documents, are not subject to release by the court in custody; and (iii) the assertion of third-party property and privacy interests precludes release of the tapes to the public.

As we assume for the purposes of this case (see text above) that the common-law right of access is applicable, we do not reach or intimate any view as to the merits of these various contentions by petitioner.

. . .

privacy claims. [ ] Respondents add that aural reproduction of actual conversations, reflecting nuances and inflections, is a more accurate means of informing the public about this important historical event than a verbatim written transcript. Petitioner disputes this claim of "accuracy," emphasizing that the tapes required 22 hours to be played. If made available for commercial recordings or broadcast by the electronic media, only fractions of the tapes, necessarily taken out of context, could or would be presented. Nor would there be any safeguard, other than the taste of the marketing medium, against distortion through cutting, erasing, and splicing of tapes. There would be strong motivation to titillate as well as to educate listeners. Petitioner insists that this use would infringe his privacy, resulting in embarrassment and anguish to himself and the other persons who participated in private conversations that they had every reason to believe would remain confidential.

Third, petitioner argues that our decision in United States v. Nixon, 418 U.S. 683 (1974), authorized only the most limited use of subpoenaed Presidential conversations consistent with the constitutional duty of the judiciary to ensure justice in criminal prosecutions. The Court of Appeals concluded, however, that the thrust of our decision in that case was to protect the confidentiality of Presidential conversations that were neither relevant nor admissible in the criminal proceeding; it did not relate to uses of conversations actually introduced into evidence. Since these conversations were no longer confidential, [ ], Presidential privilege no longer afforded any protection.

Finally, petitioner argues that it would be improper for the courts to facilitate the commercialization of these White House tapes. The court below rejected this argument, holding it a "question of taste" that could not take precedence over the public's right of access. [ ] Petitioner rejoins that such matters of taste induce courts to deny public access to court files in divorce and libel litigation. [ ] Moreover, argues petitioner, widespread publication of the transcripts has satisfied the public's legitimate interests; the marginal gain in information from the broadcast and sale of aural copies is outweighed by the unseemliness of enlisting the court, which obtained these recordings by subpoena for a limited purpose, to serve as the vehicle of their commercial exploitation "at cocktail parties, . . . in comedy acts or dramatic productions, . . . and in every manner that may occur to the enterprising, the imaginative, or the antagonistic recipients of copies." [ ]

C.

At this point, we normally would be faced with the task of weighing the interests advanced by the parties in light of the public interest and the duty of the courts.[14] On respondents' side of the scales is the

14. Judge Sirica's principal reason for refusing to release the tapes—fairness to the defendants, who were appealing their convictions—is no longer a consideration. All appeals have been resolved.

incremental gain in public understanding of an immensely important historical occurrence that arguably would flow from the release of aural copies of these tapes, a gain said to be not inconsequential despite the already widespread dissemination of printed transcripts. Also on respondents' side is the presumption—however gauged—in favor of public access to judicial records. On petitioner's side are the arguments identified above, which must be assessed in the context of court custody of the tapes. Underlying each of petitioner's arguments is the crucial fact that respondents require a court's cooperation in furthering their commercial plans. The court—as custodian of tapes obtained by subpoena over the opposition of a sitting President, solely to satisfy "fundamental demands of due process of law in the fair administration of criminal justice," United States v. Nixon, supra, at 713—has a responsibility to exercise an informed discretion as to release of the tapes, with a sensitive appreciation of the circumstances that led to their production. . . .

We need not decide how the balance would be struck if the case were resolved only on the basis of the facts and arguments reviewed above. There is in this case an additional, unique element that was neither advanced by the parties nor given appropriate consideration by the courts below. In the Presidential Recordings Act, Congress directed the Administrator of General Services to take custody of petitioner's Presidential tapes and documents. The materials are to be screened by Government archivists so that those private in nature may be returned to petitioner, while those of historical value may be preserved and made available for use in judicial proceedings and, eventually, made accessible to the public. Thus, Congress has created an administrative procedure for processing and releasing to the public, on terms meeting with congressional approval, all of petitioner's Presidential materials of historical interest, including recordings of the conversations at issue here.[15]

. . .

Considering all the circumstances of this concededly singular case, we hold that the common-law right of access to judicial records does not authorize release of the tapes in question from the custody of the District Court. We next consider whether, as respondents claim, the Constitution impels us to reach a different result.

III.

Respondents argue that release of the tapes is required by both the First Amendment guarantee of freedom of the press and the Sixth Amendment guarantee of a public trial. Neither supports respondents' conclusion.

15. Both sides insist that the Act does not in terms cover the copies of the tapes involved in this case. . . .

A.

In Cox Broadcasting Corp. v. Cohn, 420 U.S. 469 (1975), this Court held that the First Amendment prevented a State from prohibiting the press from publishing the name of a rape victim where that information had been placed "in the public domain on official court records." Id., at 495. Respondents claim that *Cox Broadcasting* guarantees the press "access" to—meaning the right to copy and publish—exhibits and materials displayed in open court.

This argument misconceives the holding in *Cox Broadcasting.* Our decision in that case merely affirmed the right of the press to publish accurately information contained in court records open to the public. Since the press serves as the information-gathering agent of the public, it could not be prevented from reporting what it had learned and what the public was entitled to know. [ ] In the instant case, however, there is no claim that the press was precluded from publishing or utilizing as it saw fit the testimony and exhibits filed in evidence. There simply were no restrictions upon press access to, or publication of any information in the public domain. Indeed, the press—including reporters of the electronic media—was permitted to listen to the tapes and report on what was heard. Reporters also were furnished transcripts of the tapes, which they were free to comment upon and publish. The contents of the tapes were given wide publicity by all elements of the media. There is no question of a truncated flow of information to the public. Thus, the issue presented in this case is not whether the press must be permitted access to public information to which the public generally is guaranteed access, but whether these copies of the White House tapes—to which the public has never had *physical* access—must be made available for copying. Our decision in *Cox Broadcasting* simply is not applicable.

The First Amendment generally grants the press no right to information about a trial superior to that of the general public. "Once beyond the confines of the courthouse, a news-gathering agency may publicize, within wide limits, what its representatives have heard and seen in the courtroom. But the line is drawn at the courthouse door; and within, a reporter's constitutional rights are no greater than those of any other member of the public." Estes v. Texas, 381 U.S. 532, 589 (1965) (Harlan, J., concurring). Cf. Saxbe v. Washington Post Co. [ ]; Pell v. Procunier [ ].

B.

Respondents contend that release of the tapes is required by the Sixth Amendment guarantee of a public trial.[19] They acknowledge that the trial at which these tapes were played was one of the most publicized in history, but argue that public understanding of it remains

19. We assume, *arguendo,* that respondents have standing to object to an alleged deprivation of a defendant's right to a public trial. But see Estes v. Texas [ ].

incomplete in the absence of the ability to listen to the tapes and form judgments as to their meaning based on inflection and emphasis.

In the first place, this argument proves too much. The same could be said of the testimony of a live witness, yet there is no constitutional right to have such testimony recorded and broadcast. Estes v. Texas [ ]. Second, while the guarantee of a public trial, in the words of Mr. Justice Black, is "a safeguard against any attempt to employ our courts as instruments of persecution," In re Oliver, 333 U.S. 257, 270 (1948), it confers no special benefit on the press. Estes v. Texas, 381 U.S., at 583 (Warren, C.J., concurring); id., at 588–589 (Harlan, J., concurring). Nor does the Sixth Amendment require that the trial—or any part of it—be broadcast live or on tape to the public. The requirement of a public trial is satisfied by the opportunity of members of the public and the press to attend the trial and to report what they have observed. Ibid. That opportunity abundantly existed here.

IV.

We hold that the Court of Appeals erred in reversing the District Court's decision not to release the tapes in its custody. We remand the case with directions that an order be entered denying respondents' application with prejudice.[20]

[Justice White, joined by Justice Brennan, reading the Presidential Recordings Act to authorize the Administrator to receive copies as well as originals, would have directed the District Court to deliver the copies in question to the Administrator.

Justice Marshall dissented on the grounds that the Act covered only "original tape recordings" and that both sides had agreed that the Act did not apply. He would have affirmed the court of appeals.

Justice Stevens dissented. Unlike the majority, he read the proceedings in the trial court as indicating that but for the existence of the appeal, the judge would have allowed access and that this had been upheld by the court of appeals. The Supreme Court should not overturn the lower courts in the absence of a showing of abuse of discretion. Here the trial was of "great historical interest" and full disclosure was warranted.]

Notes and Questions

1. Is *Cox Broadcasting* adequately distinguished?

2. On the public trial point, do the later cases of *Gannett, Richmond Newspapers,* or *Chandler* affect the Court's analysis?

3. *Copying Tapes.* The lower courts appear to be split on the standard by which to judge requests by media to copy audio and video tapes that have already been admitted in evidence or that are played for jurors

20. According to the Manual for Clerks of the United States District Courts, § 207.1 (1966), clerks of the District Courts should "obtain a direction, standing order or rule that exhibits be returned [to their owners] or destroyed within a stated time after the time for appeal has expired."

and the court. Courts involved in the ABSCAM prosecutions in the early 1980s tended to permit the copying in the absence of strong countervailing interests. See United States v. Criden, 648 F.2d 814, 7 Med.L.Rptr. (3d Cir. 1981) and United States v. Guzzino, 766 F.2d 302, 11 Med.L.Rptr. 2215 (7th Cir. 1985) (improper for trial judge, who has decided that fair trial is not an issue, to consider poor quality of tapes and fear that public might misunderstand events).

Other courts, however, have begun to treat the matter more as one of trial judge discretion and seem more ready to accept denials of access. See, e.g., United States v. Webbe, 791 F.2d 103, 12 Med.L.Rptr. 2193 (8th Cir. 1986), in which the court said, "We decline to adopt in toto the reasoning of the Second, Third, Seventh, and District of Columbia Circuits in recognizing a 'strong presumption' in favor of the common law right of access. . . . We favor the approach of the Fifth Circuit [which] gave deference to the determination of the district court." The court accepted the trial judge's concern that one of defendant's convictions was on appeal and that a reversal in that case would necessitate impaneling another jury. See also United States v. Beckham, 789 F.2d 401, 12 Med.L.Rptr. 2073 (6th Cir. 1986), accepting the trial judge's denial of access to certain items: "His decision may appear overly cautious, but the primary responsibility for the orderly administration of a criminal trial rested on his shoulders."

4. In the libel case brought by William Tavoulareas, the president of Mobil Oil, against the Washington Post, discovery produced several documents that belonged to Mobil. Claiming that the documents were confidential, Mobil fought press efforts to obtain certain documents and depositions. The trial judge used some of these in denying a defense motion for summary judgment. The judge then denied the public and press access to these documents, without making "a document-by-document determination" of the validity of the claim. This decision was upheld on appeal. In re Reporters Committee for Freedom of the Press, 773 F.2d 1325, 12 Med.L.Rptr. 1073 (D.C.Cir.1985). The panel unanimously concluded that no constitutional right of access to depositions and discovery documents existed until after the trial had ended and judgment had been entered. Over a dissent, the majority reached the same conclusion as to trial exhibits, in part because of the difficulty of conducting a trial and having to make case-by-case adjudications about confidentiality at the time each exhibit is introduced. The dissent stressed the importance of contemporaneous public access to exhibits used in a trial.

5. Another basis for sealing records, as it is for closing court proceedings, is the desire to avoid publicizing trade secrets. Recall the toxic shock case, p. 679, supra.

6. At the same time, it is clear that the simple desire of the parties to a litigation will not justify sealing the record. In Wilson v. American Motors Corp., 759 F.2d 1568, 11 Med.L.Rptr. 2008 (11th Cir.1985), a personal injury case arising out of a Jeep accident had been settled

after a jury's special verdict. The trial judge sealed the record. A plaintiff in another Jeep case wanted to see that record for possible use as offensive collateral estoppel. The court assumed that the earlier case would not have settled if the defendant had known that the record could be opened up. Nonetheless, the court now finds no good reason to seal the earlier record and orders it opened. Judicial efficiency was thought to favor opening the record, even though the result may be to discourage settlements.

Although the decision to open the record was based on common law, the court observed that the Third and Sixth Circuits have found constitutional bases for access to civil proceedings and to the information from them. See p. 679, supra.

In S.A.R.L. Orliac v. Berthe, 765 F.2d 30, 11 Med.L.Rptr. 2287 (2d Cir.1985), the parties to a commercial dispute sought to make all the appellate papers and documents confidential. The judge to whom the order was presented, refused to sign it:

> Despite the wealth of detail the parties have provided as to the procedures by which they wish to restrict and to control access to papers filed on this appeal, they have failed to provide any information about the nature of the material they seek to protect from public view or why that information warrants protection. Apparently, the parties have assumed that since they have stipulated to secrecy, the court would routinely ratify their desire without inquiry into its necessity. Their assumption is unwarranted.

The request was denied without prejudice to further application that would demonstrate the necessity of any requested relief.

7. The lower courts have not been receptive to efforts to use First Amendment claims to obtain information in government files. E.g., Capital Cities Media, Inc. v. Chester, 609 F.Supp. 494 (M.D.Pa.1985) (no First Amendment right to obtain reports of the state environmental agency); Matter of Roger B., 85 Ill.App.3d 1064, 407 N.E.2d 884 (1980), aff'd 84 Ill.2d 323, 418 N.E.2d 751, 49 Ill.Dec. 731 (1981), appeal dismissed for want of a substantial federal question 454 U.S. 806 (1981) (no First Amendment violation to bar adopted person, now an adult, from seeing sealed record to learn his biological history). Justices Brennan and Stevens would have set the case for oral argument.

8. In one case television broadcasters applied to view and copy some three hours of tapes that had been received in evidence in a criminal case. The tapes were part of nine hours of color videotape that the defendant made while he kidnapped and later raped a victim. Although tapes of the actual rapes were not shown, tapes of conversations preliminary to the rapes were admitted. During these scenes the victim was seen lying on a blanket on the floor, blindfolded, with her hands and feet bound.

Relying on the Abscam cases, the broadcasters sought the tapes for copying and possible presentation. The victim and the prosecutor objected to the release and the judge denied release. Relying on *Warner Communications,* he concluded that copying evidence was not an absolute right and that these tapes came within the exclusion permitting denial when the records would promote public scandal or be disgusting. Release would further injure the victim and would not further any legitimate public interest. Moreover, release would give judicial approval to commercial exploitation of a voice and photographic display "catering to prurient interests without proper public purpose or corresponding assurance of public benefit."

The Abscam cases were distinguishable because they involved wrongdoing by elected public officials—and those officials would not suffer further humiliation from the showing of the tapes. The rape victim allowed the tapes to be played in court to help the prosecution. "To now expose [the victim] to public humiliation and degradation by releasing the tapes for public dissemination would, at best, be unseemly and shameless; it would constitute an unconscionable invasion of her privacy." The information on the tapes was already public, and the First Amendment required no more. In re Application of KSTP, 504 F.Supp. 360, 6 Med.L.Rptr. 2249 (D.C.Minn.1980).

9. The state positions have varied from what appear to be views of absolute constitutional rights of access to fairly circumscribed positions. The cases are collected in Annot., Restricting Public Access to Judicial Records of State Courts, 84 A.L.R.3d 598 (1978).

10. Occasionally, the denial of access to admitted evidence involves a concern about prejudicial publicity. For example, photographic exhibits have been admitted in A's trial. Trials of B and C for the same offense are to follow. The court may permit the press to inspect the photos and other evidence—but not to copy them, presumably until after B and C are tried. Hearst Corp. v. Vogt, 62 A.D.2d 840, 406 N.Y.S.2d 567 (1978). The court relied on *Warner Communications* in holding that there is no unrestrained right to gather information. The proper exercise of discretion was to deny copying "at this time." The press was free to go back to the trial court when conditions had changed.

SEATTLE TIMES CO. v. RHINEHART

Supreme Court of the United States, 1984.
467 U.S. 20, 104 S.Ct. 2199, 81 L.Ed.2d 17, 10 Med.L.Rptr. 1705.

[Rhinehart was spiritual leader of the Aquarian Foundation, a religious group with fewer than 1,000 members, most of whom lived in the state of Washington. He and other members of his group sued some local newspapers for libel. The papers answered and "promptly initiated extensive discovery." In response to questions about damages, plaintiff responded that the Foundation had experienced a drop in membership and concurrent drop in contributions. Plaintiff refused to identify the Foundation's donors or members. The newspapers filed a motion to compel discovery. Plaintiffs filed affidavits asserting that disclosure of members and donors would lead to harm and harassment of those named. The state court, invoking Rule 26(c), patterned after Federal Rule 26(c), issued a protective order prohibiting the papers from "publishing, disseminating, or using the information in any way except where necessary to prepare for and try the case." The order did not apply to information obtained by means other than the discovery process. The relevant part of the rule provided that "for good cause shown, the court . . . may make any order which justice requires to protect a party or person from annoyance, embarrassment, oppression, or undue burden or expense . . . ." On the appeal by the papers from the protective order, the Supreme Court of Washington affirmed.]

JUSTICE POWELL delivered the opinion of the Court.

. . .

The Supreme Court of Washington recognized that its holding conflicts with the holdings of the United States Court of Appeals for the District of Columbia in In re Halkin, 598 F.2d 176 (1979),[11] and applies a different standard from that of the Court of Appeals for the First Circuit in In re San Juan Star Co., 662 F.2d 108 (1981).[12] We granted certiorari to resolve the conflict.[13] We affirm.

III

Most states, including Washington, have adopted discovery provisions modeled on Rules 26 through 37 of the Federal Rules of Civil Procedure. [ ]. Rule 26(b)(1) provides that a party "may obtain discovery regarding any matter, not privileged, which is relevant to the subject matter involved in the pending action." It further provides that discovery is not limited to matters that will be admissible at trial so long as the information sought "appears reasonably calculated to lead to the discovery of admissible evidence." [ ]

The rules do not differentiate between information that is private or intimate and that to which no privacy interests attach. Under the

11. See note 6 supra [which is reproduced at this point:

6. The *Halkin* decision was debated by the courts below. Prior to *Halkin,* the only federal court of appeals to consider the question directly had understood that the First Amendment did not affect a trial court's authority to restrict dissemination of information produced during pretrial discovery. See International Paper Products v. Koons, 325 F.2d 403, 407–408 (CA2 1963). *Halkin* considered the issue at length. Characterizing a protective order as a "paradigmatic prior restraint," *Halkin* held that such orders require close scrutiny. The court also held that before a court should issue a protective order that restricts expression, it must be satisfied that "the harm posed by dissemination must be substantial and serious; the restraining order must be narrowly drawn and precise; and there must be no alternative means of protecting the public interest which intrudes less directly on expression." Id., at 191.]

12. In *San Juan Star,* the Court of Appeals for the First Circuit considered and rejected *Halkin's* approach to the constitutionality of protective orders. Although the *San Juan* court held that protective orders may implicate First Amendment interests, the court reasoned that such interests are somewhat lessened in the civil discovery context. The court stated: "In general, then, we find the appropriate measure of such limitations in a standard of 'good cause' that incorporates a 'heightened sensitivity' to the First Amendment concerns at stake. . . . " 662 F.2d, at 116.

13. The holding of the Supreme Court of Washington is consistent with the decision of the Court of Appeals for the Second Circuit in International Products Corp. v. Koons, 325 F.2d 403, 407–408 (1963).

rules, the only express limitations are that the information sought is not privileged, and is relevant to the subject matter of the pending action. Thus, the rules often allow extensive intrusion into the affairs of both litigants and third parties. If a litigant fails to comply with a request for discovery, the Court may issue an order directing compliance that is enforceable by the Court's contempt powers. [ ]

Petitioners argue that the First Amendment imposes strict limits on the availability of any judicial order that has the effect of restricting expression. They contend that civil discovery is not different from other sources of information, and therefore the information is "protected speech" for First Amendment purposes. Petitioners assert the right in this case to disseminate any information gained through discovery. They do recognize that in limited circumstances, not thought to be present here, some information may be restrained. They submit, however, that:

> "When a protective order seeks to limit expression, it may do so only if the proponent shows a compelling governmental interest. Mere speculation and conjecture are insufficient. Any restraining order, moreover, must be narrowly drawn and precise. Finally, before issuing such an order a court must determine that there are no alternatives which intrude less directly on expression." Petitioners' Brief 10.

We think the rule urged by petitioners would impose an unwarranted restriction on the duty and discretion of a trial court to oversee the discovery process.

IV

It is, of course, clear that information obtained through civil discovery authorized by modern rules of civil procedure would rarely, if ever, fall within the classes of unprotected speech identified by decisions of this Court. In this case, as petitioners argue, there certainly is a public interest in knowing more about respondents. This interest may well include most—and possibly all—of what has been discovered as a result of the court's order under Rule 26(b)(1). It does not necessarily follow, however, that a litigant has an unrestrained right to disseminate information that has been obtained through pretrial discovery. For even though the broad sweep of the First Amendment seems to prohibit all restraints on free expression, this Court has observed that "freedom of speech . . . does not comprehend the right to speak on any subject at any time." American Communications Assn. v. Douds, 339 U.S. 382, 394–395 (1950).

The critical question that this case presents is whether a litigant's freedom comprehends the right to disseminate information that he has obtained pursuant to a court order that both granted him access to that information and placed restraints on the way in which the information might be used. In addressing that question it is necessary to consider whether the "practice in question [furthers] an important or substantial governmental interest unrelated to the suppression of expression" and whether "the limitation of First Amendment freedoms [is] no greater than is necessary or essential to the protection of the particular governmental interest involved." Procunier v. Martinez, 416 U.S. 396, 413 (1974); see Brown v. Glines, 444 U.S. 348, 354–355 (1980); Buckley v. Valeo, 424 U.S. 1, 25 (1976).

A

At the outset, it is important to recognize the extent of the impairment of First Amendment rights that a protective order, such as the one at issue here, may cause. As in all civil litigation, petitioners gained the information they wish to disseminate only by virtue of the trial court's discovery processes. As the rules authorizing discovery were adopted by the state legislature, the processes thereunder are a matter of legislative grace. A litigant has no First Amendment right of access to information made available only for purposes of trying his suit. Zemel v. Rusk, 381 U.S. 1, 16–17 (1965) ("The right to speak and publish does not carry with it the unrestrained right to gather information."). Thus, continued court control over the discovered information does not raise the same spectre of government censorship that such control might suggest in other situations. See In re Halkin, 598 F.2d, at 206–207 (Wilkey, J. dissenting).[18]

Moreover, pretrial depositions and interrogatories are not public components of a civil trial.[19] Such proceedings were not open to the public at common law, Gannett Co. v. DePasquale, 443 U.S. 368, 389 (1979), and, in general, they are conducted in private as a matter of modern practice. See id., at 396 (BURGER, C.J., concurring); Marcus, Myth and Reality in Protective Order Litigation, 69 Cornell L.Rev. 1 (1983). Much of the information that surfaces during pretrial discovery may be unrelated, or only tangentially related, to the underlying cause

18. Although litigants do not "surrender their First Amendment rights at the courthouse door." In re Halkin, 598 F.2d, at 186, those rights may be subordinated to other interests that arise in this setting. For instance, on several occasions this Court has approved restriction on the communications of trial participants where necessary to ensure a fair trial for a criminal defendant. See Nebraska Press v. Stuart, 427 U.S. 539, 563, (1976); id., at 601 and n. 27 (BRENNAN, J., concurring): Oklahoma Publishing Co. v. District Court, 430 U.S. 308, 310–311 (1977); Sheppard v. Maxwell, 384 U.S. 333, 361 (1966). "In the conduct of a case, a court often finds it necessary to restrict the free expression of participants, including counsel, witnesses, and jurors." Gulf Oil Co. v. Bernard, 452 U.S. 89, 104 n. 21 (1981).

19. Discovery rarely takes place in public. Depositions are scheduled at times and places most convenient to those involved. Interrogatories are answered in private. Rules of civil procedure may require parties to file with the clerk of the court interrogatory answers, responses to requests for admissions, and deposition transcripts. See Fed.Rule Civ.Proc. 5(d). Jurisdictions that require filing of discovery material customarily provide that trial courts may order that the materials not be filed or that they be filed under seal. See ibid.; Wash.Super.Ct.C.R. 26(c). Federal district courts may adopt local rules providing that the fruits of discovery are not to be filed except on order of the court. See, e.g., C.D.Cal.R. 6(d); S.D.N.Y.Civ.R. 19. Thus, to the extent that courthouse records could serve as a source of public information, access to that source customarily is subject to the control of the trial court.

of action. Therefore, restraints placed on discovered, but not yet admitted, information are not a restriction on a traditionally public source of information.

Finally, it is significant to note that an order prohibiting dissemination of discovered information before trial is not the kind of classic prior restraint that requires exacting First Amendment scrutiny. See Gannett Co. v. DePasquale, 443 U.S., at 399 (POWELL, J. concurring). As in this case, such a protective order prevents a party from disseminating only that information obtained through use of the discovery process. Thus, the party may disseminate the identical information covered by the protective order as long as the information is gained through means independent of the court's processes. In sum, judicial limitations on a party's ability to disseminate information discovered in advance of trial implicates the First Amendment rights of the restricted party to a far lesser extent than would restraints on dissemination of information in a different context. Therefore, our consideration of the provisions for protective orders contained in the Washington Civil Rules takes into account the unique position that such orders occupy in relation to the First Amendment.

B

Rule 26(c) furthers a substantial governmental interest unrelated to the suppression of expression. *Procunier,* 416 U.S., at 413. The Washington Civil Rules enable parties to litigation to obtain information "relevant to the subject matter involved" that they believe will be helpful in the preparation and trial of the case. Rule 26, however, must be viewed in its entirety. Liberal discovery is provided for the sole purpose of assisting in the preparation and trial, or the settlement, of litigated disputes. Because of the liberality of pretrial discovery permitted by Rule 26(b)(1), it is necessary for the trial court to have the authority to issue protective orders conferred by Rule 26(c). It is clear from experience that pretrial discovery by depositions and interrogatories has a significant potential for abuse.[20] This abuse is not limited to matters of delay and expense; discovery also may seriously implicate privacy interests of litigants and third parties.[21] The Rules do not

20. See Comments of the Advisory Committee on the 1983 Amendments to Fed. Rule Civ.Proc. 26. In Herbert v. Lando, 441 U.S. 153, 176 (1979), the Court observed: "[T]here have been repeated expressions of concern about undue and uncontrolled discovery, and voices from this Court have joined the chorus. But until and unless there are major changes in the present Rules of Civil Procedure, reliance must be had on what in fact and in law are ample powers of the district judge to prevent abuse." Id., at 176, 177 (citations omitted); see also id., at 179 (POWELL, J., concurring). But abuses of the Rules by litigants, and sometimes the inadequate oversight of discovery by trial courts, do not in any respect lessen the importance of discovery in civil litigation and the government's substantial interest in protecting the integrity of the discovery process.

21. Cf. [ ]; Cox Broadcasting Corp. v. Cohn, 420 U.S. 469, 488–491 (1975). Rule 26(c) includes among its express purposes the protection of a "party or person from annoyance, embarrassment, oppression or undue burden or expense." Although the Rule contains no specific reference to privacy or to other rights or interests that may be implicated, such matters are im-

distinguish between public and private information. Nor do they apply only to parties to the litigation, as relevant information in the hands of third parties may be subject to discovery.

There is an opportunity, therefore, for litigants to obtain—incidentally or purposefully—information that not only is irrelevant but if publicly released could be damaging to reputation and privacy. The government clearly has a substantial interest in preventing this sort of abuse of its processes. Cf. Herbert v. Lando, 441 U.S. 153, 176–177 (1979); [ ]. . . . The prevention of the abuse that can attend the coerced production of information under a state's discovery rule is sufficient justification for the authorization of protective orders.[22]

C

We also find that the provision for protective orders in the Washington rules requires, in itself, no heightened First Amendment scrutiny. To be sure, Rule 26(c) confers broad discretion on the trial court to decide when a protective order is appropriate and what degree of protection is required. The legislature of the State of Washington, following the example of the Congress in its approval of the Federal Rules of Civil Procedure, has determined that such discretion is necessary, and we find no reason to disagree. The trial court is in the best position to weigh fairly the competing needs and interests of parties affected by discovery. The unique character of the discovery process requires that the trial court have substantial latitude to fashion protective orders.

V

The facts in this case illustrate the concerns that justifiably may prompt a court to issue a protective order. As we have noted, the trial court's order allowing discovery was extremely broad. It compelled respondents—among other things—to identify all persons who had made donations over a five-year period to Rhinehart and the Aquarian Foundation, together with the amounts donated. In effect the order would compel disclosure of membership as well as sources of financial support. The Supreme Court of Washington found that dissemination of this information would "result in annoyance, embarrassment and even oppression." 654 P.2d, at 690. It is sufficient for purposes of our decision that the highest court in the state found no abuse of discretion in the trial court's decision to issue a protective order pursuant to a constitutional state law. We therefore hold that where, as in this case,

plicit in the broad purpose and language of the Rule.

22. The Supreme Court of Washington properly emphasized the importance of ensuring that potential litigants have unimpeded access to the courts: "[A]s the trial court rightly observed, rather than expose themselves to unwanted publicity, individuals may well forgo the pursuit of their just claims. The judicial system will thus have made the utilization of its remedies so onerous that the people will be reluctant or unwilling to use it, resulting in frustration of a right as valuable as that of speech itself," 654 P.2d at 689. [ ]

a protective order is entered on a showing of good cause as required by Rule 26(c), is limited to the context of pretrial civil discovery, and does not restrict the dissemination of the information if gained from other sources, it does not offend the First Amendment.

The judgment accordingly is affirmed.

[Justice Brennan, joined by Justice Marshall, concurred specially to observe that the majority has recognized that this kind of protective order is "subject to scrutiny under the First Amendment" because the Court looks at the state interests and at whether the limit is greater than necessary. "I agree that the respondents' interests in privacy and religious freedom are sufficient to justify this protective order and to overcome the protections afforded free expression by the First Amendment. I therefore join the Court's opinion."]

Notes and Questions

1. Is the analysis influenced by the fact that the defendant is a newspaper? What if the defendant were a large corporation, and plaintiff feared that the information revealed would be used in some harmful way that did not involve publication?

2. Would the case be different if a broadcaster approached a nonmedia defendant who was under a similar court order, to try to obtain information?

3. The Rhinehart case also sheds light on situations involving so-called gag orders in criminal cases in which the justification for ordering parties and their attorneys not to speak is couched in terms of fair trial.

In Levine v. United States District Court, 764 F.2d 590, 11 Med.L. Rptr. 2289 (9th Cir.1985), an FBI agent was awaiting trial in Los Angeles for espionage. The government's motion to bar counsel from discussing the case was denied, though the judge alerted counsel to his desire to "maintain an atmosphere in which a fair trial could be conducted." Defense counsel advised the court that they might "at some future time deem it necessary in the interest of our client to make a statement outside the courtroom."

Two months later, defense counsel were quoted at length in an article in the Los Angeles Times setting forth their contentions and their theories of the case. The article reported that the prosecutor refused to respond to the defense comments because "a judge has asked all parties in the case to avoid public discussion of the evidence."

The government renewed its motion for a restraining order. After a hearing, the trial judge found that the interviews and resulting article had created a "serious and imminent threat to a fair trial." Though unable to assess the motivation behind the interview and article, he concluded that it was "quite reasonable to expect that such publicity has been and will become even more pervasive, creating in effect a lobbying effort by counsel on behalf of their clients. The public has a right to expect a fairer trial than that."

The judge ordered all attorneys in the case and their representatives "not [to] make any statements to members of the news media concerning any aspect of this case that bears upon the merits to be resolved by the jury." (Language that originally covered parties and witnesses was removed later.) Defense counsel sought mandamus. The court of appeals granted the writ and ordered the district judge to define the scope of the order.

The court began by recognizing that this case did not involve a prior restraint on media or deny the press access to a judicial proceeding. Although media might argue that their rights to gather news had been infringed, no media organization had challenged the order. The court also held that the attorneys lacked standing to raise the claims on behalf of the media. The court treated the case as one involving freedom of speech rather than press.

Since the order was a prior restraint on counsel, it could be upheld only if the party seeking it could establish (1) that the activity restrained "poses either a clear and present danger of a serious and imminent threat to a protected competing interest"; (2) that the order was narrowly drawn; and (3) that less restrictive alternatives were not available. Surveying other results, the court concluded that the "overwhelming majority" of courts have upheld this type of order.

Turning to the first element, the court noted that *Sheppard* had directed district judges to take affirmative steps to provide fair trials to defendants:

> The sixth amendment is a limitation on the government and does not give the prosecution the right to a fair trial. [ ] It does not follow, however, that the need to restrict publicity is lessened when the publicity is caused by the actions of the defense, rather than the prosecution. . . . Society has the right to expect that the judicial system will be fair and impartial to all who come before it. . . .
>
> We do not mean to imply that the government has an absolute right to an impartial jury. Indeed, it is appropriate for the defense, within certain limits, to seek a jury that is partial to the defendant. The right to a partial jury, however, is not guaranteed by the Constitution. The ability of the defendant to seek a partial jury must be limited by the legitimate expectation of the government and the public that the judicial system will produce fair results. Accordingly, the judiciary cannot escape the task of fixing the limits within which a defendant may attempt to create publicity.

Since this was not a prior restraint, the restrictions did not have to meet the test of being essential to the selection of an impartial jury. Here, the court distinguished the CBS case, p. 545, supra. "Even if an impartial jury could be selected, intense prejudicial publicity during and immediately before trial could allow the jury to be swayed by extrajudicial influences. More importantly, the circus-like environment that surrounds highly publicized trials threatens the integrity of the judicial system."

Turning to the "narrowness" issue, the court thought the order overbroad. Many statements bearing on the "merits" of a case carry no danger to the administration of justice. On remand, the judge must consider which statements carry such dangers. As for the government, the court thought it would be appropriate for the judge to order the government to observe its self-imposed limitations of 28 C.F.R. § 50.2(b) (1984). For the defense, it "would be appropriate to proscribe statements relating to one or more of the following subjects":

> (1) The character, credibility, or reputation of a party;
>
> (2) The identity of a witness or the expected testimony of a party or a witness;
>
> (3) The contents of any pretrial confession, admission, or statement given by a defendant or that person's refusal or failure to make a statement;
>
> (4) The identity or nature of physical evidence expected to be presented or the absence of such physical evidence;
>
> (5) The strengths or weaknesses of the case of either party; and
>
> (6) Any other information the lawyer knows or reasonably should know is likely to be inadmissible as evidence and would create a substantial risk of prejudice if disclosed.

These were drawn from various ABA standards and the Model Rules of Professional Conduct.

Finally, the court reviewed the less restrictive alternatives. The trial court's rejection of a searching voir dire was upheld. Although this might eliminate bias from pretrial publicity, it "cannot eliminate prejudice caused by publicity during the trial. Moreover, voir dire cannot alleviate the harm to the integrity of the judicial process caused by the extrajudicial statements of trial participants."

Jury instructions were inadequate because they could not address the threat to judicial integrity. Change of venue and continuance would not help here because neither addressed the "problem of curbing unwarranted statements by counsel." Finally, the district court found sequestration inadequate because jurors "should not bear the brunt of counsels' transgressions." Also, the "resentments and . . . harassment which derives from sequestration can often impede calm and rational deliberation. In this court's judgment, sequestration is a remedy clearly more drastic than the restraining order being issued today."

Judge Nelson, concurring in part and dissenting in part, did not see a sufficiently clear and present danger to justify the lower court's order. The size of the Central District made it unlikely that an impartial jury could not be selected. "I do not mean to suggest that [this type of order] will never be permissible in this particular case. Once the jury is empaneled, the district court will be faced with a different situation. Even then, however, the court must examine closely the alternatives to issuance of an order restricting speech. The viability [of the various alternatives] must be reexamined in light of the degree and nature of publicity at that time. The court should also examine whether any proposed order will be effective in curbing prejudicial publicity." Since much publicity is likely to attend this case even if the court restricts the attorneys' comments, the court must consider "whether the benefits to the Sixth Amendment will outweigh the costs to the First before resorting to a prior restraint on speech."

Judge Nelson observed that one "would hope that rules governing such conduct would emanate first from the bar, lessening or eliminating the need for courts to consider imposing prior restraints on speech. The enforcement of relevant rules of professional conduct would of course be after-the-fact remedies, admittedly less effective but far safer than prior restraints."

Is there a difference between ordering those more clearly under the jurisdiction of the court not to speak, and ordering members of the press and public not to ask these persons certain questions?

A suggestion for rehearing en banc was denied over five dissents. 775 F.2d 1054, 12 Med.L.Rptr. 1458 (9th Cir. 1985). Judge Norris, writing for the dissenters, called the issue "extraordinarily important" and said this case was the first in any circuit "to approve a gag order on defense attorneys under the 'clear and present danger' standard." Implicit in the prevailing opinions was the view "that there is something improper and perhaps even unethical about a lawyer who refuses to limit his client's defense to in-court statements. This, I submit, is a myopic view of the role of a lawyer when he is carrying out what may be the noblest calling of our profession, representing a person charged by the state with a crime. . . . Marshalled against an accused is not only the awesome resources and prestige of the United States Government, but also the power of the media to disseminate the government's charges. I cannot accept the proposition that a person charged by his government with a crime should be denied the opportunity to defend himself publicly through his chosen spokesman."

The Supreme Court denied certiorari, 106 S.Ct. 2276 (1986).

4. Most states follow some version of DR 7–107 of the ABA Model Code of Professional Responsibility in regulating the ability of lawyers to comment on pending cases. A few follow Rule 3.6 of the newer Model Rules of Professional Conduct. The comments to Rule 3.6 state that it is similar to DR 7–107 except in three particulars. First, Rule 3.6 adopts the general standard of "substantial likelihood of materially prejudicing an adjudicative proceeding" to describe the impermissible conduct. This is a more rigorous standard that most courts in fact used in DR 7–107 cases. Second, Rule 3.6 "transforms the particulars in DR 7–107 into an illustrative compilation that gives fair notice of conduct

ordinarily posing unacceptable dangers to the fair administration of justice." Third, Rule 3.6 omits a part of DR 7–107 that authorized a lawyer to reveal "at the time of seizure, a description of the physical evidence seized, other than a confession, admission or statement." DR 7–107 is extensively discussed in Hirschkop v. Snead, 594 F.2d 356, 4 Med.L.Rptr. 2599 (4th Cir. 1979), and cases cited therein.

5. There is some doubt about the ability of the court to order the defendant in a criminal case not to say certain things. See Hamilton v. Municipal Court, 270 Cal.App.2d 797, 76 Cal.Rptr. 168 (1969).

6. *Identifying Jurors.* If a judge cannot prevent the press from reporting the names of jurors that have become public, the next step might be to try to prevent the names from becoming public in a state in which jurors' names are not public property. This was approved in a criminal prosecution of major narcotics suspects in New York City. The trial judge gave each prospective juror a number and never released their names or addresses. The judge did conduct a voir dire based on his own questions and some submitted by counsel. He asked jurors, among other things, the county of their residence and whether they were prejudiced against blacks (14 defendants were black). He asked about education and group memberships, but he refused to ask the jurors about their own ethnic or religious backgrounds.

After conviction, the defendants appealed, asserting, as one ground, that they had been deprived of a meaningful opportunity to use their challenges in selecting a jury. The lack of name and address meant that the defendants could not question neighbors and learn on their own about the prospective jurors.

The defendants relied in part on a 1936 statement by Clarence Darrow that a juror's "nationality, his business, religion, politics, social standing, family ties, friends, habits of life and thought; the books and newspapers he likes and reads . . . [his] method of speech, the kind of clothes he wears, the style of haircut" were important subjects for questioning.

The court affirmed the convictions. United States v. Barnes, 604 F.2d 121 (2d Cir.1979), certiorari denied 446 U.S. 907 (1980). The judge had grounds to fear threats of retaliation against the jury if it convicted. Since possible prejudice was explored, the court could see no added benefits from asking jurors about their own ethnic backgrounds. As to names and addresses, the defendants argued that "jurors must publicly disclose their identities and publicly take responsibility for the decisions they are about to make." The court disagreed. Jurors who fear retribution cannot be impartial. If an anonymous juror feels less pressure as the result of anonymity, "this is as it should be—a factor contributing to his impartiality." As to religion, "our jury selection system was not designed to subject prospective jurors to a catechism of their tenets of faith."

Defendants are entitled to a fair and impartial jury and must have enough information to enable them to use their challenges sensibly. In this case the defendants had enough information to meet their needs. "Clarence Darrow's ideal has already yielded to what has been thought to be the greater necessity, i.e., the need to streamline the *voir dire* process by resting the control of it in the district judge [ ], subject to the demand that the essentials of the case should be the subject of inquiry." (The court noted that a federal statute required that the names and addresses of prospective jurors in capital cases be disclosed three days before trial.)

An editorial in the New York Times observed that the dangers to jurors in certain types of cases "are real; but the decision is disturbing." It referred to situations in which the public loses because it cannot learn about jury behavior. The best-known example is the 1975 bribery trial of John Connally in the District of Columbia. The judge impounded the jurors' names. After acquittal, he refused to release them, in order to protect the jurors from harassment. The Times noted that the judge's decision "left the public guessing why the jury had so quickly acquitted" Connally. N.Y. Times, May 10, 1979 at A22.

Trials conducted under this approach raise some of the same questions that arose when sequestration was invoked. Defense counsel contend that "It's a red flag over a case. . . . It screams that this is a special case." Others respond that the practice is no more damaging than "posting guards in the courtroom." In recent cases in New York City involving charges tied to organized crime, the judges told the jurors that anonymity was being used to protect them from any interference because of the publicity in the case. They were not told about safety or fears of jury tampering. One critic observed that "I don't think judges should lie to jurors. It becomes contagious, and he's not fooling anyone anyway." See Smothers, A Mixed Verdict on Anonymous Jurors, N.Y. Times, Oct. 13, 1985, § 4, p. 6.

7. *Interviewing Jurors.* In In re El Paso Times, 713 F.2d 1114, 9 Med. L.Rptr. 2113 (5th Cir.1983), certiorari denied 465 U.S. 1041 (1984), the judge who had presided over a highly publicized murder trial entered the following order:

> 1. No juror has any obligation to speak to any person about this case, and may refuse all interviews or comment.
>
> 2. No person may make repeated requests for interviews or questioning after a juror has expressed his or her desire not to be interviewed.
>
> 3. No interviewer may inquire into the specific vote of any juror other than the juror being interviewed.
>
> 4. No interview may take place until each juror in this case has received a copy of this order, mailed simultaneously with the entry of this order.

On appeal, the court upheld the order. Quoting an earlier case in that circuit, the court said that "jurors, even after completing their duty, are entitled to privacy and to protection against harassment. [ ]" Further, the court recognized that "at *some* point repeated importunings of one who has declined to be interviewed become harassment and an improper invasion of privacy." The question then became one of how many to allow. "The trial judge concluded that one request made after a known refusal to be interviewed was enough to allow and that more—repeated requests—were too many. We cannot say that in so concluding he abused his discretion." A juror who later changed his mind was "always free to initiate an interview. The court's order does no more than forbid nagging him into doing so."

Item (2) was upheld as not unduly vague. Item (3) was upheld on the ground, quoting a Supreme Court decision, that "[F]reedom of debate might be stifled and independence of thought checked if jurors were made to feel that their arguments and ballots were to be freely published to the world." Is there a big difference between ordering jurors not to reveal this type of information and ordering the press not to ask jurors this type of information?

Compare United States v. Sherman, 581 F.2d 1358 (9th Cir.1978), in which the judge, after a highly publicized armed robbery case, ordered the jurors not to discuss the case with anyone, told them they would be protected from harassment, and, as the court of appeals put it, ordered "everyone, including the news media, to stay away from the jurors." The court treated the order as a "prior restraint" and began with a "heavy presumption against its constitutional validity." Since the trial had ended, there could be no concern about a fair trial. The trial judge defended the order as meant to "enable the jurors to serve on future jury panels and to protect the jurors from harassment."

But these goals could be achieved more narrowly. If a juror's impartiality is challenged in a future trial because of what the juror said to the press after an earlier trial, the juror could be excused. Alternatively, the judge might have excused all jurors from future service after this experience. Finally, some jurors might not be harassed by interviews. If they were, the trial judge might then properly act to correct "the actual intrusion suffered."

A different situation arises if the trial judge, fearing for the safety of jurors in a forthcoming trial, seeks to protect them in the first instance by not identifying them in open court. This, of course, cannot be effective in a small community where anyone walking into the courtroom would recognize some or all the jurors. But in large urban areas, the practice may work.

In Haeberle v. Texas International Airlines, 739 F.2d 1019 (5th Cir. 1984), a local district court rule barred questioning "any juror, relative, friends or associate thereof" during or after the trial "with respect to the deliberations or verdict of the jury . . . except on leave of Court granted upon good cause shown." After a jury returned a defense verdict in a civil case, the plaintiff's attorney sought leave to interview the jurors to learn some lessons from what had happened—but explicitly not to urge a new trial because of improper jury behavior. The trial judge's denial of leave was affirmed.

Although the court saw some constitutional aspect to the desired flow of information, this case differed from the Express-News case because that one involved public receipt of the information. Although the interests of self-education are "not without first amendment significance, they are not 'paramount' like the public's right to receive information necessary for informed self-government. The petitioners' access to information from jurors carries far less weight in the first amendment scale than a restriction on access to information that affects political behavior."

Moreover, attorneys undertake to comply with the rules of any court district to which their litigation might be transferred. "By voluntarily assuming the special status of trial participants and officers of the court, parties and their attorneys subject themselves to greater restraints on their communications than might constitutionally be applied to the general public." Where do jurors fit in the spectrum that runs from litigants and attorneys to reporters and members of the general public?

While the case was on appeal, the district court rule was changed to restrict juror interviews only when their purpose was to obtain evidence of improprieties in the jury deliberations.

8. At this point, it is appropriate to seek an overview of questions raised by the various ways in which courts seek to protect the accused's right to a fair trial. We have considered attempts at prior restraint by barring the press from reporting what it has already found out; efforts to keep the press out of the courtroom to keep it from learning the feared information; and now orders addressed to litigants and their counsel to stop them from conveying information to the press. Finally, and more indirectly, we have limits on discussions with jurors. Looking at the entire package, what are your reactions?

Part Four

BROADCASTING

Chapter XIII

INTRODUCTION TO BROADCASTING

Our discussion so far has dealt largely with print media, rather than with users of the broadcast spectrum, to the extent that legal controls for the two differ. This Chapter explores how broadcasting operates. In Chapter XIV, we consider what differences might lead to legal regulation quite unlike that of the print sector.

A. NATURE OF THE SPECTRUM

The electromagnetic spectrum is a unique natural resource. Utilization does not use it up or wear it out. It does not require continual maintenance to remain usable. It is subject to pollution (interference), but once the interference is removed the pollution totally disappears. The value of the spectrum lies primarily in its use for conveying a wide variety of information at varying speeds over varying distances: in other words, for communication.

All electromagnetic radiation is a form of radiant energy, similar in many respects to heat, light, or X-radiation. All of these types of radiation are considered by physicists to be waves resulting from the periodic oscillations of charged subatomic particles. All radiation has a measurable frequency, or rate of oscillation, which is measured in cycles per second, or hertz. One thousand cycles per second equals one kilocycle per second, or one kiloHertz (1 kHz); 1,000 kilocycles per second equals one Megacycle per second (1 MHz); and 1,000 Megacycles per second equals one Gigacycle per second (1 GHz). The frequencies of electromagnetic radiation that make up the radio spectrum span a wide range, from 10 kHz to 3,000,000,000,000 cycles per second (3,000 GHz), all of which are nearly incomprehensibly rapid. Present technology allows use of the spectrum up to around 40 GHz.

The radio spectrum resource itself has three dimensions: space, time, and frequency. Two spectrum users can transmit on the same frequency at the same time if they are sufficiently separate physically; the physical separation necessary will depend on the power at which each signal is transmitted. They then occupy different parts of the spectrum in the spatial sense. Similarly, the spectrum can be divided in terms of frequency, dependent on the construction of the transmitting and receiving equipment; or in a temporal sense, dependent largely on the hours of use.

The spectrum is subject to the phenomenon of interference. One radio signal interferes with another to the extent that both have the same dimensions. That is, two signals of the same frequency that occupy the same physical space at the same time will interfere with each other (co-channel interference). Signals on adjacent channels may also interfere with each other. Interference usually obscures or destroys any information that either signal is carrying: the degree to which two signals occupy the same physical space depends on the intensity of the radiated power at a given point, which in turn depends on the construction of the transmitting equipment and antenna.

The spectrum is divided into numbered bands, extending from Very Low Frequencies (VLF) to Very, Ultra, Super, and Extremely High Frequencies (EHF) and beyond. AM radio is located in the range between 300 and 3,000 kHz, known as the Medium Frequency band (MF). FM radio and VHF television (channels 2–13) are in the Very High Frequency band (VHF), from 30 to 300 MHz. The Ultra High Frequency band, from 300 to 3,000 MHz, is the location of UHF television (channels 14–69). Still higher frequencies are used for microwave relays and communication satellites.

The effective limitations on use of the radio spectrum are defined by (1) the propagation characteristics of the various frequencies, and (2) the level of interference, already discussed. Low frequency radio waves are best suited to long distance communications. In the lowest frequency bands the radio waves propagate primarily along the ground or water and follow the curvature of the earth. The attenuation of these "ground waves" generally increases with frequency; VLF waves may be propagated for thousands of miles, which makes them valuable for point-to-point communication.

Sky wave propagation is important up to the start of the VHF band. These radio waves tend to depart from the earth's surface and are reflected by the ionosphere, an electrically charged region of the atmosphere 35 to 250 miles above the earth. The amount of reflection depends on the level of daily solar activity, the time of day, the season, geographical location, the length of the signal path, and the angle at which the waves strike the ionosphere. The reflection of sky waves is much greater at night, when they may be transmitted over great distances. Above 30 MHz, radio waves tend to pierce the ionosphere rather than being reflected, and line of sight transmission becomes increasingly necessary. As frequency increases above 30 MHz, surface objects absorb radiation at an increasing rate until a clear unobstructed line of sight becomes necessary at 1 GHz. In the very highest frequencies, the waves are subject to substantial absorption by water vapor and oxygen in the atmosphere and cannot be used for communication.

Standard (AM) broadcasting propagates its waves by "amplitude modulation." The sound waves vary in power, producing variations in the height of the waves that are transmitted. The receiving unit decodes these height variations, reproducing the original sounds. AM transmissions occur in the MF band and thus have a long range primary service through ground waves, particularly near the lower end of the band. AM also can utilize sky waves to provide a secondary service at night.

FM broadcasting utilizes "frequency modulation" rather than "amplitude modulation." In this system the height of the wave is held constant but the frequency of the waves transmitted is varied. This type of broadcasting provides higher-quality service with less interference than does AM, but it serves smaller areas, since the waves of the VHF band do not follow the surface of the earth and are not reflected by the ionosphere. This also means that FM service is unaffected by skywave interference at night.

Television utilizes separate signals for the visual and the sound components. The picture is transmitted by amplitude modulation and the sound by frequency modulation. (Television uses an enormous amount of spectrum compared to radio. One VHF channel uses six mHz—six times more than the entire AM band.) Since the transmissions are either in the VHF or UHF bands, the range of the signal is short and television cannot utilize either long ground waves or sky waves.

B. ALLOCATION OF THE SPECTRUM

1. Introduction

The method of dividing the spectrum resource among prospective users is enormously complex and highly controversial. The general term "allocation policy" includes three separate but not always distinct processes, each of which involves both technical and nontechnical considerations. The allocation process is the division of the spectrum into blocks of frequencies to be used by specified services or users. Thus, the television service is allocated certain frequencies in the VHF and UHF bands, microwave users are allocated certain frequencies in the UHF and SHF bands, and so on. The second process, allotment, involves the distribution of spectrum rights within allocated bands to users in various geographical areas. The third process, assignment, denotes the choice among potential individual users of allocated and alloted channels or frequency bands. We usually refer to all three processes under the general label of "allocation policy."

Perhaps the most important consideration in formulating an allocation policy is the technical usability of the spectrum itself. Technical usability is dependent primarily on three factors: the propagation characteristics of each frequency range, interference problems and their resolution, and limitations imposed by the communications system itself, especially the transmitting and receiving equipment. In other words, it is dependent on the physics of radio waves, other users of the spectrum, and the technical state of the electronics industry.

Frequency characteristics themselves seldom pose significant problems, for although there are optimal frequency ranges for various services, these tend to be broad. Consequently, there is usually considerable flexibility in the initial choice of a frequency for a given service except for whatever priority is given to those already utilizing the space.

The problem of crowding in the broadcasting industry began early in the 1920s. The episode is recounted by Justice Frankfurter in his opinion for the Court in National Broadcasting Co. v. United States, 319 U.S. 190 (1943), a case to which we return later:

> Federal regulation of radio begins with the Wireless Ship Act of June 24, 1910, [ ] which forbade any steamer carrying or licensed to carry fifty or more persons to leave any American port unless equipped with efficient apparatus for radio communication, in charge of a skilled operator. The enforcement of this legislation was entrusted to the Secretary of Commerce and Labor, who was in charge of the administration of the marine navigation laws. But it was not until 1912, when the United States ratified the first international radio treaty, [ ], that the need for general regulation of radio communication became urgent. In order to fulfill our obligations under the treaty, Congress enacted the Radio Act of August 13, 1912, [ ]. This statute forbade the operation of radio apparatus without a license from the Secretary of Commerce and Labor; it also allocated certain frequencies for the use of the Government, and imposed restrictions upon the character of wave emissions, the transmission of distress signals, and the like.
>
> The enforcement of the Radio Act of 1912 presented no serious problems prior to the World War. Questions of interference arose only rarely because there were more than enough frequencies for all the stations then in existence. The war accelerated the development of the art, however, and in 1921 the first standard broadcast stations were established. They grew rapidly in number, and by 1923 there were several hundred such stations throughout the country. The Act of 1912 had not set aside any particular frequencies for the use of private broadcast stations; consequently, the Secretary of Commerce selected two frequencies, 750 and 833 kilocycles, and licensed all stations to operate upon one or the other of these channels. The number of stations increased so rapidly, however, and the situation became so chaotic, that the Secretary . . . established a policy of assigning specified frequencies to particular stations. The entire radio spectrum was divided into numerous bands, each allocated to a particular kind of service. The frequencies ranging from 550 to 1500 kilocycles (96 channels in all, since the channels were separated from each other by 10 kilocycles) were assigned to the standard broadcast stations. But the problems created by the enormously rapid development of radio were far from solved. The increase in the number of channels was not enough to take care of the constantly growing number of

stations. Since there were more stations than available frequencies, the Secretary of Commerce attempted to find room for everybody by limiting the power and the hours of operation of stations in order that several stations might use the same channel. The number of stations multiplied so rapidly, however, that by November, 1925, there were almost 600 stations in the country, and there were 175 applications for new stations. Every channel in the standard broadcast band was, by that time, already occupied by at least one station, and many by several. The new stations could be accommodated only by extending the standard broadcast band, at the expense of the other types of services, or by imposing still greater limitations upon time and power. The National Radio Conference which met in November, 1925, opposed both of these methods and called upon Congress to remedy the situation through legislation.

[During 1926, courts held that the Secretary of Commerce lacked the power to stem the tide, and his pleas for self-regulation went unheeded by the burgeoning new industry.]

From July, 1926, to February 23, 1927, when Congress enacted the Radio Act of 1927, [ ], almost 200 new stations went on the air. These new stations used any frequencies they desired, regardless of the interference thereby caused to others. Existing stations changed to other frequencies and increased their power and hours of operation at will. The result was confusion and chaos. With everybody on the air, nobody could be heard. . . .

2. THE FEDERAL COMMUNICATIONS COMMISSION

In 1927, Congress had no ability or time or desire to unravel the mess that had developed on the airwaves. The basic decision, in retrospect, was whether to decree a system of private ownership for the airwaves and allow the courts to unravel the matters through lawsuits invoking property law, to opt for outright public ownership, or to create an administrative body that would develop and enforce an allocation system to bring order from the chaos. Congress chose the last of these and created a five-member Federal Radio Commission to rationalize the radio spectrum and make allocations.

Congress had no specific idea how the Commission should proceed. It stated in § 303 simply that "Except as otherwise provided in this Act, the Commission from time to time, as public convenience, interest, or necessity requires shall . . . ." The list that followed included powers to assign bands of frequencies to the various classes of radio stations and assign individual frequencies; decide the times each station may operate; establish areas to be served by any station; regulate the apparatus used with respect to the sharpness of the transmissions; suspend licenses upon a showing that the licensee violated any statute or regulation; and require licensees to keep records.

Note that all these powers are conditioned on a showing that "public convenience, interest or necessity requires" them, a rather vague guideline. As we shall see, the Commission has rarely been barred from acting on the ground that the public interest did not authorize the particular regulation.

In 1934, the agency was expanded to seven members, given jurisdiction over telephone and telegraph communication as well, and renamed the Federal Communications Commission. In 1982, Congress voted to return to a five-member commission. Each member is now appointed by the President for a five-year term, subject to Senate confirmation. No more than three members may be from the same political party. The terms are staggered so that no more than one expires in any year. If a member resigns in the middle of a term, the new appointment is only for the unexpired portion of that term. One consequence is that many of those appointed do not have the independence of beginning with a seven-year term. The chairman, chosen by the President, is the chief executive officer and has the major administrative responsibilities including the setting of the agenda.

Of the several offices and bureaus that perform the agency's various functions, the most important for our purposes is the Mass Media Bureau (formed by the 1982 merger of the Broadcast Bureau and the Cable Bureau), which receives all applications for licenses, renewals and transfers. Under delegated authority from the Commission, the Bureau's staff is authorized to issue some licenses and renew others. In cases in which it has no such power, it may still recommend to the Commissioners which applications to grant and which to deny, thus acting as an advocate within the agency. In addition, complaints of violations of the fairness doctrine or of the equal opportunities provision of § 315 are processed through the Mass Media Bureau. A chart of the FCC's organization appears at p. 965, infra.

3. Radio Allocation

The Federal Communications Commission has the sole power to allocate the radio spectrum, to establish general standards of operations, and to license persons to use designated parts of the spectrum. Many services must be placed, but some critics of Commission policies charge undue reliance on the bloc allocation concept, which calls for allocating discrete frequency bands to classes of users essentially without regard to geographical location, and maintaining a relatively strict segregation among allocations. This can lead to such anomalous results as marine bands in Nebraska and forestry bands in New York City. These problems are exacerbated by the general administrative difficulty of changing an allocation once made: the start-up costs are so great and the capital investment is usually so heavy that there is a strong economic incentive not to move users from one frequency band to another. Thus, as new uses develop, they are allocated higher and higher frequencies, with little consideration of which frequencies are best suited technically for which services. For example, location of radio broadcasting in the AM band (535–1605 kHz) may be inefficient. Local broadcasting might be moved to the current FM band (88–108 MHz), which is much better suited technically to local radio, and long distance broadcasting might be moved to frequencies below 500 kHz to take advantage of the long distance ground wave propagation characteristics at those frequencies.

Another claim is that area coverage by broadcasting stations would require less spectrum if the Commission were to drop its so-called "local station" goal. High-powered stations in major urban centers could serve the entire country in only one-third the spectrum space presently used. Yet local stations are important; they are outlets for local news and local views, they serve local advertisers, and they provide such local services as weather reports (which might be critical in areas subject to flash flooding or sudden tornadoes or storms).

a. *AM Broadcasting.* AM broadcasting occupies slightly more than 1 MHz of spectrum in the Medium Frequency band between 535 kHz and 1605 kHz. This is now divided into 107 assignable channels, each with a bandwidth of 10 kHz. AM stations are divided into four major classes: Class I "clear channel" stations are high-power stations designed to provide primary (groundwave) service to a metropolitan area and its environs and secondary nighttime (skywave) service to an extended rural area. Class II stations also operate on clear channels but must usually avoid causing interference within the normally protected service areas of Class I or other Class II stations. Class III stations are medium-power and are designed to provide service primarily to larger cities and contiguous rural areas. Class IV stations are low-power and operate on local channels to provide service to a city or town and contiguous areas.

The Commission proceeded by establishing general engineering constraints, such as maximum interference standards, and by allocating each of the frequencies to a class of stations. Within these general constraints, the Commission adopted a first-come-first-served approach. An applicant who could find a promising community could apply for a license to serve that community if it could find a channel that would satisfy the various general constraints. An applicant had to show that it would not interfere excessively with the signals of existing stations nor expose too many of its new listeners to interference beyond certain acceptable limits.

Clear Channels. As noted earlier, because of the skywave phenomenon, powerful AM stations can be received at great distances at night. In the 1930s, an experiment permitted a Cincinnati station to broadcast at 500 kilowatts of power (500 kw). The experiment was terminated and a limit of 50 kw imposed for all stations. In the 1940s, with an estimated 20 million persons uncovered by local radio service at night, the FCC created a group of 25 powerful stations operating at 50 kw. Each station shared its daytime channel frequency with other stations around the country. But at sundown all the others left the air so that the channel was clear except for the powerful station, which could reach distant and remote areas of the country.

With the development of FM radio and a surge in interest in AM radio, more remote areas were served and the FCC began to doubt the clear-channel policy. After two decades of debate, the Commission acted decisively in 1980. The number of persons unserved by nighttime local radio was down to four million, and applicants were clamoring for space on the AM spectrum. The Commission decided to end the clear channel concept but to protect those stations from interference for a radius of 750 miles. This would still permit them to reach larger areas than ordinary stations but it would permit an additional 125 stations to broadcast at night.

Expanding the Band. A second way to increase the number of AM stations is to expand the part of the spectrum available for such broadcasting. This occurred in 1979, when the World Administrative Radio Conference (held once every 20 years) met and decided to increase the AM band in the western hemisphere so that it will run from 525 to 1705 kHz. Part will be used exclusively for AM radio; other parts will be shared, in a manner to be decided at Regional Administrative Radio Conferences. Regular use of the extended part of the band is unlikely to begin before late 1989.

b. *FM broadcasting.* FM broadcasting, which began around 1940, is located in the VHF band. It occupies the frequencies between 88 and 108 MHz, which are excellent for aural broadcast service and allow an effective range of 30 to 75 miles. That spectrum space is divided into 100 assignable channels, each 200 kHz wide. The lowest 20 channels are reserved for noncommercial educational stations; the remaining 80 are for commercial use.

Commercial FM channels are divided into several classes, ranging from those serving small towns to those powerful enough to serve cities and large surrounding areas. Commercial FM assignments are based on a Table of Assignments, in which communities are assigned a specific number of FM stations of specified power on specific channels. Licenses are given only for stations within the communities listed in the Table of Assignments or within a 15-mile radius—unless a formal application to change the table is granted.

In the late 1970s the demand for FM licenses increased dramatically as FM outlets started to overcome the traditional dominance of AM stations. The superior quality of the FM signal and the availability of stereo were the keys to this change. In an effort to meet the increased demand for FM stations, the FCC, in 1983, adopted a drop-in rulemaking allowing new FM stations to be started if they could avoid interfering with existing broadcasters.

In late 1984, the FCC approved a list of 689 locations, an initial step in the omnibus rulemaking process. Most of the new availabilities are Class A licenses in the southeast. The Commission initiated the application process in mid-1985, but is staggering the applications for different channels over the next three years.

Who are the likely beneficiaries of these attempts to increase the number of broadcast outlets? In radio, daytime AM broadcasters have argued forcefully that they deserve the opportunity to obtain full-time outlets. Meanwhile, the Commission has long been concerned that minority groups are woefully underrepresented among the owners of broadcast licenses. Although minority ownership does not necessarily mean that a station's programming will take minority tastes into special account, the FCC believes that minority ownership itself is important—and that the other may follow. (Other demonstrations of the FCC's concern about minorities in broadcasting are discussed elsewhere in this and later Chapters.) In the FM drop-in rulemaking, the Commission voted to give preference both to AM daytime broadcasters and to minority applicants.

4. Television Allocation

The first licensing of television stations in this country, in 1941, involved 18 channels. The first assignment plan was developed in 1945, based solely on the VHF channels. It involved the assignment of about 400 stations to 140 major market centers. Early comers quickly preempted the choice assignments. In 1948, because of unexpected problems with tropospheric interference and concern that the 1945 assignment plan could cause problems, the Commission ordered a freeze on channel assignments.

The freeze ended in 1952. The Commission rejected the idea of moving all television to the UHF band. Instead, the 12 VHF channels were retained and 70 new UHF channels were added. A Table of Assignments was created that placed 620 VHF and 1400 UHF stations around the country.

The Commission generated the Table of Assignments from its hierarchy of priorities: (1) to provide at least one television service to every part of the United States; (2) to provide each community with at least one television station; (3) to provide a choice of at least two television services to all parts of the country; (4) to provide each community with at least two television stations; and (5) to assign remaining channels to communities on the basis of population, geographical location, and the number of television services already available to that community. Note the emphasis on "local" outlets. Is this a sound hierarchy?

In making these assignments the Commission decided to "intermix" VHF and UHF channels as a single service in the same markets. Many observers warned that the newer UHF channels could not survive, but the Commission apparently believed that the demand for VHF would overflow into the UHF band. It also feared that failure to intermix would relegate UHF stations to markets overshadowed by VHF outlets in nearby metropolitan areas, or to remote rural areas. In any event, the Table of Assignments called for combined VHF and UHF channels in the following pattern: 6 to 10 for cities with population over 1,000,000; 4 to 6 for cities with 250,000 to 1,000,000; 2 to 4 for those with populations between 50,000 and 250,000; and 1 or 2 for communities under 50,000.

Because the Table tended to allot three VHF stations to most markets with only a few getting more than three, the three major networks could now program almost entirely through VHF affiliates. This gave them strong audience and advertiser support. Without adequate set penetration, UHF stations found it difficult if not impossible to secure advertising revenues and network affiliation. By the end of 1956, there were 395 VHF stations and 96 UHF stations on the air. Dumont, a fourth network, had collapsed. By 1960 only 75 (15 percent) of the 575 commercial stations on the air were UHF, even though 70 percent of the total channel assignments were UHF. (As late as 1971, 108 of the nation's 207 television markets, covering 58 percent of the nation's television households, could receive the three networks but no VHF independent stations.)

The Commission recognized that intermixture was not working. In 1956, while considering broader solutions such as the transfer of all television to the UHF band, the Commission adopted deintermixture as an "interim" measure in several communities, making them all-UHF. In 1961, the Commission planned to deintermix eight more communities. This time, however, the opposition from established VHF stations was formidable. After a fierce battle, Congress entered the fray and enacted a compromise: the All Channel Receiver Act of 1962. The Act authorized the Commission to order that all sets shipped in interstate commerce be capable of receiving both VHF and UHF signals. The VHF interests gave their support to the proposal in exchange for the Commission's indefinite suspension of deintermixture proposals. The Commission did require "all-channel" receivers and declared a moratorium on most pending deintermixture proposals. The Commission's regulation came too late for many of the UHF pioneers of the 1950s.

The continued underutilization of UHF spots led the FCC to begin to reallocate UHF frequencies to competing uses of the airwaves. Channels 70–83 have been reassigned for land mobile use. In some cities Channels 14 to 20 are being used by land mobile operators and are being shared elsewhere. In 1980, 63 percent of the television assignments were UHF. The vacancy rates were as follows: 61 of the 578 commercial VHFs; 266 of the 648 commercial UHFs; 23 of the 136 noncommercial VHFs; and 374 of the 570 noncommercial UHFs. In the top 100 markets vacancies existed on 86 UHF channels but on no commercial VHF. In the top 200 markets, the comparable figures were 176 and 6.

In addition to their intermixture problem, UHF stations are also more expensive to operate because it takes ten times as much power for a UHF transmitter to reach the same area as a VHF transmitter.

Because of the inferior wave-propagation qualities of UHF signals compared with VHF signals, UHF stations are permitted to operate at a power of 5,000 kw, compared with 100 or 316 kw for VHF stations. But the energy costs are so high that few UHF stations operate at maximum permitted power.

Since so many network programs, the most popular, are on VHF stations, viewers in intermixed communities have had little incentive to seek out UHF, even though by 1983, 96 percent of all homes with television could receive UHF. Until "click" dialing became common—in 1971 the FCC ordered it for all UHF receivers—some viewers trying to use UHF found it difficult to tune in the desired station.

During 1979, the future of UHF suddenly brightened.* Applicants sought stations that had gone begging since 1952; existing stations were sold at increasingly higher prices, and major broadcast owners became interested in UHF for the first time. The change in climate was apparently due to a variety of independent factors coming into play at the same time. Viewers were finding "click" dialing or newer digital dialing more attractive, and cable television was improving the reception of the UHF stations. Another temporary boost came from the introduction on UHF channels of Subscription Television (STV), an over-the-air pay television system in which viewers who wish to buy the service are offered decoders that unscramble the signal transmitted. Although little original programming was being provided, the prospect of uncut motion pictures without commercials was sufficiently attractive to make the venture appear profitable.

Now, however, the long-term viability of STV is in serious doubt. Hurt by increasing cable penetration, piracy of signals, and increasing interest in Multi-channel Multipoint Distribution Service (MMDS), discussed in Chapter XVII, the STV subscriber base has dropped from 1.4 million in 1981 to about 25,000 in 1986, and only two STV stations remain in operation.

A few UHF stations have become profitable as the result of developments in cable television. Because of changes in FCC rules governing cable systems, it is possible for a single television station to become, in effect, a network by supplying its programs by satellite to cable systems throughout the country. The operation of these "superstations" is described more extensively in the discussion of cable television in Chapter XVII.

New Television Outlets. In 1982, the FCC approved a new television service of perhaps as many as 4,000 low-power television (LPTV) stations throughout the country. These stations may operate at a power sufficient to reach viewers within a radius of 10 to 15 miles. It is

* The press caught the change in mood. Compare "UHF's Broadcasting Struggles: F.C.C. Help for Ailing Stations," N.Y. Times, Jan. 1, 1979, at 29, with "Picture Turns Bright for UHF: Stations Draw High Prices in Heated Bidding," N.Y. Times, Dec. 20, 1979, at D1.

up to the applicants to find spots on the VHF and UHF bands in which such stations will not interfere with existing stations.

LPTV operators are permitted to join together by satellite to set up networks. Neither the duopoly or one-to-a-market rules, which we will discuss in Chapter XVI, apply to LPTV. There is no limit on the number of LPTV licenses one entity can own. Programming restrictions are also minimal. The fairness doctrine and section 315 (see Chapter XV) apply only to licensee-originated programming.

In 1983, the Commission adopted a lottery procedure for initial licensing of LPTV to deal with the rush of applications. The backlog was estimated at 23,000 by 1985.

During this period, the Commission approved four controversial drop-ins on specific VHF channels in specific cities. These would be full-power stations that the Commission decided would provide enough new service to viewers to outweigh any loss of service to some persons in areas near existing stations on the same channel. The drop-in is required to reduce its power in the direction of existing stations, but it would be far more powerful than a low-power station. Challenges to these drop-ins were rejected in Springfield Television of Utah v. Federal Communications Commission, 710 F.2d 620, 53 R.R.2d 1139 (10th Cir. 1983).

The FCC is still considering a general VHF drop-in plan that could add up to 140 more drop-ins. Fear that the plan as originally proposed would not provide sufficient protection for existing television service has delayed action.

As of mid-1986, there are 10,002 radio stations on the air: 4,838 commercial AM, 3,917 commercial FM, and 1,247 noncommercial FM stations. There are a total of 1,262 television stations on the air: 547 commercial VHF, 415 commercial UHF, 113 noncommercial VHF, and 187 noncommercial UHF stations. In addition, there are 248 VHF and 160 UHF low-power stations.

5. Other Agencies

Several administrative agencies besides the FCC are important to the electronic mass media. Although some, such as the FTC, the NLRB, and the EEOC, function in broadcasting much as they function elsewhere, others have special roles.

a. The National Telecommunications and Information Administration (NTIA) was established in 1978 as part of the Commerce Department. NTIA is headed by an Undersecretary of Commerce. The reorganization that established NTIA combined within the new unit the former Office of Telecommunications Policy, which had been part of the Executive Office of the President, and the Office of Telecommunications of the Commerce Department. There had been concerns about excessive presidential influence on the Office of Telecommunications Policy during the Nixon administration.

NTIA's role is to formulate policies to support the development and growth of telecommunications, information, and related industries; to further the efficient development and use of telecommunications and information services; and to provide policy and management for federal use of the electromagnetic spectrum. In essence, NTIA is the telecommunications policy research department of the government. It does long-term studies into the effects of and need for telecommunications regulation. NTIA also advises the President on telecommunications policy issues.

b. The Copyright Royalty Tribunal (CRT) was created by the Copyright Act of 1976, which took effect in 1978. Among its duties is overseeing the compulsory licensing scheme governing cable retransmission of broadcast signals. Under this scheme, money is collected from cable systems and distributed to motion picture producers, program syndicators, broadcasters, sports teams, and others. We examine this licensing mechanism in Chapter XVII.

The Tribunal also makes determinations concerning the adjustment of copyright royalty rates for records and jukeboxes. In addition, it has established, and makes determinations concerning, terms and rates of royalty payments for the use by public broadcasting stations of published nondramatic compositions and pictorial, graphic, and sculptural works.

Factors involved in Tribunal decisions include existing economic conditions, impact on copyright owners and users, and maximizing the availability of creative works to the public.

c. International Agencies. Since radio and television signals obviously do not stop at international borders, neighboring countries' telecommunications concerns overlap. The problem is not a new one—Napoleon III called a conference in Paris in 1865 to take collective action to deal with technical standards, codes, and tariffs for telegraph. Out of that conference came the International Telegraph Union (ITU), which has been called "the first genuine international, intergovernmental organization to see the light of day."

Today's ITU is a direct descendant of the group formed in Paris, but its interests go far beyond the "electric telegraph." Much of the technology of today and tomorrow—communications satellites, sea cables, fiber optics, mass data storage and processing facilities—has and will have international implications. The constitution, statutes, administrative rules and regulations, and case law of any single country obviously cannot govern the international traffic messages, and international agreements are of increasing importance.

A reflection of that is the growth of the ITU. Based in Geneva, it has more than 150 member nations. Among its varied activities are the registration and management of frequencies and the collection and dissemination of massive amounts of information concerning telecommunications throughout the world.

The ITU Convention, which sets forth its rules of procedure, permits world and regional administrative conferences. A World Administrative Radio Conference (WARC) may have the authority to revise most of the regulations or may have jurisdiction only in a limited area. Such conferences in Geneva in 1959 and 1979 and in Atlantic City in 1974 had very broad jurisdiction. Examples of WARCs with more limited jurisdiction include the Broadcasting Satellite WARC, the WARC on the Aeronautical Mobile, and the WARC for Space Telecommunications. There are also Regional Administrative Radio Conferences (RARCs), which have jurisdiction over the three geographical regions. The western hemisphere is in region 2.

Chapter XIV

JUSTIFICATIONS FOR GOVERNMENT REGULATION

A. "PUBLIC INTEREST" AND "SCARCITY"

When the government entered broadcast regulation in 1927, the first question was which regulatory standard to use. Constitutional considerations did not loom large because, even for print media, the First Amendment doctrine in place in 1927 did little more than frown on "prior restraints." Recall that the Court had been confronting the World War I cases for less than a decade, discussion about clear-and-present danger was emerging slowly, and Near v. Minnesota was not decided until 1931.

Although Congress, in 1927, was confident that regulation was needed to remedy the chaos that had overtaken the airwaves, it was quite uncertain what standard to use for this new and uncharted activity. Apparently, the key phrases "public interest, convenience and necessity" and "public interest, convenience or necessity" were suggested by a young lawyer who had been loaned to the Senate by the Interstate Commerce Commission, because they were used in other federal statutes. N. Minow, Equal Time 8–9 (1964).

Judge Henry Friendly, in The Federal Administrative Agencies 54–55 (1962), comments on the standard:

> The only guideline supplied by Congress in the Communications Act of 1934 was "public convenience, interest, or necessity." The standard of public convenience and necessity introduced into the federal statute book by Transportation Act, 1920, conveyed a fair degree of meaning when the issue was whether new or duplicating railroad construction should be authorized or an existing line abandoned. It was to convey less when, as under the Motor Carrier Act of 1935, or the Civil Aeronautics Act of 1938, there would be the added issue of selecting the applicant to render a service found to be needed; but under those statutes there would usually be some demonstrable factors, such as, in air route cases, ability to render superior one-plane or one-carrier service because of junction of the new route with existing ones, lower costs due to other operations, or historical connection with the traffic, that ought to have enabled the agency to develop intelligible criteria for selection. The standard was almost drained of meaning under section 307 of the Communications Act, where the issue was almost never the need for broadcasting service but rather who should render it.

In using this standard to perform its first task, clearing the cluttered airwaves, the Federal Radio Commission announced in 1928 that "as between two broadcasting stations with otherwise equal claims for privileges, the station which has the longest record of continuous service has the superior right." On the other hand, if there was a "substantial disparity" in the services being offered by the stations, "the claim of priority must give way to the superior service." The Commission was soon evaluating service in terms of program content. Great Lakes Broadcasting Co., 3 F.R.C.Ann.Rep. 32 (1929), modified on other grounds 37 F.2d 993 (D.C.Cir.1930), certiorari dismissed 281 U.S. 706 (1930).

The other major section of the 1927 Act was a restatement of the antipathy toward "prior restraints." Section 29, reenacted as § 326 of the 1934 Act, provided in relevant part:

> Nothing in this Act shall be understood or construed to give the licensing authority the power of censorship over the radio communications or signals transmitted by any radio station, and no regulation or condition shall be promulgated or fixed by the licensing authority which shall interfere with the right of free speech by means of radio communication. . . .

When the FRC began denying renewals because of program content, the losers argued that the FRC was violating § 29. The argument was rejected in a case in which the licensee, a physician, used the station to sell his patent medicines for over an hour each day. In affirming the denial of renewal, KFKB Broadcasting Association v. Federal Radio Commission, 47 F.2d 670 (D.C.Cir.1931), the court denied that forbidden censorship had occurred:

> There has been no attempt on the part of the commission to subject any part of appellant's broadcasting matter to scrutiny prior to its release. In considering the question whether the public interest, convenience, or necessity will be served by a renewal of appellant's license, the commission has merely exercised its undoubted right to take note of appellant's past conduct, which is not censorship.

In Trinity Methodist Church, South v. Federal Radio Commission, 62 F.2d 850 (D.C.Cir.1932), certiorari denied 288 U.S. 599 (1933), the controlling figure was the minister of the church, Dr. Shuler, who regularly defamed government institutions and officials, and attacked labor groups and various religions. The Commission's denial of renewal was affirmed. The court concluded that the broadcasts "without facts to sustain or to justify them" might fairly be found not to be within the public interest:

> If it be considered that one in possession of a permit to broadcast in interstate commerce may, without let or hindrance from any source, use these facilities, reaching out, as they do, from one corner of the country to the other, to obstruct the administration of justice, offend the religious susceptibilities of thousands, inspire political distrust and civic discord, or offend youth and

innocence by the free use of words suggestive of sexual immorality, and be answerable for slander only at the instance of the one offended, then this great science, instead of a boon, will become a scourge and the nation a theater for the display of individual passions and the collusion of personal interests. This is neither censorship nor previous restraint, nor is it a whittling away of the rights guaranteed by the First Amendment, or an impairment of their free exercise. Appellant may continue to indulge his strictures upon the characters of men in public office. He may just as freely as ever criticize religious practices of which he does not approve. He may even indulge private malice or personal slander—subject, of course, to being required to answer for the abuse thereof—but he may not, as we think, demand, of right, the continued use of an instrumentality of commerce for such purposes, or any other, except in subordination to all reasonable rules and regulations Congress, acting through the Commission, may prescribe.

In 1934, Congress restructured the regulatory apparatus and replaced the FRC with the FCC. The basic regulatory standards, however, did not change. The FCC soon became concerned about the relationship between the individual licensees and the emerging networks. After conducting a study of business practices and ownership patterns of radio networks in 1941, the FCC concluded that the networks (CBS and NBC) exerted too much control over the broadcast industry through contractual rights to control local programming. To correct this situation, the Commission issued the Chain Broadcasting Regulations, which restricted the networks' ability to control affiliates' time and network ownership of stations. The goal was achieved by barring renewals to stations that entered contracts with a disfavored provision. NBC challenged the Commission's authority to adopt regulations controlling licensee behavior not related to technical and engineering matters. The Supreme Court rejected the challenge. National Broadcasting Co. v. United States, 319 U.S. 190 (1943).

The first claim was that Congress had not authorized the FCC to adopt these regulations. Section 303 of the Act provided that the Commission "as public interest, convenience, or necessity requires, shall . . . have authority to make special regulations applicable to radio stations engaged in chain broadcasting. . . . " NBC argued that the "public interest" language was to be read as limited to technical and engineering aspects of broadcasting—and that these were not the basis for the FCC's regulations in this case.

The Court noted that several sections of the Act authorized the FCC in furtherance of the "public interest, convenience, or necessity" to do such things as "study new uses for radio, . . . and generally encourage the larger and more effective use of radio in the public interest" and to provide a "fair, efficient and equitable distribution [of licenses] among the states." Building from these several grants of power, the Court rejected NBC's claim:

> The Act itself establishes that the Commission's powers are not limited to the engineering and technical aspects of regulation of radio communication. Yet we are asked to regard the Commission as a kind of traffic officer, policing the wave lengths to prevent stations from interfering with each other. But the Act does not restrict the Commission merely to supervision of the traffic. It puts upon the Commission the burden of determining the composition of that traffic. The facilities of radio are not large enough to accommodate all who wish to use them. Methods must be devised for choosing from among the many who apply. And since Congress itself could not do this, it committed the task to the Commission.
>
> . . .
>
> . . . If the criterion of "public interest" were limited to [technological matters], how could the Commission choose between two applicants for the same facilities, each of whom is financially and technically qualified to operate a station? Since the very inception of federal regulation of radio, comparative considerations as to the services to be rendered have governed the application of the standard of "public interest, convenience, or necessity." [ ]
>
> . . .
>
> . . . Suppose, for example, that a community can, because of physical limitations, be assigned only two stations. That community might be deprived of effective service in any one of several ways. More powerful stations in nearby cities might blanket out the signals of local stations so that they could not be heard at all. The stations might interfere with each other so that neither could be clearly heard. One station might dominate the other with the power of its signal. But the community could be deprived of good radio service in ways less crude. One man, financially and technically qualified, might apply for and obtain the licenses of both stations and present a single service over the two stations, thus wasting a frequency otherwise available to the area. The language of the Act does not withdraw such a situation from the licensing and regulatory powers of the Commission, and there is no evidence that Congress did not mean its broad language to carry the authority it expresses.

The Court then turned to NBC's constitutional claims. A vagueness claim was rejected in reliance on an earlier broadcasting case that had concluded that the phrase "is as concrete as the complicated factors for judgment in such a field of delegated authority permit." The phrase is not to be interpreted as giving the FCC "unlimited power." Finally, in a single paragraph, the Court rejected NBC's First Amendment claim:

> We come, finally, to an appeal to the First Amendment. The Regulations, even if valid in all other respects, must fall because

they abridge, say the appellants, their right of free speech. If that be so, it would follow that every person whose application for a license is denied by the Commission is thereby denied his constitutional right of free speech. Freedom of utterance is abridged to many who wish to use the limited facilities of radio. Unlike other modes of expression, it is subject to governmental regulation. Because it cannot be used by all, some who wish to use it must be denied. But Congress did not authorize the Commission to choose among applicants upon the basis of their political, economic or social views, or upon any other capricious basis. If it did, or if the Commission by these Regulations proposed a choice among applicants upon some such basis, the issue before us would be wholly different. The question here is simply whether the Commission, by announcing that it will refuse licenses to persons who engage in specified network practices (a basis for choice, which we hold is comprehended within the statutory criterion of "public interest"), is thereby denying such persons the constitutional right of free speech. The right of free speech does not include, however, the right to use the facilities of radio without a license. The licensing system established by Congress in the Communications Act of 1934 was a proper exercise of its power over commerce. The standard it provided for the licensing of stations was the "public interest, convenience, or necessity." Denial of a station license on that ground, if valid under the Act, is not a denial of free speech.

The Supreme Court did not again consider the FCC's power until 26 years later, in *Red Lion*. Since this case affects everything else that follows, we consider it at the outset of our exploration of broadcasting law. The case involves the personal attack part of the broader fairness

doctrine. It also refers to the "equal opportunities" rule (sometimes incorrectly called the "equal time" rule), which applies during election campaigns. Although we look at each of these doctrines in detail in Chapter XV, each is introduced now so that *Red Lion* can be fully appreciated.

As part of the 1927 Communications Act, Congress passed what is now § 315, which requires any broadcaster who sells or gives time for a candidate's use to treat all other candidates for the same office equally. This means that a broadcaster who sells 15 minutes of prime time to a candidate for Congress must be prepared to sell each opponent of that candidate the same amount of prime time at equivalent prices.

The fairness doctrine, on the other hand, was not imposed by Congress. Developed by the Commission on its own in the 1940s, the doctrine has two separate parts. One part requires the broadcaster to air issues that "are so critical or of such great public importance that it would be unreasonable for a licensee to ignore them completely." Much more attention has been paid to the second part of the doctrine: that if a broadcaster does cover a "controversial issue of public importance" it must take steps to assure that important contrasting views are also presented. These views may be presented by the licensee itself or by speakers chosen by the licensee.

The personal attack aspect of the fairness doctrine emerged in decisions in which the FCC ordered stations that, during a discussion of a controversial issue of public importance, had broadcast attacks on a person's character, to inform the person and offer him time to present his side. *Red Lion* arose from such a situation.

As *Red Lion* was being litigated, the FCC promulgated a rule to make the personal attack doctrine more precise and more readily enforceable. The personal attack rule was to apply when "during the presentation of views on a controversial issue of public importance, an attack is made upon the honesty, character, integrity, or like personal qualities of an identified person or group." Notice and an opportunity to respond (without charge if necessary) were required.

At the same time, the FCC promulgated a formal "political editorial" rule providing that when a licensee editorially endorsed a candidate for political office, other candidates for the same office were to be advised of the endorsement and be offered a reasonable opportunity (without charge if necessary) to respond. The same opportunity was to be extended to any candidate who was attacked in an editorial.

As soon as these two formal rules were announced, the Radio and Television News Directors Association (RTNDA) sued to have the rules declared unconstitutional. The Court of Appeals for the Seventh Circuit held that the rules violated the First Amendment. The Supreme Court heard both cases together and decided them in the same opinion.

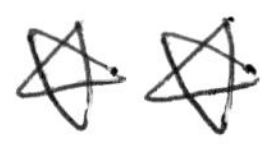

RED LION BROADCASTING CO. v. FEDERAL COMMUNICATIONS COMMISSION

Supreme Court of the United States, 1969.
395 U.S. 367, 89 S.Ct. 1794, 23 L.Ed.2d 371.

Noted, 15 S.D.L.Rev. 172, 58 Ky.L.J. 392.

MR. JUSTICE WHITE delivered the opinion of the Court.

The Federal Communications Commission has for many years imposed on radio and television broadcasters the requirement that discussion of public issues be presented on broadcast stations, and that each side of those issues must be given fair coverage. This is known as the fairness doctrine, which originated very early in the history of broadcasting and has maintained its present outlines for some time. It is an obligation whose content has been defined in a long series of FCC rulings in particular cases, and which is distinct from the statutory requirement of § 315 of the Communications Act that equal time be allotted all qualified candidates for public office. Two aspects of the fairness doctrine, relating to personal attacks in the context of controversial public issues and to political editorializing, were codified more precisely in the form of FCC regulations in 1967. The two cases before us now, which were decided separately below, challenge the constitutional and statutory bases of the doctrine and component rules. *Red Lion* involves the application of the fairness doctrine to a particular broadcast, and *RTNDA* arises as an action to review the FCC's 1967 promulgation of the personal attack and political editorializing regulations, which were laid down after the *Red Lion* litigation had begun.

I.

A.

The Red Lion Broadcasting Company is licensed to operate a Pennsylvania radio station, WGCB. On November 27, 1964, WGCB carried a 15-minute broadcast by the Reverend Billy James Hargis as part of a "Christian Crusade" series. A book by Fred J. Cook entitled "Goldwater—Extremist on the Right" was discussed by Hargis, who said that Cook had been fired by a newspaper for making false charges against city officials; that Cook had then worked for a Communist-affiliated publication; that he had defended Alger Hiss and attacked J. Edgar Hoover and the Central Intelligence Agency; and that he had now written a "bock to smear and destroy Barry Goldwater." When Cook heard of the broadcast he concluded that he had been personally attacked and demanded free reply time, which the station refused. After an exchange of letters among Cook, Red Lion, and the FCC, the FCC declared that the Hargis broadcast constituted a personal attack on Cook; that Red Lion had failed to meet its obligation under the fairness doctrine as expressed in Times-Mirror Broadcasting Co., 24 P & F Radio Reg. 404 (1962), to send a tape, transcript, or summary of the broadcast to Cook and offer him reply time; and that the station must provide reply time whether or not Cook would pay for it. On review in the Court of Appeals for the District of Columbia Circuit, the FCC's position was upheld as constitutional and otherwise proper. [ ]

B.

[The Court summarized the RTNDA's challenge of the rules.]

C.

Believing that the specific application of the fairness doctrine in *Red Lion,* and the promulgation of the regulations in *RTNDA,* are both authorized by Congress and enhance rather than abridge the freedoms of speech and press protected by the First Amendment, we hold them valid and constitutional, reversing the judgment below in *RTNDA* and affirming the judgment below in *Red Lion.*

II.

The history of the emergence of the fairness doctrine and of the related legislation shows that the Commission's action in the *Red Lion* case did not exceed its authority, and that in adopting the new regulations the Commission was implementing congressional policy rather than embarking on a frolic of its own.

A.

Before 1927, the allocation of frequencies was left entirely to the private sector, and the result was chaos. It quickly became apparent that broadcast frequencies constituted a scarce resource whose use could be regulated and rationalized only by the Government. Without government control, the medium would be of little use because of the cacophony of competing voices, none of which could be clearly and predictably heard. Consequently, the Federal Radio Commission was established to allocate frequencies among competing applicants in a manner responsive to the public "convenience, interest, or necessity."

Very shortly thereafter the Commission expressed its view that the "public interest requires ample play for the free and fair competition of opposing views, and the commission believes that the principle applies . . . to all discussions of issues of importance to the public." . . . After an extended period during which the licensee was obliged not only to cover and to cover fairly the views of others, but also to refrain from expressing his own personal views, Mayflower Broadcasting Corp., 8 F.C.C. 333 (1940), the latter limitation on the licensee was abandoned and the doctrine developed into its present form.

There is a twofold duty laid down by the FCC's decisions and described by the 1949 Report on Editorializing by Broadcast Licensees, 13 F.C.C. 1246 (1949). The broadcaster must give adequate coverage to public issues, [ ] and coverage must be fair in that it accurately reflects the opposing views. [ ] This must be done at the broadcaster's own expense if sponsorship is unavailable. [ ] Moreover, the duty must be met by programming obtained at the licensee's own initiative if available from no other source. . . .

. . . [The personal attack and political editorial doctrines and rules] differ from the general fairness requirement that issues be presented, and presented with coverage of competing views, in that the broadcaster does not have the option of presenting the attacked party's side himself or choosing a third party to represent that side. But insofar as there is an obligation of the broadcaster to see that both sides are presented, and insofar as that is an affirmative obligation, the personal attack doctrine and regulations do not differ from the preceding fairness doctrine. The simple fact that the attacked men or unendorsed candidates may respond themselves or through agents is not a critical distinction, and indeed, it is not unreasonable for the FCC to conclude that the objective of adequate presentation of all sides may best be served by allowing those most closely affected to make the response, rather than leaving the response in the hands of the station which has attacked their candidacies, endorsed their opponents, or carried a personal attack upon them.

B.

The statutory authority of the FCC to promulgate these regulations derives from the mandate to the "Commission from time to time, as public convenience, interest, or necessity requires" to promulgate "such rules and regulations and prescribe such restrictions and conditions . . . as may be necessary to carry out the provisions of this chapter . . . ." 47 U.S.C. § 303 and § 303(r). The Commission is specifically directed to consider the demands of the public interest in the course of granting licenses, [ ]; renewing them, [ ]; and modifying them. [ ] Moreover, the FCC has included among the conditions of the Red Lion license itself the requirement that operation of the station be carried out in the public interest, 47 U.S.C. § 309(h). This mandate to the FCC to assure that broadcasters operate in the public interest is a broad one, a power "not niggardly but expansive," National Broadcasting Co. v. United States, 319 U.S. 190, 219 (1943), whose validity we have long upheld. It is broad enough to encompass these regulations.

The fairness doctrine finds specific recognition in statutory form, is in part modeled on explicit statutory provisions relating to political candidates, and is approvingly reflected in legislative history.

In 1959 the Congress amended the statutory requirement of § 315 that equal time be accorded each political candidate to except certain appearances on news programs, but added that this constituted no exception *"from the obligation imposed upon them under this Act to operate in the public interest and to afford reasonable opportunity for the discussion of conflicting views on issues of public importance."* [ ] (emphasis added). This language makes it very plain that Congress, in 1959, announced that the phrase "public interest," which had been in the Act since 1927, imposed a duty on broadcasters to discuss both sides of controversial public issues. In other words, the amendment vindicated the FCC's general view that the fairness doctrine inhered in the public interest standard. Subsequent legislation declaring the intent of an earlier statute is entitled to great weight in statutory construction. And here this principle is given special force by the equally venerable principle that the construction of a statute by those charged with its execution should be followed unless there are compelling indications that it is wrong, especially when Congress has refused to alter the administrative construction. Here, the Congress has not just kept its silence by refusing to overturn the administrative construction, but has ratified it with positive legislation. . . .

The objectives of § 315 themselves could readily be circumvented but for the complementary fairness doctrine ratified by § 315. The section applies only to campaign appearances by candidates, and not by family, friends, campaign managers, or other supporters. Without the fairness doctrine, then, a licensee could ban all campaign appearances by candidates themselves from the air and proceed to deliver over his station entirely to the supporters of one slate of candidates, to the exclusion of all others. . . .

. . .

In light of the fact that the "public interest" in broadcasting clearly encompasses the presentation of vigorous debate of controversial issues of importance and concern to the public; the fact that the FCC has rested upon that language from its very inception a doctrine that these issues must be discussed, and fairly; and the fact that Congress has acknowledged that the analogous provisions of § 315 are not preclusive in this area, and knowingly preserved the FCC's complementary efforts, we think the fairness doctrine and its component personal attack and political editorializing regulations are a legitimate exercise of congressionally delegated authority. . . .

III.

The broadcasters challenge the fairness doctrine and its specific manifestations in the personal attack and political editorial rules on conventional First Amendment grounds, alleging that the rules abridge their freedom of speech and press. Their contention is that the First Amendment protects their desire to use their allotted frequencies continuously to broadcast whatever they choose, and to exclude whomever they choose from ever using that frequency. No man may be prevented from saying or publishing what he thinks, or from refusing in his speech or other utterances to give equal weight to the views of his opponents. This right, they say, applies equally to broadcasters.

A.

Although broadcasting is clearly a medium affected by a First Amendment interest, United States v. Paramount Pictures, Inc., 334 U.S. 131, 166, 68 S.Ct. 915, 933, 92 L.Ed. 1260 (1948), differences in the characteristics of new media justify differences in the First Amendment standards applied to them. [ ] For example, the ability of new technology to produce sounds more raucous than those of the human voice justifies restrictions on the sound level, and on the hours and places of use, of sound trucks so long as the restrictions are reasonable and applied without discrimination. [ ]

Just as the Government may limit the use of sound-amplifying equipment potentially so noisy that it drowns out civilized private speech, so may the Government limit the use of broadcast equipment. The right of free speech of a broadcaster, the user of a sound truck, or any other individual does not embrace a right to snuff out the free speech of others. Associated Press v. United States, 326 U.S. 1, 20, 65 S.Ct. 1416, 1424, 89 L.Ed. 2013 (1945).

When two people converse face to face, both should not speak at once if either is to be clearly understood. But the range of the human voice is so limited that there could be meaningful communications if half the people in the United States were talking and the other half listening. Just as clearly, half the people might publish and the other half read. But the reach of radio signals is incomparably greater than the range of the human voice and the problem of interference is a massive reality. The lack of know-how and equipment may keep many from the air, but only a tiny fraction of those with resources and intelligence can hope to communicate by radio at the same time if intelligible communication is to be had, even if the entire radio spectrum is utilized in the present state of commercially acceptable technology.

It was this fact, and the chaos which ensued from permitting anyone to use any frequency at whatever power level he wished, which made necessary the enactment of the Radio Act of 1927 and the Communications Act of 1934, as the Court has noted at length before. [*NBC*] It was this reality which at the very least necessitated first the division of the radio spectrum into portions reserved respectively for public broadcasting and for other important radio uses such as amateur operation, aircraft, police, defense, and navigation; and then the subdivision of each portion, and assignment of specific frequencies to individual users or groups of users. Beyond this, however, because the frequencies reserved for public broadcasting were limited in number, it was essential for the Government to tell some applicants that they could not broadcast at all because there was room for only a few.

Where there are substantially more individuals who want to broadcast than there are frequencies to allocate, it is idle to posit an unabridgeable First Amendment right to broadcast comparable to the right of every individual to speak, write, or publish. If 100 persons want broadcast licenses but there are only 10 frequencies to allocate, all of them may have the same "right" to a license; but if there is to be any effective communication by radio, only a few can be licensed and the rest must be barred from the airwaves. It would be strange if the First Amendment, aimed at protecting and furthering communications, prevented the Government from making radio communication possible by requiring licenses to broadcast and by limiting the number of licenses so as not to overcrowd the spectrum.

This has been the consistent view of the Court. . . .

By the same token, as far as the First Amendment is concerned those who are licensed stand no better than those to whom licenses are refused. A license permits broadcasting, but the licensee has no constitutional right to be the one who holds the license or to monopolize a radio frequency to the exclusion of his fellow citizens. There is nothing in the First Amendment which prevents the Government from requiring a licensee to share his frequency with others and to conduct himself as a proxy or fiduciary with obligations to present those views and voices which are representative of his community and which would otherwise, by necessity, be barred from the airwaves.

This is not to say that the First Amendment is irrelevant to public broadcasting. On the contrary, it has a major role to play as the

Congress itself recognized in § 326, which forbids FCC interference with "the right of free speech by means of radio communication." Because of the scarcity of radio frequencies, the Government is permitted to put restraints on licensees in favor of others whose views should be expressed on this unique medium. But the people as a whole retain their interest in free speech by radio and their collective right to have the medium function consistently with the ends and purposes of the First Amendment. It is the right of the viewers and listeners, not the right of the broadcasters, which is paramount. See FCC v. Sanders Bros. Radio Station, 309 U.S. 470, 475, 60 S.Ct. 693, 697, 84 L.Ed. 869 (1940); FCC v. Allentown Broadcasting Corp., 349 U.S. 358, 361–362, 75 S.Ct. 855, 857–858, 99 L.Ed. 1147 (1955); 2 Z. Chafee, Government and Mass Communications 546 (1947). It is the purpose of the First Amendment to preserve an uninhibited marketplace of ideas in which truth will ultimately prevail, rather than to countenance monopolization of that market, whether it be by the Government itself or a private licensee. Associated Press v. United States, 326 U.S. 1, 20, 65 S.Ct. 1416, 1424, 89 L.Ed. 2013 (1945); New York Times Co. v. Sullivan, 376 U.S. 254, 270, 84 S.Ct. 710, 720, 11 L.Ed.2d 686 (1964); Abrams v. United States, 250 U.S. 616, 630, 40 S.Ct. 17, 22, 63 L.Ed. 1173 (1919) (Holmes, J., dissenting). "[S]peech concerning public affairs is more than self-expression; it is the essence of self-government." Garrison v. Louisiana, 379 U.S. 64, 74–75, 85 S.Ct. 209, 216, 13 L.Ed.2d 125 (1964). See Brennan, The Supreme Court and the Meiklejohn Interpretation of the First Amendment, 79 Harv.L.Rev. 1 (1965). It is the right of the public to receive suitable access to social, political, esthetic, moral, and other ideas and experiences which is crucial here. That right may not constitutionally be abridged either by Congress or by the FCC.

B.

Rather than confer frequency monopolies on a relatively small number of licensees, in a Nation of 200,000,000, the Government could surely have decreed that each frequency should be shared among all or some of those who wish to use it, each being assigned a portion of the broadcast day or the broadcast week. The ruling and regulations at issue here do not go quite so far. They assert that under specified circumstances, a licensee must offer to make available a reasonable amount of broadcast time to those who have a view different from that which has already been expressed on his station. The expression of a political endorsement, or of a personal attack while dealing with a controversial public issue, simply triggers this time sharing. As we have said, the First Amendment confers no right on licensees to prevent others from broadcasting on "their" frequencies and no right to an unconditional monopoly of a scarce resource which the Government has denied others the right to use.

In terms of constitutional principle, and as enforced sharing of a scarce resource, the personal attack and political editorial rules are indistinguishable from the equal-time provision of § 315, a specific enactment of Congress requiring stations to set aside reply time under specified circumstances and to which the fairness doctrine and these constituent regulations are important complements. That provision, which has been part of the law since 1927, [ ], has been held valid by this Court as an obligation of the licensee relieving him of any power in any way to prevent or censor the broadcast, and thus insulating him from liability for defamation. The constitutionality of the statute under the First Amendment was unquestioned. Farmers Educ. & Coop. Union v. WDAY, 360 U.S. 525 (1959).

Nor can we say that it is inconsistent with the First Amendment goal of producing an informed public capable of conducting its own affairs to require a broadcaster to permit answers to personal attacks occurring in the course of discussing controversial issues, or to require that the political opponents of those endorsed by the station be given a chance to communicate with the public.[18] Otherwise, station owners and a few networks would have unfettered power to make time available only to the highest bidders, to communicate only their own views on public issues, people and candidates, and to permit on the air only those with whom they agreed. There is no sanctuary in the First Amendment for unlimited private censorship operating in a medium not open to all. "Freedom of the press from governmental interference under the First Amendment does not sanction repression of that freedom by private interests." Associated Press v. United States, 326 U.S. 1, 20, 65 S.Ct. 1416, 1425, 89 L.Ed. 2013 (1945).

C.

It is strenuously argued, however, that if political editorials or personal attacks will trigger an obligation in broadcasters to afford the opportunity for expression to speakers who need not pay for time and whose views are unpalatable to the licensees, then broadcasters will be irresistibly forced to self-censorship and their coverage of controversial public issues will be eliminated or at least rendered wholly ineffective. Such a result would indeed be a serious matter, for should licensees actually eliminate their coverage of controversial issues, the purposes of the doctrine would be stifled.

At this point, however, as the Federal Communications Commission has indicated, that possibility is at best speculative. The communications industry, and in particular the networks, have taken pains to present controversial issues in the past, and even now they do not assert that they intend to abandon their efforts in this regard. It would be better if the FCC's encouragement were never necessary to induce

18. The expression of views opposing those which broadcasters permit to be aired in the first place need not be confined solely to the broadcasters themselves as proxies. "Nor is it enough that he should hear the arguments of adversaries from his own teachers, presented as they state them, and accompanied by what they offer as refutations. That is not the way to do justice to the arguments, or bring them into real contact with his own mind. He must be able to hear them from persons who actually believe them; who defend them in earnest, and do their very utmost for them." J. Mill, On Liberty 32 (R. McCallum ed. 1947).

the broadcasters to meet their responsibility. And if experience with the administration of those doctrines indicates that they have the net effect of reducing rather than enhancing the volume and quality of coverage, there will be time enough to reconsider the constitutional implications. The fairness doctrine in the past has had no such overall effect.

That this will occur now seems unlikely, however, since if present licensees should suddenly prove timorous, the Commission is not powerless to insist that they give adequate and fair attention to public issues. It does not violate the First Amendment to treat licensees given the privilege of using scarce radio frequencies as proxies for the entire community, obligated to give suitable time and attention to matters of great public concern. To condition the granting or renewal of licenses on a willingness to present representative community views on controversial issues is consistent with the ends and purposes of those constitutional provisions forbidding the abridgment of freedom of speech and freedom of the press. Congress need not stand idly by and permit those with licenses to ignore the problems which beset the people or to exclude from the airways anything but their own views of fundamental questions. The statute, long administrative practice, and cases are to this effect.

Licenses to broadcast do not confer ownership of designated frequencies, but only the temporary privilege of using them. 47 U.S.C. § 301. . . . In determining how best to allocate frequencies, the Federal Radio Commission considered the needs of competing communities and the programs offered by competing stations to meet those needs; moreover, if needs or programs shifted, the Commission could alter its allocations to reflect those shifts. . . .

D.

The litigants embellish their First Amendment arguments with the contention that the regulations are so vague that their duties are impossible to discern. Of this point it is enough to say that, judging the validity of the regulations on their face as they are presented here, we cannot conclude that the FCC has been left a free hand to vindicate its own idiosyncratic conception of the public interest or of the requirements of free speech. . . .

We need not and do not now ratify every past and future decision by the FCC with regard to programming. There is no question here of the Commission's refusal to permit the broadcaster to carry a particular program or to publish his own views; of a discriminatory refusal to require the licensee to broadcast certain views which have been denied access to the airwaves; of government censorship of a particular program contrary to § 326; or of the official government view dominating public broadcasting. Such questions would raise more serious First Amendment issues. But we do hold that the Congress and the Commission do not violate the First Amendment when they require a radio or television station to give reply time to answer personal attacks and political editorials.

E.

It is argued that even if at one time the lack of available frequencies for all who wished to use them justified the Government's choice of those who would best serve the public interest by acting as proxy for those who would present differing views, or by giving the latter access directly to broadcast facilities, this condition no longer prevails so that continuing control is not justified. To this there are several answers.

Scarcity is not entirely a thing of the past. Advances in technology, such as microwave transmission, have led to more efficient utilization of the frequency spectrum, but uses for that spectrum have also grown apace. Portions of the spectrum must be reserved for vital uses unconnected with human communication, such as radio-navigational aids used by aircraft and vessels. Conflicts have even emerged between such vital functions as defense preparedness and experimentation in methods of averting midair collisions through radio warning devices. "Land mobile services" such as police, ambulance, fire department, public utility, and other communications systems have been occupying an increasingly crowded portion of the frequency spectrum and there are, apart from licensed amateur radio operators' equipment, 5,000,000 transmitters operated on the "citizens' band" which is also increasingly congested. Among the various uses for radio frequency space, including marine, aviation, amateur, military, and common carrier users, there are easily enough claimants to permit use of the whole with an even smaller allocation to broadcast radio and television uses than now exists.

Comparative hearings between competing applicants for broadcast spectrum space are by no means a thing of the past. The radio spectrum has become so congested that at times it has been necessary to suspend new applications. The very high frequency television spectrum is, in the country's major markets, almost entirely occupied, although space reserved for ultra high frequency television transmission, which is a relatively recent development as a commercially viable alternative, has not yet been completely filled.[25]

25. In a table prepared by the FCC on the basis of statistics current as of August 31, 1968, VHF and UHF channels allocated to and those available in the top 100 market areas for television are set forth:

Commercial

Market Areas	Channels Allocated		Channels On the Air, Authorized, or Applied for		Available Channels	
	VHF	UHF	VHF	UHF	VHF	UHF
Top 10	40	45	40	44	0	1
Top 50	157	163	157	136	0	27
Top 100	264	297	264	213	0	84

The rapidity with which technological advances succeed one another to create more efficient use of spectrum space on the one hand, and to create new uses for that space by ever growing numbers of people on the other, makes it unwise to speculate on the future allocation of that space. It is enough to say that the resource is one of considerable and growing importance whose scarcity impelled its regulation by an agency authorized by Congress. Nothing in this record, or in our own researches, convinces us that the resource is no longer one for which there are more immediate and potential uses than can be accommodated, and for which wise planning is essential. This does not mean, of course, that every possible wavelength must be occupied at every hour by some vital use in order to sustain the congressional judgment. The substantial capital investment required for many uses, in addition to the potentiality for confusion and interference inherent in any scheme for continuous kaleidoscopic reallocation of all available space may make this unfeasible. The allocation need not be made at such a breakneck pace that the objectives of the allocation are themselves imperiled.

Even where there are gaps in spectrum utilization, the fact remains that existing broadcasters have often attained their present position because of their initial government selection in competition with others before new technological advances opened new opportunities for further uses. Long experience in broadcasting, confirmed habits of listeners and viewers, network affiliation, and other advantages in program procurement give existing broadcasters a substantial advantage over new entrants, even where new entry is technologically possible. These advantages are the fruit of a preferred position conferred by the Government. Some present possibility for new entry by competing stations is not enough, in itself, to render unconstitutional the Government's effort to assure that a broadcaster's programming ranges widely enough to serve the public interest.

In view of the scarcity of broadcast frequencies, the Government's role in allocating those frequencies, and the legitimate claims of those unable without governmental assistance to gain access to those frequencies for expression of their views, we hold the regulations and ruling at issue here are both authorized by statute and constitutional.[28] The

25. Continued:

Noncommercial

Market Areas	Channels Reserved		Channels On the Air, Authorized, or Applied for		Available Channels	
	VHF	UHF	VHF	UHF	VHF	UHF
Top 10	7	17	7	16	0	1
Top 50	21	79	20	47	1	32
Top 100	35	138	34	69	1	69

1968 FCC Annual Report 132–135.

28. We need not deal with the argument that even if there is no longer a technological scarcity of frequencies limiting the number of broadcasters, there nevertheless is an economic scarcity in the sense that the Commission could or does

judgment of the Court of Appeals in *Red Lion* is affirmed and that in *RTNDA* reversed and the causes remanded for proceedings consistent with this opinion.

It is so ordered.

Not having heard oral argument in these cases, MR. JUSTICE DOUGLAS took no part in the Court's decision.

Notes and Questions

1. The Court states that the differences among media in their technical aspects warrant different regulatory treatment. In this section we are considering only those differences involving the use of the spectrum. In the next section we consider other distinctions.

2. The Court states that only a tiny fraction of those who want to broadcast are able to do so "even if the entire radio spectrum is utilized." Who decided how much of the spectrum to allocate to radio? Could a "niggardly or inefficient" allocation of radio space justify government exercise of its regulatory power? The notion of "scarcity" plays a major role in the Court's analysis. Consider what the term appears to mean in the following contexts: (a) all 3 FM outlets allocated to a community are being used; (b) of the 5 FM outlets allocated 3 are being used; (c) all 40 FM outlets allocated to an urban area are being used; (d) 7 of the 40 outlets are vacant. In considering these examples, would it matter how many television channels existed in each case, or whether the city had competing newspapers?

3. In terms of the Court's discussion of what "triggers . . . time sharing," is there a critical difference between (a) what the FCC did in *Red Lion*; (b) declaring that all stations in an area must go off the air between 6 p.m. and midnight every day so that a different broadcaster might use each frequency during that period; and (c) requiring all stations to have an open mike between 10 p.m. and midnight every Tuesday?

4. Does Justice White's next-to-last paragraph suggest that the reality of scarcity in the past will be enough to justify continuing regulation even if it were determined that no scarcity exists today?

5. Justice White says that "It is the right of the viewers and listeners, not the right of the broadcasters, which is paramount. [ ] It is the purpose of the First Amendment to preserve an uninhibited market-

limit entry to the broadcasting market on economic grounds and license no more stations than the market will support. Hence, it is said, the fairness doctrine or its equivalent is essential to satisfy the claims of those excluded and of the public generally. A related argument, which we also put aside, is that quite apart from scarcity of frequencies, technological or economic, Congress does not abridge freedom of speech or press by legislation directly or indirectly multiplying the voices and views presented to the public through time sharing, fairness doctrines, or other devices which limit or dissipate the power of those who sit astride the channels of communication with the general public. Cf. Citizen Pub. Co. v. United States, 394 U.S. 131 (1969).

place of ideas in which truth will ultimately prevail, rather than to countenance monopolization of that market, whether it be by the Government itself or a private licensee." What philosophical strands are being brought together here? Why don't these notions apply to print media as well?

6. When Justice White says that the "right" involved in the case belongs to "the public" and that this "right may not constitutionally be abridged either by Congress or by the FCC," is he suggesting that it might be unconstitutional for the government *not* to take steps to protect the public's ability to "receive suitable access to social, political, esthetic, moral and other ideas and experiences"?

7. There is reason to believe that Fred Cook's demand for reply time was part of a broader effort to use the fairness doctrine to soften attacks on the Kennedy administration by right-wing political commentators. The plan was to monitor right-wing programs and then to demand balance under the general fairness doctrine. F. Friendly, The Good Guys, The Bad Guys and the First Amendment (1976). If the result was that licensees cancelled several right-wing commentators, would that affect your reaction to the *Red Lion* decision? Did Cook misuse the doctrine?

8. In *Tornillo*, p. 433, supra, the Court did not mention *Red Lion*. Are the two cases consistent? Is it relevant that there are approximately four to five times as many radio stations in this country as there are daily newspapers? Or that fewer than thirty cities in the entire country have more than one daily newspaper? Is there a difference between technological and economic scarcity?

Abrams, In Defense of *Tornillo*, 86 Yale L.J. 361 (1976), argues that *Red Lion's* dismissal as "speculative" of the claim that the fairness doctrine would result in self-censorship is "utterly irreconcilable" with its conclusions in *Tornillo* that "under the operation of the Florida statute, political and electoral coverage would be blunted or reduced" and that a government-enforced right of access "inescapably dampens the vigor and limits variety of public debate." Do you agree?

The relationship between *Red Lion* and *Tornillo* is discussed at length in B. Schmidt, Jr., Freedom of the Press v. Public Access (1976).

9. The Supreme Court returned to the question of forced access again in Columbia Broadcasting System, Inc. v. Democratic National Committee, 412 U.S. 94 (1973), in which it decided that broadcasters were not obligated to accept paid advertisements from "responsible" individuals and groups. The majority relied upon *Red Lion*. (The case is discussed in detail at p. 739, infra.)

Justice Stewart, concurring separately, stated, "I agreed with the Court in *Red Lion*, although with considerable doubt, because I thought that that much Government regulation of program content was within the outer limits of First Amendment tolerability."

In another concurring opinion, Justice Douglas stated of *Red Lion:* "I did not participate in that decision and, with all respect, would not support it. The Fairness Doctrine has no place in our First Amendment regime." He argued that the uniqueness of the spectrum was "due to engineering and technical problems. But the press in a realistic sense is likewise not available to all. Small or 'underground' papers appear and disappear; and the weekly is an established institution. But the daily papers now established are unique in the sense that it would be virtually impossible for a competitor to enter the field due to the financial exigencies of this era. The result is that in practical terms the newspapers and magazines, like TV and radio, are available only to a selected few."

10. In Federal Communications Comm'n v. National Citizens Committee for Broadcasting, 436 U.S. 775, 3 Med.L.Rptr. 2409 (1978), the Court upheld regulations designed to bar newspapers from acquiring broadcast licenses in cities in which they publish papers. The case is considered in greater detail in Chapter XVI. We consider here the Court's unanimous response to an argument that the regulation violated the First Amendment rights of the newspapers—a claim pressed by the National Association of Broadcasters (NAB) and the American Newspaper Publishers Association (ANPA):

> Petitioners NAB and ANPA also argue that the regulations, though designed to further the First Amendment goal of achieving "the widest possible dissemination of information from diverse and antagonistic sources," Associated Press v. United States, 326 U.S., at 20, nevertheless violate the First Amendment rights of newspaper owners. We cannot agree, for this argument ignores the fundamental proposition that there is no "unabridgeable First Amendment right to broadcast comparable to the right of every individual to speak, write, or publish." [*Red Lion*].
>
> The physical limitations of the broadcast spectrum are well known. Because of problems of interference between broadcast signals, a finite number of frequencies can be used productively; this number is far exceeded by the number of persons wishing to broadcast to the public. In light of this physical scarcity, Government allocation and regulation of broadcast frequencies are essential, as we have often recognized. [ ] No one here questions the need for such allocation and regulation, and, given that need, we see nothing in the First Amendment to prevent the Commission from allocating licenses so as to promote the "public interest" in diversification of the mass communications media.
>
> NAB and ANPA contend, however, that it is inconsistent with the First Amendment to promote diversification by barring a newspaper owner from owning certain broadcasting stations. In support, they point to our statement in Buckley v. Valeo, 424 U.S. 1 (1976), to the effect that "government may [not] restrict the speech of some elements of our society in order to enhance the relative

voice of others," id., at 48–49. As *Buckley* also recognized, however, "'the broadcast media pose unique and special problems not present in the traditional free speech case.'" Id., at 50 n. 55, quoting Columbia Broadcasting System v. Democratic National Committee, 412 U.S., at 101. Thus efforts to "'enhanc[e] the volume and quality of coverage' of public issues" through regulation of broadcasting may be permissible where similar efforts to regulate the print media would not be.

11. In one case a licensee sought to transfer the license for a radio station that had been offering specialized programming to a new licensee who might not preserve the present program format. A group of listeners asked the FCC to consider in its transfer proceeding the impact of a change in format. The FCC, adhering to a Policy Statement it had issued on the subject, refused to do so on the ground that entertainment formats were not matters for FCC concern. The court of appeals reversed. The Supreme Court in turn upheld the FCC's position. Federal Communications Comm'n v. WNCN Listeners Guild, 450 U.S. 582 (1981), considered in Chapter XVI in connection with the licensing process. It is relevant here, however, because in a final paragraph the Court rejected the listener group's constitutional argument based on *Red Lion*:

> Although observing that the interests of the people as a whole were promoted by debate of public issues on the radio, we did not imply that the First Amendment grants individual listeners the right to have the Commission review the abandonment of their favorite entertainment programs. The Commission seeks to further the interests of the listening public as a whole by relying on market forces to promote diversity in radio entertainment formats and to satisfy the entertainment preferences of radio listeners. This policy does not conflict with the First Amendment.

12. In Federal Communications Comm'n v. League of Women Voters of California, 468 U.S. 364 (1984), a noncommercial broadcaster (Pacifica), a listener, and the League challenged the first sentence of § 399 of the Public Broadcasting Act of 1967, as amended in 1981, as unconstitutional. The section provided:

> No noncommercial educational broadcasting station which receives a grant from the Corporation for Public Broadcasting . . . may engage in editorializing. No noncommercial educational broadcasting station may support or oppose any candidate for public office.

The trial judge had declared the sentence unconstitutional and the case was on direct appeal. (Most of the justices thought the two sentences severable.) The first issue was whether to judge the statute under the "compelling" governmental interest standard adopted by the lower court or a less rigorous standard offered by the Commission because of the "special characteristic" of spectrum scarcity and the unique role of noncommercial broadcasting. Justice Brennan's opinion for the majority made several important observations in footnotes.

First, in note 11, the Court noted that the "prevailing rationale for broadcast regulation based on spectrum scarcity has come under increasing criticism in recent years. . . . We are not prepared, however, to reconsider our long-standing approach without some signal from Congress or the FCC that technological developments have advanced so far that some revision of the system of broadcast regulation may be required."

Second, the Court adverted to the view that the fairness doctrine "advanced the substantial governmental interest in ensuring balanced presentations of views in this limited medium and yet posed no threat" that a broadcaster would be denied permission to carry its own views. At this point, the Court inserted note 12, which recognized that a year earlier the FCC had observed that the fairness doctrine "impeded, rather than furthered, First Amendment objectives." The Court then asserted that "the Commission may . . . decide to modify or abandon these rules, and we express no view on the legality of either course. As we recognized in *Red Lion*, however, were it to be shown by the Commission that the fairness doctrine 'has the effect of reducing rather than enhancing' speech, we would then be forced to reconsider the constitutional basis of our decision in that case."

The Court concluded that "although the broadcasting industry plainly operates under restraints not imposed upon other media, the thrust of these restrictions has generally been to secure the public's First Amendment interest in receiving a balanced presentation of views on diverse matters of public concern. . . . But . . . these restrictions have been upheld only when we were satisfied that the restriction is narrowly tailored to further a substantial governmental interest, such as ensuring adequate and balanced coverage of public issues. [ ] Making that judgment requires a critical examination of the interests of the public and broadcasters in light of the particular circumstances of each case."

We return to the merits of the League case at p. 743, infra.

13. The FCC responded quickly to the Court's opening in the League case. In its Fairness Report (1985), 102 F.C.C.2d 143, 58 R.R.2d 1137 (1985), the FCC asserted that scarcity no longer existed and also concluded that the fairness doctrine did indeed impede rather than enhance speech. These positions are explored in greater detail at p. 818, infra.

14. The fairness doctrine is being challenged in two cases that are working their way through the courts. We explore these cases at p. 816, infra.

15. For a strong rejection of the scarcity rationale, see Telecommunications Research and Action Center v. Federal Communications Commission, No. 85–1160 (D.C.Cir.1986), in which Judges Bork, Scalia, and

MacKinnon assert that the line between print and broadcast media based on "scarcity" is "a distinction without a difference" and expressing the hope that the Supreme Court will either reject the distinction or come up with another that "is more usable than the present one." Since teletext uses broadcast frequencies, it must be regulated as a broadcast facility.

Broadcasting as Government Action. The issues raised in *NBC, Red Lion,* and *League of Women Voters* revolve around the broadcaster's claim that the First Amendment protects it from government regulation. Sometimes claims in the name of the First Amendment are made by private citizens against the media. In *Tornillo,* the citizen's claim failed. But a new element enters when such a claim is made against broadcast media. When government undertakes to provide a forum for discussion, or a street for parades, it must not discriminate among prospective users according to their views. Government must be neutral in such situations. If too many want to parade or use the forum, government might develop a lottery system or a queueing system; but it could not prefer those views it liked, or condition access to the forum on a promise to offer opposing arguments. Some have argued that this analysis applies to commercial broadcasters—that they are so closely related to, and regulated by, government that their actions are government action and thus bound by the neutrality principle.

The Supreme Court avoided this question in Columbia Broadcasting System, Inc. v. Democratic National Committee, supra. The DNC wanted to buy commercial time to urge financial support for the party, but had been thwarted in the past. Another group, Business Executives' Move for Vietnam Peace (BEM), sought to buy time to oppose the war in Vietnam, but was denied. The broadcasters' refusal to sell time was based on the claim that the proposed commercials did not fit into the type of programming the broadcasters wanted to present. The DNC and BEM asked the FCC to order the broadcasters to take their commercials—at least as long as they were accepting commercials from other sources. The FCC refused. The Supreme Court upheld the FCC's refusal.

The DNC–BEM claim that the broadcasters should be treated as government fragmented the Court and produced several extended opinions. Three justices (Chief Justice Burger and Justices Stewart and Rehnquist), met it head on and rejected it. They were concerned that the "concept of journalistic independence could not co-exist with a reading of the challenged conduct of the licensee as government action" because a government medium could not exercise editorial judgment as to what content should be carried or excluded.

Three other justices (Justices White, Blackmun, and Powell) concluded that even if government action were involved in the case, there was no violation of the groups' rights under the First Amendment. They therefore refused to pass on the question of government involvement.

Justice Douglas, the seventh concurring vote, did not decide the question. He noted that if a licensee is considered a federal agency it would "within limits of its time be bound to disseminate all views." If a licensee is not considered a federal agency "I fail to see how constitutionally we can treat TV and radio differently than we treat newspapers." He agreed that "The Commission has a duty to encourage a multitude of voices but only in a limited way, *viz.,* by preventing monopolistic practices and by promoting technological developments that will open up new channels. But censorship or editing or the screening by Government of what licensees may broadcast goes against the grain of the First Amendment."

In dissent, Justice Brennan, with whom Justice Marshall concurred, asserted:

> Thus, given the confluence of these various indicia of "governmental action"—including the public nature of the airwaves, the governmentally created preferred status of broadcasters, the extensive Government regulation of broadcast programming, and the specific governmental approval of the challenged policy—I can only conclude that the Government "has so far insinuated itself into a position" of participation in this policy that the absolute refusal of broadcast licensees to sell air time to groups or individuals wishing to speak out on controversial issues of public importance must be subjected to the restraints of the First Amendment.

The dissenters then concluded that the absolute refusal did violate the First Amendment. "The retention of such absolute control in the hands of a few Government licensees is inimical to the First Amendment, for vigorous, free debate can be attained only when members of the public have *some* opportunity to take the initiative and editorial control into their own hands." The emergence of broadcasting as "the public's prime source of information," has "made the soapbox orator and the leafleteer virtually obsolete."

The case, however, indicates only that the Constitution does not create a right of access to broadcasting. It does not address the question of whether Congress might enact a statute requiring broadcasters as a condition of their licenses to give a certain period of time per day or week to members of the public. How might those who wish to speak be selected? Would such a statute be valid? Might the Commission issue a rule to the same effect? Even if such a statute or rule would be constitutional, would it be sound? What does this controversy say about the "agenda-setting" role of media?

In the parts of the case yielding a majority view, Chief Justice Burger's opinion stated that "great weight" was to be given decisions of the FCC:

> That is not to say we "defer" to the judgment of Congress and the Commission on a constitutional question, or that we would hesitate to invoke the Constitution should we determine that the Commission has not fulfilled its task with appropriate sensitivity to the

interests in free expression. The point is, rather, that when we face a complex problem with many hard questions and few easy answers we do well to pay careful attention to how other branches of government have addressed the same problem.

Even if the First Amendment applied to this case, the groups were not entitled to access. One argument was that "[w]ith broadcasting, where the available means of communications are limited in both space and time, the admonition of Professor Alexander Meiklejohn that '[w]hat is essential is not that everyone shall speak, but that everything worth saying shall be said' is peculiarly appropriate." In the course of its discussion, the majority observed:

> Nor can we accept the view . . . that every potential speaker is "the best judge" of what the listening public ought to hear or indeed the best judge of the merits of his or her views. All journalistic tradition and experience is to the contrary. For better or worse, editing is what editors are for; and editing is selection and choice of material. That editors—newspaper or broadcast—can and do abuse this power is beyond doubt, but that is no reason to deny the discretion Congress provided. Calculated risks of abuse are taken in order to preserve higher values. The presence of these risks is nothing new; the authors of the Bill of Rights accepted the reality that these risks were evils for which there was no acceptable remedy other than a spirit of moderation and a sense of responsibility—and civility—on the part of those who exercise the guaranteed freedoms of expression.
>
> It was reasonable for Congress to conclude that the public interest in being informed requires periodic accountability on the part of those who are entrusted with the use of broadcast frequencies, scarce as they are. In the delicate balancing historically followed in the regulation of broadcasting Congress and the Commission could appropriately conclude that the allocation of journalistic priorities should be concentrated in the licensee rather than diffused among many. This policy gives the public some assurance that the broadcaster will be answerable if he fails to meet its legitimate needs. No such accountability attaches to the private individual, whose only qualification for using the broadcasting facility may be abundant funds and a point of view. To agree that debate on public issues should be "robust, and wide-open" does not mean that we should exchange "public trustee" broadcasting, with all its limitations, for a system of self-appointed editorial commentators.

Note that this discussion of the role of editors precedes *Tornillo* by a year. In the second paragraph the Court justifies complete broadcaster discretion to accept advertising on the ground that it may make it easier to hold the broadcaster "answerable" in case of a failure to meet the public's "legitimate needs." Are the two paragraphs consistent?

Recall the separate opinions of Justices Douglas and Stewart in CBS v. DNC, discussed in note 9.

B. "PUBLIC INTEREST" AND OTHER CONSIDERATIONS

We have just considered government regulation of broadcasting that is justified on the basis of "scarcity." Each form of communication raises separate questions, however, even when "scarcity" is not involved. As Justice Jackson put it in his concurring opinion in Kovacs v. Cooper, 336 U.S. 77, 97 (1949): "The moving picture screen, the radio, the newspaper, the handbill, the sound truck and the street corner orator have differing natures, values, abuses and dangers. Each, in my view, is a law unto itself. . . . "

Consider some other differences between print communication and broadcasting, such as the amounts of information transmitted because of the difference between the speed of reading and the slower speed of the speaking voice, the ability to skim a newspaper, and the ability to skip printed material that is not of interest. Do any of these differences justify the regulations discussed in *Red Lion?*

What of the fact that broadcasting is an inelastic medium? In order to carry a response by the subject of a personal attack, the 24-hour broadcaster must drop other programming. A newspaper can add pages. Does this difference justify greater regulation of one medium or the other?

Another difference between the print and electronic media is the greater impact of broadcasting in conveying certain types of information. The vivid field telecasts during the Vietnam War may have been a strong factor in the shift of public attitude against that war, beyond the potential of any print journalism. Another major difference is the role of sound in broadcasting, which makes it possible to use songs and jingles effectively in teaching and in advertising. In discussing the broadcasting of cigarette commercials, one court observed:

> Written messages are not communicated unless they are read, and reading requires an affirmative act. Broadcast messages, in contrast, are "in the air." In an age of omnipresent radio, there scarcely breathes a citizen who does not know some part of a leading cigarette jingle by heart. Similarly, an ordinary habitual television watcher can *avoid* these commercials only by frequently leaving the room, changing the channel, or doing some other such affirmative act. It is difficult to calculate the subliminal impact of this pervasive propaganda, which may be heard even if not listened to, but it may reasonably be thought greater than the impact of the written word.

Banzhaf v. Federal Communications Commission, 405 F.2d 1082, 1100–01 (D.C.Cir.1968), certiorari denied 396 U.S. 842 (1969), cited with approval in the DNC–BEM case. Does this suggest an additional basis for regulating some aspects of broadcasting?

Still other differences are explored in the following case.

FEDERAL COMMUNICATIONS COMMISSION v. PACIFICA FOUNDATION

Supreme Court of the United States, 1978.
438 U.S. 726, 98 S.Ct. 3026, 57 L.Ed.2d 1073, 3 Med.L.Rptr. 2553.

Noted, 27 Clev.St.L.Rev. 465, 1979 U.Ill.L.F. 969, 41 U.Pitt.L.Rev. 321, 32 Vand.L.Rev. 1377.

[George Carlin, a "satiric humorist," recorded a 12-minute monologue entitled "Filthy Words" before a live audience in a California theater. The theme was "the words you couldn't say on the public, ah, airwaves. . . . " Carlin then proposed a basic list: "The original seven words were shit, piss, fuck, cunt, cocksucker, motherfucker, and tits. Those are the ones that will curve your spine, grow hair on your hands and (laughter) maybe, even bring us, God help us, peace without honor (laughter) um, and a bourbon." Carlin then discussed "shit" and "fuck" at length, including the various phrases that use each word. The following passage gives some idea of the format:

> Now the word shit is okay for the man. At work you can say it like crazy. Mostly figuratively. Get that shit out of here, will ya? I don't want to see that shit anymore. I can't *cut* that shit, buddy. I've had that shit up to here. I think you're full of shit myself. (laughter) He don't know shit from Shinola. (laughter) You know that? (laughter) Always wondered how the Shinola people felt about that? (laughter) Hi, I'm the new man from Shinola. (laughter) Hi, how are ya? Nice to see ya. (laughter) How are ya? (laughter) Boy, I don't know whether to shit or wind my watch. (laughter) Guess I'll shit on my watch. (laughter) Oh, *the* shit is going to hit *de* fan. (laughter) Built like a brick shit-house. (laughter) Up, he's up shit's creek. (laughter) He's had it. (laughter) He hit me, I'm sorry. (laughter) Hot shit, holy shit, tough shit, eat shit. (laughter) Shit-eating grin. Uh, whoever thought of that was ill. (murmur laughter) He had a shit-eating grin! He had a what? (laughter) Shit on a stick. (laughter) Shit in a handbag. I always like that.

One Tuesday afternoon at 2:00 p.m., Pacifica's FM station in New York City played the monologue during a discussion about society's attitude toward language. The station warned that the monologue included language that might offend some listeners. A man who apparently did not hear the warning heard the broadcast while driving with his young son, and complained to the Commission. In response to an inquiry from the Commission, Pacifica responded that Carlin was a "significant social satirist" who "like Twain and Sahl before him, examines the language of ordinary people. . . ." Apparently, no one else complained about the broadcast.

The Commission ruled that Pacifica's action was subject to administrative sanction. Instead of imposing a formal sanction, it put the order in the file for possible use if subsequent complaints were received. The Commission asserted four reasons for treating broadcasting differently from other media: access by unsupervised children; since radio receivers are in the home, privacy interests are entitled to extra deference; unconsenting adults may tune in without a warning that offensive language is being used; and scarcity of spectrum space requires government to license in the public interest. Further facts are stated in the opinions.]

MR. JUSTICE STEVENS delivered the opinion of the Court (Parts I, II, III and IV–C) and an opinion in which THE CHIEF JUSTICE and MR. JUSTICE REHNQUIST joined (Parts IV–A and IV–B).

This case requires that we decide whether the Federal Communications Commission has any power to regulate a radio broadcast that is indecent but not obscene.

. . .

. . . [T]he Commission found a power to regulate indecent broadcasting in two statutes: 18 U.S.C. § 1464 which forbids the use of "any obscene, indecent, or profane language by means of radio communications," and 47 U.S.C. § 303(g), which requires the Commission to "encourage the larger and more effective use of radio in the public interest."

The Commission characterized the language used in the Carlin monologue as "patently offensive," though not necessarily obscene, and expressed the opinion that it should be regulated by principles analogous to those found in the law of nuisance where the "law generally speaks to *channeling* behavior more than actually prohibiting it. . . . [T]he concept of 'indecent' is intimately connected with the exposure of children to language that describes, in terms patently offensive as measured by contemporary community standards for the broadcast medium, sexual or excretory activities and organs at times of the day when there is a reasonable risk that children may be in the audience." 56 F.C.C.2d, at 98.[5]

. . .

After the order issued, the Commission was asked to clarify its opinion by ruling that the broadcast of indecent words as part of a live newscast would not be prohibited. . . . The Commission noted that its "declaratory order was issued in a specific factual context," and

5. Thus, the Commission suggested, if an offensive broadcast had literary, artistic, political, or scientific value, and were preceded by warnings, it might not be indecent in the late evening, but would be so during the day, when children are in the audience. [ ]

declined to comment on various hypothetical situations presented by the petition.[7]

The United States Court of Appeals for the District of Columbia Circuit reversed, with each of the three judges on the panel writing separately. . . .

Having granted the Commission's petition for certiorari, [ ] we must decide: (1) whether the scope of judicial review encompasses more than the Commission's determination that the monologue was indecent "as broadcast"; (2) whether the Commission's order was a form of censorship forbidden by § 326; (3) whether the broadcast was indecent within the meaning of § 1464; and (4) whether the order violates the First Amendment of the United States Constitution.

I

The general statements in the Commission's memorandum opinion do not change the character of its order. Its action was an adjudication. . . . The specific holding was carefully confined to the monologue "as broadcast."

. . . Accordingly, the focus of our review must be on the Commission's determination that the Carlin monologue was indecent as broadcast.

II

The relevant statutory questions are whether the Commission's action is forbidden "censorship" within the meaning of 47 U.S.C. § 326 and whether speech that concededly is not obscene may be restricted as "indecent" under the authority of 18 U.S.C. § 1464 (1976 ed.). The questions are not unrelated, for the two statutory provisions have a common origin. . . .

The prohibition against censorship unequivocally denies the Commission any power to edit proposed broadcasts in advance and to excise material considered inappropriate for the airwaves. The prohibition, however, has never been construed to deny the Commission the power to review the content of completed broadcasts in the performance of its regulatory duties.

. . .

There is nothing in the legislative history to contradict this conclusion. . . .

7. The Commission did, however comment:

" '[I]n some cases, public events likely to produce offensive speech are covered live, and there is no opportunity for journalistic editing.' Under these circumstances we believe that it would be inequitable for us to hold a licensee responsible for indecent language. . . . We trust that under such circumstances a licensee will exercise judgment, responsibility, and sensitivity to the community's needs, interests and tastes." [ ] . . .

We conclude, therefore, that § 326 does not limit the Commission's authority to impose sanctions on licensees who engage in obscene, indecent, or profane broadcasting.

III

The only other statutory question presented by this case is whether the afternoon broadcast of the "Filthy Words" monologue was indecent within the meaning of § 1464. Even that question is narrowly confined by the arguments of the parties.

The Commission identified several words that referred to excretory or sexual activities or organs, stated that the repetitive, deliberate use of those words in an afternoon broadcast when children are in the audience was patently offensive, and held that the broadcast was indecent. Pacifica takes issue with the Commission's definition of indecency, but does not dispute the Commission's preliminary determination that each of the components of its definition was present. Specifically, Pacifica does not quarrel with the conclusion that this afternoon broadcast was patently offensive. Pacifica's claim that the broadcast was not indecent within the meaning of the statute rests entirely on the absence of prurient appeal.

The plain language of the statute does not support Pacifica's argument. The words "obscene, indecent, or profane" are written in the disjunctive, implying that each has a separate meaning. Prurient appeal is an element of the obscene, but the normal definition of "indecent" merely refers to nonconformance with accepted standards of morality.

Pacifica argues, however, that this Court has construed the term "indecent" in related statutes to mean "obscene," as that term was defined in Miller v. California, 413 U.S. 15. [Pacifica relied on cases interpreting a statute regulating what matter might be mailed. Since the mail statute dealt with "printed matter enclosed in sealed envelopes" and § 1464 dealt with public broadcasts, it was "unrealistic to assume that Congress intended to impose precisely the same limitations on the dissemination of patently offensive matter by such different means."]

. . .

Because neither our prior decisions nor the language or history of § 1464 supports the conclusion that prurient appeal is an essential component of indecent language, we reject Pacifica's construction of the statute. When that construction is put to one side, there is no basis for disagreeing with the Commission's conclusion that indecent language was used in this broadcast.

IV

Pacifica makes two constitutional attacks on the Commission's order. First, it argues that the Commission's construction of the statutory language broadly encompasses so much constitutionally protected speech that reversal is required even if Pacifica's broadcast of the "Filthy Words" monologue is not itself protected by the First Amendment. Second, Pacifica argues that inasmuch as the recording is not obscene, the Constitution forbids any abridgment of the right to broadcast it on the radio.

A

The first argument fails because our review is limited to the question whether the Commission has the authority to proscribe this particular broadcast. As the Commission itself emphasized, its order was "issued in a specific factual context." [ ] That approach is appropriate for courts as well as the Commission when regulation of indecency is at stake, for indecency is largely a function of context—it cannot be adequately judged in the abstract.

. . .

It is true that the Commission's order may lead some broadcasters to censor themselves. At most, however, the Commission's definition of indecency will deter only the broadcasting of patently offensive references to excretory and sexual organs and activities.[18] While some of these references may be protected, they surely lie at the periphery of First Amendment concern. Cf. Bates v. State Bar of Arizona, 433 U.S. 350, 380–381. [ ] Young v. American Mini Theatres, Inc., 427 U.S. 50, 61. [ ] The danger dismissed so summarily in *Red Lion,* in contrast, was that broadcasters would respond to the vagueness of the regulations by refusing to present programs dealing with important social and political controversies. Invalidating any rule on the basis of its hypothetical application to situations not before the Court is "strong medicine" to be applied "sparingly and only as a last resort." Broadrick v. Oklahoma, 413 U.S. 601, 613. We decline to administer that medicine to preserve the vigor of patently offensive sexual and excretory speech.

B

When the issue is narrowed to the facts of this case, the question is whether the First Amendment denies government any power to restrict the public broadcast of indecent language in any circumstances.[19] For if the government has any such power, this was an appropriate occasion for its exercise.

The words of the Carlin monologue are unquestionably "speech" within the meaning of the First Amendment. It is equally clear that the Commission's objections to the broadcast were based in part on its

18. A requirement that indecent language be avoided will have its primary effect on the form, rather than the content, of serious communication. There are few, if any, thoughts that cannot be expressed by the use of less offensive language.

19. Pacifica's position [would mean that anything] that could be sold at a newsstand for private examination could be publicly displayed on television.

. . .

content. The order must therefore fall if, as Pacifica argues, the First Amendment prohibits all governmental regulation that depends on the content of speech. Our past cases demonstrate, however, that no such absolute rule is mandated by the Constitution.

The classic exposition of the proposition that both the content and the context of speech are critical elements of First Amendment analysis is Mr. Justice Holmes' statement for the Court in Schenck v. United States:

> "We admit that in many places and in ordinary times the defendants in saying all that was said in the circular would have been within their constitutional rights. But the character of every act depends upon the circumstances in which it is done. . . . The most stringent protection of free speech would not protect a man in falsely shouting fire in a theatre and causing a panic. It does not even protect a man from an injunction against uttering words that may have all the effect of force. . . . The question in every case is whether the words used are used in such circumstances and are of such a nature as to create a clear and present danger that they will bring about the substantive evils that Congress has a right to prevent."

Other distinctions based on content have been approved in the years since *Schenck*. The government may forbid speech calculated to provoke a fight. See Chaplinsky v. New Hampshire, 315 U.S. 568. It may pay heed to the " 'commonsense differences' between commercial speech and other varieties." Bates v. State Bar of Arizona, supra, 433 U.S., at 381. It may treat libels against private citizens more severely than libels against public officials. See [*Gertz*]. Obscenity may be wholly prohibited. Miller v. California, 413 U.S. 15. And only two Terms ago we refused to hold that a "statutory classification is unconstitutional because it is based on the content of communication protected by the First Amendment." Young v. American Mini Theatres, Inc., 427 U.S., at 50, 52.

The question in this case is whether a broadcast of patently offensive words dealing with sex and excretion may be regulated because of its content. Obscene materials have been denied the protection of the First Amendment because their content is so offensive to contemporary moral standards. Roth v. United States, 354 U.S. 476. But the fact that society may find speech offensive is not a sufficient reason for suppressing it. Indeed, if it is the speaker's opinion that gives offense, that consequence is a reason for according it constitutional protection. For it is a central tenet of the First Amendment that the government must remain neutral in the marketplace of ideas. If there were any reason to believe that the Commission's characterization of the Carlin monologue as offensive could be traced to its political content—or even to the fact that it satirized contemporary attitudes about four-letter words [22]—First Amendment protection might be required. But that is simply not this case. These words offend for the same reasons that obscenity offends.[23] Their place in the hierarchy of First Amendment values was aptly sketched by Mr. Justice Murphy when he said: "Such utterances are no essential part of any exposition of ideas, and are of such slight social value as a step to truth that any benefit that may be derived from them is clearly outweighed by the social interest in order and morality." Chaplinsky v. New Hampshire. [ ]

Although these words ordinarily lack literary, political, or scientific value, they are not entirely outside the protection of the First Amendment. Some uses of even the most offensive words are unquestionably protected. See, e.g., Hess v. Indiana, 414 U.S. 105. Indeed, we may assume, *arguendo,* that this monologue would be protected in other contexts. Nonetheless, the constitutional protection accorded to a communication containing such patently offensive sexual and excretory language need not be the same in every context. It is a characteristic of speech such as this that both its capacity to offend and its "social value," to use Mr. Justice Murphy's term, vary with the circumstances. Words that are commonplace in one setting are shocking in another. To paraphrase Mr. Justice Harlan, one occasion's lyric is another's vulgarity. Cf. Cohen v. California, 403 U.S. 15, 25.

In this case it is undisputed that the content of Pacifica's broadcast was "vulgar," "offensive," and "shocking." Because content of that character is not entitled to absolute constitutional protection under all circumstances, we must consider its context in order to determine whether the Commission's action was constitutionally permissible.

C

We have long recognized that each medium of expression presents special First Amendment problems. Joseph Burstyn, Inc. v. Wilson, 343 U.S. 495, 502–503. And of all forms of communication, it is broadcasting that has received the most limited First Amendment protection. Thus, although other speakers cannot be licensed except under laws that carefully define and narrow official discretion, a broadcaster may be deprived of his license and his forum if the

22. The monologue does present a point of view; it attempts to show that the words it uses are "harmless" and that our attitudes toward them are "essentially silly." [ ] The Commission objects, not to this point of view, but to the way in which it is expressed. The belief that these words are harmless does not necessarily confer a First Amendment privilege to use them while proselytizing, just as the conviction that obscenity is harmless does not license one to communicate that conviction by the indiscriminate distribution of an obscene leaflet.

23. The Commission stated: "Obnoxious, gutter language describing these matters has the effect of debasing and brutalizing human beings by reducing them to their mere bodily functions . . . ." 56 F.C.C.2d, at 98. Our society has a tradition of performing certain bodily functions in private, and of severely limiting the public exposure or discussion of such matters. Verbal or physical acts exposing those intimacies are offensive irrespective of any message that may accompany the exposure.

Commission decides that such an action would serve "the public interest, convenience, and necessity." Similarly, although the First Amendment protects newspaper publishers from being required to print the replies of those whom they criticize, [*Tornillo*], it affords no such protection to broadcasters; on the contrary, they must give free time to the victims of their criticism. [*Red Lion*].

The reasons for these distinctions are complex, but two have relevance to the present case. First, the broadcast media have established a uniquely pervasive presence in the lives of all Americans. Patently offensive, indecent material presented over the airwaves confronts the citizen, not only in public, but also in the privacy of the home, where the individual's right to be left alone plainly outweighs the First Amendment rights of an intruder. Rowan v. Post Office Dept., 397 U.S. 728. Because the broadcast audience is constantly tuning in and out, prior warnings cannot completely protect the listener or viewer from unexpected program content. To say that one may avoid further offense by turning off the radio when he hears indecent language is like saying that the remedy for an assault is to run away after the first blow. One may hang up on an indecent phone call, but that option does not give the caller a constitutional immunity or avoid a harm that has already taken place.[27]

Second, broadcasting is uniquely accessible to children, even those too young to read. Although Cohen's written message might have been incomprehensible to a first grader, Pacifica's broadcast could have enlarged a child's vocabulary in an instant. Other forms of offensive expression may be withheld from the young without restricting the expression at its source. Bookstores and motion picture theaters, for example, may be prohibited from making indecent material available to children. We held in Ginsberg v. New York, 390 U.S. 629, that the government's interest in the "well-being of its youth" and in supporting "parents' claim to authority in their own household" justified the regulation of otherwise protected expression.[28] The ease with which children may obtain access to broadcast material, coupled with the concerns recognized in *Ginsberg,* amply justify special treatment of indecent broadcasting.

It is appropriate, in conclusion, to emphasize the narrowness of our holding. This case does not involve a two-way radio conversation between a cab driver and a dispatcher, or a telecast of an Elizabethan comedy. We have not decided that an occasional expletive in either

27. Outside the home, the balance between the offensive speaker and the unwilling audience may sometimes tip in favor of the speaker, requiring the offended listener to turn away. See Erznoznik v. Jacksonville, 422 U.S. 205.

28. The Commission's action does not by any means reduce adults to hearing only what is fit for children. Cf. Butler v. Michigan, 352 U.S. 380, 383. Adults who feel the need may purchase tapes and records or go to theaters and nightclubs to hear these words. In fact, the Commission has not unequivocally closed even broadcasting to speech of this sort; whether broadcast audiences in the late evening contain so few children that playing this monologue would be permissible is an issue neither the Commission nor this Court has decided.

setting would justify any sanction or, indeed, that this broadcast would justify a criminal prosecution. The Commission's decision rested entirely on a nuisance rationale under which context is all-important. The concept requires consideration of a host of variables. The time of day was emphasized by the Commission. The content of the program in which the language is used will also affect the composition of the audience,[29] and differences between radio, television, and perhaps closed-circuit transmissions, may also be relevant. As Mr. Justice Sutherland wrote, a "nuisance may be merely a right thing in the wrong place,—like a pig in the parlor instead of the barnyard." Euclid v. Ambler Realty Co., 272 U.S. 365, 388. We simply hold that when the Commission finds that a pig has entered the parlor, the exercise of its regulatory power does not depend on proof that the pig is obscene.

The judgment of the Court of Appeals is reversed.

MR. JUSTICE POWELL, with whom MR. JUSTICE BLACKMUN joins, concurring.

I join Parts I, II, III, and IV–C of MR. JUSTICE STEVENS' opinion. . . .

. . . Because I do not subscribe to all that is said in Part IV, however, I state my views separately.

I

It is conceded that the monologue at issue here is not obscene in the constitutional sense. [ ] Nor, in this context, does its language constitute "fighting words" within the meaning of Chaplinsky v. New Hampshire [ ]. Some of the words used have been held protected by the First Amendment in other cases and contexts. [ ] I do not think Carlin, consistently with the First Amendment, could be punished for delivering the same monologue to a live audience composed of adults who, knowing what to expect, chose to attend his performance. See Brown v. Oklahoma, 408 U.S. 914 (1972) (POWELL, J., concurring in result). And I would assume that an adult could not constitutionally be prohibited from purchasing a recording or transcript of the monologue and playing or reading it in the privacy of his own home. Cf. Stanley v. Georgia, 394 U.S. 557 (1969).

But it also is true that the language employed is, to most people, vulgar and offensive. It was chosen specifically for this quality, and it was repeated over and over as a sort of verbal shock treatment. The Commission did not err in characterizing the narrow category of language used here as "patently offensive" to most people regardless of age.

29. Even a prime-time recitation of Geoffrey Chaucer's Miller's Tale would not be likely to command the attention of many children who are both old enough to understand and young enough to be adversely affected by passages such as: "And prively he caughte hire by the queynte." G. Chaucer, *The Miller's Tale* 1.3276 (c. 1386).

The issue, however, is whether the Commission may impose civil sanctions on a licensee radio station for broadcasting the monologue at two o'clock in the afternoon. The Commission's primary concern was to prevent the broadcast from reaching the ears of unsupervised children who were likely to be in the audience at that hour. In essence, the Commission sought to "channel" the monologue to hours when the fewest unsupervised children would be exposed to it. [ ] In my view, this consideration provides strong support for the Commission's holding.

The Court has recognized society's right to "adopt more stringent controls on communicative materials available to youths than on those available to adults." Erznoznik v. Jacksonville [ ]. This recognition stems in large part from the fact that "a child . . . is not possessed of that full capacity for individual choice which is the presupposition of First Amendment guarantees." Thus, children may not be able to protect themselves from speech which, although shocking to most adults, generally may be avoided by the unwilling through the exercise of choice. At the same time, such speech may have a deeper and more lasting negative effect on a child than on an adult. For these reasons, society may prevent the general dissemination of such speech to children, leaving to parents the decision as to what speech of this kind their children shall hear and repeat . . . . The Commission properly held that the speech from which society may attempt to shield its children is not limited to that which appeals to the youthful prurient interest. The language involved in this case is as potentially degrading and harmful to children as representations of many erotic acts.

In most instances, the dissemination of this kind of speech to children may be limited without also limiting willing adults' access to it. Sellers of printed and recorded matter and exhibitors of motion pictures and live performances may be required to shut their doors to children, but such a requirement has no effect on adults' access. See [*Ginsberg*]. The difficulty is that such a physical separation of the audience cannot be accomplished in the broadcast media. During most of the broadcast hours, both adults and unsupervised children are likely to be in the broadcast audience, and the broadcaster cannot reach willing adults without also reaching children. This, as the Court emphasizes, is one of the distinctions between the broadcast and other media to which we often have adverted as justifying a different treatment of the broadcast media for First Amendment purposes. [ ] In my view, the Commission was entitled to give substantial weight to this difference in reaching its decision in this case.

A second difference, not without relevance, is that broadcasting—unlike most other forms of communication—comes directly into the home, the one place where people ordinarily have the right not to be assaulted by uninvited and offensive sights and sounds. . . . The Commission also was entitled to give this factor appropriate weight in the circumstances of the instant case. This is not to say, however, that the Commission has an unrestricted license to decide what speech, protected in other media, may be banned from the airwaves in order to protect unwilling adults from momentary exposure to it in their homes.[2] Making the sensitive judgments required in these cases is not easy. But this responsibility has been reposed initially in the Commission, and its judgment is entitled to respect.

II

As the foregoing demonstrates, my views are generally in accord with what is said in Part IV–C of MR. JUSTICE STEVENS' opinion. [ ] I therefore join that portion of his opinion. I do not join Part IV–B, however, because I do not subscribe to the theory that the Justices of this Court are free generally to decide on the basis of its content which speech protected by the First Amendment is most "valuable" and hence deserving of the most protection, and which is less "valuable" and hence deserving of less protection. [ ][3] In my view, the result in this case does not turn on whether Carlin's monologue, viewed as a whole, or the words that constitute it, have more or less "value" than a candidate's campaign speech. This is a judgment for each person to make, not one for the judges to impose upon him.[4]

The result turns instead on the unique characteristics of the broadcast media, combined with society's right to protect its children from speech generally agreed to be inappropriate for their years, and with the interest of unwilling adults in not being assaulted by such offensive speech in their homes. Moreover, I doubt whether today's decision will prevent any adult who wishes to receive Carlin's message in Carlin's own words from doing so, and from making for himself a value judgment as to the merit of the message and words. . . .

MR. JUSTICE BRENNAN, with whom MR. JUSTICE MARSHALL joins, dissenting.

I agree with MR. JUSTICE STEWART that . . . the word "indecent" in 18 U.S.C. § 1464 must be construed to prohibit only obscene speech. [Although that would normally be sufficient], I find the Court's misapplication of fundamental First Amendment principles so patent, and its attempt to impose *its* notions of propriety on the whole of the American people so misguided, that I am unable to remain silent.

2. It is true that the radio listener quickly may tune out speech that is offensive to him. In addition, broadcasters may preface potentially offensive programs with warnings. But such warnings do not help the unsuspecting listener who tunes in at the middle of a program. In this respect, too, broadcasting appears to differ from books and records, which may carry warnings on their face, and from motion pictures and live performances, which may carry warnings on their marquees.

3. The Court has, however, created a limited exception to this rule in order to bring commercial speech within the protection of the First Amendment. See Ohralik v. Ohio State Bar Assn., 436 U.S. 447.

4. For much the same reason, I also do not join Part IV–A. I had not thought that the application *vel non* of overbreadth analysis should depend on the Court's judgment as to the value of the protected speech that might be deterred. . . .

I

For the second time in two years, see Young v. American Mini Theatres, the Court refuses to embrace the notion, completely antithetical to basic First Amendment values, that the degree of protection the First Amendment affords protected speech varies with the social value ascribed to that speech by five Members of this Court. . . . Yet . . . despite our unanimous agreement that the Carlin monologue is protected speech, a majority of the Court nevertheless finds that, on the facts of this case, the FCC is not constitutionally barred from imposing sanctions on Pacifica for its airing of the Carlin monologue. . . .

A

Without question, the privacy interests of an individual in his home are substantial and deserving of significant protection. In finding these interests sufficient to justify the content regulation of protected speech, however, the Court commits two errors. First, it misconceives the nature of the privacy interests involved where an individual voluntarily chooses to admit radio communications into his home. Second, it ignores the constitutionally protected interests of both those who wish to transmit and those who desire to receive broadcasts that many—including the FCC and this Court—might find offensive.

. . . I believe that an individual's actions in switching on and listening to communications transmitted over the public airways and directed to the public at large do not implicate fundamental privacy interests, even when engaged in within the home. Instead, because the radio is undeniably a public medium, these actions are more properly viewed as a decision to take part, if only as a listener, in an ongoing public discourse. [ ] Although an individual's decision to allow public radio communications into his home undoubtedly does not abrogate all of his privacy interests, the residual privacy interests he retains vis-à-vis the communication he voluntarily admits into his home are surely no greater than those of the people present in the corridor of the Los Angeles courthouse in *Cohen* who bore witness to the words "Fuck the Draft" emblazoned across Cohen's jacket. Their privacy interests were held insufficient to justify punishing Cohen for his offensive communication.

Even if an individual who voluntarily opens his home to radio communications retains privacy interests of sufficient moment to justify a ban on protected speech if those interests are "invaded in an essentially intolerable manner," [*Cohen*], the very fact that those interests are threatened only by a radio broadcast precludes any intolerable invasion of privacy; for unlike other intrusive modes of communication, such as sound trucks, "[t]he radio can be turned off," Lehman v. Shaker Heights, 418 U.S. 298, 302 (1974)—and with a minimum of effort. . . . Whatever the minimal discomfort suffered by a listener who inadvertently tunes into a program he finds offensive during the brief interval before he can simply extend his arm and switch stations or flick the "off" button, it is surely worth the candle to preserve the broadcaster's right to send, and the right of those interested to receive, a message entitled to full First Amendment protection. . . .

The Court's balance . . . permits majoritarian tastes completely to preclude a protected message from entering the homes of a receptive, unoffended minority. No decision of this Court supports such a result. . . .

B

Most parents will undoubtedly find understandable as well as commendable the Court's sympathy with the FCC's desire to prevent offensive broadcasts from reaching the ears of unsupervised children. Unfortunately, the facial appeal of this justification for radio censorship masks its constitutional insufficiency. . . .

Because the Carlin monologue is obviously not an erotic appeal to the prurient interests of children, the Court, for the first time, allows the government to prevent minors from gaining access to materials that are not obscene, and are therefore protected, as to them. . . . [3]

In concluding that the presence of children in the listening audience provides an adequate basis for the FCC to impose sanctions for Pacifica's broadcast of the Carlin monologue, the opinions of my BROTHER POWELL, and my BROTHER STEVENS, both stress the time-honored right of a parent to raise his child as he sees fit—a right this Court has consistently been vigilant to protect. [ ] Yet this principle supports a result directly contrary to that reached by the Court. . . . As surprising as it may be to individual Members of this Court, some parents may actually find Mr. Carlin's unabashed attitude towards the seven "dirty words" healthy, and deem it desirable to expose their children to the manner in which Mr. Carlin defuses the taboo surrounding the words. Such parents may constitute a minority of the American public, but the absence of great numbers willing to exercise the right to raise their children in this fashion does not alter the right's nature or its existence. Only the Court's regrettable decision does that.[4]

3. It may be that a narrowly drawn regulation prohibiting the use of offensive language on broadcasts directed specifically at younger children constitutes one of the "other legitimate proscription[s]" alluded to in *Erznoznik*. . . . To the extent that such a regulation is viewed as a regulation based on content, it marks the outermost limits to which content regulation is permissible.

4. The opinions of my Brothers POWELL and STEVENS rightly refrain from relying on the notion of "spectrum scarcity" to support their result. As Chief Judge Bazelon noted below, "although scarcity has justified *increasing* the diversity of speakers and speech, it has never been held to justify censorship." See [*Red Lion*]

C

As demonstrated above, neither of the factors relied on by both the opinion of my BROTHER POWELL and the opinion of my BROTHER STEVENS—the intrusive nature of radio and the presence of children in the listening audience—can, when taken on its own terms, support the FCC's disapproval of the Carlin monologue. These two asserted justifications are further plagued by a common failing: the lack of principled limits on their use as a basis for FCC censorship. No such limits come readily to mind, and neither of the opinions constituting the Court serve to clarify the extent to which the FCC may assert the privacy and children-in-the-audience rationales as justification for expunging from the airways protected communications the Commission finds offensive.

. . .

. . . [6]

II

. . .

. . . The idea that the content of a message and its potential impact on any who might receive it can be divorced from the words that are the vehicle for its expression is transparently fallacious. A given word may have a unique capacity to capsule an idea, evoke an emotion, or conjure up an image. Indeed, for those of us who place an appropriately high value on our cherished First Amendment rights, the word "censor" is such a word. Mr. Justice Harlan, speaking for the Court, recognized [this] when he warned that "we cannot indulge the facile assumption that one can forbid particular words without also running a substantial risk of suppressing ideas in the process." [*Cohen*]. Moreover, even if an alternative phrasing may communicate a speaker's abstract ideas as effectively as those words he is forbidden to use, it is doubtful that the sterilized message will convey the emotion that is an essential part of so many communications.

. . .

The Court apparently believes that the FCC's actions here can be analogized to the zoning ordinances upheld in Young v. American Mini Theatres, supra. For two reasons, it is wrong. First, the zoning ordinances found to pass constitutional muster in *Young* had valid goals other than the channeling of protected speech. [ ] No such goals are present here. Second, . . . the ordinances did not restrict the access of distributors or exhibitors to the market or impair the viewing public's access to the regulated material. [ ] Again, this is not the

6. Although ultimately dependent upon the outcome of review in this Court, the approach taken by my BROTHER STEVENS would not appear to tolerate the FCC's suppression of any speech, such as political speech, falling within the core area of First Amendment concern. The same, however, cannot be said of the approach taken by my BROTHER POWELL, which, on its face, permits the Commission to censor even political speech if it is sufficiently offensive to community standards. A result more contrary to rudimentary First Amendment principles is difficult to imagine.

situation here. Both those desiring to receive Carlin's message over the radio and those wishing to send it to them are prevented from doing so by the Commission's actions. Although, as my Brethren point out, Carlin's message may be disseminated or received by other means, this is of little consolation to those broadcasters and listeners who, for a host of reasons, not least among them financial, do not have access to, or cannot take advantage of, these other means.

. . .

III

[Justice Brennan found "equally disturbing" the Court's] depressing inability to appreciate that in our land of cultural pluralism, there are many who think, act, and talk differently from the Members of this Court, and who do not share their fragile sensibilities. It is only an acute ethnocentric myopia that enables the Court to approve the censorship of communications solely because of the words they contain.

. . . The words that the Court and the Commission find so unpalatable may be the stuff of everyday conversations in some, if not many, of the innumerable subcultures that compose this Nation. Academic research indicates that this is indeed the case. . . . Cf. Keefe v. Geanakos, 418 F.2d 359, 361 (CA1 1969) (finding the use of the word "motherfucker" commonplace among young radicals and protesters).

Today's decision will thus have its greatest impact on broadcasters desiring to reach, and listening audiences composed of, persons who do not share the Court's view as to which words or expressions are acceptable . . . .[8]

MR. JUSTICE STEWART, with whom MR. JUSTICE BRENNAN, MR. JUSTICE WHITE, and MR. JUSTICE MARSHALL join, dissenting.

. . .

. . . The Commission held, and the Court today agrees, that "indecent" is a broader concept than "obscene" as the latter term was defined in Miller v. California, [ ], because language can be "indecent" although it has social, political, or artistic value and lacks prurient appeal. [ ] . . . But this construction of § 1464, while perhaps plausible, is by no means compelled. To the contrary, I think that "indecent" should properly be read as meaning no more than "obscene." Since the Carlin monologue concededly was not "obscene," I believe that the Commission lacked statutory authority to ban it. Under this construction of the statute, it is unnecessary to address the difficult and important issue of the Commission's constitutional power

8. Under the approach taken by my BROTHER POWELL, the availability of broadcasts *about* groups whose members constitute such audiences might also be affected. Both news broadcasts about activities involving these groups and public affairs broadcasts about their concerns are apt to contain interviews, statements, or remarks by group leaders and members which may contain offensive language to an extent my BROTHER POWELL finds unacceptable.

to prohibit speech that would be constitutionally protected outside the context of electronic broadcasting.

. . .

Notes and Questions

1. Does any rationale command a majority?

2. In Columbia Broadcasting System, Inc. v. Democratic National Committee, p. 739, supra, one part of the Chief Justice's opinion for the Court relied on the view that "in a very real sense listeners and viewers constitute a 'captive audience.' [ ] [This] was recognized as early as 1924, when Commerce Secretary Hoover remarked . . . that 'the radio listener does not have the same option that the reader of publications has—to ignore advertising in which he is not interested—and he may resent its invasion of his set.' As the broadcast media became more pervasive in our society, the problem has become more acute. . . . It is no answer to say that because we tolerate pervasive commercial advertisements we can also live with its political counterparts."

Is this "captive audience" notion relevant in *Pacifica*?

3. Is the "risk" of tuning in an offensive program on radio or television any greater than the risk of encountering offensive language on a person's clothing on the streets? Or offensive films being shown on an outdoor movie screen that is visible from the street, as in Erznoznik v. City of Jacksonville, 422 U.S. 205 (1975)? If averting your eyes is an adequate remedy in those cases, why is turning off the radio or television set not adequate here? Is the fact that one may occur in the home relevant?

4. In some countries programs that might be found offensive carry a white dot in a corner of the picture so that a viewer can know the nature of the programming instantly. Would this solve our problems so far as television is concerned? Is there a similar technique that can be used for radio? Is it enough that certain stations become known as likely to present certain kinds of material offensive to some? What more could the licensee have done here to warn adult listeners? See Glasser and Jassem, Indecent Broadcasts and the Listener's Right of Privacy, 24 J. Broadcasting 285 (1985).

5. There are now devices available to control what programs can be seen on a television set. Using a weekly schedule, a parent can enter the day, time, channel number, and duration of time of each program the parent wishes a child to be able to see. If the set is turned to a channel that is not cleared for that day and time, no picture or sound will appear. A key permits changes to be made. If this were standard equipment on all television sets (and radios) might it meet some of the concerns in *Pacifica*?

6. It has long been agreed that Congress has preempted the matter of obscenity on radio and television—both of which are within "radio

communication." Thus, a state may not impose its movie censorship scheme on films shown on television.

7. In a clarification sought by the Radio and Television News Directors Association, the FCC announced that its decision in the Pacifica case was not meant to impinge on the coverage of news events in which offensive speech is sometimes uttered without a chance for editing: "Under these circumstances we believe that it would be inequitable for us to hold a licensee responsible for indecent language." Pacifica Foundation, 59 F.C.C.2d 892, 36 R.R.2d 1008 (1976). What if there is time for editing the dialogue but to do so would change the impact of the event? Can this be handled by an announcer who says "At this point the speaker launched into a stream of obscenities"?

Vice President Nelson Rockefeller used a finger gesture generally considered "indecent" when replying in kind to a heckler during a campaign rally. Most newspapers ran the photograph, but some did not. Would the decision be different for television stations? Are the considerations different for the 6 P.M. and the 11 P.M. news? Does the fact that it was in the course of a live news event make a difference?

8. Shortly after *Pacifica,* the Commission rejected a petition to deny renewal to a television station. The petitioners contended that the station had broadcast programs containing obscenities and had carried programs with unacceptable themes, such as a Masterpiece Theater episode that was said to approve of adultery. The Commission stated that its role in reviewing programs at renewal time "is and must be limited to determining whether the licensee's *overall* programming has served its service area, and not whether a particular program is 'appropriate' for broadcast." Nor can the subjective views of groups of listeners be considered.

The Pacifica case afforded "no general prerogative to intervene in any case where words similar or identical to those in *Pacifica* are broadcast over a licensed radio or television station. We intend strictly to observe the narrowness of the *Pacifica* holding." The FCC noted that in *Pacifica,* it had stressed the "repetitive occurrence" of the words and that Justice Powell had stressed the same feature in his opinion. "It was certainly not our intent . . . to inhibit coverage of diverse and controversial subjects by licensees, whether in news and public affairs or in dramatic or other programming contexts." WGBH Educational Foundation, 69 F.C.C.2d 1250, 43 R.R.2d 1436 (1978).

9. Recall the refusal of the Supreme Court to declare unconstitutional all motion picture censorship. Might the Court be concerned about the explicit and vivid depiction of sexual or violent episodes—and fear the impact of the medium on viewers more than it fears the printed page in such circumstances? Might such a concern with motion pictures apply to television? Recall that 47 U.S.C. § 326 bans the Commission from "censorship" of programming.

10. Some are concerned that a person who knows that he is appearing on television may alter his behavior because of it. This concern is most

apparent in the issue of television in courtrooms. As we have seen, p. 640, supra, the Supreme Court has ruled that such televising does not per se invalidate a criminal trial. Nonetheless, might states decide to prohibit television coverage of criminal trials for fear that witnesses, jurors, attorneys, the judge, or the defendant might behave in a way that will distort the trial process?

11. From a different perspective some have asserted that the televising of trials would not be desirable. One analyst of television violence argues that if real trials are telecast, the result will not be to educate the public. "Once in the courtroom, TV controls the message." Trials will be "picked and edited to fit and confirm [the Perry Mason] ritual." A trial must proceed as "independently as possible from conventional moral pressures and popular clamor. Televising trials can only erode judges' ability to do justice in each case." Television "is not neutral. It presents a coherent world of images and messages serving its own institutional interests. Plugging courtrooms into the TV system can make them appendages of that system." Gerbner, It's 11:30. And Heeeeere's Justice, N.Y. Times, Apr. 23, 1980, at A27.

12. Columnist Tom Wicker wrote that when four Republican candidates for President debated in Chicago in 1980, most in the live audience thought that Ronald Reagan had been the winner, in large part because of his "relaxed and witty performance." But many experienced political reporters who had watched the debate on television thought that John Anderson had won. They said that Anderson, who was being attacked by the other three speakers, had appeared to defend himself well and had profited from the concentration of attention, while Reagan, "who took the least part in the attack, had seldom been on camera."

Wicker observed that the impact of television had made it the principal instrument of American politics. Its ability to create illusions "cannot really be 'reformed.' Its use might be limited, or differently controlled and financed, but its 'impact' is here to stay and will always be open to manipulation. And in politics, as at the Oscar show, it's the illusion, the version on the screen, that matters." Wicker, How Pseudo The Event?, N.Y. Times, Apr. 18, 1980, at 31.

13. In CBS, Inc. v. Federal Communications Comm'n, 453 U.S. 367, 7 Med.L.Rptr. 1563 (1981), the Carter-Mondale Presidential Committee, in October, 1979, requested 30 minutes of prime time on one of four days in early December. The request to buy time, addressed to all three commercial networks, stated that several candidates had already declared for the Presidential nomination in 1980 and that delegates to conventions were being selected beginning in January. Each network rejected the request. CBS asserted that several candidates had already declared and that sale of prime time to the Carter Committee would obligate the network under § 315 to treat other Democratic aspirants equally. ABC responded that it had not yet decided when to begin selling time for the 1980 Presidential campaign, though it subsequently

stated that time would be sold starting in January, 1980. NBC responded that December was too early.

In response to a complaint from the Carter Committee, the FCC held, 4–3, that the networks had violated § 312(a)(7), which provides that the FCC may revoke a broadcaster's license for "willful or repeated failure to allow reasonable access to or to permit purchase of reasonable amounts of time for the use of a broadcasting station by a legally qualified candidate for Federal elective office on behalf of his candidacy."

The court of appeals affirmed; so did the Supreme Court, by a vote of 6–3. After rejecting claims that Congress had not authorized the FCC's action and other statutory and administrative arguments (which are considered in Chapter XV), the Court, in an opinion by Chief Justice Burger, rejected attacks on the statute's constitutionality:

> Finally, petitioners assert that § 312(a)(7) as implemented by the Commission violates the First Amendment rights of broadcasters by unduly circumscribing their editorial discretion. . . . Petitioners argue that the Commission's interpretation of § 312(a)(7)'s access requirement disrupts the "delicate balanc[e]" that broadcast regulation must achieve. We disagree.
>
> A licensed broadcaster is "granted the free and exclusive use of a limited and valuable part of the public domain; when he accepts that franchise it is burdened by enforceable public obligations." Office of Communication of the United Church of Christ v. FCC, 359 F.2d 994, 1003 (1966). This Court has noted the limits on a broadcast license:
>
> > "A license permits broadcasting, but the licensee has no constitutional right to be the one who holds the license or to monopolize a . . . frequency to the exclusion of his fellow citizens. There is nothing in the First Amendment which prevents the Government from requiring a licensee to share his frequency with others . . . ." [*Red Lion*].
>
> See also FCC v. National Citizens Comm. for Broadcasting, 436 U.S. 775, 799–800 (1978). Although the broadcasting industry is entitled under the First Amendment to exercise "the widest journalistic freedom consistent with its public [duties]," [CBS, Inc. v. DNC], the Court has made clear that:
>
> > "*It is the right of the viewers and listeners, not the right of the broadcasters which is paramount.* It is the purpose of the First Amendment to preserve an uninhibited marketplace of ideas in which truth will ultimately prevail, rather than to countenance monopolization of that market . . . . It is the right of the public to receive suitable access to social, political, esthetic, moral, and other ideas and experiences which is crucial here." [*Red Lion*] (emphasis added).

The First Amendment interests of candidates and voters, as well as broadcasters, are implicated by § 312(a)(7). We have recognized that "it is of particular importance that candidates have the . . . opportunity to make their views known so that the electorate may intelligently evaluate the candidates' personal qualities and their positions on vital public issues before choosing among them on election day." [Buckley v. Valeo]. [ ] Indeed, "speech concerning public affairs is . . . the essence of self-government." [Garrison v. Louisiana] The First Amendment "has its fullest and most urgent application precisely to the conduct of campaigns for political office." [Monitor Patriot Co. v. Roy] Section 312(a)(7) thus makes a significant contribution to freedom of expression by enhancing the ability of candidates to present, and the public to receive, information necessary for the effective operation of the democratic process.

Petitioners are correct that the Court has never approved a *general* right of access to the media. [ ] Nor do we do so today. Section 312(a)(7) creates a *limited* right to "reasonable" access that pertains only to legally qualified federal candidates and may be invoked by them only for the purpose of advancing their candidacies once a campaign has commenced. The Commission has stated that, in enforcing the statute, it will "provide leeway to broadcasters and not merely attempt *de novo* to determine the reasonableness of their judgments . . . ." If broadcasters have considered the relevant factors in good faith, the Commission will uphold their decisions. See 629 F.2d, at 25. Further, § 312(a)(7) does not impair the discretion of broadcasters to present their views on any issue or to carry any particular type of programming.

Section 312(a)(7) represents an effort by Congress to assure that an important resource—the airwaves—will be used in the public interest. We hold that the statutory right of access, as defined by the Commission and applied in these cases, properly balances the First Amendment rights of federal candidates, the public, and broadcasters.

14. If no reasons for different treatment of broadcast and print media are found, must we decide which one to treat like the other, or create a different level of protection for both groups? Another approach might be to take advantage of the existing legal differences. Professor Bollinger has suggested that society benefits from having a printed press that is exceptionally free under cases like *Tornillo,* while at the same time having another major medium obligated to be responsible and to allow access in certain situations. As Bollinger put it, "the very similarity of the two major branches of the mass media provides a rationale for treating them differently." Bollinger, Freedom of the Press and Public Access: Towards a Theory of Partial Regulation of the Mass Media, 75 Mich.L.Rev. 1 (1976). See also, Nimetz, Controlling the Content of Print and Broadcast, 58 S.Cal.L.Rev. 1349 (1985).

C. NONCOMMERCIAL BROADCASTING

---

1. INTRODUCTION

Most of our attention so far has been devoted to commercial broadcasting. Most of the litigation and regulation has involved commercial broadcasters, and, in terms of viewers, commercial broadcasting dominates the scene. But it is not the only part. AM broadcasting developed too early for the Commission to be able to reserve spots for noncommercial educational stations. In allocating FM and television, however, the Commission was able to plan in advance and reserved certain spots for educational broadcasters. These are usually operated by academic institutions, by governmental groups, or by groups organized by private citizens.

An academic institution may operate a station only in a community in which it has a bona fide full-time school; private and governmental organizations may qualify for stations in any community as long as they demonstrate an educational goal and a commitment to the advancement of an educational program. A station run by a sectarian academic institution may be eligible for a reserved educational spot in the community in which the school is located. If an organization's central purpose is religious, it is not eligible for a reserved channel. We will return to the issue of religious broadcasting later in this Chapter.

Although many of the Commission's rules apply equally to commercial and noncommercial licensees, we shall discover that there are some differences. The development and structure of noncommercial broadcasting are considered in the following case.

ACCURACY IN MEDIA, INC. v. FEDERAL COMMUNICATIONS COMMISSION

United States Court of Appeals, District of Columbia Circuit, 1975.
521 F.2d 288.
Certiorari denied, 425 U.S. 934, 96 S.Ct. 1664, 48 L.Ed.2d 175 (1976).

Before BAZELON, CHIEF JUDGE, LEVENTHAL, CIRCUIT JUDGE, and WEIGEL, UNITED STATES DISTRICT JUDGE for the Northern District of California.

BAZELON, CHIEF JUDGE.

Accuracy in Media, Inc. (AIM) filed two complaints with the FCC against the Public Broadcasting Service (PBS) concerning two programs distributed by PBS to its member stations. AIM alleged that the programs, dealing with sex education and the American system of criminal justice, were not a balanced or objective presentation of each subject and requested the FCC to order PBS to rectify the situation.

The legal basis for AIM's complaints was . . . 47 U.S.C. § 396(g)(1)(A) (1970). . . .

Section 396(g)(1)(A) is part of the Public Broadcasting Act of 1967, an act which created the Corporation for Public Broadcasting (CPB) and authorized it to fund various programming activities of local, noncommercial broadcasting licensees. Section 396(g)(1)(A) qualifies that authorization in the following language:

> In order to achieve the objectives and to carry out the purposes of this subpart, as set out in subsection (a) of this section, the Corporation is authorized to—
>
> > (A) facilitate the full development of educational broadcasting in which programs of high quality, obtained from diverse sources, will be made available to noncommercial educational television or radio broadcast stations, with strict adherence to objectivity and balance in all programs or series of programs of a controversial nature. . . .

AIM contends that since the above-mentioned PBS programs were funded by the CPB, pursuant to this authorization, the programs must contain "strict adherence to objectivity and balance", a requirement AIM contends is more stringent than the standard of balance and fairness in overall programming contained in the Fairness Doctrine. AIM alleges that the two relevant programs did not meet this more stringent standard of objectivity and balance.

. . . [T]he Commission wrongly concluded that it had no jurisdiction to enforce the mandate of § 396(g)(1)(A) against CPB. . . .

The Organization of Public Broadcasting in the United States

Resolution of the issues raised by AIM's petition requires an understanding of the operation of the public broadcasting system. There are three tiers to this operation, each reflecting a different scheme of governmental regulation. The basic level is comprised of the local, noncommercial broadcasting stations that are licensed by the FCC and, with a few exceptions, subject to the same regulations as commercial licenses. . . . [T]he FCC has reserved exclusive space in its allocation of frequencies for such noncommercial broadcasters. Other than this specific reservation, noncommercial licenses are still subject to the same renewal process and potential challenges as their commercial counterparts.

Such was the state of the public broadcasting system until the passage of the Educational Television Facilities Act in 1962. The Act added the element of government funding to public broadcasting by establishing a capital grant program for noncommercial facilities. This second level of the system was reorganized and expanded by the Public Broadcasting Act of 1967, which created the Corporation for Public Broadcasting (CPB). The Corporation, the product of a study made by the Carnegie Commission on Educational Television, was established as a funding mechanism for virtually all activities of noncommercial broadcasting. In setting up this nonprofit, private corporation, the Act specifically prohibited CPB from engaging in any form of "communication by wire or radio."

The third level of the public broadcasting system was added in 1970 when CPB and a group of noncommercial licensees formed the Public Broadcasting Service (PBS) and National Public Radio. The Public Broadcasting Service operates as the distributive arm of the public television system. As a nonprofit membership corporation, it distributes national programming to approximately 150 educational licensees via common carrier facilities. This interconnection service is funded by the Corporation (CPB) under a contract with PBS; in addition, much of the programming carried by PBS is either wholly or partially funded by CPB. National Public Radio provides similar services for noncommercial radio. In 1974, CPB and the member licensees of PBS agreed upon a station program cooperative plan [14] to insure local control and origination of noncommercial programming funded by CPB. Though PBS is the national coordinator under this scheme, it is not a "network" in the commercial broadcasting sense, and does not engage in "communication by wire or radio," except to the extent that it contracts for interconnection services.

II. *FCC Jurisdiction Over the Corporation for Public Broadcasting*

With the structure of the public broadcasting system in view, we turn to AIM's contention that the FCC should enforce the mandate of § 396(g)(1)(A) against the CPB. Since the Section is clearly directed to the Corporation and its programming activities, we have no doubt that the Corporation must respect the mandate of the Section. However, we conclude that nothing in the language and legislative history of the Federal Communications Act or the Public Broadcasting Act of 1967 authorizes the FCC to enforce that mandate against the CPB.

Section 398 of the Communications Act expresses the clear intent of Congress that there shall be no direct jurisdiction of the FCC over the Corporation. . . .

Congress desired to establish a program funding agency which would be free from governmental influence or control in its operations. Yet, the lawmakers feared that such complete autonomy might lead to biases and abuses of its own. The unique position of the Corporation is the synthesis of these competing influences. . . .

. . .

14. The Station Program Cooperative (SPC) is a unique concept in program selection and financing for public television stations. Though the idea of public television as a "fourth network" had been proposed at various times, the 1974 plan reversed this trend toward centralization. Under the SPC, certain programming will be produced only if the individual local stations decide together to fund the production. The local licensees will be financed through the CPB and other sources . . . . Through this plan the local stations will eventually assume the responsibility for support of the cooperative and the Corporation will concentrate on new programming development. [ ]

AIM maintains that this view of FCC jurisdiction to enforce § 396(g)(1)(A) renders the Section nugatory and hence ignores the Congressional sentiment that biases and abuses within the public broadcasting system should be controlled. We do not view our holding on the FCC's jurisdiction as having that effect. Rather, we take notice of the carefully balanced framework designed by Congress for the control of CPB activities.

The Corporation was established as nonprofit and non-political in nature and is prohibited from owning or operating "any television or radio broadcast station, system or network, community antenna system, or interconnection, or production facility." Numerous statutory safeguards were created to insure against partisan abuses. Ultimately, Congress may show its disapproval of any activity of the Corporation through the appropriation process.[29] This supervision of CPB through its funding is buttressed by an annual reporting requirement. . . .

A further element of this carefully balanced framework of regulation is the accountability of the local noncommercial licensees under established FCC practice, including the Fairness Doctrine in particular. This existing system of accountability was clearly recognized in the 1967 legislative debates as a crucial check on the power of the CPB. . . .

. . . The framework of regulation of the Corporation for Public Broadcasting we have described—maximum freedom from interference with programming coupled with existing public accountability requirements—is sensitive to the delicate constitutional balance between First Amendment rights of the broadcast journalist and the concerns of the viewing public struck in [CBS v. DNC]. There the Supreme Court warned that "only when the interests of the public are found to outweigh the private journalistic interests of the broadcasters" will governmental interference with broadcast journalism be allowed. The Court on the basis of this rule rejected a right of access to broadcast air time greater than that mandated by the Fairness Doctrine as constituting too great a "risk of an enlargement of Governmental control over the content of broadcast discussion of public issues."

It is certainly arguable that FCC application of the standard—whatever that standard may be—of § 396(g)(1)(A) could "risk [an] enlargement of Government control over the content of broadcast discussion of public issues" [by requiring balance within each individual program and by using the term "objective" to replace the "most limited scrutiny into the factual accuracy of programming" now undertaken.] Both of these potential enlargements of government control of programming, whether directed against the CPB, PBS or individual noncommercial licensees, threaten to upset the constitutional balance struck in *CBS.* We will not presume that Congress meant to thrust upon us the substantial constitutional questions such a result would raise. We thus

29. Section 396(k) assures that most of the CPB's operating budget be derived through the Congressional appropriation process.

construe § 396(g)(1)(A) and the scheme of regulation for public broadcasting as a whole to avoid such questions.

. . . We hold today only that the FCC has no function in this scheme of accountability established by § 396(g)(1)(A) and the 1967 Act in general other than that assigned to it by the Fairness Doctrine. Therefore, we deny the petition for review and affirm the Commission's decision rejecting jurisdiction over the Corporation for Public Broadcasting.

Notes and Questions

1. What is the difference between the fairness doctrine and AIM's reading of § 396(g)(1)(A)? Why would one call for more Commission intervention in programming than the other?

2. Why would it be incorrect to think of PBS as a "fourth network"?

3. Despite the ruling in the AIM case, the Commission retains several controls over public noncommercial broadcasters. The primary power is to be found in the licensing process. A fundamental dispute over the proper role of educational stations emerged when a renewal application for WNET in New York was challenged. Commissioner Hooks dissented from the renewal on the ground that the station was programming for a very small elite minority and essentially neglecting the needs of larger groups in the community that would benefit from language, vocational, and remedial programs. Puerto Rican Media Action and Educational Council, 51 F.C.C.2d 1178, 32 R.R.2d 1423 (1975). Elitist programming is defended on the ground that the noncommercial stations do not get enough money from public sources and must solicit funds from their communities. It is thought that a station that presents culturally high-level programs for the wealthier segments of the community will have better success at raising the funds necessary to keep the station going. Is this a problem? How might the situation be changed?

4. Concern about adequate funding for public broadcasting has increased over the past few years as a result of decreases in federal funding. In 1981, Congress created the Temporary Commission on Alternative Financing for Public Telecommunications (TCAF). Chaired by Commissioner Quello of the FCC, TCAF was directed as part of its investigation of alternative funding to oversee an 18-month experiment allowing some public broadcasters to sell advertising. Nine public television stations participated in the experiment. Although the advertising experiment generated significant income for the participants, it was not extended.

TCAF has recommended to Congress that advertising not be allowed, but that enhanced underwriting (allowing identification of contributors to include product identifications and slogans) be approved. What are the risks of allowing advertising on noncommercial stations? What other funding mechanisms should be considered?

5. In keeping with these recommendations and the Public Broadcasting Amendments Act of 1981, the Commission reconsidered its 1982 ruling prohibiting the inclusion of brand names in donor acknowledgements. Under the new rules "donor acknowledgments utilized by public broadcasters may include (1) logograms or slogans which identify and do *not* promote, (2) location, (3) value neutral descriptions of a product line or service, (4) brand and trade names and product or service listings." Noncommercial Educational Broadcasting Stations, 55 R.R.2d 1190 (1984).

6. Section 399(b), requiring public broadcasters to make and retain for 60 days (to allow inspection by government or public) audio tapes for all programs "in which any issue of public importance is discussed," was held unconstitutional on equal protection grounds in Community-Service Broadcasting of Mid-America, Inc. v. Federal Communications Commission, 593 F.2d 1102 (D.C.Cir.1978) (en banc).

2. Content Regulation

One of the more troublesome questions in the 1967 Act involved § 399, discussed at p. 737, supra, in the note on the League of Women Voters case. We turn now to the discussion of the merits of that case.

FEDERAL COMMUNICATIONS COMM'N v. LEAGUE OF WOMEN VOTERS OF CALIFORNIA

Supreme Court of the United States, 1984.

468 U.S. 364, 104 S.Ct. 3106, 82 L.Ed.2d 278, 10 Med.L.Rptr. 1937.

Noted, 71 Cornell L.Rev. 453, 39 U. Miami L.Rev. 573, 31 Wayne L.Rev. 1103.

Justice Brennan delivered the opinion of the Court.

. . .

III

We turn now to consider whether the restraint imposed by § 399 satisfies the requirements established by our prior cases for permissible broadcast regulation. Before assessing the government's proffered justifications for the statute, however, two central features of the ban against editorializing must be examined, since they help to illuminate the importance of the First Amendment interests at stake in this case.

A

First, the restriction imposed by § 399 is specifically directed at a form of speech—namely, the expression of editorial opinion—that lies at the heart of First Amendment protection. . . . As we recently reiterated in NAACP v. Claiborne Hardware Co., 458 U.S. 886 (1982), "expression on public issues 'has always rested on the highest rung of the hierarchy of First Amendment values.'" . . .

The editorial has traditionally played precisely this role by informing and arousing the public, and by criticizing and cajoling those who hold government office in order to help launch new solutions to the problems of the time. Preserving the free expression of editorial opinion, therefore, is part and parcel of "our profound national commitment . . . that debate on public issues should be uninhibited, robust, and wide-open." New York Times v. Sullivan, 376 U.S. 254, 270 (1964). As we recognized in *Mills v. Alabama,* supra, the special place of the editorial in our First Amendment jurisprudence simply reflects the fact that the press, of which the broadcasting industry is indisputably a part, United States v. Paramount Pictures, Inc., 334 U.S. 131, 166 (1948), carries out a historic, dual responsibility in our society of reporting information and of bringing critical judgment to bear on public affairs. . . . Because § 399 appears to restrict precisely that form of speech which the Framers of the Bill of Rights were most anxious to protect—speech that is "indispensable to the discovery and spread of political truth"—we must be especially careful in weighing the interests that are asserted in support of this restriction and in assessing the precision with which the ban is crafted. Whitney v. California, [ ] (Brandeis, J., concurring).

Second, the scope of § 399's ban is defined solely on the basis of the content of the suppressed speech. A wide variety of non-editorial speech "by licensees, their management or those speaking on their behalf," [ ] is plainly not prohibited by § 399. Examples of such permissible forms of speech include daily announcements of the station's program schedule or over-the-air appeals for contributions from listeners. Consequently, in order to determine whether a particular statement by station management constitutes an "editorial" proscribed by § 399, enforcement authorities must necessarily examine the content of the message that is conveyed to determine whether the views expressed concern "controversial issues of public importance." [ ]

As Justice Stevens observed in Consolidated Edison Co. v. Public Service Commission, 447 U.S. 530 (1980), however, "[a] regulation of speech that is motivated by nothing more than a desire to curtail expression of a particular point of view on controversial issues of general interest is the purest example of a 'law . . . abridging the freedom of speech, or of the press.' A regulation that denies a group of persons the right to address a selected audience on 'controversial issues of public policy' is plainly such a regulation." [ ] Section 399 is just such a regulation, for it singles out noncommercial broadcasters and denies them the right to address their chosen audience on matters of public importance. . . .

B

. . . [T]he Government urges that the statute was aimed at preventing two principal threats to the overall success of the Public Broadcasting Act of 1967. According to this argument, the ban was necessary, first, to protect noncommercial educational broadcasting stations from being coerced, as a result of federal financing, into becoming vehicles for government propagandizing or the objects of governmental influence; and, second, to keep these stations from becoming convenient targets for capture by private interest groups wishing to express their own partisan viewpoints. By seeking to safeguard the public's right to a balanced presentation of public issues through the prevention of either governmental or private bias, these objectives are, of course, broadly consistent with the goals identified in our earlier broadcast regulation cases. But, in sharp contrast to the restrictions upheld in *Red Lion* or in [CBS v. FCC, p. 760, supra], which left room for editorial discretion and simply required broadcast editors to grant others access to the microphone, § 399 directly prohibits the broadcaster from speaking out on public issues even in a balanced and fair manner. The Government insists, however, that the hazards posed in the "special" circumstances of noncommercial educational broadcasting are so great that § 399 is an indispensable means of preserving the public's First Amendment interests. We disagree.

(1)

When Congress first decided to provide financial support for the expansion and development of noncommercial educational stations, all concerned agreed that this step posed some risk that these traditionally independent stations might be pressured into becoming forums devoted solely to programming and views that were acceptable to the Federal government. That Congress was alert to these dangers cannot be doubted. It sought through the Public Broadcasting Act to fashion a system that would provide local stations with sufficient funds to foster their growth and development while preserving their tradition of autonomy and community-orientation. . . .

The intended role of § 399 in achieving these purposes, however, is not as clear. . . . [A]s the House Committee Report frankly admits, § 399 was added not because Congress thought it was essential to preserving the autonomy and vitality of local stations, but rather "out of an abundance of caution." [ ]

More importantly, an examination of both the overall legislative scheme established by the 1967 Act and the character of public broadcasting demonstrates that the interest asserted by the Government is not substantially advanced by § 399. First, to the extent that federal financial support creates a risk that stations will lose their independence through the bewitching power of governmental largesse, the elaborate structure established by the Public Broadcasting Act already operates to insulate local stations from governmental interference. Congress not only mandated that the new Corporation for Public Broadcasting would have a private, bipartisan structure, [ ], but also imposed a variety of important limitations on its powers. The Corporation was prohibited from owning or operating any station, [ ], it was required to adhere strictly to a standard of "objectivity and balance" in disbursing federal funds to local stations, [ ], and it was prohibited from contributing to or otherwise supporting any candidate for office, [ ].

The Act also established a second layer of protections which serve to protect the stations from governmental coercion and interference. Thus, in addition to requiring the Corporation to operate so as to "assure the maximum freedom [of local stations] from interference with or control of program content or other activities," [ ], the Act expressly forbids "any department, agency, officer, or employee of the United States [from] exercis[ing] any direction, supervision, or control over educational television or radio broadcasting, or over the Corporation or any of its grantees or contractors . . . ," § 398(a). . . .[19]

Even if these statutory protections were thought insufficient to the task, however, suppressing the particular category of speech restricted by § 399 is simply not likely, given the character of the public broadcasting system, to reduce substantially the risk that the Federal Government will seek to influence or put pressure on local stations. An underlying supposition of the Government's argument in this regard is that individual noncommercial stations are likely to speak so forcefully on particular issues that Congress, the ultimate source of the stations' Federal funding, will be tempted to retaliate against these individual stations by restricting appropriations for all of public broadcasting. But, as the District Court recognized, the character of public broadcasting suggests that such a risk is speculative at best. [Since there are] literally hundreds of public radio and television stations in communities scattered throughout the United States and its territories, [ ] . . . it seems reasonable to infer that the editorial voices of these stations will prove to be as distinctive, varied, and idiosyncratic as the various communities they represent. More importantly, the editorial focus of any particular station can fairly be expected to focus largely on issues affecting only its community.[20] Accordingly, absent some showing by the Government to the contrary, the risk that local editorializing will place all of public broadcasting in jeopardy is not sufficiently pressing to warrant § 399's broad suppression of speech.

Indeed, what is far more likely than local station editorials to pose the kinds of dangers hypothesized by the Government are the wide variety of programs addressing controversial issues produced, often

19. Furthermore, the risk that federal coercion or influence will be brought to bear against local stations as a result of federal financing is considerably attenuated by the fact that CPB grants account for only a portion of total public broadcasting income [23.4% in fiscal 1982]. The vast majority of financial support comes from state and local governments, as well as a variety of private sources, including foundations, businesses, and individual contributions . . . .

20. This likelihood is enhanced with respect to public stations because they are required to establish community advisory boards which must reasonably reflect the "diverse needs and interests of the communities served by such station[s]." . . .

with substantial CPB funding, for national distribution to local stations. . . .

Furthermore, the manifest imprecision of the ban imposed by § 399 reveals that its proscription is not sufficiently tailored to the harms it seeks to prevent to justify its substantial interference with broadcasters' speech. Section 399 includes within its grip a potentially infinite variety of speech, most of which would not be related in any way to governmental affairs, political candidacies or elections. Indeed, the breadth of editorial commentary is as wide as human imagination permits. But the Government never explains how, say, an editorial by local station management urging improvements in a town's parks or museums will so infuriate Congress or other Federal officials that the future of public broadcasting will be imperiled unless such editorials are suppressed. Nor is it explained how the suppression of editorials alone serves to reduce the risk of governmental retaliation and interference when it is clear that station management is fully able to broadcast controversial views so long as such views are not labelled as its own. [ ]

The Government appears to recognize these flaws in § 399, because it focuses instead on the suggestion that the source of governmental influence may well be state and local governments, many of which have established public broadcasting commissions that own and operate local noncommercial educational stations.[22] The ban on editorializing is all the more necessary . . . , the argument runs, because the management of such stations will be especially likely to broadcast only editorials that are favorable to the state or local authorities that hold the purse strings. The Government's argument, however, proves too much. First, § 399's ban applies to the many private noncommercial community organizations that own and operate stations that are not controlled in any way by state or local government. Second, the legislative history of the Public Broadcasting Act clearly indicates that Congress was concerned with "assur[ing] complete freedom from any *Federal Government Influence.*" . . .

Finally, although the Government certainly has a substantial interest in ensuring that the audiences of noncommercial stations will not be led to think that the broadcaster's editorials reflect the official view of the government, this interest can be fully satisfied by less restrictive means that are readily available. To address this important concern, Congress could simply require public broadcasting stations to broadcast a disclaimer every time they editorialize, which would state that the editorial represents only the view of the station's management and does not in any way represent the views of the Federal Government or any of the station's other sources of funding. Such a disclaimer—similar to

22. [A]t least two-thirds of the public television broadcasting stations in operation are licensed to (a) state public broadcasting authorities or commissions, in which commission members are often appointed by the governor with the advice and consent of the state legislature, (b) state universities or educational commissions, or (c) local school boards or municipal authorities. [ ]

those often used in commercial and noncommercial programming of a controversial nature—would effectively and directly communicate to the audience that the editorial reflected only the views of the station rather than those of the government. . . .

In sum, § 399's broad ban on all editorializing by every station that receives CPB funds far exceeds what is necessary to protect against the risk of governmental interference or to prevent the public from assuming that editorials by public broadcasting stations represent the official view of government. . . .

(2)

Assuming that the Government's second asserted interest in preventing noncommercial stations from becoming a "privileged outlet for the political and ideological opinions of station owners and management," [ ] is legitimate, the substantiality of this asserted interest is dubious. The patent over- and underinclusiveness of § 399's ban "undermines the likelihood of a genuine [governmental] interest" in preventing private groups from propagating their own views via public broadcasting. [*Bellotti*] If it is true, as the government contends, that noncommercial stations remain free, despite § 399, to broadcast a wide variety of controversial views through their power to control program selection, to select which persons will be interviewed, and to determine how news reports will be presented, [ ], then it seems doubtful that § 399 can fairly be said to advance any genuinely substantial governmental interest in keeping controversial or partisan opinions from being aired by noncommercial stations. . . .

We therefore hold that even if some of the hazards at which § 399 was aimed are sufficiently substantial, the restriction is not crafted with sufficient precision to remedy those dangers that may exist to justify the significant abridgement of speech worked by the provision's broad ban on editorializing. The statute is not narrowly tailored to address any of the government's suggested goals. Moreover, the public's "paramount right" to be fully and broadly informed on matters of public importance through the medium of noncommercial educational broadcasting is not well served by the restriction, for its effect is plainly to diminish rather than augment "the volume and quality of coverage" of controversial issues. [*Red Lion*] Nor do we see any reason to deny noncommercial broadcasters the right to address matters of public concern on the basis of merely speculative fears of adverse public or governmental reactions to such speech.

IV

Although the Government did not present the argument in any form to the District Court, it now seeks belatedly to justify § 399 on the basis of Congress' Spending Power. Relying upon our recent decision in Regan v. Taxation With Representation, 461 U.S. 540 (1983), the Government argues that by prohibiting noncommercial educational stations that receive CPB grants from editorializing, Congress has, in the proper exercise of its Spending Power, simply determined that it "will not subsidize public broadcasting station editorials." [ ] In *Taxation With Representation,* the Court found that Congress could, in the exercise of its Spending Power, reasonably refuse to subsidize the lobbying activities of tax-exempt charitable organizations by prohibiting such organizations from using tax-deductible contributions to support their lobbying efforts. . . .

In this case, however, . . . a noncommercial educational station that receives only 1% of its overall income from CPB grants is barred absolutely from all editorializing. [In contrast to the political group in *Taxation With Representation,*] a station is not able to segregate its activities according to the source of its funding. The station has no way of limiting the use of its Federal funds to all non-editorializing activities, and, more importantly, it is barred from using even wholly private funds to finance its editorial activity.

Of course, if Congress were to adopt a revised version of § 399 that permitted noncommercial educational broadcasting stations to establish "affiliate" organizations which could then use the station's facilities to editorialize with non-federal funds, such a statutory mechanism would plainly be valid under the reasoning of *Taxation With Representation.* . . . But in the absence of such authority, we must reject the Government's contention that our decision in *Taxation With Representation* is controlling here.

V

In conclusion, we emphasize that our disposition of this case rests upon a narrow proposition. We do not hold that the Congress or the FCC are without power to regulate the content, timing, or character of speech by noncommercial educational broadcasting stations. Rather, we hold only that the specific interests sought to be advanced by § 399's ban on editorializing are either not sufficiently substantial or are not served in a sufficiently limited manner to justify the substantial abridgement of important journalistic freedoms which the First Amendment jealously protects. Accordingly, the judgment of the District Court is affirmed.

JUSTICE REHNQUIST, with whom THE CHIEF JUSTICE and JUSTICE WHITE join, dissenting.

All but three paragraphs of the Court's lengthy opinion in this case are devoted to the development of a scenario in which the government appears as the "Big Bad Wolf" and appellee Pacifica as "Little Red Riding Hood." In the Court's scenario the Big Bad Wolf cruelly forbids Little Red Riding Hood from taking to her grandmother some of the food that she is carrying in her basket. Only three paragraphs are used to delineate a truer picture of the litigants, wherein it appears that some of the food in the basket was given to Little Red Riding Hood by the Big Bad Wolf himself, and that the Big Bad Wolf had told Little

Red Riding Hood in advance that if she accepted his food she would have to abide by his conditions. Congress in enacting § 399 of the Public Broadcasting Act, 47 U.S.C. (Supp. V) § 399, has simply determined that public funds shall not be used to subsidize noncommercial, educational broadcasting stations which engage in "editorializing" or which support or oppose any political candidate. I do not believe that anything in the First Amendment to the United States Constitution prevents Congress from choosing to spend public monies in that manner. Perhaps a more appropriate analogy than that of Little Red Riding Hood and the Big Bad Wolf is that of Faust and Mephistopheles; Pacifica, well aware of § 399's condition on its receipt of public money, nonetheless accepted the public money and now seeks to avoid the conditions which Congress legitimately has attached to receipt of that funding.

. . .

. . . Congress has rationally determined that the bulk of the taxpayers whose monies provide the funds for grants by the CPB would prefer not to see the management of local educational stations promulgate its own private views on the air at taxpayer expense. Accordingly Congress simply has decided not to subsidize stations which engage in that activity.

. . .

This is not to say that the government may attach *any* condition to its largess; it is only to say that when the government is simply exercising its power to allocate its own public funds, we need only find that the condition imposed has a rational relationship to Congress' purpose in providing the subsidy and that it is not primarily "aimed at the suppression of dangerous ideas." [ ] In this case Congress' prohibition is directly related to its purpose in providing subsidies for public broadcasting, and it is plainly rational for Congress to have determined that taxpayer monies should not be used to subsidize management's views or to pay for management's exercise of partisan politics. Indeed, it is entirely rational for Congress to have wished to avoid the appearance of government sponsorship of a particular view or a particular political candidate. Furthermore, Congress' prohibition is strictly neutral. In no sense can it be said that Congress has prohibited only editorial views of one particular ideological bent. Nor has it prevented public stations from airing programs, documentaries, interviews, etc. dealing with controversial subjects, so long as management itself does not expressly endorse a particular viewpoint. And Congress has not prevented station management from communicating its own views on those subjects through any medium other than subsidized public broadcasting.

. . . In [*Speiser v. Randall,*] California's decision to deny its property tax exemption to veterans who would not declare that they would not work to overthrow the government was plainly directed at suppressing what California regarded as speech of a dangerous content.

And the condition imposed was so unrelated to the benefit to be conferred that it is difficult to argue that California's property tax exemption actually subsidized the dangerous speech.

. . .

JUSTICE WHITE: Believing that the editorializing and candidate endorsement proscription stand or fall together and being confident that Congress may condition use of its funds on abstaining from political endorsements, I join JUSTICE REHNQUIST'S dissenting opinion.

JUSTICE STEVENS, dissenting.

The court jester who mocks the King must choose his words with great care. An artist is likely to paint a flattering portrait of his patron. The child who wants a new toy does not preface his request with a comment on how fat his mother is. Newspaper publishers have been known to listen to their advertising managers. Elected officials may remember how their elections were financed. By enacting the statutory provision that the Court invalidates today, a sophisticated group of legislators expressed a concern about the potential impact of government funds on pervasive and powerful organs of mass communication. One need not have heard the raucous voice of Adolph Hitler over Radio Berlin to appreciate the importance of that concern.

As Justice White correctly notes, the statutory prohibitions against editorializing and candidate endorsements rest on the same foundation. In my opinion that foundation is far stronger than merely "a rational basis" and it is not weakened by the fact that it is buttressed by other provisions that are also designed to avoid the insidious evils of government propaganda favoring particular points of view. The quality of the interest in maintaining government neutrality in the free market of ideas—of avoiding subtle forms of censorship and propaganda—outweigh the impact on expression that results from this statute. Indeed, by simply terminating or reducing funding, Congress could curtail much more expression with no risk whatever of a constitutional transgression.

. . .

Neither the fact that the statute regulates only one kind of speech, nor the fact that editorial opinion has traditionally been an important kind of speech, is sufficient to identify the character or the significance of the statute's impact on speech. Three additional points are relevant. First, the statute does not prohibit Pacifica from expressing its opinion through any avenue except the radio stations for which it receives federal financial support. It eliminates the subsidized channel of communication as a forum for Pacifica itself, and thereby deprives Pacifica of an advantage it would otherwise have over other speakers, but it does not exclude Pacifica from the marketplace for ideas. Second, the statute does not curtail the expression of opinion by individual commentators who participate in Pacifica's programs. Third, and of greatest significance for me, the statutory restriction is completely neutral in its operation—it prohibits all editorials without any distinction being drawn concerning the subject matter or the point of view that might be expressed.[5]

II

. . .

In my judgment the interest in keeping the Federal Government out of the propaganda arena is of overriding importance. That interest is of special importance in the field of electronic communication, not only because that medium is so powerful and persuasive, but also because it is the one form of communication that is licensed by the Federal Government.[8] When the government already has great potential power over the electronic media, it is surely legitimate to enact statutory safeguards to make sure that it does not cross the threshold that separates neutral regulation from the subsidy of partisan opinion.

. . .

Members of Congress, not members of the Judiciary, live in the world of politics. When they conclude that there is a real danger of political considerations influencing the dispensing of this money and that this provision is necessary to insulate grantees from political pressures in addition to the other safeguards, that judgment is entitled to our respect.

The magnitude of the present danger that the statute is designed to avoid is admittedly a matter about which reasonable judges may disagree.[10] Moreover, I would agree that the risk would be greater if other statutory safeguards were removed. It remains true, however, that Congress has the power to prevent the use of public funds to subsidize the expression of partisan points of view, or to suppress the propagation of dissenting opinions. No matter how great or how small

5. Section 399's ban on editorializing is a content based restriction on speech, but not in the sense that the majority implies. The majority speaks of "editorial opinion" as if it were some sort of special species of opinion, limited to issues of public importance. . . . The content which is prohibited is that the station is not permitted to state its opinion with respect to any matter. In short, it may not be an on-the-air advocate if it accepts government funds for its broadcasts. The prohibition on editorializing is not directed at any particular message a station might wish to convey. . . . Paradoxically, section 399 is later attacked by the majority as essentially being underinclusive because it does not prohibit "controversial" national programming that is often aired with substantial federal funding. . . . Next, § 399's ban on editorializing is attacked by the majority on overinclusive grounds—because it is content-neutral—since it prohibits a "potentially infinite variety of speech, most of which would not be related in any way to governmental affairs, political candidacies or elections." . . .

8. We have consistently adhered to the following guiding principles applicable to First Amendment claims in the area of broadcasting, and they bear repeating at some length: [quoting from (Red Lion)].

10. The majority argues that the Government's concededly substantial interest in ensuring that audiences of educational stations will not perceive the station to be a government propaganda organ can be fully satisfied by requiring such stations to broadcast a disclaimer each time they editorialize stating that the editorial "does not in any way represent the views of the Federal Government. . . . " [ ]. This solution would be laughable were it not so Orwellian: the answer to the fact that there is a real danger that the editorials are really government propaganda is for the government to require the station to tell the audience that it is not propaganda at all!

the immediate risk may be, there surely is more than a theoretical possibility that future grantees might be influenced by the ever present tie of the political purse strings, even if those strings are never actually pulled. . . .

I respectfully dissent.

Notes and Questions

1. Recall the majority's approach to the question of the applicable standard. Is that decision crucial to the result? What standard is each dissent using?

2. Does the case help in analyzing the nature of "content" distinctions? How do they differ from "viewpoint" distinctions? What is the importance of that distinction in the majority opinion?

3. How realistic are the fears of the dissenting justices? (President Nixon once vetoed the CPB budget because of dissatisfaction with CPB programming.) Are noncommercial licensees likely to be influenced by the "power of the purse"? How can Congress insulate noncommercial licensees from government control?

4. The crucial difference between commercial and non-commercial broadcasting involves the question of the licensee's ability to control content and to reject programming. In *League of Women Voters,* the Court was faced with the problem of indirect control of PBS stations through the CPB funding mechanism. But more than 140 PBS stations are under some form of government ownership. What effect should that have on the ability of those licensees to control content and reject programming? Consider the following case.

MUIR v. ALABAMA EDUCATIONAL TELEVISION COMMISSION

United States Court of Appeals, Fifth Circuit, en banc, 1982.
688 F.2d 1033, 8 Med.L.Rptr. 2305.

Certiorari denied, 460 U.S. 1023 (1983).

Noted, 13 Cumb.L.Rev. 397, 4 Miss.C.L.Rev. 133, 36 U.Miami L.Rev. 779.

[In this case, decided by the old Fifth Circuit before it was split, 22 judges participated in the decision. Judge Hill's opinion, referred to by all as the majority opinion, has the implicit support of ten judges. Five others wrote separately but joined Judge Hill. The seven dissenters wrote three opinions. The opinions in this case offer an intellectual challenge commensurate with the size of the bench.]

Before BROWN, CHARLES CLARK, RONEY, GEE, TJOFLAT, HILL, FAY, RUBIN, VANCE, KRAVITCH, FRANK M. JOHNSON, HENDERSON, REAVLEY, POLITZ, HATCHETT, ANDERSON, RANDALL, TATE, SAM D. JOHNSON, THOMAS A. CLARK, WILLIAMS and GARWOOD, CIRCUIT JUDGES.

JAMES C. HILL, CIRCUIT JUDGE:

I. *Introduction*

The two appeals before this Court on consolidated rehearing raise the important and novel question of whether individual viewers of public television stations, licensed by the Federal Communications Commission to state instrumentalities, have a First Amendment right to compel the licensees to broadcast a previously scheduled program which the licensees have decided to cancel. For the reasons stated below we find that the viewers do not have such a right.

Both cases before us concern the decisions of the licensees not to broadcast the program "Death of a Princess." In Muir v. Alabama Educational Television Commission, 656 F.2d 1012 (N.D.Ala.1980), the District Court for the Northern District of Alabama denied the plaintiff viewers' motion for a preliminary injunction requiring the defendant licensee, Alabama Educational Television Commission (AETC), to broadcast the program. The district court found: (1) that the likelihood of success on the merits criterion for an injunction had not been shown; (2) that the First Amendment protects the right of broadcasters, private and public, to make programming decisions free of interference; and (3) that viewers have no First Amendment right of access to the Alabama educational television network sufficient to compel the showing of "Death of a Princess." The court granted summary judgment for AETC.

In Barnstone v. University of Houston, 514 F.Supp. 670 (S.D.Tex. 1980), the District Court for the Southern District of Texas reached a different conclusion and granted the injunction requested by the plaintiff viewers and ordered the defendant licensee, University of Houston, to broadcast the program. . . .

On appeal a panel of this court affirmed the District Court's decision in *Muir*. The panel held that the plaintiffs had no constitutional right to compel the broadcast of "Death of a Princess," and that AETC's refusal to broadcast the program was a legitimate exercise of its statutory authority as a broadcast licensee and was protected by the First Amendment. In *Barnstone* another panel of this court found that the decision in *Muir* required that the panel reverse the judgment of the District Court for the Southern District of Texas and dissolve the injunctive relief which had been granted the plaintiffs.

We [affirm *Muir* and reverse *Barnstone*.]

II. *Factual Background*

The *Muir* case arose when AETC decided not to broadcast "Death of a Princess," which had been scheduled for broadcast on May 12, 1980 at 8:00 P.M. The program, one of thirteen in the series "World," is a dramatization of the investigation by the program's director, producer and co-author into the motivations and circumstances which were said to have led to the July 1977 execution for adultery of a Saudi Arabian princess and her commoner lover.

[AETC, organized under state law, has the duty of controlling and supervising the use of channels reserved by the FCC to Alabama for noncommercial, educational use. It operates a statewide network of nine noncommercial, educational television stations licensed by the FCC. AETC is funded through state legislative appropriations matching federal grants through CPB, and private contributions. It is a member of PBS and the Station Program Cooperative. "Membership in SPC entitles licensees to participate in the selection and funding of national public television programs distributed by PBS. Only those licensees who contribute to a program's cost have a right to broadcast it. Those who contribute are free to broadcast or not to broadcast the program." The series "World" was funded by 144 public television licensees, including AETC, through the SPC. "During the week prior to the scheduled broadcast of 'Death of a Princess' AETC received numerous communications from Alabama residents protesting the showing of the program. The protests expressed fear for the personal safety and well-being of Alabama citizens working in the Middle East if the program was shown. On May 10 AETC announced its decision not to broadcast the film as scheduled."]

Appellants, Muir, Buttram and Faircloth, residents of Alabama who had planned to watch "Death of a Princess," brought this action on May 12, 1980 under the First and Fourteenth Amendments and 42 U.S.C. § 1983, seeking to compel AETC to broadcast the film, and preliminary and permanent injunctions against AETC's making "political" decisions on programming.

The *Barnstone* case arose in a factual context similar to that of *Muir.* The University of Houston is a co-educational institution of higher learning funded and operated by the State of Texas. [ ] The university funds and operates KUHT–TV, a public television station licensed to the university by the F.C.C. As a member of the SPC, KUHT–TV contributed to the funding of the "World" program series. KUHT–TV scheduled "Death of a Princess" for broadcast on May 12, 1980 at 8:00 P.M.

On May 1, 1980 KUHT–TV announced that it had decided not to broadcast the program. This decision was made by Dr. Patrick J. Nicholson, University of Houston Vice-President for Public Information and University Relations. Dr. Nicholson had never previously made a programming decision such as this, though as the university official charged with the responsibility of operating KUHT–TV he had the power to do so. In a press release announcing the cancellation Dr. Nicholson gave the basis of his decision as "strong and understandable objections by the government of Saudi Arabia at a time when the mounting crisis in the Middle East, our long friendship with the Saudi government and U.S. national interests all point to the need to avoid exacerbating the situation." Dr. Nicholson also expressed a belief that the program was not balanced in a "responsible manner." [5]

Upon learning of Dr. Nicholson's decision, on May 8, 1980, plaintiff Barnstone brought suit to require KUHT–TV to air "Death of a Princess." Ms. Barnstone argued that as a subscriber to and regular viewer of KUHT–TV her First and Fourteenth Amendment rights were violated by the decision to cancel the program.

III. *The First Amendment Does Not Prohibit Governmental Expression*

The central argument advanced by the plaintiffs on appeal is that their First Amendment rights were violated when the defendants, as state actors, denied the plaintiffs an opportunity to view "Death of a Princess" on the public television stations operated by the defendants. We are thus called upon to determine whether the First Amendment rights of viewers impose limits on the programming discretion of public television stations licensed to state instrumentalities.

The First Amendment operates to protect private expression from infringement by government. Such protection applies both to the right to speak and the right to hear and is operative in a variety of contexts. The amendment prohibits government from controlling or penalizing expression which has been singled out by government because of the expression's viewpoint. The First Amendment also prohibits government from taking certain actions which impermissibly constrict the flow of information or ideas.

The plaintiffs emphasize that the protection of the First Amendment extends only to private expression and not to governmental expression. They assert that the amendment serves only to confer duties on government—not rights. While this argument of the plaintiffs may be essentially correct it in no way resolves the issue before us. To find that the government is without First Amendment protection is not to find that the government is prohibited from speaking or that private individuals have the right to limit or control the expression of government. Even without First Amendment protection government may "participate in the marketplace of ideas," and "contribute its own views to those of other speakers." [ ] As Justice Stewart aptly noted

5. In addition to the reasons cited in the press release, the District Court, upon consideration of Dr. Nicholson's testimony, found four other reasons why the cancellation decision may have been made. First, Dr. Nicholson testified that he considered the program to be "in bad taste." Second, Dr. Nicholson expressed concern that some members of the public might believe that the "docu-drama" was a true documentary. Third, Dr. Nicholson testified that the University of Houston had previously entered into a contract with the Saudi Arabian royal family to instruct a particular princess. Finally, Dr. Nicholson testified that he had been in charge of fund raising activities for the university from 1957–1978 and that a significant percentage of the university's private contributions came from major oil companies and from individuals in oil related companies.

in [*CBS v. DNC*] (Stewart, J., concurring) (hereinafter *CBS*), "[g]overnment is not restrained by the First Amendment from controlling its own expression . . . '[t]he purpose of the First Amendment is to protect private expression and nothing in the guarantee precludes the government from controlling its own expression or that of its agents.' " [12]

. . . In the absence of a violation of a constitutional right inhering in the plaintiffs, AETC and the University of Houston are free to make whatever programming decisions they choose, consistent with statutory and regulatory requirements. The fundamental question before us is whether in making the programming decisions at issue here, the defendants violated the First Amendment rights of the plaintiffs.

IV. *The Regulatory Framework Enacted by Congress*

Our inquiry into the constitutional issue at hand is aided by a brief review of the broadcast legislation enacted by Congress. . . .

. . .

The picture which emerges from the regulatory scheme adopted by Congress is one which clearly shows broadcast licensees endowed with the privilege and responsibility of exercising free programming control of their broadcasts, yet also charged with the obligation of making programming decisions which protect the legitimate interests of the public. [ ] Under the existing statutes public licensees such as AETC and the University of Houston possess the same rights and obligations to make free programming decisions as their private counterparts; however, as state instrumentalities, these public licensees are without the protection of the First Amendment. This lack of constitutional protection implies only that government could possibly impose restrictions on these licensees which it could not impose on private licensees. The lack of First Amendment protection does not result in the lessening of any of the statutory rights and duties held by the public licensees. It also does not result in individual viewers gaining any greater right to influence the programming discretion of the public licensees.

12. Government expression, being unprotected by the First Amendment, may be subject to legislative limitation which would be impermissible if sought to be applied to private expression. Yet there is nothing to suggest that, absent such limitation, government is restrained from speaking any more than are the citizens. Freedom of expression is the norm in our society, for government (if not restrained) and for the people. Freedom of speech is not good government because it is in the First Amendment; it is in the First Amendment because it is good government.

V. *KUHT–TV and AETC are not Public Forums*

It is clear that Congress did not deem it necessary for viewers to be accorded a right of access to television broadcast stations in order for the public's First Amendment interests in this medium to be fully realized. Indeed it is clear that Congress concluded that the First Amendment rights of public television viewers are adequately protected under a system where the broadcast licensee has sole programming discretion but is under an obligation to serve the public interest. In spite of this Congressional scheme the District Court in *Barnstone* found that KUHT–TV was a public forum because it was operated by the government for public communication of views on issues of political and social significance. The court held that as a public forum the station could not deny access to speakers who wished to be heard in the forum, unless the requirements for prior restraint were satisfied. [ ]

The plaintiffs now urge that we affirm the District Court's ruling that public television stations are public forums. The plaintiffs, unlike the District Court, however, do not argue for a public right of access to the stations. Instead the plaintiffs contend that as public forums the stations are prohibited by the First Amendment from making programming decisions motivated by hostility to the communicative impact of a program's message and stemming from a specific viewpoint of the broadcaster.

We find both the holding of the District Court and the argument of the plaintiffs to be incorrect. The Supreme Court has recently rejected the theory adopted by the District Court that because a government facility is "specifically used for the communication of information and ideas" it is *ipso facto* a public forum. United States Postal Service v. Council of Greenburgh Civic Ass'ns, 453 U.S. 114 (1981) [holding that a mailbox was not a public forum]. A facility is a public forum only if it is designed to provide a general public right of access to its use, or if such public access has historically existed and is not incompatible with the facility's primary activity.

. . . The pattern of usual activity for public television stations is the statutorily mandated practice of the broadcast licensee exercising sole programming authority. The general invitation extended to the public is not to schedule programs, but to watch or decline to watch what is offered.[25] It is thus clear that the public television stations involved in the cases before us are not public forums. The plaintiffs

25. Similarly producers of television programs are extended no invitation to air their programs on the public television stations. Producers are, of course, free to submit their programs to the stations with a request that they be broadcast, but they have no right to compel such broadcast. . . . [The district court in *Barnstone*] thus erred in finding that the producers of "Death of a Princess" had a right of access to station KUHT–TV to broadcast the film.

have no right of access to compel the broadcast of any particular program.

. . .

VI. *The Decision to Cancel Death of a Princess was not Governmental Censorship*

The plaintiffs argue that even if we decline to characterize KUHT–TV and AETC as public forums we should nonetheless find that the defendants violated the plaintiffs' First Amendment rights by "censoring" "Death of a Princess." The plaintiffs contend that censorship, in violation of the First Amendment, occurs when state officials in charge of state operated public television stations decide to cancel a scheduled program because of the officials' opposition to the program's political content.

. . .

The plaintiffs concede that state officials operating public television stations can exercise some editorial discretion. They contend, however, that in exercising this discretion the officials must be "carefully neutral as to which speakers or viewpoints are to prevail in the marketplace of ideas." . . .

The plaintiffs' analysis fails to recognize a number of essential differences between typical state regulation of private expressive activity and the exercise of editorial discretion by state officials responsible for the operation of public television stations. When state officials operate a public television station they must necessarily make discriminating choices. As the Supreme Court pointed out in *CBS,* [ ] "[f]or better or worse, editing is what editors are for; and editing is selection and choice of material." . . .

The plaintiffs . . . suggest that while it is a proper exercise of editorial discretion for a licensee initially to decide not to schedule a program, it is constitutionally improper for the licensee to decide to cancel a scheduled program because of its political content. In support of their view the plaintiffs cited decisions holding that school officials may be free initially to decide which books to place in their school libraries but that a decision to remove any particular book may be subject to constitutional challenge. We are not persuaded, however, that the distinction urged upon us is valid or that the school library cases are applicable.

The decision to cancel a scheduled program is no less editorial in nature than an initial decision to schedule the program. [ ] Both decisions require the licensee to determine what will best serve the public interest, and, as we noted earlier, such a determination is inherently subjective and involves judgments which could be termed "political."

School libraries are distinguishable from broadcast stations in a number of important ways. There are limited hours in a day for broadcasting, and broadcast licensees are constantly required to make sensitive choices between available programs. Cf. Board of Education v. Pico, 457 U.S. 853, 875, n. 1 (1982) ("The school's finite resources—as well as the limited number of hours in the day—require that educational officials make sensitive choices between subjects to be offered . . . .") (Blackmun, J., concurring in part). The maintenance of one volume on a library shelf does not (absent space limitations) preempt another. In broadcast, only one transmission of information, entertainment, or other message can occur at any one time. A library constantly and simultaneously proffers a myriad of written materials. . . . [T]here is no counterpart, vis-a-vis libraries, to the Federal Communications Commission's "Fairness Doctrine." When a television broadcaster finds that it has scheduled a program espousing one view, it may have unwittingly encumbered its limited broadcast hours with a requirement that equal time be devoted to other viewpoints which might touch upon an issue of limited interest in its viewing area. But the maintenance of one volume espousing one side of an issue does not invoke government regulation requiring that shelf space be made available for all other views. Finally, a school would be expected to furnish only one library for its student population. The residents of a state may expect a choice of a number of television stations, often with the publicly owned facility attracting the smallest number of viewers.

The right to cancel a program is, furthermore, far more integral a part of the operation of a television station than the decision to remove a book from a school library. Libraries typically have at least the opportunity to review a book before acquiring it, therefore, there may be "few legitimate reasons why a book, once acquired, should be removed from a library not filled to capacity." [ ] In comparison, television stations frequently do not have the chance to see a program until after the station's schedule has been printed, and there are numerous legitimate reasons why a station may decide to cancel a program it has initially scheduled. Indeed FCC regulations specifically require that licensees retain the power to reject any program which the licensee has already contracted for if the licensee determines that the program is "unsatisfactory or unsuitable or contrary to the public interest." 47 C.F.R. § 73.658.

We conclude that the defendants' editorial decisions to cancel "Death of a Princess" cannot be properly characterized as "censorship." Had the states of Alabama and Texas sought to prohibit the exhibition of the film by another party then indeed a question of censorship would have arisen. . . .

VII. *The Plaintiffs Can Seek Remedial Relief from the FCC*

Our holding that the defendants did not violate the plaintiffs' First Amendment rights does not preclude the plaintiffs from challenging the propriety of the defendants' programming decisions with the FCC. Our decision is limited to the constitutional issue presented. We offer no opinion as to whether or not the actions of AETC and the University of Houston comport with their statutory and regulatory obligation.

. . .

Notes and Questions

1. Judge Garwood joined the majority's opinion. He agreed that, although it was not desirable, editorial decisions will often be content-based. This is essential to the operation of a conventional television station. He also noted that the cases did not involve claims that the stations' overall programming was one-sided. Nor did the cases involve the question of the stations' obligation if they had broadcast the program.

Judge Rubin, joined by three other judges, agreed with Judge Garwood's opinion. The fact that the state held the license did not control the station's function. "The state may elect the station's mission, so long as this mission is consistent with the state's license and the Constitution." The powers of the staff are in part determined by the mission selected. A station featuring call-in shows will be run differently from one that emphasizes educational purposes. Neither station in these cases was shown to be a magazine of the air or a general forum. "Each appears to serve instead a diet that differs from commercial television primarily in appeal to a somewhat more sophisticated audience, the absence of commercials, and efforts to raise funds from viewers."

Similarly, government agencies publish such things as alumni newsletters, law reviews, and newspapers for the armed forces. In these activities that, "like television broadcasting to the general public, depend in part on audience interest, appraisal of audience interest and suitability for publication or broadcast inevitably involves judgment of content." On the other hand, if the state "is conducting an activity that functions as a marketplace of ideas, the Constitution requires content neutrality."

Seven judges dissented. Judge Johnson, joined by four judges, asserted that the majority made a "serious error" in permitting government officials who operate a public television station to censor views on the basis of the point of view presented. The proper inquiry was whether the actions of state officials abridged the free expression of the speakers and listeners protected by the First Amendment. The majority "commits fundamental error when it permits state broadcasters to ride on the coattails of their private counterparts. Even when the majority admits that state broadcasters 'are without the protection of the First Amendment,' it offers no principled reason why this 'implies only that government could possibly impose restrictions on these licensees which it could not impose on private licensees'."

Moreover, the FCC remedy was illusory because the FCC "steadfastly refuses to depart from its 'longstanding policy of deferring to licensee discretion.' . . . Because the FCC does not distinguish between private and public broadcasters in its regulation of the airwaves, [ ] it provides no protection from the kind of state censorship alleged in these cases."

In discussing the library case, Judge Johnson concluded that the "editorial discretion of a state broadcaster is more circumscribed than that of a school board member. Moreover, the facts of both *Muir* and *Barnstone* reveal dramatic departures from established editorial practice in direct response to the urgings or implied threats of a foreign government."

As to procedure, Judge Johnson, drawing on Mt. Healthy City School District v. Doyle, 429 U.S. 274 (1977), suggested that once the plaintiff proved that the message had been silenced because of its content, the government's decision "becomes presumptively unconstitutional. The government should then be allowed to demonstrate that it would have taken the same action on the basis of legitimate reasons."

Judge Kravitch, dissenting, agreed with Judge Johnson except for his procedural analysis. On that point, the plaintiff should have to show "improper motivation" in addition to a content-based decision.

Judge Reavley, dissenting, argued that in this case there was "no justification for pretending that the state is not relaying messages into the idea marketplace." On the other hand, state television stations should be given some leeway to "pursue excellence, to build viewing audiences, to respond to what viewers want, and to consider the effect of their programs upon that audience." The only decisions that would violate First Amendment neutrality would be those "based on viewpoint alone" without regard to "any opinion as to program value or effect."

2. What is the question before the court?

3. The impact of *Pico* is unclear because no majority view emerged in the Supreme Court. If we assume that a majority of the Court would find censorship implications in both the decision to remove a book and in the decision not to acquire it, what relevance might that have for government broadcasting?

4. What if the Court in *Pico* had concluded that a refusal to acquire a book raised no constitutional questions but that removal did?

5. What would you advise a public broadcaster that decided to use a call-in format?

6. Given the difficulty in finding alternative funding and the difficulty of insulating recipients of government funding from interference—either direct or indirect—in their programming policies, what changes should be made in the public broadcasting scheme?

3. Religious Broadcasting

Religious institutions may be eligible for reserved educational channels. The test used by the Commission to determine such eligibility is "whether the primary thrust is educational, albeit with a religious aspect to the educational activity. Recognizing that some overlap in purposes is, or can be, involved, we look to the application as a whole to determine which is the essential purpose and which is incidental." Bible Moravian Church, Inc., 28 F.C.C.2d 1, 21 R.R.2d 492 (1971) (rejecting an application for a reserved educational spot).

Religious institutions that do not meet the educational qualifications are able to apply for spots as noncommercial licensees. In such instances, the rules applicable to other broadcasters are applicable to religious broadcasters as well. In addition, the Commission will apply the "fair break" doctrine by inquiring as to "whether the applicant, whatever his own views, is likely to give a 'fair break' to others who do not share them." Noe v. Federal Communications Commission, 260 F.2d 739, 742 (D.C.Cir.1958). See generally Way of the Cross of Utah, Inc., 58 R.R.2d 455 (F.C.C.1985).

The Commission has made one major exception to its general rules in allowing a religious broadcaster to consider an applicant's religion for employment, but only for "those persons hired to espouse a particular religious philosophy over the air." In King's Garden, Inc. v. Federal Communications Commission, 498 F.2d 51 (D.C.Cir.1974), certiorari denied 419 U.S. 996 (1974), the Commission rejected the claim that a religious licensee could make religion a qualification of employment for all its staff positions: "A religious group, like any other . . . takes its franchise 'burdened by enforceable public obligations.' "

In its early days of reallocating frequencies, when there were no spots reserved for educational broadcasting, the Radio Commission had occasion to consider the value of a station emphasizing religious programming. It decided that such programming was usually aimed at too narrow a base of listeners and this "discriminated against" the rest of the listeners. "In rare cases it is possible to combine a general public-service station and a high-class religious station in a division of time which will approximate a well-rounded program. In other cases religious stations must accept part time on inferior channels or daylight assignments . . . ." Great Lakes Broadcasting Co., 3 F.R.C.Ann.Rep. 32 (1929), modified on other grounds 37 F.2d 993 (D.C.Cir.1930), certiorari dismissed 281 U.S. 706 (1930). As the spectrum expanded, religious broadcasting gained a more secure footing.

Some have argued that even today religious programming provides too narrow a base to justify the allocation of a license. An effort to persuade the Commission of this failed in 1975. Multiple and Religious Ownership of Educational Stations, 54 F.C.C.2d 941, 34 R.R.2d 1217 (1975). Two persons requested a "freeze" on all grants of reserved educational FM and television channels to religious institutions pending a study of their value. The Commission thought this would violate its obligation of "neutrality" toward sectarian applicants. The Commission concluded that no new policies were needed and decided to continue ad hoc enforcement of its existing policies, such as the fairness doctrine and "the principle that a broadcast station may not be used solely to promote the personal or partisan objectives of the broadcaster."

Whether the content of religious programming raises special questions under the fairness doctrine is discussed in Chapter XV.

Chapter XV

LEGAL CONTROL OF BROADCAST PROGRAMMING

In this Chapter we consider direct regulation of content, but not necessarily prohibitions on speech. We begin, for example, with Congressional legislation to provide access and fairness in the electoral process. No speech is prohibited. Rather, broadcasters are told that they must allow certain candidates to use the station's facilities. In addition, if a candidate for an office is allowed to use the facilities, the candidate's opponents must be allowed equal opportunities.

We then turn to doctrines developed by the Commission itself that require a broadcaster who has allowed dissemination of views on a certain topic to expose listeners or viewers to contrasting viewpoints on that topic. In each case consider whether the regulations, although not prohibitory, may nonetheless indirectly influence broadcasters to air or not to air certain types of content.

A. EQUAL OPPORTUNITIES AND ACCESS IN POLITICAL CAMPAIGNS

---

1. EQUAL OPPORTUNITIES—SECTION 315

In the Radio Act of 1927, § 18 provided:

> If any licensee shall permit any person who is a legally qualified candidate for any public office to use a broadcasting station, he shall afford equal opportunities to all other such candidates for that office in the use of such broadcasting station; . . . *Provided,* That such licensee shall have no power of censorship over the material broadcast under the provisions of this paragraph. No obligation is hereby imposed upon any licensee to allow the use of its station by any such candidate.

This became § 315 of the 1934 Act. Although the Commission has explicit rulemaking power to carry out the provisions of § 315(a), few rules have been promulgated. Since most of the problems involve requests in the heat of an election campaign, few decisions have been reviewed by the courts until recently.

a. General Application

Section 315 applies only to "legally qualified" candidates for public office. According to § 73.1940(a) of the Commission's rules, a legally qualified candidate is one who:

(i) has publicly announced his or her intention to run for nomination or office;

(ii) is qualified under the applicable local, state or federal law to hold the office for which he or she is a candidate; and

(iii) has met the qualifications set forth in either subparagraphs (2), (3) or (4) below.

These subparagraphs require the candidate either to have qualified for a place on the ballot or to have made a public commitment to seeking election by the write-in method as well as a substantial showing of being a bona-fide candidate for the office.

Efforts to expand the "candidate" category have generally failed. Senator Eugene McCarthy announced early that he was a candidate for the 1968 Democratic nomination for President against the incumbent, Lyndon Johnson. In 1967, during a traditional year-end interview with television reporters, President Johnson criticized Senator McCarthy and made several political statements. McCarthy claimed rights under § 315, but the Commission denied the request on the ground that the President had not announced that he was a candidate for reelection and thus did not come within the statute or the Commission's rules on who is a "legally qualified candidate" for office. Eugene McCarthy, 11 F.C.C.2d 511, 12 R.R.2d 106 (1968). On appeal, the Commission's position was affirmed. McCarthy v. Federal Communications Commission, 390 F.2d 471 (D.C.Cir.1968). In fact, in early 1968, President Johnson unexpectedly announced that he would not seek reelection.

For many years it has been clear that § 315 does not apply to uses of a broadcast facility on behalf of a candidate unless the candidate appeared personally during the program. This meant that friends and campaign committees could purchase time without triggering § 315. Felix v. Westinghouse Broadcasting Co., 186 F.2d 1 (3d Cir.1951). This raised a separate set of problems discussed at p. 822, infra.

Another basic question regarding § 315 was resolved in Farmers Educational & Cooperative Union v. WDAY, Inc., 360 U.S. 525 (1959), when the Court unanimously held that a licensee was barred from censoring the comments of a speaker exercising rights under § 315. The Court also held, 5–4, that the section preempted state defamation law and created an absolute privilege that protected the licensee from liability for statements made by such a candidate. Neither party challenged the constitutionality of § 315. Although the station is protected from liability for defamation, the person who utters the statements may be subject to liability for defamation.

Other content problems under § 315 are rare, but do arise. Among the candidates running in 1972 for the Democratic nomination for Senator from Georgia, one was broadcasting the following spot announcement:

I am J.B. Stoner. I am the only candidate for U.S. Senator who is for the white people. I am the only candidate who is

> against integration. All of the other candidates are race mixers to one degree or another. I say we must repeal Gambrell's civil rights law. Gambrell's law takes jobs from us whites and gives those jobs to the niggers. The main reason why niggers want integration is because the niggers want our white women. I am for law and order with the knowledge that you cannot have law and order and niggers too. Vote white. This time vote your convictions by voting white racist J.B. Stoner into the run-off election for U.S. Senator. Thank you.

Several groups asked the Commission to rule that a licensee may, and has the responsibility to, withhold announcements under § 315 if they "pose an imminent and immediate threat to the safety and security of the public it serves." The groups alleged that the spot had created racial tension and that the Mayor of Atlanta had urged broadcasters not to air the advertisement. Letter to Lonnie King, 36 F.C.C.2d 635, 25 R.R.2d 54 (1972). The Commission refused to issue the requested order:

> The relief requested in your letter would amount to an advance approval by the Commission of licensee censorship of a candidate's remarks. By way of background, we note that Constitutional guarantees do not permit the proscription of even the advocacy of force or of law violation "except where such advocacy is directed to inciting or producing imminent lawless action and is likely to incite or produce such action." Brandenburg v. Ohio, 395 U.S. 444, 447 (1969). And a prior restraint bears a heavy presumption against its constitutional validity. [ ] While there may be situations where speech is "so interlaced with burgeoning violence that it is not protected," [ ] and while a similar approach might warrant overriding the no-censorship command of Section 315, we need not resolve that difficult issue here, for we conclude on the basis of the information before us that there is no factual basis for the relief you request. Despite your report of threats of bombing and violence, there does not appear to be that clear and present danger of imminent violence which might warrant interfering with speech which does not contain any direct incitement to violence. A contrary conclusion here would permit anyone to prevent a candidate from exercising his rights under Section 315 by threatening a violent reaction. In view of the precise commands of Sections 315 and 326, we are constrained to deny your requests.

In a primary election for governor of Georgia, Stoner, a legally qualified candidate, speaking under § 315, made broadcast messages using the word "nigger." Black groups asked the Commission to bar such language as indecent under the *Pacifica* principle. The Broadcast Bureau rejected the request. First, it ruled that the word was not "language that describes in the broadcast medium, sexual or excretory activities and organs, at times of the day when there is reasonable risk that children may be in the audience," quoting the Commission's language in *Pacifica*. Also, the Commission had already announced that "we intend strictly to observe the narrowness of the *Pacifica* holding." Even if the Commission were to find the word obscene or indecent, under § 315 the candidate could not be prevented from using the word during his "use" of the licensee's facilities. Julian Bond, 69 F.C.C.2d 943, 43 R.R.2d 1015 (Bd.Bur.1978).

During the 1980 Presidential campaign, one radio commercial began as follows: A man says "Bullshit!" After a woman says "What?", the man's voice replies: "Carter, Reagan, and Anderson. It's all Bullshit! Bullshit!" Then the Citizens Party's candidate says, "Too bad people have to use such strong language, but isn't that what you think too? That's why we started an entirely new political party, the Citizens Party." The FCC, which received many complaints and inquiries, responded that the precedents were quite clear that no censorship was possible—at least unless a candidate created a clear and present danger of riot or violence.

The campaign director said that for six months the media had been covering only the three major candidates "despite the fact that they have little to say of substance about the problems of the nation. . . . It's a sad commentary on the media that we received more attention as a result of using that word than we've received in the last six months combined."

In 1983, Hustler magazine publisher Larry Flynt was reported to be intending to use clips from X-rated films in television ads supporting his presidential candidacy. Legislation was introduced in the Senate to allow broadcasters to refuse to air pornographic political announcements despite the non-censorship provision of § 315. Subsequently, the FCC indicated that it would not apply the no-censorship provision to obscene or indecent political announcements. The issue never arose as Flynt chose not to run.

b. Exemptions

During its early years the statute apparently caused few serious problems. The advent of television, however, changed matters dramatically. In 1956, the Commission issued two major rulings during the presidential campaign. In one it ruled that stations carrying President Eisenhower's appearance in a three minute appeal on behalf of the annual drive of the United Community Funds would be a "use" of the facility by a candidate that would trigger the equal opportunities provision. The section did not exempt "public service" nor did it require the appearance to be "political." Columbia Broadcasting System (United Fund), 14 R.R. 524 (F.C.C.1956). One week before the election, President Eisenhower requested and received 15 minutes of free time from the three networks to discuss the sudden eruption of war in the Middle East. His Democratic opponent's request for equal time was rejected by the networks. One day before the election, the Commission, without opinion and with one dissent, upheld the networks' position. Columbia Broadcasting System (Suez Crisis), 14 R.R. 720 (F.C.C.1956).

This response to an incumbent speaking as President rather than as candidate was unusual for the Commission, which had interpreted "use" very broadly. It did so again in 1959 when a third-party candidate for mayor of Chicago, Lar Daly, asked equal time on the basis of two series of television clips of his opponents, incumbent Mayor Daley and the Republican challenger. One group of clips showed the two major candidates filing their papers (46 seconds), Mayor Daley accepting the nomination (22 seconds), and a one-minute clip asking the Republican why he was running. A second group of clips included "nonpolitical" activities such as a 29-second clip of Mayor Daley on a March of Dimes appeal and 21 seconds of his greeting President Frondizi of Argentina at a Chicago airport. Relying on the words "use" and "all" in the statute, the Commission ruled that both groups of clips required equal time. Columbia Broadcasting System, Inc. (Lar Daly), 26 F.C.C. 715 (1959). The issue of who initiated the appearance (such as the March of Dimes asking the Mayor to appear) was irrelevant. Although formal campaigning was the most obvious way of putting forward a candidacy, "of no less importance is the candidate's appearance as a public servant, as an incumbent office holder, or as a private citizen in a nonpolitical role." Such "appearances and uses of a nonpolitical nature may confer substantial benefits on a candidate who is favored."

Congressional response was swift—and negative. Hearings began within days after the decision and resulted in an amended version of § 315:

> Sec. 315. (a) If any licensee shall permit any person who is a legally qualified candidate for any public office to use a broadcasting station, he shall afford equal opportunities to all other such candidates for that office in the use of such broadcasting station: *Provided,* That such licensee shall have no power of censorship over the material broadcast under the provisions of this section. No obligation is hereby imposed upon any licensee to allow the use of its station by any such candidate.* Appearance by a legally qualified candidate on any—
>
> (1) bona fide newscast,
>
> (2) bona fide news interview,
>
> (3) bona fide news documentary (if the appearance of the candidate is incidental to the presentation of the subject or subjects covered by the news documentary), or
>
> (4) on-the-spot coverage of bona fide news events (including but not limited to political conventions and activities incidental thereto),

* In 1971 Congress amended this sentence by adding "under this subsection" after the word "imposed." The reason is explained when we consider § 312(a)(7) shortly.

shall not be deemed to be use of a broadcasting station within the meaning of this subsection. Nothing in the foregoing sentence shall be construed as relieving broadcasters, in connection with the presentation of newscasts, news interviews, news documentaries, and on-the-spot coverage of news events, from the obligation imposed upon them under this chapter to operate in the public interest and to afford reasonable opportunity for the discussion of conflicting views on issues of public importance.

Recall the significance of this episode in *Red Lion,* p. 723, supra.

In 1960, Congress suspended the operation of § 315 so that stations could give time to national candidates without creating a § 315 obligation. This permitted the Kennedy-Nixon debates to be held without need to provide free time for the many minority candidates. There was no incumbent and no major third-party candidate—two factors that made the debates politically possible.

In subsequent years, the Commission tended to interpret the 1959 amendments narrowly. In 1962, for example, it held that television coverage of a debate between two candidates held before the Economic Club of Detroit was not "on-the-spot" coverage of a bona fide news event because the debate had been planned for a long time and had been built around the two candidates. In 1964, it held generally that press conferences of the incumbent President and those of his main challenger were not exempt.

Two weeks before the 1964 election, the three networks granted President Johnson free time to comment on two events that had just occurred: a sudden change of leadership in Moscow, and the explosion of a nuclear device in China. The Commission adhered to its 1956 ruling that this was not a "use" and also upheld a network claim that this program came within § 315(a)(4) as a bona fide news event. Republican National Committee (Dean Burch), 3 R.R.2d 647 (F.C.C.1964). The court of appeals affirmed 3–3, without opinion, and a petition for certiorari was denied, Goldwater v. Federal Communications Commission, 379 U.S. 893 (1964). Justice Goldberg, joined by Justice Black, dissented on the ground that the case presented substantial questions and that the Commission seemed not to be consistent in its own decisions.

Through the 1960s and 1970s, nothing came of Congressional efforts to amend or repeal § 315. But in 1975, the Commission responded dramatically to two petitions. It overruled its 1962 approach and now concluded that, in 1959, Congress had intended to run the risks of political favoritism among broadcasters in an effort to allow broadcasters to "cover the political news to the fullest degree." Debates were exempt if controlled by someone other than the candidates or the broadcaster, and if judged to be bona fide news events under § 315(a)(4).

In a companion ruling, the Commission overruled its 1964 decision on press conference coverage. It decided that full coverage of a press conference by any incumbent or candidate would come within the exemption for on-the-spot coverage of a bona fide news event if it "may be considered newsworthy and subject to on-the-spot coverage." But the Commission refused to bring a press conference within the exemption for bona fide news interviews because the licensee did not "control" the format and the event was not "regularly scheduled." Petitions of Aspen Institute and CBS, Inc., 55 F.C.C.2d 697, 35 R.R.2d 49 (1975).

Appeals were taken from both 1975 rulings. The main contentions were that the Commission had not followed the Congressional mandate when it permitted the candidate to "become the event" under the (a)(4) exemption, and that the statute did not allow the Commission to uphold licensee decisions if only they are in "good faith"—that it is for the Commission to make these judgments. By a vote of 2–1, the court affirmed both rulings, Chisholm v. Federal Communications Commission, 538 F.2d 349 (D.C.Cir.1976). The opinions disagreed over the significance of the complex legislative history, with the majority concluding that the Commission's interpretation was "reasonable." Rehearing en banc was denied. A petition for certiorari was denied, 429 U.S. 890 (1976) White, J., dissenting.

Electoral Debates. Seizing on the Commission's rulings, the League of Women Voters set up "debates" between the two major Presidential candidates in 1976. They were held in auditoriums before invited audiences. The candidates were questioned by panelists selected by the League after consultation with the participants. Television was allowed to cover the events—but the League imposed restrictions against showing the audience or any audience reactions. Although the networks complained about the restrictions and about the way the panelists were selected, they did carry the programs live and in full.

Again, in 1980, the League took steps to sponsor debates among the major candidates. It decided that John Anderson's showing in public opinion polls was sufficiently strong to warrant his inclusion in a three-way debate. When President Carter refused to participate in a debate with Anderson, the League went ahead anyway and staged an Anderson-Reagan debate. If networks decided to cover the event, as CBS and NBC did, the coverage would be exempt under (a)(2) because the networks and licensees were making the judgment it was a bona fide news event even without the President.

After Anderson's ratings fell to around 10 percent, the League invited Carter and Reagan to debate. Both accepted the invitation and held a single head-to-head debate a week before the election.

In Petitions of Henry Geller et al., 54 R.R.2d 1246 (1983), the FCC reversed itself and permitted broadcasters themselves to sponsor exempt debates between political candidates without having to invite all candidates. The Commission concluded that its previous interpretations neither represented the outer bounds of its legislated authority under the statute nor met the overriding Congressional mandate to encourage broadcast coverage of electoral issues. Third-party sponsorship was not the *sine qua non* of impartiality. For example, the risks of favoritism in the news interview format were thought to be no different than in the debate format and therefore disparate treatment was not justified. The FCC rejected the argument of the League of Women Voters that this approach created too great a risk of favoritism. The risks inherent in broadcaster-sponsored debates were no greater than the *Chisholm* court had understood the 1959 amendments to be willing to accept.

The Commission also noted that in many cases a broadcaster may be "the ideal, and perhaps the only, entity interested in promoting a debate between candidates for a particular office, especially at the state or local level." Exempting broadcaster-sponsored debates would therefore increase the number of debates and ultimately benefit the public. Finally, the critical issue was the news value of the debate and not its sponsorship. The Commission stressed that its new interpretation of § 315(a)(4) did not authorize licensees to favor or disfavor any candidate.

The League's expedited appeal was rejected without opinion. League of Women Voters v. FCC, 731 F.2d 995 (D.C.Cir.1984).

As of 1986, an appeal brought by Sonia Johnson, Presidential candidate of the Citizens Party in 1984, was pending in the court of appeals. She claimed that televised debates unconstitutionally discriminated against candidates of other parties.

Kennedy I. In 1980, just before the primaries began, President Carter, seeking renomination as Democratic candidate for President in the face of a challenge by Senator Edward M. Kennedy, held a press conference that was carried live in prime time by the three commercial networks and the Public Broadcasting Service. Senator Kennedy, claiming that President Carter had used more than five minutes on that occasion to attack him and to misstate several of his positions, sought relief from the FCC.

In Kennedy for President Committee v. Federal Communications Commission, 636 F.2d 432 (D.C.Cir.1980) (*Kennedy I*), the Senator claimed time under § 315 to respond to the "calculated and damaging statements" and to "provide contrasting viewpoints." The FCC's denial was affirmed on appeal.

The press conference was exempt under § 315(a)(4) so long as the broadcasters reasonably believed that the conference was a "bona fide news event." The Commission said, in a passage approved by the court, that an incumbent President "may well have an advantage over his opponent in attracting media coverage" but "absent strong evidence that broadcasters were not exercising their bona fide news judgment, the Commission will not interfere with such judgments." The Senator was free to hold a press conference the next day to rebut the charges. Indeed, generally, Senator Kennedy was getting substantial media coverage.

The court thought that the "only inquiry now in order is whether there was anything so peculiar about the February 13 presidential press conference as to remove it from the ambit of *Aspen* and *Chisholm.*" The court found no reason to doubt the broadcasters' good faith. It also concluded that the actual content of the event could not control the question of exemption. In addition to the difficult judgments about the content, context, and impact of particular statements that the Commission and the courts would have to make, the goal of the exemptions would be defeated if broadcasters could not know until after an event whether it was exempt.

Senator Kennedy then argued that the First Amendment required that he be granted time to respond, even if the statute did not. The court concluded that the First Amendment permits Congress to enforce the public's primary interests by using broadcasters as public trustees, and CBS v. DNC shows that no one has a constitutional right to broadcast his own views on any matter.

Subdivision (1). The other subdivisions, (a)(1) and (a)(3), have given rise to fewer problems. In 1976, supporters of Ronald Reagan complained when a Miami television station broadcast six-minute interviews with President Ford on five consecutive evening newscasts. The complaint asserted that the segments were from a single half-hour interview that had been broken up into five parts. The Commission held that even if the 30-minute interview would not have been exempt under § 315, inclusion of the segments within newscasts would not preclude "exempt status pursuant to § 315(a)(1) unless it has been shown that such a decision is clearly unreasonable or in bad faith." Even though this was broadcast during the last week of a primary campaign and might benefit President Ford, the complainants "have not shown that the licensee in deciding to air them, considered anything other than their newsworthiness." Citizens for Reagan, 58 F.C.C.2d 925, 36 R.R.2d 885 (1976).

The FCC has granted general exemptions under (a)(1) to such programs as "Today" and "Good Morning America." In each case, the FCC was influenced by the fact that the program was regularly scheduled and involved regular coverage of current news, supplemented by interviews, commentary, and discussions. The determinations of what to cover are made in the exercise of news judgment and not to further a particular candidate's advantage.

c. *Nonpolitical Appearances*

The Commission appears to be holding firm to its earlier decisions broadly defining "use" in cases of "nonpolitical" appearances. Thus, in United Way of America, 35 R.R.2d 137 (F.C.C.1975), which was decided at about the same time as the *Aspen-CBS* petitions, the Commission, 4–3, adhered to its earlier rulings that an appearance by candidate Ford opening an annual charity fund drive came within § 315. The Commission has also adhered to its view that appearances by television personalities or film stars after they have announced their candidacy for office constitutes a "use" under § 315. In Adrian Weiss, 58 F.C.C.2d 342, 36 R.R.2d 292 (1976), the Broadcast Bureau ruled that the showing of old Ronald Reagan films on television would create claims for his opponents under § 315. The Bureau stressed that nonpolitical uses can be very effective. The Commission refused to review the Bureau's decision, with two Commissioners concurring separately and two dissenting. These four all thought that common sense dictated exempting movies made before Reagan actively entered politics, but the two concurring Commissioners thought that any change should be made by Congress.

In Pat Paulsen, 33 F.C.C.2d 297, affirmed 33 F.C.C.2d 835, 23 R.R. 2d 861 (1972), affirmed 491 F.2d 887 (9th Cir.1974), the Commission rejected a comedian's argument that applying § 315 to his efforts to run for office would deprive him of due process and equal protection by forcing him to give up his livelihood in order to run for public office. The FCC's interpretation was held permissible "to achieve the important and legitimate objectives of encouraging political discussion and preventing unfair and unequal use of the broadcast media."

In 1985, the Commission turned down a petition by William Branch, a California TV reporter, asking for a ruling that appearing on the air as a journalist would not trigger § 315. The Commission also refused to declare that § 315 violated the First Amendment. Appeals are pending. Broadcasting, July 28, 1986, at 94.

d. *"Lowest Unit" Rate*

In 1971, as part of legislation concerning election campaigning, Congress passed two statutes that affect broadcasting during political campaigns. One, § 312(a)(7), is discussed below. The second requires that candidates using broadcast facilities during the 45 days before a primary and the 60 days before a general election be charged rates not to exceed "the lowest unit charge of the station for the same class and amount of time for the same period. . . ." At all other times, candidates are not to be charged more than "the charges made for comparable use of such station by other users thereof." 47 U.S.C. § 315(b).

The major difference between the two quoted passages is that during the 45- and 60-day periods, the candidate pays the rate that the highest-volume advertiser would pay for that time. At other times, the candidate pays the rates charged to those who advertise as little or as much as the candidate does. Section 315(b) is discussed extensively in Hernstadt v. Federal Communications Commission, 677 F.2d 893, 49 R.R.2d 359 (D.C.Cir.1980).

In KVUE, Inc. v. Moore, 709 F.2d 922, 54 R.R.2d 224 (5th Cir.1983), Texas law set year-round limits on the prices to be charged political advertisers. The statute also set standards for identifying sponsors of advertising addressed to both state and federal races. The court held that the provisions setting maximum rates and the provisions about identifying sponsors of advertising discussing federal races were preempted. The Supreme Court affirmed without argument and without opinion. 465 U.S. 1092 (1984) (Rehnquist, Stevens, and O'Connor JJ., would have noted probable jurisdiction and set the case for oral argument).

2. Reasonable Access—Section 312(a)(7)

In 1971, at the same time it passed the lowest unit rate provision, Congress adopted § 312(a)(7), providing that the Commission may revoke a license:

> (7) for willful or repeated failure to allow reasonable access to or to permit purchase of reasonable amounts of time for the use of a broadcasting station by a legally qualified candidate for Federal elective office on behalf of his candidacy.

The legislative history indicates that one purpose of the overall legislation was to "give candidates for public office greater access to the media so that they may better explain their stand on the issues and thereby more fully and completely inform the voters."

It was only in 1980 that cases involving the section began to reach the courts. The major case was CBS, Inc. v. Federal Communications Commission, discussed at p. 760, supra, involving the efforts of the Carter-Mondale Committee to buy time from the networks. The nonconstitutional aspects are discussed in the passage below.

CBS, INC. v. FCC

Supreme Court of the United States, 1981.
453 U.S. 367, 101 S.Ct. 2813, 69 L.Ed.2d 706, 7 Med.L.Rptr. 1563.

Noted, 48 Brooklyn L.Rev. 355, 1982 Det.C.L.Rev. 147, 95 Harv.L.Rev. 221, 1982 Utah L.Rev. 641.

Chief Justice Burger delivered the opinion of the Court.

[The Chief Justice agreed with the FCC and the court of appeals that Congress had intended to create "an affirmative, promptly enforceable right of reasonable access to the use of broadcast stations for individual candidates seeking federal elective office," rather than simply codifying prior policies that the FCC had developed under the general public interest standard. He relied on the specific language of the statute itself, the legislative history, and what the Court found to be the FCC's consistent administrative interpretation of the language since the statute's enactment. Perhaps the "most telling evidence" of Congressional intent was the contemporaneous change in § 315 from a statement that "No obligation is imposed upon any licensee to allow the use of its station by" a candidate to the statement that no such obligation "is imposed under this subsection."]

III

A

Although Congress provided in § 312(a)(7) for greater use of broadcasting stations by federal candidates, it did not give guidance on how the Commission should implement the statute's access requirement. Essentially, Congress adopted a "rule of reason" and charged the Commission with its enforcement. . . . The Commission has issued some general interpretative statements, but its standards implementing § 312(a)(7) have evolved principally on a case-by-case basis and are not embodied in formalized rules. . . .

Broadcasters are free to deny the sale of air time prior to the commencement of a campaign, but once a campaign has begun, they must give reasonable and good-faith attention to access requests from "legally qualified" candidates for federal elective office. Such requests must be considered on an individualized basis, and broadcasters are required to tailor their responses to accommodate, as much as reasonably possible, a candidate's stated purposes in seeking air time. In responding to access requests, however, broadcasters may also give weight to such factors as the amount of time previously sold to the candidate, the disruptive impact on regular programming, and the likelihood of requests for time by rival candidates under the equal opportunities provision of § 315(a). These considerations may not be invoked as pretexts for denying access; to justify a negative response, broadcasters must cite a realistic danger of substantial program disruption—perhaps caused by insufficient notice to allow adjustments in the schedule—or of an excessive number of equal time requests. Further, in order to facilitate review by the Commission, broadcasters must explain their reasons for refusing time or making a more limited counteroffer. If broadcasters take the appropriate factors into account and act reasonably and in good faith, their decisions will be entitled to deference even if the Commission's analysis would have differed in the first instance. But if broadcasters adopt "across-the-board policies" and do not attempt to respond to the individualized situation of a particular candidate, the Commission is not compelled to sustain their denial of access. [ ] Petitioners argue that certain of these standards are contrary to the statutory objectives of § 312(a)(7).

(1)

The Commission has concluded that, as a threshold matter, it will independently determine whether a campaign has begun and the obligations imposed by § 312(a)(7) have attached. [ ] Petitioners assert that, in undertaking such a task, the Commission becomes improperly involved in the electoral process and seriously impairs broadcaster discretion.

However, petitioners fail to recognize that the Commission does not set the starting date for a campaign. Rather, on review of a complaint alleging denial of "reasonable access," it examines objective evidence to find whether the campaign has already commenced, "taking into account the position of the candidate *and the networks* as well as other factors." [ ] (emphasis added). . . . Such a decision is not, and cannot be, purely one of editorial judgment.

. . . By confining the applicability of the statute to the period after a campaign commences, the Commission has limited its impact on broadcasters and given substance to its command of *reasonable* access.

(2)

Petitioners also challenge the Commission's requirement that broadcasters evaluate and respond to access requests on an individualized basis. In petitioners' view, the agency has attached inordinate significance to candidates' needs, thereby precluding fair assessment of broadcasters' concerns and prohibiting the adoption of uniform policies regarding requests for access.

While admonishing broadcasters not to " 'second guess' the 'political' wisdom or . . . effectiveness" of the particular format sought by a candidate, the Commission has clearly acknowledged that "the candidate's . . . request is by no means conclusive of the question of how much time, if any, is appropriate. Other . . . factors, such as the disruption or displacement of regular programming (particularly as affected by a reasonable probability of requests by other candidates), must be considered in the balance." [ ] Thus, the Commission mandates careful consideration of, not blind assent to, candidates' desires for air time.

Petitioners are correct that the Commission's standards proscribe blanket rules concerning access; each request must be examined on its own merits. While the adoption of uniform policies might well prove more convenient for broadcasters, such an approach would allow personal campaign strategies and the exigencies of the political process to be ignored. A broadcaster's "evenhanded" response of granting only time spots of a fixed duration to candidates may be "unreasonable" where a particular candidate desires less time for an advertisement or a longer format to discuss substantive issues. . . .

[The Court concluded that the Commission's actions were a "reasoned attempt to effectuate the statute's access requirement, giving broadcasters room to exercise their discretion but demanding that they act in good faith." These ground rules were sufficiently clear in late 1979 to permit the FCC to rule that the networks had violated the statute by failing to grant "reasonable access."]

IV

[Here the Court rejected the constitutional challenges to the section, as reported at p. 760, supra, and then affirmed the judgment of the court of appeals.]

[Justice White, joined by Justices Rehnquist and Stevens, dissented on the grounds that the Commission and the Court had failed to give sufficient weight to a "long-standing statutory policy of deferring to editorial judgments that are not destructive of the goals of the Act." As a result, the Commission had read § 312(a)(7) much too broadly. Congress had intended only "to codify what it conceived to be the pre-existing duty of the broadcasters to serve the public interest by presenting political broadcasts."]

[In a separate dissent, Justice Stevens argued that the result created "an impermissible risk that the Commission's evaluation of a given refusal by a licensee will be biased—or will appear to be biased—by the character of the office held by the candidate making the request." He was concerned about the fact that the four Democratic Commissioners had voted for the Carter-Mondale request and the three Republicans had dissented.]

Notes and Questions

1. From the text alone who appears to have the better of the argument over proper reading of § 312(a)(7)? The opinions in the case argue the legislative history at great length.

2. Is it significant that the FCC split along party lines in deciding the case?

3. The relationship between § 312(a)(7) and § 315 was central to Kennedy for President Committee v. Federal Communications Commission, 636 F.2d 417 (D.C.Cir.1980) (*Kennedy II*). On March 14, 1980, President Carter made a 30-minute speech in the afternoon and held a press conference from 9:00 to 9:30 p.m. that night. The three major commercial networks carried both programs live, except that ABC delayed the press conference for three hours. Senator Kennedy charged that these programs saturated the public with the President's views on the economy only four days before the Illinois primary. He asked for free time to reply under § 312(a)(7). The networks denied the request, the Commission refused to order that time be granted, and the court affirmed.

The court began by noting that Congress, in 1971, enacted § 312(a)(7) and § 315(b)(1) because Congress was concerned about the rising cost of candidates' televised appearances:

> It was believed that the informational and educational aspects of political broadcasting would be greatly enhanced by ensuring that more time would be made available to candidates at lower rates. This expectably would encourage less dependence on thirty- to sixty-second "spots"—necessarily little more than slogans—in favor of longer, more illuminating presentations; it would also enable more candidates to afford the television appearances so instrumental to present-day electioneering.

The court concluded that the "most straightforward reading" of § 312(a)(7) "is that broadcasters may fulfill their obligation thereunder either by allotting free time to a candidate *or* by selling the candidate time at the rates prescribed by Section 315(b)." Considering the legislative history, the FCC's consistent administrative interpretations, and the apparent statutory scheme of the various provisions, the court concluded that § 312(a)(7), although seeking to assure federal candidates access to broadcasting, did not "confer the privilege of using the broadcaster's facilities without charge." The choice of giving or selling time is for the broadcaster:

> Should Section 312(a)(7) be construed as automatically entitling a candidate to responsive broadcast access whenever and for whatever reason his opponent has appeared on the air, Section 315(a)'s exemptions would soon become meaningless. Statutes are to be interpreted, if possible, to give operation to all of their parts, and to maintain them in harmonious working relationship.

Since Kennedy never claimed that he had not been given an opportunity to buy time, he could not invoke § 312(a)(7). Nor had he sought relief under § 315.

4. In 1981, the National Conservative Political Action Committee (NCPAC) sought a ruling that independent political action committees (PACs) had a right of reasonable access similar to that granted candidates for federal office by § 312(a)(7). The Broadcast Bureau rejected NCPAC's request, finding nothing in either the language of § 312(a)(7) or its legislative history that would support a right of access for anyone other than a candidate for federal office. The Commission upheld the Bureau's action, citing CBS v. DNC. National Conservative Political Action Committee (NCPAC), 89 F.C.C.2d 626, 51 R.R.2d 233 (1982).

5. In June 1985, Senators Jack Danforth (R-Mo.) and Ernest Hollings (D-S.C.) introduced the Clean Campaign Act of 1985 (S. 1310). The bill, among other things, would require candidates attacking their opponents in radio, television or cable advertisements to appear personally in the advertisements. Any broadcaster airing an advertisement that violated that requirement would have to provide free response time to the opponent who was attacked. Would this be constitutional?

B. THE FAIRNESS DOCTRINE

1. IN GENERAL

Although equal opportunities has a statutory origin, the fairness doctrine was created by the Commission itself. The Commission has been concerned with fairness and the exposure of varying views since its earliest days. In 1928, the Radio Commission indicated as much in a discussion of the implications of the limited spectrum. It observed that there was not room "for every school of thought, religious, political, social, and economic, each to have its separate broadcasting station, its mouthpiece in the ether." Such ideas "must find their way into the market of ideas by the existing public-service stations, and if they are of sufficient importance to the listening public the microphone will undoubtedly be available. If it is not, a well-founded complaint will receive the careful consideration of the commission in its future action with reference to the station complained of." Great Lakes Broadcasting Co., 3 F.R.C.Ann.Rep. 32 (1929), modified on other grounds 37 F.2d 993 (D.C.Cir.1930), certiorari dismissed 281 U.S. 706 (1930).

The doctrine evolved through case law until it became the subject of a major report in 1949. The doctrine has two separate parts. One part requires the broadcaster to air issues that "are so critical or of such great public importance that it would be unreasonable for a licensee to ignore them completely." Much more attention has been paid to the second part of the doctrine—that if a broadcaster does cover a "controversial issue of public importance," it must take steps to assure that significant contrasting views are also presented. These views may be presented by the licensee itself or by speakers chosen by the licensee.

In 1959, when § 315 was amended, p. 794, supra, the phrase "nothing in the foregoing sentence shall be construed as relieving broadcasters . . . from the obligation under this chapter to operate in the public interest and to afford reasonable opportunity for the discussion of conflicting views on issues of public importance" was understood by some as codifying the fairness doctrine in the Communications Act.

IN THE MATTER OF THE HANDLING OF PUBLIC ISSUES UNDER THE FAIRNESS DOCTRINE AND THE PUBLIC INTEREST STANDARDS OF THE COMMUNICATIONS ACT (FAIRNESS REPORT)

Federal Communications Commission, 1974.
48 F.C.C.2d 1, 30 R.R.2d 1261.

By the Commission: . . .

[The Commission first restated its commitment to the goal of "uninhibited, robust, wide open" debate on public issues and the need to recognize that achievement of this goal must be compatible with the public interest in "the larger and more effective use of radio," § 303(g). "[O]urs is a commercially-based broadcast system," it observed, and the Commission's policies "should be consistent with the maintenance and growth of that system." The Commission then quoted a critical passage from its Report on Editorializing, 13 F.C.C. 1246, 1249 (1949), in which the fairness doctrine was formally announced:

> It is axiomatic that one of the most vital questions of mass communication in a democracy is the development of an informed public opinion through the public dissemination of news and ideas concerning the vital public issues of the day. . . . The Commission has consequently recognized the necessity for licensees to devote a reasonable percentage of their broadcast time to the

presentation of news and programs devoted to the consideration and discussion of public issues of interest in the community served by the particular station. And we have recognized, with respect to such programs, the paramount right of the public in a free society to be informed and to have presented to it for acceptance or rejection the different attitudes and viewpoints concerning these vital and often controversial issues which are held by the various groups which make up the community. It is this right of the public to be informed, rather than any right on the part of the Government, any broadcast licensee or any individual member of the public to broadcast his own particular views on any matter, which is the foundation stone of the American system of broadcasting.

The Commission noted that in 1970 it had described the two parts of the fairness doctrine "as the single most important requirement of operation in the public interest—the *sine qua non* for grant of a renewal of license." The Commission denied that imposition of these two duties could be inhibiting:

> 18. . . . When a licensee presents one side of a controversial issue, he is not required to provide a forum for opposing views on that same program or series of programs. He is simply expected to make provision for the opposing views in his *overall programming.* Further, there is no requirement that any precisely equal balance of views be achieved, and all matters concerning the particular opposing views to be presented and the appropriate spokesmen and format for their presentation are left to the licensee's discretion subject only to a standard of reasonableness and good faith.
>
> 19. As a matter of general procedure, we do not monitor broadcasts for possible violations, but act on the basis of complaints received from interested citizens. These complaints are not forwarded to the licensee for his comments unless they present *prima facie* evidence of a violation. Allen C. Phelps, 21 FCC2d 12 (1969). Thus, broadcasters are not burdened with the task of answering idle or capricious complaints. By way of illustration, the Commission received some 2,400 fairness complaints in fiscal 1973, only 94 of which were forwarded to licensees for their comments.
>
> 20. While there may be occasional exceptions, we find it difficult to believe that these policies add significantly to the overall administrative burdens involved in operating a broadcast station. . . .

As to the first duty imposed, the Commission noted:

> We have, in the past, indicated that some issues are so critical or of such great public importance that it would be unreasonable for a licensee to ignore them completely. [ ] But such statements on our part are the rare exception, not the rule, and we have no intention of becoming involved in the selection of issues to be

discussed, nor do we expect a broadcaster to cover each and every important issue which may arise in his community.

26. We wish to emphasize that the responsibility for the selection of program material is that of the individual licensee. That responsibility "can neither be delegated by the licensee to any network or other person or group, or be unduly fettered by contractual arrangements restricting the licensee in his free exercise of his independent judgments." Report on Editorializing, 13 FCC at 1248. . . .

The Commission then turned to the second, and more frequently litigated, aspect of the fairness doctrine.

2. A Reasonable Opportunity for Opposing Viewpoints

. . .

28. It has frequently been suggested that individual stations should not be expected to present opposing points of view and that it should be sufficient for the licensee to demonstrate that the opposing viewpoint has been adequately presented on another station in the market or in the print media. [ ] While we recognize that citizens receive information on public issues from a variety of sources, other considerations require the rejection of this suggestion. First, in amending section 315(a) of the Communications Act in 1959, Congress gave statutory approval to the fairness doctrine, including the requirement that broadcasters themselves provide an opportunity for opposing viewpoints. See *BEM,* 412 U.S. at 110, note 8. Second, it would be an administrative nightmare for this Commission to attempt to review the overall coverage of an issue in all of the broadcast stations and publications in a given market. Third, and perhaps most importantly, we believe that the requirement that *each* station provide for contrasting views greatly increases the likelihood that individual members of the public will be exposed to varying points of view. . . .

a. What is a "Controversial Issue of Public Importance"?

29. [Because of "the limitless number of potential controversial issues and the varying circumstances in which they might arise," the FCC has been unable to develop] comprehensive guidelines to aid interested parties in recognizing whether an issue is "controversial" and of "public importance." . . . For this very practical reason, and for the reason that our role must and should be limited to one of review, we will continue to rely heavily on the reasonable, good faith judgments of our licensees in this area.

30. Some general observations, however, are in order. First of all, it is obvious that an issue is not necessarily a matter of significant "public importance" merely because it has received broadcast or newspaper coverage. "Our daily papers and television broadcasts alike are filled with news items which good journalistic judgment would classify as newsworthy, but which the same editors would not characterize as

containing important controversial public issues." Healey v. FCC, 460 F.2d 917, 922 (D.C.Cir.1972). Nevertheless, the degree of media coverage is one factor which clearly should be taken into account in determining an issue's importance. It is also appropriate to consider the degree of attention the issue has received from government officials and other community leaders. The principal test of public importance, however, is not the extent of media or governmental attention, but rather a subjective evaluation of the impact that the issue is likely to have on the community at large. If the issue involves a social or political choice, the licensee might well ask himself whether the outcome of that choice will have a significant impact on society or its institutions. It appears to us that these judgments can be made only on a case-by-case basis.

31. The question of whether an issue is "controversial" may be determined in a somewhat more objective manner. Here, it is highly relevant to measure the degree of attention paid to an issue by government officials, community leaders, and the media. The licensee should be able to tell, with a reasonable degree of objectivity, whether an issue is the subject of vigorous debate with substantial elements of the community in opposition to one another. . . .

b. What Specific Issue Has Been Raised?

32. One of the most difficult problems involved in the administration of the fairness doctrine is the determination of the *specific* issue or issues raised by a particular program. This would seem to be a simple task, but in many cases it is not. . . .

. . .

c. What is a "Reasonable Opportunity" for Contrasting Viewpoints?

. . .

37. [This obligation] cannot be met "merely through the adoption of a general policy of not refusing to broadcast opposing views where a demand is made of the station for broadcast time." Report on Editorializing, 13 FCC at 1251. The licensee has a duty to play a conscious and positive role in encouraging the presentation of opposing viewpoints.[13]

. . .

38. In making provision for the airing of contrasting viewpoints, the broadcaster should be alert to the possibility that a particular issue may involve more than two opposing viewpoints. Indeed, there may be

13. This duty includes the obligation defined in Cullman Broadcasting Co., 40 FCC 576, 577 (1963) . . . .

We do not believe that the passage of time since *Cullman* was decided has in any way since diminished the importance and necessity of this principle. If the public's right to be informed of the contrasting views on controversial issues is to be truly honored, broadcasters must provide the forum for the expression of those viewpoints at their own expense if paid sponsorship is unavailable.

several important viewpoints or shades of opinion which warrant broadcast coverage.

. . .

41. In providing for the coverage of opposing points of view, we believe that the licensee must make a reasonable allowance for presentations by genuine partisans who actually believe in what they are saying. The fairness doctrine does not permit the broadcaster "to preside over a 'paternalistic' regime," *BEM,* 412 U.S. at 130, and it would clearly not be acceptable for the licensee to adopt a "policy of excluding partisan voices and always itself presenting views in a bland, inoffensive manner. . . ." . . .

42. This does not mean, however, that the Commission intends to dictate the selection of a particular spokesman or a particular format, or indeed that partisan spokesmen must be presented in every instance. We do not believe that it is either appropriate or feasible for a governmental agency to make decisions as to what is desirable in each situation. In cases involving personal attacks and political campaigns, the natural opposing spokesmen are relatively easy to identify. This is not the case, however, with the majority of public controversies. Ordinarily, there are a variety of spokesmen and formats which could reasonably be deemed to be appropriate. We believe that the public is best served by a system which allows individual broadcasters considerable discretion in selecting the manner of coverage, the appropriate spokesmen, and the techniques of production and presentation.

43. Frequently, the question of the reasonableness of the opportunity provided for contrasting viewpoints comes down to weighing the *time* allocated to each side. Aside from the field of political broadcasting, the licensee is not required to provide equal time for the various opposing points of view. Indeed, we have long felt that the basic goal of creating an informed citizenry would be frustrated if for every controversial item or presentation on a newscast or other broadcast the licensee had to offer equal time to the other side. . . . Similarly, we do not believe that it would be appropriate for the Commission to establish any other mathematical ratio, such as 3 to 1 or 4 to 1, to be applied in all cases. We believe that such an approach is much too mechanical in nature and that in many cases our preconceived ratios would prove to be far from reasonable. In the case of a 10-second personal attack, for example, fairness may dictate that more time be afforded to answer the attack than was given the attack itself.

. . .

E. Fairness and Accurate News Reporting

58. In our 1949 Report on Editorializing, we alluded to a licensee's obligation to present the news in an accurate manner:

> It must be recognized, however, that the licensee's opportunity to express his own views . . . does not justify or empower any licensee to exercise his authority over the selection of program

material to distort or suppress the basic factual information upon which any truly fair and free discussion of public issues must necessarily depend. . . . A licensee would be abusing his position as public trustee of these important means of mass communication were he to withhold from expression over his facilities relevant news or facts concerning a controversy or to slant or distort the presentation of such news. No discussion of the issues involved in any controversy can be fair or in the public interest where such discussion must take place in a climate of false or misleading information concerning the basic facts of the controversy.

It is a matter of critical importance to the public that the basic facts or elements of a controversy should not be deliberately suppressed or misstated by a licensee. But we must recognize that such distortions are "so continually done in perfect good faith, by persons who are not considered . . . ignorant or incompetent, that it is rarely possible on adequate grounds, conscientiously to stamp the misrepresentations as morally culpable. . . ." J.S. Mill, On Liberty 31 (People's ed. 1921). Accordingly, we do not believe that it would be either useful or appropriate for us to investigate charges of news misrepresentations in the absence of substantial extrinsic evidence or documents that on their face reflect deliberate distortion. See The Selling of the Pentagon, 30 FCC2d 150 (1971).

. . .

Notes and Questions

1. In 1976, the Commission denied reconsideration of the Report. 58 F.C.C.2d 691, 36 R.R.2d 1021 (1976). This time, Commissioner Robinson dissented because he doubted the value of the efforts involved and was concerned about the intrusion into editorial decisions. He noted that in 1973 and 1974, of 4,280 formal fairness complaints, only 19 resulted in findings adverse to the licensee. These included seven in the political editorial area, seven cases of personal attack, and five general fairness complaints. Of the 19 violations, only eight resulted in financial penalty to the licensee—seven political editorializing cases and one personal attack case involved forfeitures under § 503. Since this sanction is available only for violations of formal rules, it is not available for violations of the uncodified general doctrine.

2. Commissioner Robinson asserted that so long as *Red Lion* was the law the Commission could not eliminate the fairness doctrine completely. He favored a suggestion made by the Committee for Open Media, under which a licensee might choose to meet its obligations under the fairness doctrine by allowing access to its facilities. The proposal was to allow 35 one-minute messages per week scheduled at different times, including prime time. Half the spots would be allocated on a first-come, first-served basis; the other half would use "a representative spokesperson" system. If an excessive number wanted to speak, Commissioner Robinson suggested that speakers might be chosen by lot or

by queueing, so as to minimize licensee bias. Efforts would be made to prevent monopolization by any single group. Commissioner Robinson thought few licensees would choose to relinquish control in this way, but he thought it offered the Commission an opportunity to avoid judging content and he urged offering this alternative to licensees. For a study of the operation of Free Speech Messages in San Francisco, see Harris, Free Speech Messages: When the Public Gets Access, What Does It Say?, Access 34 at 20 (1976).

In a separate statement Chairman Wiley attacked the access proposal on the grounds that it encouraged licensees to abdicate editorial control and emphasized a single programming technique: the access announcement. "In my opinion a more varied, interesting and informative coverage would be possible if professional journalists played a conscious and positive role in the process."

3. After the Commission's denial of reconsideration of the Fairness Report, the court of appeals generally affirmed that ruling. National Citizens Committee for Broadcasting v. Federal Communications Commission, 567 F.2d 1095 (D.C.Cir.1977). The court upheld the Commission's decision to stop applying the fairness doctrine to most commercial advertisements—a result already reached in the snowmobile case, discussed at p. 839, infra. The court did remand two issues to the Commission for additional consideration. One was the COM proposal. The other was a proposal from Henry Geller that the Commission order each licensee to "list annually the ten controversial issues of public importance, local and national, which it chose for the most coverage in the prior year, set out the offers for response made, and note representative programming that was presented on each issue."

The parties that were dissatisfied with the commercial advertisement part of the decision sought Supreme Court review but certiorari was denied. 436 U.S. 926 (1978).

On the remand, the Commission adhered to its earlier views. 74 F.C.C.2d 163, 46 R.R.2d 999 (1979). It rejected the COM proposal on the ground that "any system which has its emphasis on speakers rather than on ideas is at cross-purposes to that of the Fairness Doctrine. Since the goal of the Fairness Doctrine is to inform the public, any substitute means of compliance must do this." Studies of access usage in various cities provided no assurances that important and timely public issues would be discussed, that presentations on issues would be balanced, or that they would be informative and comprehensible. Even time assigned to spokespersons for issue-oriented groups might not be devoted to the discussion of important public issues.

Despite the acknowledged attractions of the access proposal, such as the opportunity for "true partisans" to express their views, and the use of spot announcements "to reach larger and more diverse audiences than through program-length public affairs broadcasts," the defects were held to outweigh the potential gains.

Licensees who might choose to institute an access program must still comply with the fairness doctrine. "How the licensee achieves this mandate depends, as we have always stated, upon the journalistic discretion of each participating station."

The Commission again rejected the Geller "ten issues" proposal because it would not "necessarily enhance" coverage of controversial issues. The existing rules already required television licensees "to keep in their public inspection file a listing of no more than ten significant problems of the area served by the station during the preceding twelve months and to indicate typical and illustrative programming broadcast in response to those problems and needs." At renewal time the listings for the relevant years were sent to the Commission. In the absence of any showing that television licensees were not already covering controversial issues, the added burden was unwarranted.

Moreover, Geller's proposal was inconsistent with the goal of reviewing fairness doctrine complaints as they arose rather than waiting until renewal when the issues might have become stale.

4. In 1984, the Central Intelligence Agency filed a fairness complaint against ABC based on a news story alleging CIA involvement in an assassination. ABC subsequently admitted the allegations were false. The Commission denied the complaint, but ruled that government agencies do have the right to file fairness complaints. Central Intelligence Agency, 58 R.R.2d 1544 (1985). The dismissal has been appealed.

5. *The Affirmative Duty to Raise Issues.* In 1976, for the first time, the Commission applied the first part of the fairness doctrine. A Congresswoman sent an 11-minute tape opposing strip mining to West Virginia radio stations to counter a presentation in favor of strip mining that had been distributed to many stations by the U.S. Chamber of Commerce. WHAR refused to play the tape. It had not presented the first program and had presented nothing on the issue except items on regular newscasts taken from the AP news service. Several persons and groups complained to the Commission contending that in this part of West Virginia at this time the question of strip mining was of vital importance.

The Commission asserted that although a violation of the first part of the fairness doctrine "would be an exceptional situation," this was such a case and demonstrated an "unreasonable exercise" of discretion. It was irrelevant that nobody had asked for such programming because "it is the station's obligation to make an affirmative effort to program on issues of concern to its community." That WHAR broadcast some AP news items did not matter. "Where, as in the present case, an issue has significant and possibly unique impact on the licensee's service area, it will not be sufficient for the licensee as an indication of compliance with the fairness doctrine to show that it may have broadcast an unknown amount of news touching on a general topic related to the issue cited in a complaint." The station was ordered to tell the

Commission within 20 days how it intended to meet its fairness obligations. Rep. Patsy Mink, 59 F.C.C.2d 987, 37 R.R.2d 744 (1976).

What is the justification for requiring each station in a community to present vitally important issues? Why is it not enough if the spectrum as a whole provides such content? Are the answers the same for the first part and the second part of the fairness doctrine?

6. *The Duty to Present Contrasting Views.* At one point the Commission quotes a court to the effect that not everything that is thought newsworthy by journalists necessarily presents a controversial issue of public importance. What are some examples of divergence between the two?

The Commission has never declared the fairness doctrine "applicable to issues involving the interpretation of religious doctrine." When a group complained that the program "In Search of Noah's Ark" presented one side of the issue of whether the Ark exists, and gave mistaken impressions about the attitudes of historians, archaeologists, and scholars, the Broadcast Bureau responded: "While such issues may be widely and vigorously disputed in the religious community, they generally do not rise to the level of a controversial issue of public importance. . . . Although the issue has received media coverage in that the film itself was broadcast, you have not shown that government and community leaders have taken positions on the issue. Nor have you demonstrated that the issue has any particular impact on the community at large." The network's determination that the fairness doctrine did not apply was not unreasonable. Religion and Ethics Institute, Inc., 42 R.R.2d 1657 (Bd.Bur.1978).

7. *Defining the "Issue."* In American Security Council Educational Foundation v. Federal Communications Commission, 607 F.2d 438 (D.C. Cir.1979), the ASCEF analyzed a full year's news programming of CBS. It transcribed all CBS news reports, broke them into sentences, and then determined whether each was relevant to four topics: "United States military and foreign affairs; Soviet Union military and foreign affairs; China military and foreign affairs; and Vietnam affairs." Each relevant sentence was put into one of three categories: Viewpoint A was that the "threat to U.S. security is more serious than perceived by the government or that the United States ought to *increase* its national security efforts. Viewpoint B was that the government's perception is essentially correct. Viewpoint C was that the threat is less serious than perceived and national security efforts should be decreased. The ASCEF analysis put 3.54 percent of the content into viewpoint A; 34.63 percent into viewpoint B, and 61.83 percent into viewpoint C. Based on these results and claimed similar disparities for later years, ASCEF filed a fairness complaint with the FCC asking that CBS be ordered to provide a reasonable opportunity for the expression of "A viewpoints."

Without asking CBS to respond, the FCC dismissed the complaint on the ground that it did not identify "the particular issue of a controversial nature" that was involved. The court, 6–3, affirmed:

> We affirm the Commission's decision that ASCEF failed to base its complaint on a particular well-defined issue because (1) the indirect relationships among the issues aggregated by ASCEF under the umbrella of "national security" do not provide a basis for determining whether the public received a reasonable balance of conflicting views, and (2) a contrary result would unduly burden broadcasters without a countervailing benefit to the public's right to be informed.

Since the fairness doctrine is issue-oriented, it is essential that the "issue" be clearly identified. Here "national security" was a term used to cover too many issues that were only tangentially related, such as detente with China, America's commitment to NATO, SALT, and response to the Soviet Union's role in the Middle East.

Acceptance of ASCEF's approach would also burden broadcasters. "An editor preparing an evening newscast would be required to decide whether any of the day's newsworthy events is tied, even tangentially, to events covered in the past, and whether a report on today's lead story, in some remote way, balances yesterday's, last week's or last year's." Certiorari was denied, 444 U.S. 1013 (1980).

8. A potentially significant case involved a complaint that a network documentary about the failure of some private pension plans had been unfairly one-sided. The network responded that the program was about "some problems in some pension plans." The Commission concluded that the network had presented a one-sided program on the operation of the overall pension system and had to provide balance. On appeal, the court, 2–1, reversed the Commission on the ground that the Commission was wrong in thinking that it was the proper body to decide the subject of the program. Instead, the court held that it was for the network to decide what the program was about. The Commission could reject the network's characterization only if it was found to be unreasonable. Since that was not the case here, the Commission's order could not stand. There must be "primary reliance on the journalistic discretion of the licensee, subject to supervision by the government agency only in case he exceeds the bounds of his discretion. . . . The FCC's function becomes that of correcting the licensee for *abuse* of discretion, as our function on judical review is that of correcting the agency for *abuse* of discretion."

The entire court voted to review the panel's decision en banc. But at that stage the Commission asked that the case be remanded to be dismissed. That was done and the panel decision vacated. All the action is reported in National Broadcasting Co. v. Federal Communications Commission, 516 F.2d 1101 (D.C.Cir.1974–75). An effort to reinstate the case failed when the Court denied a petition for certiorari. 424 U.S. 910 (1976).

Although the Pensions case was mooted, subsequent cases have reiterated the court's ruling that licensee discretion is central to fairness doctrine questions. The Commission is limited to judging the reasonableness of a licensee's determination. Thus, the Commission refused even to review a Broadcast Bureau ruling denying a fairness doctrine complaint in which the controversial issue of public importance was alleged to be whether or not the FBI was responsible for actress Jean Seberg's problems. The Bureau had accepted the licensee's assertion that the broadcasts did not concern a controversial issue of public importance. Accuracy in Media, Inc. v. CBS Television Network, 94 F.C.C.2d 501, 54 R.R.2d 518 (1983).

One upshot of this approach is that when the Commission accepts the licensee's view of the matter, "it will be a rare case indeed when [judicial] reversal is warranted." Georgia Power Project v. Federal Communications Commission, 559 F.2d 237 (5th Cir.1977).

9. In Council on Religion and the Homosexual, 68 F.C.C.2d 1500, 43 R.R.2d 1580 (1978), the Commission rejected a San Francisco licensee's determination that programs advocating defeat of gay rights legislation elsewhere did not present a controversial question of public importance. Although the discussion was of "primary importance to the homosexual community . . ., the issue has had and continues to have a significant impact on the public at large."

The next question was balance. The licensee had presented eight hours of programs (half original and half rebroadcasts) featuring Anita Bryant and others arguing against the proposed Dade County, Florida, ordinance barring discrimination on grounds of sexual preference. These programs were presented over a period of four months, with one and a half hours in prime time. The licensee presented a one-hour tape supporting gay rights, nine times over a period of four days, never in prime time. The complainants argued that this did not afford a reasonable opportunity for the presentation of opposing viewpoints. The Commission disagreed. It noted that the gay rights position had received more total time than the other side. Also, the licensee had advertised only the pro-gay talks in local newspapers.

When complainants objected to equating a single one-hour tape with more varied presentations on the other side, and four months on one side with four days on the other, the Commission noted that its role was "not to substitute our judgment for that of the licensee but merely to review that judgment for reasonableness." The Commission could not, and would not, "make the subjective determination of the relative impact of the pro- or anti-gay rights programming presented on the station." The licensee's judgment could not be deemed unreasonable.

10. How helpful is the Commission's test for determining balance? It provides great flexibility, but does it provide sufficient guidance? The absence of more specific guidelines has proved troubling for reviewing courts. For an extensive discussion, see Public Media Center v. Federal Communications Commission, 587 F.2d 1322 (D.C.Cir.1978).

11. Occasionally, entertainment programming may raise problems under the fairness doctrine. One typical example would be a story in which a character considers whether to seek an abortion. See Diocesan Union of Holy Name Societies, 41 F.C.C.2d 297, 28 R.R.2d 545 (1973) (involving a pro-abortion theme). Must contrasting views be presented? If so, must it be by other entertainment programming or will an interview program suffice? What about implicit presentations, such as a series featuring a happily married couple of different faiths? Must the licensee provide for contrasting views against interfaith marriages? The cases are collected and discussed in Rosenfeld, The Jurisprudence of Fairness: Freedom Through Regulation in the Marketplace of Ideas, 44 Ford.L.Rev. 877, 901–04 (1976).

12. The owner of a station in the same county as WXUR, which was denied renewal in *Brandywine-Main Line,* p. 889, infra, wrote that his station presented two guests on a call-in show on consecutive days. The first day Dr. McIntire, the principal figure behind WXUR, appeared. Every question called in was favorable to his position. The next day, the guest was an opponent, who believed strongly in the fairness doctrine and who attacked the operation of WXUR. He did not receive a single supportive call. The owner's point was that "liberal intellectuals" are most comfortable with each other and shy away from the less educated. When the "average liberal-intellectual" listens to radio he seeks out classical music or an all-news or educational station. "If he should tune in to a talk station and listen to some of the 'drivel' broadcast, he would become furious and switch to a station with which he is more at home." The conclusion was that a liberal who hopes to convert others to that viewpoint must become a proselytizer, and call-in shows are an easy way to reach large numbers of voters. Tannen, Liberals and the Media, The Progressive, April, 1974, at 11. Is this report an accurate picture of "liberal" attitudes? If so, does that affect your view of the fairness doctrine?

13. The application of the fairness doctrine to commercial advertising is discussed at p. 838, infra.

14. *Syracuse Peace Council.* In December, 1983, a rare successful fairness complaint was filed against a Syracuse television licensee for a series of commercials discussing a proposed nuclear power plant. Syracuse Peace Council, 57 R.R.2d 519 (1984). According to the Syracuse Peace Council (SPC) the controversial issue of public importance was "whether the Nine Mile II plant is a sound investment for New York." The station, WTVH, contended that the issues discussed in the advertisement were "the need to eliminate dependence on foreign oil" and "the need for electricity." WTVH further argued that "[t]he advertisements [were] institutional in nature and merely [sought] to portray a favorable image of the new Nine Mile Point nuclear energy plant." As such they did not take a position on a controversial issue of public importance. The Commission rejected WTVH's definition of the issue:

15. . . . To determine whether the licensee was reasonable in its determination as to what issue was actually discussed during the advertisement, we carefully examined the texts of the advertisements. It is noteworthy that U.S. dependence on foreign oil was mentioned only in the first two advertisements while only the last advertisement mentioned "needed electricity." On the other hand, all three advertisements ended with the tag line "Nine Mile Point . . . a *sound investment* for New York's future." (Emphasis added.) All three advertisements are framed in terms of problems facing New York—unemployment, dependence on foreign oil, and the need for electricity—and a solution to these problems—the Nine Mile II plant. In this regard, the plain thrust of each of the advertisements is whether continued construction of Nine Mile II is desirable; the need for electricity and the elimination of foreign oil dependency are the reasons given by the Energy Association as to why this question should be answered affirmatively. Under these circumstances, we cannot find that the licensee's definition of the issue was reasonable. We recognize that different parties may reach different conclusions concerning the issue addressed by a broadcast, and that, unless the facts are so clear that reasonable people could not differ as to the issue in question, a licensee's characterization of a broadcast will govern. However, we cannot find that reasonable people could differ on the conclusion that the issue discussed and the point to be made by each of these ads is that the Nine Mile II plant is an economically sound investment and, therefore, an answer to New York's economic and energy problems. In this instance, the licensee's characterization of the issues simply falls beyond the bounds of a licensee's wide zone of discretion.

The Commission then turned to the question of the reasonableness of WTVH's determination that "whether the Nine Mile II plant is a sound investment for New York" was neither controversial nor of public importance. "The key issue here is whether the issue is the subject of vigorous debate with substantial elements of the community in opposition to one other." Based on newspaper articles submitted with the complaint, the Commission found that the ads did present one side of a controversial issue of public importance. This brought the FCC to the question whether WTVH's overall programming had been fair:

23. As noted above, there is no mathematical formula or mechanical requirement for achieving fairness. [ ] However, there are a number of factors that are relevant considerations in determining whether a "reasonable opportunity" has been afforded for the presentation of contrasting viewpoints on the controversial issue of public importance. We have stated that in order to determine whether an unreasonable imbalance exists, three factors must be considered—(1) the total amount of time afforded to each side, (2) the frequency with which each side is presented, and (3)

> the size of the listening audience during the various broadcasts. By applying these to the facts of a particular case, we determine "whether the public has been left uninformed." An unreasonable imbalance in the presentation of contrasting views results "from the sheer weight on one side as against the other." We will not apply formulae so specific and detailed that they can lead to excessive intrusion into licensee judgment. . . .

Finding a 9 to 1 ratio in total time allotted to the two points of view and a 13 to 1 ratio in terms of frequency of presentation, the Commission found an unreasonable imbalance in the presentation of the contrasting points of view. In so doing the Commission rejected an argument by WTVH that most of the pro-Nine Mile II speech was commercial and should thus be discounted because " '[a]s a general principle, the public is more likely to place credibility in the information it receives from news stories and public affairs programming than it does in commercial.' "

Commissioner Dawson dissented, claiming that the decision was "a departure from consistent Commission precedent." In Dawson's opinion the issue raised by the commercials was anything but clear, and thus she believed that the licensee's determination should have been accepted. She also argued that there was insufficient proof to override the licensee's determination that the issue was not a controversial issue of public importance and that the proof that was offered was not sufficiently "contemporaneous with the broadcast." As she pointed out, over half the articles submitted were published more than six months after the commercials had been aired.

The Commission imposed no requirement of presenting programming because, during the pendency of the matter, the licensee notified the Commission that it had determined that the matter had recently become controversial—and had offered two groups 103 spots to present contrasting views. (Since the FCC did enter a finding that Meredith had violated the fairness doctrine, Meredith claims that the failure to order programming does not render the case moot.)

Meredith filed an appeal in the Court of Appeals for the District of Columbia. It argued that the FCC had failed to follow its own precedents in determining whether the matter was controversial at the time claimed by the Syracuse Peace Council. Specifically, it attacked the FCC's reliance on newspaper clippings to show controversiality on the ground that only two of the clippings came from dates within two months of the time the ads were run. Primarily, however, Meredith challenged the constitutionality of the fairness doctrine.

15. *The 1985 Fairness Report.* As noted earlier, p. 738, supra, in 1985 the FCC returned to the question of the role of the fairness doctrine. Fairness Report of 1985, 102 F.C.C.2d 143, 58 R.R.2d 1137 (1985). This time it concluded that the doctrine was no longer justified. Although it did not question "the interest of the listening and viewing public in obtaining access to diverse and antagonistic sources of information,"

the FCC thought that the doctrine was neither a "necessary or appropriate means by which to effectuate this interest." The interest in "viewpoint diversity is fully served by the multiplicity of voices in the marketplace today." Moreover, "the intrusion by government into the content of programming occasioned by the enforcement of the doctrine unnecessarily restricts the journalistic freedom of broadcasters" and "actually inhibits the presentation of controversial issues of public importance to the detriment of the public and in degradation of the editorial prerogatives of broadcast journalists."

On the scarcity point, the FCC asserted that since *Red Lion* there had been a 48 percent increase in radio outlets and a 44 percent increase in television outlets. By 1984, 96 percent of television households received five or more signals. During that period the networks' share of the market had declined from 90 percent to 76 percent and the number of independent television stations had risen from 90 to 214. Other electronic distribution systems, such as cable and multichannel multipoint distribution systems, had exploded. Finally, the FCC pointed to the continued availability of over 1,700 daily newspapers and the increase in the number of periodicals from 6,960 in 1950 to 10,688 in 1982. The Commission concluded that "the dynamics of the information services marketplace overall insures that the public will be sufficiently exposed to controversial issues of public importance."

On the inhibition point, the Commission stressed that the fairness doctrine reduced the amount of diverse views reaching the public. The reasoning began with the fact that enforcement of the first prong of the doctrine was virtually nonexistent. But the responsive programming requirement of the second prong came into play whenever a licensee undertook to present controversial programs even if beyond what was required under the first prong. The result was that broadcasters were being encouraged "to air only the minimal amount of controversial issue programming sufficient to comply with the first prong. By restricting the amount and type of controversial programming aired, a broadcaster minimizes the potentially substantial burdens associated with the second prong of the doctrine."

Broadcasters were burdened by being found in violation of the second prong because of the remote risk of nonrenewal and the greater risks of being ordered to present programs without compensation or of having to defend against the charges and incurring legal expenses. The Commission cited the Spokane station that spent $20,000 in legal fees in successfully defending a fairness charge and NBC's expense of more than $100,000 in the Pensions case.

The answer was not to enforce the first prong more rigorously because that "would increase the government's intrusion into the editorial decisionmaking process of broadcast journalists. It would enlarge the opportunity for governmental officials to abuse the doctrine for partisan political purposes."

The FCC also noted that it was inextricably involved in the "dangerous task of evaluating the merits of particular viewpoints" as it tried to distinguish statements that are "significant enough to warrant broadcast coverage" and those that "do not rise to the level of a major viewpoint of sufficient public importance that triggers responsive programming obligations."

If a responsive obligation is imposed, the Commission must then consider the content offered by the licensee to show that it has met its obligation. In addition, the Commission noted how much of its staff time is needed to deal with inquiries and complaints related to the doctrine—6,787 in 1984. Finally, the Commission cited examples in which the fairness doctrine was misused by White House administrations intent upon gaining political advantage.

All of these costs were said to be unnecessary because of the recent increase in available information sources. To the argument that the doctrine was useful to provide broadcasters with a protection against outside pressures, the Commission responded that broadcasters were not asking for such protection and that print journalists did not need such protection.

Despite all the negative points made in the Report, the Commission did not eliminate the doctrine. Instead, it deferred action until Congress had an opportunity to review the report—and announced that it would continue to enforce the doctrine. The proceeding was terminated. Commissioner Quello asserted that the fairness doctrine had been codified by the 1959 amendments to § 315 and thus could not be repealed by the Commission.

The Radio and Television News Directors Association has appealed from the Commission's refusal to stop enforcing the fairness doctrine. Although it argues primarily constitutional matters, it also argues that the 1959 amendments "merely preserved commission policy" and did not codify the doctrine. The doctrine is being defended by groups ranging across the political spectrum. They have moved to dismiss the appeal on the ground that the FCC has taken no final action from which an appeal can be taken. The case is to be argued with the Meredith case in late 1986. (In Telecommunications Research and Action Center v. Federal Communications Commission, No. 85–1160 (D.C.Cir.1986), Judges Bork and Scalia concluded that the 1959 amendment of § 315 did not make the fairness doctrine "a binding statutory obligation.")

See Ferris and Kirkland, Fairness—The Broadcaster's Hippocratic Oath, 34 Cath.U.L.Rev. 605 (1985), and Krattenmaker and Powe, The Fairness Doctrine Today: A Constitutional Curiosity and an Impossible Dream, 1985 Duke L.J. 151.

2. Personal Attack Rules

As we saw in *Red Lion,* p. 723, supra, the personal attack part of the general fairness doctrine has been crystallized into a rule, 47 C.F.R. § 73.123:

(a) When, during the presentation of views on a controversial issue of public importance, an attack is made upon the honesty, character, integrity or like personal qualities of an identified person or group, the licensee shall, within a reasonable time and in no event later than 1 week after the attack, transmit to the person or group attacked (1) notification of the date, time and identification of the broadcast; (2) a script or tape (or an accurate summary if a script or tape is not available) of the attack; and (3) an offer of a reasonable opportunity to respond over the licensee's facilities.

(b) The provisions of paragraph (a) of this section shall not be applicable (1) to attacks on foreign groups or foreign public figures; (2) to personal attacks which are made by legally qualified candidates, their authorized spokesmen, or those associated with them in the campaign, on other such candidates, their authorized spokesmen, or persons associated with the candidates in the campaign; and (3) to bona fide newscasts, bona fide news interviews, and on-the-spot coverage of a bona fide news event (including commentary or analysis contained in the foregoing programs, but the provisions of paragraph (a) of this section shall be applicable to editorials of the licensee).

The first point to note is that the episode must occur "during the presentation of views on a controversial issue of public importance." This limitation means that personal attacks unrelated to such a discussion do not invoke the rule—and presumably are left exclusively to defamation suits. Why is this distinction drawn?

Sometimes it is difficult to determine what constitutes "during the presentation of views on a controversial issue of public importance." In Straus Communications, Inc. v. Federal Communications Commission, 530 F.2d 1001 (D.C.Cir.1976), the Commission rejected a licensee's argument that time for reply was not justified because the attack did not take place during such a discussion. On appeal, the court ruled that the Commission had used the wrong standard when stating that it "believed" that the comment was sufficiently related to an earlier discussion of a meat boycott to justify the conclusion that the personal attack occurred during a continuation of that discussion. The proper approach was for the Commission to judge "the objective reasonableness of the licensee's determination" that the meat boycott discussion had long since ended.

See also Polish American Congress v. Federal Communications Commission, 520 F.2d 1248 (7th Cir.1975), certiorari denied 424 U.S. 927 (1976), in which the complainants had claimed that a skit of Polish jokes on television violated the personal attack part of the fairness doctrine. The Commission rejected the complaint. On appeal, the court stated that the order must be upheld "if the Commission properly determined that ABC's conclusion that the broadcast did not involve a controversial issue of public importance was not unreasonable or in bad faith." The court concluded that "the Commission was correct in ruling that ABC did not overstep its discretion in failing to find a controversial issue of public importance." This was true whether the issue was stated to be (1) whether "Polish Americans are inferior to other human beings in terms of intelligence, personal hygiene, etc." or (2) whether "promulgating" Polish jokes by broadcasting them is desirable. If the former, ABC could reasonably conclude that even if some people felt that way they had not generated enough support to create a controversial issue of public importance. Had they done so, ABC could still conclude that the skit presented did not constitute a "discussion" of this issue. If the issue was the latter, no controversy was shown.

Another issue raised in *Polish American Congress* (although it was not addressed because of the lack of a controversial issue of public importance) was the size of the group attacked. Should group libel aspects of defamation law apply to the personal attack rule when the attack is on a large group rather than on an individual or on a small group? In Diocese of Rockville Centre, 50 F.C.C.2d 330, 32 R.R.2d 376 (Bd.Bur.1973), a licensee had broadcast a statement that perhaps an earlier writer was correct when he stated, "The Roman Church is filled with men who were led into it merely by ambition, who though they might have been useful and respectful as laymen, are hypocritical and immoral." The Commission ruled that the group is not sufficiently "identified" unless the licensee "could reasonably be expected to know exactly who or what finite group" is best able to present the contrasting viewpoint. The reference to "men" who fill the "Roman Church" was found too vague.

Similarly, a personal attack claim was rejected where the complainant organization was one of several discussed during a program. The program noted there were many differences among the groups and made no explicit allegations against complainant's church. The Commission concluded that the claimant had not met the burden of showing an attack on an identified person or group. Disciples of the Lord Jesus, 93 F.C.C.2d 7, 53 R.R.2d 319 (1983).

The Commission has also employed a very narrow definition of what constitutes a personal attack. In *Straus,* the FCC decided that calling a Congressman a coward did not constitute a personal attack. Similarly, the rule was held inapplicable to remarks reflecting on a journalist's personal competence. Rev. Lester Kinsolving, 67 F.C.C.2d 157, 41 R.R.2d 573 (1977).

The Commission has made clear that attacks during discussion of controversial issues of public importance are not misbehavior. Wide-open debate is encouraged—so long as the rules are followed. (See the KTYM case, p. 891, infra.)

3. Fairness in Political Campaigns

The fairness doctrine enters into political issues in two ways. The first involves the use of broadcasting by the party in power, particularly the President, between political campaigns. The courts have taken the view that when the President speaks on an issue of national concern, the major party out of power has no automatic right to reply. The only exception occurred when the President delivered five speeches during a seven-month period about the war in Indochina. Since broadcast coverage of that conflict had otherwise been roughly in balance, the FCC decided that the networks were obligated to provide free time for a spokesman from the other side of the issue.

But that instance aside, the courts have considered the speeches of a President just one factor to weigh in deciding whether the required rough balance in the presentation of contrasting views has been achieved. As usual, the FCC will generally defer to the views of the licensees, and the courts will generally defer to the views of the FCC. The subject is explored extensively in Democratic National Committee v. Federal Communications Commission, 481 F.2d 543 (D.C.Cir.1973) (unsuccessful attempt to obtain free reply time to counter President's speeches on economic policy).

The second role of the fairness doctrine in politics involves the campaign itself. Since § 315 was construed not to cover appearances by anyone other than candidates, and since the section also does not cover ballot propositions, many important political campaign broadcasts must be regulated under provisions much less precise than § 315. Not surprisingly, as television has become increasingly important in election campaigns, questions not covered by § 315 have arisen more frequently.

Uses by Supporters. Turning first to a close parallel situation, what are the controlling principles when Candidate A's friends or campaign committee purchase time to further his candidacy or to attack Opponent B? In its Letter to Nicholas Zapple, 23 F.C.C.2d 707, 19 R.R.2d 421 (1970), the Commission stated that the 1959 amendment to § 315 had explicitly recognized the operation of the fairness doctrine when the candidate's own appearance was exempted from § 315. The doctrine was thought equally applicable here.

Moreover, when a candidate is supported or his opponent attacked, although the licensee has the responsibility of identifying suitable speakers for opposing views, "barring unusual circumstances, it would not be reasonable for a licensee to refuse to sell time to spokesmen for or supporters of candidate B comparable to that previously bought on behalf of candidate A." But there was no obligation to provide B's supporters with free time. Although usually requiring that time be given away, if necessary, to get contrasting views before the public, the Commission thought this unsound in the political arena. To hold otherwise would require licensees, or other advertisers, to subsidize B's campaign. The rejection of subsidization meant that even if A's friends mounted a personal attack on B, B would not get free time. The Commission has adhered closely to the *Zapple* ruling, which is sometimes referred to as the "quasi equal opportunities" or "political party" corollary to the fairness doctrine.

In 1979, the Commission decided that Congress intended that "uses" under § 315 and *Zapple* were to be mutually exclusive of the fairness doctrine. The Commission concluded that licensees should not be responsible for "uses" since they have no control over them. As a result, the personal attack rule was rewritten to provide that it did not apply to personal attacks occurring during uses under § 315 or those occurring in *Zapple* situations.

More generally, the fairness doctrine was declared not to apply to issues raised during "uses." The Commission believed that issues raised during "uses" were likely to be of such public interest that other views would be aired in due course without the goad of the fairness doctrine. Personal Attacks and Applicability of the Fairness Doctrine to Section 315 "Uses," 78 F.C.C.2d 457, 45 R.R.2d 1635 (1979).

A new problem emerged in 1980 involving groups organized by friends of Ronald Reagan but not controlled by the candidate. These groups are not bound by federal election spending limits that may bind the candidates themselves. When these groups began to buy time on broadcast stations, the Carter campaign committee complained to the FCC that the stations selling time to these "independent expenditure groups" should be required to make equal, and free, opportunities available to the Carter campaign (and presumably to all other campaigns). These should be free, the Carter committee asserted, because it and the Reagan campaign were each limited to $29.4 million for campaigning because they agreed to accept federal funds. As a result, they could not match both the money Reagan was spending and that being spent by the independent groups.

The FCC rejected the claim on the ground that friends of Carter could start comparable groups to match the expenditures being made by the Reagan groups. To allow the Carter campaign free time would put the Commission in the position of benefitting one of the candidates at the expense of the other, whose friends had been required to pay for his time. Carter/Mondale Reelection Comm., 81 F.C.C.2d 409, 48 R.R. 2d 414 (1980).

In an effort to apply the *Zapple* ruling outside campaign periods, CBS and others asked the FCC to declare that "when a licensee sells broadcast time for political advertisements by a political party, independent political committee or other supporters of a candidate, whether during or outside a campaign period, the *Cullman* doctrine does not apply and thus, the licensee has no obligation to provide free time to opposing groups." The FCC refused on the ground that Congress had shown that § 315 was to apply only during campaign periods and that *Zapple* was designed to supplement the statute only during the same periods. At other times, *Cullman* applied. CBS, Inc., 95 F.C.C.2d 1152 (1983).

In *Kennedy II*, p. 803, supra, after rejecting the candidate's claims under § 312 and § 315, the court turned to the role of the fairness doctrine in political campaigns. The Broadcast Bureau and the Commission had found three fatal flaws in Kennedy's reliance on the fairness doctrine in this case—and the court agreed. First, he had failed to define the particular controversial issue involved with sufficient specificity. Second, there was no showing that the networks had failed to present contrasting viewpoints on the national economy in their overall programming. The fairness doctrine "does not operate with the dissective focus of" § 315(a). "Intelligent assessment of the nature and caliber of a broadcaster's overall programming obviously cannot be confined to one program, or even to one day's presentations, so a failure to show some fairness deficiency on the whole is necessarily fatal."

Even if imbalance were established, the third flaw was that Senator Kennedy had no "individual right to broadcast his views on the current economic crisis." Kennedy did not show that he was "uniquely and singularly qualified to represent those who dispute the President's economic leadership or strategies."

Note, finally, that the fairness doctrine extends to political campaigns since the question of which candidate should be elected may be considered a "controversial issue of public importance." This means that even if no requests for time are made under § 315 or § 312, a broadcaster might be required to introduce the issue under the first part of the fairness doctrine. If some views are expressed about the forthcoming campaign during non-uses, the licensee would be obligated under the second part of the doctrine to provide coverage of contrasting views. In determining what views should get how much time, the licensee must make good faith judgments about the importance of the race and the significance of each candidate.

The Commission's dismissal of a fairness complaint alleging unbalanced coverage of economic matters was upheld in Democratic National Committee v. Federal Communications Commission, 717 F.2d 1471, 54 R.R.2d 941 (D.C.Cir.1983). Disparities approximating 3 to 1 and 4 to 1 in favor of the pro-Administration economic view occurred on the networks. Compliance with fairness doctrine obligations was to be measured by a standard of good faith and reasonableness, not by reference to "rough approximations of equality." Since the disparities were not "glaring," and the audiences were not shown to be very different in size, the Commission's dismissal of the complaint was reasonable. Although the court cited data showing that fairness complainants prevail in roughly 1 in 1,000 cases, it rejected Commission statements that fairness complaints will inevitably be futile. (This was before the Syracuse case, p. 816, supra.)

Political Editorials. In a section of the personal attack rules, now 47 C.F.R. § 73.1930, the Commission covered political editorials:

(a) Where a licensee, in an editorial,

(1) Endorses or,

(2) Opposes a legally qualified candidate or candidates, the licensee shall, within 24 hours after the editorial, transmit to, respectively,

(i) The other qualified candidate or candidates for the same office or,

(ii) The candidate opposed in the editorial,

(A) Notification of the date and the time of the editorial,

(B) A script or tape of the editorial, and

(C) An offer of reasonable opportunity for the candidate or a spokesman of the candidate to respond over the licensee's facilities. Where such editorials are broadcast on the day of the election or within 72 hours prior to the day of the election, the licensee shall comply with the provisions of this paragraph sufficiently far in advance of the broadcast to enable the candidate or candidates to have a reasonable opportunity to prepare a response and to present it in a timely fashion.

. . .

Be sure to note that a single editorial on behalf of one candidate creates an opportunity to respond for *each* opposing candidate. This is true regardless of the number of opposing candidates. Friends of Howard Miller, 72 F.C.C.2d 508, 45 R.R.2d 1142 (1979).

Ballot Propositions. In an omitted part of the 1974 Fairness Report, the Commission concluded that such matters as referenda, initiative and recall propositions, bond proposals, and constitutional amendments were to be regulated under the fairness doctrine. The area was thought closer to general political discussion not involving elections than it was to the election of individuals to office. Thus, the *Cullman* doctrine, requiring the licensee to present contrasting views, by the use of free time if necessary, was applicable. One argument against the *Cullman* doctrine was that some groups might spend their available money on nonbroadcast media, wait for the other side to buy broadcast time, and then insist on free time under *Cullman* to counter their adversary. The Commission was not persuaded. First, this concern can always be raised against *Cullman,* but the Commission thought it most important that the public have access to contrasting views. On the tactical level, the Commission noted that the fairness doctrine does not guarantee equality of exposure of views nor who will be chosen as speakers. Those who rely solely on *Cullman* "have no assurance of obtaining equality by such means." Fairness Report, 48 F.C.C.2d 1, 33, 30 R.R.2d 1261, 1302 (1974).

Putting § 315, § 312, *Zapple,* the political editorial rule, and the general fairness doctrine together, does a coherent package result? What changes would you advocate?

C. DISTORTION

There is no policy on distortion in the fairness doctrine, nor has Congress enacted specific legislation to address it. The distortion policy descends from the broadcaster's duty to serve "the public interest." The FCC's policy on distorting the news did not emerge until Hunger in America, 20 F.C.C.2d 143, 17 R.R.2d 674 (1969). The developments since then are traced in the following case.

GALLOWAY v. FEDERAL COMMUNICATIONS COMMISSION

United States Court of Appeals, District of Columbia Circuit, 1985.
778 F.2d 16.

Before WRIGHT, MIKVA, and FRIEDMAN, CIRCUIT JUDGES.

WRIGHT, CIRCUIT JUDGE.

Petitioner Carl Galloway, who was mentioned during a CBS News broadcast about insurance fraud, complained to the Federal Communications Commission that the broadcast had violated both the Commission's Personal Attack rule and its policy against deliberate news distortion. Petitioner asked the Commission to revoke the licenses of intervenor CBS's owned-and-operated stations. The Commission denied Galloway's request and he appeals to this court, challenging both the policies and their application. Because petitioner has failed to make the necessary showings on either his personal attack or deliberate distortion complaint, we affirm the Commission's ruling.

I. Background

On December 9, 1979 the CBS News program *60 Minutes* broadcast a story entitled "It's No Accident," about an allegedly widespread fraudulent insurance scheme. According to the program, doctors, lawyers and "victims" would conspire to submit reports of accidents that had never occurred (or were greatly exaggerated) and submit bills for medical treatment that had never been rendered. The program said that such schemes cost insurers more than $1 billion a year, that much of the cost was passed on to honest policyholders in the form of higher premiums, and that the insurance companies were not as vigorous as they might be in investigating fraudulent claims "because it's cheaper to settle than to investigate." [ ]

In the course of preparing the broadcast CBS sent an insurance investigator to a clinic suspected of participating in the fraudulent schemes. "[She] was instructed to tell the clinic that one month earlier she had been in a minor accident, had not been hurt, but needed back-dated full medical bills as the basis for an insurance claim." [ ] She received a bill listing 19 visits that never occurred for treatment that was never administered. In describing that bill CBS Correspondent Dan Rather said, "It was signed by Carl A. Galloway, M.D." [ ]

Although the clinic figured prominently in the broadcast, no other mention was made of Galloway.

Galloway sued CBS for libel in the state courts of California, claiming that his name had been forged on the fraudulent bill. Galloway lost at trial on a general jury verdict that is currently the subject of a separate appeal in the California courts. During discovery for the libel suit Galloway received a great deal of information, including film or tape that was shot for the broadcast but never aired ("outtakes"). This material formed the basis of his complaint to the FCC.

Galloway's FCC complaint alleged two separate violations by CBS. First, he said he had been the victim of a personal attack and had been denied an opportunity to reply. Second, he said that CBS "violated Commission policy by deliberately distorting, slanting, falsifying and staging" the broadcast at issue. We will consider these two issues separately.

. . .

III. The Deliberate Distortion Complaint

A. *The FCC Policy*

The FCC's policy on rigging, staging, or distorting the news was developed in a series of cases beginning in 1969.[2] In the first of these, Hunger In America, CBS had shown an infant it said was suffering from malnutrition, but who was actually suffering from another ailment. The Commission found that

> [r]igging or slanting the news is a most henious act against the public interest—indeed, there is no act more harmful to the public's ability to handle its affairs. In all cases where we may appropriately do so, we shall act to protect the public interest in this important respect. But in this democracy, no government agency can authenticate the news, or should try to do so.

Hunger In America, 20 FCC2d 143, 151 (1969). As in all the subsequent cases, the FCC made a crucial distinction between deliberate distortion and mere inaccuracy or difference of opinion.

The Commission realized that news events can be "staged" by the participants as well as by reporters. The behavior of the subjects of news reports is often affected by the presence of television cameras, and in a real sense every news conference is a staged event. In the years since 1969 "media events" from protest demonstrations to "photo opportunities" have become more sophisticated and more pervasive. The technological imperatives of TV news may also require a certain

2. See Hunger In America, 20 FCC2d 143 (1969); WBBM–TV, 18 FCC2d 124 (1969) (allegations that college pot party was staged for camera crew); Democratic National Convention Television Coverage, 16 FCC2d 650 (1969) (concerning aspects of coverage of demonstrations outside the 1968 convention in Chicago); Hon. Harley O. Staggers, 25 Rad.Reg.2d (P & F) 413 (1972) (policy statement in response to a congressional subcommittee investigating the staging of news events).

amount of stage managing, for example, shooting "reverses." [3] These were not the kinds of practices that concerned the Commission. "The Commission viewed its proper area of concern to be with those activities which are not a matter of journalistic judgment or a gray area, but rather constitute the deliberate portrayal of a 'significant "event" which did not in fact occur but rather is "acted out" at the behest of news personnel.' " Hon. Harley O. Staggers, 25 Rad.Reg.2d (P & F) 413, 414 (1972).

The key elements of this standard are, first, that the distortion or staging be deliberately intended to slant or mislead. It is not enough to dispute the accuracy of a news report [ ] or to question the legitimate editorial decisions of the broadcaster, [ ]. The allegation of deliberate distortion must be supported by "extrinsic evidence," that is, evidence other than the broadcast itself, such as written or oral instructions from station management, outtakes, or evidence of bribery. [ ]

Second, the distortion must involve a significant event and not merely a minor or incidental aspect of the news report. The Commission has refused to investigate "inaccurate embellishments concerning peripheral aspects" of news reports or "attempts at window dressing which concerned the *manner* of presenting the news" as long as "the essential facts of the news stories to which these presentational devices related were broadcast in an accurate manner." [ ] "[T]he real criterion with respect to staging is whether the public is deceived about a matter of significance." [ ] In one of its early descriptions of news staging and distortion, the Commission said:

> For example, the licensee's newsmen should not, upon arriving late at a riot, ask one of the rioters to throw another brick through a store window for its cameras. First, if the window is already broken, it is staging a news event—one which did not in fact occur, but is acted out at the request of the news personnel; the licensee could fairly present such a film only with the full disclosure of its nature.

WBBM–TV, 18 FCC2d 124, 132–133 (1969). More recently, however, the Commission tolerates such practices unless they "affect[ ] the basic accuracy of the events reported." WPIX, Inc., [68 FCC2d at 386]; see also Oscar B. White, 87 FCC2d 954, 959–960 (1981). As with the Personal Attack rule, the Commission's practice in this respect has given its policy against news distortion an extremely limited scope. But within the constraints of the Constitution, Congress and the Commission may set the scope of broadcast regulation; it is not the role of this court to question the wisdom of their policy choices.

3. "Because documentary interviews are normally filmed by a single camera, the film crew typically will train the camera on the individual being interviewed during a question and answer series, and then run through a second 'take', known as a 'reverse', with the camera focused on the interviewer in order to get film footage of his questioning." [ ]

B. *The Specific Allegations of Distortion.*

1. *The Johnson interview.* The *60 Minutes* broadcast included tape CBS purportedly made when "we observed [insurance investigator Milton Crawford] interrogating insurance claimant Montenette Johnson." At first Johnson is seen telling Crawford that she was involved in an accident. Then Rather says, "Crawford suspects Johnson is lying. * * * After some hard questioning, Johnson changed her story." Johnson then admits that she had filed a fraudulent claim, "[b]ecause somebody told me that if I did it that I would get paid a certain amount of money." [ ]

Crawford actually "interrogated" Johnson at least twice in succession for CBS cameras, and both times she at first professed the legitimacy of her claim and later (without being confronted with contradictory evidence or the like, but simply being asked again, "Now was it true that you were involved in an accident?" and "Were you really involved in an accident on that date?") she confessed her participation in the fraud. [ ] Interviews of another woman, not broadcast, followed a similar pattern. [ ] Galloway alleges that this "clearly shows that what CBS maintained were spontaneous interrogations were, in reality, staged interviews performed for the benefit of and at the behest of CBS news personnel. * * * They were simply giving CBS another 'take' for the 'docudrama' CBS had previously scripted." [ ]

The Commission disposed of this allegation in a footnote, in which it described this matter as an exercise of "editorial judgment," lacking sufficient evidence of deliberate distortion. [ ] We think this is mistaken. The Commission is unlikely to find better circumstantial evidence that an interview is staged, and intervenor CBS never explicitly denied that these "interrogations" were staged. The interrogation was clearly an " 'event' which did not in fact occur but is 'acted out' at the behest of news personnel." [ ] And "all staging as [so] defined * * * involves distortion." [ ]

On appeal the FCC no longer argues that the evidence of distortion is insufficient. Instead, it asserts that the distortion is not significant. "Galloway did not allege that any of the statements made by the interviewee in the broadcast were false or that the broadcast misrepresented her participation in an insurance fraud scheme. * * * Whether or not this individual 'confessed' to involvement in a fraudulent scheme because of 'hard questioning' or for other reasons is not, however, a significant matter." Brief for respondents at 17. Since Ms. Johnson actually *did* participate in the fraud and *did* confess, even if not in precisely the manner portrayed, the "basic accuracy of the events reported," [ ] has not been distorted. Whatever we may think of this playacting as a journalistic practice, it does not violate FCC rules as currently applied.

2. *The Petty interview.* One of those interviewed for the broadcast was Robert Petty, an attorney who once participated in insurance fraud

and now faced disbarment. Rather asked Petty, "If I were an attorney and I sought to specialize in these kind of cases, could I make a quarter of a million dollars a year, half-million dollars a year?" [ ] During the filming, Petty's answer began, "So long as you were successful," and after discussing the dangers inherent in maintaining a fraudulent scheme concluded, "It's simply not worth it." [ ] Rather asked the question again for a reverse shot, and this time Petty's (off-camera) answer was "Quite easily." [ ] In the actual broadcast, CBS used a shot of Petty responding to a completely different question, saying simply, "Yes."

Galloway alleged that CBS had substituted an affirmative answer for a negative one. We think Petty's answer . . . was clearly affirmative, notwithstanding his warnings about the risks involved. The decision not to include Petty's cautionary remarks is more "a matter of editorial discretion . . . than an act of deliberate distortion." [ ] While the substitution of an answer to another question may fairly be considered distortion *per se*, when it does not affect the "basic accuracy" of the answer it is not "significant" enough to violate FCC rules.

. . .

4. *Anonymous doctor interview.* During the broadcast Rather interviewed an unidentified doctor who said he had once been involved in fraudulent insurance claims. In the narration Rather said, "This doctor . . . confided that he used to conspire with 15 different lawyers. He has never been in jail, has never been suspended from practice; indeed, his medical business is booming, and he is respected throughout his profession." [ ]

The statement *was* somewhat misleading in that it implied the doctor had never been caught. In fact, as the outtakes show, the doctor had struck a plea bargain for turning state's evidence. (It was only when confronted with this fact that he "confided" in Dan Rather.) It is technically accurate, however, that the doctor was never in jail or suspended from practice. . . .

C. *Repeal by Non-Enforcement*

Galloway argues that even if the decision in his case is consistent with the Commission's stated policies, the Commission's threshold requirements for complaints "are so excessive that, as a practical matter, they are unreachable and have produced a *de facto* nullification of a valid Act of Congress." These arguments about the Commission's hostility to the Fairness Doctrine owe more to ideology than to law.

First, this court has upheld the FCC policy of requiring a substantial prima facie case before proceeding against a broadcaster. See American Security Council Education Foundation v. FCC, 607 F.2d 438 (D.C.Cir.1979) (*en banc*). This policy reflects an appropriate respect for First Amendment values. Second, it is difficult to determine precisely what "Act of Congress" is being "nullifi[ed]." The Commission's policies on staging and distortion are *not* part of the Fairness Doctrine, but simply an attempt to particularize the statutory duty of broadcasters to "operate in the public interest." 47 U.S.C. § 315(a) (1982). Perhaps the broad public interest standard would justify a stricter policy, but neither the language nor the legislative history of the statute demand it. Congress has shown concern with the danger of distortion in television news,[5] but it has never enacted more particular regulation of the practice. This court will not presume to do so.

IV. Conclusion

Whatever one may think of the production techniques employed by *60 Minutes,* especially in the Johnson and Petty interviews, these techniques are not violations of FCC rules. The Commission's decision on the complaint is therefore

Affirmed.

Notes and Questions

1. Is the juxtaposition of questions with answers to different questions ever justifiable?

2. Which of the matters discussed in the case are attributable to news judgment? Which to technical problems of the medium?

3. In the Westmoreland v. CBS libel case, in violation of internal CBS guidelines, the producer gave only friendly interviewees some idea in advance of the questions to be asked, allowed one friendly interviewee to be interviewed a second time so that he could come across better, and may have photographed friendly witnesses from a distance, giving them a "halo" effect, while zooming in close on unfriendly witnesses so that their images looked more like mug shots and they could be seen perspiring. Should government be involved in investigating these practices or in imposing sanctions for their use?

D. OBSCENITY AND INDECENCY

The subject of obscenity did not become a problem on radio and television until recently. In the earlier years of these media, the licensees apparently had no practical reason to want to test the limits of permissible communication and were unsure what the Commission might legally do to licensees who stepped over the line.

In the 1934 Act, § 326, the prohibition on censorship, also contained a passage forbidding the use of obscene or indecent speech in

5. See, e.g., Inquiry Into Alleged Rigging of Television News Programs, H.R. Rep. No. 96, 92d Cong., 2d Sess. (1972):

> When film and sound recording of an actual event is presented, the public has a right to expect that the events have been filmed and recorded as they actually took place, unless there is an appropriate disclosure to the contrary. If this is not done, then the public's attention and interest is being gained under false pretenses . . . [and] people are given manufactured evidence upon which to base their conclusions on matters which vitally affect their lives and those of their children.

Id. at 3 (statement of Rep. Staggers); [ ].

broadcasting. In 1948, that provision was moved to the general criminal law in 18 U.S.C. § 1464:

> Whoever utters any obscene, indecent, or profane language by means of radio communication shall be fined not more than $10,000 or imprisoned not more than two years, or both.

Several other sections empower the Commission to impose sanctions for violation of § 1464.

In 1964, the Commission considered renewal of several stations belonging to the Pacifica Foundation. Five programs had produced complaints: two poets reading their own works; one author reading from his novel; a recording of Edward Albee's "Zoo Story"; and a program "in which eight homosexuals discussed their attitudes and problems." All were aired late at night except one of the poetry readings. The Commission indicated that it was "not concerned with individual programs" but with whether there had been a pattern of programming inconsistent with the public interest. Although it found nothing to bar renewal, the Commission discussed the five programs because it would be "useful" to the "industry and the public."

The Commission found three of the programs were well within the licensee's judgment under the public interest standard. The Commission recognized that provocative programming might offend some listeners. To rule such programs off the air, however, would mean that "only the wholly inoffensive, the bland, could gain access to the radio microphone or TV camera." The remedy for offended listeners was to turn off the program. The two poetry readings raised different questions. One did not measure up to the licensee's standards for presentation but it had not been carefully screened because it had come from a reputable source. The other reading, involving 28 poems, was broadcast at 7:15 p.m. because the station's editor admitted he had been lulled by the poet's "rather flat, monotonous voice" and did not catch unidentified "offensive words" in the 19th poem. The errors were isolated and thus caused no renewal problem. Pacifica Foundation, 36 F.C.C. 147, 1 R.R.2d 747 (1964). For a history of Pacifica's struggle in 1964, including the fact that no broadcaster came to its defense, see Barton, The Lingering Legacy of Pacifica: Broadcasters' Freedom of Silence, 53 Journ.Q. 429 (1976).

Another episode involved a taped interview on a noncommercial FM station with Jerry Garcia, leader of the Grateful Dead. Garcia apparently used "various patently offensive words as adjectives, introductory expletives, and as substitutes for 'et cetera.' " The Commission imposed a forfeiture of $100 for "indecency" and apparently hoped for a court test of its powers. Eastern Educational Radio (WUHY–FM), 24 F.C.C.2d 408, 18 R.R.2d 860 (1970). The licensee paid the fine and the case was over.

Next came charges of obscenity leveled at "topless radio," midday programs consisting of "call-in talk shows in which masters of ceremonies discuss intimate sexual topics with listeners, usually women." The format quickly became very popular. The Commission responded to complaints by ordering its staff to tape several of the shows and to present a condensed tape of some of the most offensive comments. The next day, Chairman Dean Burch condemned the format in a speech to the National Association of Broadcasters. Two weeks later the Commission issued a Notice of Apparent Liability proposing a forfeiture of $2,000 against one licensee. Sonderling Broadcasting Corp. (WGLD-FM), 27 R.R.2d 285 (F.C.C.1973). The most troublesome language was apparently:

> Female Listener: . . . of course I had a few hangups at first about—in regard to this, but you know what we did—I have a craving for peanut butter all that [sic] time so I used to spread this on my husband's privates and after a while, I mean, I didn't even need the peanut butter anymore.
>
> Announcer: (Laughs) Peanut butter, huh?
>
> Listener: Right. Oh, we can try anything—you know—any, any of these women that have called and they have, you know, hangups about this, I mean they should try their favorite—you know like—uh. . . .
>
> Announcer: Whipped cream, marshmallow . . . .

In addition, the host's conversation with a complaining listener was thought to be suffused with "leering innuendo." The Commission thought this program ran afoul of both the "indecency" and "obscenity" standards of § 1464. On the other hand, the Commission disclaimed any intention to ban the discussion of sex entirely:

> We are emphatically not saying that sex *per se* is a forbidden subject on the broadcast medium. We are well aware that sex is a vital human relationship which has concerned humanity over the centuries, and that sex and obscenity are not the same thing. In this area as in others, we recognize the licensee's right to present provocative or unpopular programming which may offend some listeners, Pacifica Foundation, 36 FCC 147, 149 (1964). Second, we note that we are not dealing with works of dramatic or literary art as we were in *Pacifica.* We are rather confronted with the talk or interview show where clearly the interviewer can readily moderate his handling of the subject matter so as to conform to the basic statutory standards which, as we point out, allow much leeway for provocative material. . . . The standards here are strictly defined by the law: The broadcaster must eschew the "obscene or indecent."

Again the Commission sought a test: "we welcome and urge judicial consideration of our action." Commissioner Johnson dissented on several grounds, including the view that the Commission had no duty to act in these cases and should leave the matter to possible prosecution by the Justice Department. Sonderling denied liability but paid the fine. Two citizen groups asked the Commission to reconsider on the ground that listeners' rights to hear such programs had been disregarded by the Commission's action. The Commission reaffirmed its action, 41 F.C.C.2d 777, 27 R.R.2d 1508 (1973), indicating that it had based its order "on the pervasive and intrusive nature of broadcast radio, even if children were left completely out of the picture." It went on, however, to point out that children were in the audience in these afternoon programs and there was some evidence that the program was not intended solely for adults. "The obvious intent of this reference to children was to convey the conclusion that this material was unlawful, and that it was even more clearly unlawful when presented to an audience which included children."

The citizen groups appealed but lost. Illinois Citizens Committee for Broadcasting v. Federal Communications Commission, 515 F.2d 397 (D.C.Cir.1975). The court refused to allow the petitioners to make certain procedural arguments that it thought were open only to the licensee itself. On the merits:

> The excerpts cited by the Commission contain repeated and explicit descriptions of the techniques of oral sex. And these are presented, not for educational and scientific purposes, but in a context that was fairly described by the FCC as "titillating and pandering." The principles of Ginzburg v. United States, 383 U.S. 463 (1966) are applicable, for commercial exploitation of interests in titillation is the broadcaster's sole end. It is not a material difference that here the tone is set by the continuity provided by the announcer rather than, as in *Ginzburg*, by the presentation of the material in advertising and sale to solicit an audience. We cannot ignore what the Commission took into account—that the announcer's response to a complaint by an offended listener and his presentation of advertising for auto insurance are suffused with leering innuendo. Moreover, and significantly, "Femme Forum" is broadcast from 10 a.m. to 3 p.m. during daytime hours when the radio audience may include children—perhaps home from school for lunch, or because of staggered school hours or illness. Given this combination of factors, we do not think that the FCC's evaluation of this material infringes upon rights protected by the First Amendment.
>
> The FCC found Sonderling's broadcasts obscene . . . .
>
> . . .
>
> Petitioners object that the Commission's determination was based on a brief condensation of offensive material and did not take into account the broadcast as a whole, as would seem to be required by certain elements of both the *Memoirs* and the *Miller* tests. The Commission's approach is not inappropriate in evaluating a broadcasting program that is episodic in nature—a cluster of individual and typically disconnected commentaries, rather than an integrated presentation. It is commonplace for members of the radio audience to listen only to short snatches of a broadcast, and

programs like "Femme Forum" are designed to attract such listeners. . . .

The court explicitly did not rely upon the Commission's argument that it had latitude to hold things "indecent" that are not obscene.

Next came FCC v. Pacifica Foundation, reprinted in Chapter XIV.

E. SAFETY—VIOLENCE AND PANIC

Although the Surgeon General has issued reports on the relationship between violence and television, and other academic studies have addressed the issue primarily in connection with children, the Commission has never attempted to regulate the area in any substantive way. It has been asked several times but each time has refused.

In 1972, for example, the Commission was asked to analogize the area to cigarette smoking because of the actions of the Surgeon General in the two areas. George Corey, 37 F.C.C.2d 641, 25 R.R.2d 437 (1972). As we shall see, p. 838, infra, the FCC held the fairness doctrine applicable to cigarette advertising. Soon thereafter, Congress eliminated all broadcast advertising for cigarettes. The complainant sought to use the fairness approach in the violence context by having the FCC order three Boston stations to carry a public service notice at appropriate times: "Warning: Viewing of violent television programming by children can be hazardous to their mental health and well being." The Commission rejected the request on two grounds. First, it stated any action should come by rule rather than a move against a few stations. Second, the Commission rejected the contention that the fairness doctrine was applicable to violent programming. The cigarette episode was discussed:

> [I]t could not reasonably or logically be concluded that the mere viewing of a person smoking a cigarette during a movie being broadcast on television constitutes a discussion of a controversial issue of public importance thus raising a fairness doctrine obligation. Similarly, we cannot agree that the broadcast of violent episodes during entertainment programs necessarily constitutes the presentation of one side of a controversial issue of public importance. . . . Were we to adopt your construction that the depiction of a violent scene is a discussion of one side of a controversial issue of public importance, the number of controversial issues presented on entertainment shows would be virtually endless (e.g., a scene with a high-powered car; or one showing a person taking an alcoholic drink or cigarette; depicting women in a soft, feminine, or light romantic role). Finally, we note that there are marked differences in the conclusiveness of the hazard established in this area as against cigarette smoking. [ ]
>
> The real thrust of your complaint would appear to be not fairness in the discussion of controversial issues but the elimination of violent TV children's programming because of its effect on children. That issue is being considered particularly by appropri-

ate Congressional committees and agencies such as HEW. [ ] It is a difficult, complex, and sensitive matter. But whatever its resolution, there is no basis for the action along the line proposed by you.

In its Report on the Broadcast of Violent, Indecent, and Obscene Material, 51 F.C.C.2d 418, 32 R.R.2d 1367 (1975), the Commission explained to Congress that the violence area was unlike the obscenity area because of the totally different statutory framework involved. In the absence of any prohibitions on violence in programming, "industry self-regulation is preferable to the adoption of rigid governmental standards." The Commission took this position for two reasons. First, it feared the constitutional questions that would emerge from such an intrusion into program content. Second, the judgments concerning the suitability of certain programming for children are "highly subjective." A speech by Chairman Richard Wiley was quoted to the effect that such things as slapstick comedy, an episode in Peter Pan when Captain Hook is eaten by a crocodile, and the poisoning of Snow White by the witch, all raise judgmental questions for which there is no objective standard.

Mass Hysteria. Another substantive problem involves programs that frighten the listening public. At 11:00 p.m. on Oct. 30, 1974, a radio station in Rhode Island presented a contemporary version of H. G. Wells's famous "War of the Worlds," which had been presented on that same night in 1938. A meteorite was reported to have fallen in a sparsely populated community, killing several people; later, "black-eyed, V-shaped mouthed, glistening creatures dripping saliva" were reported to have emerged from what turned out to be a capsule, and other landings were reported. Telephone calls from frightened, and later from angry, listeners flooded the station, police, and other public service departments.

The licensee had taken several steps before the program to inform state public safety officials in the listening area of the station. The state police in turn sent notices to all their stations in the area alerting them to the program. Approximately once an hour from noon until 10:00 p.m. the licensee broadcast the following promotional announcement: "Tonight at 11:00 p.m., WPRO invites you to listen to a spoof of the 1930s, a special Hallowe'en presentation. . . . " The last was made about an hour before the program. Three announcements were made during the program—after 47, 48, and 56 minutes. The reason for the timing was said to be that the first 30 to 35 minutes of the show involved what seemed to be a meteor crashing in a remote spot, and the arrival of creatures was not reported until 30 minutes into the program. What steps would you expect the licensee to take before presenting such a program—or is it inappropriate to present such material at any time?

The Commission told the licensee that it had not met its responsibility to operate in a manner consistent with the public interest. The warnings were inadequate because "it is a well known fact that the radio audience is constantly changing. The only way to assure adequately that the public would not be alarmed in this case would be an introductory statement repeated at frequent intervals throughout the program." One Commissioner dissented because intrusion into presentations of drama should be made with "utmost caution" and the licensee's precautions "were not in my opinion unreasonable." Capital Cities Communications, Inc., 54 F.C.C.2d 1035, 34 R.R.2d 1016 (1975).

Would the Commission's suggestions impinge on the dramatic effect sought by the licensee? Is that relevant? Can you think of other ways to meet the Commission's concern? Recall the greater ease of warning an unwilling audience about possibly offensive programs over television as opposed to radio.

On April 1, 1980, a Boston television station's local news program was interrupted by a bulletin that a 635-foot mound in suburban Milton had just blown its top and erupted. The reporter indicated that the disaster was traceable to a chain reaction set off by the earlier eruption of Mount St. Helens in Washington. After 98 seconds, the reporter held up a sign saying "April Fool."

"But by then it was too late. Local police and civil-defense officials were deluged with calls from more than a hundred frantic Milton residents trying to find out the best evacuation routes." Newsweek, April 14, 1980, at 35. The executive producer of the program was fired.

In 1985, as part of its ongoing attempt to remove "regulatory underbrush," the Commission rescinded earlier policy statements about hoaxes and public safety. To issue a Public Notice cautioning all broadcast licensees against engaging in hoaxes such as announcing that "amoebas" are invading a city was "overreaction." Alternative remedies were adequate to protect the public interest in these areas. These remedies include civil suits, criminal statutes prohibiting disturbing the peace, maintaining a public nuisance, or making harassing phone calls. The Commission did note, however, that a broadcast of something similar to "War of the Worlds" without adequate cautionary language would still be a violation of the general duty to program in the public interest. Unnecessary Broadcast Regulation, 57 R.R.2d 939 (1985).

F. MISCELLANEOUS CONSTRAINTS

1. Advertising and Commercial Practices

a. The Fairness Doctrine

In the 1960s, the Commission, for the first time, decided that advertisements might be covered under the fairness doctrine. It ruled that a licensee carrying advertising for cigarettes had to present some programming on the dangers of smoking. This ruling was upheld in Banzhaf v. Federal Communications Commission, 405 F.2d 1082 (D.C.

Cir.1968), certiorari denied 396 U.S. 842 (1969). Although the licensee could decide how to meet this requirement, most licensees presented material that had been prepared by the American Cancer Society and similar organizations.

The Commission attempted to treat the cigarette case as unique. Thus, when opponents of high-powered automobiles wanted the FCC to require licensees to present contrasting views on the value of such cars, the FCC refused. On appeal, the court of appeals could not distinguish the cigarette situation from the high-powered car situation and ordered the FCC to be consistent. Friends of the Earth v. Federal Communications Commission, 449 F.2d 1164 (D.C.Cir.1971).

In 1974, the Commission, in part of its Fairness Report, rethought the question of applying the doctrine to commercials. It decided to divide commercials into those that simply try to sell products and those that present a "meaningful statement which obviously addresses, and advocates a point of view on, a controversial issue of public importance." The latter, also called "editorial" or "advocacy" advertisements, give rise to obligations under the fairness doctrine. If an advertisement is false or misleading, it might precipitate some action by the Federal Trade Commission or by competitors, but the fairness doctrine was not the appropriate way to handle commercials that do not address public issues.

In a challenge to the policy, involving commercials for snowmobiles, environmental groups contended that the commercials showed only one side of the controversial issue of the desirability of snowmobiles. The Commission rejected the complaint on the ground that, although the environmental effects of snowmobiles might involve a controversial issue of public importance, the commercials themselves were not devoted to an obvious or meaningful discussion of that issue.

The court of appeals affirmed. Public Interest Research Group v. Federal Communications Commission, 522 F.2d 1060 (1st Cir.1975), certiorari denied 424 U.S. 965 (1976). The court upheld the Commission's power to retreat from earlier rulings: "In the absence of statutory or constitutional barriers, an agency may abandon earlier precedents and frame new policies." Congress had not frozen the fairness doctrine in any particular form.

Finally, the appellants argued that the First Amendment itself required that the fairness doctrine be rigorously enforced so that the airwaves would be true public forums for the presentation of divergent views. The court rejected this argument. Although the *Red Lion* approach might be furthered by extending the fairness doctrine to all advertising, the court did "not view that question, in the short and long run, as so free from doubt that courts should impose an inflexible response as a matter of constitutional law. We believe that the first amendment permitted the Commission not only to experiment with full-scale application of the fairness doctrine to advertising but also to retreat from its experiment when it determined from experience that the extension was unworkable."

b. Other Regulation

Although broadcasters are of course subject to advertising regulation applicable to the mass media in general, they are also subject to special restrictions.

The NAB Codes. As we have seen, indirect regulation of the content of broadcast programs occurred through the NAB Codes. Since the three major networks adhered to the Codes, affiliates that did not themselves belong would be carrying only material acceptable under the Code whenever they carried network programming.

Code provisions included several restrictions on advertising. Advertising of products such as hard liquor and contraceptives were prohibited. Limits on the total number of advertising minutes per hour were part of the code, as was a ban on connected thirty-second advertisements for two or more unrelated products ("split 30's"). In 1979, the Justice Department brought an action against the NAB charging that certain of the commercial time restrictions violated the antitrust laws. In 1982, the prohibition against split-30's was held to be an antitrust violation. United States v. National Association of Broadcasters, 536 F.Supp. 149 (D.D.C.1982). As a result, the NAB negotiated a consent decree with the Justice Department that prohibited the NAB from adopting any rule respecting the quantity, placement, or format of advertising or other nonprogram material. In addition, although not as a requirement of the settlement, the NAB cancelled the advertising standards of the Television and Radio Codes and dissolved the Code Boards of Directors. Broadcasting and Government, January 1, 1985, at 138–39.

Commercial Practices. The Commission has long taken an interest in the commercial practices of broadcast licensees. In 1985, however, the Commission eliminated many of these rules and proposed deletion of others. Among the regulations deleted were those covering distortion of audience ratings; selection of sports announcers; conflicts of interest; promotion of nonbroadcast business of a station; concert promotion announcements; and false, misleading, or deceptive advertisements. The regulations proposed for deletion apply to fraudulent billing practices, network clipping, and joint sales practices. As in the other "underbrush" proceedings, the Commission asserted that the subjects eliminated "relate to areas which often are not within this Commission's area of expertise and where either alternate remedies exist to deter the activity addressed by the particular policy or where marketplace forces will correct the particular abuse." Unnecessary Broadcast Regulation, 57 R.R.2d 913 (1985).

In addition, the Commission will no longer hear complaints regarding distortion of a station's ratings or inaccurate signal coverage maps. It did state that the filing of a misleading coverage map would imply unacceptable character and could place a station's renewal at risk. Unnecessary Broadcast Regulation (Advertising Misrepresentations), 54 R.R.2d 705 (1983).

2. CIGARETTES AND ALCOHOL—AND COMMERCIAL SPEECH

After the *Banzhaf* decision, supra, Congress confronted the cigarette commercial issue. In 1969, it adopted 15 U.S.C. § 1335: "After January 1, 1971, it shall be unlawful to advertise cigarettes on any medium of electronic communication subject to the jurisdiction of the Federal Communications Commission."

The statute was challenged by broadcasters—but not by cigarette manufacturers. It was upheld by a three-judge court in Capital Broadcasting Co. v. Mitchell, 333 F.Supp. 582 (D.D.C.1971), affirmed without opinion 405 U.S. 1000 (1972).

The court rejected the argument that this amounted to censorship in violation of § 326 because licensees were still free to present pro-smoking messages—except to the extent that Congress had forbidden commercial messages. The Commission was leaving that decision to the licensees. Moreover, some aspects of anti-smoking messages might still be found to invoke the fairness doctrine—but health danger was not one of them. Also, it was permissible to consider at renewal time whether a licensee carried programs on the dangers of smoking—not because it was a controversial issue, but because one aspect of meeting the public interest is to warn about dangers to health and safety, even if they are obvious and non-controversial.

The dissenting judge in the lower court suggested that the cigarette manufacturers were not at all unhappy to be ordered to stop advertising on radio and television because it had become unprofitable as a result of the anti-smoking messages.

What might the Commission do at renewal time if it found a licensee had presented several debates on cigarette smoking in which half the speakers argued that there was no health hazard in smoking? Is there a tension between saying that licensees are free to program pro-smoking material if they wish and that they will be judged at renewal time on how they have programmed on matters of health and safety?

Commercial Speech Doctrine. What impact might the new developments in commercial speech, discussed in Chapter VIII, have on broadcast advertising? Before this development, limits on broadcast advertising were not thought to raise a constitutional problem. Although the special status of broadcasting contributed to the lack of constitutional protection, the primary reason was that commercial speech generally was thought to be outside the protection of the First Amendment.

In addition to the inevitable reliance on *Red Lion* and the scarcity rationale, several arguments for allowing more extensive restrictions on the broadcast media have been advanced. Relying on *Pacifica*, advocates of regulation argue that the greater impact of broadcasting, its unique accessibility to children, and its intrusion into the home all mandate less constitutional protection for broadcast advertising than for print advertising. Others contend that the restricted format of broadcast advertising—thirty- or sixty-second commercials—makes it inherently deceptive and misleading.

Faced with a state ban on cable advertising of alcoholic beverages, the Court invalidated the statute on preemption grounds and did not address the commercial speech issue. Capital Cities Cable, Inc. v. Crisp, 467 U.S. 691 (1984).

3. Drugs

A 1973 case involving a licensee's playing of "drug oriented" music raised questions regarding the duty of broadcasters to have prior knowledge of their programming, so as to evaluate the desirability of broadcasting music pertaining to drug use. Yale Broadcasting Co. v. Federal Communications Commission, 478 F.2d 594 (D.C.Cir.1973).

The appellant in this case argued that the imposition of this duty was an unconstitutional burden on its freedom of speech. The court responded that only a reasonable understanding of what was being broadcast was required. Obscure, incoherent, or ambiguous lyrics would not necessarily put a station on notice.

The court accepted that a licensee would not be expected to know in advance the content of a network program, a free-flowing live discussion, or an audience participation program. However, the Commission was empowered to order broadcasters of "canned music" to "make a reasonable effort to know what is in the 'can.'" The Commission is "not required to allow radio licensees, being freely granted the use of limited air channels, to spew out to the listening public canned music, whose content and quality before broadcast is totally unknown."

Judge Bazelon dissented from the denial of rehearing en banc. Among other things, he questioned the ability of the FCC to regulate content that could not be regulated in the print media. The Supreme Court denied certiorari, 414 U.S. 914 (1973). Justice Brennan would have granted the writ and set the case for argument. Justice Douglas dissented along the lines sketched by Chief Judge Bazelon below. He noted that the Commission majority apparently had intended to ban drug-related lyrics from the air and that at a Congressional hearing the Chairman testified that if a licensee were playing songs that the Commission thought promoted the use of hard drugs, "I know what I would do, I would probably vote to take the license away." Even though a ban on drug lyrics might not cause great concern, Justice Douglas cautioned that "next year it may apply to comedy programs, and the following year to news broadcasts." He concluded that

> The Government cannot, consistent with the First Amendment, require a broadcaster to censor its music any more than it can require a newspaper to censor the stories of its reporters. Under our system the Government is not to decide what messages, spoken or in music, are of the proper "social value" to reach the people.

Could Congress ban pro-drug broadcasts—whether of songs or of normal speech? Are your views here consistent with your views about Congressional power to ban cigarette commercials?

4. CHILDREN'S PROGRAMMING

Over the years, several groups have voiced displeasure with programs aimed at children. Three major themes have dominated: the content of such programs, the paucity of children's programs, and the commercial practices on the programs.

The first concern was about early evening programs that stressed violence and sexual innuendo. As a result of such complaints and negotiations, the networks and the National Association of Broadcasters promulgated the "family viewing policy" that caused these programs to be moved to later in the evening. The story of the creation of the policy is traced in G. Cowan, See No Evil: The Backstage Battle over Sex and Violence in Television (1979). The policy and the way in which it was formulated led to extensive litigation, summarized in Writers Guild of America v. Federal Communications Commission, 609 F.2d 355 (9th Cir. 1979), certiorari denied 449 U.S. 824 (1980). A settlement was reached in 1984.

The second concern, the lack of programs aimed for children, was addressed by the Commission in a 1974 policy statement that asked licensees to make an effort to increase such programs. In 1979, the Commission concluded that children's programming per station had not increased in the five years—and it proposed several possible steps. In Children's Television Programming, 55 R.R.2d 199 (1984), the Commission rejected mandatory steps. It doubted that quotas were permissible and, in any event, quotas would create difficult definitional problems. At renewal time, a licensee must show that it had considered the needs of children in its viewing area, but might consider alternative program sources available in the area, such as noncommercial stations and cable. This approach was affirmed on appeal, Action for Children's Television v. Federal Communications Commission, 756 F.2d 899, 57 R.R.2d 1406 (D.C.Cir. 1985).

Citizen groups have also failed in attempts to deny renewal to stations that had no regularly scheduled children's programs. The Commission need not prefer a station that regularly scheduled cartoons to one that presented educational specials. Washington Association for Television and Children v. Federal Communications Commission, 712 F.2d 677, 54 R.R.2d 293 (D.C.Cir. 1983).

Finally, efforts to ban commercials on children's programs have failed. Action for Children's Television v. Federal Communications

Commission, 564 F.2d 458 (D.C.Cir. 1977). The Commission's actions—such as banning program hosts from endorsing products and ordering clear separations between programs and advertising—were held an adequate response to the matter. The Commission has also rejected a requirement that all commercials be introduced and terminated by an inaudible signal that would permit parents to buy devices to blank out the commercials. The Commission was concerned that this would erode the advertising base for children's programming. Children's Advertising Detector Signal, 57 R.R.2d 935 (1985).

5. LOTTERIES AND CONTESTS

Another specific substantive limitation has been 18 U.S.C. § 1304, prohibiting broadcast of "any advertisement of or information concerning any lottery . . . ." What is the basis for this statute? As with the specific obscenity statute, the Commission has taken the view that it has responsibility for enforcement. This has been bolstered by the provisions in the Communications Act that provide for revocation of license and for forfeitures against those who violate § 1304. See §§ 312(a)(6), 312(b), 503(b)(1)(E).

A lottery is defined as anything containing three elements: chance, consideration, and a prize. If all three are present, the broadcaster cannot air any information, either as an advertisement or public service announcement. Even news coverage is limited to situations where the lottery is deemed newsworthy. It is irrelevant whether the beneficiary of the lottery is a commercial enterprise or non-profit. Technically, a licensee can be punished for announcing that a church bingo game will still be held despite bad weather.

When states began running their own lotteries, new questions arose concerning the ban on lottery information. After a conflict between New York State Broadcasters Association v. United States, 414 F.2d 990 (2d Cir.1969) and New Jersey State Lottery Commission v. United States, 491 F.2d 219 (3d Cir.1974), the Supreme Court granted review in the New Jersey case. After argument but before decision, Congress passed a statute providing that § 1304 shall not apply to "an advertisement, list of prizes, or information concerning a lottery conducted by a State acting under the authority of State law . . . broadcast by a radio or television station licensed to a location in that State or an adjacent State which conducts such a lottery." 18 U.S.C. § 1307(a)(2). The Court remanded the New Jersey case for consideration of whether it had become moot. 420 U.S. 371 (1975). The opinion on remand is reported at 34 R.R.2d 825 (3d Cir.1975).

The only other significant case in this area involved whether so-called "give-away" programs on radio and television ran afoul of § 1304 as lotteries. The Supreme Court construed the statute narrowly and held that requiring contestants to listen to the program did not constitute a "valuable consideration." Thus, the Commission had no basis for prohibiting the programs. Federal Communications Commission v. American Broadcasting Co., 347 U.S. 284 (1954).

6. OTHER CONSTRAINTS

a. Payola and Plugola

In the late 1950s, big-money quiz shows such as "The $64,000 Question," "Tic Tac Dough," and "Twenty One" constituted one of the most popular forms of prime-time programming. In 1959, however, testimony before a House subcommittee proved that the shows were fixed. At approximately the same time evidence also surfaced that many disc jockeys and program directors were accepting bribes to play specific records on their stations. This latter practice became known as "payola." (Technically, "payola" is accepting or receiving money or other valuable consideration for the inclusion of material in a broadcast without disclosing that fact to the audience. "Plugola" is promoting goods or services in which someone responsible for selecting the material broadcast has a financial interest.)

Congress and the Commission reacted quickly to the quiz show scandal and amended Section 317 of the Communications Act and added two new sections, 508 and 509. These sections, as well as rules adopted by the Commission, sought to prevent the public from being deceived as to the commercial nature of sponsored material.

b. Sports Blackouts

In 1973, Congress passed a statute to resolve the clamor raised by the refusal of professional football teams to permit televising of a home game that was being televised to other parts of the country (47 U.S.C. § 331). It provided that professional sports telecasts could not be barred if all the tickets had been sold 72 hours before game time, and spelled out the conditions under which the rights to telecast could be made available. The statute expired by its own terms in 1975. A permanent anti-blackout statute was blocked in 1976, but the National Football League agreed to follow the expired statute.

c. Other Underbrush

In further attempts to delete unnecessary restrictions, the Commission in 1983 eliminated restrictions on liquor advertisements in dry areas, on broadcasts of foreign language programs, and on astrology information, as well as music format service agreements, repetitious broadcasts, call-in polls, private interest broadcasts, the use of sirens and sound effects, and rules regarding harassing and threatening phone calls resulting from broadcasts. Unnecessary Broadcast Regulation, 54 R.R.2d 1043 (1983). In 1984 the FCC also eliminated restrictions on horse racing programming and advertising. Unnecessary Broadcast Regulation, 56 R.R.2d 976 (1984).

Chapter XVI

BROADCAST LICENSING

In this Chapter we consider substantive and procedural aspects of the licensing activities of the Federal Communications Commission. We begin by considering a general concern that the Commission considers in various ways during the licensing process—the goal of maximizing diversity of ownership of broadcast stations.

A. MEDIA CONCENTRATION

As we saw in the NBC case, p. 720, supra, the Commission has long been concerned about excessive concentration of control over the process of deciding what programs to present. There are several ways to attack the problem. One, utilized in that case, is to prevent the networks from imposing their power on the licensees. Another is to order licensees to obtain their programs from non-network sources for certain periods of the day, as in the Prime Time Access Rules, to be discussed shortly. Still another, which gets at this problem indirectly but also attacks other problems, is to attempt to diversify the ownership of broadcast facilities.

The Commission can also use its rulemaking powers to achieve diversity of control—perhaps because the subject lends itself to quantitative definition, such as how many stations a person should be allowed to control in a particular area. It is important to realize, however, that even though the Commission may adopt specific rules to meet a problem, it must always consider requests for waivers of that rule if the public interest might be furthered by the waiver. The 1934 Act grants the Commission powers to act in the public interest, and although a rule may operate in the public interest most of the time, some exceptions may be in the public interest.

In 1980, for example, a radio station licensee in Alaska sought a license for a vacant television channel in the same community. A rule barred the same licensee from controlling radio and VHF stations in the same community. The community had three vacant VHF frequencies. If the FCC adhered to its rule, the community might not get any television service for several years. The Commission granted a waiver of its rule to meet the needs of the community.

Note, however, that the Commission might be able to argue in some situations that the overriding public interest may be better served by rigorous adherence to a firm rule that all know will be followed than by granting waivers that undercut a major rule.

1. Local Concentration

---

a. Duopoly

Local concentration of control of mass media facilities has been a problem for the Commission at least since 1938, when it received an application for a standard (AM) broadcasting station in Flint, Michigan, from applicants who controlled another corporation that already operated a standard broadcasting station in the same area. Although there were no rival applicants, the Commission refused to grant the second facility without a compelling showing that the public interest would be served in such a situation.

This was the beginning of the so-called "duopoly" rule, which the Commission later formalized in a general rule that it would not grant a license to any applicant who already held a similar facility or license so located that the service areas of the two would overlap.

In the 1960s, the Commission returned to this subject and recognized that the dwindling number of American newspapers made the impact of individual broadcasting stations "significantly greater." This reinforced the Commission's resolve to rarely grant a duopoly.

During this period, however, the Commission was granting to the same applicant one AM, one FM, and one television station in the same locality because this was not a duplication of facilities in the same service area. In 1970, the Commission moved the next step and proposed the "one-to-a-customer" rule. In the Matter of the Rules Relating to Multiple Ownership, 22 F.C.C.2d 306, 18 R.R.2d 1735 (1970). Under this rule licensees would be limited to one broadcast station in any given market regardless of the type of broadcast service involved. The Commission viewed this as a logical extension of its earlier diversification rules:

> 21. Application of the principles set forth above dictates that one person should not be licensed to operate more than one broadcast station in the same place, and serving substantially the same public, unless some other relevant public interest consideration is found to outweigh the importance of diversifying control. It is elementary that the number of frequencies available for licensing is limited. In any particular area there may be many voices that would like to be heard, but not all can be licensed. A proper objective is the maximum diversity of ownership that technology permits in each area. We are of the view that 60 different licensees are more desirable than 50, and even that 51 are more desirable than 50. In a rapidly changing social climate, communication of ideas is vital. If a city has 60 frequencies available but they are licensed to only 50 different licensees, the number of sources for ideas is not maximized. It might be the 51st licensee

that would become the communication channel for a solution to a severe social crisis. No one can say that present licensees are broadcasting everything worthwhile that can be communicated. We see no existing public interest reason for being wedded to our present policy that permits a licensee to acquire more than one station in the same area.

The Commission rejected an argument "that the good profit position of a multiple owner in the same market results in more in-depth informational programs being broadcast and thus, in more meaningful diversity. We do not doubt that some multiple owners may have a greater capacity to so program, but the record does not demonstrate that they generally do so."

The Commission was persuaded, however, that UHF stations presented a special problem in that they were still weak competitively and few would go on the air unless affiliated with an established radio station. Therefore, the Commission refused to adopt a firm rule against radio-UHF combinations but would review those on a case-by-case basis. Finally, the Commission announced that the rules would be prospective only; no divestitures would be required, due to the large number of existing combinations and a sense that ordering divestiture for such a large group might very well create instability.

The rules as originally adopted would have banned not only VHF-radio combinations, but also AM–FM combinations, even though traditionally FM had been weak as a competitive force and indeed the Commission during the 1950s had encouraged AM stations to acquire FM stations. On reconsideration, the Commission decided that although FM stations were becoming more powerful competitors and increasingly profitable, most AM–FM combinations might still be "economically and/or technically interdependent." Concerned that the rules as originally adopted might hinder the development of FM service, the FCC modified them to permit the formation of new AM–FM combinations. Multiple Ownership of Standard, FM and TV Broadcast Stations, 28 F.C.C.2d 662, 21 R.R.2d 1551 (1971). Thus, only VHF-radio combinations were flatly banned by the new rules.

b. *Crossownership*

When the Commission adopted its one-to-a-customer rules, it also proposed the adoption of a set of rules that would proscribe common ownership of newspapers and broadcast facilities serving the same area, and require divestiture of prohibited combinations. Although the Commission had flirted with such a regulation in the early 1940s, it had abandoned the attempt. The basis for the reconsideration in 1970 was an awareness that 94 television stations were affiliated through common control with a newspaper in the same city. In addition, "some newspapers own television stations in other cities, which also serve the city in which the newspaper is located." The Commission thought this situation was very similar to the joint ownership of two television stations in the same community, something the Commission had very rarely permitted. "The functions of newspapers and television stations as journalists are so similar that their joint ownership is, in this respect, essentially the same as the joint ownership of two television stations."

After extensive consideration, the Commission in 1975 amended the Multiple Ownership Rules to include daily newspapers. 50 F.C.C.2d 1046, 32 R.R.2d 954. The rules barred the grant of a license for a television or radio station to any applicant who already controls, owns, or operates a daily newspaper serving the same area, and required existing broadcast-newspaper combinations to be dissolved by 1980 in all communities in which the only newspaper of general circulation and the only radio or television station in the community were under common ownership. For radio-newspaper combinations, however, divestiture was not required if a separately owned television station served the same community. Nine radio-newspaper and seven television-newspaper combinations were affected by these provisions. If combinations for which divestiture was not required are sold in the future, the newspaper and broadcast facilities must each be sold to a different party. Finally, the Commission stated that it would not consider individual challenges against these combinations in renewal proceedings unless antitrust violations or specific abuses were alleged.

The Supreme Court unanimously upheld the Commission's rules. Federal Communications Comm'n v. National Citizens Committee for Broadcasting, 436 U.S. 775 (1978). In an opinion by Justice Marshall, the Court first held that the Commission had acted within its statutory and constitutional authority in promulgating a rule that prospectively barred newspaper owners from holding broadcast licenses in the same community. The statutory authority came from § 303(r) of the 1934 Act, which permitted the Commission to promulgate rules and regulations to give effect to the provisions of the Act. "It was not inconsistent with the statutory scheme . . . for the Commission to conclude that the maximum benefit to the 'public interest' would follow from allocation of broadcast licenses so as to promote diversification of the mass media as a whole." Even though the record was not conclusive on the point, the Commission "acted rationally in finding that diversification of ownership would enhance the possibility of achieving greater diversity of viewpoints." It was also permissible for the Commission to make diversification the controlling factor in selecting new applicants.

At this point the Court dealt with the Commission's constitutional power to exclude a class of applicants from holding licenses. This portion of the opinion was discussed in Chapter XIV.

Second, the Court upheld the Commission's decision to order divestiture in 16 "egregious" cases of small communities in which the newspaper owned the only television station or, if there was no television station, the only radio station. The danger in these situations was sufficient to warrant divestiture. Third, the Supreme Court found that the Commission had adequately explained that diversification was not its only concern:

> The Order identified several specific respects in which the public interest would or might be harmed if a sweeping divestiture requirement were imposed: the stability and continuity of meritorious service provided by the newspaper owners as a group would be lost; owners who had provided meritorious service would unfairly be denied the opportunity to continue in operation; "economic dislocations" might prevent new owners from obtaining sufficient working capital to maintain the quality of local programming; and local ownership of broadcast stations would probably decrease. [ ] We cannot say that the Commission acted irrationally in concluding that these public interest harms outweighed the potential gains that would follow from increasing diversification of ownership.

The result, then, was to permit continuation of all but 16 existing combinations, but to bar future newspaper-broadcast co-located combinations.

The Court noted that the Commission's study of "existing co-located newspaper-television combinations showed that in terms of percentage of time devoted to several categories of local programming, these stations had displayed 'an undramatic but nonetheless statistically significant superiority' over other television stations."

The Court observed that remaining combinations still could be challenged on an individual basis. Diversification "will be a relevant but somewhat secondary factor." A challenger might also show that a common owner has "engaged in specific economic or programming abuses" attributable to the existence of its combination.

2. National Concentration

The Commission has been equally concerned about the effects of concentration of ownership across different markets. Are the issues raised by national concentration different from those presented by local concentration? Is the marketplace of ideas in one city affected by a company's media holdings in other cities? Are there any potential benefits of a company's owning stations in other communities?

a. Multiple Ownership Rules

Beginning in 1940, the Commission adopted rules limiting the number of stations that might be held by a single owner. In 1953, the Commission concluded that the rules should prohibit the ownership or control, directly or indirectly, by any party of more than seven AM stations, seven FM stations, and seven television stations—of which not more than five could be VHF. The Commission explained its position as follows:

> The vitality of our system of broadcasting depends in large part on the introduction into this field of licensees who are pre-

> pared and qualified to serve the varied and divergent needs of the public for radio service. Simply stated, the fundamental purpose of this facet of the multiple ownership rules is to promote diversification of ownership in order to maximize diversification of program and service viewpoints as well as to prevent any undue concentration of economic power contrary to the public interest. In this connection, we wish to emphasize that by such rules diversification of program services is furthered without any governmental encroachment on what we recognize to be the prime responsibility of the broadcast licensee. (See Section 326 of the Communications Act.) . . .

The Commission chose an equal number of AM and FM stations because at that time, 538 of the 600 FM stations were owned by AM licensees. This was the result of a conscious Commission policy to encourage AM stations to put FM stations on the air since most of those operating FM stations alone were finding it extremely unprofitable. The number seven was chosen "in order that present holdings of such stations be not unduly disrupted." Very few owners had holdings in excess of seven, and the Commission planned to hold a divestiture hearing for each of them. Rules and Regulations Relating to Multiple Ownership, 18 F.C.C. 288 (1953).

The rules were upheld in United States v. Storer Broadcasting Co., 351 U.S. 192 (1956). The Court rejected Storer's argument that § 309 of the Communications Act always required a full hearing to determine whether granting additional licenses to the applicant would be in the public interest:

> We do not read the hearing requirement . . . as withdrawing from the power of the Commission the rulemaking authority necessary for the orderly conduct of its business. As conceded by Storer, "Section 309(b) does not require the Commission to hold a hearing before denying a license to operate a station in ways contrary to those that the Congress has determined are in the public interest." The challenged Rules contain limitations against licensing not specifically authorized by statute. But that is not the limit of the Commission's rulemaking authority.
>
> This Commission, like other agencies, deals with the public interest. [ ] Its authority covers new and rapidly developing fields. Congress sought to create regulation for public protection with careful provision to assure fair opportunity for open competition in the use of broadcasting facilities. Accordingly, we cannot interpret § 309(b) as barring rules that declare a present intent to limit the number of stations consistent with a permissible "concentration of control." It is but a rule that announces the Commission's attitude on public protection against such concentration. . . .

The opinion did state, however, that the Commission's responsibility to behave in the public interest required it to grant a hearing to an applicant who had already reached the maximum number of stations but nonetheless asserted sufficient reasons why the rule should be waived in its particular case.

In early 1984, the Commission voted to expand the limits on multiple ownership from 7–7–7 to 12–12–12 with a six-year sunset provision (eliminating the rules entirely at the end of six years). The new rule made no distinction between VHF and UHF television. Faced with mounting criticism of the new rule and threatened Congressional action, the Commission delayed implementation of the television portion of the order and reconsidered it. The revised order contained several new provisions.

Upon reconsideration, the Commission found that relaxing the numerical cap from seven to twelve stations would not prohibit a single group owner from increasing its audience substantially by making acquisitions in the largest markets. Therefore, an additional ownership limit based on audience reach was in order.

The Commission settled on a 25 percent limit on audience reach to combine with its stated numerical limits. This limited the growth of the largest group owners without requiring any divestiture or grandfathering. (Metromedia had the largest combined reach at 23.89 percent.) The Commission also eliminated the sunset provision.

The FCC then turned to requests for special treatment for both UHFs and minorities. Due to the physical limitations inherent in the UHF band, UHF stations cannot compete with VHF stations on an equal basis. The original rules' stricter limitation on VHF ownership was part of the Commission's longstanding efforts to foster the development of UHF.

Agreeing that added UHF incentives were warranted in the context of the audience-reach limit, the Commission structured the change to recognize the physical handicaps confronting UHF television. Owners of UHF stations would be treated as reaching only 50 percent of the potential audience within the relevant ADI market. This discount approach would provide some measure of the actual handicap UHF owners face, and such an approach would be consistent with diversity objectives.

Noting that the multiple ownership rules were not intended to function primarily as a vehicle for promoting minority ownership in broadcasting, the Commission observed that various other policies such as tax certificates, distress sale benefits, and lottery preferences were all instituted to promote minority ownership. Although those policies should serve as the primary mechanisms for that purpose, the Commission recognized that the national multiple ownership rules may, in some circumstances, play a role in fostering minority ownership. This led to the adoption of a rule that permits group owners of television and radio stations to have holdings in a maximum of 14 stations, provided that at least two of the stations are minority controlled.

Extending this policy to the audience-reach limit for television, a group owner having cognizable interests in minority-controlled television stations would be allowed to reach a maximum of 30 percent of the national audience, provided that at least 5 percent of the aggregate reach of its stations was derived from minority-controlled stations.

Two Commissioners objected to using the multiple ownership rules to promote minority ownership. Commissioner Dawson stated that she did not see how national "concentration is in any way ameliorated by the race of [an] entity's owners." Commissioner Patrick asked, "If the public interest is threatened by concentrating ownership of 14 stations in a single owner, how is that threat obviated by the race of that owner?"

b. Conglomerates in Broadcasting

Occasionally the concentration problem has been raised not in terms of multiple ownership of competing media, but in terms of other businesses in which a prospective licensee is engaged. The prime example is a merger that was proposed in 1966 between ABC, which in its capacity as group owner owned 17 broadcasting stations, and International Telephone and Telegraph, a vast conglomerate with manufacturing facilities, telecommunication operations, and other activities in 66 countries throughout the world.

Critics were concerned that ITT would use the broadcasting facilities to further the interests of the parent corporation in ways that might include distorting the news and making editorial decisions on grounds other than the criteria used by professional journalists. The Commission rejected these concerns on the ground that "it is too late in the day to argue that such outside business interests are disqualifying. . . . We cannot in this case adopt standards which when applied to other cases would require us to restructure the industry unless we are prepared to undertake that task. We could not, in good conscience, forbid ABC to merge with ITT without instituting proceedings to separate NBC from RCA, both of which are bigger than the respective principals in this case." The Commission granted the application for transferring of the 17 licenses by a 4–3 vote. Memorandum Opinion and Order 7 F.C.C.2d 245, 9 R.R.2d 12 (1966).

While an appeal by the Justice Department on antitrust grounds was pending, the parties abandoned their proposed merger. Would there be any problem if, for example, General Motors sought to acquire a television station in Detroit? Are different questions raised if a book publisher or motion picture producer seeks a television license?

The Gannett-Combined Communications Merger. In 1979, the FCC approved what was at that time the largest deal in broadcasting history. The parties were Gannett, which at the time published 77 daily and 32 weekly newspapers and owned one VHF station, and Combined Communications Corp., which at the time owned newspapers in Cincinnati and Oakland, plus five VHF, two UHF, six AM, and six

FM stations. In addition, Gannett owned Louis Harris and Associates, the polling firm, and Combined was a major supplier of outdoor advertising. The deal called for $370 million in Gannett stock to go to Combined. After spin-offs to meet the FCC's cross-ownership policies, Gannett had 79 daily newspapers, seven television stations and 12 radio stations.

The final result, because of the spin-offs, violated no concentration rule. Nonetheless, the Commission considered whether granting the applications to transfer ownership of the stations would be in the "public interest." The majority concluded that the deal was not likely to adversely affect competition or raise antitrust concerns.

The First Amendment issue, however, raised harder questions. The FCC noted that Gannett had represented that "local autonomy will be the touchstone for the operation of each newspaper and broadcast property" and that the newspapers would operate separately from the broadcast properties. For example, Gannett asserted that in 1976, of its 35 papers that made endorsements, 22 endorsed Gerald Ford and 13 endorsed Jimmy Carter. Decentralized operation was the goal, although everyone recognized that under § 310 of the 1934 Act, Gannett had to retain ultimate control of its stations.

Some concern was voiced that the size of the combination would lead advertisers and stock market investors to exercise more control over management than would occur with less centralized control. Presumably, a large communications entity might "harm diversity of information and opinion through its institutional pressures rather than by any intentional acts of its corporate leadership."

The FCC stressed countervailing considerations: "Media chains may have more freedom and might be inclined to take more risks in their reporting of news and opinion because their financial health allows a degree of independence from the political views of their major advertisers." The size of the organization might permit more coverage of national news in competition with the wire services, the television networks, and the largest newspapers and magazines.

Since all of these newspapers and stations face "substantial local mixed-media competition," even if a "Gannett" view entered a new market it was not eliminating other views available in that market. Affirmatively, the Commission noted that the deal had resulted in the break-up of cross-ownership interests in Phoenix and St. Louis, as well as sale of Gannett's VHF (in Rochester, N.Y.) to a buyer controlled by a minority group. This made it the first network-affiliated major market television station controlled by a minority group. The merger was approved, 5–1.

The dissenter was greatly concerned by the "trend" toward placing "organs of information and news and opinion in this country in fewer and fewer hands. This is an unhealthy thing for a democracy: absentee ownership, on a vast scale, of newspapers and broadcasting stations. . . . Where are the William Allen Whites of 1979? Too many of them have been bought out, one by one, by the chains. They've been made offers they could not refuse."

The Capital Cities Communications-American Broadcasting Companies Merger. In 1985, Capital Cities Communications (CCC) announced plans to acquire American Broadcasting Companies, Inc. (ABC) for $3.5 billion. This transaction, by far the largest in broadcast history, has resulted in the formation of a new company, Capital Cities/ABC Inc.

For the new company to meet the various FCC ownership rules, over $1 billion worth of properties were sold. Although CCC and ABC own only 12 AM stations, 12 FM stations, and 12 TV stations between them, the total reach of the TV stations was 28.59 percent, and steps were taken to bring that figure down to the 25 percent maximum, and to comply with the duopoly and other rules.

The *GE–RCA Deal.* In 1985, General Electric announced the purchase of RCA for more than $6 billion. Among RCA's subsidiaries is NBC.

c. *Minority Ownership*

Distress Sales and Minority Broadcasters. One of the FCC's concerns in recent years has been the dearth of minority broadcasters. In 1978, in an effort to meet two concerns at once, the Commission announced steps to allow licensees whose renewals might be in jeopardy to sell their stations to minority groups for more than the value of the buildings and equipment but less than the going concern value. Statement of Policy on Minority Ownership of Broadcast Facilities, 68 F.C.C.2d 979, 42 R.R.2d 1689 (1978). The Commission announced that it would permit "licensees whose licenses have been designated for revocation hearings, or whose renewal applications have been designated for hearing on basic qualification issues . . . to transfer or assign their licenses at a 'distress sale' price to applicants with a significant minority ownership interest, assuming the proposed assignee or transferee meets our other qualifications."

In a clarification, the Commission stated that the opportunity for distress sales applied only when no competing applicant was involved in the hearing.

The distress sale option has been attractive to licensees who are ordered to hearings. As we shall see, the fact that allegations have been thought serious enough to warrant a hearing is a dangerous warning. To litigate and lose the renewal would leave the licensee with nothing except the buildings and equipment that it owns. The distress sale may yield the owner as much as 75 percent of the fair appraised value of a viable business.

The immediate social result of the distress sale policy has been to allow minority groups to enter the broadcasting industry in greater numbers. If the FCC's efforts to develop new stations work as expected, many minority broadcasters will use that route, and the relatively limited distress sale route will become less important.

The distress policy explicitly limited "minority" to specific ethnic groups, but indicated that "other clearly definable groups, such as women, may be able to demonstrate that they are eligible for similar treatment." But in Petition for Issuance of Policy Statement or Notice of Inquiry, 69 F.C.C.2d 1591, 44 R.R.2d 1051 (1978), the Commission ruled that although it had on occasion recognized female involvement as a merit in certain proceedings, it would not extend the minority policy to women because it had "not concluded that the historical and contemporary disadvantagement suffered by women is of the same order, or has the same contemporary consequences" as those involving groups covered in the original policy statement. As noted shortly, the Commission policy giving preferential treatment to women in comparative licensing proceedings has been struck down by Steele v. Federal Communications Commission, 770 F.2d 1192, 58 R.R.2d 1463 (D.C.Cir. 1985), rehearing granted en banc, and the Commission has also eliminated the preference for women in lottery license selection processes. Lottery Selection (Reference for Women), 58 R.R.2d 1077 (1985).

The FCC has developed other techniques for encouraging minority entry into broadcasting. In its 1978 Statement, the Commission announced that it would grant tax certificates to owners who sell their stations to groups controlled by members of minority groups. These certificates permit the seller to defer payment of capital gains taxes. Minority groups also have been given preferences in connection with the FM openings recently created by the Commission.

3. NETWORKS

Concentration of control problems are not limited, however, to ownership issues. Because broadcast networks supply much of the programming in the country, their influence extends far beyond the stations they own. The two primary legal devices available to control or limit the actions of the networks are application of conventional antitrust laws and FCC regulation.

A few antitrust actions have been begun in recent years. In 1978, for example, after six years of defending against an antitrust action, NBC entered into a consent decree that prohibited it from acquiring syndication rights from independent producers and entering reciprocal dealings with the other networks, and placed other limitations on dealings with independent producers. The other networks signed similar consent decrees.

But most of the control has been through FCC regulation. In the late 1930s the three national network companies (NBC, CBS, and Mutual) had almost half of the entire broadcast business in the country. In 1938, concerned by this concentration of control, the Commission began an inquiry into the need for special regulations to curb the power of the networks by prohibiting certain common network practices. In

1941, after extensive public hearings, the Commission adopted a series of regulations pertaining to chain broadcasting.

The networks then brought suit to enjoin enforcement of the chain broadcasting rules. We examined the Commission's authority to regulate broadcasting at p. 720, supra. The Court in *NBC* recognized the role these rules played in the development of radio:

> . . . Chain broadcasting makes possible a wider reception for expensive entertainment and cultural programs and also for programs of national or regional significance which would otherwise have coverage only in the locality of origin. [Advertisers have incentive to finance the production of these programs.] But the fact that the chain broadcasting method brings benefits and advantages to both the listening public and to broadcast station licensees does not mean that the prevailing practices and policies of the networks and their outlets are sound in all respects, or that they should not be altered. . . .

Among other things, the rules limited the exclusive affiliation of stations, regulated terms of affiliation, and protected the ability of affiliates to reject network programs.

In 1977, the Commission re-examined the application of the Chain Broadcasting Regulations to radio and concluded that, due to the high degree of competition that now existed, virtually all of the regulations were unnecessary, and they were eliminated.

In television, the Commission's concern about network power manifested itself in efforts to prevent the networks from programming all four hours of evening prime time. This led to local and non-network syndications during the 7–8 p.m. hour in most parts of the country. The story of the various rules can be found in Mt. Mansfield Television, Inc. v. Federal Communications Commission, 442 F.2d 470 (2d Cir. 1970) (upholding the constitutionality of the first rule); Independent Television Producers & Distributors v. Federal Communications Commission, 502 F.2d 249 (2d Cir. 1974) (upsetting the second rule); and Independent Television Producers & Distributors v. Federal Communications Commission, 516 F.2d 526 (2d Cir. 1975) (generally upholding the third rule). See Krattenmaker, The Prime Time Access Rule: Six Commandments for Inept Regulation, 7 COMM/ENT L.J. 19 (1984).

When it first adopted the prime time approach, the FCC also adopted rules designed to eliminate the networks from much of domestic sydication, and to restrict their activities in foreign markets to distribution of programs of which they were the sole producers. FCC efforts in 1983 to abandon these financial interest and syndication restrictions ran into fierce opposition from motion picture companies and other originators of programs. As a result, no action was taken.

Although several groups have tried to develop a "fourth network," all have failed. The latest effort is that of Rupert Murdoch, who is using his ownership of the group of 20th Century Fox television stations. With these as a base, Fox began lining up other groups and individual independent stations. Program delivery will be done by satellite. The service began in late 1986 with a late night one-hour program featuring Joan Rivers. The plans call for one or two nights per week of prime time programming by early 1987.

B. INITIAL LICENSING

---

1. THE ADMINISTRATIVE PROCESS AT WORK

At the outset, we examine the process by which the Commission grants licenses to applicants. An applicant for a broadcast frequency first asks the Commission for a construction permit to build the facility. If the construction permit is granted, the license will then follow almost automatically if the facility is constructed on schedule.

The application is filed initially with the Mass Media Bureau, whose staff reviews the papers to identify any deficiency. If the case is routine, the Commissioners have authorized the Bureau staff to issue the license. But if the application raises any of a variety of questions of fact or law, a more complex procedure is required.

Section 309(a) of the Communications Act provides that if, after examining an application, the Commission concludes that the "public interest, convenience, and necessity" will be served, it shall grant the application. But subsection (e) provides that "if a substantial and material question of fact is presented or the Commission for any reason is unable to make the finding specified in [subsection (a)], it shall formally designate the application for hearing . . . and shall forthwith notify the applicant . . . of such action and the grounds and reasons therefor, specifying with particularity the matters and things in issue. . . ."

The "hearing" mentioned in the statute is conducted by a member of the FCC's staff called an Administrative Law Judge (ALJ) (formerly called a hearing examiner), who functions much as does a regular judge presiding over a trial—except that there is no jury and the issues to be explored at the hearing are designated in advance by the Commission. If the application seems to raise no problem except the question of whether the applicant is adequately financed, for example, the Commission will order the ALJ to conduct a hearing limited to that fact question.

Does the applicant have to face an adversary at the hearing? The answer is that if the Mass Media Bureau has raised a question about the applicant's answers, the Mass Media Bureau itself may take part in the hearing to oppose the applicant. If the fact dispute is resolved in favor of the applicant, and the rest of the application is proper, the ALJ may grant the permit. If the Mass Media Bureau thinks the ALJ has made a mistake, it may appeal within the agency—sometimes to a "review board" of senior civil servants and sometimes to the Commissioners themselves. Similarly, if the judge's ruling favors the Bureau, the losing applicant may appeal within the agency.

If the Commission eventually decides against issuing a license or a construction permit, the unsuccessful applicant may then appeal to the courts—usually to the United States Court of Appeals for the District of Columbia. In this situation, the adversary is the Commission itself, represented by its general counsel's staff. However the court of appeals may decide, the losing side may seek Supreme Court review by filing a petition for a writ of certiorari.

An indication of how the courts view their role in reviewing broadcast licensing is found in Greater Boston Television Corp. v. Federal Communications Commission, 444 F.2d 841, 850–53 (D.C.Cir. 1970), certiorari denied 403 U.S. 923 (1971), to which we return shortly (footnotes citing a wealth of authorities have been excluded):

> Assuming consistency with law and the legislative mandate, the agency has latitude not merely to find facts and make judgments, but also to select the policies deemed in the public interest. The function of the court is to assure that the agency has given reasoned consideration to all the material facts and issues. This calls for insistence that the agency articulate with reasonable clarity its reasons for decision, and identify the significance of the crucial facts, a course that tends to assure that the agency's policies effectuate general standards, applied without unreasonable discrimination. . . .
>
> Its supervisory function calls on the court to intervene not merely in case of procedural inadequacies or bypassing of the mandate in the legislative charter, but more broadly if the court becomes aware, especially from a combination of danger signals, that the agency has not really taken a "hard look" at the salient problems, and has not genuinely engaged in reasoned decision-making. If the agency has not shirked this fundamental task, however, the court exercises restraint and affirms the agency's action even though the court would on its own account have made different findings or adopted different standards. Nor will the court upset a decision because of errors that are not material, there being room for the doctrine of harmless error. . . .

This brief description has assumed that it was possible for the Commission, or the Mass Media Bureau, to deny an application for a vacant frequency or channel—even though no one else has applied for it. As we shall see, this does occasionally happen.

But the most complex cases before the Commission are those in which more than one applicant seeks a single vacant frequency or channel. These are called "mutually exclusive" applications because only one can be granted. These cases almost always raise serious fact questions that must be resolved in a hearing. These hearings can be very time-consuming, because each of two or more (sometimes a dozen) parties attempts to show not only why it should get the spot, but also presents evidence attacking each of the other applicants.

In these cases there may be specific questions, such as whether one of the applicants is an alien, or is inadequately financed, or proposes to use inadequate engineering equipment. But even if all the applicants meet every basic qualification, a hearing is still needed to determine which qualified applicant should get the award.

We might note now that the same hearing procedure may be required at other stages in the licensing process. When a licensee applies for a renewal, if claims are made that the licensee has misbehaved in some way and should not get the license renewed, any fact questions to be resolved will be explored at a similar hearing conducted by an ALJ.

In the interests of simplicity, the foregoing description of the administrative process has assumed that when the FCC decides to grant or renew a license to an applicant who had no competitors, that is the end of the process. If the applicant had beaten out challengers, they could carry the fight into the courts. But if the applicant had no challenger and the Commission decided in its favor, the Bureau—even if it had disagreed with that result—could not attack the decision of its agency.

Competitors. Other parties, however, do have standing to participate. For example, existing licensees can object to the granting of a new license on the grounds that it will cause technical interference with existing stations. A more difficult question is raised when a competitor wishes to argue that there is not enough potential advertising revenue in the community to support an additional station. Initially, the Commission was receptive to claims of economic injury. See Carroll Broadcasting Company v. Federal Communications Commission, 258 F.2d 440 (D.C.Cir.1958):

> [W]e think it is not incumbent upon the Commission to evaluate the probable economic results of every license grant. Of course, the public is not concerned whether it gets service from A or from B or from both combined. The public interest is not disturbed if A is destroyed by B, so long as B renders the required service. The public interest is affected when service is affected. We think the problem arises when a protestant offers to prove that the grant of a new license would be detrimental to the public interest. The Commission is equipped to receive and appraise such evidence. If the protestant fails to bear the burden of proving his point (and it is certainly a heavy burden), there may be an end to the matter. If his showing is substantial, or if there is a genuine issue posed, findings should be made.

The FCC was able to limit the number of *Carroll* doctrine complaints by ruling that when such a complaint is made and the FCC agrees that the community cannot support both stations, the existing licensee's renewal application will be heard together with the new application.

Citizen groups. The Commission firmly rejected all efforts of listeners or citizen groups to take a formal part in the licensing process. In 1966, however, the court of appeals ordered that citizen groups be allowed to participate in these proceedings. Office of Communications of United Church of Christ v. Federal Communications Commission, 359 F.2d 994 (D.C.Cir.1966). In this case (to which we return in the section on license renewals) the opinion by then Circuit Judge Burger stated:

> The argument that a broadcaster is not a public utility is beside the point. True it is not a public utility in the same sense as strictly regulated common carriers or purveyors of power, but neither is it a purely private enterprise like a newspaper or an automobile agency. A broadcaster has much in common with a newspaper publisher, but he is not in the same category in terms of public obligations imposed by law. A broadcaster seeks and is granted the free and exclusive use of a limited and valuable part of the public domain; when he accepts that franchise it is burdened by enforceable public obligations. A newspaper can be operated at the whim or caprice of its owners; a broadcast station cannot. After nearly five decades of operation the broadcast industry does not seem to have grasped the simple fact that a broadcast license is a public trust subject to termination for breach of duty.
>
> The theory that the Commission can always effectively represent the listener interests . . . is one of those assumptions we collectively try to work with so long as they are reasonably adequate. When it becomes clear, as it does to us now, that it is no longer a valid assumption which stands up under the realities of actual experience, neither we nor the Commission can continue to rely on it. . . .
>
> . . .
>
> Public participation is especially important in a renewal proceeding, since the public will have been exposed for at least three years to the licensee's performance, as cannot be the case when the Commission considers an initial grant, unless the applicant has a prior record as a licensee. In a renewal proceeding, furthermore, public spokesmen, such as Appellants here, may be the only objectors. In a community served by only one outlet, the public interest focus is perhaps sharper and the need for airing complaints often greater than where, for example, several channels exist. Yet if there is only one outlet, there are no rivals at hand to assert the public interest, and reliance on opposing applicants to challenge the existing licensee for the channel would be fortuitous at best. Even when there are multiple competing stations in a locality, various factors may operate to inhibit the other broadcasters from opposing a renewal application. An imperfect rival may be

thought a desirable rival, or there may be a "gentleman's agreement" of deference to a fellow broadcaster in the hope he will reciprocate on a propitious occasion.

He also noted that the fears of regulatory agencies that they will be flooded with applications are rarely borne out.

Since this case, citizen groups have been playing a more active part in the regulatory processes of the Commission than before. Their most common legal action is the filing of a petition to deny a renewal application on the ground that the applicant has failed to meet the required level of public service.

Negotiation and Agreement. In order to avoid the expense (and minor uncertainty) of defending against petitions to deny renewals, a broadcaster may enter into an agreement with the challenging citizen group. In return for withdrawal of the challenge, a broadcaster typically undertakes to make certain changes in its station's operation. The broadcaster may promise to change its employment policies, to support local production of broadcast programming, or to attempt to expand certain types of programming.

The Commission generally allows broadcasters to enter into such agreements if the licensee maintains responsibility at all times for determining how best to serve the public interest. Does recognition of private agreements serve the public interest? Does it allow a broadcaster to "buy off" citizen groups who may be in the best position to point out programming deficiencies? Section 311 regulates reimbursement of legal expenses or payments of money in the case of negotiated settlements.

2. Introduction to Basic Qualifications

In the 1934 Act, Congress empowered the Federal Communications Commission to grant licenses to applicants for radio stations for periods of up to three years "if public convenience, interest, or necessity will be served thereby." § 307(a). (In 1981, the maximum term was extended to five years for television and seven years for radio.) Section 307(b) requires the Commission to make "such distribution of licenses, frequencies, hours of operation, and of power among the several states and communities as to provide a fair, efficient, and equitable distribution of radio service to each of the same."

As we have seen, the Commission responded by allocating a portion of the spectrum for standard (AM) radio service and then subdividing that space further by requiring very powerful stations to use certain frequencies and weaker stations to use others and some stations to leave the air at sundown. The Commission used its rulemaking powers to develop these allocations and it then set engineering standards of separation and interference. The 1934 Act empowered the Commission to promulgate "such rules and regulations and prescribe such restrictions and conditions, not inconsistent with law, as may be necessary to carry out the provisions of this chapter. . . . " § 303(r). The Commission did not allocate the AM frequencies to particular cities. Instead, it left it to those interested in broadcasting to determine whether they could organize an AM broadcast facility in a given location that complied with the various allocation and interference rules. With FM and television, the Commission assigned particular frequencies to particular cities. An applicant for one of these licenses must apply for the assigned frequency in the listed, or a nearby, community or must seek to change the frequency assignments through an amendment of the rules.

In addition to requiring proof that a grant will serve the "public convenience, interest, or necessity," § 307(a), the Act also requires that each applicant demonstrate that it meets basic "citizenship, character, and financial, technical, and other qualifications," § 308(b). An applicant who fails to satisfy any one of the following "basic qualifications" is ineligible to receive a license.

a. *Legal Qualifications.* An applicant for a license must comply with the specific requirements of the Communications Act and the Commission's rules. For example, § 310(b) restricts the power of aliens to hold radio and broadcast licenses. Prior revocation of an applicant's license by a federal court for an antitrust violation precludes grant of a new application. § 313. An application will be denied if its grant would result in violation of the Commission's multiple ownership or crossownership rules or its chain broadcasting regulations.

b. *Technical Qualifications.* An applicant for a broadcast station must also comply with the Commission's standards for transmission. These standards include such issues as interference with existing or allocated stations and efficiency of operation, gains or losses of service to affected populations, structure, power and location of the antenna, coverage and quality of the signal in the areas to be served, and studio location and operating equipment utilized.

c. *Financial Qualifications.* Although the applicant must show it has an adequate financial base to commence operations, it need not demonstrate that it can sustain operations indefinitely. Generally, the applicant must have sufficient funds to operate for three months without advertising revenue. The Commission may also inquire into the applicant's estimates of the amounts that will actually be required to operate the station and the reliability of its proposed sources of funds, such as estimated advertising revenues.

d. *Character Qualifications.* Until very recently, character issues considered by the Commission included past criminal convictions of the applicant, trafficking in broadcast licenses, failure to keep the Commission informed of changes in the applicant's status, and other situations that raised questions as to the integrity or reliability of the applicant in the broadcasting function. In 1985, as a result of the RKO case (p. 886, infra) and in keeping with the move toward deregulation, the Commission narrowed the scope of character examinations. The Commission will now confine its interest to three areas: misconduct involving violations of the Act or Commission rules; misrepresentations or lack of candor before the Commission; and fraudulent programming.

Other than those issues, the Commission will consider as relevant only criminal fraud convictions, adjudicated cases of broadcast-related antitrust or anticompetitive misconduct, and felony convictions substantially related to operating as a broadcaster in a manner consistent with Commission rules and policies. (Although Commission-related misconduct by a corporate parent may generally be held against a broadcast subsidiary, misconduct by a corporate parent unrelated to the FCC will generally be held against a broadcast subsidiary only if a close relationship exists between the parent and the subsidiary and they share principals involved in day-to-day broadcast operations.) Character Qualification in Broadcast Licensing, 59 R.R.2d 801 (1985).

e. The final category of basic qualifications, "other," is likely to overlap with public interest considerations.

3. Substantive Considerations

If an applicant has met the basic qualifications, how does the Commission decide whether granting the application will serve the "public interest, convenience or necessity"? In this section we discuss the substantive considerations in the process, starting with the single applicant for the single vacancy.

As noted earlier, even though an applicant has met the basic qualifications and is the only applicant for the license, that applicant may not get the license. *NBC* recognized that the FCC may act as more than a traffic policeman, and may consider the public interest. Sometimes the public interest might be better served by leaving a spot vacant to await a good applicant rather than taking the first comer.

This, of course, requires that the FCC be able to identify a "good" applicant. From the very beginning the Commission has confronted the tension between using criteria that directly address programming considerations and the concern that too close a look at proposed programming may amount to government control.

In its 1929 Annual Report, the FRC asserted that the "entire listening public within the service area of a station, or of a group of stations in one community, is entitled to service from that station or stations." Specialized stations were entitled to little or no consideration. In the Commission's opinion, "the tastes, needs, and desires of all substantial groups among the listening public should be met, in some fair proportion by a well-rounded program, in which entertainment, consisting of music of both classical and lighter grades, religion, education and instruction, important public events, discussions of public questions, weather, market reports and news, and matters of interest to all members of the family find a place." Recognizing that communities differed and that other variables were relevant, the Commission did not erect a "rigid schedule."

In 1946, the Commission issued a report entitled "Public Service Responsibility of Broadcast Licensees" (known generally as the "Blue Book"). The Commission stressed that although licensees bore the primary responsibility for program service, the Commission would still play a part: "In issuing and in renewing the licenses of broadcast stations, the Commission proposes to give particular consideration to four program service factors relevant to the public interest." One category was the carrying of "sustaining" (unsponsored) programs during hours "when the public is awake and listening." This would provide balance by allowing the broadcast of certain types of programs that did not invite sponsorship, including experimental programs. Second, the Commission called for local live programs to encourage local self-expression. Third, the Commission expected "programs devoted to the discussion of public issues." Finally, the Commission, expressing concern about excessive advertising, announced that "in its application forms the Commission will request the applicant to state how much time he proposes to devote to advertising matter in any one hour."

In 1960, the Commission changed direction. In its Report and Statement of Policy Re: Commission En Banc Programming Inquiry, 25 Fed.Reg. 7291, 20 R.R. 1901 (1960), the FCC asserted that "the principal ingredient of the licensee's obligation to operate his station in the public interest is the diligent, positive and continuing effort . . . to discover and fulfill the tastes, needs and desires of his service area, for broadcast service." Broadcasters were advised to meet this obligation in two ways: they were to consult with members of the listening public who could receive the station's signal and with a variety of community leaders. The distinction between sustaining and sponsored programs was explicitly abandoned.

In 1971, the Commission elaborated upon and clarified the applicant's obligation. The Primer on Ascertainment of Community Problems by Broadcast Applicants, 27 F.C.C.2d 650, 21 R.R.2d 1507 (1971), standardized the Commission's policy with respect to ascertainment of, and programming for, community needs. It placed specific ascertainment requirements upon all commercial applicants for new broadcast stations, modification of existing facilities, and renewals. The Primer required that an applicant determine the economic, ethnic, and social composition of the communities it proposed to serve, and that principals or management-level employees consult with leaders from each significant community group. The applicant was also to consult with a random sample of members of the general public. Finally, the applicant had to set forth in its license application program proposals designed to meet community problems identified. The process of ascertainment had to take place within six months prior to the application.

The courts readily accepted the Commission's emphasis on the importance of the ascertainment process. In Henry v. Federal Communications Commission, 302 F.2d 191 (D.C.Cir.1962), certiorari denied 371 U.S. 821 (1962), Suburban Broadcasters filed the sole application for a permit to construct the first commercial FM station in Elizabeth, New Jersey. Although Suburban was found legally, technically, and financially qualified, the Commission found that Suburban had made no inquiry into the characteristics or programming needs of Elizabeth and was "totally without knowledge of the area." Suburban's program proposals for Elizabeth were identical to those submitted in its application for an AM station in Berwyn, Illinois, and in the application of two of its principal stockholders for an FM station in Alameda, California. Although acknowledging the community's "presumptive need" for its first FM service, the Commission denied the permit, finding that a grant would not serve the public interest.

On appeal, the Commission's denial was upheld on the ground that an applicant may be required to "demonstrate an earnest interest in serving a local community by evidencing a familiarity with its particular needs and an effort to meet them."

The ascertainment process was designed to allow the FCC to consider proposed programming from the standpoint of the community rather than the Commissioners' own ideas of "good" programming, and was part of the Commission's continued emphasis on localism. In 1976, the FCC amended the ascertainment regulations to require interviews with community segments and institutions, including agriculture, business, charities, religion, the elderly, youth, and women. Some groups, particularly from the homosexual and physically handicapped communities, claimed that broadcasters were not interviewing them and asked to be added to the list. The FCC rejected that approach because its studies indicated that gay and handicapped persons were not significant elements in all or most communities. Amendment of the Primers on Ascertainment of Community Problems, 76 F.C.C.2d 401, 47 R.R.2d 189 (1980).

Deregulation. In January, 1981, the FCC adopted a set of proposals reducing the regulations affecting commercial radio licensees. Deregulation of Radio, 84 F.C.C.2d 968, 49 R.R.2d 1 (1981). Among the changes was the elimination of formal ascertainment requirements. Others included the elimination of quantitative programming guidelines and those for commercialization. The order applying this deletion to all radio broadcasters was upheld in Office of Communication of the United Church of Christ v. Federal Communications Commission, 707 F.2d 1413, 53 R.R.2d 1371 (D.C.Cir.1983). In June, 1984, the Commission adopted a similar set of changes in the regulations for commercial television. Deregulation of Commercial Television, 98 F.C.C.2d 1076, 56 R.R.2d 1005 (1984), reconsideration denied, 60 R.R.2d 526 (1986) (except on logging), appeals pending. We will look more closely at deregulation in the section on renewals.

4. The Comparative Proceeding

If two or more applicants file for use of the same or interfering facilities the Commission must hold a comparative hearing among all qualified applicants to determine which will best serve the public interest. An applicant in a comparative proceeding must not only meet minimum qualifications but must also prevail when judged on the Commission's comparative criteria. These criteria differ from those used in the non-comparative proceeding.

POLICY STATEMENT ON COMPARATIVE BROADCAST HEARINGS

Federal Communications Commission, 1965.
1 F.C.C.2d 393, 5 R.R.2d 1901.

By the Commission: Commissioners HYDE and BARTLEY dissenting and issuing statements; Commissioner LEE concurring and issuing a statement.

[The Commission noted that choosing one from among several qualified applicants for a facility was one of its primary responsibilities. The process involved an extended hearing in which the various applicants were compared on a variety of subjects. The "subject does not lend itself to precise categorization or to the clear making of precedent. The various factors cannot be assigned absolute values. . . ." Moreover, the membership of the Commission is continually changing and each member has his or her own idea of what factors are important. Thus, no statement is binding and the Commission is not obligated to deal with all cases "as it has dealt with some that seem comparable." Nonetheless, it is "important to have a high degree of consistency of decision and of clarity in our basic policies." The policy statement was to "serve the purpose of clarity and consistency of decision, and the further purpose of eliminating from the hearing process time-consuming elements not substantially related to the public interest." The Commission declared that this statement "does not attempt to deal with the somewhat different problems raised where an applicant is contesting with a licensee seeking renewal of license." The Commission then turned to the merits and identified "two primary objectives:" "best practicable service to the public" and "maximum diffusion of control of the media of mass communications."]

Several factors are significant in the two areas of comparison mentioned above, and it is important to make clear the manner in which each will be treated.

1. *Diversification of control of the media of mass communication.* Diversification is a factor of primary significance since, as set forth above, it constitutes a primary objective in the licensing scheme.

. . .

2. *Full-time participation in station operation by owners.* We consider this factor to be of substantial importance. It is inherently desirable that legal responsibility and day-to-day performance be closely associated. In addition, there is a likelihood of greater sensitivity to an area's changing needs, and of programing designed to serve these needs, to the extent that the station's proprietors actively participate in the day-to-day operation of the station. This factor is thus important in securing the best practicable service. It also frequently complements the objective of diversification, since concentrations of control are necessarily achieved at the expense of integrated ownership.

We are primarily interested in full-time participation.

Attributes of participating owners, such as their experience and local residence, will also be considered in weighing integration of ownership and management. While, for the reasons given above, integration of ownership and management is important per se, its value is increased if the participating owners are local residents and if they have experience in the field. Participation in station affairs on the basis described above by a local resident indicates a likelihood of continuing knowledge of changing local interests and needs. . . .

. . .

3. *Proposed program service.* . . . The importance of program service is obvious. The feasibility of making a comparative evaluation is not so obvious. Hearings take considerable time and precisely formulated program plans may have to be changed, not only in details but in substance, to take account of new conditions obtaining at the time a successful applicant commences operation. Thus, minor differences among applicants are apt to prove to be of no significance.

. . .

Decisional significance will be accorded only to material and substantial differences between applicants' proposed program plans. [ ] Minor differences in the proportions of time allocated to different types of programs will not be considered. Substantial differences will be considered to the extent that they go beyond ordinary differences in judgment and show a superior devotion to public service. . . .

In light of the considerations set forth above, and our experience with the similarity of the program plans of competing applicants, taken with the desirability of keeping hearing records free of immaterial clutter, no comparative issue will ordinarily be designated on program plans and policies, or on staffing plans or other program planning elements, and evidence on these matters will not be taken under the standard issues. The Commission will designate an issue where examination of the applications and other information before it makes such action appropriate, and applicants who believe they can demonstrate significant differences upon which the reception of evidence will be useful may petition to amend the issues.

No independent factor of likelihood of effectuation of proposals will be utilized. The Commission expects every licensee to carry out its proposals, subject to factors beyond its control, and subject to reasonable judgment that the public's needs and interests require a departure from original plans. If there is a substantial indication that any party will not be able to carry out its proposals to a significant degree, the proposals themselves will be considered deficient.

4. *Past broadcast record.* This factor includes past ownership interest and significant participation in a broadcast station by one with an ownership interest in the applicant. It is a factor of substantial importance upon the terms set forth below.

A past record within the bounds of average performance will be disregarded, since average future performance is expected. Thus, we are not interested in the fact of past ownership per se, and will not give a preference because one applicant has owned stations in the past and another has not.

We are interested in records which, because either unusually good or unusually poor, give some indication of unusual performance in the future. . . .

. . .

5. *Efficient use of frequency.*[12] In comparative cases where one of two or more competing applicants proposes an operation which, for one or more engineering reasons, would be more efficient, this fact can and should be considered in determining which of the applicants should be preferred. . . .

6. *Character.* . . .

7. *Other factors.* As we stated at the outset, our interest in the consistency and clarity of decision and in expedition of the hearing process is not intended to preclude the full examination of any relevant and substantial factor. We will thus favorably consider petitions to add issues when, but only when, they demonstrate that significant evidence will be adduced.[13]

. . . [I]t may be well to emphasize that by this attempt to clarify our present policy . . . we do not intend to stultify the continuing process of reviewing our judgments on these matters. . . .

DISSENTING STATEMENT OF COMMISSIONER HYDE

. . .

The proposed fiat as to the weight which will be given to the various criteria—without sound predication of accepted data and when considered only in a vacuum and in the abstract—must necessarily result in a degree of unfairness to some applicants and in the fashion-

12. This factor as discussed here is not to be confused with the determination to be made of which of two communities has the greater need for a new [AM] station. See Federal Communications Commission v. Allentown Broadcasting Corp., 349 U.S. 358 (1955).

13. Where a narrow question is raised, for example on one aspect of financial qualification, a narrowly drawn issue will be appropriate. In other circumstances, a broader inquiry may be required. This is a matter for ad hoc determination.

ing of an unnecessary straitjacket for the Commission in its decisional process. How can we decide in advance and in a vacuum that a specific broadcaster with a satisfactory record in one community will be less likely to serve the broadcasting needs of a second community than a specific long-time resident of that second community who doesn't have broadcast experience? How can we make this decision without knowing more about each applicant? . . .

. . .

DISSENTING STATEMENT OF COMMISSIONER ROBERT T. BARTLEY

I believe that our comparative hearings should be expedited by eliminating what has amounted to extensive bickering in the record over minutiae.

As I see it, however, the Commission majority is attempting the impossible here when it prejudges the decisional factors in future cases. My observation is that there are no two cases exactly alike. There are so many varying circumstances in each case that a factor in one may be more important than the same factor in another. Broadcasting—a dynamic force in our society—experiences constant change. I have expressed it differently on occasions by saying, "There's nothing static in radio but the noise." If we are to encourage the larger and more effective use of radio in the public interest, we must avoid becoming static ourselves.

CONCURRING STATEMENT OF COMMISSIONER ROBERT E. LEE

. . .

Over the years I have participated in decisions in hundreds of "comparative proceedings" and candor compels me to say that our method of selection of the winning applicant has given me grave concern. I realize, of course, that where we have a number of qualified applicants in a consolidated proceeding for a single facility in a given community, it is necessary that we grant one and deny the others. The ultimate choice of the winner generally sustains the Commission's choice despite the recent rash of remands from the court. Thus, it would appear that we generally grant the "right" application. However, I am not so naive as to believe that granting the "right application" could not, in some cases, be one of several applications.

The criteria that the Commission now says will be decisive—assuming all other things are substantially equal—in choosing among qualified applicants for new broadcast facilities in comparative broadcast hearings are not new. However, the policy statement does tend to restrict the scope somewhat of existing factors and if undue delay is thus prevented, some good will have been accomplished.

I wish to make clear that my concurrence here does not bind me with respect to the weight I might see fit to put upon the various criteria in a given case. . . .

Historically, a prospective applicant hires a highly skilled communications attorney, well versed in the procedures of the Commission. This counsel has a long history of Commission decisions to guide him and he puts together an application that meets all of the so-called criteria. There then follows a tortuous and expensive hearing wherein each applicant attempts to tear down his adversaries on every conceivable front, while individually presenting that which he thinks the Commission would like to hear. The examiner then makes a reasoned decision which, at first blush, generally makes a lot of sense—but comes the oral argument and all of the losers concentrate their fire on the "potential" winner and the Commission must thereupon examine the claims and counterclaims, "weigh" the criteria and pick the winner which, if my recollection serves me correctly, is a different winner in about 50 percent of the cases.

The real blow, however, comes later when the applicant that emerged as the winner on the basis of our "decisive" criteria sells the station to a multiple owner or someone else that could not possibly have prevailed over other qualified applicants under the criteria in an adversary proceeding. It may be that there is no better selection system than the one being followed. If so, it seems like a "hell of a way to run a railroad," and I hope these few comments may inspire the Commission to find that better system even if it requires changes in the Communications Act.

Notes and Questions

1. In 1985, the Commission curtailed the scope of character considerations for comparative proceedings, as it did for single applicant cases. See p. 863, supra. The only issues now relevant are those that raise concerns about basic qualifications. Other character issues tended to lengthen comparative hearings with meager results. Misrepresentations to Commission inquiries are now prohibited by a rule adopted at the same time.

2. The 1965 Policy Statement eliminated three specific criteria—staffing and related plans, likelihood of effectuation of proposals, and proposed studios and equipment—that had formerly been used for comparison.

3. Does choosing licensees on the basis of proposed programming violate either the First Amendment or § 326 of the Communications Act? How far can the Commission go in examining applicants' programming proposals? These questions were discussed in Johnston Broadcasting Co. v. Federal Communications Commission, 175 F.2d 351, 359 (D.C.Cir.1949):

> As to appellant's contention that the Commission's consideration of the proposed programs was a form of censorship, it is true that the Commission cannot choose on the basis of political, economic or social views of an applicant. But in a comparative consideration, it is well recognized that comparative service to the listening public is the vital element, and programs are the essence of that service. So, while the Commission cannot prescribe any type of program (except for prohibitions against obscenity, profanity, etc.) it can make a comparison on the basis of public interest and, therefore, of public service. Such a comparison of proposals is not a form of censorship within the meaning of the statute. . . .

4. When is a comparative hearing required? In Ashbacker Radio Corp. v. Federal Communications Commission, 326 U.S. 327 (1945), the Commission had held a hearing on an application for a construction permit while an application for license modification in a nearby community was pending. The grant of the construction permit precluded the license modification. The Court held that the second applicant was denied its § 309(e) right to a hearing by the granting of the first application. As a result, the *Ashbacker* doctrine requires that whenever mutually exclusive applications are pending, the Commission must hold a single comparative hearing on all of the applications before granting any of them.

5. We consider Commissioner Lee's point about the transferability of licenses at p. 905, infra.

6. Although the Commission has emphasized localism, there has always been an undercurrent of doubt. In the early 1960s, when the Commission appeared to favor not only local programs but also live presentations, Judge Friendly observed, "I wonder also whether the Commission is really wise enough to determine that live telecasts, so much stressed in the decisions, e.g., of local cooking lessons, are always 'better' than a tape of Shakespeare's Histories." Friendly, The Federal Administrative Agencies: The Need for Better Definition of Standards, 75 Harv.L.Rev. 1055, 1071 (1962). This concern was restated in a different context by a Commissioner Hyde:

> [T]he automatic preference accorded local applicants disregards the possibility that, depending on the facts of a particular case, a competitor's proposed use of a professional employee-manager from outside the community might very well bring imagination, an appreciation of the role of journalism, and sensitivity to social issues far exceeding that of a particular local owner-manager.

Hyde, FCC Policies and Procedures Relating to Hearings on Broadcast Applications, 1975 Duke L.J. 253, 277 (1975).

7. For a recent example of the process referred to in note 12 of the Commission's statement—choosing between two communities—see WHW Enterprises, Inc. v. Federal Communications Commission, 753 F.2d 1132 (D.C.Cir.1985) (approving Commission's decision of assigning new facility to city of 34,000 with one daytime-only radio station rather

than to city of 86,000 with three full-time and two daytime-only stations).

8. *Minority Ownership.* New issues may reflect changes in licensing policy. In TV 9, Inc. v. Federal Communications Commission, 495 F.2d 929 (D.C.Cir.1973), rehearing and rehearing en banc denied, certiorari denied 419 U.S. 986 (1974), Comint Corp., Mid-Florida Television Corporation, and six other applicants sought a construction permit for Channel 9 in Orlando, Florida. In making the award to Mid-Florida, the Commission rejected Comint's contention that it was entitled to special consideration because two of Comint's principals were local black residents and 25 percent of those to be served by Channel 9 were black. The Commission's position was that the Communications Act was "color blind" and did not permit considerations of color in the award of licenses. The court disagreed and ruled that the ownership interests and participation of the two black residents gave Comint an edge in providing "broader community representation and practicable service to the public by increasing diversity of content, especially of opinion and viewpoint."

In Radio Jonesboro, Inc., 57 R.R.2d 1564 (1985) the Commission ruled that integration of minority owners is an enhancement factor equal to that of integration of local residents, declining to elevate the status of minority ownership as a comparative factor. The Commission noted that both kinds of integration of active participants can be expected to have a beneficial effect on programming. The Commission also reiterated its policy that minority ownership is significant only in the context of integration of ownership and management, and should not also be considered in the diversification context.

9. *Ownership by Women.* In 1985, the court of appeals, 2–1, overturned a 1978 Commission rule that granted women a preference in comparative licensing proceedings. In Steele v. Federal Communications Commission, 770 F.2d 1192 (D.C.Cir.1985), the rule was held to exceed the Commission's statutory authority. Preferences for women could not be justified on the same grounds as those for ethnic minorities because women "transcend ethnic, religious, and cultural barriers" and "appear to be just as divided among themselves as are men." The dissenting judge argued that although women are not uniform in their beliefs or life styles, "neither are blacks." The court has granted a rehearing en banc.

In a related matter, the Commission refused to grant preferences to women applicants in the lotteries being held to award LPTV licenses. Lottery Selection (Preference for Women), 58 R.R.2d 1077 (1985), appeal pending sub nom. Pappas v. Federal Communications Commission.

10. The "recent rash of remands from the court" referred to by Commissioner Lee was caused by the revelation that an FCC Commissioner had been bribed in the late 1950s to vote in certain ways in licensing proceedings. Since the outcomes of these comparative hearings were not readily predictable, it was relatively easy for a Commis-

sioner to vote one way in a particular case without being embarrassed by any votes cast in previous licensing cases. The incentive to offer bribes came from the fact that a license is awarded without charging the applicant the value of the part of the spectrum being licensed. In addition, since renewals have been virtually automatic, television channels in large cities have acquired great value. (In the 1980s a VHF in Los Angeles was sold for $510 million and a Boston VHF brought $450 million.)

After the bribes came to light, the court of appeals remanded virtually every licensing decision the FCC had made for a second look by what was then an FCC with some new faces.

11. Although the following is technically a renewal case, it is appropriately considered here because, for reasons to be seen at p. 904, infra, the court of appeals remanded an earlier decision in this matter to the Commission. On this remand, the Commission is treating the incumbent as though he were competing for a new station. Discussion of Geller's past record at WVCA–FM might be treated as though it was addressed to his performance at some other station he owned—and used for whatever predictive value it might have on his qualifications for this new license. The case is useful here as a short checklist of the current status of the comparative factors. The competitors are Simon Geller and Grandbanke Corp.

APPLICATION OF SIMON GELLER

Federal Communications Commission, 1985.
102 F.C.C.2d 1443, 59 R.R.2d 579.

BY THE COMMISSION:

. . .

11. The Court of Appeals affirmed the Commission's denial of a renewal expectancy to Geller. Accordingly, that finding will not be revisited on remand, and Geller will receive no renewal expectancy in the overall comparative analysis.

PROPOSED PROGRAMMING

12. Geller proposes to continue his present format, broadcasting 99.52% symphonic music, no news, 0.24% public affairs, and 0.24% other nonentertainment programming. Grandbanke proposes to devote 16.9% of its broadcast time to news, 5.9% to public affairs, and 5.9% to other nonentertainment programming, with 55% of its news to be local and regional. Unlike Geller, Grandbanke proposes that its informational programming will be directly related to ascertained community needs and interests. Whereas Geller proposed a 44-hour 27-minute-a-week program schedule, Grandbanke proposes to broadcast 136 hours of programming a week.

13. The Commission concluded that Grandbanke deserved a substantial preference for proposed programming for its demonstrated superior devotion to public service. This preference arose from Grandbanke's superior attention to presenting informational programming responsive to ascertained community needs and interests and was enhanced by the significant discrepancy between the applicants' proposed hours of operation and the relative restrictiveness of Geller's programming.

14. As it did with respect to the renewal expectancy, the court affirmed the award of a substantial preference to Grandbanke for its proposed programming. Thus, this finding will not be revisited on remand.

EFFICIENT USE OF FREQUENCY

15. Because of differences between their engineering proposals, Grandbanke's facilities will have greater coverage than Geller's. Grandbanke's 1 mV/m contour will cover more than 300 square miles, providing a signal to nearly 360,000 people, as opposed to Geller's 73 square miles and 43,000 people. All relevant areas are served by at least five other aural signals.

16. The Commission awarded Grandbanke a slight preference based on the superiority of its coverage. Only a slight preference was warranted since the areas in question are already well served by at least five other aural signals.

17. The court did not specifically address this issue. Grandbanke will therefore continue to receive a slight preference.

INTEGRATION OF OWNERSHIP INTO MANAGEMENT

18. Geller is WVCA–FM's sole owner and employee and will devote full time to the operation of the station. He has been a resident of Gloucester for 13 years. Grandbanke proposes that its 66% owner Edward Mattar will serve as the station's general manager. Mattar has had 3 years of broadcast experience and proposes to move to Gloucester in the event Grandbanke's application is granted.

19. The Commission previously held that despite Geller's technical advantages under the integration criterion, Geller merited only a slight preference over Grandbanke. The Commission reasoned that the rationale of the integration criterion was that an integrated owner would tend to be more sensitive to an area's changing needs and that Geller's poor past broadcast record detracted from these assurances.

20. The court criticized the Commission's conclusions in this regard. In the court's view, the Commission had failed to reconcile its integration analysis in this case with past precedent. . . . The court noted that the Commission did not make, as it usually does, an explicit analysis of the quantitative and qualitative aspects of integration. Moreover, the court noted that the Commission does not customarily reduce the merit accorded for a quantitative integration advantage

unless the applicant has committed misconduct. The court speculated that the Commission may have engaged in the type of "functional analysis" of the essentially structural characteristic of integration, which was previously disapproved by the court. . . .

. . .

22. Having reexamined the integration aspect of this case pursuant to the court's remand, we conclude that our prior treatment of this issue constituted the type of functional analysis previously criticized by the court.[27] We will therefore reevaluate the integration criterion using our ordinary analytical approach. This approach encompasses a weighing of the customary quantitative and qualitative factors, without attempting to factor in other considerations . . . .

23. Turning first to the quantitative aspect of integration, we agree with Grandbanke that, consistent with precedent, an applicant proposing 100% integration deserves a moderate preference over an applicant proposing 66% integration. Qualitatively, Geller's integration is enhanced by his long term local residence, which outweighs Grandbanke's proposal that Mattar will move to Gloucester prospectively and Mattar's limited broadcast experience. Geller will therefore receive a qualitatively enhanced moderate integration preference to be taken into account in the overall comparative analysis.

DIVERSIFICATION OF MEDIA OWNERSHIP

24. Geller owns no media interests other than WVCA. On the other hand, Grandbanke's principals have interests in other broadcast stations. Edward Mattar, Grandbanke's 66% owner, has a 100% interest in station WINQ–FM, Winchendon, Massachusetts. Stockholders with a 34% interest in Grandbanke have a 100% interest in Station WNCS–FM, Montpelier, Vermont.

25. The Commission awarded Geller a moderate preference for diversification. In the Commission's view, based on the degree of media ownership alone, Geller would have been entitled to a substantial preference. However, the Commission believed that Geller's preference should be diminished because of his failure to present substantial amounts of informational programming. The Commission reasoned that the rationale of diversification was to present the public with diverse and antagonistic points of view. Since Geller had virtually abandoned his role as an information source, the Commission concluded that he did not qualify as a diverse and antagonistic voice or deserve full credit for diversification.

26. The court rejected the Commission's analysis. The court held that the crux of the diversification issue is ownership, based on the probability that diverse ownership will lead to a diversity of views. Moreover, the court held that a direct evaluation of the content of a

27. Central Florida Enterprises, Inc. v. FCC, 598 F.2d 37, 56 (D.C.Cir.1978), cert. dismissed, 441 U.S. 957 (1979).

broadcaster's views would be questionable under the First Amendment. In this vein, the court indicated that there was no basis for inferring that the amount of informational programming presented necessarily represented the broadcaster's value as a diverse voice. On remand, the court required, at minimum, that the Commission adequately explain its apparent departure from established principles.

. . .

28. Having reexamined our diversification analysis pursuant to the court's mandate, we conclude that it must be revised. As in the case of integration, we believe that our prior discussion relied on an improper functional analysis. In accordance with the court's ruling, we will not look behind the presumption that underlies the diversification criterion. Our prior conclusion that, based on considerations of media ownership alone, Geller deserves a substantial preference stands unabridged. In line with the court's views, no other considerations are relevant in this assessment. Accordingly, Geller will receive a substantial preference for diversification.

OVERALL COMPARATIVE ANALYSIS

. . .

30. In his Comments, Geller maintains that once his integration and diversification preferences are given their proper weights, undiminished by "multiple counting" of his past broadcast record, these advantages are decisive. Grandbanke, which considers Geller's integration and diversification advantages to be moderate, submits on the other hand that its advantages for proposed programming and efficient use of frequency are dispositive. Grandbanke continues to assert that Geller's failure to provide substantial amounts of informational programming responsive to local needs and interests should weigh heavily in the comparative balancing.

31. The framework for the comparative evaluation of broadcast applicants is provided by the Commission's 1965 Policy Statement on Comparative Broadcast Hearings. There, the Commission enunciated two primary objectives: (1) best practicable service to the public, and (2) diversification of control of the media of mass communications. The former objective encompasses several factors of which those relevant here are: (1) integration of ownership into management, (2) proposed programming, and (3) efficient use of frequency. Under the best practicable service to the public criterion, we have concluded that Grandbanke deserves a substantial preference for proposed programming and a slight preference for efficient use of frequency, while Geller deserves an enhanced moderate preference for integration. On balance, we believe Grandbanke should receive a moderate preference for best practicable service. As to diversification, the other primary criterion, Geller receives a substantial preference. Thus, we are faced with a situation in which each applicant is superior to the other with respect to one of the primary objectives of the comparative process. However,

the substantial preference awarded to Geller for diversification clearly outweighs the moderate preference awarded to Grandbanke for best practicable service. For this reason, we believe that Geller is ultimately the preferred applicant.

. . .

Notes and Questions

1. How are the various pluses compared?

2. The bribery episode noted earlier raises the question whether there are better ways to decide comparative cases than through the approach developed in the Policy Statement. Is it that Congress gave the FCC a difficult, if not impossible, task?

Some critics have suggested that the Commission emphasize one or two factors, such as diversity, and use these as the major bases for decision. Others have suggested using more factors but giving each a preannounced weight, so that results would become more predictable. See Anthony, Towards Simplicity and Rationality in Comparative Broadcast Licensing Proceedings, 24 Stan.L.Rev. 1 (1971), commenting on the incongruity of comparing a group of factors that are not even relevant in cases of unopposed applicants. He argued that if they were so important they should be considered basic qualifications. If they were not, they should not be used as tie-breakers. He proposed comparing only two or three subject areas and giving each a predetermined number of points. For example, an applicant who had no other media interest would receive three credits in the area of diversification of control, while an applicant with an interest in any medium located more than 100 miles from the community to be licensed would receive two credits.

3. *Lotteries.* Still another suggestion is to award the license to the winner of a lottery among equally qualified applicants. The theory of this approach is that sometimes there simply is no superior applicant and it is unrealistic, if not dishonest, to announce a single winner on the merits. The lottery idea could be applied to all applicants who meet the basic tests, or only to those who also offered maximum diversification or some other added criteria, or only to those who emerged from a regular comparative hearing too closely matched for a clear winner to be identified.

In 1980, the FCC voted, 4–3, to order its staff to prepare a decision that would award the license by lottery to one of two applicants who were both judged superior to a third but equal to each other. Two dissenters complained that one applicant should win on the merits because of the full-time participation of a black woman who was a 5% owner. The third dissenter argued that the action was "an impermissible abdication of the Commission's statutory responsibilities and an improper denial of the hearing rights of the applicants." The FCC had an obligation to make "public-interest judgments" rather than using lotteries. Broadcasting, June 9, 1980, at 30. In early 1981, the FCC abandoned the idea of a lottery, but shortly thereafter Congress amended § 309 of the Communications Act to authorize the use of lotteries.

In response to that amendment, the Commission developed lottery procedures for some licensing proceedings, including Low Power Television (LPTV). These procedures gave preferences (additional chances) for minority ownership and diversity. Then, in 1984, the Commission decided that even though the lottery statute did not authorize the use of lotteries to resolve ties in the usual comparative proceedings, the general public interest standard gave the FCC the authority to adopt such a system. Thus, where the Commission finds applicants who "are in true equipoise on comparative factors" it will use a lottery to decide which applicant will be awarded the license. Lottery Selection Among Applicants, 57 R.R.2d 427 (1984).

4. Another system suggested to speed up the process of choosing applicants and put money into public coffers is to auction scarce channel space to the highest bidder. Broadcast media, and licenses already assigned for other media, would be exempted from this plan, proposed by the Commission. Even the lottery process involves evaluating applications to ensure that potential operators meet minimum qualifications. In the case of the recently initiated mobile "cellular" telephone assignments, this meant examining 5,000 applications. Many contend that this time-consuming task was of no value in finding "worthy" applicants and that the time has come to recognize the market value of the spectrum now being given out by the government to private interests.

An editorial in the New York Times, May 9, 1985, at 24, asserted that the auction system "would eliminate the time-consuming charade of choosing the most qualified applicant—who could then sell to any other qualified applicant." The "one shortcoming" is that it may be too late to recoup the value of licenses already assigned. "But it would be a shame to sacrifice the good in a faint hope of obtaining the best. The sooner Congress approves spectrum auctions, the sooner the public will profit."

C. RENEWAL OF LICENSES

1. INTRODUCTION

The initial license period was limited to three years by § 307(d), and the Commission considered renewal applications from about one-third of all licensees each year. In 1981, Congress changed license terms to five years for television and seven years for radio. At the outset, as it sought to unclutter the AM spectrum, the Commission frequently denied renewals. After the initial flurry, however, this rarely occurred unless the broadcaster's behavior fell far below par. A study of denials and their reasons is discussed at p. 888, infra. The

FCC staff cannot fully investigate the performance of each renewal applicant. Instead, the Commission has relied increasingly on informal complaints from citizens or citizen groups, on petitions to deny renewal, which became possible after the United Church of Christ case, p. 861 supra, and on issues raised when a new applicant challenges an incumbent. Section 307(d) authorizes renewals only on the same terms as initial grants—when the public interest, convenience, and necessity will be served. (To the extent that challenges involved the incumbent's programming, challengers could study the logs kept at the station, and the licensee's regular submission to the Commission of the log for a "composite week." The Commission would randomly specify a Sunday, a Monday, etc., from the prior year and ask licensees to submit their programming for those days. This eliminated the need to study an entire year's programs.)

When a petition to deny is received, the Commission must follow a set procedure.

As indicated in Citizens for Jazz on WRVR, Inc. v. Federal Communications Commission, 775 F.2d 392, 59 R.R.2d 249 (D.C.Cir.1985), the process requires three separate analytical steps:

> *First,* the Commission must determine whether the petition to deny sets forth "specific allegations of fact sufficient to show that . . . a grant of the application would be prima facie inconsistent with [the public interest, convenience, and necessity]." 47 U.S.C. § 309(d)(1) If it does not meet this threshold requirement, it can form no basis for an evidentiary hearing. [ ] Even if it does meet the requirement, however, the Commission must determine, *second,* whether "on the basis of the application, the pleadings filed, or other matters which [the Commission] may officially notice," "a substantial and material question of fact is presented." 47 U.S.C. § 309(d)(2). If not, no evidentiary hearing need be held. *Third,* whether or not an evidentiary hearing is held, the Commission must make the ultimate determinations of whether the facts establish that the "public interest, convenience, and necessity will be served by the granting [of the application.]." 47 U.S.C. § 309(a).

In reviewing the Commission's determination that a question of fact is not "substantial" enough to warrant a hearing, the court's stance is "particularly deferential, not only because it is . . . inherently the sort of judgment akin to the 'probable cause' determination made by prosecutors, [ ] but also because 'Congress intended to vest in the FCC a large discretion to avoid time-consuming hearing in this field whenever possible.' [ ]."

OFFICE OF COMMUNICATION OF THE UNITED CHURCH OF CHRIST v. FEDERAL COMMUNICATIONS COMMISSION

United States Court of Appeals, District of Columbia Circuit, 1985.
779 F.2d 702, 59 R.R.2d 895.

Before WRIGHT, MIKVA and GINSBURG, CIRCUIT JUDGES.

J. SKELLY WRIGHT, CIRCUIT JUDGE: Petitioner challenges an order of the Federal Communications Commission (FCC) revising its regulations governing the contents of the public files of commercial radio broadcasters. The new rule requires broadcast licensees to maintain a list of at least five to ten community issues addressed by the station's programming during each three-month period. This new rule was enacted pursuant to our remand in Office of Communication of United Church of Christ v. FCC, 707 F.2d 1413 (D.C.Cir.1983) (UCC III). Our remand was predicated on the FCC's failure to explain adequately its replacement of its logging requirements with an illustrative issues/programs list. We were concerned that the FCC's new rule left the public with insufficient information to evaluate the programming of broadcast licensees. [ ] at 1442. Unfortunately, the FCC's latest effort provides only cosmetic improvements on its previous design. As in *UCC III,* we find that a merely illustrative issues/program list does not further the Commission's stated regulatory goal of relying on effective public participation in the license renewal process. [ ] Moreover, the Commission has failed to provide an adequate explanation for its rejection of an alternative proposal, duly submitted during the notice and comment proceedings, that would advance its stated goal. We therefore vacate the Commission's order as arbitrary and capricious and remand the case for further proceedings.

I. BACKGROUND

In 1981 the FCC initiated a sweeping deregulation of the radio industry. Specifically, it (1) deleted guidelines encouraging radio licensees to present a certain quantity of nonentertainment programming responsive to community needs, (2) abolished the ascertainment procedures by which the licensees identified community needs, (3) eliminated guidelines that limited the amount of broadcast time devoted to commercials, and (4) repealed the requirement that radio stations maintain program logs that recorded information about each program or commercial aired during the broadcast day. *See Report and Order, Deregulation of Radio,* 84 FCC2d 968 (1981) (*First Report*). At about the same time the FCC moved to simplify its license renewal process, replacing its previous long application forms with a "postcard" application. [ ]

The FCC's salutary purpose in enacting this deregulatory program was to reduce the paperwork burden borne by licensees. [ ] Mindful that the Commission has ample discretion to articulate policy within the broad framework of the Communications Act, we upheld the bulk of these changes when they were challenged before this court. In Black Citizens For A Fair Media v. FCC, 719 F.2d 407 (D.C.Cir.1983), *cert. denied,* 467 U.S. 1255 (1984), we upheld the new streamlined renewal process. In *UCC III* this court upheld the elimination of the ascertainment requirements, the minimum nonentertainment programming requirement, and the limit on commercials. [ ][1]

The public file regulation, however, presented special difficulties. In its *First Report* the FCC had eliminated the requirement that licensees maintain a log of every program aired. Instead, the Commission merely required licensees to provide an annual "issues/programs list." This list would enumerate five to ten issues of concern to the community and provide examples of the programs presented in efforts to address those issues. [ ] In evaluating this rule we noted that the agency's stated goals required a more comprehensive recordkeeping requirement. Specifically, we noted that the FCC's new faith in voluntary public participation could only function effectively if the public were assured an adequate flow of information. [ ] We then found that the Commission had failed to provide an adequate explanation of its new recordkeeping regulations and remanded the issue to the FCC.

. . . When the Commission issued its new order, however, it once more endorsed the concept of a merely illustrative issues list. . . .

. . . Instead of an annual report the Commission now requires quarterly reports. And instead of establishing a maximum of 10 issues, the new rule leaves licensees free to determine the maximum number of issues on which they wish to report. The five-issue minimum, however, was retained. [ ]

Petitioner United Church of Christ challenges the Commission's revised recordkeeping requirement as arbitrary and capricious. We sustain that challenge.

. . .

II. THE MERITS

There is no question but that the Commission has the statutory authority to require whatever recordkeeping requirements it deems appropriate. Review therefore proceeds under the "arbitrary and capricious" standard. Particularly because this is an instance of administrative change in policy, this court must scrutinize the agency's actions to ensure that the Commission has rationally considered significant alternatives. [ ] Rational decisionmaking also dictates that the agency simply cannot employ means that actually undercut its own purported goals. [ ] The Commission's action in this case fails to pass muster under either of these criteria.

1. In a related case, Nat'l Black Media Coalition v. FCC, 706 F.2d 1224 (D.C.Cir. 1983), this court approved the decision of the FCC to exempt small radio and television licensees from the requirement of conducting formal surveys to ascertain the needs and interests of the community they served.

A. *The Irrationality of an Illustrative Issues List*

1. *The role of the public file regulations in the current regulatory scheme.* In our case the requirement that the agency's means not undermine its purported goals translates into a requirement that the FCC's rules governing the content of licensees' public files not contradict its stated policy of relying on public participation in the license renewal process. . . .

The Communications Act, 47 U.S.C. § 309(d)(1) (1982), requires a petitioner seeking to deny a license renewal to bear the burden of making a prima facie case indicating that the licensee has failed to meet its public interest responsibilities under the Act. In making a prima facie case a petitioner must file affidavits making "substantial and specific allegations of fact which, if true, would indicate that a grant of the application would be prima facie inconsistent with the public interest." . . .

After the petitioner has filed its affidavits, the applicant for renewal can file counter-affidavits. [ ] After considering such counter-affidavits, the Commission must determine whether there is a "substantial and material question of fact" concerning the adequacy of the applicant's programming. Only if it finds such a significant dispute on this ultimate issue will it order a hearing. . . .

Exactly, *what* constitutes a violation of the public interest standard in general or the community issue programming test in particular is largely committed to the discretion of the agency. In *UCC III,* however, this court found that a petitioner to deny must show that the "overall" programming efforts of a licensee had failed to adequately respond to issues of community concern. . . .

Petitioner argues that for all practical purposes the issues list will be the sole basis for building a prima facie case in a petition to deny. [ ] Petitioner's argument is supported by this court's observation that the new streamlined renewal process "is premised, in part, on the Commission's belief that sufficient information is available in the public file" to facilitate petitions to deny. . . .

. . .

If the Commission's goal is public participation in the license renewal process, the least it can do is assure that public files contain the minimum amount of information required to begin the process outlined in 47 U.S.C. § 309(d) (1982). The threshold requirement of that section is that the petitioner make a prima facie case. Indeed, enabling a petitioner to deny the ability to make a prima facie case is to ensure very little. The FCC retains the authority under 47 U.S.C. § 309(d)(2) to refuse to grant a hearing even where a petitioner has satisfied the prima facie case requirements of 47 U.S.C. § 309(d)(1). And even a petitioner to deny who has obtained a hearing is still far from a victory on the merits. . . .

In sum, we conclude that the petition to deny plays a critical role in the current regulatory scheme. Moreover, we believe that an adequate public file is essential to proper functioning of the procedures governing the petition to deny. Specifically, the agency's public file requirements must be sufficient to enable a petitioner to make a prima facie case under 47 U.S.C. § 309(d)(1). The current public file regulations do not meet this test.

2. *The inadequacy of the illustrative issues/program list.* As noted, the illustrative issues lists identify the issues covered by a station and describe how the station treated each issue, including specific examples of programs responsive to each issue. The lists must also identify the time, date, and duration of broadcast for each program listed. By the time a license comes up for renewal, there will be 28 quarterly lists available. Although such lists will therefore contain a non-trivial quantity of data, they will not assure a petitioner to deny the ability even to come close to making a prima facie case.

. . .

B. *The Rejection of Reasonable Alternatives*

. . .

2. *The "significant treatment" alternative.* . . . During the notice and comment period following our remand at least one commentator suggested that the agency require licensees to list the programs that had provided "significant treatment" of community issues during the relevant time period. *See* Comments of ABC, Inc. [ ] Under this proposal a petitioner to deny would not rely solely on a merely illustrative list. Instead, the petitioner would rely on a list that the broadcaster *itself* had certified to include those programs in which the broadcaster had provided "significant treatment" of issues of community concern.

The relative benefits of such a list are obvious. By referring to this list a petitioner to deny would be able to determine whether a broadcaster had provided significant coverage of some set of issues of community concern. The petitioner would be able to assert that by the *broadcaster's own admission* the programs on this list represented the most significant treatment by that broadcaster of issues that the broadcaster itself thought to be of community concern. If the petitioner could submit affidavits explaining why such programs failed to meet the most minimum qualitative standards, serious doubt would be cast on the overall adequacy of the broadcaster's programming. For if the broadcaster's *best* programs (i.e., its listed programs) were inadequate, it is questionable whether the broadcaster's unlisted programming would pass muster. Although the Commission would retain substantial discretion in each case to evaluate the probative value of such a showing, common sense suggests that a petitioner to deny would usually come quite close to showing that such a record made renewal of a license prima facie inconsistent with the public interest.

. . .

This court does not insist that the agency consider *every* conceivable option. [ ] But the "significant treatment" option would seem tailor-made to the agency's new "qualitative" standard for evaluating petitions to deny. The Commission's failure to provide a single word of explanation for its rejection of an option that appears to serve precisely the agency's purported goals suggests a lapse of rational decisionmaking.

IV. CONCLUSION

The FCC has stated that it now primarily relies on petitions to deny in enforcing the statutorily mandated public interest requirement of the Communications Act. Yet the Commission's revised issues list fails to provide an adequate basis for a prima facie showing in a petition to deny. This court has repeatedly noted that its approval of the FCC's deregulation of the license renewal process hinges, in part, on the development of adequate recordkeeping requirements by the Commission. Because the Commission's new recordkeeping requirements fail to advance the Commission's own purported goals in a rational manner, and because the Commission has failed to explain adequately its rejection of one of the most serious options before it, the order of the Commission must be vacated. The case is remanded so that the agency may reconsider the specified alternative or develop another adequate means of assuring petitioners to deny the basis for stating a prima facie case.

Vacated and remanded.

Notes and Questions

1. What is the major difference between the requirement the FCC developed on remand from *UCC III* and the "significant treatment" approach?

2. As the court notes, the rest of the FCC's deregulation of commercial radio has been accepted. The FCC's efforts to deregulate television are on appeal. During this appellate process, the Commission has adjusted its public-file requirements for television in an effort to satisfy the court of appeals.

3. The FCC has been generally reluctant to deny renewals except in egregious cases because denial is such a drastic step when VHF stations may be worth $500 million or more, and radio stations may be worth tens of millions of dollars.

4. *Penalties and Short Renewals.* Before 1960 the Commission had few weapons for dealing with misbehavior, since Congress assumed that denial of renewal would suffice in most cases, with revocation during the term to handle the most serious violations. But the Commission came to view denial of renewal as too harsh for all but the most serious violations of rules or other misbehavior. (In cases of extreme misconduct or danger, the Commission is authorized to revoke licenses in

midterm under § 312. See Sea Island Broadcasting Corp. v. Federal Communications Commission, 627 F.2d 240 (D.C.Cir.1980), certiorari denied 449 U.S. 834 (1980), requiring that the case for revocation must meet the "clear and convincing" standard. There "is a 'security' of interest during a license term even assuming there is none at the end of a term.")

In the 1960 amendments to the Communications Act, Congress explicitly authorized shorter renewals by amending § 307(d), but this could not be utilized until the end of the license period. To fill the gap, Congress responded with § 503(b) et seq. to provide the Commission with "an effective tool in dealing with violations in situations where revocation or suspension does not appear to be appropriate." Under § 503(b), the Commission could impose a fine—called a forfeiture—against a licensee who had violated a specific rule. The maximum penalty is now "$2,000 for each violation. Each day of a continuing violation shall constitute a separate offense," but the total penalty shall not exceed $20,000 for licensees or cable operators. (In 1986, the Commission asked Congress to increase this amount to $1,000,000—to permit a greater range of forfeitures and to take into account the longer license terms now available.)

The added array of sanctions reduced the likelihood that the denial of renewal would be used for what the Commission perceived to be lesser transgressions of the rules. The Commission has resorted extensively to the short-term renewal. The expectation is that if the licensee performs properly during that period it will then return to the regular renewal cycle. In addition to the probationary impact, a short renewal imposes burdens of legal expenses and administrative effort in preparing and defending the application.

5. After years of warning against fraudulent conduct involving advertising, or conducting rigged contests, and punishing violators with forfeitures and other penalties, the Commission began to deny license renewals to violators. The courts upheld the shift. See White Mountain Broadcasting Co. v. Federal Communications Commission, 598 F.2d 274 (D.C.Cir.1979) (upholding denial of renewal where the practice had continued for 5½ years with full knowledge of the president and sole shareholder of licensee). In the 1980s, however, the Commission again changed its attitude toward enforcing these regulations. In early 1985, as part of an ongoing attempt to reduce overly restrictive regulations as well as those that duplicate other federal or state law, the Commission eliminated the rules on fraudulent billing. Elimination of Unnecessary Broadcast Regulation (Business Practices), 59 R.R.2d 1500 (1986).

6. Perhaps the most significant nonrenewal decision based on nonspeech conduct involved RKO General's sixteen licenses, including several VHFs in major cities. The situation is recounted in RKO General, Inc. v. Federal Communications Commission, 670 F.2d 215, 7 Med.L.Rptr. 2313 (D.C.Cir.1981). Petitions for certiorari to review the part of the case involving the Boston VHF were denied. 456 U.S. 927

(1982). Hearings were ordered on the New York and Los Angeles VHFs to determine whether the lack of candor that cost RKO its Boston station should also deprive it of the other stations.

While the New York part of the case was on remand, Congress added § 331 to the Communications Act to require that the Commission renew the license of any VHF licensee willing to relocate to a state with no commercial television stations. After RKO notified the FCC in 1982 that it would move WOR–TV from New York City to Secaucus, New Jersey, its license was renewed. RKO General, Inc. (WOR–TV), 53 R.R. 2d 469 (1983). The grant of the five-year license to RKO without a hearing, pursuant to § 331, was unanimously affirmed in Multi-State Communications, Inc. v. Federal Communications Commission, 728 F.2d 1519, 55 R.R.2d 911 (D.C.Cir.1984), certiorari denied 105 S.Ct. 431 (1984).

2. Substantive Grounds for Nonrenewal

---

a. Non-Speech Considerations

Just as the Commission may deny an uncontested application for a vacant channel, it may also deny renewal when no other applicant seeks the spot and even when no complaint has been made. The Mass Media Bureau may argue against renewals when it believes that they would not serve the public interest.

Lying to the Commission may be the clearest basis for denying renewal. In its early years, the FCC did not treat dishonesty toward the Commission with heavy sanctions, which tended to encourage such behavior. Finally, the Commission denied the renewal of a license for a station whose general manager for twelve years had concealed from the Commission the fact that a vice-president of a network secretly owned 24 percent of the station's stock. The station appealed on the grounds, among others, that the harsh treatment came without warning and that there was no indication that the FCC would not have renewed the station's application even if it had known the truth.

The Supreme Court upheld the denial of renewal. The fact that the FCC had previously dealt more mildly with similar cases did not prevent it from changing course without warning. Also, the "fact of concealment may be more significant than the facts concealed. The willingness to deceive a regulatory body may be disclosed by immaterial and useless deceptions as well as by material and persuasive ones." The fact that stockholders of a majority of the shares had no knowledge of the dishonesty did not bar the FCC from acting: "the fact that there are innocent stockholders cannot immunize the corporation from the consequences of such deception." Federal Communications Commission v. WOKO, Inc., 329 U.S. 223 (1946).

Sometimes the Commission has held that the manager's deceit is the licensee's responsibility because of its failure to exercise adequate control and supervision consistent with its responsibilities as a licensee. Continental Broadcasting, Inc. v. Federal Communications Commission, 439 F.2d 580 (D.C.Cir.1971), certiorari denied 403 U.S. 905 (1971).

Since the license is issued to the licensee, the licensee must meet the standards of the Communications Act and the FCC. Misbehavior of the officers may show that the licensee knew of the misbehavior or may show a serious failure to control the station. In an appropriate situation, either may justify denial of renewal.

b. Speech Considerations

As we have seen, p. 719, supra, in its early days the Commission was not hesitant about denying a renewal when it disapproved of the speech being uttered. The potential implications of that practice were not tested because the situation eased after the famous Mayflower Broadcasting Corp., 8 F.C.C. 333 (1940), in which the Commission renewed a license but appeared to criticize the licensee for editorializing: "A truly free radio cannot be used to advocate the causes of the licensee. . . . In brief, the broadcaster cannot be an advocate." The case apparently deterred controversial discussion and therefore reduced the need for the Commission to judge speech directly. The situation changed after the Commission's Report on Editorializing by Broadcast Licensees, 13 F.C.C. 1246, 1 R.R. pt. 3, § 91.21 (1949), which directed licensees to devote a reasonable portion of their broadcast time to the discussion of controversial issues of public importance and to encourage the presentation of various views on these questions. This has also affected renewal cases.

One study indicates that 64 radio and television licenses were revoked or not renewed between 1970 and 1978, compared with 78 during the years from 1934 to 1969. Weiss, Ostroff, and Clift, Station License Revocations and Denials of Renewal, 1970–1978, 24 J. Broadcasting 69 (1980). The authors analyzed the grounds for revocation or nonrenewal in the 64 cases. Multiple grounds were common, and 110 reasons were listed. The most common were misrepresentations to the FCC (18), failure to pursue the renewal procedure (16), fraudulent billing practices (11), departure from promised programming (11), and unauthorized transfer of control by the licensee (10).

Very few of the 64 involved speech grounds. Even those that did commonly involved other derelictions as well because the Commission was reluctant to single out a speech basis for nonrenewal. For example, although the study shows that four licenses were lost for "news slanting," all four of these stations were also listed under "misrepresentations to the Commission." Three others were listed under character qualifications, and the fourth was also listed under failure to prosecute renewal. Similarly, although three cases listed "fairness" violation as grounds for nonrenewal, one of these was also one of the group of four listed above and had four separate reasons for nonrenewal. A second was also listed for misrepresentation. The third, the Brandywine case, is discussed shortly.

The situation is not surprising. First, a station that senses that it may be doing something wrong may seek to hide the matter without realizing that misrepresentation to the Commission may be much more serious than its substantive misbehavior. Recall the WOKO case. Second, misbehavior sometimes occurs because the licensee has not exerted sufficient control over management or employees. In such a case, the FCC combines the misbehavior with inadequate supervision as grounds for the denial of renewal. Third, the posture of the courts has not encouraged the FCC to deny renewals on pure speech grounds—as a few examples will make clear.

In one case, the FCC found that a disc jockey had been using vulgar and suggestive language. When the FCC began to investigate, the licensee denied all knowledge of the offending conduct. Because of the history of complaints, the Commission found that denial incredible, which raised a question about the licensee's character qualifications. After renewal was denied, the court affirmed, but did so explicitly on the character ground, refusing to pass on whether the speech alone would have justified nonrenewal. Robinson v. Federal Communications Commission, 334 F.2d 534 (D.C.Cir.1964), certiorari denied 379 U.S. 843 (1964).

Another kind of deception was attempted by a minister whose initial efforts to acquire a station for his seminary were challenged by groups that believed his past record showed he would not honor the fairness doctrine or his other obligations. The prospective licensee responded by promising to provide balanced programming. Within ten days of obtaining the license, the licensee began drastically altering its format and groups complained that the licensee was not living up to its obligations. The Commission denied renewal on two grounds: alleged violations of the fairness doctrine, and deception practiced on the Commission in obtaining the license. On appeal, the court affirmed, 2–1. Although the majority agreed on the deception ground, the dissenter found that ground "too narrow a ledge" for decision. He thought that the Commission had really denied renewal because of the speech uttered on the station and he concluded that this was impermissible. Brandywine-Main Line Radio, Inc. v. Federal Communications Commission, 473 F.2d 16 (D.C.Cir.1972), certiorari denied 412 U.S. 922 (1973), Douglas, J. dissenting.

In United Television Co., 55 F.C.C.2d 416, 34 R.R.2d 1465 (1975), the Commission denied renewal to a station accused of violating 18 U.S.C. § 1304 by broadcasting information concerning lotteries. This was done by ministers who "broadcast programs offering three-digit scripture citations in return for monetary donations." The licensee conceded that the language used in the broadcasts referred to numbers games. This behavior alone was held to warrant denial and to bar

United from a comparative hearing. In addition to this misbehavior, the licensee was found to have engaged in false and misleading advertising as well as violations of technical rules.

United's appeal failed. United Broadcasting Co. v. Federal Communications Commission, 565 F.2d 699 (D.C.Cir.1977). The court, however, refused to accept the speech ground. It noted that the FCC's order cited several independent reasons for nonrenewal, including technical violations: "In our view, the long history of persistent violations of those rules was a sufficient reason for disqualification. The Commission's decision is therefore affirmed on the basis of its discussion of this issue, and we reach no other question tendered by this appeal." Certiorari was denied, 434 U.S. 1046 (1978).

In Trustees of the University of Pennsylvania, 69 F.C.C.2d 1394, 44 R.R.2d 747 (1978), the Commission denied a renewal application from a university. Listeners had complained for some time that announcers on the station had frequently used obscenity and that entire programs had been obscene. The University took few steps to meet the problem until after the FCC began inquiries and ordered a hearing on the renewal application. The Commission denied renewal, exclusively on the ground that the licensee had totally abdicated its control over the station's management. The FCC refused to accept the argument that noncommercial licensees should not be held to the same level of accountability as commercial licensees. Corrective action could not mitigate the situation since it was undertaken only after it became clear that the license was in jeopardy.

A dissenting Commissioner argued for a short-term renewal on the ground that the FCC had been renewing university stations for years although it knew that they "were not as tightly controlled as commercially operated stations." He was distressed that the University and the community should suffer because of the actions of a "few immature, irresponsible students" who "should have been spanked long ago and the matter ended there."

The most dramatic nonrenewal on speech grounds involved the station in Jackson, Mississippi, that was the subject of the United Church of Christ case at p. 861, supra. Strangely, the case did *not* involve a Commission decision not to renew. Groups claimed that the station had violated the fairness doctrine, had failed to air contrasting viewpoints on racial matters, had given blacks inadequate exposure, had generally been disrespectful to blacks, had discriminated against local Catholics, and given inadequate time to public affairs. Blacks constituted 45 percent of the population of the station's primary service area. The FCC gave the licensee a short renewal and ordered it to honor its obligations.

After the FCC had been ordered to allow the citizen groups to participate and to reconsider the case, it decided that the station deserved renewal because the allegations had not been proven.

On a second appeal, the court reversed on the ground that the FCC's decision was not supported by substantial evidence. The FCC's errors included placing the burden of proof on the citizen groups rather than on the renewal applicant and failing to accept uncontradicted testimony about the station's practices, including cutting off national programs that showed blacks in a favorable light or discussed racial issues. Sometimes the licensee falsely blamed technical difficulties for the interruptions in service. Office of Communication of United Church of Christ v. Federal Communications Commission, 425 F.2d 543 (D.C.Cir.1969).

Rather than remand again, the court itself vacated the license and ordered the FCC to invite applications for the now vacant channel—and to provide for interim operation of the facility. Finally, the station was taken over by a different licensee.

Surely the most wide-scale nonrenewal occurred when the Commission refused to renew licenses for eight educational stations in Alabama as well as an application for a construction permit for a ninth. Alabama Educational Television Commission, 50 F.C.C.2d 461, 32 R.R.2d 539 (1975). The Commission found that "blacks rarely appeared on AETC programs; that no black instructors were employed in connection with locally-produced in-school programs; and that unexplained decisions or inconsistently applied policies caused the preemption of almost all black-oriented network programming." The Commission concluded that the "licensee followed a racially discriminatory policy in its overall programming practices and, by reason of its pervasive neglect of a black minority consisting of approximately 30 percent of the population of Alabama, its programming did not adequately meet the needs of the public it was licensed to serve." Although a station need not meet minority needs by special programming, the licensee "cannot with impunity ignore the problems of significant minorities in its service areas."

ANTI-DEFAMATION LEAGUE OF B'NAI B'RITH v. FEDERAL COMMUNICATIONS COMMISSION

United States Court of Appeals, District of Columbia Circuit, 1968.
403 F.2d 169.

Certiorari denied, 394 U.S. 930 (1969).

[The FCC granted renewal without a hearing to a radio station over objections from citizen groups that the station had broadcast several programs, including some by Richard Cotten, that the Commission found "made offensive comments concerning persons of the Jewish faith, equating Judaism with Socialism and Socialism with Communism."]

Before WILBUR K. MILLER, SENIOR CIRCUIT JUDGE, and BURGER and WRIGHT, CIRCUIT JUDGES

BURGER, CIRCUIT JUDGE.

. . .

. . . Two broadcasts, one on October 7, 1964, and one on May 27, 1965, were singled out and transcripts of those programs were before the Commission. The League's complaint is that the Licensee did nothing to remedy these programs until the programs were called to its attention and then declined either to cancel the program or to control Cotten in any way. The Licensee then offered the League free equal time to respond to Cotten's paid broadcasts or use the time in any way it desired. The League advised the Commission that it would not accept the tender of free time.

In granting renewal of the KTYM license without conducting an evidentiary hearing on the content of Cotten's programs, the Commission explained that no dispute of fact as to the content of the Cotten program existed and no issue as to KTYM's performance was raised apart from the Cotten programs. The Commission determined that as to a specific attack by Cotten on Arnold Forster, General Counsel of the League, KTYM had violated the "fairness doctrine" because the station had failed to give advance notice of the facts to Forster or the League. However, the Commission concluded that this was an isolated violation which neither afforded a basis for denying the license renewal nor necessitated an evidentiary hearing since the station had offered free time for a reply. That offer was still outstanding when the Commission acted.

The Commission considered the broad issue raised by the League that Cotten's utterances were so contrary to the public interest that a Licensee carrying such programs should be disqualified for renewal. The Commission declared that its historic policy in conformity with Congressional authority precluded censorship of programs:

> The Commission has long held that its function is not to judge the merit, wisdom or accuracy of any broadcast discussion or commentary but to insure that all viewpoints are given fair and equal opportunity for expression and that controverted allegations are balanced by the presentation of opposing viewpoints. Any other position would stifle discussion and destroy broadcasting as a medium of free speech. To require every licensee to defend his decision to present any controversial program that has been complained of in a license renewal hearing would cause most—if not all—licensees to refuse to broadcast any program that was potentially controversial or offensive to any substantial group. More often than not this would operate to deprive the public of the opportunity to hear unpopular or unorthodox views. . . .

Appellant's primary argument is that "recurrent bigoted appeals to anti-Semitic prejudice" and tolerance of personal attacks without notice to those attacked, constituted a basis for denial of license renewal and required an evidentiary hearing on those issues.

. . .

Our examination of the record satisfies us that the Commission acted within its authority in denying an evidentiary hearing as to the undisputed facts which formed the basis of Appellant's claims. The disposition of Appellant's claims turned not on determination of facts but inferences to be drawn from facts already known and the legal conclusions to be derived from those facts.

The First Amendment aspect also deserves some comment. . . .

Commissioner Loevinger, while concurring fully with the decision of the Commission, restated some basic propositions which seem to us unanswerable:

> For the FCC to promulgate rules regarding permissible and impermissible speech relating to religion would be not only an egregious interference with free speech in broadcasting, but also an unconstitutional infraction of the free exercise clause and the establishment clause of the First Amendment.
>
> . . .
>
> It is not only impractical—and impossible in any ultimate sense—to separate an appeal to prejudice from an appeal to reason in this field, it is equally beyond the power or ability of authority to say what is religious or racial. There are centuries of bloody strife to prove that man cannot agree on what is or is not "religion."
>
> . . .
>
> Nevertheless these subjects will and must be discussed. But they cannot be freely discussed if there is to be an official ban on the utterance of "falsehood" or an "appeal to prejudice" as officially defined. All that the government can properly do, consistently with the right of free speech, is to demand that the opportunity be kept open for the presentation of all viewpoints. Yet this would be impossible under the rule espoused by the ADL. The present case illustrates the matter. The assailed commentator here does not ostensibly attack the Jews as a religious group, but does attack Zionists and the ADL because the latter is conducting a campaign against "right wing extremists" which is said to include that commentator. But if anyone is permitted to express views favorable to Zionism or the ADL, or unfavorable to "right wing extremists" or the assailed commentator, then the Fairness Doctrine requires that someone representing the contrary viewpoints be given the opportunity to reply. This, of course, is precisely what the ADL contends cannot be permitted. If what the ADL calls "appeals to racial or religious prejudice" is to be classed with hardcore obscenity, then it has no right to be heard on the air, and the only views which are entitled to be broadcast on matters of concern to the ADL are those which the ADL holds or finds acceptable. This is irreconcilable with either the Fairness Doctrine or the right of free speech.
>
> Talk of "responsibility" of a broadcaster in this connection is simply a euphemism for self-censorship. It is an attempt to shift

the onus of action against speech from the Commission to the broadcaster, but it seeks the same result—suppression of certain views and arguments. Since the imposition of the duty of such "responsibility" involves Commission compulsion to perform the function of selection and exclusion and Commission supervision of the manner in which that function is performed, the Commission still retains the ultimate power to determine what is and what is not permitted on the air. So this formulation does not advance the argument either constitutionally, ideologically or practically. Attempts to impose such schemes of self-censorship have been found as unconstitutional as more direct censorship efforts by government. [ ]

While the Commission has the power and indeed the duty to consider a pattern of libelous conduct in a license renewal hearing, the First Amendment demands that it proceed cautiously and Congress, as we have noted, limited the Commission's powers in this area. We hold that the record reflects substantial evidence in support of the Commission's decision.

Affirmed.

J. SKELLY WRIGHT, CIRCUIT JUDGE, concurring:

Subject to the following observations, I join the court's opinion in this case.

The Anti-Defamation League charges that Station KTYM, knowingly and on repeated occasions, allowed to be broadcast a series of programs containing false and defamatory statements about Jews in general and on one occasion about some Jewish individuals in particular. Two types of program content are thus challenged—libeling an individual and attacking a group—and different approaches are required for each.

With respect to individual libel, I start with the premise that a license to run a radio station is not a license to libel. False defamatory statements, made knowingly or with reckless disregard of their falsity, cannot claim the shelter of the First Amendment. New York Times Co. v. Sullivan, [ ]. A radio station, like a newspaper, cannot claim immunity from libel laws.[2]

Thus when a station allows a series of programs in which individuals are repeatedly defamed and the station is put on notice (for example, by the complaint of an offended individual) that such programs contain false and unsubstantiated statements, in a renewal proceeding involving that station's license the Commission should: (1) determine whether the station knew of the falsity of the material or

2. . . .

There is one narrowly drawn exception: a radio station is not responsible for libelous statements made in a political broadcast by a candidate for public office. Farmers E. & C. Union, etc. v. WDAY, 360 U.S. 525 (1959). This is so because § 315(a) of the Federal Communications Act precludes a station from deleting any of the material from such a speech. The station here, however, is under no such disability. . . .

allowed it to be broadcast in reckless disregard of its truth or falsity (the standard of New York Times Co. v. Sullivan), and (2) consider whether such programming is in the public interest. Neither the First Amendment nor a policy of encouraging stimulating and constructive radio broadcasting would preclude the Commission from refusing to renew a license because of repeated individual libels; nor would the Commission be prevented from cancelling the license of a broadcaster who persisted in such a course of programming.[3] In the instant case there is no pattern of repeated individual libels. Therefore I concur in affirming the Commission.

Attacking a group presents a harder problem. Under the law of libel, defamation of a broad group or class is not usually actionable. And this kind of speech, detestable as some of its anti-Semitic and racist aspects may be, approaches the area of political and social commentary. To this extent it makes a stronger claim for First Amendment protection.[5] I share the desire of the Commission and the court to foster free and full debate on political and social issues. For this reason, broadcasters should not be so burdened in this area that they would shy away from presenting controversial issues.

Station KTYM offered the Anti-Defamation League substantial time to reply to the anti-Semitic broadcasts. This application of the "fairness doctrine" will have to suffice. To go further, requiring stations to check the truth of all commentary attacking a group or class, might result in a "chilling effect," constraining stations to steer clear of controversial material. However, as this case illustrates, there is a substantial flaw in the theory of the fairness doctrine. Not surprisingly, the Anti-Defamation League refused to dignify or exacerbate the attack by replying. It is likely that other groups would similarly refuse to reply. Under such circumstances, the Commission may decide to require a licensee to seek with reasonable diligence exponents of other views when it presents one side of a controversial issue in which a group or class is attacked.[6]

. . .

3. This would not be prohibited "censorship," 47 U.S.C. § 315 (1964), any more than would the Commission's considering on a license renewal application whether a broadcaster allowed "coarse, vulgar, suggestive, double-meaning" programming; programs containing such material are grounds for denial of a license renewal. Palmetto Broadcasting Co., 23 Pike & Fischer R.R. 483, 484 (1962), affirmed 334 F.2d 534, certiorari denied 379 U.S. 843 (1964).

5. In Beauharnais v. People of State of Illinois, 343 U.S. 250 (1952), a divided Supreme Court upheld a conviction under a statute outlawing defamation of a racial or religious group. However, far from spawning progeny, *Beauharnais* has been left more and more barren by subsequent First Amendment decisions, to the point where it is now doubtful that the decision still represents the views of the Court.

6. Nothing I have said would preclude the Commission from finding that a station was not in the public interest whose regular programming consisted solely of views slanted toward one side of a controversial issue or issues, even if the station allowed the other side time to reply. The Commission could conclude that a station which offered more rounded programming better served the public.

Notes and Questions

1. What are the disagreements between the majority and the concurring judge?

2. What is the relevance of New York Times v. Sullivan in this context?

3. The concurring judge suggests that some groups will not dignify arguments by responding to them. Should that affect the analysis?

4. Does this case suggest that no speech uttered by a broadcaster can be grounds for denial of renewal unless it is specifically prohibited, such as obscenity, or the broadcaster fails to observe the fairness doctrine and its personal attack part?

5. *Promise v. Performance.* If the Commission "encourages" promises of certain types of programs, how should it treat disparities between the promise and the actual performance? The Commission's general reluctance to deny renewals originally led it to overlook disparities. The subject is discussed extensively in Moline Television Corp., 31 F.C.C.2d 263, 22 R.R.2d 745 (1971), dealing with an assertion that an applicant obtained a station by lavish promises and failed to carry them out. The Commission noted that for some years it had "not awarded a preference to any applicant based on proposed programming. The door to a sorry episode has been firmly closed."

In 1976, the Commission adopted a quantitative guideline for the "promise versus performance" issue in renewals. Matter of Revision of FCC Form 303, Application for Renewal of Broadcast Station Licenses, 59 F.C.C.2d 750, 37 R.R.2d 1 (1976). The Commission's guideline was that an actual decrease of 15 percent in such categories as news or public affairs or a 20 percent decrease overall had to be explained to the Commission. "This refers to decreases between the composite week performance and the amount promised in the applicant's last renewal application. . . ."

In West Coast Media, Inc., 79 F.C.C.2d 610, 47 R.R.2d 1709 (1980), a petition to deny renewal was filed against a San Diego FM station for failing to comply with its promises to the FCC. After a hearing, the FCC denied renewal. The Commission stressed that it had not set minimum program requirements to qualify for renewal. Instead, the licensee is obliged to comply substantially with its promises for future performance. "Insubstantial variations do not raise a question of the licensee's ability" to serve the public interest. Here the licensee fell far below its promises. In such cases "the Commission confines its review of programming performance to a determination of whether the licensee made reasonable and good faith efforts to effectuate its proposal. Moreover, the licensee must show that its programming has been appropriately responsive to community problems, needs and interests."

After reviewing the record, the Commission concluded that the record showed that the licensee failed to make "reasonable and good faith efforts to effectuate its proposal." This order was upheld in West

Coast Media, Inc. (KDIG) v. Federal Communications Commission, 695 F.2d 617, 52 R.R.2d 1295 (D.C.Cir.1982), certiorari denied 464 U.S. 816 (1983).

In *Deregulation of Television,* p. 866, supra, the Commission eliminated quantitative programming guidelines, including those dealing with promise versus performance. This action was based on studies showing that commercial television stations were carrying nonentertainment programming that far exceeded the percentages set up by the Commission.

3. Comparative Renewal Proceedings

In the early years of regulation of each medium, except perhaps AM, so many vacant frequencies existed that few applicants tried to oust incumbents. When such a challenge did occur, the Commission undertook the difficult comparison of the incumbent's actual performance and the challenger's proposed operation. In a major case involving renewal of the license of a Baltimore AM station, the Commission's analysis showed some reasons favoring the incumbent and others favoring the challenger. Hearst Radio, Inc. (WBAL), 15 F.C.C. 1149, 6 R.R. 994 (1951). The incumbent's failure to have integrated ownership and management did not matter because its actual performance was now available for review. Similarly, although the incumbent also controlled an FM station, a television station, and a newspaper in Baltimore, it had not abused its power, so this was not a serious problem. The Commission found little difference in proposed programming, and concluded:

> We have found that both of the applicants are legally, technically, and financially qualified and must therefore choose between them as their applications are mutually exclusive. We have discussed at some length why the criteria which we may sometimes consider as determining factors when one of the applicants is not operating the facilities sought and where the applicants have not proved their abilities, are not controlling factors in the light of the record of WBAL. The determining factor in our decision is the clear advantage of continuing the established and excellent service now furnished by WBAL and which we find to be in the public interest, when compared to the risks attendant on the execution of the proposed programming of Public Service Radio Corporation, excellent though the proposal may be.

This decision was thought to give renewal applicants such an advantage that prospective challengers sought entry by other means, such as buying an existing facility or seeking available, though less desirable, vacant frequencies. In its 1965 Policy Statement on Comparative Broadcast Hearings, p. 867, supra, the Commission noted that it was not attempting to deal with "the somewhat different problems raised where an applicant is contesting with a licensee seeking renewal of a license." Yet, later that year, in a case in which two applicants were challenging the incumbent, the Commission, on further consideration, "concluded that the policy statement should govern the introduction of evidence in this and similar proceedings where a renewal application is contested. . . . However, we wish to make it clear that the parties will be free to urge any arguments they may deem applicable concerning the relative weights to be afforded the evidence bearing on the various comparative factors." Seven (7) League Productions, Inc., 1 F.C.C.2d 1597 (1965).

Although the Commission might have developed a special set of standards governing renewal cases, it has found it quite difficult to do so. This was not a serious problem so long as few applicants challenged renewal applicants. But in the 1960s and early 1970s, those who wished to get into broadcasting were faced with virtually no vacancies on the spectrum (except UHF) and greatly increasing prices for existing stations. Despite the warning of *Hearst,* applicants began increasingly to challenge incumbents. Whether because the incumbents were superior—or at least equal—or because the denial of renewal imposed a serious financial penalty, the Commission continued to favor renewal applicants.

In 1969, after a complex 15-year proceeding, the Commission awarded a license for Channel 5 in Boston to BBI, over the claims of WHDH, Inc., which had been broadcasting on that channel for years. Although some contended that this was a denial of renewal, the FCC insisted that the peculiar facts of the case, including an episode of possible bribery, had warranted approaching the case as if it involved initial applicants. This approach was affirmed in Greater Boston Television Corp. v. Federal Communications Commission, 444 F.2d 841 (D.C.Cir.1970), certiorari denied 403 U.S. 923 (1971).

The Commission tried to assuage industry concern with a Policy Statement providing that in a hearing between an incumbent and a challenger, the incumbent would obtain a conclusive preference by demonstrating "substantial past performance without serious deficiencies." 22 F.C.C.2d 424, 18 R.R.2d 1901 (1970).

The court of appeals invalidated the policy in Citizens Communication Center v. Federal Communications Commission, 447 F.2d 1201 (D.C.Cir.1971) on the ground that it was inconsistent with the 1934 Act, which nowhere created a presumption in favor of incumbents. At the hearing each party had to be allowed to present its case. The incumbent's past performance would be a critical part of the hearing—and "superior performance should be a plus of major significance." In all cases, however, the challenger's application had to be compared with that of the incumbent.

Legislation to give incumbents greater protection nearly passed in 1974. For the next few years, although it purported not to be doing so, the Commission appeared to be giving incumbent licensees a controlling preference for "superior" or even "substantial" service. One such case involved Cowles Florida Broadcasting, Inc.'s application for renewal of the license for its television station in Daytona Beach, Florida. The administrative law judge, in recommending renewal, characterized Cowles's performance as "thoroughly acceptable." The Commission granted renewal, 4–3. The majority, after its own study of the record, concluded that the performance was "superior" and warranted renewal even though the challenger, Central Florida Enterprises, Inc., had gained advantages on several other issues, including diversification, integration, and minority participation, and the incumbent received a demerit for having moved its main studio location in violation of an FCC regulation. The majority also chose to disregard mail fraud allegations against other subsidiaries of Cowles's parent company.

One dissenter thought that the majority had distorted the record to find "superior" service. He thought it only "solid." He would have held that enough to justify renewal but felt constrained to dissent because the court of appeals had set a higher standard. Another dissenter followed much the same path.

In an order "clarifying" its earlier opinion, a majority of the Commission explained that its previous use of "superior" was not meant to suggest "exceptional when compared to other broadcast stations" in the area or elsewhere. Rather, the intention was to distinguish "between the two situations—one where the licensee has served the public interest but in the least permissible fashion still sufficient to be renewed in the absence of competing applications, and the other where the licensee has done so in a solid, favorable fashion." The licensee was said to be in the second group. The majority shifted from "superior" to "substantial."

The court of appeals reversed the renewal and remanded. Central Florida Enterprises, Inc. v. Federal Communications Commission, 598 F.2d 37 (D.C.Cir.1978). The court's final position (after an original opinion, an order amending that opinion, and a supplemental opinion denying a petition for rehearing), rejected the Commission's entire approach to comparative renewal proceedings—and found inadequacies in its dealings with specific issues. The court observed:

> [The Commission] found favorably to Central [the challenger] on each of diversification, integration, and minority participation, and adversely to Cowles on the studio move question. Then simply on the basis of a wholly noncomparative assessment of Cowles' past performance as "substantial," the Commission confirmed Cowles' "renewal expectancy." Even were we to agree (and we do not agree) with the Commission's trivialization of each of Central's advantages, we still would be unable to sustain its action here. The Commission nowhere even vaguely described how it aggregated its findings into the decisive balance; rather, we are told that the conclusion is based on "administrative 'feel.'" Such intuitional forms of decision-making, completely opaque to judicial review, fall somewhere on the distant side of arbitrary.

On remand the Commission again awarded the license to Cowles. Central Florida appealed once more.

CENTRAL FLORIDA ENTERPRISES, INC. v. FEDERAL COMMUNICATIONS COMMISSION

United States Court of Appeals, District of Columbia Circuit, 1982.
683 F.2d 503.

Certiorari denied 460 U.S. 1084 (1983).

Before ROBINSON, CHIEF JUDGE, WILKEY, CIRCUIT JUDGE, and FLANNERY, DISTRICT JUDGE for the District of Columbia.

WILKEY, CIRCUIT JUDGE:

. . .

In its decision appealed in *Central Florida I* the FCC concluded that the reasons undercutting Cowles' bid for renewal did "not outweigh the substantial service Cowles rendered to the public during the last license period." Accordingly, the license was renewed. Our reversal was rooted in a twofold finding. First, the Commission had inadequately investigated and analyzed the four factors weighing against Cowles' renewal. Second, the process by which the FCC weighed these four factors against Cowles' past record was never "even vaguely described" and, indeed, "the Commission's handling of the facts of this case [made] embarrassingly clear that the FCC [had] practically erected a presumption of renewal that is inconsistent with the full hearing requirement" of the Communications Act. We remand with instructions to the FCC to cure these deficiencies.

On remand the Commission has followed our directives and corrected, point by point, the inadequate investigation and analysis of the four factors cutting against Cowles' requested renewal. The Commission concluded that, indeed, three of the four merited an advantage for Central Florida, and on only one (the mail fraud issue) did it conclude that nothing needed to be added on the scale to Central's plan or removed from Cowles'. We cannot fault the Commission's actions here.

We are left, then, with evaluating the way in which the FCC weighed Cowles' main studio move violation and Central's superior diversification and integration, on the one hand, against Cowles' substantial record of performance on the other. This is the most difficult and important issue in this case, for the new weighing process which the FCC has adopted will presumably be employed in its renewal proceedings elsewhere. We therefore feel that it is necessary to scrutinize carefully the FCC's new approach, and discuss what we understand and expect it to entail.

For some time now the FCC has had to wrestle with the problem of how it can factor in some degree of "renewal expectancy" for a broadcaster's meritorious past record, while at the same time undertaking the required comparative evaluation of the incumbent's probable future performance versus the challenger's. As we stated in *Central Florida I*, "the incumbent's past performance is some evidence, and perhaps the best evidence, of what its future performance would be." And it has been intimated—by the Supreme Court in FCC v. National Citizens Committee for Broadcasting (NCCB) and by this court in *Citizens Communications Center v. FCC* and *Central Florida I*—that some degree of renewal expectancy is permissible. But *Citizens* and *Central Florida I* also indicated that the FCC has in the past impermissibly raised renewal expectancy to an irrebuttable presumption in favor of the incumbent.

We believe that the formulation by the FCC in its latest decision, however, is a permissible way to incorporate some renewal expectancy while still undertaking the required comparative hearing. *The new policy, as we understand it, is simply this: renewal expectancy is to be a factor weighed with all the other factors, and the better the past record, the greater the renewal expectancy "weight."*

> In our view [states the FCC], the strength of the expectancy depends on the merit of the past record. Where, as in this case, the incumbent rendered substantial but not superior service, the "expectancy" takes the form of a comparative preference weighed against [the] other factors . . . . An incumbent performing in a superior manner would receive an even stronger preference. An incumbent rendering minimal service would receive no preference.

This is to be contrasted with Commission's *1965 Policy Statement on Comparative Broadcast Hearings*, where "[o]nly unusually good or unusually poor records have relevance."

. . .

The reasons given by the Commission for factoring in some degree of renewal expectancy are rooted in a concern that failure to do so would hurt broadcast *consumers*.

> The justification for a renewal expectancy is three-fold. (1) There is no guarantee that a challenger's paper proposals will, in fact, match the incumbent's proven performance. Thus, not only might replacing an incumbent be entirely gratuitous, but *it might even deprive the community of an acceptable service and replace it with an inferior one.* (2) Licensees should be encouraged through the likelihood of renewal to make investments *to ensure quality service. Comparative renewal proceedings cannot function as a "competitive spur" to licensees if their dedication to the community is not rewarded.* (3) Comparing incumbents and challengers as if they were both new applicants could lead to a haphazard restructuring of the broadcast industry especially considering the large number of group owners. *We cannot readily conclude that such a restructuring could serve the public interest.*

We are relying, then, on the FCC's commitment that renewal expectancy will be factored in for the benefit of the public, not for incumbent broadcasters. . . . As we concluded in *Central Florida I*, "[t]he only legitimate fear which should move [incumbent] licensees is the fear of their own substandard performance, and that would be all to the public good."

There is a danger, of course, that the FCC's new approach could still degenerate into precisely the sort of irrebuttable presumption in favor of renewal that we have warned against. . . . [M]uch will depend on how the Commission applies it and fleshes it out. Of particular importance will be the definition and level of service it assigns to "substantial"—and whether that definition is ever found to be "opaque to judicial review," "wholly unintelligible," or based purely on "administrative 'feel.' " [27]

In this case, however, the Commission was painstaking and explicit in its balancing. The Commission discussed in quite specific terms, for instance, the items it found impressive in Cowles' past record. It stressed and listed numerous programs demonstrating Cowles' "local community orientation" and "responsive[ness] to community needs," discussed the percentage of Cowles' programming devoted to news, public affairs, and local topics, and said it was "impressed by [Cowles'] reputation in the community. Seven community leaders and three public officials testified that [Cowles] had made outstanding contributions to the local community. Moreover, the record shows no complaints . . . ." The Commission concluded that "Cowles' record [was] more than minimal," was in fact " 'substantial,' i.e., 'sound, favorable and substantially above a level of mediocre service which might just minimally warrant renewal.' "

The Commission's inquiry in this case did not end with Cowles' record, but continued with a particularized analysis of what factors weighed against Cowles' record, and how much. The FCC investigated fully the mail fraud issue. It discussed the integration and diversification disadvantages of Cowles and conceded that Central had an edge on these issues—"slight" for integration, "clear" for diversification. But it reasoned that "structural factors such as [these]—of primary importance in a new license proceeding—should have lesser weight compared with the preference arising from substantial past service." [31] Finally,

27. [ ] We think it would be helpful if at some point the Commission defined and explained the distinctions, if any, among: substantial, meritorious, average, above average, not above average, not far above average, above mediocre, more than minimal, solid, sound, favorable, not superior, not exceptional, and unexceptional—all terms used by the parties to describe what the FCC found Cowles' level of performance to have been. We are especially interested to know what the standard of comparison is in each case. "Average" compared to all applicants? "Mediocre" compared to all incumbents? "Favorable" with respect to the FCC's expectations? We realize that the FCC's task is a subjective one, but the use of imprecise terms needlessly compounds our difficulty in evaluating what the Commission has done. We think we can discern enough to review intelligently the Commission's actions today, but if the air is not cleared or, worse, becomes foggier, the FCC's decisionmaking may again be adjudged "opaque to judicial review."

31. . . .

Here we have a caveat. We do not read the Commission's new policy as *ignoring* integration and diversification considerations in comparative renewal hearings. In its brief [ ] the Commission states that "an incumbent's meritorious record should

with respect to the illegal main studio move, the FCC found that "licensee misconduct" in general "may provide a more meaningful basis for preferring an untested challenger over a proven incumbent." The Commission found, however, that here the "comparative significance of the violation" was diminished by the underlying facts. . . . The FCC concluded that "the risk to the public interest posed by the violation seems small when compared to the actuality of depriving Daytona Beach of Cowles' tested and acceptable performance."

Having listed the relevant factors and assigned them weights, the Commission concluded that Cowles' license should be renewed. We note, however, that despite the finding that Cowles' performance was " 'substantial,' i.e., 'sound, favorable and substantially above a level of mediocre service,' " the combination of Cowles' main studio rule violation and Central's diversification and integration advantages made this a "close and difficult case." Again, we trust that this is more evidence that the Commission's weighing did not, and will not, amount to automatic renewal for incumbents.

We are somewhat reassured by a recent FCC decision granting, for the first time since at least 1961, on *comparative* grounds the application of the challenger for a radio station license and denying the renewal application of the incumbent licensee.[38] In that decision the Commission found that the *incumbent deserved no renewal expectancy* for his past program record and that his application was inferior to the challenger's on comparative grounds. Indeed, it was the *incumbent's* preferences on the diversification and integration factors which were overcome (there, by the challenger's superior programming proposals and longer broadcast week). The Commission found that the incumbent's "inadequate [past performance] reflects poorly on the *likelihood of future service in the public interest.*" Further, it found that the incumbent had no "legitimate renewal expectancy" because his past performance was neither "meritorious" nor "substantial."

We have, however, an important caveat. In the Commission's weighing of factors the scale mid-mark must be neither the factors themselves, nor the interests of the broadcasting industry, nor some other secondary and artificial construct, but rather the intent of Con-

outweigh in the comparative renewal context a challenging applicant's advantages under the structural factors of integration and diversification." Ceteris paribus, this may be so—depending in part, of course, on how "meritorious" is defined. But where there are weights on the scales other than a meritorious record on the one hand, and integration and diversification on the other, the Commission must afford the latter two *some* weight, since while they alone may not outweigh a meritorious record they may tip the balance if weighed with something else. See *Citizens*, [ ].

That, of course, is precisely the situation here, since the main studio move violation must also be balanced against the meritorious record. The Commission may not weigh the antirenewal factors separately against the incumbent's record, eliminating them as it goes along. It must weigh them all simultaneously. . . .

38. In re Applications of Simon Geller and Grandbanke Corp., FCC Docket Nos. 21104–05 (Released 15 June 1982). We intimate no view at this time, of course, on the soundness of the Commission's decision there; we cite it only as demonstrating that the Commission's new approach may prove to be more than a paper tiger.

gress, which is to say the interests of the listening public. All other doctrine is merely a means to this end, and it should not become more. If in a given case, for instance, the factual situation is such that the denial of a license renewal would not undermine renewal expectancy *in a way harmful to the public interest,* then renewal expectancy should not be invoked.[40]

Finally, we must note that we are still troubled by the fact that the record remains that an incumbent *television* licensee has *never* been denied renewal in a comparative challenge. American television viewers will be reassured, although a trifle baffled, to learn that even the worst television stations—those which are, presumably, the ones picked out as vulnerable to a challenge [42]—are so good that they never need replacing. We suspect that somewhere, sometime, somehow, some television licensee *should* fail in a comparative renewal challenge, but the FCC has never discovered such a licensee yet. As a court we cannot say that it must be Cowles here.

We hope that the standard now embraced by the FCC will result in the protection of the public, not just incumbent licensees. And in today's case we believe the FCC's application of the new standard was not inconsistent with the Commission's mandate. Accordingly the Commission's decision is

Affirmed.

Notes and Questions

1. Is the latest Commission explanation of its comparative renewal standards clear? Exactly how much renewal expectancy is there? Has the Commission adequately justified the need for a strong renewal expectancy?

2. Was the court too deferential in its review?

3. Ironically, less than a year later, when the court was presented with the Commission's action in denying renewal to Simon Geller, it refused to affirm. Geller had been operating a one-man classical music FM station in Gloucester, Massachusetts, since the early 1960s. In 1981, Grandebanke Corporation filed a competing application. The Commission held that because less than 1 percent of the station's programming was of a nonentertainment nature and the station broadcast no news, editorials, or locally produced programming, Geller was not entitled to the benefit of renewal expectancy. Simon Geller, 91

40. Thus, the three justifications given by the Commission for renewal expectancy, [ ] should be remembered by the FCC in future renewal proceedings and, where these justifications are in a particular case attenuated, the Commission ought not to chant "renewal expectancy" and grant the license.

42. Counsel for the FCC conceded at oral argument, "I grant you, [competitors] wouldn't challenge the [incumbent] they thought was exceptional or far above average." The dissent from the Commission's decision declared it a "readily apparent fact that competing applicants file against only the ne'er-do-wells of the industry." [ ]

F.C.C.2d 1253, 52 R.R.2d 709 (1982). The Commission awarded the radio license to Grandbanke.

On appeal, the FCC's action was vacated and the case remanded. The court began by characterizing it as "yet another meandering effort by the [FCC] to develop a paradigm for its license renewal hearings."

> For years this court has urged the FCC to put some bite into its comparative hearings. [ ] Indeed, we have too long hungered for just one instance in which the FCC properly denied an incumbent's renewal expectancy. Unfortunately, in the process of seeking to respond to this court's signals with regard to renewal expectancy, the FCC ignored its own precedents as to the other factors that must be considered in conducting a comparative analysis.

The court of appeals agreed that Geller was entitled to no renewal expectancy because his programming did not even attempt to respond to ascertained community needs and problems. The FCC then properly turned to the comparative criteria. Here, however, the court concluded that the FCC had improperly diminished the value of Geller's obvious advantages of diversification and integration of ownership and management because it tied each to its view of Geller's programming. The FCC thus failed to accord Geller the importance it had generally attached to diversification and integration in prior cases. The case was remanded for further consideration. Committee for Community Access v. Federal Communications Commission, 737 F.2d 74 (D.C.Cir.1984). As we have seen, p. 874, supra, on that remand Geller was renewed. That renewal is now on appeal.

4. In its inquiry aimed at streamlining the renewal process, the Commission has been considering eliminating "content orientation" from the comparison. One proposal would base renewal expectancy solely on compliance with statutory obligations and nonprogramming-related FCC rules. Broadcasting, April 15, 1985 at 7. How might the comparative aspect of the proceeding be preserved?

Some would argue that it is impossible to devise an adequate system of comparing incumbents and new applicants and that comparative renewals should be eliminated completely. What are the pros and cons of such a proposal?

D. TRANSFER OF LICENSES

In part because of the Commission's renewal policies, radio and television licenses have acquired substantial value. When a licensee decides to leave broadcasting altogether or to switch services or locations at the end of a license period, it loses the chance to make a profit. To reap profits, the licensee must seek renewal and, during the term, sell the facilities and goodwill and assign the license to a prospective buyer. In some ways this "transfer" procedure resembles the sale of any business, but the Commission's rules substantially affect the transaction.

Section 310(d) of the Communications Act requires the Commission to pass on all transfers and find that "the public interest, convenience, and necessity will be served thereby." But it also provides that in deciding whether the public interest would be served by the transfer the Commission "may not consider whether the public interest . . . might be served by the transfer . . . to a person other than the proposed transferee or assignee." Why might Congress have imposed this limitation?

When a transferee applies for its first full term, should it be judged as an original applicant who must compete in a comparative hearing without any advantage of incumbency, or as a renewal applicant? What are the justifications for each view?

Despite the possible objections to transfer applications, most are granted, usually with little or no delay. This kind of turnover suggests a problem for the Commission. If licenses acquire substantial value a tendency may develop to build up stations and then sell them at a profit. This might be viewed as undermining the "public interest" philosophy of the licensing process. On the other hand, the public may benefit when someone builds up a station, even though that person's motive is to sell it for a profit.

In 1962, the Commission adopted a rule prohibiting licensees from transferring a broadcast license during the first three years after acquisition unless a hardship waiver—usually upon a showing of financial loss—is granted. Frequent changes in ownership were viewed as disruptive and thus contrary to the public interest. Applications for Voluntary Assignments or Transfer of Control, 32 F.C.C. 689 (1962).

Twenty years later, the Commission reversed its position on this issue after concluding that a willing buyer was more likely to serve the public interest than an unwilling owner prohibited from selling the station. The three-year rule was abolished, but a one-year requirement was instituted for licenses acquired through the comparative hearing process. Applications for Voluntary Assignments or Transfer of Control, 52 R.R.2d 1081 (1982). Subsequently the one-year rule was extended to licenses obtained through the minority ownership policy.

Until 1970, the foregoing summary would have covered most of the major problems related to transfers, but then the question of format change arose, plaguing the courts and the Commission until 1981 when the Supreme Court resolved the issue. The problem arose when a prospective transferee of a radio license proposed to change the station's distinctive programming format.

In Federal Communications Comm'n v. WNCN Listeners Guild, 450 U.S. 582 (1981), the Court, 7–2, reversed the court of appeals and upheld the Commission's approach. The FCC had concluded that "reliance on the market is the best method of promoting diversity in entertainment formats." The court of appeals had insisted on review of formats when "there is evidence that market forces have deprived the public of a 'unique' format." For the Court, Justice White concluded that the FCC had rationally explained why it had determined that examining format proposals before granting transfers would be administratively difficult, would inhibit experimental formats, and would not advance the welfare of the radio-listening public.

Justice White noted that the Court's "opinions have repeatedly emphasized that the Commission's judgment regarding how the public interest is best served is entitled to substantial judicial deference." Furthermore, diversity is not the only policy that is to be furthered under the statutory obligation to promote the "public interest." The FCC's position "reflects a reasonable accommodation of the policy of promoting diversity in programming and the policy of avoiding unnecessary restrictions on licensee discretion." The legislative history and the FCC's interpretations were consistent with its position.

The critical dispute boiled down to whether the FCC was obligated to examine each individual transfer application to see if it was in the public interest, or whether it could adopt a general policy that, by refusing to permit individual examinations of the question, might lead to grants of individual transfers that were not in the public interest, although the general policy might be. The Court upheld the FCC's view that individual examinations would require judgment on such matters as the preferences of the community, the intensity with which each preference is held, and on diversity within similar formats as well as diversity among very different formats.

Finally, in a passage set forth at p. 737, supra, the Court rejected respondents' contention that the policy statement conflicted with the First Amendment right of listeners.

Justice Marshall, joined by Justice Brennan, dissented. The thrust of their argument was that the 1934 Act requires the Commission to assure itself that each transfer is in the public interest. If a party asserts that a particular transfer would not serve the public interest, the FCC must consider that claim on the merits and may not contend that the general refusal to look at entertainment formats does more good than harm overall. Beyond that, the dissenters argued that the FCC was clearly wrong in asserting that it was unable to do a good job of considering individual cases on the merits.

In 1985, the Commission reaffirmed its position of nonintervention in format controversies. WEAM Radio, Inc., 58 R.R.2d 141 (1985).

Chapter XVII

CABLE TELEVISION AND NEW TECHNOLOGIES

Our discussion until this point has been addressed solely to broadcasting. Some programs reached the public through radios and others through television sets. In this Chapter we will examine other forms of communication that do not necessarily involve broadcasting—though the end product does emerge through the television set. It is important to recognize at the outset that although broadcasting and the television set have been joined, new technology permits the television set to be used for communications that have not been broadcast. The most obvious example is the use of video cassette players and recorders, which permit the owner of a television set to buy or rent a video cassette at a store and play it on a television set at home—all without any use of the spectrum. That activity closely resembles the showing of movies at home.

A. THE DEVELOPMENT OF CABLE TELEVISION

Cable television, the first of the "new" communication technologies, involves the transmission of electrical signals over wires to television sets in homes or elsewhere. The technique involves a studio, called the "head-end," and coaxial cables that physically connect the head-end with the television set of every user of the system. A single cable is capable of carrying such a wide range of electrical signals that it can simultaneously carry signals sufficient for fifty-five or more television channels. (As the signals are carried along the cable they become weaker and must be amplified along the way.)

It is possible to transmit certain signals in scrambled form that require decoders, while others can be received by all users. It is also possible, as Warner Communications first showed with QUBE in Columbus, Ohio, to run a system in which the users are able to send signals back to the head-end: voting on a question asked on a program, ordering merchandise, or telling a quarterback what plays to call in a semiprofessional football game.

The programming sent out from the head-end can come from many sources. The system owner might send out a variety of motion pictures he has bought or rented; he might send a camera crew out to cover the local high school football game; he might present live programs from his own studio; he might carry programs prepared by others specially for cable, which he receives by wire or by satellite; or he might seek to transmit over his system the signals and programs broadcast by television stations. This last source of programming raises serious questions of the relationship between cable and over-the-air television. So long as the cable system carries only programming from other sources, cable television is simply another competitor of broadcasting, along with movies, phonograph records, books and other communication sources. In fact, however, cable has been intimately involved with broadcasting since its inception—and that has produced substantial conflict.

Cable transmission was first used in the 1950s to provide television reception to remote locations that otherwise would have received none. For example, a community located in the mountains of West Virginia constructed an antenna on high ground to receive the signals of nearby television stations and transmit them through cable to households in the community. Such systems were called CATV for "community antenna television." Since cable was the only means of bringing television service to these remote areas, television broadcasters welcomed the additional viewers.

It was soon realized, however, that cable could do more than merely provide television service to remote areas. In 1961, a cable operator began serving San Diego, a city already served by three VHF network affiliates. The cable operator erected an antenna capable of picking up signals from Los Angeles, 120 miles away. In addition to the three networks received locally, cable offered four independent stations that served Los Angeles with sports, old motion pictures, and reruns of network shows. The San Diego experience demonstrated that the three channels offered by over-the-air signals were not enough to satisfy the audience and that viewers were willing to pay for more diversified programming through importation of distant signals. In effect, cable television service filled in the uneven pattern of FCC station allocation. Since cable offered a service alternative to that offered by local, over-the-air stations, television broadcasters began to view cable transmission as a competitive threat.

The spread of color television also provided new impetus to cable development. VHF signals tend to bounce off large obstacles rather than bending around them. Hence a tall building can be a weak transmitter, rebroadcasting the television signal at the same frequency as the station from which the signal originates. The result is interference, barely noticeable on a black-and-white set, but more pronounced on a color set. Cable provided the residents of large cities something that an over-the-air television signal could not—a high-quality color picture. Thus, cable television invaded large cities that already had a full complement of VHF signals.

Finally, cable began to originate programming not available to viewers of network or independent television. Cable systems offered entertainment programming, sports events, and special programs designed to meet the interests of discrete groups. Communication satellites made nationwide distribution of this programming economically feasible. The discovery that viewers were willing to pay a few dollars more per month for programming not available on over-the-air television led to the development of pay cable service.

Pay cable involves the cable distribution of non-broadcast programming for which the subscriber is charged an additional program or channel fee beyond the regular monthly fee for the system's television signal reception service. The systems for distributing pay cable vary technically. The simplest method is to distribute the programming on one or more channels of a cable television system in scrambled form. System subscribers who wish to receive the additional programming are supplied with a device that converts the programming transmission so that it can be understood. It is technically possible, but more expensive, to use systems that permit a separate charge to be made for each program viewed. Here the subscriber must either purchase a ticket for each program in advance, which, when inserted into a decoding device in the subscriber's home, provides access to the programming, or utilize the return communications capacity of a cable system or a telephone connection to activate a central computer facility that releases the programming through the subscriber's decoding device (addressable converters) and performs the billing functions.

Most cable systems utilize a fee structure known as "tiering." A relatively low monthly fee gives the subscriber access to the local over-the-air television stations as well as any community access or local origination channels. Access channels carry programming produced by citizens or community groups, and the cable operator may originate some local programming, such as local news, sports, and public affairs programs. Sometimes advertiser-supported services, such as the Entertainment and Sports Programming Network (ESPN), the Cable News Network (CNN), and over-the-air signals, are imported from other parts of the country.

An additional monthly fee gives the subscriber access to other specialized programming services ranging from children's programs to adult entertainment. These services are usually bundled together in groups called "tiers." Thus, the subscriber must often take several unwanted program services to obtain one desired service. Often a higher tier includes all the programming available in lower tiers.

The range of programming available via cable has grown greatly. In the New York area, for example, cable companies include more than ten services in the basic monthly fee, such as programming directed to racial and religious groups, all-news and all-sports channels, live coverage of Congress, children's programming, and "superstations" (discussed infra). For an extra monthly charge, subscribers may obtain an equal number of additional services, such as movie and entertainment channels, adult movies, and cultural programming.

Cable, then, has had a variety of roles. It began as a way of bringing to a community programming that would have been available but for geographical barriers. Then, it imported programs from communities beyond the reach of normal reception. Later, it became a service for those who wished to improve reception of their local signals. These features have been combined with each other as well as with the origination of new programming on cable. Now it is possible to obtain the origination without any of the other features—and this origination may be local or part of a network that programs specially for cable subscribers.

By 1985, cable systems had been installed in 36.1 million (42.9 percent) of the nation's 84 million television homes. Systems varied in size from a few hundred homes to some in larger cities with hundreds of thousands of subscribers. The largest multiple system operators (MSOs) own hundreds of systems. Pay cable reached 25 million of these subscribers. The pay systems ranged from Home Box Office with 14.5 million subscribers to specialized services with only a few thousand subscribers.

B. FCC JURISDICTION OVER CABLE

When the first CATV systems emerged in the late 1950s, rural television stations became concerned about their local dominance. The FCC rejected requests that it assume jurisdiction over the activities of these new enterprises. The problem was thought trivial and no different from a request for protection against motion picture theaters or publishers who also compete with broadcasting.

In 1962, however, the FCC changed direction and began to deny cable systems permission to carry broadcast signals that might adversely affect local television. The Commission had two main concerns. First, it believed that if cable systems were allowed to import distant signals this would fragment the audience available to local stations, erode their revenue bases, affect their programming, and perhaps cause the stations to leave the air—to the public's detriment.

The second concern was that a cable system's use of retransmitted broadcast programming, for which the cable system had paid nothing, gave it an unfair competitive advantage over local television stations since the latter had to pay considerable sums to those who held the copyrights on particular programs. We will discuss the copyright decisions allowing cable to retransmit without paying later in this Chapter.

These two concerns—fragmentation and program costs—led the FCC to embark on a series of regulations designed to keep cable systems subordinate to over-the-air broadcasting. Recall that this was the period of weak UHF stations, for which audience fragmentation might well have been fatal.

One of the restrictions imposed was a ban on importing distant signals (those from outside the market area) into a top-100 market unless the cable system could prove that the importation would not hurt UHF development in that market. This restriction resulted in the first court challenge to the FCC's authority to regulate cable. United States v. Southwestern Cable Co., 392 U.S. 157 (1968). The Commission relied on § 152(a) of the Communications Act: "The provisions of this Act shall apply to all interstate and foreign communication by wire or radio . . . ." 47 U.S.C. § 152(a). Southwestern argued that "§ 152(a) does not independently confer regulatory authority upon the Commission, but instead merely prescribes the forms of communication to which the Act's other provisions may separately be made applicable." Since there were no specific cable provisions in the Act, Southwestern contended the Commission had no authority to regulate it.

The Court rejected that argument as an overly restrictive reading of the Act. Relying on *National Broadcasting Co.,* the case involving the chain broadcasting rules, the Court held that Congress had delegated "not niggardly but expansive powers" over electronic media to the Commission and that a broad reading of the Act was required.

Although *Southwestern Cable* established that the Commission did have jurisdiction over cable, it left unanswered the boundaries of that jurisdiction. The next challenge arose from the promulgation, in the late 1960s, of rules requiring larger cable systems to originate a certain amount of programming from their own resources. This requirement was upheld, 5–4, by the Supreme Court in United States v. Midwest Video Corp. (Midwest Video I), 406 U.S. 649 (1972), on the ground that the regulation was "reasonably ancillary" to the FCC's obligations to regulate over-the-air television. Since cable operators had become enmeshed with television broadcasting, the FCC could require them to engage in the functional equivalent of broadcasting. Chief Justice Burger, concurring, concluded that the FCC's regulation "strains the outer limits of even the open-ended and pervasive jurisdiction that has evolved by decisions of the Commission and the Courts." Within two years, the FCC eliminated the origination requirement because it concluded that quality local programming could not be obtained by government mandate.

Instead, the Commission issued rules requiring new cable systems to allocate four of their 20 channels to public, educational, local government and leased access. The systems had to make equipment available for studio use by the public and could not control who might use the facilities or what they might say. Charges for use of the facilities were controlled. Once again the Court was asked to define the limits of the Commission's jurisdiction in the case that has come to be called Midwest Video II. Federal Communications Commission v. Midwest Video Corporation, 440 U.S. 689 (1979). Justice White defined the central issue as follows:

> whether these [access] rules are "reasonably ancillary to the effective performance of the Commission's various responsibilities for the regulation of television broadcasting," United States v. Southwestern Cable Co., [ ] and hence within the Commission's statutory authority.

The Court agreed with the respondents that recognition of agency jurisdiction to promulgate the access rules would require an extension of its prior decisions. The origination rule did not abrogate the cable operators' control over the composition of their programming, as did the access rules. The use of access rules transferred control of the content of access cable channels from cable operators to members of the public "relegating cable systems, *pro tanto,* to common-carrier status." A common-carrier service in the communications context is one that "makes a public offering to provide [communications facilities] whereby all members of the public who choose to employ such facilities may communicate or transmit intelligence of their own design and choosing. . . . " A common carrier does not "make individualized decisions, in particular cases, whether and on what terms to deal."

The Court resolved the case on a statutory basis by relying on § 3(h) of the Communications Act (47 U.S.C. § 153(h)), which provided that "a person engaged in . . . broadcasting shall not . . . be deemed a common carrier":

> The provision's background manifests a congressional belief that the intrusion worked by such regulation on the journalistic integrity of broadcasters would overshadow any benefits associated with the resulting public access. It is difficult to deny, then, that forcing broadcasters to develop a "nondiscriminatory system for controlling access . . . is precisely what Congress intended to avoid through § 3(h) of the Act." [ ]

Although noting that the court below suggested that the Commission's rules might violate the First Amendment rights of cable operators, the Supreme Court emphasized that it was deciding this case on statutory grounds. It expressed no view on the constitutional question "save to acknowledge that it is not frivolous and to make clear that the asserted constitutional issue did not determine or sharply influence our construction of the statute."

In the early 1980s, there were no serious challenges to the Commission's jurisdiction over cable, perhaps because the Commission changed its regulatory posture towards cable. As we will discuss later in this Chapter, the Commission began, in the late 1970s, to eliminate its regulations restricting cable.

The elimination of the Commission's mandatory access channels did not eliminate access channel requirements. Filling the vacuum were state and municipal requirements. Most cities demanded access channels and studios as a prerequisite for obtaining a cable franchise. Often these demands were more extensive than the FCC's had been.

In October 1984, the jurisdictional question was settled when Congress passed the Cable Communications Policy Act of 1984. One of the provisions of the Cable Act amended a jurisdictional section of the Communications Act of 1934 to include specifically "cable service to all persons engaged within the United States in providing such service, and to the facilities of cable operators which relate to such service, as provided in Title VI." 47 U.S.C. § 152. At the same time, Title VI, Cable Communications, was added to the Communications Act of 1934. 47 U.S.C. §§ 601–639. We will consider some of these provisions later in this Chapter. Thus, the Commission no longer has to derive its jurisdiction over cable from its jurisdiction over broadcasting, and courts no longer have to determine whether a Commission rule is reasonably ancillary to its jurisdiction over broadcasting.

In the Cable Communications Policy Act of 1984, Congress provided express authorization for access channel requirements. Section 611 states that access channels for public, educational, and governmental use can be required as part of a franchise proposal or a proposal for renewal. In addition, § 612 requires all systems with 36 or more activated channels to set aside some channels for commercial use by persons unaffiliated with the operator. The number of channels that must be set aside varies according to the size of the system. Now that Congress has authorized mandatory access, it seems virtually certain that, one way or another, the constitutional question will reach the Supreme Court.

C. SIGNAL CARRIAGE RULES AND COPYRIGHT PROBLEMS

The Commission's signal carriage restrictions have produced major challenges to the Commission's jurisdiction over cable. Each of these rules was designed to protect local broadcasting from cable competition. We have already discussed the mandatory access requirements. Let us now turn to the other signal carriage rules.

1. Leapfrogging and Superstations

One of the earliest restrictions, called the anti-leapfrogging rule, provided that when it was permissible to import distant signals, the system had to select from among those nearest to the city in which the system was operating. The FCC deleted this rule in 1976. One result was the emergence of the so-called "superstation"—an independent television station that makes its programs available to cable systems throughout the country, via satellite transmission.

The most famous superstation is Ted Turner's Channel 17 in Atlanta, which has access to 200 live sporting events each year. By 1985, the station was distributing its programs nationwide to 8,000 cable systems with more than 31 million subscribers. The satellite company charged the cable systems 10 cents per subscriber per month. The cable systems made the programs available as part of their basic monthly charge to attract subscribers.

Channel 17 prospered by increased charges for advertising on its programs, which were now reaching up to 30 million more viewers than previously. As a result, Channel 17's local advertisers were soon replaced by those marketing national products. Program suppliers have increased charges to Channel 17 because the program is reaching a much larger audience than it did before and cable distribution may result in reduced licensing fees or even preclude sales to local television stations in cities receiving the cable program.

Other superstations have followed, but they lag behind the Atlanta enterprise, which had a two-year head start. Some, using wires instead of satellites, have become regional stations.

2. Exclusivity

To protect the local station when it was carrying network programs, the FCC promulgated exclusivity rules (formerly called nonduplication rules) to prevent cable from carrying an imported distant signal that was offering the same network program as the local network affiliate. First, the FCC required the cable system to black out the distant signal if the program was being broadcast on the same day it was being presented by the local affiliate. Later, the FCC changed the rule to require blackout only if the two showings were at the same hour.

In the mid-1970s the Commission modified the blackout requirement, permitting cable systems to show the local station's signal (and its commercials) simultaneously on both the local channel and on the channel that normally carries the distant signal, even though the local station might suffer if the local audience stays with the distant station after the program is over. This more limited protection survives.

Another regulation protecting local stations had provided that cable systems in large markets could not carry distant signals showing programs to which a local station had acquired exclusive future local rights. The obvious concern underlying the syndicated program exclusivity rule was that the increased availability of the program would fragment the audience for the show. This rule was terminated in 1980.

3. Copyright Problems

One of the major factors influencing the Commission in its decisions governing signal carriage has been the application of copyright law to the retransmission of broadcast signals by cable operators. The question has always been whether or not cable operators should have to compensate either the broadcasters or the program producers for retransmission and, if so, how the compensation should be determined.

The issue first reached the Supreme Court in Fortnightly Corp. v. United Artists Television, Inc., 392 U.S. 390 (1968). The Court held that retransmission was not a "performance" and thus, there was no infringement. The Court was unable to find a real distinction between a viewer's antenna system and the cable company's equipment. Both were designed to improve reception of the broadcast signals.

When cable systems started using microwaves to import signals from around the country, there was some question whether this would change the copyright issue. The Supreme Court decided that the fact that there was no way a non-cable subscriber could receive these signals using existing technology did not make a difference. The "reception and rechanneling of these signals for simultaneous viewing is essentially a viewer function, irrespective of the distance between the broadcast station and the ultimate viewer." Teleprompter Corporation v. Columbia Broadcasting System, 415 U.S. 394 (1974).

These copyright rulings greatly increased the importance to local broadcasters of the FCC restrictions. It meant little to local broadcasters to have their signal carried elsewhere because their local advertisers had little or no interest in reaching consumers in other parts of the country. Meanwhile, the signals being imported into the community fragmented the local audiences, reducing the number of viewers they could offer to local advertisers.

There also was an apparent inequity in the system. Broadcasters had to pay royalties or license fees for much of their programming. Cable operators were paying nothing to distribute the exact same programming and were collecting a fee for doing so. The Copyright Act of 1976 addressed the situation by defining retransmission of broadcast signals by cable systems as copyright infringement. But simultaneous retransmission, "secondary transmission," of broadcast signals is protected by a complex compulsory licensing scheme.

Section 111 provides, in effect, that cablecasters need pay no royalties for programs on "local" (or "must carry") stations that they were required to carry until September, 1985. (The must-carry rules are discussed at p. 918, infra.) Cablecasters are permitted to carry the copyrighted programs of "distant" (or "may carry") stations without the owner's consent in return for the payment of a compulsory royalty fee. This fee is fixed by statute and depends on the size of the cable system and whether the distant station is commercial or educational. The Act represented a compromise between the interests of broadcasters and cable operators. Although cable operators now had to pay for the right to retransmit broadcast programming, broadcasters could not withhold the right to carry the programming.

Because of this inability to refuse transmission consent, certain stations found themselves unwilling superstations. As previously noted, the only way for such a broadcaster to benefit is to shift to national advertisers from local or regional advertisers. But there are several disadvantages to being a superstation, although Turner for one found them outweighed by the advantages. Program acquisition costs increase as a result of the increased audience. In addition, certain sports programming is unavailable because the importation of that programming into other areas of the country will violate agreements between the syndicator and the league or conference. For example, Atlanta's WTBS was unable to carry baseball playoff games involving the Atlanta Braves, even though the station that carries a team during the regular season is normally entitled to carry that team's playoff games. Importation of the games on WTBS into other markets would have conflicted with an agreement between the networks and professional baseball giving the networks exclusivity outside the markets of the teams participating in the playoffs.

The enactment of the Copyright Act of 1976 was soon followed by a change in the Commission's attitude toward cable. In 1980, the FCC repealed the distant signal limitations and syndicated program exclusivity rule. The Commission argued that there was no real evidence that repeal of the rules would seriously harm broadcasters. Furthermore, the new copyright act now provided compensation for the retransmission of those programs. Finally, with regard to syndicated program exclusivity, the viewers' interest in "time-diversity"—seeing programs when they wanted—was more compelling than the local station's interest in the exclusive programming. Deletion of the old rule would not reduce the supply of programs for television. The deletion of the rules was upheld in Malrite T.V. of New York v. Federal Communications Commission, 652 F.2d 1140 (2d Cir.1981), certiorari denied 454 U.S. 1143 (1982).

As a result of the FCC's repeal of the distant signal rules, the Copyright Royalty Tribunal raised the rates cable operators must pay for distant signals effective March 15, 1983. Large cable systems became liable for a compulsory license fee of 3.75% of their basic revenues for each distant signal added since June 24, 1981. This increase was upheld in National Cable Television Association v. Copyright Royalty Tribunal, 724 F.2d 176, 55 R.R.2d 387 (D.C.Cir.1983). In response, some cable operators dropped distant signals to reduce their copyright liability. Superstations were the major casualties.

As a result of these changes fee distribution has also become more complicated. There are now three funds at stake: the basic royalties fund, the 3.75% fund which contains the fees for distant signals added after June 24, 1981, and the "syndex" fund which contains a surcharge adopted as a result of the repeal of the syndicated program exclusivity rules.

Broadcasters maintain that cable's contribution to the fund is tiny when compared with the fact that commercial television broadcasters spend some 35 percent of their budgets on program acquisition. Cable operators claim the current fees, after the recent rate hikes, are already prohibitive. Meanwhile, the FCC has asserted that any economic problem for the broadcasters derives from the Copyright Act or the Tribunal's allocation—and relief must come from those sources.

For years, the compulsory license and royalty provision has been under attack in Congress. The recent decision in the Quincy Cable case, p. 918, infra, has only intensified the pressure. The problem is that the 1976 Act did not contemplate the changes in FCC rules that have permitted the growth of superstations and increased carriage of distant signals. The result is that an increasing amount of cable programming is coming from distant sources, leaving the program suppliers with less control over geographical distribution of their products. Complaints are also being heard from major sports leagues because, for example, an Atlanta baseball game may be shown on a Boston area cable system at the same time another game is being played in Boston. As a result, the teams carried on the major superstations have agreed to pay the other league teams annual fees.

Broadcasters have argued that the compulsory license should be abolished and replaced by a negotiated agreement between the cable system and the originating broadcaster (who, under contract, would need the consent of the copyright owner). This need not lead to individual negotiations—the matter could be handled the way song writers grant licenses and collect royalties: through such groups as ASCAP and BMI that grant bulk licenses for a fee and then distribute the proceeds according to a formula.

4. Must-Carry Rules

One of the earliest signal carriage rules was a requirement that cable systems retransmit the signal of any local television station or "significantly viewed" station that requested carriage. Cable systems were allowed to request a waiver of the rule where it created hardship, but the process was a slow one and few waivers were granted. The "must-carry" rules imposed a special hardship on the smaller cable systems, which could find most of their channels occupied by must-carry channels. Due to overlapping signals, some systems were forced to carry several affiliates of the same network, or similarly duplicative stations, to the exclusion of other non-duplicative services.

As with the other rules, the purpose was to protect local broadcasters, especially UHF stations, whose picture quality was noticeably inferior to that provided by cable. There was also concern that cable subscribers would remove their television antennas or, at the very least, fail to maintain them, and that this would put broadcasters not carried by the cable system at a great competitive disadvantage.

When the compulsory scheme was enacted in the Copyright Act of 1976, many thought it a trade-off for the must-carry rules. Although the legislative history on this issue is inconclusive, many cable operators were reluctant to challenge the must-carry rules for fear of losing the compulsory license.

In 1980, however, Turner Broadcasting System petitioned the Commission to institute rulemaking proceedings to delete the must-carry rules. TBS argued that the rules violated the First Amendment rights of cable operators and that, at the very least, extensive changes in the broadcast and cable industries since the promulgation of the rules required a re-examination. The Commission denied the TBS petition.

Meanwhile, Quincy Cable Television Inc., operator of a cable system in Quincy, Washington, was ordered to carry the signals of various Spokane, Washington, television stations and was fined $5,000 for failing to do so. Quincy Cable's appeal of the order and the fine was consolidated with TBS's appeal.

In Quincy Cable TV, Inc. v. Federal Communications Commission, 768 F.2d 1434 (D.C.Cir.1985), certiorari denied, 106 S.Ct. 2889 (1986), the court concluded that the must-carry rules, as drafted, violated the First Amendment. The court thought that the Commission's rules created "undifferentiated protectionism," and that the Commission had failed "to determine whether the evil the rules seek to correct 'is a real or merely a fanciful threat.' " (quoting Home Box Office v. FCC, p. 921, infra). The central purposes and effects of the regulation were never supported by sufficient data and factual analysis. Neither the "scarcity rationale" nor the "natural monopoly characteristics" of cable could provide justification for lesser First Amendment scrutiny. The rules were more than an incidental burden on speech because they both coerced speech, through requiring the operator to carry other signals regardless of their content, and imposed a limitation on the operator's discretion to select the programming it may offer its subscribers. Even if the court were to assume that the rules had only to pass muster under the lower *O'Brien* standard of "furthering an important or substantial governmental interest," they imposed a restriction greater than was essential to that interest.

The rules were "grossly" and "fatally" overbroad in protecting each and every broadcaster, regardless of the quantity of local programming available generally or already provided by the cable operator. The regulations were not finely tuned enough to serve the asserted interest of assuring an adequate amount of local broadcasting in the community. "At some point the goal of preserving localism becomes undifferentiated protectionism. Until the Commission makes some effort to demonstrate the contrary, the blunderbuss approach of the rules in their current form makes inescapable the conclusion that that point has been passed." The court concluded:

> Regulation of emerging video technologies requires a delicate balancing of competing interests. On the one hand, a regulatory framework that throttles the growth of new media or otherwise limits the number and variety of outlets for expression is likely to run afoul of the First Amendment's central mission of assuring the "widest possible dissemination of information from diverse and antagonistic sources," [ ]. On the other hand, unfettered growth of new video services may well threaten other deeply ingrained societal values. In particular, the complete displacement of expressive outlets attuned to the needs and concerns of the communities they serve not only would contravene a long-standing historical tradition of a locally oriented press but might itself disserve the objective of diversity.
>
> . . .
>
> We stress that we have not found it necessary to decide whether any version of the mandatory carriage rules would contravene the First Amendment. We hold only that in their current form they can no longer stand. . . . Should the Commission wish to recraft the rules in a manner more sensitive to the First Amendment concerns we outline today, it is, of course, free to do so.

We would consider the constitutionality of the product of that effort at the appropriate time.

In *Quincy,* the court suggested that even if the *O'Brien* test had been met, a stricter standard of review might be applicable. Applying a newspaper standard of review to the Cable Act might well be fatal for a number of the provisions of the act, involving public, educational and government access; commercial leased access; and the imposition of franchise fees, among others. If the *O'Brien* test is used, those provisions may well survive, with the possible exception of the statutory franchise fee, which might be more difficult to justify by substantial government interests. The more cable is likened to the print medium, the more the franchising and renewal system itself is threatened as well.

After months of discussion, the FCC, in August, 1986, promulgated a new must-carry rule that will expire in five years. Cable systems with fewer than 20 channels need carry no local stations. Those with 21 to 27 channels must devote seven to local stations. Those with more than 27 channels must set aside 25 percent of the total for local stations. Regardless of size, all cable systems must carry one noncommercial educational station. Finally, cable systems must make available to subscribers a switch that enables them to obtain both cable and conventional over-the-air television broadcasts. This will permit viewers to receive a local station that is not being carried by the local cable system. It is virtually certain that this new rule will be appealed.

5. The Anti-Siphoning Rules

After an erratic early history, the Commission began to regulate pay systems' programs. The first major challenge of these regulations involved subscription television (STV), an over-the-air pay system that developed in the late 1960s. In defending the regulations, the Commission noted that they were the result of a two-year test in Hartford, Connecticut. The rules generally barred STV from showing any sports events that were regularly carried on conventional television and also restricted showing of feature films that were more than three but less than ten years old. Also, commercials were barred and no more than 90 percent of the programming could be movies and sports.

The Commission decided that although it had the authority to allocate scarce channels to a pay service, such a service would not be justifiable unless it presented programs that were not readily available on conventional television. A second concern was that revenues from subscription operations might be sufficient to permit pay systems to bid away the most popular programs on conventional television, thus reducing the quality of conventional programming. These regulations were upheld in National Ass'n of Theatre Owners v. Federal Communications Commission, 420 F.2d 194 (D.C.Cir.1969), certiorari denied 397 U.S. 922 (1970).

The next major development was the promulgation of similar restrictions for pay cable origination. These regulations, similar to those just mentioned for STV, were overturned in a lengthy opinion in Home Box Office, Inc. v. Federal Communications Commission, 567 F.2d 9 (D.C.Cir.1977), certiorari denied 434 U.S. 829 (1977). In the consolidated proceeding, involving 15 cases, the Commission's pay cable regulations, previously aimed at preventing cable from "siphoning" programs from "free" commercial television, were now said to be intended to prevent the "migration" of such programs from "free" television to cable.

The court in *Home Box Office* found that the connection between the perceived threat to broadcasting and the anti-siphoning rules was insufficient to justify them under the "reasonably ancillary to broadcasting" standard. This meant the rules were beyond the Commission's jurisdiction. Although this ruling alone would have invalidated the Commission's action, the court decided to consider the merits of the rules.

Here the court found insufficient evidence to support the claim that pay cable would bar popular programs to the conventional audience. Rather, the court assumed that pay cable would sell these programs for use by conventional broadcasters. The court was more concerned about the problem of the poor since pay cable would demand exclusive rights—at least for first presentation. But the court concluded that it was not clear that the popularity of films declined "with an increase in the interval between first theater exhibition and first television broadcast." The conclusion was that as to movies, at least, migration would not hurt the poor "very much." Also, the court noted that the Commission's exclusion of advertising on pay cable hurt the poor because it prevented cablecasters from experimenting with a combined revenue system that allowed lower program fees together with some advertising. But all this was speculation; the record was silent and could not support these restrictions on cable.

Addressing the constitutional question, the court started by rejecting the contention that cable's First Amendment rights were governed by *Red Lion.* This left the question of what constituted permissible restrictions on cable. "The absence in cable television of the physical restraints of the electromagnetic spectrum does not, however, automatically lead to the conclusion that no regulation of cable television is valid."

The court drew a distinction between regulation aimed at suppression of free speech and regulation where the restriction on speech is incidental to the purpose of the regulation. Cases involving the latter situation were governed by a test first set out in U.S. v. O'Brien, p. 46, supra: "If such regulations '[1] further an important or substantial governmental interest; . . . and [2] if the incidental restriction on alleged First Amendment freedoms is no greater than is essential to the furtherance of that interest,' . . . then the regulations are valid."

Applying the test to the anti-siphoning rules, the court found them "grossly overbroad." For example, the rules restricted the exhibition on cable of many films that were clearly unsuitable for broadcast television. Furthermore, there was no real evidence that siphoning was a serious threat to broadcasting. "Where the First Amendment is concerned, creation of such a rebuttable presumption of siphoning without clear record support is simply impermissible."

D. FEDERAL v. STATE REGULATION OF CABLE

1. Preemption

Cable, unlike broadcasting, is regulated by both federal and state government. State and local jurisdiction was originally based primarily on the cable operator's use of the city streets and other rights of way. Federal jurisdiction grew out of the FCC's jurisdiction over broadcasting. Gradually a conflict arose over where the line between state and federal jurisdiction should be drawn.

The majority of cable operators preferred to restrict state and local jurisdiction as much as possible. They believed that some cities were making impossible demands in return for their franchises and imposing heavy burdens on the cable operators once the franchises were awarded. They also feared that franchise renewal in cable would not carry the same level of expectancy that has developed in broadcasting.

At the same time the FCC was gradually asserting the right to preempt more and more state and local regulation. When these issues reached the courts, the Commission's position generally prevailed. In mid-1984, the Commission received strong support for its asserted right to preempt in a case in which it was not directly involved.

The combination of FCC regulatory attention to cable and the copyright aspects of cable television led the Supreme Court to protect cable operators from state regulation in Capital Cities Cable, Inc. v. Crisp, 467 U.S. 691, 56 R.R.2d 263, 10 Med.L.Rptr. 1873 (1984). Although it is lawful to consume alcoholic beverages in Oklahoma, it is a crime to advertise such beverages except by certain on-premises signs. Local television stations have been barred from carrying such advertising and have been required to block it out of national network programming. The state Attorney General had ruled that because of the difficulty involved, the statutory ban did not apply to ads for alcoholic beverages appearing in newspapers, magazines, and other publications printed outside the state but distributed within the state. Until 1980, a similar policy protected cable operators. Then the state Attorney General concluded that retransmission of an out-of-state commercial over cable television would violate the statute. Respondent Crisp, director of the Oklahoma Alcoholic Beverage Commission, thereupon warned cable operators of their potential criminal liability.

Cable operators sued for declaratory and injunctive relief. The District Court granted a preliminary injunction that was reversed by the Court of Appeals for the Tenth Circuit. Both courts addressed the matter as a commercial speech question. In the Supreme Court the parties were asked specifically to brief and argue the question whether the state law was preempted by federal regulation of the cable industry. In an opinion by Justice Brennan, the Court unanimously found preemption.

The Court recognized that cable provides its subscribers with a variety of signals, including those picked up over the air from local and nearby television stations, those from distant television stations brought in by communications satellites, "and non-broadcast signals that are not originated by television broadcasting stations, but are instead transmitted specifically for cable systems by satellite or microwave relay." Then the Court concluded that the "FCC has unambiguously expressed its intent to pre-empt any state or local regulation of this entire array of signals carried by cable television systems." The Court cited FCC statements to the effect that it has preempted "signal carriage, pay cable, leased channel regulations, technical standards, access, and several areas of franchisee responsibility. . . . Non-federal officials have responsibility for the non-operational aspects of cable franchising including bonding agreements, maintenance of rights-of-way, franchisee selection and conditions of occupancy and construction."

Although the FCC has relaxed its regulation of importation of distant signals, this was done to foster the Commission's goal of according viewers additional viewing options. "Clearly, the full accomplishment of such objectives would be jeopardized if state and local authorities were now permitted to restrict substantially the ability of cable operators to provide these diverse services to their subscribers." In this part of the opinion, the Court concluded that "to the extent it has been invoked to control the distant broadcast and nonbroadcast signals imported by cable operators, the Oklahoma advertising ban plainly . . . trespasses into the exclusive domain of the FCC."

Apart from this general preemption, the Court found conflicts with specific federal regulations. First, the "must-carry" rules require Oklahoma cable systems to carry some stations from neighboring states "in full, without deletion or alteration of any portion." 47 CFR § 76.55(b). Second, the FCC encourages cable systems to bring in distant stations, including the so-called "superstations," to offer subscribers greater choice. It was not disputed that cable operators who carry such signals "are barred by Commission regulations from deleting or altering any portion of those signals, including commercial advertising."

Third, the Court asserted that the Oklahoma statute would affect cable operators who "transmit specialized nonbroadcast services to their subscribers. This source of programming, often referred to as 'pay cable,' includes such advertiser-supported national cable programming as the Cable News Network (CNN) and the Entertainment and Sports Programming Network (ESPN)." The Court concluded that the FCC "has explicitly stated that state regulation of these services is completely precluded by federal law." Local cable systems generally receive these programs by antenna, microwave, or satellite and retransmit them by wire. Unlike local television stations, which transmit only one signal and receive advance notice about content from the network, local cable systems receive and transmit a variety of signals from many sources "without any advance notice about the timing or content of commercial advertisements carried on those signals." Monitoring each signal and deleting forbidden commercials would be a "prohibitively burdensome task." This burden would be "wholly at odds with the regulatory goals contemplated by the FCC." Although some may disagree with the FCC's determination "that only federal pre-emption of state and local regulation can assure cable systems the breathing space necessary to expand vigorously and provide a diverse range of program offerings to potential cable subscribers, . . . that judgment . . . plainly represents a reasonable accommodation of the competing policies committed to the FCC's care and we see no reason to disturb the agency's judgment."

Finally, the Court observed that under the 1976 Copyright Act's compulsory licensing of cable retransmitters, the cable operator must refrain from deleting or altering commercial advertising on these broadcast signals. Thus, Oklahoma has put the cable operator in the position of either violating state law or being unable to take advantage of the federal compulsory license. Dropping these programs entirely would avoid this problem but would be totally inconsistent with the federal goal of encouraging the importation of distant signals.

Oklahoma's argument that what might otherwise be preempted is protected under the 21st Amendment was rejected. The FCC's interests were great. Oklahoma's were modest since the ban did not go to consumption but only to advertising—and even then out-of-state print media were excluded from the ban. In addition, beer may be advertised. On balance, "it is clear that the state's interest is not of the same stature as the goals identified in the FCC's rulings and regulations."

The Court explicitly refrained from addressing the question whether the Oklahoma ban was an "invalid restriction on protected commercial speech." It also declined, in note 6, to consider the state's argument that the FCC's regulation of cable violated the cable operators' First Amendment right to control the editorial content of the signals they carry—and thus should not be considered as a basis for preemption. The state lacked standing to object to the violation of an adversary's rights when that adversary has made no such claim.

2. FRANCHISING

Cable systems operate under franchise authority granted by a municipality, though state agencies also may grant permission to operate. See, e.g., Clear Television Cable Corp. v. Board of Public Utility Commissioners, 85 N.J. 30, 424 A.2d 1151 (1981). A franchise gives the cable operator access to city streets and other rights-of-way within a defined area for specific periods of time. Franchises usually are awarded after competitive bidding by several companies in response to a request for proposals outlining the requirements of the franchising authority. In practice they are almost always exclusive. After a franchise is awarded a franchise agreement is signed specifying services the system must provide, construction schedules, and franchise fees. Many also specify fees the operators may charge subscribers, although much of this rate regulation has now been preempted by the FCC.

For a while, the competition among cable operators for city franchises was quite intense. At the height of the franchising rush, operators were willing to promise almost anything to obtain a franchise. For example, in 1981, Denver attracted bids from three firms, one offering a 215-channel system including a 107-channel home network. The three offered basic home services for monthly fees ranging from nothing to $3.95.

Unfortunately, once they had obtained the franchises, some operators discovered that cable wasn't necessarily the goldmine they had anticipated. These operators are now asking cities to renegotiate the franchise agreements and eliminate some of the promised services or are selling the franchises to other operators. Companies that promised 108 channels are now persuading cities to accept 56 channels.

Around 1980, when franchising competition was at its peak, cities were able to demand far more than large numbers of channels. Access channels, studios, mobile vans, financial contributions to access foundations, and free wiring of public buildings were commonly sought—and offered. In many cities, cable companies ended up providing benefits totally unrelated to cable service, ranging from building new libraries to planting trees along the roads.

Spurred on by cable industry hype and franchising fever, the cities kept increasing the cost of obtaining franchises. Gradually, the FCC expanded its limitations on state and local regulation of cable. Among the more important restrictions imposed by the Commission were a prohibition of rate regulation of premium services and a ceiling on franchise fees. Further restrictions were under consideration when the Cable Communications Policy Act of 1984 was enacted.

a. *The 1984 Policy Act*

The FCC's increasingly aggressive policy of preemption had already led the National League of Cities (NLC) to pursue legislative relief. Lengthy negotiations between NLC and the National Cable Television Association (NCTA) had not produced a compromise satisfactory to both constituencies. Perhaps given new impetus by Court decisions such as *Crisp*, a compromise bill was drafted and presented to Congress with the backing of both groups. In late 1984, this bill was enacted into law as the Cable Communications Policy Act of 1984.

Franchising. Under the Cable Act, franchising is still primarily the province of state and local governments. The most important restriction is the prohibition on regulating cable service as a common carrier. At the same time anyone wishing to offer cable service must obtain a franchise. 47 U.S.C. § 621. Franchising authorities are prohibited from specifying video programming or other information services in requests for proposals. 47 U.S.C. § 624.

Franchise Fees. Section 622 of the Act prohibits franchising authorities from charging more than five percent of gross revenues as a franchise fee. In the case of existing franchises, money used to support community access channels will not be covered by the five percent limit. 47 U.S.C. § 622. (The Commission repealed its rule that had limited franchise fees to three percent without waiver.)

Concentration Rules. The Cable Act essentially codified existing FCC cross-ownership restrictions. A television broadcast licensee may not own a cable system within its primary signal coverage area. 47 U.S.C. § 613(a). A telephone company may not own a cable system within its telephone service area except in rural areas. 47 U.S.C. § 613(b).

The Commission is permitted to issue further ownership restrictions, but state regulation is pre-empted. Some states previously had more restrictive cross-ownership rules. In some states, for example, cross-ownership of cable and a newspaper, daily or weekly, had been prohibited.

Renewals. One of the great fears of cable operators was nonrenewal. Specific guidelines for franchise renewal are set out in great detail in § 626 of the Communications Act. 47 U.S.C. § 626. A denial of renewal must be based on a finding that the operator failed to comply substantially with the existing franchise agreement; that the quality of the operator's service was unreasonable in light of community needs; that the operator lacks necessary technical, financial, or legal ability to fulfill the promises made in its proposal; or that the operator's proposal is not reasonable in terms of meeting the future needs of the community. This appears to create a strong renewal expectancy. The full impact of this section will, of course, not be clear until it has been in effect for several years.

Rate Regulation. The new law allows regulation only of rates for basic cable service, and then only in the absence of effective competition. Somewhat more extensive regulation of existing franchises was permitted until the end of 1986. 47 U.S.C. § 623. This provision is viewed as a major victory for cable operators, who have long argued that rate regulation was unnecessary due to competition from other communication technologies. Opponents of the provision contended that cable is effectively a monopoly and that cable rates are not subject to adequate pressure from competition.

The Commission has defined effective competition as the availability of three or more off-the-air television signals in the market. It rejected the suggestion that the availability of the three major networks be part of the definition. Cable Communications Act Rules, 58 R.R.2d 1 (1985).

b. *Constitutional Questions*

During this period there were no serious challenges to the cities' authority to extract everything possible from the cable companies by running what was, in essence, an auction, with the franchise going to the highest bidder. Probably, most companies were loath to start a fight with the cities for fear of being denied franchises. As a result serious questions remained unanswered: What is the connection between a city's control of public rights of way and authority over cable programming? Is awarding a franchise based in part on programming promises a violation of the First Amendment? If there is room for more than one company's cables, is awarding an exclusive franchise a First Amendment violation?

CITY OF LOS ANGELES v. PREFERRED COMMUNICATIONS, INC.

Supreme Court of the United States, 1986.
476 U.S. ___, 106 S.Ct. 2034, 90 L.Ed.2d 480, 12 Med.L.Rptr. 2244.

JUSTICE REHNQUIST delivered the opinion of the Court.

Respondent Preferred Communications, Inc., sued petitioners City of Los Angeles (City) and the Department of Water and Power (DWP) in the United States District Court for the Central District of California. The complaint alleged a violation of respondent's rights under the First and Fourteenth Amendments, and under §§ 1 and 2 of the Sherman Act, by reason of the City's refusal to grant respondent a cable television franchise and of DWP's refusal to grant access to DWP's poles or underground conduits used for power lines. The District Court dismissed the complaint for failure to state a claim upon which relief could be granted. [ ] The Court of Appeals for the Ninth Circuit affirmed with respect to the Sherman Act, but reversed as to the First Amendment claim. [ ] We granted certiorari with respect to the latter issue, [ ].

Respondent's complaint against the City and DWP alleged, inter alia, the following facts: Respondent asked Pacific Telephone and Telegraph (PT & T) and DWP for permission to lease space on their utility poles in order to provide cable television service in the South Central area of Los Angeles. [ ] These utilities responded that they would not lease the space unless respondent first obtained a cable television franchise from the City. [ ] Respondent asked the City for a franchise, but the City refused to grant it one, stating that respondent had failed to participate in an auction that was to award a single franchise in the area. [ ][1]

1. California authorizes municipalities to limit the number of cable television operators in an area by means of a "franchise or license" system, and to prescribe "rules

The complaint further alleged that cable operators are First Amendment speakers, [ ] that there is sufficient excess physical capacity and economic demand in the South Central area of Los Angeles to accommodate more than one cable company, [ ] and that the City's auction process allowed it to discriminate among franchise applicants based on which one it deemed to be the "best." [ ] Based on these and other factual allegations, the complaint alleged that the City and DWP had violated the Free Speech Clause of the First and Fourteenth Amendments, §§ 1 and 2 of the Sherman Act, the California Constitution, and certain provisions of state law. [ ]

The City did not deny that there was excess physical capacity to accommodate more than one cable television system. But it argued that the physical scarcity of available space on public utility structures, the limits of economic demand for the cable medium, and the practical and esthetic disruptive effect that installing and maintaining a cable system has on the public right-of-way justified its decision to restrict access to its facilities to a single cable television company. [ ]

The District Court dismissed the free speech claim without leave to amend for failure to state a claim upon which relief could be granted. [ ] It also dismissed the antitrust claims . . . . Finally, it declined to exercise pendent jurisdiction over the remaining state claims.

The Court of Appeals for the Ninth Circuit affirmed in part and reversed in part. [ ] It upheld the conclusion that petitioners were immune from liability under the federal antitrust laws. [ ] But it reversed the District Court's dismissal of the First Amendment claim, and remanded for further proceedings. [ ] It held that, taking the allegations in the complaint as true, [ ] the City violated the First Amendment by refusing to issue a franchise to more than one cable television company when there was sufficient excess physical and economic capacity to accommodate more than one. [ ] The Court of

and regulations" to protect customers of such operators. [ ] Congress has recently endorsed such franchise systems. [ ] Pursuant to the authority granted by the State, the City has adopted a provision forbidding the construction or operation of a cable television system within city limits unless a franchise is first obtained. [ ] A city ordinance provides that franchises are to be allotted by auction to the bidder offering "the highest percentage of gross annual receipts" derived from the franchise and "such other compensation or consideration . . . as may be prescribed by the Council in the advertisement for bids and notice of sale." [ ]

In October 1982, the City published an advertisement soliciting bids for a cable television franchise in the South Central area of Los Angeles. The advertisement indicated that only one franchise would be awarded, and it established a deadline for the submission of bids. [ ] It also set forth certain nonfinancial criteria to be considered in the selection process, including the degree of local participation in management or ownership reflecting the ethnic and economic diversity of the franchise area, the capacity to provide 52 channels and two-way communication, the willingness to set aside channels for various public purposes and to provide public access facilities, the willingness to develop other services in the public interest, the criminal and civil enforcement record of the company and its principals, the degree of business experience in cable television or other activities, and the willingness to engage in creative and aggressive affirmative action. [ ] Respondent did not submit a bid in response to this solicitation, and the franchise was eventually awarded to another cable operator.

Appeals expressed the view that the facts alleged in the complaint brought respondent into the ambit of cases such as Miami Herald Publishing Co. v. Tornillo, [ ], rather than of cases such as Red Lion Broadcasting Co. v. FCC, [ ] and Members of the City Council v. Taxpayers for Vincent, 466 U.S. 789 (1984). [ ]

We agree with the Court of Appeals that respondent's complaint should not have been dismissed, and we therefore affirm the judgment of that court; but we do so on a narrower ground than the one taken by it. The well pleaded facts in the complaint include allegations of sufficient excess physical capacity and economic demand for cable television operators in the area which respondent sought to serve.[2] The City, while admitting the existence of excess physical capacity on the utility poles, the rights-of-way, and the like, justifies the limit on franchises in terms of minimizing the demand that cable systems make for the use of public property. The City characterizes these uses as the stringing of "nearly 700 miles of hanging and buried wire and other appliances necessary for the operation of its system." [ ] The City also characterizes them as "a permanent visual blight," [ ] and adds that the process of installation and repair of such a system in effect subjects City facilities designed for other purposes to a servitude which will cause traffic delays and hazards and esthetic unsightliness. Respondent in its turn replies that the City does not "provide anything more than speculations and assumptions," and that the City's "legitimate concerns are easily satisfied without the need to limit the right to speak to a single speaker." [ ]

We of course take the well-pleaded allegations of the complaint as true for the purpose of a motion to dismiss, [ ]. Ordinarily such a motion frames a legal issue such as the one which the Court of Appeals undertook to decide in this case. But this case is different from a case between private litigants for two reasons: first, it is an action of a municipal corporation taken pursuant to a city ordinance that is challenged here, and, second, the ordinance is challenged on colorable First Amendment grounds. The City has adduced essentially factual arguments to justify the restrictions on cable franchising imposed by its ordinance, but the factual assertions of the City are disputed at least in part by the respondent. We are unwilling to decide the legal questions posed by the parties without a more thoroughly developed record of proceedings in which the parties have an opportunity to prove those disputed factual assertions upon which they rely.

We do think that the activities in which respondent allegedly seeks to engage plainly implicate First Amendment interests. Respondent alleges:

2. They also include allegations that the City imposes numerous other conditions upon a successful applicant for a franchise. It is claimed that, entirely apart from the limitation of franchises to one in each area, these conditions violate respondent's First Amendment rights. The Court of Appeals did not reach these contentions, and neither do we.

"The business of cable television, like that of newspapers and magazines, is to provide its subscribers with a mixture of news, information and entertainment. As do newspapers, cable television companies use a portion of their available space to reprint (or retransmit) the communications of others, while at the same time providing some original content." [ ]

Thus, through original programming or by exercising editorial discretion over which stations or programs to include in its repertoire, respondent seeks to communicate messages on a wide variety of topics and in a wide variety of formats. We recently noted that cable operators exercise "a significant amount of editorial discretion regarding what their programming will include." FCC v. Midwest Video Corp., 440 U.S. 689, 707 (1979). Cable television partakes of some of the aspects of speech and the communication of ideas as do the traditional enterprises of newspaper and book publishers, public speakers and pamphleteers. Respondent's proposed activities would seem to implicate First Amendment interests as do the activities of wireless broadcasters, which were found to fall within the ambit of the First Amendment in [*Red Lion*] even though the free speech aspects of the wireless broadcasters' claim were found to be outweighed by the government interests in regulating by reason of the scarcity of available frequencies.

Of course, the conclusion that respondent's factual allegations implicate protected speech does not end the inquiry. "Even protected speech is not equally permissible in all places and at all times." [ ] Moreover, where speech and conduct are joined in a single course of action, the First Amendment values must be balanced against competing societal interests. See, e.g., Members of the City Council v. Taxpayers for Vincent, supra, at 805–807; United States v. O'Brien, 391 U.S. 367, 376–377 (1968). We do not think, however, that it is desirable to express any more detailed views on the proper resolution of the First Amendment question raised by the respondent's complaint and the City's responses to it without a fuller development of the disputed issues in the case. We think that we may know more than we know now about how the constitutional issues should be resolved when we know more about the present uses of the public utility poles and rights-of-way and how respondent proposes to install and maintain its facilities on them.

The City claims that no such trial of the issues is required, because the City need not "generate a legislative record" in enacting ordinances which would grant one franchise for each area of the City. [ ] "Whether a limitation on the number of franchises . . . is 'reasonable,'" the City continues, "thus cannot turn on a review of historical facts." [ ] The City supports its contention in this regard by citation to cases such as United States Railroad Retirement Board v. Fritz, 449 U.S. 166, 179 (1980), and Schweiker v. Wilson, 450 U.S. 221, 236–237 (1981). [ ]

The flaw in the City's argument is that both *Fritz* and *Wilson* involved Fifth Amendment equal protection challenges to legislation, rather than challenges under the First Amendment. Where a law is subjected to a colorable First Amendment challenge, the rule of rationality which will sustain legislation against other constitutional challenges typically does not have the same controlling force. But cf. Ohralik v. Ohio State Bar Ass'n, 436 U.S. 447, 459 (1978). This Court "may not simply assume that the ordinance will always advance the asserted state interests sufficiently to justify its abridgment of expressive activity." Taxpayers for Vincent, 466 U.S., at 803, n. 22; Landmark Communications, Inc. v. Virginia, 435 U.S. 829, 843–844 (1978).

We affirm the judgment of the Court of Appeals reversing the dismissal of respondent's complaint by the District Court, and remand the case to the District Court so that petitioners may file an answer and the material factual disputes between the parties may be resolved.

It is so ordered.

JUSTICE BLACKMUN, with whom JUSTICE MARSHALL and JUSTICE O'CONNOR join, concurring.

I join the Court's opinion on the understanding that it leaves open the question of the proper standard for judging First Amendment challenges to a municipality's restriction of access to cable facilities. Different communications media are treated differently for First Amendment purposes. [ ] In assessing First Amendment claims concerning cable access, the Court must determine whether the characteristics of cable television make it sufficiently analogous to another medium to warrant application of an already existing standard or whether those characteristics require a new analysis. As this case arises out of a motion to dismiss, we lack factual information about the nature of cable television. Recognizing these considerations, [ ] the Court does not attempt to choose or justify any particular standard. It simply concludes that, in challenging Los Angeles' policy of exclusivity in cable franchising, respondent alleges a cognizable First Amendment claim.

Notes and Questions

1. What relevant facts might be developed on remand—and how might they help clarify the legal issues?

2. Might some standard between the current newspaper standard and the current broadcasting standard be a useful resolution of the issue? If so, what might it look like?

3. Shortly after the court of appeals' ruling in *Preferred* was announced, a similar result was reached in Tele-Communications of Key West, Inc. v. United States, 757 F.2d 1330 (D.C. Cir.1985). The case arose when, in 1973, the Air Force solicited bids from various companies to provide cable service to Homestead Air Force Base. After the bids were submitted a company was chosen and TCI, which had been providing cable service to the base for ten years was ordered to remove

its equipment. TCI sought injunctive relief arguing that the Air Force order violated its First Amendment rights. The trial court's dismissal of TCI's complaint was reversed on appeal.

The court of appeals held that by alleging "that there were *no* reasons, practical or legal, why two cable television companies could not simultaneously use the cable rights-of-way on Homestead Air Force Base," TCI's complaint stated a claim. The court also found that TCI had stated an adequate Fifth Amendment cause of action. If there were indeed no reasons for refusing to allow two cable operators to provide service, then the selection of another operator and the exclusion of TCI might constitute a denial of equal protection.

4. In both *Preferred* and *TCI*, the courts assumed for the purposes of their decision that there was adequate space on the poles or other rights of way to accommodate all interested cable companies. What if there are more cable companies wishing franchises than can be accommodated? Under the rationale of *Preferred* and *TCI*, what methods of choosing applicants would be constitutional?

5. Section 621(a)(3) of the Cable Communications Policy Act states:

> In awarding a franchise or franchises, a franchising authority shall assure that access to cable service is not denied to any group of potential residential cable subscribers because of the income of the residents of the local area in which such group resides.

Can a franchising authority require a cable system to offer service to an area that it does not wish to serve as a prerequisite to the right to serve a more attractive area?

6. In Florida Power Corporation v. Federal Communications Commission, 772 F.2d 1537, 12 Med.L.Rptr. 1409 (11th Cir.1985), the court held unconstitutional the Pole Attachments Act, under which the FCC regulates the rates utility companies may charge for cable attachments to their poles. The court held that the statute violated the Fifth Amendment ban against "taking" without just compensation. The Supreme Court has noted probable jurisdiction, 106 S.Ct. 2273 (1986).

E. CONTENT REGULATION OF CABLE

Because of the early view that cable television was merely an enhancement of broadcast television, many of the same restrictions on content that were developed for broadcasting were applied to cable. Very few cases address these restrictions.

1. POLITICAL SPEECH

Many of the political access rules have also been applied to origination cablecasting. The equal opportunities provision applicable to cable is essentially identical to that which governs broadcasting. There is also an equivalent lowest-unit-rate provision. 47 C.F.R. § 76.205. The Commission has also adopted rules applying the fairness doctrine, including the personal attack and political editorial rules, to origination cablecasting. 47 C.F.R. § 76.209.

Because the cable operators are not responsible under these rules for secondary transmissions or mandated access channels, and since many of the premium cable channels do not carry political programming, there have been no real tests of the application of the rules. Also contributing to the lack of cases is the limited size of the audience for many cable programs.

2. Nonpolitical Speech

Among the restrictions on nonpolitical speech are a prohibition on cablecasting lottery information and a requirement for sponsorship identification. These provisions mirror the broadcasting rules. Also, the ban on cigarette advertising applies to cable. The most common controversy has involved attempts to ban indecent programs or nudity. The following case is illustrative.

CRUZ v. FERRE

United States Court of Appeals, Eleventh Circuit, 1985.
755 F.2d 1415, 57 R.R.2d 1452.

Before Hatchett and Clark, Circuit Judges, and Stafford, Chief District Judge, Northern District of Florida.

Stafford, District Judge. This cause involves a challenge to the constitutionality of a Miami ordinance regulating the distribution of obscene and indecent material through cable television. [The lower court invalidated the ordinance.]

. . .

. . . The relevant portions of this ordinance provide:

> Section 1. No person shall by means of a cable television system knowingly distribute by wire or cable any obscene or indecent material.
>
> Section 2. The following words have the following meanings:
>
> . . .
>
> (f) The test of whether or not material is "obscene" is: (i) whether the average person, applying contemporary community standards, would find that the work, taken as a whole, appeals to the prurient interest; (ii) whether the work depicts or describes, in a patently offensive way, sexual conduct specifically defined by the applicable state law; and (iii) whether the work, taken as a whole, lacks serious literary, artistic, political or scientific value.
>
> (g) "Indecent material" means material which is a representation or description of a human sexual or excretory organ or function which the average person, applying contemporary community standards, would find to be patently offensive.

. . .

Appellees did not challenge the Miami ordinance's definition of "obscene" material or the city's constitutional authority to regulate obscenity on cable television. (The ordinance's definition of obscenity is in fact closely derived from the test set forth in *Miller.*) Rather, appellees challenged the provisions of the ordinance which attempt to regulate "indecent" materials. The ordinance's definition of indecent materials goes beyond the *Miller* definition of obscenity in two significant respects. First the ordinance does not require that the challenged materials, "taken as a whole, appeal to the prurient interest in sex." [ ] Second, the ordinance does not inquire whether the materials, "taken as a whole, do not have serious literary, artistic, political, or scientific value." [ ] Therefore, if materials falling within the ordinance's definition of "indecent" are to be regulated, the city's authority to do so must be found somewhere other than in the Supreme Court's obscenity cases.

Appellants' primary argument on appeal is that authority for the city's regulation is found in [*Pacifica*]. . . . Five members of the Court concluded that broadcasting of indecency could be regulated by the FCC under certain circumstances. The Court noted that "of all forms of communication, it is broadcasting that has received the most limited First Amendment protection." Id. at 748. The Court found two factors regarding broadcasting to be of particular relevance . . . . First, the Court found relevance in the fact that "the broadcast media have established a uniquely pervasive presence in the lives of all Americans" and that "[p]atently offensive, indecent material presented over the airwaves confronts the citizen, not only in public, but also in the privacy of the home, where the individual's right to be left alone plainly outweighs the First Amendment rights of an intruder." Id. Second, the Court found that "broadcasting is uniquely accessible to children, even those too young to read." Id. at 749. The Court was concerned with "[t]he ease with which children may obtain access to broadcast material," and also recognized "the government's interest in the 'well-being of its youth' and in supporting 'parents' claim to authority in their own household' . . . ." Id. at 749–50 (quoting *Ginsberg v. New York*, [ ]).

. . .

Although we recognize the complicated and uncertain area of constitutional interpretation which we are entering and the importance of the interests asserted by the city, we are persuaded that *Pacifica* cannot be extended to cover the particular facts of this case. . . . The Court's concern with the pervasiveness of the broadcast media can best be seen in its description of broadcasted material as an "intruder" into the privacy of the home. Cablevision, however, does not "intrude" into the home. The Cablevision subscriber must affirmatively elect to have cable service come into his home. Additionally, the subscriber must make the additional affirmative decision whether to purchase any "extra" programming services, such as HBO. The subscriber must make a monthly decision whether to continue to subscribe to cable, and if dissatisfied with the cable service, he may cancel his subscription. The Supreme Court's reference to "a nuisance rationale," id. at 750, is not applicable to the Cablevision system, where there is no possibility that a non-cable subscriber will be confronted with materials carried only on cable. One of the keys to the very existence of cable television is the fact that cable programming is available only to those who have the cable attached to their television sets.[6]

Probably the more important justification recognized in *Pacifica* for the FCC's authority to regulate the broadcasting of indecent materials was the accessibility of broadcasting to children. "The ease with which children may obtain access to broadcast material . . . justif[ies] special treatment of indecent broadcasting." Id. at 750. This interest, however, is significantly weaker in the context of cable television because parental manageability of cable television greatly exceeds the ability to manage the broadcast media. Again, parents must decide whether to allow Cablevision into the home. Parents decide whether to select supplementary programming services such as HBO. These services publish programming guides which identify programs containing "vulgarity," "nudity," and "violence." Additionally, parents may obtain a "lockbox" or "parental key" device enabling parents to prevent children from gaining access to "objectionable" channels of programming. Cablevision provides these without charge to subscribers.

Because we determine that under the facts of the instant case the interests of the City of Miami are substantially less strong than those of the FCC in *Pacifica,* we believe that we must hold *Pacifica* to be inapplicable to this case.

. . .

Even if we were to find the rationale of *Pacifica* applicable to this case, we would still be compelled to strike the ordinance as facially overbroad. As the district judge noted, the ordinance "prohibits far too broadly the transmission of indecent materials through cable television. The ordinance's prohibition is wholesale, without regard to the time of day or other variables indispensable to the decision in *Pacifica.*" [ ] The ordinance totally fails to account for the variables identified in *Pacifica*: the time of day; the context of the program in which the material appears; the composition of the viewing audience. In ignoring these variables, the ordinance goes far beyond the realm of permissible regulation envisioned by the *Pacifica* Court.

[The court also upheld the district court's determination that the enforcement provisions of the ordinance violated due process. These provisions authorized the city manager to initiate complaints, conduct

6. Appellants seem to want to extend Justice Steven's "pig in the parlor" analogy. *See* Brief of Appellants at 16 ("it makes no difference whether the pig enters the parlor through the door of broadcast, cable, or amplified speech: government is entitled to keep the pig out of the parlor"). It seems to us, however, that if an individual voluntarily opens his door and allows a pig into his parlor, he is in less of a position to squeal.

hearings on complaints, determine the admissibility of evidence, make findings based on the hearing, and impose sanctions. "[C]oncentrating the functions of complainant, jury, judge and 'executioner' in one person" created a "risk of arbitrary or capricious governmental action [which] under these circumstances is intolerably high."]

[Affirmed.]

Notes and Questions

1. At about the same time, another federal court struck down a Utah statute on similar grounds. Community Television of Utah, Inc., v. Wilkinson, 611 F.Supp. 1099 (D.Utah 1985). The Cable Television Programming Decency Act authorized the filing of nuisance actions against anyone who continuously and knowingly distributed indecent material over cable television. Material was defined as indecent if it was "presented in a patently offensive way for the time, place and manner, and context in which the material is presented." The court held that the statute was unconstitutionally vague and overbroad. The Tenth Circuit affirmed per curiam in September, 1986.

2. The Cable Communications Policy Act provides that anyone who "transmits over any cable system any matter which is obscene or otherwise unprotected by the Constitution of the United States shall be fined not more than $10,000 or imprisoned not more than two years." 47 U.S.C. § 639. As a result of this provision, the Commission eliminated its regulation banning obscene or indecent cable programming. Cable Communications Act Rules, 58 R.R.2d 1 (1985).

3. The Act also provides that cable operators must, upon request, sell or lease lock-out devices to subscribers. 47 U.S.C. § 624(2)(a).

4. What is the difference between buying a television set—certainly a prerequisite to bringing broadcast service into the home—and subscribing to cable? What if basic cable service is provided free of charge? Would a statute banning nudity on basic cable then be subject to the *Pacifica* rationale?

F. NEW COMMUNICATION TECHNOLOGIES

As we have seen, at one time cable was seen as the ultimate communications technology. At the height of the franchising battles, operators were promising that cable would provide everything to everybody. Not only were those promises unfulfilled, but cable is no longer even the "new" technology. A proliferation of new delivery systems such as multipoint distribution service (MDS), direct broadcast satellites (DBS), and satellite master antenna television (SMATV) are fighting for their share of the communications marketplace.

As each of these services has developed, new regulatory questions have arisen. In developing regulatory frameworks for new technologies, the FCC must work within the context of the Communications Act. Originally, the Act provided two basic models for regulation—the "broadcast" model and the "common carrier" model. If the technology does not fit either of these models, the FCC's regulatory authority is in doubt. This was a major issue in the regulation of cable. In *Midwest Video I*, p. 912, supra, the Commission's jurisdiction over cable was upheld as being ancillary to its jurisdiction over broadcasting. The exact limits of this jurisdiction, however, were never clear.

Common carriers are regulated under Title II of the Communications Act. The key element of common carrier regulation is that the "content is separated from the conduit" so that, unlike broadcasters, common carriers have no editorial discretion. Instead, they must provide, in a non-discriminatory manner, the facilities for transmission of the customer's message. National Association of Regulatory Utilities Commissioners v. Federal Communications Commission (NARUC I), 525 F.2d 630 (D.C.Cir.), certiorari denied 425 U.S. 992 (1976).

There are a number of other important distinctions between broadcasters and common carriers. The federal government has preempted state regulation of broadcasting. In contrast, common carriers are regulated on both the state and federal levels. Interstate service is regulated by the Federal Communications Commission, and intrastate service is regulated by state agencies.

Sometimes, however, the Commission will decide to preempt the states and regulate a service on a strictly federal basis. When the Commission decides to preempt state regulation it does not necessarily imply that the Commission will choose to regulate to the same extent. Instead, the FCC may choose to "preempt and forbear." This means that the Commission will eliminate the state regulations without substituting any of its own because the Commission believes that any regulation is unwise.

The regulations most commonly subject to preemption are entry requirements and rate regulation. When a common carrier wishes to provide a service, it is usually required to demonstrate a need for the service. Some states require that, in addition to showing need, an applicant demonstrate that current carriers are either unable to or unwilling to provide the additional needed service. These requirements can effectively bar any new entrants into a given type of service.

Because common carriers often enjoy either a natural or government-created monopoly, they are often subject to rate regulation by either the FCC or appropriate state agencies. Rate regulation is usually eliminated when there is a finding of sufficient effective competition in the services provided.

Traditionally, the Commission assigned services to one of the two regulatory models based on the method of transmission. Because this led to anomalies, the Commission has begun imposing regulations based on the service provided as opposed to the method of transmission. In some cases the Commission has even left the initial choice of regulatory model up to the licensee. In other words, licensees can decide for themselves which regulatory model would be most appropriate for the type of service they wish to offer.

Obviously, the flood of new communications technologies has presented the FCC with serious problems as it tries to fit them into the traditional regulatory models. We now turn to some of these new communication technologies and examine how the Commission has attempted to resolve these problems.

1. MULTIPOINT DISTRIBUTION SERVICE (MDS)

MDS transmits microwave signals over super high frequencies within a range of about 25 miles. The signal is received by a small microwave antenna, usually located on a rooftop. The signal is then converted to a broadcast frequency and shown on a vacant VHF channel. Originally, MDS was intended to be used to transmit data, but some operators found that a more profitable use was distribution of video programming to hotels and other multi-unit buildings. As the cost of converters and antenna systems dropped, it even became feasible to distribute programming to single-family dwellings. In some urban areas in which cable is not available, MDS has been distributing HBO programming.

MDS is regulated as a common carrier because the Commission viewed it as a point-to-point service. In a 1977 decision, the Commission preempted state and local regulation that might hinder the development of MDS. This was affirmed in New York State Commission on Cable Television v. Federal Communications Commission, 669 F.2d 58, 50 R.R.2d 1201 (2d Cir.1982). In essence, the case preempted state and local government attempts to impose entry restrictions.

In 1983, the FCC reallocated 8 of the 28 instructional television fixed service (ITFS) microwave channels to MDS, making four-channel multichannel multipoint distribution service (MMDS) available. ITFS (MDS Reallocation), 54 R.R.2d 107 (1983). MMDS operators may also obtain extra channel capacity by leasing an ITFS operator's excess capacity. Subscribers then might receive HBO, a superstation, CNN, and ESPN.

The Commission decided to use a lottery system to award licenses for the ITFS channels reallocated to MDS. The court of appeals ordered the FCC either to postpone the MDS lottery until rulemaking on women's preferences was completed or to protect women applicants until the rulemaking was completed. Steele v. Federal Communications Commission, 770 F.2d 1192 (D.C.Cir.1985) rehearing en banc granted. The Commission postponed the lottery. The next month the Commission voted to give women no preference in MDS lotteries and rescheduled the lottery. Appeals are pending.

2. DIRECT BROADCAST SATELLITES (DBS)

DBS is a system of broadcasting directly from studio to home via satellite. The technology involves the usual transmission to a satellite and the return to earth, where the signal is collected by a receiving dish two or three feet in diameter placed on the roof of the home of the subscriber.

The first communications satellites were not suitable for DBS because their relatively weak signals could be received only by very large, expensive dishes. By the late 1970s, however, the technology had improved to the point where a commercial DBS system appeared feasible. It was now possible to build systems that would allow the use of small, inexpensive dishes for home reception.

At the 1979 World Administrative Radio Conference (WARC–79) the 12 GHz band was allocated to DBS. Decisions on specific orbital locations and frequency assignments were left for later decision. In 1982, the Commission granted Satellite Television Corporation's (STC) application to construct an experimental DBS system offering subscription television service to the eastern United States. Both the FCC's Interim DBS Regulations and the grant of STC's application were appealed. The court brushed aside suggestions that authorizing DBS violated Congressional legislation embedding the concept of localism in all broadcasting.

The court, however, did reject the extent of the FCC's efforts to protect DBS from having to meet certain statutory obligations, such as the equal opportunities section. Under the FCC's approach, DBS operators that did not retain control over the content of their transmissions would be treated as common carriers rather than broadcasters. But these common carriers would not have been subject to statutory obligations, nor would those who leased the satellite channels. This meant that where the functions were divided between the two parties, neither one would have the statutory obligations to which broadcasters are subject. (An operator that retained control over content would have been regulated as a broadcaster.) The court of appeals thought that these statutory obligations could not be avoided by the simple expedient of dividing the functions. When DBS signals are going straight to the public, "such transmissions rather clearly fit the definition of broadcasting." If the common carrier satellite leases its channels to a broadcaster programmer, "someone—either the lessee or the satellite owner—is broadcasting." The case was remanded to change the rules in this respect. National Assn. of Broadcasters v. F.C.C., 740 F.2d 1190, 56 R.R.2d 1105 (D.C.Cir.1984). The first DBS system began operating in 1983 but folded in 1985.

3. Satellite Master Antenna Television

SMATV involves setting up one or more earth stations on a large building or complex and distributing by wire or cable the programming received. The distinction between SMATV and cable television is that no city streets or rights of way are used. This prevents cities from subjecting SMATV operators to a franchising process. It also limits SMATV systems to large apartment houses and hotels where a large number of subscribers can be reached without crossing city streets.

Although SMATV resembles MMDS in that multiple channels are distributed to receiving systems usually set up on rooftops, there are some distinctions. SMATV uses large, expensive earth stations to receive the programming directly from satellites, whereas MMDS receives the satellite feeds at some central location and then redistributes them by microwave to the customer. Since the more expensive satellite receiving equipment must be located at each building served by SMATV, it is viable only for large buildings. In contrast, a single earth station facility allows MMDS to serve every building in an approximately twenty-five mile radius. Because the equipment needed at a customer's location is relatively inexpensive—a small microwave antenna and a converter—MMDS can economically serve single-family homes.

On the other hand, SMATV has some advantages over MMDS. SMATV systems can offer essentially unlimited channels since the transmission from central facility to actual customers is through wires. MMDS is limited to the number of separate microwave channels available. Recall that until two years ago that meant a single channel.

SMATV's freedom from franchising requirements has long concerned cable operators, who argue that it gives SMATV an unfair competitive advantage. Although cable companies must compete through a long and expensive process and often are required to pay franchise fees and make expensive concessions for the right to do business, SMATV operators can just set up a dish and start delivering service. Furthermore, cable companies are required to offer service to everyone within their franchise areas. SMATV operators are free to choose their customers.

To counter this perceived inequity cable operators tried to persuade state and local governments to regulate SMATV by imposing strict entry requirements similar to those applied to cable television. The FCC's preemption of SMATV was affirmed in New York State Commission on Cable Television v. Federal Communications Commission, 749 F.2d 804, 57 R.R.2d 363 (D.C.Cir.1984).

The court noted that the Commission had become increasingly more reliant on market forces to regulate the entry of new cable systems and that the petitioners advanced no credible argument why the marketplace would be an inappropriate tool to use here. It dismissed the contention that the harmful impact of competition on existing cable franchises was contrary to the purposes of the Communications Act. Such an approach would only ensure "a regulatory regime frozen into maintaining the status quo. We cannot read into the Communications Act a congressional intent to so prevent innovative technologies from conferring substantial benefits upon the viewing public."

What if, as a result of SMATV competition, some cable systems failed, leaving many people with no service at all?

4. Home Satellite Dishes

In 1979, the Commission decided to eliminate a licensing requirement for receive-only satellite dishes. Regulation of Domestic Receive-Only Satellite Earth Stations, 74 F.C.C.2d 205, 46 R.R.2d 698 (1979). Over the next few years, the cost of receive-only satellite dishes dropped from over $10,000 to under $1,000. As a result of this deregulation and sudden affordability, a rapidly increasing number of homeowners bought dishes to obtain access to the hundreds of video signals being transmitted by communications satellites. These include many of the cable programming services and programs fed by the broadcast networks to their affiliates. In addition, the dishes can pick up unedited video, e.g. news feeds.

The dishes became very controversial because the dish owners were paying nothing for the programming. The cable programming companies argued that the dish owners were pirates, stealing the signals. The dish owners claimed that they were willing to pay for the service, but that the programming companies refused to sell to them. Most of the ensuing litigation favored the programmers. E.g., California Satellite Systems v. Seimon, 767 F.2d 1364 (9th Cir.1985).

A compromise solution to the controversy was included in the Cable Communications Policy Act of 1984. Section 605, now redesignated § 705, of the Communications Act, was amended to authorize receipt of any non-encrypted signal for private viewing, unless a system for marketing the programming service for private viewing had been established. Cable programming services began to scramble their signals in 1986 to prevent any unauthorized reception, and to sell their services to subscribers.

In 1986, the FCC ruled that cities could not ban satellite receiving dishes as a way of promoting the growth of cable television. At the same time, though, the FCC stated that cities could ban dishes if they interfered with public health or safety or if they conflict with "reasonable and clearly defined" aesthetic values. Matter of Preemption of Local Zoning or Other Regulation of Receive-Only Satellite Earth Stations, 59 R.R.2d 1073 (FCC 1986).

5. Electronic Publishing

Electronic publishing puts pages of information, both text and images, on television sets or other display tubes. Teletext is a one-way system with signals flowing only from the computer to the screen. It operates by sending a continuous cycle of information to home television screens during the regular vertical blanking interval (VBI) of a television signal (the black horizontal line that appears when the vertical hold is not properly adjusted). A user chooses the desired "page" of information from a published index, and instructs the receiver terminal to "grab" the page as it goes by. When the user is finished the page is released from the screen. Teletext can be delivered by either broadcasting or cable.

Another system, called "videotex," is a two-way system in which the computer holds a much larger data base and the user signals which information he wants to obtain. The selected pages are then transmitted to the user. This system requires telephone lines or cable.

When the Commission authorized teletext service, in 1983, it ruled that the licensee should choose the appropriate regulatory model. Teletext Transmission, 53 R.R.2d 1309 (1983).

The Commission also decided that, even in the case of broadcast-related services, teletext would be exempt from content restrictions such as § 315 and the fairness doctrine. In response to petitions for reconsideration filed by various parties, the Commission reaffirmed its position. Teletext Transmission (Reconsideration), 57 R.R.2d 842 (1985). The important point was that "the changing nature of the industry due both to competitive and technological flux requires us to give primary concern to the First Amendment implications of our actions":

> We consider teletext clearly as an ancillary service not strictly related to the traditional broadcast mode of mass communication. First, the very definition of teletext confined the service to traditional print and textual data transmission. [ ] Thus, although these data will be transmitted at some point through the use of the electromagnetic spectrum, its primary and overriding feature will be its historical and cultural connection to the print media, especially books, magazines and newspapers. Users of this medium will not be listening or viewing teletext in any traditional broadcasting sense, but instead will be *reading* it, and thus be able to skip, scan and select the desired material in ways that are incomparable to anything in the history of broadcasting and broadcast regulation. In this light, we believe that the content regulations created for traditional broadcast operations are simply out of place in this new print-related textual data transmission medium. . . .

The Commission continued the analogy to print media by noting that modern newspapers are often written and edited in one location and then transmitted by satellite to other locations for printing. Relying on Miami Herald v. Tornillo, p. 433, supra, the Commission concluded that application of content restrictions to teletext would serve "neither the letter nor the purpose of the First Amendment." In Telecommunications Research and Action Center v. Federal Communications Commission, No. 85–1160 (D.C.Cir.1986), the court upheld the FCC's decision not to apply § 312(a)(7) or the fairness doctrine to teletext, but rejected the FCC's decision not to apply § 315.

At the time of the Commission's original authorization of teletext service, the most controversial part of the ruling was the decision to allow cable systems to remove the teletext portion of the signal from any broadcast transmissions they carried.

Despite the Commission's ruling and *Quincy Cable,* cable operators are not free to remove all teletext from the vertical blanking interval of secondary transmissions of broadcast signals. In WGN Continental Broadcasting Co. v. United Video, Inc., 693 F.2d 622 (7th Cir.1982), the court of appeals held that under some circumstances, stripping teletext constitutes a copyright violation. According to the court, main-channel programming and program-related teletext constitute a single, copyrighted work. Deletion of the teletext, not only is infringement, but it removes the signal from the protection of the compulsory license normally applicable to secondary transmissions.

*

STATUTORY APPENDIX

COMMUNICATIONS ACT OF 1934

48 Stat. 1064 (1934), as amended, 47 U.S.C.A. § 151 et seq.

TITLE I—GENERAL PROVISIONS

PURPOSES OF ACT; CREATION OF FEDERAL COMMUNICATIONS COMMISSION

Sec. 1. [47 U.S.C.A. § 151.]

For the purpose of regulating interstate and foreign commerce in communication by wire and radio so as to make available, so far as possible, to all the people of the United States a rapid, efficient, Nationwide, and world-wide wire and radio communication service with adequate facilities at reasonable charges, for the purpose of the national defense, for the purpose of promoting safety of life and property through the use of wire and radio communication, and for the purpose of securing a more effective execution of this policy by centralizing authority heretofore granted by law to several agencies and by granting additional authority with respect to interstate and foreign commerce in wire and radio communication, there is hereby created a commission to be known as the "Federal Communications Commission," which shall be constituted as hereinafter provided, and which shall execute and enforce the provisions of this Act.

. . .

APPLICATION OF ACT

Sec. 2. [47 U.S.C.A. § 152.]

(a) The provisions of this Act shall apply to all interstate and foreign communication by wire or radio and all interstate and foreign transmission of energy by radio, which originates and/or is received within the United States, and to all persons engaged within the United States in such communication or such transmission of energy by radio, and to the licensing and regulating of all radio stations as hereinafter provided . . . . The provisions of this Act shall apply with respect to cable service to all persons engaged within the United States in providing such service, and to the facilities of cable operators which relate to such service as provided in title VI.

. . .

TITLE III—PROVISIONS RELATING TO RADIO

LICENSE FOR RADIO COMMUNICATION OR TRANSMISSION OF ENERGY

Sec. 301. [47 U.S.C.A. § 301.]

It is the purpose of this Act, among other things, to maintain the control of the United States over all the channels of interstate and foreign radio transmission; and to provide for the use of such channels, but not the ownership thereof, by persons for limited periods of time, under licenses granted by Federal authority, and no such license shall be construed to create any right, beyond the terms, conditions, and periods of the license. No person shall use or operate any apparatus for the transmission of energy or communications or signals by radio (a) from one place in any Territory or possession of the United States or in the District of Columbia to another place in the same Territory, possession, or district; or (b) from any State, Territory, or possession of the United States, or from the District of Columbia to any other State, Territory, or possession of the United States; or (c) from any place in any State, Territory, or possession of the United States, or in the District of Columbia, to any place in any foreign country or to any vessel; or (d) within any State when the effects of such use extend beyond the borders of said State, or when interference is caused by such use or operation with the transmission of such energy, communications, or signals from within said State to any place beyond its borders, or from any place beyond its borders to any place within said State, or with the transmission or reception of such energy, communications, or signals from and/or to places beyond the borders of said State; or (e) upon any vessel or aircraft of the United States; or (f) upon any other mobile stations within the jurisdiction of the United States, except under and in accordance with this Act and with a license in that behalf granted under the provisions of this Act.

. . .

GENERAL POWERS OF THE COMMISSION

Sec. 303. [47 U.S.C.A. § 303.]

Except as otherwise provided in this Act, the Commission from time to time, as public convenience, interest, or necessity requires shall:

(a) Classify radio stations;

(b) Prescribe the nature of the service to be rendered by each class of licensed stations and each station within any class;

(c) Assign bands of frequencies to the various classes of stations, and assign frequencies for each individual station and determine the power which each station shall use and the time during which it may operate;

(d) Determine the location of classes of stations or individual stations;

(e) Regulate the kind of apparatus to be used with respect to its external effects and the purity and sharpness of the emissions from each station and from the apparatus therein;

(f) Make such regulations not inconsistent with law as it may deem necessary to prevent interference between stations and to carry out the provisions of this Act: *Provided, however,* That changes in the frequencies, authorized power, or in the times of operation of any station, shall not be made without the consent of the station licensee unless, after a public hearing, the Commission shall determine that such changes will promote public convenience or interest or will serve public necessity, or the provisions of this Act will be more fully complied with;

(g) Study new uses for radio, provide for experimental uses of frequencies, and generally encourage the larger and more effective use of radio in the public interest;

(h) Have authority to establish areas or zones to be served by any station;

(i) Have authority to make special regulations applicable to radio stations engaged in chain broadcasting;

(j) Have authority to make general rules and regulations requiring stations to keep such records of programs, transmissions of energy, communications, or signals as it may deem desirable;

. . .

(m)(1) Have authority to suspend the license of any operator upon proof sufficient to satisfy the Commission that the licensee—

> (A) has violated any provision of any Act, treaty, or convention binding on the United States, which the Commission is authorized to administer, or any regulation made by the Commission under any such Act, treaty, or convention; or
>
> . . .
>
> (D) has transmitted superfluous radio communications or signals or communications containing profane or obscene words, language, or meaning. . . .
>
> . . .

(r) Make such rules and regulations and prescribe such restrictions and conditions, not inconsistent with law, as may be necessary to carry out the provisions of this Act, or any international radio or wire communications treaty or convention, or regulations annexed thereto, including any treaty or convention insofar as it relates to the use of radio, to which the United States is or may hereafter become a party.

(s) Have authority to require that apparatus designed to receive television pictures broadcast simultaneously with sound be capable of adequately receiving all frequencies allocated by the Commission to television broadcasting when such apparatus is shipped in interstate commerce, or is imported from any foreign country into the United States, for sale or resale to the public.

. . .

ALLOCATION OF FACILITIES; TERM OF LICENSES

Sec. 307. [47 U.S.C.A. § 307.]

(a) The Commission, if public convenience, interest, or necessity will be served thereby, subject to the limitations of this Act, shall grant to any applicant therefor a station license provided for by this Act.

(b) In considering applications for licenses, and modifications and renewals thereof, when and insofar as there is demand for the same, the Commission shall make such distribution of licenses, frequencies, hours of operation, and of power among the several States and communities as to provide a fair, efficient, and equitable distribution of radio service to each of the same.

. . .

(d) No license granted for the operation of a television broadcasting station shall be for a term longer than five years . . . and any license granted may be revoked as hereinafter provided. Each license granted for the operation of a radio broadcasting station shall be for a term of not to exceed seven years. Upon the expiration of any license, upon application therefor, a renewal of such license may be granted from time to time for a term of not to exceed five years in the case of television broadcasting licenses, for a term of not to exceed seven years in the case of radio broadcasting station licenses, and for a term of not to exceed five years in the case of other licenses, if the Commission finds that public interest, convenience, and necessity would be served thereby. . . .

(e) No renewal of an existing station license in the broadcast or the common carrier services shall be granted more than thirty days prior to the expiration of the original license.

APPLICATIONS FOR LICENSES . . .

Sec. 308. [47 U.S.C.A. § 308.]

. . .

(b) All applications for station licenses, or modifications or renewals thereof, shall set forth such facts as the Commission by regulation may prescribe as to the citizenship, character, and financial, technical, and other qualifications of the applicant to operate the station; the ownership and location of the proposed station and of the stations, if any, with which it is proposed to communicate; the frequencies and the power desired to be used; the hours of the day or other periods of time during which it is proposed to operate the station; the purposes for which the station is to be used; and such other information as it may require. . . .

. . .

ACTION UPON APPLICATIONS; FORM OF AND CONDITIONS ATTACHED TO LICENSES

Sec. 309. [47 U.S.C.A. § 309.]

(a) Subject to the provisions of this section, the Commission shall determine, in the case of each application filed with it to which section 308 applies, whether the public interest, convenience, and necessity will be served by the granting of such application, and, if the Commission, upon examination of such application and upon consideration of such other matters as the Commission may officially notice, shall find that public interest, convenience, and necessity would be served by the granting thereof, it shall grant such application.

. . .

(d)(1) Any party in interest may file with the Commission a petition to deny any application. . . .

(2) If the Commission finds on the basis of the application, the pleadings filed, or other matters which it may officially notice that there are no substantial and material questions of fact and that a grant of the application would be consistent with subsection (a), it shall make the grant, deny the petition, and issue a concise statement of the reasons for denying the petition, which statement shall dispose of all substantial issues raised by the petition. If a substantial and material question of fact is presented or if the Commission for any reason is unable to find that grant of the application would be consistent with subsection (a), it shall proceed as provided in subsection (e).

(e) If, in the case of any application to which subsection (a) of this section applies, a substantial and material question of fact is presented or the Commission for any reason is unable to make the finding specified in such subsection, it shall formally designate the application for hearing on the ground or reasons then obtaining and shall forthwith notify the applicant and all other known parties in interest of such action and the grounds and reasons therefor, specifying with particularity the matters and things in issue but not including issues or requirements phrased generally. . . .

. . .

(h) Such station licenses as the Commission may grant shall be in such general form as it may prescribe, but each license shall contain, in addition to other provisions, a statement of the following conditions to which such license shall be subject: (1) The station license shall not vest in the licensee any right to operate the station nor any right in the use of the frequencies designated in the license beyond the term thereof nor in any other manner than authorized therein; (2) neither the license nor the right granted thereunder shall be assigned or otherwise transferred in violation of this Act; (3) every license issued under this Act shall be subject in terms to the right of use or control conferred by section 606 of this Act.*

. . .

LIMITATION ON HOLDING AND TRANSFER OF LICENSES

Sec. 310. [47 U.S.C.A. § 310.]

(a) The station license required hereby shall not be granted to or held by any foreign government or representative thereof.

(b) No broadcast or common carrier . . . license shall be granted to or held by—

(1) Any alien or the representative of any alien;

(2) Any corporation organized under the laws of any foreign government;

. . .

(d) No construction permit or station license, or any rights thereunder, shall be transferred, assigned, or disposed of in any manner, voluntarily or involuntarily, directly or indirectly, or by transfer of control of any corporation holding such permit or license, to any person except upon application to the Commission and upon finding by the Commission that the public interest, convenience, and necessity will be served thereby. Any such application shall be disposed of as if the proposed transferee or assignee were making application under section 308 for the permit or license in question; but in acting thereon the Commission may not consider whether the public interest, convenience, and necessity might be served by the transfer, assignment, or disposal of the permit or license to a person other than the proposed transferee or assignee.

SPECIAL REQUIREMENTS WITH RESPECT TO CERTAIN APPLICATIONS IN THE BROADCASTING SERVICE

Sec. 311. [47 U.S.C.A. § 311.]

. . .

(c)(1) If there are pending before the Commission two or more applications for a permit for construction of a broadcasting station, only one of which can be granted, it shall be unlawful, without approval of the Commission, for the applicants or any of them to effectuate an agreement whereby one or more of such applicants withdraws his or their application or applications.

(2) The request for Commission approval in any such case shall be made in writing jointly by all the parties to the agreement. Such request shall contain or be accompanied by full information

* [Section 606 grants substantial powers to the President to utilize communications facilities during wartime or a national emergency.]

with respect to the agreement, set forth in such detail, form, and manner as the Commission shall by rule require.

(3) The Commission shall approve the agreement only if it determines (A) that the agreement is consistent with the public interest, convenience, or necessity; and (B) no party to the agreement filed its application for the purpose of reaching or carrying out such agreement. If the agreement does not contemplate a merger, but contemplates the making of any direct or indirect payment to any party thereto in consideration of his withdrawal of his application, the Commission may determine the agreement to be consistent with the public interest, convenience, or necessity only if the amount or value of such payment, as determined by the Commission, is not in excess of the aggregate amount determined by the Commission to have been legitimately and prudently expended and to be expended by such applicant in connection with preparing, filing, and advocating the granting of his application.

. . .

ADMINISTRATIVE SANCTIONS

Sec. 312. [47 U.S.C.A. § 312.]

(a) The Commission may revoke any station license or construction permit—

(1) for false statements knowingly made either in the application or in any statement of fact which may be required pursuant to section 308;

(2) because of conditions coming to the attention of the Commission which would warrant it in refusing to grant a license or permit on an original application;

(3) for willful or repeated failure to operate substantially as set forth in the license;

(4) for willful or repeated violation of, or willful or repeated failure to observe any provision of this Act or any rule or regulation of the Commission authorized by this Act or by a treaty ratified by the United States;

(5) for violation of or failure to observe any final cease and desist order issued by the Commission under this section;

(6) for violation of section 1304, 1343, or 1464 of title 18 of the United States Code; * or

* [Relevant provisions read as follows:

§ 1304. Broadcasting lottery information

Whoever broadcasts by means of any radio station for which a license is required by any law of the United States, or whoever, operating any such station, knowingly permits the broadcasting of, any advertisement of or information concerning any lottery, gift enterprise, or similar scheme, offering prizes dependent in whole or in part upon lot or chance, or any list of the prizes drawn or awarded by means of any such lottery, gift enterprise, or scheme, whether said list contains any part or all of such prizes, shall be fined not more than $1,000 or imprisoned not more than one year, or both.

(7) for willful or repeated failure to allow reasonable access to or to permit purchase of reasonable amounts of time for the use of a broadcasting station by a legally qualified candidate for Federal elective office on behalf of his candidacy.

(b) Where any person (1) has failed to operate substantially as set forth in a license, (2) has violated or failed to observe any of the provisions of this Act, or section 1304, 1343, or 1464 of title 18 of the United States Code, or (3) has violated or failed to observe any rule or regulation of the Commission authorized by this Act or by a treaty ratified by the United States, the Commission may order such person to cease and desist from such action.

(c) Before revoking a license or permit pursuant to subsection (a), or issuing a cease and desist order pursuant to subsection (b), the Commission shall serve upon the licensee, permittee, or person involved an order to show cause [at a hearing] why an order of revocation or a cease and desist order should not be issued. . . .

(d) In any case where a hearing is conducted pursuant to the provisions of this section, both the burden of proceeding with the introduction of evidence and the burden of proof shall be upon the Commission.

. . .

APPLICATION OF ANTITRUST LAWS; REFUSAL OF LICENSES AND PERMITS IN CERTAIN CASES

Sec. 313. [47 U.S.C.A. § 313.]

(a) All laws of the United States relating to unlawful restraints and monopolies and to combinations, contracts, or agreements in restraint of trade are hereby declared to be applicable to the manufacture and sale of and to trade in radio apparatus and devices entering into or affecting interstate or foreign commerce and to interstate or foreign radio communications. Whenever in any suit, action, or proceeding,

Each day's broadcasting shall constitute a separate offense.

§ 1343. Fraud by wire, radio, or television

Whoever, having devised or intending to devise any scheme or artifice to defraud, or for obtaining money or property by means of false or fraudulent pretenses, representations, or promises, transmits or causes to be transmitted by means of wire, radio, or television communication in interstate or foreign commerce, any writings, signs, signals, pictures, or sounds for the purpose of executing such scheme or artifice, shall be fined not more than $1,000 or imprisoned not more than five years, or both.

§ 1464. Broadcasting obscene language

Whoever utters any obscene, indecent, or profane language by means of radio communications shall be fined not more than $10,000 or imprisoned not more than two years, or both.

§ 1307. State-conducted lotteries

(a) The provisions of sections 1301, 1302, 1303, and 1304 shall not apply to an advertisement, list of prizes, or information concerning a lottery conducted by a State acting under the authority of State law—

(1) contained in a newspaper published in that State, or

(2) broadcast by a radio or television station licensed to a location in that State or an adjacent State which conducts such a lottery. . . .]

civil or criminal, brought under the provisions of any of said laws or in any proceedings brought to enforce or to review findings and orders of the Federal Trade Commission or other governmental agency in respect of any matters as to which said Commission or other governmental agency is by law authorized to act, any licensee shall be found guilty of the violation of the provisions of such laws or any of them, the court, in addition to the penalties imposed by said laws, may adjudge, order, and/or decree that the license of such licensee shall, as of the date the decree or judgment becomes finally effective or as of such other date as the said decree shall fix, be revoked and that all rights under such license shall thereupon cease: *Provided, however,* That such licensee shall have the same right of appeal or review, as is provided by law in respect of other decrees and judgments of said court.

(b) The Commission is hereby directed to refuse a station license and/or the permit hereinafter required for the construction of a station to any person (or to any person directly or indirectly controlled by such person) whose license has been revoked by a court under this section.

. . .

FACILITIES FOR CANDIDATES FOR PUBLIC OFFICE

Sec. 315. [47 U.S.C.A. § 315.]

(a) If any licensee shall permit any person who is a legally qualified candidate for any public office to use a broadcasting station, he shall afford equal opportunities to all other such candidates for that office in the use of such broadcasting station: *Provided*, That such licensee shall have no power of censorship over the material broadcast under the provisions of this section. No obligation is imposed under this subsection upon any licensee to allow the use of its station by any such candidate. Appearance by a legally qualified candidate on any—

(1) Bona fide newscast,

(2) Bona fide news interview,

(3) Bona fide news documentary (if the appearance of the candidate is incidental to the presentation of the subject or subjects covered by the news documentary), or

(4) On-the-spot coverage of bona fide news events (included but not limited to political conventions and activities incidental thereto), shall not be deemed to be use of a broadcasting station within the meaning of this subsection. Nothing in the foregoing sentence shall be construed as relieving broadcasters, in connection with the presentation of newscasts, news interviews, news documentaries, and on-the-spot coverage of news events, from the obligation imposed upon them under this Act to operate in the public interest and to afford reasonable opportunity for the discussion of conflicting views on issues of public importance.

(b) The charges made for the use of any broadcast station by any person who is a legally qualified candidate for any public office in connection with his campaign for nomination for election, or election, to such office shall not exceed—

(1) During the 45 days preceding the date of a primary or primary runoff election and during the 60 days preceding the date of a general or special election in which such person is a candidate, the lowest unit charge of the station for the same class and amount of time for the same period; and

(2) At any other time, the charges made for comparable use of such station by other users thereof.

(c) For the purposes of this section:

(1) The term "broadcasting station" includes a community antenna television system.

(2) The terms "licensee" and "station licensee" when used with respect to a community antenna television system, mean the operator of such system.

(d) The Commission shall prescribe appropriate rules and regulations to carry out the provisions of this section.

MODIFICATION BY COMMISSION OF CONSTRUCTION PERMITS OR LICENSES

Sec. 316. [47 U.S.C.A. § 316.]

(a) Any station license or construction permit may be modified by the Commission either for a limited time or for the duration of the term thereof, if in the judgment of the Commission such action will promote the public interest, convenience, and necessity, or the provisions of this Act or of any treaty ratified by the United States will be more fully complied with. No such order of modification shall become final until the holder of the license or permit shall have been notified in writing of the proposed action and the grounds and reasons therefor, and shall have been given reasonable opportunity, in no event less than thirty days, to show cause by public hearing, if requested, why such order of modification should not issue. . . .

(b) In any case where a hearing is conducted pursuant to the provisions of this section, both the burden of proceeding with the introduction of evidence and the burden of proof shall be upon the Commission.

ANNOUNCEMENT WITH RESPECT TO CERTAIN MATTER BROADCAST

Sec. 317. [47 U.S.C.A. § 317.]

(a)(1) All matter broadcast by any radio station for which any money, service or other valuable consideration is directly or indirectly paid, or promised to or charged or accepted by, the station so broadcasting, from any person, shall, at the time the same is so broadcast, be announced as paid for or furnished, as the case may be, by such person:

Provided, That "service or other valuable consideration" shall not include any service or property furnished without charge or at a nominal charge for use on, or in connection with, a broadcast unless it is so furnished in consideration for an identification in a broadcast of any person, product, service, trademark, or brand name beyond an identification which is reasonably related to the use of such service or property on the broadcast.

. . .

FALSE DISTRESS SIGNALS; REBROADCASTING . . .

Sec. 325. [47 U.S.C.A. § 325.]

(a) No person within the jurisdiction of the United States shall knowingly utter or transmit, or cause to be uttered or transmitted, any false or fraudulent signal of distress, or communication relating thereto, nor shall any broadcasting station rebroadcast the program or any part thereof of another broadcasting station without the express authority of the originating station.

. . .

CENSORSHIP . . .

Sec. 326. [47 U.S.C.A. § 326.]

Nothing in this Act shall be understood or construed to give the Commission the power of censorship over the radio communications or signals transmitted by any radio station, and no regulation or condition shall be promulgated or fixed by the Commission which shall interfere with the right of free speech by means of radio communication.

PROHIBITION AGAINST SHIPMENT OF CERTAIN TELEVISION RECEIVERS

Sec. 330. [47 U.S.C.A. § 330.]

(a) No person shall ship in interstate commerce, or import from any foreign country into the United States, for sale or resale to the public, apparatus described in paragraph(s) of section 303 unless it complies with rules prescribed by the Commission pursuant to the authority granted by that paragraph: *Provided,* That this section shall not apply to carriers transporting such apparatus without trading in it.

. . .

TITLE V—PENAL PROVISIONS—FORFEITURES

FORFEITURES

Sec. 503. [47 U.S.C.A. § 503.]

. . .

(b)(1) Any person who is determined by the Commission, in accordance with paragraph (3) or (4) of this subsection, to have—

(A) willfully or repeatedly failed to comply substantially with the terms and conditions of any license, permit, certificate, or other instrument or authorization issued by the Commission;

(B) willfully or repeatedly failed to comply with any of the provisions of this Act or of any rule, regulation, or order issued by the Commission under this Act or under any treaty convention, or other agreement to which the United States is a party and which is binding upon the United States;

(C) violated any provision of section 317(c) or 509(a) of this Act; or

(D) violated any provision of sections 1304, 1343, or 1464 of Title 18, United States Code;

shall be liable to the United States for a forfeiture penalty. A forfeiture penalty under this subsection shall be in addition to any other penalty provided for by this Act; except that this subsection shall not apply to any conduct which is subject to forfeiture under . . . section 507 of this Act.

(2) The amount of any forfeiture penalty determined under this subsection shall not exceed $2,000 for each violation. Each day of a continuing violation shall constitute a separate offense, but the total forfeiture penalty which may be imposed under this subsection, for acts or omissions described in paragraph (1) of this subsection and set forth in the notice or the notice of apparent liability issued under this subsection, shall not exceed:

(A) $20,000, if the violator is (i) a common carrier subject to the provisions of this Act, (ii) a broadcast station licensee or permittee, or (iii) a cable television operator; or

(B) $5,000, in any case not covered by subparagraph (A).

The amount of such forfeiture penalty shall be assessed by the Commission, or its designee, by written notice. In determining the amount of such a forfeiture penalty, the Commission or its designee shall take into account the nature, circumstances, extent, and gravity of the prohibited acts committed and, with respect to the violator, the degree of culpability, any history of prior offenses, ability to pay, and such other matters as justice may require.

. . .

PROHIBITED PRACTICES IN CASES OF CONTESTS OF INTELLECTUAL KNOWLEDGE, INTELLECTUAL SKILL OR CHANCE

Sec. 509. [47 U.S.C.A. § 509.]

(a) It shall be unlawful for any person, with intent to deceive the listening or viewing public—

(1) To supply to any contestant in a purportedly bona fide contest of intellectual knowledge or intellectual skill any special

and secret assistance whereby the outcome of such contest will be in whole or in part prearranged or predetermined.

(2) By means of persuasion, bribery, intimidation, or otherwise, to induce or cause any contestant in a purportedly bona fide contest of intellectual knowledge or intellectual skill to refrain in any manner from using or displaying his knowledge or skill in such contest, whereby the outcome thereof will be in whole or in part prearranged or predetermined.

. . .

TITLE VI—CABLE COMMUNICATIONS

PURPOSES

Sec. 601. [47 U.S.C.A. § 601.]

The purposes of this title are to

(1) establish a national policy concerning cable communications;

(2) establish franchise procedures and standards which encourage the growth and development of cable systems and which assure that cable systems are responsive to the needs and interests of the local community;

(3) establish guidelines for the exercise of Federal, State, and local authority with respect to the regulation of cable systems;

(4) assure and encourage that cable communications provide and are encouraged to provide the widest possible diversity of information sources and services to the public.

(5) establish an orderly process for franchise renewal which protects cable operators against unfair denials of renewal where the operator's past performance and proposal for future performance meet the standards established by this title; and

(6) promote competition in cable communications and minimize unnecessary regulation that would impose an undue economic burden on cable systems.

. . .

[Until 1984, Sec. 605 dealt with unauthorized publication or use of communications. For the current provisions, see Sec. 705.]

CABLE CHANNELS FOR PUBLIC, EDUCATIONAL OR GOVERNMENTAL USE

Sec. 611. [47 U.S.C.A. § 611.]

(a) A franchising authority may establish requirements in a franchise with respect to the designation or use of channel capacity for public, educational, or governmental use only to the extent provided in this section.

(b) A franchising authority may in its request for proposals require as part of a franchise, and may require as part of a cable operator's proposal for a franchise renewal, subject to section 626, that channel capacity be designated for public, educational, or governmental use, . . .

(c) A franchising authority may enforce any requirement in any franchise regarding the providing or use of such channel capacity. Such enforcement authority includes the authority to enforce any provisions of the franchise for services, facilities, or equipment proposed by the cable operator, which relate to public, educational, or governmental use of channel capacity, whether or not required by the franchising authority pursuant to subsection (b).

. . .

(e) Subject to section 624(d), a cable operator shall not exercise any editorial control over any public, educational, or governmental use of channel capacity provided pursuant to this section.

. . .

GENERAL FRANCHISE REQUIREMENTS

Sec. 621. [47 U.S.C.A. § 621.]

(a)(1) A franchising authority may award, in accordance with the provisions of this title, one or more franchises within its jurisdiction.

. . .

(3) In awarding a franchise or franchises, a franchising authority shall assure that access to cable service is not denied to any group of potential residential cable subscribers because of the income of the residents of the local area in which such group resides.

. . .

(c) Any cable system shall not be subject to regulation as a common carrier or utility by reason of providing any cable service.

. . .

FRANCHISE FEES

Sec. 622. [47 U.S.C.A. § 622.]

(a) Subject to the limitation of subsection (b), any cable operator may be required under the terms of any franchise to pay a franchise fee.

(b) For any 12-month period, the franchise fees paid by a cable operator with respect to any cable system shall not exceed 5 percent of such cable operator's gross revenues derived in such period from the operation of the cable system.

. . .

REGULATION OF RATES

Sec. 623. [47 U.S.C.A. § 623.]

(a) Any Federal agency or State may not regulate the rates for the provision of cable service except to cable subscribers only to the extent provided under this section. Any franchising authority may regulate the rates for the provision of cable service or any other communications service provided over a cable system to cable subscribers, but only to the extent provided under this section.

(b)(1) Within 180 days after the date of the enactment of this title, the Commission shall prescribe and make effective regulations which authorize a franchising authority to regulate rates for the provision of basic cable service in circumstances in which a cable system is not subject to effective competition. Such regulations may apply to any franchise granted after the effective date of such regulations. Such regulations shall not apply to any rate while such rate is subject to the provisions of subsection (c).

(2) For purposes of rate regulation under this subsection, such regulations shall—

(A) define the circumstances in which a cable system is not subject to effective competition; and

(B) establish standards for such rate regulation.

. . .

(c) In the case of any cable system for which a franchise has been granted on or before the effective date of this title, until the end of the 2-year period beginning on such effective date, the franchising authority may, to the extent provided in a franchise—

(1) regulate the rates for the provision of basic cable service, including multiple tiers of basic cable service;

(2) require the provision of any service tier provided without charge (disregarding any installation or rental charge for equipment necessary for receipt of such tier); or

(3) regulate rates for the initial installation or the rental of one set of the minimum equipment which is necessary for the subscriber's receipt of basic cable service.

. . .

RENEWAL

Sec. 626. [47 U.S.C.A. § 626.]

(a) During the 6-month period which begins with the 36th month before the franchise expiration, the franchising authority may on its own initiative, and shall at the request of the cable operator, commence proceedings which afford the public in the franchise area appropriate notice and participation for the purpose of—

(1) identifying the future cable-related community needs and interests; and

(2) reviewing the performance of the cable operator under the franchise during the then current franchise term.

(b)(1) Upon completion of a proceeding under subsection (a), a cable operator seeking renewal of a franchise may, on its own initiative or at the request of a franchising authority, submit a proposal for renewal.

(2) Subject to section 624, any such proposal shall contain such material as the franchising authority may require, including proposals for an upgrade of the cable system.

(3) The franchising authority may establish a date by which such proposals shall be submitted.

(c)(1) Upon submittal by a cable operator of a proposal to the franchising authority for the renewal of a franchise, the franchising authority shall provide prompt public notice of such proposal and, during the 4-month period which begins on the completion of any proceedings under subsection (a), renew the franchise or, issue a preliminary assessment that the franchise should not be renewed and, at the request of the operator or on its own initiative, commence an administrative proceeding after providing prompt public notice of such proceeding in accordance with paragraph (2) to consider whether—

(A) the cable operator has substantially complied with the material terms of the existing franchise and with applicable law;

(B) the quality of the operator's service including signal quality, response to consumer complaints, and billing practices, but without regard to the mix, quality, or level of cable services or other services provided over the system, has been reasonable in light of community needs;

(C) the operator has the financial, legal, and technical ability to provide the services, facilities, and equipment as set forth in the operator's proposal; and

(D) the operator's proposal is reasonable to meet the future cable-related community needs and interests, taking into account the cost of meeting such needs and interests.

. . .

(3) At the completion of a proceeding under this subsection, the franchising authority shall issue a written decision granting or denying the proposal for renewal based upon the record of such proceeding, and transmit a copy of such decision to the cable operator. Such decision shall state the reasons therefor.

(d) Any denial of a proposal for renewal shall be based on one or more adverse findings made with respect to the factors described in subparagraphs (A) through (D) of subsection (c)(1) . . . .

. . .

OBSCENE PROGRAMMING

Sec. 639. [47 U.S.C.A. § 639.]

Whoever transmits over any cable system any matter which is obscene or otherwise unprotected by the Constitution of the United States shall be fined not more than $10,000 or imprisoned not more than two years, or both.

UNAUTHORIZED PUBLICATION OR USE OF COMMUNICATIONS

Sec. 705. [47 U.S.C.A. § 705.]

(a) Except as authorized by Chapter 119, Title 18, no person receiving, assisting in receiving, transmitting, or assisting in transmitting, any interstate or foreign communication by wire or radio shall divulge or publish the existence, contents, substance, purport, effect, or meaning thereof, except through authorized channels of transmission or reception, (1) to any person other than the addressee, his agent, or attorney, (2) to a person employed or authorized to forward such communication to its destination, (3) to proper accounting or distributing officers of the various communicating centers over which the communication may be passed, (4) to the master of a ship under whom he is serving, (5) in response to a subpoena issued by a court of competent jurisdiction, or (6) on demand of other lawful authority. No person not being authorized by the sender shall intercept any radio communication and divulge or publish the existence, contents, substance, purport, effect, or meaning of such intercepted communication to any person. No person not being entitled thereto shall receive or assist in receiving any interstate or foreign communication by radio and use such communication (or any information therein contained) for his own benefit or for the benefit of another not entitled thereto. No person having received any intercepted radio communication or having become acquainted with the contents, substance, purport, effect, or meaning of such communication (or any part thereof) knowing that such communication was intercepted, shall divulge or publish the existence, contents, substance, purport, effect, or meaning of such communication (or any part thereof) or use such communication (or any information therein contained) for his own benefit or for the benefit of another not entitled thereto. This section shall not apply to the receiving, divulging, publishing, or utilizing the contents of any radio communication which is transmitted by any station for the use of the general public, which relates to ships, aircraft, vehicles or persons in distress, or which is transmitted by an amateur radio station operator or by a citizens band radio operator.

(b) The provisions of subsection (a) shall not apply to the interception or receipt by any individual, or the assisting (including the manufacture or sale) of such interception or receipt, of any satellite cable programming for private viewing if—

(1) the programming involved is not encrypted; and

(2)(A) a marketing system is not established under which—

(i) an agent or agents have been lawfully designated for the purpose of authorizing private viewing by individuals, and

(ii) such authorization is available to the individual involved from the appropriate agent or agents; or

(B) a marketing system described in subparagraph (A) is established and the individuals receiving such programming have obtained authorization for private viewing under that system.

(c) For purposes of this section—

(1) the term "satellite cable programming" means video programming which is transmitted via satellite and which is primarily intended for the direct receipt by cable operators for their retransmission to cable subscribers;

(2) the term "agent," with respect to any person, includes an employee of such person;

(3) the term "encrypt," when used with respect to satellite cable programming, means to transmit such programming in a form whereby the aural and visual characteristics (or both) are modified or altered for the purpose of preventing the unauthorized receipt of such programming by persons without authorized equipment which is designed to eliminate the effects of such modification or alteration;

(4) the term "private viewing" means the viewing for private use in an individual's dwelling unit by means of equipment, owned or operated by such individual, capable of receiving satellite cable programming directly from a satellite; and

(5) the term "private financial gain" shall not include the gain resulting to any individual for the private use in such individual's dwelling unit of any programming for which the individual has not obtained authorization for that use.

(d)(1) Any person who willfully violates subsection (a) shall be fined not more than $1,000 or imprisoned for not more than 6 months or both.

(2) Any person who violates subsection (a) willfully and for purposes of direct or indirect commercial advantage or private financial gain shall be fined not more than $25,000 or imprisoned for not more than 1 year, or both, for the first such conviction and shall be fined not more than $50,000 or imprisoned for not more than 2 years, or both, for any subsequent conviction.

(3)(A) Any person aggrieved by any violation of subsection (a) may bring a civil action in a United States district court or in any other court of competent jurisdiction.

(B) The court may—

(i) grant temporary and final injunctions on such terms as it may deem reasonable to prevent or restrain violations of subsection (a);

(ii) award damages as described in subparagraph (C); and

(iii) direct the recovery of full costs, including awarding reasonable attorneys' fees to an aggrieved party who prevails.

(C)(i) Damages awarded by any court under this section shall be computed, at the election of the aggrieved party, in accordance with either of the following subclauses;

(I) the party aggrieved may recover the actual damages suffered by him as a result of the violation and any profits of the violator that are attributable to the violation which are not taken into account in computing the actual damages; in determining the violator's profits, the party aggrieved shall be required to prove only the violator's gross revenue, and the violator shall be required to prove his deductible expenses and the elements of profit attributable to factors other than the violation; or

(II) the party aggrieved may recover an award of statutory damages for each violation involved in the action in a sum of not less than $250 or more than $10,000, as the court considers just.

(ii) In any case in which the court finds that the violation was committed willfully and for purposes of direct or indirect commercial advantage or private financial gain, the court in its discretion may increase the award of damages, whether actual or statutory, by an amount of not more than $50,000.

(iii) In any case where the court finds that the violator was not aware and had no reason to believe that his acts constituted a violation of this section, the court in its discretion may reduce the award of damages to a sum of not less than $100.

(4) The importation, manufacture, sale, or distribution of equipment by any person with the intent of its use to assist in any activity prohibited by subsection (a) shall be subject to penalties and remedies under this subsection to the same extent and in the same manner as a person who has engaged in such prohibited activity.

(5) The penalties under this subsection shall be in addition to those prescribed under any other provision of this title.

(6) Nothing in this subsection shall prevent any State, or political subdivision thereof, from enacting or enforcing any laws with respect to the importation, sale, manufacture, or distribution of equipment by any person with the intent of its use to assist in

the interception or receipt of radio communications prohibited by subsection (a).

(e) Nothing in this section shall affect any right, obligation, or liability under Title 17, United States Code, any rule, regulation, or order thereunder, or any other applicable Federal, State, or local law.

FEDERAL COMMUNICATIONS COMMISSION

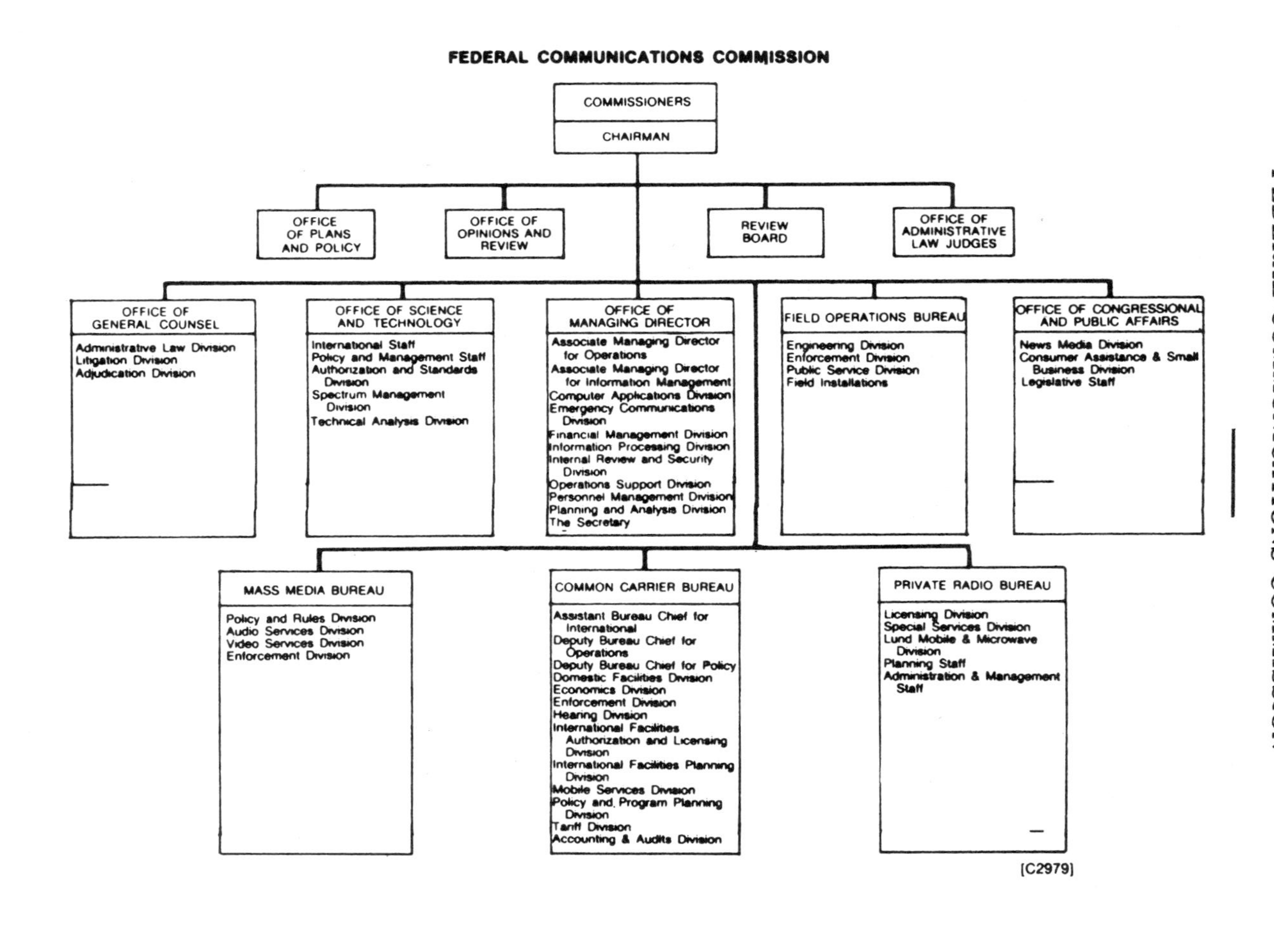

*

INDEX

References are to Pages

†